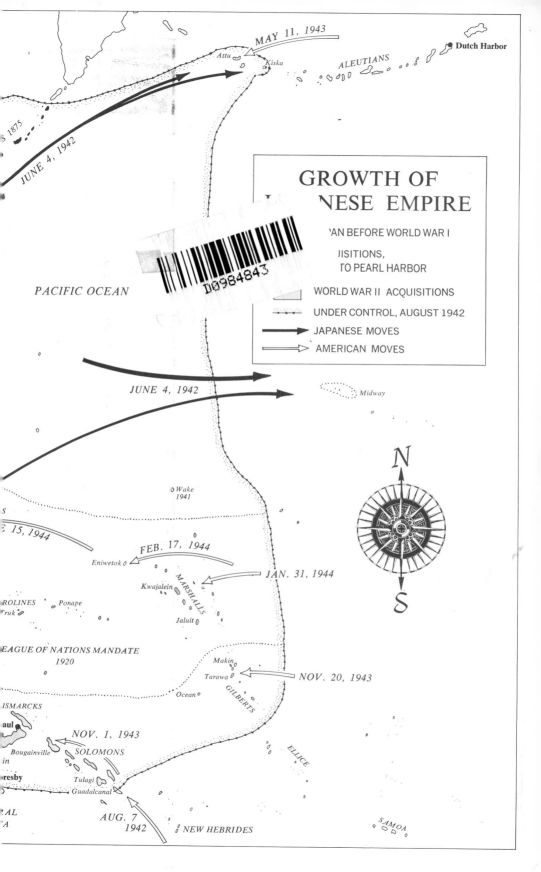

MAY 11, 1943

Attu   Kiska   ALEUTIANS   ● **Dutch Harbor**

JUNE 4, 1942

PACIFIC OCEAN

GROWTH OF

NESE EMPIRE

'AN BEFORE WORLD WAR I

JISITIONS,
ΓO PEARL HARBOR

WORLD WAR II ACQUISITIONS

UNDER CONTROL, AUGUST 1942

JAPANESE MOVES

AMERICAN MOVES

JUNE 4, 1942

Midway

N

S

○ *Wake*
1941

E 15, 1944

FEB. 17, 1944

Eniwetok ○

Kwajalein   *MARSHALLS*   *JAN. 31, 1944*

ROLINES   *Ponape*
ruk ○

Jaluit ○

EAGUE OF NATIONS MANDATE
1920

Makin
Tarawa ○   *NOV. 20, 1943*

Ocean ○   *GILBERTS*

ISMARCKS

aul ●

Bougainville   *NOV. 1, 1943*
in   *SOLOMONS*

resby   *Tulagi*

Guadalcanal   *ELLICE*

AL
A   *AUG. 7*
1942   ○ *NEW HEBRIDES*   *SAMOA*

S 1875

JAPAN'S
IMPERIAL
CONSPIRACY

JAPAN'S
IMPERIAL
CONSPIRACY

BY DAVID BERGAMINI

William Morrow and Company, Inc., New York

19 71

Photo Credits:
REGENT HIROHITO: *Underwood & Underwood.* THE WEIGHT OF TRADITION: Sadako, Hirohito, wife in coronation robes, *Underwood & Underwood.* TRIP ABROAD: Yamagato, Hirohito & Prince of Wales, Asaka on mountain, in car, *Underwood & Underwood*; Higashikuni, *United Press International.* HELPFUL KINSMEN: Kanin, Kaya & wife, *United Press International*; Fushimi, Yamashina, Kuni & wife, Takamatsu, *Underwood & Underwood*; Chichibu, Mikasa, *Pix, Inc.* FAVORITE ADVISORS: Sugiyama, Yamamoto, *Underwood & Underwood*; Suzuki Tei-ichi, Kido, Tojo, *Carl Mydans, LIFE Magazine © Time Inc.*; Konoye as Hitler, Konoye's body, *Wide World Photos.* LOYAL OPPOSITION: Araki, *Foto Notori from Black Star*; Ugaki, *Domon-ken from Black Star*; Honjo, *Hara Shobo*; Saionji & Harada, *Iwanami Shoten.* VILLAINS AND VICTIMS: Inukai, *Underwood & Underwood.* JAPANESE AGGRESSION: Siege gun, *Underwood & Underwood*; three commanders, *United Press International*; killing prisoners, *Carl Mydans, LIFE Magazine © Time Inc.* TRIUMPH AND DEFEAT: Hirohito on horseback, in railway car, *Wide World Photos.* SARTOR RESARTUS: *Wide World Photos.*

Printed in the United States of America by
Quinn & Boden Company, Inc., Rahway, N.J.

Designed by Paula Wiener

Maps by Dyno Lowenstein

Library of Congress Catalog Card Number 74-102686

To Jack, a U.S. Marine, and Kino-san, a Japanese nursemaid, who both perished in a clash of cultures and aspirations which might have been averted but for the proud deceptions and lazy ignorance of many on both sides.

CONTENTS

PART FIVE—DISCIPLINING THE LEGIONS

PART SIX—TRIUMVIR OF ASIA

PART SEVEN—ARMAGEDDON

INTRODUCTION

The work at hand resurveys an area of history which I once explored in a judicial capacity. Whilst Chief Justice of the Australian state of Queensland and later a justice of the High Court of Australia, I headed the bench of eleven judges from eleven nations known as the International Military Tribunal for the Far East, which sat in Tokyo from May 1946 to November 1948. After that two-and-a-half-years' trial, which was commended for its fairness even by the Japanese vernacular press, the Tribunal sentenced twenty-five Japanese leaders to death or imprisonment for having conspired to wage aggressive war and for being responsible for the conventional war crimes—the atrocities—which had been committed by their subordinates.

When David Bergamini's manuscript, *Japan's Imperial Conspiracy,* arrived in my mail I picked it up with alacrity. I had been led to expect much from the author because of his journalistic and scholarly qualifications and his years of research with source documents. Now, on reading the result of his labors, I find that my expectations have been exceeded.

Japan's Imperial Conspiracy is a tremendous achievement. I have read few histories which weave so many intricate situations into an engrossing story and at the same time present, with logic and lucidity, a challenging thesis as to the nature of the historical process. The author's insistence upon dealing with history as the deeds of men and women, and not as the dark workings of complex sociological and economic pressures, is refreshing. It may take years for this work to find its proper place in the evaluation of scholars. More than half the information in it is new to the English-speaking public and some of the interpretation is sure to be controversial. I would judge, however, that the book has the highest importance and will cause a major readjustment in Western views of Oriental history.

To a large extent, *Japan's Imperial Conspiracy* supplements and complements the findings of the Tribunal of which I was president. Indeed it indicates that those findings could have been based on evidence of guilt even more convincing than that tendered by the Prosecution. This is not surprising, as the trial began on May 3, 1946, only eight months after Japan's surrender, and a large part of the author's source materials did not become available in Japan until after 1960. The judges at the Tribunal could be sure that much evidence existed which was not tendered by the Prosecution or the Defense and which was not readily accessible to the Prosecution or Defense; but the Tribunal had no power of its own motion to order investigations and researches.

The work at hand departs from the facts known to the Tribunal in its appreciation of the role of the Emperor. With much fascinating detail drawn from the diaries of Hirohito's courtiers, Mr. Bergamini holds the Emperor responsible not only for authorizing Japan's 1941 attack upon the West, but also for instigating it. I can comment on this point of view, without acting extrajudicially, because the Emperor was not on trial before the Tribunal.

The Tribunal used the Anglo-American form of trial. That form had, for centuries, worked well in English-speaking countries and seemed likely to ensure just results. In Anglo-American jurisprudence, however, the right to present an indictment belonged exclusively to the prosecution. The Prosecution at the Tribunal indicted lesser Japanese leaders but specifically exempted the Emperor from the Tribunal's jurisdiction.

Before the trial began I took the view that the Emperor, as an absolute monarch, was responsible prima facie for authorizing the war, and at the request of my government I advised accordingly. I added that if the Emperor were indicted I would have to disbar myself because I gave that advice. The evidence brought out at the trial confirmed my a priori finding and revealed that the Emperor had, indeed, authorized the war and so was responsible for it.

The question of the Emperor's part became an important matter when it came time to award punishment to the accused. Inasmuch as the accused were only subordinates who had obeyed orders and inasmuch as their leader had escaped trial, strongly extenuating circumstances had to be taken into account in awarding punishment. The Prosecution's evidence left room to believe that the Emperor had authorized the war with reluctance. I was not entirely convinced by this evidence, but it had some probative value.

An entry made on November 30, 1941, in the diary of Marquis Kido, the Emperor's Lord Privy Seal, revealed that the Emperor authorized the war with some hesitation. It also revealed that this hesitation was not due to his dedication to peace but to a fear of defeat which was dispelled by what the Emperor called "the altogether satisfactory assurances" given by the Navy Minister and the Navy Chief of Staff.

Japan's 1941 Prime Minister, General Tojo, who was one of the accused at the trial, first testified that he had never acted against the wishes of the Emperor and then returned to the stand to say that he had done his best to persuade the Emperor to authorize the war. Neither of his statements added much to the effect of Marquis Kido's diary entry.

Admiral Okada, who as Prime Minister in 1936 had barely survived an assassination attempt by military extremists, gave evidence to the effect that the Emperor was a man of peace. Had the Emperor been in the dock, Okada's statement would certainly have been received in mitigation as going to the general character of the Emperor.

Since the extent of the Emperor's guilt or innocence lay outside the competence of the Tribunal, these shreds of evidence were incidental. Nevertheless the Prosecution had opened a wide church door of doubt as to the authority of the accused in initiating the crimes with which they were charged. To avoid any possibility of injustice, I proposed that no capital punishment be imposed on any of the accused, and that they be sentenced instead to imprisonment under conditions of hardship in some place or places outside Japan. However, seven of the accused were sentenced to death by hanging.

As I could not say that the death sentences were manifestly excessive— the test applied by the High Court of Australia in reviewing sentences on appeal—I did not press my dissent, and pronounced the death sentences as well as the sentences of imprisonment.

Japan's Imperial Conspiracy reassures me that, with the possible exception of the hanging of Matsui Iwane, none of these sentences was a miscarriage of justice and that the men hanged were indeed responsible for, although they might have deplored, the wanton murders and barbarous inhumanities which they did little or nothing to prevent. In regard to the Emperor himself, the decision not to try him had been reached, at a high political level, in the U.S. and other Allied governments. At my government's request for advice on the Emperor's case, I advised that it should be dealt with at the political or diplomatic level.

It may seem rather quaint for an alliance of democratic governments to wage war upon an autocratic government at great expense in life and material, and then leave the chief autocrat of that government in a position of leadership. But Hirohito was not only an individual; he was a symbol. However culpable he may have been individually, he was also the spiritual embodiment of his entire nation. In 1945 a majority of Japanese believed, as a matter of religious faith, that Japan and the Emperor were indivisible and must live or die together.

During the thirty months in which I sat upon the bench in Tokyo, I was frequently struck by the solicitude and reverence of witnesses toward the Japanese monarch, and by their earnestness and sense of rectitude in pleading their case. I sometimes asked myself what right we had to condemn

Japan for having resorted to belligerency in 1941. I perceived much justice and extenuation in the able arguments of Defense counsel that Japan was a tiny land of 90,000,000 and 15 per cent cultivable soil, and that she had been subjected to severe trade restrictions and limitations from without. I pondered how the United States or Britain would have reacted in that situation, and indeed how their peoples would have wanted them to react.

The United States and Britain in a situation like Japan's in 1941 might well have had recourse to war. I recall Daniel Webster's address to the Bar Association in London over a century ago in which that notable American jurist acclaimed the expansion of little England into a great empire in these words:

> Her morning drumbeats beginning with the Sun and keeping company with the hours encircle the globe with one unbroken strain of the martial airs of England.

The expansion was not wholly the result of peaceful negotiation.

Until the twentieth century the right to wage war was a sovereign right exercised by all nations without any check except the fear of defeat. Losers paid indemnities in money or territory, and rough rules of chivalry were applied in judging international right and wrong. After World War I, however, all the major powers made an effort to agree upon standards of war conduct and upon principles of international law which might be used in judging those who initiated war. Finally in 1928 sixty-three nations signed the Pact of Paris condemning recourse to war as an instrument of national policy except in self-defense. Japan was one of these nations. Ironically her government specifically informed fellow signatories that she was signing in the name of the Imperial Throne and not, as others had done, in the name of her people.

The Pact of Paris did not explicitly state that the war leaders of a signatory nation could be held individually responsible if that nation broke the pact. Some international jurists of standing have taken the view that the Pact did not impose individual liability. However, I cannot attribute to sixty-three nations—some of whom signed the Pact only after years of deep consideration of their national interests—such futility as to subscribe to an international law for the breach of which no individual human being could be punished. In any case Japan explicitly acknowledged, in the Instrument of Surrender which was signed on behalf of Emperor Hirohito on September 2, 1945, that the Allied nations had the right to try individual Japanese war leaders for crimes against international law. Entries for August 1945 in the diary of Marquis Kido, the Emperor's Lord Privy Seal, reveal that Hirohito understood "war criminals" to include all those responsible for the war, even, perhaps, himself.

Briefly and simply then this was the legal position at the opening of the Tribunal: if Japan was guilty of aggressive war according to the Pact of

Paris and the Instrument of Surrender of Japan which she had signed, her political, military and other war leaders were individually liable. The only defense which she could make was "self-defense." The Tribunal considered this defense and rejected it; it could not succeed. Japan had attacked nations like Thailand and the Commonwealth of the Philippines which had never in any way threatened her. In short her making of war was not merely an Act of State for which the customary punishment was indemnity or cession of territory. It was a Delict of State for which we could find her war leaders guilty as criminals.

After hearing evidence, pro and con, for two and a half years the Tribunal did so find. Tempering justice with mercy, we saw sufficient extenuation in 18 of the 25 cases before us to impose only prison terms. In the other seven cases the Tribunal imposed capital punishment because, on the basis of the evidence, the accused were responsible not only for aggressive war but also for leadership which had allowed otherwise well disciplined Japanese troops to commit pillage, rape and murder in areas outside the forward field of battle.

It is Mr. Bergamini's view, implicit if not stated, that we should have sentenced no Japanese leader to death without also trying the Emperor. I can sympathize with this view even though I do not concur in it. The Emperor, by Mr. Bergamini's account, had a somewhat theoretical, scientific and cloistered appreciation of the realities. He may have been, as the author suggests, no puppet but a robust and intelligent leader of his gifted and energetic people. He lived, however, on a plane above some of his ministers. He seems to have been a patriot, acting in a spirit of self-sacrifice and for the good of his people. He may have played the role of a hawk and may have plotted war on the West for decades before 1941. But I suspect that, had Hirohito sat in the dock in 1946–1948, I would have had a higher regard for his character than I had for that of most of the other Japanese war leaders. Indeed the worth of Hirohito as a statesman appears from the position of his nation today which, under his rule, has reacted to war and defeat by making herself the third industrial power on earth.

Offenders who turn King's evidence or otherwise assist the rule of law have always been treated with a degree of leniency. So it was with Hirohito. He survived the threat of indictment and the humiliation of defeat to make Japan a stable force in Asia. He asserted his supreme authority as an absolute monarch to terminate hostilities which had escalated into nuclear warfare. It is true that he did so only as Japan reeled in the shock of the atomic blasts at Hiroshima and Nagasaki; but he did it at some personal risk as is revealed by Mr. Bergamini's account of the curious happenings in and about the Palace on the night of August 14–15, 1945.

Mr. Bergamini presents a strong case for believing that Hirohito schemed and plotted to lead Japan to the conquest of Asia. Under the circumstances my feeling that the Emperor was worth saving may seem cynical and

Machiavellian. But so may the author's evident admiration for Hirohito. And so may the decision to grant the Emperor immunity which was concurred in by statesmen of such disparate views as Truman, Churchill, Attlee and Stalin.

Hirohito was Japanese. He grew up in a peculiarly insular world which had developed for centuries in isolation from other nations. Anthropologists, poets, priests and diplomats, each in their own fields, have found, on study, that the Japanese world contains a logic and a beauty of its own. Now Mr. Bergamini, after long research in source documents, presents the political side of that world. He does so in lucid Western terms but he succeeds in projecting the Japanese viewpoint. On putting down his book, I was convinced that any Japanese who had grown up in the Imperial Palace would have tried to do what Hirohito did and that few would have succeeded in doing it so well. In short, having tried war and nearly succeeded in it, Hirohito was better qualified to profit by the lessons of defeat and to lead his people in new directions than any other Japanese.

In driving the reader to this realization, Mr. Bergamini adopts a realism toward Japan which, in my experience, is new. On the one hand he rejects the wartime hate of the Japanese as cold and calculating schemers. On the other hand he deplores the postwar apology for the Japanese as fanatic emotional blunderers. In Mr. Bergamini's view, the Japanese were always rational and succeeded in terrifying the rest of the world by using well the few material resources which they possessed. At the same time they were loving parents and children and fought for a way of life which to them was all firelight and comfort. It included the matting floor, the scalding tub, the backlighted paper-screened doorways and windows, the pickled radishes and steaming rice. In my years in Tokyo I never adopted any of those Japanese institutions but Mr. Bergamini almost makes me wish that I had. In reading his pages I found myself identifying so well with the protagonists of his story that I was hanging upon the success of their enterprises.

Because of his insistence upon appreciating Japanese values and Japanese accomplishments, without accepting obfuscations or apologies, Mr. Bergamini has had to reinterpret Japanese history. His pages offer fresh ideas about events A.D. 50 as well as A.D. 1945. I find his insights extraordinarily coherent and persuasive and I can only say: "Reader, read on."

SIR WILLIAM FLOOD WEBB

Brisbane, Australia

AUTHOR TO READER

"Of course I want the Japanese to win," I said. "The Japanese are clean and the Chinese are dirty. The Japanese work and the Chinese beg. The Japs make machines and the Chinese only break them."

"I should say you're a bloody Nazi," remarked the English boy. And at that, the two of us were rolling on the playground, muddying our gray flannel shorts and school blazers and knocking our heads against the sandbag emplacement put up a week earlier after the first Japanese air raid. It was October of 1937. We were both nine-year-old students at a small British school for white boys in the central Chinese city of Hankow. The fight was my first at Hankow Private and it was to be repeated with other members of my class, for the same cause, several times in the next two months. I had been born in Japan and my family had brought me to China from Japan less than a year earlier. Now Japan had attacked China and Japanese troops were driving swiftly on Nanking, the Chinese capital.

Almost a year later, in September of 1938, I sat with my father at the mouth of a cave used as a temple by the chanting, sandaled, Buddhist monks of the sacred Chinese mountain of Lushan. In summertime Lushan —halfway down the Yangtze River from Hankow toward Nanking—was a resort for Westerners. Through our field glasses, my father and I looked down the steep slopes, 5,000 feet, into the front lines of Japanese-occupied China. At our distance we could just make out individual Japanese soldiers. They were conducting a reprisal raid against a Chinese farm village, bayoneting its inhabitants and systematically burning its huts. The smoke of the village streamed into the sky, blotting out the plumes from the fires of the charcoal makers who worked rain or shine, war or peace, in the wooded foothills. Tomorrow there would be a fresh influx of refugees to our mountaintop, orphaned children for the most part, toddlers with cruel bayonet wounds carried piggyback by elder sisters only a few years older than they were. And then tomorrow night the Chinese guerrillas who held the summit of the mountain would make a fresh sortie into the flatlands and bring back a few Japanese heads to mount on bamboo poles and carry in their victory parade.

I was no longer a Japanese sympathizer. The gentle, thoughtful, courteous, good-natured people among whom I had grown to boyhood were now transformed, hideously and most puzzlingly. Here on the battlefield, the Japanese soldiers did not merely wage war: they strutted and slapped faces; they commandeered food from the starving, bedrolls from the homeless, coppers from the destitute; they raped little girls, cut open pregnant women, threw infants into the air and caught them on bayonets; they recognized no truth except the confessions of the tortured, no art of government except intimidation. I did not understand why they acted as they did but I came to take Japanese behavior for granted. Some of my father's friends blamed the famous "Japanese inferiority complex." The Chinese general who lived down the street said it was Japanese leadership that was at fault. Japan, he said, was governed by an unworthy emperor who hoped to conquer the world. I tended to accept the general's explanation because it was simple.

In early 1939 my family and other Westerners were evacuated from the mountaintop of Lushan, through the Chinese and Japanese lines, and taken on a Japanese ship to Shanghai. During the three-day voyage down the Yangtze River, the Japanese commissary served nothing but bread, butter, sardines, and coffee. I discovered that there was plenty of Japanese-style food aboard and was soon eating rice, soya sauce, and pickled radish with the cooks and the guards in the kitchen. Outside the war zone I found with surprise that the Japanese soldiers were the same cheerful, considerate people that I remembered. Most of them knew the big Tokyo hospital of St. Luke's which my father had built. They seemed genuinely grateful for the years he had devoted to architecture in Japan.

Two days after Christmas, 1941, I was once again on a mountaintop with my family—this time in the resort town of Baguio in the Philippines. Again we were refugees, living from suitcases. We were waiting at the local American school, in a body with some 300 other Americans, to be officially captured by the Japanese and declared prisoners of war. A local Japanese immigrant who had worked for my father as a carpenter came to the headmaster's home, where my family was camped out on mattresses on the floor, and informed us with great politeness that at last the Japanese Army had arrived. We gathered to greet it on one of the school tennis courts.

A sound truck, escorted by two weapons carriers, screeched up the drive in the dusk and lurched to a halt. Light machine guns turned back and forth to cover us. A Japanese Methodist minister leapt from the sound truck and began a harangue. By the heroism of the Japanese Army, he announced, an Asia for the Asiatics had at last been realized. We were prisoners of the Co-Prosperity Sphere of Greater East Asia. "You wirru prease surrender your guns." Our elected spokesman told him that we had already made sure that none of us had any guns. The minister did not believe us. He threatened to have his men conduct a search and shoot a man for every gun they found. Then he threatened to shoot ten men for every gun found. Finally he declared: "If we find one gun, we wirru shoot orr of you."

A second-grader came forward trembling, holding out an air-compression BB pistol. "Please," he sobbed, "don't shoot Mom." The Japanese soldiers in the weapons carriers guffawed. The rest of us relaxed. The Methodist minister scowled and turned away. We were herded into one of the school dormitories and left there, hungry but unmolested, for two days while the Japanese secured the town of Baguio and decided where to intern us for the duration. As a thirteen-year-old, I made a mental note of the fact that, even in a war zone, Japanese soldiers might retain some of their sentimental fondness for children.

It also struck me that we were to be treated with speeches rather than bayonets—not at all like Japanese prisoners in China. Was Japanese brutality all calculated, all obedience to policy dictated from above? My question was answered a few days later when Baguio's community of expatriate Chinese shopkeepers was interned in a building next to ours. In a matter of hours the same Japanese soldiers who were guarding us had tied one of the Chinese to a post and beaten him senseless in front of his fellow nationals. The Chinese, I perceived, fell under internal Asian policy whereas we were items classified under external policy toward the West.

Eventually we settled in a former U.S. Army post. There we learned to grow thin on two bowls of rice and one serving of vegetable stew a day and became accustomed to living communally on one six-by-three-foot oblong of barracks floor apiece. One day a Japanese guard approached our Executive Committee, suggesting that arrangements might be made for opening a school in the camp. Like most of the adult internees, the members of the committee anticipated a short war. Preoccupied with immediate problems of survival, they paid little attention to the suggestion. The guard, however, was persistent. He approached one of the older teen-age boys in camp and offered to help get books. Finally he loaded five of us into a truck, covered us with a tarpaulin, and secretly drove past his own guardhouse to Brent School where we had studied before the war.

We found the doors sealed with notices which announced: "Property of the Imperial Japanese Army. Looters will be shot." We broke the seals, loaded the truck with school books, and took them back into the concentration camp. Finding that our assumed birthright of an education might be denied us, most of us read those school books dog-eared in the years which followed. As a result, only one of the score of high-school-age internees lost much educational ground because of his three years in camp, and two of us actually managed to gain a year. After five hours on a work gang each day, our stomachs empty, we had little strength left anyway for anything but reading. I remember lying on my bunk with a geometry book, slightly dizzy as usual before the afternoon meal, puzzling over the fanatic belief in education which gave Japan a literacy rate of over 99 per cent and which had prompted our guard to conspire with us in getting the books.

Mine and a dozen other families which had been registered residents of Baguio before the war were released from camp for a few months in 1942 in a Japanese attempt to make the native Filipinos feel that life had returned to normal. In those months of liberation, we borrowed money, bought food, and had enough to eat. Baguio had been made a convalescent center for Japanese troops wounded on Bataan. The town crawled with soldiers, and most of us stayed close to home except for a weekly expedition to the stalls of the open-air food market in the town plaza. On those trips downtown I made a hobby of collecting proclamations written in English and posted in the market by the Japanese high command. I did not dare to be seen transcribing them in public so I read and reread them until I had memorized the words, then wrote them down as soon as I was home in the little house where we were living. These proclamations struck me because they showed the gulf between Japanese and other languages and the awkward light in which the Japanese appeared whenever they tried to express themselves in English. I remember one poster in particular:

> Still the Igorot peoples living in and about Baguio continue to put the fire on or to loot something from the properties in and about Baguio. This is not good behaviour anyway. When the Imperial Japanese Army finds out those who intend to do so, it will shoot them by guns.
>
> > signed,
> > Affectionately yours,
> > Lt. Col. Kanmori

A year and a half later I was sitting after dark on the split-cane porch of one of the huts satellite to the barracks of our concentration camp. Each of us had just received our first and only Red Cross package of the war. Mine contained ten packages of cigarettes which were not edible. That afternoon, during my daily chore and privilege of passing through the fence to remove the garbage from the kitchen in the Japanese guardhouse, I had spoken to one of the guards—a clean-looking, open-faced mechanic from the Japanese city of Nagoya—offering him a pack of cigarettes for two hands of bananas. I had given him ten cigarettes in advance and he had secreted one hand of bananas at the bottom of one of the garbage cans I was to carry away. Now, as I sat on the tiny porch, I heard a hiss in the darkness beyond. I moved out warily from the puddle of light surrounding the hut and there in the darkness confronted the guard from Nagoya, thrusting a huge hand of bananas at me.

"We have been ordered out," he said.

"Can you come back to the men's barracks with me?" I asked. "I have the cigarettes at my bunk there."

"Do not think of them," he assured me. "We are already equal. I have a son in Japan who is also hungry."

I thanked him and asked him where he was going.

"To the Southern Area," he replied.

That probably meant New Guinea, so I wished him health.

"No," he said fatalistically, "we must all die. There is no way but to die for the Emperor." He bobbed his head in a short but punctilious bow and hurried toward the guardhouse before he could be caught fraternizing. The sadness and despair of his voice lingered after him. Most of them, I thought, hated it as much as we did. They were just waiting to have it over with, to obey the final order and die. If the guard had had the orders, he would probably have killed his own son. With a baffled tug, I adjusted the G string, which was all I was wearing, settled my toes firmly against the soles of my clumsy wooden clogs, and turned my mind to the problem of smuggling my bananas into the men's barracks.

In early 1944 a new commandant was sent to us from Tokyo. He let it be known that he suffered from tertiary syphilis and was subject to savage fits of temper. He quickly showed us that he liked nothing better than to belabor a man about the head with a baseball bat. He might have killed some of us with his beatings if it had not been for the presence of a Japanese civilian attached to our camp as an observer. This civilian was the son of the famous General Mazaki who had sponsored a rebellion against Emperor Hirohito in 1936 and earlier had opposed an imperial policy decision to "Strike South," that is, to prepare for ultimate seizure of the British colony of Malaya, the Dutch colony of the East Indies, and if necessary the U.S. colony of the Philippines. Because of his father's opposition to imperial wishes, our young Mazaki had not been allowed to join the Army, but because of his father's former prestige, he knew how to talk to Army men. His ability to stand up to our mad commandant saved us many concussions and at least one death.

One day while tending to the garbage at the officers' quarters near the gate, I overheard Mazaki pleading with the commandant about our right to have light bulbs with which to read until lights-out at 9:30 P.M. The commandant said that he had orders from Tokyo to be tough, that there was no place for us in the New Order, that we must ultimately die. Mazaki replied that of course we might die under those circumstances, but that if wrong was done there might some day, after the war, come a time of payment. Then, sternly, he reminded the commandant that the name of the Imperial Throne must never be sullied by impropriety in international dealings.

Young Mazaki, our benefactor, was later killed when an American plane strafed a Japanese truck convoy. The convoy had just delivered a life-saving shipment of food to 6,000 interned Westerners at a camp south of Manila. The camp had been cut off from supplies during the confusion which followed the first American landings in Luzon in 1945. In later years, when I knew the history of the Mazaki family, I was impressed by the fact that those who had tried to keep Japan from waging an unjust war were brave men who had continued their struggle to the end.

In December of 1944 our concentration camp was moved in trucks to Manila for the denouement of the war. We lived on chicken corn, weeds, and snails for a month and a half. And then, unexpectedly, came the U.S. 1st Cavalry. MacArthur had received a tip from an unknown Japanese— a correct tip as we were told later by a member of our camp committee— that Tokyo had ordered concentration camp commandants to dispose of their prisoners rather than surrender them. Our executions were scheduled for Monday morning, February 5, 1945. On Saturday afternoon, February 3, the 1st Cavalry tanks made a dash across the swamps north of Manila. They arrived in the city at dusk. We were housed on the concrete floors of the Bilibid Prison hospital, a bleak white building shuttered with sheets of corrugated iron and surrounded by the thick mossy walls of an old Spanish fortress. From our roof the Disney cartoon emblems on the sides of the tanks could not be made out for what they were. They looked like Japanese characters. Only scattered rifle fire greeted the tanks at first, but then a Japanese battery on a building across the avenue opened up and sent us all scuttling downstairs to lie low on the concrete ground floor. No one could tell whether the Americans had finally arrived or whether the Japanese were putting down a guerrilla insurrection. A few wealthy internees laid bets pro and con with their last hoarded ounces of Philippine tobacco and peanut butter.

Four objectives were red-circled on the tank crews' maps: our Bilibid Prison, the bigger internment center at Santo Tomas University, and two breweries. While waiting for reinforcements, the tanks began circling the four city blocks containing these four objectives. Only a skeleton force of Japanese soldiers remained in the city, and they were concentrated in the old Spanish citadel to the south of us. This skeleton force had been supplemented at the last minute by a landing party of Imperial Marines—aristocratic kinsmen of the Emperor—and at the instigation of these newcomers was now preoccupied with a death-throe orgy of rape and murder in the Filipino slums. As a result, except for fires set by infiltrators and a few small shells lobbed in from knee mortars, action in our area was light. A Japanese munitions dump which was being destroyed several blocks away lit the night with carnival fireworks. The tanks went round and round our compound with a monotonous grinding sound. We still did not know for sure that they were American.

Then, one of the gold miners of the Benguet Company, who was interned with us, crawled upstairs and peered over the parapet on the roof to see what the tanks were doing. While he stood watch, two of the tanks stopped and opened up their turrets for the men to smoke a cigarette. One of the drivers yelled something to the other. The miner crawled back downstairs and passed on his story. It reached me by an excited missionary spinster in her fifties: "Hey, Casey, haven't we been up this fricking street before?" And so we knew that bets could be paid off, that the last little hoards of food could be eaten, that the tanks were American.

Next morning the Japanese officers in charge of our Formosan and Korean guards carried machine guns and Molotov cocktails up the stairs to our roof where they prepared to make a last stand. My father was asked by the chairman of our Executive Committee to stand watch over the meager possessions we had left on the deserted second floor. After shooting at the tanks for a while, the officers of the guard were signaled from the prison gate that the tank crews outside had agreed to Japanese terms: release of all P.O.W.'s and internees unharmed in exchange for a jeep ride to the city limits and freedom to join Japanese forces outside Manila. Our Japanese officers then came down from the roof. They found my father sitting alone at the head of the stairs on the second floor. Knowing nothing of the agreement made at the gate, he assumed that they were going out to die and might well shoot him in passing. In his confusion he politely muttered *sayonara,* good-bye. The first of the retreating officers turned on him with a look of hate. "Hope I see you all soon in Tokyo," added my father brightly. The second officer smiled, opened his coat, took something from an inner pocket, and thrust into my father's lap a bottle of beer.

In a moment the Japanese had withdrawn from the building. My dazed father was left surrounded by half-empty flasks of brandy and bottles of beer—tokens of the Japanese hopes for the future. Our own American tankmen drove the Japanese guard out into the suburbs and let them off at a place where Filipino irregulars were waiting to gun them down. I did not feel sorry for the officers at the time, but I was grateful for their bureaucratic propriety. They had let us live because our executions were not scheduled for another twenty-four hours.

Twenty years later, with degrees from Dartmouth and Oxford and ten years of experience on *Life* magazine, I was finishing my fifth book, a volume about the philosophy of science. My agent suggested to me that the editors of William Morrow and Company would be interested in a book about the Japanese side of World War II, based on Japanese documents.

The thought of unriddling my childhood puzzlement about the double nature of the Japanese appealed to me strongly. I spent almost a year studying in U.S. libraries. I learned how to speak Japanese again, still badly, and for the first time how to read it—slowly. I worked my way through 140,000 pages of collateral reading in English, French, and German, 50,000 pages of testimony presented at the postwar Tokyo war crimes trials, and another 30,000 pages of captured Japanese documents and U.S. Intelligence reports. Then I moved my wife, my four children, and 272 reference books to a small Japanese-style house overlooking the experimental fields of the agricultural faculty of the old Imperial University in Kyoto, the ancient capital of Japan.

On an afternoon in September of 1965, I was eating seaweed-wrapped rolls of vinegared rice and raw fish across a table from a retired Japanese Naval Air Force commander. He was one of a handful of air aces who had survived both Japan's war with China and her war with the United States. I had had an uneasy feeling ever since my arrival a few weeks earlier that nothing had changed in Japan except the size of the buildings, and I was prepared to dislike the commander cordially. Half his face had been blown away and was covered with purple scar tissue. He was gentle and spoke English. Learning that I had spent thirty-nine months in a Japanese concentration camp, he said that he was ready to help me in any way that he could, for his people "owed me a debt." He told me that he had dive-bombed over both the mountaintops where I had seen Japanese fire as a child. We compared dates and discovered that I had probably seen his plane hurtling down out of the sky on both occasions: once in 1938 and again in 1941. He had even spent time on Guam, where my elder brother, a U.S. Marine on his way to liberate the concentration camps in the Philippines, had died before a Japanese machine-gun blast in 1944.

Strangely, I soon found myself talking animatedly with this former enemy. Despite his blasted face, he had no bitterness. War was a profession and a game to him. He interested me in it and gave me introductions to several old retired generals who had not already been bored with interviews and interrogations. I became something of an authority on Japanese battle-grounds and Japanese World War II strategic concepts. Soon I realized that I was being passed from hand to hand to hear incidental stories of Japanese heroism and tactical genius. I was not bored by the stories, nor did I disbelieve them, but I came to feel more and more strongly that anecdotes and actions do not a war make. I was still haunted by my childhood question: What had made the delightful, intelligent, artistic Japanese people turn to war and run amok over half of Asia?

The stock answer to my question was militarism, a mass madness which was supposed to have been stirred up in the Japanese public during the 1930's by a handful of conniving, ambitious generals. I studied the soldiers

I was interviewing. Most of them had ended the war as lieutenant generals. All of them were intelligent men who had gone on to staff college after military academy and so had served for years in the nerve center of Japanese militarism, the offices of the Army General Staff in Tokyo. All of them were enthusiastic military technicians, full of recommendations about the conduct of the war in Viet Nam. None of them seemed to be gifted politically. When they felt they could not give straightforward answers to my questions, they said nothing: they looked blank and professed ignorance, or they looked arch and pleaded continuing security restrictions.

On occasion they let slip previously unknown facts of great significance. A retired general of seventy-six, for instance, proudly told me that in August of 1938 he had been put in charge of devising air-to-ground communications and given detailed maps of the terrain for the Nomonhan war with Russia. Evidently he did not realize that this war, which began in May of 1939, was still represented officially by the Japanese government as a spontaneous border incident and his superiors had testified at the war crimes trials to being unable, at the outbreak of the "incident," to find a map in the files of the General Staff which would show them where Nomonhan was.

I could hardly believe, I said, that there were no radios in most Army Air Force planes before 1938. Was the general absolutely sure of his dates? He rummaged in his papers in the next room and triumphantly returned with a volume of his diary. He showed me the dated entry in it where he had recorded his assignment. Two Japanese witnesses were present at my interview with him, and when it was over, I questioned them both to make sure that I had made no mistake about what he had said. They assured me that I had not, but one of them showed curiosity as to why I laid such stress on the date.

Later that week the seventy-six-year-old general traveled over 500 miles, up to Tokyo and back, to see an aged colleague who was a consultant for Japan's modern Self-Defense Forces. When he returned he called me to say that he had been mistaken, that he had carelessly confused the 1938 and 1939 volumes of his diary. Since I had seen the year, *Showa jusannen,* clearly written outside and inside the volume in question, I dismissed the matter as trivial and did my best to save the general's face.

I had an opportunity to see most of my generals in the company of a man of aristocratic birth. I was impressed by their deference to him. They knew their place. Clearly they had been mere cogs in the machine of Japanese society. They did not have the social caste and with it the self-assurance to have forced militarism on Japan—not without the tacit support of their betters in Japan's social hierarchy.

With all of my generals I discussed the atrocities which I had seen committed by Japanese soldiers in China and to a lesser extent in the Philippines. I wanted to discover whether they stemmed from a latent vengeful cruelty in the Japanese or from a well-considered policy of terror which the Japanese soldier carried out under orders. Most of my generals had little to say on the subject except to insist that Japanese troops committed no more casual brutalities than the troops of any other nation. They cited old military police reports and Chinese newspapers to persuade me that, ordinarily, in taking a town Japanese soldiers had committed about two murders and twenty rapes for every thousand troops engaged. I was prepared to believe that similar figures might hold for any army.

In addition to casual brutalities, however, the Japanese had frequently massacred entire villages in China. One of my generals admitted that this was true. He explained that every realistic commander, who had to hold a wide territory with a few troops, was forced on occasion to conduct disciplined reprisals against villages as object lessons to neighboring villages. He maintained cynically that this practice, too, was common to all armies. Indeed, a good commander, he said, kept his special "dirty" reprisal units apart from the rest of his men so that corruption would not spread through the ranks.

I persisted that there had been occasions like the Bataan death march and the rape of Nanking on which the Japanese Army had committed at one time not ten murders out of casual brutality and not a hundred murders in a reprisal raid but thousands and even tens of thousands of murders. All of my generals confessed that they had heard of such "bad things" but only my one exceptionally candid general would make a comment. "Those were the politicians' murders." He wrinkled his face and would say no more.

It was the "politicians' " murders which interested me and I began to study seriously the machinery of prewar Japanese civilian decision making.

In Kyoto I had acquired an excellent research assistant, an honest, politically moderate young student leader taking a master's degree at Doshisha University. Hijino Shigeki bought and read and underlined for me some 30,000 pages of Japanese memoirs and background histories. He worked for me purely in a research capacity and is not responsible for any of the views or judgments expressed herein. A born politician, he gave me insights into Japanese politics. He recruited for me an army of research assistants which I would never have been able to mobilize for myself. His indefatigable staff scanned and culled for me the whole of Japan's voluminous war literature. In the editorials and novels of the late 1920's which my research group collected, I found no evidence of any trend toward militarism. On the contrary I found a popular desire for peace, a repudiation of the hoary warrior cult of the samurai. In the staid economic and military journals of the period, however, I found every evidence of planning for war—planning without popular support but directed and centralized from the pinnacles of the Japanese aristocracy.

I had an introduction at the Imperial Court from General MacArthur's nephew, Douglas MacArthur II, a former U.S. ambassador to Tokyo. I used it to test my growing suspicions in interviews with courtiers who had been close to Hirohito. What a contrast they were to my generals: charming, devious, knowledgeable, never at a loss. Surely here were the real leaders of Japan.

Two of the courtiers inserted into their conversations with me a number of stories about the ruler of Japan since 1926, Emperor Hirohito. These stories had never been reported in print, and I dismissed them at first as Court gossip. But they assumed considerable importance when I later assembled the full context for them. I was told, for instance, that Hirohito had listened to shortwave transmissions from Malaya on the night of Pearl Harbor; that he had once been induced to have a son by artificial insemination; that his own birth was rumored to have taken place a year earlier than commonly stated.

In the anecdotes told to me, I perceived that Hirohito, at the very least, was not the passive dupe of history that he had been made out to be. From the mouths of his own chamberlains he emerged as a powerful autocratic protagonist. He was said to have extraordinary intelligence. Until 1945 he was said to have kept up with every detail of government, to have consulted constantly with officials of all sorts, and to have maintained always an over-all view of world affairs. His powers—civil, military, and religious—were acknowledged to have been absolute, but he was said to have exercised them only ceremonially and to have rubber-stamped the recommendations of his state ministers. Yet in anecdote after anecdote he was shown keeping abreast of his ministers' deliberations and putting in a word now and then to steer them toward recommendations which would be acceptable to him. It was even admitted that he had occasionally decided between opposing viewpoints, accepted a minority viewpoint, or disregarded a recommendation altogether.

I realized that I must go back to the beginning of my research and start all over again. Emperor Hirohito had signed the declaration of war with the United States. It was said that he had done so unwillingly, but this assertion did not appear in the record until made by a retired prime minister, Prince Konoye, many months after the war had started. It was also said that Hirohito might have been assassinated if he had tried to prevent the war. This assertion seemed farfetched, for it was generally admitted that privates and generals were all ready to die for him and that the only Japanese irreverent enough to assassinate him would have been the few Westernized bankers and diplomats who opposed the war.

Emperor Hirohito had stamped the orders sending troops into north China in 1937. It was later said that he did so unwillingly, yet he went on two months later to stamp orders for the dispatch of troops to central and south China as well. He reluctantly postponed execution of the south-China orders on the advice of hesitant "militarists" in the Japanese General

Staff. He opened an Imperial Headquarters in his palace so that he could personally supervise the fighting. He became so immersed in war planning that the prime minister at the time complained of his preoccupation. Finally his own uncle assumed command of the attack in Nanking, the Chinese capital, and moved into a hotel in Nanking, to look on while his troops murdered over 100,000 defenseless military and civilian prisoners there. It was the first act of genocide in World War II, but when the uncle returned to Tokyo, Hirohito went out of his way to confer decorations and honors upon him.

Earlier still, in 1931–32, Hirohito had sanctioned the conquest of Manchuria. Again it was said afterward that he had acted reluctantly, but the records of the time simply indicated that he had been reluctant to have the full responsibility for the venture borne by the sacred institution of the Throne which he represented. Again, when the conquest was complete, he honored the conquerors, making the general in charge his chief aide-de-camp and military advisor.

From such obvious facts, I concluded that there was a great disparity between the deeds of Emperor Hirohito and the words which were said about him in later years. I reviewed and reconsidered all the notes I had taken in my reading of source documents, and I became convinced that the modern history of Japan, as presented since World War II, was a skillfully contrived illusion fabricated late in the war, partly by counter-intelligence specialists in the General Staff and partly by high-ranking palace courtiers.

The logic of the Japanese cover story was so topsy-turvy that sequels were sometimes cited as causes for what had already happened. Again and again the documents of the time showed that events attributed to chance or spontaneous mass action had actually been discussed at high official levels months or years in advance. The Emperor's chief political advisor, the lord privy seal, routinely named the next prime minister and described "his mission" weeks or months before the onset of the Cabinet crisis which would topple the prime minister already in office. Conversations were even on record in which the lord privy seal correctly foresaw the personnel and accomplishments of the next two governments.

I began to meet my Japanese contacts with a fresh attitude, interviewing them informally and asking for flesh-and-blood details of the countless stick figures who scurried across the pages of the testimony, the diaries, the reminiscences which I had read. I was rewarded with responsive answers, still cautious and indirect, but now full of anecdote and illustration. The vignettes given to me were subtle and ironic, as fragile as butterfly wings, as difficult to pin down as the snide remarks of a consummate hostess. But I began to glimpse the real world inside Japan's closed prewar society.

It was a nightmare world in which everyone spoke politely in well-modulated voices while living with the secrecy and involuted double-thinking of eternal intrigue. The men in the limelight always represented more powerful figures in the shadow. In assessing the role a man played, his deeds had to be counted for more than his words and his associations and loyalties for more than his personal character. State policy was framed in back rooms behind back rooms and the people had no voice in it. Even the party politicians, even the great industrial magnates were usually out on the edges of the national web of string pulling and influence peddling. The masses were nothing more than a mob, swayed this way and that by a venal press and a system of public relations and rumor mongering which had been in use for more than a thousand years.

As my understanding of prewar Japanese society grew, I became increasingly uncomfortable in the Japanese society of 1966. I harbored blasphemous thoughts about the man who from 1926 to 1945 had been worshipped by all Japanese as a god. It did not ease my sense of dangerous knowledge to discover that most of the Japanese who befriended me in Kyoto had been World War II intelligence agents. Two of my best informants in Tokyo asked to have their final interviews with me surreptitiously in small out-of-the-way cafés where they would not be known. My mail from the United States showed signs of having been opened by the local postmaster. While my luggage lay awaiting shipment on a Kobe dock, two notebooks and a roll of film marked "Rape of Nanking" disappeared from one of my six book lockers.

When our ship cleared harbor, taking my family and me on the first leg of our journey home to the United States, I watched the receding coastline of Japan with mingled relief and regret: relief from the oppressive feeling that I was being watched; regret that the book I envisaged writing would not make me welcome again in the land of my birth.

I had with me eight thick loose-leaf folders of cards inscribed with the personnel records of 932 leading Japanese bureaucrats and military officers, 2,000 pages of closely scribbled notebooks, a hundred issues of various Japanese magazines, 60 volumes of Japanese diaries and reminiscences, and 240 hours of interviews and impressions on magnetic tape.

I added to this mass of material by interrupting our journey home for ten days in Singapore and five weeks in Australia. In Singapore I was able to read the complete files of a wartime newspaper, the *Syonan Times,* published by the Japanese occupation authorities in English. In Canberra, Australia, I was kindly given access to some World War II Australian civil intelligence reports; to the papers of the Far Eastern Commission, which was supposed to advise General Douglas MacArthur in the postwar administration of Japan; and to the memoranda and letters of Queensland's Chief Justice Sir William Webb who had presided over the eleven-nation Allied tribunal which had tried Japan's Class-A war criminals in Tokyo from 1946 to 1948. I was relieved to discover in the Canberra archives that at war's end Australian, New Zealand, and Chinese officials had all agreed that Emperor Hirohito was the master of Japan and should head any list of Japanese responsible for the war. They had later bowed to a decision by General MacArthur—a decision which I myself thought sensible—to use the Emperor for the rehabilitation of Japan rather than try him as a criminal under international law.

On return to my home in Connecticut, I began to assimilate and arrange the mountain of half digested information I had brought back with me from abroad. From my eight volumes of individual personnel records I distilled a large wall chart of the men who had occupied key posts in the Army, the Court, and the bureaucracy. From Japanese biographical dictionaries I drew up scores of pedigrees of aristocratic families.* From old Japanese newspapers and from 5,613 pages of diaries kept by the highest officials in the Japanese state, I compiled a day-by-day chronology of events, covering 8,125 days of the most intimate Japanese history. Gradually I learned to separate spear carriers from principals. Patterns emerged— factions and tongs which maintained consistent positions year after year and decade after decade. Countless "incidents" which had once seemed unfathomably Oriental began to make hard, rational sense. Everything fell into place and reinforced my simple perception of the obvious: that Hirohito had, indeed, been Emperor.

The picture of Hirohito which emerged from my evidence differed from the official portrait of biographers as a photographic negative from a photographic positive. By my account Hirohito was a formidable war leader: tireless, dedicated, meticulous, clever, and patient. He had inherited from his great-grandfather a mission, which was to rid Asia of white men. Since his people were reluctant and backward, he had skillfully manipulated them for twenty years before the war in order to prepare them psychologically and militarily for their task. By contrast the official portrait—in many ways less attractive—represented Hirohito as a cultured, secluded biologist who left the management of his realm to generals and admirals and devoted all his energy to puttering about with fungi and small wormlike marine organisms.

Skillful mythmaking, of which I had uncovered many examples in Imperial Court press releases, could account for the imprinting of a false image, but I was perplexed by the ease with which the true image had been obliterated. It was difficult for me to believe that an entire people, plus foreign observers, could suffer consistently from mass blindness. Could an Emperor really strut about naked while everyone, including envoys from other nations, admired the quality and refinement of his clothes? Apparently

---

* I discovered with wonderment that neither in Japanese nor English had a complete list ever been printed of the living members of the imperial family. Even during World War II, when Japanese were calling their Emperor a god and committing suicide for him by the legion, no Western analyst had traced the careers of the Japanese generals who were his uncles and cousins.

he could, for in 1967 I witnessed a convincing demonstration of the phenomenon.

In January of that year, as I neared the end of my researches, a small Tokyo publishing firm, Hara Shobo, came out with the memoranda of Japan's wartime Army Chief of Staff, General Sugiyama Hajime, as jotted down in his daybook between 1940 and 1944. Here was an unimpeachable handwritten source document by the highest military official in the Japanese state. Sugiyama had committed suicide in 1945, at the time of Japan's surrender, and had had no opportunity to dress up his notes in any way. Most of them were concerned with dull military details or duller militaristic cant. A few of them, however, were verbatim accounts of conversations with Hirohito. They revealed Hirohito asking detailed questions about military and economic planning in the months before Pearl Harbor. They directly refuted statements which General Douglas MacArthur said that Hirohito had made to him after the war, professing ignorance of all military and economic matters in 1941.

Most surprising, the *Sugiyama Memoranda* stated that in January 1941, eleven months before the outbreak of war with the United States, Hirohito had personally ordered a secret evaluation to be made of the feasibility of a surprise attack on Pearl Harbor. Previously Western historians had believed that Hirohito had known nothing of the surprise-attack plan until at least November 1941. The 1941 grand chamberlain, Admiral Suzuki Kantaro, was even on record stating flatly, after the war, that Hirohito had been ignorant of the Pearl Harbor plan until it had been already executed.

The *Sugiyama Memoranda* revealed that Hirohito had participated in the Pearl Harbor planning a full six months before any of his official military advisors were informed of it. Evidence taken before the Allied judges of the International Military Tribunal for the Far East, and verified by witnesses under oath and cross-examination, demonstrated conclusively that none of the "militarists" who were supposed to have dragged Hirohito to war knew of the Pearl Harbor plan until August 1941. General Tojo, the arch "militarist" who headed Japan's wartime Cabinet, was not told of the plan until November 1941.

This, then, was a major historical revelation. Its hypothetical equivalent in U.S. terms would be a newly discovered note in the handwriting of Secretary of War Henry L. Stimson asserting that in the summer of 1941 President Roosevelt had secretly ordered a study to be made of the possibility of keeping obsolescent battleships at conspicuously ill-protected moorings in Pearl Harbor in order to lure Japan into making an attack and providing an excuse for American entry into World War II.

I could imagine what a front-page sensation such a documentary discovery would create in the United States, and I watched with fascination the Japanese reaction to the publication of the *Sugiyama Memoranda*. The leading Japanese newspapers all noted, on back pages, that Chief of Staff

Sugiyama's papers had been published in two handsome volumes. But not one newspaper carried a review of the set or commented on it in any way. As a result U.S. newspapers never got the story, and Hirohito's personal part in the Pearl Harbor planning had not yet reached the pages of *The New York Times* as this book went to press in 1971.

The silence which greeted the *Sugiyama Memoranda* convinced me that the Japanese, even today, remain extraordinarily discreet in matters touching the Emperor, and that Western observers in Japan, beset as ever by linguistic and cultural confusions, can fail to notice anything that is not deliberately pointed out to them. To see this demonstrated erased a last doubt in my mind. It was the summer of 1967. I had just finished reviewing the last of the plots and assassinations of the 1930's and had satisfied myself that Hirohito had had a hand in many of them. I wrote finis to a 300,000-word rough draft which I had been writing of all that was new and problematic in my research. It was not a book but a legal brief which examined all the evidence available to me. It assured me that all events fitted my interpretation and that all the historic protagonists were consistently motivated.

I laid my rough draft aside for a month to consider its implications. The story that emerged from its densely packed pages was strange and new. It was unkind to both Japanese and Americans. More than half of my information had never before been reported in English. And the burden of it all was that Hirohito had not only led his nation into war by stamping military orders but, through his coterie, had also intimidated those who opposed him by conniving in bizarre Oriental intrigues, including religious frauds, blackmails, and assassinations.

I realized that it would be difficult for anyone to believe that what I had written was true when it was largely unknown to Western specialists on Japan and when much of it would be new even to well-informed Japanese. So many prior considerations had to be taken into account by the incredulous reader before he could suspend his disbelief. He had to know that ancient religious taboos still clung to the person of the Japanese Emperor; that until 1945 no Japanese plebeian ever dared utter the syllables *Hi-ro-hi-to;* that until 1945 Japanese commoners never looked at the Emperor except slyly from an almost prostrate position on the curb beside an imperial progress; that Japanese courtiers from time immemorial had been inventing artful stories to conceal the active participation of their masters in controversial affairs of state. The concept of god-king had passed out of memory in the West centuries ago, and Western observers in Japan had never had reason to put together all available scraps of information about the imperial family; they had readily accepted the conventional assertion that Hirohito was a ceremonial figurehead, for they had preconceptions about "constitutional monarchs" based on such figures as Queen Victoria. No firsthand records of day-to-day dealings with Hirohito had been published in Japan until 1966. And most important, General

Douglas MacArthur, in hopes of recasting Japanese character in an American mold, had decided in 1945 to use the Emperor and to whitewash him rather than depose and expose him.

It would take pages of particulars, I felt, to make others understand these bizarre circumstances, and I foresaw that my pages might be roundly abused before the general reader would have a chance to look at them. Only twenty-five years ago millions of Japanese had died with a prayer on their lips of *Banzai,* "May the Emperor live ten thousand years." Since then Japan in 1967 had passed West Germany in gross national product to become the third-ranking nation on earth.

Yet as late as 1961, when a Japanese magazine published a fantasy about a robber who broke into a palace and beheaded a fictional emperor, the publisher found himself terrorized for having committed lèse majesté. Hired "patriots" from one of the underworld gangs forced their way into his print shop and smashed up his presses. Then they went on to his home, shot one of his servants dead, and wounded his wife. The Grub Street scribbler who had written the fantasy disappeared. Reportedly he went underground and some say that he emigrated to Brazil.

Through no virtue of my own, I had happened to revisit Japan during a period of historical re-evaluation in which some of the first important papers of the Imperial Court were published. These cast a new light on the rest of the documentation, a light which was particularly illuminating to anyone like me, going over the whole mass of materials freshly at one time.

The re-evaluation—so I was told later by a senior Japanese diplomat—had been launched by Hirohito himself. In the fall of 1963, at a palace banquet in support of literature, Hirohito had suggested to the writers at his end of the table that it was time to overleap the trauma of Hiroshima and to begin re-creating the true spirit of Japan's prewar and wartime history. World War II no longer seemed the colossal blunder it had in 1946 but a positive piece of statesmanship which had hastened the complete industrialization of Japan. The year 1965 would be the twentieth anniversary of the end of that war, and 1966 would be the twenty-fifth anniversary of the beginning of that war.

The historical re-evaluation begun in Japan in 1965 was conducted with extreme circumspection and aimed mainly at the knowledgeable Japanese audience. I had to make its implications explicit for the American audience. I had to explain feelings and motives which Japanese took for granted—especially the feelings and motives of Emperor Hirohito. In so doing, I would have to enter dark corners of Hirohito's life wherein I would have to hunt down clues and rely on circumstantial, as well as verbal and documentary, evidence.

Moreover, since history is continuous, I would have to offer to fit my interpretation into the whole course of Japanese history. I could not possibly make myself as much of an authority on the years 1866 to 1911 as I was on the years 1931 to 1945, but I would have to say what I knew about those years because it had not been said before and because the burden of my book related as much to the nineteenth, the seventeenth, or the twenty-first centuries as it did to the twentieth.

Also, I would have to present Hirohito as the leader of a "conspiracy," a word which, through overuse and jingoism, had become universally suspect. The International Military Tribunal for the Far East had handed down a verdict of "conspiracy to wage aggressive war" against Japanese war leaders and had uncovered no less than eight important conspiracies which had directed the course of Japan between 1928 and 1936. Conspiracy had an old and honored place in Japanese culture. Each of Japan's territorial armies in prewar days had had a team of staff officers which was officially called "the plot section." I had added six conspiracies to the list compiled by the Allied judges and had connected them all with Hirohito's central, imperial-family conspiracy. Hirohito had worked with a minority, in secret, first to lead Japan to war with the West and then, in defeat, to obscure the record.

Resolutely I entitled my work *Japan's Imperial Conspiracy*. I set out to select the most pivotal events from my research and to bring them alive with light and color. Wherever I felt I had enough information to work with, I did my best to make the reader feel that he was present. If I knew from my own experience what a landscape looked like at a certain time of year, I re-created that landscape if it came up at that time of year. If I knew what brand of cigarettes a man smoked, I mentioned it when I reported that he was smoking. If I knew a man cracked his knuckles idiosyncratically, I took the liberty of saying that he cracked his knuckles at this or that juncture.

I also used certain rhetorical devices which may irritate some readers already familiar with Japan. To overcome the difficulty and confusion of Japanese names I tagged some of them, repetitively, with touchstone adjectives. I did this because I found that even specialists often lost track of minor characters in the cast of Japanese history and kept in mind no over-all picture of their careers.

Between 1967 and 1970, while I worked on my final manuscript, I received much help from Japanese who came to see me. I was honored by visits from an influential banker's son, a leading publicist, an in-law of the Japanese imperial family, and an important diplomat. All of these men were friends or children of Hirohito's closest advisors. Passing through New York, they breathed the freedom—or the social informality—of the United States and spoke much more candidly than even the best of my informants in Japan. Only one of them volunteered information to me, but I now had detailed knowledge of many of their relatives and close associates, and I was able to draw them out. In response to trivial questions they unburdened themselves.

They gave me many of the grace notes I needed and, more important, they assured me that I was right. They corroborated my interpretation and encouraged me to think that I was presenting a true view of an Oriental ideology during an era when Americans were preoccupied with European communism and fascism.

It seems to me that Western historians have gone too far in portraying the Japanese as creatures of mass hysteria. Japan's economic record belies such a patronizing attitude. Only a century ago, in 1868, Japan's economic development resembled that of England when Henry VII came to the throne in 1485. The transformation of the last century was not wrought by inscrutable madmen but by a most industrious and intelligent people. I have had the awe and pleasure of knowing them all my life. It is a basic premise of this book that Japanese leaders—and their Western counterparts also—have been very smart men.

When Allied armies overran Germany in 1945, they captured millions of pages of the highest state papers. By contrast, when the Allies began their negotiated Occupation of Japan, the war had been over for two weeks and the only papers of any consequence which fell into American hands were placed there voluntarily by the Japanese themselves. The minutes of the meetings of Imperial Headquarters, presided over by Emperor Hirohito in his palace from 1937 to 1945, had all, it was said, been incinerated. So had most of the files of the Army General Staff, the Navy General Staff, and the secret police.

In my bibliography and source notes I have cited about a thousand books and documents which have provided me with items of information. Most of them, however, have given me a single detail or a single insight. Only a score of them have been extensively helpful and all but two of that score were not published in Japan until after 1960.

The only significant primary source documents turned over after the war to Allied Occupation authorities were diaries. Every Japanese in an important position kept a record of his official life in order to defend himself against the threats of blackmail or charges of irresponsibility which were likely to be made against him in the normal course of Japanese politics. All such daybooks were of course written with an eye to the public and to posterity. They might at any time be seized and produced in chambers by the secret police. They might in later years be published by impecunious grandchildren. And in the case of palace officials they might always be requisitioned for research or recreational reading by Hirohito himself.

Two of these carefully written journals, by men in the highest policy-making circles, were placed in American hands during the first two years of the Occupation. One was the *Kido Diary,* 1930–1945, written by Marquis Kido Koichi who had been lord privy seal and chief civilian advisor to Hirohito in the years 1940–1945. Less than a tenth of it, selected for point-making reasons, was translated either by the prosecution or the defense and placed in evidence at the International Military Tribunal for the Far East. Another nine tenths of the diary, as it is presently available, were not released until 1966 when they were published by Tokyo University Press. Even in this form the diary still seems to be incomplete because the most eventful days in the period which it covers are filled with the notation "nothing to report." *

The second journal made available to the American Occupation forces has come to be known as the "Saionji-Harada Memoirs." These were ostensibly the notes of Japan's most eminent liberal statesman, Prince Saionji, who had the duty, until November 1940, when he was ninety-one years old, of recommending to the Emperor the name of the man to appoint as prime minister in each successive Japanese government. Actually the memoirs were composed by Saionji's political secretary, Baron Harada, a sly gossip and opportunist who acted as agent for Hirohito in Saionji's staff.

An English version of the Saionji-Harada memoirs was produced in twenty-five mimeographed volumes by a volunteer Japanese task force in 1946–47 for use by the defense at the International Military Tribunal. The translation was stylish but inexact. For instance, at several critical junctures it converted the lord privy seal or *naidaijin,* the Emperor's chief civilian advisor, into the home minister or *naimudaijin,* a Cabinet bureaucrat in charge of police.

The Japanese text of the Saionji-Harada memoirs was published in eight volumes in Tokyo between 1952 and 1956 under the title *Saionji-ko to Seikyoku* [Prince Saionji and the Political Situation]. The British scholar who undertook to read it on behalf of the Western academic community apparently glanced at it and then wrote two books which quote exclusively from the careless translation prepared for the defense section of the International Military Tribunal.

In 1956 a ninth volume of the Saionji-Harada memoirs was published in Japan, in a limited edition. It contained the notes of Harada on which the other eight volumes were based, and an index which made the other eight volumes useful. So far as I have been able to determine, few Western scholars except myself have made much use of this expensive, difficult-to-obtain ninth volume.

Twenty-two years after the end of the war, in 1967, two more important journals were published in Japan: the diaries of General Honjo Shigeru, written during the years 1931–1936 in which he led the conquest of Manchuria and in which he served Hirohito as chief aide-de-camp and military

---

* As far as I have been able to discover, no one except for myself has read the complete text of the diary critically, comparing the terse entries with events recorded elsewhere. A graduate student of Japanese ancestry at the University of Washington has translated the previously untranslated bulk of the diary and his gloss, which I have not seen, will no doubt be put out by a university press in due course.

advisor; and the memoranda of General Sugiyama Hajime, written in the years 1940–1944 when he served at Imperial Headquarters as chief of the Japanese Army General Staff. Until 1970, neither of these primary source documents had been digested by Western scholars of Japan or much cited in Western scholarly journals. Yet they contained the stories of Hirohito's military advisors and greatly supplemented the two journals of the civilian advisors, Kido and Harada, which had been partially available since 1946.

These four diaries, of Kido, Harada, Honjo, and Sugiyama, contain more than half of all that is known of the highest deliberations of Japanese leaders in the years 1930–1945.

In addition I have reviewed most of the police files, personnel records, position papers, and military orders which were captured by American intelligence officers during the opening months of the Occupation. I have been through the 200,000-odd pages of testimony, proceedings, and collateral documentation put in the record by Japanese and Western sources at the International Military Tribunal for the Far East. I have scanned bushel-baskets of subsidiary exposés and reminiscences published in Tokyo in the late 1940's and early 1950's.

With more care, I have also examined some 300,000 pages of memoirs, journalistic reconstructions, and "lost" documents in anthologies which have emerged from Japanese presses since the end of the Occupation in 1952. I have found several thousand pages of this material worth reading word by word, especially the journalistic reconstructions based on extensive interviewing. I believe that the best of the Japanese secondary evidence stems from highly authoritative sources and is more honest than some of the primary material.* In addition there is a wealth of information available verbally from old men of importance who survived the war and are still alive.

I made wary but exhaustive use of all these materials. In handling them I gave high credence to chronology and cause-and-effect logic. I relied heavily on the indisputable record of deeds done by Japanese, as recorded in back files of newspapers, and of positions occupied by Japanese, as recorded in personnel records.† The color and much of the explanation with which I filled in my narrative were supplied almost entirely by word of mouth. Some of my informants pledged me to nonattribution, some did not. A few

---

* In particular the two volumes of reminiscences by retired Major General Ohtani Keijiro of the secret police; a short tract privately printed by the Empress's brother; an as yet unpublished 5,000-page opus by retired Lieutenant General Tanaka Taka-yoshi of Army Intelligence; and the volumes of Murofushi Tetsuro, Takahashi Masae, Fujishima Taisuke, Shimada Toshihiko, Hata Ikuhiko, Oyake Soichi, Agawa Hiroshi, and Kuroda Hisata.

† Most of the latter were kindly made available to me by Hata Ikuhiko, a civilian employee of Japan's modern Self-Defense Forces. Mr. Hata is the author of *Nichu Senso-shi,* The History of the Sino-Japanese War, and of *Gun Fuashizumu Undoshi,* The Record of Fascist Movements in the Japanese Army.

asked me to conceal the fact that I had interviewed them at all. I have kept these promises because of the danger which still exists for those who speak too freely in modern Japan.

There was one extraordinary Japanese aristocrat in his sixties who said to me, in English: "Why, I believe you are leading me on. What do you wish me to say? I knew Hirohito as a boy. He was a romantic warlike idiot then and I suppose he still is. But I have been out of things for several decades. I do not wish to be disturbed in my old age. If you quote me by name I shall deny that I ever met you."

Strict historians do not approve of using information from privileged sources. In dealing with American or European history they are certainly right in so feeling. For Japanese history—and perhaps for all Asiatic history—a case can be made for greater latitude. In most parts of the Orient, the very idea of a public record does not exist. To a far greater degree than in the West, state records belong to the statesmen who made them. The tradition of a free press has no deep roots. Even the written contract in financial transactions has only begun to supplant the verbal agreement based on word of honor.

However, I think that any thoughtful scholar who takes the trouble to go through the source notes at the end of this volume will find that the essential facts of the story which I have told come from written diaries, memoranda, and memoirs. I have relied on privileged word-of-mouth sources primarily to corroborate my assessments of the facts, characters, and motives revealed in the primary source documents and to re-create as closely as possible the physical settings in which events took place. I have invented nothing but I have put together much. And I trust that from total immersion in the day-to-day, week-by-week record of Japanese history, I have gained an understanding of circumstances and nuances which has enabled me to shed more insights than I have committed errors.

So many people have helped me with this book that I cannot list them without fear of forgetting a few. I am especially grateful to the librarians of the Beinecke and Law School libraries at Yale, of the Doshisha and Kyoto University libraries in Kyoto, of the War Memorial Museum in Canberra, Australia, of the Fergusson Library in Stamford, Connecticut, and of the U.S. National Archives' War Documents Center in Alexandria, Virginia. There I would like to call attention to Thomas E. Hohmann as the most knowledgeable, unbureaucratic expediter of information flow whom I have ever encountered inside or outside of government.

Kitagawa Hiroshi, Koizumi Shinzo, Henry R. Luce, Douglas MacArthur II, and my father were all particularly helpful in opening doors to me in Japan. Historian Hata Ikuhiko made available to me personal notebooks which he had compiled over a fifteen-year period. Retired Major General Tanaka Takayoshi allowed me to read part of his 5,000-page unpublished memoirs. Aso Shigeru, Lester Brooks, Don Brown, Robert J. C. Butow,

Chiang Kai-shek, Otis Cary, William Craig, James Crowley, Grace Fox, Fujimoto Kazu, Fujisawa Shigezo, Frank Gibney, Giga Soichiro, Hashimoto Hirotoshi, Arthur Hummel, Inoki Masamichi, Inoue Ichiro, Kajiura Ginjiro, Kagami Mideo, Kawamata Yoshiya, Kobayashi Yoshiaki, Kotani Hidejiro, Matsumoto Shigeharu, Morishige Yoshi, Walter Nichols, R. K. Ochiai, Ogawa Masao, Okumiya Masatake, Oya Soichi, Edwin O. Reischauer, Sato Yoshijiro, Osamu Shimizu, Roy Smith, Sung Yueh, Tachibana Yoshimori, Takahashi Shun, Takata Ichitaro, Takata Motosaburo, Tanaka Katsumi, Tsurumi Shunsuke, Uemura Kazuhiko, Elizabeth Gray Vining, William P. Woodard, Chitoshi Yanaga, all have given me their time and their kind and courteous attention. I am indebted to Hillel Black, John Cuneo, Alan Fraser, Lawrence Hughes, Peter Leavitt, Elizabeth Lucas, and Mary Newman for invaluable help and criticism in reducing my manuscript to its present form. My dear wife has lived with me and typed each of these pages more than once in the last six years. Finally I wish to express particular gratitude to a Buddhist priest and an innkeeper in Kyoto, to four retired Japanese generals, to three former members of Hirohito's Court, and to three second-generation members of Hirohito's circle of intimates without whose information this book would have been stillborn.

In writing the names of Japanese citizens, I have followed the native Oriental custom: that is, last name first and first name last. To do otherwise would be inconsistent, for the ruler of Republican China is known as Chiang Kai-shek, and it would be confusing to Westernize the order of his names by calling him Kai-shek Chiang. In dealing with Westerners, modern Japanese usually reverse the order of their names whereas most modern Chinese do not. In these pages the reader is asked to remember that family names are given first and personal names second according to the familiar bureaucratic formula, "Doe, John."

In daily life the second or personal name of a Japanese male adult is almost never spoken. Even good friends do not address one another as Jim or Harry but always as Mr. Jones or Mr. Smith. Moreover, the ideographs in which given names are written often have exotic pronunciations. In every case there is a right reading which was used by the man's parents when he was a child, but even the man's close associates in later life may not know what it is. The notorious World War II prime minister, Tojo, for instance, was listed for years in *Who's Who in Japan* as Tojo Eiki when in fact his name was Tojo Hideki. Many of these misreadings have become permanent fixtures of the historical record as it is set down in English. In the chapter which follows, for example, Lieutenant General Tada Hayao is known in most other books as Tada Shun. Throughout this work I have tried to give people the names their mothers actually called them. I have undoubtedly made or perpetuated some mistakes, for which I apologize in advance both to readers and to mothers.

Finally, I dedicate this work to a rather simple, old-fashioned proposition: that history is not determined by blind economic and demographic forces; that the much maligned masses of countries play little part in it; that the responsibility for it belongs primarily to a few willful individuals who take upon themselves the professional duties of government. Except in tiny city-state democracies or in broken-down societies, prey to anarchy, the people do not make policy. The leaders who do make policy are, I believe, enthusiastic patriots who come to identify their personal advancement with the national interest. They are open to persuasion only when they hope to get the best of a bargain or when they fear that their leadership position may be destroyed before the eyes of their followers. My story deals with leaders who recognize such homely truths; with leaders who look upon themselves as institutions rather than individuals; with leaders of a society which has a longer record of uninterrupted successful domestic political development than any other in the world.

PART ONE

VENGEANCE OF WAR

" 'The Emperor is sacred and inviolable' (Constitution, Art. 3). He cannot be removed from the Throne for any reason, and he is not to be held responsible for over-stepping the limitations of law in the exercise of his sovereignty. All responsibility for the exercise of his sovereignty must be assumed by the Ministers of State and other organs. Thus, no criticism can be directed against the Emperor, but only against the instruments of his sovereignty. Laws are not to be applied to the Emperor as a principle especially criminal laws, for no court of law can try the Emperor himself and he is not subject to any law."

Page 117, *The Japan Yearbook 1944–45*, published by The Foreign Affairs Association of Japan, an organization financed by the Japanese government.

1

RAPE OF NANKING

SHRINE OF REMORSE

High on a green hillside of gnarled pines and weathered rocks, some fifty miles down the coast from Tokyo, stands a more-than-life-sized statue of Kanon, the Buddhist goddess of mercy. She looks southwest toward China across the blue waters and white sands of Atami, a beach resort celebrated for its baths and its courtesans. She is made crudely of clay baked to a mud-gold glaze. Half of the clay is native Japanese soil; the other half came in sacks from China in 1938, dug from the banks of the great muddy Yangtze River. If you scramble up the rock on which the goddess stands and work your way around her pedestal, you find a four-foot clearing in the underbrush immediately behind her flowing robes. There, where they cannot be seen from the path below, seven slender boards of graying unpainted wood are stuck in the earth, each with a name lettered on it in black Japanese characters: Tojo Hideki, Itagaki Seishiro, Doihara Kenji, Hirota Koki, Kimura Heitaro, Muto Akira, Matsui Iwane. They are the names of the men hanged by the Allies after a two-year trial in 1948 as the Hitlers, Himmlers, and Goerings of Japan.

Nearby, on a terrace poised over the sparkling bay a thousand feet below, stands a small shrine. Its eaves are hung with ropes of colored paper—token presents to the spirits of the dead. On a lectern, at one end of the prayer rail that runs across the shrine entrance, is a guest book. Members of the families of each of the hanged men on the hill have signed it every month or two since the early 1950's. Inside the shrine, mementos of Japanese war dead hang on one wall and of Chinese war dead on the opposite wall. Between them at the altar, on most days most of the time, kneels the shrine priestess chanting prayers and lamentations. As she chants she

3

strikes musically on a polished stick and weeps. She says, if you speak to her, that it is her duty to weep and that she has been weeping since 1938.

Beside the shrine is a tea pavilion for pilgrims who need to catch their breath after the steep climb up the hillside. It is hung with testimonials to the ideal of Pan-Asianism and with posterlike paintings of Chinese and Japanese toiling together in harmony. Along one wall of the tea pavilion runs a minutely detailed panorama of the monumental roofs and towers which once adorned the skyline of the Chinese city of Nanking. It was for Nanking that the priestess first began to weep—Nanking which for a decade in the 1920's and 1930's was the showpiece capital of China, Nanking where a brief experiment in republicanism intervened between the totalitarian eras of old Imperial Peking and new Communist Peking. The priestess weeps for Nanking because she is engaged to do so by her family, the Matsuis, on whose estate the shrine stands; because the name of her kinsman, General Matsui Iwane, is one of those on the markers up on the rock behind the goddess of mercy; because it was for Nanking that Matsui was hanged in 1948.

In 1937 Matsui's army, in a brilliant, brutal four-month campaign, smashed its way 170 miles up the Yangtze Valley from the port of Shanghai, captured Nanking, and subjected it to six weeks of gruesome, graduated terror. Between 100,000 and 200,000 Chinese were executed. At least 5,000 women, girls, and children were raped before they were killed. Everything of value in the city was pillaged and whole sections of it were systematically put to the torch. Before Warsaw, before Buchenwald, Nanking was the great atrocity. It convinced many Americans, for the first time, that the governments siding with Germany in the Anti-Comintern Pact were genuinely evil.

The goddess of mercy on the slope above Atami, built half of Yangtze and half of native clay, was already standing, in 1938, in acknowledgment of Japan's national guilt for Nanking. A decade later, after many more atrocities and the war with the United States, the markers for the seven hanged men were added secretly behind the statue. The markers were put there not to condemn the shades of the men to eternal penitence for Nanking but rather to signify that Japan's war criminals, like the Chinese murdered in Nanking, were considered sacrificial victims. In the eyes of most Japanese, they were not guilty in the sense charged by the international tribunal of jurists which had sentenced them. They were not evil conspirators who had forced Japan to war, not mad individualists like Hitler and his cohorts, but loyal servants of the Emperor, responsible officials of the government, symbolic scapegoats elected from the ruling circle to satisfy the requirements of Western justice. As such they deserved the mercy of the goddess and the special prayers of all those pilgrims who felt that they too had participated in the nation's crime.

Although Japanese almost unanimously condemn the sentence handed down at the war crimes trial in 1948, they do not therefore maintain that Japan went to war by majority choice or even that Japanese soldiers raped and killed without official encouragement. They say only that Japan is a collective family society and that it is impossible for any seven men to have been mainly responsible. They say that Japan is a hierarchic society and that none of the seven men hanged came from the topmost layers of the aristocracy. They say that Emperor Hirohito declared the war and that he is still the master of the Japanese nation. The priestess at Atami says that her shrine is a reminder "to the Emperor and the great vassals of the debt which they owe the people and the dead."

"It is not only for the former time," she explains, "but for today and the time to come that I remain at my post in prayer."

JAPAN AND CHINA

In 1937, when the crime of Nanking did not yet burden the Japanese conscience, Japan had been wresting territory from China for over forty years: the island of Taiwan and the peninsula of Korea in 1896; a New-England-sized piece of Manchuria in 1931; the remaining Texas-sized piece of Manchuria in 1932; the Kansas-sized province of Jehol in 1933; and Montana-sized Inner Mongolia in 1935. Then in the summer of 1937 Japan went on to launch a full-scale invasion of all that was left of China, the populous heartland of some 500 million souls extending from the Great Wall in the north to the borders of Indochina, Siam, Burma, and India to the south. First, in July, Japanese armies captured Peking, the old imperial capital in North China. Then, in August, Japanese forces began to fight at the mouth of the Yangtze River for the huge port of Shanghai which laid claim, with New York, London, and Tokyo, to being the largest city in the world. Shanghai was the doorway to Central China. Once unlocked, it would open an easy passage to Nanking, the Chinese capital, which lay 170 miles inland up the Yangtze River.

Ostensibly the war with China began because a Japanese private left his unit for a few minutes while he went into the bushes to urinate. While he was gone his comrades heard shooting. They were men of the Japanese regiment garrisoned by treaty in the northern Chinese city of Tientsin. They were out on night maneuvers near the ancient Marco Polo Bridge outside Peking.[1] Their commander said, "I heard Chinese Communist shots"— and ordered a roll call. Finding that the soldier who was urinating did not answer the roll call, the commander advanced on the Chinese fort at one end of the Marco Polo Bridge and demanded that it open its gates so that the Japanese could search it for their missing comrade. When the Chinese

[1] A bridge decorated with stone lions which the Venetian traveler, six hundred and fifty years earlier, had called "unequaled by any other in the world."

commander refused, the Japanese commander started shelling the fort. The absent soldier had long since rejoined his battalion, but the war had begun.

Although two million Chinese were to die in it and one million Japanese were to fight in it, the Japanese government insisted, throughout the eight years that it lasted, on calling the war the "China Incident." To this day, some Western historians maintain that it really was an incident, beginning in an accidental brush between Chinese and Japanese troops and escalating into a major conflict as a matter of military honor on both sides. In reality Emperor Hirohito of Japan had directed his General Staff to plan the war in early 1935. In March of 1936, still more than a year before the war broke out, Hirohito reviewed the plans which had been made. They were so detailed that they included even a description of the provocation which would be staged at the Marco Polo Bridge.

In the inner circles of Japanese government, the war was a controversial issue from the moment it was first planned. It was opposed, in particular, by the Japanese Army. A majority of the officers in the General Staff wanted to fight Russia, not China. The most zealous of them sought to change Hirohito's views by supporting an insurrection of junior officers in the streets of Tokyo in February of 1936. Hirohito refused to be swayed. Exercising his full powers as commander-in-chief, national high priest, and divine descendant of the sun goddess, he put down the insurrection and dismissed from the Army the ringleaders of the Strike-North or Fight-Russia faction.

Hirohito insisted on fighting China not because he bore any animosity toward the Chinese but because war with China had become a necessary part of the national program which he had inherited from his grandfather and great-grandfather. After Commodore Perry of the United States in 1853 had forced Japan at gun point to open her ports to Western commerce and settlement, Hirohito's great-grandfather had sworn an oath with his great vassals. The "redheaded barbarians" must be driven from Japan's sacred soil and Japan must "expand overseas" in order to create a buffer zone which would prevent any further profanation.

By the 1920's, Hirohito and his own great vassals had decided that the national program could not be fulfilled until Japan had added the East Indies to her empire. Except in the East Indies there was no adequate source of petroleum in Asia. And without petroleum for ships and airplanes, Japan could not hope to keep the "barbarians" at bay. To control the East Indies Japan needed ports and staging areas along the South China coast.

In the early 1930's Chiang Kai-shek, the ruler of China and a former protégé of Japan, ceased to co-operate with Hirohito. Like the Japanese Army, he insisted that the first enemy of Asian traditionalists was Russia and communism. It followed as the night the day that the necessary staging areas and dock facilities in southern China must be taken by force. At first

Hirohito and his intimates thought to bring Chiang Kai-shek to reason by only threatening war. But in December of 1936, on a visit to a town in western China, Chiang Kai-shek was kidnapped by a group of his own soldiers. As a condition for his release, Chiang agreed to stand up to Japan and grant the Japanese no more concessions.

When the urinating soldier disappeared and Japan began pouring troops into North China, Chiang held to the political pledge he had made to his kidnappers and refused Hirohito's offered terms of peace. When Japan extended the fighting from the Peking area in North China to Shanghai in Central China, Chiang committed his best divisions to an all-out defense of Shanghai. At that point Hirohito and his advisors decided to make China get rid of Chiang Kai-shek and accept a more accommodating leader. The capture of Nanking was planned in the innermost recesses of the Imperial Palace in Tokyo to bring about Chiang's ouster.

MATSUI'S COMMAND

The eerie arrangements for the rape of Nanking began to be made on August 15, 1937. On that day General Matsui Iwane, the kinsman of the weeping priestess at the shrine for war criminals in Atami, the man who would go down in history as "the butcher of Nanking," was summoned by Emperor Hirohito to the Imperial Palace in Tokyo. Matsui's official car approached the great moat from the southwest. Beyond it rose a massive, mortarless, fifty-foot wall of gray granite erected in the sixteenth century. Atop the battlements grew pine trees. The corners of the tile-and-copper roofs on the white watchtowers curved up at their tips like wings about to fly. Beyond could be seen the crowns of giant hardwoods in the Emperor's private park, the Fukiage Gardens. There in a landscape of trees and rocks and ponds—perhaps the most carefully tended garden in the world—rambled the one-story buildings of unpainted weathered wood in which Emperor Hirohito lived. General Matsui had never seen them at close quarters. He had been no farther into the Inner Palace than the courtyard of white pebbles and the ghostly white wood Shrine of the Sacred Mirror where Hirohito worshipped his ancestors. Few but servants and members of the imperial family went farther.

Matsui's car threaded its way between the office buildings of government ministries on his right and the southwest wall of the palace on his left. Rounding the southernmost corner of the wall he crossed through Cherry Field Gate into the imperial public gardens. Thence across the moat, through Foot-of-the-Slope Gate, he arrived at the cluster of office buildings where clerks of the Imperial Household Ministry toiled over investment of the Emperor's hundred-million-dollar private fortune. Outside the office of the imperial aides-de-camp, Matsui alighted and saluted a fellow officer, an aide, who would lead him into the Imperial Presence. His samurai sword knocking against his ankle, Matsui followed the aide through a checker-board of raked pebble courtyards, miniature gardens of dwarfed trees, and sundry outbuildings. Some of these unpretentious palace shacks were only kitchens; others were tiny research centers and libraries, the repositories of imperial family codes, genealogies, and contracts.

Emerging once more into open park, Matsui and the Emperor's aide passed the sprawling banquet hall and Privy Council chamber and came to the east entrance of the Outer Palace reserved for ceremonial functions. Here, a quarter of a mile from Hirohito's residence and from the Western-style study where he did most of his paper work, were the official audience chambers and anterooms in which Japanese history was, if not made, at least formalized.

General Matsui mounted a flight of stone steps, passed through a quiet reception area of muted gold screens and coffered ceilings, marched down a plain straight corridor, and stiffly saluted the Emperor's chief aide-de-camp who stood at the door of the Emperor's audience chamber. In accordance with ancient custom, Matsui untied his ancestral samurai sword and handed it to his guide, the junior aide, to keep for him while he was in the Emperor's presence. Then, he strode forward into the magnificent audience chamber, the Phoenix Hall. It was so named for the motif of fiery mythological birds which could be picked out everywhere in the par-quet, brocade, lacquer, chased silver, and carved wood of its floors, walls, and ceilings.

The Phoenix Hall was empty. Matsui bowed double and remained bow-ing while he waited for Emperor Hirohito to show himself. In this room Hirohito was a god-king who could make no mistakes. In this room Hiro-hito never exercised the absolute power he was acknowledged to possess. In this room Hirohito acted only on the advice of his advisors. Beside Matsui bowed the chief aide-de-camp, waiting to advise.

Matsui had been sounded out by the chief aide-de-camp the previous day and knew that Hirohito was about to offer him a command in China. It was a great honor for him to be reactivated from the reserve for such an appointment. It was especially gratifying to him because he was a pro-ponent of friendship with China. Only two months ago he had been hatching subversive plots to prevent an all-out war with China. He did not know it, but a secret-police report to that effect had recently crossed the Emperor's desk.[2] Two years ago, in August of 1933, when Matsui had first heard about the proposed conquest of China, he had asked to be retired from active Army command and had gone on a tour of Asiatic capitals seeking leaders who would support his personal dream of a united Asia.

---

[2] His fellow conspirator, according to the secret-police report, was General Honjo Shigeru who will be met with in the pages that follow as the conqueror of Manchuria, then as the Emperor's chief aide-de-camp, then as a sympathizer with the Army rebels who tried unsuccessfully in 1936 to change the Emperor's mind.

In Peking, he had tried vainly to establish a local branch of the *Toa Renmei* or East Asia League, a society which he had helped to found in Japan two years earlier.

Now that war between China and Japan was a reality, Matsui felt compelled, out of patriotism, to change his line somewhat. For the past month, in his public speeches for the East Asia League, he had been advocating a bold drive up the Yangtze River on Nanking, the Chinese capital. Swift capture of Nanking, he said, followed by humane occupation policies and an honest municipal administration, would persuade the Chinese masses to forsake Chiang Kai-shek and throw in their lot with the leaders of Japan.

That Hirohito, knowing Matsui's convictions, should be giving him a command in China was a good sign—a sign, perhaps, that Hirohito was beginning to understand the advantages of a negotiated settlement with China. Matsui would have felt happier, however, if his impending audience with the Emperor had been called in the concrete Imperial Library on the fringe of the Inner Palace. There in his workroom Hirohito was acknowledged to be a man and fallible. There he talked to other men. There he expressed opinions and invited discussion. Here in the magnificent Phoenix Hall he usually uttered only predictable formulas in the high-pitched official voice belonging to his position as national Shinto high priest.

As a devout Buddhist, the sixth son of a wealthy scholar of Chinese classics, Matsui paid only lip service to the state religion of Shinto ancestor worship. This bowing and waiting in the August heat made him feel older than his sixty years. After all, he was not a well man. His weight was down to one hundred pounds and that was too little even for his slight, five-foot frame. His medal-encrusted full-dress uniform stifled him. The humiliating tics in his right face and arm began to work uncontrollably. He felt as if one of his fevers might be coming on. His mind drifted. He entertained a brief vision of East Asia awakening under benevolent Japanese leadership—and felt somewhat better.

Suddenly the Emperor was present. With words of extraordinary solicitude he begged Matsui to stand at ease and come forward. He regretted that he had kept the general waiting and asked him how he was recuperating from his tuberculosis. Matsui straightened and marched unsteadily ahead. He saw his thirty-seven-year-old monarch standing before him in a plain unadorned khaki uniform, rumpled and slightly sweat-stained but buttoned to the neck. Hirohito had not been seen out of military uniform, now, for a year and a half.

Before Matsui had begun to answer the Emperor's question about his health, the chief aide-de-camp interrupted to remind Hirohito of his next appointment. Hirohito nodded and told Matsui that the latest flare-up of fighting in the port city of Shanghai, the gateway to Nanking, had reached a critical juncture. Hirohito had decided to dispatch a relief force of two divisions to assist the Marine garrison which was endeavoring to protect

Japanese property in the port. He understood, he said, that General Matsui would be willing to lead such an expedition.

Matsui bowed low and, still feeling faint, began to explain the honor that he felt and also the convictions that he held as to the enlightened methods which must be used in bringing the Chinese over to the Japanese cause. Hirohito nodded approvingly and unrolled an official scroll of rice-paper parchment. At Matsui's first pause, the Emperor began to read in his high-pitched official voice. At a nudge from the chief aide-de-camp Matsui knelt. Hirohito proclaimed him commander-in-chief of Japanese forces in Central China and bestowed upon him a baton symbolic of his new command.

Matsui might have reflected that a retired general in his state of health, with his nervous frailties and somewhat mystic convictions, was an extraordinary choice for the duty which Hirohito had conferred upon him. Matsui, however, was in a daze. A few moments later he found himself riding out of the palace grounds sharing a car with the highest ranking of Hirohito's hereditary counselors, the lanky, cynical, effete Prince Konoye. At forty-six, after seventeen years as Hirohito's chief back-room crony, Prince Konoye had finally been appointed by Hirohito, just two months previously, as the nation's constitutional figurehead, the prime minister.

"There is no solution," said little General Matsui to Konoye in the car, "except to break the power of Chiang Kai-shek by capturing Nanking. That is what I must do."

At a farewell dinner given by his fellow directors of the East Asia League on the eve of his departure for China two days later, General Matsui explained, "I am going to the front not to fight an enemy but in the state of mind of one who sets out to pacify his brother."

MIRED IN SHANGHAI

As Japanese Intelligence well knew, Matsui would have a hard time of it. Chiang Kai-shek had saved his best troops from commitment in the war in North China and was pouring them into the action in Central China at Shanghai. Ordinary tactical considerations were complicated by the fact that Shanghai was the world's most cosmopolitan city. The United States, Great Britain, and France all maintained military garrisons there in addition to the Japanese and Chinese. English clubs, American hotels, French cafés, Russian bakeries, German rathskellers, and Japanese geisha houses, together with branch offices of all the largest commercial concerns on earth, rubbed walls with opium dens and brothels—the unparalleled poverty of China's worst slums.

When Matsui received his orders from Emperor Hirohito, the Japanese Marines stationed in Shanghai were fighting for their lives. Chiang Kai-shek's troops outnumbered the Marines ten to one and had collectively about half the fire power of the Marines. A Japanese fleet of destroyers, cruisers, and battleships lay out in the mouth of the Yangtze River pouring shells into the Chinese rear. A tiny Chinese air force, commanded by Madame Chiang Kai-shek, was doing its best to sink the Japanese fleet with ten- and twenty-pound bombs. A minority of the Chinese pilots had been trained in America and were harassing the Japanese fleet effectively. A majority of the Chinese pilots had been trained by an Italian mission sent to Chiang Kai-shek by Mussolini. They were greatly confusing issues by dropping bombs near Western ships in the harbor and even on the crowded streets of the International Settlement. The pursuit planes of the Japanese Naval Air Force were fighting back effectively and gradually knocking the Chinese pilots out of the sky. The bombers of the Japanese Army Air Force were raining down explosives on the Chinese slums with a carnage that was appalling.

By international agreement Japan was pledged, in waging war, to avoid all deliberate killing of civilian noncombatants. Quaint as it may seem today, the bombing of civilians was a novelty, little practiced before except in Spain's civil war and in Mussolini's aggression in Ethiopia. Japan's violation of the convention had begun on August 14, 1937. On August 13 Emperor Hirohito's uncle, Prince Higashikuni, had been appointed chief of the Japanese Army Air Force. In aristocratic Japanese circles, Prince Higashikuni was known as one of the boldest and most unscrupulous of Hirohito's retinue—a man with a long, unsavory record of Army Intelligence work, blackmail, and religious fraud.

Into this complicated military, political, and diplomatic situation, little General Matsui brought some 35,000 fresh troops on August 23, eight days after his audience with Hirohito. As he was landing his men, a hidden Chinese artillery emplacement opened fire on the Japanese docks and killed several hundred Japanese before it was silenced. One of those who fell was a cousin of Hirohito's wife, Empress Nagako.[3] It was little General Matsui's first setback and a foretaste of things to come. Chiang Kai-shek's troops fought with a reckless courage that was unexpected. Against their human-sea tactics every step of advance was taken over a hill of corpses. After five days of action General Matsui had to be reinforced by another regular division and two reservist divisions which had been forehandedly reactivated months earlier.

Even with five divisions at his disposal, Matsui could not break out of the street fighting in Shanghai to drive upriver on Nanking. His progress was made doubly cautious by the presence of the English, American, and French forces nearby who were entrusted with protection of their own nationals in Shanghai's International Settlement and French Concession.

---

[3] Prince Fushimi Hiroyoshi. He recovered from his wounds but died of complications a year later. The Chinese exulted, for his father, a cousin once removed of Empress Nagako, was the chief of the Japanese Navy General Staff.

Japanese intellectuals in Army uniform who hoped to incite Western intervention caused almost daily incidents with Western Marines and policemen
along the borders of the various zones of foreign settlement. The Chinese
Air Force, in the same spirit, had already bombed two of the largest Western hotels and, with remarkable accuracy, had killed some forty-odd foreign
nationals.

General Matsui took extreme pains to keep his men from lobbing shells
over the foreign settlements or from taking tactical advantage of foreign
leasehold soil. Although he spoke pigeon English haltingly and pronounced
French unintelligibly, he became a favorite source of Western newsmen and
was invited to dinner at some of the best homes in the foreign community.
Little by little his five divisions advanced out of the Japanese sector and
moved on, street by street and barricade by barricade, into the native slums
to the west. But it took time, and when two months had passed, Matsui was
still battling his way out through the suburbs.

From the beginning Matsui's sluggish pace disappointed Hirohito and he
began to feel that he must take more personal charge of the war. Up to that
time he had supervised operations through two channels: over-all strategy
through his wife's great-uncle Prince Kanin, chief of the Army General
Staff; and detailed tactics through his cadre of aides-de-camp who shuttled
back and forth between the palace and the General Staff Operations office
three hundred yards from the palace wall. All divisional movement orders
had to be signed by him ultimately, and he liked to be in on tactical deliberations before they arrived on his desk as fully developed plans. He had
found in the past that unless he expressed his wishes early in every process
of policy formulation he could not object to a detail later without making
some underling lose face and tender his resignation.

In early September, Hirohito requested the creation of a Grand Imperial
Headquarters inside the palace at which he could supervise staff planning
personally. The membership and protocol of the headquarters, doing business as it would in the Imperial Presence—the presence of a god—naturally
took some working out, and the Imperial H.Q. did not become a reality
until mid-November. Hirohito insisted on it partly because of the stalemate
in Shanghai and partly because he had learned in early September that
some of his instructions to the General Staff were being filed and forgotten
in the in-basket of the chief of the Operations Department, Major General
Ishiwara Kanji.

Ishiwara was a brilliant strategist and had drawn up the plans for the
conquest of Manchuria six years earlier, but he was also an idealist. With
Matsui, the little tubercular general in Shanghai, he was co-founder of the
East Asia League, the *Toa Renmei*. The League espoused war in order to
create a united Asia in which Japanese would be equal partners with other
Asian nationals. It stood in contrast to the Asia Development Union, the

Koa Domei, which espoused absolute Japanese mastery and exploitation of Asia for "war eternal" with the other races. The founder of the Asia Development Union was Tojo, chief of staff of Japanese forces in Manchuria and later notorious as Japan's prime minister in World War II. Tojo was Ishiwara's most bitter enemy. Five days after Hirohito discovered that Ishiwara was not transmitting all his imperial instructions, Ishiwara was posted to Manchuria to become Tojo's assistant.

In the weeks that followed, a new chief of operations—appropriately named Shimomura Sadamu, or Shimomura the "Peace-Fixer"—drew up plans for a second expeditionary force to Central China which would outflank the stubborn Chinese defense of Shanghai and push on to Nanking. The development and realization of these plans were entrusted to members of the Emperor's own cabal of officers. These were colonels and generals in their forties who had become liegemen of one or another of the Emperor's uncles at the Military Academy and Staff College between 1905 and 1915.[4] Most of them had pledged themselves to Hirohito personally in 1921 in Europe when they were embassy Intelligence officers and he was a crown prince on a grand tour. Most of them had attended political indoctrination classes at a school in the palace in 1922–1924 and had become converts there to the idea that Japan's destiny lay to the south in the Indies.

As soon as plans for the Nanking operation were completed in October, the two young officers on the cabal who had been responsible for drafting the plans were assigned as assistants to General Matsui's staff in Shanghai to see that the plans were well understood and executed. At the same time one of the Emperor's kinsmen, his favorite aide-de-camp,[5] left Hirohito's side to take charge of the all-powerful Military Affairs Bureau which ran the War Ministry. Also at the same time, the most talented of the Emperor's cabal, Major General Suzuki Tei-ichi, was attached to the command of the 16th Division which would actually conduct the great rape.

Suzuki was one of the two or three young Army men whom Hirohito knew best and relied on most. His name will crop up so often in these pages that, to distinguish him from other Suzukis (other Smiths), he will be called the "ubiquitous" Suzuki. He had the keen, lean, professorial air of many successful stockbrokers: long face, high forehead, close-cropped hair, spectacles, and thoughtful creases around the jaw. As chief of the Cabinet Planning Board, he would become the czar of Japan's legislation and economic mobilization during World War II. After ten years in Allied prison,

---

[4] Emperor Hirohito had no true blood uncles, but Empress Nagako, his wife and distant cousin, had six uncles and nine avuncular first cousins. Two of her uncles and two of her uncle-cousins married Hirohito's blood aunts. The term "Hirohito's uncle" as used in these pages refers regularly to one or the other of his two double-uncles-in-law.

[5] Machijiri Kazumoto. He and the Emperor's uncle, Prince Higashikuni, on a trip to Paris in 1920, had been the two original founders of the cabal.

he remains at eighty-one, in 1970, one of Japan's best dressed, best spoken, best informed citizens.

The ubiquitous Suzuki supervised the rape of Nanking largely by radio from a desk at the home headquarters of the 16th Division in the old Japanese capital city of Kyoto. He probably supplemented his desk work by lightning plane trips to and from the front lines, but testimony as to the times and frequency of his inspections is confused and contradictory. He had known Chiang Kai-shek at Military Academy in Tokyo thirty years ago, and he had been used as Hirohito's personal emissary to Chiang on several past occasions. In addition he was the Army's leading economic expert. Thus he was equipped to fulfill a double function. On the one hand he would play the intermediary in secret radio negotiations between Chiang Kai-shek and Prime Minister Prince Konoye while the rape of Nanking was in progress. On the other hand, to defray invasion costs, he would direct his 16th Division in a systematic looting of Nanking.

When his most trusted minions in the Army had taken their ominous places, Hirohito issued an imperial rescript in October explaining that Japan was unleashing her military might "to urge grave self-reflection upon China and to establish peace in the East without delay." Prince Konoye and little General Matsui, the commander in Shanghai, both expanded on this thesis to itemize the political objectives of a drive on Nanking. They made two principal points: the Chinese must appreciate "the price they will have to pay" for "continued nationalism" and "anti-Japanese sentiments"; they must forsake the cause of Chiang Kai-shek and of his party, the Kuomintang or KMT.

RED TENTS

When the fourteenth-century Mongol conqueror Tamerlane invested a city, he is supposed to have camped before it in a white tent on the first day of the siege as a sign of mercy, in a red tent on the second day as a sign of mercy to women and children, in a black tent on the third day as a sign of mercy to no one. Matsui's expeditionary force to Shanghai had been Japan's white tent. Now in late October, when Chiang Kai-shek did not respond to Hirohito's edict, a second flotilla gathered in North Chinese and Japanese ports. It carried four and a half fresh divisions, some 80,000 men. It sailed in two shifts, a "red" and a "black." It struck at two ill-protected shorelines, the first well south and the last well north of the fighting in Shanghai. Logistically both landings were triumphs of amphibious technique on hostile beaches and deserve place in military annals beside the exploits of Napoleon in Egypt or of Caesar in Britain. They foreshadowed the landings of the later war in the Pacific.

The experts who presided over the amphibious technicalities had been working in Taiwan for three years, assigned to study the problems associated with the possibility of a Japanese attack on offshore islands like

Java or Luzon. Half the men in the two armadas had been purged from the Army by Hirohito's order in the ideological struggles of the previous twelve years. The over-all commander, who personally led the major southern prong of the task force, was himself a reactivated general, a small, bald, studious-looking strategist named Yanagawa Heisuke. He had been cast into the reserve as one of the three Army figureheads of the unsuccessful rebellion against Hirohito in 1936. General Yanagawa had been in Paris to greet Hirohito in 1921 when the then crown prince had made his first and only trip beyond the borders of his homeland. Yanagawa had been in and out of the palace at all hours as the vice minister of war between 1932 and 1934. In late 1935 he had taken charge of the Japanese army stationed in Taiwan and had superintended the development of many of the amphibious techniques which were to be tried out this day. Like most of his men he was hungry to re-establish himself in imperial favor. When recalled to command in September, he had written to his wife: "It is as if I were recrossing the Styx out of Hades; I can see light ahead."

Early on the morning of November 5, 1937, Yanagawa's task force steamed under radio silence into Hangchow Bay, a finger of the China Sea some 40 miles south of Shanghai which reached into the China coastline along the underbelly of Chiang Kai-shek's southern flank. The transports, with over 60,000 men aboard, hove to and waited for dawn off the water-front of the little walled town of Chin-shan-wei, Bastion of the Golden Mountain. On the muted ships, over the grumble of taut anchor chains and the squeak of the winches which were lowering assault boats, could be heard the work chants of the awakening town, the "heya-hoa" of coolies shouldering produce and refuse to and from the central market place.

First light revealed a dawn fog clinging to the yellow waters of the bay. General Yanagawa decided to wait for it to lift. This low-lying green shore beyond the fog was the southern edge of the swarming, industrious bayou land of the Yangtze River delta; it was laced with sampan canals which would cause confusion and casualties unless his men could see the whole lay of the terrain. To the rhythmic knocking of the assault boats against the metal hull of the ship, Yanagawa wrote two bleak *tanka* (thirty-one-syllable poems):

> The mist of morning
> has still not dissipated.
> Enveloped by it,
> I wait out ninety minutes
> that seem interminable.

> By the Emperor's
> inexorable mandate,
> the road that I take
> is like today's scenery
> washed entirely in tears.

When the effluvia of the bay began to melt under the rising sun, Yanagawa donned a white surgical mask, such as Japanese regularly wore in those days to prevent the catching or spreading of colds. His common soldiers, hastily mustered under his command, did not yet know that he was the former vice minister of war, and he thought it best that they should not recognize him now. Yanagawa stepped onto the nets above the waiting assault boats and ordered the first wave to cast off and make for the beaches.

The Chinese soldiers in the area were taken completely unawares. By noon most of Yanagawa's three and a half divisions were ashore and had invested the Bastion of the Golden Mountain. The next morning Yanagawa had clouds of advertising balloons wafted aloft on an onshore breeze. They dangled scrolls of false intelligence: "A million Japanese soldiers have landed at Hangchow Bay." Provincial Chinese levies melted away before the news. Those that stayed at their posts were quickly overrun by the Japanese 6th Division which spearheaded the thrust north from the beach-heads. Its commander, Lieutenant General Tani Hisao, later executed as a war criminal, is described by a contemporary Army commentator as beginning the advance by "galloping off in eight directions in the fog with the fury of the demon Ashura."

Three days after the landing, the 6th Division had burned and blasted its way twenty-five of the forty miles to the outskirts of Shanghai. On the third day it occupied the suburban city of Pine Bay or Sungchiang. Nine weeks later a British correspondent managed to see what was left of Pine Bay. "There is hardly a building standing," he wrote, "which has not been gutted by fire. Smouldering ruins and deserted streets present an eerie spectacle, the only living creatures being dogs unnaturally fattened by feasting on corpses. In the whole of Sungchiang, which should contain a densely packed population of approximately 100,000, I saw only five Chinese, who were old men, hiding in a French mission compound in tears."

BLACK TENTS

With their southern flank turned, the Chinese outside of Shanghai began to pull back to a line of pillboxes across the Yangtze delta which had been planned by Chiang Kai-shek's German military aides for this very eventuality. Then the Japanese 16th Division, the "black" fleet from North China, steamed up the Yangtze estuary under cover of darkness and landed at a place called Paimou Inlet on the Chinese northern flank just behind the line of pillboxes. The second "black" half of Japan's seaborne pincer had closed. The executioners of Nanking had arrived. The new division was commanded from Kyoto by the ubiquitous Suzuki and in the field by Lieutenant General Nakajima Kesago, fifty-five, a small Himmler of a man, a specialist in thought control, intimidation, and torture. It was Nakajima who would superintend in detail over the Nanking atrocities. Like most of the other officers recently reposted to take charge of the Nanking operation, Nakajima had been in France as a member of Army Intelligence in 1921 and had then had the honor of being presented to Crown Prince Hirohito. Since the Army mutiny in Tokyo in 1936, Hirohito had employed Nakajima to keep peace in the capital as chief of the secret police or *kempei*.

Although Japanese officers rarely criticize one another in front of foreigners, they make an exception in Nakajima's case. In their words, Nakajima was a "hard man of sadistic personality."

"He is such an expert marksman," wrote one, "that he finds duckhunting 'ridiculous' and prefers to stand by a waterfall shooting robins as they come over in the downdraft. Now [in 1939] in North Manchuria, where he has been sent to preserve peace after the sacred war with China, there are no more 'bandits' to suppress and . . . he is no doubt morose. It must be a catastrophe for the robins of Manchuria."

"Nakajima drank too much French civilization," said another. "He fancied himself a Robespierre or Danton. He came to Nanking bringing special Peking oil for burning bodies."

"After we broke out of Shanghai," recalled a third, "my 11th Division advanced on a parallel course with Nakajima's 16th which had just landed. Every night from my sleeping floor I could see the glare of the villages they were firing. . . . Burned houses make bad billets. Only cowards are involved in such incidents."

After the war, Chiang Kai-shek's government charged that Nakajima's 16th Division, together with the 6th under "demon Ashura" Tani, took 390,000 lives in their advance on Nanking.

STOP LINE FARCE

In the trident of Nakajima hooking down from the north, Yanagawa stabbing up from the south, and Matsui thrusting out towards Nanking from Shanghai to the east, the retreat of Chiang Kai-shek's troops turned into a rout. The necklace of pillboxes scientifically strung across the Yangtze delta by German military engineers was abandoned with hardly a fight. Dark rumors circulated in China that it had been bought out with Japanese gold, and so in part it may have been, but in an over-all sense it fell to Japanese technique and daring.

After the Chinese retreat began, the Japanese divisions in the field did not pause in their pursuit. The General Staff in Tokyo made a great show for the Western press of drawing lines on the map and announcing that here the advance was to stop. At each line the men regrouped and then moved on as soon as they received secret orders from the Emperor to do so. The existence of such orders was not revealed until their publication by a group of retired generals in 1964.

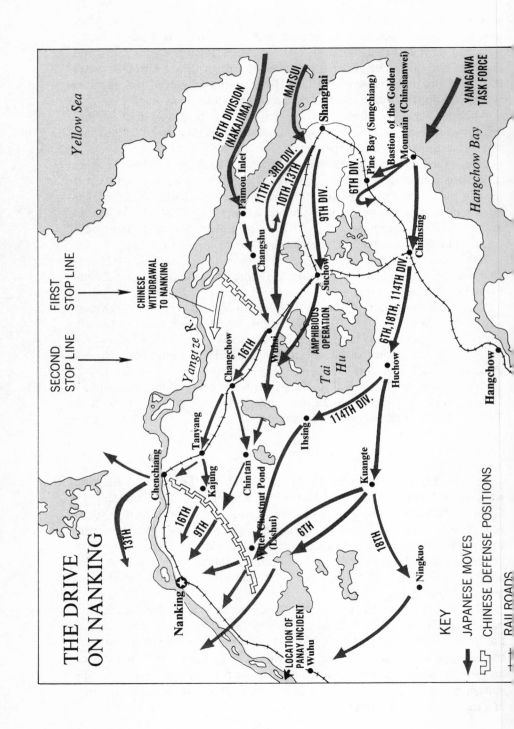

THE DRIVE
ON NANKING

KEY

JAPANESE MOVES

CHINESE DEFENSE POSITIONS

RAILROADS

At the time an impression was carefully created for foreign observers that the men at the front were out of hand and could not be controlled. The truth was that they had never been more scrupulously obedient, for they knew that a Grand Imperial Headquarters was being established in the palace and that their deeds would be watched by the sacred Emperor in person. The first stop line was drawn across the Yangtze delta on November 7. When all divisions had arrived at it on November 24, it was dissolved by the Emperor's order. The General Staff drew a second stop line that same day fifty miles farther west. Hirohito dissolved it unofficially three days later and officially seven days later.

By that four-day interval between unofficial and official orders hangs a typical palace tale. The vice chief of the General Staff in Tokyo, Lieutenant General Tada Hayao, disapproved of the attack on Nanking because he knew of the campaign of terror that was planned for the Chinese capital and felt that it would undermine Army morale. He steadfastly refused to advise Hirohito to give it imperial sanction. Just as steadfastly Hirohito insisted that Tada must so advise—and must countersign the necessary orders—because he was the vice chief of the General Staff. The task of persuading Lieutenant General Tada fell to the new, biddable chief of the General Staff's Operations Department, Major General Peace-Fixer Shimomura. He coaxed and threatened all week long from Monday, November 22, to Saturday, November 27. At midweek, on Wednesday, November 24, Peace-Fixer Shimomura met privately with Emperor Hirohito after a session of the Grand Imperial Headquarters staff and arranged with him to have all formalities and seals and counterseals ready so that the orders could be put through the Court machinery instantaneously when Tada once capitulated. On Saturday, nearing despair, Shimomura sent out a most irregular pair of cables, one official to General Matsui in Shanghai, the other unofficial to the staff officers from Hirohito's cabal who had been injected into Matsui's command the month before. The first cable to Matsui said:

KEEPING A FIRM DETERMINATION TO ATTACK NANKING WE ARE ENGAGED IN THIS DEPARTMENT IN STEADY DISCUSSION. HOWEVER, WE HAVE NOT YET OBTAINED A FINAL DECISION. ONLY REST ASSURED, PLEASE, THAT NO MATTER WHAT, WE ARE COMING AROUND.

The second cable—to the staff officers under Matsui—was marked confidential and sent special priority. It said:

ALTHOUGH I HAVE NOT YET OBTAINED A DECISION FROM OUR SUPERIOR OFFICER, THE CENTER OF THIS DEPARTMENT IS ENTHUSIASTIC FOR THE ATTACK ON NANKING. WITH THIS UNDERSTANDING, THEREFORE, PLEASE ABANDON YOUR PREVIOUS OCCUPATIONS AND GO AHEAD WITH IT.

The only "center of this department," aside from Major General Shimomura who signed the cables, was Emperor Hirohito. The "superior officer" was, of course, the embattled Lieutenant General Tada.

As soon as staff officers at the front received the second cable, they had their troops bugled out of bistros and brothels in the two principal cities on the second stop line and made ready to plunge onward. The stubborn Tada in Tokyo was threatened with the possibility that the troops would move without orders—a stain on Army honor for which he, as vice chief of staff, would be made to take the responsibility. Faced with retirement and disgrace on the one hand and on the other promises of a prosperous future, Tada gave in on the evening of the day the cables were sent. He stipulated that the orders be dated December 1, four days hence—a peculiarly Japanese way of putting on record the fact that he was acting under duress. He also asked that Emperor Hirohito acknowledge his responsibility for the orders by promulgating them in the form of an imperial edict to the whole people of Japan.

Tada conceded that he would carry the orders to the front himself and that they need not mention the second stop line but should merely say, "Take Nanking." An imperial edict required imprimatur by the Great Seal of State and by the counterseals of chamberlains who were ordinarily scattered about in villas and spas all over Japan. Usually the formalities took a week or more. Now, to Tada's astonishment, all arrangements had been made in advance; Emperor Hirohito, in perfect propriety, was able to affix the Great Seal to them the next morning, Sunday, November 28. Tada then completed his demonstration of dissent by taking three days to deliver the written orders to Shanghai, a one-day flight away. However, the orders were radioed to the front immediately, and the troops poured over the second stop line minutes after receiving them. Some of the men were under the impression that they were ordered to "take Nanking, effective December 1," which meant that they had more than 100 miles to go in three days.

The "white" divisions of Matsui and the "red" divisions of Yanagawa now began a race to see which could reach Nanking first. Matsui's men made a brilliant start by an amphibious flanking thrust across the Tai-Hu or Big Lake which lies just west of the Yangtze delta, about halfway between Shanghai and Nanking. Yanagawa's men, skirting the same lake on the south, more than kept pace. On the northernmost front, the "black" 16th Division of the sadistic Nakajima, who was to conduct the Rape, loafed along in the rear. On December 1, when the Emperor's orders to take Nanking arrived officially, all forces were running well but all had over fifty miles to go before they could comply.

The campaign had cost the Japanese 70,000 casualties already and would cost them another 40,000 before Nanking was taken. In the decimated forward regiments battle fever propelled the men on nerves alone. Inter-unit rivalries had always run fierce in the Japanese Army, making mortal combat out of the traditional barroom brawl. But now, according to surviving veterans, the chase up the Yangtze delta had brought the men to such a competitive pitch that they were burning villages, slaughtering cattle, and carrying off girls solely to deprive men from other units of billets, food, and entertainment. Their mood may be gauged from an item passed by the censor and printed on December 7 by the *Japan Advertiser*.

SUB-LIEUTENANTS IN RACE
TO FELL 100 CHINESE
RUNNING CLOSE CONTEST

Sub-Lieutenant Toshiaki Mukai and Sub-Lieutenant Takeshi Noda, both of the Katagiri unit at Kuyung, in a friendly contest to see which of them will first fell 100 Chinese in individual sword combat before the Japanese forces completely occupy Nanking, are well in the final phase of their race, running almost neck to neck. On Sunday [December 5th] . . . the "score," according to the *Asahi,* was: Sub-Lieutenant Mukai, 89, and Sub-Lieutenant Noda, 78.

A week later, the day after Nanking had already fallen, the *Advertiser* went on to tell that the goal had been extended to 150 because referees had not been able to determine which contestant had reached 100 first. "Mukai's blade," it reported, "was slightly damaged in the competition. He explained that this was the result of cutting a Chinese in half, helmet and all. The contest was 'fun' he declared."

After moving 120 miles in a week, against the grain of the few motor roads in the region, the "red" men of the eager, disgraced Yanagawa occupied Lishiu, or Water-Chestnut Pond, on Saturday, December 4. From there it was only thirty miles north along a good highway to the Nanking city walls. There, however, a last-ditch line of resistance had been improvised by fresh provincial Chinese levies who were defending their own homes and paddies. Yanagawa's weary soldiers could not make a breakthrough and were held up for almost three days. Farther north, Matsui's "white" troops reached the same stubborn line two days later and proceeded to blast through the Chinese entrenchments with a salvo of all-out infantry charges. Still farther north, the sadistic Nakajima and his "black" forces cut out cross-country after a ride along the Shanghai-Nanking railway tracks and, meeting little resistance, began to catch up with their fellow runners.

CHIANG CORNERED

Within the walls of Nanking, Chiang Kai-shek had lived through a month of bitter disillusionment. At his request, on September 12, the League of Nations had called a conference of law-professing nations which had met from November 4 to November 24 in Brussels. The conference had closed without taking action except to censure Japan mildly. Chiang Kai-shek's German advisors had asked for more support from Berlin and had learned that the faction of Foreign Minister Ribbentrop, favoring Japan, had won Hitler's ear. Russia, caught in the toils of Stalin's latest purge, could send only a few more planes and pilots to Chiang. The United States sent retired Air Force General Claire Chennault and a score of flying adventurers, but American planes, already bought and shipped, were being off-loaded and held in Californian ports. On December 2 Chiang Kai-shek met with his generals and agreed to accede to Japanese terms. From a Japanese point of view, they were moderate, amounting to no more than official Chinese recognition of *de facto* realities: an autonomous Inner Mongolia; an enlargement of the international demilitarized zone around Shanghai; an alliance with Japan against Russia; demilitarization of a two-hundred-mile-wide strip along the Manchurian frontier which would include the old capital of Peking; appointment therein of officials friendly to Japan.

On accepting the terms in principle, Chiang learned on December 5 that the situation had changed and that Japan was no longer willing to offer any peace terms. Chiang therefore told his neutral negotiator, the German ambassador to China, Oscar Trautmann, that further negotiations were impossible in the military predicament of the moment. Chiang proceeded to evacuate the last skeletal bureaus of his government from Nanking. He and his staff followed on December 7, when he flew to Hankow, 350 miles farther upriver, and there established a new temporary capital.

HIROHITO'S UNCLE

By December 7, 1937, the 300,000 troops remaining between the Japanese forces and their goal, Nanking, were in complete disarray, and the Chinese capital was effectively naked of any defense except its own ancient brick walls. Four divisions of weary, overstrung Japanese soldiers were converging on the city across a cold, ravaged countryside: Yanagawa's "red" 6th and 114th, Matsui's "white" 9th and Nakajima's "black" 16th. As the bloodthirsty troops closed in, General Matsui lay bedridden with a tubercular fever at his field headquarters in Suchow in the Yangtze delta. On December 2, five days earlier, Emperor Hirohito had relieved him of personal supervision of the men in the field and had moved him up to over-all command of the Central China theater. In his place as commander-in-chief of the Army around Nanking, Hirohito appointed his own uncle, Prince Asaka.

Despite the fact that he was a member of the imperial family, Prince Asaka was a tough professional soldier and in his thirty-year rise from cadet to lieutenant general had enjoyed few favors or sinecures. A lean, silent aristocrat of fifty, he walked with a pronounced limp which he had acquired in a car crash outside of Paris in 1923 during his three-year posting there

—with his present helpmeets Yanagawa and Nakajima—as a military intelligence officer. Once a versatile athlete, he had concentrated on golf since his accident and now played one of the best games in Japan. He used it along with his fluent French to entertain most of the luminaries who visited Tokyo from Paris in the 1930's. During the Army mutiny of February 1936, at an emergency meeting of the Council of Princes of the Blood, he had sided with Emperor Hirohito's brother Chichibu in urging consideration of the grievances of the Army's Strike-North or Fight-Russia faction. Afterwards,. in a memorandum for the palace rolls, Hirohito had singled him out for censure as the one imperial kinsman whose attitude was "not good." He had been given this present disagreeable duty at Nanking as an opportunity to make amends. When he had performed it, as he would perform it, all too well, he would return to imperial favor.

Prince Asaka's appointment to the front, overriding all other authority in a wave of imperial influence, gave the sick General Matsui premonitions that his command was about to be abused. He ordered his armies to pull up and regroup three to four kilometers outside the Nanking city walls, to go into the city with only a few well-disciplined battalions, and to make sure that the occupation was carried out in such a way as "to sparkle before the eyes of the Chinese and make them place confidence in Japan." Then he called the staff officers of his legions together at his sickbed in Suchow and issued them a most extraordinary tablet of moral commandments:

> The entry of the Imperial Army into a foreign capital is a great event in our history ·. . . attracting the attention of the world. Therefore let no unit enter the city in a disorderly fashion. . . . The units entering the walled city shall be the ones especially chosen for that purpose by the divisional commanders concerned. Let them know beforehand the matters to be remembered and the position of foreign rights and interests in the walled city. Let them be absolutely free from plunder. Dispose sentries as needed. Plundering and causing fires, even carelessly, shall be punished severely. Together with the troops let many military police and auxiliary military police enter the walled city and thereby prevent unlawful conduct.

Prince Asaka left Tokyo by plane on Sunday, December 5, and arrived to take command at the front three days later. He found his old companion of Paris days, the sadistic Nakajima, installed in an abandoned Chinese country villa near advanced field headquarters some ten miles southeast of Nanking. Nakajima was laid up with a painful flesh wound in the left buttock received that Sunday. He reported to his former princely patron that the Japanese forces had broken through everywhere at the outer Nanking perimeter and that some 300,000 Chinese troops were about to be surrounded and pinned against the Nanking city walls. Preliminary negotiations indicated that they were ready to surrender. After Prince Asaka had heard this summary, a set of orders went out from his headquarters, under his personal seal, marked "secret, to be destroyed." They said simply, "Kill all captives." The Chinese soldiers sensed a change in attitude and fled for the walls of Nanking. At least three quarters of them lived to fight another day. The remaining 75,000 men were later trapped in Nanking and contributed substantially to the fatality statistics compiled by Western observers in the city during the rape. Prince Asaka's staff officer for Intelligence, a lieutenant colonel, claimed to friends that he had forged the "kill" orders on his own initiative. If he did, it is remarkable that he was not court-martialed but continued his fighting career until June of 1945 when he died, a lieutenant general, in the caves of Okinawa.[6]

THE PANAY DIVERSION

After Prince Asaka's dispatch to the front, during the final days before the capture of Nanking, Emperor Hirohito is described by one of his courtiers as "taking no recreation and exercising a wide intensive supervision of military operations." Prince Konoye, the prime minister and long the specialist in domestic politics within Hirohito's coterie of young men, feared that the Emperor might be losing his perspective in a welter of military detail. Though a prince, the lanky cynical Konoye belonged not to the imperial family but to the equally ancient and aristocratic Fujiwara clan whose duty it had been for thirteen hundred years to stand around the Throne as "ministers on the left" and "ministers on the right" and protect emperors from the consequences of their own cloistered enthusiasms. No courtier knew better than Konoye how to humor Hirohito. With no other palace familiar did the young Emperor feel more equal—more free to argue, to talk personalities, to bandy criticism.

On November 20, when Hirohito established his Grand Imperial Headquarters, Prince Konoye had stormed into the palace to protest the fact that he was not included in the headquarters even as an observer. Hirohito assured him that it would be a purely military conclave, of great stiffness, in which a politician would have no interest. Konoye replied that military decisions were always of political interest. "I would like to resign," he declared, "before this second strategy in China begins." Accustomed to such dramatic outbursts from his favorite, Hirohito begged Konoye to remain in office and soothed him with a promise: "I myself will keep you fully informed on military operations."

Konoye had voiced no previous objections to the war with China. On the contrary, if Japan became embroiled deeply enough in China she might be prevented from making a disastrously premature attack on Russia to the

---

[6] Cho Isamu. Earlier, in 1931, he had helped to organize, under palace auspices, a pair of fake coups d'etat which served to confuse issues and ease settlements during the domestic political crises attendant upon the conquest of Manchuria.

north or on the United States and Great Britain to the south. All autumn long Konoye had been fighting a running battle with officers in the General Staff who wished to fight Russia and avoid involvement in China. They had opposed the expeditionary force to Shanghai, opposed reinforcing it, opposed the additional landings south and north of Shanghai, and opposed the orders to take Nanking. Most recently they had sought to accept Chiang Kai-shek's offer of conditional capitulation, and Konoye had been hard put to it to increase the severity of Japanese demands so that Chiang would not accept them. It was difficult for a politician to stand against militarists when they wanted to make peace.

Now "this second strategy in China" threatened Konoye's objectives in a different way. He had helped to persuade Hirohito that no acceptable deal could be worked out with Chiang. He had urged, without much personal conviction, that the capture of Nanking would cause Chiang's generals to desert him and would make possible the establishment of a puppet Chinese regime co-operative toward long-range Japanese aims. But this new strategy which was to be pursued at Nanking gave Konoye pause. He may not have known much about it, but he knew enough to feel squeamish about presiding over it as prime minister. If terror and destruction at Nanking were carried far enough, they might even succeed in toppling Chiang Kai-shek. Then the problem would be to prevent Hirohito and the Navy from proceeding too fast with plans for an attack on Malaya and the Indies.

On December 7, after another audience with the Emperor, Konoye felt that his worst fears were coming true. He knew from his sources in Chiang Kai-shek's suite that the Chinese leader had fled Nanking that day. The troops were closing in. And Hirohito was entirely absorbed in long-term military planning. Konoye complained to Marquis Kido, another of the Emperor's intimates: "I just met with the Emperor and he is talking of strategy all the way up to next March. He mentioned sending a division to Canton, which surprised me because I had heard nothing of such a strike before." Canton lay only fifty-seven miles from the British crown colony of Hong Kong. Hirohito had already signed the orders to attack it. "If things go on this way," continued Konoye, "I cannot take the full responsibility. I told the Emperor that after observing the results of the capture of Nanking, I may have to ask for a change of Cabinet. The Emperor seems to have no objections."

Five days after Konoye's audience with Hirohito, an old crony of the prime minister, a reactivated reserve colonel of artillery named Hashimoto Kingoro, torpedoed the plans to attack Canton by singlehandedly instigating a celebrated international incident, the sinking of the U.S. gunboat *Panay*. Shortly after Chiang Kai-shek fled his capital, Hashimoto's artillery regiment had reached the Yangtze by an overland route sixty miles upstream from Nanking. There, near the town of Wuhu, he had laid out a two-mile gauntlet of heavy field pieces along the river bank in order to cut off fugitives attempting to escape up the river from Nanking. Late on Saturday, December 11, he had shelled a ferryboat load of British refugees and a British gunboat, the *Lady Bird,* and killed a British sailor. On the following morning he learned that a second convoy of Western refugees, consisting of three Socony-Vacuum tankers and the little U.S. gunboat *Panay,* was waiting out the occupation of Nanking at a safe anchorage downriver, halfway between the battery and the beleaguered city. Colonel Hashimoto commanded a squadron of naval aircraft which had been attached to his unit to help him blockade the river. He ordered his naval pilots to attack the U.S. ships. The pilots, although they were not commissioned officers, questioned Colonel Hashimoto's orders and took off only after long argument.

At 1:30 P.M. ordinary Sunday routine was being observed aboard the *Panay*. Eight of her officers were off visiting with the civilians on the three nearby tankers. It was a fine clear day. The two huge American flags painted on the *Panay*'s decks glistened in the bright sunlight. At 1:38 three twin-motor planes in V-formation were seen coming in at a considerable height from the southwest. Red circles on their underwings proclaimed them Japanese, which was reassuring, because the Japanese had been notified of the *Panay*'s position, and Japanese pilots, unlike their Chinese counterparts, were not known for dropping bombs by mistake. Then suddenly black dots detached themselves from the bellies of the three planes and a moment later, in what was for that time a miracle of precision bombing, the *Panay* was mortally damaged. One bomb scored a direct hit on her bow and a second stove a hole in her starboard side. The engines were knocked out. The three-inch gun was disabled. The pilot house, sick bay, and radio shack were demolished. The captain went out of action with a hipful of shrapnel.

Before the crew could recover from this instant devastation, six single-engine biplane fighters bore in from the south, unloading smaller anti-personnel bombs. The executive officer, who had just assumed command, took a piece of shrapnel in the throat and could not speak. He continued to issue orders, scribbling them on slips of paper. The slow biplane fighters wheeled and climbed and came in singly for a second and third run of dive bombing. The crew of the 30-caliber machine gun on the afterdeck collected itself and began to return fire. Two of the planes answered in kind. After twenty minutes of bombing and strafing, the *Panay* was listing to starboard and slowly settling, and the attacking planes turned their attention to the three Socony tankers.

Every one of the *Panay*'s line officers was wounded along with almost every member of the crew. At 2:00 P.M. the mute executive officer scrawled an order to abandon ship. As the wounded were being ferried ashore, one of the planes returned briefly to strafe the open lifeboat. By 3:00 P.M. the decks of the *Panay* had been emptied and were awash with the yellow waters of the great septic river. When she did not sink at once, two mates rowed back to her to take off provisions and medical supplies. A Japanese launch approached the *Panay,* swept her decks with machine-gun fire, and put aboard an inspection crew. A moment later the Japanese seamen could be seen leaping back into their boat and hurrying away. Five minutes later, at 3:54 P.M., the *Panay* rolled onto her starboard side and sank. Two of the tankers were burning and the third had been grounded on a mud bank. Their passengers and crews, together with the men of the *Panay,* hid out for three days in the rushes of the riverbank. They were finally rescued by the U.S. gunboat *Oahu.* In all, two Americans were dead, one dying and fourteen others critical litter cases. A considerable number of the Chinese crewmen of the tankers had also been killed or wounded but could not be counted because many of the survivors had fled into the countryside.

On the day after the sinking of the *Panay,* President Roosevelt unofficially requested the Japanese ambassador in Washington to transmit his "shock and concern" directly to Emperor Hirohito. It was an unprecedented step which disregarded the façade of Japan's official government. Chamberlains with diplomatic experience encouraged Hirohito to think that it might presage a declaration of war by the United States. Ambassador Joseph Grew in the American Embassy a few blocks from the palace had servants start packing his trunks and let it be known that the situation reminded him of Berlin in 1915 when the *Lusitania* had been sunk. Japanese Foreign Minister Hirota Koki immediately offered apologies and promised an indemnity for the families of the bereaved and wounded. Japanese private citizens flocked to the American Embassy and stopped embassy staff members on the streets to express their regrets. One well-dressed Japanese woman cut off a tress of her hair in the embassy lobby and submitted it with a carnation to signify that she felt as if she had lost a husband. So much unsolicited condolence money poured in to the embassy that Grew finally rounded it out and contributed $5,000,000 to Japanese charity. Vice Navy Minister Yamamoto Isoroku, who would later lead the attack on Pearl Harbor, publicly accepted the full responsibility for the incident and privately fumed because he could not force the Army to discipline its Colonel Hashimoto who had ordered the *Panay* to be sunk.

Through Konoye's patronage, the guilty Hashimoto enjoyed impunity. He continued in command of his artillery regiment until March of 1939. When he finally doffed his uniform, Prince Konoye was organizing a one-party system for Japan—an Imperial Rule Assistance Association which would serve as a reasonable facsimile of the Nazi party in Germany or of the Communist party in Russia. Konoye made Hashimoto executive director of the new monolithic party.

By sinking the U.S.S. *Panay* and shelling H.M.S. *Lady Bird,* Colonel Hashimoto did succeed in making the planned attack on the Hong Kong

area too dangerous for execution. On December 20, eight days after the
Panay incident, 30,000 Japanese troops were embarked on transports in
harbors along the southwestern coast of Taiwan. Two days later, at Konoye's urging, Hirohito reluctantly ordered them back ashore and postponed the attack on Canton for ten months. A strong presumption exists
that Konoye sent a messenger to China to ask Hashimoto to sink the
Panay. It is reinforced by the fact that a few days after the *Panay* sinking,
an emissary of Konoye, sent to feel out Chinese politicians on a puppet
regime which might replace Chiang Kai-shek's government, was mistakenly
apprehended by the Japanese secret police in the port of Osaka and prevented from leaving Japan in time to keep his appointments on the
continent.

On the day of the *Panay* sinking, December 12, Konoye moved into a
new villa in the suburb of Ogikubo. At the housewarming he told one of his
guests, "I can no longer bear it. When Nanking falls, Chiang Kai-shek's
government must fall. If it does not, I am to issue a statement of non-
recognition of Chiang and to refuse to deal with him. I think that is the
time for me to withdraw. I shall resign then." A statement to the effect
that Japan would refuse to deal with Chiang Kai-shek and would found
its own puppet government in China had already been drafted by Hirohito's
kinsman and favorite aide-de-camp, Machijiri. Konoye did finally issue a
version of the statement a month later when the rape of Nanking was
reaching its final stages. But neither Konoye nor Chiang Kai-shek resigned, and Konoye's new home at Ogikubo came to be known in the
Japanese vernacular as the "Hate-China" Villa. By the uninformed Japanese masses, in short, Konoye was held responsible as prime minister for
the butchery at Nanking.

THE ELEVENTH HOUR

In the bleak winter landscape of resting rice paddies outside Nanking,
the little mud-walled villages of farmers' huts were almost empty. By
December 10, three days after Chiang Kai-shek had left the capital, almost
800,000 of the 1,000,000-odd inhabitants of the city had fled upriver.
Eighteen million refugees from the Yangtze delta had passed through the
environs of the city and most of them, too, were now on their way into
the hinterlands. The Chinese rearguard of about 100,000 soldiers bundled
any civilians remaining in the suburbs inside the city walls; in accordance
with "a scorched-earth policy of resistance" enunciated two months earlier
by Chiang Kai-shek, they proceeded to burn every outlying field and roof
that might be of use to the invader.

As the sound of cannon fire approached, the Chinese troops manned
the great brick walls and waited. Twenty feet thick and fifty feet high,
the notched medieval battlements presented a substantial impediment

even to modern artillery. Within them the old medieval city had been razed during a peasant rebellion eighty years earlier. Now, except for several dense Chinese residential and commercial areas, it was a monumental government park, studded with new public buildings and full of open vistas in which pheasants nested. As the Chinese troops waited to be attacked, they respected the republican dream embodied in the city. They stole a few bicycles and broke into a few shops but connoisseurs of warfare in China were struck by their exemplary discipline, their solemn good behavior.

American, German, and British residents remaining in the city organized a safety zone, a noncombatant area of one and a half square miles around the major missionary, university, and hospital properties. The fleeing Chinese government had turned over to the zone's administrative committee of foreigners 450 policemen, 10,000 sacks of flour, $400,-000 in cash, and four million pounds of rice. It was hoped that in the zone Chinese civilians might find refuge for a few nights until the Japanese had completed their occupation and re-established law and order. Such a scheme had been tried in Shanghai and had been welcomed by the Japanese. General Matsui had contributed almost $3,000 out of his own pocket to help defray its expenses.

But in the case of Nanking, the Japanese refused in advance to sanction a safety zone. And before attacking, they advised that all non-Chinese should leave the area. Consular officials and most Western businessmen complied under orders from their head offices. Some retired to Western gunboats on the river like the *Panay,* others to a huge floating wharf of transit sheds and check-out shacks maintained by the British Jardine-Matheson Steamship Company. Twenty-two university professors, doctors, missionaries, and businessmen, however, remained inside the walls, including fifteen Americans and six Germans. Because of their presence the occupation of Nanking was carefully documented as the occupation of other cities west of Shanghai had not been. The Germans in particular had a chance to see all, for they felt protected by the Anti-Comintern Pact and walked about freely wearing swastika arm bands.

On Thursday, December 9, two battalions of Matsui's 9th Division drove to within a trench line of the southeastern walls. General Matsui had leaflets dropped from planes, promising clemency and suggesting truce procedures for handing over the reins of civil government. At midday on Friday two of Matsui's staff officers stood for three hours outside the Mountain Gate in the eastern wall, waiting to see if the Chinese would send out a delegation under flag of truce to cede the city. When none came, Hirohito's uncle Prince Asaka ordered a general assault. According to Tokyo's *Asahi* newspaper, the next day, Prince Asaka stood Napoleonic on a hill to the east and "watched the fall of the city surrounded by clouds of gunsmoke." In the morning commoners in Tokyo were rewarded

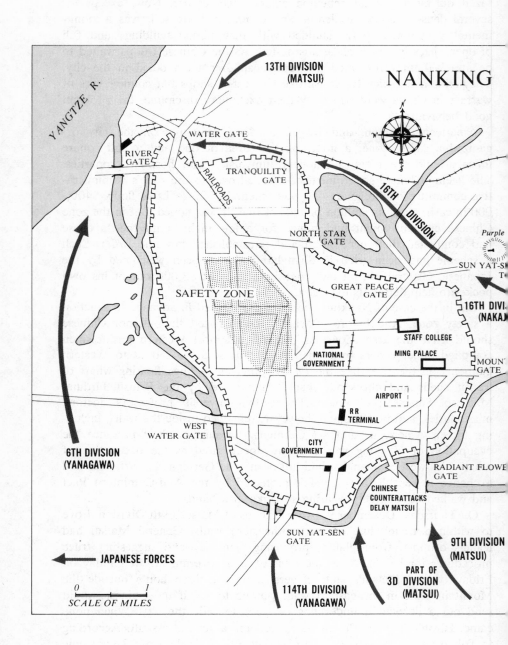

with the opportunity of eating specially decorated dishes of *Nanking soba,* Nanking noodles.

The news and noodles were premature, however. Late on Friday, December 10, the men of Matsui's 9th Division had managed to plant the flag of the rising sun on the southeastern walls only to be driven off by counterattacks during the night. Prince Asaka ordered the three other divisions under his command to cut short their mopping-up activities in outlying areas and make a thorough investiture of the city. The terrible 16th under secret-police sadist Nakajima was to circle around on the eastern side, the brutal 6th to fight its way up the western side along the river, and the reservist 114th to join the attack on the southern walls.

Black-booted but still limping from the bullet in his buttock, Nakajima was detained during Saturday, December 11, by resistance on the hump of the Purple Mountain northeast of the walls. It was a wooded suburban area noted for its fine villas and for the acre-large, granite-stepped mausoleum of Sun Yat-sen. The mausoleum was laid out on the upper slopes of the mountain in the shape of an ancient Chinese crossbow pointing toward the summit. Sun Yat-sen, once a protégé of Japan, was revered by Chinese republicans as a George Washington. With the aid of spotters in two blimps which hovered unmolested over his head, Nakajima was able to capture the tomb unscratched and to burn the nearby homes of China's rich on a selective political basis.

Yanagawa's 6th and 114th Divisions were also held up that day, by a bloody action on the Rain Flower Plateau south of Nanking. However, by Sunday, the following day, all units had fought their way clear. Nakajima spurred his men west toward the Yangtze along the northern walls of the city while Yanagawa's 6th Division hunted down Chinese soldiers in the marshes along the riverbank and headed north along the western walls. When the pincer of the two divisions closed at the northwest corner of town, it would shut off Nanking from the Yangtze and block the last avenue of escape. Chinese troops manning the walls began to desert their posts in panic. The Chinese commander made belated gestures toward arranging a truce through German intermediation, then abruptly joined the fugitives.

The last way out of the city was the Ichiang or Water Gate on the Yangtze to the northwest. In the approaches to this gate, according to a letter written twelve days later by Nanking's regional Y.M.C.A. secretary George Fitch, "Trucks and cars jammed, were overturned, caught fire; at the gate more cars jammed and were burned—a terrible holocaust—and the dead lay feet deep. The gate blocked, terror-mad soldiers scaled the wall and let themselves down on the other side with ropes, puttees and belts tied together, clothing torn to strips. Many fell and were killed. But at the river was perhaps the most appalling scene of all. A fleet of junks

was there. It was totally inadequate for the horde that was now in a
frenzy to cross to the north side. The overcrowded junks capsized, then
sank; thousands drowned."

Some of the fugitive junks and sampans survived the panic at the Water
Gate to make a start upstream. Above Nanking they were overhauled by
fast Japanese naval launches which had followed the Army's advance all
the way up the Yangtze from Shanghai. The duck hunt which ensued was
not in the finest traditions of the aristocratic British-style Japanese Navy,
and on some of the boats generous rations of saké were issued to keep the
sailors happy with their work. In and out the launches darted, ramming
and machine-gunning until the river was clear.

FALL OF THE CITY

That night, Sunday, December 12, Nanking was captured at last. The
storming of the walls resembled some scene from the brush of Hieronymus
Bosch. It was not yet moonrise, and the only light was the hellish flicker
of grenade bursts and flares. The Chinese fought with antiquated muskets
and great two-handed Manchurian swords from a parapet that had been
deeply furrowed by artillery fire; the Japanese machine-gunned their way
up scaling ladders which were set up, overthrown, and set up again. The
cadences of rattling, whining, thudding high explosive were punctuated by
the splashes of bodies falling into the waters of the ancient moat. At
about midnight men of the 114th Division—most of them disgraced rebels
like their commander, Yanagawa—scrambled to a slippery foothold
atop the battlements, raised a Japanese flag, and fought their way down
the stairs within to open the Sun Yat-sen Gate at the southernmost extremity of the city. A few minutes later the Wakizaki unit of Matsui's 9th
Division blasted their way through the Radiant Flower Gate farther to the
east.

By early Monday morning retreating Chinese soldiers, with nowhere to
run, were taking off their uniforms and begging the German businessmen
and American professors in charge of the unrecognized safety zone for
admission and concealment. The innocent Westerners disarmed several
hundred of them, assured them that they would be treated as war prisoners
by the Japanese, and quartered them all together in one building where
they could be turned over to the occupation troops in a body. Many of
them then proceeded to filter out of the building and mingle with the rest
of the refugee throng in the safety zone.

According to a report unearthed years later in occupied Berlin—a report written by General Alexander Ernst von Falkenhausen who was attached to the German Embassy as a military advisor for Chiang Kai-shek—
the attitude of the first Japanese soldiers entering the city that Monday

was "very correct." [7] Pushing north, unresisted through the half-deserted slums in the southern part of town, men of Yanagawa's division were first reported in the safety zone at eleven o'clock on Monday morning. Three members of the zone committee met them and explained to them the purpose of the zone. According to the American Y.M.C.A. man Fitch, "They showed no hostility, though a few moments later they killed twenty refugees who were frightened by their presence and ran away from them."

Throughout the rest of the day patrols from Matsui's and Yanagawa's divisions wandered through the city exploring, sightseeing, and occasionally shooting. One of Matsui's staff officers entered the Mountain Gate on the east and checked the route over which Matsui would ride on horseback when he presided at the official triumphal entry planned for four days later. Around the Radiant Flower Gate where fighting had been heaviest, the Wakizaki unit tidied up, cremating Chinese corpses and assembling and marking Japanese ones. All day and through the night Buddhist chaplains chanted prayers beside the rows of bodies.

That night a few picked garrison battalions and a number of AWOL drunks remained in the city. The bulk of the men who had entered in the morning returned as ordered to the 9th and 114th Division encampments outside the walls—to cold tents, poor food, and scarce water. They took with them as solace about a dozen Chinese women whom they had seized in the city. During the night the patrols left in the town shot at any Chinese seen abroad, and the drunk and disorderly went on a bender in the southern slums in the course of which they murdered eight men and boys in one household and raped, murdered, and mutilated a woman and two girls in a family of thirteen. The next day an American missionary, on a walk through the downtown area, was disgusted to find a "civilian Chinese corpse on almost every block."

According to a survey made three months later by an American sociologist, three hundred civilians had died during the capture of the city, fifty of them by stray bullets, bombs, and shells in the military action, the rest by wanton shooting and bayoneting after the military action was over. As war went in China in those days it was an ordinary toll. A few hundred killed, a few dozen raped—such had been the statistics in Tientsin, Peking, Shanghai, and all other major cities occupied in China by Japanese troops in previous weeks.

Not knowing that the casualties would be deliberately multiplied a hundredfold in the month to come, Western newsmen made plans that Monday

[7] Falkenhausen was a Prussian Junker who had his own strict views as to what was correct and what not. He served as military governor for the Third Reich in Belgium in World War II, conspired in the plot to assassinate Hitler, and ended the war first in Gestapo prison, then in Allied prison. He was judged guilty of war crimes at Nuremberg but because of extenuating circumstances the execution of his prison sentence was indefinitely suspended.

night to return to Shanghai and file their stories. A dozen of them left the city walls early the next morning and fretted out the next few days on docks or over beer in Japanese regimental field H.Q.s waiting for transportation. Only one, Yates McDaniel of the Associated Press, remained in the city long enough to witness the onset of the terror.

THE RAPE BEGINS

Late on Tuesday morning, when Nanking had been in Japanese hands for thirty-six hours, former Tokyo secret-police chief Nakajima and his 16th Division rolled into town through the Water Gate in trucks and armored cars. He had been delayed by the capture of some 10,000 prisoners at the last moment. All through the night his men had been busy herding the prisoners drove by drove to the edge of the Yangtze. They had worn their fingers to the bone pressing machine-gun triggers. At least 6,000 of the prisoners had died. Now in the flat drear light of the next noon, Nakajima's men began a systematic search inside Nanking for Chinese soldiers who had run away, taken off their uniforms, and vanished. The orders from Prince Asaka, the Emperor's uncle, were explicit: kill all captives. There were supposed to be 300,000 captives; less than 10,000 had been killed. Chiang Kai-shek's advisor, the Junker General von Falkenhausen, in his report to Berlin, notes that thereafter he saw a "complete change in attitude" in the Japanese.

"The Japanese troops," he wrote, "which had been insufficiently supplied because of their rapid advance were let loose in the town and behaved in a manner which was almost indescribable for regular troops."

Secret policeman Nakajima came to Nanking with an appointment in his pocket from Prince Asaka putting him in charge of the "maintenance of public peace." Thereafter public peace was sedulously destroyed. With Nakajima came Colonel Muto Akira, a member of the imperial cabal; he was charged by Prince Asaka with the "responsibility for billeting Japanese troops in the Nanking area." Thereafter the troops found their own billets. Muto announced that their camps outside the walls were inadequate and invited all hands in all four divisions to enter town and bed down where they pleased.

In defense of the Muto-Nakajima administration it was submitted at war crime tribunals a decade later that Nakajima had only fourteen secret policemen to assist him in maintaining public peace. The facts are that he had just come from the supreme command of all the secret police in Tokyo; that he had planes available for transporting staff officers to and from the homeland; and that Western observers saw those secret policemen which he did have in Nanking supervising looting and standing guard for soldiers who had entered homes to rape the women.

Colonel Muto, at his trial, made cynical fun of the proceedings by an equally absurd excuse; he pleaded that divisional encampments outside the city on the banks of the great Yangtze were "inadequate due to shortage of water." When the horde of soldiers were moved into town, they subsisted largely on water which they boiled and filtered and which was carried in to them by coolies from the Yangtze. The Nanking municipal water plant had been put out of commission by a bomb or shell on December 9. Damage to it was described as slight. Muto had at his disposal the 6th Field Epidemic Control Unit and a part of the 8th Field Engineers. Yet water was not turned on again in Nanking until January 7 when the Japanese had been there for over three weeks.

The 80,000-odd soldiers turned loose in Nanking by Muto, Nakajima, and Prince Asaka would have raped, killed, stolen, and burned if left to their own devices. In the event they acted under the guidance of their officers; they worked at being drunk and disorderly; they ran amok, but systematically. Their rape of Nanking began when Nakajima entered the city on December 14; it continued for six weeks; and it was not stopped, despite world-wide protest, until Prince Konoye admitted to Hirohito that there was no longer any hope of it unseating Chiang Kai-shek.

The full tale of crimes conveys a numbing insistent horror which beggars summation. It is recorded in some four thousand pages of notes, letters, and diaries written at the time by Y.M.C.A. man Fitch, General von Falkenhausen, and several others including an American surgeon and two American university professors. In addition the Safety Zone Committee filed 444 carefully authenticated "cases" of murder, mass murder, rape, arson, and pillage with Prince Asaka's staff officers while the terror was in progress. Finally the Reverend John Magee, postwar chaplain of Yale University and father of Ian Magee, the war poet, documented the sights he saw with a movie camera. His black-and-white film—which he later protested did not do justice to the "black-and-red realities"—was smuggled home to the United States. Its parade of mutilated corpses, blood-spattered rooms, and babies on bayonets was considered too revolting to exhibit except to a few limited audiences. Ironically enough, sections of the film were given their widest circulation by America First organizations intent on demonstrating the futility of foreign involvements.

On the afternoon of his arrival in town, Tuesday, December 14, sadist Nakajima had bills posted advising Chinese soldiers who had gone into hiding to give themselves up and trust to "the mercy of the Imperial Japanese Army." One of Nakajima's subordinates called on the Safety Zone Committee to inform it that 6,000 discarded Chinese uniforms had been found inside the walls. Unless the soldiers who had worn them surrendered quickly, they would sacrifice their rights as prisoners of war and would be subject to the death penalty as spies. The Western committeemen circulated the Japanese argument by word of mouth through the zone shelters and advised Chinese that it was legally correct. The next day thousands of

Chinese soldiers and coolies who had served in labor battalions gave themselves up. "How foolish I had been," wrote Y.M.C.A. man Fitch a fortnight later, "to tell them the Japanese would spare their lives."

Throughout Wednesday, December 15, the prisoners of war were assembled in city squares, trussed hand to hand and man to man with signal
corps telephone wire, and marched off to pens along the riverbank to be
"interned." That night a command orgy was held beside the pens. The
captives were brought out group by group, surrounded on all sides by
soldiers, and used as dummies for bayonet charges. Kerosene was poured
on the heaps of bodies and ignited. More prisoners were led out to be
prodded into the flames of the pyres. Officers with sabers gave decapitation
demonstrations. A trial was made of old samurai swords in which it was
demonstrated that none had the virtue of being able to split a man from
pate to groin at a stroke.

On Thursday the performance was repeated. For lack of military prisoners Nakajima's men requisitioned any able-bodied Chinese civilian they
could lay hands on. They took the staff which was laboring to turn on the
power again at the electrical plant. They took ninety policemen and forty-
seven volunteer policemen employed by the safety zone. They took a quota
of fathers and sons from most of the refugee camps. Once again novel
forms of execution were tried out in an effort to heighten the terror and
relieve the sickening monotony of bayonet and bonfire. According to
photographs snapped by Japanese officers—and later copied by Chinese
technicians in Shanghai studios where the films were brazenly brought for
development—men were bound hand and foot and planted neck deep
in earth. In the third century B.C., the Chinese emperor who built the
Great Wall of China had executed a band of proscribed Confucian scholars
in this way. Generations of Chinese and Japanese schoolboys had read the
old horror tale with flesh crawling. Its re-enactment at Nanking must have
struck some staff officer as a clever way to exploit cultural traditions, but
in the staging the psychological effect was mitigated by overembellishment
and impatience. In antiquity the protruding heads of the victims had had
to endure the kicks and catcalls of passers-by until the bodies below
ground began to waste away. In 1937 the victims were all dead long
before the onset of starvation and maggots—some jabbed with bayonets,
some trampled by horses, some doused with boiling water, some crushed
under tank tracks.

Between their nocturnal duties as devils on the riverbank, the Japanese
soldiers were employed by day for looting. According to sociologist Lewis
Smythe, one of the American professors in Nanking, the pillage began as
private enterprise. "Japanese soldiers," he wrote, "needed private carriers
to help them struggle along under great loads." But already on the day
after Nakajima's arrival, Smythe also saw "systematic destruction of shop-
front after shop-front under the eyes of Japanese officers." He added,

"Scores of refugees in camps and shelters had money and valuables removed from their slight possessions during mass searches." The great bulk of the booty found its way not into privates' knapsacks but into official Army warehouses. Three months later one of the zone committee tried to track down a piano which had been looted from his home. He was politely conducted by a Japanese officer to an Army storage shed containing two hundred pianos. Other warehouses were filled with rugs and paintings, mattresses and blankets, antique screens and chests. Some high officers, including Nakajima, were able to keep small fortunes for themselves in jade and porcelain and silver, but most of the plunder was later sold and the money used to defray over-all Army expenses.

It was the same day, December 15, that the crime for which Nanking is most remembered became an organized pastime. The raping started when trucks commanded by well-spoken officers made the rounds of the safety-zone refugee camps and took away loads of young women for "questioning." In some instances the pretext was belied on the spot by the soldiers who raped the girls in full public view even before loading them on the trucks. Women of beauty and some education were usually culled from each catch to serve with others of their own quality in the harems of colonels or major generals. Less fortunate creatures were shipped off to the various public buildings and auditoriums where soldiers were barracked. Some were raped for a night by ten or twenty men and then released in the morning, to be called for again and again by other trucks in days to come. Some were violated and then executed. Many immature girls were turned loose in such a manhandled condition that they died a day or two later. Sturdy wives were often assigned as slaves to platoons or entire companies and were expected to wash clothes all day and perform as prostitutes all night. Many young women were simply tied to beds as permanent fixtures accessible to any and all comers. When they became too weepy or too diseased to arouse desire, they were disposed of. In alleys and parks lay the corpses of women who had been dishonored even after death by mutilation and stuffing.

The mass abductions of December 15 and 16 caused panic and wholesale immigration of women and children into the safety zone. Most came stealthily by night; some painted sores and rashes on their faces and skulked in along back alleys by day. The population of the zone climbed from 50,000 to 200,000 in seventy-two hours. Only a quarter of the refugees could fit into the various schools and dormitories where the Zone Committee had organized staffs and kitchens. The rest camped where they could, as close to the organized shelters as possible. They thereby gained a little protection from the zone's policemen and from the nearby presence of Nanking's twenty-two Westerners.

Nevertheless, the Japanese raided the buildings of the zone regularly for more victims. Night after night soldiers climbed over walls into the various compounds, brandished pistols, and had their way with as many cowed women as they wanted. Westerners retained remarkable authority under the circumstances and could usually prevent rape when they came on it in person. Thus Minor Searle Bates, a history professor with degrees from Oxford, Yale, and Harvard, succeeded on five occasions in breaking up acts of rape already in progress. But there were many women in the zone, many buildings, many lascivious soldiers, and the indignant Western missionaries and professors could not be everywhere. Moreover they themselves were sometimes held at bayonet point and made to look on helplessly.

On Thursday night, when the rabble of unkempt, laughing, drunken conquerors had unbuttoned their collective lust for two full days, the members of the Safety Zone Committee met to compare notes. Some of them broke down and wept while trying to tell what they had seen. They estimated that a thousand women were being raped that night and that almost as many had been raped that day. The next morning one of them took into his compound a dazed creature who said that she had been abused by thirty-seven men in turn. Another decided to leave on his lawn undisturbed a baby who had cried and been smothered by a soldier who was raping the child's mother.

In Nakajima's first three days of terror, his men had been ruthless but not efficient in the later Nazi sense. To save machine-gun bullets they had used bayonets for most of the killing, and an astonishing number of victims crawled away to recover. So many thousands of men and women had been submitted to the crude Japanese techniques of genocide that the hundreds who survived are not statistically surprising. But individually the tales of hardihood which some of them recounted at postwar tribunals seem miraculous. Men who quickly threw themselves flat sometimes survived machine-gunning, bayoneting, and burning with kerosene. Men run through with bayonets and "buried" in the river clung to reeds for hours, waiting for the Japanese to go away. Men "beheaded"—their thick carrying-pole shoulder muscles severed but not their spinal cords—recovered untended in river-bank hovels. A few men even lived to tell of scrabbling up out of shallow mass graves. The Chinese peasant who survived his septic childhood had a hardy constitution and an uncomplicated will to live.

TRIUMPHAL ENTRY

On Friday morning, December 17, the rape of Nanking slackened during the ceremonial entry into the city of little General Matsui. Still feverish after the latest flare-up of his chronic tuberculosis, Matsui was brought up-river in a naval launch, put into a car, and driven around to the battered triple archway of the Mountain Gate on the eastern side of the city. There he mounted a fine chestnut with a narrow white stripe or race on its nose.

While he waited at the gate for the triumphal procession to form up behind him, he mused sorrowfully on his old friend Sun Yat-sen, the founder of Republican China, who lay buried in the great mausoleum up the hill to his rear. It was more than twenty years now since Matsui and Sun had first talked dreams together of Oriental unity and brotherhood. It was already eight years since Sun's entombment there on the Purple Mountain. The other Japanese who had attended the entombment as mourners were all dead or discredited. Of all the old group espousing Sino-Japanese co-operation only Matsui still held a position of authority.

Matsui was distracted in his meditations by a stir behind him. He turned and saw that the second place in his cavalcade had been taken by Colonel Hashimoto Kingoro who had sunk the *Panay*. It was a calculated insult. Matsui had tried to discipline Hashimoto after the *Panay* attack only to discover that he was protected by influential friends and that Prince Asaka would not even reprimand him. To make the indignity more pointed, Hashimoto rode a larger, finer horse than Matsui's, a thoroughbred bay with a full blaze on its nostrils. The pleasure went out of the afternoon; the laurels of the conqueror seemed faded and empty. This was Prince Asaka's command territory, and Matsui could do nothing about the affront without merely calling attention to his own loss of face. He was reduced to complaining of the incident a week later to—of all people—the American correspondent of *The New York Times*.

A fanfare of ill-blown bugles sounded and General Matsui led Hashimoto and the entourage of Prince Asaka into the conquered capital. The boulevard before him was lined with tens of thousands of soldiers. He reared his horse and wheeled it smartly to face the palace in Tokyo far and away to the northeast. Nearby the announcer for Japan Radio quickly, softly, tensely told his microphone: "General Matsui will lead a triple banzai for the Emperor."

General Matsui broke in at once in a thin straining voice: "Dai Gen-sui Heika (Great Field Marshal on the Steps of Heaven)—banzai—ten thousand years of life."

A great banzai came roaring back but it ended—he could hardly believe it of Japanese troops on review—in a hideous cackle of drunken laughter.

"Banzai," he ventured more shrilly—and a thousand voices shouted.

"Banzai," he quavered a third time—and a radio technician had to turn down his controls to avoid overloading and distortion. The words were conventional enough but the voices of the men, preserved on tape by Japan's National Broadcasting Company, would have done credit to the legions of Genghis Khan or Attila. Matsui headed his horse down the boulevard and proceeded along a carefully cleared route, past thousands of cheering soldiers, until he arrived at the Metropolitan Hotel in the north of town.

From the shouts and look of the men at the parade and from hints dropped during the feasting at the Metropolitan that evening, Matsui gleaned a shrewd suspicion of what had been happening in Nanking. His specific instructions to quarter only a few picked battalions in the city had been flagrantly disregarded. He cut short the banquet and called a staff conference. According to officers who were present, he dressed down Nakajima and Muto and ordered them to have all unnecessary troops moved out of the city. Billeting officer Muto promised to take a fresh look at accommodations in the countryside.

On awakening in the Metropolitan next morning, Matsui was melancholy. One of his civilian aides asked him why and he replied, "I now realize that we have unknowingly wrought a most grievous effect on this city. When I think of the feelings and sentiments of many of my Chinese friends who have fled from Nanking and of the future of the two countries, I cannot but feel depressed. I am very lonely and can never get in a mood to rejoice about this victory."

Even in his press release that morning, though he dutifully trumpeted official Tokyo policy, Matsui let a note of sadness creep into the bombast: "Future Army operations will depend entirely on what attitude Chiang Kai-shek and the Nationalist Government take. I personally feel sorry for the tragedies to the people, but the Army must continue unless China repents. Now, in the winter, the season gives time to reflect. I offer my sympathy, with deep emotion, to a million innocent people."

All that day Matsui remained lugubriously intent upon the dead. He visited the tomb of Sun Yat-sen, on the Purple Mountain, and sat for hours at a memorial service at the Nanking city airport just inside the southeastern walls. During the ceremony, he composed one of those short, cryptogrammic "Chinese poems" which have been cultivated as a separate art by Japanese literati for so many centuries that they are difficult to understand either for a Japanese or a Chinese. It was addressed to the soul of Sun Yat-sen:

> In the gold-purple tomb
> was he present or absent
> the departed spirit,
> my friend of former years,
> in the ghastly
> field-colors of the dusk?
>
> Memories of past meetings
> on the battlefield
> came back to pierce my heart
> as I sat, head bowed,
> astride my war horse
> under the Mountain Gate.

In the latter part of the memorial service, Matsui delivered a substantial address on the awakening of "Greater East Asia" and the brotherhood of Chinese and Japanese. He spoke of conducting a service for the dead Chinese warriors which would immediately follow the ceremony for the fallen Japanese. However, Prince Asaka told him that since it was growing late the service for the Chinese would have to be held some other time. Matsui was upset; according to the account he gave to his Buddhist confessor shortly before his hanging in 1948: "Immediately after the memorial services, I assembled the higher officers and wept tears of anger before them. . . . Both Prince Asaka and Lieutenant General Yanagawa . . . were there. . . . I told them . . . everything had been lost in one moment through the brutalities of the soldiers. And can you imagine it, even after that, these soldiers laughed at me."

The next day billeting expert Muto reported that he still could find no adequate facilities for troops outside Nanking. And so Matsui, exercising his full powers as commander of the Central China Theater, issued operational orders which would send three of the four divisions in Nanking out on new campaigns across the Yangtze or back toward the coast. The remaining division was Nakajima's "black" 16th, and that Matsui could not touch because it was already assigned to Nanking by Imperial Headquarters in Tokyo. Prince Asaka's retinue of European-educated staff officers, thinking it best to humor Matsui, assured him that his orders would be carried out promptly.

Later that Sunday morning, when Matsui expressed a wish to inspect the whole of Nanking, a group of them drove him up to the observatory on Chinling Hill. There he made them "look curiously at one another"; he studied the destroyed areas of the city intently through field glasses and said, "If General Chiang [Kai-shek] had been patient for a few years longer and avoided hostilities, Japan would have understood the disadvantage of trying to solve the issue between the two countries by the use of arms." On the way down the hill from the observatory, Matsui abruptly asked to talk to some of the Chinese refugees in Nanking. After a brief delay a suitable group was herded together for him, and he went about among them asking questions and offering words of comfort and reassurance.

That afternoon Matsui was removed to Prince Asaka's headquarters outside of Nanking, to be put on a destroyer a day later and sent back to Shanghai.

RAPE RENEWED

While Matsui conducted his sentimental visit to the conquered capital, the terror had subsided. Even in the western half of town which he did not visit, only a few dozen men were executed during his stay and only a few score women raped. As soon as he had left the city, however, terror was resumed. And by midnight the committeemen of the safety zone had set down that Sunday as "the worst yet." For the first time they themselves felt threatened. They continued with impunity to haul soldiers from the bodies of Chinese women, but they were also forced to watch Chinese husbands, who had stirred in defense of their wives, killed out of hand. Matsui in reproving his staff officers had said too much about the danger of antagonizing foreign powers and about the shame of Japan before the world. The men involved in the shame felt compelled to flaunt their indifference. They made a hero out of Colonel Hashimoto who had sunk the *Panay*. They went out of their way to dare the West to intervene. One American was shot at that day and several others were jostled and shoved. Western homes marked and sealed as neutral property were broken into and looted. Chinese caretakers at deserted Western embassies were killed. Star-Spangled Banners and Union Jacks were torn down and trampled. Uniformed Japanese toughs went out of their way to murder in front of white witnesses. A mandarin in a long silk gown was overtaken by two Japanese soldiers under a balcony where two Americans and two Russians were standing watching. One of the Americans later testified: "He was trying to get away, hastened his pace to get away, around a corner in a bamboo fence, but there was no opening. The soldiers walked in front of him and shot him in the face. . . . They were both laughing and talking as if nothing had happened, never stopped smoking their cigarettes and talking, killed him with no more feeling than one taking a shot at a wild duck."

That night the confused devil soldiers were rallied and regimented for a new destructive duty that could be laid out for them in plans like a campaign of battle. The objective was to complete the looting of Nanking's shops and home industries and then, alley by alley and section by section, to burn them systematically to the ground. The arson squads were given trucks in which to load everything of value before a building was put to the torch. For kindling they were issued black sticks of Thermit and strips of paper impregnated with another incendiary chemical. It was cold in Nanking and the men went to work with a will. The first fires bloomed at dusk a few hours after Matsui had left the city. By the next night Y.M.C.A. man Fitch, looking from his bedroom window, could count fourteen districts all blazing at once.

If anyone doubted that the rape was to continue, he was disabused on Friday morning, December 24, when Nakajima advised the Safety Zone Committee that the number of Chinese soldiers who had doffed their uniforms and gone into hiding was not 6,000 as previously estimated but 20,000. Equally ominous, it was noted that the molestation of women had begun to take new and extreme forms—grandmothers over seventy, girls under twelve, and mothers in the last month of pregnancy.

After Matsui had gone, his staff officer Colonel Muto, the billeting expert, stayed on in Nanking "overseeing the enforcement of Matsui's orders." There was "some delay" in withdrawing the surplus divisions. By Thursday, December 23, Yanagawa's renegade 114th, the brutal 6th, and Matsui's own 9th had withdrawn from the city. Thereafter only Nakajima's 16th was left to superintend over the longest, most disciplined stage of the rape. Nanking was already a picked carcass; only a sharp knife could cut more flesh from it.

ASAKA'S LAST OUNCE

Prince Asaka, the Emperor's uncle, moved his headquarters into Nanking on Christmas Day. He remained within the walls all through January while rape and murder continued to ladle off blood from the city into a graduated chemical flask. It was not until the last hope of frightening or shaming the Chinese into capitulation had vanished—the last little girl been violated—that he finally started back toward Tokyo on February 10.

In Shanghai little General Matsui heard of new atrocities in Nanking every day. He remained powerless to stop them and so he "worried greatly" about Prince Asaka's reputation. On Christmas, the day that Asaka moved into Nanking, Matsui voiced his worries in an interview with *New York Times* correspondent Hallett Abend—whom he struck as "likeable" and "pathetic." Having little hope that this indirect plea to Emperor Hirohito, through the pages of *The New York Times,* would do any good, he followed it up the next day by sending a message to Prince Asaka's chief of staff. "It is rumored," he wrote, "that unlawful acts continue. . . . Especially because Prince Asaka is our commander, military discipline and morals must be that much more strictly maintained. Anyone who misconducts himself must be severely punished." Privately, over a New Year's toast, Matsui told a Japanese diplomat, "My men have done something very wrong and extremely regrettable." Asked later if the men had thrown over the traces and gone berserk, he pointedly said, "I considered that the discipline was excellent but the guidance and behavior were not."

Despite Matsui's protests it remained a commonplace to stumble on new bodies in the fetid streets or to see queues of soldiers waiting their turn outside a doorway where some Chinese woman had at last been run to earth. All the men remaining in the city were registered by Nakajima's secret police, and a few score of them were selected each afternoon for that night's beheading party. The city remained without light, water, garbage disposal, police, or firemen. The Safety Zone Committee warned Prince Asaka's headquarters of the danger of plague. Asaka's staff officers replied by offering to take over the feeding of the 100,000 Chinese who were being kept alive by the zone's daily rice dole. With this responsibility, of course, the Japanese Army would assume control of the zone's rice warehouses and international relief funds. The Zone Committee refused the offer. Western newspapers were beginning to print their first eyewitness accounts of what had happened in Nanking.

Prince Asaka's engineers finally turned on the city's public utilities on January 7. Three days later Prince Kaya, a cousin of Hirohito's Empress—one who had served in previous years as an admiring emissary to Adolf Hitler—paid Nanking a ceremonial visit and "talked earnestly to second lieutenants." On January 16, after Prince Kaya's report home to the Throne, the lanky, cynical Prince Konoye played his last trump and announced that the Japanese people no longer recognized Chiang Kai-shek as the representative of the Chinese people, that war to the death would continue to be waged against the Chiang regime, and that a Japanese-sponsored government would soon be available to all Chinese who wished to give their allegiance to peace and Pan-Asianism.

Konoye's threat to continue the war indefinitely was a threat to kill China; the rape of Nanking had been the preliminary torture supposed to make Chinese believe the threat and fear it. But police technique, usually so successful against individual Chinese, failed to work on the Chinese nation as a whole. Konoye's declaration elicited no response. Indeed the Chiang Kai-shek government had never been more popular than in its present fugitive state in Hankow. And so the unsuccessful policy was gradually abandoned. Corpses were cleared from the streets and ponds and the systematic burning of the city ceased. The last abuse protested by the Safety Zone Committee—the rape of a twelve-year-old girl—took place on February 7, fifty-seven days after the Japanese had completely occupied the city and quelled all resistance. General von Falkenhausen, the German, continued his meticulous account a little further, up to March 19 when he noted that a girl was raped by a Japanese soldier in the U.S. missionary compound.

FINAL TOLL

In all, according to figures accepted after two years of hearings by a panel of eminent jurists from many lands, the International Military Tribunal for the Far East which sat in Tokyo from 1946 to 1948, 20,000 women were raped in Nanking and its vicinity and over 200,000 men, at least a quarter of them civilians, were murdered.[8] A third of the city was

---

[8] Many Japanese maintain that the figures accepted by the tribunal are grossly exaggerated, being based in part on Chinese claims. The author, after reviewing the original data and weeding out Chinese statistics, believes it fair to say that not less than 100,000 war prisoners and 50,000 civilians were executed within thirty-seven miles of Nanking and that at least 5,000 women were raped, many of them repeatedly or on several occasions.

destroyed by fire. Everything of value was removed from the ruins and placed in Japanese Army warehouses. The Nanking shopkeeper and the farmer outside the walls were economically wiped out. According to a survey conducted in March 1938 by sociologist Smythe and his university students on a 2 per cent sample of the population, the farmer had lost in money and goods the equivalent of 278 days of labor, the city dweller the equivalent of 681 days of labor. Since both at the best of times lived at subsistence level, the wherewithal to begin life anew did not exist. There were few stores of seed grain for replanting, few savings with which to stock shops. Thousands of utterly hopeless women and children had no future except the day-to-day dole of rice provided by international relief funds. It would be a year before capital filtering back into Nanking from other parts of China began to create employment opportunities and a semblance of economic revival.

REWARD AND PAYMENT

The tally of lives taken at Nanking was obviously no accident. It would not be easy for 100,000 men to kill 200,000 in the course of routine carelessness, drunkenness, and disorder. But despite world-wide protest against the crime, none of the criminals were in any way punished by the Japanese government of the time. It was official Tokyo doctrine that the troops in the field had gone berserk and that nothing could be done about them. When the Nanking veterans first returned home, however, many of them told a different story—a story of disgust at what they had seen and done. They complained that they had "learned nothing in the Army but rape and burglary"; that they had had to shoot prisoners merely to test the efficiency of machine guns; that they had been ordered by their officers, in dealing with Chinese girls, "Either pay them money or kill them in some out-of-the-way place after you have finished." In February 1939, the War Ministry issued orders to suppress such "improper talk" which may "give rise to rumors" and "impair the trust of the people in the Army." Even today Nanking is regularly referred to by retired Japanese Army officers as "the ten-year shame" or "the great dishonor." Except in the most vague theoretical terms, it remains impossible to talk about Nanking with any Japanese who participated in the deeds done there.

After Japan's defeat in 1945, Japanese government spokesmen claimed at the war crime tribunals that an Army officer had been court-martialed and put to death for responsibility in the Nanking fiasco. They did not give his name or rank. They said that a noncommissioned officer had even been sentenced to prison "for stealing a Chinese lady's slipper." They said that many of the principals in the rape had been "severely reprimanded."

True 1937 Japanese attitudes toward Nanking are not reflected in such dubious latter-day assertions. More relevant facts are these: that on the day after the capture of Nanking Emperor Hirohito expressed his "extreme satisfaction" to Prince Kanin, his wife's grand-uncle, who was chief of the Army General Staff; that Prince Kanin sent a telegram of congratulations to General Matsui, telling him that "not since history began has there been such an extraordinary military exploit"; that in late January Prince Kaya, the Empress's fascistic cousin, returned from Nanking and gave the Emperor a full report on what he had seen there; that a month later, on February 26, Emperor Hirohito received the febrile Matsui, the princely Asaka, and the eager Yanagawa at the imperial summer villa in Hayama and rewarded each of them with a pair of silver vases embossed with the imperial chrysanthemum.

Matsui retired to build his shrine of remorse at Atami, Prince Asaka to play golf. No longer in disgrace, General Yanagawa was appointed by the Emperor to run the economy of occupied China and then serve as minister of justice, no less, in the Japanese Cabinet. He finally died of disease as proconsul in Sumatra in 1944. Billeting expert Muto rose steadily to become a major general and chief of the powerful Military Affairs Bureau in 1939, lieutenant general and commander of the 2d Imperial Guards in 1942, and later Yamashita's chief of staff in the Philippines in 1944–45. The ubiquitous Major General Suzuki Tei-ichi, who had done the cerebral desk work in Kyoto for the terrible 16th Division in the field, remained as always Hirohito's personal envoy and troubleshooter in the Army, moving about with breathtaking versatility from one delicate appointment to the next. As for the sadistic Nakajima, who had dirtied himself most in the rape, he was allowed to retire from the Army in 1939 and to live out his life in comfort on the spoils which he had brought back from Nanking.

Hirohito honored all the criminals, punished none of them, and remains to this day on cordial terms with his kinsman Prince Asaka. If Hirohito had any feeling at the time that Prince Asaka had sullied the family name, he gave no sign of it. He continued to play golf with Asaka, to attend weekly showings of newsreels with him, to grant him private audiences, to sit with him on the exclusive *Gokazoku Kaigi* or Council of Princes of the Blood. If Hirohito had any feeling that Prince Asaka had been deceived or exploited by his Army subordinates at Nanking, he gave no sign of that either. On the contrary he appointed three other members of the imperial family to important Army commands in the six months after the rape of Nanking.

It is the crowning irony of Nanking that the man who finally shouldered all the blame was little tubercular General Matsui. He was tried, along with the other six leaders enshrined at Atami, by the International Military Tribunal for the Far East. Scattered through the 150,000-page record of the trial may be found the gist of Matsui's part in the rape as it has been recounted here. Nowhere in the record is there any evidence that Matsui issued secret orders for the rape to take place. Nowhere did the Allied attorneys for the prosecution ever impeach his sincerity or catch him out in even one lie.

On the other hand, there is also no explicit statement by Matsui or his defense lawyers that his authority as Central China commander-in-chief was overridden at Nanking by the imperial authority of Prince Asaka. Instead, in one of the most fuzzy defense presentations in the annals of jurisprudence, Matsui's lawyers allowed him to discourse about Sino-Japanese friendship in a windy manner that could only impress his judges as hypocritical. He wound himself in a noose of Buddhist piety and mysticism. He buried himself in pompous platitudes. His judges were naturally impressed by eyewitness accounts of Nanking bestialities. When they heard him offer no adequate excuses for the fact that he had been in over-all command in Central China they assumed that he must be worthy of hanging. Matsui himself did not disagree. After a decade of introspection, he felt that he should have done more to guide Prince Asaka and the Emperor and that it was his religious duty now to die in protection of the Throne.

"I am happy to end this way," he said. "After things turning out this way, I am really eager to die at any time."

Memoirs, orders, and diaries which have come to light in Japan since the trial tend to corroborate Matsui's story. Moreover, the conduct of the trial itself, as an honest quest for truth, is open to question, and has been questioned by every single Western historian who has since had occasion to review it. It is an incredible fact of the Matsui case that Prince Asaka, who was in direct command at Nanking and physically present there during most of the rape, was never summoned into court to testify even as a witness, much less as a defendant. The judges, who knew his position of command and listened to many less important stories at tedious length, would not have been averse to hearing his account of the rape of Nanking. They were prevented from doing so by the terms of the political equation which held in Japan immediately after the dropping of the atomic bombs and the Japanese surrender.[9]

History is not merely enacted and recorded but made and remade by later events and later points of view. After Nanking, Japan went on to invade South China and then Russian Mongolia. In the year that followed, 1940, Japan remodeled herself domestically as a one-party police state totally mobilized for modern warfare. In early 1941, Japan made a satellite of French Indochina and began to train troops seriously for the conquest of British Malaya, of the Dutch East Indies, and, contingently, of the Philippines. That summer President Roosevelt cut off Japan's supplies of strategic materials, particularly oil. In the negotiations which followed, Japan expressed herself willing to accept all of Roosevelt's conditions, except the

[9] This point is taken up in detail in Chapter 3.

most important: withdrawal from China and from the bases there which could be used against the Philippines and other points south. Emperor Hirohito ordered the attack on Pearl Harbor to be prepared, and when Roosevelt persisted in calling the Japanese hand, Hirohito overrode voices of caution and procrastination and ordered the attack to be launched.

In the next six months Singapore, the Philippines, Borneo, Sumatra, Java, and a dozen other islands of immense natural wealth fell to Japan in an Army-Navy operation of unexpected brilliance and ferocity. The atrocities of Nanking were repeated again and again—at the Bataan Death March, in the building of the Burma-Thailand railway, in the final desperate rape of Manila in 1945. Then came the counter-atrocities, the appalling incendiary raids on the wood-and-paper cities of civilian Japan, and the atomic bombings of Hiroshima and Nagasaki.

When Japan had been effectively defeated, the Japanese dream of an Asiatic empire lay buried under four million corpses. If the Emperor ordered it, the Japanese people were prepared to add their own seventy million bodies to the carnage heap before admitting the defeat. America's war, however, had been waged against fascism, not the Japanese people. To stay the slaying, peace had to be made at any price. How it was made will be told in the next two chapters. The price paid was a polite international lie, a falsification of history. It was not a high price, but historical lies have to be corrected if anything is to be learned from the lessons of life on earth. From the fourth chapter onward, this book presents a previously untold story: the inner workings of the Japanese government during its attempt to conquer the world.

If a grievous miscarriage of justice was delivered by the United States and her Allies in the hanging of General Matsui in 1948, it is at least not thought of that way by most Japanese today. Rather, they see Matsui's death as a noble suicidal sacrifice in the interests of peace and the saving of Japanese and American face. The musical stick of lamentation, struck daily by the weeping priestess at the shrine in Atami, tolls in her own ears not merely for her kinsman general, nor merely for the other war criminals on the hill above her, not merely for Japan alone, but for all men everywhere.

2

A-BOMB

HIROSHIMA

You will proceed to a rendezvous at Iwo with two other B-29's. One plane will carry it.

The other planes will carry instruments and photographic equipment. You three will not contact each other, but will maintain the strictest radio silence.

Weather observation planes will be returning from over the Empire and the area of the targets. They will not address you directly, but speak as if addressing the base at Tinian. You will naturally take extreme care in hearing their reports. If they are not understood you will not break radio silence to ask repeat. They will be repeated as prearranged.

You will approach the target at a ground speed around 300 mph, and maintain a steady bombing platform at about 30,000 feet.

Bombing will be visual. If the city of choice is not clear, proceed at your discretion to another target.

As bomb is released, you will immediately turn at a 150-degree angle.

You must not, repeat, not follow standard bombing procedure by proceeding as usual to fly over the target . . . You will not fly over this explosion.

After bombs away, turn sharply so as not to be over Ground Zero when the device explodes. You may even wish to lose altitude to put more distance between yourself and zero.

Following these specifications, planes of the 509th Composite Group had practiced for seventeen days dropping oddly shaped "punkins" of Torpex explosives on various Japanese cities. Japanese plane spotters had grown used to the sight of B-29's that came in harmless threesomes and dropped a single bomb. Japanese radio propagandists had even picked up enough idle radio chatter from American ground crews in Tinian to taunt the 509th because its men put on airs of importance and secrecy. Tokyo Rose said that they had been trained in America's last desperate resort: "magic."

On August 6, 1945, however, the 509th's *Enola Gay* was not carrying magic or pumpkins but a "Thin Boy," a long slender container in which small pieces of uranium-235 waited at one end to be fired at a large piece held at the other—in short, an atomic bomb. Six and a half hours from take-off in Tinian, at exactly 8:15:17 A.M. Hiroshima time, the special bomb-bay doors opened and the bomb and its parachute were toggled out. Colonel Paul W. Tibbets took back the control from bomb-run pilot Major Thomas W. Ferebee, put the plane into a violent turn, and at full throttle headed down and out. About two minutes later—fifteen miles away—the fleeing *Enola Gay* leapt like a bronco. Captain Robert Lewis who was keeping the flight log had last written, "There will be a short intermission while we bomb our target." Now he entered the simple exclamation, "My God!"

The bomb had burst in a clear blue sky about 1,500 feet over the northwest center of the city and of its 245,000 inhabitants. For an instant a ball of fire 250 feet in diameter had hung in the air like a piece out of the heart of the sun. And in the next instant some 64,000 Japanese civilians had been set aflame or crushed. Another 26,000-odd were scorched and riddled with neutrons and gamma rays. They died within the following minutes, days, weeks, and months.

A great light sparked the land out to 100 miles. An intense thud of sound leveled 6,820 buildings at a clap and could be heard over ten miles away. The whole center of the city, a mile wide, burst into flame. A titanic spout of air and ashes—ash of buildings, ash of people—shot into the upper atmosphere and flattened into a mushroom head against the floor of space. Around the foot of the fiery cloud, cold air rushed in to fill the vacuum, gradually picking up speed until two and three hours after the explosion it roared in to fan the flames with a 30- to 40-mph gale. Around the outer eddies of the fire storm, where the initial heat wave had parched everything to tinder, more fires sprang up as if licks of flame were breaking through the earth from below. In a few hours four square miles were burning.

The pall of airborne rubbish hanging over the city darkened the crackling streets. Hail-sized drops of muddy water, taken up as vapor from Hiroshima's rivers, sporadically fell out of the cloud in a kind of rain. The ionized air had a pervasive electric smell such as one scents near a lightning stroke or a welder's arc. Small tornadoes played around the edges of the storm, disturbing the ruins and toppling still-standing trees.

Stunned human beings, finding escape holes from collapsed buildings near the center of the blast, joined processions of horribly burned ghosts who had been caught in the open but were still alive enough to try to walk away. Mildly burned and irradiated outsiders hovered on the perimeter of the inferno looking for relatives. They saw and never forgot the bodies stumbling out, flayed by the heat, skin black or bubbled or hanging in gray strips. The three rivers flowing out of the heart of the city became clogged with corpses of adults and notably of children who had quenched their seared lives in the water.

As the fire spread it caught many mildly injured people trapped under wreckage. Passing evacuees extricated some and ignored others. Men in search of their own families were even said to have stopped and apologized for obeying what they considered to be their first duty. Some sections of the city became entirely ringed with flames and the survivors in them huddled in open parks and gardens. In these sanctuaries, the dying died. Those destined to live fought fires that crept in on them, went about distributing cups of water from broken pipes and running streams, told stories for the children, swapped theories about what had happened, and spread rumors about what would happen next. A low-flying plane caused terror of strafing. The queerness of the rain suggested that the city was being sprayed with gasoline for final immolation. Soldiers went about searching for American parachutists.

For the first thirty hours most survivors wandered about digging in ashes, staring at horrors, unwittingly picking up roentgens. Electricity was out, water pipes had been broken in 70,000 places. Of forty-five hospitals, three were left standing and of their staffs only twenty-eight out of 290 doctors and 126 out of 1,780 nurses remained uninjured. Yet life did go on. It was determined later that earthworms, even in the immediate area of ground zero, continued to crawl only a few inches beneath the surface of the soil.

Gradually above ground, too, a semblance of order was restored. On the day after the bomb the governor of the prefecture called for "rehabilitation of the stricken city and an aroused fighting spirit to exterminate the devilish Americans." The Japanese Army, which for all its faults was a relatively modern and efficient organization, took charge of relief. Casualties were herded into hospitals. Army stockpiles of food and blankets were distributed. Heaps of corpses were soaked with gasoline and incinerated. The fires burned out in three days, the embers smouldered for a few days more.

By final count six months later, over 90,000 civilians and almost 10,000 soldiers had perished. Another thousand-odd were to die in the decade ahead of leukemia and other radiation diseases.

NAGASAKI

The U.S. had a second type of atomic bomb ready to drop on Japan: "Fat Boy." A prototype of it had already been exploded atop a test tower in the New Mexican desert. Fat Boy depended for its power on an extremely fissile element, plutonium, which was not found in nature but was man-made at a plant on the Columbia River in the state of Washington. Atoms of the plutonium were distributed more or less evenly throughout a compressible medium which kept them apart and prevented them from engaging in chain reactions. They were encased on the outside in a spherical shell of conventional explosive charges. When the charges were sparked and detonated, the plutonium atoms would be blown in on one another and for a fraction of a second would be held together so tightly that a far more universal splitting of the atoms would take place than in the shotgun type of uranium bomb used at Hiroshima. Indeed, the Fat Boy was expected to pack at least three times the bang of the Thin Boy.

Since Fat Boy was the second atomic bomb, everyone involved in dropping it knew that he was making awesome history. Casualty estimates had already been broadcast concerning Hiroshima. Radios crackled with commentary and speculation about the significance of the atomic age a-dawning. Japan must surrender soon. Not even the suicidal kamikaze pilot could stand on his honor while his entire homeland was being erased city by city. Moreover, the U.S.S.R. was massing tanks on the Russo-Manchurian border in order to snap up the continental fragments of Japan's collapsing empire. The Soviet offensive was launched at midnight on August 8, Tokyo time. President Truman was informed of it an hour later, and the news was broadcast. Bomb crews in the Pacific, preparing for early morning take-offs, took it in with their coffee and briefings.

Fat Boy was scheduled to be dropped on Japan on August 11. A few hours before the Russian drive started, on the afternoon of August 8, the Fat Boy bomb crew were out dropping a practice "punkin" in the Pacific. That evening when their B-29, named *Bock's Car,* touched down at the U.S. air base on the Pacific island of Tinian, the crew were abruptly notified to be ready to fly again that night—this time in earnest. A wide storm center was forming out in the Pacific. Southern Japan was expected to cloud over the next day and to remain closed in for five days thereafter. To avoid any chance of a mistake, President Truman had ordered that the Fat Boy be cast visually, not by radar. General Thomas Farrell, the Tinian commander who had discretionary powers as to when the next A-bomb should be dropped, had decided to move up the date from the eleventh to the morning of the ninth. William Laurence, *The New York Times* science reporter who was to accompany *Bock's Car* in one of its attendant camera planes, observed dryly, "I'll bet those weather forecasts came all the way from Potsdam."

From the beginning the crew members of *Bock's Car* seemed dogged by hard luck. To be ready for early morning take-off they were allowed only two hours of sleep. Awakened at 11 P.M., they were briefed until midnight, then ate a light meal and stood by during the loading of the bomb and the complex checkout of all its mechanisms. At the last minute the flight engineer discovered that an auxiliary fuel pump was out of action and that a

600-gallon tank of reserve gasoline would not be available for use during the long flight home. "To hell with it," decided Major Charles Sweeney, the *Bock's Car*'s pilot. He took off at 1:56 A.M., Tokyo time.

An hour later the crew of the *Bock's Car* were disturbed by an extraordinary breach of radio silence from headquarters in Tinian. One of the two attendant photographic planes had left behind a physicist who was supposed to run a scientifically important high-speed camera. For thirty excruciating minutes everyone including, it was feared, Japanese radio monitors listened while the operation manual for the unmanned camera was read out over the airwaves. An hour and a half later, the black box which monitored and controlled the Fat Boy began to flash a red light which indicated that all firing circuits were closed. For another tense half hour the crew waited in fear of fission while the lieutenant in charge of electronics delved into the black box. It turned out that a faulty switch had lit the warning light meaninglessly. Another hour and a half of napping and routine passed. Then at 8:12 A.M. *Bock's Car* rendezvoused with one of its two camera planes off the southern tip of Japan. The second camera plane, the one which had left behind its physicist, was cruising at a higher altitude a little to the north. For forty minutes the planes circled in search of one another, passing again and again just out of sight. At 8:56 Pilot Sweeney decided that the fuel supply was too short for further search and headed north toward his target. Weather planes up ahead reported conditions excellent: dawn haze clearing, blue skies shining through.

The primary target that morning was not Nagasaki but Kokura, a manufacturing town of 170,000 inhabitants on the north coast of Kyushu, the southernmost of Japan's main islands. Kokura had been little bombed previously and was an ideal target. It lay in a plain and nudged so closely against the industrial cities of Tobata, Wakamatsu, and Yawata that the four have since been amalgamated as a single megalopolis, Kitakyushu, the fifth city of Japan. Had *Bock's Car* unloaded Fat Boy on Kokura that morning, it is estimated that at least 300,000 of the 610,000 people in the four cities would have been killed.

As Major Sweeney approached Kokura at 9:30 A.M., he was pleased to see that the weather held, the sky was clear, the visibility excellent. As the plane passed over its target, however, Bombardier Kermit Beahan reported that he could not see the arsenal which he was supposed to use as aiming point; it was obscured by the smoke of factory chimneys.[1] Major Sweeney

---

[1] *New York Times* correspondent William L. Laurence, in an eyewitness account which was delayed by censorship and not printed until September 9, wrote that there was "no opening in the thick umbrella of clouds that covered" Kokura. This was the official story for many years but now crewmen of the bomb plane deny it. By September 1945, when his article appeared, Mr. Laurence was extremely busy, being given a whirlwind Air Force tour of atomic installations in the United States as background for an exclusive series of articles on the manufacture and testing of atomic bombs.

circled and came in for a second bomb run. Once again the city fled past below. Once again the river and other landmarks near point zero could be seen clearly but not the arsenal. Once again Bombardier Beahan called out, "No drop." On the third bomb run members of the crew murmured that Japanese antiaircraft gunners were beginning to get the range and that Japanese fighters were climbing from below. For the third time Bombardier Beahan failed to see his bull's-eye and shouted, "No drop." Circling and surveying the white puffs of the flak over the city, Major Sweeney announced that he was giving up and proceeding to the secondary target, Nagasaki, ninety miles to the southwest. By now the fuel situation was critical. There was no possibility of returning to Tinian. The plane would have to refuel at Iwo Jima or at the airstrip on recently secured Okinawa.

Bock's Car thundered in toward Nagasaki a few minutes before eleven in the morning. The edgy crew saw clouds ahead and begged for a radar drop. Navy Commander Fred Ashworth, who had over-all charge of the bomb, at first refused. Major Sweeney assured him, "I'll guarantee we come within a thousand feet of the target." As there was not enough fuel left to carry the heavy bomb back to Okinawa the only alternative would be to jettison Fat Boy over the ocean. After a moment's hesitation Commander Ashworth decided to disregard President Truman's orders and gave his consent.

Nagasaki stands at the head of a V-shaped bay. Its two heavily built-up strips of harbor front meet at the center of the city and extend inland up two narrow valleys. The distinctive X-shape of the city showed up clearly on the radarscope. Ground zero was supposed to be the center of the X. But as *Bock's Car* bore in on it, Bombardier Beahan suddenly sighted a stadium through a rift in the clouds, a stadium which he recognized from reconnaissance photographs. "I'll take it," he shouted. He asked for a correction to the right and received it. Less than a minute later, at 10:58 A.M., Tokyo time, he released the bomb visually and *Bock's Car* jumped as Fat Boy fell from the bomb bay. Major Sweeney banked his plane sharply and hared away to the south toward a forced landing on Okinawa two hours later.

Behind him, dangling from its parachute, drifted the "gimmick" as it was known to the fliers—the *pikadon* or "thunder-and-lightning" as it would be dubbed by the men on the ground. It had been released not 1,000 feet off target but 11,000 feet or more than two miles. It was descending over the bowl-shaped valley of Urakami, which housed Nagasaki's most important war factory, the Mitsubishi Ordnance Works. Through the valley ran another valuable objective, the railway line which linked the big peninsular port city to the rest of Japan. All of the dozen Japanese who looked up, and lived to write about it later, remember searching a clear blue sky. Several of them saw the plane; two of them saw the bomb and its parachute. At their lathes, turning out torpedoes and small arms, the workers in the

Mitsubishi plant heard nothing. The congregation at the Friday morning mass in the nearby Our Lady of the Immaculate Conception, the largest Roman Catholic cathedral in the Orient, saw nothing. The roar of machinery, the opacity of stained glass saved them from fear before they died.

Four minutes after release, at a point approximately 1,540 feet above the ground and 200 feet east of the railway line, the bomb went off. Directly under it, destruction was complete, more complete than at Hiroshima, and death was instantaneous. But the bowl of the Urakami Valley shielded the rest of Nagasaki from direct radiation. There were no fire storms, no strange falls of muddy rain. The valley's two-mile strip of city had simply been crushed flat. The immense thunderclap echoed from the surrounding hills, overtaking the fleeing *Bock's Car* and jolting it with no less than five separate head-jerking shocks. By a count made six months later, 39,214 men, women, and children had died.[2]

ATOMIC DECISION MAKING

The two atomic bombings took 140,000 lives in all. The rape of Nanking, eight years earlier, had taken approximately the same number. Japan's conquest of Asia had begun and ended in horror. An eye for an eye and a tooth for a tooth had been meted out to an uncanny jot and tittle by the whirling scythe of war. Unlike Nanking, the A-bomb has become one of the most completely documented events in history. The unknown terrors of radiation, the horror of death by flame, the large number of victims who lingered on to die weeks later have all combined to give humane men and women everywhere an uneasy conscience. Many have wondered whether an act of vengeance or even cold-blooded racism was not committed. Bertrand Russell, the British mathematician and political idealist, went so far as to call Hiroshima "a wanton act of mass murder." It is difficult to face the skulls of Hiroshima and Nagasaki objectively. Cautious Ph.D.'s, however, have searched and searched again through the records of the decision-making process which led to the A-bombing of Hiroshima and Nagasaki, and have found little to cavil with.

At the time of the bomb decision the statesmen of three nations were

[2] Had it not been for Bombardier Beahan's lucky two-mile miss, another 50,000 to 75,000 would have been killed. Beahan does not maintain that the miss was entirely accidental. He says guardedly that he knew where he was dropping the bomb and that the stadium which he sighted through the rift in the clouds was an "alternate aiming point." It may be, then, that the humane miss was authorized at a high level in General Carl Spaatz's Strategic Air Command. Wasting the kill power of such an expensive weapon would have been sufficient reason at that time for hushing up the story. Five minutes after dropping the bomb the radio operator on *Bock's Car* flashed Tinian: "Results technically successful but other factors involved make conference necessary before taking further steps."

pitted against one another in a triangular negotiation, conducted through curtains of national security and self-interest. For U.S. leaders the concern was to find a surrender formula that would make it possible after the war to revolutionize Japanese culture, root out the cherished cults of samurai and Emperor worship, and cure Japan of the wish to spread ruin, ever again, through the Far East. The Emperor and the men around him had narrower objectives. They wanted to keep as much as possible of the Japanese Empire, to protect themselves from execution or imprisonment as war criminals, and above all to preserve the institution of the imperial family which had become, in modern Shinto, the be-all and end-all of Japan's spiritual life. The third party in the surrender struggle was Russia, represented by Stalin. And in Stalin's eyes the self-interest of the U.S.S.R. lay simply in acquiring for communism as much territory and influence as possible.

To achieve its ends each of the three parties had certain powers which encouraged it and certain fears which inhibited it. The United States had the strength to invade and crush Japan utterly, but could not revolutionize the governing process in Japan without the co-operation of the people and particularly of their leader and god, the Emperor. Consequently the United States needed not only to keep the Emperor as an agent but also to keep him in doubt about his future status so that he would be a helpful agent. Where Russia was concerned, the United States was in a position either to offer or withhold sanction for land grabs which the Soviet Army could and would make, with or without authorization, among the pieces of Japan's vast continental empire. The United States also had some power, through threat of landing troops on the China coast, to see that the government of China was turned back to Chiang Kai-shek rather than to Communist Mao Tse-tung.

The power of Japan's leaders lay in their ability to command a fanatic last-ditch battle from hill to hill and cave to cave which would have cost the United States 250,000 to 1,000,000 G.I. lives, would have decimated Japan, and for the future, would have deprived U.S. policy of the most viable, most stable, and most progressive nation in postwar Asia. In addition the Japanese could, at last resort, give the U.S.S.R., unopposed, the fair provinces of Manchuria, Korea, and China in return for continued neutrality and war materials with which to fight U.S. invasion.

As for the U.S.S.R., her veteran armies, in co-operation with those of Mao Tse-tung, had the brute strength to make Manchuria and most of China safe for communism. She might do this without casualties and without honor by making a deal with "fascist" Japan, or if the war lasted long enough, she might gain Anglo-American blessing to do it by force. Though depleted, the Japanese armies on the Continent were still dangerous. To defeat them would take manpower needed for the reconstruction of war-ravaged western Russia. Moreover, the U.S.S.R. had a nonaggression treaty with Japan which would not expire until 1946. On the other hand, to make a deal with Japan would be to incur the disapproval of Communists everywhere and the instant antagonism of the United States and Britain. Russia could, in fact, do nothing at all if she wished. She had much to gain and nothing to lose simply by a policy of watchful opportunism. Therefore, when Berlin fell in May 1945, the U.S.S.R. began to move the Red Army east to await developments on the doorstep of the Japanese Empire.

When the bomb burst in this triangle of power politics, it disrupted all the equations of statesmanship. Japanese leaders had no inkling of its presence until Hiroshima was actually hit in August. Stalin was far better informed. Soviet espionage had revealed to him the existence of the bomb project in early 1945. He knew that it was nearing success. When his troops had captured atomic research laboratories in Germany, he had been briefed on their purpose and told the potential military significance of the bomb. But as subsequent events were to show, Stalin did not fully appreciate the new weapon until it was used. To him it was only a bigger bomb. And in his lifetime he had seen bombs enlarged from one kilogram to a thousand without upsetting the basic power balances between nations.

As the guardians and bankers for the international group of physicists who had built the bomb, U.S. leaders had been the first to wrestle with the implications of the new weapon. The far-sighted War Secretary Henry Stimson notified the new President Harry S Truman on April 25, 1945: "The world in its present state of moral advancement, compared with its technical development, would be eventually at the mercy of such a weapon. In other words, modern civilization might be completely destroyed." Truman noted in his memoirs that Stimson "seemed at least as much concerned with the role of the atomic bomb in the shaping of history as in its capacity to shorten this war."

On April 7 a new Cabinet had taken office in Japan. The State Department had analyzed it as a "peace cabinet," but as yet it had sounded no overtures to peace. On May 1 Under Secretary Joseph C. Grew, the prewar ambassador to Japan, met with the Navy and War Secretaries to urge that the United States offer some face-saving token that would serve as an opening for negotiations. Both Stimson and Navy Secretary James Forrestal were sympathetic. "How far and how thoroughly," asked Forrestal, "do we want to beat Japan?" Enough to make Japan a law-abiding nation was the accepted answer, but no one was sure how much of a thrashing that answer implied. Former Ambassador Grew wished to assure the Japanese that they could keep their Emperor, but a number of other State Department officials, including Assistant Secretaries Dean Acheson and Archibald MacLeish, the poet, argued that the ills of Japan might not be curable as long as the Emperor remained even as titular head of state.

After Grew's meeting with Stimson and Forrestal on May 1, President

Truman on May 8 faced up to the obdurate belligerence of Japan and told the press that the United States would fight on "until the Japanese military and naval forces lay down their arms in unconditional surrender." He called for "termination of the influence of the military leaders who have brought Japan to the present brink of disaster." He promised that the United States did not want "extermination or enslavement of the Japanese people" but only a "return of soldiers and sailors to their families, their farms, their jobs." His words were, of course, beamed to Japan by radio and were dismissed by many of the Japanese privileged to hear them as mere propaganda. A few days later Truman wrote home to his family:

> I know that Japan is a terribly cruel nation in warfare but I can't bring myself to believe that, because they are cruel, we should ourselves act in the same manner. For myself, I certainly regret the necessity of wiping out whole populations because of the "pigheadedness" of the leaders of a nation and, for your information, I am not going to do it unless it becomes absolutely necessary. My object is to save as many American lives as possible, but I also have a humane feeling for the women and children in Japan.

Throughout May, the humane Truman waited in vain for any Japanese response. In Moscow, on May 28, Stalin suggested to Presidential Envoy Harry Hopkins that it might be possible to accept a conditional surrender from the Japanese and then, after occupying Japan, to escalate gradually the severity of American demands; in other words, according to Hopkins, "to agree to milder peace terms but once we get into Japan to give them the works."

This was the world of sharks and gentlemen in which, on May 31 and June 1, the leading political strategists of the United States met with the top atomic scientists of the United States to discuss policy regarding the big new bomb being perfected at Los Alamos. The group was called the Interim Committee and included Presidential representative James Byrnes, War Secretary Stimson, Chief of Staff George C. Marshall, A-bomb Project Director Major General Leslie R. Groves, and representatives of the Navy and State Departments.

On the scientific side, the meeting was staffed by Vannevar Bush, James Conant, and Karl Compton and was assisted by the expert testimony of three Nobel Prize winners: Karl's brother Arthur Compton, Enrico Fermi, and Ernest O. Lawrence, the cyclotron builder. All three advisors were pioneers in nuclear research, fission, and chain reactions, and they had been living with the vague theoretical threat of the bomb since the early 1930's. They had with them J. Robert Oppenheimer, the physicist whose charm and political ability had played a major role in enabling generals, scientists, and industrialists to pull together in production of the bomb.

Stimson, the white-haired Secretary of War who had shaped U.S. policy in the Orient since the Japanese conquest of Manchuria in 1931, swept the gathering with his burning eyes and declared the purpose of the meeting:

> Our great task is to bring this war to a prompt and successful conclusion. We may assume that our new weapon puts in our hands overwhelming power. It is our obligation to use this power with the best wisdom we can command. . . . To us now the matter of first importance is how our use of this new weapon will appear in the long view of history.

Technical questions followed Stimson's opening. Though still untested, the bomb would almost certainly work. Two bombs would be available for use early in August. Thereafter an additional bomb would be ready for delivery every few weeks.

Throughout the morning session, it was assumed that the bomb would be used. At lunch Arthur Compton suggested that it might be most humane to hold a demonstration of the bomb for the Japanese before using it on a target. War Secretary Stimson enthusiastically agreed. But over dessert the idea foundered in a sea of practical difficulties. Without killing anyone or devastating a city, what demonstration in America would impress an observation team of Japanese generals? On a mesa or bleak salt flat, the big firecracker would be startling but it would do little visible harm to the surface of the earth. How make the generals pace off the distances, learn to trust the wind gauges and seismographs, and compute the difference between this bomb and other bombs? How persuade them that it was not all some kind of gigantic materialistic Yankee stunt?

To stage an announced demonstration in an uninhabited section of Japan also seemed futile and quixotic. Under combat conditions many things could go wrong: the bomb might not work or the plane and its bomb load might be captured by the enemy. The President's representative, James Byrnes, feared with good reason that the Japanese, if warned in advance, might assemble an army of American and British P.O.W.'s to stand shackled as viewers and victims of any demonstration.

For the statesmen present, time was of the essence. If the scientists could really deliver their goods, Japan might surrender before Russia gobbled up China. The daily toll of Japanese lives taken by conventional bombs— 80,000 in a single incendiary raid over Tokyo on May 10—might cease. The bomb offered an opportunity, in Churchill's words, to "end the whole war in one or two violent shocks"; and in Stimson's words, to "save many times the number of lives, both American and Japanese, that it would cost."

The Interim Committee, including all the scientists present, finally voted against demonstration and for military use of the bomb. At the same time the scientists were asked by Stimson to consider the matter further and "prepare a report as to whether we could devise any kind of demonstration that would seem likely to bring the war to an end without using the bomb against a live target." The scientists' answer was delivered on June 16. It said, in a sentence that Stimson underlined in his own copy, "We can propose no technical demonstration likely to bring an end to the war; we see no acceptable alternative to direct military use."

A group of equally distinguished atomic physicists, who did not sit on the Interim Committee but had also worked on the bomb, disagreed vehemently. At a series of meetings conducted by Nobel Prize winner James O. Franck at the University of Chicago, they drew up the Franck report, a strong idealistic plea not to use the bomb in warfare. Their protest, which was submitted in Washington but never reached the highest levels of government, was couched in strategic, moral, and political terms. They foresaw the possibility of "suitcase warfare," that is "a Pearl Harbor disaster repeated in thousandfold magnification in every one of our major cities." They recommended that the United States demonstrate the bomb before representatives of the United Nations and then turn it over to an international control commission. After demonstration, they said, the bomb might be used against Japan with the sanction of the United Nations.

At a time when the United Nations was just being organized and the Russians were beginning to show their postwar colors, internationalization of the bomb was not an idea calculated to appeal to U.S. statesmen. The one scientific question at issue, that of staging an effective demonstration of the bomb for Japanese leaders, was begged by the Franck report. It should perhaps have been considered more deeply. That perennial political loner, Edward Teller, who later masterminded the H-bomb, has since asserted: "I was positive then and I am positive now, that we made a mistake dropping the bomb without a previous bloodless demonstration. We could have used the bomb to end the war without bloodshed by exploding it high over Tokyo at night without prior warning. If it had been exploded at an altitude of 20,000 feet, instead of the low altitude of 2,000 feet . . . there would have been a minimum loss of life, if any, and hardly any damage to property, but there would have been tremendous sound and light effects. We could then have said to the Japanese leaders: 'This was an atomic bomb. One of them can destroy a city. Surrender or be destroyed!' "

Such a demonstration might very well have been effective. Indeed it might have impressed the leaders in Tokyo more than the actual obliteration of provincial Hiroshima. The technical difficulties of getting the dropplane away from the burst at such an altitude could have been solved readily. The uncertainties of a night attack, so long as it were made without warning, would have been minimal. The fact is, however, that the suggestion was never put forward in government circles.

After the Interim Committee had met on June 1 and voted to use the bomb militarily, the decision was never changed. It was, however, kept open to change. In the six weeks that followed, President Truman was preparing for the last of the wartime conferences with Stalin and Churchill.

It was to be held at Potsdam in the Soviet Zone of Germany. There the decision to use the bomb would be made final. Up to the last minute Truman watched Japan. Through radio monitoring and code breaking, he had access to all messages which passed between Tokyo and Japanese embassies in neutral countries. He was also privy to the reports of Army, Navy, and O.S.S. agents. Though not all of this intelligence has yet been made public, he cannot have found in it much hope that Japan was about to accept unconditional surrender because the actual deliberations in Tokyo at that time were a study in procrastination and bluff.

JAPAN'S DILEMMA

The majority of Japanese officials had long recognized the need to surrender but their will to act was frozen. They did not know how to admit to one another that they were beaten. They only knew what they had done in their own conquests, and they feared vengeance in kind. Theirs was not the Washington world of brusque, explicit proposals and of statesmen concerned with moral issues but a murky political atmosphere of guarded allusions and feudal allegiances, of time-consuming etiquette and prickly samurai honor.

Emperor Hirohito had been reminding his ministers to miss no chance for concluding an advantageous peace ever since the Japanese capture of Singapore in February 1942. Indeed, a Navy peace mission, equipped with special code machines and clerks, had been installed in Switzerland in 1941 even before the attack on Pearl Harbor. It was charged with keeping channels of negotiations open and maintaining contact with U.S. Intelligence. To Hirohito's dismay, however, the Japanese mission discovered that U.S. leaders had no interest in a negotiated peace. The Americans remained confident of final victory even at the lowest ebb in their fortunes. They took the position that they had been forced into war by Japan's surprise attack and that they did not mean to cease fighting until they had divested Japan of her empire and made her into a peace-loving nation. In October of 1942, Hirohito had the Army dispatch to Europe its own corps of peace experts. The major general in charge of the mission, Okamoto Kiyotomi, was an intimate friend of the Emperor's brother Prince Chichibu, who enjoyed a reputation in the West for pro-British attitudes. Nevertheless, in Sofia, Ankara, Vichy, and Berne, Okamoto and his three fellow officers found that neutral mediators held out little hope.

Six months before Pearl Harbor Hirohito had had the Naval General Staff make a study of war prospects. When the results were submitted to him, he had ordered that the study be made again by a separate group of staff officers. The second analysis corroborated the conclusion of the first: that Japan could wage war successfully on the United States for eighteen months, or until June of 1943. After that Japan must negotiate a peace or she would gradually lose everything. When the deadline passed and Japanese envoys still reported no hope of arranging a settlement, both Army and Navy had new studies made of the war outlook. By the end of 1943 the Navy's had been completed and the Army's was nearing final draft. The Navy's concluded that Japan had lost the war and would be forced to give up all the territorial acquisitions which she had made since 1880. The Army study concurred and went a step further: Japan might be able to attach only two conditions to surrender, that the homeland be spared from ravage and that the imperial dynasty be left on the Throne.

The chilling conclusions of the two staff studies were difficult to accept. Hirohito's forces still held a vast empire, an area of the globe wider than Canada and almost as long as South America. Prime Minister Tojo assured Hirohito that the cold figures of war production and war losses could lie; much could happen. But Hirohito understood figures. The staff conclusions might not be inevitable but he must still make some provision for the eventuality of defeat. He therefore asked his closest civilian advisor, Lord Privy Seal Marquis Kido Koichi, to study the problems of peace from his standpoint as a specialist in opinion making and domestic political control.

Kido committed his first thoughts to paper on January 6, 1944, precisely nineteen months before the bomb fell on Hiroshima. The war, he conceded in essence, is lost. We must make a realistic peace proposal before Germany capitulates. We should ask the U.S.S.R., as a neutral in the Pacific War, to act as our go-between and convoke a "commission of the principal Pacific nations" to dispose of our conquests. We must be ready to let them all go, either returning them to China or giving them their independence as "permanent neutral nations like Switzerland." Then, "in view of the terrible attrition we have suffered," we must "preserve and cultivate our power for one hundred years." Above all we must "keep the Anglo-Saxons from destroying us as a colored race." We around the Throne "will have to retain our actual power in the state secretly."

If the Throne was to keep its power in secret and Japan was to lie low for one hundred years, the people of the country would have to be carefully prepared. The fighting men had staked their honor on victory or suicide, and hundreds of thousands had died in the Emperor's name. If peace were declared prematurely, patriots would say that Hirohito lacked courage to fight the war through. Widows and orphans would blame him for letting their loved ones die in vain. To save the nation's face, then, the war must be continued until everyone had suffered from it and was eager to see it finished. At that point the people could be made to feel that they had fought poorly and let the Emperor down. At that point, if Hirohito declared peace, the people would feel obligated to him.

Kido discussed his ideas with other members of the Emperor's Young Set—all in their fifties now—and found that they had been thinking along similar lines. According to an ancient metaphor, the Emperor lived "above the clouds like a crane," surveying the whole state of his nation and leaving the routine of government to his appointed officials. On those rare occasions of national crisis when he felt compelled to issue direct commands to his people, his intervention was known as "the Voice of the Crane." The members of the imperial cabal all agreed that, when the right moment came to announce a surrender, the Emperor should do it personally and suddenly, as if on an impulse of pity for the sufferings of his subjects. Then his act could be romanticized at home and abroad as "a sacred decision" enunciated by the Voice of the Crane. It might even be effective to break with all precedent and broadcast his voice on the radio.

To make Japanese absolve Hirohito would be difficult, but to make the democratizing conquerors accept the Emperor would be a problem of incalculable difficulty. Personally Hirohito did not care what happened to himself. If he lost the war—and he did not admit that he had lost it yet— he would gladly abdicate. It was the imperial institution, the bequest of his divine ancestors, which must be protected. With this one proviso, Hirohito encouraged Kido in his peace plans and returned to his preoccupation of the moment, the defense of the Marshall Islands.

Having gained the tacit consent of the Emperor, Kido delegated the task of contingency planning for defeat to a group headed by the lanky, cynical Prince Konoye, the prime minister at the time of the rape of Nanking. The group called itself the "Peace Faction." It included Japan's living ex-prime ministers, half a dozen of her leading diplomats, and several of her best strategic minds from the Army and Navy General Staffs. It met secretly at first in Konoye's home, the "Hate-China" Villa, where he had lived since the fall of Nanking in 1937. Later in 1944 it hired a regular secretarial staff and rented space in the Dai Ichi Insurance Building overlooking the southeastern gate of the palace. This location was ideal. In the basement Japan Broadcasting Corporation had its secret emergency radio station. On the sixth floor were the headquarters of the Tokyo Area Army and a switchboard controlling direct lines to the palace, to the various police headquarters, and to all military barracks in the city.

The duty of the Peace Faction was not to promote peace, as its name implied, but to salvage as much as possible from surrender. Analysis of American propaganda broadcasts to Japan revealed that Americans tended to exaggerate the dominance of "the military clique" in Japan. As a former foreign minister explained it to Lord Privy Seal Kido: "In the United States they think there is a confrontation between moderates and extremists. They think the extreme group suppresses the moderate one." Hoping to exploit this misapprehension, the Peace Faction created cover stories and remade public images for the century of enforced quiescence which Kido envisaged after defeat. Army and Navy officers were sought out who would be willing to take the part of extremists and lead mock mutinies against the Emperor when it came time for him to surrender. Men with reputations as moderates were coached in the roles they would have to play as postwar cabinet ministers. Still other moderates were recruited from the business world to take charge of hidden imperial assets and care for them as their own property. Since true moderates were in short supply, make-believe moderates were manufactured by the simple expedient of having the secret police keep dossiers on them as possible subversives. In this fashion even Prince Konoye, who had led the nation to war in 1937, hoped to create dove's clothing for himself.

In early 1945, Lord Privy Seal Kido had the secret police imprison four hundred members of the Peace Faction and keep them in detention for forty days. He apparently did so without consulting them, but as they were well treated they did not hold it against him. Many of them had once been leading advocates of war with the United States and Great Britain. Now they were cleared in Western eyes and would be enabled to hold government posts during the American Occupation. Indeed one of them, Yoshida Shigeru, was to serve for seven years as a postwar prime minister. Since 1933 he had been an unabashed proponent of the Strike-South policy, against the United States, Britain, and the Netherlands. Now, overnight, in a well-appointed prison cell, he became a certifiable hero of the resistance movement. His sudden transformation was all the more bewildering to the silent populace because he was the son-in-law of Count Makino, the Emperor's chief advisor from 1926 to 1935. Makino had been implicated in all of the assassinations and fake coups d'etat of that era which had turned Japan's military zeal from the U.S.S.R. towards the United States.

The staff officers of the Peace Faction saw the second great weakness in American political psychology as an obsessive fear of communism. By playing on it, they felt that they could make Americans look at modern Japanese history in a new and more sympathetic light. The assignment fell to Prince Konoye. He qualified as something of an expert because his son, "Butch," who later died as a prisoner of war in Russia, had attended Princeton. Konoye set about his task by creating "notes" and "diaries" which would explain the events of his own three years as prime minister. He discovered that the forgeries were more difficult to write than he had anticipated. He knew too much about the complexities of Japanese politics to frame straightforward arguments. Throughout the summer of 1944 his false starts piled up in his secretary's files. One of them, a specially composed "diary," turned up as late as 1967 at one of the inns to which he used to take assorted male and female companions.[3]

---

[3] Japanese, who are ordinarily tolerant about such matters, shake their heads over Konoye's sex life. They complain that he had a taste for men and women of the lowest classes and that he would give entire weekends to the bizarre experiences which they devised for him. A geisha who knew him has defended his aberrations as "a natural expression of his speculative mind."

Finally Prince Konoye wrote a long, implausible "memorial to the Throne" which he later turned over to Allied Intelligence. To give it standing as a document of state, he actually read the memorial to Hirohito on February 14, 1945. He and the Emperor must have chuckled over some of the allegations in it. Konoye accused the Communists, "as part of a purposeful plan," of inciting militarism in Japan "ever since the Manchurian incident" of 1931. The Reds, he said, had brought "the country to its present plight" in order to create conditions for lower-class revolution in "the confusion that will arise out of defeat." Unfortunately for Konoye's thesis, all Communists and most leftists of any description in Japan had been in prison since the late 1920's. The only civilians agitating for militarism had always been hired bullies belonging to Court-sponsored "patriotic societies." To cope with these awkward facts, Konoye went on to explain that "our right-wingers are nothing more than Communists masquerading."

Throughout the planning of peace, Lord Privy Seal Kido encouraged Hirohito to maintain a bold public front of fight-to-the-finish. Only thus could the honor of the samurai be satisfied. Only thus could the people be kept at their jobs. Only thus could the enemy be made to appreciate the expense involved in reducing Japan's island strongholds. Only thus, finally, could the Americans be persuaded that the real power in Japan lay not with calculating civilians of the highest caste but with soldier fanatics from one of the lower castes.

In the spring of 1944 Hirohito approved construction of a labyrinth of tunnels under three mountains in the wild Nagano Alps. He let it be believed that there, if worst came to worst, he would preside over the final Imperial Headquarters and fight to the death with his best troops. Six miles of concrete galleries were ultimately completed and 75,000 men employed on them at a cost of $20 million. Even Hirohito's personal bathtub was installed. But he never expected to use it. He acknowledged to intimates that if he ever left Tokyo the people's will to resist would collapse.

Later, in the autumn of 1944, Hirohito sanctioned the manufacture of "special attack weapons," kamikaze planes and torpedoes designed specifically for suicide missions. He put his seal on plans for fire lanes across the major cities, swathes of houses cut down to minimize the effectiveness of incendiary bombing. He supported, in his edicts and rescripts, a campaign of domestic propaganda calculated to persuade the people that the U.S. government meant to rape and destroy Japan thoroughly in the event of defeat.

A year passed in which Japan lost battle after desperate battle. When Saipan and the Marianas fell in June of 1944, Hirohito was persuaded that perhaps a new prime minister would tempt the U.S. government into making a peace offer. Hirohito therefore withdrew his support from Prime

Minister Tojo, who was supposed in the United States to be the archmilitarist, and smoothly replaced him with a less notorious member of the imperial cabal, reserve General Koiso Kuniaki. Although he had masterminded much of the plotting for the conquest of Manchuria in 1931, Koiso was little known outside Japan. Wizened and narrow-eyed, the new prime minister looked more like a Chinese opium den proprietor than a Japanese head of state. He was known in Japan as a man of guile, a specialist in counterespionage rather than combat. His appointment signified that Japan was no longer trying to win by conventional force of arms but only to salvage what she could by intrigue. It was under Prime Minister Koiso's guidance that Japan now resorted to human bombs, human torpedoes, and banzai charges. Though they made U.S. victories costly, the kamikaze tactics could do no more than slow the leapfrog approach of American task forces.

THE GREAT BLUFF

On January 6, 1945, exactly a year after admitting to his diary that the war could not be won, Lord Privy Seal Kido, the Emperor's chief civilian advisor, was thumbing papers and digesting lunch in his book-lined study on the third floor of the Imperial Household Administration Building. He was a slightly built, owlish man of fifty-five—short sparse hair, spidery utilitarian glasses, a Hitler mustache. To those who were his friends he was known for his dapper grooming, his light-colored waistcoats, and his "hunted animal look," a disarming expression of puzzled astonishment with which he greeted all news, whether of rain outside or of a city destroyed. To those who were not his friends, Kido was known for theatrical fits of hysteria in which he would shriek threats at social inferiors who thwarted him. His detractors liked to point out that he kept a pack of savage chows and police dogs locked in separate cages along the front of his villa and that he had fed them red meat throughout the period of wartime rationing. Behind the mask of Kido's driven personality worked a mind which friend and foe alike conceded to be the coolest, quickest, and soundest in the counsels of government. Emperor Hirohito, who had known Kido all his life and had worked with him closely since 1922, valued his judgment and held a genuine affection for him. When Kido was put on trial as a war criminal in 1946, Hirohito let it be known that he would abdicate if Kido were sentenced to death.[4]

Now, when the telephone rang, it was the Emperor asking Kido to come over and talk to him. Kido summoned his charcoal-burning limousine and

[4] Kido was released from Allied prison in 1956. Thereafter he lived in a villa outside the palace, shunning all publicity. At late as 1968 neighbors said that he looked as frail and aristocratic as fine rice parchment but remained lively, saw many visitors, and read many books.

went downstairs to wait for it. The Imperial Household Building, once a dazzling concrete symbol of Court modernization, looked dingy under its protective wartime stripes. The watery winter sun did not flatter it. When the car came, it drove Kido along the northern outbuildings of the ceremonial Outer Palace where Matsui had received his baton of command for the offensive against Nanking in 1937. The car continued up a drive flanked on the left by the moat and wall of the Inner Palace enclosure. On the other side of the wall were scattered the facilities dedicated to the personal use of the Emperor and Empress: Hirohito's biological laboratory and experimental rice field; Empress Nagako's silkworm house; the Imperial Shrine in its courtyard of white pebbles; the severely Japanese Residential Palace in which Hirohito no longer lived. All were surrounded by an artful sea of vegetation, the woodland of the Fukiage Gardens. It had suffered little from the austerity care of wartime. Its surprise turnings still surprised; its perfect vistas still satisfied. Fewer cranes and peacocks strutted the paths but there remained the arching bridges, the rock gardens, the hidden lotus pools, the tiny greenhouses containing dwarf trees, some a thousand years old.

Kido's car took a sharp left, crossed the moat on a causeway, and passed through a gate into the inner enclosure. A short driveway did scant justice to the wonders of the gardens. Through the trees on the left Kido could glimpse the gables of the English-style country house where the Empress and her chief ladies had their wartime quarters and where Emperor and Empress entertained close personal friends. It was known officially by the colorful old name of Ka-in Tei, the Pavilion of Concubines, but no concubines had been kept there during the two decades of Hirohito's reign.

Straight ahead at the end of the drive rose a squat rectangle of concrete known as *Obunko,* the Honorable Imperial Library. Hirohito had built it as a work place and over the busy years it had become his home. Now, in addition to his office, it consisted of a complex of anterooms, and sixty feet below, in the hill on which it stood, an air raid shelter. The concrete walls of the bunker, twenty feet thick, enclosed ventilating machinery, cubby-holes for attendants, a comfortable Western-style living room and bath, and a long monastically furnished audience chamber. The walls were pierced by two sloping shafts. The tunnel from the audience chamber led up a staircase to a steel bulkhead in the hillside behind the library. The shaft from the living quarters came out to a concealed door in Hirohito's above-ground workroom.

As Kido made his way into the library, past guards and chamberlains, he reviewed the arrangements with satisfaction. Hirohito was waiting for him. "The American fleet," Hirohito said, without prologue, "has begun to shell the beaches of Lingayen Gulf. I am told that they will land and that it will be difficult to defend Luzon." Luzon was the main island of the Philippines, and Hirohito's information was accurate and up-to-date. Soft-

ening up of the beaches had begun that morning in preparation for a
landing three days later. "The situation," continued the Emperor, "is extremely grave and I wonder if the time has not come for me to consult the
elder statesmen. What do you think?"

Hirohito was telling Kido that he was ready to order his government and
people to surrender. He never consulted the elder statesmen, the former
prime ministers of Japan, unless he was about to take a momentous step.
The last time he had seen them had been before Pearl Harbor. The majority of them then had advised him against war with the United States
and he had disregarded their counsel. In offering to consult them again now,
he was admitting that his course of conquest had been wrong from the
beginning; that his life, in effect, was a failure. Kido knew how difficult it
must be for him. The forty-three-year-old Hirohito was no longer the taut
ambitious prince of 1922. He felt himself middle-aged now, growing fat
and puffy from overwork and lack of exercise. His people murmured
against him. As he paced his study, his drooping mustache quivered and
his short legs shuffled jerkily as they always did when he was nervous. He
cut a sad figure, as symbolic of Japan in defeat as he had once been,
in his scrubbed callow youth, symbolic of the aspiring opportunistic Japan.

"As you say," said Kido, "the war situation in the Philippines is extremely grave, and as it develops we may have to reconsider seriously our
guidance of the war. But before we do I beg of you to stand back and
await developments for a while. I think you should sound out the real
convictions of the two chiefs of staff on a thoroughly informal basis. Then
later call in the members of the Cabinet. Finally, if you deem it necessary
to decide on a change in the fundamental imperial policy, summon a joint
meeting of the Cabinet and the elder statesmen in the Imperial Presence."

It was no part of Kido's peace plan to have the Emperor admit his
mistakes or blurt out his declaration of peace prematurely. First he must
give up his direct personal supervision of military operations and ask the
chiefs of staff to take all the responsibility for further defeats. Then he
must warn the members of the Cabinet of his change of heart so that they
could make necessary political arrangements. Then finally, when the public
mind was prepared, he should simply announce his decision to the elders.
Hirohito gladly took Kido's advice and from that day on he became a
willing cog in the machinery which Kido had been designing for the past
year.

Lord Privy Seal Kido, as chief advisor to the Throne, had assumed the
dread responsibility of deciding when the moment was ripe for the imperial decision. His final meticulous arrangements went forward at an
excruciating snail's pace. It would be disastrous to declare for peace too
early. Kido could not be sure that his plan would work at all. It must have
the benefit of perfect timing. The nation must be reduced to war-weariness.
The soldiers must sate their sense of honor. If possible, the enemy must
begin to feel shame and pity.

The B-29's came almost nightly. Men on whom Kido counted disappeared in the air raids. Men lost sleep in shelters. Men had to be pushed. Hirohito, himself, sometimes wavered and had to be encouraged. On January 22, 1945, Kido wrote a heartening poem for him:

> If a hedge of plum
> can survive a winter
> of sear and fallow,
> the heart of the warrior
> can also bloom again.

While Kido waited for the perfect moment, 200,000 Japanese died.

From the last week of January until early in April, 1945, Hirohito gave private audiences, one by one, to each of the admirals and generals in the top echelons of the military bureaucracy, to each of Japan's former prime ministers, and to a number of lawyers, professors, cartel owners, and mouthpieces for slum gang lords. By mid-March there was hardly a man of influence who had not pledged his silent unselfish co-operation in the plan for national survival. As each of them emerged from the Imperial Library or from the audience chamber in the bunker below, he had further conversation with Lord Privy Seal Kido and learned what specific service he might render.

While the political muster continued, so did the military bluster and bluff. Nine thousand obsolescent planes were hidden in forest airstrips. Suicide pilots were put in training to man them. Gangs of peasant volunteers drove stakes and dug entrenchments along Japan's sacred beaches. Exhibits of hoes, rakes, axes, bamboo spears, and other rustic secret weapons were mounted in such public places as the lobby of the prime minister's residence. The last concrete was poured at the headquarters of final resort under the Japanese Alps. The Americans were promised a "final decisive battle" if they ventured to land, as anticipated, in the coming autumn.

On March 24, 1945, the wizened Prime Minister Koiso, in whose help Hirohito had been led to expect subtlety and sophistication, came to the library, in agitation after a stormy Cabinet session. He requested an immediate audience, and asked Hirohito's approval for plans to make the government a complete military dictatorship. Hirohito did not intend to give the Army more power than it already possessed. He feared that if he did Japan would be committed to a suicide course. He had hoped that Prime Minister Koiso would be able to remain in power until the summer, by which time the nation and the armed forces might be fully prepared for peace. But events had moved too swiftly and Koiso already found the political pressures on him intolerable. The Emperor, he said, must either let him prepare for war to the last or replace him with a true surrender Cabinet.

Hirohito listened in silence while his prime minister described the deterioration of national morale and the psychological need for drastic political reorganization. Out the window it was another fine spring afternoon. The sun smiled down as if in mockery on the Fukiage Gardens. It had been a month of unrelieved disaster. In two weeks more than 100,000 Tokyo residents had burned to death in the great fires of the enemy's first incendiary raids. In four weeks Iwo Jima had fallen. It was the first island to be lost on Japan's inner defense perimeter, the first home island where Japanese fishermen had lived for centuries. With Iwo had perished 20,000 soldiers and any hope that the new kamikaze tactic of despair would do more than postpone the inevitable. All those 20,000 men had vowed to die and take as many Americans with them as possible. They had had eight months to dig tunnels and develop the natural caves of the rocky island. And in the end they had killed less than 7,000 Americans and held out for less than five weeks. Their failure was a preview of the fate in store for Hirohito if he accepted the Army's plan and became a chieftain of guerrilla werewolves in the Nagano Alps. Prime Minister Koiso came to the end of his report.

"I appreciate the painful service that you have rendered," said Hirohito. "Since you have offered it, I will accept your resignation. But I must ask you to keep it confidential and remain at your post until I have appointed a suitable successor for you."

Imperial advisor Kido spent the next two weeks in difficult negotiations. The prime minister and principal Cabinet members who were to succeed the Koiso government had been chosen tentatively, as part of the peace plan, during the previous autumn. But now many of them felt that it was too early for their appointment. The high command of the secret police could give no assurance that the armed forces were ready yet to accept a peace cabinet. The government might discover on surrendering that it spoke for only a part of the country and had become a "Badoglio regime" like the one in Italy. Nevertheless, having weighed the risks and consulted the elders, Lord Privy Seal Kido finally advised the Emperor to proceed according to plan.

Hirohito accepted Kido's recommendation and on April 7, 1945, invested as the next prime minister Suzuki Kan-taro, a retired admiral of eighty. Mrs. Suzuki had helped to take care of Hirohito as a little boy and the admiral himself had served from 1929 to 1936 as Hirohito's grand chamberlain, one of his four principal advisors.[5] No man had done more to turn the Emperor's eyes south toward the wealth of the Indies. No

---

[5] The other three were the lord privy seal, who specialized in domestic political intrigue; the chief aide-de-camp, who handled liaison with the Army; and the imperial household minister who took care of the Emperor's intricate finances. It was the grand chamberlain's function to counsel the Emperor in personal, religious, and diplomatic matters.

man had done more to furnish him with an image as a peace-loving constitutional monarch. No man knew him more intimately. "To Suzuki,"
Hirohito once said, "I could pour out my heart."

Despite his years, the old admiral-chamberlain maintained a droll façade
of youth. He had big ears, a puckish face, and an elfin sense of humor.
He smoked as many cigars as the defense effort would allow him. Whenever he had a spare moment, he produced a volume of Taoist philosophy
and appeared to immerse himself in it. He larded his talk with ancient
Chinese aphorisms. He never disagreed with anyone and almost never
expressed an opinion. "The art of government," he liked to say, "lies in
non-government."

Prime Minister Suzuki opened his term of office with a call on the people
to fight and die to the last. His words, as he later explained, were an
exercise in *haragei,* belly acting or belly talk, the art of saying one thing
and meaning the opposite which has been cultivated by Japanese ever
since the nation became an efficient police state in the tenth century A.D.
Suzuki knew that he would be considered at home and abroad "a peace
prime minister." At his investiture ceremony, according to his recollection
later, he was "given to understand" that he must end the war.

After searching his soul and talking with Lord Privy Seal Kido, Suzuki
saw his mission in the terms of an old Japanese romance. A baron who had
been defeated in battle and had lost the flower of his knights was called on
by the enemy to surrender his castle. His surviving retainer besought him
to seek terms and save his life. He refused. He retreated to the castle,
dismissed the retainers, opened the gates wide, and stood exposed on the
drawbridge all alone. When the enemy came in sight, he shouted, "If you
want to come, come." The enemy, fearing a trick, retired, and the shrewd
baron was left to rebuild his fief. This was the stratagem which Hirohito
was to use in surrendering his Imperial Throne to the conquering Americans.

In Washington former Ambassador Grew correctly interpreted the appointment of the Suzuki Cabinet as a peace gesture. He responded, as
Suzuki would have wished, by asking for Japan to be reassured that she
could keep her Emperor system. When the suggestion was not accepted
by President Truman, Prime Minister Suzuki's vigil on the drawbridge
became a nightmarish test of nerve. Japan's ally, the Third Reich, was
collapsing with terrifying abruptness. By mid-April 1945, a month after
crossing the Rhine into German territory, Eisenhower's armies had driven
to within sixty miles of Berlin. To the east the Red Army had broken
out from its bridgeheads on the Oder River and was even closer to the
German capital. The idea that troops could perform miracles when
fighting on their native soil lay exposed. Japan's hope of winning a decisive battle on her home beaches began to look foolish. The home minister
in charge of police and the education minister in charge of propaganda

consulted with Lord Privy Seal Kido on means of suppressing popular unrest. On April 29 Hirohito's forty-fourth birthday was marred by news that his former ally Mussolini had been executed at Lake Como the day before and his corpse mutilated and left in the gutter by a mob of angry Italians.

On May 1, Hirohito warned Lord Privy Seal Kido of the imminent capitulation of Germany and discussed it with him for fifty minutes. On the following day they discussed the suicide of Adolf Hitler. In his initial peace planning sixteen months earlier, Kido had hoped to negotiate a peace before the fall of Germany. Now that the Allies had both hands free to strangle Japan, the last hope of negotiating terms had vanished and unconditional surrender became inevitable. But Japan must appear to be an irrational nation. Otherwise there would be no need for the Emperor to intervene and speak with the Voice of the Crane. More than ever, therefore, Japan must show that she was ready to hold out insanely. On May 7, the day of Germany's official surrender, Kido went through his family strong room to remove from it all documents and mementos which might incriminate the Throne.

Two days later an operational dispatch in code, stamped "urgent, confidential, top military secret," arrived at the Navy Building across the street from the plaza outside the main south gate of the palace. It came from Commander Fujimura Yoshiro who had sat out the war as the head of the Navy's peace-seeking mission in Switzerland. Desperately worried about his nation's plight, Fujimura had recently redoubled his efforts. Now he proudly reported that Allen Dulles, the head of O.S.S. in Europe, had offered his services in case Japan should wish to arrange a termination of hostilities. Fujimura followed his first cable with six others in the next ten days. He described the havoc which Nazi diehards had brought to Germany. He enumerated the Allied forces which were being diverted from Europe to the Pacific Theater. He relayed intelligence that Russia would soon join in the war against Japan. He described the part which Allen Dulles had played in bringing peace to northern Italy and preserving it from destruction.

Fujimura's cables from Switzerland continued to arrive at the Navy Building. Pressure mounted on the two principal officers of the Navy General Staff to give some kind of answers. On May 18, when five cables had accumulated in in-baskets, Hirohito's brother Prince Takamatsu, a captain on the Navy General Staff, came to the palace to discuss the cables with Hirohito and Lord Privy Seal Kido. It was unthinkable for the Emperor to make peace directly with the Americans—not after ordering the attack on Pearl Harbor, not after the Americans had scorned earlier offers of negotiated peace. But perhaps—and Prince Takamatsu merely raised the possibility—perhaps, after all, Hirohito should abdicate in favor of his eleven-year-old son and leave others to assume the responsibility and chagrin of capitulating to the Americans. Kido disagreed sharply. Abdication would be not only cowardice but an admission of guilt. It would discredit the Throne in the eyes of the people and make democratization easy for the conquerors. Hirohito agreed.

Rumors that an American peace feeler had been rejected brought Hirohito's popularity in the Tokyo bureaucracy to an all-time ebb. When the senior member of the imperial family, Prince Kanin, died on May 21, three days after Prince Takamatsu's visit to the palace, the cause of his death—hemorrhoids—was the subject of disrespectful jokes. Nevertheless, the next day, Commander Fujimura in Switzerland was sent a cable warning him that the O.S.S. offer "contains certain points indicative of an enemy plot. Therefore we advise you to be extremely cautious." [6]

In a week during which 193 kamikaze pilots were hurling themselves to death at Okinawa, the chief and vice chief of the Navy General Staff felt that they could not shoulder the responsibility for refusing Dulles's mediation. Hirohito accepted their resignations on May 25 and replaced them a few days later with admirals tough enough to ignore further cables from Switzerland.

On the evening of the resignations, May 25, wagging tongues were stilled by catastrophe. American bombardiers, who had a fine record for missing hospitals, universities, and the palace, neatly cleaned out an area south of the palace walls with incendiaries. It was a calculated escalation. Other fire raids had taken more lives but this one burned out the aristocracy and singed the Throne. It destroyed the principal ministries of the government and ninety-one villas belonging to the most distinguished families in Japan. Seven Imperial Princes and uncounted chamberlains had to flee their burning homes and take refuge within the palace moat.

Hours after the raid was over the ceremonial Outer Palace caught fire. Chamberlains explain, with a snide sense of poetic justice, that during the burning of the War Ministry half a mile away, old contingency planning papers were lofted into the night air and came down smoldering on the tiled palace roofs. Some 5,000 Imperial Guardsmen and several hundred officials were encamped within the moat that night, but the flames spread quickly. Hastily organized bucket brigades succeeded in wetting down the Imperial Household Ministry and preserving it untouched, but the older buildings which stood wall to wall with it were all burned to the ground: the lovely Phoenix Hall and banqueting chamber, the villa of the crown prince, and many outbuildings including several storehouses for imperial

[6] Later, on June 20, when a month had passed, the zealous Fujimura was informed that his problem had been referred to the foreign ministry and that in future he would kindly submit his proposals through channels at the Japanese diplomatic office in Berne. The O.S.S. at once dropped Fujimura as a cold contact. The Japanese diplomatic codes had been broken by every major nation. To deal further with Fujimura would be to talk to Tokyo over a line tapped in Moscow.

records. Some firemen who took all the responsibility for failing to check
the flames were later found shot nearby. As the embers cooled, Hirohito
announced from his concrete library in the Fukiage woods, "I am glad to
share the sufferings of my people."

The American attempt to bring the war home to Japan's richest and
most influential citizens only caused the great feudal vassal families to draw
in closer to the Throne. It was clear now that the Americans were ready,
if need be, to topple the entire social hierarchy. They would not consider
Hirohito's personal abdication an adequate expiation of war guilt. The
elite must survive or perish together. Lord Privy Seal Kido, the Emperor's
principal advisor, discovered that he had new supporters. A dawn of com-
prehension gleamed in other aristocratic eyes when he spoke of the elaborate deceptions envisaged in his peace plan. Three days after the fire,
when the minister of war sought to resign in apology for the destruction
of the palace, Hirohito was widely quoted, with approval, as saying,
"Please stay at your post; you will be needed this fall when it comes time
for the survival or obliteration of our nation."

Now, at last, in the first week of June, the official leaders of the Japanese government were recruited to carry out the first phase of Kido's
peace plan and to decide publicly on the need for surrender. Their performance, as staged, was a masterpiece of belly acting which said one
thing to the world audience and another to the exclusive audience of
political connoisseurs on the domestic front. On June 7 the Cabinet resolved not to desert the capital before the final decisive battle. This meant
that Hirohito had given up the idea of fighting to the last in the Nagano
Alps. It meant that there would be no final battle because Japan would
surrender first.

With this understanding the Cabinet and representatives of the General
Staff met at the Imperial Household Ministry on the following day for a
full-dress council in the Imperial Presence. Before the meeting each man
present was handed a pair of documents prepared by the General Staff.
One reviewed the "World Situation," the other "The Present State of Our
National Power." In the most pessimistic phrases, the most chilling statistics, the two studies revealed that the war had taken "an ominous turn"
and that "insurmountable difficulties" stood in the way of continuing it.

After the Emperor and the others in the room had glanced through the
two gloomy background papers, a declaration was read aloud and passed
unanimously. It called on the nation to fight to the last of its 70 million
men, women, and children. It announced that this was the "fundamental
policy to be pursued henceforth in the prosecution of the war." Then it
gave one minuscule hint that the policy being decided was really one for
prosecution of the peace: "The enemy is also facing its own concealed difficulties and is desperate in its efforts to terminate the war soon. . . . We
must resolutely take every political and military step to grasp the god-sent

opportunity." In other words, Japan must exploit the distrust between the United States and Russia in order to negotiate a surrender. Without a word being said explicitly about peace, everyone in the room understood that peace was the issue. As Hirohito later explained to one of his chamberlains: "A concealed clause, which we may call clause X, was contained in the proposals laid before the imperial conference of June 8. This clause was a peace clause."

As soon as the meeting had adjourned imperial advisor Kido drafted a written plan for implementing the peace resolution. His idea was that the United States could be made to concede terms out of fear that, otherwise, Japan would give China to Russia. He proposed therefore that Japan should begin conversations with Russia at once on two separate topics: what bribe Russia would take to remain a neutral; and what terms Russia, as mediator, would be willing to try to get for Japan in a peace settlement. Kido proposed that Japan should hold out for two conditions: preservation of the Emperor system of government and some face-saving statement by the enemy that Japan had won peace with honor. Hirohito approved Kido's plan the next day, June 9, and Foreign Minister Togo [7] at once promised to press home negotiations with the Russian ambassador in Tokyo. Hirohito urged Togo "not to be too prudent." One of Togo's envoys had been talking to Russia's Ambassador Malik for a week. As yet the two men had not passed the point of drinking tea together and swapping stories about the lack of understanding for the Russian character in Japanese provincial areas.

POTSDAM ULTIMATUM

This was the state of cold fear and colder cunning which immobilized Japan in June when President Truman began to prepare for the Potsdam Conference in mid-July. It was a state unknown to any American at the time and not one which would have aroused much sympathy if it had been known. As yet the Japanese government had made no official offer to surrender. On June 18, President Truman approved plans for Operation Olympic which would have sent a million Americans into the beachheads of southern Japan in the coming November. To support the invasion Chief of Staff Marshall in Washington was expecting to need—for "tactical use" —no less than nine of the new untried atomic bombs.

By coincidence, on that same day, June 18, Hirohito began to feel that his ministers were dawdling over the task of salvaging an honorable peace. That afternoon Lord Privy Seal Kido arranged a meeting of the Big Six— the chiefs of staff; Army, Navy, foreign, and prime ministers—and had

---

[7] Not to be confused with Japan's notorious World War II Prime Minister Tojo, spelled with a *j*.

them adopt a timetable for ending the war. They agreed that negotiations must be opened in Moscow before the middle of July and that the target date for cease-fire should be September. Their plan was confirmed at a meeting in the Imperial Presence four days later. It was an unusual meeting in that Hirohito spoke individually to the ministers requiring their active co-operation in the humiliating task ahead. The next day Hirohito asked his advisor Kido to have work begun on the imperial rescript which would have to be issued explaining defeat to the people.

A week later, on June 29, the Japanese foreign ministry finally made its first written proposal to the U.S.S.R. Through an intermediary,[8] Foreign Minister Togo offered Soviet Ambassador Malik a neutral Manchuria, no more special Japanese fishing privileges, favorable consideration of other Russian requests—this pittance in exchange for a pledge by Russia that she would refrain from joining in the war against Japan. No mention was made of Japan surrendering. On the contrary the Japanese emissary suggested that perhaps the U.S.S.R. would like to throw in some oil and aviation gas in order to weaken the common enemy, the United States. Soviet Ambassador Malik fidgeted and seemed hardly to be listening. The Japanese were not offering enough to tempt Russia nor asking enough to help themselves. Malik stifled a yawn and promised routinely to study the proposal. For the next two weeks he put off increasingly desperate Japanese representations. He was sick in bed, he said, with Japanese dysentery.

On Independence Day, the British government concurred jovially in what it termed the "independent" U.S. decision to use the bomb.

In Tokyo that day leaders were discussing fresh intelligence from Switzerland. It came this time from Lieutenant General Okamoto, the head of the Army "peace mission" there. Through a third party Okamoto had sounded out Allen Dulles, the chief of the O.S.S. in Europe, as to what terms, if any, the United States would give Japan. Dulles had replied that "if Japan surrenders" it was the "understanding" of the United States that the Allies would allow the Emperor system of government to be continued. It was the one condition which Japanese leaders months earlier had agreed to settle for if worst came to worst. But no one knew how much trust to put in it. Japanese spy agencies had offered such reassurances routinely in China without any intention of honoring them. Moreover, on July 2, Senator Homer Capehart of Indiana had told Congress that "Japan's capitulation is imminent" and that "only the Emperor's status remains to be decided."

Analysis of foreign broadcasts had brought it home to Hirohito that Allied leaders at their scheduled Potsdam meeting in mid-July were about to decide the fate of the Orient. To save American lives, Truman might invite Russia and even China to contribute troops for the assault on Japan.

---

[8] Hirota Koki, a former prime and foreign minister.

The thought of a Russian invasion was terrifying enough, but the thought of a Chinese revenge raised cold sweats. Hirohito decided to go over the head of "sick" Ambassador Malik in Tokyo and begin direct conversations with Molotov in Moscow. He summoned Prime Minister Suzuki on July 7 and told him, "We are wasting precious time feeling out the belly of Russia. How would it be if we ask her frankly to act as go-between and offer to send an envoy to Moscow with an imperial letter?" Suzuki accepted the suggestion "gratefully."

Hirohito, anguished over the decision he had made, began to have second thoughts. On July 10 his old Army minion, the ubiquitous Suzuki Tei-ichi, who had manned the home headquarters of the division which raped Nanking, came to the palace to discuss Japan's ability "to end and start again." Finally, two days later, imperial advisor Kido noted that "the Emperor has now reached a state of determination." Kido at once arranged a private audience for Prince Konoye. Konoye assured Hirohito that the nation must, indeed, surrender. In his description of conditions outside the palace, he went so far as to say, "The people all want to find a way out. Some are even of the opinion that the Emperor should be rebuked."

"Is it your conviction then that we should end the war at once?" asked Hirohito bleakly.

"It is," replied Konoye.

"So be it," said Hirohito. "There may be occasion to send you to Russia. Please be ready to act on your convictions." And with that the Emperor left the room.

Prince Konoye went directly to a meeting with Foreign Minister Togo and Togo cabled at once to Ambassador Sato in Moscow: SEE MOLOTOV BEFORE HIS DEPARTURE FOR POTSDAM. . . . CONVEY HIS MAJESTY'S STRONG DESIRE TO SECURE A TERMINATION OF THE WAR. . . . UNCONDITIONAL SURRENDER IS THE ONLY OBSTACLE TO PEACE. . . .

That night at 11:25 Ambassador Sato cabled back: THERE IS NO CHANCE OF WINNING THE SOVIET UNION TO OUR SIDE AND OF OBTAINING HER SUPPORT ON THE BASIS SET FORTH IN YOUR CABLES. . . . JAPAN IS DEFEATED. . . . WE MUST FACE THAT FACT AND ACT ACCORDINGLY. . . .

Sato's message crossed en route with a second cable from Foreign Minister Togo. It contained the news that Prince Konoye, bearing a letter in Hirohito's own hand, would come to Moscow to work out the details of surrender: PLEASE ARRANGE IMMEDIATELY TO OBTAIN AN ENTRY PERMIT FOR PRINCE KONOYE AND HIS PARTY. . . . HAVE A SOVIET PLANE MEET THEM AT TSITSIHAR OR MANCHOULI.[9]

There followed as sad a correspondence with death as history has ever

[9] Manchouli or Lupin is a town on the Russo-Manchurian border near the eastern corner of Mongolia. Tsitsihar or Lungkiang, which is inside of Manchuria 220 miles from the border, had a better airport.

recorded. Ambassador Sato Naotake in Moscow cabled home on July 13 that Molotov "could not find time to see me." So Sato saw Molotov's subordinate instead and begged him for a quick response to the proposed Konoye visit. Late that night Ambassador Sato was told over the phone that "the Soviet answer will be delayed because of the departure of Stalin and Molotov" for Potsdam. Throughout the Potsdam Conference Sato called every morning at the Soviet Foreign Ministry to relay further clarifications from Tokyo as to the purpose of Konoye's mission. Every afternoon and evening he composed cables itemizing the latest Soviet requests for still more clarification. Hirohito seemed relieved at the Russian procrastination. When he received Foreign Minister Togo in audience on July 18, he said, "The fate of our proposal is now beyond your control. It depends on the response of the other side and on the national destiny ordained by the divine ancestors."

On July 19 Ambassador Sato in Moscow finally received an ordinary postal letter from a member of Molotov's staff, stating that the Japanese proposals, as yet, were too vague to warrant an answer. Sato relayed this opinion to Tokyo and accompanied it with an impassioned plea for a realistic surrender note which would spare his beloved country. Foreign Minister Togo consulted with Hirohito and felt able to give Sato little further clarification. It was Prince Konoye's mission, he cabled, to bring specific surrender proposals to Moscow and to arrange a peace short of unconditional surrender.

Unknown to Stalin, unknown to Hirohito, the telegraphic correspondence between Togo and Sato was being intercepted by U.S. Intelligence; it was decoded, translated, and submitted to Secretary of State Byrnes. It revealed clearly that Japan was desperate to surrender. It did not reveal the minimal face-saving terms which Lord Privy Seal Kido and members of the General Staff had agreed to accept months earlier. It did not show any willingness on the part of the Japanese to settle for the one condition which had already been granted through O.S.S. Chief Dulles. U.S. Intelligence analysts tended to see Japan as a brutal police state under the control of a few tough fanatic generals like Tojo. The analysts did not know that Tojo was only an obedient servant of the Throne. They did not know that the Emperor's civilian advisors were at least as influential as his military aides. The power of the Japanese Army was judged by its arrogant totalitarian behavior in conquered countries overseas. It was not fully appreciated that most Japanese soldiers were of humble birth and that this made them subservient to aristocratic civilians at home.

Secretary of State Byrnes was advised, accordingly, that the Togo-Sato cables appeared to be an attempt on the part of the Japanese military to make a deal with Russia and thereby attach conditions to surrender, conditions which might enable the military clique to evade punishment and stay in power. Russian analysts took an equally inappropriate view: that Japa-

nese capitalism was attempting to perpetuate its hold on the Japanese proletariat. The fact that capitalists had given their factories and that generals
had given their lives in order to serve Hirohito as a god-king seemed
beyond understanding in the practical-minded West.

In the U.S. State Department a group of men around former Ambassador
Grew shared an affection for Japan and understood some of the complexities of Japan's savage heart. They demanded that the unconditional surrender policy enunciated at the height of the war be restudied so that American
statesmen might know the various interpretations which could be placed on
it. They succeeded in securing an agreement that unconditional surrender
should be explained as unconditional surrender of soldiers and guns, not of
women and private property. Before President Truman left for Potsdam,
they also exacted from him a reassurance that he would try to incorporate
in the Potsdam Declaration a warning of the atomic holocaust which would
be visited on Japan if she did not surrender soon. Grew, and to some extent
Stimson, wanted to include in the warning a clear statement of the bomb's
existence and a reassurance as to the person of the Emperor. But other
presidential advisors saw no reason to tell Russia, in effect, we are going to
A-bomb Japan, so you had better hurry in your attack on Manchuria. And
still others saw no reason to assure the Emperor that he and his family
could remain in the saddle, riding out a token Allied Occupation that would
make no basic changes in Japan's class and power structure.

On July 14, Washington time, when the Allied leaders were all in transit
to Potsdam, the first A-bomb was hoisted atop a tower in the New Mexico
desert for a test. Early on July 17, the morning of the Potsdam Conference,
Truman heard the first news of results: "Baby satisfactorily born." On the
following day details came in: "Baby's scream" was strong enough to be
heard from the Capitol in Washington to Interim Committee Secretary
George Harrison's house in Upperville, Virginia. The "light in baby's eyes"
was bright enough to shine from the Capitol to Stimson's home in Highhold,
Long Island. The bomb was far more powerful than anyone had anticipated.
In a pre-test pool conducted by the physicists in New Mexico, guesses as
to the yield of the explosion in terms of TNT equivalent had ranged from
18,000 tons down to a skeptical "zero" tossed in by Dr. Lee DuBridge,
director of U.S. wartime radar research. The actual yield was 20,000 tons.
After reading the full report of the test, Churchill on July 22 leaned forward
in his chair, waved his cigar in emphasis, and rumbled oracularly: "Stimson! What was gunpowder? Trivial. What was electricity? Meaningless. This
atomic bomb is the Second Coming in wrath."

Churchill was to add later: "The decision whether or not to use the
atomic bomb to compel the surrender of Japan was never even an issue."
In Truman's mind, however, it was a source of uneasiness. On July 18, the
day the President received details of what the bomb could do, he consulted
with his military advisors and with anyone else whose opinion might be

valuable. General Eisenhower, who was visiting in Potsdam that day, remembered in later years that he had been sounded out by the President and had "expressed the hope that we would never have to use such a thing . . . take the lead in introducing into war something as horrible and destructive."

Stimson, however, maintained that the bomb might be the excuse the Japanese were waiting for, and he urged that it be used "in the manner best calculated to persuade the Emperor to submit to our demand for what is essentially unconditional surrender." Churchill and other statesmen sided with Stimson. And so on July 24, while still at Potsdam, the President issued the operational order to General Carl Spaatz that the first "special bomb" should be dropped by the "509 Composite Group as soon as weather will permit" after about August 3.

The same day, as Truman recalled later, "I casually mentioned to Stalin that we had a new weapon of unusual destructive force. The Russian premier showed no particular interest. All he said was that he was glad to hear it and hoped we would make 'good use of it against the Japanese.' " Stalin almost certainly knew that this was the atomic bomb which Red Army Intelligence had been warning him about, but he gave no sign of knowing; later, when the bomb was used at Hiroshima, the Red Army was to require almost two days before it was ready to scramble across the border into Manchuria. Instead of commenting on the bomb, Stalin four days later revealed to Truman that he had been asked by Tokyo to act as a peace mediator. He added, more or less truthfully, that Tokyo had not made any specific proposal. It was Truman's turn to look innocent, and he agreed that the Japanese peace feelers as yet had been too tentative to warrant much attention.

On July 26, after the wording had been hammered out between the Allied leaders and their staffs, Japan was given the warning of the Potsdam Declaration: "We call upon the government of Japan to proclaim the unconditional surrender of all Japanese armed forces. . . . The alternative for Japan is prompt and utter destruction." Japanese Foreign Office analysts noticed with appreciation that the Allies had defined unconditional surrender as applying only to the "armed forces." They did not notice anything more than ordinary propaganda in the phrase "prompt and utter destruction." Two days after the Potsdam Declaration had been issued, Prime Minister Suzuki declared that it offered no change in the Roosevelt policy of unconditional surrender laid down at the Cairo Conference in December 1943 and that "to us its meaning does not seem of great worth, just something to be ignored."

Several historians and several participants in the history of that decade, including General Eisenhower, have complained that the Potsdam Declaration was inadequate. It did not tell the Japanese why destruction would be "prompt and utter" nor how relatively pleasant might be the prospect of unconditional surrender and U.S. occupation. Captain Ellis M. Zacharias of U.S. Naval Intelligence did as well as he was permitted in a Japanese and English broadcast on July 28 that was beamed into Japan on the medium wave band which could be picked up by the radio sets of ordinary Japanese citizens.[10] "Japan," he said, "must make a choice. One alternative is prompt and utter destruction. . . . Centuries of sweat and toil will be brought to naught in a cataclysmic end. . . . The other alternative is the end of war. One simple decision will allow tranquility again to return to the city and the countryside. . . . The homeland of Japan will be saved to continue a sovereign existence under a peacefully inclined and responsible government."

On August 2, Foreign Minister Togo begged his ambassador in Moscow to extract from the Soviet government some answer to the proposal that Prince Konoye fly to Russia for talks. Togo now promised that Konoye would be empowered to accept the Potsdam Declaration as "the basis for a study regarding terms." At the Soviet Foreign Ministry, Japanese Ambassador Sato learned that Molotov was still on his way home from Potsdam and would see him in a few days. Russia delayed. Japan waited. The Thin Boy was flown to Tinian and assembled. On August 6 Ambassador Sato was informed that Molotov had returned and would see him two days later at 5:00 P.M. That same morning, August 6, Ambassador Sato heard that Hiroshima had disappeared in a puff of flame.

THE GOD SPEAKS

When most of Hiroshima vanished from the map, it was the switchboard operators in Tokyo who first noticed that something was missing. Minutes later incoherent phone calls began to come in from the Hiroshima area. The Army General Staff at once responded by sending out wires for more information. On the following morning, Tuesday, the vice chief of staff received an angry, terrifying confirmation of his worst fears: "The whole city of Hiroshima was destroyed instantly by a single bomb." The Army General Staff sent out more wires, and planes as well, to find out what sort of bomb had been dropped and how many had been killed.

While the generals waited, Emperor Hirohito and his advisor Lord Privy Seal Kido already knew the answers. When they met in the Imperial Library that afternoon, both had seen Naval Intelligence analyses and reports from physicists at Tokyo Imperial University. The claims being broadcast from the United States were almost certainly honest. It had been an atomic bomb. Emperor Hirohito had received remarkably accurate statistics as to the casualties: "130,000 killed and wounded." Unlike most of his countrymen

---

[10] All radios were registered by the secret police and periodically inspected to see that they could not pick up short wave. Zacharias's broadcasts were made possible only by U.S. relay ships steaming in perilously close to the Japanese coast.

Hirohito understood what *genshi bakudan,* atomic bomb, signified. Until a few months previously, he had patronized Japan's own atomic research effort. It had come to a disastrous end when a physicist, some technicians, and two buildings full of apparatus had been mysteriously blown up. Under pressure to save Japan from defeat, the work had been pushed ahead too fast and safety precautions had been neglected.[11]

In the glare of Hiroshima, Kido and Hirohito knew that they could conspire to delay no longer: the time had come to put Kido's peace plot to its final test. Man and god, they set to work that afternoon seeing key functionaries and giving them final instructions. By the next afternoon, Wednesday, August 8, the machinery was primed and ready. Kido took advantage of an air alert to join the Emperor in his bunker under the Imperial Library. Kido urged the Emperor to speak the word which would set the machinery in motion. Hirohito at once summoned Foreign Minister Togo and told him, "Now that a weapon of this devastating power has been used against us, we should not let slip the opportunity. . . . Tell Prime Minister Suzuki that it is my wish that the war be ended as soon as possible on the basis of the Potsdam Declaration." In the unforeseen and unanswerable bomb, Hirohito saw a face-saving excuse for Japan's fighting men, one which could be used to ease the humiliation of defeat and smooth the pathway to surrender.

It was that Wednesday night, six hours after Hirohito had spoken, that the bomb, in the words of Wisconsin's Senator Alexander Wiley, "blew Joey off the fence." Japan's Ambassador Sato in Moscow had an appointment at 11 P.M. Tokyo time, 5 P.M. Moscow time, to see Foreign Minister Molotov. He went to the appointment expecting to learn at last whether Russia would receive Konoye and help in arranging Japan's surrender. Instead, he was handed a declaration of war. Molotov coolly explained to him that the Russo-Japanese nonaggression treaty had been canceled years before by Japan's assistance of Germany. Stalin had promised Truman at Potsdam that, before entering the Pacific war, he would reach agreement with Chiang Kai-shek on the future of China. The Red Army chief of staff had told his opposite number at Potsdam that Russian operations would not begin against Japan until the second half of August. Now, ahead of schedule on all counts, after only two days of preparation, the Soviet forces were surging forward into Manchuria. It was the next morning, eighteen hours after Hirohito had spoken, that the bomb fell, tragically, on Urakami—and blessedly spared Kokura and most of Nagasaki. The Japanese had had three full days to think since Hiroshima. No American knew that Emperor Hirohito had already decided to accept the Potsdam Declaration.

On Thursday morning, August 9, when the second bomb was scoring its

---

[11] The physicist was named Odan, thirty-eight years old; the explosion was probably caused by careless handling of liquid gases.

merciful two-mile miss, the Big Six of the Japanese Government had just gathered in the prime minister's air raid shelter outside the palace to debate the Emperor's wish to accept unconditional surrender. They had been summoned the previous evening, but some of the military members of the group had made themselves unreachable. During the night, however, pressure for instant action had mounted when the secret police circulated news of a "confession" made by a B-29 pilot shot down the day before off Osaka.

Already bruised and bloodied by his interrogators, Lieutenant Marcus McDilda had been threatened with death unless he revealed what he knew about the atomic bomb. Knowing nothing, he decided to tell all. "As you know," he began in his Florida drawl, "when atoms are split, there are a lot of plusses and minuses released. Well, we've taken these and put them in a huge container and separated them from each other with a lead shield. When the box is dropped out of a plane, we melt the lead shield and the plusses and minuses come together. When that happens, it causes a tremendous bolt of lightning and all the atmosphere over a city is pushed back. Then when the atmosphere rolls in again, it brings about a tremendous thunderclap, which knocks down everything beneath it.

"I believe," added McDilda under prodding, "that the next two targets are to be Kyoto and Tokyo. Tokyo is supposed to be bombed in the next few days."

As the war minister and the two chiefs of staff sat down with the other members of the Big Six to discuss Hirohito's request in the sweltering air raid shelter, they exchanged information about McDilda's confession and felt oppressed by the thought that Tokyo and the Emperor, or Kyoto and the tombs of past Emperors, might soon be turned to ash. At the same time, they also feared an end to the war. They still had at their disposal in the home islands 2.5 million combat-equipped troops and 9,000 kamikaze planes. These men had been told for years that death was preferable to surrender. For months they had been promised "a final decisive battle" on the shores of Japan, a battle so costly to the enemy that it might be possible afterwards to negotiate a conditional surrender and win an honorable peace. To surrender these men without a fight evoked visions of unbearable future shame—of the veteran in rags who would spit on any general he passed on the street and feel justified in doing so.

General Anami, the war minister, carried the argument for his fellow soldiers. The Emperor wished to surrender. Japan must surrender. But it was foolish not to bargain. Japan should signify her willingness to accept the Potsdam Declaration on four conditions: that her soil be spared the tread of occupation troops; that her fighting men be disarmed and disbanded by their own officers; that her war criminals be tried in her own courts; and most important, that the Emperor system of government be guaranteed. Everyone agreed to the last proviso as an unquestionable article of religious faith. Only the two chiefs of staff, however, would back the war minister on the other three provisos. The prime, foreign, and Navy ministers argued that to surrender unconditionally on one condition might be possible but that to surrender unconditionally on four conditions could only invite an atomic attack on Tokyo. The 3–3 deadlock was not broken when news of the Nagasaki bombing was brought into the council chamber about 11:30 A.M. At one in the afternoon Prime Minister Suzuki opened his eyes, pushed away his teacup, stamped out his cigar, and recessed the meeting for an hour.

War Minister Anami returned to his own ministry to see if anything important had come up in the business of the morning. A group of his most militant subordinates clustered around him to ask about the Big Six meeting. He put them off with generalities and a promise that he had taken a strong stand. One of them, his own brother-in-law, warned him, in a loud voice, "If you are going to accept the Potsdam Declaration, you had better commit hara-kiri."

"A cruel thing to say," remarked Anami to his secretary as they climbed back into the car. "They don't know how easy hara-kiri is for an old man of sixty like me." His secretary thought he looked tired and deflated as he spoke. The car drove on to the official residence supplied Anami by the government. There he took out his old samurai bow and target and tested the state of his nerves in the back yard. It took him seventeen shots to group five arrows in the center of the mark. Usually ten or eleven sufficed. Aware of his tension and his limitations, he went inside for a hurried lunch of rice and pickles and returned to the prime minister's residence.

For the afternoon session Prime Minister Suzuki had called in the rest of the Cabinet. Now instead of six there were fourteen at the deliberations. Two voted with War Minister Anami for the stiffest conditions, five with Foreign Minister Togo for a moderate response, and five others opted to accept unconditional surrender in any wording that would still leave a little room for bargaining. The meeting continued from 2:30 P.M. to 5:30 P.M. and resumed after dinner at 6:30 P.M.

As the sun moved over the lotus pools and lengthened the shadows of the artfully grotesque trees in the palace garden, Hirohito waited in the Imperial Library to give the divine command which would end all argument. It was his unique privilege to vouchsafe peace to the war-weary, his dangerous responsibility to withhold honor from the fanatics. At intervals during the afternoon Lord Privy Seal Kido came to the library to reassure him and beg him to be patient. It was a matter of plan that the meeting in progress should fail to reach unanimous agreement, but the ministers were duty bound to exhaust every avenue of argument before conceding a deadlock. Only then could they legitimately appeal to Hirohito and invoke the Voice of the Crane.

The task of protracting the proceedings and of preventing the weary negotiators from reaching a compromise rested on the broad shoulders of

War Minister Anami. He performed it willingly enough because it helped him save face before his subordinates. He was known as an advocate of surrender, but of conditional surrender. For months he had been promising his men that he would wrest an honorable peace from the Allies or die in the attempt. He had made a similar pledge to the Emperor.

Of the cabal of young officers who had served Hirohito since the early 1920's, the sleek, burly Anami was the most dedicated and loyal, the most perfect exemplar of the samurai ideal. His archery was only one of the ancient knightly exercises by which he kept himself fit; he had also attained the fifth degree in *kendo,* the traditional Japanese swordsmanship. Contemptuous of money, careless of personal comfort, he cultivated a relaxed frame of mind, what the Japanese call "a belly that knows how to sit down." He was no intellectual and had twice failed the entrance examinations for military academy. But he knew how to lead men. In combat he was renowned for his nerves of steel. Out of combat he was beloved for his even temper, his affable storytelling, and his hard drinking.

Having gone through military academy with Prince Asaka and Prince Higashikuni, the Emperor's uncles, Anami had come into the palace circle naturally at the outset of his career and had been a part of it ever since. He had served as an aide-de-camp for the Emperor from 1926 to 1932. On the very day of Hirohito's accession to the Throne, December 25, 1926, Anami had represented the palace at a meeting with Tojo and other members of the cabal, a meeting which had resolved on the "liberation" of Manchuria from Chinese sovereignty. Many sensitive assignments later, Anami had found himself in 1944 attempting to perform miracles in New Guinea where the Japanese garrisons were cut off from outside help. When the situation had become equally desperate in Tokyo in December 1944, Hirohito, at the instigation of his two uncles, had had Anami flown home.

At 10:00 P.M., eleven hours after the second atomic bomb had been dropped, the sturdy Anami was still finding arguments against unconditional surrender. His opponents, who did not fight a bout and fill a clout each day, were all exhausted. Prime Minister Suzuki, Hirohito's old grand chamberlain, decided that enough of a gesture had been made. He called a recess and left the other members of his government to enjoy the hospitality of his residence while he drove to the palace. It was a clear night. The moon had not yet risen. Tokyo lay blacked out. As his car groped along behind its hooded headlights, Suzuki admired the silhouettes of the great trees on either side of the palace malls.

The old admiral-chamberlain-prime minister found Hirohito sitting up waiting for him in the library. He reported the deadlock in deliberations and advised the Emperor to break it by calling an immediate council in the Imperial Presence. Hirohito consented instantly and asked his attendants to phone Lord Privy Seal Kido and make the necessary arrangements. By prior agreement with Kido, Suzuki then asked the Emperor if

Baron Hiranuma might be invited to the council. Hirohito winced and nodded his assent with downcast eyes. Few men in Japan had tried harder than Baron Hiranuma to turn Hirohito from the path to Pearl Harbor; few had more right to say, "I told you so."

At eighty, Baron Hiranuma represented the traditional pre-fascist variety of right-wing nationalism in Japan. He had the backing of other mossback aristocrats and also of many slum gang leaders and shape-up bosses. From 1929 to 1936 he had directed the affluent National Foundation Society or *Kokuhonsha,* an equivalent in U.S. terms of a combined Mafia headquarters and New York Athletic Club. Through his underworld connections he claimed to represent labor, and through labor, the people. In the early years of Hirohito's reign, Baron Hiranuma had supported the Strike-North faction in the Army which wished to direct Japanese aggression against Russia. In addition, as a legal authority, he had taken the position that Hirohito should not be above the law in act unless he were willing to avow himself above the law in name as well. After long conflict, Hirohito had conceded the point in 1936 when he personally and openly purged the Strike-North faction from the Army and turned on China. At the same time he had reached an understanding with Hiranuma and appointed him to the presidency of the Privy Council, an advisory body which met with Hirohito every Wednesday morning. In 1939 Baron Hiranuma had gone on to preside as prime minister over the Nomonhan Incident, a limited exploratory attack on Russia. It had turned into a fiasco and Baron Hiranuma had withdrawn into brief retirement. He had sprung back as a Cabinet minister in 1941 and had survived an assassination attempt by a hired gunman who tried to murder him for his outspoken opposition to war with America. Since then he had helped Prince Konoye to organize the Peace Faction.

When Lord Privy Seal Kido arrived at the library a few minutes later, he assured Hirohito that Baron Hiranuma would cause no trouble. He and Kido had had a long talk the day before; there was an understanding. Hirohito nodded gratefully. The baron certainly had a sharp legal mind. And he had proved his pertinacious loyalty even as an opponent. It was probably no more than just that he should assist at these final fateful deliberations. Hirohito waited restlessly for them to begin. It was 11:00 P.M. before the members of the Cabinet and High Command began to arrive at the library. Lord Privy Seal Kido bustled about having a word with each of them. Chamberlains and equerries then escorted them one by one around to the hillside entrance of the imperial bunker and down the steps into the hill, sixty feet into it horizontally, fifty feet into it vertically, to the anteroom outside the subterranean audience chamber. It was 11:20 P.M. before they were all briefed and assembled.

At 11:25 P.M. Kido had a last twelve-minute meeting with Hirohito, and then the Emperor proceeded down into the bunker through his own private door by his own stairway. He looked into the subterranean living room where some of his children and nieces and nephews were camped out asleep on the rugs and sofas. He spoke briefly with his chief aide-de-camp. He passed inspection by his wife, Empress Nagako. Then at ten minutes to midnight, his hair noticeably unkempt, his eyes unusually deep-set and haggard-looking, he entered the hot, damp 30-by-18-foot chamber. Voices hushed and there were sighs of astonishment at his disheveled appearance. He sat down behind a table, covered like an altar with a cloth of golden chrysanthemum brocade.

At Hirohito's back extended a magnificent, six-gate, golden screen. Before him, behind two narrow tables along the walls, sat eleven tired men. Four were civilians, four were generals, and three were admirals. The gathering was an accurate cross-section of the hierarchy which took turns administering Hirohito's police state. All were of the inner clique and had been privy to high conspiratorial affairs since the late 1920's. All knew now that the great gamble of war had been lost. Suicide or prison closed in ahead of them. The stuffy air of the shelter seemed, in the words of one of them, "to buzz with the spirits of the dead." A mood of bitter spiritualistic *Weltschmerz* engulfed the room.

Prime Minister Suzuki's secretary, Sakomizu Hisatsune, had the uncanny feeling that he and his companions in the bunker had already passed over into the other world. A nimbus seemed to surround the Emperor. Military Affairs Bureau Chief Yoshizumi Masao, sitting next to Sakomizu, bore an eerie resemblance to another Military Affairs Bureau chief, Nagata Tetsuzan, who had been stabbed to death exactly ten years ago by an assassin sent to him from Hirohito's two uncles, Prince Asaka and Prince Higashikuni. It seemed only right that Nagata should have returned now. Until a month before his murder, he had been the leader of the Emperor's Army cabal. He had fallen out with Hirohito over plans for the war with China and had embarrassed Hirohito through security leaks. He had been offered a chance to save himself by resigning or taking a leave of absence, but he had chosen instead to remain at his post and to become a sacrificial victim.

The haunting presence of Nagata's spirit in the bunker seized so strongly on Secretary Sakomizu's mind that years later his vision was incorporated in a painting of the surrender scene which he commissioned for the memorial museum to Prime Minister Suzuki. By subtly strengthening the chin and filling out the lips of the real man in the bunker, the artist re-created a startling likeness of Nagata as he looked at a conference in 1935 shortly before his death. The men across from him seem to be eyeing him warily but he does not look back at them. His eyes appear to be closed. And on his full lips plays a distant half smile, half sneer of sardonic satisfaction. Thousands of Japanese visit the Suzuki Museum each year and silently file past the painting.

In the real bunker, that evening of August 9, 1945, the cynical, impres-

sionable Secretary Sakomizu saw the ghostly proceedings open with a ceremonial recitation of all the anguished arguments of the preceding days.
Hirohito sat listening mute and immobile, ramrod stiff at the altar before
the golden screen. Foreign Minister Togo and Navy Minister Yonai reviewed the inescapable reasons for accepting unconditional surrender. War
Minister Anami and Army Chief of Staff Umezu begged—for the honor
of the living and the dead—to fight a final battle.

Then Prime Minister Suzuki called on the octogenarian lawyer, Baron
Hiranuma. The room rustled as the others in it whispered to one another,
asking why Baron Hiranuma should speak and what he was doing there in
the first place. They soon learned. Baron Hiranuma was to act as prosecutor on behalf of Japan. He was to remind each of them, even Hirohito,
of his responsibilities and past irresponsibilities. As the old man rose, his
long equine face was blank, then he pursed his lips judiciously, narrowed
his eyes, and began.

"Have you ever made proposals to the U.S.S.R. on concrete matters?" he
demanded in his cross-examination of Foreign Minister Togo. "Is a defense
against these bombs possible?" he asked War Minister Anami. "It seems
to me that the enemy do as they please and that there are absolutely no
counterattacks against enemy air raids." He turned on the Navy minister
and naval chief of staff: "Does the Navy have any countermeasures against
enemy task forces?" Having no ships left to speak of, Naval Chief of Staff
Toyoda spoke lamely of new types of kamikaze planes. "In view of the
present deterioration of the general situation in Japan," cut in Hiranuma
relentlessly, "we can suppose that continuation of the war will create greater
domestic disturbance then ending of the war."

Finally, Hiranuma turned his eyes on the Emperor. "The wording of the
reservation to be sent to the Allies must be revised. To accept the Potsdam
Declaration *'on the understanding that it does not include any demand for
a change in the status of the Emperor under the national laws'* is inappropriate. . . . The sovereignty of the Emperor is not derived through state
law, nor is it provided for by the Constitution. It is only referred to in the
Constitution. If the wording is changed to read 'the said declaration does
not comprise any demand which prejudices the prerogatives of His Majesty
as a sovereign ruler,' I would then have no objection."

When Hirohito had nodded his assent to Foreign Minister Togo that he
would accept this definition of his power and responsibility in the surrender
note, Hiranuma closed his case: "In accordance with the legacy bequeathed
by the ancestors, Your Imperial Majesty is also responsible for preventing
unrest in the nation. I should like to ask Your Majesty to make your decision with this point in mind."

Baron Hiranuma sat down. The naval chief of staff briefly took the
floor. Then Prime Minister Suzuki seconded the suggestion of Hiranuma:

"For hours we have discussed these matters and come to no decision. We cannot afford to waste even a minute. I propose to seek the imperial guidance. His Majesty's wish must settle the issue." Suzuki took a step toward the altar where Hirohito sat and there was a gasp at his boldness.

Without rising Hirohito replied in the high-pitched, senile-sounding Court monotone which was reserved for state pronouncements: "I will state my opinion. I agree with the foreign minister. My reasons are as follows: I have concluded that to continue this war can only mean destruction of the homeland. I cannot bear to have my innocent people suffer further. I was told by the Army chief of staff that in June the defenses at Ninety-nine League Beach would be complete. . . . It is now August and the fortifications are not complete. It was officially reported to me that one of the newly created divisions had been fully equipped. I find that as yet the men have not been supplied even with bayonets. . . . Some advocate a decisive battle in the homeland. . . . In my experience, however, there has been a discrepancy between the plans and the achievements of the fighting services. . . . I am afraid that in the face of present circumstances the Japanese people may be doomed. But I wish to hand on the country of Japan to our descendants; I wish to see as many as possible of our people survive and rise again. . . . It gives me great pain to think of the faithful soldiers and sailors who have been wounded or killed on distant battlefields and of the families who have lost everything in air raids at home. . . . Disarmament of my brave and loyal men is painful to me. Painful, too, that my devoted vassals should be considered war criminals. . . . But the time has come to bear the unbearable. . . . It does not matter what happens to me. . . . I have decided to bring the war to an end. That is why I agree with the foreign minister's proposal."

The men in the bunker were all weeping. Hirohito rose. Prime Minister Suzuki quickly said, "The imperial decision has been expressed and is thereby made the conclusion of this conference. Meeting adjourned."

It was 2:20 A.M. Hirohito turned to the door which was opened for him by his chief aide-de-camp, who had remained standing in a corner throughout the proceedings. When the Emperor had returned into the depths of the bunker, the other leaders mounted the steps into the Fukiage Gardens. The moon had risen during their stay underground, and the beauty of the garden in the moonbeams somewhat restored their despondent spirits. Hirohito reported briefly to his wife and Lord Privy Seal Kido. The Cabinet adjourned to Prime Minister Suzuki's residence where with food and drink, in a fourth and last meeting of a long and bitter day, they voted unanimously to accept the imperial decision. They broke up and went home about 4:00 A.M. Foreign Minister Togo worked on until 7:00 A.M. when his diplomatic note to Sweden and Switzerland, announcing Japan's unconditional surrender on one condition, had been duly coded and tapped out.

AMERICA RESPONDS

Seven o'clock in the morning in Tokyo is eleven o'clock the night before in Stockholm and Berne. By the time Japan's surrender offer had been decoded by Japanese diplomats in those capitals, it was past midnight. The diplomats waited politely until morning before transmitting the note to Swiss and Swedish foreign offices. By then it was past midnight in Washington. Thus when Truman and his advisors met to discuss the note at 9:00 A.M. on Friday, August 10, Washington time, sixteen anxious hours had passed in Tokyo. Moreover in Australia, which had been the most important fighting ally of the United States in the Pacific War, it was once again midnight. Japan was trying to surrender against the clock. Her note to the Allies stated:

> THE JAPANESE GOVERNMENT ARE READY TO ACCEPT THE TERMS ENUMER-
> ATED IN THE JOINT DECLARATION WHICH WAS ISSUED AT POTSDAM ON JULY
> 26, 1945 . . . WITH THE UNDERSTANDING THAT THE SAID DECLARATION DOES
> NOT COMPRISE ANY DEMAND WHICH PREJUDICES THE PREROGATIVES OF HIS
> MAJESTY AS A SOVEREIGN RULER.
>
> THE JAPANESE GOVERNMENT SINCERELY HOPE THAT THIS UNDERSTANDING IS
> WARRANTED AND DESIRE KEENLY THAT AN EXPLICIT INDICATION TO THAT
> EFFECT WILL BE SPEEDILY FORTHCOMING.

Truman and the new British Prime Minister Clement Attlee were disposed to accept the Japanese reservation about the Emperor. As far as anyone knew in the West, the Emperor was only a figurehead. Later that afternoon, however, when dawn came "down under," Australia was heard from. First Canberra cabled London:

> WE WOULD INSIST THAT THE EMPEROR AS HEAD OF STATE AND COMMANDER
> IN CHIEF OF THE ARMED FORCES SHOULD BE HELD RESPONSIBLE FOR THE JAPA-
> NESE ACTS OF AGGRESSION AND WAR CRIMES AND WOULD THUS DEMAND HIS
> REMOVAL.

As the motherland of the British Commonwealth, the United Kingdom had been allowed hitherto to speak for Australia in most wartime policy making. Now, however, when London replied with vague reassurances, the Australian government was not to be reassured. It rebelliously shot off a second cable, this time directly to Washington:

> . . . THE EMPEROR SHOULD HAVE NO IMMUNITY FROM RESPONSIBILITY FOR
> JAPAN'S ACTS OF AGGRESSION. . . . THE VISIBLE DETHRONEMENT OF THE SYS-
> TEM IS A PRIMARY MEANS OF SHAKING THE FAITH OF THE JAPANESE IN THE
> HEAVENLY CHARACTER OF THE EMPEROR IN WHOSE NAME THEY HAVE COM-
> MITTED MANY ATROCITIES. UNLESS THE SYSTEM GOES, THE JAPANESE WILL

REMAIN UNCHANGED AND RECRUDESCENCE OF AGGRESSION IN THE PACIFIC
WILL ONLY BE POSTPONED TO A LATER GENERATION.

AT YOUR REQUEST WE POSTPONED PUBLICATION OF THE REPORT WHICH IS
NOW BEFORE THE WAR CRIMES COMMISSION. . . . IN OUR VIEW IT DISCLOSES
A DELIBERATE SYSTEM OF TERRORISM AND ATROCITY WHICH MUST HAVE BEEN
KNOWN TO THE SUPREME AUTHORITIES IN JAPAN NOT EXCLUDING THE EM-
PEROR. IT WOULD BE A VERY DIFFICULT MATTER TO JUSTIFY DISCRIMINATION
IN THIS RESPECT AS BETWEEN HITLER AND HIS ASSOCIATES ON THE ONE HAND
AND HIROHITO AND HIS ASSOCIATES ON THE OTHER.

FOR THESE REASONS WE ARE OPPOSED TO THE ACCEPTANCE OF SURRENDER
ON THE UNDERSTANDING WHICH THE JAPANESE ARE ATTEMPTING TO ATTACH
TO THE POTSDAM TERMS. . . . IT SHOULD BE CLEARLY UNDERSTOOD BY THE
JAPANESE . . . THAT THE PERSON OF THE EMPEROR IS TO BE REGARDED AS AT
THE DISPOSAL OF THE ALLIED GOVERNMENTS IN THE SAME WAY AS EACH AND
EVERY OTHER PERSON OF THE SURRENDERING ENEMY STATE.

Truman and his Secretary of State James Byrnes wished to humor Australia if at all possible. Australia had contributed almost as much sweat and
blood to the defeat of Japan as had the United States. Moreover, Australia
had been excluded from the inner counsels at Potsdam. On the other hand,
Great Britain and China had already approved a U.S. draft of the reply to
Japan. So had the Soviet Union, but with a warning that the Red Army
would continue its drive into Manchuria until Japan ceased to fight. Secretary of State Byrnes, therefore, made minor modifications in the U.S. note
on the evening of August 10 and, pleading the urgency of the situation,
begged the Australian government to be satisfied with them. The two significant paragraphs, over which Japanese would agonize, were the second
and fifth:

FROM THE MOMENT OF SURRENDER, THE AUTHORITY OF THE EMPEROR AND
THE JAPANESE GOVERNMENT TO RULE THE STATE SHALL BE SUBJECT TO THE
SUPREME COMMANDER OF THE ALLIED POWERS, WHO WILL TAKE SUCH STEPS
AS HE DEEMS PROPER TO EFFECTUATE THE SURRENDER TERMS. . . .

THE ULTIMATE FORM OF GOVERNMENT OF JAPAN SHALL, IN ACCORDANCE
WITH THE POTSDAM DECLARATION, BE ESTABLISHED BY THE FREELY EXPRESSED
WILL OF THE JAPANESE PEOPLE.

The phrasing was masterful. On the one hand it assured Japanese that
the Emperor would retain authority "to rule the state"; on the other it
assured Australians that he would be "subject" to the Allied commander,
MacArthur. Early on the morning of August 11, Byrnes received grudging
approval of his wording from the Australian government, and at 10:45 A.M.,
Washington time, the note was broadcast to Japan. There it was now a
quarter to one, Sunday morning, August 12, exactly forty-one hours forty-
five minutes since Japan had announced her surrender.

In Tokyo the vice foreign minister and half a dozen seasoned diplomats with knowledge of English were at once routed from their beds and set to work translating the note and studying it. Their initial reaction was gloomy. The wording seemed excessively harsh and straightforward. There were none of those polite hypocrisies with which Japan had always honeyed her communications to conquered peoples. The note stated flatly that "the armed forces of the Allied Powers will remain in Japan until the purposes set forth in the Potsdam Declaration are achieved." Those purposes included complete disarmament, removal of all obstacles to democracy, "exaction of just reparations," and "stern justice . . . to all war criminals." Not even before the capture of Nanking had Japan sent a note of such severe tone. Anyone without firsthand experience of gruff Western ways would be led to expect wholesale rape, pillage, and butchery. The people might not accept the prospect without civil strife.

For the time being, then, the text of the note would have to be kept out of the newspapers. It could not be prevented, however, from circulating in the upper levels of the bureaucracy. There, the vice foreign minister observed, the problem would be to have the note "swallowed without chewing." The troublesome phrase would be the one, "government . . . established by the freely expressed will of the . . . people." That was arrant republicanism. It went against the ancestral precepts handed down in every family of the warrior caste. Rather than submit to it, there were those who would prefer to see the whole Japanese race pass over into the spirit world. From a Valhalla in Hades, said some devout Shintoists, the ghosts of samurai would wreak vengeance for the rest of eternity, causing fearful accidents to befall barbarians who ventured to set foot in the empty sacred isles of the homeland.

At 5:30 A.M. that morning the ranking officials of the Foreign Office took the American note, and the problems which they felt it presented, to Foreign Minister Togo at his residence. In the car one of them suggested that perhaps a diversion could be created to distract patrician attention from the "will of the people" clause. Togo's German wife was away in the mountains, and the foreign minister greeted them personally in his sleeping kimono. In this informal Japanese attire he seemed more relaxed than usual—more approachable than in the striped shirts, French cuffs, and Savile Row suits he wore to the office. Nevertheless his subordinates bowed to him with a depth and formality that exceeded required courtesy. Their feelings for him ranged from fearful respect to cool dislike. One of them noticed that his hand, as he took the American note, was completely steady.

Until a few years ago Foreign Minister Togo had been a heavy drinker and had smoked three packs of Turkish cigarettes a day. Then, at a word from his doctor, as he neared his sixtieth birthday, he had given up both in a single stroke of self-discipline. He was, without doubt, an intellectual of great brilliance and considerable inward sensitivity, but the walls of his psyche bristled with spears. His sarcasms punctured and his punctilios drew blood. His one failure as an ambassador had been scored in Germany during the mid-Thirties when he persistently referred to Hitler as "that upstart." One of the principal reasons that Hirohito had appointed him foreign minister in the Suzuki Cabinet was that he had the daring to call generals "idiots" to their faces. Now, as Togo patted out the wrinkles in his kimono and fitted on his heavy black-rimmed spectacles, he had never looked more human.

Togo read the note once, slowly. "This is the problem," he said, putting his finger on the "will of the people" clause. "In the long run it will not be an insurmountable problem from a practical standpoint, but emotionally it is difficult to accept. I do not think that the people will vote against the Emperor in a plebiscite, and until then the Emperor's 'authority to rule the state' is specifically acknowledged." Togo knew that the concept of free will was religious anathema to all but the tiny minority of Japan's 300,000 Christians. As for free expression, it had been successfully controlled for more than a thousand years.

"On this basis," continued Togo, "I think the Emperor will rise above personal feelings and accept the humiliation of being declared 'subject' to a foreigner. Still, it is an extremely hard note. Do any of you have any suggestions for softening its impact? At this time of crisis, it is most important for the whole nation to maintain perfect harmony and a united front."

The other foreign officers present broached the idea of creating a distraction. Vice Foreign Minister Matsumoto suggested that the Emperor's submission to "subject" status could be considered from one point of view as an awesome act of self-sacrifice made for the sake of the nation. Indeed the supreme humiliation could be used to make him seem a hero in his own eyes and in the eyes of the people. Togo seized on the idea with enthusiasm. All attention must be focused on the pathos and nobility of the Emperor's position. The meeting broke up shortly after dawn, and before breakfast the necessary diversion was being created.

Within the hour a captain in the Navy's Political Strategy Section, who happened also to be a minor member of the imperial family, called on the foreign editor of Domei, the state-controlled press service.[12] Despite the fact that the press had not published—and for three days would not publish—anything about the surrender negotiations, the captain asked the editor for a translation of the American note. The Navy, he said, did not feel sure enough of its own English to make a correct translation. Since hundreds of Naval officers had studied in England and even served as midshipmen in the British fleet, Domei's editor understood that a game was being played. After feeling out the requirements of the captain, he gave him a Domei News translation of the American note which described the

[12] Captain Arima Takayasu and Editor Hasegawa Saiji.

Occupation status of the Emperor as that of "a menial belonging to the Supreme Allied Commander."

At the same time the Foreign Office was running off a translation of the note which described the Emperor's Occupation status as "limited by the Supreme Allied Commander." The foreign editor at Domei immediately sent a special messenger with the translation he had made for the Navy to Prime Minister Suzuki's office. The prime minister's secretary proceeded to call key offices throughout the bureaucracy in order to advise them that the Navy was circulating an unauthorized translation of the note which differed from the official one put out by the Foreign Ministry. By the time that most bureaucrats arrived at their offices to face another day of shortages and air alarms, it was common knowledge in official Tokyo that the Americans were turning all their spite on Hirohito personally and that the men in striped pants at the Foreign Ministry were trying to hide the fact.

At 8:20 A.M., that same Sunday morning, Army and Navy chiefs of staff met with one another to discuss the situation and went on to call at the Imperial Library. They told Hirohito that in their view the U.S. note was rude in the extreme and that the Army and Navy stood ready to a man to die if Hirohito wished to reject it. Hirohito's chief aide-de-camp noted that the chiefs of staff seemed uncomfortable in their protestations, as if they were making a polite gesture suggested by their subordinates. Hirohito thanked them for their loyalty and assured them that he would study the note carefully when he received the official text from Sweden. At 11:00 A.M., while the Tokyo grapevine buzzed with gossip and concern over the Emperor's humiliation, Foreign Minister Togo motored to the palace. He reported to the Throne that, in his view as a diplomat, the American note was honest and as lenient as could be expected. Hirohito agreed and asked that the Cabinet officially endorse his acceptance of it.

SAMURAI'S COMPACT

The Cabinet and the chiefs of staff debated the American note throughout Sunday afternoon and all day Monday. War Minister Anami, who had had a lengthy audience with Hirohito on Saturday, once again led the anti-surrender faction. Baron Hiranuma, who had previously played peace advocate, was received in audience by Hirohito on Sunday and had thereafter supported Anami and supplied him with legal arguments. U.S. aircraft had not bombed Japan since Friday, and both men could be reasonably sure that there would be no more atomic attacks for the time being.

The Japanese masses, however, had no such certainty. They were forbidden by law to listen to foreign broadcasts. And as yet the domestic press, though it had mentioned "the new type of bomb," and finally "the atomic bomb," dropped on Hiroshima and Nagasaki, had printed not a word about the surrender note sent to Washington. Dark rumors spread of atomic horrors, and the inhabitants of every city wondered fatalistically if they would be next. While Anami sought to impress the enemy with Japan's continuing will to fight, the fierce kamikaze spirit was, in reality, oozing from the nation's heart and leaving only apathy and despair.

In addition to reasons of state, War Minister Anami had a strong personal motive for prolonging the surrender debate. He had encouraged a group of his favorite subordinates to stage a rebellion at the moment of Japan's surrender, and he had tacitly promised them that, if they would make this last suicidal gesture, he would go with them to the spirit world by committing hara-kiri. It was a feudal bargain of a type unknown in the West since the days of chivalry—a death pact between a knight and his liegemen in service to their king. In Japan such romantic deeds of self-sacrifice had a recognized place in government, and careful preparations were made to see that the victims were honored and their lives were not wasted.

War Minister Anami's suicide plan had first acquired official standing on July 27, a few hours after Japan received the Potsdam Declaration. That day orders under Anami's seal were radioed out to Taiwan recalling to Japan a lieutenant colonel of the secret police, Tsukamoto Makoto. Tsukamoto had recommended himself to imperial attention in 1934 when he had helped other Court agents uncover a subversive plot of the Strike-North or Fight-Russia faction at the military academy. He had then served under the Emperor's uncle Prince Higashikuni in various intrigues in Osaka during 1935, one of them the murder of the Military Affairs Bureau chief who appears as a ghostly anachronism in the Suzuki Museum's painting of Hirohito's bunker. Promoted to the rank of captain—a high one in the secret police—Tsukamoto had gone on in 1937 to assist Prince Asaka, the other of the Emperor's uncles, at the rape of Nanking. Now, when Lieutenant Colonel Tsukamoto received his orders in Taiwan he saw that they contained a built-in official disclaimer of the type reserved for special assignments. That is, they attached him, for the record, to the secret-police force in Kyoto, but they asked him to report in Tokyo. Moreover, they gave him top transportation priority.

Planes out of Taiwan were almost nonexistent and Okinawa blocked any direct flights to Japan. Tsukamoto had to proceed by many short hops, first to Canton, then up the China coast to Shanghai, then across to Kyushu and along the main island of Honshu. It was August 6 before he was able to report in Tokyo to the supreme commandant of the secret police. The commandant professed complete bafflement as to why Tsukamoto had been ordered home but added, "Since you are here you may as well take a temporary assignment. The other day War Minister Anami was over worrying about unrest among his subordinates. He instructed me to look into talk of a coup d'etat. He wants me to watch over these people and report on their plans." Old plotter Tsukamoto understood at once. He renewed acquaintance with a former messmate on Anami's staff and through him made friends with Anami's other subordinates.

The arrival of Tsukamoto gave the fanatics on Anami's staff an official witness. This was important to them because it meant that their deeds would be recorded, and, if they died, they would be given a fair hearing by their ancestors in the spirit world. In Japan's tightly organized homogeneous family society, it was common for political plotters to end their cell meetings with a report to the local police box. Like the priests or psychiatrists of other lands, the police could be relied on to treat such confessions as privileged communications. They would advise as to penalties and even sound out superiors as to official policy and attitudes. But their meticulous records would not be accessible except to other policemen. The act of confession and its recording on the tablets of life were considered a sacramental end unto itself. The crime and the punishment, being ordained by fate, were secondary. If a confession was made before the fact, that was a sign of sincerity and was usually considered mitigating. If a confession was made after the fact, that was satisfactory and gave a man a place again in the family of his ancestors. But if a confession was not made voluntarily, then one had to be extorted even if it meant torturing a man to death. The best Japanese police took the same attitude and assumed the same heavy responsibility as the inquisitors of the Church in medieval Europe.

Having been joined by police witness Tsukamoto, a group of the most patriotic majors and lieutenant colonels at the War Ministry now did begin, in earnest, to plot a coup d'etat. Before surrender became final they would seize the palace, they said, and save the Emperor from the evil counselors who advised him to accept dishonor. War Minister Anami's brother-in-law assured them that Anami supported them and would commit suicide if their plot failed. On several occasions they discussed their ideas with Anami directly. Though always noncommittal, he took pains to seem sympathetic to their cause. They also sounded out the commander of the Imperial Guards Division and the commander of the Tokyo Area Army. These two generals responded with appropriate remarks about the importance of Army discipline but otherwise did nothing to stop the conspirators. On Sunday, August 12, when the U.S. reply was received, the plotters drew up final plans for a rising on the following night. Secret-police Colonel Tsukamoto at once reported the plans in full to his chief, the supreme commandant. When the appointed evening arrived, the rebels came to War Minister Anami to tell him that they planned to act that night. They begged him to join them. Anami reviewed their schemes and found fault with their arrangements for cutting palace telephone lines. He advised them to wait a day and they agreed that they would.

JAPAN'S LONGEST DAY

On Tuesday morning, as the Emperor's chief advisor, Lord Privy Seal Kido, was surfacing from the last dreams of the night, a chamberlain burst into his study on the third floor of the Imperial Household Building and shook him where he lay on his pallet on the floor. The chamberlain was waving a leaflet which had just been dropped in the palace grounds. It was one of five million which had been unloaded by B-29's over Japan's principal cities that morning. It informed the populace that "the Japanese government has offered to surrender." Kido sprang to his feet and, according to his own account, was "stricken with consternation." He ordered that the chief of the civilian police be phoned immediately to make sure that they were having the leaflets picked up as fast as possible. The people had standing orders to turn in the devilish B-29 pamphlets without reading them and most citizens obeyed, but there were always those who kept the pamphlets and spread the rumors they contained. Right now was the worst possible moment for the masses to learn that Japan had surrendered. They must hear it from the Emperor's own mouth. Otherwise the doves would not feel grateful to him and the hawks might rise in unsolicited rebellions.

Kido phoned the library and was received in audience at 8:30 A.M. Hirohito agreed that the great gesture of debate must be stopped at once. Prime Minister Suzuki arrived at the library while Hirohito and Kido were talking, and at 8:45 A.M. Hirohito instructed him to call together Japan's leaders at once for a conference in the Imperial Presence. Imperial advisor Kido emphasized the urgency of the situation by stipulating that the usual Court attire of frock coat or cutaway would not be required. Two hours later, wearing the most presentable coats and ties which they could borrow in the offices where the summons reached them, the ministers and generals gathered.

Presiding once more in the underground audience chamber—a sweltering inferno that fine August morning—Hirohito again overrode all differences of opinion and ordered his vassals to accept surrender. He spoke so movingly of the unbearable humiliation which he and Japan must endure for the sake of national survival that he began to weep. With him wept the leaders who had ravaged half of Asia.

When Hirohito emerged at noon from the bunker, up the private staircase into his study, he found Lord Privy Seal Kido waiting for him. Still wracked by sobs, Hirohito asked that the remarks he had just made be used as the basis for the imperial rescript of surrender which he would read over the radio on August 15, the next day. Kido relayed the Emperor's thoughts to the secretary of the Cabinet and he in turn wrote up a draft. Two scholars translated it into suitable archaic Chinese-style Japanese and labored to give it the required singsong cadences.

Before the meeting in Hirohito's air raid shelter, that Tuesday morning, August 14, War Minister Anami had told his subordinates to abandon their coup d'etat plans. During the meeting, however, Lord Privy Seal Kido received a visit from Hirohito's brother, twenty-nine-year-old Prince Mikasa, an Army lieutenant colonel. And after the meeting, when the senior members of the conspiracy refused to have anything to do with the coup plans, a major who had been a close friend of Prince Mikasa at the military academy tried to revive the plot. He spent the rest of the afternoon making the rounds of important generals' offices in an effort to muster support.

Late that afternoon Prince Konoye got wind of the coup in the air and called on Lord Privy Seal Kido to discuss rumors of "unrest in the First Imperial Guards Division." The commander of the guards, Lieutenant General Mori Takeshi, was a friend, protégé, and distant in-law of Prince Konoye. He was one of those who had been sounded out by the rebels and asked to give his support to the rebellion. At 6:00 P.M. Lieutenant General Mori came himself to the palace to find out what was expected of him. As he drove down the mall from guard headquarters to the Imperial Household Building he saw his men posted outside every one of the gates to the Fukiage Gardens. It was all most unprecedented. Two of the three guards battalions had been called out together to stand watch in the Inner Palace Enclosure and he, their commander, did not know why. He had a shrewd suspicion that Japan was facing the crisis of surrender, for he had seen the pamphlets dropped that morning by the B-29's, but he knew nothing specific. At the Imperial Household Ministry he saw the Emperor's chief aide-de-camp and sought to feel him out as to what was brewing. The most that he could elicit from Hirohito's chief military advisor, however, was a typical piece of Court advice: "The ultimate test has come. Unless it is made to go with great circumspection, it will not go at all." Mori, who was a simple, studious man, went on to see General Tanaka, in charge of Tokyo Area Defense. Tanaka told him frankly of the Emperor's decision to surrender. Imperial Guards Commander Mori returned to his headquarters in the north of the palace immersed in thought. Late that night he was to behave so circumspectly that it was to cost him his life.

General Tojo, the former prime minister, was also worried by rumors of a coup. His son-in-law Major Koga Hidemasa was involved in it. The day before, son-in-law Koga had paid a brief visit to his suburban home next door to the Tojos' and had asked Tojo's daughter if she had recent clippings of his hair and nails. It was the duty of every soldier's wife to keep such things to put in a box on the prayer shelf and worship in case her husband died. Mrs. Koga, Tojo's daughter, bade adieu to her husband in the belief that he was about to die. With the Spartan stoicism of a good Japanese wife she calmly told her mother at supper what Koga had said. Her father, Tojo, at once drove in to Tokyo to find out what was happening. He returned greatly relieved to discover that his son-in-law had been involved in a coup d'etat plan but that it had been suspended.

The next afternoon, however, Tojo heard further rumors and at 6:30 P.M. on Tuesday, August 14, he was again in Tokyo talking to War Minister Anami as he took a bath during a brief Cabinet recess. Anami, whom Tojo had known for twenty years as a junior member of Hirohito's cabal of young officers, was strangely preoccupied and reticent. But Tojo understood enough from his belly talk to stress vociferously that the way to deal with the American conquerors was not to try to deceive them but to stand up to them honestly. "After the surrender," he said, "we will all of course be tried by a military court as war criminals. That goes without saying. What we must do when the time comes is all stand together. We must be forthright in stating our belief that the Greater East Asia War was necessary. What we fought was a defensive war." War Minister Anami agreed abstractedly, got out of his tub, put on his clothes, and returned to the Cabinet meeting, leaving Tojo to go home despondent.

While Mori, the general in command of the Imperial Guards, was seeing the Emperor's chief military advisor and Tojo was seeing the war minister, Hirohito was taking his evening stroll in the Fukiage Gardens. The junior chamberlain who walked in respectful silence behind him was alarmed to see "soldiers in the garden where they had never been seen before." Hirohito nodded to the men lounging about under the trees and returned in silence to the Imperial Library. There he found Prime Minister Suzuki waiting for him apologetically to make a report on the progress of the Cabinet. The draft of the imperial rescript of surrender, which Hirohito had approved in the middle of the afternoon, had been debated for two hours and was still not ready for Hirohito's signature. The phrase about "preservation of sacred national treasures" had been deleted because the minister of agriculture felt "it might lead to disagreeable inquiries by the Occupation forces." Hirohito impatiently approved this amendment and several other small word changes. The one remaining problem, continued Prime Minister Suzuki, was a tiny difference of opinion between War Minister Anami and Navy Minister Yonai. Anami insisted that the words "war situation has daily deteriorated" be changed to "war situation has not developed to Japan's advantage." Navy Minister Yonai branded this change an attempted evasion of Army responsibility and refused to endorse it. Could the Emperor, asked Prime Minister Suzuki, please give the Cabinet some guidance on this unfortunate little detail? Indeed Hirohito could and asked Suzuki to tell Navy Minister Yonai that there was no objection to the war minister's proposal.

Before the Cabinet meeting reconvened at 7:00 P.M. that Tuesday evening, one of Prime Minister Suzuki's secretaries communicated the Emperor's wishes to Navy Minister Yonai in the washroom of the prime minister's residence. Yonai turned without a word into one of the booths there and only sighed expressively as he urinated. At 8:30 P.M. Prime Minister Suzuki was back at the Imperial Library with a Cabinet-approved version of the surrender rescript. Hirohito made one or two tiny stylistic changes and strengthened Anami's insertion to read: "The war situation has developed not necessarily to Japan's advantage." Then Hirohito sent a copy of the historical document over to the palace office of the *Court Gazette*. At 11:00 P.M. the *Gazette* would begin running off an extra which would be circulated among the aristocracy and would give advance warning to the nation of Hirohito's radio address, scheduled for the morrow.

THE LONGEST EVENING

During the Cabinet recess between 8:30 and 9:30 P.M., War Minister Anami drove to his office to collect personal belongings from his desk. He noted with a sense of bleak poetry that the sunset that night—the setting of Japan's sun—was obscured by a heavy mist. It entirely enveloped the War Ministry, which had been housed, since the incendiary raid of May 25, in a complex of buildings around the old military academy. Anami found everything in the Ministry at sixes and sevens. During the afternoon the parade ground had blazed in the heat as men shuttled back and forth between files and bonfires burning the documents of Grand Imperial Headquarters. Now the embers of the fires still glowed but there was no one to tend them except a few soldiers who were drunk. Most of the officers had put on civilian clothes and set out for their home villages. The corridors of the War Ministry were deserted. War Minister Anami's footfalls echoed with emptiness and loneliness as he made his way to his office. His desk was littered with copies of cables he had ordered written and dispatched that afternoon to secret police units everywhere in Asia preparing for surrender. He sat down wearily and began to sort out the papers to be kept and those to be thrown away. An adjutant drifted in like a piece of the fog from outside and was ordered to summon the rest of the staff, particularly Colonel Arao, the senior member of the coup d'etat group. While waiting, Anami drafted a note of resignation to Prime Minister Suzuki and a cable to commanders overseas explaining the surrender.

Colonel Arao of the projected coup d'etat finally made his appearance at 9:30 P.M. He had been waiting by mistake to see War Minister Anami at his residence instead of the ministry. Anami dismissed the rest of his staff members who by now had gathered to help and watch him. "This war has been given up," he said. "Please leave me with what remains to be done." His secretaries and orderlies filed from the room, bowing. Arao remained to talk with him in private.

"It is the duty of you officers," Anami said, "to live and work for the rebuilding of Japan." Whatever else he may have said, this in itself was sufficient belly talk for Arao. It meant that Anami no longer numbered himself among "you officers" but among the dead. It meant that the war minister no longer hoped to fight a decisive battle against the Americans but merely to impress them with his high-level fanaticism by committing suicide.

Arao wept and promised to carry out the war minister's intentions. Anami took a bundle of cigars which he had brought back from New Guinea out of a desk drawer and began to wrap them in newspaper. Then, as if on impulse, he handed two of them to Arao. "I'd like you to have these," he said, with his kindest smile. And then gathering up a few souvenirs in a *furoshiki,* a carrying cloth, and tucking his ceremonial shortsword in its polished cherry scabbard under his arm, Anami bowed curtly in the professional manner of the Japanese officer. "I'll see you on the other side," he said and turned on his heel to return to his limousine.

By his cryptic words to Arao, War Minister Anami had sanctioned a reactivation of the suspended coup d'etat plans. Now, however, the coup was to be a fake one, staged as realistically as possible but no longer intended as a genuine effort to prolong the war. All that mattered was a gesture which would convince outside observers, especially Americans, that the sacred Emperor had been victim rather than villain of Japanese militarism. The busy conferences of the afternoon, the circumspect words of Hirohito's aide-de-camp, Hirohito's own walk in the Fukiage Gardens—all had been contrived to convey through belly talk the need for this final gesture.

The man most responsible for reviving the coup plans and converting them into fake coup plans was a certain Lieutenant Colonel X, an officer who has been regularly identified as unidentifiable by all the witnesses of that night's work. Lieutenant Colonel X was first noticed at 8:30 P.M., talking with junior officers of the Imperial Guards at the Double Bridge, the sacred entrance to the palace used only by the Emperor on state occasions. He had with him Major Hatanaka, War Minister Anami's pet firebrand, who would be the ringleader in the high-wire acts which followed.

Now, no military man ever presented himself at a palace gate—least of all at the Double Bridge—without giving his name and showing his credentials. The identity of Lieutenant Colonel X, in short, was not genuinely unknown to the officers of the Imperial Guards nor to the surviving members of the guards who have written about him since. In gossipy Japan only the imperial taboo which gives anonymity to the private acts of members of the Emperor's immediate family could account for such an unidentifiable personage in the Inner Palace enclosure at such a crucial juncture in Japanese history. The presumption is strong that Lieutenant Colonel X was Lieutenant Colonel Mikasa, the Emperor's youngest brother. Mikasa was a classmate of the junior officers participating in the coup that night. Mikasa had called on Hirohito and his chief advisor Kido twice that afternoon. The performance of Mikasa's classmates that night was to be so gruesomely realistic that it could not have been staged, not even as a hopeless samurai gesture of honor, without high priestly, imperial sanction.

A few minutes after 9:30 P.M., when War Minister Anami left his office in his limousine, Lieutenant Colonel X and his firebrand protégé, Major Hatanaka, visited the colonel in charge of the two battalions of Imperial Guards waiting in the Fukiage Gardens. Earlier in the day this same colonel had refused to subscribe to Major Hatanaka's coup plans. Now, when presented to Lieutenant Colonel X, the colonel said, "It seems I have changed my mind."

While Major Hatanaka and Lieutenant Colonel X were making their rounds in the palace, War Minister Anami, alone in his car, gazed out at the ruins of Tokyo on his right and the ancient, unchanging walls of the palace on his left. He had ordered his last young men to die. He had thrown his last dust in the eyes of the enemy. He returned to the Cabinet meeting at the prime minister's residence to approve the wording of the note which would be sent that night to the Allies: "His Majesty the Emperor has issued an imperial rescript regarding Japan's acceptance. . . . His Majesty the Emperor is prepared to authorize and insure the signature by his government and the Imperial General Headquarters of the necessary terms."

Anami listened apathetically, without comment, to the main text of the note. Then Foreign Minister Togo began to read a lengthy postscript which he planned to send in a second cable, and Anami opened his eyes wide with interest. "It is earnestly solicited that . . . the number of points in Japanese territory to be designated by the Allies for occupation be limited . . . ; that . . . the Japanese forces be allowed to disarm themselves . . . ; that . . . the honor of the soldiers will be respected, permitting them, for instance, to wear swords . . . ; that reasonable time be allowed before the cessation of hostilities . . . ; that the Allies will be good enough quickly to take necessary steps or extend us facilities for the shipment of indispensable foodstuffs and medical supplies to Japanese forces in distant islands."

"If I had known you were going to deal with the matter that way," exclaimed Anami, "I would not have felt compelled to speak so zealously earlier." Foreign Minister Togo bowed stiffly in acknowledgment of the apology.

The Cabinet sat on, reminiscing as to what might have been and speculating as to the next phase of Lord Privy Seal Kido's peace plan. When the ministers finally adjourned, about 11:30 P.M., War Minister Anami tarried for a last word with Prime Minister Suzuki. "I am afraid I have caused you a great deal of trouble," Anami said—and handed the prime minister the newspaper-wrapped package of precious cigars which he had brought from his office.

"I fully appreciate your painful position," answered Suzuki. "As His Majesty is extremely punctilious in the worship of his ancestors, however, and performs the rites required of him each spring and autumn, I am sure that the gods will show us their grace. I have not lost hope for the future of Japan."

Anami smiled and bowed and turned on his heel. "He came to say good-bye," observed Suzuki to his secretary. Anami drove to his residence and prepared for his last sentimental duty. He steeped himself in a scalding Japanese wooden tub, allowed his household maid to inject in his arm a last vitamin shot, donned a comfortable kimono, poured himself a drink, and sat down beside his telephone, with paper, ink, and writing brush, to frame his final testaments. His secretary passed in and out of the room, giving him news and scraps of conversation. The maid stole in silently from time to time with a freshly warmed pitcher of saké.

Earlier that Tuesday evening, at 10:00 P.M., U.S. B-29's had returned to Tokyo after a four-day bombing pause. When the air raid alert sounded, Emperor Hirohito decided not to wait for the adjournment of his Cabinet but instructed his chamberlains to make preparations at once for the promulgation of the surrender rescript. At 11:25 P.M., wearing the uniform of an Army field marshal, he drove across the palace park, through the blackout, to the Imperial Household Administration Building. There, in the audience hall on the second floor, a team of technicians from Japan National Broadcasting were waiting for him, and he intoned his rescript into a microphone. At the first reading, though no one presumed to remark on it, his voice trembled.

"It sounds too low and husky," he said, when he listened to the playback. "Let me try again."

On the second take his voice was clearer, more correctly high-pitched and nasal, and more nervous. He was not entirely satisfied and offered to make a third take. But the room was stifling and the technicians were awed to the point of suicide by the discomfort to which they were putting him. They assured him that a third take would not be necessary. Hirohito took them at their word and at 12:05 A.M. returned to his library.

Two records had been cut of each reading, one for playback and one for possible broadcast. After repeated hearings, the technicians judged the first reading to be far the most moving and discovered that there was a good reason to reject the second: Hirohito had left out a conjunction. All four pressings, however, were packed in cans and cotton bags and given to a chamberlain for safekeeping. After careful thought the chamberlain hid them in a safe behind the books in a room on the first floor of the Imperial Household Building belonging to one of the Empress's ladies-in-waiting.

THE FINAL GESTURE

During Hirohito's recording session and War Minister Anami's farewell to his Cabinet colleagues, the long and gingerly incubated coup d'etat was finally taking shape. At 10:00 P.M., when the air raid sirens were sounding for the first time, one of the principals in the coup, Lieutenant Colonel Ida Masataka, was lying on his bunk in the staff quarters at the War Ministry, gazing at the ceiling in romantic gloom. Ida was the member of Anami's staff whom Tsukamoto of the secret police had first contacted on his return from Taiwan. For a week Ida had been the coup's most enthusiastic booster, but since Hirohito's final decision in the bunker that morning Ida had obediently given up the scheme. He had told the young firebrand major, Hatanaka, not to count on him and had devoted himself all afternoon to a new idea: the mass suicide of the Japanese Army officer corps. If enough officers would take their lives and so demonstrate their responsibility for fighting a losing war, it would save the honor of Japan and at the same time exonerate the Emperor in American eyes. But when Ida conducted a poll of the officers at the War Ministry, he found that only 20 per cent were willing to kill themselves. Another 10 per cent thought it would be better to go underground. The remaining 70 per cent had no opinion. Ida had been so disgusted by the results of his poll that he had retired to his quarters to prepare himself for his own suicide.

When the air raid sirens shrieked out, Lieutenant Colonel Ida lay still in his bunk and hoped that a bomb would fall on him. Suddenly his friend Major Hatanaka burst into his bedchamber to give him the exciting news of Anami's commitment to suicide and of the agreement of the colonel in the Fukiage Gardens to support the coup with his two battalions of guards. Unlike Ida, Hatanaka was not troubled by subtle, palsied casts of thought. He was a man of action. Handsome, serious, slight, athletic, he had the look of a man who would make a good soldier if he ever survived his thirty-fifth birthday.

Lieutenant Colonel Ida listened to him morosely, shook his head, and told his eager young friend that the coup would never impress Americans as much as mass hara-kiri. Major Hatanaka swiftly explained that the two plans could be dovetailed. After the coup the conspirators could commit suicide. Lieutenant Colonel Ida brightened somewhat at this thought, and Major Hatanaka pressed home his argument. Without Ida's participation, he said flatteringly, the coup could not even begin. Ida was a kinsman of Lieutenant General Mori who had over-all command of the Imperial Palace Guards. Without Ida's help it would be impossible to talk to Lieutenant General Mori and persuade him to issue the necessary orders for the coup. Ida proudly saw the logic of this argument and agreed to play his part.

The two conspirators set out on their bicycles to pedal a mile through the sultry night from the War Ministry to the Imperial Guards headquarters in the northernmost salient of the palace. Ida's bicycle sprang a flat tire, and Hatanaka had to stop and help the unmechanical colonel fix it. The two arrived at the North Gate of the palace at 11:00 P.M. and asked to be taken at once to Lieutenant General Mori. Mori, however, sent out word asking them to wait a while. All evening Mori had been considering the words about circumspection delivered to him five hours earlier by the Emperor's chief aide-de-camp. Now he was consulting his brother-in-law from Hiroshima and was hearing for the first time an eyewitness account of the effects of the atomic bomb.

Lieutenant General Mori kept the conspirators waiting for an hour and a half and did not admit them to his presence until almost 12:30 A.M. By then he knew that Hirohito had returned from his recording session to the safety of the Imperial Library. Firebrand Hatanaka demanded that Mori call out his Imperial Guards, seize the palace, cut off the Imperial Library, and issue instructions in the Emperor's name for the Army and Navy to continue the war. Hatanaka asserted that he spoke for War Minister Anami. Lieutenant General Mori insisted that Hatanaka must be mistaken. At 12:45 A.M. Hatanaka agreed to go back to Anami and seek confirmation. He left Mori talking to his kinsman, Lieutenant Colonel Ida.

Five minutes later the courtiers at the Imperial Household Building were informed by telephone that the Emperor and Empress had gone to bed. At that moment, at his residence to the south of the palace, War Minister Anami was preparing for suicide. Tokyo Area Commander Tanaka was napping at his desk upstairs from Peace Faction headquarters in the Dai Ichi Insurance Building. Secret Policeman Tsukamoto from Taiwan, the watchdog of the coup, dozed in the police headquarters outside the North Gate of the palace, where he happened to have the duty that night. A stone's throw away, inside the North Gate at the guards' headquarters, Lieutenant General Mori and Lieutenant Colonel Ida were engaged in earnest conversation. At some time between 12:50 and 1:00 A.M. they were joined by the mysterious Lieutenant Colonel X.

Major Hatanaka had commandeered a staff car and set out to seek reassurance on the other side of the palace from War Minister Anami's brother-in-law, Lieutenant Colonel Takeshita. He arrived at his destination about 1:00 A.M. and implored Takeshita to see Anami and have the war minister telephone Guards Commander Mori. Takeshita promised to see what he could do, and Major Hatanaka started back for the command post of the Imperial Guards. Takeshita went off at the same time to drive down the block to his brother-in-law's. He found Anami struggling to write a poem of farewell to life. "I am thinking of committing suicide tonight according to plan," said Anami.

"Does it have to be tonight?" asked Takeshita.

"I'm glad you do not oppose the idea," replied Anami.

"Why don't you use the poem you wrote before you went to the front in China?" suggested Takeshita.

Anami laughed and ordered the maid to bring beer mugs to put the saké in. "It's all right," he said. "The revolt won't amount to anything because General Tanaka and the Tokyo Area Army will refuse to support it."

Takeshita telephoned Imperial Guards headquarters to say that Anami was going ahead with suicide according to plan. Then he and Anami settled down for a last bout of serious drinking together.

Firebrand Hatanaka returned to guards' headquarters shortly after 1:00 A.M. He found Lieutenant General Mori, Lieutenant Colonel Ida, and Lieutenant Colonel X still discussing suicide and the destiny of Japan. At Hatanaka's reappearance Lieutenant Colonel Ida bowed himself from the room and left Hatanaka, Lieutenant Colonel X, and a newcomer, an Army Air Force captain, to finish the conversation. A few minutes later firebrand Hatanaka shot dead Mori, the commander of the Imperial Guards. The Air Force captain, Uehara Shigetaro, scion of one of the greatest military families in Japan, drew his sword and decapitated Mori's brother-in-law from Hiroshima.

In the quiet of the night and the blackout expectant ears throughout the palace area heard the gunshot. War Minister Anami heard it a mile away and realized that his colleague Lieutenant General Mori had met a meaningful end. The chamberlains at the Imperial Household Ministry also heard the shot. So did Secret Policeman Tsukamoto at his headquarters outside the North Gate.

Lieutenant Colonel X stepped from the room where the murders—the courted ceremonial self-sacrifices—had taken place and nodded to the junior officers waiting outside. He then disappeared, insofar as the records reveal, into the palace night. Firebrand Hatanaka and Air Force Captain Uehara followed him out of the murder room, glassy-eyed and spattered with blood. Tojo's son-in-law Koga and other majors entered the room, took the seals from the gory, kimono-clad general on the floor, and used them to stamp orders, which Koga had prepared earlier, for the Imperial Guards to seize the palace. As several hundred of the sleepy guardsmen were being mustered from their barracks, Lieutenant Colonel Ida told the overwrought Major Hatanaka to take charge of himself and the men while Ida went to the Dai Ichi Insurance Building and gave the signal for general uprising to the Tokyo Area Army. Ida drove to the Dai Ichi Building, reported to the Tokyo area commander, and was back at the North Gate of the palace at 2:45 A.M. The blood-stained Major Hatanaka was waiting for him. Hatanaka had successfully deployed the Imperial Guards and had seized all major checkpoints in the palace compound. He had apprehended a Cabinet minister attempting to enter the North Gate of the palace and now had him under lock and key. But Lieutenant Colonel Ida had no solace to offer. The Tokyo Area Army, Ida reported, would definitely not support the uprising.

Major Hatanaka set off, eyes glazed, to see what could be salvaged with the troops who now occupied the southern grounds of the palace. Lieutenant Colonel Ida offered to remain behind at the North Gate to preserve discipline. Hatanaka found that his rebel forces had captured the radio technicians of National Broadcasting and locked them in the keep at the southeastern gate. The technicians had lingered at the Household Ministry drinking toasts to the Voice of the Crane after their historic recording session and had been apprehended weaving an unsteady course home. Now Hatanaka's fellow officers were grilling them as to their business so late at night in the palace.

Hatanaka's men had also succeeded in cutting the main communication cables connecting the palace with the outside world. They did not know it but they had missed two secret cables: one from the chief naval aide-de-camp's office in the Imperial Household Building, the other from the chief Army aide-de-camp's office in the bunker under the Imperial Library. Over these the chamberlains of the Outer and Inner Palaces were keeping in touch with Tokyo Area Commander Tanaka in the Dai Ichi Insurance Building across the moat. At about the same moment that Hatanaka joined his men, the chamberlains learned that General Tanaka was in full command of the situation and was prepared to prevent anything serious from happening. He had just seen Lieutenant Colonel Ida and sent him back to supervise developments at the North Gate. Tsukamoto, at secret-police headquarters outside the gate, was fully informed and ready to move with his men at an instant's notice. As yet, however, Tsukamoto did not believe that secret-police intervention was warranted and feared that it might only be dangerous.

Having resolved to stage a realistic coup d'etat, the firebrand Major Hatanaka needed a military objective in the palace on which to focus the attention of his noncoms and soldiers. The logical objective was the Emperor. It would have been a simple matter to surround the Imperial Library, take the Emperor hostage, and force Japan to continue the war. Instead Hatanaka wasted two hours in meaningless comings and goings, making sure that all the guards at palace gates and checkpoints acknowledged the authority of the forged orders which had been issued. When the soldiers began to grow restless and apprehensive, Hatanaka declared that the purpose of the coup was to seize the surrender recording which the Emperor had made and prevent it from being broadcast to the people.

At 3:00 A.M. Hatanaka's troops surrounded the Imperial Household Ministry Building and demanded that the chamberlains on night duty there surrender the recording. The chamberlains parleyed. Hatanaka's men entered the building and began to question the chamberlains individually. They all agreed that someone must have the recording but that he was "a taller man with a bigger nose" than any of the soldiers' prime suspects. All the chamberlains wore the drab blue wartime *koku-fuku* or national uniform for civilians, a Nehru jacket and unstriped pants. It was difficult to tell one chamberlain from another. All had the air of expert butlers. Hatanaka's soldiers felt that they were being made fun of. They began to look increasingly frustrated and potentially violent.

At 3:20 A.M., fearing that Hatanaka's men were about to conduct a search of the building, one of the chamberlains aroused Lord Privy Seal Kido from his pallet and advised him that the soldiers were in a vicious mood and might kill him if they found him. Kido flushed secret documents in his room down the toilet and repaired to the great steel bank vault under the building where the paper assets of the imperial fortune were stored. Together with the imperial household minister and a number of secretaries and guards, he spent the rest of the night there, locked in like some gilt-edged security. The vault opened by a staircase into a cupboard in the anteroom for ladies-in-waiting outside the audience chamber on the third floor. It was provided with peepholes and intercoms which made it possible for the two prisoners to keep in touch with much of what was happening in the rest of the building.

Once Kido was safely hidden, the chamberlain who had put away the phonograph records set out to investigate reports that the Imperial Library was surrounded and cut off. His name, Tokugawa Yoshihiro, guaranteed his safety, for the Tokugawas had supplied ancient Japan with military dictators and the scions of the family still held a place second only to the Emperor's in the esteem of soldiers.[13] Chamberlain Tokugawa negotiated the rebel guard lines with sure aristocratic poise. At the library he learned that the Emperor was fast asleep. The Emperor, according to his own later account, was not asleep but listening with amusement through the paper walls from his nearby bedroom. At the adjoining English-style country house, the Concubines' Pavilion, Chamberlain Tokugawa was told that Empress Nagako was equally oblivious. He had the iron shutters of both dwellings closed as a precaution and then walked back through the dark gardens and through a newly built tunnel under a hill celebrated for its maples.

At the Imperial Household Building, Chamberlain Tokugawa found that the rebels had begun a room-to-room search for the imperial recording. The soldiers were slashing upholstery and breaking open fine Chinese camphor-

---

[13] Tokugawa Yoshihiro was the son of Tokugawa Yoshichika who will be met with later as the financier of the March Plot, an intrigue which prepared the domestic political scene in 1931 for the conquest of Manchuria.

wood chests. They were angry that the style of furnishing was almost entirely Western. Tokugawa followed them about scalding them with patrician sarcasms. A desperate sergeant [14] finally slapped him in the face, and a lieutenant sat him down and threatened him with a sword unless he would reveal the whereabouts of the recording. Tokugawa went to the aide-de-camps' common room to inquire indignantly what the Army was doing to restore discipline. The naval aide-de-camp took him aside and whispered that he had just spoken on his secret telephone with the Tokyo Area Army HQ and everything was well in hand. Tokyo Area Commander Tanaka had set out from his headquarters by staff car shortly after 4:00 A.M. to begin the task of suppressing the revolt. A little later he had been joined at the North Gate by secret-police Colonel Tsukamoto, the rebellion's watchdog.[15]

LIVES FOR THE EMPEROR

At 3:30 A.M., when the soldiers entered the Imperial Household Building, Lieutenant Colonel Ida deserted his post at the North Gate of the palace to report to War Minister Anami. He found Anami still drinking saké by the mugful with his secretary and his brother-in-law. He had wound his belly in a white sash and put on a white shirt given him by the Emperor. Ida reported on the gesture of rebellion being made in the palace and sat down to join in the carouse. About 4:00 A.M. Air Force Captain Uehara called to relate ecstatically his part in the murder of Guards Commander Mori. Anami remarked, "Something else to make amends for," and went on drinking. A little later his brother-in-law Takeshita asked the war minister if he might not be drinking too much. Anami discounted the idea by reminding Takeshita that saké helped the blood to flow and that a fifth-degree swordsman could hardly fail in his suicide. Nevertheless Anami shortly dismissed them all and asked to be alone.

Lieutenant Colonel Ida went outside to wait. He later said that he waited on the curb for a passing Army vehicle which would take him back to the palace. But he could have called for a car easily enough. What he meant was that he was waiting to make sure that Anami would fulfill his part of the pledge and commit suicide. Ida, after all, had stood by patriotically, outside the door, while his own kinsman, Lieutenant General Mori of the guards, was being shot.

In bold, childlike calligraphy, Anami was completing the two memorials

---

[14] Sergeant Wakabayashi, fifteen years later, made himself known to Chamberlain Tokugawa, presenting him with an apologetic teapot made out of an ancient bronze mirror, the most cherished possession of his family.

[15] Tanaka's aide, Major Tsukamoto Kiyoshi, was also present. The two Tsukamotos have sometimes been confused in Western reporting of the record.

over which he had agonized earlier. The first was the poem which he had written years ago, before going to China:

> Having received from
> His Imperial Majesty
> many great favors,
> I have no final statement
> to make to posterity.

The second was a single new sentence in prose: "In the conviction that our sacred land will never perish, I offer my life to the Emperor as an apology for the great crime." By the great crime most surviving officers believe that he meant the Army's crime in being defeated. Having completed his literary chores, he sat down with his brother-in-law for one or two more drinks. Amid the distractions of the modern world it was hard for a fifty-eight-year-old bowman to follow the ancient formulas of honor.

At 5:30 A.M. the supreme commandant of the secret police called at Anami's residence to inform him that Tokyo Area Commander Tanaka was now in the Imperial Guards compound in the northern corner of the palace, rescinding the false orders given earlier and calling the soldiers back to their barracks. The rebellion was over. Being no great friend of Anami, the commandant of the secret police was not privileged to see the war minister but delivered his report to Anami's brother-in-law.

For War Minister Anami the time had come. His death, like that of Mori's earlier, was required to show that the insurrection was not all play-acting. He walked to the veranda of his bedroom and laid out the two memorials he had written, together with a picture of his son who had died in battle the year before. He took a kneeling position, shortsword in his right hand, dagger in his left. He stared at the beams of the rising sun stealing in through the cracks of the closed blackout shutters of the porch. He listened for a moment to the tread of the guards in the garden outside. He sank the shortsword into his muscular belly below the lowest rib on the left. He wrenched the sword to the right, through his stomach and then sharply upward. Having followed the painful prescribed formula, he found himself still alive. With the dagger in his left hand he reached around to the right side of his neck and felt about for the area of the carotid artery.

His brother-in-law came back into the room, ran to kneel at his side, and assured him that the rebellion had served its purpose. "May I have the honor of assisting you?"

Anami shook his head and dug the dagger into his neck. It missed the carotid artery but cut the cervical vein. He remained kneeling, swaying from side to side, for almost an hour. Then he fainted forward and continued to bleed and writhe, unconscious on the floor. His brother-in-law sat out the long vigil waiting for him to die. About 7:30 A.M. one of several visiting officers finally called in a medical corpsman to dispatch him with a hypodermic.

Within the palace, half a mile to the northeast of Anami's bedroom, Tokyo Area Commander Tanaka was driving from checkpoint to checkpoint sending the soldiers back to their barracks. His eyes flashed. His magnificent mustache, which he had first cultivated as an undergraduate years ago at Oxford, heaved and twisted expressively. His riding crop slapped savagely against his riding boots as he itemized and emphasized his admonitions. It was his noblest hour, for he too had now resolved on suicide. As a classmate and old friend and rival of Anami he could do no less. He would blow his brains out nine days later when he felt sure that the Army would obey the Emperor and accept surrender in a disciplined manner. Now, in the palace, the soldiers followed his instructions instantly. In a matter of minutes there was no disturbance within the sacred precincts but the dawn twitter of birds.

Left without troops, the young rebel officers of Anami's staff withdrew to the offices of the Japan Broadcasting Company two blocks outside the moat. There they sought to turn on the transmitters so that they could make their own last statement to the nation. When they failed, they disbanded and went out to lose themselves in the early morning crowds of people going to work.

Other attacks were made that night on the homes of Hirohito's accessories in the peace plot. This was a tried and true stratagem, a standard method of operation. In three previous sham coups d'etat staged in the 1930's, simultaneous attacks had always been made on the homes of the master plotters. Now, on the night of August 14, 1945, secret policemen attacked the home of Hirohito's chief advisor, Lord Privy Seal Kido, and had to be driven off by other secret policemen. Groups of venal civilian patriots, seasoned by the leadership of a few soldiers, burned the private residences of Prime Minister Suzuki and of Baron Hiranuma, the two great impresarios of the peace scenes in the imperial bunker. Before both fires the victims were given adequate warning and allowed to escape. Some of Baron Hiranuma's own stout right-wing partisans participated in the burning of his home.

At Prime Minister Suzuki's, a comedy of fate overtook the droll old philosopher. His getaway limousine refused to start. It was loaded with family and valuables and proved too heavy for servants to push. His entire bodyguard, which was large enough to repel an army, had to be summoned from neighborhood retreats to carry the car to the top of a gradient. Everyone enjoyed the farce, including Prime Minister Suzuki. And when the car's engine finally sparked, going down the hill, the bodyguard turned back uproariously to mingle with the incendiary mob gathering at Suzuki's home.

No one was later tried for the acts of arson, but Suzuki and Hiranuma both collected a little devaluated insurance. More to the point, the public was satisfied. Both men had saved face. They had established their innocence of the anti-peace coup in the palace and they had paid a little for their pro-peace coup at the counsel tables.

At 7:21 A.M., Wednesday, August 15, the Japan National Broadcasting Company, having repaired its cables cut by the rebels, went back on the air to announce: "The Emperor at noon today will graciously broadcast, in person. This is a most gracious act. All the people are requested to listen respectfully to the Emperor. Electricity will be supplied to districts not normally supplied during daylight hours." After the events of the previous weeks and the leaflets dropped the day before, few Tokyo residents had any doubt as to what the Emperor would announce. All morning long the park of the Imperial Plaza, outside the southeastern palace gate near the Household Ministry Building, filled up with relieved and sorrowful people. At noon the loudspeakers there and at every other city square in the country vibrated with the Emperor's voice:

> We declared war on America and Britain out of Our sincere desire to ensure Japan's self-preservation and the stabilization of East Asia, it being far from Our thought either to infringe upon the sovereignty of other nations or to embark upon territorial aggrandizement. But now the war has lasted for nearly four years. Despite the best that has been done by everyone . . . the war situation has developed not necessarily to Japan's advantage, while the general trends of the world have all turned against her interest. Moreover, the enemy has begun to employ a new and most cruel bomb, the power of which to do damage is indeed incalculable. . . . Should We continue to fight it would . . . result in an ultimate collapse and obliteration of the Japanese nation. . . . Such being the case, how are We to save the millions of Our subjects; or to atone Ourselves before the hallowed spirits of Our Imperial Ancestors? This is the reason why We have ordered the acceptance of the provisions of the Joint Declaration of the Powers. . . .
>
> Let the entire nation continue as one family, from generation to generation. . . . Unite your total strength to be devoted to the construction for the future. . . . Work with resolution so as ye may enhance the innate glory of the Imperial State and keep pace with the progress of the world.

The throngs in the squares wept with humiliation, incredulity, and weary relief. Men prostrated themselves and knocked their heads on the pavements. Here and there someone drove a dagger or bullet into himself. The crowds bowed to each corpse, muttered words of prayer for each departing spirit and dispersed in silence to their homes. In all, 376 Army men from general to private, 113 Navy men from admiral to seaman, and 37 nurses and civilians died by their own hands that week, a grand total of only 526.[16]

The scores who killed themselves on the precincts of the palace in Tokyo included firebrand Hatanaka, General Tojo's son-in-law, and one other leader of the hopeless coup the night before. A fourth rebel, Air Force Captain Uehara who had murdered General Mori's brother-in-law, shot himself two days later. Four more of the rebel officers may still be found alive in Tokyo today. One presides over the Historical Section of Japan's modern Self-Defense Forces. A second, General Anami's brother-in-law, runs the Self-Defense Staff College. A third, Arao, is president of an automobile agency. A fourth, Lieutenant Colonel Ida, has changed his name to Iwata. He has divorced his wife because she was ashamed of him for not committing suicide. He works in an advertising agency for Colonel Tsukamoto Makoto, the secret policeman from Formosa, the official witness of the coup, who in years gone by had assisted Prince Asaka at the rape of Nanking.

Through Hirohito's broadcast the Japanese became the last people in the world to learn that the war was over. Others had heard the news the previous afternoon when Domei, the Japanese news service, at 2:49 P.M. Tokyo time, had beamed a message to the American operator on Okinawa: FLASH FLASH TOKYO AUGUST 14 IT IS LEARNED THAT AN IMPERIAL MESSAGE ACCEPTING THE POTSDAM DECLARATION IS FORTHCOMING SOON. By the time that Japanese were going home from the Emperor's broadcast to "eat stones and drink gall," as they said, London's first V-J Day celebration was spending itself in walk-up flats. In New York surging crowds of sailors, soldiers, and girls in Times Square were waiting for the magical stroke of midnight.

The Allies had laid down the terms. The bomb had enforced them. The Emperor had accepted them. The Allies had obviated an inch-by-inch conquest of Japan and postponed for a few years the communization of China. They had won a chance to cure Japan of her proud tribalism and to harness the vast powers of the Emperor for the task. Vengeance need not stand in the way of construction, for vengeance had already been taken. The 140,-000 corpses of Hiroshima and Nagasaki had paid for Nanking, and the 166,000 killed in the fire raids on Tokyo had more than paid for American, Australian, and British war prisoners who had been starved and beaten to death in Japanese concentration camps. Only ignorance and suspicion remained to be conquered. The exact arithmetic of war had to be replaced by the conversational arts of peace. Vague foreign concepts like Shinto and

---

[16] The over-all suicide rate that year dropped dramatically from the norm of 2.5 per ten thousand to 1.5, an all-time low even in the postwar period. Apparently the honor of the few was more than discounted by the need to survive of the many.

Emperor system, or like Christianity and democracy, had to acquire flesh-and-blood meaning. A few hundred Americans and a few thousand Japanese who spoke one another's language had to fill out the blank checks of "unconditional" surrender.

In the palace, Lord Privy Seal Kido and Emperor Hirohito waited with apprehension. They hoped that the enemy would demonstrate Christian kindness; they prayed that the enemy would fail to democratize. Unless they could preserve the Emperor system, they would not be able to answer to their ancestors. Without aristocracy and hierarchy, the society of the living would cease to be at one with the spirit world of the dead. Up to now the peace plot had worked with the vanquished; now it must work with the victors.

3

DEFEAT

RECEPTION CABINET

The Japanese were the only people on earth who had lived in their homeland from prehistoric times and never been conquered by outsiders. Many of them, however, had studied surrender subterfuges from the greatest masters, the Chinese. And now, after surrender in 1945, Japan had two weeks in which to prepare before the first American Occupation troops would unload from their planes onto Japanese soil. Dazed and disheartened as they were, the people demonstrated extraordinary discipline and, in the words of one newspaper, "complete compliance with the imperial will." From palace on down to police box, they moved with zeal to implement the well-considered plans of the Peace Faction. Millionaires gave millions "to save the nation," and aristocratic ladies prepared to contribute even their virtue if it was required of them.

Fighting off a mood of inanition and despair, Hirohito worked early and late to set his people an example. He reviewed most of the peace preparations personally and saw a steady stream of "experts" who had ideas for handling the Americans. No rigid policy could be laid down in advance for the attitude which the people should take toward the conquerors, but tentatively one of cautious politeness and obedience was agreed upon as the best initial approach. This recommendation was transmitted to the masses by an amazingly efficient word-of-mouth system perfected during the war. Each of ten men was responsible for telling ten other men and each of them, in turn, for relaying the message to ten more. The superstructure of the pyramid was Japan's single monolithic political party, the Imperial Rule Assistance Association, which had been organized by Prince Konoye in the late 1930's in emulation of the Nazi and Communist parties of Germany and

115

Russia. The base of the pyramid consisted of "neighborhood association" leaders who doubled as police informers and air raid wardens.

More than most people under such circumstances, the Japanese needed to be told how to behave. In their own highly structured society, they had elaborate rules of etiquette for dealing with all grades of superiors and inferiors in all types of situations. But they had no universal code of behavior to apply to human beings from outside their society. Defeat was an unthinkable situation and foreigners had no place or rank in the national family. In their bewilderment Japanese might fawn upon the Americans or might attack them with knives. Japanese soldiers who had been knocked unconscious in battle and so had fallen alive into enemy hands had almost always surprised Allied interrogators by their pliability as prisoners. Ready one day to cut out American hearts and eat them, they found themselves the next in another life, glad to be breathing but sure that they were dead to their own society. Now it was feared that the whole nation might react in the same way; that in the hunger, misery, and relief of defeat, the people might overnight forget their Japanese heritage.

To give the populace the clearest possible leadership in dealing with the conquerors, Hirohito called to office the first Cabinet in Japan's history headed by an imperial prince of the blood. Prime Minister Suzuki, the old cigar-smoking Taoist philosopher, submitted the resignation of his own Cabinet three hours after the surrender broadcast. Hirohito at once summoned his advisor, Lord Privy Seal Kido, to the library and asked him to proceed according to plan in recommending a successor.

Before making his nomination, Kido broke with all precedent and consulted only one of the elder statesmen, the canny old lawyer Baron Hiranuma. It was a symbolic gesture meant to indicate that the two greatest political camps in Japan, patrician and plebeian, had joined ranks in the hour of national crisis. Hiranuma could speak for the village mayors who controlled the peasants, for the gang leaders who ruled the urban poor, and for the majority in the Army who had wanted to fight Russia rather than the United States.

In response to Kido's summons, Hiranuma walked over immediately from the Privy Council Office where he worked to the Imperial Household Building. "My teeth got burned up with my house this morning," he mumbled as he entered Kido's office. "Now I'll have to buy another house and another set of teeth."

In less than an hour, he and Kido had agreed to recommend a slate of Cabinet ministers headed by Prince Higashikuni, the Emperor's uncle. It was Higashikuni, figuratively, who was to stand on the bridge outside the palace and shout to the Americans, "If you want to come, come." The people would understand that the imperial family was bravely accepting responsibility for defeat. And the Americans would see that Japan considered her imperial princes to be men of peace.

Emperor Hirohito accepted the nomination of Prince Higashikuni as a matter of prearrangement, but Higashikuni himself had last-minute objections. During the 1860's, after the Americans had forced their way into Japan the first time, his father, he complained, had undertaken a similar role as a peacemaker for Hirohito's great-grandfather. And for this loyal service he had later been disgraced and banished from Court. Prince Higashikuni wanted assurance that the same thing would not happen to him now. The next morning, August 16, Hirohito talked privately with Higashikuni for twenty minutes in the library and promised him a lifelong place in the imperial favor. Higashikuni later said that he was much moved by the Emperor's haggard appearance. Lord Privy Seal Kido was summoned to witness the bargain, and Higashikuni formally accepted the imperial mandate to form a government.

Higashikuni designed a Cabinet which would look like an apology to the people and a gesture of defiance to the Allies, particularly to the Chinese. He indicated the Emperor's contrition for the disastrous adventure in the South Seas by including as ministers several members of the Fight-Russia or Strike-North Faction ousted in the 1930's. At the same time he took as his chief minister of state Prince Konoye, who had led the nation into war with China, and as war minister General Shimomura Sadamu who had forced the plans for the rape of Nanking through the General Staff in 1937. As special Cabinet advisor, Higashikuni chose a retired Lieutenant General Ishiwara Kanji who had conducted the strategic planning for the conquest of Manchuria in 1929–1931.

To those in the inner circle of Japanese leadership, the most cynical feature of Higashikuni's Peace Cabinet was Prince Higashikuni himself. There were nine other eligible princes in the ranks of Hirohito's immediate family who might have stood more sincerely for peace. The bold, affable Higashikuni had played a conspicuously active role behind the scenes in the last twenty-five years. And if the Allies could but know it, he was better qualified than most for the label of Class A war criminal. As a privileged Army Intelligence officer in Paris in 1921, he had helped to recruit a private, unofficial cabal of Army officers for Hirohito. In 1927 he had helped to persuade Hirohito to prepare for the conquest of Manchuria. Between 1930 and 1936, as part of the terror which silenced Japanese moderates, he had been involved in no less than eight fake coups d'etat, four assassinations, two religious hoaxes, and countless threats of murder and blackmail. He alone among princes of the blood had taken active measures in 1936 to help his nephew Hirohito to suppress Strike-North or Fight-Russia insurgents. A year later Higashikuni had assumed command of the bombing of civilian China. In 1941, after Hirohito had approved plans for the attack on Pearl Harbor, Higashikuni had stood ready to lead Japan into the war as prime minister. Only the caution of men like Lord Privy Seal Kido, who considered the possibility of defeat and worried about

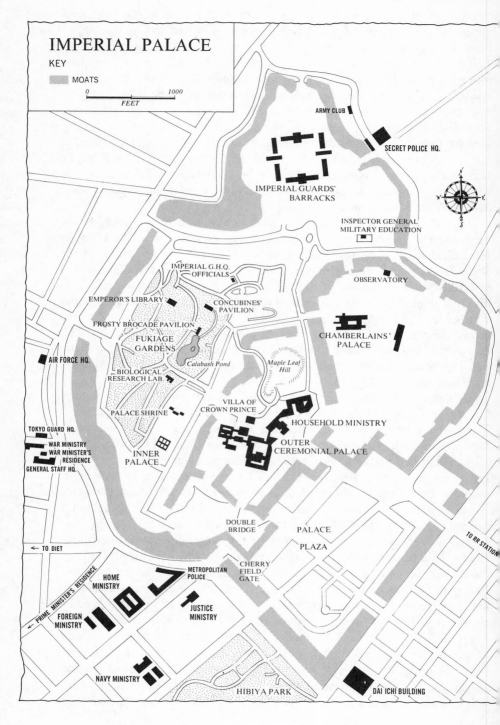

IMPERIAL PALACE

KEY

▨ MOATS

0 ————————————— 1000
FEET

ARMY CLUB

SECRET POLICE HQ.

IMPERIAL GUARDS'
BARRACKS

INSPECTOR GENERAL
MILITARY EDUCATION

IMPERIAL G.H.Q.
OFFICIALS

OBSERVATORY

EMPEROR'S LIBRARY

CONCUBINES'
PAVILION

FROSTY BROCADE PAVILION

CHAMBERLAINS'
PALACE

FUKIAGE
GARDENS

AIR FORCE HQ.

Calabash Pond

*Maple Leaf
Hill*

BIOLOGICAL
RESEARCH LAB.

VILLA OF
CROWN PRINCE

PALACE SHRINE

HOUSEHOLD MINISTRY

TOKYO GUARD HQ.

OUTER
CEREMONIAL PALACE

WAR MINISTRY
WAR MINISTER'S
RESIDENCE

INNER
PALACE

GENERAL STAFF HQ.

DOUBLE
BRIDGE

PALACE

← TO DIET

PLAZA

TO RR STATION

CHERRY
FIELD
GATE

METROPOLITAN
POLICE

HOME
MINISTRY

PRIME MINISTER'S RESIDENCE

JUSTICE
MINISTRY

FOREIGN
MINISTRY

NAVY MINISTRY

HIBIYA PARK

DAI ICHI BUILDING

the future of the imperial family, induced Hirohito to nominate General Tojo as prime minister instead.

More than any other prince of the blood, Higashikuni had always been able to work smoothly with Hirohito. The attraction between the two men —the Emperor was only thirteen years younger than his uncle—was one between complementary opposites, between a tough, unscrupulous man of the world and a hothouse product of the finest education which could be given in a palace. Nephew Hirohito was an intellectual who always strove to be more knowledgeable and rational than those about him. Uncle Higashikuni professed to be a simple, manly, religious fellow. Hirohito liked to attack problems by working from general principles; Higashikuni began all his thinking in terms of personalities and how to use them. Hirohito valued statistics; Higashikuni considered them details best left to subordinates. Hirohito surrounded himself with propriety and punctilio; Higashikuni had built up an undeserved reputation for himself as an easygoing wastrel who played the devil with fast cars, hot planes, and French mistresses. Hirohito was known for being gruff, open, and to the point, Higashikuni for his ability to speak deviously, impressively, and at length without ever committing himself to a single definite statement. Hirohito knew how to charm men of culture and breeding, Higashikuni how to manipulate violent, superstitious men of a type with whom Hirohito had no contact.

Like his brother Prince Asaka, who had had command at the capture and rape of Nanking, Higashikuni was a fully professional soldier with thirty-one years of experience, including seven in Japanese Army Intelligence in Europe. Bull-necked and flat-faced, with a high forehead and a drooping, twisted mouth, he had an air of shamelessness—totally blithe and bland— that was the fear and envy of his lower-class associates. A close friend of his once said that he looked on human beings "not as men, but as smells" —smells of human weakness which could be used to flavor his stews of intrigue. His forte was religious humbug. He knew and protected some of the best confidence men and charlatans in Japan. They reciprocated by recruiting credulous mystics to serve in his elaborate plots or by extracting information at séances which he could use for purposes of political blackmail.

GIRLS AND WEREWOLVES

In preparing Japan to greet the American invaders, Prince Higashikuni and his chief Minister of State Prince Konoye gave their first attention to the domestic problem of keeping the people's loyalty. On the day of surrender the Cabinet ordered that there should be a "disposal of government goods." Weapons themselves must be turned over to the Allies but everything else stockpiled for the "final decisive battle" could be given away. Approximately ten billion dollars' worth of cars, trucks, gasoline, rubber, tin, scrap iron, silver wire, copper, shoes, blankets, uniforms, banknotes, and blasting powder were distributed to the populace from Army warehouses. Years later the Diet—the Japanese equivalent of Congress—tried to investigate the profit-takers in the giveaway and succeeded in recovering only two million dollars. The other 9.998 billion had gone to repay old Army henchmen for services rendered or to bind them against services anticipated.

Special Cabinet Advisor Ishiwara Kanji, the retired strategist of Manchuria, was detailed to go from town to town explaining the defeat. He was a popular hero, with a rabid following of Buddhist zealots in rural areas. Special trains were laid on everywhere by the government to bring the peasants in to the provincial centers where he spoke. He seldom addressed a crowd of less than 10,000. The burden of his message was simple: former Prime Minister Tojo caused the war; no one else is responsible. Ishiwara and Tojo had worked together as bitter rivals for imperial favor in the early 1930's. Tojo had triumphed, and no one knew better than Ishiwara the details which would make Tojo seem a fit scapegoat. At his home in Tokyo, where he had been living in retirement for more than a year, Tojo accepted the vilification stoically and privately told his friends that it was his wish to take full responsibility for the war. His friends respected his desires but many of his former subordinates and servants protested. The porter at the prime minister's official residence, for instance, was widely quoted as saying that Tojo had been the most human and considerate being who had occupied the building in twenty years.

Having bribed the masses and indoctrinated them with an official explanation of war responsibility, Prince Higashikuni and his ministers turned to the external threat. In case the Occupation Forces came to wreak vengeance, there should be a *maquis* organized to make vengeance costly. Japanese officers created a web of cultural clubs, research institutes, and gymnasiums to serve as fronts for resistance work. With the connivance of the Ministry of Agriculture they founded a number of veterans' farm communes on which gunless tanks were used for tractors and the men held in tight discipline for service at a moment's notice. Pistols and grenades were cached in mountain caves. Temples became repositories for airplane engines. Uninhabited islets off the coast were heaped with camouflaged guns and ammunition. Two billion dollars' worth of gold and platinum was flown home from Korea, encased in lead and sunk in Tokyo harbor. There it remained until April 1946 when, with MacArthur's blessing, it was dredged up and returned to the economy.

Physical education instructors at middle schools were entrusted with blueprints for the resurrection of a weapons technology in case Japan's present factories were all razed. In the island of Kanawa, just offshore from the Japanese Naval Academy, a veritable time capsule of twentieth-century Japanese civilization was stored away on shelves along hundreds of subterranean tunnels. The horde included one neatly labeled example of almost every useful object known to man: bolts of cloth, Siberian furs, Chinese porcelain, and Mongolian leather; all manner of meters and motors; cameras and lenses; radio and recording gear; chemical reagents; hoes, crucibles, welding torches, and metal presses.

The romantic arrangements for werewolf resistance were expected to be useful, as a latent threat, in later bargaining with General MacArthur. More homely measures were needed to minimize the immediate ravages of American Occupation troops. Even the most sophisticated Japanese feared that the "stern justice" promised by the Potsdam Declaration would be reflected in a vindictive racist attitude on the part of the G.I.'s. A rumor made the rounds that President Roosevelt had always opened his letters with a paper knife made from the bone of a Japanese soldier. Wartime propaganda stories were recalled about secret U.S. plans "to emasculate every man and rape every woman" in Japan. Now, journalists reversed themselves and wrote reassuring essays about American civilization. But they coupled these with suggestions on the handling of G.I.'s that were sometimes less than reassuring:

"Wear old clothes and be careful not to smile; your politeness will be misunderstood."

"Be careful not to bare your breasts in public; Americans are not used to seeing the female form uncovered. They have no public baths in America and many of the women do not nurse their babies."

"When in danger of being raped, show the most dignified attitude. Do not yield. Cry for help."

Remembering the exploits of their own soldiers, town elders called mass meetings to advise that virtuous wives and daughters be evacuated to rural areas. Many municipalities offered severance pay to employees to use as escape money. Tens of thousands of women complied and fled to remote mountain villages. But thousands more refused to go and made fun of government efforts. Fifteen years of propaganda had failed to frighten them. They called the evacuation scheme "a face-saving distraction in the hour of defeat." They intimated that municipal officials were attempting to get rid of superannuated secretaries. At some town meetings cosmopolitan school teachers even had the courage to say that they would feel safer on the streets when American troops arrived than they did now when their neighborhoods teemed with half-demobilized Japanese soldiers.

While the women fled to the hills or stood defiantly by their hearths, the men sought to avoid America's "stern justice" by a wholesale reshuffling and falsification of records. Never a simple language, Japanese could be exploited as a private code. Any name written in ideographs could be read with several different pronunciations. A man could change his ideographs without changing what he was called. Then he could say, "I am not that Sato Hiroshi but this one." Or conversely, he could change the pronunciation of his name and say, "Those are my name characters but they are

read Sato Makoto in my family." Other Japanese when questioned would
agree that he could be telling the truth. The success of such tactics may
be seen from the fact that, two years after the war was over, more than
a hundred of the Japanese witnesses who testified at the Class A War
Criminal trials in Tokyo were able to go down in the record under ap-
pellations by which they had never been known at home.

All the names and numbers of combat units had been changed a few
weeks prior to surrender. Now many of the officers were transferred to new
commands where subordinates would not know their past careers. In a
move suggested to the Emperor on August 19, four days after Hirohito's
broadcast to his people, and reported to him again on its completion six
days later, secret policemen and thought policemen were given new credentials as civilian detectives and traffic cops. Many who had been guards
at concentration camps were allowed to change their names and vanish
into civilian life as if their military careers had never existed. A sadist,
whose victims at Omori Prison Camp called him only by the fearful code
name of Mr. Brown, was never found by Allied investigators after the
war—and this despite the fact that he was well known by name and long
association to Hirohito's brother's brother-in-law, Tokugawa Yoshitomo,
who had served at the prison camp as an "observer" for the Japanese Red
Cross. A notorious secret police major, who also escaped the Allied War
Criminal Prosecution Section, caters today to an almost exclusively American clientele of tourists at his old pottery store on Kyoto's main shopping
street.

"The flames of burning documents of a defeated nation preparing for
the occupation of the enemy were full of sadness and sorrow," recalls one
patriot. He saw them as a "glare of big fires" as he returned to Tokyo on
the morning of August 16 after informing the wife of the commander of
the Kamikaze Corps that her husband had just committed suicide. Every
town in Japan was blazing that night with bonfires of paper. The order to
destroy, from Imperial Headquarters, was itself marked "to be destroyed,"
and only fragments of it were later picked up in city dumps. Prefectural
libraries did away with all books giving biographical information on possible war criminal suspects, including even *Who's Who*'s and their Japanese equivalents *Daijinmei Jiten*. In some libraries the books were burned;
in others only their file catalogue cards were destroyed and the books
themselves were taken home for safekeeping by the librarians. Few if any
important documents were entirely lost. They may be found in yellowed
stacks of paper surrounding former generals and statesmen interviewed
today. They are still considered secret and withheld from foreign hands.
But the old gentlemen who keep them are usually willing to refer to them,
to answer questions about them, and to do so with specifics that have the
air of authority. When Allied language officers first fanned out to look for
such documents a generation ago, they found few. They were expected to

look up the unequivocal truth of history in black and white, but instead they pondered a nightmare record of gray lies and half truths.

If the Occupation forces came to Japan with good intentions rather than a lust for vengeance, that too was a contingency to be prepared for. There must be facilities ready for welcoming them and for divesting them as quickly as possible of war hate. Hirohito's sixty-one-year-old mother, the handsome Empress Dowager Sadako, had been consulted on the entertainment problem by her kinsman, Prince Konoye, many months previously. Although she was a severe critic of the war and had been on strained terms with Hirohito since Pearl Harbor, she had promised that ladies of rank would do all they could to help the Peace Faction in its patriotic efforts. Now in the days immediately before and after surrender, Konoye and the police put into effect a number of the Court ladies' suggestions. Foreign embassies which had been closed for over three years were inspected and their former staffs of servants were reassembled, where possible, to re-create a semblance of convivial days gone by.[1] The plaque near Yokohama, commemorating Commodore Perry's opening of Japan at gunpoint in 1853, had been torn down by overzealous patriots during the war. Now it was put up again by the Yokohama prefectural police in the polite secrecy of a dark night.

On the day of surrender, August 15, Prince Konoye called Ban Nobuya, the superintendent of the Tokyo Metropolitan Police, and told him: "We must protect the daughters of Japan. I want you to see to it personally." The staid middle classes were hiding their women in the hills and giving them cyanide capsules to take in an emergency. In the villas of the aristocracy, where the ladies had been brought up to understand the political requirements of their fathers and husbands, less dire prospects were being contemplated with equanimity if not positive pleasure. In the slums remained thousands of women who had never had the right to be virtuous nor the time to think of themselves patriotically as national assets. Now was their hour. Police Superintendent Ban convoked the leaders of the major entertainment guilds in Tokyo—the keepers of hotels, restaurants, mah-jongg parlors, geisha tea houses, hostess bars, and ordinary brothels. By August 23, these worthies had founded a Recreation and Amusement Association, the R.A.A., for Allied enlisted men. It was capitalized at $2 million through a stock issue floated among friends of the Emperor by the Hypothec Bank. In a matter of weeks the R.A.A. could offer the services of thirty-three establishments in Tokyo, five in the provinces, and two hospitals for women. Under separate management a large munitions factory in downtown Tokyo was converted into a hotel. Never was sword more profitably beaten into plowshare. Before the place was finally declared off

---

[1] But the rain water which had come in through a bomb hole in the roof was pointedly left standing on the floor in the chancellery of the American Embassy.

limits, "Willow Run," as it came to be called, had a production line of 250 girls and an average quota of 3,750 G.I.'s a day.

The R.A.A. and kindred organizations were promoted and guaranteed by a group of industrialists who offered their services to the Throne as "one-yen-a-year" men. They were recruited and directed by Yamashita Taro, a chemicals and shipping magnate who had been sitting in on Peace-Faction councils and conferring frequently with Lord Privy Seal Kido for the past ten months. Yamashita and his associates put together a fund of 200 million yen, or about $14 million, and offered it to the Emperor as a contribution. Some reciprocal favors were implied by the gift because Lord Privy Seal Kido took two days to negotiate its acceptance.

Of the many tasks undertaken by Yamashita and his one-yen-a-year men, the most delicate was liaison with MacArthur and his aides. The ladies at Court advised that relations with Allied G.H.Q. would go most smoothly if the incompetent services of insular police interpreters could be dispensed with and replaced by those of cosmopolitan gentlewomen who had real ability as linguists. Accordingly, a group of princesses and marchionesses who had lived in Paris and London agreed to merge forces with a group of businessmen who had good contacts in the United States. Money was laid aside to buy new kimonos for war widows whose conservatively invested fortunes had been wiped out by depreciation. Family villas were inspected and rated according to their chic and their entertainment facilities. Private clubs were created in imitation of those which had been observed in Occidental capitals. Some groups of wealthy blue-stockings invited famous geisha to address them on the art of entertaining men.

The nervous bustle of peace preparations was punctuated by the violence of diehards who still protested against surrender. Prince Takamatsu, the Emperor's brother, had to go down to Atsugi Air Base near Yokohama to pacify a group of dissident kamikaze pilots who were dropping leaflets on Tokyo calling for continuance of the war. Two hundred men of a provincial garrison mutinied and marched on Tokyo. Twelve extreme rightists of the Revere-the-Emperor-and-Expel-the-Barbarians Society blew themselves up with hand grenades atop a hill in Tokyo's Shiba Park.

MISSION TO MANILA

As the cult of death died and the plans to live developed at fever pace, Japan had no communication with the conquerors except by radio. The future invaders remained faceless, giving instructions and hints of their own diabolical planning by Morse code. On August 19, four days after the Emperor announced Japan's surrender and in compliance with orders from MacArthur in Manila, Army Vice Chief of Staff Kawabe Torashiro flew to Okinawa by Japanese bomber and thence by American bomber to Nichols Field southwest of Manila. After twelve hours of flying, he and his aides disembarked into a sea of American olive drab, of men who pointedly ignored hands extended for shaking, of cameras which ground ceaselessly to record every wince and twitch of shame on the impassive faces of the Japanese delegation, of crowds of Filipinos who stood beyond the police lines and screamed curses learned in years past from Japanese soldiers. The drive into town led through a corner of the Spanish citadel which had been thoroughly laid waste, looted, raped, and butchered by suicidal young Japanese aristocrats of the Imperial Marines only six months previously. The drive ended at the Rosario Apartments overlooking Manila Bay. There the accommodations were comfortable but once again the associations were not, for a group of Japanese Marines and of Filipino women seized as hostages had spent their last hours there.

After an American dinner served with frigid punctilio, the Japanese delegation went on to an eight-hour, all-night meeting at MacArthur's headquarters in the half-ruined Manila City Hall. MacArthur was represented by his chief of staff, General Richard Sutherland. Kawabe and his aides spent the night turning over to Sutherland, item by item, the maps and lists of Japanese troop dispositions in the Orient. Then the Americans submitted to the Japanese MacArthur's instructions for the reception and billeting of U.S. troops in Japan. The first American transport planes were to touch down at Atsugi Air Base on August 23, a scant eighty hours hence.

General Kawabe begged for more time: "The Japanese side would sincerely advise you not to land so quickly. At least ten days are needed to prepare." He elaborated on the unrest among the kamikaze pilots at Atsugi. He did not mention the fact that the field at Atsugi was full of holes and would require an all-out construction effort before it could be safely used.

General Sutherland agreed to a five-day postponement and told Kawabe to have the New Grand Hotel in Yokohama ready for occupancy by MacArthur and a fleet of fifty automobiles in running order for staff transportation. Kawabe agreed to do what he could but left the meeting warning that a week of preparation would be insufficient. "You are the winners," he said, "and so your decision is almighty, but to our way of thinking, there remains some uneasiness."

Back at the Rosario Apartments the members of the Japanese delegation watched the sun come up and read over some of the other American requirements. Three maids for every U.S. officer of general or admiral class, two for everyone of colonel class, one for everyone of lieutenant class—did the Americans think they were dealing with Chinese? Then there was a statement prepared in Washington which was to be issued in the Emperor's name. The Japanese text of it had the Emperor using the ordinary humble pronoun *I*. Everyone knew that the Emperor, when referring to himself, used the old Chinese imperial pronoun *Chin,* meaning moon that speaks to heaven. Before going to bed, Kawabe had his dissatisfaction with these and other small points made known to the U.S. guard unit at the Rosario Apartments. By the time he awoke four hours later, Allied translators had prepared a new packet of instructions for Tokyo in which offensive pronouns and servant requirements had been suppressed.

Kawabe took off at 1:00 P.M., highly elated by the success of his mission. Hours later as his Betty-type bomber approached Japan, it sprang a leak in a fuel line. The pilot changed course to hug the Japanese coast. About midnight the last drop of gas was gone and he brought the lumbering craft down to a crash landing a few yards from a beach in central Honshu. The buffeted members of the delegation waded ashore and found themselves looking up in the moonlight at Mount Fuji, Mount Fortunate Warrior, the volcanic symbol of Japan. It was more than a hundred miles to Tokyo, and by the time that the delegates had roused villagers, summoned a truck, and negotiated the pockmarked roads to the capital it was late in the morning.

General Kawabe reported at once to the prime minister's residence and Prince Higashikuni drove with him to the palace. Emperor Hirohito received them at 1:15 P.M. and heard a full report of Kawabe's exhausting ordeal. It closed with the assurance that "in general the enemy attitude is unexpectedly good." The next day a capable labor racketeer, who was a friend of Prince Takamatsu, the Emperor's brother, put to work his truckers and construction men to repair the Atsugi kamikaze base for the American landing. Werewolf preparations were almost abandoned. Destruction of documents and briefing of girls was pushed forward frantically to meet with the new early date of American arrival.

Lights also burned late that week at MacArthur's headquarters in Manila and at the State Department in Washington. Throughout the war the sages of American foreign policy had had mixed emotions about the war with Japan. In Roosevelt's inner councils Japan had been considered a tool and the Pacific a secondary war theater. As a result the degree of severity with which Japan should be punished had never been fully decided. Here was a nation which had shown the way in savagery to its European partners, a nation which some said was not merely sick like Germany but innately predatory. Then again, here was a society little understood, a cultural relic of an earlier, more barbaric age, a country which had developed apart and then had been forced to join the modern world by Commodore Perry and the United States.

The Japanese had succeeded beyond Roosevelt's wildest nightmares in conquering the Pacific, and the road back had been a long one. But from the beginning the American government had known it would win and had debated what it would do with its victory: reduce Japan to a pastoral state as many Australians advocated? Remake Japanese society from the bottom up and thoroughly re-educate the people as some New Deal intellectuals demanded? Trust a chastened, demilitarized Japan to carry out her own moral reformation as many old Japan hands urged? Or simply take away

Japan's colonies and post observers in her ports as her former allies the British proposed?

Each of the suggestions entailed a predictable amount of expense and moral commitment. To pastoralize Japan an army would have to carry out a brutal pacification campaign and then remain in oppressive occupation for many years to come. Indeed the population would have to be decimated many times before it could be expected to subsist on agriculture alone. To remake Japanese society in the Western image might be a more humane goal, but it too would require a long occupation of several decades. To suppose that Japan had learned her lesson and could reform herself seemed foolhardy in the light of past experience. Merely to penalize Japan heavily and leave her to struggle up again out of abject poverty seemed equally shortsighted.

To choose intelligently between the various possibilities was virtually impossible because there was no information to work with. The government of Japan was a box within a box, a closed corporation within a closed and secretive society. No one knew how Japan's aggressive policy decisions had been made nor who had made them. The Emperor was said to be a ceremonial nonentity. The parliament or Diet had only limited budgetary powers. The Cabinet was always changing. During F.D.R.'s presidency Japan had had eleven different prime ministers. The bureaucracy of "militarists" in the General Staff who supposedly controlled the Japanese juggernaut shifted about so frequently that it was rare for one man to occupy the same post for more than two years. But some man or group of men surely did have hold of the helm, for Japan's aggressive policies had developed consistently. Moreover, everyone who had ever visited Japan agreed that the people themselves were gentle, courteous, and law abiding and that the domestic administration of the country was as orderly and efficient as any in the world.

Western scholars who had studied Japan and men of affairs who had lived there could cast little light on the puzzle. Only a handful were fluent in Japanese, and the rest could not speak authoritatively about any part of Japan except the white man's ghetto world where everyone knew English. Linguists who had studied Japanese institutions more closely portrayed a society which did not fit comfortably into Western frames of reference. Knights rode side by side with secret policemen. Great industrial combines were built on feudal allegiances and run like fiefs. It was not clear whether atrocities like the rape of Nanking should be thought of as Buchenwalds or Deerfield Massacres. Japan presented the sinister twentieth-century façade of a highly industrialized fascist state but was also, in MacArthur's words, "something out of the pages of mythology."

Of the various proposals for dealing with the Japanese enigma, the tolerant British plan and the vindictive Australian program were alike in that they both treated the whole Japanese people as if they were responsible for the actions of the government. Such an idea did not appeal to the idealistic American mind nor fit the known facts. It was the U.S. point of view that some element in Japanese society had misled the people and could be cut out like a cancer. The New Deal intellectuals in the State Department, led by Dean Acheson and Archibald MacLeish, believed that reform and democratization could be achieved only through overthrow of the entire Establishment, the hereditary ruling caste of imperial high priests, of professional bureaucrats and police administrators, of warriors and generals, of medieval merchant families and modern cartel owners. A less intellectual and more tolerant group of former diplomats and businessmen, who had lived in Japan, allied themselves with ex-Ambassador Grew. They argued cogently that the ruling caste were the only Japanese who knew how to govern their country or had any experience with the outside world. If a reform was contemplated, they must be the ones reformed; they must be the cornerstone for rebuilding. Otherwise Japan would become an anarchy and the United States would be forced to administer her indefinitely as an American possession.

The debate finally resolved itself into disagreement on one central question: what to do with the Emperor who ruled the ruling class. Some experts said he should be tried as a war criminal, others that he should be deposed, still others that he should be left to rule as a constitutional monarch. In the absence of any dependable information about Hirohito, the issue was argued hotly. The last two *New York Times* correspondents in Japan, drawing on the same *Times* morgue of translations and dispatches, wrote books on opposite sides of the question, Hugh Byas opting for the Emperor and Otto Tolischus against. The dispute could not be settled because the problem was logically insoluble. Could Japan be reformed without destroying her god-king? And then again, could Japan be reformed without the god-king's co-operation? The answer to both queries was patently, "No." And so Roosevelt, early in the war, decided that the best course might be to hold the Emperor as a hostage. Skillfully handled, he might be used to sponsor reform and at the same time to undercut the foundations of his own prestige and power. As early as 1942 the Office of War Information and the Office of Strategic Services spread the suggestion, through the many publicists, journalists, and authors on O.W.I.-O.S.S. payrolls, that American cartoonists should concentrate their attention on bespectacled General Tojo rather than Hirohito on his white horse.

In August of 1945 President Truman wisely decided to delegate the execution of Roosevelt's tentative policy for dealing with the Emperor to General of the Army Douglas MacArthur whose memos had helped to formulate it. MacArthur had the stature domestically to override American dissent and the experience in the Orient to carry out such a policy with flexibility and an ear tuned to changing circumstances. Truman appointed MacArthur proconsul in Japan on August 14, the day that Japan's surrender note was received. Thereafter Truman supported MacArthur in a virtuoso solo role unparalleled in American history. For five years MacArthur was to rule absolute in Japan. He was to disregard almost all suggestions from other Allied governments, and Truman was to back him up. Seldom since the days of Scipio Africanus has a proconsul had such power over a conquered people. Never has one been so popular as MacArthur was with almost 80 million Japanese.

MacArthur had been in and out of Japan since 1904 when his father, General Arthur MacArthur, had had charge of pacifying the Philippines after the Spanish-American War. MacArthur was a brilliant man: first in his class at West Point, youngest divisional commander in U.S. history, and youngest chief of staff. He had retired from the U.S. Army in 1937 to become a field marshal in the Philippine Army. He had been recalled to active duty—the defense of the Philippines in July 1941—by his close personal friend and political antagonist, Franklin Delano Roosevelt. Throughout World War II, in defeat and victory, MacArthur had commanded the American Army in the Pacific.

On August 14, 1945, as soon as MacArthur heard of his appointment to the military governorship of Japan, he instructed his staff and intelligence officers in Manila to work out the logistics of occupation and to submit ideas on the best approach to use in taming and exploiting the Emperor. MacArthur's Chief of Intelligence Charles A. Willoughby brainstormed the problem with his assistants and advised that the Emperor should be harnessed tactfully and gradually. Willoughby recommended that Hirohito should be surrounded by "liberal advisors" and made to feel that he was a "symbol" for the "regeneration of Japan." MacArthur himself had already given long thought to the problem and had his own shrewd perceptions of what would be required. He did not consider himself an expert on any Oriental country save the Philippines. He knew few of the details of modern Japanese history and did not want to know them. Bygones, he felt, should be bygones. If Americans tried to pit their detective work against Japanese deceptive cunning, he was sure that the Japanese would win and that no one would be the better for it. The solution to the problem of Japan did not exist except in some prescription—any prescription—which had the authority of a good doctor behind it. The Japanese must cure themselves.

As early as September of 1944, when he had landed at Morotai, an island in the eastern East Indies, MacArthur had expressed his considered views on the sickness and cure of Japan. He termed the disease "a type of national savagery at strange variance with many basic impulses of the Japanese people." The cure, he felt, would be automatic: "The Japanese citizen will cease his almost idolatrous worship of the military" when he discovers that "the military has failed him in this, his greatest hour of need." MacArthur either did not know or did not choose to know that a majority of the Japanese electorate had never idolized the military and as late as 1937 still had the courage to say so at the polls. Perhaps as a result of childhood association with Indians at a U.S. Army post in Arkansas, MacArthur saw the Japanese as a tribal people who would lose their proud sense of identity as soon as their false gods were broken. His view was a patronizing one, but it grew out of sincere Christian convictions and he was willing to gamble his life on its correctness. When the first surrender note arrived on August 10, he proposed that he and a small airborne detachment should be landed immediately at Tokyo airport to help the Emperor surrender. It would have been a theatrical gesture of a type which both he and the Japanese loved. More than likely no harm would have come to him if he had been allowed to try it.

The officers to whom MacArthur would delegate the execution of his policy for Japan were all with him in Manila and were all thoroughly educated in what he would expect of them. Three of the most important of them were Eichelberger, Willoughby, and Whitney. Lieutenant General Robert Eichelberger, a kindly, intelligent man, was to be MacArthur's hands. He was to have command of the Eighth Army which would manage the nonpolitical, physical half of the Occupation. It would be his men who would fan out into the Japanese countryside, his M.P.'s who would execute the raids and arrests decided on by MacArthur's inner brain trust.

MacArthur's Chief of Intelligence, Major General Charles A. Willoughby —a crude, witty, gargantuan son of a German aristocrat named Tscheppe-Weidenbach—was to be MacArthur's eyes and ears. To keep his command as autonomous as possible, MacArthur had always banned from his theater of operations the Washington-centered O.S.S. and O.W.I., and Willoughby was his sole source of background research. It was Willoughby who would teach MacArthur what he knew of the past careers of the Japanese leaders with whom he dealt, Willoughby who would be in part responsible for the United States being caught by surprise when the Chinese entered the Korean War.

Despite thirty years in the American Army, Willoughby retained a Prussian view of world affairs. In a book called *Maneuver in War,* published in 1939, he had admired almost every aspect of Japan's strike for *Lebensraum* in China except her "yellow fingers clawing at white women." "Historical judgment," he had written, "freed from the emotional haze of the moment, will credit Mussolini with wiping out a memory of defeat by re-establishing the traditional military supremacy of the white race for generations to come." He was, in brief, a straightforward military man. He admired Mussolini's exploits in Ethiopia and, grudgingly, those of other conquerors including the Japanese. His knowledge of campaigns in out-of-the-way colonial wars was encyclopedic. Having helped to form MacArthur's plan for Japan, Willoughby touted it as a "shatteringly simple formula" for resolving "the terrific tension" in Japan by "utilizing the existing Japanese government, the person of the Emperor, and the psychic force of tradition."

Brigadier General Courtney Whitney, the chief of the Occupation's Government Section, was MacArthur's mouth and writing hand. A tough, nimble-witted lawyer who had made a small fortune for himself in Manila during the 1930's, he was to conduct the political negotiations with Japanese leaders, dictate the reform of the Japanese government, and write most of MacArthur's personal utterances. In describing MacArthur's policy for Japan, he later minced no words: "We blackmailed Japan. . . . Discussion concerning the Emperor . . . was designed to encourage action toward a speed-up in essential reforms."

In the week that intervened between General Kawabe's visit to Manila and the landing of the first U.S. Occupation troops at Atsugi kamikaze base, couriers and cables shuttled back and forth between Washington and Manila; MacArthur's ideas were integrated with those of State Department officials to become the official policy of the U.S. Government. The document that resulted was entitled "United States Initial Post-Surrender Policy for Japan." Its final text was radioed to MacArthur on August 29 after he had already started for Japan and was stopping over for a night in Okinawa. It instructed him as follows:

> The ultimate objectives of the United States in regard to Japan . . . are . . . to insure that Japan will not again become a menace . . . [and] to bring about the eventual establishment of a peaceful and responsible government which will respect the rights of other states. . . . It is not the responsibility of the Allied Powers to impose upon Japan any form of government not supported by the freely expressed will of the people. . . . In view of the present character of Japanese society and the desire of the United States to attain its objectives with a minimum commitment of its forces and resources, the Supreme Commander will exercise his authority through Japanese governmental machinery and agencies, including the Emperor. . . . The policy is to use the existing form of government in Japan, not to support it.

There followed a blueprint of the social reforms which MacArthur was to carry out: disarmament; punishment of war criminals; breakup of landlord and industrialist holdings; emancipation of religion, press, labor, and women.

U.S. TOUCHDOWN

For five days after General Kawabe's return to Tokyo from Manila, rain drummed down on the tiled roofs of the palace and branches tossed in the Fukiage Gardens. Late each afternoon Hirohito walked to the Palace Shrine, stood beneath the dripping eaves, and meditated on the ordeals ahead. Curtains of white mist enclosed the shrine, making its lustrous white-pebbled courtyard seem more private, more infinite, more close to the dead than ever before. Hirohito was not alone in his brooding; men waited in anxiety throughout the Orient. An officer at Atsugi kamikaze base, preparing to greet the Occupation troops, implored his men to kill themselves before taking offense at any action of the conquerors. Far to the south in Manila a G.I. cleaned his gun and muttered: "A people can't be turned off and on like a hot water faucet." He was one of a few hundred detailed to go into Japan with the U.S. advance party—to land in the midst of the enemy camp where 2.5 million fanatic Japanese soldiers were waiting to be disarmed.

On August 27 the weather cleared, and a single American daredevil from the carrier *Yorktown* astonished Japanese ground crews by landing at Atsugi unauthorized, a full day ahead of schedule. As General MacArthur would have predicted, he was courteously treated. Indeed he was helped to put up signs which said, "Welcome U.S. Army from the Third Fleet." As soon as he had taken off, the ground crews removed the signs lest they give offense to the serious Occupation forces due to arrive on the morrow.

At dawn the next morning a line of forty-five C-47's snaked in over the head of the giant bronze Buddha at Kamakura and landed at Atsugi in rapid succession. As an evasive precaution they came in with the wind behind them and so pulled up at the end of the airport where the Japanese least expected them. By the time that the reception committee had started a truck and raced the length of the field, the Americans were out of their planes with carbines on the ready. Greetings were exchanged stiffly and a long walk led back to the reception booth at the other end of the runway. There the Japanese had ready pitchers of freshly squeezed orange juice. It was said to be the favorite American drink, but these Americans would not so much as sip it until they had seen their hosts drink first. Into the atmosphere of tense suspicion, the Japanese commander introduced a Russian naval attaché whom he had brought with him from Tokyo expressly for the purpose. As anticipated the rival white man shamed the Americans out of their jitters. Soon Japanese and American officers were swapping cigarettes and working together smoothly. A U.S. naval group set out in Japanese vehicles to visit nearby Allied prisoner-of-war camps. Lunch, complete with fruit and wine, was served by the Japanese on white tablecloths.

After lunch the American commander, Colonel Charles Tench, was consulted on the case of an American prisoner of war who had come down with appendicitis. The Japanese said that he was in the hands of a capable physician such as attended P.O.W.'s routinely, but added that perhaps, since the Americans were now in charge, they might wish to take over the care of their countryman or send a doctor to assist at the appendectomy. Colonel Tench replied that he had full confidence in the Japanese surgeons who had been handling the case. He did not know the reputation of the Shinagawa P.O.W. hospital north of Yokohama to which the prisoner had been taken. It had one model wing which was used for inspections and would have been used for the appendectomy if an American observer had been sent. The rest of the hospital was a horror house of lice and excrement. The doctor in charge was later hanged for senseless experiments in sadism. Healthy men he had bled to death for their plasma. Sick men he had killed with strange injections. He had shot soy bean milk and urine into their veins. He had administered bile from dysentery patients to TB cases and serum from malaria victims to those with beriberi. Late that night the Japanese commander at Atsugi came to Colonel Tench incensed because a U.S. naval party under the command of Harold Stassen, the later presidential contender, had raided Shinagawa Hospital and spirited away the appendicitis case to an American hospital ship in the harbor.

The speed with which the Americans worked astonished the Japanese. In the first four days some 5,000 ragged, emaciated, ecstatic war prisoners were evacuated from camps in the Tokyo-Yokohama area to Allied ships offshore. A new fifteen-mile oil pipeline was laid to Yokohama and was operating in a week. All through the second day, August 29, U.S. C-54's swooped down on Atsugi, landing at two-minute intervals and disgorging almost the entire 11th Airborne Division by nightfall. Japanese fliers stood by watching with rueful admiration. That same afternoon the whole of the 4th Marine Regiment came ashore in Yokohama. One of its members described it as being made up "entirely of admirals trying to get ashore before MacArthur."

On the third day MacArthur himself arrived with his retinue of staff officers and war correspondents. "Of all the amazing deeds of bravery of the war," wrote Winston Churchill a few years later, "I regard MacArthur's personal landing at Atsugi as the greatest of the lot." MacArthur deplaned with a corncob pipe in his mouth, embraced fellow General Robert Eichelberger, and said, "This is the payoff, Bob." He climbed into a decrepit Lincoln supplied by the Japanese government and started for Yokohama fifteen miles away. Some forty cars, most of them charcoal-burners, started with him. At the head of the procession moved an old red fire engine which sometimes started and sometimes stopped. Smartly caparisoned Japanese staff officers cast down their eyes at American complaints and humbly insisted that these were the best vehicles left in Japan.

Along the entire fifteen-mile route stood armed Japanese soldiers, their backs to the roadway, watching the fields on either side for any hint of trouble. This was a security precaution normally accorded only to the Emperor. MacArthur was so delighted by it that he took the rest of the two-hour automobile burlesque in good part. Moreover, he dispensed with bodyguards throughout his remaining five years in Japan and forbade any officer walking or riding with him ever to wear a sidearm. The Japanese so justified his confidence in them that not a rock was ever thrown at him.

That night at the Edwardian New Grand Hotel in Yokohama's waterfront park, the manager provided MacArthur and his staff with an excellent steak dinner. He could not promise an egg for breakfast, however, and one of MacArthur's generals sent out a search party. In the entire ruin of Yokohama, a city the size of Baltimore, the hunt uncovered precisely one egg. MacArthur was so impressed by the people's hunger that he ordered all U.S. personnel to live entirely on their own rations, and he had his commissary contribute twenty-one truckloads of food to the Yokohama municipal government.

The American war correspondents who had landed with MacArthur proceeded by public transportation to make their way inland and occupy Tokyo. People on trams and trains looked at them curiously and then made room for them with calm civility. A Japanese Domei reporter, who had greeted them at Atsugi and warned them to be cautious, arrived back in Tokyo to find them in his office using his typewriters. Russell Brines of the Associated Press had gone directly to the Aztec-style Imperial Hotel designed by Frank Lloyd Wright in the early 1920's. In the cool cave of the volcanic-stone lobby, the manager was standing as if waiting for him. "So glad to see you," said the manager. "Do you want a room?"

OVERTURES

On the afternoon of August 28, when the first police reports on the behavior of the Occupation troops arrived in Tokyo, they were taken at once to the palace. Hirohito was impressed and summoned Prince Higashikuni. After the audience Higashikuni rescinded previous orders to give away Army stockpiles and issued instructions to buy back any munitions which might have been distributed by mistake. The behavior of the American soldiers remained exemplary. By August 31 when there were almost 50,000 Occupation troops in the Yokohama area, the police had reported only 216 complaints against them, and of these 167 had been lodged, over matters of jurisdiction, by the police themselves. Most of the remaining 49 cases were alleged thefts. By September 5, after nine days of Occupation, the G.I. crime rate, as reported by the Japanese police, had fallen to an average of two offenses a day and the cumulative total up to that date included only one murder and six cases of "complete and incomplete rape."

During the five-day rainstorm which had preceded the U.S. landings, Hirohito had pondered the various fates which might lie in store for him. He was not afraid of being hanged. Martyrdom would insure the loyalty of the people to his son. Nor was he afraid of being shorn of power and made a constitutional monarch. As long as the Throne survived, his heirs would have a chance to recoup. What most disturbed him was the possibility that the Allies would systematically discredit him in the eyes of his people. If they forced him to preside over their own acts of vengeance—their reparations and war crime tribunals—then the people might become disillusioned. They might turn to democratic forms of government. They might even renounce all things Japanese and allow themselves to become wholly Americanized.

Hirohito had always minimized the danger of democratic sentiments taking hold in Japan. He felt that the Anglo-American type of government was too individualistic to be compatible with Japanese society. In a democracy each voter needed a conscience of his own and an absolute scale of right and wrong. But in Japan these prerequisites did not exist. Every act, from casting a ballot to committing a murder, could be right or wrong depending on whether or not it was in the interest of the family or clan or nation. The highest justification which any Japanese ever sought for an action was *taigi meibun,* "individual share in large righteousness." And for many Japanese the largest conceivable righteousness was mere feudal loyalty—loyalty to the next man higher on the totem pole. During the early years of his reign, Hirohito had made a point of impressing on every man to whom he gave an office or assignment that *taigi meibun* meant sharing in national rather than clan or family righteousness. The idea of an individual striving to transcend the morality of his group by reference to a universal frame of reference struck Hirohito as a Western hypocrisy. Individualism, he felt, could only lead to misery and bad government.[2]

The early reports on American behavior at Atsugi made it clear that MacArthur intended to complete the conquest of Japan by kindness. Prince Konoye warned Hirohito to be wary. As Emperor he had had little experience in negotiation and compromise, but he had had the final power of decision. Now, as MacArthur's puppet, he would have no power, only a bargaining position. MacArthur would seek his seal of approval for American "reform" programs. Some of them might redound to Hirohito's credit, but most of them would undercut his authority and destroy his popularity. Konoye recommended that the safest course would be for Hirohito to abdicate. No one would hold his eleven-year-old son responsible for being manipulated by the Americans. And in due course the Americans would return to their own country.

Hirohito seized on Konoye's advice to abdicate and in the weeks ahead repeatedly offered—almost threatened—to take it. If he was to be MacArthur's puppet, he wished to make it clear at every step of the way that he was acting under duress for the sake of the nation and not for any selfish motive of his own. On August 29, after sleeping on the first reports from Atsugi, he called his special advisor, Kido, to the library in the Fukiage Gardens and told him: "To pick men responsible for the war and hand them over to the Allies hurts me more than I can bear. I am wondering if it might not go well in translation if I myself, as the one man responsible, clear the books by abdicating."

[2] Hirohito's convictions, as here summarized, are taken from his recorded conversations with his former chief aide-de-camp, General Honjo Shigeru.

"Your magnificent sentiments do you the utmost credit," replied Kido, "but I would venture to surmise from the attitudes and preconceptions of the Allies at present that it would be rather difficult to secure agreement on a step of that sort. Then too, since foreign ways of thinking are seldom the same as our own, a proclamation of abdication would create the impression that the foundations of the Throne had been shaken. The result would be a democratic reorganization of the state structure—in short, republicanism. We should beware of arousing discussion of that type. The important point for Your Highness is to adopt a relaxed and studious façade and watch the moves of the other side with all due prudence."

Hirohito nodded noncommittally, and the next day his uncle Prince Higashikuni paid a courtesy call, as prime minister, on General MacArthur at the New Grand Hotel in Yokohama. The meeting was purely formal, but MacArthur took the opportunity to suggest that the Japanese Establishment would greatly improve its reputation in America if it would show some signs of progressive leadership. It might begin, for instance, by revising the Japanese Constitution.

Hirohito considered the Japanese Constitution a sacred document. Over the years he had used it and interpreted it freely but he was not willing to change it. It had been promulgated by his deified grandfather Meiji, and it gave the Throne a more absolute power than the Roman Senate had ever voted to Nero or Caesar Augustus. It enumerated at length the duties which devolved upon subjects and carefully restricted the rights which it conceded them: freedom of speech "within the limits of law"; freedom of religion "within limits not prejudicial to peace and order and not antagonistic to the duties of subjects." Its over-all flavor may be sampled in a deliciously Japanese clause on petitions: "Japanese subjects may present petitions, by observing the proper forms of respect, and by complying with the rules specially provided for the same."

Since Hirohito would not even consider a change in the Constitution, his courtiers cast about for other sops to throw to the American reformers. MacArthur for his part maintained a frigid reserve and made no effort to follow up Prince Higashikuni's overture. Some of his staff recommended that he summon Hirohito and tell him what would be required of him. But MacArthur assured his aides that the Emperor would make his own advances in his own good time. Meanwhile there was more than enough to do. Over 10,000 Americans were being landed in Japan each day and were fanning out to look for records and arms caches, give away chocolate bars, and make friends with children.

On both sides leaders were preparing for the official surrender ceremonies aboard the battleship *Missouri* in Tokyo Harbor on September 2. The Allies flew in General Jonathan Wainwright and General Arthur Percival, the senior American and British officers who had just been released from Japanese prison camps. Both were walking skeletons. Both had sat as losers at previous surrender tables, Wainwright in the Philippines and Percival in Malaya. The duty of meeting with them was so humiliating that it was difficult to find Japanese of suitable rank to accept it. Hirohito began the trouble himself by asking that no member of the imperial family be expected to sign the surrender documents. Several Army officers followed suit by announcing that they would commit suicide if asked to attend the ceremony. Chief of Staff Umezu was finally induced to represent the Japanese Army, but Hirohito did not give his personal approval to the text of the instrument of surrender until 1:00 A.M. of the day on which it was to be signed.

The weather was so clear that Mount Fuji, the Fortunate Warrior, could be seen sixty miles away. The sun sparkled on the white uniforms of American sailors. Tokyo Bay overflowed with Allied vessels of war—the greatest armada ever assembled. MacArthur delivered an oration and used five pens to sign the surrender instrument. The Japanese signatories walked and talked as stiffly as mechanical dolls. As soon as possible they climbed back down to the launch provided for them and made for shore. They went directly to the palace and reported to the Emperor. The next morning Hirohito and his closest advisors repaired to the Palace Shrine to announce officially the end of the war to his ancestors and the sun goddess.

That afternoon, September 3, negotiations began in earnest to find out what MacArthur meant to do to Japan. Foreign Minister Shigemitsu called on him at the New Grand Hotel in Yokohama and informed him that the last of Japan's munitions factories had now been shut down. MacArthur said he was delighted. If the Japanese government continued to co-operate so well with Occupation policy, he said, it might be possible after all to work through the local authorities rather than replace them with American officials. MacArthur had never intended to do anything else, but the implied threat was effective and the foreign minister expressed his gratitude. MacArthur followed up his advantage by suggesting that if the Japanese government would also co-operate in rounding up war criminals and revising the Constitution, it should be possible to preserve the Emperor system.

Foreign Minister Shigemitsu reported MacArthur's terms to the palace that same evening. Hirohito heard them without recorded comment, but the next day in a public address to an emergency session of the Diet Hirohito obliquely reminded MacArthur that Japan had accepted unconditional surrender on certain understandings. Politely avoiding the word "defeat" and substituting for it "termination of hostilities," he told the people that if they would abide peacefully by the terms of the Potsdam Declaration it should be possible for Japan to rebuild and keep her "national structure" or Emperor system. The next morning, September 5, Foreign Minister Shigemitsu resumed his negotiations with MacArthur in Yokohama and delicately pointed out that the Emperor's statement had an obverse: if the people were not allowed to keep their national structure, they might abide by the Potsdam Declaration unpeacefully. MacArthur genially ignored the suggestion and once more sent Shigemitsu away empty handed.

The following day, September 6, Prince Konoye was sent down to Kyoto, the ancient capital of Japan, to arrange suitable retirement quarters for Hirohito in case he should decide to abdicate. In old Japan, before Perry's coming, abdication had been a routine imperial tactic. In those days the Emperor had exercised little but religious power and had delegated his political and military authority to the shogun or chief general of the nation. If the shogun failed to respect imperial wishes, however, the Emperor would set one of his children on the Throne and retire as an abbot and regent to one of Kyoto's great Buddhist monasteries. Thence he could continue to control the Throne, and free of all ceremonial duty and responsibility could devote himself full time to the plotting of intrigues which would embarrass the shogun.

It was with such a thought in mind that on September 7 Prince Konoye left the lovely old inn of his previous night's entertainment and motored west through the narrow colorful streets of the Gion, Kyoto's entertainment district, where the arts of pleasing men had been developed and handed down for a thousand years. In the northwestern suburbs at the end of a green lane he left his car and walked into the white courtyards of the great Zen temple of Ninna-ji. The chief bonze conducted him up a hillside through a park of pines and cryptomerias to the Omuro Imperial Villa. Konoye admired the fine views over Kyoto in one direction and over a little river gorge in the other. The place would be ideal for Hirohito in his old age. Konoye gave instructions for repairs and improvements and drove back to Kyoto to worship at his mother's grave.

During Konoye's trip south, MacArthur made his ceremonial entry into Tokyo. On September 6 one of his press officers had asked American reporters to leave the capital because "it is not American military policy for correspondents to spearhead the Occupation." On September 7, all Japanese troops had been withdrawn to the north, leaving only about one division of Imperial Guards who remained behind secretly, in civilian clothes, to protect the palace. MacArthur set out from Yokohama on the following morning. He had instructed the Japanese government to take no security precautions. When his car broke down on the road, however, a crowd of police and plainclothesmen materialized out of nowhere to stand about helpfully until a new car was brought up from the rear. Then MacArthur pushed on through a wasteland of war damage to the Tokyo town line. There the veteran jungle fighters of the U.S. 1st Cavalry Division were drawn up waiting, dressed for parade. At a word they rolled forward into the enemy capital, leading the way to MacArthur's future residence, the American Embassy. By nightfall they had taken up positions all around the great gray-walled palace of Hirohito. The hub of the Japanese Empire was secure. Two days later, on September 10, Lord Privy Seal Kido felt it safe to leave the palace and sleep in his own home for the first time in a month.

SEIZING TOJO

With almost 100,000 U.S. troops ashore now, MacArthur could begin, gingerly, to impose Occupation policies on the Japanese government. Politically the most pressing order of business was war criminals. Atrocity stories told by the 30,000 Allied P.O.W.'s found in Japanese concentration camps made prompt arrests mandatory. In the last week the State Department and its Australian counterpart had both supplemented the tales of the prisoners by releasing previously classified files on Japanese deeds in other theaters earlier in the war. American airmen had been cooked and eaten by Japanese generals on Pacific islands. Sixteen thousand Allied P.O.W.'s had been beaten, starved, and worked to death in the construction of a jungle railway from Thailand to Burma. The Japanese secret police had kept pens of naked Western men and women in the cellars under the torture chambers of Bridge House in Shanghai. The Japanese public knew nothing of such brutalities except what had been whispered by a few disgusted Japanese soldiers who had returned home. Now, as the horror stories were printed, public incredulity turned to fear and shame, and Japanese leaders grew nervous waiting for MacArthur to outline the terms of Western vengeance.

On September 9, two members of Prince Higashikuni's brain trust told reporters: "The Allies should announce their war criminal list soon so the Japanese people can consider it and perhaps add a few names. Prince Konoye, the deputy prime minister, and Mr. Shigemitsu, the foreign minister, should be included on it." This strange accusation, which suggested bitter hatreds within the Higashikuni cabinet, was really no more than a statement of fact. Konoye and Shigemitsu had helped to lead Japan to Pearl Harbor, and both had promised Hirohito that they would take responsibility and serve as scapegoats.

The United States had had a War Crime Subcommission making lists of Japanese suspects in Chungking since November of 1944. With Chinese help the difficult Oriental names had been sorted out but not the guilt. Sometimes it seemed that all Japanese were guilty, sometimes that no one was guilty. There was no outstanding group of leaders like the Goering-Goebbels-Himmler gang in Germany. Nor was there any clearcut party like the Nazis by which to judge affiliations. Every Western expert seemed to know a different faction which was supposed to be the keystone of Japanese fascism.

Prodded by Washington and by the anxious Japanese themselves, MacArthur approached the problem of war guilt with caution. He had his giant Germanic Intelligence chief, General Willoughby, in co-operation with

General Eichelberger's M.P.'s, establish a War Crimes Board. The board worked out of Willoughby's advance headquarters in Tokyo in the old secret police building outside the North Gate of the palace. On September 10 the board issued its first tentative list of war criminal suspects who were to be arrested.

The first name on the list was that of General Tojo, the Pearl Harbor prime minister. American correspondents at once threaded their way by jeep from police box to police box, through the maze of blasted, burned-out Tokyo streets, to Tojo's suburban home. They found the bald mustachioed little man in gray knee socks, white shorts, and shirt, playing the part of a gentleman truck farmer in his garden. Unlike Konoye, Shigemitsu, or Prince Higashikuni, General Tojo was a man of conviction: straightforward, sharp, logical, and irrascible. When he saw that he could not fob off the reporters, he sat down with them on a garden bench, offered them cheap wartime Hope cigarettes and told them what he thought. "I believe," he said, "that Japan's war was a just one. Although I know your country will not accept that, history will decide who was right. As for me, I accept full responsibility for the war."

A week earlier General Tojo had been summoned by War Minister Shimomura, the general who had forced the Nanking attack plans through the General Staff in 1937. On behalf of the government the war minister asked Tojo to submit to arrest if necessary and to forego suicide until he had had a chance to persuade the Allies that he, rather than the Emperor, was responsible for the war. Tojo promised to continue to do everything in his power to shield the Emperor but warned that he might feel compelled to commit suicide for the sake of honor. He would voluntarily turn himself in on request at any prison in Japan, but he would not submit to being seized like a captive on the battlefield. He was a soldier and had vowed never to be captured alive. War Minister Shimomura thanked him and intimated that whatever happened the Tojo family would be taken care of financially.

On the afternoon of September 11, when U.S. correspondents had been staked out in the Tojo front yard all day, the M.P.'s finally came to make their arrest. Tojo questioned them out his study window. What did they want? Did they have a warrant? Would the American officer in charge present his credentials? After each answer Tojo ducked back into his study to consider the next question. "It's beginning to look like the balcony scene from *Romeo and Juliet*," cracked one of the U.S. correspondents. Finally Tojo asked them to wait a moment while he opened the front door. His wife, whom he had dismissed at the approach of the jeeps, stood watching the house from a neighbor's garden. She had put on a pair of peasant-woman trousers so that she would not be noticed. It was her duty to report as many particulars as she could to the rest of the Tojo family.

Inside the house, Tojo had seated himself in his favorite red armchair and picked up a 32-caliber Colt automatic pistol taken from a downed American pilot during the war. It was the same weapon which his son-in-law Major Koga had used to kill himself after the rising in the palace on the night of the surrender. Tojo unbuttoned the top of his shirt. On his chest the outline of a heart had been drawn in charcoal a day or two earlier by the doctor who lived next door. Tojo aimed carefully at the target area and fired. The bullet went through him and buried itself in the upholstery. By an irony of anatomy it barely missed his heart, an abnormally long and slender one. Instead it punctured his lung and the two holes it had made in his skin alternately frothed and sucked as he gasped for breath. The American M.P.'s kicked in the door, found him alive and conscious, and summoned a doctor.

For two hours Tojo bled and begged to die while American correspondents photographed him from every conceivable angle and dipped souvenir handkerchiefs in his blood. "I am very sorry it is taking so much time to die," he said. "I would not like to be judged in front of a conqueror's court. I wait for the righteous judgment of history." Finally the American doctor arrived, sutured the holes in his chest and back, and administered plasma. Tojo responded well. The doctor moved him to a hospital and there, after several transfusions from G.I. donors, he recovered to stand trial and go to the gallows.

The day after Tojo's arrest, September 12, the Cabinet voted to preempt Allied justice by having war criminal suspects arrested and tried by native Japanese law agencies. Prince Higashikuni, the prime minister, hurried to the Imperial Library for Hirohito's endorsement of the subterfuge and was met with refusal. "All the so-called war criminals," said Hirohito, "wanted by the enemy, particularly those said to be responsible for causing the war, are men who spent themselves in loyal honest service to me. To judge them in my name puts me in an intolerable position. I will ask you therefore if there is not some room for reconsideration." If the Americans insisted on vengeance, Hirohito meant to let the blood be on their own hands. Lives might be saved by nominal Japanese justice, but Hirohito trusted the accused to prefer martyrdom and honor at American hands.

MacArthur had ordered twenty-four other Japanese leaders to be apprehended including all members of the 1941 Pearl Harbor Cabinet. The prickly foreign minister who had spoken for surrender in the imperial air raid shelter on August 9 was on the list. So was the ubiquitous Suzuki Tei-ichi, who had recruited most of Hirohito's cabal of young officers in the 1920's. MacArthur had his M.P.'s carry out their arrests on a leisurely, one-man-a-day schedule. Some said that he was indulging his sense of theater; some that he hoped the war criminals would commit suicide if given enough time; some that he was waiting for Hirohito to agree to punish the war criminals himself.

On September 12, the M.P.'s knocked at the door of Admiral Shimada

Shigetaro, Tojo's opposite number in the Navy. In the entryway, where invited guests would have taken off their shoes, they were greeted by Mrs. Shimada. She knelt at the edge of the raised floor of the interior and touched her head to the matting. Then wreathed in polite smiles, she asked to see their credentials. She bowed again and promised that her husband would be with them in fifteen minutes. The American M.P.'s, stamping and chafing in the doorway, heard the sounds of a last meal being hastily served inside. When the fifteen minutes had passed, a nisei or second-generation American of Japanese ancestry took off his shoes and entered the house. At the end of twenty minutes Admiral Shimada finally appeared dressed in a new green uniform still freshly crinkled from the tailor's box. Shimada asked to see the M.P.'s credentials. "Tell him to get his shoes on and get going," said the American major in charge. "Tell him to quit this nonsense." Shimada laughed and put a hand on the major's shoulder. "Be quiet," he said in broken English, "I don't suicide." As he put on his shoes, his wife and two daughters knelt on the matting in deep obeisance. The daughters were weeping. Shimada bid them live bravely, turned and walked away with the M.P.'s to seven years in jail.

At about the moment that Shimada was being ushered from his home, Field Marshal Sugiyama Hajime, the highest ranking commoner in the Army, who had served as chief of staff from 1940 to 1944, blew his brains out. His wife took cyanide and plunged a dagger into her throat. In an effort to save a few necks for the hangman, MacArthur's headquarters issued an extraordinary statement claiming that the Japanese government of General Prince Higashikuni approved of the arrests. Overlooking the six admirals and generals in the Cabinet, MacArthur's spokesman declared: "The government is made up principally of nonmilitary elements which have been trembling under threats from the Black Dragon and other supposedly secret organizations."

The name of the Black Dragon Society had caught the fancy of Western journalists in the 1930's. It was supposed to be, and once had been, one of the most powerful subversive tongs in the Orient. The 1911 revolution which overthrew the throne of the Manchus and brought republicanism to China had been subsidized by it. The Kuomintang party of Sun Yat-sen and Chiang Kai-shek which rules Taiwan today had held its first meeting in Black Dragon headquarters in Tokyo in 1905. Western observers had always been encouraged by their upper-class Japanese friends to think of the Black Dragon as a crime syndicate, akin to the Mafia of Sicily. But in reality the Black Dragon was first of all a revolutionary cell dedicated to Pan-Asianism and xenophobia. Its sinister name referred not to some monster of the underworld but to the Black Dragon River, the Amur, which separates Manchuria from Siberia. During the 1890's and 1900's the name had stood for Japan's determination to prevent Russia from extending her empire south of the Amur. When Japan seized control of Manchuria in 1932, the Black Dragon Society persisted in calling the main enemy Russia. It backed the Strike-North Faction in the Japanese Army and lost. After 1936 when Hirohito singlehandedly overruled the expansion plans of the Strike-North Faction, the Amur River Society ceased to be a force. It held its last public meeting in October 1935 to protest Mussolini's white invasion of black Ethiopia.

Ten years later, on September 13, 1945, MacArthur's headquarters ordered the immediate dissolution of the Black Dragon Society and the arrest of seven of its leaders. Two of the men mentioned had never belonged to the society. A third had headed the organization and had died of old age in 1938. A fourth had been forced to commit suicide by the order of Tojo in 1943. Three others had renounced their affiliations with the Black Dragon in early manhood and had since served Hirohito as responsible Cabinet ministers.

Distressed by the out-of-date intelligence in the hands of MacArthur's Intelligence agents, Deputy Prime Minister Konoye sped down to Yokohama on September 13 and tried to explain matters. He phoned back that he was having difficulty in making himself understood through MacArthur's personal interpreter, Colonel Sidney Mashbir. Foreign Minister Shigemitsu at once followed Konoye to Yokohama and late that afternoon transmitted in English a message which could cross the language barrier: if MacArthur's men would consult with the Cabinet on war criminals to be arrested, the suspects would turn themselves in voluntarily at specified Allied detention points. Shaken by Tojo's suicide attempt and by the embarrassment of having tried to arrest dead men, MacArthur's War Crimes Board readily agreed. The Cabinet for its part persuaded Hirohito that it would be no treachery for him to save old retainers from the indignity of forcible arrest. General Eichelberger at once issued orders for the Japanese police to "deliver Japanese war criminals in good health."

HIROHITO'S OUTING

The five days that followed rubbed sensibilities raw on both sides. The remaining twenty-three war criminal suspects named by MacArthur's staff in its first sweep turned themselves in alive and well. The most important of them were given words of imperial comfort by Lord Privy Seal Kido's secretary before they reported for imprisonment. *New York Times* columnist Hanson Baldwin in Washington accused MacArthur of accepting the Emperor "as a sort of junior partner in the Occupation." On September 14 the glib Prime Minister Higashikuni, in answer to a questionnaire mailed him by the Associated Press, raised a storm in the United States by asking: "People of America, won't you forget Pearl Harbor? We Japanese people will forget the picture of devastation wrought by the atomic bomb and will start entirely anew as a peace-loving nation. America has won and Japan

has lost. The war is ended. Let us now bury hate." General Eichelberger
was criticized in Washington for telling reporters: "If the Japs continue
acting as they are now, within a year this thing should be washed up." Mac-
Arthur was criticized in Washington for announcing that Allied Occupation
forces would be cut from 500,000 to 200,000. State Department employees
continued to publish evidence of Japanese wartime atrocities. It was leaked
that the Australian and Chinese governments headed their war criminal
lists with the name Hirohito. Japanese newspapers published stories of G.I.
murders and rapes which were unreported by the Japanese police. Mac-
Arthur personally accused the press of "lack of good faith in handling the
news." The sly old Taoist philosopher Suzuki Kantaro took his cigar from
his mouth to tell U.S. reporters an outrageous lie: "The Emperor did not
know that Japan had attacked Pearl Harbor until the Japanese militarists
told him." Several American correspondents submitted demands to the
palace that they be allowed to interview the Emperor personally.

Palace officials were frankly worried. The Emperor showed no inclination to save himself, and MacArthur's investigators now seemed intent on
getting at the truth without respect for persons or rank. At the same time
MacArthur himself seemed eager to believe the best of Hirohito. A dignified,
idealized account of the Emperor's role in ending the war was prepared by
one of the palace public relations experts and accepted gratefully by Mac-
Arthur's Chief of Intelligence General Willoughby. "Based on personal
confidence rather than official pressure," Willoughby later wrote, "American
Intelligence in Tokyo obtained confidential notes and observations by one
of the highest functionaries in the imperial entourage." Repeatedly Mac-
Arthur told visitors that he was weary of dealing through middlemen and
would like to get to the point. Hirohito, too, was dissatisfied with the results
brought back by his envoys from MacArthur's New Grand Hotel headquarters in Yokohama.

As a Japanese, Prime Minister Higashikuni assumed that the cause of all
the unpleasantness must lie in the quality of the go-betweens being used.
On September 17, he relieved Shigemitsu of his duties as foreign minister
and replaced him with Yoshida Shigeru, the former Strike-South advocate
who had been arrested by the secret police a few months earlier as a member of the Peace Faction. A short, scowling, cigar-chewing gnome of a man,
Yoshida was an ideal emissary to use with American generals. He spoke
good English and with a gruff directness most unusual in a Japanese. He
needed no instruction in the inner workings of palace politics for he was the
son-in-law of Hirohito's chief advisor and Lord Privy Seal from 1925 to
1935. In serving his father-in-law, Yoshida had built his career on work
behind the scenes, with the result that he had held no incriminating public
offices. His last public appointment, in fact, had been ambassador to the
Court of St. James in the period 1936 to 1938. And although an advocate
of expansion into the South Seas, he had never felt that it was absolutely

necessary to attack the United States. In 1941 he had felt that attack on the United States was still to be avoided. Painstakingly groomed and trained, he now came into his own at the age of sixty-seven. MacArthur and his generals liked him so well that from 1946 to 1954 he would be five times prime minister and would be remembered as the architect of postwar Japan.

On September 18, the day of Yoshida's investiture as foreign minister, MacArthur and his staff moved up from Yokohama to Tokyo and opened for business on a more or less permanent basis. At the American Embassy which MacArthur took for his home, the entire prewar staff of servants reappeared one by one without being summoned. They stole in by the rear entrance, went up to the attic, unpacked their brown staff kimonos from trunks, and resumed service as if the four years of war had never been. For his place of work MacArthur took the white-columned, marble-and-granite Dai Ichi Insurance Building where the Peace Faction and the Tokyo Area Army had had their offices a few weeks earlier. Here were security facilities unequaled elsewhere in Japan, including shoot-the-chute tubes for personnel to use in reaching the ground floor in the event of fire. Here, from a phone-less, walnut-paneled room on the sixth floor, MacArthur would preside over Japan for five and a half years. Here he would organize an entire second government for Japan, a sprawling bureaucracy of American officers and civilians who would ultimately require a 278-page phone book and would be known collectively as SCAP, Supreme Commander Allied Powers. Here, from his sixth-floor window, MacArthur looked directly out, across a moat and plaza, onto the walls and watchtowers of Hirohito's palace. Probably never in history have two adversaries, holding such absolute power over the same land, worked so near one another.

On SCAP's first day in Tokyo, the prime minister, General Prince Higashikuni, held his first press conference for American reporters. One of them later doubted that any man "of comparable political status in any country of the world has ever been subjected to such blunt questioning by news correspondents." Rakishly dressed in a tan silk suit, Higashikuni fielded the insulting questions with bland sangfroid. Yes, he intended to broaden democratic processes. He expected soon to abolish the War and Navy Ministries and to curtail sharply the influence of the House of Peers. Yes, he would submit all his plans for approval to MacArthur, but he hoped that his Cabinet would be able to keep many of the contemplated reforms in its own hands. For example, the prosecution of war criminals—it had begun long before the entry of American forces, and men were already being punished for their roughness with Allied prisoners. No, on the spur of the moment he could not give the names of those convicted nor the sentences against them, but he would make a list of them available through SCAP.

The next morning, September 20, newspapers reported that Senator Richard Russell of Georgia had asked the U.S. Senate to resolve that the Emperor be tried as a war criminal along with Tojo. With Hirohito's approval Prince Higashikuni at once paid a courtesy call on MacArthur in his new office in the Dai Ichi Building. He told MacArthur that he was prepared to resign whenever MacArthur or Hirohito requested it. He also indicated, guardedly, that the Emperor, in the interests of liberalism and democracy, would like to emerge from his cloistered life in the palace and play a more personal part in public affairs. MacArthur had the false impression, gleaned from newspapers, that the Emperor had never been interviewed, never delivered a public speech, never even used a telephone. And so he endorsed Higashikuni's suggestion with enthusiasm. He added by way of reminder, however, that Hirohito's emergence would not be accepted as a substitute for constructive steps towards reform on the part of the Japanese government.

Hirohito began his career as an extrovert on September 25, 1945. Many other Japanese remember it as the day that they were allowed to unstrap the short-wave bands on their radios and for the first time since prewar days listen again to broadcasts from overseas. Hirohito remembers it as the day that he gave ten-minute interviews to two U.S. newspaper correspondents. On being ushered into the audience chamber of the Imperial Household Building, Frank Kluckhohn of *The New York Times* strode briskly across to the dais where the Emperor was standing, reached out aggressively and shook the Emperor's hand. Hirohito showed no surprise at the unprecedented familiarity but in Kluckhohn's words "looked directly into my eyes, giving a sincere impression." He told Kluckhohn that he approved of constitutional monarchy and that he relied greatly on General MacArthur. "Once the Japanese people have been fed and clothed," he declared, "it will be comparatively easy to carry out the needed reforms within Japan." Kluckhohn also understood the Emperor to say that Tojo had acted against imperial wishes and had misused the Grand Seal of State in attacking Pearl Harbor before delivering a declaration of war.

"Hirohito in Interview Puts Blame on Tojo in Sneak Raid," headlined *The New York Times* the next day. The story drew a quick disavowal from the palace in which Hirohito pretended disingenuously that he had not known in advance the details of the Pearl Harbor attack plan. "It was usual," he declared irrelevantly, "for the High Command to handle the details of attacks. I meant Tojo to declare war in advance." In actuality both he and Tojo had meant to give the United States a few minutes' warning but had failed to do so because of a series of tragicomic accidents.

Hirohito followed his chats with American reporters by making an appointment to call on MacArthur. The historic first meeting took place at 10:00 A.M. September 27 within the clean white plaster walls of the American Embassy. Hirohito had rehearsed and discussed the role he planned to play with his favorite advisor Lord Privy Seal Kido for two hours and forty-five minutes the previous day. He was ready to take an extremely "low position," to be humble and even ludicrous if necessary, in order to win

MacArthur's sympathy. He could afford to cut such a figure because, in Japan, there was an old and honorable tradition of playing the fool while waiting for revenge. It went so deep that every man in the Japanese Army had for decades cultivated a slovenly bumpkin appearance in order to seem weak and undisciplined in the eyes of potential spit-and-polish Western enemies. Japanese drill masters had taught privates to drag their heels on parade, to go unshaven, to leave buttons undone. Hirohito, who had worn Army uniforms for years, understood well this Spartan samurai mystique. And the drab disguise, the self-effacing air, became him well.

A Saladin in rags, Hirohito confronted one of the last knights to imagine himself armed in shining Christian chivalry. MacArthur came to the meeting determined to be as magnanimous as possible. He was under orders from Washington to punish Japan's war criminals, but it was a duty which he disliked, one that served no useful purpose but to satisfy vengeful voters in the United States and Great Britain. In MacArthur's view all Japanese had behaved badly, but as pagans rather than criminals. Now they needed to be enlightened, not punished. The Emperor, he believed, was a weak and ineffectual man who had the power to lead his people but no will except to be led.

Hirohito arrived at the American Embassy in one of the oldest limousines in the imperial garages, a plum-colored Daimler of World War I vintage. He had doffed his field marshal's uniform weeks ago and now, like the lowliest chamberlain in his suite, he was dressed in shabby prewar morning clothes. At the embassy steps he was met by Brigadier General Bonner Fellers. To Fellers's astonishment Hirohito held out his hand, and Fellers automatically took it and shook it. Then Hirohito and his attendants were led into the foyer and introduced to a group of MacArthur's aides. U.S. officers noticed that the Emperor seemed highstrung and trembling—almost as if he had been given an early-morning stimulant. The impression was highlighted by the fact that one of the courtiers with him was introduced as his personal physician. By prior arrangement, at Hirohito's own insistence, the meeting was to be entirely private and only Hirohito and his interpreter were ushered into MacArthur's presence.

MacArthur met Hirohito at the door of the embassy library dressed in sharply pressed khaki trousers and plain open-necked khaki shirt. He was at his most charming and genial. As he led Hirohito to a chair he recalled that in 1905, when twenty-five, he had had the privilege of being received with his father, General Arthur MacArthur, by Hirohito's deified grandfather, Emperor Meiji. He offered an American cigarette to Hirohito—ordinarily a nonsmoker—and noticed how the Emperor's "hands shook as I lighted it for him." There followed a thirty-eight-minute conversation. No minutes were kept of it but both MacArthur and Hirohito later gave accounts of what was said.

Hirohito thanked MacArthur for the excellent conduct of his troops.

MacArthur thanked Hirohito for the excellent conduct of his people. MacArthur added that he had heard of Hirohito's decisive role in ending the war and was grateful for it.

Hirohito objected modestly that he had not ended the war singlehandedly. "The public was not correctly informed," he said, and it was difficult "to bring about an end to the war without a shock to public opinion. . . . The peace party did not prevail until the bombing of Hiroshima created a situation which could be dramatized."

MacArthur said he was puzzled how it was that an Emperor powerful enough to end the war had not been powerful enough to prevent it.

"I felt my heart was breaking," replied Hirohito, "when I gave the word for war against the British royal family. They treated me with great kindness when I visited Europe as a crown prince. But the idea of gainsaying my advisors in those days never even occurred to me. Besides, it would have done no good. I would have been put in an insane asylum or even assassinated."

"A monarch must be brave enough to run such risks," said MacArthur sternly.

Hirohito replied instantly. His well-modulated nasal voice rose slightly. His eyes turned attentively on the interpreter whose English seemed suddenly hushed and hesitant: "It was not clear to me that our course was unjustified. Even now I am not sure how future historians will allocate the responsibility for the war." MacArthur was surprised. He had expected Hirohito to disassociate himself from Pearl Harbor and lay the blame for it on Tojo. Instead he heard Hirohito say: "General MacArthur, I have come to you to offer myself to the judgment of the powers you represent as the one to bear sole responsibility for every political and military decision made by my people, every action taken in the conduct of the war."

"This courageous assumption of responsibility implicit with death . . ." wrote MacArthur later, "moved me to the very marrow of my bones. He was an Emperor by inherent birth but in that instant I knew I faced the First Gentleman of Japan in his own right." Beaming paternally, MacArthur explained that the punishment of war criminals was a political necessity dictated by Washington which he, as a soldier, found distasteful. He added, however, that there could be no harm in punishing those who, for personal ambition, had given the Throne evil counsel. "I believe," he said, "that the Emperor of Japan knows best about the important men in the Japanese political world. Therefore I want to get your advice from now on on various matters."

Delighted, Hirohito promised to advise MacArthur in any way that he could. He would be ready, he said, to come to the embassy in person or send over the lord privy seal or grand chamberlain whenever he could be of assistance.

MacArthur promised to consult him often and on this cordial note their first tête-à-tête adjourned. A cameraman was summoned to record the historic moment. His photograph, showing the hulking general in fatigues towering over the tiny Emperor in striped pants, was so unflattering to Hirohito that Japanese editors did not publish it until ordered to do so by SCAP. Then it captured a curious place in the affections of the populace. The public humiliation of the little Emperor in striped pants became a symbol for the self-pity of the entire nation in defeat. Hirohito was brought close to his people as never before.

Hirohito returned to the palace and at once told Lord Privy Seal Kido of the understanding reached with MacArthur. "And this," he said, with glee, "was volunteered from MacArthur's side." Two days later, when Kido told him that the latest press clippings from America were almost all hostile to the Throne, Hirohito struck an indignant pose and threatened to go right over to his friend General MacArthur and have the criticism stopped. Kido owlishly warned him "to bottle up his resentment and keep silent." Kido's warning was reinforced by a member of MacArthur's War Crimes Board who indicated that the board had not yet decided whether or not to try the Emperor. To wile away the hours of uncertainty, Hirohito worked on a personal account of the events of his reign, a document in his defense which, unfortunately for historians, he was never called upon to produce in evidence. By October 3 he had brought his account up to the year 1929.

FIRST QUARREL

Any sense of cozy safety which Hirohito had brought away with him from his meeting with MacArthur was shattered on October 4 by a directive known as JCS 10 from the Joint Chiefs of Staff in Washington. It demanded reform of the Japanese police system; abolition of the thought police which had dealt with political crimes; amnesty for all political prisoners, including Communists; and complete freedom of the press—freedom even to criticize the Emperor. Hirohito received an intercept of the directive and Prince Konoye, a minister without portfolio in the Cabinet, at once called at the Dai Ichi Building to find out from MacArthur what it would mean. Konoye returned with the unsettling intelligence that MacArthur saw no harm in Communists, freed from jail, making speeches from soapboxes. Further, MacArthur intended to repeal the 1936 law making "thought criminals" liable to preventive arrest and the 1939 law requiring Japanese Christians to subordinate their faith to Shintoism. In addition, all commercial transactions between Japan and the outside world must now be approved by SCAP. Finally, Prime Minister Higashikuni's home minister must be dropped from the Cabinet because he had formerly been a thought policeman. That afternoon an official copy of JCS 10 was delivered to Prince Higashikuni at the prime minister's residence.

MacArthur worked late that night and emissaries shuttled back and forth between the prime minister's residence, the palace, and the Dai Ichi Building. Prince Higashikuni first suggested that he and his Cabinet should resign in protest to the directive and should then return to power with a new home minister. MacArthur, however, told a go-between: "I have the highest regard for Prince Higashikuni and I know of no one better qualified to carry out the terms of my directive, but if the Cabinet resigns *en masse* tomorrow it can only be interpreted by the Japanese people to mean that it is unable to implement my directive. Thereafter Prince Higashikuni may be acceptable to the Emperor for reappointment as prime minister, but he will not be acceptable to me." [3]

Prince Konoye then suggested that Foreign Minister Yoshida Shigeru form a Cabinet. He had, after all, been groomed for the post by his membership in the Peace Faction and by his incarceration at the hands of the secret police. Hirohito and his favorite advisor, Lord Privy Seal Kido, however, were not sure that it was time yet for a Yoshida Cabinet. The sixty-seven-year-old Yoshida had been "saved" for the prime ministership for so many years that it would be foolish to waste him now. Until the proud warriors of Japan became accustomed to American authority, until MacArthur had finished arresting war criminals, until the first hungry humiliating winter of the Occupation was over, it might be best to exploit a more expendable man. By bedtime, Hirohito and Kido had agreed that the ideal person would be Baron Shidehara Kijuro, seventy-three. In the 1920's Shidehara had been sorely used and abused as a diplomatic front man for Japan. Perennially foreign minister, perennially castigated by soldiers as "the weak-kneed diplomat," he had persuaded the world that Japan was a peaceful nation, and then, after the conquest of Manchuria, he had been put to pasture.

The next day, October 5, when the Emperor and his advisors were all agreed on what must be done, Prince Higashikuni made a great face-saving show by storming into the palace and declaring that he could not remain in office another moment after receiving such an insulting Allied directive as that of the previous evening. Foreign Minister Yoshida immediately saw MacArthur and sounded him out on the candidacy of old "weak-kneed" Baron Shidehara. "Isn't he rather old?" asked MacArthur. "Can he speak English?" Assured that he could, MacArthur nodded approvingly and said that he had no intention of interfering in domestic Japanese politics.

And so it was decided that Shidehara would be Japan's next prime minister. Persuading him to accept the post was not easy. He saw no honor in being MacArthur's lackey, and after his shoddy treatment in years gone by he felt he owed Hirohito no favors. All morning on October 6, chamber-

---

[3] MacArthur in his *Reminiscences* remembers saying this of Prime Minister Shidehara during a later purge in January 1946. The story as told here follows Japanese sources.

lains and Cabinet ministers at the Imperial Household Building wooed Shidehara in vain. At Kido's suggestion, Hirohito sent a special lunch over to him from the imperial kitchen. After lunch Hirohito sat down with him in private, dispensed with the usual Court formalities, and spoke to him not as sovereign to subject but as man to man. In an hour Shidehara was persuaded to do his disagreeable duty.

Every new prime minister of Japan always had a clearly recognized mission to perform. Hirohito and his advisors usually formulated the mission and selected the man for it weeks and even months in advance. Indeed, those close to the Throne could sometimes see so far into the future as to know who would be the prime minister after next. Prince Higashikuni's mission as prime minister had been to see that the Japanese Armed Forces obeyed the Imperial Will and demobilized peaceably. In addition, by resigning, he was able to signify to the nation that the imperial family disassociated itself from the rest of MacArthur's program. Shidehara's mission, by contrast, was to give in to MacArthur, to "bend like the young bamboo." He was to carry out American reforms as a gesture, at the same time making it clear that he acted without commitment and was only a figurehead. On his first day in office he promised to back MacArthur and added sarcastically, "I hope I am not a war criminal, but if I turn out to be one, that's all right too; we all helped to fight the war." Three days later he attributed the war with the United States to a "succession of minor incidents." Seven weeks later, when petitioned by members of the Diet to appoint a board of inquiry to fix responsibility for starting the war, he rejected the suggestion with the words, "I would rather ask you all to continue inquiring into the causes of defeat."

The Cabinet of Prime Minister Shidehara began its truculent co-operation with MacArthur by dissolving officially the secret police which had retained a skeletal organization since the surrender. Before complying with MacArthur's demand that political prisoners be released from Japanese prisons, one of Shidehara's aides came up with the alarming information that 957,000 convicts were about to be let loose on the Japanese population. Investigation, however, soon showed that this figure represented the total number of arrests made in Hirohito's reign for all types of crime. Next it was said that 10,000 desperate leftists would have to be released. But this figure, too, turned out to be somewhat exaggerated. It was the number of leftists picked up in a mass arrest in April of 1929. Of the 10,000, only 1,200 had been held in jail after 1935. Of these, seven had been executed after due process, 200 had been beaten to death, and 200 had died of malnutrition and disease. A little over 700 had been released into labor battalions during the war or simply sent home on probation after American bombing began. Finally, when all the facts were in, twenty-five political agitators were released from prison, sixteen of them Communists.

The sixteen Communists celebrated their freedom by leading 500 idle citizens in a noisy hunger demonstration under MacArthur's windows on the Imperial Plaza between the Dai Ichi Building and the palace. The next morning, Columbus Day, MacArthur held his first meeting with the new prime minister, Shidehara, and urged him to press forward with other reforms: to give the people a bill of rights, to emancipate women, to allow labor to organize, to eradicate cant and mythology from textbooks. In his hereditary capacity as advisor to the Throne, the lanky Prince Konoye countered the following day with a statement to the effect that the Emperor would not object to being made a constitutional monarch but was seriously concerned over other suggested changes in the Constitution. Abdication, said Konoye, was a possibility which Hirohito had not yet ruled out. On October 14 the Cabinet voted to give women the franchise and to decrease the voting age from twenty-five to twenty. Two days later the Japanese General Staff was dissolved. On the following day the demobilization of the Japanese Army and Navy was proclaimed complete. Veterans still overseas would be mustered out as they arrived home in Japanese ports.

The reform programs of Prime Minister Shidehara had at least two happy results. Thousands of politically suspect Japanese were restored to first-class citizenship and so were enabled to clear their family escutcheons of dishonor. And in the election the following spring, thirty-eight women were elected to the Diet. Imperial advisor Kido's son-in-law at once called on MacArthur to tell him with gleeful mock horror that one of the new representatives was a famous prostitute.

"How many votes did she get?" asked MacArthur.

"Two hundred and fifty-six thousand," sighed Kido's son-in-law.

MacArthur, who was later to give different versions of his reply to some audiences, smiled and said, "She must be a hard-working woman."

BLOOM OF ROMANCE

When Prime Minister Shidehara's "reform" Cabinet had been in office a week, SCAP announced that the majority of the Occupation forces were no longer combat veterans but fresh recruits from the United States. The Occupation was no longer a military operation but a social experiment. MacArthur feared that it now faced its greatest test. He had commanded the Rainbow Division in the occupation of the Rhineland after World War I, and he maintained that never in history had there been a successful peacetime occupation army. Under combat conditions, he felt, men retained discipline and respected the enemy, but in the slothful toils of peace conquerors grew overweening and veterans lost their starch. He feared that the boys from home would soon be subjugating women to make up for the heroics of real conquest which they had missed.

Japan was fully prepared to take up the psychological slack which Mac-

Arthur anticipated in his troops. The Peace Faction's Recreation and Amusement Association had mobilized the nation's seductive powers for that very purpose. From the first when U.S. armor began rolling into Tokyo, occupying assigned barracks and factories and setting up checkpoints, the men were astonished by trucks of girls that were unloaded at their road-blocks with interpreters in train to explain: "Courtesy of the Recreation and Amusement Association." These initial advances were all rebuffed and the truckloads of presents sent home unopened. But in a matter of weeks, when fear of Japanese treachery subsided, the Americans began to thaw. Soon MacArthur was expressing "grave concern and deep distress over published reports suggestive of an existing widespread promiscuous relationship be-tween members of the occupying forces and Japanese women of immoral character."

In prewar days Japanese prostitutes had enjoyed an international reputa-tion for their petite figures, their unabashed hedonism, and the tasteful illusion they created of self-respect and honest feeling. They lived and worked in ornate walled ghettos on the peripheries of the major cities. The most famous of their compounds was Tokyo's Yoshiwara, forty well-policed acres of winking lanterns and narrow teeming streets, of gilt dragons and red-lacquer archways, of costumed pimps and tumblers and vendors of sweetmeats, of pools and gardens glimpsed through lattice gates, of girls on balconies and girls in cages—of concentrated Oriental glamour and vice. MacArthur's M.P.'s knew of the Yoshiwara by report and on their first day in Tokyo headed for it directly to post "Off Limits" signs. They found only a ruin gutted by incendiaries.

The girls who had survived the bombing were scattered over the whole metropolitan and suburban area. Those who could speak a little English had been recruited by the R.A.A. and were waiting to serve at quaint old inns in the outskirts or in the new cabarets and brothels which the R.A.A. was building downtown. Eventually American demand would create such mani-fest hotspots as the Big Tits Bar in Yokohama or the Hard On Café in Tokyo, but now, less than a month after the Occupation had commenced, the girls were being trucked about discreetly to emerge, as if by chance, wherever it seemed that they might be welcomed.

Some of the G.I. encounters from those earliest days read like opium dreams. A former Eighth Army sergeant, who roved the Japanese country-side looking for caches of arms to destroy, gave an account of a day in late October of 1945.

He and his companions parked their jeep in the dusty plaza of a small seaside town east of Tokyo. As the men unpacked their K-rations for lunch, a gentleman in black, wearing a top hat, came to beg them in halting Eng-lish to take their repast in the shade of his humble roof. Standing on the back bumper of their jeep, he directed them up a dirt road to a bluff over-looking the sea. Then he stopped them at a bamboo grove and led them down a path to an old inn on the edge of a cliff. In the entryway four delicate creatures in kimono helped them off with their shoes and led them upstairs to a room floored with mats and furnished with one low lacquered table. Cushions were brought for them to sit upon, and one wall was slid away to reveal a magnificent view of the crashing surf below. Maids slipped in with bottles of beer, tubs of steaming rice, and various hors d'oeuvres to add to the K-rations. The girls made uproarious mistakes in English and hand-fed the G.I.'s with chopsticks. The girls taught the G.I.'s to play parlor games with fingers and matchsticks and beer bottles—games which transcended language. Warm saké was brought in tiny pitchers and drunk from tiny pottery cups. Soon food and communication were almost exhausted and one of the girls said, "Take bath now."

Down two flights of stairs, the incredulous G.I.'s were ushered into a grotto room in the cliff. The stone floor slanted gently to a wall which opened on the sea. In the center of the floor was a sunken tiled pool of steaming water. The girls disrobed and firmly began to undress the men. Then they poured small wooden buckets of scalding water over themselves. The performance was repeated, with the G.I.'s the delighted victims. When everyone was washed and rinsed, the girls slipped into the bath. Little by little the men were induced to follow them and were taught the trick of sitting completely still, neck deep in the 120-degree water, until it no longer seemed to scald. As the girls mopped the G.I.'s brows with tiny towels, they fed them small glasses of beer from bottles brought in by the maids. In the distance the shadow of the cliff lengthened on the Pacific swell below.

When everyone was well steeped, the maids brought clean cotton sleeping kimonos, and the men learned to knot the sashes in front and pull them around so that the sash ends hung in back. Then the girls led the G.I.'s upstairs to private rooms where thick mattresses were laid out on the matting floors and more bottles of beer were standing on the low tables. "Show me American love," said a girl to the sergeant as she curled herself up against him. And the sergeant, who a moment before felt stuffed, swamped, and steeped, found himself too proud to refuse. In the morning he awoke alone. Arousing his companions in nearby rooms, he pooled money with them in a worried effort to find out if they could pay for their sumptuous entertainment. The maids brought them tea and rice, and after breakfast they consulted their host in the black suit. He told them that the cost of their entertainment would be two packs of American cigarettes from each of them. In the foyer their mistresses of the night before waited with shoe horns, all smiles and bows, to see them on their way.

Memories and stories of such early liaisons made it impossible for American M.P.'s ever to begin to enforce the official Occupation policy of nonfraternization. By the time the veterans of jungle fighting had all returned "stateside," the girls knew their way around U.S. billets and around periodic clean-up campaigns. In many of the former Japanese Army barracks and converted munition factories occupied by Allied personnel, lights-out became a mysterious witching hour of tapping heels and wafted scents, sighing and creaking. At the once dignified Peers Club in Tokyo, which had been requisitioned as quarters for members of MacArthur's staff, twenty-two chambermaids and switchboard operators had to be fined for spending their nights in the officers' rooms. Before the Occupation was six months old, it was conservatively estimated that more than half the American officer corps had Japanese mistresses.

It was about the time that Prime Minister Shidehara's Cabinet took office in October that the recruits of the Recreation and Amusement Association began to distinguish between American enlisted men and officers and to urge that the entire Occupation army of 500,000 could not all be entertained in the same handsome fashion. From that date began the cheap hostess bars for noncoms and the "Willow Runs" for privates. The fine old inns were increasingly reserved for officers. By no means were all of them fully appreciated, however. Some lovely villas with exquisite gardens were fitted out with American-style bathrooms and then all but forgotten. Most popular with the American officer class turned out to be private clubs, open only by invitation, in the neon-lighted heart of Tokyo.

The most popular of the clubs was the Dai-An or Great Satiated Repose run by an effusive war profiteer, Ando Akira, who was a crony of Hirohito's second brother, Naval Captain Prince Takamatsu. A leader in the trucking and construction rackets, Ando had recommended himself by his rapid repair work at Atsugi Air Base before the touchdown of the first Occupation troops. At his Dai-An club he introduced high-ranking American officers to vivacious English-speaking noblewomen and nightly gave away strings of Mikimoto pearls as table favors. His lavish operations nudged him repeatedly to the verge of bankruptcy and repeatedly he recouped through killings on the black market. After finally serving a brief prison term, he retired to honored comfort.

Outside of the clubs, the most successful entertainments were held at the villas of Cabinet Secretary Narahashi Wataru and of former Prime Minister Prince Higashikuni himself. Not much has ever been recorded of Higashikuni's parties, but Narashashi's were such brazen seductions that they make old American generals blush to this day. Narahashi had his villa at Atami, the beautiful, vulgar beach resort which also houses the goddess of mercy erected by General Matsui after the rape of Nanking. Atami's bay and mountains and celebrated baths and hostesses needed no special lore to be appreciated, and Narahashi was an excellent host. A wealthy lawyer, he had spent the war years running the largest, most lucrative listening-post hotel in Peking. One of his staff, Viscountess Torio, became the mistress of an officer who served under Brigadier General Courtney Whitney. Whitney ran the Government Section of SCAP where the reform legislation for Japan was being drafted. Old hotel keeper Narahashi boasted that he and "his princesses" would ultimately "capture" the whole of Whitney's staff.

To the sex bribe were added many extraordinary investment opportunities. Colonel Harold R. Ruth, MacArthur's fiscal officer, reported that occupationaires were sending home eight million more dollars each month than they were being paid. Many of the objets d'art which the Japanese had looted from China, as well as some native Japanese treasures, made their way in duffel bags to the United States. Prince Higashikuni himself, the Emperor's uncle, went into the antique business and liked to say later that he had bankrupted himself providing bargains for influential American officers. Years afterwards, when the Diet sought to make political profit out of alleged "jewel theft" by American officers, the investigation fell flat because it consisted of little more than a pooling of knowledge as to who had helped which American to what.

PALACE HOSTAGES

By dispensing gifts and favors, the Japanese bought little except information: gossip about personality clashes in the Dai Ichi Building, advance notice of American antitrust clampdowns, and, most important, the latest listing of war criminal suspects. Laws could be repealed after the American Occupation, business alliances could be remade and wealth returned to its rightful owners, but men hanged could not be brought back to life. Hirohito and MacArthur met at least three times during October and November of 1945 to discuss the war criminal issue in complete secrecy. MacArthur considered the punishment of a handful of discredited leaders to be of little moment in his over-all program for Japan. Hirohito, on the other hand, felt acute personal shame at the thought that others should have to suffer taking his responsibility. After first meeting Hirohito on September 27, MacArthur cabled the Joint Chiefs of Staff an account of the interview and suggested that, since the Emperor accepted all blame for the war, it might not be wise to charge others with it. The reply from Washington arrived on October 6, the day that Prime Minister Shidehara began forming his Cabinet. It was brief and explicit: "Proceed at once with the prosecution of war criminals. . . . Take no action against the Emperor without further consultation."

Saddled with a small vengeance of which he did not approve, MacArthur made the best of a bad situation and used the threat of war criminal arrests to extract concessions from Hirohito in other areas. At first he gave Hirohito the impression that Japanese co-operation might make a token punishment of war criminals sufficient. Retiring Prime Minister Higashikuni leapt at the bait and tried to swallow the fisherman: he told a farewell press conference that "Japan has already tried her war criminals and it may be assumed that their punishment has taken place." As evidence for this assertion, he submitted the names of two Japanese officers who had received prison terms, he said, for brutality during the construction of the Burma-Thailand railway. Inasmuch as 16,000 Allied P.O.W.'s and 60,000 East Indian coolies had died as slaves along that 200-mile length of railway track, it was an unusually brazen statement even for Higashikuni.

Unmoved by Higashikuni's protestations, SCAP continued to add names to its list of Class A war criminals. These were the men to be charged not with torturing prisoners but with "conspiracy" to "plan aggressive war" and commit "crimes against peace." They were to be the principals in a show-piece trial which, it was hoped would open the eyes of the Japanese people to the evils of militarism. For American purposes the men tried did not need to be the most culpable in bringing about the war; almost any leader would serve as long as there was sufficient evidence to make a good case against him. It did not matter whether he was a righteous Japanese gentleman who had always done his best to obey the demigod on the Throne or a cynical opportunist who had sought to use the ambitions of Hirohito for his own advancement. More than enough of both sorts were put on SCAP lists, and it was left to Hirohito to rule out as many as he could. Lord Privy Seal Kido's secretary, Matsudaira Yasumasa, went over the lists, felt out the supposed criminals as to their willingness to stand trial, and indicated to Kido and the Emperor which men could be relied on and which, if possible, should be kept out of court. Neither MacArthur nor Hirohito had to keep up with every sordid detail of these transactions, but they did have to review the results and agree on them. Every few weeks SCAP published a new roster of men who should report for imprisonment.

Each list was more difficult than the one before for Hirohito to accept. The first consisted of Tojo and his Cabinet ministers. The second included former Prime Minister Hirota Koki, a whelp of the Black Dragon who, in 1936, had betrayed his tong to throw Hirohito the support of one dissident tail of it. The list of November 3 took in the 1944 Prime Minister Koiso, the 1941 Foreign Minister Matsuoka, and three important generals of the Strike-North or Fight-Russia Faction who had last enjoyed Hirohito's full confidence in 1934. One of them, General Honjo Shigeru, the conqueror of Manchuria, had served from 1933 to 1936 as Hirohito's chief aide-de-camp. Having fallen out with Hirohito in 1936 over the issue of fighting Russia to the north or the Western colonial powers to the south, General Honjo felt that he could not, in good conscience, serve the Emperor as a defendant in court. When he received the summons to present himself at Sugamo Prison, he held his tongue in the only way he knew by ripping open his belly with a shortsword.

The fourth list, published December 3, branded no less than fifty-nine individuals. It was so objectionable to Hirohito that it temporarily disrupted liaison between palace and Dai Ichi Building and had to be completed without benefit of Japanese advice. As a result it contained some curiosities.

It called for the arrest of General Tada Hayao who had struggled vainly as vice chief of staff to prevent the rape of Nanking. And it left General Shimomura Sadamu, who had forced through the Nanking attack plans, at large as the Shidehara government's demobilization board director. The list also indicted the learned Dr. Okawa Shumei, a dangerous man to put on trial because, in the 1920's, he had given indoctrination lectures in the palace to Hirohito's cabal of young officers, and in the 1930's, he had served a token prison term for organizing the assassination of a financier, an industrialist, and a prime minister who opposed Hirohito's policies. A third controversial name on the list was that of Arima Yoriyasu, the "Socialist Count." Arima had recruited left-wing backing for Konoye's wartime one-party system but he was also a cousin-in-law of the Empress.

Most insupportable of all, the December list included seventy-one-year-old Prince Nashimoto Morimasa, the senior member of the imperial family. Elder brother of the Emperor's two scheming uncles, Prince Higashikuni and Prince Asaka, Nashimoto was the highest ranking of the four field marshals of the Japanese army. He was also the chief priest of Ise, Japan's cardinal shrine where dwelt the spirit of Amaterasu, the ancestral sun goddess. It was Nashimoto who had journeyed to Manchuria in June of 1937 to arrange with Tojo the outbreak of war with China. In this sense, he was the author of the whole eight years of hellish war, but whether or not SCAP's investigators knew it has never been revealed. No charges were ever pressed against Nashimoto. He was merely held in Sugamo Prison for five months until Hirohito had agreed to all of MacArthur's legislative reforms for Japan. In the eyes of the Japanese people, it was good for the image of the Throne to have a member of the imperial family bearing some share in the punishment for the war. But the indignity was monumental. Venerable prince and chief priest though he was, Nashimoto cleaned toilets at Sugamo Prison along with the rest of the Class A war criminal suspects. A heavy old man of porcine, jovial features, he went about his menial chores with a philosophical good humor that was put down to his credit.

On December 6, three days after the December list had been published, SCAP announced a codicil of two more names to be added to the roster. They were those of Lord Privy Seal Kido and Prince Konoye, Hirohito's two most intimate advisors. The decision to take them had been made in SCAP's war crimes section during early November. By the time that the public announcement was made, Hirohito had already reconciled himself to it and resumed his bitter relationship with the conqueror. Kido's diary reveals that the arrests were handled with exquisite deliberation and ceremony, making it as easy on Hirohito as possible.

Kido had advised the Emperor in October that he would be willing to serve as a war criminal. He asked only that his office of lord privy seal might be abolished with him. On October 14, he arranged to borrow a particularly beautiful suburban villa from a wealthy industrialist to live in during his last days of freedom. For the next month, however, he was too busy to occupy it and was spending from one to three hours every day in private audience with Hirohito. Finally on November 10 he submitted to a three-hour interrogation by a SCAP investigating team at the Meiji Building. He returned to the palace to accompany Hirohito to Ise Shrine and the old capital of Kyoto.

At Ise the roofs are like those of palm-thatched South Sea island huts—steeply gabled in the ancient imperial style with rafters crossing and extending outward in V's against the sky. Hirohito walked alone into the inner shrine where only he and other anointed priests and priestesses of his family are allowed. There he remained for an hour apologizing for losing the war to his supposed ancestress, Amaterasu the sun goddess. In Kyoto he repeated the apology at the shrines of his grandfather Meiji and of the supposed first Emperor Jimmu. Kido noted with great relief that the spectators along the imperial progress seemed reverent and respectful as they had been before the war. There were no great crowds of children and factory workers marshaled by the police as there had been in prewar days, but old men and women sat on mats beside the railway tracks and bowed as the train passed.

On the days that followed, members of the imperial family went on pilgrimages to the tombs of the other one hundred twenty-one Emperors who had ruled in Japan. On November 20, Kido accompanied Hirohito to Yasukuni Shrine in Tokyo, the Valhalla for the souls of warriors who had died away from home in battle. Four days later, after seeing to innumerable last-minute details, Kido went to the palace for his last day in office. He drank champagne with the Emperor and thanked him for various farewell gifts including a box of canned goods, a barrel of saké, an antique inkstone, a vase, a scroll, and two checks totaling $8,000.

On Tuesday, November 27, Kido cleaned out his safe deposit vault. On Wednesday he returned to Ise Shrine and Kyoto for his own report to the gods. The following Monday he was back in Tokyo and finally took up residence in the exquisite suburban villa he had borrowed. He devoted Tuesday and Wednesday to reading books, a pastime which he had been promising himself for twenty years. On Thursday, December 6, the radio announced that SCAP had ordered his and Konoye's arrest, effective December 16. "Having expected it," he wrote in his diary, "I heard the news with a calm heart." For the next ten days—his last days of freedom —he made an almost ostentatious display of his tranquility. He strolled in the gardens of his villa, wrote poems, played croquet, and performed a service at his household god shelf to explain to the family spirits their removal to new and temporary domicles.

The day after the announcement that Kido would be arrested, a petty chamberlain called at his retirement villa to bring him news from the palace.

The Emperor had told his grand chamberlain, "I would like to call Kido to the palace for a last visit."

The grand chamberlain, an admiral, had replied, "Kido is now a war criminal suspect so he may hesitate to come out of politeness. Possibly it is better for Your Highness not to see him at the present time."

"From the American point of view," said the Emperor, "Kido may be a war criminal, but from our nation's point of view he is a man to be acclaimed."

On hearing of this conversation from the petty chamberlain Kido felt deeply moved. "If the Emperor summons me," he declared, "I will come."

And so at 6:00 A.M. on December 10 Kido received an order to present himself at the palace that evening. He put on his old working clothes of striped pants and cutaway, stopped to worship at the tomb of his grandfather, and presented himself at his old office in the Imperial Household Ministry at 5:00 P.M. A chamberlain was there to greet him: "The Emperor is waiting for you. Please go to the Imperial Library at once."

Kido drove across the neglected gardens where the maple leaves lay unraked in windfalls. "As usual," he wrote, "I met the Emperor in his private study."

Hirohito was in a sentimental mood. "At this season I am filled with regrets," he said. "Please take care of your health. I think you understand my feelings completely, for we had talked to one another always. So please explain fully to the others in prison."

"I swear I will follow the Imperial Will," said Kido thickly. And Hirohito, in his most charming manner, at once took the conversation off into pleasant byways of reminiscence, "telling stories," as Kido wrote, "in all directions." After the tête-à-tête Empress Nagako came in and presented Kido with a precious antique table. A group of Kido's former colleagues joined the royal gathering with more presents, and wines and dinner followed. At about eight o'clock the Empress bestowed on Kido, as a last parting gift, a tray of doughnuts which she had baked with her own hand. Then, slightly tipsy, he retired from the Imperial Presence and returned to the Imperial Household Ministry to pay his farewells to the other chamberlains. He retired for the night to the home of a friend's mistress.

Before he went to bed, his son-in-law, Harvard graduate Tsuru Shigeto, a specialist in American law, called on him and told him: "It will seem to Americans that the Emperor is guilty if his privy seal tries to accept responsibility and take all blame for the war upon himself. Conversely, if the privy seal maintains his innocence, then the opposite impression will be made and the Emperor, in American eyes, will be judged not guilty. This is their way of thinking, so it is necessary to consider well the matter of lawyers for you." Kido thanked his son-in-law, asked him to get the best lawyers, and, if possible, to talk to the chief American prosecutor.

Tsuru succeeded in having lunch with the prosecutor on December 15. On hearing his report Kido prepared cheerfully to present himself the next morning for incarceration at Omori, a former prison camp for Allied P.O.W.'s.

Prince Konoye, who was supposed to accompany Kido to prison, held a party that night at his luxurious suburban Hate-China Villa, which he had christened precisely eight years earlier during the rape of Nanking. The close friends and relatives who were his guests reported afterwards that he was his usual languid, cynical, witty self. When they had gone, he put on pajamas and a silken robe. On the low table beside his bed, he laid out some of his favorite books and the best of the essays he had written for the Peace Faction in exoneration of the Emperor. One of the books was a morocco-bound copy of Oscar Wilde's *De Profundis*. And one of the passages he had marked in it for posterity was this: "I must say to myself that I ruined myself and that nobody great or small can be ruined except by his own hand."

The one paper on the table which SCAP released to news reporters explained Konoye's motives for suicide: "I have been gravely concerned over the fact that I have committed certain errors in handling state affairs since the outbreak of the China Incident. I believe my real intentions are even now understood and appreciated by my friends, including not a few friends in America. The winner is too boastful and the loser too servile. World public opinion, which is at present full of overexcitement . . . will in time recover calmness and balance. Only then will a just verdict be rendered." A few hours later Prince Konoye took poison, dying as sybaritically as he had lived. He had failed to steer Hirohito from an unsuccessful war. He had proved himself a failure in the stratagems of defeat. He did not trust himself to shield the Emperor under cross-examination in court. And most important, perhaps, he was a snob and could not bear the thought of sharing a cell with a commoner like Tojo.

Half blind without his glasses, the myopic Lord Privy Seal Kido stood naked before an American doctor in the infirmary at Omori prison camp. Disinfectant was squirted over him, his clothes and possessions were catalogued by American M.P.'s, and finally he was allowed to dress and join his fellow war criminal suspects. At that moment the barons and marquises who had attended Konoye's soiree the night before were telephoning one another to transmit the intelligence that Prince Konoye had really gone through with his boast and was now dead. The last arrests had been made. More than one hundred of Hirohito's loyal retainers were in American hands. How many would be tried, how many hanged, would depend now on the alacrity with which Hirohito and the Cabinet of Prime Minister Shidehara made laws to reform Japan. MacArthur told the courtier who had had charge of negotiating the war criminal lists: "Now that the dead wood has been removed, Emperor Hirohito can be a real Emperor."

GOD IS DEAD

Land reform, disestablishment of state Shinto, women's suffrage, antitrust legislation—these were reforms which would be presented to the Diet and passed without murmur. Landlords, priests, politicians, and industrialists could be trusted to find their own loopholes in the new laws, their own ways of maintaining the status quo. The Emperor himself was willing to give away much of his personal wealth. But the fundamental charter of the land, the description of the Japanese way of government, the Constitution—that was different. To be forced to accept an imitation of the American constitution was a humiliation and danger which no one in the ruling classes could bear. While war criminal suspects languished in prison camp, the possibility of constitutional reform was tabled in committee and studied and studied again. In its place Hirohito sought to compromise and temporize by accepting a redefinition of his religious status. The suggestion came from a curious quarter, a former American Y.M.C.A. leader.

In the first week of September, when the palace was still looking for effective go-betweens to use in dealing with MacArthur, Prince Konoye had enlisted the help of Japan's most eminent native-born American, William Merrell Vories. Vories was an evangelist, an architect, and a millionaire. Kansas bred, he had come to Japan for the Y.M.C.A. in 1905 and had stayed to make a fortune selling the patent ointment Metholatum. At the same time he had designed and built many of Japan's largest modern buildings, had founded a thriving Christian sect, the Omi Brotherhood, had married the daughter of Viscount Hitotsu Yanagi, and had become a naturalized Japanese citizen. Hirohito considered Vories a friend because, shortly before the outbreak of the Pacific War, he had arranged to give Vories an "accidental" private audience. A Court chamberlain had visited Vories and suggested to him that he would find it rewarding to go to the Kyoto Palace at a specific hour on a specific day and wait there beside a specific flowering bush in the palace garden. When he did as he was told, the Emperor, down in Kyoto on a visit, chanced to pass that way on a stroll and stopped to chat with him. They talked about Japan and religion for almost an hour. Hirohito was impressed by Vories' patriotism for his adopted country and his command of the Japanese language.

On September 7, 1945, while inspecting abdication quarters for Hirohito in Kyoto, Konoye had asked Vories to visit MacArthur and sound out his intentions. Vories agreed to do what he could, but two days later, when he went to SCAP headquarters in Yokohama, he was treated like a collaborator. MacArthur refused to see him and sent word through an aide that if Konoye or Hirohito had anything to say they should say it directly without use of emissaries; also, that if they hoped for concessions, they should come bearing specific proposals for reform. Vories reported his rebuff to Konoye and was asked to stay in Tokyo and help think of a suitable reform.

On September 12 Vories awoke in the Imperial Hotel a block and a half south of the Dai Ichi Building with what he considered to be a godsent idea. Let the Emperor publicly renounce his divinity. Educated Japanese, including Hirohito himself, had never considered the Emperor a god in the omnipotent, omnipresent Western sense. Rather, he was a *kami* or immortal spirit. All things Japanese, even rocks and trees and women, were thought to possess some share of *kami*. The Emperor had the largest and most potent share. To the Japanese mind there was nothing superhuman or moral about *kami;* it was the distilled essence of a man, his special charm and efficacy. The spirit world to which it belonged was an exact shadow of the real world. No god ruled over it. It was animated entirely by worldly spirits. Japan's social hierarchy extended into it, and the Emperor when he died joined the souls of other Emperors in presiding over it. Holding such beliefs, the Emperor would find it easy and meaningless to renounce his Western-style title to divinity.

Vories transmitted his idea to Konoye who took it to the Emperor. A dictionary revealed that the English word "God" meant "the Spirit of monotheism; the Master Craftsman of all things." Hirohito acknowledged that he was neither of these and Konoye the next day visited MacArthur. He found that SCAP welcomed Vories' suggestion with enthusiasm. During the next two months, however, the idea hung fire. It was revived in November to use as a poker chip in the final negotiations about war criminal lists. Then, in December, when Prince Nashimoto, the senior member of the imperial family, and Lord Privy Seal Kido, the Emperor's chief advisor, were safely in Allied hands, SCAP submitted a draft of a "non-divinity proclamation" such as it would like Hirohito to make. Hoping that it might serve in place of a new constitution, Hirohito had the Imperial Household Ministry draw up a counterdraft. After discussion the two drafts were dovetailed. Hirohito and MacArthur personally edited the respective Japanese and English texts, and an approved version was submitted to Prime Minister Shidehara for consideration by the Cabinet. The prime minister found the wording "too Japanese in spirit." He revised it in his best Gettysburg Address English and had it translated back into stilted Japanese.

Hirohito approved the Japanese version, MacArthur the English one, and both were issued together as the Emperor's New Year's message to his people on January 1, 1946. The key sentences were buried at the end of a long rescript in which Hirohito reiterated the charter oath made by his grandfather, Emperor Meiji, in the spring of 1868: to govern the nation through deliberative assemblies according to public opinion; to unite the land in single-minded pursuit of the national interest; to give every individual the opportunity to pursue the calling of his choice; to abolish "all base customs of former times" and follow "the laws of heaven and earth"; "to seek knowledge in every corner of the earth in order to extend the foundations of the Empire." This much was belly talk to tell the people that Japan had slipped back to the humble position of 1868 and that it might be a hundred years before Japan could rise again. Then came the crucial sentences which had gone through so much editing. Buried as they might be, couched as they might be in an alien phraseology, they were a revelation to most Japanese:

> The ties between Us and Our people have always stood on mutual trust and affection. They do not depend upon mere legends and myths. They are not predicated upon the false concept that the Emperor is divine and that the Japanese people are superior to other races and fated to rule the world.

When Hirohito published his annual thirty-one-syllable *tanka* for the New Year's poetry contest a few days later, he suggested to his subjects that they must not be confused by the frosting of dissimulation forced upon them by circumstances:

> Courageous the pine
> that does not change its color
> under winter snow.
> Truly the men of Japan
> should be a forest of pines.

DICTATING DEMOCRACY

While the senior kinsman of the blood, the venerable, seventy-one-year-old Prince Nashimoto continued each night to lay his bald head on a prison pallet, Hirohito and MacArthur, through their respective intermediaries, fought a bitter battle over the Japanese Constitution. Consideration of constitutional reform had begun on October 8, 1945. Then Lord Privy Seal Kido, Prince Konoye, and Prime Minister Shidehara had agreed, first, that the old Constitution could not be improved except possibly by changing a few words in it; and, second, that SCAP would take unilateral action unless the Japanese changed far more than a few words. Prime Minister Shidehara felt it would be "easiest to surrender and keep the documents of negotiation" in order to repudiate the imposed MacArthur constitution at some later date. Hirohito had a higher view of his responsibilities and felt that he must make it clear from the beginning that he would not be an accomplice in changing a sacred document handed down to him from his grandfather. Accordingly, two committees were set up: one of courtiers, headed by Prince Konoye; the other of Cabinet ministers and scholars, headed by an expert on constitutional law, Matsumoto Joji. When the moat, figuratively speaking, froze over between the Dai Ichi Building and the palace in mid-November, Prince Konoye and his committee submitted a report to the Throne that the old Constitution needed no substantial changes and then made a great public show of resigning. Having thus washed his hands of responsibility for reform, Hirohito directed the Cabinet's committee on constitutional reform to pursue "detailed studies."

Months passed while the Cabinet committee used a thesaurus to rewrite the Constitution in new words with the same old meanings. Finally in late January, under great pressure from SCAP, the Cabinet committee submitted a "Gist" and an "Explanation" of the changes it proposed. MacArthur found the changes insufficient. He noted that the Emperor was no longer "sacred and inviolable" but "supreme and inviolable"; also that too many clauses ended with the loophole "except as otherwise provided by law." Accordingly MacArthur penciled a note on the minimal provisions which he expected to find in the new document: "The Emperor's rights and duties . . . will be exercised in accordance with the constitution and [be] responsible to the basic will of the people as provided therein. . . . War as a sovereign right of the nation is abolished . . . and no rights of belligerency will ever be conferred upon any Japanese force. . . . The feudal system of Japan will cease."

On February 3, 1946, after MacArthur assured himself that the Japanese Court and Cabinet would not be able to meet his demands without detailed coaching, he handed his scribbled notes to General Whitney and told him to have his Government Section mount a crash program and draft a sample constitution of the sort that would be acceptable. Whitney delegated the task to his right-hand man, Colonel Charles L. Kades.

Nine days later, the American constitution for Japan was ready. General Whitney laid it before the Cabinet Constitutional Reform Committee at a meeting at Foreign Minister Yoshida's residence that afternoon. "Gentlemen," he said, "the Supreme Commander has found your proposals for revising the constitution inacceptable. Your draft falls far short of the broad and liberal reorganization of the government structure . . . which the Allied Powers could regard as significant evidence that Japan has learned the lessons of war and defeat and is prepared to act as a responsible member of a peaceful community. Accordingly the Supreme Commander has had a detailed statement prepared of the principles he deems basic. We are presenting this statement to you in the form of a draft constitution. I advise you to give it your fullest consideration and I propose that you use it as a guide in renewed efforts to prepare a revised constitution. Of course there is no compulsion upon you . . . but the Supreme Commander is determined that the constitutional issue shall be brought before the people well in advance of the general elections in April. . . . If the Cabinet is unable to prepare a suitable and acceptable draft before that time, General MacArthur is prepared to lay this statement of principles directly before the people. I suggest, therefore, that you read it here and now while we wait outside."

For a moment there was no sound except a peculiarly Japanese hiss of intaken breath. The tiny, barrel-shaped Foreign Minister Yoshida, dressed in white, scowled a black Niebelung scowl. Then Shirasu Jiro, his live-in assistant and for twelve years a golfing crony of imprisoned Lord Privy Seal Kido, ushered Whitney and his aides outside into the artfully landscaped garden. He showed them to a little pavilion where they could be comfortable and left them with the sarcastic, bitter words of the vanquished, "Please bask in the atomic sunshine." Almost an hour later he returned to summon them, apologizing profusely for the long wait. "Not at all, Mr. Shirasu," said Whitney. "We have enjoyed your atomic sunshine very much." At that moment a B-29 happened to roar over, lending weight to his retort. The committee promised to use the statement of principles as the basis for a new attempt at constitutional revision.

Two days later, on February 14, Shirasu, the foreign minister's assistant, sent Whitney a letter explaining, "Your way is so American in the way that is straight and direct. Their way must be Japanese in the way that is roundabout, twisted and narrow." In the same letter Shirasu reminded Whitney, "I am afraid that I have already accelerated the paper shortage by writing this mumble but I know you will forgive me for my shortcomings for which my late father is also partly responsible."

Four days later Whitney received another letter from the committee by which he learned that "some of the roses of the West, when cultivated in Japan, lose their fragrance"; also that his brain child, the American version of the constitution, had not yet been translated into Japanese. Whitney saw MacArthur and MacArthur saw Hirohito. On Washington's Birthday, Whitney met again with the committee and ordered it to present the American draft immediately at the palace for consideration by the Emperor. Foreign Minister Yoshida did as told that same afternoon and was astonished to hear Hirohito say, albeit stiffly, "Upon these principles will truly rest the welfare of Our people and the rebuilding of Japan."

The committee obediently fussed over the translation of Whitney's constitution, made a few changes in it, and had it inscribed on fine parchment. It was submitted to MacArthur on March 4 and approved with minor qualifications. Whitney organized another crash program to edit it and reconcile the Japanese and English texts. For thirty-six hours his Government Section sat with the Japanese committee and an army of translators to thrash out the final wording. K-rations and five-gallon cans of coffee were served continuously. At 5:30 on the afternoon of March 5, 1946, MacArthur approved the completed text. The next day he announced to newsmen the "decision of the Emperor and the government of Japan to submit to the Japanese people a new and enlightened constitution."

The general election at which the people were to pass upon the Constitution was scheduled for April 10. As the campaigning reached its noisiest, Hirohito quietly submitted to another concession which he had struggled to evade ever since it had first been suggested to him by Prince Higashikuni the previous October. It was that all members of the imperial family should give up their titles and become commoners except Hirohito and his immediate sons and brothers. Four days before the election, Prime Minister Shidehara called on Hirohito at his vacation palace at Hayama on the seashore to tell him that the first step had been taken: the Cabinet had accepted the resignation of fifteen princes of the blood from the House of Peers. The process would be completed two years later in October of 1947 when Hirohito attended a great wake in the palace at which fifty-one sisters and cousins and aunts met to drink a last bitter cup of commiseration at their downgrading to the ranks of plain citizens. With their titles went most of their emoluments. The vast imperial family fortune had been impounded and returned to the people. Imperial forests and gardens had been made national parks. Imperial treasures had been turned over to museums. Many of the imperial stocks and bonds and an unknown quantity of gold and silver had been secretly given to loyal friends of the Throne who could be trusted to handle it astutely and return it with the accrued gains at the end of Kido's suggested one-hundred-year period of quiescence. Investigators of SCAP's Economic Section traced some of these underground reserves, and the rest must have been depleted by the postwar inflation which dropped the exchange rate of the yen from 15 to 50 to 270 and finally to 360 per dollar.

On April 10, 1946, a record turnout at the polls expressed favor for the Constitution. "Oh? Has it been translated into Japanese already?" joked the voters. But they voted for it enthusiastically, and on November 3, Hirohito would declare it the law of the land. It stated in part: ". . . The Japanese people forever renounce war as a sovereign right of the nation. . . . Land, sea, and air forces, as well as other war potential, will never be maintained. The right of belligerency of the state will not be recognized." This was MacArthur's own favorite clause, put in at his insistence, but in three years he felt compelled by the Soviet menace to betray it, to give Japan a lesson in the interpretation of constitutions, to insist that Japan build up forces for self-defense: an Army and Air Force of police which in twenty short years would grow to be the most highly skilled and up-to-date military establishment in Asia. By 1970 it would have a morale-lifting tradition all its own. Instead of answering to the traditional banzai with a great roar of "Banzai!"—May the Emperor live 10,000 years!—it would respond only to a materialist catechism: "Do you all want color television?"

"Hai!"

"Do you all want electric rice cookers?"

"Hai!"

Sometimes in drill, when no Americans are watching, the men of the Self-Defense Forces re-enact a scene that took place years ago when the new American order, "Eyes right," was first screamed at a regiment on parade. Eyes turn right, as if to ogle a passing girl, but chins and noses remain pointing straight ahead in perfectly disciplined cynicism.

IMPERIAL BARGAIN

As soon as the Japanese people had endorsed the American constitution, old Prince Nashimoto was finally released from his four months of unexplained detention in prison. The days of imperial insecurity were over. The Emperor had paid his ransom. He had given up most of his wealth, all of his favorite retainers, many of his family's privileges and titles, his claim to divinity, and now his supreme power under the Constitution. It was an enormous price but having made his bargain Hirohito would not renege on it. He would tour the country making friends with the people. He would become known to them as Mr. Ah-so-desuka, Mr. Oh-is-that-so. Everyone would remember his visit to Hiroshima, on an anniversary of its bombing, when he said dryly, "There seems to have been considerable destruction here." Finally, when personal appearances were no longer necessary, Hirohito would retire behind a façade of penitence to become the senior national consultant. He would let it be known that he was giving himself entirely to his hobby of marine biology, and, with the help of his laboratory assistant, would publish a serious scientific book, the beautifully illustrated *Opisthobranchia of Sagami Bay*. Domestic Japanese politics had never much interested him, and now, for several decades, Japan would have little voice in her role in international politics.

It was MacArthur's part of the bargain to keep the Emperor out of court at any cost. On May 3, twenty days after Prince Nashimoto's release from prison, the International Military Tribunal for the Far East would arraign twenty-eight of Hirohito's retainers as Class A war criminals, thereby beginning a trial of them that would last for two and a half years. It was to be a unique experiment in controlled historical research, and great effort had gone into making it a political success. While cajoling, bribing, and blackmailing the Imperial Court into co-operating with Occupation therapy for Japan, MacArthur at the same time had been fighting for the Emperor's life. More than Hirohito knew and far more than he could believe, there was a genuine desire on the part of many Americans and most of the Allied governments to treat him as a common criminal.

The various national positions on his case had been communicated to the United States at the time of surrender. Nationalist China, whose analysts had the best grasp of the historical facts and also the most reason to feel vengeful, demanded flatly that Hirohito be hanged. Communist Russia had doctrinaire theories against emperors in general but voiced surprisingly little objection to the American policy of keeping Hirohito in power as a necessary tool for renovation. Australia advised "that international law should not give immunity to sovereigns"; that Japanese "breaches of the laws of war" were "so terrible" and "so widespread that the Emperor and his ministers must have learned of them" and "abetted them if they did not take steps to prevent them"; "that it would be a travesty of justice seriously reflecting on the U.N. to punish the common Japanese or Korean guard while granting immunity to others perhaps even more guilty." The government of New Zealand concurred but in more moderate language.

MacArthur, having inherited the Emperor's absolute power in Japan, could afford to disregard the positions of the Allies but the U.S. State Department could not. It argued successfully, however, that the choice of war criminals to be tried should be made by the U.S. intelligence agents who were "studying the evidence in Japan." Only the disgruntled Australians refused to be put off by such assurances. The files in Canberra are full of complaints from officials and journalists who visited Japan in the early months of the Occupation. They professed shock to find that MacArthur knew little about prewar Japanese history and took little interest in the fragmentary information being turned up by his War Crimes Board. They rightly guessed that the only evidence tending to exonerate the Emperor was of words rather than of deeds. They felt that MacArthur was showing a cynical disregard for historical truth and legal justice. MacArthur, on the other hand, felt that the Australians were more interested in the past than the future, more intent upon revenge than rehabilitation. He believed that the Emperor, if he had fangs at all, could be emptied of venom, rendered harmless, and used.

If MacArthur had had his way he would have extended to all Japanese leaders the same clemency that he felt obliged to show the Emperor. Politicians in both Washington and London, however, needed scapegoats to punish for the mass killings and tortures of the Japanese concentration camps. MacArthur bowed to their political necessity, but the inconsistency of punishing subordinates and pardoning superiors troubled him. As he was to write later, "The principle of holding criminally responsible the political leaders of the vanquished in war was repugnant to me."

When in October of 1945, at the insistence of the Dean Acheson group in the State Department, the Joint Chiefs of Staff ordered MacArthur to begin prosecuting war criminals, he countered with "urgent and repeated appeals" that "any criminal responsibility attached to Japanese political leaders . . . should be limited to an indictment for the attack on Pearl Harbor." His stratagem was to stage a quick trial of Tojo and the members of his 1941 Cabinet and thus avoid an investigation of wider scope that might implicate the Emperor and jeopardize the Occupation program of reform. When the Joint Chiefs insisted on a full showpiece trial, MacArthur asked to be "relieved of all responsibility having to do with the actual trial procedure." Having been assigned the formidable task of reforming Japanese society, he did not wish to impair his image as an inspirational leader in the eyes of the Japanese people.

On November 14, therefore, the trials were put in the charge of a U.S. prosecutor to be sent from Washington. And on November 25, when the palace had temporarily severed relations with the Dai Ichi Building over selection of those to be arrested, SCAP's information officers released to the Japanese press a detailed account of MacArthur's struggles with Washington on the war criminals' behalf. The press release served a double function. It cleared MacArthur with the Japanese, and it warned Hirohito that if he did not co-operate SCAP would leave him to the tender graces of the trial prosecutor. Hirohito promptly capitulated and the names of Lord Privy Seal Kido and Prince Konoye were put on the wanted list the very day that the U.S. prosecutor arrived in Tokyo.

RIGGING JUSTICE

The prosecutor who took the burden of the trials from MacArthur's conscience was a politicians' lawyer, a former assistant attorney general, Joseph Berry Keenan. In the early 1930's Keenan had made a name for himself by sending Machine Gun Kelly to the penitentiary and framing the Lindbergh Kidnapping Law. But a decade of Washington whiskey, politics, and poker had taken their toll. By the time he came to Japan he was described by one of his friends as "a florid, aggressive but not unkindly man." His enemies pointed out that in court he did not always have command of the facts at his disposal, that his language was often imprecise and full of Fourth of July oratory, that his delivery, especially in afternoon sessions, was sometimes thick and blurry.

On November 15, before leaving Washington, Keenan had discussed "his mission" with President Truman and Attorney General Tom C. Clark. On December 7, the day after his arrival in Tokyo, Keenan spent the morning with MacArthur and declared when he emerged from the Dai Ichi Building that he had found "decided harmony" in the views of the President and the Supreme Commander. Less than a week later he announced to the press that he and MacArthur "had sifted the Emperor's war record" and found nothing incriminating in it. He hoped, he said, for a speedy trial of Tojo and his clique for their guilt in the events which had transpired since July 1937, the opening of the war with China. He saw that it was a convenient date, because it marked the beginning of Tojo's rise to positions of policy-making responsibility. Three days later he conceded that he had been hasty in naming it and that SCAP had ordered the Japanese government to produce police and trial records for five prior incidents which had occurred between 1932 and 1937.

On December 15, Keenan had lunch with Lord Privy Seal Kido's son-in-law and gave him a message which cheered Kido on the eve of his imprisonment. A few days later Keenan made the acquaintance of Kido's successor in the Throne Room and former secretary, Matsudaira Yasumasa. By now Matsudaira was an expert on every phase of the war criminal issue. From the beginning he had handled all liaison on the subject between SCAP and the palace and had interviewed each of the Class A suspects before they had given themselves up. He now helped Keenan to find a suitable Japanese secretary with whom he could conduct business. The offered helper turned out to be a young aristocratic professor of German and English philosophy who had been a petty propagandist during the war—one of those denizens of the literary demimonde in Japan who arrange meetings between writers and stories. Keenan had brought with him from Washington a staff of twenty-four lawyers and fourteen assistants who were to be the nucleus of the American Prosecution Section at the tribunal. He had inherited the files of SCAP's War Crimes Board and the suspects it had arrested. Now through the good offices of his new secretary he would inherit most of the board's contacts as well. Men and women of the Peace Faction who had trooped to Yokohama in the opening days of the Occupation to renew acquaintance with old Japan hands on MacArthur's staff were obliged to repeat the performance and ask for an introduction to Keenan. The prosecutor enjoyed his popularity and welcomed the assistance given him. He needed documents to put in evidence and witnesses to testify in court. To stage any sort of trial, fair or foul, would be no mean accomplishment, he felt, in Japan's closed society.

By New Year's Day 1946, when Hirohito was proclaiming himself a common mortal and MacArthur was still waiting for the Japanese to submit an acceptable draft of a new constitution, Keenan and his lawyers had put down their roots in Tokyo and were hard at work preparing for the great trial ahead. MacArthur, through the State Department, sent out invitations to the other principal nations which had fought against Japan asking them to participate and send legal brains to preside. The panel of judges was announced in Washington on January 18. Each name on it was one of the most highly respected in the legal ranks of each of the Allied nations. There were to be eleven countries represented: the United States, Great Britain, the Netherlands, France, Canada, Australia, New Zealand, Russia, China, the Philippines, and India.

In writing stories about preparations for the trial, correspondents in Tokyo inevitably suggested to U.S. readers that MacArthur was shielding the Emperor. European lawyers and judges in transit through the United States on their way to the Tokyo trials were all asked their opinions on Hirohito's guilt. The Dean Acheson faction in the State Department renewed pressure on the Joint Chiefs of Staff, demanding that everything about the forthcoming trials be scrupulously aboveboard and fair.

MacArthur, on January 27, made a straight face of it and reassured his chiefs: "There is no specific or tangible evidence to connect the Emperor with responsibility for any decision of the Japanese government during the past ten years. The Japanese people would regard indictment of the Emperor as a grave betrayal. They understood the acceptance of the Potsdam terms as preserving the position of the Emperor. Trial of the Emperor would lead to an upheaval. There would be action by resistance groups. This could be held in check by the Occupation forces but it is not unlikely that there would be a complete breakdown of Japanese governmental machinery. The whole plan of occupation would have to be changed." MacArthur added that he would "make no recommendation concerning the Emperor," but advised strongly that, if it were decided to try him, a million troops should be stationed in Japan and it would be necessary in addition to have 20,000 or more civilian administrative personnel. "Plans should be made at once."

Two days after filing this recommendation, MacArthur was visited in the Dai Ichi Building by the Far Eastern Commission, the Allied board which sat in Washington to advise the United States on the Occupation of Japan. The commission had come to Tokyo for its first on-the-spot look at Occupation progress. The Australian members of the commission sent home a detailed report on MacArthur's reasons for holding the Emperor guiltless:

> His views, he stated, were based mainly on personal talks with the Emperor himself. MacArthur gave a description of the Emperor's personality in which such phrases as "good blood," "wears his clothes easily," "cultured man," "gentleman" occurred. . . . He summed up the Emperor's position as that of a stooge who had never had a positive thought in his life. The Emperor's sense of duty was high. If held responsible for Japan's aggression, he would accept his fate. Nothing in his life would become him like the leaving of it. . . . His execution would have the effect of making him a martyr with incalculable effect on the Japanese attitude.

The Far Eastern Commission went on its way grumbling, newspapermen turned to other stories, and MacArthur and Keenan faced the next hurdle: the arrival of the Allied judges. To guide eleven sharp legal minds from eleven different national backgrounds through a millrace of half-hidden Japanese history and bring them out in a serene pond of unanimity was a challenge of an order which Keenan had never faced before—not even in Al Capone's Chicago. It was agreed that the men whom Keenan would place on trial should be charged with "conspiracy to wage aggressive war" and with responsibility for "organized crimes against humanity," that is, atrocities. That the deeds had been done was beyond question. That they were crimes, however, was not felt by more than a tiny minority of Japanese. And that the selection of men in the dock were particularly responsi-

ble for them—more than any other group of leaders who had advised Hirohito in the last twenty years—was a doubtful proposition that would be
exceedingly difficult to prove. The most that could be said by thoughtful
Japanese was that Tojo had assumed responsibility for advising the Emperor to take the losing gamble against the United States in 1941. The
Japanese soldiers who had committed the atrocities did not usually blame
their superiors in the German fashion. Nor did they seem, for the most
part, to have found any sadistic satisfaction in their crimes. Rather, they
said that they had done what their society expected them to do.

For any jurist the Japanese attitude posed disquieting questions—social
and philosophical as well as legal. Not a single one of the twenty-eight
defendants, with the possible exception of Hashimoto Kingoro who had
sunk the *Panay* in 1937, was a small bourgeois gangster of Hitler's caliber.
Nor was there any ideological common denominator between them except
their lifelong loyalty to Hirohito. They had all served obediently under the
very best families, the most polite, wealthy, English-speaking people in all
Japan.

Fortunately for Keenan, Japanese atrocities had been committed on the
persons of citizens of every one of the nations which would be represented
by the judges. By parading witnesses to horrors, he could at least distract
the judges' attention from the unsettling questions, why the Japanese
felt no Germanic guilt and why they did not blame their superiors. Japan's
proven atrocities had begun at the outset of Hirohito's reign in a massacre
at the Chinese town of Tsinan in 1928. At that time none of the accused
had been in a position to take leadership responsibility but at least most of
them had been colonels. Tojo, awkwardly enough, had led an outwardly
blameless life as an Army bureaucrat until 1935 when he had assumed
charge of the secret police in Manchuria. To establish leadership responsibility for the policy of terror which Japan had pursued since 1928 would
require, rightly speaking, an intensive investigation of Japanese history
since at least 1910 when the leaders of 1928 were young. Keenan could
forsee a trial interminably mired in complexity if he went back that far. He
felt that he must assert his authority at once to establish boundaries and
ground rules for the investigation.

With the backing of Washington, Keenan had it understood by all judges
when they accepted their appointments that his Prosecution Section would
have the exclusive right to choose the men to be put on trial and the
evidence to be presented against them. This was a right of the prosecution
in most civilized countries and was accepted without demur. Having established it and having "sifted the evidence," Keenan proceeded arbitrarily to
restrict testimony about "the criminal conspiracy" charged against "Tojo's
military clique" to the period of atrocities since 1928. Whether Keenan
knew it or not, he was thus excluding from consideration the most truly

conspiratorial years. Before 1928, as will be particularized later in this book, Tojo and other members of the imperial cabal had appeared to be harmless junior officers who went freely in and out of the Imperial Palace. After 1928, when they became busy bureaucrats and important colonels and generals—when they began to organize military adventures abroad— they severed open connections with the palace and maintained a seemly distance from Hirohito.

To Keenan's 1928-and-after restriction on behalf of the prosecution, a further obfuscation was added by the defense. Every one of the accused was represented by one American lawyer and at least one Japanese lawyer. The American defenders were mostly able, if somewhat quixotic, volunteer lawyers from the ranks of the American Army. Because of their knowledge of English and of Anglo-American legal procedure, they were to do most of the speaking for the defense in court. They depended, however, on Japanese defense lawyers for the substance of their briefs. All the Japanese members of the defense were graduates of Tokyo or Kyoto Imperial University Law Schools and thus classmates and cousins of the leaders in Hirohito's bureaucracy. Most of them had assisted at rigged trials during the 1930's to defend the assassins and plotters of coups d'etat who had terrorized the Japanese nation into accepting the overlordship of Hirohito's militaristic cabal.

In early 1946, before the war criminal trials began, these Japanese lawyers for the defense met in secret to draw up rules which might guide them in presenting evidence on behalf of Tojo, Kido, and their other clients. They considered two propositions: whether or not to use evidence favorable to their clients but "disturbing" to the Emperor; whether or not to use evidence favorable to their clients but "prejudicial to the honor of the Japanese nation." They agreed to exclude all evidence which they judged to be unfavorable to the Emperor, but they voted down the second proposition on the grounds that it would be a "breach of human rights" to sacrifice their clients for the reputation of the country as a whole. They pledged instead "not to forget the importance of saving the nation." The American lawyers for the defense were not told of these resolutions by their colleagues nor given other reason to question the selection of information fed to them.

While Keenan restricted the evidence which could be presented for the prosecution and Japanese lawyers restricted evidence which could be presented for the defense, both parties worked with a common aim to find men willing to testify in court. The clearing ground for all evidence was the palace. The office of the former lord privy seal approved all defense witnesses and steered most prosecution witnesses into Keenan's hands. Because Japanese soldiers considered it treason to reveal information to the former enemy and because they might be easily trapped into telling the truth by their combined hostility and sense of samurai honor, it was no easy matter to provide witnesses who would serve. Men were needed who could reveal as much Japanese history as it had been decided to reveal, who could do so with accurate convincing detail, and who were smart, knowledgeable, and even-tempered enough to avoid being caught in contradictions. General Eichelberger of the Eighth Army, on landing in Yokohama, had told one of his first visitors, an old retired Japanese lieutenant general whom he had known in Siberia in 1920, that he feared it would be difficult to find witnesses for the inevitable war criminal trials. And so the word had gone out through the ranks of Peace Faction courtiers to find the best man in Japan for the job.

The ideal was discovered in retired Major General Tanaka Takayoshi—Tanaka Top-luck, as his name may be translated. Tanaka was a shambling, Rabelaisian giant of a man with a ribald sense of humor and an enormous, shaven, egg-shaped head four times the size of most men's. He kept in it a voluminous, almost comprehensive file of Japanese Army intrigues between 1921 and 1945. As a former operative in Army Intelligence, he had played a role in many of them personally. In 1923 he had attended special indoctrination classes inside the sacred walls of the palace. In 1928 he had helped plan the assassination of the ruler of Manchuria. In 1931 he had become the lover of Japan's leading girl spy, a Manchu princess, and with her had created the provocations for a small smokescreen war in Shanghai in 1932. Later, in 1938, he had helped Hirohito stop an unauthorized Army probe into Russia, the Lake Khassan Incident. "Monster Tanaka," as his messmates called him, had instant access to his vast memory and an intelligence quick enough to use and sift the information it provided according to the needs of the occasion. Most of all, Tanaka was brave; Tanaka was loyal to the Emperor; Tanaka hated Tojo. In 1942 he had fallen out with Tojo over the attack on America and had lived out the war years in retirement.

With the approval of Lord Privy Seal Matsudaira Yasumasa, the new imperial advisor, Tanaka was turned over to Keenan's interrogators in February of 1946. As soon as he overcame his hate for the conquerors, he became Keenan's most valuable asset, a loyal retainer of MacArthur and the Emperor, who would testify indifferently for the prosecution or the defense and could maintain his accuracy and affability even when produced as a hostile witness. In two years of service, under merciless attack from all quarters, asked to remember details of events ten and twenty years past, he made only one mistake and that of a single day in citing a date. Small wonder that, in 1970, Monster Tanaka was still considered by Japanese to enjoy the protection of the American Embassy in Tokyo as well as of the palace.

The hulking Tanaka soon became a familiar and bodyguard of Chief Prosecutor Keenan. The two shared a common language, French, and Tanaka learned to enjoy bourbon almost as much as if it were "Super-

Express," the best saké. According to Tanaka's published reminiscences, which are nothing compared to the voluminous notes which he has written but not published, Keenan used Tanaka as his guide to Japanese life. If Keenan wanted feminine companionship, he had only to insert the remark, *"Je suis fort,"* into a conversation and Tanaka would be on the phone making arrangements. Tanaka, in fact, was so knowledgeable that he could arrange places of entertainment where Keenan could stride in over the delicate *tatami* (matting) floors without going to the trouble, which he hated, of taking off his shoes. Keenan disapproved of the liaisons between American officers and Japanese noblewomen. "I like a little fun, too," he used to say, "but I don't mess around with amateurs. It's no good."

While the script was being written, while the actors were learning their lines, while Director Keenan and Producer MacArthur were sedulously humored by the Japanese playwrights and prompters, a set was designed to impress all with the seriousness and high purpose of the trial. The tribunal's two-and-a-half-year run was mounted in the old Japanese Military Academy auditorium on Ichigaya Heights next door to the building where War Minister Anami had spent his last days. The witness box occupied the center of the darkly paneled auditorium and was surrounded by tables for Japanese and American lawyers. At the right of the witness box, as one entered the room, stood a stepped, three-tiered dock for the defendants. At the left, in dark solemnity, towered an unusually high polished bench for the judges. Rimming the walls were balcony seats for spectators and glass-fronted boxes for correspondents and translators. Miles of wire gave everyone headphones over which the proceedings could be heard in simultaneous translation in a language of choice: French, Russian, Chinese, English, or Japanese. Sixty floodlights made the floor brighter than day. Hundreds of translators and lawyers were to put almost 200,000 pages of testimony, debate, correction, and collateral exhibits into the murky record before Tojo, Matsui, and five others were to be hanged. The case for the prosecution was to begin on June 13, 1946. The case for the defense was to run from February 1947 until April of 1948. The judges were to pronounce sentence on November 12, 1948. And the sentences were to be executed on December 23, 1948.

SOUR VERDICT

Of the eleven tribunal judges only one could be allowed to speak in court. Otherwise the trial would have become a babel. The others would have to pass their questions and suggestions in notes along the bench. By prior political arrangement the speaking role of tribunal president was awarded, on February 14, 1946, to the Australian judge, Sir William Webb, chief justice of Australia's vast northern state of Queensland. He had had almost two years of experience trying Japanese war criminals in New Guinea and

Rabaul, and he already knew so much about Japanese atrocities in those areas that American lawyers for the defense unsuccessfuly moved that he should disqualify himself as prejudiced.

Tribunal President Webb was a large, indefatigable, implacably keen man. His blue eyes stung from beneath his heavy dark brows. Deep lines bracketed his mouth. His nose was massive and his command of English Churchillian. He had a high sense of the dignity, integrity, and independence of his profession. If his secretary was not picked up by the jeep on time to come to work or if Webb's own driver was given a questionable traffic ticket by the American M.P.'s, then SCAP had to reckon with a trenchant legal memo. If the air conditioning or earphone system broke down in court, that too would be the subject of a Webb brief. There was hardly room for two prose styles the size of Webb's and MacArthur's in all Tokyo.

Webb was convinced that the Emperor—the man MacArthur was trying to build up as a "fine liberal gentleman"—was in actuality the first war criminal of Japan. In early 1945, responding to a request from his government, Webb had cabled the Australian foreign minister, Dr. H. V. Evatt: "Although there is a *prima facie* case against the Emperor, his case should be dealt with at the highest political and diplomatic level." For having so advised, before any trial took place, Webb also informed his government that he would feel obliged to disqualify himself from judgment at any trial of the Emperor. When he did preside at a trial from which the highest political and diplomatic levels had excluded the Emperor, he found himself champing at a bit he had put in his own mouth.

Webb's views towards the proceedings were partly shared by the most articulate of the lawyers present, Mr. Arthur Strettell Comyns Carr. Comyns Carr was the head of the British section for the prosecution. He was a bencher at Gray's Inn, a renowned London barrister of forty years' experience. Tall and thin, with a lined face full of intelligence and kindly humor, he had great courtroom charm: a lock of brown hair that kept falling over his forehead, a mellow voice, a wit that seemed gentle until it had sat a while and begun to etch. Comyns Carr had drawn up the original indictment of the twenty-eight accused. Like President Webb, he was thoroughly familiar with the known historical facts. Like Webb he was used to the Anglican style of court business. Unlike the American lawyers, who worked for Keenan to prosecute, or for the accused to defend, he had no special interest in shielding the Emperor. He and President Webb indulged in a game of gentle mockery concerning Hirohito. Comyns Carr would touch on incriminating circumstances, spin them out with fine irony, and then, when he went too far, would be called good-naturedly to order by Webb. At one point he went so far as to suggest that SCAP had suppressed a captured copy of the minutes of Hirohito's wartime Imperial Headquarters meetings. Such a document, had it still existed, would have proved beyond question the Emperor's war guilt or innocence. Yet no attempt was made in court to deny its existence. Comyns Carr merely dropped his suggestion and passed on to other matters when he was ruled out of order. His remarks were later stricken from the proceedings and can only be found in early unedited versions of the trial transcript.

Tribunal President Webb and British Prosecutor Comyns Carr early took a dislike to Chief Prosecutor Keenan of the United States, and to his style of law, his style of oratory, and most of all to the self-righteousness with which he went about his task of saving the Emperor. Soon the "Keenan-Webb feud" as it was dubbed by the American press began to break through professional decorum into open exchanges in court. Keenan had the worst of the stiff legal repartee, but he plunged through the chill winds of Webb's sarcasm and remained doggedly buoyant. Every month or two he called a news conference and announced once more that there was no evidence against the Emperor.

With a united Japan behind him and no opposition except the well-disciplined kidding of Webb and Comyns Carr, Keenan survived the first months of the trial unscathed. But as the trial went on and evidence mounted, U.S. journalists renewed old criticisms and asked increasingly difficult questions. To quiet them Keenan tried, on September 25, 1946, to elicit from witness Okada, a retired Japanese admiral and former prime minister, some evidence that the Emperor had had no foreknowledge of Pearl Harbor plans late in 1941. He succeeded in drawing from Okada a statement that the Emperor "disliked war," was unable to avoid it, and "was not concerned with winning or losing" it.

"I fail to see the relevance of that in this trial," interjected Tribunal President Webb.

KEENAN: Mr. President . . . the relevancy is the contention that these accused were engaged in the conspiracy and that they seized the power of Japan. They defrauded the people of Japan into believing that the Emperor was behind the war with the rescript that he issued a few days after or instantly—a few hours after—the attack that constituted lawlessness in Japan as well as a part of the breach of international law, too.
WEBB: This is the first time in this lengthy trial that that has been suggested and it is contrary to the prosecution's evidence.
KEENAN: Mr. President, I respectfully call this Tribunal's attention, as chief prosecutor appointed under this charter, to the fact that the accused who are in dock, are the people we believe are really responsible for the war. If there had been anyone else, they would have been in the dock, too.

Webb snorted and made no reply. As he had often pointed out in chambers, Lord Privy Seal Kido's diary showed that eight days before Pearl Harbor, Hirohito had rejected a last-minute plea from his brother, Prince Takamatsu, to reconsider the attack plans. He had done so after seeking reassurance from the chiefs of the General Staff that Japan had a good chance of winning or at least of negotiating an advantageous peace. From a variety of evidence Webb knew that Hirohito had reviewed the attack plan on Pearl Harbor in detail, had approved it, and of his own volition had signed the necessary declaration of war well in advance of the attack. Webb also knew that his government in Canberra had conceded to the American prosecution section the right to choose the men who would stand trial. Keenan, for his part, had staked the honor of the United States on the implausible proposition that no one in Japan had had any serious responsibility for the war except the handful of defendants in the dock. Thousands of Japanese who knew better and had done worse went about their free and gainful pursuits sniffing politely.

The next day, out of court, Keenan told the press for the hundredth time, "A thorough investigation has convinced the prosecution that there is no evidence available to support a charge that the Emperor participated in the conspiracy."

Webb responded by leaking to his own newsmen the statement: "Quite early when decisions were being made as to who should be indicted and who not, it was decided not to bring the Emperor to justice. It must always be a matter of opinion as to whether this was justified for if the doctrine is to be maintained that the head of state is responsible for the acts of his ministers then at the very least he should have been made to stand trial."

As the trial drew to a close and the incidental matter of sentencing the men in the dock to hanging, imprisonment, or freedom became pressing, Keenan found his position increasingly difficult. In December of 1947 wartime Prime Minister Tojo himself took the stand in his own defense. Willing scapegoat though he was, he had been abused almost beyond endurance since the surrender. The Emperor himself had been reported in the newspapers accusing Tojo falsely of disobedience. Japanese editorial writers had called Tojo a coward for using a pistol instead of a sword and then failing in his suicide attempt. Tojo's family were being treated like lepers by their Japanese neighbors and were short of money. His brother had been arrested two months earlier for stealing a bag of rice on the elevated railway.

Tojo, in short, had a grievance and could be expected to voice it. He had an awkwardly logical, almost Western way of thinking. He might well dash his accepted cup of hemlock on the courtroom floor and spatter everyone. American prosecution lawyer John W. Fihelly had conducted the interrogations of Tojo in prison and knew the complex ins and outs of his case. Since there was much political glory to be gained in examining Tojo in court and leading him correctly, Keenan decided to displace Fihelly and conduct Tojo's cross-examination personally. To be precise, he requested that he be allowed to open the cross-examination and let Fihelly pursue it in detail, but the court, Justice Webb dissenting, ruled that it was most fair to have only one cross-examiner for each accused. Keenan accepted the full responsibility for himself, and Fihelly resigned from the prosecution in protest.

On the last day of 1947, lawyer Logan for the defense, in direct examination of Tojo, asked the following question: "Do you know of any instance whatsoever where Marquis Kido acted or gave any advice contrary to the Emperor's wishes for peace?"

> TOJO: In so far as I know there was no such instance whatsoever and I further wish to add that there is no Japanese subject who could go against the will of His Majesty, more particularly among high officials of the Japanese government or of Japan.
>
> LOGAN: That concludes the examination on behalf of Marquis Kido.
>
> THE PRESIDENT (WEBB): Well, you know the implications from that reply.

Indeed everybody did know. Keenan called his star witness Top-luck Tanaka back from vacation at his home by Lake Yamanaka near Mount Fuji and had him go at once to see Tojo in Sugamo Prison. Tojo would not yield, so Tanaka went to the palace and explained the situation to Matsudaira Yasumasa, Kido's former secretary and his successor as imperial advisor. Matsudaira, in turn, consulted with his fellow chamberlains and obtained permission from Hirohito to send a message to former Lord Privy Seal Kido in prison. Kido, who shared a cell next to Tojo's, began a negotiation. He spoke at length to Tojo around the M.P.-guarded partition. He talked to Tojo directly as they jogged through their courtyard exercises. Kido promised betterment in the position of the Tojo family, and Tojo had to listen because the myopic little Kido, even in prison fatigues, was Hirohito's representative. After two days of conversations, Tojo gave in. He returned to the courtroom and under continued cross-examination by Keenan was brought to admit that he had persuaded the Emperor to go to war and that, in so doing, he might have forced Hirohito to act against his personal inclinations.

Thereafter, on January 8, 1948, Keenan was given a truly Oriental night out. The place was a millionaire's villa in the seaside pleasure resort of Atami. General Matsui's goddess of mercy looked down from the hillside over the bay, shimmering with moonbeams. Two former prime ministers, a former war minister, and the mayor of Atami were on hand to entertain Keenan. *"Je suis très fort,"* said Keenan. The mayor called for girls after the banquet and the old men who had been statesmen of Japan gave Keenan first choice. "The host always pays on such occasions," said Keenan to Tanaka later that night. And on the way home to Tokyo, in the first gray of dawn, he gave his chauffeur $100 for racing a train and beating it to a crossing. Tanaka, too, was rewarded. He was invited to dinner by Imperial Advisor Matsudaira inside the palace. His double role at the War Crimes Tribunal was explained to the Emperor. *"Ah sore wa kekko desu,"* said Hirohito—"Oh well, that's all right then."

Three months later the defense rested its case, and Webb and the other ten judges retired to ponder the evidence, draft a judgment, and agree on sentences. The more Webb reviewed the facts, the more worried he became that only half the truth had been brought out in court. On February 11, 1948, in answer to a *Life* magazine allegation of a "Keenan-Webb feud," he explained in a letter to MacArthur:

My Dear Supreme Commander,
. . . I told the Chief of Counsel [Keenan] on one or two occasions that the question whether the Emperor was guilty or not was irrelevant as he was not on trial. I also pointed out to him that the Prosecution's evidence implicated the Emperor.

As spring passed into summer, Webb's doubts multiplied and he began to wonder whether it would be just to exact the death penalty of men who were clearly obsessed with loyalty and would tell lies against themselves in order to protect their lord. He conceived the idea of treating them instead like Napoleons and of remanding them to the Allied powers for exile on distant islands. He so recommended in his own first draft of a judgment, adding that death sentences, under the circumstances, would seem "vindictive" and that the defendants themselves would prefer "swift spectacular death to banishment to some remote part of the earth."

Webb amplified on his position in his second draft of a judgment, circulated among the other members of the tribunal on September 17, 1948:

. . . The great authority of the Emperor was proved beyond question when he ended the war. The outstanding part played by him in starting as well as ending it was the subject of unimpeachable evidence led by the Prosecution and of necessary findings in the general conclusions as to Japan's war guilt. But the Prosecution also made it clear that the Emperor would not be indicted. This immunity of the Emperor, as contrasted with the part he played in launching the war in the Pacific, is something which this Tribunal must take into consideration in imposing sentences on the accused. It is, of course, for the Prosecution to say who will be indicted; but a British Court in passing sentence would I believe, take into account, if it could, that the leader in the crime, though available for trial, had been granted immunity. If, as in cases of murder, the court must by law impose capital punishment, the prerogative of mercy would probably be exercised to save the lives of the condemned. . . .

The suggestion that the Emperor was bound to act on advice is contrary to evidence. He was not a limited monarch. If he acted on advice it was because he saw fit to do so. That did not limit his responsibility. . . .

I do not suggest the Emperor should have been prosecuted. His case was, no doubt, decided at the highest level in the best interests of all the Allied Powers.

Justice requires me to take into consideration the Emperor's immunity when determining the punishment of the accused found guilty; that is all.

A majority of Webb's colleagues felt that these scrupulous paragraphs would only be misinterpreted by Japanese apologists on the one hand and by Communists on the other. After being repeatedly outvoted, Webb gracefully capitulated, and on November 4, 1948, he began reading in court a majority judgment which did not contain his cherished escape clause concerning the role of the Emperor. He concurred in the judgment because, as president of the tribunal, he felt he must set an example of compromise to discourage his colleagues from each handing down a separate opinion. Even as it was, only four of the eleven judges concurred wholeheartedly and, of the seven who did not, four wrote their own independent judgments. The justices of Russia and Nationalist China, like Webb, signed the "majority" document cynically, suppressing their misgivings because they saw no other choice. Justices Jaranilla of the Philippines and Boling of the Netherlands, whose national territories had been occupied by the Japanese during the war, wrote concurring opinions in which they spoke for heavier sentences to most of the accused. Justice Pal of India, whose land had not been overrun and who shared in the Buddhist religious heritage of the Japanese, dissented entirely because he could not see his way clear to condemning Japan for having waged war on the West. Justice Bernard of France dissented for the same reasons which had given President Webb such pause.

"It cannot be denied," he wrote, that the war "had a principal author who escaped all prosecution and of whom, in any case, the present defendants could only be considered as accomplices."

Keenan, when he heard the sentences which he had rhetorically asked for, went out for an evening of drinking with his star witness, Top-luck Tanaka. "Stupid," he said in his cups, "the sentences are stupid." The penalty to which he most objected was death for Matsui, the pathetic little general whose command had been abused at the rape of Nanking.

So it was that seven of the Emperor's most "loyal retainers" were hanged, eighteen others imprisoned for the duration of the Occupation, and the Emperor himself left on the Throne and called a "fine liberal gentleman." At midnight on December 22, 1948, before mounting the scaffold, Tojo, Matsui, and the other five men to be hanged all joined in a banzai for the Emperor, a last wish that Hirohito's dynasty might remain on the Throne eternally. Allied diplomats who were obliged, in line of duty, to witness the executions were all impressed by the stoic good humor with which the condemned went to their deaths.

In the lonely years that followed the trials, MacArthur's policy of letting bygones be bygones took hold with astonishing thoroughness. When the Occupation came to an end in 1952, the unhanged "war criminals" were first given home visiting privileges, then one by one released permanently from prison. By 1956 all were free again and most were already back in back-room politics. The dead had been brought home from the islands of the Pacific and put to rest in Arlington National Cemetery or in Tokyo's Yasukuni Shrine. The U.S. imagination occupied itself with the terrors of creeping communism and of domestic Hiroshimas. Japan rose from her ashes to become, in 1968, the third most powerful nation in the world, boasting a gross national product second only to those of the United States and Soviet Russia. The majority of Japanese came to think of themselves, however unwillingly, as allies of their former American enemies. The ruling minority of Japanese watched Communist China grow to become a menace and took sardonic satisfaction in the fact that the United States bore the bulk of expense for defending Japan.

Only Hirohito lived on and remembered. He was protected at home by the reverence which the elder generation still felt for him. No longer was his name, Hirohito, a taboo that could not be spoken aloud, but the occasional rudeness of a Socialist Dietman was not condoned by the populace and did not have to be taken seriously. At first the role of retiring constitutional monarch amused Hirohito. For four years after the war he insisted upon sharing in the misery of his people by wearing only threadbare prewar suits. Then in 1949, at the insistence of chamberlains who said that American newspapers reported him walking about in rags, he condescended to have a new suit made for his twenty-fifth wedding anniversary. A few years later when a lady novelist, Koyama Itoko, wrote a book about Empress Nagako, she ended it with an account of the new suit. The Emperor was fond of Aesop and Andersen, and she knew that he would be pleased by her allusion to the *Emperor's New Clothes*.

Hirohito's new clothes, in a figurative sense, were embroidered throughout the 1950's. The crass suspicions of Western jurists and journalists in the 1940's were forgotten. For lack of records, the handful of American historians interested in Japanese history depended heavily for their viewpoint upon the verbal information of a small, accessible coterie of elder Japanese statesmen. The same informants were interviewed again and again and their stories became more charming, circumstantial, and convincing with each telling. Schooled by centuries of experience in a frugal, authoritarian, densely populated society, all Japanese are masters at creating pleasant illusions and at believing them to be reality. One carefully tended shrub and one carefully selected rock in every tiny urban front yard suggest to their proud owner all the beauty of a forest and a mountain. A fragile paper screen drawn between one room and another gives its occupant privacy and prohibits the occupants of adjoining rooms from taking note of what is said behind it.

About 1960, however, Japanese historians and journalists, writing in their own language, began discreetly to suggest certain transparencies in the Emperor's new clothes. They began to draw on "lost" records: on courtiers' diaries, on admirals' logs and generals' daybooks, on the minutes and transactions of various political societies, on law court transcripts, and even on resurrected secret police files. Men who had previously held their peace began guardedly to reminisce. For the sake of the sacred ancestors and of the sacred children of the future, the proud truth of Japan's attempt—Hirohito's attempt—to conquer the world had to be set down in writing. It has been coming out in snatches, much of it in small editions by small publishing houses, much of it in private printings or in manuscripts circulated from hand to hand. From this new material, this new truthfulness of the Japanese, emerges a story to which Western historians have as yet paid little attention. It is a bizarre tale of Oriental *Realpolitik,* intrigue, and murder. Perhaps never has there been a detective story of such monumental proportions nor a hoax so rooted in antiquity. To trace its origins we go back no less than two thousand years.

PART TWO

LAND OF THE
SUN GODDESS

4

IMPERIAL HERITAGE

(A.D. 50–1642)

VIKING EMPERORS

The stained and crooked carpet of imperial purple that was trod by Hirohito in the twentieth century had been unrolled for him in centuries gone by. His was an ancient house, governed by precedents and aspirations as hoary as the hills. It was literally at about the time of the coming of the first Emperor, two thousand years ago, that the sacred volcano of Mount Fuji arose out of the Eastern Plain in a single fiery night of earthquake. Ever since then the Emperor's relationship with his people and his method of government had been developing in picturesque isolation from the rest of the world. Part figurehead and chief executive, part war chief and king, part high priest and pope for his people, he was invested in heavy seals of state, heavier coats of mail, and still heavier religious robes. In the Western world there had been nothing like him, as a political institution, since the time of the pharaohs.

The first people came to Japan about 100,000 years ago. They were pre-Mongolian Asiatics, similar to the aborigines of Australia today—wandering hunters with pale complexions and heavy beards of varying color and curliness. For the next 90,000 years, during the last of the ice ages, Japan was usually linked to the Asiatic mainland by land bridges and island chains. Hokkaido, the northernmost island, was accessible to Siberia. Kyushu, the southernmost island, was accessible to Taiwan and Southeast Asia. Then, about 10,000 years ago, the oceans were swelled by the melting of the glaciers, and Japan was cut off from the Continent by straits twice as wide as those at Dover. She became a land beyond land's end, out of sight of the mainland even on a clear day.

In her isolation Japan developed the unique qualities which set her apart

187

from other nations of Asia or of the world. There were two cultures each with its own language, a Siberian one in the north and a Southeast Asian one in the south. The northern language survives today in Hokkaido as Ainu, a distant relative of some of the tongues of the Siberian tundra. The southern language has developed into modern Japanese. In its most homely and presumably ancient words—words for *mother, father, oyster,* or *belly*— it bears slight resemblances to the dialects of some Polynesians and of some hill tribes in the Malayan area. It is probably a branch of the family of languages spoken by ancient Southeast Asians before they were overrun by advanced Mongolian Stone-Agers out of Central Asia.

During the last 8,000 years before Christ, the aggressive, pale-faced, black-bearded bear hunters of the northern Ainu culture of Japan maintained their racial integrity and extended their hunting domains down into the central Japanese island of Honshu. By contrast, the southern aborigines —speaking a form of Japanese and leading rather sedentary lives as shellfish eaters—began to be replaced gradually, from about 500 B.C., by the Mongolian type of people associated with modern Japan. Traces of the aborigines' curly hair, gray eyes, brown or even red beards may still be found in upland valleys away from the Japanese coast, but their principal contribution to modern Japan seems to have been their language.

No archaeological evidence exists to suggest that the Mongolian race invaded southern Japan. Apparently they trickled in, raft by raft, canoe by canoe, and wreck by wreck. Each new boatload learned to speak the existing native dialects. Each new boatload brought with it new techniques from the Continent which made living easier—improved stone implements, thatched roofs, potters' wheels, elementary ideas of agriculture. Such arts, known to all fisherfolk on the outskirts of Chinese civilization, enabled the Mongolian newcomers to thrive in Japan—to have large families and gradually to push back the aborigines into the hills.

About 300 B.C. traders began to arrive in southern Japan, introducing bronze, iron, and the rice plant. The colonies of castaways assimilated the innovations easily and profited by them. In the last century B.C. a relatively small Mongolian castaway population in the southern island of Kyushu multiplied so rapidly as agriculturists that they took over all the arable land in Kyushu. Some of the pre-Mongolian hunters became serfs of the agriculturists and swiftly died out. Others retired to the hills whence they continued to trouble the farmers for centuries with their warlike outbursts. The new Kyushu agricultural community was organized as a loose confederacy of villages, each ruled by its matriarch or fertility mother. The matriarch of the most powerful town was called the sun goddess. The accounts of the earliest Chinese travelers called her Pime-ko, a Chinese pronunciation of Hime-ko, Sunshine Child.[1]

[1] In modern Japanese *hime* has come to have two meanings: sunshine and princess.

At about the time of Christ, the Kyushu sun goddess, being sorely pressed by one of the hill tribes, the Kumaso, allied herself with a marauding pirate-trader from Korea. This was the grandfather of Japan's first Emperor and the direct ancestor, seventy-one generations removed, of Emperor Hirohito. Legends, archaeology, and old Chinese and Korean annals combine to suggest that Hirohito's forebear was the Oriental equivalent of a Viking. His home port was a buccaneers' enclave called Karak at the tip of the Korean peninsula where Pusan stands today. The records of nearby Korean kingdoms show that Karak, or Mimana as the Japanese later called it, was recognized as an independent Japanese city state from A.D. 42 until 562. Like the Normandy of England's William the Conqueror, it was itself only a way station. The original Scandinavia from which Japan's imperial Vikings had come was probably far to the south in the Malayan area. That was the vicinity which, a century or two earlier, had launched the great Polynesian seafarers who discovered and populated the islands of the Pacific. Some historians think that the navigational enterprise of the region had been stimulated by the breakup of the great fleet which Alexander the Great had assembled in the Persian Gulf for the conquest of India at the time of his sudden death in 323 B.C.

In an episode reminiscent of Dido and Aeneas, Hirohito's forebear had a son by a granddaughter of the Kyushu sun goddess. The son was allowed to grow up with the pirates and assist in their campaigns against the unregenerate Stone-Age Kumaso. He and his son, Jimmu, the first Emperor, ranged widely up the Inland Sea, exploring and provisioning along the southern Honshu coast.

As soon as he came of age, Jimmu, Hirohito's ancestor sixty-nine generations removed, resolved to carve out his own kingdom in Japan. The Kumaso had been beaten back into the Kyushu hills, and there was no longer any room for a male military leader in the matriarchal Kyushu society. Jimmu moved his entire pirate fleet—ships, warriors, women, and utensils—across the Inland Sea from Kyushu to Honshu. He anchored in what is now Osaka harbor in central Japan, 260 miles west-southwest of modern Tokyo. There a fertile plain, extending forty miles inland, lay waiting to be planted with rice. There the shellfishing aborigines needed help against the hairy Ainu-speaking hunters of the interior. Perhaps most important, Jimmu's warriors found in the hills around Osaka an iron ore which contained the right impurities for making steel. Within a few generations his swordsmiths would pass directly from the bronze age into the steel age and would turn out blades unsurpassed elsewhere in the world for centuries to come.[2]

---

[2] Precious metals, by contrast, were not discovered in Japan for centuries. Native silver began to be mined A.D. 674 and native gold A.D. 701. The first copper coins were minted A.D. 708.

After three years of campaigning, about A.D. 50,[3] Jimmu proclaimed himself Emperor of the fertile plain around Osaka Bay, together with its approaches in the surrounding mountains. His kingdom included the sites of modern Osaka, Kobe, and Kyoto. He called it Yamato, which is still the chauvinists' name for Japan.

Emperor Jimmu charged his three ablest lieutenants—Nakatomi, Inner Companion; Mononobe, Swordsmith; and Otomo, Mighty Friend—to govern wisely for him and to push on against the pale, hirsute hunters of the interior. He designated Nakatomi and his seed as the ceremonialists of his realm who would execute state business. He assigned to the Mononobe family the care and provision of weapons and the responsibility of enforcing state decisions. To the Otomo he gave the privilege of guarding his palace and person. Today most Japanese of any affluence claim descent either from Jimmu's progeny or from one of these three lieutenant families. Prince Konoye, for instance, who led Japan to war in 1937, considered himself the senior Konoye of the senior Fujiwara branch of the Nakatomi family.

At first Emperor Jimmu's kingdom of Yamato was only one of a hundred similar settlements reported by traders to contemporary Chinese chroniclers. Jimmu and his son, however, soon made it the most powerful. Jimmu brought to the natives a military leadership and discipline more Spartan than Sparta's. He and his kinsmen practiced a savage puritanism which equated godliness with cleanliness and required them to perform countless ceremonies of ritual purification. Like the Greeks at Thermopylae they bathed and combed their hair before battle. They also bathed after battle, after eating, after sexual intercourse, after slaying a stag—after any act which they felt to be unclean. To this day the Emperor's bath is one of the most sacred pieces of furniture in the palace, and total immersion in water at 110–130 degrees Fahrenheit is a daily ritual in the life of every Japanese.

Once having settled in Yamato, Jimmu and his men were terrified of succumbing to the pollution of death and the sloth of a sedentary life. When a man died, his home was burned. When a monarch passed away, the entire capital was moved to a new site. Nor was this a passing fancy. For more than six hundred years, the capital was studiously looked upon as a field headquarters and was moved at the end of every reign. Only A.D. 710, when the bureaucracy had become so large that a sizable city had to be destroyed and rebuilt every generation, did the Court finally settle down and accept a permanent capital city. To this day behind the great outer

---

[3] Official Japanese dating, adopted for ideological purposes in the nineteenth century, places Emperor Jimmu's ascension to the Throne at 660 B.C. Most scholars agree that this is six hundred to eight hundred years too early. Until after A.D. 200 the Japanese employed a lunar calendar which made Methuselahs of the first nine Emperors. The chronology used here follows that of the archaeologist J. Edward Kidder.

walls of the various imperial palaces, most of the buildings are simple wooden structures of one or two stories. Other Japanese have followed the Court example and most of them still live traditionally in flimsy homes of paper and wood. Until the advent of modern construction, it was a practical style well geared to easy moves and small losses in Japan's recurrent earthquakes.

On the animism, the local spirit worship of the natives, Jimmu built the basis for later Shintoism. He added the Continental worship of ancestral ghosts—and most particularly of the ghosts of his own ancestors who had been born, he said, by the sun goddess. He showed the shellfishers a bronze mirror, a bright sword, and a string of semiprecious stones, rubbed smooth in the fetal shape of cashew nuts, and warned them that these were the talismans of his divinity, bestowed on him in person by the sun goddess.

Jimmu gave purpose to their placid lives by making them all doughty foot soldiers and by telling them that his mission was "to encompass the eight corners of the earth under one roof." His phrase, "eight corners, one canopy," would become a slogan nineteen hundred years later for Hirohito's propagandists. Decade by decade Emperor Jimmu and his descendants led out his adopted people to conquer adjoining villages and kingdoms and drive back the Ainu.

Like the fertility cultists of the sun goddess in Kyushu, Jimmu and his retainers were careful not to mix their blood with that of the aborigines. They sought instead to replace the aborigines by having enormous families of their own. For five generations they imported women of their own race —whom they called Sacred Ones—from the home fief in Korea. Each prince and vassal, according to his wealth and power, had as many wives as he could afford. The old records tell of families with a hundred children. Such proliferation soon converted Jimmu's few boatloads of retainers into a population of thousands. After five generations, Jimmu's Court progeny began to marry their own cousins, the Great Children. The inbreeding was great, but the original stock had been healthy. A large percentage, probably a majority, of modern Japanese are descended from it.[4]

In the reign of the tenth Emperor, between 200 and 250, Jimmu's mirror of knowledge and sword of power were enshrined outside the palace for all to see and admire. Emperor Sujin felt secure in retaining only the jewels of divinity in his own keeping. The sword of power found its way to Atsuta Shrine in Nagoya, in an area newly wrested from the hairy barbarians of the north. The mirror of knowledge was housed closer to Yamato, at a shrine called Ise, overlooking the sea. Today Ise Shrine is the cardinal holy

---

[4] If the Japanese ever cease to consider their excellent genealogical records as sacred and private and begin to use them in conjunction with blood-type and chromosome analysis, Japan should prove to be the perfect laboratory for human genetic studies.

place of Japan to which every Cabinet minister reports before assuming office.

The twelfth Emperor, Keiko, who probably reigned from 280 to 316, and who sired no less than seventy-two sons, felt so sure of his power that he left Yamato in the care of his ministers and returned for six years to the kingdom of the sun goddess in the southern island of Kyushu. There he and one of his sons rid the Kyushu queens of a savage tribe of aborigines which had been molesting them and succeeded in negotiating a permanent merger between Yamato and Kyushu.

By about 400, the descendants of Jimmu and the sun goddess had subjugated most of southern Japan and their captains were fighting the hairy men of the north in the vicinity of Tokyo. The earliest state document out of Yamato, a report delivered by the Yamato ambassador to the Chinese Imperial Court in 478, asserted: "From of old our forebears have clad themselves in armor and helmet and gone across the hills and waters, sparing no time for rest. In the east they conquered fifty-five countries of hairy men and in the west they gained the homage of sixty-six countries of assorted barbarians."

While so boasting, the Japanese emissaries to China also told their hosts that Yamato, the name of their homeland, meant Great Peace. It was thus inscribed in the Chinese chronicles, and when Japan officially adopted the Chinese method of writing a few decades later, *Dai Wa* or Great Peace became the name of the country. In Japan, however, the Chinese characters for *Dai Wa* were given an exceptional double reading which flouted all rules. As every literate Japanese knew, the characters spelled *d-a-i w-a* when pronounced in front of a Chinese and *y-a-m-a t-o* when pronounced domestically. The truth was that Yamato really meant "mountain road" or path to new conquests—but it would have been undiplomatic to suggest as much to the emperor of China.

THE GRAVEDIGGERS

As Yamato grew and the Emperors waxed all-powerful, they began to construct vast mausolea which attest not only to the slave labor which they could recruit but also to the fact that their Shintoism, their belief in the ghostly presence of their ancestors, had become a cult of death. Their divine descent "in a line unbroken for ages eternal" from Amaterasu, the sun goddess, took a terrible toll of their adherents.

The eighth Emperor, Kogen, who lived about 200, had a small artificial hill built to memorialize his sarcophagus. It was only 180 feet long and only a few score of his retainers were laid to rest along its slopes, but it signified the beginning of a burial madness which possessed the Emperors for the next three hundred years. Each successive ruler demanded a bigger tumulus and a larger company of victim vassals to accompany him to the spirit world. Legend has it that Suinin, the eleventh Emperor, was troubled by the wailing of retainers who were being buried alive during the obsequies for his brother, a mere prince. He therefore decreed that at his own interment clay figurines should be substituted for live victims. His humanitarian impulse wrought no lasting change, however, and the practice of retainer sacrifice continued by force up to the sixth century and sporadically by choice of the retainers themselves up to the death of Emperor Meiji in 1912.

The imperial tombs still play an important role in Japanese government. Even now in 1970 the aged Hirohito continues to send Court messengers to them to report important events like the signing of treaties. The earliest of the tombs, following the style of Emperor Kogen, are keyhole-shaped mounds, like great gourds or butternut squashes half buried in the ground. They are said by some savants to be related to a cult of gourd worship, then popular in Korea, and to represent enormous beached boats reminiscent of the ship mounds being thrown up by Norse adventurers in England at about the same time. The imperial mausolea or *misasagi,* however, are far larger than any of the Viking monuments. Indeed some of them, in sheer amount of earth moved, rival the pyramids.

That of Nintoku, the sixteenth Emperor, who probably reigned A.D. 395–427, is a moat-girt artificial mountain, 80 acres in area, more than half a mile long and, after fifteen hundred years of weathering, still over 100 feet high. As built, it is reputed to have had twin peaks and to have been planted and terraced and set about at its approaches with graceful archways in the shape of the Greek letter *pi.* Twenty years in construction, it was built by conscripted labor. As the Court chronicles point out, obliquely, of another of Nintoku's architectural efforts, "the people, without superintendence, supporting the aged and leading by the hand the young, transported timber, carried baskets [of earth] on their backs, and worked their hardest without distinction of night or day." [5]

The most ferocious of the tomb-building Emperors was Nintoku's grandson, Yuryaku, who reigned from 457 to 479. He is reported by the later chroniclers to have been a particularly monstrous sadist who executed every male member of the imperial family that he could lay hands on. It pleased

[5] Perhaps the most amazing feature of Nintoku's tomb is the fact that modern Japanese refrain from noticing it. It sprawls like New York's Central Park across the valuable real estate of Osaka's suburbs but no guide books mention it, and none but Court ceremonialists ever cross its three concentric moats to climb its wooded slopes. The skeleton of Emperor Nintoku is still supposed to lie in a stone vault inside, surrounded by his favorite possessions. Hungry antiquarians from the West have noted from afar that the sides of the mound are strewn with bones. For more than forty years they have eyed a fine stone sarcophagus peeping out from the rubble left by a landslide. But whenever they suggest an official scientific investigation to their Japanese colleagues, they are met evasively with a sudden change of subject. Nintoku's tomb is the private, sacred property of Hirohito's family.

him to put courtiers up in high trees and practice archery on them until they eventually slipped or were shot down. Pregnant peasant women were supposedly brought to him so that he could enjoy the sensation of tearing them open with his bare hands. After Yuryaku's death, Court advisors saw to it that Emperors did not mate with their aunts and half-sisters, or if they did, that crown princes be chosen from the broods of concubines only distantly related to the mainstream of the imperial family.

LIGHT FROM CHINA

The fourth-century union of the Yamato patriarchy of the Emperors with the Kyushu matriarchy of the sun goddesses led to three hundred years of cultural strife at Court. The Kyushu women espoused the advanced, ancient civilization of China, closer ties with the Continent, and an all-out effort to extend the Yamato empire into northern Korea. The Yamato male retainers —especially the old lieutenant clans of the Nakatomi, Mononobe, and Otomo—spoke for war against the Ainu and extension of Yamato into northern Honshu. About 400, the Chinese system of ideographic writing began to interest Court intellectuals. And Chinese Buddhism began to sap conviction in Shinto.

The Buddhism brought to Japan was an agnostic, almost atheistic creed, full of ceremony, mysticism, and homilies. It undermined the morbid superstition and sublime family confidence of the early Emperors and sowed in their minds the Confucian ideal of good government. According to Buddhist doctrine, a man's high birth could not be used as a passport to paradise. No matter how aristocratic his family, his spirit after death might pass into a peasant or a dog if he did not live wisely according to the teachings of the Hindu prophets. Only by submerging individualism in meditation and by achieving gentle unimpassioned enlightenment could a soul finally break out of the weary round of transmigration and escape into the oneness of the universe, the blessed nonexistence of Nirvana.

The Chinese system of ideographs—of characters or *kanji*—was almost equally pernicious to imperial pretensions because it made written laws and records a fact to be reckoned with. Fortunately for the Emperors, however, it was not an alphabet, and its idea pictures, which had been developed for the monosyllabic uninflected utterances of Chinese, were not easily adapted to the polysyllabic, highly inflected words of Japan.[6] Phonetic symbols had to be invented to express Japanese word endings, and long experimentation was required before general agreement could be reached on the correct matching of the Chinese idea symbols with spoken

---

[6] The spoken languages of China and Japan are totally unrelated and mutually unintelligible. Modern Chinese and Japanese, however, can communicate through writing because their word pictures have meaning independent of sound.

Japanese words. More than two hundred years passed before the Chinese writing system became a dangerous vehicle for Japanese thought. In those two hundred years Court scribes would have adequate time to develop an acceptable account of the past, pleasing to their masters.

It was the ladies who finally won the cultural battle. The imperial family, in 562, lost its ancient Korean fief of Karak to neighboring Korean kingdoms sponsored by China. The prestige of Chinese civilization soared. In 587 Emperor Bidatsu, the thirty-first sovereign, embraced Buddhism on his deathbed. The clan of Court armorers, the Mononobe, rebelled. The Kyushu ladies' faction at Court exterminated the Mononobes, and then, in a typical Japanese compromise, brought to power the son of a Mononobe mother, Prince Shotoku Taishi. Shotoku agreed to co-operate in a Chinese-ifying program for the reform and strengthening of the nation.

Prince Shotoku was a child prodigy who had mastered the difficult Chinese system of writing by the age of seven. He instituted an ambitious research into Chinese laws and letters with a view to adopting them in Japan. The scholars of his study groups wrote the first histories, geographies, grammars, and legal codes of Japan and drew up the first orderly plans for census taking, land surveys, and equitable conscription and taxation. Most important, Shotoku worked out the first accommodation between his family's cult of Shintoism and the new religion of Buddha. Buddhist monks came to accept the Shinto pantheon of ancestors and nature spirits as mani-festations—*bodhisattva*—of Buddha himself. It was understood that Emperors would be spared the humiliation of transmigration and given an automatic dispensation when they died to go straight to Nirvana.

While most of his plans for reform were still on paper, Shotoku Taishi died in 621, at the age of forty-nine. Without his leadership the Shinto princes allied with the imperial family and the Buddhist princes allied with the Kyushu sun goddesses quickly fell out. A small war in the streets of the capital made the Soga family of the Kyushu ladies' faction the dictators of the country. Twenty-four years later, in 645, a crown prince and one of the last of the Nakatomi family, the Inner Companions, carried out a carefully planned countercoup. They slew some Soga princes in the Throne room in the very presence of the Empress and drove the rest out of the Capital. The leader of the Soga clan retired to his walled villa, set a fire, and burned himself to death. He took with him most of his retainers and most of the research papers and records which had been compiled by Shotoku Taishi.

VEILING THE THRONE

Crown Prince Tenji and Nakatomi Kametari of the Inner Companions followed up their victory by reconstructing from memory the lost programs of Shotoku Taishi and inaugurating a thorough overhaul of Japanese government. In the great Taika Reforms of 645–655, the country was given a bureaucracy on the Chinese model and with it provincial governors, a census, a land survey, and the right of petition to the Throne. Arms were collected forcibly into armories, for use only in time of war. Now, at last, after centuries of strife, a man could walk a day's journey without fear of being set upon by brigands.

In 670 the wise old reformer Nakatomi lay dying. To honor him, Emperor Tenji, his patron and disciple, presented him with an imperial concubine who was already full with child. "If it's only a girl," said the Emperor, "then of course I will take the responsibility for her sustenance, but if it's a boy, you will want to keep him yourself." It *was* a boy, and Emperor Tenji, before he died a year later, bestowed on the child the name of Fujiwara. It was this bastard imperial clan, the Fujiwaras, who were to take the place of the Nakatomis as Inner Companions and serve as the Emperors' most intimate counselors for the next 1,275 years. When the Fujiwara Prince Konoye, who led Japan to war in 1937, took poison in 1945, he was the last of a kind.

During the eighth and ninth centuries, as ministers on the left, ministers on the right, and ministers on the inside, the Fujiwaras turned Court life into a pageant of ceremonies and costumes. Everywhere in the courtyards of the palace walked fat old men, stiffly. The cut and color of their robes, the depth of their bows, were all prescribed. On their heads they wore shallow skull caps of stiff black silk, rather like academic mortarboards but topped with various shapes and sizes of black lacquered phallic symbols denoting their rank. In the big square Throne room, on a floor of white mats, the Emperor took on increasingly the appearance of a rouged and gilded doll, squatting motionless in the center of a gravely comic surrealist ballet. His person became so taboo and awe-inspiring that he was no longer called Emperor but identified by euphemisms such as Dawn in the Palace, Forbidden Closet, Steps to Heaven, or The Great Great. One of his names was Worshipful Gateway, the "Mikado" of Gilbert and Sullivan.

As the Fujiwaras institutionalized the Emperor, they gradually assumed responsibility for all advice given to him. Theirs was the first veil in what is known to Japanese as the Emperor's "government from behind the curtains." The Emperor lurked somewhere behind the last veil but, except on those rare occasions when he spoke with the Voice of the Crane, he did nothing overt. He accepted the advice of his ministers or asked them to reconsider it. He presided and sanctioned but never—officially—did he initiate. Thus, if state policies turned out badly, the Fujiwaras took all the blame and the imperial family was exempted from criticism or threat of violence. In a land of volatile honor and pride this responsibility was a dangerous one. The Fujiwaras accepted it partly for influence and wealth and partly out of a genuine religious conviction that the Throne must be shielded.

Through the masterful, illusion-creating stage management of the Fujiwaras, the people of Japan came gradually to believe in a head of state who was a paradox: a mortal god, a zero infinity, an impotent omnipotence. By long tradition Japanese government had always been a family matter, and the Fujiwaras simply persuaded the nation that the Emperor was the head of the national family. Everyone had a voice in family councils according to the weight of his position in the social hierarchy. The Emperor, as father, had the most weight—so much, in fact, that everyone must try to spare him from ever being proved wrong. To be born into his national family was to incur an "unlimited obligation" to him: to obey him and take responsibility for him with the fierce, unquestioning family pride of a child. His desires were binding, but under Fujiwara tutelage he cultivated a dark, oracular style of speech which was always open to interpretation. It was the duty of the subject to act in the interests of the national family according to the unexpressed will of the Emperor. No need always to ask explicit instructions; need only to take all the blame if the imperial wishes turned out to have been misunderstood.

The Fujiwaras occupied the most important positions at Court, advising or manipulating Emperors from 670 to 1945. Until 1165 they actively headed the administration of the nation's government. Over the centuries, they imparted to Japanese politics a special quality of subtlety which reflected their own temperament—their own family tradition and genetic make-up—rather than an inherent trait of the Japanese public. Almost without exception, the Fujiwaras, like their close kin the Emperors, never showed much taste for supervising civil servants or for constructing a body of workable laws. To rule, in their way of thinking, was less a science than an art—a game of skill to be played with living pieces, as if each move was a unique aesthetic experience. They unrolled history as if it were a moving tapestry which they themselves were weaving. They loved ceremony and intrigue. Ungloved might appalled them; they preferred deft assassinations. Sensitive, refined, amorous, and highly literate, also superstitious, cynical, and unscrupulous, they ran Japan to preserve the godhood of their imperial cousins and to indulge their own patrician tastes.

The bedrock on which the Fujiwaras' influence rested was not so much their own statesmanship as it was the hereditary good looks and carefully inculcated seductiveness of their sisters and daughters. For thirteen hundred years, more than three quarters of the wives and concubines who minced their way in and out of the palace were Fujiwaras. Many of them learned the arts of love before they were ten and bore princes before they were fifteen. Over the centuries they were to set an astonishing genetic record by bearing no less than fifty-four of the seventy-six Emperors between 724 and Hirohito's birth in 1900. In a Court where there were usually a score of noblewomen enjoying the imperial favor at any one time and where epidemics decimated the ranks of retainers every decade, the hygiene, charm, sensuality, intelligence, and genuine devotion of the Fujiwara ladies must be counted nothing less than heroic.

From 670 to 950 the Fujiwaras ran Japan skillfully, gradually strengthening the government, extending it into northern Japan and holding civil strife at a minimum. Under the professional management of Fujiwara ministers and mistresses, the Emperors lost their splendid barbarism and cultivated the arts. They wrote poetry and studied the mysteries of Buddhism. They accepted a permanent capital for their sacerdotal administration—first, in 710, the town of Nara in the center of the original Yamato kingdom, and then, in 794, when Nara became too infested with Buddhist priests, Kyoto, eighteen miles north of Nara.[7] Under the patronage of their brilliant Court grew up most of the handcrafts for which Japan is still celebrated: the lovely subdued silks, the fragrant unvarnished woodwork, the delicate porcelains, the gaudy lacquers, and the painted paper screens.

The very cookery of Japan was largely a product of the Kyoto Court. In those days such modern staples as rice, pork, beef, and fowl were caviar to the general. The peasants subsisted mostly on barley, millet, fish, oysters, seaweed, beans, radishes, wild herbs, and ferns. Only the Court noblewomen had the ingredients with which to experiment and create variety. Their wealth allowed them to waste vats of rice, radish, fish, and flour and to invent an unsurpassed variety of salt and rice-vinegar pickles and of soya-bean yogurts and cheeses. Their warrior husbands kept bow and sword hand in practice by daily hunts in the hills. They brought back wild boar and venison and pheasant, and many uncultivated vegetables such as bamboo shoots, mushrooms, and lotus roots. From these the Court ladies created the characteristic meat cookery of Japan such as survives in the popular sukiyaki of modern restaurants. The masses did not know even that it existed. Buddhism proscribed the eating of meat and courtiers encouraged the people to be pious. For a thousand years imperial princes served as high priests at all the great Buddhist temples but privately patronized clandestine Kyoto guilds of butchers and meat cooks. When carnivorous customs resurfaced in the nineteenth century and began to be practiced on prime Western steers in the stockyards of Kobe, most Japanese beefeaters thought that the novel Japanese recipes they followed had been freshly invented.[8]

Although the Emperors at first took a cynical view of the new Buddhist religion and studied it only to control its converts, many courtiers and Court ladies fell prey to its permissive mysticism. At length the Emperors

[7] Kyoto means Capital Capital. Tokyo, the modern administrative center of Japan, means Eastern Capital. In the early days Kyoto was called Heian, Unruffled Peace, and Tokyo was called Edo, Navvies' Doorway.

[8] Then, and only then, did imports from Southeast Asia make rice the staple of the nation, driving millet and barley from the plebeian menu.

themselves became engrossed in its theological fine points and began to rely excessively on the advice of Buddhist confessors. Empress Koken, who reigned from 749 to 758, grew so intimate with her priest that she is said to have made him her lover and plotted to put him on the Throne. This may be a canard, however, invented to justify the action of her Fujiwara ministers when they finally prevailed upon her to abdicate. In their eyes she had more foolish offenses to her discredit: she had issued a decree against the killing of any animals, and she had interested herself in yet another new religion—the teachings of a group of Nestorian Christians who visited the capital from China. With her deposition, Christian influence disappeared from Japan for eight hundred years.

The curtain which the Fujiwaras hung around the Throne was meant only to protect it, not to stifle its occupant. If an Emperor showed a talent for politics and the real exercise of power, he was not supposed to indulge it while he remained Emperor, but if he abdicated and put his infant son on the Throne, it was deemed proper that he give full autocratic play to his abilities from behind the scenes. It became standard practice for every strong Emperor to retire young to a monastery, set up his own Court and administrative offices there, and run the Fujiwaras who ran the nation. Sometimes he would outlive his successor and manipulate a whole series of reigns. Sometimes, too, his successor would abdicate and compete with him in the arts of stage management. In 1301 there were to be no less than five retired Emperors, each doing his best to govern Japan from the temple of his choice.

The city of Kyoto, which was the capital from 794 to 1868, soon grew to be even more priest-ridden than Nara before it. More than a thousand Buddhist temples were built atop the steep, pine-clad, natural fortress of Mount Hiei—Mountain of Wisdom to be Compared with the Emperor's—and from it belligerent monks regularly descended in incendiary raids on government offices which offended them. The imperial family's cult of Shinto fell into disuse. After 946 the Emperors gave up the regular practice of sending messengers to announce important events at the tombs of their ancestors. When they themselves died, they no longer built huge burial mounds but allowed themselves to be cremated and interred in little white boxes under tidy stone slabs in neat rectangular Kyoto parks. Their learned skepticism, however, was not fully shared by the common people, and periodically folk superstitions would reinfect the Court and produce a brief Shinto revival.

The days and years and centuries slipped by in an afternoon doze of sexual intrigue, poems, paintings, new concubines, and occasional duels. The people responded well to Fujiwara direction. They wore cotton pants and wide conical straw hats, tilled their paddies, and paid their tithes in much the same way that they do in rural Japan today. Little by little the valleys of Honshu, the large, central Japanese island, succumbed to cultivation, and only in crossing the mountain ranges might an agriculturist still meet with his savage Stone-Age brethren who persisted in living by the hunt. The Cains of the land, however, were coming into the possession of good steel swords and these, added to their fleet arrows, made them formidable. Outlaws banished from the strict hierarchy of society provided them with leadership.

A growing caste of nobles found use for hardy cutthroats. The Emperors and the Fujiwaras had many children, and second sons had to be provided for. They were granted provincial fiefs and lived in discontent because of their rustication from the capital. They gradually took over all the ancient clans until hardly a region in Japan did not have a member of the imperial family in its manor house. But giving second sons tax-free estates and allowing them to own the aboriginal citizens as serfs had certain inevitable drawbacks. The Ainu people of the northern culture repeatedly rebelled and had to be almost exterminated. The nobles themselves grew overproud of their provincial prowess and wanted to meddle in Kyoto affairs. Worst of all, land to give away to talented second sons grew scarce and tax-free estates kept the growing income of the nation from meeting the growing expenses of government.

The Emperors, shortsightedly, had always considered the whole land their own fief and had set aside no special crown lands for income but only a few scenic estates for pleasure. By about 950 they began to find themselves dependent upon the Fujiwaras for money to make up Court deficits which could not be covered by the dwindling tax take. The nation was falling apart into baronial estates. The barons were members of the imperial family who could not be dealt with like the old clan lords because they were relatives and had their own Iron-Age companies of soldiers. Even the Kyoto branches of the Fujiwara family, who had seen to it that they did own some estates, found themselves dangerously dependent on professional soldiers and policemen to keep the peace. No longer did a few hired braves suffice to preserve and equalize political balances; allegiances had to be made with provincial kinsmen who could provide whole armies led by skilled generals.

THE SHOGUNS

In 1192, after a war with a group of southern princes who sought to supersede the Fujiwaras as manipulators of the Throne, the princes of the north converted a makeshift council which they had established in Kamakura near Tokyo into a permanent headquarters or "tent government" for the administration of the northern half of the nation. Upon their chief, Emperor Go-Toba conferred the title *Sei-i Dai Shogun,* Great Barbarian-suppressing General. The title would be abbreviated in later years to shogun and would come to mean in Western dictionaries, "military governor ruling Japan." In reality the shoguns never did entirely rule Japan, for they remained subjects of the Throne, ostensibly loyal and often obedient. They did, however, rule northern Japan and for the next seven hundred years they usually controlled the armies which held the military balance of power in the nation.

Thus came into being the third layer of government from behind the curtain: someone to take responsibility for the Fujiwara chief minister at Court, and for the Emperor behind him. With the third veil descended also the fourth. The shoguns were rusticated imperial princelings, and the real power in their "tent government" lay with tough practical bureaucrats: either chiefs of staff or military police chiefs. Most of these soldier administrators at the fourth level of government were also distant kinsmen of the Emperor. They enriched themselves, they killed their own brothers for power, but none of them ever tried to seize the Throne or depose the godlike senior kinsman who sat on it.

Outside the immediate environs of Kyoto, where the Court ruled supreme, the military administration of the shogun or field marshal, and of his chiefs of staff, secret agents, and soldiers, policed the clan lords and collected the taxes. They soon monopolized the temporal power of Japan and left the Emperors nothing but the spiritual power. As high priests, however, the Emperors always retained the authority to confer and bless all high-level appointments. They successfully insisted that they were the overseers of the nation's welfare and that they must be consulted on all matters of national importance. In particular, they claimed absolute authority over Japan's foot soldiers. Though tenuous, their claims were never denied.

In the new fourfold system of government, all offices on the ladder swiftly became hereditary. The Kamakura chiefs of staff would resign in favor of their sons or brothers in the event of a lost battle; the Kamakura shoguns would resign under the same terms for a lost war; a Fujiwara minister of state in Kyoto would resign for a losing policy; and the Emperor would abdicate only for personal reasons or as a gesture of national ceremonial purification after a particularly severe earthquake.

In 1221, Go-Toba, who was now the retired Emperor, grew jealous of the growing power of the shogun, whom he had rusticated to Kamakura, and plotted to outlaw him. While laying his plans and collecting his recruits, Go-Toba resorted to a traditional Japanese ruse: he pretended to be a voluptuary, not worthy of surveillance. At his strategy sessions, watered saké was served copiously by Court beauties in transparent kimonos. The shogun's spies admired what they saw but were not deceived. The shogun marched on Kyoto, forced Go-Toba's juvenile puppet Emperor to abdicate, and replaced him with another juvenile puppet Emperor, Go-Toba's nephew. From that day Kyoto ceased to be the main center of power in the nation and the Tokyo area, in the north, took its place. The imperial family, however, was treated handsomely and was preserved in its Kyoto sinecure as the national high priesthood.

KUBLAI KHAN

During the supremacy of the first shogun family, the Genji, the neighboring land of China was overrun by Mongol horsemen from the Russian steppes. In 1268 envoys from Kublai Khan, the new ruler in Peking, whose grandfather Genghis had swallowed most of Asia, arrived in Japan with a letter ordering "the king of your little country" to submit to Mongol suzerainty or suffer invasion. The letter was carried posthaste to the shogun in Kamakura. He deemed it so important that he decided to disturb the celestial peace of the Court and refer the letter to the Emperor.

In Kyoto a careful note was drafted, rejecting Kublai Khan's demands. This reply was forwarded to Kamakura for the shogun to consider and transmit if he saw fit. He was incidentally reminded that he was responsible for the defense of the nation. The shogun decided that the Emperor's note was unrealistic—both too proud and too humble—and sent the Chinese envoys back to Kublai Khan without a reply or even an acknowledgment. Kublai Khan indignantly ordered his vassal kings in Korea to construct a great fleet. The Koreans diplomatically kept the Japanese informed of Kublai's intentions.

For six years both nations made preparations. Finally, in 1274, 15,000 Mongols and 8,000 Koreans embarked from Korean ports and made sail for southern Japan. They first assaulted two little islands off the Kyushu coast. The Japanese garrisons on the islands established a heroic precedent by dying to the last man.

Next the Mongol fleet landed at Hikata, southeast of Kokura, the lucky primary target which would narrowly escape atomic destruction 671 years later. The Japanese fought a savage holding action at the beaches while the warriors waiting in central Kyushu were called to join in the fray.[9] That night a storm blew up and the Korean captains of the invasion ships urged a withdrawal. The Mongol generals of the landing force were nothing loath to seize the excuse. Their losses had been enormous. By the time they had regained the mainland and taken stock, they found that they had lost 13,-000 of their 23,000 men.

Kublai Khan accepted the excuse of weather but not the rebuff to his pride. He coolly sent more envoys to Japan the next year, ordering the Japanese to surrender before he began to fight in earnest. The shogun had the envoys' heads cut off and secured imperial approval for an all-out na-

---

[9] The heroic commander was Shimazu Hisatsune, a scion of the imperial family and of the local matriarchy of sun goddesses. His descendants and the descendants of his powerful Satsuma clansmen would staff the "Kyushu clique" which plotted Japan's aggressive Strike-South policy in the 1920's.

tional defense effort. Kublai Khan was preoccupied with wars in southern China and it would be six more years before he would launch his thrust.

The Japanese prepared for it feverishly. They built a "vast cloud of firefly boats," with which to harass the Chinese war junks, and a stone wall more than a hundred miles long, with which to contain the most likely beachheads. Every man, woman, and child contributed money or labor toward the national armory.

Kublai descended in his full wrath in 1281. He impressed all the junks of Canton and Korea into his service and floated an army of 140,000 troops—some 40,000 of them his own redoubtable northern warriors. They were landed all along the perimeter of the stone wall which the Japanese had constructed and in greatest strength at the two ends where it seemed most possible to turn the Japanese flanks. For fifty-three days desperate hand-to-hand combat continued without letup, particularly at the two ends of the long wall. Then at last came the divine wind—the kamikaze—which ravaged the Mongol fleet for forty-eight hours, August 15 and 16 in the year 1281.[10] When the skies cleared, less than half of the great Chinese host of 140,000 men survived to touch foot again on the mainland.

SCHISM

After their great victory the warriors of Japan relaxed and fought aimlessly with one another. The rule of the shoguns in Kamakura deteriorated, and the imperial family in Kyoto split into two factions. From 1339 to 1392, there were two Imperial Courts, a southern one in the mountains south of Kyoto where an Emperor wished to rule in his own right and a northern one in Kyoto itself where an Emperor was willing to delegate all but religious power to the military strongmen, the shoguns.[11] Confirmed Shintoists considered the true Court to be the southern one because it had possession of the imperial regalia—the mirror, sword, and necklace. The northern Court in Kyoto, the capital, was said to be occupied by traitorous pretenders, not anointed with the holy oil. In point of fact the northern Emperors had a better right under the rules of primogeniture to occupy the Throne, but since they lacked the talismans of divine power, they never felt sure of themselves and were to live down their usurpation for centuries to come. Hirohito himself was to be sorely vexed in the 1930's by detractors who pointed out that he came of the northern dynasty.

To substantiate their claims during the schism, the southern Emperors revived Shintoism at Court and cleansed it of many of its accumulated

[10] Those same August days in which, 664 years later in 1945, many devout Japanese waited expectantly and accusingly at their family shrines, asking when the kamikaze would blow again.

[11] Coincidentally there were two popes during the same period in Europe, one in Rome and the other in Avignon.

Buddhist trappings. Thereafter—down to Hirohito's time—it became a rule of thumb that Emperors who emphasized Shinto and ancestor worship in their priestly functions were restorationists who wished to exercise power in their own right, and that Emperors who preached ethics and devoutly chanted Buddhist sutra were ceremonialists, satisfied with being figureheads.

In 1392 the princes of the southern dynasty accepted a handsome financial settlement and returned to Kyoto as a branch house of the imperial family. Their capitulation, however, brought no lasting peace. From 1467 to 1600 civil war raged incessantly. Clans and clan lords struggled like Scottish sheep thieves to extend or hold their fiefs. The hereditary warrior caste of the samurai, who were descended from Emperor Jimmu and his pirate lieutenants and who were allowed, therefore, to bear arms, wear mail, and ride horses, oppressed the peasants sorely. They observed a Spartan knightly ethic which prevented them from touching money and therefore from selling their services. But their extreme loyalty advantaged only their lords. Since it was taboo for them to touch gold or silver—in the nineteenth century Japanese Army officers still accepted their pay on an outstretched fan and passed it to their adjutants—the samurai were entitled to live off the land and expect free hospitality wherever they lodged. They had the right to kill any serf or farmer without having to answer for their crime except to the samurai or clan lord who protected that commoner. They also had the right to kill one another in duels, subject only to the laws of vendetta between samurai families.

When the entire family of a clan lord was exterminated in one of the wars, his fighting retainers became masterless samurai or *ronin*—literally, wave men—who rode the billows of fortune and sold their services wherever they could. The same term, wave men, had been used to describe masterless warriors in Anglo-Saxon England eight hundred years earlier. In England wave men became mercenary brigands and pirates of the salt sea. So they also did in Japan. In the early sixteenth century Japanese wave men terrorized the coast of China and plied the seas as far away as Bangkok Bight and Manila Bay. By 1550 the kings of Burma, Siam, and Cambodia all employed stalwart Japanese cutthroats for their personal bodyguards.

Although the common folk suffered by the interminable marching of armies in Japan, it was the warriors who died, the clan lords who were bankrupted and dispossessed. Such statistics as there are show that the nation as a whole prospered in the civil war. The population rose from an estimated 15 to 25 million, making Japan almost twice as populous as France at the same time, almost four times as populous as Spain, and fully five times as populous as England. The artisan and merchant class, though considered materialists, beneath contempt by the samurai, had grown fat on war profits. Japanese lacquer and steel ware were the best in the world. Japanese traders did a thriving business in them as far away as Batavia and Calcutta. Japan was the leading exporter of arms in the Far East. Her sword blades were known and envied by Moorish craftsmen in Toledo.

The Kyoto region was hardest hit by the civil war because most of the great lords maintained their own private troops in the capital. Each lord hoped to gain imperial sanction for a campaign of extermination against his neighbors. The imperial family, however, could offer little leadership because it remained riven between princes of restorationist tendencies and princes who preferred to wield only ceremonial and religious power. The family arguments were at best academic because in that evil era the Emperors could not be sure of commanding square meals for their noble retainers much less the square miles of their domain. For years at a time they received no allowance from the office of shogun, and the country around Kyoto was so unsettled that they had difficulty collecting rents from their few crown parks and forests. Many of the lesser Court nobles, who were not closely related to the Emperor of the moment or to his Fujiwara minister of state, had to return to their home fiefs to be sure of a decent living.

Emperor Go-Tsuchi-Mikado, in 1500, lay unburied for forty-four days while the Court was shaming the shogun into putting up enough money for the traditional obsequies. His successor, Go-Kashiwabara, claimed to be so poor that, for financial reasons, he postponed his official coronation for twenty-two years. The next Emperor, Go-Nara, who reigned from 1526 to 1557, made a pitiful show of penury by having samples of his calligraphy peddled on the Kyoto streets. By such protestations he raised enough money from loyalists to build a fine new palace and bring back from the provinces many of his poverty-stricken courtiers.

BARBARIAN

It was at this juncture, when imperial fortunes had reached their lowest ebb, that the first Europeans came to Japan. They were not accustomed to associating poverty with power—not even with spiritual power. They therefore gained and reported a poor first impression of the Throne—one that was not corrected later because the Emperors soon came to fear Christians and made all knowledge of themselves increasingly inaccessible to outsiders. To most Japanese, foreigners were not human beings from another land but creatures in human form who might as well have come from another planet. They were called *ebisu* which meant, in the original murderous, insular Greek sense of the word, barbarian. By the priestly rulers in Kyoto, they were regarded as unclean vermin who would pollute the sacred soil and anger the spirits interred in it.

The existence of human creatures across the seas, more distant than the Koreans or the Chinese, had been realized in Japan since the sixth century and reported at first hand by pirates since the twelfth century. For at least a century before 1521, when circumnavigator Magellan laid claim to the Philippines for Spain, Japanese seafarers had been serving and colonizing in the Sulu sultanate of Mindanao in the southern Philippines. After 1510 Japanese adventurers were rubbing shoulders with Portuguese at Goa on the west coast of India. In 1529 Japanese buccaneers sent home some Indians to be inspected and interrogated by the Court officials in Kyoto. Pirate news of the world was regularly sent to Prince Shimazu of the Satsuma clan in southern Kyushu—the descendant of the hero of the Mongol repulse of 1274—and he relayed it, for analysis, to the shogun and Emperor in Kyoto.

In 1542 the first Portuguese ships began to call at ports in Kyushu, the southern island. Japanese officialdom, which had long expected their coming, arranged for them to be treated hospitably and given no offense. For six years intercourse with the West was sporadic, friendly, and safe. Then, in 1549, the first Christian missionaries arrived in Nagasaki. They were led by the illustrious Jesuit, Francis Xavier, later to be declared a saint. The authorities followed Saint Francis's movements closely. By full-time application he quickly acquired a working knowledge of the Japanese language, which he described, because of its difficulty, as "a contrivance of a conciliabulum of devils."

After two years of study, he extracted the taboo intelligence that there was an Emperor in Japan above the shogun. He made a painful journey to Kyoto, mostly on foot, and asked for an audience with Emperor Go-Nara. He was told that his request could not be referred through channels because the shogun was out of town and that, in any case, the Emperor—the one who sold his penmanship—was living in retreat. The streets of Kyoto were so full of dueling samurai that Saint Francis saw no hope for a useful mission there, and after a few days, set out to return to southern Japan. He never did see the Emperor and referred to him in letters as a powerless spiritual leader "called Emperor" who maintained his establishment in Kyoto. No other Westerner saw the Emperor for more than three hundred years thereafter and his very existence was forgotten in the West.

The carefully watched Europeans brought to war-torn Japan two powerful pacifiers: fear of invasion and knowledge of firearms. When three Portuguese adventurers arrived on a Chinese cargo ship in 1543 at Tanega, an island off the southern tip of Kyushu, the lord of the island promptly hired them to teach him the use of their weapon, the gun. After a month of lessons, he was so impressed that he bought the two matchlocks they had with them for the staggering sum of 2,000 taels—approximately the wages that a Japanese working man could expect to earn in thirty years, or roughly $180,000 by modern American standards.[12] The lord gave the guns to his master swordsmith to copy. The latter, having trouble with the spring in the breech, gave his daughter to the captain of the next Portuguese vessel that called in Tanega a few months later and received lessons in return from the ship's gunsmith.

Once the knack of gunmaking was learned, it spread quickly. The Japanese craftsmen, who already made the best sword steel in the world, were soon able to widen the bore and breech of the matchlock so that it would carry farther and kill more certainly. To quantity buyers, they suggested use of a serial firing technique. They packaged their wares in handsome waterproof lacquer boxes that protected them from powder's greatest enemy, the rain. In Europe at that time firearms were still special equipment, used to supplement the standard tools of war. In Japan they were so swiftly improved and employed that some military historians say the first modern infantry and infantry tactics were developed there. Within a decade every Japanese clan lord's armorer was making guns and cannon, and the samurai wars of the previous two centuries were to end in a clap of gunpowder.

THE GREAT MUSKETEER

One of the first to whose ears the crackle of musket fire sounded musically was a fifteen-year-old boy who had been prematurely elevated to the leadership of his sub-clan by the death of his father. In 1535, when the palace had been half destroyed by one of Kyoto's periodic fires, the father had contributed handsomely to a palace repair subscription. For this reason the son, at an early age, was blessed with Court favor and information. His fief was only a small one in the province of Owari, between Kyoto and Tokyo, but it included the port of Nagoya which housed the shrine of Atsuta, containing the sacred sword of Japan, the third item in the imperial regalia.

Oda Nobunaga, as the boy was called, came of both imperial and Fujiwara forebears. He had been a wild youth and had spent all his time with his father's soldiers instead of his books. When his father died, leaving the Oda castle to him, his tutor committed suicide and bequeathed to him a note advising him to mend his ways. Young Oda had listened to the boastful stories of foot soldiers who had wielded the earliest matchlocks in battle, and his first act on succeeding his father was to put in an order for no less than five hundred of the new weapons to the gunsmith on Tanega. This was in 1549 when the Tanega gunsmith had been in business for less than six years.

---

[12] Only about $65,000 by modern Japanese standards, but the Japanese working man's salary is far lower today in relation to the world at large than it was in 1545.

Young Oda turned out to be a military genius. Other lords had gun-bearing foot soldiers but only Oda seemed able to employ them success-fully. By 1559, when he was twenty-five, he had taken over his entire home province of Owari. In 1562, when he was twenty-eight, Emperor Ogimachi sent him a secret message bidding him come and rid Kyoto of its brawling samurai. Not until 1568, when Oda had defeated all the major clan lords between Tokyo and Kyoto, was he able to comply. Then, however, he entered the capital with perfectly disciplined troops, deposed the shogun, put a puppet shogun in his place, and began to build Emperor Ogimachi a magnificent new palace. It became a familiar sight for the workmen to see Oda walking proudly at the Emperor's side, giving advice on the placement of a shrub, rock, or moon-pool. A disarmingly vain man, he wore a cloak made of Chinese tiger skins and preened a twisted, upturned hairline mustache.

With the Emperor's sanction, Oda set out to destroy Japan's feuding barons and unify the country. He coolly ordered entire families of noble-men to commit suicide. Politically-minded Buddhist priests, whom he abhorred, he implacably roasted on spits. He razed all the armed monas-teries of Kyoto and Osaka except one sacred mountain out in the country. That one he spared, after laying seige to it, because he received a request to do so from the Emperor.

With Christians, however, he remained lenient, and lived to see 15,000 converts and 200 churches in the Kyoto area. The pure logic and pure living of the Portuguese Jesuits fitted his conception of the holy man, and the Jesuitical view of killing as God's business, not a sport, tallied exactly with his own feelings. He found the Christian teaching as straight and prac-tical as a bullet. It fired the hearts of some of his most Spartan warriors. They went into battle with Christian crosses and emblems hanging at their necks, and Oda found them more dependably fanatic at their posts than the best Shintoists.

In 1575, at the age of forty-one, Oda met the lords of the north coast in the biggest battle of his career. By this time he commanded an army of over 100,000 men, including many cannon and 10,000 matchlocks. His opponents had more men, far more samurai on horseback, and almost as many guns. But Oda had been perfecting the tactical use of firearms for twenty-six years. He picked out his 3,000 most disciplined musketeers—all men of low caste—and placed them in three ranks behind a zigzag palisade in the center of battle where he expected to meet the most heroic cavalry charges. He had trained the men to fire successively in three cadres of a thousand each, one pulling their triggers while the next was lighting their tinder and the third was stuffing powder and shot down their muzzles. It had been doctrine previously that a cavalry charge could always break a cluster of missile launchers. But at the battle of Narashino, Oda's three ranks of plebeian musketeers knelt and aimed and fired so rapidly, one after another, that no samurai on horseback ever came in sword's length of them. Almost 16,000 riders, the flower of northern chivalry, died on the field in front of the palisades. There was to be no battle to compare with it in Europe for almost a hundred years.

In 1582, seven years after the battle of Narashino, Oda was forty-eight and had reached the zenith of his power. He began to move his men south to conquer the southern island of Kyushu, the kingdom of the sun goddess. On his last night in Kyoto one of his most trusted generals, for unknown motives, with unknown instigation, assassinated him. The general was hunted down a few days later and died without betraying his patrons. To the mind of someone in a position of power, Oda's pride and cruelty had grown excessive. He had served his purpose. During his meteoric career the population of Kyoto, the capital, had climbed back from a low of 20,000 in 1550 to almost 500,000.

JAPAN'S NAPOLEON

Oda's place was immediately taken by the most talented of his staff chiefs, Hideyoshi. Unlike Oda or the shoguns before him, Hideyoshi was a commoner, the son of a peasant foot soldier. He had risen in Oda's army by his ability, in many campaigns, to win battles. He had a genius for engineering and had found ways to sap or flood the most impregnable strongholds. Like Oda, he gave the Emperor reverent allegiance. His administration of sixteen years, from 1582 to 1598, was to be the one period of Japanese history up to 1945 in which the real rule of the nation would be delegated to a man outside the wide pool of imperial blood.[13]

Hideyoshi completed the unification of Japan. He forced all the clan lords to come to Kyoto and renew their vows of allegiance to the Throne. He took hostages from families of dubious loyalty and held them in the capital as privileged guests. He remapped the fiefs of Japan for tax purposes and in the process gerrymandered them to break up old rebellious alliances. In a totally fraudulent gush of religious emotion, he requisitioned most of the non-government sword steel in Japan to build the largest statue of Buddha in the world. Finally, to provide employment for idle sword hands, he resolved on a course of overseas conquest. He spoke grandly of seizing Korea, the Philippines, Malaya, Siam, Burma, and India. He decided to begin modestly with Korea.

Transported to Europe, Hideyoshi's hordes of well-trained, well-

---

[13] Years later many Japanese were to say that Hirohito could abide General Mac-Arthur because he saw in him another Hideyoshi, another military genius from outside the family circle, to whom revolutionary changes could be entrusted without commitment. The comparison was to be fortified by the similarity in the experiences of Hideyoshi and of MacArthur in Korea.

equipped fighting men would have been more than a match for any army in Christendom. In crossing to Korea, however, he was challenging China, the wealthiest and most populous nation in the world at that time. The kingdom of Korea was a tributary of China, and Hideyoshi knew that, if he attacked it, the Chinese would not stand idly by. In 1591, therefore, he went straight to the point and demanded that the Korean king give Japanese troops uncontested lines of march to the Chinese border so that he could move directly on Peking. The king of Korea decided that 150 million Chinese were a more lasting menace than 25 million Japanese and refused Hideyoshi's proposal.

In the spring of 1592, after elaborate preparations, Hideyoshi dispatched an expeditionary force of 205,000 men to Pusan, the lost Japanese fief of Karak. Most of the Japanese force landed without mishap but Hideyoshi, being a dry-land general, had overlooked the importance of sea power and had relied overmuch on Japanese buccaneers and traders to keep open his supply lines. The Japanese pirate craft were basically coastal vessels designed for conditions in the calm Inland Sea between Kyushu and Honshu. The Koreans, by comparison, had large ships, armed with cannon, and a brilliant admiral, named Yi, who made driftwood out of Japanese supply convoys.

Despite severed lines of communication, the Japanese army, once it was ashore in Korea, advanced from Pusan to the Yalu River in less than six months. Then, as anticipated, China launched a massive counterattack. At the height of her effort, she was to put more than a million troops in the field, the equivalent of at least four million in the more tightly populated world of today. Letters sent home to estate managers by samurai who had previously scorned the use of firearms are notable because they sound one refrain: "Send us more guns." Japanese garrisons, outnumbered five to one, no longer cared for sport or honor but only for efficient killing.

After a three-year stalemate, Hideyoshi, in 1594, unleashed a second expeditionary force on Korea which again swept the southern half of the peninsula. Having suffered almost half a million casualties, China put into the field fully twice as many reinforcements. In danger of losing control of the sea, the canny Korean Admiral Yi, two hundred fifty years before the *Monitor* and *Merrimac,* devised the world's first ironclad. Designed in elegant Oriental baroque to look like a fierce turtle, it glided majestically under oar power through the wooden fleets of the Japanese—and cannonaded and rammed with impunity. Once again Hideyoshi's soldiers found their supply lines severed and their backs to the sea. Garrisons of Japanese Christians and Buddhists vied with each other to see which could hold out the longest. The Chinese suffered terrible losses and once again conceded a draw.

In 1598, as negotiations toward a peace were resumed, Hideyoshi died. In his last hours he tried to make an old comrade in arms, Tokugawa

Ieyasu, the guardian and regent for his five-year-old son. Tokugawa promised to see that Hideyoshi's child grew up but refused to play regent. Instead he agreed to rule the realm as one of a council of five of Hideyoshi's generals. In anticipation of a power struggle at home, the five generals accepted an immediate and barely face-saving peace treaty with China and withdrew their armies from Korea. The war was over. For sheer carnage it had surpassed anything that Europe would see until the campaigns of Napoleon more than two hundred years later.

TOKUGAWA TYRANTS

Tokugawa Ieyasu was an icy, unlovable man with the heavy face and blood-shot eyes of a bulldog, but he had a gift for administration, a prodigious patience, and, unlike Hideyoshi, royal blood flowing in his veins. Fourteen months after Hideyoshi's death, Tokugawa fought a decisive battle with his rival generals on a plain sixty miles west of Kyoto. Through the machinations of Fujiwara allies at Court, several of his enemies changed sides at the last minute, enabling him to win an easy victory. He went on to make himself and his heirs the new shoguns of Japan.

He spared the lives of his enemies, judiciously sliced provinces from their fiefs, and gave the parings to his own henchmen. He repaired the road and established new stage houses and garrisons along the great south coast trade route between Kyoto and Tokyo. He brought order to Japan's chaotic finances by creating a dependable currency of freshly minted gold coins. He provided employment for masterless samurai in a new national police network. In two years he had imposed peace on the countryside and made Japan into a beneficently efficient police state. A British merchant who ran a trading post in Nagasaki compared Tokugawa's autocracy with that of James I in England and concluded that Japan had "the greatest and most puissant tyranny that the world has ever known."

In 1603 Tokugawa Ieyasu met with young Emperor Go-Yozei and conferred on him a decent share of the tax take. It was Tokugawa's aim to put the Emperor in a gilded cage where he would live well, would be treated with respectful reverence, and would avoid embroiling himself in intrigues against Tokugawa's heirs. Except in military theory, he could no more have deposed the Emperor and seized the Throne for himself than the king of France could have declared himself Pope. Instead, Tokugawa pressed Emperor Go-Yozei to accept a Tokugawa granddaughter as a daughter-in-law.

Emperor Go-Yozei contended that such a base alliance would be impossible for a member of the imperial family unless Tokugawa could find some way to resume the offensive and drive the twin threats of white supremacy and Christianity from Japan's door. Tokugawa did not feel strong enough domestically to lead Japan in a foreign crusade and so Emperor Go-Yozei, in 1611, abdicated in protest. Then in 1614, after further negotiation, ex-Emperor Go-Yozei consented to the Tokugawa-imperial marriage, and Tokugawa Ieyasu, for his part, issued an edict ordering the deportation of foreign priests, the demolition of churches, and the renunciation of faith by all those Christians who seek "to change the government of the country and obtain possession of the land."

In making this concession to the xenophobia of the high-priestly Emperor, Tokugawa was influenced by the views of a practical Protestant layman who had no love for Portuguese Jesuits and Spanish friars. This was Will Adams, an Englishman from Kent, who had arrived in Japan in 1600 as a virtual castaway—the pilot of a Dutch vessel which had lost three quarters of her crew through storm, hunger, thirst, and beriberi. As Tokugawa's prisoner, Adams had built two European-style ships for the Japanese and had been elevated to the rank of samurai and given an estate. Though prohibited from leaving Japan, he regularly sent money home to his family in England and found his Japanese household much to his liking. "It is like unto a lordship in England," he wrote, "with 80 or 90 husbandmen that be as my slaves."

Adams eventually died in 1620 in the arms of his Japanese wife, but his spirit is still worshipped by Japanese Shinto pilgrims who visit the shrine built for him on the hill above his former estate. During his lifetime Adams enjoyed the right of informal access to Shogun Tokugawa and, as a Protestant, constantly warned him against the territorial ambitions of Spain and of her advance agents, "the Papists." As a result, Tokugawa tended to look upon all Spanish missionaries and most of the Portuguese Jesuits as fifth columnists bent on subversion.

Antagonistic as he was to the minions of Rome, Adams had no desire to see all Christian missionaries deported from Japan. Nor was Tokugawa so eager to please the Emperor that he wanted to stop the profitable flow of Western trade and knowledge which came in the wake of the missionaries. And so, on Adams's advice, Tokugawa encouraged Protestant merchants from Holland and England and used his edict against Christianity merely as an unenforced warning to the friars and Jesuits.

Tokugawa Ieyasu died in 1616—the same year as William Shakespeare. Behind him he left a dynastic system of administration centered in Tokyo, or Edo as it was then called, which would keep his heirs in office for 252 years. They would be called the "emperors" or "kings" of Japan in most foreign lands and only taboo-struck native sons would know that there were true Emperors above the shoguns. Tokugawa's thirty-seven-year-old son had been titular shogun for a decade and his fifteen-year-old grandson was already groomed to succeed his father.

In 1617 Emperor Go-Mizu-no-O succeeded to real power in the Kyoto Court. Go-Mizu-no-O was a vigorous, scholarly young man of twenty-two who would direct the highest affairs of state until his death as an octogenarian ex-Emperor sixty-three years later in 1680. At long last, in 1620, with great pomp and ceremony, Go-Mizu-no-O married the young shogun's sister. The shogun reciprocated by instituting a vigorous persecution of Christians. Hideyoshi, in the last wrathful year before his death, 1597, had set the precedent by ordering an experiment in what he understood to be the Christian form of execution. He had had six Spanish friars from the Philippines and twenty of their Japanese converts nailed to crosses and exhibited while they died. Now, between 1620 and 1635, some 6,000 Christians were crucified, many of them upside down like Saint Peter.

The menace which the Emperor saw in the Christians was, from his point of view, a real one. In seventy years, by 1620, the new religion had captured the minds of one out of every fifty Japanese.[14] The majority of the converts were peasants and many of them were foot soldiers who knew how to use guns. They had learned in the wars how to shoot down their betters at a distance, and they now had the leadership of half a dozen Christian clan lords. They set little store by the society of ghosts and spirits which surrounded other Japanese. They were ready to die for inhuman abstractions which they said were above the Emperor.

After the Tokugawa take-over in 1600, many Christians who had fought on the losing side refused to commit suicide, as Tokugawa magnanimously suggested, and insisted, instead, on being ignominiously beheaded in public execution. The defiant honesty of these martyrs appealed to all Japanese, and the shogun found eradication of Christianity a politically difficult duty. After promising the Emperor in 1620 to perform it, the young shogun continued to move cautiously. He spent thousands on anti-Christian propaganda and pennies on headsmen and police work. He sought to get at the root of the evil by rigorously curtailing and supervising foreign trade. He kept new foreign priests from being smuggled into the country, and those old missionaries, whom he allowed to remain under the protection of powerful native converts, he rendered ineffective by constant police harassment. Nevertheless, by the clandestine efforts of Japanese priests, the runaway, subversive creed continued to spread.

In addition to Christians, there were anti-Tokugawa partisans aplenty left over from the wars. The system of police and informers designed by Tokugawa Ieyasu functioned smoothly, but more than enough discontent simmered beneath the surface of his totalitarian state for another civil war. To quash it, the Tokugawas needed the support, however token, of the imperial family. And the Emperor and his kin continued to sulk because the Tokugawas had not yet reinstated them at the top of an unthreatened, unchristian nation of peaceful reverence. To gain imperial sanction for a realistic gradual policy of pacification, the shogun at first tried to bend the Emperor by force. An officer of the shogun's government was sta-

---

[14] In 1970 less than one out of every 300 Japanese professes Christianity.

tioned in Kyoto and the Emperor was not supposed to leave the palace without his consent.

Emperor Go-Mizu-no-O, despite his Tokugawa wife, rebelled. In 1629, after many protests, he abdicated and put a seven-year-old girl on the Throne, the first Empress since 769. It was a sign to the nation that the Tokugawas were infringing on the imperial power and were fit to manage no one but little girls. Shogun Tokugawa Iemitsu decided to call the imperial bluff, graciously accepted the girl puppet, and settled a meager income of a million pounds of rice a year on the abdicating Go-Mizu-no-O. The latter resolved to make it do and retired to a temple to plot. For the next five years the Tokugawas led the perilous lives of tyrants.

SECLUSION

In 1634 Shogun Tokugawa Iemitsu came from Tokyo to Kyoto to parley. He came in peace, but with a tremendous show of pomp and power. No less than 307,000 retainers escorted him down the 300 miles of the great stage route, the East Sea Road, to Kyoto. Their officers overflowed the inns for miles around and their encampments filled the Kyoto plain up to the horizon. Never had the courtesans and jugglers from the city's pleasure district, the minstrels and sweetmeat makers and rollers of dice, done such business as they did around the nightly campfires. In the capital the shogun entertained the adolescent Empress, her father the retired Emperor, and all their courtiers at Nijo Castle, built by Oda Nobunaga.

During great feasting and the giving of magnificent gifts, Shogun Iemitsu and retired Emperor Go-Mizu-no-O withdrew from time to time for serious conversation in a back room. Go-Mizu-no-O called for *burei,* suspension of usual etiquette, and the two squatted as equals on straw mats across a low table from one another. The shogun had with him the globe on which Will Adams had formerly given lessons in geography to Ieyasu, the shogun's grandfather. After many hours of belly talk, of careful, noncommittal, exhaustive indirection, they had examined Japan's position in the world from every angle and reached a meeting of minds. It was to determine Japan's highest state policy for the next 233 years. Its specifics were unwritten and secret but its general tenor may be judged from its results.

On returning to Tokyo, the shogun adopted a course of stringent conservatism such as has never been matched in the history of any other nation. In 1635 he required all clan lords to live in Tokyo one year out of every two and to leave their wives and children there as hostages when they were absent. He made rebellion virtually impossible. The next year he ordered all merchants to trade only within Japan; he forbade Japanese dockyards to construct oceangoing vessels; he divested all Japanese living abroad of their citizenship and promised death to any of them who ever returned to the homeland; finally he proscribed all practice of the alien Christian religion on pain of death. Thus he found a substitute for Hideyoshi's policy of overseas expansion; thus he satisfied the imperial wish to keep Japan safe for Shintoism; thus he sealed Japan off from the rest of the world.

When the law against Christianity was enforced and half a million converts were ordered to renounce their faith, many Japanese built their own crosses and waited to be nailed to them. Thousands were imprisoned to think things over while hundreds were being crucified as examples. Jesuit fathers who lived in hiding had to warn their parishioners against the pride of suicidal martyrdom. Tens of thousands of parishioners nevertheless died. One Christian community of 37,000, which withdrew to the headland and castle of Shimabara in Kyushu, was butchered to the last man, woman, and child. Tens of thousands of other Christians went underground, and several congregations were to resurface in Kyushu and on the north coast of Honshu 235 years later.

In 1638 the shogun's police rounded up the last Portuguese priests and deported them. Thereafter one or two Catholic priests were smuggled in, hunted down, and executed, and all ships from Catholic countries were turned away at gunpoint. A Portuguese vessel, which called in 1640 to plead the cause of commerce, was sent home bearing as message to the outside world the corpses of sixty-one of its crewmen who had been decapitated. Toward the Protestant Dutch and English, Ieyasu's advisor Will Adams had given the authorities a somewhat more lenient attitude. As late as 1673 a British ship which called to trade was received civilly. The shogun was even inclined to let it discharge its cargo—or was until he learned that Charles II of England was married to Catherine of Braganza and that Catherine was Portuguese. After that all deals were off and the British East Indiaman was sent away with threats.

Only a small Dutch trading post was allowed to remain in Japan, and its staff had to pay a high price for their profits. To prove their religious neutrality they had had to provide the ships and cannon-fire which reduced the Christian fortress of Shimabara in 1638. After 1641 they were cooped up on the tiny island of Deshima in Nagasaki harbor. To comply strictly with the Emperor's feelings about the sanctity of Japanese soil, it was an artificial island only 300 paces long. Annually the Dutch traders had to walk to Tokyo, kiss the feet of the shogun, perform scientific tricks and buffoonery for him, and give him a written résumé of historical events in the world outside. Periodically they also had to perform a ritual trampling of the crucifix.

In 1642, the year Isaac Newton was born, the last Japanese priest had been crucified and Japan had closed like an oyster. She would not relax enough to be opened again for 211 years. She took the step deliberately after a debate which had lasted for 90 years. Hideyoshi's attempt to conquer a buffer zone to put between Japan and the outside world had failed, and now Japan, in isolation, planned to improve her inner world and make it spiritually impregnable. At a time when she might still have run rough-shod over Southeast Asia, it was a philosopher's decision, a decision for peace. The scholarly ex-Emperor Go-Mizu-no-O, who was largely responsible for making it, could hardly foresee that the Great Outside would undergo an industrial revolution while Japanese craftsmen were making better sword blades and fans. He could hardly guess that Japan, which went into seclusion as one of the two or three strongest nations on the globe, would emerge from it, centuries later, as a distinctly second-class power.

REGENT HIROHITO

This photograph was released by the Imperial Household Ministry on December 18, 1926, a week before Emperor Taisho died. Having governed Japan for five years during his father's illness, Hirohito already knew what he wanted for Japan and how to go about effecting it.

THE WEIGHT OF TRADITION

On his way home from Peers' School on a day in 1913 (above left) Hirohito could tussle and laugh with one of the chamberlains who constantly attended him, but he already took seriously the burdens of ancestry and tradition which lay upon his shoulders. He had to live up to the expectations of his domineering grandfather, Emperor Meiji (above); live down the eccentric reputation of his weak, vain father, Emperor Taisho (below left); and live through years of disapproval from his religious pacifist mother, Empress Dowager Sadako (below). At his coronation ceremonies in 1928 he and his bride, Nagako, (above right) would have to wear robes almost as ancient as the huge tomb of the fifth-century Emperor Nintoku (below right). The tomb took up valuable land in the suburbs of commercial Osaka, but because it was sacred no one complained of it or even pretended to notice its existence. By the same taboo Japanese would overlook many of Hirohito's activities during the years ahead.

TRIP ABROAD

While still Crown Prince in 1921, Hirohito made a memorable visit to Europe. He did so over the objections of Army strongman Field Marshal Yamagata Aritomo (above left). In Europe Hirohito founded an anti-Yamagata movement in the ranks of military attachés at Japanese embassies. It was headed by his uncles Prince Higashikuni (above right) and Prince Asaka (below right). It suffered a temporary check in 1923 when Prince Kitashirakawa died in the car wreck below. Prince Asaka, too, was in the crash and broke his left leg. A brace is still visible as a bulge in his pants leg in the 1924 picture at far right. At near right he recuperates mountain climbing in the Rockies. In one further outcome of the tour, Edward Prince of Wales accepted an invitation to visit Japan in 1922 and finish a game of golf (above). Hirohito greatly admired and envied Edward's stylish dash and self-composure.

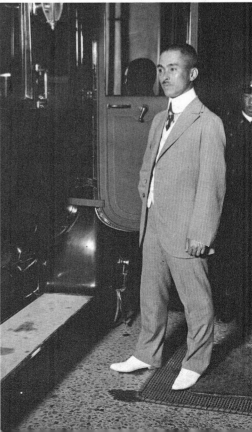

HELPFUL KINSMEN

Top left: Prince Kanin, great-uncle of Hirohito's wife, Nagako, and Army chief of staff, 1931–40. Mid-left: Prince Fushimi, Nagako's cousin and Navy chief of staff, 1932–41. Bottom left: another of Nagako's cousins, Prince Yamashina, after an audience with Hirohito in 1926. He helped develop torpedo planes as a Navy test pilot. Above: Nagako's father, Prince Kuni, and mother, Shimazu Chikako, in 1927. Kuni communicated to Hirohito a lasting enthusiasm for airplanes, tanks, and biological warfare. At right: Prince Kaya, also a cousin of Nagako, and his wife, Toshiko, a first cousin of Hirohito. They are shown passing through Los Angeles in 1934 after a goodwill visit to Hitler. Above right: Hirohito's own three brothers: Prince Chichibu, the eldest, in 1937 in London; below him, Prince Takamatsu of the Navy, in 1931; and at far right, young Prince Mikasa of the Army, as he appeared in 1935.

FAVORITE ADVISORS

Above left: World War II Chief of Staff Sugiya[m]
on his way home as a colonel in 1922 after a year a[nd]
a half as an observer and aviation specialist at [the]
League of Nations in Geneva. Above: Admiral Yam[a]
moto Isoroku when he was a captain attached to [the]
embassy in Washington in 1925. At left: Lord Pri[vy]
Seal Makino shortly before his retirement in 19[35.]
Below left: Lord Privy Seal Kido after his retireme[nt]
in 1945. Below: Economic co-ordinator Suzuki Tei-i[chi]
during his trial in 1947 as a war criminal. Oppos[ite]
page, at top, Prewar Prime Minister Konoye sitting [in]
the guise of his ally Hitler at a fancy-dress party; bel[ow]
left, after his suicide from poison in 1945. Below rig[ht,]
Wartime Prime Minister Tojo.

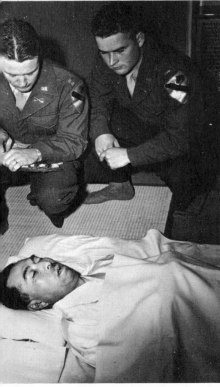

皇太子殿下御降誕
奉祝紀念撮影

LOYAL OPPOSITION

Of those who fought Hirohito hardest behind the scenes and then accepted defeat in silence, the most notable were General Araki Sadao, far left above; General Ugaki Kazushige, left above; Toyama Mitsuru, the lord of the Black Dragon Society, shown in 1927 with Chiang Kai-shek, far left; General Honjo Shigeru, left, Hirohito's chief aide-de-camp from 1933 to 1936; and finally Japan's tragic old liberal, the most long-lived of Emperor Meiji's advisors, Prince Saionji Kinmochi. Eyes ablaze with indignation, Saionji is shown above arriving at his Tokyo villa after one of the assassinations of 1932. He is greeted by Baron Harada Kumao, the Court spy who acted as his political secretary and Boswell.

VILLAINS AND VICTIMS

At left: Japan's girl spy, Eastern Jewel and her lover, Tanaka Takayoshi, shortly after they had successfully touched off the 1932 "Fake War" in Shanghai. Below left: Eastern Jewel with one of the Japanese planes in which she prepared for her missions behind Chinese lines. Above right, from left to right: Kita Ikki, the ideologist of the Strike-North Faction; Dr. Okawa Shumei, the ideologist of the Strike-South Faction and palace go-between with assassins during the terror of 1932; his minion Inoue Nisho, the leader of the Blood Brotherhood; and Tatekawa Yoshiji, the Army emissary who successfully failed to prevent the seizure of Mukden by Japanese troops in September 1931. Below: Nagata Tetsuzan, the Army leader whom Hirohito's uncles first sponsored and then, in 1935, allowed to be assassinated. At right: In a remarkable picture taken early in 1932, Prime Minister Inukai stands in the clothes and posture he had at the moment of his shooting later that spring.

JAPANESE AGGRESSION

The siege gun above, emplaced to bombard Port Arthur in the 1905 war with Russia, was later smuggled into Mukden in 1931, mounted in a recreation shed, and used to shell Chinese positions on the night of September 18. At left: Tsuji Masanobu, the staff officer who masterminded the conquest of Singapore and the Bataan Death March in 1941. Below: Japanese troops walk through the "back door" from Malaya to Singapore across an easily bridged gap in the causeway left by British demolition experts. Above right: the three commanders who took Nanking in 1937—General Matsui, Prince Asaka, and General Yanagawa—confer at field headquarters. Asaka, the Emperor's uncle, was in local command when scenes like the one at right were enacted and thousands of Chinese prisoners were bayoneted beside Nanking's walls.

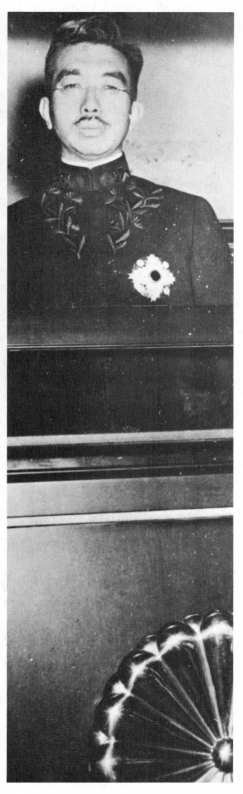

TRIUMPH AND DEFEAT

At the fall of Singapore on February 19, 1942, in a rare spontaneous popular appearance (left), Hirohito rode his horse White Snow out onto one of the palace bridges and remained motionless in the saddle for most of an hour while crowds gathered to share his moment of victory. Just as silently three years later Hirohito acknowledged imperial fault for the lost war by making his uncle Prince Higashikuni take the humiliating post of surrender prime minister. In token of his humble and contrite position Higashikuni (above) stood on a lower step out in front of his ministers in the official Cabinet portrait. In November 1945, as soon as the Occupation began to look as if it would be a success, Hirohito (right) went by train as a pilgrim to the shrine of the sun goddess at Ise. Cutting a lonely figure at the window of his imperial carriage, he wore a modified naval uniform stripped of all badges of rank save his Order of Merit, First Class.

SARTOR RESARTUS

It was years after the war before Hirohito would buy a new suit. When he did buy one, it was cut to an American pattern. Here, with Pearl Harbor now in the distant past and Japan once more a world power, Emperor Hirohito strolls in his new suit through his palace gardens.

5

THE COMING OF PERRY

(1642–1900)

THE EMPTY YEARS

In closing Japan, the Emperor and shogun needed one another and shared a common aim: to keep the Japanese social hierarchy safe and reverent for their heirs. They believed that by study and contemplation Japan could rediscover the special quality that made her "the country of the gods." Under the joint sponsorship of the Tokugawas and the Imperial Court, the scholars of Japan from 1657 to 1715 conducted an exhaustive research into the fountainheads of Japanese culture and into all things peculiarly Japanese such as gardens of raked pebbles, floors of straw matting, tea ceremonies, and prayer shelves of planed, unvarnished wood. The result of these efforts was a twenty-six-volume opus entitled *Dai Nihonshi, The Great History of Japan.* The word for Japan used in the title was the Shinto one, *Nihon* or *Nippon,* which meant sun-begot land. Throughout the pages of the book the authors stressed the divine descent of the Emperors from the sun goddess and the unique verity of the ancient spirit worship, Shinto, meaning the way of the ghosts. The authors condemned as usurpers all those shoguns who had exceeded their imperial mandate and tyrannized the Throne.

Lest the hoi polloi misunderstand such potentially inflammatory ideas, the *Great History,* on its completion, was kept out of print and circulated only in manuscript form among the aristocratic few. To imperial princes, fluttering their wings against the bars of their gilded cage, the book represented a Tokugawa promise of ultimate freedom. To Tokugawas it represented a commitment to force Japan into a perfect Japanese mold. To disgruntled warrior lords, who worried about the creeping military weakness of Japan, the book offered a prescription: arm again when the Emperors have been restored to full direct power.

Under the Tokugawas, the day-to-day government of Japan was delegated to a senate of wizened elders who were no more than half privy to the long-range national policy. All of them came of prestigious pedigrees, representing the best interests of vast tracts of Japanese soil. Too old for personal ambition, they were allowed in their wisdom to draft the routine laws which governed the state and to nominate most of its officers. The headstrong young man who happened to be shogun at any one time sometimes overruled their appointments. The headstrong young man who happened to be Emperor sometimes tabled their recommendations. Except for appointments, they asked for authority from the shogun only in high policy decisions and from the Emperor only in momentous policy decisions affecting the fate of the nation.

Between 1638 and 1853, the Tokugawa wise men—taken like a page from Plato's *Republic*—managed Japan with sterile autocratic efficiency. The deep freeze into which they put the energetic Japanese people may be measured on the tablets of life in birth and death statistics. In over two hundred years the population increased only from 26 million to 33 million. The farmers were so well taxed and policed that they exposed and abandoned all infants who could not be fitted into the national budget. At the same time the authority of the clan lords dwindled, and in most regions the villages developed a democratic independence, a town-meeting form of self-government, which enabled them to cope with the shogun's tax collectors and policemen.

For two centuries little happened. The arts became more specialized and minor. The national etiquette grew more punctilious. Everything that had been peculiarly Japanese became more so, and Japan was unified in its practice. The arts of peace were cultivated so sedulously that the arts of war were relegated to the status of antiquarian sports. After 1640 the shogun's government gradually licensed all gunsmiths and reduced the national annual output of firearms from about 5,000 to less than 200. Finally the guns that were being made were mostly art objects that went unfired into the collections of wealthy samurai. The shogun's coastal defense forces kept their shore batteries well oiled and polished but fired them only once every seven years. Then, since the cannon were all pre-1640 antiques and apt to burst, the gunners handled them gingerly, touching them off with matches on the ends of long bamboo poles.

KNOCKS ON THE DOOR

Many young noblemen who were privileged to read the Dutch news-briefs from the trading post on the tiny artificial island of Deshima complained about the nation's growing backwardness and military weakness. They received reports on the spread of English colonies in the New World, of the American Revolution, and of the rapid expansion of the United States.

They noted the appearance of Yankee vessels in the China Sea during the 1780's. Merchants from China reported the disintegration of Chinese influence in Siam and the Indies. Someday, muttered the young samurai, Japan would have to fight, and when she did, it might be too late.

The great center of samurai unrest was old southwestern Japan, the land of the sun goddess. There the clans had paid dearly for their opposition to Tokugawa rule in 1600. Two clans in particular had forfeited much land to the Tokugawas without losing any of their hereditary samurai families. Satsuma in Kyushu, with 27,000 hereditary warrior lords, and Choshu, in southwestern Honshu, with 11,000, had denser populations of unemployed swordsmen than any other region in Japan. Both clans had invested heavily in Hideyoshi's Korean campaigns and had fought strenuously against the Tokugawa policy of replacing external aggression with internal consolidation. Both clans were to play major political roles in the unleashed Japan of 1853–1945.

The Satsuma clan was governed by the branch of the imperial family named Shimazu or Island Port. Satsuma was the seagoing principality of Japan, in southern Kyushu. It had borne the brunt of the Mongol invasion in 1274. It had provided most of the ships for Hideyoshi's Korean invasion fleet in 1592. It had conquered Okinawa and the Ryukyus for the nation in 1609. It would supply more than its share of officers to the Japanese Navy in 1941. During the 1930's it would lead the fight for a Strike South against the colonies of the West in southeast Asia.

Its fellow clan, Choshu, on the main island of Honshu, was governed by another ancient branch of the imperial family, the Mori, whose name means Those Who Took Advantage of the Hairy Ones. It was a land-based power which prided itself on its provincialism and its big-handed, big-hearted family form of self-government. It despised money, cherished land, idolized the dynamic sons of the land, and held to a creed of revolutionary puritan conservatism that was strictly martial. Choshu had provided a disproportionate share of the foot soldiers who had fought with Hideyoshi in Korea and against the Tokugawas in 1600. From 1868 to 1924 its brightest spirits would control the Japanese Army and threaten to control the Japanese state. In the 1930's its partisans would lead the losing political fight for a Strike-North policy against Russia.

Being ardent loyalists, the Choshu and Satsuma swordsmen would have risen in rebellion, at any time, if they had received a word of encouragement from Kyoto. Their readiness to defy death enabled the Emperors to keep Tokugawa pride in bounds during the first century of seclusion. As Western ships and cannon became more formidable, however, Tokugawa government became more rigid, astringent, and unrealistic. The pampered Kyoto Court grew more effeminately sure of itself. In 1779 the main line of the imperial family ended without male issue and a collateral house of more vigorous cousins, the Kanins, took its place. The Kanins instituted a revival of Shinto and a more careful supervision of Tokugawa government.

About 1820 the ex-Emperor Kokaku established a school for noblemen between the ages of fifteen and forty which was to become the famous *Gaku-shu-in* or Peers' School. At the Peers' School Hirohito would learn his ABC's; at the Peers' School his son Akihito would study Western ways under Elizabeth Gray Vining, the gracious Quaker tutor recommended for him by General MacArthur. When founded, the school was meant to prepare young courtiers, who already knew how to turn a pretty verse or finger a lute, for the realities of Japanese history and government. Its noble graduates were to take over policy making in the troubled years ahead.

Year after year foreign ships poked their bowsprits vainly into Japanese harbors. Some were mere merchantmen, off course and looking for a way station in a long voyage. Many were official government vessels commissioned to open trade with Japan and put an end to her fear of foreign contamination. Russian ships began calling at Japanese fishing villages in 1739. The Tokugawa government responded by refurbishing the shore batteries along Japan's northern coasts. The first U.S. vessel came to demand trade in 1791. The shogun's government had the cannon polished on Japan's southern coasts. Illicit commerce with the West began to thrive. In 1808 the crew of a British merchantman, visiting the brothels of Nagasaki, started a brawl and called attention to the fact that it had been allowed ashore without authorization. On orders from the shogun, the mayor of Nagasaki committed suicide.

In 1837 the American brig *Morrison* approached the Kyushu coast on a carefully planned mission. In token of peaceful intent her guns had been removed. Her hold bulged with presents and trading samples of the best New England textiles. On her deck stood seven Japanese fisherman-castaways ready to be repatriated. The shogun's government had received advance warning of her mission, and the antiquated Japanese shore batteries were actually fired to drive her off before she could discharge her passengers or cargo.

The *Morrison*'s bootless voyage came at a time of growing internal crisis. The progressives of the nation had reached the end of their patience and the traditionalists on the shogun's council faced problems which they could not solve. Chinese and Dutch boats had brought a virulent form of smallpox into the country over the previous centuries and by now its ravages were endemic. Poor harvests, for several unusual years, had reduced the peasantry to starvation, stealing, and even murder. The perfect Tokugawa despotism, after two hundred years of trial, found itself bankrupt. There was a rebellion in Osaka which had to be crushed ruthlessly, and Shogun Tokugawa Ienari resigned in favor of Shogun Tokugawa Ieyoshi. The new shogun tightened purse strings and cut administrative expenses to the last ragged edge of red tape. But the depression continued. Men had to be executed as public examples for espousing free trade and an opening of the country. The Tokugawas, in their debility and desperation, had promised that soon, very soon, would come the time of paradise and imperial restoration. Young men at Court were ready to take over the responsibility.

FEAR WITHIN

The crisis of 1838–1840 broke on the nation when the first graduates of the Peers' School were approaching their mature forties. It was apparent that the Tokugawas had been lying to save face and that the millennium was not around the corner. For the first time since retired Emperor Go-Mizu-no-O's compact with the shogun in 1634, imperial princes began to plot with samurai and threaten civil war unless the Tokugawas could make good on their pledge. All the most important Buddhist temples and Shinto shrines in Kyoto were run by princely priests who were first or second cousins of the Emperor. Each temple had branches in the provinces and through these the Emperor sent secret commissions to several of the most loyal clan lords, instructing them to put pressure on the shogun and make him strengthen shore defenses. In particular the Court wooed the shogun's cousin, Lord Tokugawa Nariaki of Mito.

The loyalist Lord of Mito responded by melting down all the temple bells in his fief as cannon metal. Lord Shimazu of Satsuma in the southern island of Kyushu did likewise and soon had the most up-to-date cannon factory in Japan. The officials of the shogun became alarmed that the unauthorized preparations for war might be turned against the central government. The Lords of Satsuma and Mito were ordered to stop casting cannon, and the Tokugawa police moved in against the center of the conspiracy, the defenseless Kyoto Court. They clapped the Emperor's son-in-law, Prince Akira, into house arrest at his temple and trumped up a charge against Prince Kuniye, Akira's father, forcing him to "close his doors in disgrace."

Prince Kuniye was not a person to be trifled with in this fashion. Majestically pious, corpulent, and concupiscent, he had innumerable connections and immense influence. Neither Buddhism nor Shinto attached any stigma to bawdy, burly, worldly priests, and Priest Kuniye was as much all man as he was all aristocrat. Harlots and harlequins, hangmen and holy men jumped at his nod as quickly as the most haughty courtiers. Kuniye headed the largest of the four "imperial houses" which were entitled to provide heirs to the Throne. For generations the other houses had taxed their genes to raise one adult male per generation. At least one of their princes perished whenever the Court caught a sniffle.

Prince Kuniye's house of Fushimi, by contrast, had had at least three healthy sons in every generation for centuries. Kuniye personally had two brothers and five sons. By the time he was sixty-five he would have twelve living sons by as many mistresses. From his loins would spring the whole firmament of some fifty princelings who surrounded Hirohito in the 1930's. His son, Prince Kanin, would head the Army General Staff from 1931 to 1940. And of his grandsons, Prince Fushimi would run the Naval General Staff from 1932 to 1941; Prince Kuni would father Hirohito's wife, Empress Nagako; Prince Asaka would rape Nanking in 1937; Prince Higashikuni would hand over Japan to the Americans as prime minister in 1945; and Prince Nashimoto would be held hostage by MacArthur until the acceptance of the new Japanese Constitution in 1946.

Prince Kuniye needed no prescience to appreciate the future blackguard vigor of his family. It had always been thus. His house of Fushimi was the oldest of the collateral houses and had twigged from the main stem of the imperial family in 1372. Ever since then it had kept its place in the family and avoided demotion to commoner status by providing husbands for old-maid daughters of the Emperors. The vitality of its brood stallions matched that of the Fujiwara clan's brood mares. Fushimi princes were traditionally active men, privy to back-room policy and employed by the Throne as agents in intrigues. The very name, Fushimi, means Hidden from Sight.

The moment that Prince Kuniye and his son Prince Akira were rusticated by the Tokugawa police, two centuries of Emperor-shogun co-operation dissolved into bitter political warfare. Kuniye's uncles, brothers, and sons were all abbots at the head of the Japanese theocracy. By their preaching and purple robes they had the hearts of men and women whom the Tokugawa police could control only as bodies. From their temples they spread the insidious sermon that the Tokugawas had become disloyal subjects and impious tyrants. The Tokugawas squirmed under the attack and began to delegate their responsibilities more irresponsibly than ever. They passed about the office of shogun as if it were too hot to handle. In the next twenty years four different shoguns would occupy it and each would be a greater failure than the last.

When Japan's internal political atmosphere had become implosive as a vacuum, it happened to be the Americans, the latest intruders, who most vigorously pursued the application of external pressure. In 1844 the Yankee whaler *Manhattan* sought to win over the shogun by bringing to Tokyo a group of Japanese fishermen which it had picked up adrift in mid-Pacific. Captain Mercator Cooper was allowed to put ashore his hostages and then was turned aside by a letter from the shogun. "He thanks me for picking up their men," Cooper wrote, "and sends me word that I must not come again."

As soon as the *Manhattan* had departed, Tokugawa Nariaki of Mito resumed his manufacture of cannon in defiance of his cousin, the shogun. The shogun's army invaded Mito, put Nariaki under house arrest in his favorite temple, and had him turn over the administration of his fief to his seventeen-year-old son. Not a man to fritter away his time, Nariaki had the

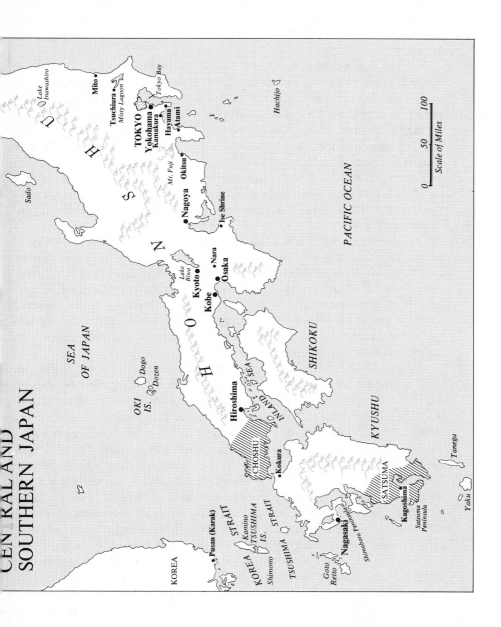

CENTRAL AND
SOUTHERN JAPAN

priests of the temple install a printing press in his apartments and began to set in type the dangerously imperial *Great History of Japan* which had circulated only in manuscript since its completion in 1715. With the help of shaven-pated assistants, the loyalist Lord of Mito was to finish setting the twenty-sixth volume in 1852, the last of his nine years of templed house arrest.

In 1846 U.S. Commodore James Biddle forced his way into Tokyo harbor with two men-of-war and demanded that the shogun sign a treaty promising American castaways good treatment and consular representation. The shogun rejected the American note politely and sent out his guard boats. As gently as they could, they surrounded the American vessels, cut their anchors, attached lines to their sprits and stays, and towed them willy-nilly back out to sea. The Yankee tars set their sails but found the breeze too light to match the oar power of two hundred men in wide straw hats pulling for dear life in their war sampans. Commodore Biddle, who was a kindly man, accepted the rebuff with equanimity and sailed home for further instructions.

Only weeks before Biddle's intrusion, the first of the Emperors who had grown up under the influence of the Peers' School ascended the Throne. Emperor Komei, as he was to be called, was a powerful, robust, handsome, haughty youth of sixteen. He had as large and high-bridged a nose, as perfectly long and oval a face, as the first Emperor, Jimmu, eighteen hundred years earlier. Emboldened by a century of neoclassical scholarship, he was an ardent Shintoist who believed in the inherent war talents of his long tamed and dormant family.

He opened his reign with a stern note to the shogun in Tokyo asking for a full report on Japan's defenses, reminding him that they must be impregnable, advising him that the policy of excluding foreigners must be upheld, and demanding that the Throne, from now on, be consulted fully on every detail of foreign policy. The shogun responded with polite meaningless promises, and young Emperor Komei was only half satisfied. He communicated frequently and secretly with Prince Kuniye, under house arrest in Nara, with the Lord of Mito, Tokugawa Nariaki, in his temple prison north of Tokyo, and with Lord Shimazu of Satsuma who was still at liberty far to the south in Kyushu. Beyond the effective reach of the shogun's police, Shimazu continued to manufacture cannon, and he built several experimental war vessels with which he hoped to match the ships of the West.

When the U.S. Navy's sloop *Preble* called in 1849, the shogun tried to keep its visit a secret and swiftly handed over to it the members of U.S. whaling crews held in Japan. Some of them had been kept and interrogated at Christian House in Tokyo, an institution which had been maintained by the police since 1640 for the de-conversion of disciples of Western philosophy.

In the summer of 1851 a gifted young Japanese fisherman named Manjiro was lowered from the Baltimore clipper *Sarah Boyd* in a small boat off the coast of Okinawa. He was returning to Japan, bent on seeing his mother before she died. By a run of incredible luck, he alone of all Japanese knew the United States. Indeed Manjiro had lived there for seven years. In 1842 he had been a poor fisher lad of sixteen caught in a terrible storm on the banks in the Japan Sea. Driven ever northeast into a world of ice, he and his four companions had been wrecked finally on one of the Aleutians. For five months they had subsisted on rain water, fish, and seaweed, and then had been miraculously rescued by the *John Howland,* a whaler out of New Bedford. Taken home to Fairhaven, Massachusetts, by the captain, Manjiro had learned English, mathematics, and basic navigation. He had signed on for a four-year whaling cruise to the South Seas and had been elected second officer by his shipmates. With his share of earnings from the cruise, he had outfitted himself as a forty-niner, had worked his way around the Horn, and had promptly stumbled on a nugget as big as an egg in the gold-fields outside San Francisco. Cashing in his winnings, he had traveled as an honored passenger on the *Sarah Boyd,* and now the boat in which he cast off from her was his own, purchased in the French-held Hawaiian port of Honolulu.

Manjiro rowed for the palm-girt coast of subtropical Okinawa with trepidation. One of the Tokugawa seclusion laws stipulated a punishment of death for any Japanese trying to return to Japan from the old Japanese settlements abroad. Manjiro relied on his tongue, his acquired wealth, and the value of his knowledge about the outside to get an exception made in his case. His shrewd judgment was rewarded. The police in Okinawa shipped him to Nagasaki, and there, after eighteen exhaustive interrogations, he performed the ritual trampling of the crucifix and was sent on to Tokyo. The shogun at once made him a government official, in charge of American intelligence. From December 1851 until July 1853, working with artists and writers, he recorded all that he had seen and heard in the lands of the barbarians. One product of his debriefing was a remarkably accurate drawing of Boston's Old North Church.

In early 1853 the head of the Dutch trading station on the artificial island of Deshima in Nagasaki harbor brought word to the shogun that an American naval officer named Perry was assembling a squadron on the coast of China in order to force his way into Japan. Manjiro urged that the American threat of force be used as a pretext for the Tokugawas to abandon the increasingly unpopular seclusion policy. The shogun's administrators listened to his advice carefully and kept him under close guard. Many of them agreed with him but felt that the Emperor must be persuaded to inaugurate any change of national policy from the summit of the state.

The issue was a delicate one, for though the Westerners were powerful and were much to be admired in some ways, they were also pernicious to the civilization of the Orient. As both Tokyo and Kyoto well knew, the

British, in 1842–43, had fought and won a war on the China coast for their traders' right to sell opium to the Chinese masses. The Chinese emperor's prestige had been so damaged by the British victory that now a rebellion to end all rebellions was in progress in China. The Taiping insurgents were a minority group of half-Christianized peasants under the command of a self-styled Chinese messiah, Hung Hsiu-ch'uan. He had set out to create a utopia of pastoral, puritanical communism in Central China. But now he and his zealots were merely killing. Before the rebellion would be suppressed in 1864 it would take five to ten million lives. Statistically—Chinese statistics always beggar the world—it would rank as the greatest war in history until World War II.

Perry's fleet was detained in 1852, doing guard duty for American trading posts on the China coast during the upheaval sweeping the Chinese hinterland. In Japan, Tokugawa Nariaki, who had just sent his first prison-printed copies of the inflammatory *Great History of Japan* to the Emperor and the shogun, was abruptly released from nine years of house arrest. So was Prince Kuniye and two of his sons in Kyoto. The officers of the shogun hoped that Emperor Komei might be persuaded by a little kindness to open Japan to foreign trade and make it unnecessary to try to resist Perry by force. Emperor Komei, however, remained as xenophobic as ever. Out of spite for the Tokugawas, he promptly appointed one of Kuniye's released sons, Prince Asahiko, as his chief advisor.

Asahiko, who was to be the father of Hirohito's two murderous uncles, Asaka and Higashikuni, was twenty-nine at the time of his appointment, just six years older than Emperor Komei himself. Through his mother's kin—all Court ladies of charm and experience—Asahiko was a near relative of Komei, some say a half brother. He resembled Komei closely except that, if anything, he was even more handsome and haughty. Unlike Komei, who was obliged to remain ceremonially closeted in the palace, Asahiko could go where he pleased. Being abbot and chief priest of the prestigious Buddhist-Shinto monastery-shrine of Shoren-In, he had business which took him all over Kyoto.

THE BLACK SHIPS

Matthew Calbraith Perry was the younger brother of the late Oliver Hazard Perry renowned for his report—"We have met the enemy and they are ours"—made after the Battle of Lake Erie in 1813. Commodore Matthew Perry had supervised the design and construction of the U.S. Navy's first steam frigate, the *Mississippi,* and had used it as his flagship in the taking of Veracruz during the war with Mexico. He was known throughout the Navy as "Old Matt," a taciturn disciplinarian with a gift for getting things done. Portly and somewhat vain about his appearance, he dressed immaculately. His double chin always puffed out over as stiff a collar and as much gold braid as the occasion would permit. He believed that America's manifest destiny—now that California in 1848 had been ceded by Mexico—extended across the Pacific. He felt that his ships, the "black ships" as they would soon be known in Japan, were "carrying the gospel of God to the heathen."

Perry's fleet consisted of two warships under sail and two side-wheelers under steam. It was calculated that the "steamers" could win a tug of war, regardless of weather conditions, against any number of guard boats that could lay a tow line on them. Perry put in first at Okinawa, a tributary island of the seagoing Satsuma clan in Kyushu. There he made a great show of discipline and firepower. His marines forced their way up the crushed-coral main street of Naha, the capital city, into the local "palace" where ruled a boy, reputed to be descended from the imperial family, under the charge of a bureaucratic "regent." After giving gifts and expressing some civilities, Perry and his men sailed on for Tokyo harbor. Perry noted with pleasure that several of the fast high-sided courier junks of the Satsuma clan's navy preceded him out of Naha harbor bearing before him the evil tidings of his coming.

On July 8, 1853, his lookouts sighted Mount Fuji rising above the horizon and soon Japanese fishing boats were seen dropping their sails in the offshore breeze, putting out their oars, and "fleeing like wild birds" for the distant coastline. At five o'clock that afternoon, when the Yankee vessels cast anchor a mile off the town of Uraga in Outer Tokyo Bay, temple bells were already ringing a tocsin throughout central Japan. In Uraga old women clapped their hands to summon the spirits at the shrines and prayed for a divine tempest to come and disperse the Yankee fleet.

In Tokyo, according to a contemporary Japanese account, "the tramp of war-horses, the clatter of armed warriors, the noise of carts, the parades of firemen, the incessant tolling of bells, the shrieks of women, the cries of children dinning all the streets of a city of more than a million souls made confusion worse confounded." Pawnbrokers and moneylenders reaped fortunes that night supplying ready cash to well-born families who wished to flee to the countryside. In his cozy private quarters behind the big draughty four-square palace in Kyoto, 300 miles to the west, Emperor Komei received news of the Americans' coming by carrier pigeon shortly after midnight.

As his ships lazed at anchor in the balmy evening breeze, Perry's first contact with the Japanese was anything but friendly. Guard boats flocked around the four Yankee vessels, and excited Japanese swarmed up lines and anchor chains to be dumped into the water by shakes, prods, and bayonet jabs. In the gathering dusk, a large official-looking junk, flying a black-and-white striped pennant, approached Perry's flagship, the side-wheeler *Susquehanna*.

"I can speak Dutch," cried a voice in faltering English.

Perry's Dutch interpreter was summoned to the rail and shouted back that Perry was prepared to see no one except the highest authority in Uraga. If the delegation was prepared to deal with Perry's subordinates, it might come aboard. Uraga's assistant police chief climbed up to the deck accompanied by an interpreter who introduced him as the vice-governor of Uraga. They were led below to the chartroom adjoining Perry's personal cabin. While Perry listened and sometimes coached from the wings, it was explained to the Japanese that the commodore was the highest officer in the U.S. Navy and could be expected to see no Japanese of lesser rank. The Japanese thenceforward referred to him always as admiral, which he found slightly embarrassing.

Perry carried with him a note from President Millard Fillmore, penned by Daniel Webster and based on a first draft scribbled by Perry himself. It demanded the opening of Japan to normal civilized intercourse and was addressed to "the Emperor." By "Emperor" the American envoys quickly made it clear that they meant "shogun." The Japanese negotiators, who were all sub-sub-officials of the Tokugawa government in Tokyo, did not disabuse the Americans but introduced all those who were to deal with Perry thereafter as "princes." Privately the Japanese compared the American ignorance unfavorably with their own knowledge of the United States which had fattened on Dutch newsbriefs since 1745. But they kept the existence of the Emperor a secret and never did reveal what he meant to them as a religious figure. When the first American consul to Japan, Townsend Harris, finally did learn of the Emperor's existence a few years later, he described it, in his journal, as "a *tabu* concealed as carefully as the *tabu* of Polynesian witchcraft."

President Fillmore's letter to the "Emperor" pointed out:

Our steamships can go from California to Japan in eighteen days. . . . If your Imperial Majesty were so far to change the ancient laws as to allow a free trade between the two countries, it would be extremely beneficial to both. . . . It sometimes happens in stormy weather that one of our ships is wrecked on your Imperial Majesty's shores. In all such cases we ask and expect, that our unfortunate people should be treated with kindness, and that their property should be protected, till we can send a vessel and bring them away. We are very much in earnest in this. . . . We understand there is a great abundance of coal and provisions in the empire of Japan. . . . We wish that our steam-ships and other vessels should be allowed to stop in Japan and supply themselves with coal, provisions and water. They will pay for them, in money, or anything else your Imperial Majesty's subjects may prefer. . . . We are very desirous of this.

The letter was written on fine vellum, sealed with the Great Seal of the United States in gold, and housed in an elegant rosewood box. The Uraga assistant chief of police was allowed to look at it. He protested that such a letter could, by law, be presented only through the authorized channel of the Dutch in Nagasaki. The unseen presence of Perry in the next room boomed that such a letter from his own emperor must be presented directly, nation to nation, at the Japanese capital—or not at all. He would give it, here in Outer Tokyo Bay, to a potentiary of his own rank and he hoped that, while he waited to do so, the Japanese would disperse the swarm of guard-boat gnats that molested his fleet. Otherwise he might shoot them out of the water.

The assistant police chief asked for time to seek further instructions and withdrew, taking most of the guard boats with him. The few that remained rowed off immediately when the *Susquehanna* launched a cutter. Night fell. As the American sailors stood watch in their nests and beside their open gun ports, the shore flickered with bonfires and signal rockets. Knights wearing shoulder-length wigs of horsehair and demon-faced helmets were riding in from all over the province, accompanied by troops of mailed swordsmen. What seemed to be great forts overlooked the harbor. Their cannon were all antiques or dummies of wood; some of their parapets were painted stage sets. Perry, peering through his telescope earlier in the evening, had pronounced them "a false show." But his men did not all share his confidence. For many it was a restless night.

At daybreak the next morning squads of samurai could be seen in split skirts, jacket-length kimonos, over-cloaks, and top-knotted hairdos practicing their exercises on the shore. They rushed at one another with staves, fenced skillfully, and uttered loud nasal grunts. Periodically they broke off their sword drill, sauntered in single file along the beach, and then, as if by common consent, suddenly set to again with their quarterstaffs. As the day brightened, several sampans approached and anchored as close as they dared to the American fleet. The Yankee sailors were astonished to see that they were full of quick-sketch artists, recording every detail of the American planking and rigging. In a week all of their drawings were being studied by the shogun's military experts and some of them were being hawked on the news-hungry, fashion-loving streets of Tokyo.

At 7:00 A.M. two large junks backed oars off the *Susquehanna* and the Uraga chief of police, presented as the governor, boarded Perry's flagship. The dialogue of the night before was repeated and confirmed and the Japanese asked for four days to send to Tokyo for instructions. They meant, of course, to Kyoto. The shogun's castle in Tokyo was only 30 miles away, or two hours by stage rider. The Kyoto Palace, on the other hand, was nearly 300 miles away—a full twenty-four-hour ride even for the fleetest couriers and horses in the government's stables. And in the present crisis the shogun would wish to send an official to Kyoto, to explain matters fully, rather than an unofficial note by carrier pigeon.

Perry, who did not know about the Emperor in Kyoto, magnanimously offered the Japanese three days in which to give him an answer. While he waited for it, he had his longboats move ahead and map Tokyo's inner harbor. Throughout their survey they were shadowed by guard boats which might easily have annihilated them.

By the appointed day, Tuesday, July 12, 1853, the shogun had received only a brief noncommittal note from the Emperor, reminding him of his duty to preserve the sanctity of Japanese soil. That morning the Uraga police chief called in his barge on Perry. He offered politely to accept President Fillmore's letter in Uraga now, provided that Perry would submit it later in Nagasaki. This was the official port for dealings with foreigners, chosen because it was a full 600 miles from Tokyo. Perry brusquely rejected the proposal and was promised that a duly accredited representative of the "Emperor" would be on hand to accept the letter on shore on Thursday, July 14.

For the next two days Japanese artisans were busy hanging drapes which would screen the huts of Uraga—and the inadequacy of the shore defenses —from the evil eye of the intruder. Miles of figured curtains bearing subtle challenges in ideographs from the samurai of the various clans were stretched between bamboo poles along the beach. At the head of the central jetty a fine ceremonial shed was constructed behind a tidy quadrangular drill ground.

On Thursday morning when Uraga's assistant police chief called at the *Susquehanna* to escort Perry ashore, he was dressed in golden trousers, wide-sleeved brocade jacket, and bright lacquer clogs. According to the official log of Perry's voyage, he had "very much the appearance of an unusually brilliant knave of trumps." Perry had ready 300 picked men who were coached in putting on a show of pomp and circumstance for the American side. As they approached the shore, it was lined with foot soldiers in ribbed armor of leather and iron, shaking clan banners of green, blue, and orange. Behind the front ranks bobbed the horned helmets of restless cavalrymen. Their jeweled hilts and inlaid scabbards flashed in the sun and their long crimson pennons dangled fluttering to the ground.

As the first marines set foot on the sacred Japanese soil, hundreds of the watching samurai grunted in anger. Perry's men relied on the cannon, run out and ready, on the ships behind them and were careful not to flinch. With a blare of silver trumpets and a clash of cymbals, the marine band struck up "Hail, Columbia" and in close order followed their vanguard ashore. Then came Perry's standard-bearer and two young ensigns carrying Fillmore's message. Behind it walked Perry, "the high and mighty mysteriousness," as the Japanese had dubbed him. He alone of all his officers was in hot dress blues, plume, and cocked hat. He was flanked by American Negroes—in the words of the log, "two of the best looking fellers of their color that the squadron could furnish." Behind him paced more marines with guns and bayonets on the ready.

The inside of the pavilion where the presentation of the letter was to be made was lined with violet silk hangings and tasseled ropes of rose, white, and blue. The Japanese emissaries, impassive as sculptured Buddhas, knelt on a dais covered with red felt. At the other end of the hall chairs were arrayed for the Americans. As far as the Japanese were concerned, chairs were Chinese artifacts, unused in Japan except by a few Buddhist priests. Since the Americans were known to sit in nothing else, however, these chairs had been collected for the occasion from Buddhist temples in the area.

As soon as Perry and his officers had sat down, the two ensigns who were serving as page boys carried the rosewood box to the edge of the dais, whence it was handed on to two dignitaries, presented as princes. They were in reality the governors of the town and of the province. The chief of police arose and read the official government acknowledgment. Its straight-forward lucidity showed clearly that the Japanese, for all their Dutch intelligence, still knew nothing of the diplomatic niceties:

> The letter of the President of the United States of North America, and copy, are hereby received, and will be delivered to the Emperor.
>
> It has been suggested many times that business relating to foreign countries cannot be done here in Uraga but only at Nagasaki. However, since we have noticed that the Admiral, in his capacity as the President's ambassador, would feel insulted by a refusal to receive the letter at this place—the justice of which has been acknowledged—we hereby receive the aforesaid letter in opposition to Japanese laws.
>
> As this is no place to negotiate with foreigners, so too we can offer you no entertainment nor hold any conference with you. The letter has been received, therefore you are able to depart.

Through his interpreters, Perry and his officers attempted to engage in some post-ceremony conversation. The Japanese dignitaries, however, responded in one-word sentences, the silences grew more long and impassive, and finally Perry had it announced that he would be back "next spring" to receive the "Emperor's answer." So saying, he turned on his heel and led his marines back through the glowering ranks of samurai to the longboats at the jetty. The phrase, "you are able to depart," rankled. Before sailing away, Perry again sent his cutters into Inner Tokyo Harbor to sound and survey. When asked by the agitated "knave of trumps" why he did not depart, he replied that he was only seeking a big enough anchorage for the large fleet he intended to bring back with him in the spring. Finally on Sunday, July 17, he sailed away, to come again eight months later.

PERRY'S RETURN

During that eight-month interval, Japan seethed inwardly. The sixty-year-old shogun took the opportunity to die of "anxiety." He was replaced by a twenty-nine-year-old nonentity. The real power passed to the new shogun's chief administrator, young Abe Masahiro, thirty-four. Abe's name meant Flattery-Department Legal-Latitude, and he lived up to it with all the statesmanly cunning at his disposal. He had been appointed with an eye to his excellent connections in the Kyoto Court. Now he sent gifts and sugary letters to Prince Asahiko, Emperor Komei's chief advisor. He appointed Asahiko's friend, Prince Shimazu Nariakira of the seagoing Satsuma clan, to the shogun's inner council. He put the loyalist Lord of Mito, newly released from his temple prison and print shop, in charge of the nation's cannon foundries.

Most important, Flattery-Department admitted that the shogun's government was baffled by the immensity of the foreign threat and needed help and counsel from the whole nation. He polled fifty-nine of the greatest of the clan lords for their advice. Almost to a man they expressed themselves, in written replies, as being opposed to the opening of the country and ready to fight if necessary. Only nineteen of them, however, favored outright rejection of Perry's demands and immediate war. Eighteen of them timorously counseled a policy of appeasement and of protracted noncommittal negotiations. The remaining twenty-two suggested that a period of foreign trade might enable Japan to acquire the arts of the West and prepare for revenge. It would be time enough, they argued, to face down the barbarians when Japan had learned the military techniques which made the barbarians so bold. This moderate position was backed by most Japanese outside the warrior caste, in particular by the despised but powerful moneylenders and merchants. The seclusion policy was now universally unpopular, for Perry's contemptuous boldness had demonstrated how far Japan, in isolation, had withered on the vine.

Fortified by the opinions of the clan lords, Flattery-Department urged the moderate position on Emperor Komei. Now twenty-two, the muscular, saturnine young Emperor was not convinced by it. Rusty as they might be after two hundred years of peace, the million samurai of Japan, in their coats of mail, on their fine Mongol ponies, with their expert swords and antique matchlocks, must still count for something. And of course Emperor Komei was right. They could have made the Yankee dream of opening Japan far too costly for any Yankee to pursue. On the other hand, Flattery-Department had broad political backing. And therefore, at the suggestion of Prince Asahiko, his chief advisor, Emperor Komei compromised. He would give no official sanction to the shogun's policy of appeasement, but unofficially, while Japan was strengthening her defenses, he would agree to give Perry courteous, noncommittal treatment.

Accordingly, when Perry returned with nine "black ships," three of them under steam, on February 11, 1854, he was met in far friendlier fashion than before. Within the violet drapes of the parley pavilion, he found men who would talk and even drink with him. Flattery-Department himself and some minor courtiers from Kyoto were there in disguise, masquerading as small officials of the shogun's government. During the six weeks of negotiations which followed, Perry presented gifts to the Japanese which he had ordered from his own country more than a year previously. They included a mile-long telegraph line over which messages could be encoded, flashed, decoded, and explained to a Japanese umpire at the receiving station long before the fastest courier could bring the same intelligence on horseback.

Still more entertaining was the black horse brought by the black ships: a miniature steam engine, about the size of a small donkey, which ran on an 18-inch track. Perry had a carnival circle of the track laid out in a field by the jetty where he and his marines were negotiating. During recesses in the talks, the Japanese delegates delighted in mounting the runt locomotive as if it were a pony. Laughing bravely and hysterically, their ceremonial skirts flowing about them, they rode the unsaddled steam monster as fast as Perry's chief fireman could run it, which was about 30 miles an hour. A Japanese student of Dutch engineering texts stood by making notes on every move of the American toy railroadman. Later, when the gift had been delivered, this studious onlooker, much to the surprise of Perry's engineering staff, succeeded in setting up and operating the locomotive merry-go-round in a Tokyo park outside the shogun's castle.[1]

When the train rides were over, Flattery-Department Legal-Latitude acceded to Perry's demands and the witnesses from Court retired to Kyoto to nurse their saddle sores and write their reports to the Emperor. While the Court reflected, the shogun's government went ahead on its own and provisionally approved the draft text of a treaty with the United States. In the months that followed, similar treaties presented by Russia and Great Britain were also accepted. Two provincial ports were to be opened to foreign intercourse; Western consular officials were to be allowed to reside in them; Western visitors who broke Japanese laws were to be tried in the treaty ports by their own consuls. This last provision, which is known as the extraterritorial-rights clause, offended Japanese officials because it implied that their own courts and police were unjust and uncivilized. If there was one institution on which Japan prided herself under Tokugawa despotism, it was the national police force.

IMPERIAL WRATH

Emperor Komei refused to approve the treaties with the West and opened a political war against the Tokugawa regime which was not to end until

---

[1] This was the beginning of a Japanese passion for railroading which has never slackened. Wherever the Japanese Army went in the first half of the twentieth century, it based its strategy on existing rail lines and built new ones. It would be for their demonic driving of slave labor in the construction of jungle railroads in Thailand, Burma, and Sumatra that many Japanese officers would be hanged as war criminals in 1946. Today the "bullet train" that routinely streaks in four hours down the 300-mile track between Tokyo and Osaka continues to testify to the thoroughness with which Japan learned its first lesson in technology from the West.

thirteen years had passed and a dozen of the ablest aristocrats in Japan had been assassinated or prompted to commit suicide. The final victim would be Emperor Komei himself.

Flattery-Department Legal-Latitude continued to negotiate with Kyoto and hoped vainly that the West would not take advantage too quickly of the concessions it had won. Commodore Perry, however, went directly from the bargaining pavilion on Tokyo Bay to spend the spring of 1854 inspecting the pretty little treaty port of Shimoda. He was disturbed to find that Shimoda, out on rugged Izu Peninsula, 80 miles from Tokyo, was entirely cut off by mountains from the rest of Japan. His seamen were shadowed and chaperoned wherever they went—even in the local brothels—by polite, inconspicuous police escorts. Japanese observers and quick-sketch artists were everywhere, looking down the muzzles of his cannon and drawing diagrams of his rigging, his dinner service, his very underwear. They even painted pictures of his own artists out painting what little they could see of the Japanese countryside.

When Perry finally sailed for home on June 28, 1854, a horde of Tokugawa officials left Shimoda at the same time to return to Tokyo. The citizens of the town breathed an anticlimactic sigh and returned to their old dull pastoral pursuits. Then in August 1856 arrived the first American consul, Townsend Harris. The local inhabitants were totally unprepared for him. It was inconceivable that he should insist on coming so soon when Perry had already been shown that he was not welcome. The villagers pointed out to Harris that no accommodations were ready for him; that the harvest had been a poor one; that there had been an earthquake; that the peasants were poorer than usual. Why not return in a few years when conditions were more settled? Consul Harris stayed. He established his consulate in an abandoned temple infested with rats, bats, and spiders, ran up the Stars and Stripes on a flagstaff, and wrote in his journal: "Grim reflections— ominous of change—undoubted beginning of the end. Query: if for the real good of Japan?" [2]

For the next three years Harris, abetted by pressure from the American, British, and Russian navies, negotiated with the Tokugawa government for a commercial treaty opening Japan fully to free trade. Flattery-Department equivocated, pressed ahead with halfhearted military preparations, and gave his main effort to negotiations with the Imperial Court. Before he opened Japan further, he needed imperial sanction for what had already been done. Emperor Komei not only refused to give it, he branded the shogun's armament efforts as spurious and questioned the shogun's reverence for the gods of the Japanese soil. Consul Harris's secretary, a young Dutch translator, noted sadly in his journal that when his Japanese counter-

[2] In later years the Japanese inscribed this journal entry on a stone monument near Harris's temple—a hint to native sightseers that the Yankees had hoped to end Japan, and had felt uneasy in conscience about it, from the start.

parts said, "We may not be able to meet again in such a pleasant manner," they sometimes meant that they had been ordered to commit hara-kiri.

Emperor Komei's advisor, Prince Asahiko, organized a subversive cell of young courtiers and clan lords. It met at Asahiko's temple, Shoren-In, which remains to this day one of the most aristocratic and inaccessible of Kyoto's holy places.[3] There, on the second floor, the acolytes built a special secret chamber for the cell meetings. No doors that looked like doors gave entrance to the room, and for exit, in the event of a police raid, there was a blind stairway, a trap door, and a tunnel leading out into the azalea garden. From this hideaway, Prince Asahiko's robed and hooded recruits disseminated a slogan that is still famous in Japan today: "Venerate the Emperor and expel the barbarians." After the clandestine meetings, Asahiko, according to one of his grandsons, often went on to the palace for further discussion. Putting the colorful canal boats and lantern-lit alleys of the Gion pleasure district at his back, he presented himself at a small postern in the southeastern wall of the palace compound and was ushered directly into the garden of Emperor Komei's private apartments. There, in his priestly robes of midnight violet,[4] he had complete freedom of access, "entering and withdrawing from the Imperial Presence even in the dead of night."

After three years of talk, intrigue, and stalemate, Flattery-Department, in 1857 found himself in an impossible position; he was caught between his promises to Emperor Komei on the one hand and on the other to internationally-minded merchants who had helped him financially. After months of negotiation with Consul Harris, his subordinates had drawn up a trade treaty with the United States which they urged him to submit to the Emperor. In vain he sent a spokesman to Kyoto to explain the advantages of world commerce. When Emperor Komei denounced the spokesman's arguments as irreligious, the thirty-eight-year-old Flattery-Department suddenly died "after a brief illness." His patron, the thirty-four-year-old shogun, fell sick and followed him to the spirit world less than eight months later.

Emperor Komei had been promised that the next shogun would be a member of the loyalist Mito branch of the Tokugawa family. The late shogun and his chief minister, Flattery-Department, had both agreed to the arrangement. But now that these two had succumbed to the overwhelming religious pressure from Kyoto, the elders of the Tokugawa council felt

[3] Unfortunately, the ninth century building in which Asahiko plotted burned down in 1893, and the present temple, what can be seen of it, is a structure of little interest, dating from 1895.

[4] At Court, as a general rule, the Emperor wore white, the color of the departed ancestors; the princes of the blood, black or deep violet, the color of secret action; the Fujiwara courtiers, crimson, the color of sex and intrigue; and lesser nobles, green, the color of the land. On some occasions the upper Court ranks could also wear yellow, the color of thought.

rebellious. In meeting to nominate a new shogun, they passed by the loyalist Lord of Mito and voted, in defiance of the Emperor, to appoint the twelve-year-old scion of another Tokugawa branch family, an unfortunate boy who will be known in these pages as Shogun Aquarius.[5]

The new chief minister who had replaced Flattery-Department and who had steered the council toward its decision was Lord I-i of Hikone, a tough, practical executive of forty-three. He proceeded at once to sign a trade treaty with Consul Harris, opening five Japanese ports to Western commerce. Emperor Komei refused to ratify the new treaty and sent it back to Tokyo with a pettish note, framed by Prince Asahiko, abdicating all responsibility for foreign relations to the government of the shogun.

A nobleman in the Kyoto Court, the thirty-three-year-old Iwakura Tomomi, who would later be called the "architect of modern Japan," promptly submitted a memorandum of protest to the Throne, advising Emperor Komei that he could not delegate his sacred authority in this fashion but must order the shogun to do his bidding. Emperor Komei was struck by the attitude of the young nobleman and elevated Iwakura to the board of imperial advisors. Iwakura was allowed to leak the news that the Emperor had abdicated his power over foreign affairs under duress and was waiting for the twelve-year-old Shogun Aquarius to reconsider. At the same time Prince Asahiko, the Emperor's principal advisor, sent north to Mito a secret commission under Emperor Komei's signature, ordering the cannon-building, *History*-publishing loyalist Lord of Mito to get rid of the shogun's objectionable new strongman. Lord I-i, the strongman, heard of the move and staged a massive counter-coup. The efficient Tokugawa police moved in on Kyoto and politely but firmly arrested more than a hundred noblemen, clan lords, and samurai who belonged to Emperor Komei's coterie of loyalists. Prince Asahiko, the chief imperial advisor, was rusticated to a little "wild" temple in the countryside outside of Kyoto, and several of his lower-ranking samurai cronies were executed. In his place, Emperor Komei took as chief advisor the idealistic young nobleman, Iwakura.

Never before had the shogun's government resorted to such a gloveless display of power. Emperor Komei warned Lord I-i that it would be civil war if he opened the ports of Kobe and Osaka—both within a day's journey of Kyoto. He coldly, flatly advised I-i: "We must assuredly keep aloof from foreigners and revert to the sound rule of seclusion." Lord I-i paid no attention. He had the young Shogun Aquarius sign the treaty in the name of Japan and in 1860 dispatched a delegation of eighteen lords and fifty-three servants to the United States to convey the instruments of ratification.

---

[5] Tokugawa Iemochi. Iemochi is an astrological given name meaning House of the Dog, or by the Western zodiac, Aquarius.

The ambassadors traveled on the U.S. *Powhatan* and took with them a Japanese escort vessel and fifty tons of baggage, including cattle, sheep, pigs, poultry, and many gifts and works of art. Their translation problems were bridged for them by Manjiro, the fisher waif who had been picked up on an Aleutian island eighteen years earlier. Wearing the traditional two swords and robes of samurai, they made a deep impression wherever they stopped —in Honolulu, Panama, Washington, Baltimore, Philadelphia, and New York. In Washington, when they went in parade to see President James Buchanan, they were cheered by a crowd estimated at 20,000. In New York they were accorded "the finest public entertainment ever given in this country"—a ball and banquet at which there were 10,000 dinner guests and five bands instructed to play all night if necessary.

The Spartan samurai were not impressed by the noise of their welcome. "There is no end to speakers," wrote one of them, "some speaking quietly, some wildly brandishing their arms." On their visit to Congress they were surprised to find a senator "making a speech at the top of his voice." They were more impressed by iced drinks and by bare-shouldered "geisha," who "hopped about" at public dances with their own husbands. But what most struck them were the massive preparations under way for the Civil War and the railroads snaking out across the huge continent toward California. In their reports later they urged emulation of Western technology but not of Western culture or religion. They found the culture "too showy" and the religion full of "good principles which are not well observed in the morality of the people."

While the shogun's scouts were reconnoitering the strength of the enemy abroad, the secluded Emperor at home plotted implacably against the minister in Tokyo who had defied him. Komei's private apartments in the Kyoto Palace became a midnight headquarters for noble recruits to the loyalist cause. There the saké cups and candles of pure wax were tended by his favorite concubine, Nakayama Yoshiko—literally Child of Joy. She was the daughter of a noble family which had suffered repeatedly at Tokugawa hands. In 1852 she had borne Komei his only healthy son, the future Emperor Meiji. Her father and brothers were all ardent believers in restoring the imperial house to direct rule. With her encouragement, Emperor Komei ordered his Chief Advisor Iwakura to recruit samurai and clan lords in western Japan for a showdown with the government in Tokyo. At her urging, Komei finally directed the loyalist Lord of Mito to do away with Strongman I-i.

Lord I-i lived in a rambling gray-tiled villa across the moat from the great palace in Tokyo. In those days the Tokyo palace was the home and fortress of the shogun. Every morning Lord I-i was carried in a sedan chair from his doorway, across the palace moat, to deliver his daily report to the adolescent Shogun Aquarius. On the morning of March 24, 1860, he began his routine as usual. An early spring had brought the cherries into bloom prematurely, and now, in an unseasonal cold wave, snow and sleet were falling with the graying petals. As Lord I-i approached the Cherry Field Gate at the southeastern corner of the palace, his bearers and bodyguards, in wide conical lacquer hats and raincoats of oiled paper, leaned against the wind as they walked. On the other side of the bridge the rear guard of Lord Shimazu of Satsuma was seen disappearing into the palace.

Lord I-i called to his bearers to make haste; he wished to be present to hear what Lord Shimazu was about to say to the young shogun. I-i's guardsmen shouldered aside a group of nondescript sightseers in cloaks who were admiring the palace keep. When his palanquin reached the throat of the bridge, seventeen of the bystanders suddenly threw off their rain capes and revealed by their crests that they were samurai of the slighted Lord of Mito.

Drawing their swords, advancing at a crouch, wheeling and leaping, they slashed their way through I-i's litter-bearers and laid them red on the snow. The shogun's guard dashed from the palace and scattered the assassins. But too late. Lord I-i of Hikone was found crumpled in his sedan chair, a headless torso. Lord I-i's head was delivered, by an assassin who escaped, to the Lord of Mito, Tokugawa Nariaki, who had ordered the deed done.[6] Nariaki spat upon the head and sent it on to Emperor Komei in Kyoto. There it was displayed for weeks on the public execution ground above a placard which stated: "This is the head of a traitor who violated the most sacred law of Japan—that which forbids the admission of foreigners into our country."

PROGRAM FOR UNITY

In the weeks that followed, handbills denouncing the shogun as a traitor were posted by night in Tokyo's main thoroughfares. Arcane scrolls of supposed great antiquity, foretelling the doom of the Tokugawa shoguns, were turned up in many parts of Japan at temples controlled by the princely high priests in Kyoto. Several notorious brigands and gamblers in the Tokugawa domains of the north were approached by noble emissaries who came in secret from Kyoto to buy their swords. Masked bands waylaid the mail on the post roads, intercepted shipments of merchant gold and distributed it to the poor. A gang of patriotic cutthroats broke into the Ashikaga mausoleum and decapitated the statues of all thirteen of the former shoguns who had ruled Japan from 1338 to 1573.

Released by their liege lords, samurai from all over the country flocked to Kyoto to offer their services to Emperor Komei. The coterie of restora-

[6] The shogun's forces claimed that this was a fake head and that Lord I-i's had been recovered after the battle at the bridge.

tionists around Komei's favorite concubine, Child of Joy, urged the Emperor to declare the shogun a usurper and to order a general uprising against the Tokugawa bureaucracy. Had Komei listened, the "restoration" would probably have taken place immediately. But Emperor Komei, influenced by conservative Fujiwara ministers, did not primarily wish to be restored—did not desire to resume direct responsibility for all civil affairs. He simply wanted the shogun to perform his office and drive out the barbarians.

Having done his duty and killed a retainer of his own Tokugawa clan, the Lord of Mito, a few months later, was found mysteriously stabbed to death in his own bathroom—a victim either of suicide or assassination. A spirit of thoughtful calm now descended on the nation. Civil war seemed hardly a sensible response to the threat of foreign invasion. For a year the country ran itself, smoothly and bureaucratically, in a political vacuum. Iwakura Tomomi, the Emperor's idealistic young advisor, spoke for reconciliation and negotiated a marriage between Emperor Komei's sister and the fifteen-year-old Shogun Aquarius. In return the shogun's bureaucracy wrung permission from Consul Harris to delay the opening of Kobe and Osaka until 1868. At the wedding the boy shogun solemnly promised the Emperor's emissaries that all foreigners would be expelled from the country by 1876.

With his sister in Tokyo Castle, Emperor Komei now felt that the Tokugawas would be respectful allies and would proceed apace with the crusade against the infidels. However Iwakura, the Emperor's advisor, knew that the problem was not so easily solved. He foresaw a long period of internal reorganization and modernization before the country would be strong enough to expel the barbarians. He was not impressed with what he had seen of the shogun's government during the marriage negotiations in Tokyo. He felt that the country needed a new form of government which would make use of all clans and factions and would rally everyone around the Throne in this time of crisis. He persuaded Emperor Komei to circularize forty-nine "outer clans" of the southwest—clans which had been excluded from any voice in the government since 1600—and ask them what programs they would recommend for Japan in her hour of need.

Most of the clans responded by pledging their loyalty to any course of action which the Emperor decided upon. But the great Choshu clan, on the southwestern tip of the main island, sent back a detailed prospectus for national unification under the Emperor and for long-range strategic planning against the barbarian enemy. First unite, modernize, and strengthen; then carry the war to the enemy by "expanding across the seas" and creating buffer zones between Japan and the West. In essence the Choshu program was that of Hideyoshi in the sixteenth century—a policy to which the Choshu clan had remained loyal throughout their two hundred and sixty-two years of banishment. With Emperor Komei's sanction, advisor Iwakura persuaded the shogun to adopt it as the long-range plan for Japan. It was to remain Japan's basic policy until 1945.

The first stage in the Choshu program, unification, was the most difficult. The decadent Court in Kyoto and bureaucracy in Tokyo were not ready for the sweeping changes which it entailed. Up to this point—early 1862—the noisiest patriots in Kyoto had been swashbuckling samurai from the seagoing Satsuma clan in Kyushu who had been given leave by their lord to go to the capital and pledge their loyalty to the imperial cause. When the program of the rival clan of Choshu was adopted by Emperor Komei, Choshu samurai also began to pour into Kyoto. In the gay streets of the geisha district, the Guion, the Satsuma men picked nightly quarrels with the newcomers. Their bloody brawls caused fires which threatened the whole city.

At Emperor Komei's order, Lord Shimazu of Satsuma came to Kyoto to suppress his troublemaking former retainers. One group of them, which had grown fond of their swaggering, masterless life, resented Shimazu's interference and plotted to assassinate their former lord. They gathered at the Teradaya Inn. It was once again the roistering season of the cherry blossoms, the spring of 1862. Lord Shimazu heard of their scheme, visited the inn in force, and in a famous melee fought entirely in darkness, killed seven of them. Sick of heart at shedding his own clansmen's blood, he resolved to rid the unification program of its Choshu leadership and the Court of its dynamic young advisor, Iwakura.

Lord Shimazu had many friends both in Tokyo and Kyoto. He was an in-law of the shogun and had sisters among the concubines at Court. He had worked with the late Lord Tokugawa of Mito in building up coastal defenses and was therefore *persona grata* to Emperor Komei. He had worked with the bureaucracy to prevent a complete rupture between Tokyo and Kyoto and was therefore *persona grata* to the Tokugawa family. After the unpleasant incident at Teradaya Inn, his first move was to have the shogun's police release Prince Asahiko, the Emperor's former first counselor—the father of Hirohito's activist uncles—from the little "wild" temple in the Kyoto suburbs where he had spent the last three years under house arrest. Then he and Asahiko had no difficulty agreeing that the first order of business was to free Emperor Komei of his upstart advisor, Iwakura, and of Iwakura's recruits, the upstart clan of Choshu.

It is a simplification but no exaggeration to say that the lines of modern Japanese history were drawn at that moment. The Army supporters of the Strike North, who wanted to turn Japanese aggression against Russia in the 1930's, were factional descendants of Iwakura and Choshu. The apostles of the Strike South, who wished to move against the West in Singapore and Manila, were to be naval admirals of Shimazu's Satsuma clan and princely sons and grandsons of Asahiko.

As the nation's highest Shinto priest, Emperor Komei was obsessed by the idea that the few foreigners on sacred soil must be driven out. Then it would be time enough to consider the problems of national fortification and reform. The charming Prince Asahiko, whose rank as a prince of the blood gave him access at all times even to Komei's bedchamber, humored the Emperor in his fixed idea and, indeed, agreed with him. For Asahiko the old order was good enough. Reform and modernization, in themselves, were not desirable.

Very different were the views of Komei's other advisor, Iwakura. He felt that the old order was stifling Japan and that the threat of suffocation from within was greater than that of desecration from without. But Iwakura, though a skillful courtier, was only one of the "New House Noblemen" and as such he was at a disadvantage—he could not see Emperor Komei without an appointment. His one bond with the Emperor was dedication. The Emperor as a religious recluse was dedicated to the preservation of his ancestral Shintoism. Iwakura, as a brilliant visionary, was dedicated to the future he saw for Japan.

In the spring of 1862, Lord Shimazu and Prince Asahiko, plotting together, finally convinced Emperor Komei that he should order the shogun to give up many of his powers and at the same time begin a terrorization of the small foreign community, thereby forcing its withdrawal from Japanese soil. On delivering this message in Tokyo, Lord Shimazu advised the ministers of sixteen-year-old Shogun Aquarius not to pay too much attention to all clauses in the Emperor's note. The important item, he said, was the intimidation of the foreign settlement. Lord Shimazu assured the shogun's faint-hearted officials that the Emperor would compromise on matters of domestic management. And the West, too, would seek terms when its bluff was called. Thousands of miles from home, without any superiority except in cannon with which to shell the fringes of the coast, what could the barbarians do?

Lord Shimazu's swordsmen, abetted by samurai from Mito, proceeded to harass the nascent foreign colony in Yokohama and to pick duels with the strongest of the shogun's administrators. They won over the shogun's advisors one by one. They slapped the faces of Frenchmen, Russians, and Americans. They set fire to the British Legation and mortally wounded two of the British consular guards.[7] Finally, when they believed that the puerile shogun understood the wishes of his brother-in-law, the Emperor, they set out once again under Lord Shimazu to return to Kyoto.

On September 14, 1862, when Lord Shimazu and his men started back down the Eastern Sea Road toward Kyoto, they encountered three Eng-

---

[7] They singled out the British as special objects of their spite because they understood that Britain was the great naval power of the West and therefore the one honorably dangerous opponent for Shimazu's seagoing Satsuma clan.

lishmen and an Englishwoman out for an early morning canter from the foreign settlement in Yokohama. The foreign sightseers blundered into Lord Shimazu's vanguard, ignorant of the fact that every Japanese, by law, was obliged to clear the road before a clan lord's progress. One of Shimazu's samurai swaggered forward and challenged the leading Englishman, a visiting merchant from Shanghai, Charles Lenox Richardson, to a duel. When Richardson failed to respond, the samurai laid him on his horse's neck with one bloody stroke. The horse of the English lady behind Richardson bolted straight into the samurai phalanx. One of the Japanese swordsmen deftly lifted his razor-sharp blade to cut off the lady's pigtails as a trophy. She galloped on, terror-stricken, to warn the English colony in Yokohama while the two untouched Englishmen behind her backed their horses, amid taunts, out of Shimazu's way.

Richardson slipped to the ground and lay bleeding at the edge of the road. When Lord Shimazu's bodyguard had ridden past, he crawled to a hut and was nursed for a few hours by a peasant. Lord Shimazu heard of what had happened and sent back a retainer to dispatch him and dispose of the body. The swordsman dismembered Richardson and ordered the peasant to bury the pieces.

What was done was done, but Lord Shimazu was not happy with his last piece of work. When he returned to Kyoto, he found that his swordsmen there had done their butchery no more artistically than their comrades in Tokyo. They had attempted and failed to exterminate the Choshu samurai from the Kyoto streets, and the old capital had become a dangerous place for him.[8] Worried about British reprisals against his provincial capital of Kagoshima, Lord Shimazu paid his respects to the Emperor and then rode hard for his home fief in Kyushu.

In his brief audience with the Emperor, Lord Shimazu complained that the sealed orders which he had taken to Shogun Aquarius in Tokyo had been less explicit about expelling barbarians than he had understood they would be. Emperor Komei, aided by his jealous advisor, Prince Asahiko, had an investigation made and discovered that unauthorized softening phrases had been written in to the final presentation copy of the orders. The Court nobleman who had physically carried them to the shogun's castle was sent in disgrace to a monastery, and advisor Iwakura, who had penned the original missive, fell under a cloud. In October, Iwakura was placed under guard in the palace, and in November, Emperor Komei issued a decree stripping him of his Court rank and offices and exiling him from Kyoto. That night, before the sentence could be executed by force, Iwakura

---

[8] During the fighting a certain Kido Koin, the adoptive grandfather of Kido Koichi, Emperor Hirohito's lord privy seal, had made a romantic name for himself by being saved from ambush by the warning of a geisha who loved him. A Choshu man by birth, he took the Satsuma side in the swordplay. He subsequently married the geisha and adopted Kido's father as his legitimate son.

obtained a disguise from his sister, who was a lady-in-waiting in the Imperial Wardrobe, and succeeded in stealing out of Kyoto. He established a hide-out in the countryside nearby, where he remained in contact with a handful of trusty Choshu samurai in the city and progressive young noblemen at Court. Emperor Komei dispatched a new emissary to Tokyo to tell Shogun Aquarius explicitly that the barbarians must be expelled forthwith.

In January 1863, the triumphant Prince Asahiko, alone now in the affections of his monarch, celebrated his thirty-ninth birthday. He had a small party at which the guests of honor were Konoye Tadahiro, the grandfather of the prime minister who would launch war on China in 1937, and Shimazu Tadayoshi, the twenty-three-year-old ward in whose name Lord Shimazu ruled over Satsuma. During the party, Prince Asahiko and the young Lord Shimazu met beside the gaunt winter skeleton of a particularly fine and sacred maple in the grounds of Asahiko's villa, and in the presence of Konoye pledged eternal friendship between their two families. This bond between the imperial house of Fushimi and the naval house of Satsuma was to remain the most dependable of the romantic feudal allegiances which would still be operative during the kaleidoscopic politics of the 1930's.

BARBARIANS UNBUDGED

During Asahiko's birthday party, the big, melancholic thirty-three-year-old Emperor was preoccupied with the scholarly problems associated with ancient imperial tombs. When the second emissary had returned from Tokyo in December, he had brought no assurance that the shogun would expel all barbarians immediately, but instead a promise that Shogun Aquarius would come to Kyoto in March to discuss the matter. With the promise was delivered a peace offering of money for the repair of the tombs of Emperor Komei's ancestors.

A Court committee had had charge of rediscovering and maintaining the old tombs ever since the beginning of the Tokugawa era in 1658, but there had never been sufficient funds for a comprehensive assault on the delicate scholarly questions of correct identification and restoration. Now the shogun's unexpected generosity, at a time when his own finances were precarious, gave the avid Shintoist Emperor a full-time diversion. The most gossipy barbarian-haters at Court, the oldest and most pettifogging Shinto neoclassicists, were set to work drawing up a list of the hundred most important mausolea and an estimate of cost for providing each with a *torii* archway, a stone lantern, a paved pathway, and a suitably inscribed marker. The day the work began a messenger was sent to announce the great event at the supposed tumulus of Jimmu, the first Emperor.

In March, the seventeen-year-old Shogun Aquarius arrived in Kyoto as promised. He planned to stay for ten days, but Emperor Komei had called a national congress of clan lords to meet with Aquarius in the Imperial Presence. As a result Aquarius's visit was to be prolonged by more than two months. In his suite of 300 retainers—a sad falling off from the 307,000 employed by the shogun under similar circumstances in 1634— he brought with him most of the men who had negotiated with Commodore Perry and Consul Harris or had firsthand knowledge of the United States. In vain they explained to the clan congress the immensity of the industrial revolution which had swept the West and the futility of barring the barbarians until Japan had undergone the same process.

The spiritualistic Emperor Komei was not impressed. Komei was at the height of his funerary enthusiasms and was living with ghosts. He persuaded a majority of the dubious clan lords to agree that a holy war should be opened against the West on June 25, 1863. Then, after much feasting and drinking of tea and saké, he accompanied the bemused adolescent shogun in a great midnight parade to the shrine of Hachiman, the god of war, atop Kyoto's Mount Otoko. There, in the flickering light of pine torches, he performed a brief, severe Shinto evocation of the shades and presented Shogun Aquarius with an ancient sword from one of the imperial troves. In bestowing it, he repeated the divine commission: rid Japan of infidels by June 25.

Early in May rumors of the song being sung by the Voice of the Crane leaked out to the peasant grapevine. The coasts of Japan were evacuated by tens of thousands of women and children. On May 5, the foreign settlers in Yokohama noted with dismay the overnight disappearance of all their Japanese servants. They attributed it to the stiffness of the indemnity— £100,000 sterling—which the British were demanding for the murder of the young Englishman, Richardson, eight months earlier.

Not long after the panic on the coasts, Shogun Aquarius and his retinue returned from Kyoto to Tokyo, outraged but outvoted. They came, not by the great Eastern Sea Road, but by ship, which somewhat restored public confidence in the possibility of peace. The shogun's ministers proceeded to negotiate with the West in a conciliatory fashion. On June 24, the day before Emperor Komei's war deadline, Shogun Aquarius—in a gesture of defiance to the Throne—acceded to British demands and paid the £100,-000. All morning long, crates of Mexican silver were carried from the Tokugawa treasure house to the British dock and counted and weighed in front of witnesses.

The news spread by carrier pigeon that the Tokugawas, the most powerful of the clans, did not intend to participate in the holy war. The other lords, reverent as they were of the Emperor as the cornerstone of their aristocratic system, did not share in his Shinto mania. The next day, when the war was to have begun, every clan remained at home except that of Choshu.

Because of its rowdy samurai in the Kyoto streets, Choshu was in disfavor at Court. Its leading noble protagonist, the former Imperial Advisor Iwakura, was in hiding. It was in order to make amends and recommend itself once more to imperial favor that Choshu now took action alone. An American ship, passing through the narrow straits of Shimonoseki, which separated Honshu from Kyushu and Choshu from Satsuma, was shelled without warning by the Choshu forts on the north bank. The American vessel barely survived the barrage and limped home to Yokohama with bloody scuppers and broken rigging.

Much excited, the consuls and attachés in Yokohama demanded that Shogun Aquarius bring the clans into line. Without ever mentioning Emperor Komei, Aquarius's ministers pleaded naval weakness and internal dissension and invited the foreign powers to seek their own satisfaction. A joint Anglo-French fleet duly sailed south in July and shelled the seventy-four cannon on the Choshu coast into silence. Then the marines of the task force went ashore and helped to put out the fires they had started. They found the natives surprisingly friendly. Choshu had made its gesture and saved face. Only about fifty of its warriors had been killed.

In early August, again with encouragement from Aquarius's ministers, a British fleet hove to off the Satsuma clan capital of Kagoshima in Kyushu to demand the surrender of Richardson's murderer to Western justice. Satsuma's Lord Shimazu refused and had his shore batteries open fire. The British flagship was, for an hour, unable to return the fire because she had the £100,000 indemnity silver stacked in cases over the hatch to her magazine. The Satsuma gunners worked with better cannon than their Choshu counterparts and succeeded in killing and wounding no less than sixty-three English sailors. Finally the British squadron began to pump incendiary rockets into Kagoshima. When half the flammable town was burning, the Satsuma marksmen deserted their posts for higher duty as fire fighters. This time the marines did not land to help. The British fleet sailed away without accomplishing its purpose. The deft swordsman who had cut Richardson down remained behind in the bosom of his people where he was to live to an honored old age.

Emperor Komei was elated by the news of heroism brought from Choshu and Satsuma and disgusted with his brother-in-law the shogun for conciliating the foreigners. Clearly the Tokugawas were no longer fit to wear the title of *Sei-i Dai Shogun,* Great Barbarian-suppressing General. And so Emperor Komei called on his loyalist samurai in Kyoto to revolt and overthrow the Tokugawa government. Three years earlier, such a rising would probably have swept the country. Now the clan lords had begun to doubt the wisdom of the Emperor's xenophobia, and Komei had to entrust his revolution to the rabid Shinto scholars at Court and to their rabble of samurai followers.

Being pedants and ceremonialists, the insurgents laid their plans with a keener sense of symbolism than of realism. They started by giving their plot the name of *Tenchu,* Heavenly Retribution. Then they decided that the signal for the uprising should be a state visit by Emperor Komei to the ancient capital of Yoshino where the schismatic restorationist Emperors of the southern dynasty had dined on pride in the fourteenth century. The brother of Child of Joy, Komei's favorite concubine, was to be ready in Yoshino with a small force of loyalists. They would proclaim "the restoration," attack the local Tokugawa police garrison, and then, because of Yoshino's historical associations, they could expect the whole countryside to rally to the imperial cause.

Optimistic as the plot was, the populace might have responded to it if Choshu and Satsuma had had any luck against the fleets sent to bombard them. In their first reports to Kyoto both clans glossed over their losses and exaggerated the damage they had inflicted. The populace, which had its grapevine, knew better, but the secluded Emperor Komei went ahead with his plans undaunted. Then, in late September 1863, on the eve of the uprising, Lord Shimazu and his retinue of Satsuma samurai galloped into Kyoto on lathered horses. Hasting to the villa of Prince Asahiko, Emperor Komei's advisor, Shimazu confessed that reports of victory over the barbarians had been grossly exaggerated. Shimazu was prepared to go before the Emperor and admit the truth. Prince Asahiko, however, proposed a way of softening the blow—of saving both his friend's face and the Emperor's.

That night a group of loyalist courtiers were closeted with Emperor Komei in his private apartments, fussing over last-minute details of their coup. The Emperor in a kimono of white silk sat cross-legged before a golden screen. His fellow conspirators knelt at the other end of the room, touching their heads to the matting as preface whenever they spoke. From time to time ladies-in-waiting brought freshly warmed saké to the door of the room. There they would kneel and press their foreheads to the floor. Also kneeling and bowing, Child of Joy, the favorite concubine, would accept the pitchers and, without ever rising from her knees, would move about the room refilling the tiny cups of her lord and his guests. The sliding doors to the veranda and garden were closed to an early nip of autumn and the room glowed in the subdued light of an aromatic oil lantern.

Suddenly the veranda doors were thrown open and Prince Asahiko burst in, prostrating himself and wearing the old priestly garments which he had not had on for two years. In a hushed voice of awe he declared that he had just had a religious vision; that he had been commanded to resume the cloth; that he had been sent to warn the Emperor against any bloodshed while the stars hung in their present configuration. It had been revealed to him, he said, that natural disasters would temporarily rob the imperial cause of its victories. His forebodings were confirmed a few hours later when Lord Shimazu unexpectedly arrived from Satsuma and told Emperor

Komei of the great fire which had swept his provincial capital after the repulse of the British fleet.

Against the will of the spirits, nothing could be done. Emperor Komei abruptly canceled his rising against the Tokugawas and exiled seven of his most firebrand restorationist nobles. His concubine's brother in Yoshino—the uncle of the ten-year-old crown prince, the future Emperor Meiji—did not hear of the cancellation in time and went ahead according to plan. He seized local government offices and set out to attack the Tokugawa police barracks. After a brief beating, the shogun's troops regrouped, summoned reinforcements, hunted down the rebels, and executed Child of Joy's brother. In Kyoto Lord Shimazu's men rounded up many troublemaking Choshu and Satsuma samurai and packed them off to the clan capitals with Emperor Komei's seven banished noblemen.

CIVIL WAR

In March 1864 at a national council of reconciliation in Kyoto, the new loyalist Lord of Mito, a Tokugawa, and the equally loyalist Lord of Choshu fell into a drunken quarrel before the Emperor. As a result a Choshu contingent marched north on Kyoto with a bill of grievances and a petition imploring the Emperor to broaden his circle of advisors. The Choshu men were driven off by the Tokugawa police, and Emperor Komei agreed half-heartedly to a Tokugawa expedition against Choshu.

Shogun Aquarius marched south with an army of 150,000 samurai. The young progressive leaders of Choshu prepared to meet him with cadres of riflemen which they had trained in the European style of warfare. At the last moment hostilities were averted by intermediaries from the neutral seagoing clan of Satsuma. The Choshu young bloods were not satisfied with the truce. They no longer believed it possible to compromise with Japanese traditionalists. Only a thoroughgoing reform and Westernization of the nation, they felt, would suffice to meet the challenge of the West. Kido Koin, the adoptive grandfather of Hirohito's lord privy seal, led a coup within the provincial Choshu government and unseated the clan elders who had agreed to accept peace.

In 1865 while the young samurai leaders of Choshu continued to prepare for civil war, a joint Anglo-French fleet stationed itself off the unopened treaty port of Kobe, in the Kyoto area, and requested menacingly that Japan hurry up in fulfilling her treaty commitments. Shogun Aquarius, still scarcely nineteen, moved his headquarters in June to Osaka to be near the Emperor in the hour of emergency. Horrified at the dissension that had settled on the nation, Emperor Komei was induced by Prince Asahiko and Lord Shimazu to give his sanction, at long last, to the treaties which had been negotiated eleven years earlier with the Western powers.

Having postponed the barbarian threat, young Shogun Aquarius took the government into his own hands and mounted a fresh expedition against Choshu to dispose of the domestic threat. Emperor Komei frowned, and none but the Tokugawa fiefs of the north would contribute troops to the expedition. Nevertheless the headstrong young shogun moved ahead into Choshu territory. His big army won ground but suffered staggering losses to Choshu riflemen who took their toll and vanished. The Choshu captains of the rifle companies were the future generals who would run the Japanese Army until the 1920's. The military advisors of Shogun Aquarius warned that the big army would be decimated before it ever met the main body of the Choshu forces. In September 1866 Shogun Aquarius, a twenty-year-old failure, abruptly died of an "abdominal disorder," presumably self-inflicted.

REGICIDE

The nation had come to a standstill. The Tokugawas, the Court nobles, and the lords of Choshu and Satsuma had all made their loyal efforts, but imperial wishes remained as unrealistic and insatiable as ever. Emperor Komei appointed the young loyalist Lord of Mito to be the next shogun and called on him to settle internal dissension and proceed with the expulsion of the barbarians. In December 1866, Emperor Komei and the new shogun called another council of the nation's clan lords. Of twenty-four lords invited to participate, only five came.

On January 15, 1867, Emperor Komei had a cold and his doctors prescribed a potion for him. One of the elder ladies-in-waiting, who performed menial palace housework, later said: "He was given smallpox poison." Japanese physicians, who were conversant with Dutch medical texts, had been experimenting with smallpox vaccines since about 1840. It may be that what the old woman called "poison" was an oral vaccine which Emperor Komei took in hopes that it would protect him from the recurrent epidemics which swept Kyoto. The next morning Emperor Komei felt "unpleasant," and against his doctors' advice insisted on performing his customary rituals at the palace shrine. By January 18 he was confined to bed, was running a high fever, could not eat or sleep, and babbled deliriously. The next day his chief physician diagnosed a case of "either smallpox or melancholy fever."

"A man full of blood and muscles, who never suffers so much as a sniffle," noted one of the courtiers in his diary. "This is indeed surprising and regrettable."

In the days that followed the vigorous young Emperor went through a typical case of smallpox. The pustules appeared on January 20. On the twenty-first he tossed with fever and from time to time vomited. On the twenty-second his doctors diagnosed smallpox definitely and gave orders that "prayers be said for him at the seven temples." By the twenty-third he was covered with oily pustules and his throat was too sore to eat anything but chilled liquids. On the twenty-fourth the pox turned purple, he ate some rice gruel and passed wastes from the "honorable eighth and ninth holes." [9] By January 26 he was so far recovered that Shogun Tokugawa Yoshinobu, Lord of Mito, visited his bedside. The doctors called the twenty-seventh and twenty-eighth the "key days of the crisis." The pus stopped oozing and the pox began to dry. On the twenty-ninth he seemed fully convalescent and ate heartily.

That night his handmaidens gave him a bath and a thimble or two of his favorite saké. The next day, January 30, 1867, he awoke in misery. The great draughty palace was unusually quiet and cold. No one was about but ladies-in-waiting. He asked that his half score of doctors be summoned and was given the chilling intelligence that every single one of them had been called from the palace that day on other business. Too weak to move, he dozed and waited. Somewhere in the distance a female attendant told one of his sisters that she could not be admitted to his sick chamber. He vomited repeatedly, "breathed like an insect," and "passed blood from the honorable ninth hole." Late in the afternoon he fell into a coma. During the evening his doctors reappeared in force, examined him, found his pulse growing weaker and his limbs colder. At 11:00 P.M. he died.

The death was not announced for four days, the funeral not held for thirty-two days. To courtiers whose diaries have been preserved, it appeared that Emperor Komei had survived a classic case of smallpox only to fall prey to a classic case of poisoning.

Iwakura Tomomi, the nobleman who had once been Emperor Komei's chief advisor and had been living for four years in exile and hiding outside the Kyoto city walls, returned to Court immediately. One week after Komei's death, when he was still locked in struggle with Komei's other advisor, Prince Asahiko, Iwakura sent a letter to one of the progressive samurai of Satsuma, one of the future leaders of Japan, with whom he had corresponded throughout the years of his rustication and plotting. In it, he wrote: "I wish to release you and the others from any responsibility or punishment. I alone am responsible." His correspondent wrote back: "Silence is the best course."

It was no light matter to do away with an Emperor. Whatever their foibles, the Emperors were gods and none of them had been assassinated since Emperor Sushun in 592. Others as well as nobleman Iwakura were surely implicated in the strange death of Emperor Komei in 1867. Possibly the devout Shintoist Emperor himself, believing that he was doomed to failure, trapped between the demands of his ancestors and the wishes of his people, had even agreed to die as an extreme form of abdication—a withdrawal to power behind the curtain in the spirit world.

[9] The first seven were eyes, ears, nostrils, and mouth.

The honorable Iwakura took all the royal blood on his own head and dedicated the rest of his life to the selfless service of Emperor Meiji, Komei's son and Hirohito's grandfather.

Iwakura returned to Court with adequate backing from young Choshu and Satsuma warriors and with a large following among the Fujiwara officials in the palace. The position of his rival advisor was parlous. Prince Asahiko tendered his resignation immediately to the new Emperor, the fourteen-year-old Emperor Meiji, and had it accepted.

As a gesture of deference to the old regime, Iwakura, who was now firmly in command, organized a fine funeral for Emperor Komei and had him buried, uncremated, in the pure Shinto fashion of the earliest "Viking" Emperors. A spur on the slopes of the pine-covered mountains east of Kyoto was cut away in a large mound 148 feet in diameter. Three terraces supported by retaining walls of cut stone led up to the grave beside which waited an immense rock of great beauty, brought from afar, to be rolled in over the coffin. Komei's body was borne to the site at eleven in the morning and placed in a stone sarcophagus. For the next five hours it inched its way up the burial mound, through countless ceremonies and symbolic barriers. At each stop priests and favorite noblemen were left behind until finally, at the top, only four pallbearers, Komei's most cherished retainers, were left to move the heavy sarcophagus into its pit and lever the great stone over the gaping hole. At four in the afternoon the last prayer was said and the loyal courtiers retired in the dusk.

A few hours later Iwakura Tomomi climbed the mound alone and knelt by the grave in the darkness. All night he remained there kneeling, praying, listening to the sighing of pine needles in the wind, explaining himself and trying to propitiate the angry imperial spirit he imagined hovering before him.

RESTORATION

Even as he prayed, Iwakura was reviewing the plans he had for a new Japan. Writing letters and receiving only night visitors at his cottage outside the city during his five years of exile, he had had much time to think. As with many other great men, a long period of enforced quiet had allowed him to solidify his ideas and accumulate a realistic program for the future. Even before the funeral he had set committees to work drafting plans for a new currency, a new capital, a new landholding system, a new way of government.

In January 1868, the juvenile Emperor Meiji issued a rescript, penned by Iwakura, abolishing the thousand-year-old system of "curtain government" and announcing reinstitution of direct rule by the imperial family. The well-administered clans of the Tokugawa in the north were dismayed at the prospect of being managed by priests from Kyoto and begged the shogun to bring the Emperor to his senses. Shogun Tokugawa Yoshinobu led a small military retinue of 30,000 toward Kyoto for a parley.

Iwakura advised the adolescent Emperor to take military action against this attempt at intimidation. Let the people see that the Tokugawas were powerless on the battlefield and that the Emperor meant to make a complete break with the past. Emperor Meiji and his family council accepted Iwakura's advice and put two princes of the blood in charge of a large army of samurai from the "outer clans" recruited by Iwakura. The imperial forces fell upon Tokugawa Yoshinobu's 30,000 retainers in the outskirts of Kyoto and routed them utterly.

With little bloodshed, against token resistance, the imperial armies drove north on Tokyo. The former shogun ceded to the Emperor his great fortress of Edo Castle, the future Imperial Palace, and retired to his home fief of Mito, which every Japanese knew to have been a center of loyalty to the Emperor for over two hundred years. There the last shogun disbanded his troops and waited. The new imperial regime in Tokyo first sentenced him to death, then to lifelong rustication, and finally invited him back to free converse in the councils of state. A few diehard retainers of other branches of the Tokugawa family continued to resist in north Japan, but after a year of ritual suicides and little real military action, the whole nation was in the hands of Iwakura and his samurai henchmen from Choshu.

With the help of another Court noble, Sanjo Sanetomi, Iwakura ran his radical young samurai as an oligarchy of comrades under strict revolutionary discipline. Each oligarch was assigned some task of reform such as breakdown of class distinctions or abolition of clan autonomy and was told to draw up a program for his project. Then, if the Emperor and the imperial family council approved it, Iwakura made the oligarch publicly responsible for putting his plan into effect. The people were encouraged to think that the Emperor signed whatever Iwakura laid before him. Thus the advantages of the old system of government were not abandoned: the oligarchy of young reformers were used in traditional fashion as a curtain, hanging like a new shogunate between the Court and the populace.

Behind the curtain stood the fifteen-year-old boy, Emperor Meiji.[10] The first and only Westerner to have a glimpse of him in his traditional Kyoto surroundings was Sir Harry Parkes, the British ambassador to Tokyo. When it was announced that henceforth the Emperor would be head of state and would sign all treaties, Parkes journeyed to Kyoto in March 1868 and requested an audience in which to present his credentials. On his way to the palace, he and his retinue were set upon by two expert

[10] Strictly speaking, Emperor Meiji in his lifetime should be called by his personal name, Mutsuhito. Meiji, Enlightened Rule, is the name he gave his reign and the name he is supposed to bear after death in the spirit world.

swordsmen, one of them a warrior monk from a temple presided over by one of Prince Asahiko's priestly brothers. Before the two crouching, leaping, slashing assassins could be stopped they had wounded eleven of Parkes's Japanese guards, one of his English infantry escort, his groom, one of the Japanese officials accompanying him, and four of the party's horses.

Nothing deterred, Parkes made a fresh appointment at the palace and a few days later was ushered into one of the long bleak audience chambers there. At the far end was a dais flanked by a carved lion in black lacquer and another in gold lacquer. Over it hung a canopy of pure white silk on a frame of slender black lacquered pillars. The white drapes were tied back with bright red sashes. Before the dais, on a lawn of green silk, knelt two princes of the blood, one a general, the other a priest. The clan lords of Choshu and Satsuma knelt in deep obeisance at one side, utterly immobile and impassive in glistening robes stamped with their clan crests. Courtiers jostled outside the doorway wearing belted, thigh-length kimonos, divided skirts, and high black-lacquered hats that looked like loaves of bread tied to their heads.

As Parkes entered, Emperor Meiji on the dais arose in a white brocade, full-sleeved, tunic-length kimono and a pair of flowing crimson culottes, cut so that the leg ends trailed in little trains behind his high black-and-gold lacquered clogs. On his head was tied a mortarboard from which towered an oblong two-foot fertility symbol of stiff black lacquered silk, stamped with a suitable inscription in red. His face was powdered mask white. His cheeks were rouged. His lips were painted red and gold. His teeth were lacquered black. In a high singsong voice, he read a scroll accepting Ambassador Parkes's credentials and the audience was over.

Behind the doll face of this pampered boy worked a strong will and a keen intelligence. Meiji had been born during the early winter of 1852 in an unpretentious cottage nestled beside the carved wooden gables of minor courtiers and courtesans under the high white wall along the north edge of the outer palace compound in Kyoto. His mother was not the official Empress, a regal Fujiwara girl, but the vivacious, dedicated Child of Joy, the favorite of Emperor Komei's score of Court-lady concubines. Because of his birth to a second-class noblewoman, Meiji had the privilege of being brought up until the age of eight by his natural mother and by her rabidly loyalist father instead of by a committee of aged chamberlains as was the wont with crown princes. On the death of the last of his half brothers in 1860, Meiji was declared heir apparent and put into normal ceremonial harness. In 1863, when the shogun visited Kyoto in state and gave money for the rehabilitation of imperial tombs, Meiji and Komei officiated together at an elaborate Shinto ceremony in the palace garden known as "worship at a distance."

Throughout the next three years, until his father's death, Meiji remained beside the Throne at all occasions of state. He came to revere the Shinto pantheon of his ancestors, to admire the free samurai spirits who swaggered in and out of the west gate of the palace, to detest the heavy robes and ceremony of state occasions, and to feel fired by the dreams of a reborn Japan, the stories of Western material progress and power, which were told him in confidence by some of the more cosmopolitan clan lords who paid homage to his father. Although not a robust child, he was sensitive and quick and had a way of endearing himself to all the strident conflicting personalities who came and went from the palace during those final tumultuous years of Emperor Komei's reign.

When Emperor Komei was killed and Iwakura returned from exile, Emperor Meiji was protected from knowledge of the sordid intrigue at Court and was soon a devoted admirer of Iwakura, the new strongman. It is likely that he had already met Iwakura, for during the final year of his banishment the revolutionary young nobleman had frequently visited the palace in secret at night. It is even said that he sometimes met with Emperor Komei, his banisher, and under flag of truce, by imperial request, aired his views on the state of the nation.

Sheltered child though he was, Emperor Meiji, even in the first year of his reign, was never a cipher. He disapproved of his father's handling of the Court, he considered many of the princely priests who were his cousins to be dangerous "madmen," and he responded to the magnetism of Iwakura. From the beginning he showed powers of decision, compromise, and realism that contrasted sharply with the sulky, conservative standing on principle of his father. Emperor Komei had been sacrificed because his words, in favor of a foolish, impossible policy, carried so much weight that there was no other way to get around them. Emperor Meiji, though he did not hear until years later of the suspicious circumstances surrounding his father's death, was careful from the first not to take upon himself too much godliness. He insisted on his right to be wrong in informal discussions, and in formal capacities he never spoke until he was sure he was right. Iwakura helped to train him in this stance and was always careful to discuss and explain all matters of state with him in great detail.

Having announced that he would rule Japan in person, young Emperor Meiji's first act was to transfer his capital from the tradition-laden city of Kyoto, where the Throne had remained since A.D. 794, and from the Western Plain of Yamato, where his "Viking" progenitors had come ashore, to the Eastern Plain and its bustling port city of Tokyo or Edo, where the shoguns had ruled for seven hundred years. Here was Japan's true center of gravity, and Iwakura, the chief of the new samurai oligarchy, was determined that Emperor Meiji should sit in it.

In November 1868, in the longest state progress of Japanese history, the entire Imperial Court wended its way, by easy stages, up the 300-mile length of the Eastern Sea Road. At every mile peasants lay prostrate along the shoulders of the highway to be present when the Being from above the Clouds passed. On November 26, 1868, twenty-three days after Meiji's sixteenth birthday, the imperial palanquin entered Tokyo. Three Westerners were on hand to watch. Meiji rode in a black lacquered sedan chair surmounted by a phoenix of gold, its head and body like a peacock's, its tail like a copper pheasant's fanned out forward over its eyes. Sixty bearers and guardsmen of the imperial blood, robed in yellow silk and wearing tiny chrysanthemum-shaped earrings of feathers, walked beside him. In front paced three aged lictors shaking fans at the assembled multitudes to warn them of the imperial approach. The crowds knelt in waves on either side of the imperial retinue, gluing foreheads to the dust until it passed.

In January 1869, from the former palace of the shoguns, Emperor Meiji decreed that commoners must no longer prostrate themselves in this fashion except before official imperial progresses. Then he ventured forth, unofficially, to inspect the first Western-style vessel built in Japan for a proposed national navy. At the same time he declared Tokyo open to foreigners and advised that henceforth foreigners should be addressed in the noncommittal polite second person which was reserved in Japanese verb forms for the occasional awkward situation in which the speaker did not know the rank of the person he was talking to. Psychologically the new form of address was a great advance over the bellicose, "Hey, you, barbarian inferior," or the obsequious "Hail, outside eminence," which had been in use previously. And since Westerners, learning Japanese, tended to speak as they were spoken to, the new form led to a great improvement in Western-Japanese relations.

The original program for dealing with the Western menace still stood as submitted to the Emperor by the Choshu clan in 1862. First Japan must grow strong; then she must expand overseas to establish a defense perimeter outside the sacred soil; then and only then should she expel the barbarians. But Emperor Meiji's edicts told every Japanese of sensitivity that the program was to be put into effect cautiously, with patience. Emperor Komei's frontal attacks had been rebuffed. The time had come to approach the cherished goal obliquely.

THE MIRACLE

Fresh edicts issued almost daily from the new palace in Tokyo. The incongruous pair, the assassin and his victim's son, worked together with astonishing wisdom and harmony. And still more extraordinary, Japan's ancient, almost fossilized tribal society responded.

Not only the common people but also the most entrenched vested in-

terests of Japan answered to the challenge. The refined sensibilities of
every member of the race—perhaps the most aesthetic, ascetic, romantic,
disciplined, highly educated people on earth at that time—had been
rubbed raw. It was as if everyone felt a personal responsibility for the
state of affairs which had led to the killing of Emperor Komei. In two
years, between 1869 and 1871, a miracle of idealism and self-sacrifice
took place. While token civil war with Tokugawa partisans was still
a-dying, all the feudal clan lords voluntarily relinquished the fiefs which
they had ruled for centuries and gave back their patrimonies to the Emperor. The samurai, who constituted 5 or 6 per cent of the population,
gave up their special rights to kill to preserve the peace and to be fed
without touching money or doing work and accepted a status under law
equal to that of other citizens. The people themselves promised to give
up their own class distinctions and behave as equals.

There was an outcast class, the Eta or Many Filthy Ones, which was
descended from the aboriginal Japanese population, augmented by "non-
men" outlaws from the criminal ranks of the rest of society. Decree gave
to the Eta—approximately 5 per cent of the population—equal rights
under the law with other citizens. And though prejudice against them
persisted—and does to this day—Emperor Meiji's edict on their behalf
was enforced with remarkable fairness.

The most leveling of all the revolutionary imperial decrees called for
the establishment of a national army and navy conscripted from the whole
population without regard for birth in or outside of the traditional warrior
caste. True, the officers were all former samurai, but in the ranks commoners and samurai mixed. Peasants and untouchables felt positively
proud to be conscripted.

As soon as the new laws had been promulgated and before they had
worked themselves out in terms of enforcement, the idealistic Iwakura
confidently turned over his Emperor and his oligarchy to the care of his
lieutenant noble, Sanjo Sanetomi, and went on a scouting trip abroad.
Officially his mission was diplomatic: to renegotiate the treaties with the
West so that Westerners, residing in Japan, would be subject to Japanese
laws and could not fall back on the tender mercies of their own consular
courts. In this official purpose Iwakura failed, for no Western nation was
ready to relegate its nationals to the inscrutable mental processes of Japanese judges and police interpreters. In the real, unofficial purpose of his
mission, Iwakura was more successful: he saw for himself what Japan
had to contend with. For two years he reconnoitered the capitals of Europe
and America as an honored visitor. In his guarded letters home he expressed dismay at the way power was used in the West, unchecked by any
of the family feeling and cohesiveness which gloved fists in Japan. He
was impressed by the dispassionate scientific quest for logic which made

possible, always, the manufacture of bigger cannon. In a later report to Emperor Meiji he dwelt in particular on an off-the-cuff lesson in *Realpolitik* which he had received from the old master, Bismarck. "The only way," said Bismarck, "for a country like Japan is to strengthen and protect herself with all her own might and set no reliance in other nations. . . . When international law is not to a nation's advantage, it is ignored and resort is made to war."

Iwakura's eyes were still opening when, in 1872, he was called home by rumors of a breakup in his oligarchy. The king of Korea was refusing to open ports to Japanese commerce. He was doing so as rudely and stubbornly as Japan had done earlier in the face of Western trade demands. During Iwakura's absence, his deputy, the nobleman Sanjo Sanetomi, had sided with the Emperor and a group of young Satsuma oligarchs in advocating a military expedition to teach Korea a lesson. Iwakura hastened home, his head swimming with the immensity of the task of modernization confronting Japan. He demonstrated to the twenty-year-old Emperor Meiji, in economic black and red, that the game was not yet worth playing; that Korea was too small and intractable, and Japan too poor, to make the prize worth the effort.

Iwakura found his reborn nation slipping back into the abyss. The economy was a chaos and the would-be conquistadors of Korea were ready for rebellion. For five years Iwakura wrestled with the situation masterfully. He gradually forced Korea, by gunboat diplomacy, to open her ports, and at the same time he checked Japan's runaway inflation. In return for promises of preferential treatment in the future—government pledges which later became the cornerstones of Japan's cartel system and the grubstake of most modern Japanese fortunes—he drew on the gold hoarded by wealthy merchants and established public confidence in his currency and bonds.

Finally, in 1877, Iwakura felt strong enough to challenge the rebels of the Conquer-Korea faction whose threat had brought him home in 1872. The rebels had withdrawn to Kyushu and had enlisted most of the samurai of the seagoing Satsuma clan. They were led by Satsuma oligarch Saigo Takamori. Iwakura set against them Satsuma oligarch Okubo Toshimichi who had grown up on the same street with Saigo but had also accompanied Iwakura to Europe and there shared with Iwakura a look at the realities of the modern world.[11] Under Okubo the nascent national army of Japan, recruited from all classes, crushed the proud samurai of Satsuma and left rebel leader Saigo to commit suicide on a mountaintop with his last 400 supporters.

[11] Okubo was the father of Count Makino Nobuaki who would be Hirohito's chief advisor and lord privy seal from 1922 to 1935. On Iwakura's European tour Okubo had been the Satsuma clan's representative. The Choshu clan representative had been Kido Koin, the adoptive grandfather of Kido Koichi who would be Hirohito's chief advisor and lord privy seal from 1940 to 1945.

THE WORKING YEARS

Now that the foreign putsch had been postponed, now that the clan lords had returned their fiefs to the Throne, now that inflation had been checked and all eager spirits taught to be patient awhile in harness, the nation for fifteen years germinated in the soil of hard work and money-making. The Japanese home craftsman became the light industrialist. The Japanese merchant became the shipping magnate. The Japanese moneylender became the financier. Tokyo, Osaka, Hiroshima, Nagasaki, and Kokura grew into industrial centers where armies of peasants from the countryside learned a new urban way of life working in mills and banks and railroad yards.

The patriotic duty of absorbing the spiritual strength of the West was practiced religiously by everyone—by tailors and musicians and dramatists as well as by technologists. As a result wave after wave of Western imitation swept over the surface of Japanese culture. Clan lords bustled about Tokyo wearing two swords, top hats, and plus fours. More than 30,000 Western "classics" were roughly translated into the Japanese language and given to the literate public to puzzle over. Painters deserted their own refined native style and took to copying the robust realism of Western masters. Audiences attuned to the dulcet harmonic vagaries of the Japanese guitar and lute, the *samisen* and *biwa,* allowed their senses to be assaulted and swamped by Beethoven and Wagner. New schools of Japanese writers threw over their classical conventions and began to tell stories in the contemporary vernacular. University students fed on Bacon, Hume, Kant, and Hegel and espoused ill-digested new systems of thought and government. Action groups began to call themselves anarchists and socialists and were relentlessly persecuted by the police.

In 1883, when Japan, in her great leap forward into modernity, had still scarcely left the ground, Iwakura Tomomi, the strongman of the oligarchy of young samurai, died of stomach cancer at forty-eight. He was attended in his last hours by Emperor Meiji's personal physician. Meiji, who had grown up to be a strikingly handsome and intelligent monarch of thirty-one, proceeded to take the reigns of the oligarchy into his own hands. His touch was light and sure. He remained always "behind the curtain," and handled his oligarchs with an easygoing sense of humor. On those rare occasions when a piece of paper came to his desk that displeased him, he would ignore it. Each morning he would carefully move it to the bottom of the pile of state business and would continue to do so until it was discreetly withdrawn and redrafted.

Under his keen eyes, not only the national family but the imperial family prospered. He gave monopolistic development rights in the new industrial Japan to merchant friends of his Court and received a share of the profits in return. Control of the nation's economy fell into the hands of three great cartel families, the Mitsuis of the Mitsui Company, the Iwasakis of the Mitsubishi Company, and the Sumitomos of the Sumitomo Company. Between them they ruled Japan's foreign trade, her heavy industry, and her banking. Because of their loyalty and indebtedness to the Throne, they acted as unofficial members of the government, co-ordinating their industrialization plans with long-range imperial policy. Past dependence upon doles from shoguns had taught the lesson that high-priestly power could no more be exercised without money than without arms. And so Emperor Meiji amassed the fourth largest concentration of capital for himself and his family. Through gifts, investments, and outright expropriations, he increased the imperial fortune from a paltry $51,000 in 1867 to approximately $40 million by the end of his reign in 1912.

To consolidate further the position of the imperial family, Emperor Meiji sent all but two of the fifteen sons and nephews of Emperor Komei's advisor, Prince Asahiko, away to Europe to study the Western arts of war. At Sandhurst and St. Cyr, Brest and Dartmouth, the Polytechnique and Göttingen, they learned military physics and gathered around them cadres of poorer Japanese students who would serve them gratefully, as familiars, later in Japan. Future field marshals and chiefs of staff shared intimately in the homesickness and bounty of the lonely princes in a way that would never have been possible inside the rank-and-etiquette-conscious structure of domestic Japanese society.

When the half-Westernized princes returned home, they joined Meiji's family council, his kitchen cabinet. Hidden from the public eye, this body advised Meiji on policy making; administration it left to the samurai cabinet of oligarchs. Unknown to the public, the cabinet also met regularly with Emperor Meiji—in an atmosphere not much more formal than that in the back rooms of the White House at the same period. Thus, in 1896, young oligarch Saionji Kinmochi got up in Emperor Meiji's presence to recommend an official Japanese representative to send to the coronation of Czar Nicholas II. He delivered the following preposterous encomium on behalf of his fellow oligarch Yamagata Aritomo, the most sly, tough, unreconstructed samurai in the room: "Instead of sending a man of prominent position or of thorough knowledge of conditions, or of great ability, it would be better to send a person whose words are not only trusted by foreign countries but who commands the implicit faith of our own land, too, as an indubitable national representative." When Meiji had recovered from his guffaws, Yamagata, scowling, was nominated by acclamation.

Saionji and Yamagata represented opposite poles of opinion in Emperor Meiji's oligarchy—two factions which were to haunt Emperor Hirohito decades later. Ramrod-stiff and straight, his shaggy mustache bristling, Yamagata was a Choshu-clan samurai, every inch the military man. At the restoration, he had been put in charge of national conscription and had built up the Army from a few ragged regiments to a formidable establishment of 250,000 men. A firm believer in Asia for the Asiatics, he saw the Choshu program of 1862 as strictly limited in its goals. If only Japan could create a buffer zone in Korea and North China, she would be able to draw in on herself once more and go back to her pursuit of disciplined one-family happiness. Yamagata believed the main obstacle to be the Russians for whom he had a deep hatred. In spirit, and by actual ties of blood and allegiance, he was the father of the Strike-North group which would try to force Hirohito in the 1930's to attack Russia instead of the United States.

Yamagata's tormentor in Emperor Meiji's councils, Saionji Kinmochi, was a blithe, graceful courtier of thirty-seven. He was no samurai but a prince, a prince of the Fujiwara family, which was second only to being a prince of the imperial blood. His faction was that of many Westernized Japanese who saw in the barbarians no threat and hoped that the Choshu program of 1862 would be abandoned. As a member of the Fujiwara clan, Saionji believed it his duty, bequeathed him by his ancestors, to preserve the institution of the imperial family and its pantheon of spirits. He hoped to do so, however, by making the Japanese god-king a powerless constitutional monarch. He meant every quip he flung at Yamagata to be a chip from the tree of tradition he hoped one day to fell. He was to be tragically disillusioned. Outliving the rest of Emperor Meiji's oligarchs, he would become, in the 1930's, Hirohito's senior advisor. He would be scorned by his monarch and used as a loyal tool. Remaining loyal nonetheless, he would do his utmost to steer Hirohito away from the disaster he saw ahead. Finally in 1940, he would die at the age of ninety-one, recognizing that all his dreams had been blasted.

In 1868, at the age of eighteen, Saionji had made a name for himself as the leader of a cavalry troop in the civil war with the Tokugawas. He had stood out then as a bright young knight, wearing a green plume and green silk over his corselet of wood and metal ribs. Being only three years older than Emperor Meiji and a nobleman of the highest hereditary Court rank, he enjoyed an intimacy with his monarch far closer than that of General Yamagata or of any of the other oligarchs. Although he was not allowed, by birth, to sit on the imperial family council, he was privileged to know more than the other oligarchs about the deliberations in that other, higher kitchen cabinet.

Saionji had gone abroad with Iwakura in 1871 as a member of the delegation sent to study Western customs. He had remained there, studying in Paris, for nine years. Unlike many of his fellow aristocrats, who felt themselves slighted in Western capitals, Saionji enjoyed himself enormously. By family tradition, he was a ladies' man. The first Saionji, in the twelfth century, had made a vow that he and his successors would never take wives but only mistresses. His excuse was that he played the lute in a way pleasing to the Emperor and that the muse of lute players was insanely jealous of wives. Ever since that time every Saionji had played the lute, had enjoyed many mistresses, and had adopted an heir from another family—often from the family of a man who had been cuckolded by a Saionji.[12]

Oligarch Saionji Kinmochi was no exception to his family tradition. He was a Tokudaiji by birth, one of the highest ranking Fujiwara families at Court. His elder brother was for many years Emperor Meiji's first Fujiwara advisor. His younger brother was adopted heir to the great cartel family of Sumitomo, the third wealthiest in Japan. Because of his excellent connections, young expatriate Saionji lacked not for money or introductions in Paris. He ingratiated himself at the finest dinner tables. He played the lute passing well. He liked the French girls and they liked him. After less than a month in Paris he had his own chic French mistress. In one of his first letters home he declared that it was far easier for him to master the difficult barbarian books he was reading with a native barbarian girl at his side than all alone.

In 1880 Saionji had returned to Japan for a year, had moved into a geisha tea house, and then had been sent abroad again to help an elder oligarch, Ito Hirobumi, draft a constitution for Japan. Ito and the young Saionji returned in 1883 with a blueprint that was 90 per cent Japanese

[12] The aristocratic families of Kyoto have many such traditions, invented as conversation pieces in courtly years gone by but now maintained as treasures of the national heritage. Many families keep temples, supported by ancient endowments, where their first sons preside as priests. One family maintains a shrine for the spirits of broken sewing needles. I know a wealthy gentleman of fifty-five, known locally as "Prince of the Night," who obeys a vow, taken at about the time of the Battle of Hastings, that every heir to the family must do proletarian work. His father spent sixteen years at French, English, and Australian universities and came home to be a farmer. The son, Prince of the Night, put in a dozen years as an Army officer on the frontiers of Manchuria, and came home to hawk noodles from a bucket on the Kyoto streets. When his day is over, he takes off the sweatband from his forehead, and the tunic and baggy cotton pants of the laborer, dons a custom-tailored sports shirt and trousers, steps into his chauffeur-driven limousine, and drives off each night to visit the score or more of bars, night clubs, and tea houses built on his property. I had the pleasure once of accompanying him on his evening rounds. We started at a modest bar at seven and went on to twelve other establishments, each more Japanese and exclusive than the last. On the way Prince of the Night acquired half a dozen new male acquaintances, three bar hostesses, and four apprentice geisha. Our last stop was an exquisite tea house. remodeled as a club, which had stayed open waiting for us from its usual closing hour of ten until our arrival at one in the morning. We left it in five rented Cadillacs which all escorted me home. A wife is a taboo item on such occasions, and mine was asleep upstairs in our Japanese-style house when the cavalcade pulled up at the curb. Prince of the Night took a package from his chauffeur and came in with me to present it as solace to the stay-at-home. When I awakened her from a sound sleep, my noble wife did me great credit in Japanese eyes by coming downstairs without a murmur to accept the gift: three teacups and saucers designed and commissioned from a local porcelain works by Prince of the Night himself. The next morning he was back on the streets in peddler's garb, crying, "Noodles, fresh noodles, all fresh, a-fresh-O."

and 10 per cent French and German in inspiration. Constitutional scholars say that its prime Western model was Bismarck's constitution for Germany. The ideas and purposes of the Constitution were debated within the oligarchy for six years.

Before considering the Constitution closely, the oligarchy hired Western jurists and interpreters to find an acceptable Western model for a legal code which would fit established Japanese police practices. Then in 1885, to test the applicability of the Constitution to the Japanese scene, Emperor Meiji appointed a national deliberative body of wise men, the Diet or Congress. Conservatives feared that the new debating society would reveal aristocratic secrets to the masses. Its powers, however, were carefully restricted in advance to legislation pertaining to increases in the annual national budget. Much to the disappointment of many gossips, the appointed delegates did not stray far from this one topic. Policy, as represented by the budgets inherited from previous years, remained beyond debate. Only the reasons for increases could be scrutinized. The Diet caused so little trouble that it was continued and the restriction on its powers was written into the contemplated Constitution.

In April 1888 Meiji ordered the senior members of his oligarchy to form a new advisory body to the Throne, the Privy Council, in order to thrash out the final text of the Constitution. For the next nine months the Privy Councillors met weekly with Emperor Meiji in the palace to argue and edit Saionji's masterpiece. Finally, on February 11, 1889, the Constitution was promulgated as a gift of the Emperor to the people. It explicitly conferred on the Emperor an unqualified, all-encompassing power that would have warmed the heart of a Catherine or Caligula:

The Empire of Japan shall be reigned over and governed by a line of Emperors unbroken for ages eternal. . . . The Emperor is sacred and inviolable. . . . The Emperor exercises the legislative power with the consent of the Imperial Diet. . . . The Emperor convokes the Imperial Diet, opens, closes and prorogues it, and dissolves the House of Representatives. . . . The Emperor gives sanction to laws, and orders them to be promulgated and executed. . . . The Emperor, in consequence of urgent necessity . . . issues . . . when the Imperial Diet is not sitting, Imperial Ordinances in the place of law. . . . The Emperor determines the organization of the different branches of the administration, and salaries of all civil and military officers, and appoints and dismisses the same. . . . The Emperor has the supreme command of the Army and Navy. . . . The Emperor determines the organization and peace standing of the Army and Navy. . . . The Emperor declares war, makes peace, and concludes treaties. . . . The Emperor confers titles of nobility, rank, orders and other marks of honor. . . . The Emperor orders amnesty, pardon, commutation of punishments and rehabilitation.

Complex feelings and disagreements had caused the long delay in issuing this extraordinary document. Its secret purpose was to persuade Western nations that Japan had an explicit social compact which could be relied upon as legally binding. Once the West was so convinced, it would be possible to renegotiate the humiliating treaties which allowed foreigners to be tried for crimes in their own courts. Once Western business interests in Japan came under Japanese jurisdiction, it would be possible to make Western statesmen accept Japan as an equal in international power politics.

Prince Akira, the elder brother of Komei's counselor and the chief advisor on foreign policy to Emperor Meiji, hoped that by treaties and alliances it would be possible to play the Great Power game and share in the anticipated dismemberment of China. In the ranks of ordinary conservative samurai, the feeling prevailed that this was a dishonorable tradesman's approach to national goals. Yamagata, the boss of the Army, encouraged such feeling. He saw no purpose in taking on Western state trappings and advocated a simple policy of armament, followed by straightforward conquest of the required buffer zone. Saionji and a few other genuine liberals espoused the Constitution enthusiastically as an opening wedge for their plan to rationalize the mystical relationship between people and Throne and make the Emperor a being under law.

Two of the oligarchs who advocated the liberal position too openly in public were silenced by mysterious acts of violence. The day that the Constitution was promulgated, Minister of Education Mori Arinori was knifed and killed by a young Shinto fanatic. The assassin had been told that Mori, on a visit to the shrine of the sun goddess at Ise, had impiously raised a bamboo curtain with the tip of his cane in order to have a look at the relics behind the curtain.

Eight months later, on October 18, 1889, Minister of Foreign Affairs Okuma Shigenobu lost a leg when a bomb was hurled into his carriage. The public was surprised to learn that Okuma had been returning to his ministry early in the morning from a heated debate about treaty revision which had been going on more or less continuously in the palace for four days—Emperor Meiji presiding over it in person. Okuma had concluded the first egalitarian treaty—with Mexico—the year before, and was in process of negotiating successfully with the United States and Great Britain. His assailant claimed to have thrown the bomb at him for the upside-down reason that the treaty inequalities which Okuma was trying to eliminate still existed.

LORD HIGH ASSASSIN

Behind both of the would-be assassins stood the dark figure of a man named Toyama, who would be known as the intermediary for important assassinations of state throughout the rest of his long life. To Western onlookers he seemed a gangster. To the great mass of Japanese he seemed a patriot—the conscience of the nation, a man of the people. He took money from ward heelers in order to fix local grievances. He took money from Army sources controlled by Oligarch Yamagata. He accepted money even from imperial princes. When the Great Powers had signed new treaties and it came time for taking the first step in Japan's expansion, he was to be entrusted with creating provocation for the step. After the imperial family, the Army, and the genuine liberals like Saionji, he was the fourth force in Japan, representing the people, especially the people of the new city slums. A singularly Japanese character, he would figure large in Western writings about Japan for the next fifty years. It would be leaders of his foster organization, the Black Dragon Society, who would be arrested first by General MacArthur's M.P.'s in 1945.

Toyama Mitsuru began his career at the time of the restoration in 1868 as a shrewd thirteen-year-old urchin peddling yams on the streets of Fukuoka in the southern island of Kyushu. Barred by his lowly birth from ever participating directly in government, he made himself a leader of labor bosses in the new industrial cities. Most of his henchmen were masterless samurai who had gravitated to the city slums and embarked on wastrel careers as poets or cutthroats. Still scornful of money, still dedicated to a strict barbaric code of honor, they were hopelessly incompetent at earning a living by peaceful arts. They still wore two swords, however, and still knew how to lead men. Toyama was the most successful of several criminal geniuses who saw that these masterless samurai, the *ronin,* had a role to play in the new order. Because of their former high rank in society, they could organize the new suburbs and shape up the new gangs of factory hands.

Toyama instinctively knew all the right whistles for making the fierce wolves of the slums his obedient sheepdogs. He represented whatever he did, no matter how shabby or savage, as a piece of patriotism in the service of the Throne. If a ward boss had to be murdered, it was because he had slurred the name of the imperial family; if a businessman had to be blackmailed, it was because some society dedicated to the imperial cause needed the funds. Having once gained the admiration of a masterless samurai by his professions of a simple warlike loyalism, Toyama could, if necessary, cement his relationship with the man by an exhibition of personal prowess as a wrestler or swordsman. He was an excellent athlete.

One of Toyama's most devoted disciples, a future Cabinet minister, explained his idol as "an example of a man who refrains from displaying his mental and physical faculties." That is, he gave an impression of unused secret strength. His antagonists often capitulated to him without investigating the weaknesses of his position.

But Toyama was nothing if not an exhibitionist. He larded his conversation with vaguely threatening parables and anecdotes. In his storytelling he was a master of the *ma,* the grunt that expresses what is inexpressible and the long, seemingly significant pause that follows it. In his facial expressions he cultivated *bo,* an absolutely blank look of sleepy indifference which might cover a genuine doze or a hand on the dagger in the sleeve of his kimono.

In his first years of success as a gang leader, Toyama sometimes made a show of standing on a street corner passing out unopened packages of bank notes to his henchmen. He would walk weeping with gifts to the home of one of his men who had been killed in a brawl. He thought nothing of striding into the office of a rival or politician with a scroll of signatures advising his host to do hara-kiri. On one occasion, after many procrastinations and pleas of business, he finally vouchsafed an interview to a Japanese newspaper reporter who had been trying to see him for days. Shown in by a maid, the reporter found Toyama atop one of his many mistresses. "Excuse me for being on my horse," he said casually—and continued his erotic exercise throughout the interview.

In Toyama's hands, the art of silent intimidation was raised to a level which is much admired in Japan to this day. Without any show of force, without breaking any of the fragile, smiling conventions of Japanese etiquette, he could come unarmed to a man's home—to the home of a Dietman or even a prime minister—and make that man tremble for his life. As a matter of face, those whom he had successfully cowed and bluffed always touted his powers thereafter. Because he seldom needed to shed blood, his services as a bully were sought and bought by the heaviest moneybags in the land. The poor recognized him as a Robin Hood and the rich as a valuable, if costly, arranger. With aristocratic backing he founded many patriotic tongs, only one of which was the famous Amur River Society or Black Dragon. It became the most powerful of his organizations largely because of its awesome-sounding name. In the minds of Japanese and Europeans alike, it evoked exotic visions of opium dens and of Chinese mandarins tugging new ecstasies of sadism out of their sparse beards.

FIRST AGGRESSION

Toyama had just established himself as a national underworld figure, just withdrawn from the hurly-burly of the streets, just begun to run the lower classes of the nation from the back garden of his home, when Japan had advanced far enough to take the first step in her program of overseas expansion. In 1893 a dramatic increase in the national military budget was debated noisily in the Diet. The debate was abruptly stilled by a special message from Emperor Meiji, explaining in grand indirections that the present state of the world required a strengthening of the nation. The message came at a time when the state of the world had been unprecedentedly peaceful—without even a minor war, anywhere, for almost twenty years. The Diet, however, passed the special military budget without further murmur. And it was then, in 1894, that Toyama was given his first big foreign assignment.

Minister of War Kawakami Soroku of the Satsuma clan, a minion of Imperial Princes Arisugawa and Yoshihisa, the two senior generals of the Army at that time, gave an interview to a delegation of Toyama's master-less samurai. They had come to see War Minister Kawakami for a trivial favor for their constituents. After granting it, he held them in his office by musing expansively on Japan in the world of 1894. The Cabinet, he said, was not officially prepared to seize Korea at that time, but if someone were to "start a fire" in Korea, the Ministry of the Army would be called in to put it out, and he, Kawakami, was prepared to play "fireman."

Toyama's men "understood his meaning" and duly reported Kawakami's remarks to Toyama. Seeing his duty at once, Toyama hand-picked a band of fifteen self-styled "fire-setters." They went to Korea, established relations with a group of ultraconservative Koreans, the Tonghaks, who were militating for closure of the country to Japanese intercourse, and helped them to start a revolution.

The Chinese Imperial Court in Peking had countered earlier Japanese infiltration of masterless samurai into Korea by the dispatch in 1883 of Yuan Shih-kai, one of China's most promising young military minds, to serve as resident general in Seoul. Yuan was to become the ruler of all China twenty years later and was to be remembered, according to the slant of the commentator, as a Japanese puppet or as a cunning subverter of Japanese plans. In 1894, when he discovered that the Japanese "fire-setters" were backing the diehard Tonghak rebellion, he made the mistake of persuading the corrupt and ineffective Korean emperor to summon the aid of Chinese troops. This was all the fire that Meiji and his oligarchs needed. When the Korean government had already suppressed the Tonghak rebellion, when the Chinese were still mobilizing their intervention, when Czar Nicholas had massed troops on the northern Korean border but had not yet sent them across, Japanese divisions suddenly arrived by sea and occupied Seoul and other strategic cities in a brilliantly executed nineteenth century blitzkrieg. The Chinese Navy sought to prevent the Japanese from sending reinforcements, and so the Chinese Navy was sunk by the Japanese Navy.

Emperor Meiji put himself in personal charge of all military operations. To escape from the distractions of routine government and be within a day's flight, by carrier pigeon, of the front, he moved himself and the General Staff to the fated town of Hiroshima in southwestern Honshu and there set up a strictly celibate headquarters, no more luxurious than those of his generals in the field. His preoccupation with the war was so intense and his discipline so Spartan that courtiers worried for his health and arranged "a chance meeting" for him with a favorite concubine who had come down from Tokyo—a 500-mile journey—to give him solace.

Almost before the first Sino-Japanese war had started, China was suing for peace. In the settlement, she gave Japan not only the right to "protect" Korea, but also a substantial indemnity, the balmy island of Taiwan or Formosa, and the southern seaside appendix of Manchuria known as the Kwantung Peninsula. Alarmed by the extent of Japan's unexpected victory, France, Russia, and Germany, in a triple intervention, at once illustrated Bismarck's earlier candid lesson to Iwakura by warning Japan that she was taking too much. Japan resentfully relinquished her rights to the Kwantung Peninsula only to see it leased for a song by Russia three years later. In acquiring Taiwan, Japan had increased her area by 10 per cent. Nevertheless, the mass of Japanese felt balked and bilked by the triple intervention, and they were not at all mollified by U.S. acquisition of the Philippines, three years later, in 1898.

Not knowing the high level at which the war had been plotted, the Japanese Cabinet approved the occupation of Korea on the understanding that it would be only temporary. In the first year of the protectorship, two enlightened Japanese administrators did their best to steer Korea into a progressive policy of Westernized nationalism and reform such as Japan had followed. They were stubbornly resisted by reactionaries ready to die for the cause of the old order.

Accordingly, the third of the Japanese ministers in Korea, General Miura Goro, a Choshu samurai who had run the Peers' School for noblemen and had many intimate connections at Court, plotted with a group of Black Dragon Toyama's men to snuff out the one vital ruling spark in the effete Korean Court, Crown Princess Bin. On October 8, 1895, while Miura's soldiers restrained the Korean Imperial Guards outside the palace, Toyama's thugs chased the princess and her ladies down corridors inside and lopped them limb from limb. The bodies were doused with oil and burned in the courtyard. Miura was haled home to stand trial for permitting the crime but was acquitted by his Japanese judges "for lack of definitive evidence." He remained an honored oracle behind the curtains of Japanese politics, and his advice was sought on most Cabinet appointments for the next thirty years.

The nonentity who was the emperor of Korea sought asylum in the Russian Embassy and called on Czar Nicholas II to protect him. Nicholas, the last of the czars, then thirty-three years old, was offended by the Japanese attempt to make Korea a colony on the borders of Russia, and ordered his subordinates to give refuge as requested by the Korean king and to mass troops once more on the Siberian-Korean border. Encouraged by Russia, Korean ultranationalists went on a rampage of assassination against the Japanese military police. With cruel efficiency the police suppressed them.

The handful of liberal statesmen who advocated an enlightened administration for Korea were discredited in Emperor Meiji's councils.

The surviving brothers of Emperor Komei's advisor, Prince Asahiko,[13] recommended that the next Japanese crusade be directed against the czar of all the Russias. The emperor of China had been put down. He could be dethroned if the emperor of Russia could be held in check. Finally both emperors might be overthrown. Then, outside of Japan, there would be no monarch claiming to rule a great empire, with imperial prerogatives, except the old lady, Victoria, who sat on the throne of England. At the turn of the century in 1900, Emperor Meiji had no advice to fall back on but that of his cousins.

At that juncture entered the protagonist of the twentieth century, Hirohito. It would be his attempt to enforce restoration of his family's rule over the nation, his attempt to expel barbarians and carry out the Choshu plan of 1862 which would lead to Nanking in 1937, Pearl Harbor in 1941, and Hiroshima in 1945. Emperor Komei had died for the cause of expelling the barbarians. Emperor Hirohito would live for it. It was a holy mission bequeathed by the imperial ancestors.

---

[13] Asahiko had died at sixty-seven in 1891. His elder brother Akira, after thirty years as the Throne's chief advisor on foreign policy, died in 1898. His younger brother, Prince Yoshihisa, had succumbed to dysentery as commander in chief of pacification forces in Taiwan in 1895. Out of the brood of twelve sons fathered by Asahiko's lusty father, Prince Kuniye, there remained alive only Prince Akihito, a priest turned Chief of Staff; Prince Sadanaru, an admiral; Count Kiyosu, a provincial governor; Prince Kanin, a colonel with a long future ahead of him; and Prince Yorihito, a Navy captain.

HOUSE OF

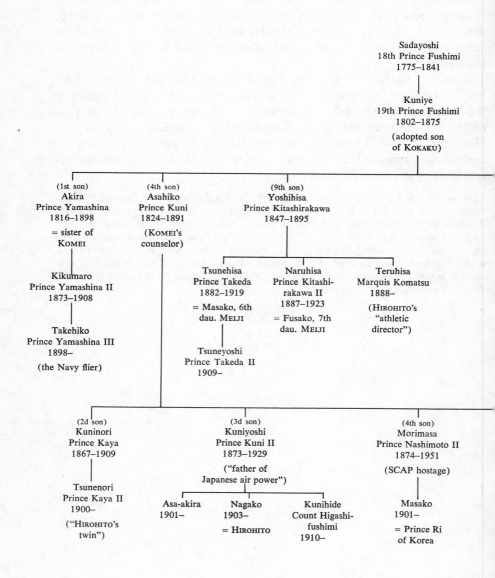

Sadayoshi
18th Prince Fushimi
1775–1841

Kuniye
19th Prince Fushimi
1802–1875

(adopted son
of KOKAKU)

(1st son)
Akira
Prince Yamashina
1816–1898

= sister of
KOMEI

Kikumaro
Prince Yamashina II
1873–1908

Takehiko
Prince Yamashina III
1898–

(the Navy flier)

(4th son)
Asahiko
Prince Kuni
1824–1891

(KOMEI's
counselor)

(9th son)
Yoshihisa
Prince Kitashirakawa
1847–1895

Tsunehisa
Prince Takeda
1882–1919

= Masako, 6th
dau. MEIJI

Tsuneyoshi
Prince Takeda II
1909–

Naruhisa
Prince Kitashi-
rakawa II
1887–1923

= Fusako, 7th
dau. MEIJI

Teruhisa
Marquis Komatsu
1888–

(HIROHITO's
"athletic
director")

(2d son)
Kuninori
Prince Kaya
1867–1909

Tsunenori
Prince Kaya II
1900–

("HIROHITO's
twin")

(3d son)
Kuniyoshi
Prince Kuni II
1873–1929

("father of
Japanese air power")

Asa-akira
1901–

Nagako
1903–

= HIROHITO

Kunihide
Count Higashi-
fushimi
1910–

(4th son)
Morimasa
Prince Nashimoto II
1874–1951

(SCAP hostage)

Masako
1901–

= Prince Ri
of Korea

FUSHIMI

(14th son)
Sadanaru
21st Prince Fushimi
1858–1923

(TAISHO's advisor)

|

Hiroyasu
22d Prince Fushimi
1875–1947

(Navy Chief of
Staff, 1932–41)

(16th son)
Kotohito
Prince Kanin
1865–1945

(Army Chief of
Staff, 1931–40)

(8th son)
Yasuhiko
Prince Asaka
1887–

(Commander
at Nanking)

= Nobuko, 8th
dau. MEIJI

(9th son)
Naruhiko
Prince Higashikuni
1887–

(Prime Minister,
Aug.–Sept., 1945)

= Toshiko, 9th
dau. MEIJI

IMPERIAL LINE AFTER 1779

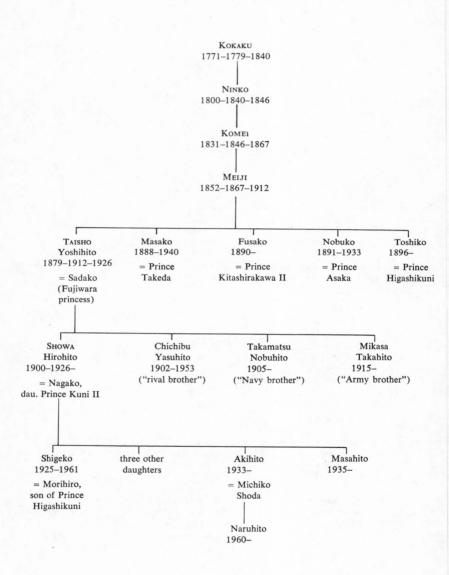

KOKAKU
1771–1779–1840

NINKO
1800–1840–1846

KOMEI
1831–1846–1867

MEIJI
1852–1867–1912

TAISHO	Masako	Fusako	Nobuko	Toshiko
Yoshihito	1888–1940	1890–	1891–1933	1896–
1879–1912–1926	= Prince	= Prince	= Prince	= Prince
= Sadako	Takeda	Kitashirakawa II	Asaka	Higashikuni
(Fujiwara				
princess)				

SHOWA	Chichibu	Takamatsu	Mikasa
Hirohito	Yasuhito	Nobuhito	Takahito
1900–1926–	1902–1953	1905–	1915–
= Nagako,	("rival brother")	("Navy brother")	("Army brother")
dau. Prince Kuni II			

Shigeko	three other	Akihito	Masahito
1925–1961	daughters	1933–	1935–
= Morihiro,		= Michiko	
son of Prince		Shoda	
Higashikuni			

Naruhito
1960–

PART THREE

YOUNG CAESAR

6

HIROHITO'S BOYHOOD

(1900–1912)

EARLY BABY

In the walled gardens of the Aoyama Palace in Tokyo, the cherry blossoms, which Japanese compare with warriors because they fall in the full pride of their bloom, had drifted from the boughs and lay scattered on the ground. Each morning, surrounded by ladies in waiting, a fifteen-year-old princess named Sadako walked the fragrant carpets of fading pink, around the moon-mirror pools, between the painstakingly stunted and gnarled pine trees, and across the rainbow bridges. She glowed with good health, for she had lived most of her life on a farm, following a regimen prescribed by Court physicians to make her a fertile mother. Now the fact that she was in the last stages of pregnancy enhanced her beauty, bringing a special quality of color and transparency to her white skin. Her high-bridged imperial nose, long neck, and slanting shoulders stamped her a Fujiwara, one of the family whose daughters had traditionally knelt beside the Emperors for over eighty reigns.

In carrying her child Sadako faced a challenge unknown to her Fujiwara forebears. Since Emperor Go-Momozono's birth in 1758, all the Emperors had been sons of imperial mistresses rather than of wives. To satisfy Western standards of propriety, Emperor Meiji had promulgated a new Imperial House Law stipulating that from now on only the official Empress could supply an heir to the Throne. As Meiji and his two most privy chamberlains [1] interpreted the new rule, it meant that only a proven heir-producer could become Empress. The future of the princess in the garden,

---

[1] Prince Tokudaiji Sanenori, the elder brother of Prince Saionji, the lute-playing Constitutionalist; Count Tanaka Mitsuaki, who would live to meddle in Hirohito's own matrimonial affairs in the 1930's.

273

therefore, depended on the gender of the child she carried. She was betrothed to Crown Prince Yoshihito, the future Emperor Taisho. If she gave him a boy, she would be married to him; if she had a girl, Meiji might give her a second chance, but only if none of the other noble mistresses of the crown prince delivered a boy first.

In due course, then, when the fallen cherry blossoms had turned almost gray, Princess Sadako's breathing quickened one morning and she retired a few weeks earlier than expected to labor in the pavilion assigned to her. That night, at ten minutes past ten, a wrinkled, premature Hirohito shouted his first cry. A trusted courtier inspected the tiny red body, whipped up his horses, and bowled across central Tokyo in his carriage to report the birth at the Imperial Palace. Emperor Meiji tabled his glass of port and the writing brush with which he had been composing a *tanka* and ordered champagne all around for the chamberlains of his bedchamber.

Princess Sadako was formally married to Crown Prince Yoshihito eleven days later, on May 10, 1900. The wedding was a small family affair, held at eight o'clock in the morning in the Shinto shrine in the private inner enclosure of the main palace. Western ambassadors in Tokyo were permitted to congratulate the newlyweds at a reception that afternoon in the semipublic halls of the outer Ceremonial Palace. The existence of Hirohito was kept a secret for almost a year, until the announcement of his first birthday on April 29, 1901. By the Oriental method of reckoning age, a child is one at the hour of his birth. The fact that, by Western standards, he is one a year later enabled the Imperial Household Ministry to represent Hirohito, without technically lying, as newly born in 1901. Thus Western propriety and Japanese practicality were both satisfied, and no honor was lost.[2]

Born in secret, Hirohito was kept out of the limelight throughout his childhood. Until 1912 he was not even declared heir apparent but shared the right of succeeding to the Throne with his younger brothers. During his first year he remained snugly hidden with his mother in the Aoyama Palace. Then, because it was an old custom, devised to protect heirs from

[2] The official date of Hirohito's birth, as acknowledged by the Imperial Household Ministry, is still 1901 rather than 1900. But the account given above, which is based upon Court gossip, has been tacitly accepted by several knowledgeable writers since the 1920's. Thus F. S. G. Piggott, who later served as translator for conversations between Hirohito and Edward, Prince of Wales, described Hirohito as "in his twenty-second year" when he visited England in May 1921. And Hirohito's personal public relations man, Count Futara Yoshinori, wrote unequivocally in 1928 that Hirohito was born "on the night of April 29, 1900." The publisher of Count Futara's account is on record elsewhere with a list of all the typographical errors concerning the imperial family for which he was ever made to apologize by the police; he does not include Count Futara's statement as one of them. Finally, the issues of Japanese newspapers for the fortnight surrounding April 29, 1901, were removed from Japanese libraries in 1945 and have remained unavailable ever since.

the recurrent dysenteries and fevers of Court life, he was put out for foster care. Princess Sadako returned demurely to the gay, Westernized, Edwardian life of the crown prince in the Akasaka Palace, and Hirohito, wrapped in purple swaddling clothes, was bundled off by coach and four. It was typically muggy Tokyo summer weather. The carriage skirted the barbarian embassies outside the western walls of the palace and rolled south through the best residential district of Tokyo, past villas belonging to Tokugawas, Fujiwaras, and princes of the blood. Finally it drew up at the home of Vice Admiral Kawamura Sumiyoshi in Azabu, about a mile and a half from its starting point.

Kawamura was a Satsuma clansman, a retainer of the Shimazu family. He had been responsible thirty years earlier for importing ten British officers to train the men of Japan's nascent navy. Now he was an elder of sixty-five, renowned for his traditionalism and his simple way of life. His neat clean house stood for all that was purest in the old Japan: planed unlacquered cryptomeria, ground cypress, paulownia, and pine; sliding paper-paned doors opening on miniature gardens; *tatami* floors for stockinged feet; charcoal braziers and throw-pillows; pallets rolled out onto the floor at dusk for sleeping; piping hot baths in a deep wooden tub; an austere alcove for prayer and meditation, where hung a single inspirational example of calligraphy.

Hirohito's foster home was an island of conservatism and taste in a sea of change. Outside the small villa's walls, shanties of plain pine crowded against one another as far south and west as the eye could see. The ancient fort town of Edo, now known as Tokyo, had become one of the largest cities in the world. Where the moon after dark had once stood over a few straight, empty, well-policed thoroughfares—illuminated fitfully by the glimmer of a geisha's lantern or the bumptious roar of a samurai's torch—there now twisted countless alleyways, draped with telegraph wires and busy under gaslight. It was a shark's ocean. No longer did the people ask favors of portly government officials in starched robes but of pimps, racketeers, and slum landlords.

In the eyes of Hirohito's foster father, even the great 240-acre palace, two miles to the northeast, had begun to suffer the modern defilement. Several of the grim battlements and moats had been leveled, pierced, or bridged in a manner which made them militarily unsound. A new ceremonial complex of buildings, completed in 1889, contained a Throne Room, audience chambers, and a banqueting hall, all designed to satisfy European ideas of magnificence.[3] Writhing roofs of glinting green copper overhung eaves and gables painted with green and blue floral patterns. In the

---

[3] Emperor Meiji began to use his $2 million Ceremonial Palace twenty-two years after Emperor Komei's death. After it was destroyed in 1945, Emperor Hirohito waited exactly twenty-two years before dedicating a $36 million replacement for it.

steam-heated interior, coffered ceilings were set with intricately carved panels, depicting birds and beasts and landscapes, lacquered in gold. On the floors of orange-wood and cedar, covered with rich carpets rather than *tatami,* stood heavy Chinese chests, Victorian sideboards, and Empire sofas. Sliding doors of the most exquisite native joinery still communicated between the rooms, but the paper panes in them were now a leathery parchment embossed with ivory and gold. In its own way every detail was a work of art, but for a Japanese of taste the beauties were too thickly encrusted for appreciative thought. In addition, the Western furniture seemed to leave little room for proper ceremonial—for ritual kneeling, backing, bowing, and prostration.

On all significant diplomatic occasions Emperor Meiji—with mustache, goatee, and deep flashing eyes—cut an imposing figure in Western uniform or evening dress in these roomfuls of evident richness. But for members of his oligarchy or family, he also had a maze of Japanese-style apartments, floored with straw mats, where he presided either in the official robes of the old Kyoto court or in loose, informal kimonos of white silk. When the palace burned down on May 26, 1945, it was said that some of its rooms had never been seen except by princes, princesses, and titled servants of high Court rank. In such rooms Meiji wrote several thousand classically Japanese poems and drank several thousand glasses of classically French burgundy. A dozen Court ladies, whose names used to be listed in the nineteenth century *Court Gazette,* had the privilege of waiting on him in the evening and of picking up the silk handkerchief which he dropped in front of his choice for the night. Though he sometimes inveighed against enervating Western customs, it was noted that he always retired, not to a draughty sleeping floor of mats, but to a heated room with a good Western bed in it.

The future Emperor Taisho, in his separate Akasaka Palace, had been even more contaminated by Western sartorial, architectural, and philosophical ideas than his father. He wore Prussian uniforms, larded his conversation with Parisian argot, cultivated the mustache of his contemporary, Wilhelm II, the German kaiser, and consorted by preference with imperial cousins of the Fushimi house who had had the opportunity denied him to go abroad and study the wonders of the Colosseum, Buckingham Palace, and the Folies Bergère. Original paintings by Monet, Manet, and Degas hung in his study and bedroom. On his banqueting table, huge candelabra in the shape of cranes illuminated the masterpieces of a French chef. In 1904 he commissioned an architect trained in Paris to rebuild his Akasaka Palace as a miniature Versailles, complete with chairs and sofas upholstered in pale rose brocade. Emperor Meiji took one look at the plans and vowed that he would never set foot in "Yoshihito's French house."

While his father idolized Western ways and his easygoing grandfather enjoyed and scoffed at them, Hirohito grew from baby to small boy in the pure Spartan Japan of Vice Admiral Kawamura's household. He was slow to walk because he inherited from his grandfather Meiji a slight motor malfunction of the legs which gave him a peculiar gait, known by irreverent Japanese as "the imperial shuffle." Lest his disability create in him an inferiority complex, Vice Admiral Kawamura kept him from associating with any other children until he was almost two years old. Then junior playmates were introduced into his world, one by one: first four toddling princes of the Fushimi house, and then a younger brother, Prince Chichibu, born in June 1902. Through his planned seniority, Hirohito learned to wear the mantle of leadership before he was three. Whenever he and his companions poked holes in the *shoji,* the paper-paned sliding doors in which all normal Japanese children poke holes, Hirohito always remained calmly on the scene of the crime and gravely accepted full responsibility. He and his friends early realized that he could not be punished and that others who set him a bad example might be punished severely. He learned to shield them under a look of puzzled innocence—and to expect favors of them in return.

Going on four, Hirohito was psychologically orphaned by the death of his naval foster father and was brought back to the semi-Westernized world of palaces where he had been born. He was installed in the Aoyama-Akasaka Palace compound, near his mother and father, in a small, especially constructed Japanese-style home called the Imperial Grandson's Abode. There he was taken care of mostly by titled servants. He saw his mother once or twice a week, his father more or less monthly, and his grandfather quarterly for a pat on the head. In moments of paternal feeling, brought on by wine, his father, Crown Prince Yoshihito, sometimes had him brought over to the Akasaka Palace at night to be dandled by merry-making sycophants. On one occasion they plied the little boy with so much saké that they made him drunk, sick, and a teetotaler for life.

The Court official in charge of Hirohito's new ménage was Kido Takamasa, the son of a samurai who had died in Emperor Komei's service in 1862. Takamasa had been adopted by one of Emperor Meiji's most popular oligarchs and sent to the United States for his education. There he had lived for a decade, studying mining techniques and cultivating his native prejudice against Commodore Perry's countrymen. A few years after his return to Japan, Kido Takamasa adopted the son, it is said, of an imperial princess. This was Kido Koichi who would become Hirohito's most trusted counselor and finally, in 1945, Hirohito's representative among the Japanese war criminals in Sugamo Prison.

At the time Hirohito moved in under the elder Kido's wing, Kido Koichi was fifteen. The owlish young man played big brother to the regal boy and introduced him early to several other teen-age "Big Brothers" who would later become the nucleus for Hirohito's cabal. All these fledgling aristocrats had been born between 1887 and 1891 and had attended the

Peers' School together: Prince Asaka, sixteen, who would rape Nanking in 1937; his half brother and near twin, Prince Higashikuni, who would become prime minister in 1945; another sixteen-year-old imperial "uncle," Prince Kitashirakawa, who would die in the course of an intelligence mission in France in 1923; Kitashirakawa's half brother, Marquis Komatsu Teruhisa, fifteen, who would oversee Naval Staff studies for the attack on Pearl Harbor; and finally a twelve-year-old hanger-on of the bigger boys, the precocious, sensitive, much teased Fujiwara prince, Konoye Fumimaro, who would lead Japan to war as prime minister in 1937.

Being typical young aristocrats of their time, the Big Brothers played soldier with Hirohito and told him war stories. They spoke constantly of Japan's mission to lead Asia out of Western bondage. They belonged to the East Asia All-One-Culture Society, a movement launched in both Japan and China by Prince Konoye Atsumaro, the father of the youngest of the Big Brothers. At the society the Big Brothers came to know and patronize a motley assortment of idealists who believed in Asia for the Asiatics and of tough adventurers who believed in Asia for the Japanese. Some were dispossessed samurai of the Black Dragon Society who scratched out a living in China as white slavers, dope importers, or common cutthroats. Others were burly undercover agents in monks' clothing who had accompanied the high priests of Hongan Temple—the temple of Hirohito's mother's family—on a 1900 pilgrimage to Thailand to bring back the ashes of the true Buddha and on a 1902 expedition to Samarkand "to explore vestiges of ancient Buddhist culture" in Central Asia. Still others were non-Japanese Asian nationalists who had taken refuge in Tokyo from troubles at home—the most notable being the revolutionary Sun Yat-sen, later known as the George Washington of China.

Sun Yat-sen had led an abortive rebellion against the Manchu throne in South China and was a fugitive from the Chinese police. He was protected in Japan by the elder Prince Konoye and by Lord High Assassin Toyama of the Black Dragon Society. In 1905, at Black Dragon headquarters in Tokyo, Sun Yat-sen met with a group of fellow Chinese exiles to form a revolutionary party which was later to become the Kuomintang or KMT. The young Chiang Kai-shek, who leads the KMT in Taiwan today, joined the party in 1907 when he came to Tokyo for postgraduate work at the Japanese Military Academy.

FELLING GOLIATH

In 1904 and 1905 Hirohito's Big Brothers of the East Asia All-One-Culture Society had one enthusiasm which excited them more than Pan-Asianism, and this was the imminent prospect of war with Russia. In the conflict of 1894–95, Emperor Meiji had bested the Dragon Throne of the

Manchus. Now it was common knowledge in the palace that he was preparing to put down the czars of Muscovy.

Planning for the new war had started before Hirohito's birth in 1900. At that time the lute-playing Prince Saionji and his mentor, Ito Hirobumi, the two oligarchs who had championed codified Western-style laws for Japan, were in favor of a straightforward agreement with Russia, acknowledging her supremacy in northern Manchuria in return for unopposed Japanese control of Korea. Army Chief Yamagata insisted that the whole of Manchuria up to the Amur River must be conquered before Japan would feel safe.[4] Emperor Meiji and the surviving brothers of Emperor Komei's advisor, Prince Asahiko, listened noncommittally and declined to set any limit to Japan's ultimate goals. Army Chief Yamagata assured them that Japan would have a sporting chance against Russia unless the French and Germans intervened to keep Japan in her place as they had done in 1896 after the war with China. Emperor Meiji decided, therefore, to seek an alliance with Great Britain which would neutralize France and Germany and enable Japan to challenge Russia hand to hand, one nation against one nation.

As a part of his campaign to prevent the Emperor from going to war, the Westernized oligarch Ito Hirobumi, in the fall of 1900, tried to enlist the voice of the people by founding Japan's first important political party, the Constitutionalists.[5] There had been other political parties before, no less than fourteen of them since 1882, but Ito had the popular support to create a lasting organization that would have the mandate of the majority of the people. For the next thirty-five years it would regularly command 45 to 60 per cent of the national vote. But it would struggle in vain against the overriding imperial powers written into the very Constitution it championed—in particular the power to appoint all officials. By contesting Army budget increases in the Diet, Ito dreamt that his party might be able to keep Japan at peace.

In the summer of 1901 Emperor Meiji sent a delegation of professional diplomats to London to negotiate the required treaty with England. Oligarch Ito at once resigned as prime minister in favor of his fun-loving protégé, Prince Saionji, and threw all his energies into selling the people on his idea of direct negotiations with Russia. At the outset of his campaign, he was visited one day by Toyama, the Lord of the Black Dragon and "Darkside Emperor" of the slums. Somewhat hard of hearing, the sixty-one-year-old Ito craned his neck, cocked his head, and professed to be unable to hear any of the gang lord's quiet threats.

---

[4] Toyama, the lord high assassin of the underworld, founded the Black Dragon Society in 1901 to support Yamagata's position. The society took as its own the Chinese name for the Amur, Black Dragon River.

[5] In full, *Rikken Seiyukai,* Constitution Political Comrades party.

"Let me sit closer to you, so that you can hear better," quoth Toyama.

"You are too close already," piped Ito, and dismissed Toyama under a cloak of indifference and senility.

A few days later Ito asked permission of Emperor Meiji to take a vacation and accept an honorary law degree from Yale University in the United States. Emperor Meiji was all too happy to be rid of him, and Ito promptly took ship for San Francisco. Then, after a quick call on President Roosevelt, Ito rewrote his itinerary and boarded the fastest available packet for Europe. Via Paris and Berlin, he went express to St. Petersburg. Czar Nicholas welcomed him, even as a private citizen, and wined and dined him magnificently. The czar's ministers were less accommodating, however, and would not give Ito all the diplomatic concessions that he had hoped for.

Ito's efforts in St. Petersburg merely hastened the drafting of an Anglo-Japanese agreement in London. The British could not endure the possibility of an alliance between Russia and Japan at the northern approaches to Shanghai and Hong Kong. Ito vainly cabled Tokyo the results of his own conversations in Moscow. The Japanese cabinet on December 9, 1901, decided that the arrangements with Great Britain were the more satisfactory. Emperor Meiji, after consulting his Privy Council, cabled his approval to London, and Ito decided to accept defeat gracefully. He hurried to England and gave his blessing to the negotiations there. The historic Anglo-Japanese pact was duly signed on January 30, 1902.

Before launching her first blow against a Western nation, Japan, at Emperor Meiji's insistence, made one other preparation. The British, by the treaty, were committed to attack any third powers which allied themselves to an adversary of Japan. There was, however, a strong possibility that Russia might trounce Japan unassisted. Therefore Emperor Meiji, through his ambassador in Washington, sought and received verbal assurances from President Theodore Roosevelt that the United States, in the event, would do everything in its power to prevent Russia from occupying and annihilating Japan.

So armed, Japan readied herself for war, and Japanese envoys in Moscow pressed belligerently for withdrawal of Russian forces from the Russian rail lines and railheads in Manchuria. The czar had already agreed several years earlier that he would remove his legions in due time, but he was now of mixed mind, and he vastly underrated Japan as a threat. British leaders, too, began to have second thoughts about their new ally and cautioned Japan that she was not strong enough to win the war.

Ignoring all warnings, the Japanese government severed relations with Russia on February 6, 1904. Thirty-six hours later the taut young Japanese Navy, manned by men of the Satsuma clan and commanded by officers trained in England, stole up on the Russian Asiatic fleet in the middle of the night and scattered it by a surprise attack with torpedo boats. The

Russian ships which remained afloat took refuge in the harbor of Port Arthur at the tip of the Kwantung Peninsula leasehold in southern Manchuria. There they were kept bottled up by Japanese battleships which waited broadside outside the harbor's mouth.

On February 10, two days after the naval engagement, Emperor Meiji issued a rescript declaring war. As he had done ten years previously during the war with China, he moved from Tokyo to Hiroshima and there presided personally at staff headquarters. The strategy of the conflict developed around two particularly tense situations. On the one hand the citadel of Port Arthur, defended according to the best Prussian science of the day by Russia's General Stössel, held out stubbornly against attack from the landward side by Japan's expeditionary force. On the other hand, Russia's large Baltic fleet was on its way around the world to avenge the havoc wrought by the Japanese torpedo boats. Unless Port Arthur could be taken in time, the Japanese would have to turn to meet the Baltic fleet, leaving the remnants of the Asiatic fleet free to emerge from their battle and attack the Japanese rear.

Great Britain helpfully denied the Baltic fleet passage through the Suez Canal and forced it to steam from the Kattegat, the strait between Sweden and Denmark, all the way around Africa. On the way it was further delayed by having to refuel only at the widely scattered ports controlled by the French. Nevertheless it did make daily progress and Port Arthur did not fall. When the Baltic fleet entered the Indian Ocean, General Nogi Maresuke, in charge of the Japanese army outside Port Arthur, was sent a personal command from Emperor Meiji in Hiroshima to take the citadel quickly, no matter what the cost. Wave after wave of Japanese advanced into withering fire and bewildering mine fields. The no man's land before the fortress writhed with wounded who could not be helped. The stench of corpses hung so heavy on the air that the Russian defenders on the ramparts wore handkerchiefs soaked in camphor.

Finally the agents of Army Chief Yamagata Aritomo, who was assisting Emperor Meiji in Hiroshima, attempted to bribe three of Stössel's officers with a promissory note for $65 million payable eleven years later and signed by Yamagata. For this enormous sum, it is said that the three officers gave their Japanese contacts a plan of the Russian mine fields. Whether or not the plan reached General Nogi outside Port Arthur and whether or not it helped him capture the fortress are debatable. The fact is that on December 6, 1904, when the war had been in progress for over nine months and the Baltic fleet was approaching the China Sea, General Nogi launched his third all-out assault on 203-Meter Hill outside Port Arthur. In previous charges he had seen both his own sons mowed down before his field glasses. Now at last he saw the Japanese flag raised on the summit of the hill and knew that the battle for Port Arthur was over. The crest commanded a fine sweep of the harbor and an easy run up a ridge to the feet of the walls of Port Arthur citadel. Trapped between the pounding of Japanese field artillery from the ridge and of Japanese battleships waiting outside the bay, the Russian fleet was sunk to a vessel.

On New Year's Day 1905, Stössel decided that the position he held was no longer either strategically useful or tactically tenable and he surrendered the 25,000 men and 500 guns remaining under his command. He was later court-martialed by the Russians and sentenced to death, but the sentence was commuted to life because he successfully maintained in court that he had been betrayed.

The bizarre aftermath of the bribe has since been recounted by an American diplomat, Post Wheeler, who knew one of the traitors and investigated the whole matter personally. In 1915, eleven years after the fact, Army strongman Yamagata was not about to ask the Emperor to pay $65 million for a fortress that had cost 20,000 Japanese lives. And so when the first of the Russian officers showed up in Nagasaki in 1915, Yamagata had him shot in the back. The death of a foreign tramp was accorded one three-line obituary in a single edition of one Nagasaki newspaper. The second Russian traitor was believed by Post Wheeler to have been killed by Japanese agents somewhere in Russia. The third put his note of hand into the trust of a British syndicate which negotiated for years with the Japanese government for a settlement of payment. Yamagata's brushwork signature on the document appeared, under the glasses of experts, to be authentic and elicited from the Japanese government contradictory explanations of why it was a forgery. In 1921, when relations between Japan and England began to deteriorate as a result of postwar peace conferences, the syndicate began to press its claim in earnest. Then, abruptly, the third Russian traitor, the one material witness, vanished without a trace in Switzerland.

After the capture of Port Arthur in 1904 and the annihilation of Russia's Asiatic fleet, Japan's Admiral Togo Heihachiro was able to turn and redeploy, with little time to spare, for the reception of the Baltic fleet. Fueling problems forced the czar's ships to make a straight dash from the friendly French port of Camranh Bay in Indochina toward the depots of Vladivostok. Togo lay in wait for them at Tsushima Strait which divides two islets in the channel between Japan and Korea. As the Russian battle wagons emerged single file from the narrow waters, Togo's ships "crossed the T" of their column, booming broadsides. When the action was over, Russia had lost almost all her fleet, including twenty capital ships sunk, five captured, and some 12,000 out of 18,000 Russian sailors drowned. Japan had lost only three torpedo boats and 116 men. When news of the catastrophe reached Russia, it helped to touch off Trotsky's abortive revolution of 1905.

PRICE OF PEACE

Once Russia had tasted the bitter fruits of disaster and overconfidence, Theodore Roosevelt offered to mediate the war. Meiji accepted the offer with alacrity. For all her outward show of success, Japan faced an internal crisis. She had lost 20,000 men at Port Arthur and almost an equal number at Mukden, the capital of Manchuria, two months later. More important, her stripling economy was strained to breaking under foreign and domestic war debts. An honorable peace had to be sought, and when President Roosevelt first entertained the emissaries of the two belligerents at Portsmouth, New Hampshire, it looked as if Japan would gain enough to have made the war worthwhile. But Count Sergei Witte, the Russian negotiator, soon sensed that the Japanese were more eager to make immediate peace than he was. Little by little, he hardened his attitude, and by the time that the negotiations were concluded, the Japanese gave up what they most needed, a hard cash indemnity, and accepted instead unquestioned supremacy in Korea, Port Arthur, and the Kwantung Peninsula, and Russian railroads and rights of way in southern Manchuria.

Emperor Meiji reluctantly approved the terms of the treaty after a long and stormy conference in the palace on August 28, 1905. But the Japanese public, which had been fed on reports of unmitigated victory and had been sweated economically to make the war possible, resented the lack of indemnity and rioted obstreperously in every major city. The violence reached such a pitch that the government proclaimed martial law and the war Cabinet of General Katsura Taro had to resign. The new government was headed by Prince Saionji, the lute-playing Constitutionalist. Having been known as an opponent of the war, he successfully soothed the angry people, but he also shouldered for his Constitutionalist party the grievous financial problems and unpopular austerity created by the war.

In retrospect only young aristocrats like Hirohito's teen-age Big Brothers exulted in the great victory Japan had won. Army Chief Yamagata warned that the war had been too much of a gamble ever to be repeated. Oligarch Ito, the founder of the popular Constitutionalist party, spread the idea that Korea could have been won by negotiation. Now that it had been won by force, he said, it was all the buffer zone Japan needed. He opposed outright annexation of it because annexation would only give the Army a new border to patrol; better, he insisted, to make Korea a friendly ally and protectorate of Japan. With this aim in view he advocated a lenient civilian colonial policy toward Korea. Emperor Meiji, with characteristic good humor and poetic justice, let him practice what he preached by making him resident governor. At the same time masterless samurai of the Black Dragon Society were encouraged to enlist in Ito's service and help him in enlightening the natives. They uncovered and savagely suppressed almost weekly insurrections, riots, and anti-Japanese murmuring campaigns, and so turned all Ito's good intentions to hate and terror.

After three and a half years of frustration the sixty-nine-year-old Ito was recalled to Japan in the summer of 1909. He was angry and ready to use his Constitutionalist party's power at the polls to change the direction of imperial policy. Three months later, he was dispatched to Manchuria on a peculiarly inconsequential diplomatic mission. There, in the city of Harbin, he was shot and killed by a Korean. Japanese Constitutionalists murmured in vain for a full investigation of the assassination. It was strange, they said, that Ito's assassin had outwitted the Japanese police, had acquired a gun, slipped out of Korea, traveled all the way to Harbin, and known where to be waiting for Ito. But the police killed the assassin during interrogation and announced that he was a fanatic, working alone. Seven months after the assassination, in May 1910, Japan formally annexed Korea.

PRINCELY ABC'S

In the triumphant years after the war with Russia, when Japan took her place as an equal beside the nations of the West, the fascist princes of the 1930's were still getting their educations. In April 1908, Hirohito began to go to the famous Peers' School. He set out each morning, usually on foot, with a chamberlain trailing along behind him. Most mornings he had for company two junior princes. It was only a ten-minute walk to the school from Hirohito's Aoyama Palace, but when the three little princes went together, they usually managed to provide a full half-hour's exercise for the nagging chamberlain who accompanied them.

Hirohito's new school was the lineal descendant of the academy for noblemen, established in Kyoto during the late eighteenth century, which had instilled in the Court the courage and independence to agitate for the restoration. In 1908 its headmaster—always a distinguished patriot—was General Nogi Maresuke, the commander who had piled up corpses outside Port Arthur and watched both of his own sons slain there. Entrusted with the planning of Hirohito's curriculum, he took an intense interest in the quiet young Emperor-to-be, and Hirohito responded by addressing him in the forms ordinarily reserved for a father.

Nogi had been born in 1849 to the traditional Spartan code of the samurai. As a child, if he complained of the cold, he was made to stand naked in the snow while his father poured buckets of well water over him. As a sixteen-year-old adolescent, learning fencing, he lost an eye. As a twenty-eight-year-old, commanding his first troops in battle, he was surrounded during the Satsuma clan's samurai uprising of 1877, crippled in one arm and one leg, and disgraced in his own mind by the capture of the imperial colors under his charge. Limping and looking out on the world through a single eye, he was probably saved from defeat in the Russian war—despite the sacrifice of his sons—only by Yamagata and Stössel's three traitors. After the war, he is said to have asked Emperor Meiji's permission to commit ritual suicide, and to have been answered with the words, "Not while I am still alive, Nogi. That is an order."

Nogi believed implicitly in the traditional samurai mystique of killing with honor, of magnanimity toward the chastened and defeated, of utter ruthlessness toward the base and mercantile, of appreciation mainly for the contrived artistic beauty of poems and paintings in life, and for the moonlight reality of the spirit world in death. This was Bushido, the way of the warrior. Out of it had come the only masculine selflessness and dedication which Japan had ever known.

While Nogi lived by command, he did all in his ken to make a good samurai out of Hirohito. He promulgated twelve rules to guide the prince and the other aristocrats under his charge. Among them:

"(4) Inquire of your parents about your ancestors, your crest and lineage, and keep them well in mind.

"(9) Be ashamed of torn clothes, but never of patched ones.

"(12) When you order your Western-style clothing, boots, and shoes, have them made larger than your present size, regardless of fashion. You will outgrow them."

On one occasion Nogi had Hirohito stand naked under a glacial waterfall. When the boy proved that he could stand still there without shivering, Nogi beckoned him out and wrapped him in a commoner's coarse winter house kimono. Nogi liked to boast that neither he nor his ward had ever known the feel of silk undergarments next to the skin.

Under Nogi's tutelage, Hirohito tackled the forbidding complexities of written Japanese. He first learned the two Japanese syllabaries of fifty-five symbols apiece and the English or *romanji* alphabet of twenty-six letters so that he could read phonetically. In Japanese, however, phonetic reading does not suffice to impart understanding, because there are too many ordinary words used in writing which all have the same ambiguous sound. When used in intellectual conversation, they have to be identified either by a lengthy explanation or by a Chinese character traced on the palm with a finger. Like other Japanese, therefore, Hirohito next embarked on the learning of Chinese characters or *kanji*. Through movement of hand and writing brush he memorized the primary and variant forms, meanings, and pronunciations of from three to four thousand characters, each consisting of one to forty-eight brush strokes. By constant drill and reading, he came to recognize 20,000 to 30,000 combinations of the characters which represented whole words. In a nation where everyone gives the best years of his life in an attempt to make the archaic system of hieroglyphs work, Hirohito learned to read and write with exceptional ease. By the age of twelve he was already trying his hand at delicate, disciplined *tanka* which,

after editing, would express his mind on ceremonial occasions and would
be read aloud at the national poetry contests held in the palace each
New Year.

Because of the imperial shuffle, Hirohito was far less gifted athletically
than he was intellectually, a fact of genetics to which he reconciled himself
only with the greatest difficulty. Living in a samurai's world, he set great
store on strength, agility, and endurance. By arduous effort he ultimately
became a powerful swimmer, good horseman, and avid golfer, but each
sporting accomplishment cost him great pain. As a small boy he had had
little opportunity to learn ways of compensating for his defect because
anxious chamberlains had forever curbed in him the normal abandon of a
child, encouraging him to walk, not run, down corridors and step, not leap,
down staircases. His tutor, Nogi, warned him repeatedly against developing a hunchback's psychology.

In spite of himself, Nogi showed a spontaneous partiality for Hirohito's
graceful, open-natured younger brother, Prince Chichibu. Chichibu was
free of the imperial affliction. Chichibu excelled at sports. Chichibu had
been publicly cuddled and privately cuffed by Hirohito ever since his birth.
Hirohito was to make Chichibu the family scapegoat for the abortive
Strike-North Army rebellion of 1936. Chichibu was to die of another
imperial weakness, tuberculosis, in 1953.

Hirohito's physical disability, together with the other peculiarities of his
childhood, left him with a defensive shyness and poise chiseled out of ice,
and an almost masochistic need to prove himself by living more simply and
working harder than anyone else. He schooled himself to become a lucid,
well-paced, and even dramatic speaker at official gatherings but he never
learned to seem completely at ease on the rostrum. He was steadfastly loyal
to all who served him but warm and vivacious with only a few of his oldest
intimates. His idea of humor was to give a pumpkin that looked like a
melon to one of his in-laws who was excessively fond of melons. By
exercise of an encyclopedic memory, he was able to appear perceptive and
even maliciously witty on occasion. But few chamberlains ever felt sure how
to take his sallies, because they came so rarely. Both he and his brothers
had been carefully trained from infancy to listen rather than speak, to encourage rather than command, to censor from their voiced thoughts every
direct expression of bias or desire, to seek and weigh the opinions of others,
and to make such advisors responsible for promoting suggestions that
seemed good.

On his way to the Peers' School each day, Hirohito often led his entourage across the northern grounds of the main palace so that he could
watch the Imperial Guards at their morning drill. Frequently he would see
one of his Big Brothers on the parade ground and stop gravely to salute
him. Prince Higashikuni, Prince Asaka, and Prince Kitashirakawa had
graduated from military academy and had been posted as sub-lieutenants to

the Imperial Guards Division in 1908 at the same time that Hirohito had entered the Peers' School. There, in the north corner of the palace, from 1908 until 1912, they were billeted with all the young lieutenants and captains who would later be known as the great fascist generals of Japan. Prince Higashikuni, for instance, has stated that in those years he came to know well the later famous Tojo who would act as shogun for Japan in the fateful years, 1941–1944. At that time Higashikuni found Tojo "a run-of-the-mill officer," who was "ambitious for advancement."

Emperor Meiji made no secret of the fact that Hirohito's Big Brothers were his own favorites, too, and were being groomed by him for missions of national importance. He was especially partial to the four of them who were grandsons of Prince Kuniye, the father of Emperor Komei's advisor Asahiko. In token of his favor he betrothed them to his daughters with an uncanny numerological precision: Kuniye's sixth grandson, Takeda, to his sixth daughter, Masako; Kuniye's seventh grandson, Kitashirakawa, to his seventh daughter, Fusako; Kuniye's eighth grandson, Asaka, to his eighth daughter, Nobuko; and Kuniye's ninth grandson, Higashikuni, to his ninth daughter, Toshiko. To make crystal clear his high hopes for these young men, Emperor Meiji put in a personal appearance at the first three of the weddings—in 1905, 1909, and 1910. He cared so little for the daughters he thus gave away that he met all three of them, for the first time in their lives, at the nuptials.

The fourth wedding, that of Meiji's ninth daughter, was delayed because Kuniye's ninth grandson, the trouble-making Higashikuni, became involved in a palace spat which caused him to be put on probation. It was Emperor Meiji's custom, whenever he had an evening free of state business, to invite a pair of the four favorite princes to eat dinner with him. Higashikuni was invariably teamed with Prince Kitashirakawa, an enthusiastic, athletic young man who always said what was expected of him and never tired of hearing Emperor Meiji, over his port, expatiate on the future greatness of Japan. Prince Higashikuni, who in those days had not yet learned to be devious, sometimes showed boredom in the after-dinner conversations.

One day in 1911, when his stomach was upset and he was studying for the entrance examinations to Staff College, Prince Higashikuni refused one of Emperor Meiji's summonses. A palace coach called for him anyway and he caused a scandal by sending it away empty. Chamberlains came to his villa to lecture him on filial piety. Higashikuni told them rebelliously that he wished he could emigrate to the West where filial piety was left to Confucius. There the matter might have rested except that Hirohito's father, the future Emperor Taisho, who was Higashikuni's elder by only eight years, took it upon himself to tell Higashikuni that he was not worthy of being a member of the imperial family. With great wounded pride, the twenty-three-year-old Higashikuni at once submitted a formal request to the Imperial Household Ministry asking leave to resign his rank as a prince and go away to live in a foreign country. Emperor Meiji had the request ignored and asked Field Marshal Yamagata, the old man of the Army, to talk some sense into the young soldier's head. Higashikuni maintained, however, that he would resign from the imperial family unless Yamagata would agree to owe him a posting abroad, payable on demand. Yamagata promised that he would, and finally Emperor Meiji called Higashikuni in for a private audience in the Imperial Study. In his genial way, he told Higashikuni not to be so prickly; there would be foreign adventures enough when Higashikuni had finished his training and was ready for them. Then, more sternly, Meiji reminded the headstrong young prince that old chamberlains were loyal retainers and must not be alienated by childish lower-class outbursts of pride.

REBELLION IN CHINA

Four hundred million strong, the Chinese, in less than a century, had fallen in their own eyes from one of the mightiest to one of the most miserable nations on earth. At least 20 million Chinese had become addicts of opium, heroin, or morphine, most of which was imported by Western traders. The China coast had become a necklace of foreign enclaves. Whole Chinese armies had been routed repeatedly by landing parties of European and American marines. Japan's victory over Russia in 1905 and annexation of Korea in 1910 only added to China's humiliation. The "Eastern pigmies," as the Japanese had long been called in China, were succeeding against the West where the Chinese had failed.

In 1911 peasant rebellions against the corrupt and bankrupt regime of the ruling Manchu emperors—the Ching dynasty—broke out in almost every province of China. For lack of any other national leadership the dissidents gave their allegiance to the Kuomintang or KMT cell of intellectual Cantonese republicans headed by Sun Yat-sen. Sun and his disciples—of whom Chiang Kai-shek was one—were all protégés of the elder Prince Konoye's East Asia All-One-Culture Society, of Hirohito's Big Brotherhood, and of Toyama's Black Dragon tong. With combined Japanese and American assistance Sun Yat-sen was able to help the peasant revolutionaries pay their armies until they had secured control of the southern half of China.

The Manchu throne was occupied at that time by a five-year-old boy, Henry Pu-Yi, later Japan's puppet emperor of Manchuria. The real power in the Manchu Court was held by the general in charge of the Manchu armies, Yuan Shih-kai. Like Japan's Army strongman, his good friend Yamagata, General Yuan believed that China must remain unified under a military dictatorship. Yuan therefore promised to betray the Manchu throne and throw the weight of his armies into the republican cause if he could become China's first president. Faced with the alternative of civil war, Sun Yat-sen agreed. So it was that in February 1912 the five-year-old

Manchu Emperor Pu-Yi was forced to abdicate, and the Chinese Republic was born.

For the first time since Genghis Khan, China had her own native government; the Mongol-Manchu conquerors from the wastelands north of the Great Wall had been finally expelled. But the peasants who had started the rebellion gained nothing. The same soldiers and tax collectors oppressed them, and the façade of democratic government—of a congress and elections—which Yuan Shih-kai gave to his regime inspired only bitter jokes. From the day he became president Yuan began to plot against China's leading parliamentarians. In two years he would have the bravest of them assassinated. In four years he would try to make himself emperor and found a new dynasty.

7

CROWN PRINCE HIROHITO

(1912–1921)

DEATH OF MEIJI

Hirohito's thirty-two-year-old father, Crown Prince Yoshihito, saw in the Chinese Revolution a heaven-sent opportunity going to waste. Had he been Emperor he would have capitalized on it to take over one or the other of the two halves of China. Instead, while Yuan in Peking was consolidating his power, Army strongman Yamagata and the surviving members of Emperor Meiji's oligarchy ruled in Japan. Emperor Meiji, that spring of 1912, had delegated to the oligarchs all his authority—for he himself lay dying of stomach cancer.

Japanese flocked by the tens of thousands to pray in the plaza outside the palace for the Emperor's recovery. They burned hundreds of thousands of symbolic paper offerings at the most important national shrines. Nevertheless, on July 29, the great Emperor Meiji died. He had had more than a dozen sons, but only one survived him, the child of a concubine, the father of Hirohito, Crown Prince Yoshihito. Yoshihito at once assumed possession of the sacred mirror, necklace, and sword and took the reign-name of Taisho, Great Correctness.

Up to this time the boy Hirohito had been merely the eldest of the imperial grandsons. Now, while the nation mourned, a new crown prince had to be nominated. Hirohito was the obvious but not the only choice. The fact that he had been born before his parents' marriage provided an excuse to pass him by, in favor of his younger brother, if his physical disability seemed to warrant it. A rump caucus of princes and chamberlains met in the palace to discuss the matter.

Emperor Taisho and most of his courtiers wished to accept Hirohito in order to avoid any outward suggestion of irregularities. To their surprise,

Hirohito's own beloved tutor, General Nogi, organized a minority which favored the election of Prince Chichibu, Hirohito's brother. Nogi had no convincing reason to urge for his stand, only a vague presentiment, a sense of something dark. He was, accordingly, outvoted and Hirohito was elected heir apparent.

In six weeks of deep mourning, wearing old-fashioned Court clothes, participating in numerous family rites of purification, the twelve-year-old Hirohito was made deeply conscious of his impending responsibilities, his coming of age. On September 9, 1912, as the progress of his grandfather's shade into the spirit world drew to a close, he was duly proclaimed heir and simultaneously appointed to the rank of lieutenant in the Army and ensign in the Navy.

Three days later, on the eve of Meiji's state funeral, General Nogi, the outvoted tutor, paid a last visit to Hirohito and to his two brothers, Chichibu, ten, and Takamatsu, seven. They received him in their private apartments at the temporary Akasaka Palace where they lived while the new one—Taisho's Versailles—was nearing completion. Nogi had recently returned from George V's coronation in London and apologized for his long absence. He apologized further that he must go out of town again, immediately, as guide to Arthur, Duke of Connaught, the emissary sent by Great Britain to Emperor Meiji's funeral. Then, earnestly, he scolded the three boys for neglecting their lessons while he had been away and reminded them that they must learn to police their own work habits if they were ever to fit themselves for the lonely task of rule.

Turning to Hirohito, Nogi discussed a recent specimen of the boy's calligraphy and said: "I ask you to study harder. You are now the crown prince, the youngest of the officers in the Army and Navy, and the future commander of the nation. I beg you to attend to your military duties. I beg you to take daily care of your health, no matter how busy you are. Remember, I shall be watching. Work well for yourself and Japan." He handed Hirohito a book of Confucian moral precepts, bowed low, and backed out of the room.

In the next hour Emperor Meiji's funeral cortege rolled out across the palace moat on the Double Bridge reserved for imperial progresses. The cannon of Tokyo harbor thundered rhythmically in the distance. Silent, prostrate Japanese lined the route which the cortege would take to Tokyo Station. There a railway car waited, paneled in new unfinished wood of ghostly whiteness, unblemished by knotholes. The next day it would arrive in the old capital of Kyoto where a heroic tumulus was being thrown up, beside the graves of the ancestors, to receive the coffin.

General Nogi watched the cortege start from the palace and then walked home to his villa in Azabu, not far from the house where Hirohito had learned to toddle. Countess Nogi was quietly waiting for him in the tiny entry hall. To the insistent tolling of the cannon the two took a bath together, put on new white kimonos, and knelt before an autographed picture of Emperor Meiji which hung in their prayer alcove.

Six centuries earlier a retainer of the southern dynasty, after surrendering his army to a general of the northern dynasty, had asked his captors to bear witness to the fact that he had surrendered for the sake of his men and not out of fear of death. Kneeling in front of them, he had deliberately cut open his belly and pulled out his entrails, explaining the while that he was dying by the most prolonged and agonizing method that he knew. Since his time the painful ceremony of *hara-kiri* or belly cutting—of *seppuku* or intestinal incision as it was called by the fastidious—had been ritualized and observed by every man of honor who wished to "prove his sincerity" before passing over into the spirit world. Women who wished to make a similar "meaningful gesture" were not supposed to do hara-kiri but might die slowly by another method, the severing of the carotid artery.

Following the prescribed formulas, Countess Nogi now drove a dagger into her neck and bled to death. When she had lost consciousness, General Nogi thrust a short sword into his bowels, gave it a pull crosswise and a final jerk upward. On the *tatami* at his side he left a note, deploring the self-indulgence of the younger generation and begging every patriotic Japanese to abide more sternly by the ancient warrior virtues. When the new crown prince, Hirohito, heard of the tragedy, he stiffened in a bow, and without any other sign of emotion said, "Japan has suffered a regrettable loss."

The story was put out for foreigners that General Nogi and his wife had committed double suicide in order to follow their liege lord, Meiji, to a new Throne beyond the grave. For the mass of Japanese, who knew that Nogi had not enough rank to consider himself an indispensable retainer, it was said that the Nogis had fulfilled a sacred pledge made to themselves and to the bereaved parents of other slaughtered sons after the costly storming of Port Arthur. It was well known that Nogi's wife had indeed taken the death of her sons much to heart. But General Nogi, according to knowledgeable aristocrats, felt most driven to suicide by pride. He had advised against the selection of Hirohito as crown prince and his advice had been spurned. He could not live to see himself rejected by his own student.

TAISHO'S COUP

On ascending the Throne at the end of July 1912, Hirohito's father, the young Emperor Taisho, sought to be an absolute monarch and an empire builder. He aspired to give Japan a "progressive" Occidental administration, patterned on that of Alexander the Great, Caesar, Louis XIV, and the German kaiser. The Japanese, he felt, were too parochial. He believed that in turning outward and making themselves a force in the world his people would require specific autocratic instruction at every step. But he did not know Japan. He understood in theory but not in feeling the web of loyalties which made the people work as one. Spoiled by diversions with polite wines and women and Western ideas, Taisho thought that he had only to issue orders. He could not imagine that the Throne would ever be disobeyed. He did not see the need for the easygoing charm and careful subterfuge practiced by Emperor Meiji. Highly intelligent but neurotically arrogant, he took no care of his public image. It was widely known that he dressed like a German hussar, waxed his mustache, and sometimes lashed out at delinquent servants on the palace grounds with his riding crop.

For all his faults, Emperor Taisho had wit and charm enough to command the allegiance of the most cosmopolitan Japanese. His immediate followers and intermediaries were six worldly-wise princes of the blood who had played uncles to him in his growing up. All but one of them had seen action in the war with Russia. Two of them were graduates of St. Cyr, the French West Point, one of Brest, the French Annapolis. Two more were graduates of Japan's own West Point. The sixth was a Shinto priest who would run the nation's religious establishment until 1937. The chief of the six was Prince Sadanaru, fifty-five, Prince Asahiko's eighth brother and Emperor Taisho's most intimate advisor. He had studied long in France, visited often in England, and attended the St. Louis World's Fair in the United States in 1904.

In traditional Japanese fashion, Taisho and his six princely advisors at once called on a loyal henchman, General Katsura Taro, to stand before them and take responsibility for their plans. General Katsura had been prime minister from 1901 to 1906 and from 1908 to 1911. He had represented the Emperor and the Army against the Constitutionalists in every election since 1900. While he was governor general of Taiwan in 1900, he had drawn up an elaborate plan for Japanese expansion southward into Malaya, Indonesia, and the Philippines. He had presented the plan to Emperor Meiji and his oligarchy and had been told that its execution would have to be postponed until the northern borders of the Empire had been secured against Russia. Now, August 1912, the war with Russia had been won, and it seemed that the time had come.

Katsura was in Russia on reconnaissance when the news of Emperor Meiji's death and the summons from Taisho reached him. He hastened home and was at once appointed by Emperor Taisho to both the chief offices in the palace: that of grand chamberlain and, concurrently, that of lord privy seal. In the one he had the duty of making appointments for all audiences with the Emperor and in the other the privilege of being in attendance, ready to answer questions, at all audiences.

The cardinal plank in Taisho's imperial program was "perfection of national defense": a major buildup of the armed forces in anticipation of trans-Korean empire building. At Emperor Taisho's and Prince Sadanaru's suggestion, the Army General Staff began to agitate for an increase of two divisions in the strength of the Army occupying Korea. The Constitutionalists, headed by Prime Minister Saionji, the lute-playing prince of the old Court clan of Fujiwaras, opposed the increase on financial grounds. The nation was still struggling with the deficit financing left over from the war with Russia eight years before. Since Saionji and the Constitutionalists had the majority at the polls, in the Diet, and in the Cabinet, they voted down the Army expansion plan handily. As a result, in early December 1912, the war minister resigned and Emperor Taisho's palace factotum, General Katsura, saw to it that no Army officer would accept the war ministership in his place.

Prime Minister Saionji had no choice but to resign, too. In the protracted government crisis which ensued, Emperor Taisho ordered no less than five statesmen to form cabinets. Each of them in turn failed, for the civilians under Saionji's command were determined to show that they could be as disciplined about refusing Cabinet portfolios as could the military men under Katsura. Finally, on December 21, 1912, Emperor Taisho exercised his full constitutional powers and simply declared that Grand Chamberlain-Lord Privy Seal Katsura was to be the new prime minister. Katsura impressed an unimposing slate of old henchmen to serve as his ministers. The Navy at first refused to supply him with a Navy minister but was brought around when the money for new Army divisions was reallocated for a naval shipbuilding program.

Emperor Taisho's coup d'etat blew up a typhoon of popular protest. His minion, General Katsura, was accused in the Diet of "hiding behind the sleeve of the dragon," which was a Japanese way of saying that the Emperor was using him in an abuse of the imperial power. In Meiji's time when prime ministers had been assailed with this charge, Dragon Meiji had always belched softly and the accusations had been withdrawn. Now, however, Emperor Taisho issued a direct order commanding the Diet to recess for three days. When, after two more recesses, the Diet remained as openly critical as before, Emperor Taisho summoned Prince Saionji and commanded him to have his Constitutionalist party cease their opposition to the imperial will. Saionji obediently called a party caucus and delivered the Emperor's request. After two days' debate, it was voted down. Never before in the history of Japan had an express imperial order been rejected outright. Liberal though he was, Prince Saionji knew his place as a Fujiwara courtier: he immediately resigned his presidency of the Constitutionalist party.

Mobs rioted in Tokyo, Kobe, and Osaka, burning newspaper offices, waging pitched battles with the police, and threatening civil war. Finally, on February 11, 1913, when the Katsura administration had lasted just fifty-three days, Emperor Taisho accepted Prime Minister Katsura's resignation. By his obedience to the Emperor's wishes, Katsura had utterly destroyed his reputation as a deft politician. He died eight months later. Army boss

Yamagata and his old rival in the oligarchy, Prince Saionji, prevailed upon Emperor Taisho to save face by accepting a military Cabinet of a different, nonpartisan sort, one headed by an admiral.

To the satisfaction of Prince Saionji and of his banker brother Sumitomo, the new Japanese prime minister, Admiral Yamamoto Gombei, cut government spending by 13 per cent and canceled most of the fat naval expansion program for which keels had already been laid during the "Army administration" of General Katsura. Emperor Taisho affixed his seal to Yamamoto's measures with a surly show of indifference. He talked of abdicating. Courtiers noted that his fits of savage temper now gave way to long moods of morose dejection and silence.

In March 1914, on the eve of World War I, the surviving elders of Emperor Meiji's oligarchy, in particular the sixty-four-year-old Saionji, persuaded Emperor Taisho to take heart and try a new approach to the realization of his imperial aspirations. Prime Minister Admiral Yamamoto was ousted from office by disclosure of a scandal involving naval procurement officers in Europe and kickbacks from Siemens Electric in Germany and Vickers Aircraft in England. Then, by prearrangement, Saionji proceeded to the palace with one of the smartest, coolest diplomats in the Japanese Foreign Service, the monocle-wearing Kato Taka-aki.[1]

Taisho, Saionji, and Kato sat down and smoked and talked together with unprecedented informality. Years later Saionji would recall that Taisho, in the bargaining, showed himself as intelligent as any of the four Emperors whom Saionji served between 1865 and 1940. At the end of the negotiations, Taisho agreed to give up, for the time being, Katsura's dream of military conquest in Malaya and Indonesia and accept in its place a shrewd mixture of economic salesmanship, watchful waiting, and diplomatic opportunism. In particular he agreed that, in the event of world war, he would throw in Japan's lot with the Western nations which had power in the Pacific: England which held Malaya, France which governed Indochina, and the United States which controlled the Philippines. It was a difficult decision for Taisho to make because he had always admired Germany most of the Western nations and had modeled himself on what he knew of the German kaiser.

Kato Taka-aki, the diplomat who sat beside Saionji in the informal smoke with Emperor Taisho, was given the key post of foreign minister in the new government. The prime ministership itself was allotted to a professorial figurehead, Okuma Shigenobu. Once a courageous liberal in the lower echelons of Emperor Meiji's oligarchy, Okuma had lost a leg to a bomb

---

[1] Kato was a partisan of the late humiliated Prime Minister Katsura. He had served as foreign minister in the Cabinets of 1900 and 1906, had been created baron for his services in concluding the Anglo-Japanese Alliance, and had taken over Katsura's minority party, the Constitutional Fellow Spirits, at Katsura's death in October 1913.

thrown by one of Toyama's underworld assassins in 1889. Now seventy-six, he was not prepared to lose another. As the "Sage of Waseda"—the president of a university which he had founded—he was popular for his easygoing fund-raising manners and for his reassuring prescription of book learning for all ills. He had acquired a respectable following in one of the minority parties but did not belong to the disloyal Constitutionalists. The people accepted him as their champion, and for two and a half years, in a time of war prosperity and full employment, he gave them a stable government.

FINISHING SCHOOL

While the Okuma Cabinet was planning Japan's new policy of smart opportunism, the embattled imperial household made peace with the nation. Prince Sadanaru, the eldest of Taisho's six family advisors, resigned the key palace post of lord privy seal, which he had taken when Katsura became prime minister, and turned it over to a commoner. Junior princes of the blood were transferred from the Imperial Guards Division in the palace to other, more plebeian units stationed in the provinces. Crown Prince Hirohito was withdrawn from the exclusive Peers' School and put in the hands of private tutors under the charge of popular war heros. A simple classroom was constructed for his studies on the grounds of the Akasaka Palace and its Spartan furnishings were publicized in the press.

Hirohito's chief tutor, entrusted with the planning of his studies, was Togo Heihachiro, the admiral who had turned in time to sink the Baltic fleet in the war with Russia. Unlike General Nogi, he was a prosaic, peace-loving man who believed in war only as a meticulously planned exercise in self-defense. He sensed that Hirohito was antagonistic to him and he left the boy's curriculum largely to two old Prussian-oriented generals. They were assisted by a preoccupied scientist who was a graduate of Yale and by a rear admiral who was a prolific propagandist for samurai ideals.

Under the planning of these staff officers, Hirohito's tutoring was conducted with strict formality and clockwork. Lessons were monitored in silence, from a kneeling position on the *tatami,* by a spritely old court gentleman who listened only for thoughts that might be disturbing or un-Japanese. The lecturers who gave the lessons came in from Tokyo University or from Army or Navy Staff headquarters; they knelt with bowed heads on a mat facing Hirohito and duly delivered themselves. The gap between crown prince and professor was so great that many of the pedagogues strove to say only what they imagined Hirohito should hear. If they became too trite, however, Hirohito himself let it be known that they were "bland as *jagaimo*" —bland as the white potatoes introduced from the West.

Army and Navy lecturers were the most interesting because they spoke boldly, as a matter of honor, and because they felt sure that any child surrounded by French- and German-speaking civilians must be out of contact with the people, the stark realities of a billet, and the verities of samurai ethics. They kept Hirohito well informed about the battles of World War I and about strategic implications for the Orient. He contracted a fascination for tactics and logistics which never left him. And he remained in touch with several of his military mentors throughout the rest of their lives.

One of Hirohito's more academic instructors, a viscount, succeeded in making him reasonably proficient in arithmetic. Another viscount, for lack of courage to ask him questions and correct his mistakes, left him with a knowledge of French inferior to that of his brother, Prince Chichibu. In history, a baron, who specialized in studies of Manchuria, taught him at length the importance of that land to Japan and sometimes bored him with mythology about the gods begetting the Japanese islands—tales which Hirohito questioned as historically unsound and biologically distasteful. Wada Isaburo, who held degrees from Johns Hopkins, M.I.T., and the University of Berlin, gave him an enthusiasm for airplanes and a firm grasp of mechanics and elementary chemistry.

Only two of the palace professors made personal friendships with Hirohito. One was Hattori Hirotaro, an effeminate little man who taught him natural history, Darwinism, and, perhaps most important, Herbert Spencer's apocrypha to Darwin. This was reduced by Hattori to two ideas: there are fit and unfit societies; the former must destroy the latter in the interests of the race as a whole. At the same time Hattori greatly enhanced Hirohito's enjoyment of life by training him to notice the smallest details of nature in the world about him. When Hirohito complained that nature was disturbed by the column of chamberlains who accompanied him on natural history walks in the countryside, Hattori arranged fishing and diving trips for him in boats too small to hold much of a Court. From these excursions on the water, Hirohito garnered the most pleasant memories of his childhood and a lifelong interest in the worms and shellfish of Japanese bays—an interest that was eventually to win him genuine international recognition as a marine biologist.

Hirohito's other favorite tutor was Sugiura Jugo, a professional jingoist who for thirty-odd years had lashed about with his writing brush in defense of Japanese culture against Western adulteration. Though a chemist by training, with a degree from the University of London, he was detailed to teach Hirohito ethics. And if Hattori distorted biology with his Spencerian asides on survival among nations, what Sugiura did to "ethics" was still more strange and flammable. He lectured at length on the three sacred treasures—the mirror, the sword, and the necklace—and also on the inner virtues of the flag, the nation, rice, shrines, guns, watches, water, and Mount Fuji. From the lecture notes of his beloved tutor, here are some samples:

In Europe there is little rice produced. In some Asian countries much rice is produced but of poor quality, incomparable with our own. Therefore, I feel sorry for the rest of the world, especially the Europeans.

Nowadays, although there are many nations on the earth, only two are strong: England and Russia. In the Western Hemisphere, the United States follows a close third. We do not yet know the outcome of the World War, of course, but it is plain that all the strong nations belong to the same Aryan clan, which comprises one nation. By contrast in Asia the large country, China, is degenerate. Therefore, China cannot be our partner and cannot stand with us against the nations of the West. Our Empire must decide to match arms with the Aryan clan all alone.

The ideas being entertained by the Russians are essentially American-European individualism. We must beware of them. Because of our growing closeness to Europe, esteem for the ancient sacred swords of Japan is declining.

Though we speak of 8,000,000 gods in Japan we really pray only to the excellent souls among the Rulers and the Ruled. Our religion is unique. In foreign lands there are fixed gods. The religion there is based on mere hypothesis.

At his *Genbuku* or coming of age in 1915, Hirohito donned the two swords of the samurai and presented himself at the palace shrine to be anointed a warrior. His father celebrated the event by sending the boy a young concubine to instruct him in the ways of love. Hirohito was shy but the girl was infinitely patient and tactful. Eventually—so Court gossips say —he satisfied his scientific curiosity. Courtiers at the time regretted that he did not seem to be a ladies' man to compare with his hearty grandfather Meiji.

WORLD WAR

In August 1914 the expected war in Europe broke out. Foreign Minister Kato Taka-aki promptly threw in Japan's lot with France and England. His object was not to help Britain but, as he frankly told his colleagues, to silence in advance any British objections to Japanese moves on China. For the next two years Japan undertook to protect British interests in Hong Kong and Shanghai. She sent troops to Singapore to quash trouble there with "the natives." Her Navy convoyed merchantmen through the Indian Ocean into the Mediterranean. She refused repeatedly, however, to contribute any troops to the bloody battlefields of Europe.

For her pittance of co-operation Japan expected a mountain of reciprocity. Foreign Minister Kato Taka-aki wanted the British government to run diplomatic interference for Japanese seizure and permanent possession of all German mandates and leaseholds in the Pacific. Hard pressed though she was, Great Britain refused to give Japan such a carte blanche.

In October 1914, two months after the war started, Japan went ahead on her own. Imperial marines poured ashore on nominally German islands all across the western Pacific, while Japanese Army divisions landed on the Shantung Peninsula, jutting out toward Korea from the north China coast, to begin a drive on the German-leased port of Tsingtao. After three months of campaigning, mostly on the sovereign territory of China, the Japanese forces not only took the German city but occupied the entire peninsula, a region roughly equivalent in area and population to the combined states of Connecticut and Massachusetts.

British diplomats talked for time. American diplomats frowned. And Yuan Shih-kai, the president of the new Republic of China, protested mildly. He knew that Western friends could not help him while the war lasted, and he hoped that divided councils in Japan herself might protect his regime until the war was over. At the end of 1914, Yuan politely told Tokyo that, since the Tsingtao campaign had ended, it was time for Japan to stop parading troops across Chinese territory and restrict them to police administration in the German leasehold. Japanese Foreign Minister Kato expressed indignation at Yuan's snide imputations and on January 18, 1915, delivered a note to China "to clarify the situation."

The note, which was amplified by a number of reference documents, has been remembered as the Twenty-One Demands. It explained fully—all too fully—what was required of China. The demands broke down into five groups, each making a separate point:

(1) As to Tsingtao: China must accept whatever settlement Japan might make with Germany and must let Japan build and operate a 200-mile railroad inland from Tsingtao to Tsinan on the Yellow River, thereby cutting China strategically into two halves.

(2) As to Manchuria: China must extend Japanese leases there to ninety-nine years and give Japan veto and first option rights in all future economic development of that region.

(3) As to financing: China must come first to Japan for all future loans and must here and now deliver, as collateral for past loans, supervisory control of the Chinese iron industry.

(4) As to the West: China must cede no more harbors, islands, or bays to the barbarians.

(5) As to the future: China must employ Japanese advisors for all important political, financial, and military development programs; must buy over 50 per cent of her army and navy supplies in Japan; must let Japan build a network of railroads in central China.

Foreign Minister Kato presented the Twenty-One Demands not to the foreign minister of China but directly to President Yuan Shih-kai, enjoining him to keep all of them, particularly the fifth group, secret. Yuan naturally leaked them as soon as possible to the American ambassador in Peking, and Kato was embarrassed by diplomatic inquiries from all over the world. Kato replied to the Western Powers with a summary of the first four points and a denial of the existence of the fifth. To China he replied with the dispatch of 30,000 reinforcements for Japan's continental garrisons. When Yuan continued to resist all the demands, Foreign Minister Kato told him on May 7, 1915, that the fifth set could be reserved for future discussion but that he had only forty-eight hours to consider the first four sets, after which China would be invaded. Yuan promptly gave in and let it be known in the West that he was acting under duress. Years later, when the peace settlements were made after World War I, Chinese diplomats regained a substantial part of the ground which Yuan had temporarily conceded.

In Tokyo old Army Chief Yamagata saw clearly from the tenor of Chinese newspapers that Foreign Minister Kato had won a Pyrrhic victory. The Chinese felt that Yuan Shih-kai had actually put up a brave stand against Japan's hated cutthroats and carpetbaggers. At seventy-seven, Yamagata still had enough political influence to force the Cabinet to resign. Prime Minister Okuma obediently formed a new Cabinet which did not contain the controversial foreign minister, Kato.

In December 1915, four months after Kato's ouster, China's President Yuan Shih-kai announced that, by popular request, he planned to crown himself emperor. It was a fatal miscalculation. The war lords who commanded Yuan's armies might not be republican idealists but neither did they want to serve under a new imperial dynasty. Rebellion spread and on June 6, 1916, Yuan died of uremia brought on by nervous prostration. He was succeeded by a nonentity who preserved the central Republican government only as a façade for many separate provincial regimes, each run by one of Yuan's former generals.

Emperor Meiji's old Army Chief Yamagata was dismayed. With Yuan went all hope of a strong Japan-China to face the West. Yamagata exerted all his influence to find a new, non-republican autocrat to govern China and a new, un-Westernized Cabinet to govern Japan. He pointed out to his pro-German Emperor, Taisho, that Japan's allies were not winning the war; that the kaiser's armies were fighting the battle of the Somme and pressing on toward Verdun; that the buffer state of Russia, which separated Germany from her lost leasehold of Tsingtao, seemed dangerously weak. After a complex political parley and, for an old man, a tremendous display of energy and influence, Yamagata succeeded, in September 1916, in toppling the Okuma government. He persuaded Emperor Taisho to appoint in its place a Cabinet headed by an Army man, General Terauchi.

Through Terauchi, Yamagata backed the war lord of Manchuria, Chang Tso-lin, as the next strongman in northern China. A peasant boy, Chang had grown up hunting hares on the Manchurian prairies to help feed himself and his ailing seamstress mother. One day, as a teen-ager, he had hid behind a clump of bushes at the sound of horses' hooves. Seeing a bandit band fleeing from the imperial Manchu constabulary, he raised his gun and shot one of the fugitives. When the chase had passed, he took possession of the dead bandit's horse. With this small grubstake he went on to become a bandit himself, the most successful in all Manchuria. During the Russo-Japanese War he and his men had served the Japanese as irregulars behind the Russian lines. After the war his troops had been accepted into the imperial Chinese Army and he had made a name for himself as a capable general. Now that Yuan was dead, Chang Tso-lin planned to fill the vacuum and make himself master of China. He took to striking Napoleonic poses and wearing a Russian greatcoat lined with otter skins.

The Six Princes of Emperor Taisho's kitchen cabinet conceived an immediate dislike for Chang Tso-lin. They did not look favorably on his plans for unifying China or on his friendship with the old Choshu clan's Army chief, Yamagata. Through their contacts with the remnants of the former Chinese imperial family, they arranged to have Chang Tso-lin's ambitions nipped in the bud. In 1916 Manchu Prince Babojab of Mongolia invaded western Manchuria with a horde of Tartar roughriders, officered by Japanese "advisors" who were all protégés of Emperor Taisho's princes. The horsemen from the steppes harassed the railroad between Peking and the Manchurian capital of Mukden. Their presence on Chang Tso-lin's flank made it impossible for Chang to prepare his contemplated invasion of China.

At the height of the Mongol invasion on October 15, 1916—six days after the formation of the Yamagata-backed Army Cabinet of General Terauchi—the youngest of Emperor Taisho's Six Princes arrived in Mukden to preside in person over an intrigue that was expected to end Chang Tso-lin's career. The prince was Kanin, the tenth brother of Emperor Komei's advisor, Asahiko, and the future Army Chief of Staff for Hirohito in the years 1932–1940. He was on his way home by rail from a state visit to Petrograd—the then capital of Russia, now Leningrad—where he had gone to assess the weakness of the czarist regime and of the crumbling Russian front against Germany. At Mukden station Prince Kanin was met by a crowd of Japanese bureaucrats and Army officers employed by the Japanese governments of the Kwantung Peninsula Leasehold and the South Manchuria Railroad Zone. The reception committee was headed by the governor of Port Arthur, a general whom Kanin had known intimately for years. The general brought with him to the station, as host, Chang Tso-lin, the war lord of Manchuria.

After the platform welcomes, the groups of dignitaries climbed into carriages and bowled off together down the dusty unpaved roads of Mukden to an Oriental feast. As they neared their restaurant in the Japanese quarter, a bystander lobbed a bomb at Chang Tso-lin's carriage, which led the cavalcade. The bomb fell short and burst amid his mounted bodyguard, killing five of them. Chang leapt swift as an alley cat from his coach, seized a cap and a horse from one of his surviving henchmen, and made off down a side street, unnoticed in the confusion. The bomb thrower was shot at once, before his affiliations could be determined, and Chang's coachman covered his master's flight by moving on gravely with the rest of the procession. Undaunted, a second bomb thrower came forward to blow the empty carriage to splinters.

The next day a horde of Babojab's Mongol horsemen, accompanied by their Japanese advisors, poured into the country west of Mukden and drove on the city. To the surprise of the Japanese, a very angry and alive Chang Tso-lin marshaled his defense forces, met the Mongolians, and routed them. When the Japanese realized that they had failed, a number of nettled officers proposed to seize Mukden anyway with regular Japanese railway guard units. The acting Japanese consul general in Mukden cabled news of the plan to Tokyo, and Prime Minister Terauchi cabled back orders that no one do anything more without authorization. Prince Kanin and his cronies were bitterly frustrated. They solaced themselves in later years by describing with relish the spectacle of Chang Tso-lin fleeing on horseback in common soldier's garb down a back alley. At length, after Hirohito came to power, Prince Kanin's minions, in 1928, would inaugurate the aggressions of Hirohito's reign by assassinating Chang Tso-lin successfully. Imperial policy might change direction but it did not forget or forgive.

SIBERIA

Shortly after Emperor Taisho's ill-conceived effort to add Manchuria to the Empire, Germany turned east from stalemate at Verdun and overran Rumania. The Russian front collapsed and with it the rule of the Romanovs. During March 1917, Czar Nicholas relinquished his crown, and the whole long underbelly of Russia became a military emptiness, preoccupied with internal rumbling. To many Japanese it appeared that any day Kaiser Wilhelm might come knocking at the door, demanding payment for the seized German leasehold of Tsingtao.

In the early months of 1917 old Army Chief Yamagata was able to align most responsible Japanese behind him against further ill-considered essays in gunboat diplomacy. Taisho retired petulantly under the face-saving cover of sickness. Then, on April 7, Tokyo time, the United States joined the Allies against Germany and Emperor Taisho felt better. The Six Princes of his kitchen cabinet began at once to tout the possibility of adding eastern Siberia to the Empire. The revolutionary regime in western Russia had not the men or money to defend Vladivostok. The Germans now would need all their strength for the western front. And what was more, the British and French governments had invited Japan several times since 1915 to move troops west from Vladivostok in order to shore up the eastern front. By accepting the invitation at this belated date Japan might not be able to annex Siberia permanently but she would at least ingratiate herself with the victors and have counters with which to bargain at the postwar peace conferences.

On June 5, 1917, Emperor Taisho appointed a Special Advisory Council on Foreign Affairs to help him consider the possibilities. At the same time he ordered the Army General Staff to prepare a detailed study of the strategic situation. The Army study, submitted in October 1917, showed that a thrust all the way to the eastern front, as requested by France and England, would overextend the Army's logistical resources, but that a simple occupation of the railheads and lines of track as far west as Lake Baikal in mid-Siberia would be completely feasible.

Army strongman Yamagata and his old oligarch rival, Prince Saionji, mustered the elders of the nation in opposition to the Siberian venture. Army agents, said Yamagata, had discovered that there were approximately 300,000 Austrian, German, Turkish, and Bulgarian prisoners of war in Siberia who would fight for the Bolsheviks in return for their freedom. Under the circumstances, a Japanese expeditionary force of less than 100,000 men would be a rash venture, courting disaster.

In late December 1917, the Central Soviet opened an administrative office in Vladivostok, and Great Britain at once announced that she was dispatching H.M.S. *Suffolk* to the port to look after British interests there and stand by to evacuate British nationals if it became necessary. Yamagata agreed that Japan would be justified in doing whatever the British did. And so on January 12, 1918, Japan sent a naval squadron to Vladivostok to make sure that the municipal government there would remain in White Russian hands.

All through the spring of 1918 Japan kept open the Vladivostok beachhead, and an intense political battle raged in Tokyo about whether or not to extend it. Almost singlehandedly the eighty-year-old Yamagata held out against unilateral Japanese action.

"We must inquire the views of the various countries," he told Emperor Taisho. "There must be a consensus and we must be fully justified."

On April 23, 1918, Emperor Taisho finally bowed to his arguments. The Japanese marines went back to their ships and on April 25 Vladivostok formed its own soviet and entered the Lenin-Trotsky fold.

Just when Yamagata had won his battle, the whole situation was changed by an about-face on the part of the United States. Fifty thousand Czech soldiers, who had earlier surrendered to the Russians in the hopes of being able to liberate their native land from the yoke of the Austro-Hungarian Empire, were now unemployed mercenaries in Russia, struggling to go home. The Allies had agreed to use them on the western front if they could find any way of getting there. They organized themselves into sixty trainloads of from 700 to 1000 men each and set off from western Russia in April 1918 to stage their way east along the Trans-Siberian railroad.

At the other end in Vladivostok they hoped they would find Allied transports ready to take them to France. As they began their journey, the British landed marines in northern Russia at Murmansk, and the German government demanded that the Bolsheviks disarm the Czechs before they could gather at this potential second front. When the Reds tried to comply, the Czech rear guard, which was still west of the Volga, rebuffed the attempt with bullets. In a matter of weeks the strung-out Czech column had seized every major railhead from the Volga to Vladivostok and their peaceful exodus had become a fighting anabasis. Seasoned soldiers, they drove off every force, Red or White, that sought to stay their passage.

The thought of 50,000 Czech patriots fighting their way across 5,000 miles of steppe and tundra was not difficult to dramatize in newspapers, and the sympathy of the American public was profoundly stirred. The romantic feeling for the Czechs was used by American interests which feared the Red plague of Bolshevism, and on July 8, 1918, the United States abruptly suggested to Japan that the two nations mount a joint intervention in Siberia. Its objectives should be limited to help for the Czechs, satisfactory disposition of the 300,000-odd prisoners of war in Siberian stockades, and retrieval of Allied war supplies stockpiled in Vladivostok.

Old Army man Yamagata chuckled cynically when he heard the news. Overnight all his opinions changed, and he became, in the days that followed, an ardent champion of intervention. By July 12 he was saying, "Since the present expedition is not to fight with Germany there is no need for our inadequacy to give anxiety." On August 3 the Japanese government announced that it would participate in the Allied expedition, and three weeks later, by arrangement with China, 30,000 Japanese troops were already marching north to the Russian border through Manchuria.

The intervention was not popular anywhere. All through August, after the decision for it was made, Japanese housewives staged riots in the major cities, burning warehouses in protest against the high price of rice. Soldiers complained that no one would come to see them off when they left for the front, and many of them wore civilian clothes so that they would not be recognized as Army men. As a result of the popular protest, the Terauchi government resigned in late September, and Emperor Taisho mollified the mobs by appointing in its place Japan's first true party government, presided over by a commoner, the president of the Constitutionalists, Hara Takashi.

American observers were no more pleased by Japan's speedy co-operation than were the mass of Japanese themselves. In American eyes, too many Japanese troops had moved too quickly. Yamagata, however, smiled innocently. The Army, he said, was always kept ready to move swiftly and with a safe margin of force. What right, he demanded brazenly, had anyone to question the Emperor's constitutional prerogative of supreme command?

As quickly as possible, President Woodrow Wilson shipped 7,000 U.S. troops to Siberia to keep an eye on the Japanese. Each side separately supported a succession of ill-conceived White Russian puppet regimes, all of which were blackened from their inception by the sundry tortures, rapes, and murders of their Cossack hangers-on. The Japanese soldiers themselves won a name for savagery by carrying out, under orders, several village massacres in reprisal for Russian terrorism.

None of the White Russian governments set up by the "Allies" won any degree of popular backing from the Siberian peasantry, and all collapsed in 1919 when Red Armies finally emerged out of the west and began to apply military pressure. Anglo-American troops developed a revulsion for the duty they were called upon to perform. In late 1919 the British withdrew their tiny contingent, and with them went a force of Canadians who were reported on the verge of mutiny. In April 1920 the last U.S. troops followed them, leaving the Japanese to their own devices. In the months that followed, over large areas of Siberia, all pretence of native government was dropped and the Japanese Army ruled by its own law.

The Czechs, who had never needed any help in the first place, except ships to carry them home, now began to be repatriated. They sailed from Vladivostok, regiment by regiment, all year long. While they waited they clashed frequently with the Japanese and sold the last and best of the White Russian puppets, Alexander Kolchak, to a Bolshevik firing squad.

The 300,000 German, Austrian, Turkish, and Bulgarian war prisoners —men who might have been repatriated in 1917 if it had not been for the intervention—were left forgotten in their stockades. Scandinavian, American, and German Red Cross teams began to take notice of their sorry plight late in 1919, but before anything effective was done for them, 100,000 had died of starvation, typhus, and smallpox. Of the survivors many were shipped home insane. The Japanese forces lingered on in Siberia until 1922. Only when the postwar peace conferences were over and their presence could no longer be represented as a force of leverage in international politics were they finally withdrawn.

PEACE AND MADNESS

The Versailles peace conference opened in January 1919. The Japanese delegation to it was headed by the once debonair lute-playing Fujiwara Prince Saionji. Saionji was now seventy years old, and he captivated the world's press by arriving in Paris with a great deal of baggage, including a pretty young apprentice geisha named Flower Child whom he unabashedly called his mistress. Whenever negotiations went badly for his delegation, he moved the baggage and Flower Child out to the lobby of the Hotel Bristol where he was staying as a sign that Japan might withdraw from the conference. Then he would take a stroll in the Bois de Boulogne and await developments. As soon as his subordinates had worked out a suitable compromise, he would re-register at the Bristol and call for his effects. French hostesses, dying to see Flower Child, invited him to all their parties, but he accepted invitations judiciously and usually left the girl back in his hotel suite.[2] He attended no sessions of the peace conference but met everyone he needed to meet at the soirees. All the Western statesmen at the conference developed a liking for him as an urbane conversationalist, a shrewd bargainer, and a convincing liberal.

Saionji's objectives at the conference were to keep the territories which Japan had taken from Germany during the war and to gain recognition for Japan as a first-class power. He succeeded in keeping the leasehold of Tsingtao and the German mandated islands in the Pacific, and he relinquished in return Japan's occupied areas in Siberia and the Shantung Peninsula. He succeeded in having Japan included, after France and Italy, in the Big Five but failed to win agreement on a resolution calling for legal equality among nations without "distinction . . . on account of their race."

In the summer of 1919, while Saionji was still in Paris, the forty-year-old Emperor Taisho suffered the first in a succession of cerebral hemorrhages or thromboses which were to incapacitate him increasingly for the rest of his life. Although the attack was kept secret and indeed has never been precisely defined by the doctors who attended him, news of it spread quickly through aristocratic circles. It was difficult for Taisho to walk now, even with a shuffle. His hands trembled. His memory of recent events was blurred. His judgment and sense of propriety were dimmed. At the annual autumn maneuvers for the Army and Navy he descended unexpectedly from the reviewing stand and with his own hands unpacked a soldier's kit to see what was in it. At the opening of the Diet two months later he rolled the message he was to read into a spyglass and peered quizzically through it at legislators who had offended him in the past. Though he seemed rational, he expressed himself with a heightened sense of whimsy and sarcasm which caused his retainers great pain. They called him mad, a diagnosis which young Hirohito never accepted.

Emperor Taisho's lapse removed the vortex from the hurricane of Japanese political life. The spry old Army spirit, Yamagata, stepped in to fill the void. Taisho's Six Princes consulted with their sworn allies of the Satsuma clan and decided that, now or never, they must launch an underground campaign to break the tightening stranglehold of Yamagata and his Choshu clan. Anti-Choshu cells must be established in the traditional Choshu strongholds of the bureaucracy, in the Home Ministry which controlled the police, in the Agriculture and Commerce Ministry which controlled long-range in-

---

[2] He made an exception for President Wilson, who acknowledged the honor by giving Flower Child a necklace which Japanese appraisers valued at over $1,000.

dustrial planning, and most important, in the Army. The nineteen-year-old Crown Prince Hirohito probably gave his consent to the scheme, for it was his favorites in the younger generation of princes and noblemen—his childhood Big Brothers—who became the most active executioners of the plot.

One of the conspirators' anti-Choshu cells, one which would cast a long shadow over Hirohito's reign, was established in the ranks of Army Intelligence. Far from the prying eyes of Yamagata's agents, it was headquartered in France and staffed by young noblemen who had arranged postings for themselves as military attachés in the various capitals of Europe. The task of recruiting this Parisian imperial cell fell to thirty-two-year-old Prince Higashikuni, the sixth and youngest of the surviving sons of Emperor Komei's advisor Asahiko and the future prime minister who would hand Japan over to General MacArthur.

By 1919 Higashikuni was far less plain-spoken than he had been eight years earlier when he had refused Emperor Meiji's dinner invitation. In 1914 he had graduated from the Army's exclusive Staff College or War College where officers had to prove their intellectual capacity in original strategic planning. In 1915 he had been finally restored to his family's good graces and allowed to marry Emperor Meiji's ninth daughter, Toshiko. Since then he had served with the 2d Division in the northern city of Sendai, taken a special course in armored cars and tanks at the Chiba Infantry School, and everywhere widened his circle of henchmen. By 1919 he was a thoroughly professional intelligence officer.

In December 1919 the Satsuma clan's senior general suggested to Choshu Army Chief Yamagata that perhaps Prince Higashikuni should be allowed to fulfill his long-cherished ambition to study at the famous military schools of Napoleon in France. The Satsuma chieftain pointed out that most of Higashikuni's best Army friends were already in Europe and that a good spy ring was needed there if Japan was to catch up on the technological secrets developed during World War I. The bright young analysts attached to the embassies would work more closely and secretly together if an imperial prince joined them in their mission and impressed them with its importance. Army Chief Yamagata, unsuspecting, called in Higashikuni for a man-to-man chat, was impressed by his patriotism, and forthwith approved the orders which posted him to France.

Higashikuni took ship with another, more peripheral member of the imperial family, the husband of his eldest niece, Army Captain Viscount Machijiri Kazumoto. Within a week of their arrival at Marseilles, Machijiri was in touch with Captain Tojo Hideki in Switzerland, the later World War II "dictator." Tojo was already a thoroughly trustworthy conspirator, for in addition to being an old friend of Higashikuni, he had served for three years as a personal aide to the war minister who had helped Prince

Kanin in the abortive 1916 Manchuria coup.[3] Using Tojo as an intermediary, Prince Higashikuni had soon established contact with a galaxy
of ambitious young non-Choshu attachés and observers all over Europe:
in Berlin with Major Umezu Yoshijiro, the future chief of staff who would
surrender in Hirohito's bunker in 1945; in Bern with Captain Yamashita
Tomoyuki, the later general who would capture Singapore; in Moscow
with Lieutenant Murakami Keisaku, the son-in-law of Prime Minister
Katsura's war minister; in Copenhagen with Lieutenant Colonel Nakamura
Kotaro, a later war minister; in Paris with Major Nakajima Kesago, the
sadist who would bring special body-burning oils to Nanking in 1937;
in Cologne with Captain Shimomura Sadamu who would force the Nanking
plans through the General Staff. To these in the early months of 1920
were added other notorious fascist generals of years to come.

COLOR-BLIND BRIDE

Vague rumors of an Emperor-Satsuma plot reached Yamagata's ears
through his private agents in the spring of 1920. He understood, he said
delicately, that young Crown Prince Hirohito's name was being used and
abused by the plotters to give their machinations a semblance of sanction.
Such impiety, as Yamagata saw it, stemmed from the marriage alliance
which Hirohito had arranged for himself. Two years earlier, on January
17, 1918, when the Navy had just sent ships to Vladivostok, the Imperial
Household Ministry had announced the betrothal of Hirohito to Princess
Nagako, the daughter of Prince Kuni Kuniyoshi. Prince Kuni was the second of the surviving sons of Emperor Komei's advisor Asahiko and one
of Taisho's Six Princes. His wife Chikako was the daughter of the Satsuma
clan lord, Shimazu, who had sworn eternal friendship with Asahiko and
his heirs in 1863. For Hirohito to marry Princess Nagako was to bring
the Throne itself into the Shimazu-Asahiko alliance.

As a Choshu man and a hereditary foe of the Satsuma clan, old Army
martinet Yamagata had not liked the marriage plans when he first heard
of them in 1917 but had said nothing because he understood that Nagako
was young Crown Prince Hirohito's own choice. Chamberlains in charge
of genealogies, rituals, and other imperial mysteries had scoured the land
in early 1917 to compile a complete list of eligible fiancées for Hirohito.
Empress Sadako, the pretty young woman who had waited with the cherry
blossoms in the garden in 1900, had insisted that her son make his selection personally. In midsummer, 1917, she had stationed the seventeen-
year-old boy in hiding behind a sliding door in her suite in the Concubines' Pavilion of the palace, enabling him to observe the eligibles through

---

[3] War Minister Oshima Kenichi, the father of Lieutenant General Oshima Hiroshi
who, as acting Japanese ambassador in Berlin in 1940, would bring Hirohito into
the Tripartite Pact with Hitler and Mussolini.

a peephole while she entertained each of them in turn at a tea ceremony. He had had time beforehand to study their photographs and their curricula vitae. Many of them he had played with in years past on the beach outside the Summer Palace at Hayama or in the bamboo groves of the mountain resort of Karuizawa. Now almost a score of girls were paraded in front of him, kneeling to drink a ceremonial cup of tea and exchange a few words with his mother. They ranged in age from Hirohito's own lofty seventeen down to a gawky eleven. Half of them, the prettiest half, were Fujiwara princesses, schooled to be charming, seductive, and obedient. The other half were princesses of the blood, culled from a smaller reservoir of eligibility, and for the most part semi-Westernized, proud, and uncertain of their rights.

Chamberlains had expected Hirohito to pick one of the faun-eyed daughters of Fujiwara Prince Ichijo or the pert fifteen-year-old princess of the blood, Masako, with whom he had once spent a pleasant summer in the mountains. Masako then had been a good rough-and-tumble tomboy of a companion; Masako now, in the chamberlains' eyes, had filled out ravishingly. What teasing trick she had played on Hirohito they could never find out, but he passed her over and three years later sanctioned a purely political match for her with a foreigner; the only match which has been contracted by the imperial family with a foreigner to this day, a match, moreover, with a Korean prince, a leader of Japan's most persecuted immigrant minority.[4]

In selecting Nagako over all the rest, Hirohito took a bright, serious, placid, chubby fourteen-year-old who could not be compared, as a woman, with most of the other candidates he saw. He made the choice out of loyalty to her uncles, his Big Brothers Prince Higashikuni and Prince Asaka, and to her fifteen-year-old brother Kuni Kunihisa who had been his companion since nursery days. She was, in short, the girl-brat who had often tagged along. He was at home with her and all her family. Even her father struck a responsive chord in him, for Prince Kuni shared Hirohito's interest in science. He was an intellectual and a visionary. He ridiculed the notion that Japan would ever make a military dent in the world by sheer force of samurai ardor and gave his enthusiasms instead to the development of the weapons of the future: the airplane, the tank, and bacteriological warfare.

In 1920 when eighty-two-year-old strongman Yamagata became suspicious of the intentions of Hirohito's fiancée's family, he struck back with pseudoscientific arguments. He planted a learned article in a Tokyo periodical tracing the hereditary course of color-blindness down through the

---

[4] After World War II, when the puppet princes of Korea became an unpleasant reminder of past glory, Masako found the condescending politeness of Japanese high society intolerable. In 1963, she took her ailing husband back to his homeland where they founded an orphanage for Japanese-Korean half-breeds.

generations of the Satsuma clan's Shimazu family. Since Nagako had a
Shimazu mother the blemish might well enter the imperial blood stream
if Hirohito went through with his marriage plans.

Yamagata's family physician convoked a medical congress to discuss
the problems of the color-blind. A former inspector general of Army
medicine devoted a lecture he had been asked to give at the "Imperial
Study"—the imperial family's standing adult self-education program—
entirely to color-blindness. Empress Sadako, whose Fujiwara nieces and
cousins had been rejected by her son, publicly stood by Nagako and
scoffed at Yamagata's allegations. Privately, however, she consulted her
kinsman, the old lute-player Prince Saionji, and asked him if there were
really any genetic danger. Saionji let Yamagata understand that he would
not stand in the way if an attempt were made to break up the engagement of Hirohito and Nagako.

Neither Yamagata nor Saionji knew their opponent. In years past both
of them had often worked out compromises with princes of the blood. But
Prince Kuni Kuniyoshi, the father of the fiancée, was a man of conscience.
He believed in his daughter as he believed in military air power. When
his uncle, Prince Sadanaru, the senior of Taisho's Six Princes, came to
him and begged him to humor Yamagata—to withdraw his Shimazu daughter Nagako in favor of his non-clan, non-controversial niece Masako—
Prince Kuni stood on principle and refused. He announced that Nagako
had been chosen through no machinations of his own, and therefore he
would take it as a point of personal honor if she should now be put aside.
It was an extremely European stand to take, but it meant, in plain Japanese, that he was prepared to kill both himself and Nagako if she were
now jilted.

Yamagata next got in touch with Sugiura Jugo, Hirohito's favorite tutor,
to see if he could persuade the boy to annul the engagement by his own
motion. Hirohito did not absolutely rebuff the feeler but mildly reiterated
that Nagako was still his preference. Sugiura then justified all the trust
Hirohito had ever placed in him by announcing that if the crown prince
were not given his way, he, Sugiura, a mere school teacher, would also
commit hara-kiri.

While Yamagata hesitated, Prince Kuni hired the powers of persuasion
of a band of Black Dragon thugs. From mid-Meiji times, Yamagata and
the Black Dragon's "Darkside Emperor" Toyama had been the upper and
lower spiders in Japan's "web society." They had often co-operated in the
past, and each owed part of his power to the other's help. But now that
Toyama, who had started life as a street urchin, found himself directly
solicited by the imperial family, he knew that his kingdom had come.
No longer need he cultivate Yamagata, who was after all a mere clan
samurai. Besides, the romantic gangsters and slum dwellers whom Toyama
controlled and represented would always favor a prince in white armor

over a sly old fox of an aristocrat like Yamagata. When Prince Kuni's bribes began to percolate down through Toyama's adept hands, an aging buck in the Diet, Otake Kanichi, sprang up to challenge Yamagata to a duel: "For old times' sake, let's assassinate each other with swords." More to the point, a Toyama henchman visited Yamagata and bowed himself out with the courteous threat: "I would be humbly honored to accept the life of Your Excellency's wife."

Yamagata had heard all these dramatic declarations before and had an old warrior's contempt for them. The police, however, who in Japan consider their function as mainly preventive intelligence rather than detective or punitive work, automatically set pickets around Yamagata's villa in the Tokyo suburb of Odawara. Yamagata was so incensed by the suggestion that he might need protection—he, a samurai who could once have routed singlehandedly a dozen ruffians with his swordplay—that he drove off the police with his cane. Thereafter, a group of his fellow Choshu clansmen took it upon themselves to guard his home, standing shifts tactfully in plainclothes.

Yamagata's personal agent at Court, Imperial Household Minister Nakamura Yujiro, who had seen to it that the trumped-up issue of color-blindness was the burning question in Court gossip, now sought an audience with Emperor Taisho and Empress Sadako. Kneeling rigidly on the *tatami,* head to the floor, he said: "I must beg miserably for Your favor after the failure of my Imperial Household Agency to discover the color-blindness in the Shimazu family of Princess Nagako's mother. Now that the defect is well known, what is your Imperial Highness's pleasure?" Emperor Taisho looked straight ahead, unspeaking, and Empress Sadako, too, was strangely silent. Nakamura looked up several times from the *tatami* and saw a bitter ghost of a smile playing around her mouth. When the tension had become extreme, the Emperor suddenly spoke in the high-pitched chanting voice which he reserved for oracular priestly occasions: "I am told that scientists, too, often make mistakes." Nakamura glanced at the Empress and saw her motioning with her eyes for him to withdraw. The audience was over.

On February 10, 1921, the Home Ministry, in charge of prefectural governments and police, announced: "Although there are rumors about Princess Nagako's marriage, no changes of plan are presently contemplated. Of this the government is absolutely certain. Also Household Minister Nakamura Yujiro has determined to tender his resignation." Previously the newspapers had carried no explicit stories about the marriage controversy but had only alluded to "a delicate situation in the imperial household." Suddenly to announce Household Minister Nakamura as the culprit of the situation, when everyone knew that Nakamura was Yamagata's protégé, was rude in the extreme. Yamagata offered ostentatiously to resign all his titles and the Throne just as ostentatiously begged him to keep them. The Emperor, it was declared, had full confidence in Yamagata as a loyal elder of the nation.

BON VOYAGE

No sooner had Yamagata retired to his corner to stanch his wounds and plan the next round than a new issue was injected into the controversy, an issue which temporarily embarrassed Hirohito and permanently discredited Yamagata in the eyes of the public. For many months Hirohito had been planning to round out his education with a trip to Europe. Tentative arrangements had been made with the British and French governments and Yamagata had expressed his approval of the plan. Responsible officials of the government all agreed that the trip might improve relations with Great Britain and make it possible to renew the advantageous Anglo-Japanese alliance. Yamagata's old friend and rival, the lute-playing Prince Saionji, however, saw deeper. He had some inkling of Prince Higashikuni's mission to the young attachés at the Japanese embassies in Europe. He had seen how Taisho's Six Princes had come back from Europe in the 1880's with their private cabals of henchmen. He could imagine the magic which Hirohito's presence in France would work on Higashikuni's efforts.

Through his son-in-law and adopted son—Saionji Hachiro, a chamberlain—Saionji leaked to the press a highly distorted account of the reasons for Hirohito's trip abroad. According to the planted story, Yamagata was sending Hirohito away to cool his ardor for Nagako and break up the engagement. Overnight Toyama's thugs, the newspapers, and the romantic Japanese masses joined in indignant opposition to the European tour. Editorialists suggested that Yamagata might have Nagako assassinated in Hirohito's absence, that Westerners would ridicule Hirohito's noisy Japanese way of drinking soup, that Korean assassins would be able to cut Hirohito down in Trafalgar Square, that Hirohito would catch cold because of "the disgusting European habit of blowing noses." Knowing nothing of the West but distrust and nothing of Hirohito but reverence, the people could not appreciate the fact that their future Emperor was better equipped by training to feel at home in Western clothes, eating frogs' legs on the Champs-Élysées, than to squat in kimono, sipping noodles on the Ginza.

Toyama Mitsuru, the elder statesman of gangland, hardly needed to be told that Hirohito genuinely looked forward to his visit abroad and would come to no harm by it. His enthusiastic underlings, however, invested much face in the struggle to stop the voyage. Before Toyama was fully aware of all the niceties of the situation, some of them had vowed to strap themselves to the railroad tracks in front of the train taking Hirohito to his port of departure. And so, when visited by a chamberlain, Toyama sighed and asked for time. The impatient young Hirohito was not prepared to give it and sent to him Count Futara, one of the Big Brothers of Hirohito's childhood and the husband of one of the nieces of Emperor Komei's advisor Asahiko. Count Futara was to become Hirohito's public relations man. He would supply an image of Hirohito to satisfy the demands of Western newsmen—the one image on which Western accounts of Hirohito's character as a young man are all based. He had a flair for words and drama. "We have gone with you this far," he told Toyama, "but now we are all resolved to go with Hirohito even to the gates of death." Toyama nodded approvingly and asked only for some little diversionary act of bravado which would make it easier for his men to back down.

A few days later, on February 27, 1920, a group of toughs forced their way into the home of Saionji's son, Hachiro. They belonged to a cell of young intellectuals within the Black Dragon Society which was patronized by Hirohito's Big Brothers and used by the Throne for private civilian intelligence work in China. They were led by Dr. Okawa Shumei, who would later win a reputation as the "Goebbels of Japan" and as the ideologist for the Strike-South faction which espoused war against Western colonies in Southeast Asia rather than war against Communist Russia.

In a nod to popular chauvinistic sentiment, the intruders first accused young Saionji, wrongfully, of advocating Hirohito's trip abroad. Then they leveled their real charges. They told Hachiro that he was suspected of having connived with Yamagata's discredited Imperial Household Minister Nakamura and of having opposed Hirohito's betrothal to Nagako. Finally they upbraided him, as a palace chamberlain, for having gossiped too much to the men of the press about Hirohito's proposed trip. For these derelictions of duty they demanded that young Saionji stand up and be chastised. Hachiro realized at once that he was about to be punished sacramentally as a scapegoat for his father, the elder statesman. In defense of the Saionji family honor, he drew his sword. Dr. Okawa's toughs seized cleat bolts from the sliding screens and held their ground. Meanwhile some of them dashed outside to fetch wooden swords which they had cached at the front entrance. Flailing the air, Hachiro retreated through a doorway at the rear of the house, turned and sought to escape through his back garden. The street bullies caught him, weaving through the trees, and thrashed him thoroughly with their mock swords. When they departed they left beside his bruised body a two-foot scroll that declared him a traitor.

Saionji Hachiro did not commit suicide, and his father and Toyama duly apologized both to one another and to the Throne. All the great nobles and princes at Court agreed with Hirohito that Yamagata must be firmly ignored. Accordingly, they decided to minimize further trouble by starting for Europe as quickly as possible. In London equerries of the British royal family scurried about rearranging schedules which had been thrown askew by the announced arrival of "that bloody little prince" a whole week earlier than anticipated.

SALT AIR

Hirohito and his fifteen-man suite of chamberlains and Army and Navy officers proceeded in state through the streets of Tokyo on the morning of March 3, 1921, boarded the battleship *Katori* off Yokohama, and steamed for the open sea with the battleship *Kajima* in escort. Before moving out of sight of the Japanese coast, the squadron hove to briefly three miles off the village of Hayama where Empress Sadako and her sick Taisho lived in seclusion on the beach at their villa known as the Summer Palace. Standing at the stern of the *Katori,* above the suddenly silenced propellors, the twenty-year-old Hirohito bowed in the direction of his father and for a few moments meditated. Then he turned on his heel, the engines throbbed again, and the two warships made for the open sea trailing ribbons of soot from their tall slender smokestacks.

Hirohito sensed that this outing across the sea would be both his last childhood adventure and his first test as a ruler. For a year now he had stood in for his father at receptions for foreign ambassadors. The doctors said that Emperor Taisho's condition was irreversible, and so when Hirohito returned from abroad he would probably have to assume the full-time leadership of his country. As yet he had not had time to formulate a program for his reign. The long voyage through the Indian Ocean and Mediterranean would give him a chance to think.

Hirohito began all considerations with a sad awareness that his father's reign had been a failure. The dream of the ancestors to rule theocratically and keep Japan sacred for the sun goddess remained unfulfilled. Hirohito had reservations about the dream. It was too insular, too mystical and unscientific. Because of his training in geography and economics, Hirohito could not think of Japan in isolation but only as a part—the leading part—of Asia. Because of his scientific training he could not accept the legend of the sun goddess at face value. He was a devout Shinto priest and believed in the ghosts of his ancestors, but not in a simple superstitious way like most of his countrymen. He would eventually rationalize his creed by grafting onto it the semiscientific spiritualism of such Western thinkers as the astrophysicist Sir James Jeans and the physiologist J. S. Haldane. Hirohito believed that the spirits were always present and even available for consultation but only as psychic wave forms permeating the ether. He doubted that they could provide physical assistance to men in battle, as many Japanese believed. No, if his country was to realize her imperial ambitions, she would have to count on armies of living men equipped with modern weapons and deployed with coolheaded statesmanship. He was inclined to agree with his father that the most natural growth for Japan would be as a sea power into the islands of Southeast Asia.[5]

To help him formulate his plans, Hirohito had with him aboard the *Katori* the four men on whom he would continue to rely most throughout the first decade of his rule: Count Makino, Count Chinda, General Nara, and Prince Kanin.

Count Makino Nobuaki would be Hirohito's lord privy seal, principal civilian advisor, and plot-maker-in-chief until the end of 1935. He was a tall, slim, nervous, thin-lipped gentleman of fifty-nine, renowned for his mercurial wit, his courtly manners, and his velvety softness of voice. He spoke excellent English, having spent eight unhappy years as a boy and teen-ager studying in the United States. From 1917 to 1919 he had served as the secretary of Emperor Taisho's Advisory Council on Foreign Policy during the debate over the Siberian intervention. In 1919 he had gone to the Versailles peace conference as Japan's active representative who attended sessions and spoke for the coyly aloof chief delegate, Prince Saionji. Makino was the son of Emperor Meiji's oligarch Okubo Toshimichi of Satsuma who had led the imperial forces against his own clansmen when they revolted in 1877.

Count Chinda Sutemi also came of a non-Choshu clan, was also American-educated, had also served under Saionji in the Japanese delegation at Versailles. Vice foreign minister in Emperor Taisho's disastrous Katsura Cabinet of 1912 and then ambassador to England from 1916 to 1920, he was supposed to help Hirohito now in renewing the Anglo-Japanese alliance. A genial sixty-five, he would remain at Hirohito's side as grand chamberlain until his death at seventy-three in 1929.

General Nara Takeji, fifty-three, a non-Choshu officer from the northern province of Tochigi, was fatherly, taciturn, and efficient. He would be Hirohito's chief aide-de-camp, in charge of all liaison between the Throne and the Army, until completion of the conquest of Manchuria in 1933.

Before the war with the United States Hirohito would have other chief aides-de-camp, other grand chamberlains, other lord privy seals, but Prince Kanin, the fourth important member of the suite aboard the *Katori,* would be with Hirohito as the senior member of the Supreme War Council until his death of severe hemorrhoids in May 1945. In 1921 Kanin was already a living anachronism. He was one of the last three remaining brothers of Emperor Komei's advisor, Prince Asahiko, and by 1924 he would be the only remaining brother. As a baby he had been adopted by Emperor Komei, which made him, by the abacus of royal adoption, the grand-uncle

---

[5] This capsule of Hirohito's ideas is drawn from many accounts, put together by many men who knew him, at different times over the next forty-five years. Possibly he did not yet entertain them all in 1921 but it is likely that he did, for in other respects his thinking, character, and even turns of speech changed little from decade to decade.

of Hirohito and the brother of the deified Emperor Meiji. Yet Kanin was still only fifty-six years old and would live to see Tokyo burning under American incendiaries. Full of vitality, he was the most active of Taisho's Six Princes and the youngest field marshal in the Japanese Army, equal in rank and superior in social position to Yamagata himself. It was Kanin who had engineered the Mukden coup of 1916, Kanin who would head the Army General Staff from 1931 to 1940 during the conquest of Manchuria, the invasion of China, the 1939 Nomonhan war with Russia, and the preparation of war with the United States. Kanin looked even younger than his age: strikingly handsome, magnificently mustached, fit and muscular, always well tailored and in spit-and-polish press. His appearance was so un-Japanese that in France he sometimes passed successfully as a Frenchman.

In addition to Makino, Chinda, Nara, and Kanin—advisors respectively on politics, diplomacy, tactics, and strategy—Hirohito had in his retinue aboard the *Katori* three of his favorite Big Brothers: his fiancée's cousin, Marquis Komatsu, who had charge of his physical education program; Komatsu's brother-in-law, Count Futara, who handled imperial publicity; and a naval aide, Commander Oikawa Koshiro, who would be Navy minister in 1941 during the preparation of the attack on Pearl Harbor. The other eight members of Hirohito's personal entourage were Saionji Hachiro, the welted but wiser son of the old lute player; Big Brother Prince Konoye's cousin, Marquis Maeda Toshinari, a major who would later direct the attack on Bataan in the Philippines in early 1942; and six other commanders and majors of noble birth with bloody futures ahead of them.

Lounging in deck chairs or playing croquet, Hirohito and his suite discussed the future of Japan. They were predominantly members or relatives of the great naval clan of Satsuma, favorable toward maritime expansion in the South Seas and antagonistic toward the Choshu clan which had provided Emperor Meiji with most of his oligarchs. In Europe they were to be joined by representatives of other non-Choshu interests. Hardly anyone outside of Choshu who prided himself on his inside information had not hurried down to the ticket office to buy a passage to Europe when Hirohito's tour had been announced. The *Mishima Maru,* which the *Katori* would overhaul off the coast of Ceylon, was booked solid. Among these spectators were in-laws and debtors through whom Hirohito could construct any conceivable alliance of interests that he wanted. He must only beware of making his father's mistake—of coming out too autocratically in front of the brocade curtain hung for him by his ancestors.

The squadron of the crown prince plunged its way through choppy seas to the southernmost point of Japan. Though many on board were seasick, Hirohito kept the deck. When the radio officer informed him that hundreds of school children lined the shores waving in his direction, he dutifully gazed back toward them through a spyglass, but, as Count Futara put it, "the distance being too great, to his regret he was unable to see the people on the coast." Two days later the battleships made port at Okinawa, and the people of the island bowed low in silence along his route—once Perry's route—while he walked into the center of Naha, the Okinawan capital, and back again. Two more days and the squadron had skimmed the last point of Taiwan and left the Japanese Empire behind. Hirohito joined Marquis Komatsu, chamberlain of the imperial exercise, in prayers for Komatsu's father, General Prince Kitashirakawa Yoshihisa, who had died of malaria during the subjugation of the island in 1895.

After another two days, the squadron was in Hong Kong for a long weekend of banquets. During the festivities, Hirohito made a special point of inspecting the reservoir on Victoria Island, which, as it turned out, in 1941 was to be the crown colony's tactical Achilles' heel. On March 13, 1921, the channel leading out of the harbor was edged by fourteen steam launches bearing fourteen huge ideograms on placards, reading "Royal send-off by the Japanese Association of Hong Kong. Banzai."

In five more days the squadron entered the bastion of Singapore where Hirohito had to stand on deck for almost an hour returning the salutes of patriotic overseas Japanese who had come out to greet him and guide him in. The schedule for the next four days was again crowded with state functions, and again Hirohito requested the insertion of a few items which interested him personally. He took in the Museum of Natural History and famous Botanical Gardens where Alfred Russel Wallace in 1857 had penned the learned paper on natural selection which forced Darwin to publish his own theories on evolution. He stopped the official clock one morning while he turned toward Japan and celebrated the vernal Shinto feast of the dead. He borrowed a yacht and circumnavigated Singapore Island, of which Count Futara noted only that it "is separated from Johore by a narrow strait."

The long twenty-five-day voyage from Singapore to Suez was broken only once by a stop at Colombo in Ceylon where Hirohito was awed and amused by native dances and a down-on-the-knees salute from forty elephants trumpeting in unison. During the days at sea he played deck golf, swam in the pool, polished up his French, and imbibed lore and gossip from the in-laws and powers of Japan who traveled with him. In the battleship's makeshift cinema he demonstrated his progressive inclinations by ordering crewmen who huddled in the back of the room to come forward and take seats immediately behind his own entourage.

WAR FRONT TOURISM

Four days in Egypt, where he had the rare raw luck to see a genuine desert sandstorm whirl through the Cairo streets; two days in Malta, where he prayed for the seventy-seven Japanese who had become spirits on World

War I convoy duty; three days at Gibralter, inspecting the cisterns and tunnels of the Rock [6]—and on May 8, Hirohito docked in Portsmouth, England. In the weeks of banquets, receptions, and parades that followed, he stood for the first and only time of his life out in front of the chrysanthemum curtain, under the full scrutiny of Western cameramen and reporters. The British press were almost universally struck by his modesty, composure, and intelligence. In the adjectives of Lord Riddell, he seemed "pleasant," "unassuming," "courteous," "appreciative," "with remarkable development above the eyes, showing, I believe, great powers of observation."

Hirohito found time in his crowded schedule to memorize the toasts and shorter set speeches he had to deliver without seeming difficulty. He learned in advance and did not forget the names and careers of the scores of officers and diplomats—Japanese and European—whom he met at receptions. On one occasion he caught up a British officer on a fine point of British Army organization: "I thought at the beginning of the Great War, England had division organization only and no army corps." He impressed everyone with the economy and directness of his speech and his absolute correctness, fairness, and good manners in dealing with subordinates. He was up every morning at six, in bed at the latest by midnight, and seemed able to react like clockwork, without any visible tension, to the minute-by-minute timing of his schedule.

Facing a large audience for the first time in his life at his reception by the Lord Mayor of London, Hirohito "calmly glanced at the whole assembly"—in Count Futara's words—"and, after lightly saluting, put his military plumed hat under his left arm, and began to unroll the written reply to the address. As the scroll was thick and stiff, it seemed difficult for him to straighten it sufficiently for reading, but without showing the slightest embarrassment, he straightened the paper calmly and continued his speech in a loud, sonorous voice, with eloquent intonation. . . . The faces of the Japanese group glowed . . . at this triumphant performance of a delicate and trying task."

As the days passed, the members of Hirohito's entourage sometimes found that their paragon had more aplomb and sophistication than they had. On May 10 in Buckingham Palace, when they were helping him dress for the evening's banquet after a day's sightseeing at Windsor Castle, there was a knock on the door and in walked George of England, unannounced and as half-dressed as Hirohito himself: in slippers, shirt, and

---

[6] There Count Futara notes that Mr. Yoshida Shigeru, first secretary to the Japanese Embassy in London, came aboard "to consult us about various arrangements then being made in England for welcoming our Prince." This was the same Yoshida who would launch the political movement for a Strike South in 1933; who would be given a new face when arrested by the secret police as a member of the Peace Faction in 1945; and who would be Japan's leading postwar prime minister.

braces. The retainers were flustered. Even the noblest of them was unsure of imperial family mores in the privacy of the back palace, and they feared that Hirohito might react with hostility to this unprecedented informality by one not of the blood. But Hirohito's eyes scarcely widened. King George put an arm around his shoulder, sat down on the bed with him, told him what a pleasure it had been having him in Buckingham Palace, and chatted with him, partly in French and partly through a nervous naval aide-interpreter, about the subject that interested Hirohito most: the recent war.

In the course of the conversation, King George mentioned that the British had lost 150,000 men at Ypres and voiced the thought that the crown prince might like to have a look at that battlefield if he found time during his stay in Belgium. Hirohito later made time and cabled the British king his impressions: "The scene before me is impressive and edifying in the extreme, reminding me vividly of the words in which Your Majesty explained to me the sanguinary character of struggle on this field of honour at Ypres."

Three days in Buckingham Palace as a guest of the king, and eight days in Chesterfield House as a guest of the British government, saw Hirohito, after a swirl of sights and ceremonies, on his way to Scotland for a week of hunting, shooting, and fishing with the Duke of Atholl at Blair Castle. He was much impressed by the system of clan democracy which brought a staff of volunteer servants to the castle to meet the taxing demands of his visit and at the same time allowed the "servants" to dance the fling one evening with the duke himself.

After his first night in a Pullman and two days inspecting aircraft and shipping companies, Hirohito was back in London on May 27 for a final four days in England as his own guest at the Japanese Embassy. There he gave a series of receptions and feasts for all the promising young commanders and captains of the Japanese Navy who had contrived to be in London to meet him.

The British phase of his trip was over. He had attended a march-past or review. He had had his picture taken in the uniform of a British general. He had carefully watched the deportment of his frequent companion, Edward, Prince of Wales, and had admired greatly—sometimes in envy, sometimes with hurt feelings—that young man's polished, carefree airs. Hirohito could understand a good deal of spoken English, and later in his trip he came to the point of carrying on conversations with some ease in French, but at this stage he and Edward relied on Japanese equerries and British intendants to translate for them. The amount of communication that took place may be gauged from a conversation reported in the memoirs of one of the British interpreters. Toward the end of a long reception Prince Edward dutifully looked in on Prince Hirohito's corner of the reception line and said, "Tell the prince that when I was on the staff of the 14th

Corps, under Lord Cavan, you [the interpreter] were in the 20th Division in the same corps, and that you lent me your horse one day." Hirohito, gravely attentive as always, asked particulars. The Prince of Wales said, "Splendid! One of the star turns of the evening!"—and drifted off.

With the *bonhomie* of King George and the *air dégagé* of Prince Edward both working in his mind, Hirohito moved on to Paris. After initial formalities, he ascended the Eiffel Tower. The next day, June 3, he took in the Louvre and the Venus de Milo "on the run," as staid *Le Temps* somewhat tartly reported, and then repaired to the tomb of Napoleon at the Hôtel des Invalides, where he gazed long and fixedly at the sword of Austerlitz. Having spent three times as long at the tomb as at the Louvre, he emerged so moved that he gave over $400 to the upkeep of Napoleon's memory—an amount which, by the normal standards of imperial family largesse, would have recompensed a village for twenty summers of hospitality to a prince or princess in Japan.

On June 4 Hirohito inspected the French Artillery School with Prince Kanin and one of Kanin's former instructors at St. Cyr, Maréchal Pétain. At the time Pétain was the hero—*ils ne passeront pas*—of Verdun. Already an admirer of D'Annunzio's Italian Black Shirts, he was to wither his garlands later as a Nazi quisling. Throughout the rest of Hirohito's stay, he acted as the young prince's guide to the military tourist attractions of France.

On June 5, Hirohito canceled a scheduled visit to Versailles and went to the races instead. The press in Japan studiously ignored this wild debauch and padded out its trip reportage the following day with general remarks as to the prince's keen interest in French culture. In point of fact, the cultural phase of Hirohito's stay in France, which lasted from May 31 to June 9, was perfunctory at best. He made token appearances at most of the routine tourist sights and reserved as much time as he could for personal matters.

On June 7, Hirohito had a long intimate lunch with Prince Higashikuni, the Big Brother of Army Intelligence who was in Paris organizing a spy ring for Yamagata and an anti-Yamagata cell for Hirohito. On that June morning, Count Futara, the imperial family publicity man, described Higashikuni simply as "studying under the incognito of Count Higashi."

Two days later, on June 9, Hirohito himself assumed incognito and for the first and only time in his life walked alone on a city street and passed money with his own hand. He stopped at several shops and bought presents for his family and fiancée back home. For himself, too, he made one purchase of a lifetime: a bust of Napoleon. It was to stand in his study thereafter, being joined in the 1920's by a head of Darwin and in 1945 by one of Lincoln. Conquer, evolve, liberate: this was to be the program imposed on his reign by fate.

On June 10, Hirohito left Paris for Brussels, and for the next ten days he was back in official harness, visiting Waterloo, Ypres, and other battle-fields of the Low Countries, and attending functions with the Dutch and Belgian royal families. When he returned to Paris on June 20, battlefields had become, it seemed, an obsession with him. He paid a brief call on the Chambre des Députés, went to the races again, inspected at his own per-sonal request the international meter stick of platinum at the Bureau of International Weights at Saint-Cloud, and had another long lunch with Prince Higashikuni. All the rest of his time—nine tenths of it—he spent in the company of Prince Kanin and Maréchal Pétain, trekking through the shell-scarred woods and meadows, inspecting military schools, and watching tank and aircraft displays. One tank maneuver that he studied was made so realistic that its commanding officer broke his pelvis when his horse bolted and threw him.

Hirohito devoted two days to Gravelotte, Saint-Privat, and Fort Saint Quentin near Metz, a day to Verdun, a day to the Somme, and a day to the fields around Reims. In the interstices of his schedule, he fitted in the old military school of French sappers and geometers, the Polytechnique, the cavalry school of Saumur, and the Military Academy of St. Cyr. On July 5 he saw Prince Higashikuni again for a morning of golf at La Boulie.

The next night, July 6, he gave his last of several parties for Japanese attachés and observers in Europe. Never before had there been so many young Japanese officers on the Continent—so many, indeed, that American, British, and French security agents had begun to watch them closely. They worked primarily in the triangle of three cities, Paris, Zurich, and Frank-furt, for here, in the factories of the Ruhr, the Saar, and Switzerland, many new industrial techniques had been worked out during the secrecy of the war years and it behooved Japan to copy them if she could. What was remarkable about these industrial spies was not their spying but the fact that in an army heavily dominated by men of the Choshu clan, none of them were from Choshu. Still more remarkable, their roster included about half of the later famous fascist Japanese generals of the 1930's and 1940's. Hirohito met all of them and honored many of them with a moment of knowledgeable conversation and exhortation.

On July 7 Hirohito boarded a special train for Toulon in the south of France where he would catch his battleships and start for home. From July 10 to 18 he visited Naples and Rome, giving cursory attention to the Colosseum and the Sistine Chapel and spending time, once again, at tank and gun demonstrations and in talk with local Japanese officials. One ob-ject caught his eye in the Vatican: a piece of calligraphy brushed by an early Japanese convert to Christianity who had journeyed to Rome and had an audience with Pope Paul V in 1613.

Perhaps Hirohito was sated with foreign exposure. As soon as he was back on his battleship his first athletic diversion was not golf or swimming but Japanese wrestling. He practiced a few falls with thirty-three-year-old

Marquis Komatsu, his athletics director, and then opened the ring to any other member of his immediate suite who cared to tussle with him. Count Futara wrote: "Time and time again His Highness struggled with his opponents, even when troubled by nose-bleeding. The *tsukidashi* or sudden thrust appeared to be his favorite trick." When Hirohito's ships stopped again at Ceylon on August 9, a British colonial matron remarked on his great increase in ease and poise since his previous visit four and a half months earlier.

HIROHITO'S TAKE-OVER

Hirohito arrived home on September 3, 1921. Old Army strongman Yamagata was sick and had only a few months to live. Prime Minister Hara of the Constitutionalists, however, had taken over Yamagata's authority behind the scenes and was loudly promising the people democracy. Known as the "Great Commoner," he ran an administration which was thoroughly venal in regard to money but was considered honest in regard to ideas. Then, two months after Hirohito's return, on November 4, 1921, at Tokyo railroad station, Prime Minister Hara was knifed to death. The assassin, Nakaoka Konichi, was a young employee of the railroad. A few weeks earlier he had bragged to his fellow workers that he intended to commit hara-kiri or belly cutting in protest against the pleasure-loving laxity and creeping Westernization of the times.

"Many talk of cutting open their *hara*," jibed one of his listeners, "but few have belly enough to carry it out."

"Ha!" screamed Nakaoka. "See if I do not cut *hara*." And so, after days of brooding, he fulfilled his pledge by cutting down Hara, the prime minister.

The murder was passed off in the press as the act of an unhappy half-wit and was quickly forgotten. Hirohito's Big Brother Prince Konoye, the future 1937 prime minister, however, told his friends that he had known of the assassination in advance; that, in fact, a member of Japan's spy service in China, a henchman of his father and of Prince Kanin, one Iogi Yoshimitsu, had come to him on the eve of the knifing with the promise that it would be done. The assassin Nakaoka was given an unusually light sentence of twelve years. On his release from Sendai Penitentiary in 1934, Iogi and other right wing "patriots" met him with a hero's welcome and provided him with a living for life.

After Prime Minister Hara's murder, the other potentates of Japan— particularly those who had been along on the European tour—agreed that Hirohito was a truly Oriental leader, worth following and if possible guiding. On November 25, 1921, they gave their support to an imperial household announcement declaring Hirohito regent for the ailing Taisho and subject only to the advice of the imperial family council composed of Kanin and the other princes of the blood.

While Hirohito was taking power in Tokyo, Prince Higashikuni in Paris was proceeding apace with the organization of his imperial cabal in the ranks of Army Intelligence. The cabal held its first historic meeting—a meeting which would determine the destiny of Japan, a meeting, moreover, which has never been described before in any Western language—on October 27, 1921, at the German spa of Baden-Baden. In obedience to the imperial taboo, the participants have refused to state whether or not Prince Higashikuni was present in person, but if not present, he was at least nearby. He was a regular member of Maréchal Pétain's entourage, and that week the maréchal was making an inspection tour of the French occupation zone of the Saar which took him through Baden-Baden on the day in question. October was out of season at Baden-Baden and prices were low. The Chinese pagoda in front of the *Konversationshaus* and the many public baths made the town as homelike for Japanese visitors as any place in Europe. The Black Forest on the heights above the Rhine and the forbidding castle of the margraves against the bleak October sky lent a suitable air of somber purpose to the proceedings. The conspirators rendezvoused in one of the private chambers at the vapor baths behind the Roman Catholic cathedral.

The three principal operatives at the meeting—Nagata Tetsuzan from Bern, Obata Toshiro from Moscow, and Okamura Yasuji, attaché-at-large—came to be known throughout the Japanese Army as the Three Crows. It was they who would make the Army a modern fighting force, they who would rid it of the samurai leadership of Yamagata's Choshu clan, they who would launch Hirohito on his dreams of glory by engineering the conquest of Manchuria. All three were non-Choshu men. All three were majors, inferior in Army rank to Prince Higashikuni who was a lieutenant colonel. They were accompanied by several less senior majors who had all served in the Imperial Guards with Prince Higashikuni in the last years of Emperor Meiji's reign. One of them, the "observer" in Leipzig, a member of the "stand-by faculty of the Staff College," was the future World War II prime minister, Tojo Hideki.

The leader of the Three Crows was Major Nagata Tetsuzan, whose ghost would later be painted into the surrender deliberations in Hirohito's air raid shelter. He was the son of a doctor who ran a Red Cross hospital in a small resort town near Lake Suwa in the Japanese Alps. In those days the Japanese Red Cross served unofficially as a branch of the Army Medical Corps, and his father's patients were able to recommend him for an appointment to the military academy. There Nagata applied himself well and graduated second in his class. He went on to Staff College in 1911 and graduated with highest honors. He served with such distinction at the embassy in Copenhagen during World War I that from June 1920 he was given a carte blanche leave of absence "to travel in Europe."

No matter how complex the intrigues surrounding him, Nagata always looked as if he knew what he was doing and what others were doing as well. On him—perhaps alone in the Japanese Army—the utterly utilitarian, perfectly circular iron frames of general-issue spectacles sat well, giving him an air of detached scholarly competence. He wore his hair closely cropped, Prussian style, and his mustache trimmed down to the silhouette of an oncoming seagull. His full lips moved easily from a slight twist, denoting amusement or friendliness, to a fine grim line of utmost sarcasm and contempt. His ears were well shaped but large. It was Nagata who carried out the early phases of the imperial program decided upon at Baden-Baden, and it would have been Nagata who commanded the nation as Hirohito's shogun in 1941, if he had not been assassinated, for opposing war with China, by a minion of Prince Higashikuni in 1935.

Major Tojo Hideki, who did become the Emperor's shogun in 1941, was Nagata's protégé, best friend, and loyal servant. When Nagata died, Tojo would step obediently into his shoes. In 1921 at Baden-Baden Tojo said little, for he was one whole military academy class behind the Three Crows. To have been too forward, according to the seniority code of the time, would have been to invite a face slapping. And so Tojo lit Nagata's cigarettes for him and periodically checked the door of the steam room to make sure that no one was listening outside.

The most voluble of the conspirators was the second of the Three Crows, Obata Toshiro, an aristocrat. In the words of his colleagues he was "skinny," "nervous," and "almost too brilliant." He paced the steam-filled room naked while the others steeped in a hot pool of Baden-Baden's famous ill-smelling waters. Fifth in the 1904 class at military academy— just behind the steady Nagata—and first in the 1911 class at Staff College—just ahead of Nagata—he was a brilliant strategist, and his mind brimmed over with possibilities at the thought of invading Manchuria. He had been stationed in Russia throughout the revolution and was convinced that Bolshevism was the number-one threat to Japan and the Throne. So intensely had he studied Marxism, however, that he developed a belief as the years passed that Japan must have her own tribal communism under which all men would share alike in mystical communion with the Emperor. These views made him a leader of the Strike-North or Fight-Russia faction in the 1930's and ultimately estranged him from the Emperor. After the Army mutiny of 1936 he would be dropped from Hirohito's inner circle. His genius as strategist and tactician, however, could not be dispensed with, and when the war broke out with China in 1937, he would be called back to handle the logistics for Japan's crack mobile blitzkrieg division, the 14th. Throughout the war years he would hover on the fringes of politics, and in 1945 would become one of the many ministers without portfolio who would organize a welcome for MacArthur in the surrender Cabinet of Prince Higashikuni.

The third of the Three Crows, Okamura Yasuji, a scion of the samurai clan which for centuries had provided the Tokugawa shoguns with their bodyguards, sat stolidly in the scalding tub and got out only to douse himself occasionally with a bucket of cold water. Without his glasses he was half blind. When he wore them, they gave him the typical look of a bespectacled Japanese officer—that of a fierce owl dazzled by the beam of a flashlight. He was unshaven as usual, for he affected the unkempt, carelessly pressed air of a field officer rather than a staff officer. The theory was that a fighting soldier, if he eschewed spit and polish, would develop in himself a laudable contempt for earthly possessions and would cause enemies to underrate his fighting trim. Behind Okamura's stubble-cheeked look of bemusement worked a keen mind. He had come in third behind Nagata and Obata in the military academy class of 1904 and, when sent belatedly to Staff College in 1913, he had worked hard, taken top honors, and been awarded a prize by Emperor Taisho. After spending World War I in Tokyo on the General Staff as an information officer, he had had the connections to be assigned for Crown Prince Hirohito's European trip to the entourage of Tokugawa Iyemasa, the ranking heir of the former shoguns' family.

When Hirohito returned to Japan, Okamura stayed on in Paris. He was often overshadowed in the years that followed by the other Crows, Nagata and Obata, but in the late 1930's when one of them had been murdered and the other disgraced, Okamura became the principal commander for the long, unrewarding war with China. In 1945, he saw to it that his forces did not simply throw down their arms where they stood but waited and sometimes fought until competent representatives of the Chiang Kai-shek government appeared on the scene to disband and replace them. As a consequence, he was held only briefly as a war criminal in a Shanghai prison and then, abruptly, elevated to serve as Chiang Kai-shek's military advisor in the struggle with the Chinese Communists. When the struggle was lost and Chiang Kai-shek had moved to Taiwan, Okamura Yasuji returned to Tokyo where he played an important part behind the scenes in organizing Japan's present American-supported Self-Defense Forces. In March 1963, nearing the age of seventy-nine, he retired as head of the Japanese Veterans Association and became an advisor to the Self-Defense Forces' "historical" or contingency planning section.

In the hot mineral water and later at the *Konversationhaus,* drinking kirsch, the Three Crows and their subordinates resolved to dedicate their lives to the fulfillment of a two-point program for Japan: make "a big window where Choshu sits today," and "renew the national strength along French lines" so that Japan, too, can fight "a total war." The plan, in other words, was to purge the Army of Yamagata and the rest of its Choshu leadership; reorganize the Army to be on a par with the triumphant French;

in particular, train the Army to fight with modern weapons such as tanks and airplanes. During the Siberian intervention, Japanese soldiers had observed that they were altogether outclassed in equipment and even tactics by the Czech veterans whom they were supposed to be rescuing. It was for this reason that Hirohito, on his tour, had been so assiduous in attending military reviews.

A third point decided at Baden-Baden was personnel. The Three Crows selected "eleven reliable men," to carry out their program. Only two were present; the other nine were then in China, Siberia, or Japan. All were members of the military academy classes of 1904 and 1905 which had graduated during the war with Russia. All were non-Choshu. All were mere majors, though talented. Several were already specialists in aviation. Three of them, Tojo, Itagaki Seishiro, and Doihara Kenji, won fame enough to be hanged as Class A war criminals in 1948. Another, Komoto Daisaku, was to finish Prince Kanin's bloody business of 1916 by assassinating the Manchurian war lord Chang Tso-lin in 1928. Isogai Rensuke, after amassing a brilliant record for himself as a lieutenant general in China, took responsibility for defeat in the Nomonhan border war with Russia in 1939, sat out World War II as the governor general of Hong Kong, and was still alive in 1970. Three others were to die betimes in China.[7] The final three were to prove not so reliable after all and were to be cashiered following the Army Mutiny of 1936.[8]

A FUNNY HAPPENING

The first order of business in realizing the Baden-Baden program was the accumulation of technical information on modern weapons' manufacture. A few weeks after the attachés had returned to their various posts in the cities of Europe, Hirohito dispatched two more of his Big Brothers from Tokyo to encourage the plotters and help Prince Higashikuni in opening doors for them into the drafting rooms of the great European munitions works. Hirohito's new envoys were Prince Kitashirakawa, who had married Emperor Meiji's seventh daughter, and Prince Asaka, the later scourge of Nanking, who had married Emperor Meiji's eighth daughter. Princes Kitashirakawa and Asaka were both trained intelligence officers. They arrived in Paris early in 1922 and all that year the spy ring grew. By 1923 it had thirty members strategically placed in the various capitals and all pledged to the anti-Choshu plan of Army reorganization. American intelligence officers who were in Paris at the time say that their Japanese

---

[7] Watari Hisao as a lieutenant general in 1939; Ogasawara Kazuo as an Air Force lieutenant general in 1938; Italian specialist Ogawa Tsunesaburo, who was the attaché in Rome in 1921, in an airplane crash.

[8] Kudo Yoshio, Matsumura Masakasu, and Yamaoka Shigeatsu.

counterparts, working in the Paris-Zurich-Frankfurt triangle, were effective in purchasing up-to-date plans for diesel engines and tanks.

Abruptly, in the summer of 1923, the spy ring shrank to normal peace-time proportions. The shrinkage was triggered by a curious automobile accident—curious because the circumstances surrounding it were later falsified by the Japanese press. At the end of March 1923, Prince Higashi-kuni flew to London on a piece of "urgent business" that forced him to cancel previous social engagements in Paris. On April 1, Prince Asaka and Prince Kitashirakawa, together with Kitashirakawa's wife and two French servants, left their residence beside the Bois de Boulogne for a "picnic" in their high-powered touring car. That afternoon at four-thirty, at Per-riers-la-Campagne, on the Cherbourg road near Bernay, 88 miles from Paris, as they were heading toward the English Channel at a speed which the police later estimated at 90 miles an hour, the picnickers struck a tree. Prince Kitashirakawa, who had checked out in small planes, was at the wheel, and the official French chauffeur was sitting beside him on the right in the traditional death seat. The chauffeur was killed instantly, and Kitashirakawa *"horriblement défiguré"*—in fact, without legs or much of a head, died twenty minutes later. In the back seat, Prince Asaka suffered compound and complex fractures in one leg, fractures from which he would still limp on the heights above Nanking in 1937. The maid who sat beside him was "gravely wounded." Kitashirakawa's wife, Emperor Meiji's daughter Fusako, in the rear right-hand seat, had two broken legs and so many other injuries that she remained in hospital for over a year.

The French government prepared elaborate obsequies, but Prince Hi-gashikuni caught the first boat train back from London and, with the help of the Japanese ambassador in Paris, canceled all the French plans. He paid off the families of the chauffeur and the maid and exercised influence to quiet the Parisian press. Prince Kitashirakawa lay in embalmed state for three weeks in a room lined with white silk at the home of the Japanese ambassador. On April 22 the corpse was shipped aboard the *Kitano Maru* in Marseilles for transport to the homeland.

Subsequently the *Japan Year Book* in its annual rundown of important events regularly reported the automobile accident—but as having taken place in the "suburbs of Paris," 80 miles off the mark. This error, and Prince Higashikuni's efforts to quash the investigations of French news-men, suggest that Prince Kitashirakawa, when he died, was driving to the English Channel on a mission connected with the intelligence network of which he was a leader. Surviving Japanese officers point out that Prince Higashikuni was in England, on the other side of the Channel. Then they grunt mysteriously. Whatever the mission that killed him, Kitashirakawa's death spelled the end of the spy ring. The number of Japanese Army offi-cers on special assignment "to travel" or "to study" in Europe suffered such a dramatic decline that the writer of this book first noticed the decline, statistically, in Japanese personnel records and only then, in the belief that something of note had happened, turned to French newspapers and discovered the occurrence of the car crash. Hirohito himself was much affected by the death of his Big Brother, Prince Kitashirakawa. He fell out of love with espionage and never again subscribed to it with enthusiastic expectations. Most important, he canceled his plans for a trip to Taiwan and refused ever afterward to leave the main islands of Japan.

8

REGENT HIROHITO

(1921–1926)

HIROHITO'S RECRUITING

It was December 1921 and Crown Prince Hirohito, now Regent of Japan, was celebrating his return from Europe and his assumption of power. Light poured from the windows of the miniature Versailles built by Emperor Taisho. The snow flakes falling on the grounds of the Akasaka Palace compound danced in the darkness to the rhythms of the latest Parisian dance records. Inside, between the pink-brocaded chairs and sofas, tripped geisha in brilliant kimonos, carrying drinks and sometimes agreeing, with a giggle, to serve as dance partners in a fox trot, a tango, or a hesitation waltz. The guests were all young men in tails—either former schoolmates of Hirohito in their twenties or intimates of his Big Brothers in their thirties. Their invitations had stipulated that the order of the evening would be *burei*, suspension of the usual laws of etiquette and precedent. Outside Hirohito's study was set up a keg of Scotch whisky given him in Scotland by the Duke of Atholl.

As the night progressed and the keg emptied, Hirohito's wish for informality was gratified. Most of the guests were typical Japanese in that they suffered from an inbred intolerance of alcohol.[1] The first sip of Scotch

---

[1] The distinction between those who do and do not have the genetic weakness is marked. The majority become flushed after a single thimble of saké or even after a rum baba. The minority can tope with the best drinkers of any nation and are much prized as negotiators for dealing with Westerners. Many and perhaps all of the minority are descended from families which immigrated from the Continent in historic times. For the majority Japanese make special allowances. Prime ministers are not held responsible for speeches made in drunkenness to the Diet, and crimes of passion are regularly excused in the law courts if intoxication can be proved in mitigation.

darkened their cheeks, loosened their tongues, and lightened their brains. Before long men were coming and going freely from the study where Hirohito sat. Voices were raised in boasting for Japan and in scoffing against the West. Plans were laid and promises made in a spirit of hilarity which many guests later regretted. Hirohito drank tea-tinted water, put up good-naturedly with many familiarities to his person, flirted with one of the geisha, and awoke the next morning clear-headed and pleased with his performance. It had been a precedent-shattering party.

On the second day after the party, the old lute player Saionji, who had galloped in green armor through the wars of the restoration fifty-three years earlier, took the two-hour train journey from his winter villa on the coast at Okitsu and paid one of his infrequent visits to Tokyo. As soon as he had moved into the town mansion kept for him by his millionaire brother, he phoned the Akasaka Palace for an audience with Crown Prince Hirohito. He had been delegated by the other chamberlains of his family— the Fujiwaras who had the hereditary duty of keeping Emperors free from incriminating responsibilities—to speak to Hirohito about his behavior. The role of moralist and censor hardly suited the pleasure-loving old statesman. Time and again he had advised Hirohito to unbend a little and take a woman or a glass of good wine. Although he dutifully scolded Hirohito for the "looseness" and "apalling familiarity" of the recent party, he was not concerned by either one. He had seen gayer bacchanals in the Akasaka Palace during Taisho's youth. Rather, what alarmed Saionji about the party was the open recruiting of stalwarts—the explicit discussion of future plans which were now the post-party gossip of Tokyo high society.

Regent Hirohito met Saionji with an innocent face, heard his remonstrances, and apologized disingenuously for sowing wild oats. Then Hirohito made a bargain with Saionji which the old man would live to rue. If Saionji would take the place of Army Elder Yamagata, who was then mortally ill, as senior advisor to the Throne, Hirohito would promise to give up overt leadership of his cabal and respect all the conventions of a constitutional monarch. Saionji took the measure of the intense young ruler before him and stared silently for a few moments at the carpet. He believed that the people of Japan had changed in the last decade and had come to accept the philosophy of constitutionalism and legalism propounded by Ito Hirobumi before his assassination in Manchuria in 1909. If the people expressed themselves clearly, Saionji thought that Hirohito would bow to majority opinion.

Hirohito, as he watched the old man turning over the proposition, waited impatiently. If the seventy-two-year-old Saionji accepted, he would make an invaluable ally and figurehead. Forty years of experience in Emperor Meiji's councils had taught him how to give a semblance of moderation and regularity to government. His peers respected him for his incisive realism. In the company of others, he had a talent for tangled, discreet utterances, even that rare gift of complete silence when it was needed. He had a sharp, subtle mind, an upright character, and only one foolish mental quirk: an absolute, overriding loyalty to the Throne.

Saionji looked up from the carpet and admitted sadly that it was his duty to accept Hirohito's proposal. He had hoped, he said, to spend the rest of his days in quiet at his little villa on the shore in the fishing village of Okitsu, reading French and Chinese novels, practicing on the lute, carving canes for himself, and walking up to Seiken Temple to watch the sunrise when he couldn't sleep. But if the nation demanded it, he must accept the responsibility. Hirohito promptly confirmed him in the status of *Genro*, a descriptive title that had long been used to designate the surviving members of Emperor Meiji's oligarchy. Literally it meant Founding Elder, but as applied to Saionji, who would soon become the one and only *Genro*, it meant Prime-Minister-Maker. It carried with it the formal duty of appearing in Tokyo whenever a Cabinet fell, of sounding out the political situation, and of taking responsibility for recommending to Hirohito the men he should appoint for the next Cabinet. Saionji would retain the title and the responsibility until his death, in bitter disillusionment, at the age of ninety-one, in 1940.

PALACE PLOT SCHOOL

Having promised Saionji to assume the discreet guise of a constitutional ruler, Hirohito immediately established an undercover organization through which to direct his widening circle of henchmen. At the eastern edge of the palace grounds, where a salient in the old fortifications had left a sequestered bulge of walls and moats, sprawled a low, weather-beaten, wooden building, the Palace Meteorological Observatory. On his way home from the Peers' School as a child, Hirohito had sometimes wandered through its rooms, inspecting the sextants, the astrological charts, the rain gauges, and the little, eighteenth century Dutch telescope.

The week after the party, Hirohito had the old observatory converted into a security-shrouded indoctrination center for young men who wished to play a part in his dreams for Japan. Here, in the precincts of the palace, were made the first rough plans for Japan's attempt to conquer half the world. Here were struck up the friendships and working relationships which governed Japan until 1945. Here studied every one of the Class A war criminals tried by Allied judges in 1946 and 1947. Here, if anywhere, was hatched the "criminal conspiracy" of which Japan's war leaders, with the exception of Hirohito, were judged guilty. Here only were all Japan's "criminals" together in one place at one time to "conspire." Yet the indoctrination center in the old observatory has never until now been mentioned in writing in English except passingly in an unpublished 1946 U.S. Army Intelligence report. This report was circulated among the Allied judges at the war crimes trials, but information regarding the indoctrination center was not introduced in evidence, presumably because it implicated the Emperor.

The center was first called the Social Problems Research Institute and later given the less suggestive code name of *Daigaku Ryo,* or University Lodging House. It was, of course, a tremendous honor for junior officers and fledgling bureaucrats to attend lectures and discussions within the sacred walls of the palace, and few who participated ever failed the Emperor in years to come. In founding the Lodging House, however, Hirohito was looking not only for loyal henchmen but also for ideas. The plot conceived at Baden-Baden had given him a cadre of Army shock troopers to work with, at a time when Adolf Schicklgruber was still struggling for control of an obscure band of brown-shirted racists in Bavaria. But Hirohito needed more: he needed skillful economic and political planners, a long-term plan, and a national ideology.

In assuming the regency in 1921, Hirohito had taken over a nation of 56 million people. It had increased 25 per cent in population and more than 100 per cent in gross national product since his birth in 1900. Though still backward in comparison with France or England, its economy was growing faster than any other in the world. It was bursting with surplus talent, energy, and ideas and demanded carefully co-ordinated direction.

Hirohito entrusted the organization of the Lodging House in the old observatory to his chief advisor, the tall, high-strung, charming Count Makino who had headed the imperial suite during the European tour. Makino, in turn, delegated the headmastership of the Lodging House to Dr. Okawa, the intellectual tough who had devised the thrashing of Prince Saionji's adopted son during the controversy before the tour. A keen-looking young man of thirty-seven, with close-cropped black hair and a sharp black mustache, Dr. Okawa enjoyed a filial intimacy with Count Makino. Some Japanese suggest that he was Makino's illegitimate son. Through Makino's patronage, Okawa had acquired eminent qualifications for the task at hand. He had worked closely for years with Hirohito's future chief of staff, Prince Kanin, and with the father of Hirohito's fiancée, Prince Kuni. He was a trusted lieutenant of gang lord Toyama and a leader of the younger generation of Pan-Asianists in Toyama's Black Dragon Society. He had had a decade of experience as a spy in China. And not least, he was a genuine scholar. He had graduated in Oriental philosophy from Tokyo Imperial University in 1911 and could read Chinese, Sanskrit, Arabic, Greek, German, French, and English.

Until he became headmaster of the Lodging House, Dr. Okawa had represented the assorted ideas of all the Pan-Asianists, spies, and nationalists with whom he had consorted for a decade. They had been joined together by a common enthusiasm for the future of Japan—a vague sense of mission which they had expressed in a collective credo published in the magazine *War Cry* in July 1920:

> The Japanese people must become the vortex of a whirlwind which will liberate mankind. The Japanese nation is destined to accomplish the revolu-

tionization of the world. The fulfillment of this ideal and the military re-organization of Japan are the work of the spirits. We believe that our duty will not end with the revolution or reform of Japan alone, but we must be content to begin with the reform of our nation because we have faith in the Japanese mission to free the universe.

When Dr. Okawa became headmaster of the Lodging House, many of his former comrades felt that he had sold out to the Establishment and betrayed the cause of revolution. In splitting with him, they chose to follow another erudite spy and political philosopher, Kita Ikki, the later ideologist of the Strike-North or Fight-Russia faction which would plague Hirohito in the 1930's. Dr. Okawa had discovered Kita in 1918 in a Shanghai garret where, on a diet of rice balls and water, he was just completing the eighth volume of a magnum opus, *The Fundamental Principles for the Reconstruction of the Nation.* In this lucid but radical tome, Kita poured Marxist wine into old saké pitchers and brewed a heady polemic which Hirohito found unpalatable and his brother, Prince Chichibu, found exciting. Kita called for a thoroughgoing reconstruction and purification of Japan: suspension of the Constitution under martial law; convocation of a national family council chosen by universal suffrage; restriction of individual capital to $500,000 and of corporate capital to $5,000,000; equal profit sharing between employers and employees; maintenance of friendship with the United States in order to develop China; hostility toward Russia and Great Britain which, in Kita's view, controlled an unfair share of the world's living space.

Kita's eight-volume work, circulated in a mimeographed edition run off by one of Prince Chichibu's best friends, made a tremendous impression on many young Japanese in search of a vision. Crown Prince Hirohito, however, looked on it with a narrow eye because, among its other reforms, it called for the surrender to the nation of all property held by the imperial household.

In January 1922, when Dr. Okawa received his invitation to become headmaster at the Lodging House in the palace, he and his friend Kita spent one last vociferous saké-steeped evening together and then went their separate ways as sworn enemies. In fear of police arrest, Kita hid at a Buddhist monastery where he compiled a special set of cautionary Buddhist sutra which he sent to Hirohito. Dr. Okawa moved into the palace and organized the faculty for the Lodging House.

Under Dr. Okawa's direction, the curriculum at the Lodging House was spiced with a little of every *ism* he knew. The young bureaucrats and military officers who were privileged to attend heard lectures on Confucian ethics, weapons development, contingency planning, Army reorganization, and the geopolitical theories—carefully excerpted—of Kita Ikki. Hirohito's chief advisor, Count Makino, gave a course on the place of the Throne, explaining the offices of the imperial household; their function in inter-mediating with loyal henchmen; the need, always, to keep the Emperor beyond the tarbrush of popular criticism. When they came home from France in January and February 1923, the Three Crows all lectured at the Lodging House. So did several of the Eleven Reliables they had chosen at Baden-Baden. So did assorted secret policemen, commercial spies, narcotics experts, pimps, terrorists, and interrogation specialists from Japan's com-plex web of paramilitary apparatuses on the Continent.

At Lodging House seminars the smartest junior members of the General Staff and of the faculties of the Army and Navy Staff Colleges came to know intimately the Big Brothers of Hirohito who had gone into the bureaucracy, the Diet, or the influential pool of literary handymen which supplied male private secretaries to Cabinet ministers. After classes they all went out sometimes to tea houses to drink and wench together. In later years one of Hirohito's Big Brothers recalled that Colonel Sugiyama, Japan's World War II Chief of Staff, did an excellent comic dance of the seven veils with napkin-sized towels. Commander Yamamoto, the later admiral who would plan and lead the attack on Pearl Harbor, did conjuring tricks and stood on his head.

In these after-school drinking sessions the chief topic of discussion was Japan's position in the postwar world. At the Washington Conference, begun in late 1921 when the Lodging House opened, Japan had been forced to agree to limit her Navy according to the formula 10:6:3.5—that is, for every 10 tons of U.S. or British warship and for every 3.5 French or Italian tons, Japan would maintain no more than 6 tons. Fortu-nately the naval ratio did not apply to submarines and torpedo boats; therefore the money saved on battleships could be applied to non-conven-tional modern weapons in which the fleet was deficient. A top-secret naval development plan, taking advantage of such treaty loopholes, was worked out in the Lodging House and in the Navy General Staff and was formally approved by Hirohito in late 1922.

Any compunction which had been felt by some naval officers about arm-ing in secret against the United States and Great Britain was overcome by resentment at anti-Japanese legislation in the West. Great Britain, in 1921, refused to renew the Anglo-Japanese Alliance. The U.S. Supreme Court in November 1922 declared, in effect, that Japanese were ineligible for natu-ralization as U.S. citizens. The U.S. Congress in May 1924 made total exclusion of Orientals an official part of U.S. immigration policy.

QUAKE

Funds had just been appropriated and building begun for the secret naval development plan, and young Regent Hirohito was just turning his attention toward the Army reorganization scheme proposed at Baden-Baden, when his national imperial program suffered a setback of such cataclysmic proportions that it would take years to recoup the loss. At exactly noon on Saturday, September 1, 1923, as charcoal braziers in almost every house were being lit under the midday meal, tremors began to register on the seismographs at Tokyo Imperial University. The first were no larger than those which rocked the needles three hundred times a year in volcanic Japan. But they kept coming, stronger and more frequent with each passing second. In a matter of minutes they merged into a great swell that inundated the instruments. The whole of the Great Eastern Plain around Tokyo was in fact billowing as if it were the surface of the Pacific. Thousands of homes pancaked. The proud new twelve-story Tokyo Tower tumbled from the sky. The colossal thirteenth century bronze figure of Buddha in Kamakura—50 feet in stature and 100 in girth—pitched from its pedestal. On the seacoast southwest of Tokyo, near the epicenter of the quake, entire villages of debris were swept away by tidal waves.

The main shock was over in five minutes, but in the splintered woodpile that remained, the buried cookstoves still burned and soon the whole of the Tokyo-Yokohama megalopolis was aflame. Fire storms or "dragon tails" swept the ruins. At the naval base of Yokosuka near Yokohama, 100,000 tons of stock-piled oil had spilled into the sea and drifted in huge puddles along the coast. Now it too caught fire and immolated countless survivors who had taken to the water to escape the infernos ashore. In the end two thirds of Tokyo and four fifths of Yokohama were destroyed, and approximately 140,000 human beings—as many as at Hiroshima and Nagasaki combined—were burned to death.

When the shock struck, the twenty-three-year-old Hirohito was at a state luncheon in the *petit* Versailles built by Taisho on the Akasaka Palace compound. It had been Japan's first large two-story structure designed specifically to withstand seismic upheavals.[2] As a result it rode out the earth waves with hardly a crack in its plaster. Hirohito and his guests ran outside into the open in obedience to the earthquake drill which every Japanese learns as a child. There they watched the rest of the city shaking apart and saw the first plumes of the great fires.

Regent Hirohito was then in direct personal charge of the government as at almost no other time in his life. The prime minister had died the week before and Hirohito had not yet appointed a successor for him. During the interregnum Hirohito elevated General Fukuda Masataro to impose martial

---

[2] A Chicago firm, E. C. and R. M. Shankland, had developed the necessary engineering concepts back in 1900. The building, 270 feet wide and 400 feet long, rested on continuous footings of concrete to which was bolted a massive steel skeleton. Every piece of masonry in the building was anchored by rods and plates to this rigid frame.

law and take charge of relief work. Throughout the next fortnight Hirohito and Fukuda conferred twice a day. The great problem was to assign responsibility for the holocaust. Many Japanese still believed that a monstrous catfish lay on the ocean bottom under Japan and stirred only when the sun goddess was angry with her son on the Throne. In ancient times the Emperor had often abdicated in token of penance after major earthquakes. In 1923 the destruction had been so great that the abdication of the ailing, impotent Emperor Taisho would have seemed insufficient.

Accordingly, a new way of assigning responsibility was introduced to the people: General Fukuda, the martial law commandant, gave them a scapegoat. His military secret police spread the rumor that Koreans and Socialists had offended the spirits before the earthquake and now, afterward, were taking advantage of the disaster by setting fires and pillaging shops. Fukuda's soldiers, aided by young vigilantes of the palace-sponsored Military Sports Clubs and by thugs of the Black Dragon Society, began to hunt down every Oriental they could find who spoke Japanese with an accent. Four thousand despised Koreans from the slums were given mock trials or simple linguistic tests and were then beheaded in the streets. Nine Socialists were dragged off to Tokyo's Kameido Jail by the military police, and when they persisted in singing labor songs from their cells, were, according to the report of the officer in charge, "stabbed . . . to death in accordance with Article 12 of Garrison Regulations."

At the height of the fire, a mob of frightened people sought entry to the cool moat-girt lawns of the Imperial Palace. Turned aside by the police and again turned by the fire, they began to surge in against the police lines. They were cheered on by a firebrand Socialist, Osugi Sakae, who shouted, "Remember Russia, and never lay down your arms!" The police had their way and the flames spared the crowd. But two weeks later when the embers no longer smouldered, Captain Amakasu of the secret police tracked down Osugi and escorted him, his wife, and seven-year-old nephew to the fearsome secret police headquarters in Tokyo's Kojimachi ward. There, on September 16, Captain Amakasu received a visit from Yuasa Kurahei, a chamberlain intimate with Hirohito, who would later become lord privy seal, the Emperor's chief advisor. That night after dark Captain Amakasu entered the cell occupied by Socialist Osugi, surprised him from the rear, and soundlessly strangled him.

Amakasu proceeded with two noncoms to the cell of Osugi's wife. Less trusting than her idealistic husband, she turned in time to face her murderer and utter a few gurgled screams before she died. The seven-year-old in the next cell heard her and began to shout in terror. And so, when Mrs. Osugi finally lay quiet, the boy too was strangled.

Because the Japanese loved children and because rumors had spread of direct imperial involvement in the Osugi case, Captain Amakasu's infanticide was the one crime committed in the ashen twilight of the earthquake which had to be punished.[8] After a showpiece trial, Amakasu was sentenced to ten years in prison which Hirohito inconspicuously commuted later to three years. On release Amakasu was given money by a self-styled "friend of the Throne" to "study in Europe." He did so with the remnants of the spy ring in Paris from 1927 to 1929. Thereafter he enjoyed various sinecures in Manchuria until August 20, 1945, when he took potassium cyanide and left a note saying, "We lost our big gamble; this is the end."

REGICIDE

Fourteen weeks after the earthquake, on December 27, 1923, Crown Prince Regent Hirohito rode through the resurrected shanty town which was then Tokyo to deliver an opening address to the new Diet. In the Toranomon district, a few blocks southwest of the palace, a young man darted from the kneeling crowd, shouldered through the bowing police cordon, leveled a gun three to five inches from the side window of Hirohito's Daimler limousine, brought the regent's head into the sights, and pulled the trigger. The bullet, according to the official story, miraculously missed Hirohito, ricocheted no less than five times from the reinforced panelwork of the plush interior, and knicked one of Hirohito's chamberlains. Knowledgeable Japanese quietly point out that three months later, Kacho Hirotada, a minor member of the imperial family who resembled Hirohito and had understudied him as a security decoy, was announced to have died suddenly of "heart attack" at the age of twenty-two.

Namba Daisaku, the man who tried to shoot Hirohito, prevented the police from immediately gunning him down by raising his hands and running along quietly behind the imperial limousine until he was arrested. The police interrogated and tortured him for eleven months but finally announced that he would give no explanation of his crime except general political dissatisfaction and sympathy for the murdered Socialist Osugi and for Osugi's seven-year-old nephew. Before his execution, according to the police, Namba shouted, "Banzai for the proletariat." It was apparent to the great majority of Japanese that he was nothing but a Bolshevik traitor.

In fact, assassin Namba was not a Communist. All the few hundred members of Japan's Communist party had been clapped in prison the previous May. Rather, Namba was a knowledgeable, well-connected dissident of the late Army strongman Yamagata's Choshu clan, which Hirohito was planning to purge from its position of influence. Namba's father was a noted liberal in the lower chamber of the Diet. He was returning by train to the protection of his clan and his constituency when he heard of his son's failure. He retired to his home, barred his front gate with slats of young

---

[8] General Fukuda relinquished his command under criticism but his son-in-law, Lieutenant Colonel Yasuda Tetsunosuke, was singled out for honor by being appointed equerry to Prince Higashikuni in Paris.

"blue bamboo" to keep out callers, and remained permanently in his room upstairs. Six months after the announcement of his son's execution, he left the room in a coffin.

For many Japanese the most symbolic feature of young Namba's case was the gun which he had used. It was a pistol, encased in a cane, which Choshu clansman Ito Hirobumi, the founder of the Constitutionalist party and mentor of Prime-Minister-Maker Saionji, had brought home from London before his assassination in Harbin in 1909. Ito had given the gun for safekeeping to one of his relations, Hayashi Fumitaro.[4] Hayashi had loaned it to his own kinsman Namba for the assassination attempt. When it failed to kill Hirohito, Ito's spirit was presumed to have lost face among the dead and the Ito-Saionji cause of constitutionalism lost a little in prestige among the living.

WAR MINISTER UGAKI

Hirohito used young Namba's attempted regicide as an excuse for appointing a new Cabinet, one which would take the political risk of pushing ahead with the Baden-Baden program, of modernizing the Army, and of smashing the influence of assassin Namba's Choshu clan. Prime Minister Admiral Yamamoto Gombei, who had formed the second government of his career only three months earlier, after the earthquake, offered his Cabinet's resignation as a purely formal gesture of apology for Namba's attack. But Hirohito unexpectedly accepted it. In Yamamoto's place Hirohito had Prime-Minister-Maker Saionji, who was unusually tractable after the bungled regicide attempt, submit the name of Viscount Kiyoura, a pliant legal hack left over from Emperor Meiji's days. Kiyoura had little to recommend him except his venerable seventy-four years of age and his experience as a minister of justice at the turn of the century.

The portfolios of the new Kiyoura Cabinet were held mostly by aged undistinguished aristocrats who seemed to emerge like lizards from cracks in the palace walls. There was, however, one exception, the minister of war, the first since 1912 who was not a samurai of Choshu. Ugaki Kazushige was his name, a man of the people from Okayama on the Inland Sea. He was a lieutenant general, fifty-four years old, ambitious and bullnecked, with a face as honest and stodgy as bean-curd paste. When Ugaki went visiting on a political errand, he always carried his own lunch with

---

[4] The Ito-Hayashi-Namba family, hailing from the southern Choshu fishing hamlet of Kumage-gun, represented the samurai element in Choshu. The ancient Choshu nobility, the Katsura-Kido-Moris of the towns of Yamaguchi and Hagi farther north, were intertwined with the imperial lineage and exempted from Hirohoto's purge plans. Their scions included Emperor Taisho's prime minister, Katsura Taro, and Hirohito's original Big Brother, the later World War II privy seal, Marquis Kido Koichi.

him—rice balls packed in an ordinary *furoshiki* or carrying cloth. He was not a clever man but the cleverest non-Choshu officer who had been deemed safe by Choshu elders to leave in the ladder of command. Hirohito knew him as a supplementary tutor who had delivered a few lectures in "The Study of the Crown Prince" during Hirohito's adolescence. Now Hirohito would use him and abuse him until he would become one of the greatest loyal dupes in Japan—second only to Saionji.

On being elevated to the post of war minister, Ugaki found that a staff plan for his term of office had been carefully prepared in advance by the Three Crows of Baden-Baden who had returned to Japan from Paris in early 1923. The plan called first of all for a cutback in the Army's sheer force of samurai numbers, a cutback which could be represented as money-saving and demilitarizing. In the course of it Ugaki was to purge the Army of its Choshu leadership and of all other henchmen of Hirohito's late antagonist, strongman Yamagata. Finally Ugaki was to strengthen the Army for war by equipping it with modern tank and air forces. Ugaki realized that such a program could be carried out only in the face of powerful opposition from Choshu clansmen in the bureaucracy and also from any Constitutionalists in the Diet who saw through the lamb's-wool wrappings. Nevertheless Ugaki accepted his assignment and wrote in his diary: "I will advance bravely and carry this sublime responsibility with high purpose. I will rush forward with a progressive attitude, intestinal fortitude, and greatness of spirit."

NUPTIALS

With carefully considered timing, on the eve of his struggle with Choshu, Crown Prince Hirohito consolidated his position in the hearts of his people by getting married. Princess Nagako, the granddaughter of Emperor Komei's advisor Asahiko, had been waiting for him, studying under special tutors at her father's villa ever since her choice as fiancée in 1917 more than six years earlier. The wedding was solemnized on January 26, 1924, a fortnight after Ugaki's appointment, a month after Namba's assassination attempt, and almost five months after the earthquake.

During the wedding a gathering of seven hundred invited guests—all of them Japanese, one of them the gang lord Black Dragon Toyama—stood attendance outside the Imperial Family Shrine in the forested area of the palace garden. In ancient Court regalia, Nagako carrying a fan, Hirohito a scepter, the couple met before the assembled witnesses at the shrine entrance. The gates swung open and Hirohito, all alone, entered the court-yard leading toward the Inner Shrine. The chamberlain of rituals chanted Shinto prayers in a high singsong. The doors of the Inner Shrine sprang open and Hirohito disappeared into his ancestors' Holy of Holies. Having done brief homage and declared his intentions to the spirits, he returned to the outer gate where Nagako was waiting. The two drank alternately, three times, from a goblet of sanctified rice wine and the ceremony was over. The ships of the fleet in Tokyo harbor crashed out a 101-gun salute, more than twice as prolonged as that accorded any other ruler on earth.

For the wedding, Hirohito's public relations expert, Count Futara, dinned home the image which he had been creating of his master since 1921. Hirohito was represented as a young liberal, full of Western ideas, playing golf in a tweed hat and plus fours with Edward, Prince of Wales, who had visited Japan in 1922. In an eagerness to learn to beat the West at its own games, Hirohito had built a nine-hole golf course on the grounds of the Akasaka Palace. In an effort to get to know his people, Hirohito had appeared on the beach to swim in public. The leading British editor in Japan described this press campaign as "sedulous care . . . to promote the idea of personal loyalty to him." But the people warmed to the campaign because they were fed up with centuries of stiff Spartan courtesy and military discipline.

PURGE

Behind the promotional stage drops, in early 1924, the Choshu samurai were making their last desperate stand. The leader of the Choshu clan, General Tanaka Gi-ichi—a simple fellow to wear the shoes of his Machiavellian predecessor, strongman Yamagata--called a meeting of Army elders at his home. "We face a Satsuma clan conspiracy. Let's break them utterly," he announced. Six months later the Choshu generals, and a few Constitutionalist allies, succeeded only in gaining a public save of face. They were allowed to topple the reptilian, dinosaurian Kiyoura Cabinet and in return they accepted the Army reorganization scheme.

In June 1924, a new cabinet, headed by the monocle-wearing diplomat Kato Taka-aki, who had served the Twenty-One Demands on China a decade earlier, made light of the Army purge as a routine economy measure and diverted public attention to a fresh issue: universal suffrage. Since 1902 all Japanese liberals had militated for abolition of the three-yen poll tax. Now Prime Minister Kato and Hirohito came out in favor of abolition and of an increase in the electorate from 3,300,000 to 14,000,000 voters, that is, to all males of twenty-five or over. The loyalist press manufactured mossbacked commentators who opposed the increase in suffrage and a great fake debate occupied the front pages.

While the nation was distracted, War Minister Ugaki stood in a small spotlight to one side, ostensibly "demilitarizing" the Army. In reality he was carrying out a complicated horse trade within the officer corps by which all the most important Choshu generals and a compensatory selection of Satsuma and other clan generals voluntarily resigned their commissions. In all some 2,000 officers were cashiered and with them, it seemed at first, some 80,000 men. Four divisions, the 13th, 15th, 17th, and 18th, were declared dissolved, but many of the companies and battalions in them were preserved intact, awaiting orders. By the time the Choshu officers had been mustered out, many of their units had been reassigned to swell the divisions which remained or to staff new auxiliary forces. The entire re-organization was juggled with the deftness of a master bookkeeper. When the ink had dried, only 33,894 men and 6,089 horses had been discharged from the Army and the other 46,000-odd men, who had seemed to be on their way out, had been reabsorbed. There were new mechanized transport groups, machine-gun squads for every infantry company, research teams to study modern weapons, fresh branches of intelligence, two new air regiments, an antiaircraft regiment, a 5,500-man tank corps, and several new specialized military schools such as the Signal Academy in Kanagawa and the Narashino School in Chiba for chemical and bacteriological war-fare.

In addition, the period of compulsory military training was shortened to six weeks so that the government could afford to give every young male some foundation to fall back on in the event of national mobilization. To compensate for the brevity of the training, a new Army educational corps of 1200 drill masters was organized and posted at leading high schools and prep schools. These physical education officers made sure that every adolescent, before his service, was already inculcated with the principles of martial spirit, parading, and sword and rifle drill. By intimidating fellow faculty members, they would gradually gain a tight hold on the curriculum in years ahead and would succeed in making Japanese education a bland exercise in indoctrinational cant.

As the Army reorganization scheme was unfolded step by step and battalion by battalion, cashiered Choshu officers grumbled privately, but publicly there was an uncanny lack of protest. Part of the silence did credit simply to the Japanese soldier's discipline in obeying orders; the other part reflected the excellent staff planning of the Three Crows. They had begun the reorganization by posting members of Hirohito's cabal of young officers in all the most sensitive posts. The chief of the Three Crows, Lieutenant Colonel Nagata Tetsuzan himself, spent four months of 1924 as an officer in one of the regiments which was to be abolished, a regiment stationed in Choshu territory and staffed by Choshu officers. By deft poli-ticking he prevented its men from staging a mutiny. Students of the in-doctrination school in the palace, the University Lodging House, were so widely dispersed on similar missions that the school was closed in late 1924, and its building, the old palace observatory, was condemned be-cause of structural damage done by the earthquake.

By March 1925 when the elimination of four divisions—of four sacred battle standards around which ancestors had died—was finally announced to the public, Crown Prince Hirohito's position was so strong that his minions in the House of Peers were able to attach a rider to the Universal

Suffrage Bill. When the latter was passed on May 5, 1925, its supporters had been pledged to vote also for a Maintenance of Public Peace Bill. This was largely the work of Hirohito's Big Brother, the gangling, effete Fujiwara Prince Konoye who would preside over Japan as prime minister a decade later during the rape of Nanking. Known by its detractors as the "Dangerous Thoughts Bill," it gave the police almost unlimited power to suppress political dissidents. It was passed by the Diet, without much protest, on May 12, 1925, a week after the Universal Suffrage Bill. Fifteen years later it would enable Prince Konoye to transform universal suffrage into universal agreement—a single mass party of reverent imperialists.

NEW STAR IN CHINA

During the enactment of the Baden-Baden program, one member of Hirohito's cabal of young officers, one graduate of the University Lodging House, was absent: the ubiquitous Suzuki Tei-ichi. He was away in China observing the early struggles and rise to power of a new Chinese strongman, a friend from cadet days at the Japanese Military Academy, Chiang Kai-shek. Since 1920, when he had first made his way into the inner counsels of Hirohito's Big Brotherhood,[5] Captain Suzuki had been detailed by General Staff Intelligence to remain constantly near Chiang Kai-shek as an advisor. To outsiders it seemed a strange assignment because, when it began in 1920, Chiang Kai-shek was a little known commodity and currency broker in Shanghai.

The gray-eyed Chiang [6] had amassed a small fortune speculating in futures during World War I and had made the acquaintance of China's greatest banking families. They respected him as a handsome, taciturn, direct, forceful, shrewd dealer. He kept a wife and a stable of mistresses but had not then met the later Madame Chiang or become a convert to Christianity. He was still fond of his adopted land, Japan, where he had attended military academy after graduation from China's own military school, Paoting. He still kept in touch with dozens of Japanese friends including Prince Asaka, who would rape Nanking; Prince Higashikuni, who would bomb Nanking; Matsui Iwane, the later general who would be hanged as the "Butcher of Nanking"; and in addition Lord of the Black Dragon Toyama, who had given refuge to Chiang's mentor, Sun Yat-sen.

---

[5] His patron was an artillery major, Big Brother Marquis Inoue Saburo, the illegitimate son of Emperor Taisho's favorite, Prime Minister Katsura Taro. Suzuki had become intimate with Marquis Inoue when the two served a one-year stint together in special economic training at the Finance Ministry in 1919.

[6] In the coastal village of Fenghua, 100 miles south of Shanghai, where Chiang had been born to a prosperous wine merchant in 1887, gossips attributed the unusual color of his eyes to a Portuguese or Dutch seaman entwined in his ancestral tree.

Indeed Chiang had met an entire generation of Asian nationalists and conquerors in Japan, a military elite to which he felt he belonged but with which he was destined to spend his life in mortal combat.

Chiang had led a Japanese-financed regiment in the Chinese Revolution of 1911 and since then had regularly attended the congresses of Sun Yat-sen's Kuomintang or KMT party. He had seen the Revolution turn sour, Yuan Shih-kai and his war lords take power in North China, and Sun Yat-sen grow old as a testy visionary among his most faithful supporters in the southern Chinese port of Canton. Having made sure of his future financially, Chiang, in 1923, gave up his brokerage in Shanghai and at the age of thirty-five retired to dedicate himself full time to the cause of Sun Yat-sen in Canton. The ubiquitous Suzuki Tei-ichi was detached by the Japanese General Staff to follow Chiang south.

Chiang found Sun Yat-sen, the "George Washington" of the original 1911 Republican Movement, bitter against the war lord regime in Peking and dying of liver cancer. He had surrounded himself with young Communists like Mao Tse-tung and Chou En-lai. He was under the influence of two Russian advisors: General Vasili Blücher, the strategic magician who had whipped together raw Red recruits to defeat the Cossacks in Siberia in 1921, and Michael Borodin, the product of a Vitebsk ghetto, best known to some Americans as Mike Berg, a soapbox orator on the corner of Division and Halstead streets in Chicago during the years before World War I. Chiang Kai-shek took brief stock of his old hero's entourage and in the fall of 1923 paid a two-month visit to Moscow to study communism at its source. In that brief visit he won the admiration and support of Joseph Stalin who was then locked in his own leadership struggle with Leon Trotsky.

On returning to Canton in December of 1923, Chiang enlisted the help of his Japanese friend and observer, the ubiquitous Suzuki Tei-ichi, to found an indoctrination center, modeled on the University Lodging House and known as Whampoa Academy. By 1925, when Lodging House graduates were foisting their program on Japan, Whampoa graduates were infiltrating the officer corps of the war lords' private armies in northern China. In March 1925, when the Baden-Baden program was passing the Diet in Tokyo, Sun Yat-sen was finally killed by his cancer and Chiang Kai-shek emerged as his successor. Chiang consolidated his position for a year. Then in March 1926, in a theatrical show of strength, he had his military police arrest all the Chinese Communists in Canton and make them agree to a military campaign against the nominally Republican warlord regime in Peking. Chiang's armies started north and swept everything before them.

Suzuki, the ubiquitous observer, was impressed by the support given Chiang's troops everywhere by the Chinese peasants. In his dispatches home to Tokyo he assessed Chiang as a genuine popular leader, capable of making China a force to reckon with. Japanese Prime Minister Kato Taka-aki, the server of the Twenty-One Demands on China in 1915, had shuffled off the coils of his cool, calculating, monocled existence on January 28, 1926, but there were other "China experts" in high places who appreciated the import of Suzuki's dispatches and brought them to the attention of Hirohito.

Accordingly, in the spring of 1926, Hirohito dispatched a pride of his lion cubs, including both officers and civilians, to join Suzuki in China and study the situation at first hand.[7] They agreed that Chiang Kai-shek was worth backing. He might not be entirely trustworthy, because he had dreams of unifying China, but at the moment he was willing to make Manchuria, Mongolia, and North China safe for Japan by allowing autonomous puppet governments to be established in those regions.

DEATH OF TAISHO

Early on Christmas morning 1926, as the waves of the Pacific lapped at the fringe of ice crystals on the beach at Hayama, the forty-seven-year-old Emperor Taisho, in the seclusion of his Summer Palace, a few yards up the strand, suffered his final stroke. The twenty-six-year-old Crown Prince Hirohito, who was sleeping nearby, was informed instantly over a telephone line which had been kept open ever since Taisho had lapsed unconscious a few weeks earlier. Hirohito's voice broke as he told the chamberlain at the other end of the wire how much he regretted being absent from his father's side in the last moments.

Less than two hours later a motorcade with sirens screaming arrived at the main Imperial Palace in Tokyo, the gates swung open, and Crown Prince Hirohito was rushed on through parks along malls to the entrance of the Imperial Family Shrine in the palace forest. Leaving his retinue at their limousines, he walked on with two princes of the blood and two witnesses from the nobility across the frosty white pebbles of the shrine courtyard. Entering alone into the Holy of Holies, he faced the three imperial regalia and began the solemn private ceremony of declaring himself to the spirits as the new Emperor of Japan. He touched first the fragile brocade bag which was supposed to hold the sacred green jewels, representing the verdant isles of Japan. He knew that inside the bag was supposed to be coiled a necklace of amethyst and turquoise, cut irregularly in comma-shaped beads, interspersed with oblong beads. He knew that the original almost certainly lay at the bottom of the Inland Sea, having gone down with Emperor Antoku at the naval engagement of Dan-no-ura A.D. 1185. Officially the beads had been found after the battle, floating safely in their box. He did not open the bag to admire them. Next he lifted

[7] One of them was diplomat Matsuoka Yosuke who would later win notoriety as Japan's chief operator in dealings with Hitler and Stalin.

a replica of the sacred sword of power, the *Excalibur* plucked from the tail of a dragon by the son of the sun goddess. He knew that the original of the sword was genuine, safely housed in the Atsuta Shrine in Nagoya. He could not guess that it would be destroyed by a bomb from a B-29 before his reign was over.

Finally he held aloft a replica of the most mighty of the regalia, the bronze mirror of knowledge. The original, dating from the first century, lay in the vaults of Ise Shrine on a peninsula overlooking the sea from which the first Emperor had come. If one could gaze into the mirror, one could see the face of the sun goddess and commune with her as through a glass darkly. But palace fires A.D. 960, 1005, and 1040 had reduced the original to a few droplets of bright metal. Hirohito held in his hands an imitation, almost a thousand years old, but still an imitation.

On emerging from the shrine, having perfunctorily touched the regalia and fervently declared his intentions to the hovering spirits, Hirohito was considered anointed by the holy oil. He would be publicly crowned Emperor for Western observers in an elaborate ceremony more than a year later in Kyoto, the old capital, but he was already crowned spiritually for all devout Japanese.

That night back at his study in the little Akasaka Versailles, from which he would have to move now that he was Emperor, Hirohito glanced through a list of names suggested for his reign and chose that of Showa, Peace Made Manifest. Its ideographs carried something of the force of "millennium in which men shall speak with tongues." [8] Then he took writing brush in hand and personally wrote the first draft of an edict describing the aspirations of his reign: "Simplicity instead of vain display, originality instead of blind imitation, progress in view of this period of evolution, improvement to keep pace with the advancement of civilization, national harmony in purpose and in action."

As Hirohito sat before the fire in his *petit* Versailles, composing his visions of the future, a group of young officers who had graduated from the University Lodging House before its demolition two years earlier were brought word of Emperor Taisho's passing by one of Hirohito's aides-de-camp. The messenger was Major Anami Korechika, the later general who would preside over the fake coup d'etat in the palace and prepare to do hara-kiri during the long night of August 14, 1945. Anami brought a purse of money with him and took all the young officers out for a spree in the student quarter of Kanda east of the palace. The headmaster of the

[8] This choice of reign-name meant that 1926, the year of his accession, would be styled in the Japanese calendar as Showa One; 1936 as Showa Eleven; 1945 as Showa Twenty. It also meant that Hirohito, at his death, would be known as Emperor Showa. The names of Emperors used in previous pages are all posthumous reign-names. Thus Komei's unspoken personal name while he lived was Osahito, Meiji's was Mutsuhito, and Taisho's was Yoshihito.

University Lodging House, Dr. Okawa, opened the celebration with a toast to Japan's future conquest of Manchuria.

Lieutenant Colonel Tojo, the later World War II prime minister, reminded him, "But we can never move troops unless the Emperor says so."

"Oh, well," boasted Okawa, "I will have my friend Lord Privy Seal Makino persuade the Emperor."

Tojo was indignant at Okawa's disrespect, and the suave Lieutenant Colonel Itagaki, the member of the Baden-Baden Eleven Reliables who would later organize the conquest of Manchuria, had to inject a pleasantry to prevent a fight.

Tojo's mentor, Lieutenant Colonel Nagata, the first of the Three Crows, quietly stated the final word: "I agree that independence for Manchuria is desirable, but not complete, perfect independence. That might bring eternal enmity between China and Japan and disrupt the future peace of the Far East. So let China keep her official sovereignty."

The young officers of the cabal went on to discuss the deplorable ebb in the nation's fighting spirit. Boarding a public conveyance, a man in uniform was likely to be greeted by such remarks as, "What use are spurs on a tram car?" or "Big swords certainly do get in the way of fellow passengers." After gloomily dwelling on such signs of the times, the conspirators broke up and, at Aide-de-Camp Anami's generous insistence, took taxicabs home to their billets. One group dropped Anami off in the plaza outside the main gates of the palace. There they saw country folk kneeling in the moonlight to pray for the new Emperor. In the words of one of them, "We felt relieved by the sight, as if the independence of Manchuria was already assured."

9

HIROHITO AS EMPEROR

(1926–1929)

IMPERIAL REGIMEN

A day or two after his father's death, Hirohito left his elegantly appointed Versailles in the separate Akasaka compound just west of the main palace and moved his manifold sources of influence and affluence into the high-walled confinement of the central battlements. Thereafter he would venture forth only a score or more times a year: for garden parties, convocations of the Diet, graduation days at the military and naval academies, fleet reviews, and Army maneuvers. Within the old picturesque fortifications, his dwelling was a prim, traditional Japanese house of sliding paper doors and straw matting floors. It was uncomfortable by Western standards, and Hirohito felt uncomfortable in it. He at once selected a large room about twenty feet square, with a low, handsomely coffered ceiling, to serve as his study and place of work. He had the room furnished in Western style, putting in a carpet, a table, some chairs, and a sofa on which he might spend the night. From the walls he stripped a number of Western masters, left by Meiji and Taisho, and substituted photographs of himself in Europe with Maréchal Pétain, the Prince of Wales, and Belgium's Crown Prince Leopold. Beside the prayer alcove he ensconced his busts of Napoleon and Darwin. At one end of the room the screens slid open onto a veranda overlooking his private park. There workmen were already breaking ground to build for him a new golf course, a roofed riding ring for rainy days, and the bomb-resistant concrete working quarters, the Imperial Library, under which he would surrender at the end of World War II.

No sooner had Hirohito occupied his new quarters as Emperor than his nose was assaulted by the stench of fish. It was an old custom for the members of the imperial family to felicitate one another on happy occasions with delicacies from the sea, but on this occasion the corridors of the palace were lined with panniers that reeked. Hirohito threw one of the few tantrums of his reign. "It is no congratulation to me," he shouted, "to receive a present of fresh fish. I find it more congratulating when I see one of them swimming free around me in the sea. This nonsensical, dirty custom must be abolished." And so it was, except that Hirohito continued to send fresh fish to his mother on festival days and princes of the blood found that they could please Hirohito by sending him occasionally live fish of rare varieties with which to stock his palace ponds.

Having corrected his kinsmen's misapprehensions about the interests of a marine biologist, Hirohito made one other change in palace customs. Formerly Emperors had worn clothes once or twice and then handed them down to their retainers. "Following the teaching of my tutor Nogi," declared Hirohito, "I feel that clothes are the product of my people's industry and should be worn for a long time. Therefore the vassals of the Throne may expect a third as many presents as formerly."

These two crotchets about fish and finery out of the way, Hirohito quickly settled down in his new surroundings to be a model master. He established for himself a punctual pattern of life which delighted his attendants and has changed little to this day. He customarily arose at six o'clock, shaved and dressed himself, prayed to his ancestors, and then, if he had time before breakfast, went outside for an exhilarating canter or a thoughtful stroll. At his summer villa on the beach at Hayama he would regularly rouse the neighborhood by vigorously chopping wood. At seven he would come in, full of gruff martinet good spirits, to sit down with Empress Nagako, not to the traditional Japanese breakfast of salt plums, fish, seaweed, soya-bean soup, rice, and tea, but to oatmeal, eggs, bacon, toast, and coffee.

Having breakfasted heartily, Hirohito would retire to his study to muse over the Toyko dailies, *Asahi* and *Mainichi,* and over the English-language *Japan Advertiser*. This homework completed, the Emperor would receive Lord Privy Seal Makino, his closest advisor, who would look in at the door of the study to pronounce the traditional noncommittal Japanese good morning salutation: "It is early." If any special plot was afoot, Makino would remind Hirohito of it in a sentence.

Then Hirohito would begin his official day by calling in his chief aide-de-camp, General Nara Takeji, to discuss the latest Army and Navy news, the list of military men seeking an audience in the near future, and the points to be stressed or avoided in the military audiences already scheduled for the day at hand. Next Hirohito would call in Count Chinda Sutemi, his grand chamberlain, who, like Nara and Makino, had been with him ever since the beginning of the trip to Europe. Chinda was a man of cosmopolitan charm and polish, with an American education and experience as an ambassador in half the capitals of the West. With him Hirohito would discuss the civilian audiences of the day. Finally, if one of the chiefs of staff had exercised his right to demand "direct access" to the Throne, Hirohito would see him on some item of urgent Navy or Army business before the start of the day's scheduled interviews.

From about ten until two o'clock, with a break for a light lunch at twelve-thirty, Hirohito would see a steady stream of ministers and officials. Many of the audiences, especially the formal ones held in the official Throne Room, the Phoenix Hall, were perfunctory affairs with relative strangers. Hirohito would merely greet his guest, hear him deliver a formal report, and then dismiss him. Other meetings with trusted or familiar ministers also began with a formal report, but after it was delivered, the Emperor frequently asked questions and drew out his informant to learn his personal opinions and concerns. During formal reports from military men, Chief Aide-de-Camp Nara was required to be present. However, by a curious custom instituted in Emperor Meiji's time, the aide-de-camp was obliged to withdraw immediately if any matter regarding personnel was brought up.[1] Thus, an officer who wished to share secrets with the Emperor could always talk of personnel shifts to secure a private audience, though with some risk of rebuff and imperial displeasure. Moreover, Hirohito, at any time after the formal report had been delivered, could direct Nara to withdraw out of earshot by a simple wave of his hand.

A similar procedure was followed with the grand chamberlain during audiences with nonmilitary petitioners. Hirohito, however, did not trust himself with civilians. He had found in the past that many of them used devious political approaches in talking to him, or else gossiped afterwards about what had been said. Therefore, when he dismissed Grand Chamberlain Chinda and gave a private hearing to a civilian, he usually had Lord Privy Seal Makino eavesdrop on the proceedings. In the old palace there were special listening closets provided for this purpose; in the new concrete library there were to be intercom devices as well. After 1930, when an official of the Railway Ministry abused a private audience to discuss a proposed government-wide salary cut, which was one of Hirohito's own pet economy measures, no more private audiences with civilians were granted except with officials of Court or ministerial rank, that is, with princes and noblemen or with Cabinet members and specially designated honorary ministers.

If state business permitted, Hirohito gave over the hours from two to four each afternoon to exercise, chiefly golf. Between strokes on the little nine-hole links, he discussed over-all situations and planning with his closest confidants. No day-to-day record of the people he played with is available,

---

[1] Supposedly, Emperor Meiji had heard that, during the Russo-Japanese War, the military aides of Czar Nicholas II made a practice of selling Russian officers promotions which the czar had already freely granted.

but some of his favorite partners were Fujiwara Prince Konoye, the Big Brother in charge of steering the House of Peers; Imperial Prince Asaka, the limping uncle who watched over Army Intelligence while the other uncle, Prince Higashikuni, remained in Paris; Marquis Inoue Saburo, the patron of Chiang Kai-shek's ubiquitous observer, Major Suzuki Tei-ichi; and Marquis Kido Koichi, the original Big Brother who was making plans to "rationalize" Japan's economy in the Agriculture and Commerce Ministry. Kido's published diary, which begins in 1930, suggests that some proficiency with a putting iron later became a requisite for Court advancement.

At four o'clock Hirohito took his *ofuro,* his "honorable wind on the backbone"—his bath. The Imperial Residence in the palace had been equipped in Meiji's time with shallow porcelain European tubs for tepid bathing as well as deep wooden Japanese tubs for tingling hot soaks. Hirohito favored the Japanese style of immersion, but in water at a precise, conservative 110 degrees Fahrenheit—ten to twenty degrees cooler than that of most Japanese baths. Warmed through and wrapped in the comfort of a kimono, he returned to his study to put his seal or brush his signature on a score or more state papers submitted by Lord Privy Seal Makino. About six he would try to call it a day. He would remind the chamberlain and aide-de-camp on night duty that they must disturb him if anything important came up. Then he would retire to his private apartments to dine and devote the rest of the evening to Empress Nagako, a good book, his diary,[2] or his hobby of biology. He drank not, neither did he smoke.

The punctilious round of Hirohito's domestic routine was varied on Wednesdays when the Privy Council sat. This body consisted of twenty-four distinguished aristocrats appointed by the Emperor for their meritorious service to the Empire, plus Cabinet ministers and princes of the blood. Its duty was to deliberate on treaties, on imperial ordinances issued when the Diet was out of session, and on any question submitted to it for an opinion by the Emperor. Hirohito invariably attended its plenary sessions on Wednesdays and kept informed on all its committee and preparatory meetings. This was the one occasion of the week in which he heard a semblance of discussion and observed conflicts of opinion and personality. Consequently, he always tried to keep his schedule for the next day as open as possible in order to consider and act upon the thoughts suggested to him by the Privy Council meeting. On Friday he cleared his mind for the weekend by meeting mainly with award-winning students, athletic heroes, and foreign ambassadors.

[2] Hirohito's own day-by-day record has been kept studiously since his adolescence. It was not subpoenaed by the war crimes investigators of the American Occupation and has not been read even by Hirohito's intimates. It has, however, been seen by some of them, and a part of it now fills a sizable safe in the bombproof vaults of the new Ceremonial Palace buildings completed in 1968.

On Saturday mornings, Hirohito indulged in his hobby of biology, an expression of his personality which has been much misrepresented and misunderstood. He was not, as some have thought, a scientific dilettante building an undeserved reputation for himself through the effort of hired assistants. The diaries of his courtiers and his own published work demonstrate clearly that he was a good naturalist, genuinely observant, interested, and knowledgeable. Nor was he, as some others have thought, a preoccupied collector of obscure marine organisms who pursued science for its own sake. The institutes which he subsidized over the years and the comments which he made to intimates show that he believed in science as a practical tool, a necessary tool of warfare, a tool in which he knew Japan to be deficient.

Thus he prided himself that his marine biological knowledge of tides and currents was of use in naval planning. Thus, too, in 1927, at a time when the very concept of biological warfare was novel in the West, a number of biologists and physicians who were his former tutors had been encouraged to devote themselves full time to war research. By 1939 tissue cultures at the Imperial University would be producing the most virulent agents of yaws, encephalitis, botulism, and bubonic plague known to medicine. After 1940 plague bombs containing bacilli, or bacilli in fleas, or bacilli in rat food would be dropped repeatedly in China in unavailing experiments to find effective germ-delivery systems. In 1945 Occupation search teams would find large stockpiles of unused viruses, spirochetes, and fungus spores in decentralized laboratories in Japanese rural areas.

Hirohito in 1927 was personally engrossed in a study of disease-causing fungi. Some of the unclassified portions of his work were later published in 1936 by Hattori, the faithful tutor who had contrived to take him out skin diving as a child. Hattori had become Hirohito's assistant. A commodious laboratory was being built for him in the palace gardens but at this moment, in 1927, he was cataloguing fungus specimens—many of them picked by Hirohito's own hand—in a converted palace potting shed. There on Saturday mornings Hirohito visited him, dressed in a Western-style business suit and carrying a brief-case of culture charts and sketches given him by Hattori the previous weekend. For two hours he would look over Hattori's work of the past week, asking questions and giving words of praise. Then he would pick up a new brief-case of homework and start back for the palace. Empress Nagako made a special point of waiting to greet him at the end of one of the garden paths when he returned. She was a practical political woman who did not fully understand the fascinations of his hobby, but her aged father, Prince Kuni, was also an enthusiast for biological warfare and she was glad of the relaxation which it gave her husband.

On the daily framework of Hirohito's life were imposed a number of set calendar obligations. Once a fortnight he saw the vice chiefs of his own personal departments of government, the Army and Navy General Staffs. The Cabinet Ministries of War and Navy, which administered the recruitment, pay, and peacetime organization of the armed forces, belonged to the elected government of the prime minister; the staffs, which directed military operations in the field and states of martial law at home and of occupation government abroad, answered directly to Hirohito and to him alone.

On the first, eleventh, and twenty-first of each month and on twenty-four annual holidays, the Emperor also had to break his diurnal scheme to officiate at religious rites: at folk festivals similar to May Day and Thanksgiving, at ceremonies for the sun goddess, at anniversaries for the worship of the most illustrious of the imperial ancestors. On these solemn occasions the courtyard of the Palace Shrine was filled with imperial and Fujiwara princes. Court musicians, kneeling on the ground in scarlet cloaks and pointed headdresses, made doleful music on archaic flutes, drums, and viols. The chamberlain of rituals chanted Shinto prayers almost as old and obscure as the fountainheads of the Japanese language itself. At the end of the explanatory or introductory part of the service, Hirohito, clad in robes of heavy white silk, would rise from an ancient lacquered throne, intone an invocation in a stylized high-pitched monotone, and then hold high an offering or heirloom to the spirits of his family or the spirits of the land. At some of the services, the entire Court of princes, each in his turn, according to his rank, would follow him to the altar and perform an individual act of reverence. Although punctilious in all these high-priestly duties, Hirohito confessed in later years that the folk festivals stirred less devout, more objective feelings in him than the prayers to his ancestors. He did find, however, that the November offering of harvest rice and saké to the earth spirits was often "an uplifting experience."

CHIANG CLEANS HOUSE

No sooner had Hirohito become Emperor than his cabal launched an aggressive campaign of secret diplomacy to take Manchuria from China without having to fight for it. The campaign ultimately failed but it had momentous side effects. It encouraged Chiang Kai-shek to break irrevocably with the Communist wing of his KMT party, thereby planting the seeds of China's future. It set Hirohito at odds with many of the elders of his nation. And finally, when it ended in disappointment, Hirohito allowed himself to become a party to his first clear-cut international crime: the vindictive assassination of Manchuria's war lord, Chang Tso-lin.

One of the masterminds of this ill-conceived effort in private diplomacy was Prince Higashikuni, the leader of the Japanese spy ring in Europe. As soon as he got word of Emperor Taisho's death, he posted home by ship from Paris. He and Emperor Taisho had never been friends, but with Hirohito, his niece's husband and his wife's nephew, Higashikuni hoped for a better relationship. He arrived in Tokyo incognito, called at the palace, and then went on to the Asiatic continent to take up new intelligence duties as an agent at large, working under an alias out of Peking.[3] It was his new secret mission to co-ordinate with palace policy the efforts of other members of the cabal in China—efforts to turn to Japan's advantage the northward march of the armies of Chiang Kai-shek.

The witches' brew that Higashikuni and his minions had to work with was a rich broth even by Chinese standards. Peking, the capital of China, was controlled by the Manchurian war lord Chang Tso-lin. Following his escape in 1916 from the dynamite thrown at him by Prince Kanin's cronies, he had given his nominal public support to Sun Yat-sen's Republic. Behind the scenes, however, he had worked for a restoration of the Manchu dynasty. He was backed in his conservatism by the deposed Manchu court, by many of the old bureaucratic class of mandarins, by elders of the discomfited Choshu clan in Tokyo, and by most Western business interests in China.

Arrayed against Chang Tso-lin were the leaders of the KMT, who now controlled all of southern China from Burma to the Yangtze. They were a motley assortment of unlettered peasant revolutionaries, of tough Comintern agents,[4] and of moderates like Chiang Kai-shek. Their common aim was to "liberate" Peking and "realize" the Republican government there which Chang Tso-lin said he was protecting.

After consultation with Chiang Kai-shek himself, Hirohito's cabal agreed, first, to a purge of Communists from the KMT, then to the establishment of Chiang Kai-shek as the one ruler in the whole of classical China, south of the Great Wall. In exchange, the Chinese provinces north of the Wall— the big, empty, potentially wealthy ones of Manchuria and Mongolia— were to be controlled by Japan. Once established, Chiang was also expected to ease out Western business interests from Shanghai and to look in future to Japan for all technical and economic assistance.

When Prince Higashikuni arrived secretly in Peking, the campaign to rid the KMT of its Communists was going well. Chiang was co-operating in it for personal reasons. He wished to persuade the wealthiest of the Shanghai bankers, C. J. Soong, to abandon the cause of his daughter, Ching-ling, and espouse that of another daughter, May-ling. Ching-ling had married Sun Yat-sen and was being used as a figurehead by the Communists in the KMT. May-ling, by contrast, was a Wellesley graduate, a Christian, an anti-Communist, and an ardent admirer of Chiang Kai-shek.

[3] His return was not officially reported by the Japanese press until January of the following year, but his presence at Taisho's funeral was noted without comment.

[4] The dedicated Communists in the KMT movement, like Mao Tse-tung, Chou En-lai, and Chu Teh, were a minority, but they enjoyed the assistance of technical advisors from Moscow.

As they drove down the Yangtze River from the hinterlands toward Shanghai, Chiang's troops rode a crest of mass chauvinism and xenophobia. At Hankow and Kiukiang they terrorized the Western settlements. Chiang blamed their excesses entirely on Bolshevik agitators, a charge which Western businessmen were predisposed to believe. C. J. Soong, the pink banker, saw that the Reds in the KMT were spoiling his reputation and impairing his interests.

In late March 1927, when Chiang's soldiers occupied Nanking, less than 200 miles from the China coast, they burned several of the foreign consulates, killed six Westerners, and manhandled a number of consular wives and secretaries. British and American gunboats in the Yangtze laid down a semicircle of protective fire around Socony Hill while Westerners, who had congregated there as refugees, were lowered on ropes from the city wall to evacuation launches. Two Japanese gunboats steamed 50 miles downriver to help but managed to arrive too late. In the days that followed, representatives of the Western nations discussed the possibility of sending an international expeditionary force to Nanking to restore order. The foreign minister of Japan, by prearrangement, aborted the expedition by refusing to participate in it.

In the KMT advance, Western colonials saw a Red spectre marching with a flail into all they considered near and dear. Over their glasses of Scotch in Shanghai clubs they grumbled that the West had invested more than $2 billion in China. These foreign holdings were represented by the "concessions" and "legation quarters," the little enclaves of Paris, London, Tokyo, and St. Petersburg which dominated the downtown areas of all the largest Chinese cities including Shanghai, Tientsin, Hankow, Nanking, and Peking. Most were leaseholds of a few thousand acres. Several of them, notably those of Shanghai and Hankow, had been marshes or mudflats originally and had become valuable only because foreigners had developed them. By the 1920's, however, native Chinese urban areas had grown up around all of them. In septic seas of tiled roofs, narrow alleyways, intrigue, violence, and disease, they stood out as blessed isles of peace, police, and cleanliness, of Western architecture and broad, arbored boulevards. In a French concession, one could always eat snails in hailing distance of an Annamese gendarme. In a British concession, there was always a tea shop or two, a busy banking district, and a Sikh bobby on every corner. The old Russian and German concessions, which had been taken over by carefully selected Chinese administrators after World War I, still had their borscht and bakeries and Wiener schnitzel. The Japanese concessions, being less Occidental, were naturally less congenial to Westerners. They teemed with people and closely set small buildings. But to a Japanese they were pure Osaka, and the policework, neighborhood organization, geisha, and sukiyaki were of the best.

After the capture of Nanking, Chiang Kai-shek used Western threats of intervention as an excuse to summon a full-dress conference of all KMT leaders in the town of Nanchang, halfway up the Yangtze between his own field headquarters downriver and the government of the KMT Left upriver in Hankow. On March 22, 1927, after interminable sessions of fruitless talk, Chiang abruptly stalked from the bargaining table and disappeared into the countryside, submerging among his own personal troops. During his disappearance a cadre of disciplined Communists under the leadership of the later famous Chinese Communist foreign minister, Chou En-lai, staged a municipal coup d'etat in the Chinese quarter of Shanghai and put the bulk of the city in Red hands, greatly alarming the Western residents in the concessions downtown.

Far to the north, on April 6, a fortnight later, Chang Tso-lin acted on a tip from one of Hirohito's Eleven Baden-Baden Reliables and ordered his police to break into the Russian Embassy in Peking. In their raid the police seized documents which showed that the left-wing government of the KMT in Hankow was being run as a front organization according to instructions from Moscow. Chang Tso-lin hoped that this revelation, added to Chiang Kai-shek's experience in Russia and friendship with Stalin, would destroy Chiang's credit with bankers and undermine his popularity with the xenophobic rank and file. Instead, as the Japanese had understood all too well, the revelations gave Chiang precisely the justification he needed to purge the Reds from the KMT without losing the support, which he also needed, of the KMT pinks.

As soon as the news of Russian subversion in the KMT made the headlines, Chiang Kai-shek resurfaced at the head of a strong force outside Shanghai. The new Communist mayor, Chou En-lai, went into hiding. Chiang seized the municipal government of the Chinese city, and on April 12, 1927—Black Tuesday as it is now remembered in mainland China— his troops hunted down all Red officials. That afternoon he had 5,000 of them beheaded in the public squares. Chou En-lai slipped through the dragnet and escaped. But he and the other Communists never forgot or forgave. The Chinese revolutionary front of the KMT was split irreparably. From then on, whenever they were not fighting Japanese, the armies of Chiang and of the Communists engaged in civil warfare. It was a struggle deeper and more bitter than the rivalries of war lords, a struggle in which brother fought against brother and father against son, a struggle which would not end until two decades later when Chiang and over a million of his partisans were forced into exile on the island of Taiwan.

Chiang Kai-shek followed up Black Tuesday by further purges of Reds in all the towns of the lower Yangtze. Then, on April 18, 1927, he set up his own government of KMT moderates in Nanking. KMT leftists maintained their separate regime in Hankow, 300 miles upriver, but cleansed it of outright Communists. Blücher and Borodin, the KMT's two Russian advisors, returned to Moscow. Mao Tse-tung and Chou En-lai withdrew into the provinces. Ching-ling, the Communist widow of Sun Yat-sen, betook her dainty self into exile in Europe.

JAPAN CHANGES HORSES

Phase One of the cabal's plan for China was now complete. Phase Two required that Chang Tso-lin be kept from interfering while Chiang Kai-shek consolidated his position south of the Great Wall and Japan made off with the provinces north of the Wall. Up to now the Japanese Cabinet had stood for nonintervention in China. Now a Cabinet was needed which would be willing to intervene if necessary. Accordingly, on April 20, 1927, two days after the founding of the Chiang government in Nanking, Hirohito followed by appointing a new government in Tokyo. The fall of the old Cabinet was engineered by exposure of a financial scandal at a Privy Council meeting presided over by Hirohito in person.

On Saionji's recommendation, Hirohito accepted as the next prime minister Tanaka Gi-ichi, the successor to the late strongman Yamagata as chieftain of the Choshu clan. To all appearances Tanaka was the perfect dupe to take responsibility for what was planned next. He was a big, bluff, hard-living sabre of a man, a tough-talking dandy infatuated with braid and dress uniforms, who had capitulated gracefully when voted down over the Army reorganization scheme by the Board of Field Marshals in 1925. Since then he had resigned voluntarily from the Army and had shown a desire to continue his career by accepting the presidency of the majority political party, the Constitutionalists. To Court analysts, he seemed to be an opportunist, ready to lead both Choshu and the Constitutionalists anywhere if it served his ambition. But the analysts were mistaken. Tanaka had become a Constitutionalist mainly to resist Hirohito and restore Choshu leadership of the nation. He would pursue his plans with an apologetic bluster and suavity which were to thwart Hirohito's cabal at every turn for the next two years.

As a condition for taking office Prime Minister Tanaka agreed to delegate the detailed administration of foreign affairs to a parliamentary vice minister recommended by Big Brother Konoye of the House of Peers.[5] In effect Tanaka agreed to take responsibility for foreign policy while giving over the making of it to others. It seemed incredible to Prime Minister Tanaka that a pack of young majors and ministry section chiefs—even though they might have the ear of the young Emperor—could pose any threat to the elders of the nation. He called a series of conferences with his friends in the upper echelons of the bureaucracy and agreed with them that a show of big get-tough-with-China talk would be enough to satisfy

[5] Mori Kaku, a brash young man of forty, who had ridden on Prince Konoye's coattails for a decade.

Hirohito. He summoned home the chief of Chang Tso-lin's Japanese military advisors and asked him to negotiate with Chang Tso-lin for the construction of five new Japanese railroads in Manchuria which might help in silencing Hirohito's young hawks. "I promise to co-operate with Chang Tso-lin in the administration of the railroads," Tanaka said. "If these plans are carried out, I can maintain order at home."

That same month, May 1927, the ubiquitous Major Suzuki left his post at the side of Chiang Kai-shek and was reassigned to Japan to help Konoye and the parliamentary vice minister of foreign affairs in implementing the second phase of the cabal's plan: the neutralization of Chang Tso-lin and the Japanese acquisition of Manchuria and Mongolia. Suzuki at once reconvoked the young Army officers who were graduates of the Lodging House and asked them to form a "study group" on the China problem.[6] The task of the Suzuki Study Group was to prepare position papers in defense of the cabal's planning—arguments which were to be laid before a full-dress conclave of Japanese elders, administrators, and colonials which the new parliamentary vice minister of foreign affairs had scheduled for late June.

While the cabal was mustering its arguments for the great debate, Prime Minister Tanaka advised Chang Tso-lin to withdraw his forces from China proper into Manchuria and make sure of his home province before it became too late. Chang Tso-lin replied indignantly:

> I myself have advanced to Peking and am waging war on Communist influences. My war is Japan's war. What am I to make of Japan's good faith when, in spite of this fact, Japan is assisting Chiang Kai-shek, who has gone Red, and is advising me to return to Manchuria?

Chang followed his words, on June 18, by inaugurating a new policy with two objectives: on the one hand, politically, to reach a compromise with Chiang Kai-shek and woo him away from the KMT; on the other hand, militarily, to smash the KMT armies in one all-out offensive.

[6] In retrospect its roster would read like a who's who of Japanese fascism. It included one of Hirohito's aides-de-camp, Viscount Machijiri, who had been with Higashikuni in Paris; aide-de-camp Anami, the quiet young major who would live to kill himself as Japan's last war minister; Hashimoto Gun, who would organize the Marco Polo Bridge Incident which opened the 1937 war with China; Ishiwara Kanji, who would plan the occupation of Manchuria in 1931–32; Kusaba Tatsumi, who would commit suicide in a Russian plane in 1945 while en route to stand trial for atrocities done during his command of the Twenty-fifth Army in Malaya in 1942; Muto Akira, who would be chief of staff in the Philippines at the time of the rape of Manila in 1945; Suzuki Yorimichi of the General Staff's Operations Squad, who would command the Army Air Force on Pearl Harbor day; Tanaka Shinichi who would be chief of staff in Burma during the completion of the infamous Burma-Thailand railroad in 1944; Yokoyama Isamu who would be executed in 1946 for beheading downed U.S. pilots. Most of the study group had been introduced personally to Hirohito in Paris in 1921.

FAR EASTERN CONFERENCE

As Chang began to move troops south for a drive on Nanking, the great debate of the elders was opened in Tokyo at the foreign minister's residence in the same garden of atomic sunshine where Japanese leaders in 1946 would accept an American-made constitution. The debate lasted from June 27 to July 7, 1929, and was attended by all Japan's proconsuls—the generals and "experts" from Korea, Manchuria, and the legation listening posts in China proper. The meetings, which are collectively known to scholars as the Far Eastern Conference, were chairmanned and keynoted by the ubiquitous Major Suzuki Tei-ichi. Only Suzuki's own recollections of his opening address to the conference have emerged from the white water of subsequent history:

> It was my aim to unify their ideas about the course that Japan should follow on the Continent. Most of us felt that Manchuria should be cut off from China proper and brought under Japan's political control. This required that Japan's whole policy—domestic, foreign, and military—should be concentrated on the achievement of this one goal. . . .
>
> Unless Japan waged war, she would find it difficult to solve her Continental problems. . . . We knew . . . no minister in Tanaka's government would support such a plan.

Prime Minister Tanaka countered the schemes of Suzuki and the cabal by laying before the conference a comprehensive long-range program for the economic infiltration and exploitation of China, a program which, though frankly rapacious, would have been merely a continuation of classical Choshu clan policies. In an effort to please Hirohito, Tanaka presented his program in the most belligerent terms possible. When he had finished, one of his old comrades in arms, General Muto Nobuyoshi, arose. Muto was commander in chief of Japan's leasehold garrison in Manchuria, the tough Kwantung Army, and was known as "Muto the Silent." He had once ridden for ten hours on a train beside his chief of staff without uttering a single word. Now, however, he spoke at some length, objecting strenuously to Tanaka's program:

"Japan must be prepared to face a world war if such a drastic program is to be carried out. To begin with, America will not tolerate it. If America will not acquiesce, neither will England nor the rest of the Powers. Are you prepared to cope with America and the eventuality of a world war?"

"I am prepared to face the consequences," Tanaka replied.

"You are sure you will not waver later on, are you?" asked Muto.

"I am all set to face the worst," answered Tanaka.

"If the government is so determined," declared Muto, "I have nothing else to add. We shall wait for the order to come and simply carry it out."

Throughout the remaining days of the conference, Muto voiced not so much as another syllable. His timely opposition to Tanaka's program of economic aggression, however, made the alternative of armed aggression unthinkable. In vain the young staff officers of the Suzuki Study Group presented their own more ambitious plans. General Muto, on behalf of the Kwantung Army, looked on silently shaking his head. Finally, when the young men had completed their presentation, the other proconsuls voted overwhelmingly to accept Tanaka's proposal as the lesser of two evils. In the final analysis they agreed only to demand of Chang Tso-lin in northern China a number of specific rights similar to those stipulated in the Twenty-One Demands of a dozen years earlier.[7]

TANAKA MEMORIAL

After the conference, on July 25, 1927, Tanaka presented a report to the Throne on the decision which had been made. Chinese intelligence agents tried to reconstruct this report by piecing together fragments which they had obtained of Tanaka's plan and of the position papers which had been delivered by members of the Suzuki Study Group. In their reconstruction the Chinese got the two points of view all mixed up. The result, which they published, became one of the most famous documents in Japanese history—a pastiche of truths adding up to a gigantic forgery. Under the title, *The Tanaka Memorial,* it was widely reprinted in the West, a few years later, as evidence of Japan's piratical aspirations. It permanently confused Western intelligence analysts, leading them to identify Tanaka and his Choshu-Constitutionalist faction with Japanese militarism.

According to the Chinese verson of Tanaka's memorial to the Throne, Tanaka advised Emperor Hirohito that "the plan left to us by Emperor Meiji" was first to conquer Manchuria and Mongolia, then to occupy China, then to "crush the United States," and finally to subjugate all Asia "in order to conquer the world." In reality, according to knowledgeable courtiers, Tanaka warned Hirohito that military conquest of Manchuria, Mongolia, and China would lead inevitably to war with the United States and that Japan could not win such a war unless she had already gained economic control of Asia's raw materials and factories.

CHIANG GOES A-WOOING

Hirohito tabled the decision of the Far Eastern Conference at the bottom of his in-basket, and Chiang Kai-shek, closely questioned by colleagues

---

[7] The right to renew all present Japanese leases in China and to supply all future loans to China; the right to provide all arms for Manchurian-Mongolian wars and all ships for Manchurian-Mongolian commerce; the unrestricted right of Japanese to travel and trade on the Continent without being subject to Chinese criminal jurisdiction; the right to build and manage a dozen new railroads which would be useful in the event of war for carrying Japanese troops to the strategic garrison towns of North China.

about his ties with Japan, dramatically resigned his presidency of the KMT and retired to his villa to sulk. Chang Tso-lin, the northern war lord, descended on Chiang's capital of Nanking with a huge army and was fought to a standstill, in an epic engagement, by the noncommunist forces remaining in the KMT. Chang fell back toward Peking and the KMT armies pursued him north. Hirohito's cabal in the Army demanded that Japan abandon Chang Tso-lin to his fate and seize his home base, Manchuria. Prime Minister Tanaka stolidly insisted: "Our government is taking the position that we negotiate with Chang Tso-lin so long as he prevails in the north and likewise with Chiang Kai-shek so long as he is in control of the south."

Emperor Hirohito called in for rebriefing the Japanese consul general from the Manchurian capital of Mukden. This was the son-in-law of Lord Privy Seal Count Makino and the future Peace-Faction leader and American-Occupation-era prime minister, Yoshida Shigeru. On instructions from the palace, Yoshida returned to Mukden and approached the commander of the Kwantung Army, Muto the Silent, with a proposition: why not deploy the Kwantung Army to cut the Peking-Mukden railroad, making it impossible for Chang Tso-lin to receive supplies from his home base or to retreat to it? Muto bluntly refused to have any part in the scheme without official orders, passed on by Prime Minister Tanaka. A week later Hirohito stamped orders recalling Silent Muto to a titular position of honor in Tokyo.

At this juncture Chiang Kai-shek, the temporarily retired president of the KMT, arrived in Japan, seeking clarification. Ostensibly he came for a personal reason: to court and marry Soong May-ling, the noncommunist Wellesley daughter of the pink banker, C. J. Soong. May-ling was summering with her family in Nagasaki and it was thither that Chiang Kai-shek traveled first. He told the Soong parents that he had divorced his former wife, given up his stable of concubines, and was prepared to lead the irreproachable life of a Western-style head of state. His future mother-in-law, Madame Soong, asked him if he would now become a Christian like the rest of her family. He replied that, no, he had no immediate conversion plans because Christianty was not a pill that a man should take at a swallow. Madame Soong was struck by his frankness.

While father and mother Soong were thinking over his proposal, Chiang left May-ling to plead his cause for him and went up to Tokyo for three months. There he negotiated a clarification of the future with the ubiquitous Major Suzuki, with the Emperor's Big Brothers, and at second hand with Hirohito himself. There, too, he visited with such old Pan-Asianist acquaintances as Chief of Army Intelligence Matsui Iwane, the general who would later be hanged unjustly as the "Butcher of Nanking." There, a photograph was taken of him squatting cross-legged on a *tatami* floor with Black Dragon Lord Toyama. Toyama, in kimono, with long white beard, was staring sagely off to his right, as if at some transcendental geometric proposition; Chiang, in Western business suit, with loud tie, was gazing directly at the camera with a smug, pucker-lipped half-smile.

At the meetings Chiang had with members of Hirohito's cabal no photographs were taken, but Chiang reconfirmed the bargain which both he and Sun Yat-sen before him had made with the Japanese: China's outer provinces of Manchuria and Mongolia in exchange for Japanese help and friendship during the unification of the Chinese heartland south of the Great Wall. Specifically, Chiang promised to make no more than token protests against Japanese actions north of the Wall if Japan would remain a friendly neutral during the civil war which he foresaw with the Communist leaders of the KMT who had survived Black Tuesday. Satisfied with the hedged manner in which he had made this compact, Chiang returned to Nagasaki to marry May-ling on December 27, 1927. In January 1928 he went back to Nanking, his new bride on his arm, and was at once re-elected to the leadership of the KMT.

Hirohito's cabal did not wait for the wedding or for Chiang's return to China to begin acting on their understanding with him. In November 1927 Big Brother Prince Konoye resigned from the Research Society in the Diet, which he had helped to found in 1921 and which had become the ruling circle in the House of Peers, and founded his own clique of twenty-one young imperialist noblemen, all close to Hirohito, which he dubbed the Tuesday Club. The Research Society, he said, had come to be dominated by reactionary old men who believed in war lords like Chang Tso-lin. It was one of the charter tenets of the Tuesday Club that alliance with Chiang Kai-shek might ultimately lead to a united Asia under Japanese leadership.

In early December 1927, Colonel Komoto Daisaku of the staff of the Kwantung Army—a member of the Suzuki Study Group and also of the Eleven Reliables chosen at Baden-Baden—superintended the dynamiting of a small railroad bridge on a branch line in Manchuria. He meant no special harm by the explosion. It was simply a dry run. He wanted to make sure that the noise and damage could be attributed to Chinese bandits. He was gratified to discover that it could be—that Russian, Japanese, and even Chinese newspapers all accepted the obvious explanation. He repeated the experiment several times on several different bridges in the months that followed. The reaction was always the same: bandits. The stage was set.

CHANG AT BAY

During Diet elections, in February 1928, agrarian reformers, labor unionists, Communists, anarchists, and shockingly emancipated *mobos* and *mogas*—"modern boys" and "modern girls"—demonstrated vociferously against militarism and authoritarianism in Japan. In March, the police arrested 5,000 of the troublemakers and held them indefinitely without trial or bail. Hirohito forthwith approved a strengthening of the Peace Preserva-

tion Law, enabling the courts to exact the death penalty of political undesirables. Even with this imperial easement the police, four years later, in
July 1932, were forced to let 4,520 of the so-called radicals go free. Of
the remaining 480, kept in jail, only 190 could ultimately be proved deserving of execution or prison sentences.

Shortly after the arrests, in May 1928, the Northern Expedition of
Chiang Kai-shek's KMT "Army of Liberation" reached the Shantung
Peninsula where some 2,000 Japanese nationals lived in and around the old
German leasehold of Tsingtao. To help his old friend Chang Tso-lin, Prime
Minister Tanaka reinforced the Japanese garrison in the area and thereby
interposed a force which would delay Chiang Kai-shek's advance. Hirohito puzzled his intimates by sanctioning the plan. To take charge of the
expedition, he appointed Lieutenant General Fukuda Hikosuke, a kinsman
of General Fukuda who had massacred Koreans after the 1923 earthquake. When Fukuda's officers met to parley with Chiang Kai-shek's
vanguard at the railhead of Tsinan in China a few days later, a Japanese
Special Service Organ agent,[8] working under the command of one of the
Eleven Baden-Baden Reliables, fired a pistol from one of the nearby roof-
tops. Fukuda's men assumed that they were being attacked and promptly
massacred 7,000 of the Chinese within easiest reach. In a nine-day reign
of terror, Fukuda thoroughly discredited Prime Minister Tanaka's "intervention."

Chiang Kai-shek had his government protest the massacre in the usual
polite terms of diplomacy. Then, knowing that it was a maneuver of domestic Japanese politics, he had his men bypass Tsinan and press on against
Peking. On May 18, 1928, Field Marshal Prince Kanin, the elder of the
imperial family, had an order sent to the Kwantung Army in Manchuria,
asking it to be ready, on twenty-four-hour alert, to seize the Manchurian
rail system and disarm Chang Tso-lin's soldiers if they attempted to retreat
to Mukden. On the same day the Japanese diplomatic representative in
Peking handed Chang his last ultimatum: either withdraw at once or be
caught between Chiang Kai-shek and a hostile Kwantung Army. The old
war-lord fox was trapped. He began to move his men secretly back to
Mukden, laid elaborate cover plans for his own personal retreat, and at the
same time shouted public defiance toward Chiang Kai-shek.

INTERNATIONAL MURDER

Assassination of another nation's political leader is a relatively simple
tactic of statecraft but one which is rarely used because it invites reprisal

[8] The Special Service Organs were branches of Army and Navy Intelligence,
specializing in political intrigue. They were attached to all Japanese garrisons overseas and were usually housed blatantly in substantial concrete buildings of their own.
As will be described later in more detail, they worked closely with all agencies of
Japanese subversion including the Opium Board, the Secret Police, Military Intelligence, and Japan's shadowy, supragovernmental Civilian Spy Service.

in kind. Hirohito turned to it in 1928 out of frustration and spite. In so doing he rounded a corner and gave Japan the name of a killer nation in the West.

On May 21, 1928, taking full advantage of Japan's ownership of the South Manchuria railroad, the headquarters of the Kwantung Army and a few crack Japanese regiments moved 250 miles north from Port Arthur into Mukden, Manchuria's capital city. There the Japanese forces, surrounded by an ocean of Chinese, waited tensely to carry out the disarming of Chang Tso-lin.

Through intermediaries, Prime Minister Tanaka informed the American Embassy in Tokyo that a flammable situation existed, and suddenly from across the Pacific, the U.S. government spoke up, warning Japan not to take unilateral action without first consulting the Powers. Prime Minister Tanaka's de facto foreign minister, the parliamentary vice minister for foreign affairs, stormed from ministry to ministry in Tokyo trying to prevent influential bureaucrats from paying heed to the American warning. The disarming of Chang Tso-lin's forces, he argued, was "a predetermined plan" and therefore could not be shelved without great sacrifice of national prestige. Many were prepared to agree with him, but that evening a general and a diplomat who were disciples of the old lute player Prince Saionji visited Prime Minister Tanaka at his villa in the suburb of Kamakura. Walking on the beach with him, they persuaded him to do his utmost to restrain the young bloods who had Hirohito's ear. The next morning, May 26, without consulting anyone, Tanaka cabled the Kwantung Army chief of staff to cancel the scheduled disarming.

Once again the Throne had suffered a rebuff. Short of a public confrontation with Prime Minister Tanaka and the elders of Japan, Hirohito could do nothing. The members of his cabal vented their collective spleen on Chang Tso-lin. Chang's son, Chang Hsueh-liang, was reputed to be an admirer of Chiang Kai-shek. Possibly, if Chang Tso-lin were dead, the son might understand Chiang Kai-shek's bargain with Japan and agree to serve as Japan's puppet.

The planning of Chang Tso-lin's murder was entrusted to Major General Tatekawa Yoshiji, a protégé of Field Marshal Prince Kanin, the imperial family elder who had presided over the previous attempt on Chang's life in 1916. Suave, chubby, inscrutable, Tatekawa was known to his friends as the "Man Snatcher" or the "Peerless Pimp." He was a charter member of the imperial cabal. During the war with Russia he had organized a group of irregulars, the Tatekawa Volunteers, to work with Chang Tso-lin and other Chinese bandits behind Russian lines. After the war he had been decorated by Emperor Meiji and had become a favorite at the palace. In March 1928 he had been transferred from the important post of European and American intelligence chief in the General Staff to that of attaché at the Japanese Embassy in Peking. In that lowly capacity he had been visiting and watching Chang Tso-lin for two months.

In May 1928 Tatekawa dispatched a fellow attaché to Mukden to advise the new commander of the Kwantung Army in Manchuria of the cabal's latest plan. Leaving the commander's office, the attaché encountered Reliable Komoto, the experimental dynamiter, who had now blown up a dozen of Manchuria's sturdiest bridges. The attaché told Komoto that Chang Tso-lin was to be assassinated by a hired cutthroat in Peking. Komoto begged leave to handle the assignment himself. It would be so much more poetic if Chang, who had escaped dynamiting in 1916, should fall by it now. The attaché promptly wired Tatekawa in Peking that Komoto had accepted the assignment.

On June 2, Chang Tso-lin circularized his commanders by telegram to let them know that he had finally decided to withdraw into his Manchurian homeland beyond the Great Wall. Major General Tatekawa, the Peerless Pimp, had a man ready in the Peking rail yards, studying the composition and routing of all trains moving north. The man was Captain Tanaka Takayoshi, later American Prosecutor Keenan's star witness at the Tokyo war crimes trials. On May 30, 1928, three days before Chang Tso-lin announced his decision to return home, the elephant-memoried Tanaka wired Komoto in Mukden a provisional report on train scheduling in Peking.

In Mukden, Komoto was prepared for any train which might pass. Outside Mukden, where the Chinese-owned Peking-Mukden rail line ran under the Japanese-owned Dairen-Mukden line, Komoto had had his men bury three bags of blasting powder, wired to a plunger on a nearby hill. Three Manchurian soldiers with a grudge against Chang Tso-lin were hired to stand sentry duty over the section of Chinese track where the charges had been planted.

After Chang Tso-lin's beaten soldiers had been pouring into Mukden for days, Chang finally boarded a train to follow them. Having heard rumors of a Japanese plot against him, he sent his "number-five wife" and other dispensable members of his suite ahead of him in a yellow train of seven coaches exactly like his own. When it had been on its way for six or seven hours, his own train left its siding in the Peking yards, at 1:15 A.M. on June 3. Three of its passengers were Japanese officers who had long been his military advisors. Two of the three got off the train when it stopped in Tientsin at daybreak. The third, Major Giga Nobuya, remained aboard. Chang knew Major Giga to be a henchman of Prince Kanin and therefore felt safe from dynamite as long as Giga was close at hand to share fate with him.

About five the following afternoon a Japanese spotter, posted by Major General Tatekawa, confirmed the passage of Chang's train through the Great Wall of China at the border town of Shanhaikwan. The men of Reliable Komoto reported it rolling through Chinchow station in Manchuria during the night. Sightings further along the line of a similar train led to momentary confusion in Mukden, and Komoto's assistants were all set to blow up the decoy. Fortunately for Chang's number-five wife, the distinction between the two trains was sorted out in time from the rising drift of intelligence telegrams, and the pretty young creature was allowed to pass unmolested into Mukden about midnight.

As Chang's train bowled through the dark across the flat Manchurian plains, he and his suite, including the Japanese Major Giga, sat up playing mah-jongg. In Mukden, where it was clear now that the train would not arrive until five or six A.M., some of the conspirators napped in town and some at their posts near the railroad overpass half a mile outside of town. By the time that the sky had begun to lighten with a promise of dawn, all of them had rendezvoused by bicycle at the bridge. On the theory that dead men tell no tales, Komoto's men stole up on the three Manchurian soldiers who had been bribed to stand sentry duty and rushed them with fixed bayonets. One escaped in the darkness. The corpses of the other two were laid by the railroad track and tricked out with forged orders from one of Chang's tributary bandit lords. In their stiffening hands were planted Russian-made bombs bought at a secondhand store in Tokyo and donated to the cause by the general in charge of the Tokyo secret police.

On the onrushing train, when it was a few miles from Mukden, the gambling game broke up and the players hurried back to their respective cars to assemble their gear for arrival. Chang Tso-lin and Governor Wu of the province of Hailar nodded over the scattered mah-jongg tiles and spent bottles of beer. Japanese Major Giga snatched a blanket from his berth, ran to the caboose, wrapped himself up, and lay down on the rear platform. On a convenient knoll nearby, Komoto's chief assistant, Captain Tomiya Tetsuo, watched tensely as the train entered the underpass, and at the precise moment that Chang's own car passed over the explosive, he pushed the plunger. There was a dramatic puff of fire and black smoke, and the car jumped shattered from the track. Chang and Governor Wu were both dead along with seventeen of their retainers. Giga, merely shaken, leapt from the caboose as the train dragged to a halt, rushed forward to the remains of Chang's carriage, and is reported to have exclaimed with great feeling, "Ah, how dreadful!"

The other conspirators, appearing at the site of the wreck, announced that they had just bayoneted the criminals responsible. It was a flimsy story at best, and the third Manchurian sentry, who had escaped in the dark, knew the truth. He found his way to Chang Tso-lin's son, Chang Hsueh-liang, and told his story. But the young Chang feared that he might push Japan into war if he caused her to lose face. Therefore he had his officials gravely bear his father's body to hospital and did not announce the success of the assassination until it seemed sure, almost two weeks later, that war could be avoided. In the meantime Peking attaché

Major General Tatekawa, the Peerless Pimp, professed to be so "shocked" at what had taken place that he burned all relevant telegrams in his possession.

IMPERIAL IMPENITENCE

Hirohito, after Chang Tso-lin's murder, was in a mood of defiant self-confidence. He had been trained from childhood to be above ordinary Japanese feelings of pride in face. He exulted in the downfall of old bandit Chang Tso-lin and expected Prime Minister Tanaka to take responsibility for it. If Tanaka was sensible he would conduct a token investigation of the assassination and mete out nominal punishment to a handful of loyal Army officers. If Tanaka was not sensible he would be condemned by the reverent, taboo-conscious Japanese electorate for trying to hide behind the sleeve of the dragon and foist off his responsibilities on the sacred Throne.

Nine days after Chang Tso-lin's assassination Hirohito gave public indication of his mood by having a banquet of celebration in the palace. The occasion was a routine one: the Feast of the Five Families, held annually to honor the five branches of the Fujiwara clan which served as the innermost veil in Hirohito's government from behind the curtain. Without precedent, however, Japanese newsmen were allowed to look in on the proceedings, to note that they were merry, and to publish the names of the six notables who sat at Hirohito's table. All six were personal acquaintances of Chang Tso-lin's assassin, the Baden-Baden Reliable, Colonel Komoto Daisaku.

Prime Minister Tanaka at once paid a call on old Prime-Minister-Maker Saionji at his seaside villa in the fishing village of Okitsu. Guardedly he told Saionji that "the Chang Tso-lin affair" must be disposed of and that some of Hirohito's most trusted Army familiars were almost certainly involved in it. How was he, the humble prime minister and front man of imperial government, to handle the matter?

The seventy-eight-year-old Saionji considered the question well before replying. As the elder of the Fujiwara family, he had the duty always of being a friend to the Throne and an apologist for it. As a pro-Western liberal who had helped to frame the Constitution, he must also disapprove of Hirohito's recent policies. All the best and brightest of Japan's heredity aristocrats looked up to him for leadership.

Prime Minister Tanaka waited patiently for an answer. Saionji had aged greatly in recent years and had suffered a succession of personal tragedies. One by one all his boon companions had died, including his younger brother, the millionaire. Moreover, Flower Child, the mistress he had taken to Versailles, had had a child by a young lover and Saionji had felt compelled to banish her from his bed and board. Now he was all alone.

Choosing his words carefully, Saionji finally replied: "Wrongdoing is wrongdoing and must be punished accordingly. It would be bad for military discipline if we did less." With this preface Saionji exhorted Prime Minister Tanaka to probe the assassination of Chang Tso-lin "to the bottom" and "do it bravely."

Tanaka asked warily if it would be proper to sound out Hirohito in person and make sure that this was also the Emperor's view. Saionji assured Tanaka that it would be "extraordinarily proper." So Tanaka did go to Hirohito, and Hirohito coolly assured him that he wanted no semblance of impropriety or of Army insubordination in his government.

At Hirohito's suggestion, Prime Minister Tanaka sent the chief of the Tokyo Secret Police, Major General Mine Komatsu, to Manchuria to make an on-the-spot investigation. Mine was an apt choice for he was already an expert on the affair, having supplied the Russian-made bombs found in the hands of the dead sentries beside the railroad track. In mid-August 1928 he submitted his preliminary findings. They were burdened with details of track measurements, train schedules, and bomb techniques but delicately vague as to the names of the assassins. Mine suggested, however, that certain officers around Colonel Komoto, the perennial bridge blower, had been remiss in seeing to the security of Chang Tso-lin's train and should perhaps be transferred and reprimanded.

Hirohito urged Prime Minister Tanaka to take the disciplinary action suggested and close the case as quickly as possible. Tanaka, however, knew the Mine report to be a whitewash and was encouraged by old luteplayer Saionji to keep the case open as long as possible.

When Tanaka failed to lay Chang's ghost, Hirohito took a step which would increase his secret power to undercut the prime minister's authority. On August 21, 1928, he had a phone installed in his study. It was a precedent-shattering innovation, with a set of push buttons, which gave him instant access to all his aides on the palace grounds. Previously he had had to delegate his communication with the outside world entirely to slow, gossipy intermediaries. Now he could phone one of the ministers of the vast imperial family fortune and exercise his influence immediately on the financial world. His various political chamberlains could be summoned individually to his study without the chamberlain on duty knowing why they had been called. Most important, the Army and Navy aides-decamp could put him through on their own private tie lines direct to the War Ministry and General Staff offices outside the palace walls. In using his new phone, Hirohito exposed himself not at all, for he never identified himself on the phone but trusted that his respondent on the other end of the line would recognize his voice.[9]

On August 27, 1928, a few days after the installation of the phone,

[9] Several American historians have used the phrase "without even a phone" to describe Hirohito's supposed isolation in the palace. The installation of the phone was reported by *Mainichi,* the great Tokyo daily, on August 22, 1928. Hirohito's use of it is described several times in the diaries of Big Brother Harada, the political secretary to Saionji.

Prime Minister Tanaka's relationship with the Throne deteriorated further when his subordinates in the Foreign Ministry signed the Kellogg-Briand Pact in Paris, outlawing war as a legitimate instrument of statecraft. It was a triumph for Saionji, Tanaka, and the Constitutionalists because they knew that Hirohito, as national high priest, could never come out openly against the idea of peace. The Tokyo press and public greeted the treaty with applause. Hirohito, however, referred it to the Privy Council over which he presided, asking that a thorough study be made of the wording of the treaty before he signed it. The loyal privy councillors quickly found a fault and attacked Prime Minister Tanaka for having allowed the pact to be signed "in the names of the respective peoples." This wording, said the councillors, violated the Japanese Constitution by enthroning the people in the Emperor's place and by denying the Emperor his explicit constitutional right to declare war in defense of the nation. Before Hirohito would sign the treaty, Tanaka was forced to notify other signatory nations that the pact was understood not to compromise Japan's right of self-defense and that the objectionable phrase "in the names of the respective peoples" did not apply to Japan.

On September 9, 1928, when Prime Minister Tanaka found himself at odds with Hirohito over the Kellogg-Briand Pact, he harkened to the pleas of old Saionji and ordered Secret Police Chief Mine back to Manchuria to conduct a more thorough investigation of Chang Tso-lin's murder. On September 22, Tanaka followed by convoking a committee of Diet Constitutionalists to deliberate on the Chang Tso-lin affair under the eyes of newspaper reporters. On October 8, while the committee was still sitting, Secret Police Chief Mine submitted his second report, "top secret." Tanaka at once recessed his political investigators and reassessed his political position. Mine's second report implicated not only Hirohito but many of Prime Minister Tanaka's own oldest and closest Army friends. Tanaka had never before appreciated fully the breadth of Hirohito's Army backing and the depth of its planning.

In the days that followed, Tanaka was given further evidence to make him hesitate and to convince him that Hirohito was in earnest. On October 10, he learned that the Army Engineering Corps at Tumen, on the northern border between Korea and Manchuria, had just completed a railroad bridge which led nowhere at the moment but which stood ready to be connected with a northern terminus of the Manchurian railroad system in the event that the Army should need a second strategic entryway into Manchuria. A few days later he heard that Lieutenant Colonel Ishiwara Kanji, the most brilliant strategist in the ubiquitous Major Suzuki's Study Group, had been posted to the Kwantung Army to begin staff planning for the conquest of Manchuria.[10]

---

[10] Strategist Ishiwara later testified at the war crimes trials that he had orders from the Emperor "to use force if necessary."

Once more Tanaka consulted Prime-Minister-Maker Saionji. Once more Saionji encouraged Tanaka to pursue his investigation of the Chang Tso-lin affair, to let the chips fall where they might, and to keep Hirohito fully informed of all implications as the case developed.

Prime Minister Tanaka returned from Saionji's villa on the beach, without making any promises. Basically a somewhat honest, simple man, never sure of himself in his role of antagonist to the Throne, he became frightened by the subtlety of the situation in which he found himself. Finally, after a week of anguish, he decided to forget the Chang Tso-lin case and smother it with inaction. He conceded warily to Hirohito that a suitable show of discipline might have to be meted out to certain Japanese Army officers. And he protested noncommittally to Saionji that nothing could be done at present because everyone in official Tokyo was preparing for the imminent ceremony of Hirohito's official enthronement in the old capital of Kyoto.

On November 10, 1928, Western correspondents followed Hirohito's progress from the Kyoto railroad station to the palace where Emperor Meiji had been born. There a few select Japanese saw him mount the antique lacquered throne of his ancestors and stood by as witnesses when he withdrew into a cluster of specially constructed ceremonial huts on the palace grounds for an all-night solitary vigil with the presence of the sun goddess. Throughout the next month, Hirohito's popularity ran high and he seemed unusually dedicated and preoccupied. Prime Minister Tanaka ignored representations from Saionji and let the Chang Tso-lin matter slumber.

THE BANDIT'S SON

Chang Hsueh-liang, the thirty-year-old son of the murdered Chang Tso-lin, was a dope addict. During a bout of influenza, a Japanese doctor had dosed him with opium and he had caught the habit. The Japanese assumed he was debilitated. He seemed to them a war-lord's spoiled child, who had traveled abroad and acquired the manners of a Western gentleman. But Chang Hsueh-liang had kept a firm grasp on the realities of politics in his homeland.

Beneath his silken exterior, Chang had the same courage, cunning, and ruthlessness as his father. In addition he had a streak of idealism in him which made him devoted to the cause of Republicanism in China, the cause ostensibly of Chiang Kai-shek. Over the years he was to become Chiang Kai-shek's conscience, a constant reminder of the ideals which Chiang Kai-shek often lost sight of in pursuit of means. A David-and-Jonathan relationship would grow up between the two. It still exists to this day, 1970, when Chang Hsueh-liang, now seventy-one, remains a pampered prisoner, under house arrest, in the Taiwan of Chiang Kai-shek, who is now eighty-two.

The strange firm friendship between these two politicians—both renowned for their harems, their evident heterosexuality—began in the fall
of 1928 when Chiang Kai-shek, at the behest of the Japanese, recognized Chang Hsueh-liang as the new ruler of Manchuria. On December 29,
1928, Chang Hsueh-liang responded by raising the KMT flag on every
government building around Mukden. In the early stages of opium addiction, burning his candle fervidly at both ends, Chang felt that Chiang must
be reminded of Manchuria's organic place in the body of China. He
realized, too, that the Japanese would consider his gesture a hostile act,
violating the spirit of their unwritten agreement with Chiang Kai-shek.

He was right. In the first week of January 1929, Japanese agents began
to post anti-Chang handbills on walls throughout the three Manchurian
provinces. The text of one of them—totally at variance with the facts—
stated in part:

> Since Chang Tso-lin captured the Three Eastern Provinces . . . good people
> have suffered from his evil government, causing the neighboring powers
> to interfere in our domestic affairs. For this reason heavenly punishment was
> inflicted upon him and he fell under a bomb. The son, Chang Hsueh-liang,
> who succeeded him is worse than his father to such an extent that the land
> has been turned red and the sufferings of the people are beyond description.

To this challenge the thirty-year-old Chang Hsueh-liang responded with
a bravado that caught up Chiang Kai-shek and carried him in its political
rip tide. Chang and Chiang both knew that the only hope for preserving
the integrity of Manchuria, short of defeating a Japanese attempt at conquest, lay in making Manchuria seem an exploitable puppet state, in effect
playing for time. Old hands in the Japanese Army had hoped to manipulate
the young Manchurian leader through a general named Yang Yu-tang and
through the chief of the Chinese railroads in Manchuria. But on January
10, 1929, young, idealistic Chang Hsueh-liang, suffering from withdrawal
during one of his earliest attempts to kick the opium habit, confounded
everyone by inviting these two worthies to an evening of mah-jongg in his
Mukden palace and having them both shot as they entered the game room.
He announced that Yang had conspired with Toyko to become the chief
executive of a Japanese-managed Manchurian Republic. At the same time
he sent 100,000 Manchurian dollars—some 40,000 U.S. ones—to Yang's
widow. Every Chinese patriot applauded his merciful dispatch and liberal
generosity.

FACE WASHING

Chiang Kai-shek was impressed by the popular support which Chang
Hsueh-liang had uncovered and refused to disassociate himself from it.
For the first time Hirohito's Big Brothers began to talk of Chiang Kai-shek
as an enemy. Bitter "re-evaluation of the Manchuria problem" filled the

front pages of Tokyo newspapers. The American manager of United Press in the Orient, Miles W. Vaughn, reported home that the only question was whether Japan's Kwantung Army would seize Manchuria at once or wait, "believing that an opportunity will soon present itself to take not only Manchuria but most of North China as well."

Colonel Komoto Daisaku, the unpunished Reliable who had murdered Chang Tso-lin, cabled a memo to Hirohito and the General Staff, stating: "Any rational and thorough disposition of outstanding issues in Manchuria and Mongolia must start with the elimination of the Nanking government [of Chiang Kai-shek], to which end a war with China must be expected, and one with the U.S., too, must be considered."

Hirohito was not yet prepared to abandon his hopes for Chiang Kai-shek or to alienate the rest of the world. Field Marshal Prince Kanin, the senior member of the imperial family, warned that Manchuria was a huge country and could not be occupied without careful military planning. Young Prince Konoye, Hirohito's chosen familiar from the Fujiwara family, warned that domestic opinion was not yet prepared for a war of conquest. Prime-Minister-Maker Saionji, the Fujiwara elder, inferior to Konoye in hereditary rank but vastly superior to him in seniority and influence, showed every inclination to cause real trouble if an attempt were made to seize Manchuria now. All through February and March of 1929 Saionji's friends spread rumors in Constitutionalist circles that, if the investigation of Chang Tso-lin's murder were pursued, Hirohito's "august face would be muddy."

Hirohito refused to be embarrassed but saw that he must proceed with caution. He let the members of the cabal know that they must plan the conquest of Manchuria thoroughly, down to the last rifle bullet. While preparations were in progress, he asked that the imperial face be cleared of all taint. Through Lord Privy Seal Count Makino, he arranged for two of the most loyal members of the cabal to shoulder some of the responsibility for the failure of the cabal's China policy. The ubiquitous Major Suzuki Tei-ichi was sent on a ten-month leave to Europe, and Big Brother Kido Koichi, at work on industrial mobilization plans in the Agriculture and Commerce Ministry, was persuaded to take a year's sabbatical in the United States. The two rustications were meant to indicate to the informed public that events in China had displeased Hirohito and that he had privately punished two of the men responsible for them. Having made these gestures, Hirohito went ahead undaunted with his secret military planning and insistently pressed Prime Minister Tanaka for a satisfactory burial of the Chang Tso-lin scandal.

In April 1929 Hirohito summoned the commanders of Japan's seventeen standing divisions for their annual individual audiences with him. This year they were known to have two worries which Hirohito sought to allay. They feared that Chang Tso-lin's murder would set a precedent of action without official imperial orders that might undermine Army discipline.

And they were excited by rumors of secret General Staff planning for a full-scale invasion of Manchuria. It was Hirohito's task to tell the division chiefs that Komoto would be punished for Chang Tso-lin's murder and to make clear to them that the General Staff's blueprints for Manchuria were contingency plans which would be used or modified according to events. As the division chiefs entered and withdrew from Hirohito's presence, Hirohito learned from an aide that he was making the right impression and that the division chiefs would support him fully.

Prime Minister Tanaka discovered that, after Hirohito had applied his magic touch, the murder of Chang Tso-lin was no longer an issue worth mentioning. Nevertheless, at Saionji's bidding, Tanaka refused to settle the dust by staging a nominal show of disciplinary action. On June 28, 1929, Hirohito finally called Tanaka to the Throne Room and asked him, disingenuously, if the Chang Tso-lin case were yet solved. Tanaka replied that, after all, despite his previous reports, no Army staff officers were implicated but only policemen and the like who could be disciplined by administrative action at a low level. In effect Tanaka was refusing to stage the mock trials which Hirohito had requested and was trying to tell the public that his investigations had led to the taboo gates of the palace.

In great displeasure Hirohito dismissed Tanaka with a wave of the hand and one icy statement of fact: "What you say now differs from your previous explanations." As soon as Tanaka had bowed himself from the audience chamber, Hirohito summoned Grand Chamberlain Suzuki Kantaro, the clever old cigar-smoking Taoist who would stand beside the Throne as prime minister during the last desperate, plot-filled months of World War II. "I cannot understand what Tanaka says," complained Hirohito to Suzuki. "I do not ever wish to see him again."

When the sentence of banishment from the Imperial Presence was repeated to Tanaka, he wept. He asked several times thereafter for an audience but was always refused. And so, three days later, without notifying his Cabinet or the Constitutionalist party whip beforehand, he abruptly had his resignation delivered to the Throne. It was accepted immediately, and no future prime minister of Japan would ever again venture to oppose Hirohito so openly.

Three months later, in the early morning hours of September 29, 1929, Tanaka died. It was widely rumored that he had committed suicide as a gesture of patriotic protest against national policy. According to a more explicit account, however, which was circulated with relish by members of the Court, he attended a political rally, got drunk, and later expired in the arms of his geisha mistress.

In May 1929, a few days after Hirohito's audiences with the Army division chiefs, War Minister Shirakawa had complied with imperial wishes and reposted Colonel Komoto, the bridge blower, to a stand-by position with the 9th Division in Kanazawa on the Japanese north coast. In July, when Tanaka resigned as prime minister, Komoto had been officially stripped of command and given a year to find himself before being mustered out into the first reserve. Token amends were thus made for Chang Tso-lin's murder, and both Hirohito and Chang Hsueh-liang pretended to be satisfied that the incident was closed. In fact Komoto had been rewarded, for he would remain in Manchuria enjoying various sinecures in the business world and amassing a small fortune. Today his son, Komoto Toshio, is a prominent industrialist, a Diet man, and an inner member of Japan's ruling Liberal Democratic party.

The other conspirators in Chang's assassination went unpunished. In August 1929, Major General Tatekawa, the Peerless Pimp, was promoted chief of the key Second Department of the General Staff: Army Intelligence.

There was one conspirator, however, whom the Chinese were not disposed to let off so easily. Giga Nobuya, the man wrapped in a blanket on the caboose of the murder train, was promoted after the killing to lieutenant colonel. Since he had been one of Chang Tso-lin's closest advisors for many years, partisans of the dead war lord felt that he had played Judas. They hunted him from Mukden in Manchuria to Hiroshima in southern Japan, to Sendai in northern Japan, to Tsitsihar on the Manchurian-Siberian frontier. In 1937 Prince Kanin's son turned over to him a walled villa in Tientsin as a secure place of hiding. But to no avail; there on January 24, 1938, after a decade's stalking, a Manchurian assassin finally reached him with a bullet. Thus young Chang made at least a token revenge to dispel the curse which, according to the Chinese Book of Rites, falls "on him who suffers his father's murderer to exist on the same earth with him."

JAPAN'S PREWAR GOVERNMENT

EMPEROR   NOBILITY   PEOPLE

Palace Institutions

Imperial Family Councillors: all adult male members of the imperial family down to fifth generation in descent from an Emperor; through most of Hirohito's reign, 25 princes; to advise Emperor on matters affecting family, e.g., property, marriages, princely peccadillos, major decisions of state

Privy Councillors: 26 elder statesmen appointed by Emperor on advice of prime minister; to advise Emperor on any question he refers to it for opinion

Lord Privy Seal: to give Emperor day-to-day political advice

Secretary and staff: to keep track of imperial seals and all documents of state to which they are affixed

Imperial tombs and shrines

Imperial archives

Peerage and Heraldry Bureau: to keep track of all noble houses

Peers' and Peeresses' Schools

Code Research Institute

Spy Service Directorship, to co-ordinate and keep track of all Japanese espionage; roughly equivalent to C.I.A.

Grand Chamberlain: to advise Emperor on matters of his personal health and recreation and, in practice, on matters

General Staffs

Army Chief of Staff

General Affairs Bureau

Organization and Mobilization Section

First Department: Operations

Second Department: Intelligence
Russia Desk
Europe-America Desk
China Desk

Special Service Organs: political counterintelligence overseas

Third Department: Transport and Communications

Kwantung Army
Korean Army
North China Army
Taiwan Army
Tokyo Guard
War College

Navy Chief of Staff

First Department: Operations

Second Department: Intelligence

Commander-in-Chief, Combined Fleet
First Fleet
Second Fleet
etc.

Naval Staff College

Inspectorships

Inspector General of Military Education

Cabinet

Prime Minister: appointed by Emperor on advice of Prince Saionji and elder statesmen; until 1932, often the head of a political party

Foreign Minister
Foreign Ministry
Ambassadors

Home Minister
Thought Police
Tokyo (Metropolitan) Police
Prefectural governors and prefectural police

Finance
Board of the Budget
Bank of Japan
Yokohama Specie Bank

War
Military Affairs Bureau
Military Affairs Section
Aviation Headquarters
Personnel Bureau
Appointments Section
Soldiers' Affairs Bureau
Army Investigation Committee
Press Relations Squad

Secret Police: semi-autonomous, responsible to commanders overseas and expected to work with Home and Justice

Prisoner of War Administration (founded 1942)

Navy: administered naval affairs through bureaucracy similar to War Minister's

Diet

Function: to approve or veto *increases* in national budget and to discuss legislation presented by prime minister to Emperor

House of Representatives (Lower House)
466 politicians elected by some 14 million eligible male voters (out of population of 70 million, 1940)

House of Peers
to guide House of Representatives; included:
66 rich men elected by the 6,000 highest taxpayers in Japan
150 of lesser nobility elected by the 1,000-odd adult male members of same
all princes and marquises
125 imperial nominees selected for erudition or meritorious service

liaison committees

Government publications and propaganda

Commerce and Industry

Agriculture and Forestry

Communications

Railways

Colonization

Prosperous Asia Institute: semi-autonomous, to administer occupied areas in China

South Sea Development Board: semi-autonomous, to administer conquests in Southeast Asia

Welfare

National health

Food rationing

Cabinet Planning Board: to write all legislation discussed by Diet (began as inspection board, 1935; became planning board, 1941, and took charge of all domestic legislation and mobilization for the war

Imperial Stables Bureau

Imperial Poetry Bureau

Imperial Recreations Board

Households of Crown Prince, Empress, Empress Dowager

Imperial Household Minister: to supervise and manage imperial fortune: investments, rents from 3.2 million acres of crown lands, upkeep of 23 secondary palaces

Imperial Treasury

Maintenance and Works Bureau

Board of Imperial Auditors

Chief Imperial Aide-de-Camp: to advise Emperor on military matters

Imperial Naval Aide-de-Camp

Other aides-de-camp

Supreme War Council: High-ranking Army and Navy officers appointed by Emperor—the military counterpart of the Privy Council

Board of Field Marshals and Fleet Admirals

Imperial Headquarters: Founded 1937 to centralize Emperor's command functions in palace; top ministers and bureau chiefs from General Staff and War and Navy ministries plus permanent palace staff to co-ordinate all war plans and maps for Emperor's reference

PART FOUR

RUBICON MANCHURIA

10

SEA POWER

(1929–1930)

CHOICE OF A LION

On the evening of July 3, 1929, the seventy-nine-year-old Prime-Minister-Maker Saionji had his chauffeur drive up past Ueno Park in Tokyo so that he could get out for a short walk among the people and the plum trees.[1] It was dusk and the plainclothesmen assigned to him hovered behind at a respectful distance. A group of office workers were picnicking under the trees, dancing tangos and Charlestons to the records of a wind-up Victrola. Two of the men, over their bottles of beer, were talking with vociferous pride about Tokyo's growing subway system, opened in 1927. Two others were acclaiming a levelheaded editorial in *Mainichi* which came out for nonintervention in China and reduction in armaments. Their girl friends, flirting and frolicking in the summer heat, seemed altogether unself-conscious in their chic Western cloche hats, silk stockings, and gauzy, high-hemmed dresses. Never had the smiling people of Tokyo appeared more peaceable, pleasure-loving, and modern.

Saionji was gratified by what he saw. "The trend of the times," as he told a friend a few days later, was running against "palace imperialism." There would be no place soon for police despotism and militarism in Japan. In the end Hirohito would have to bow to the sentiments of his people and relinquish the warlike ambitions of his youth.

Saionji had come up to Tokyo to recommend to Hirohito a successor for General Tanaka, the prime minister who had been made the villain

---

[1] This and the two succeeding vignettes of men's minds that night are based on the recollections and assumptions of friends who met the principals during the weeks following. I have added some explanatory background information to make the thoughts intelligible.

of the Chang Tso-lin killing. Tanaka was the president of the Constitutionalist party. Hirohito was accustomed to thinking of the other party,
the anti-Constitutionalists, as pliant instruments of the Throne. And so,
when Saionji had nominated the president of the anti-Constitutionalists as
the next prime minister, Hirohito had accepted with alacrity.

Saionji, however, had high hopes that the new government would show
a mind of its own. Its prime minister, Hamaguchi Osachi, was a tiny man
of humble parentage. His stubborn convictions and fiery indignation had
won him the nickname of "the Lion." He had been responsible, in 1927,
for uniting all the various anti-Constitutionalist tongs founded by friends
of the Throne in the past and for proclaiming them a new mass party,
responsive to the needs of constituents and capable of presenting the Constitutionalists with their first professionally managed political opposition.[2]
Saionji had backed and had arranged cartel financing for the new party
from its inception. He saw promise in its existence of a mature, two-party
system which might become increasingly difficult for anyone to manipulate
from the back rooms of the palace.

The foreign minister in Lion Hamaguchi's new cabinet was Baron
Shidehara Kijuro.[3] Like most diplomats he was inclined to say what was
expected of him but Saionji considered him basically a well-meaning man.
His statement on assuming office called for "co-existence and co-prosperity"
with China. Saionji had looked over the text that very afternoon and had
approved it. He could not know that the term co-prosperity, as later used
in Japan's World War II "Co-Prosperity Sphere," would acquire an infamous place in history as a byword of hypocritical propaganda.

Saionji returned the next morning to his home, Sit-and-Fish Villa, on
the seashore at Okitsu. He was pleased with the new government he had
arranged for Japan and settled back complacently into the pastimes of his
retired life: the reading of risqué French novels and the carving of sig-
nature-seals and cane handles for old friends.

YOUNG ARMY GENIUS

The same evening that Saionji took his stroll in Ueno Park to look at
the people, a group of Japanese Army officers, a thousand miles to the west,
crossed the border between Japan's leasehold on the Kwantung Peninsula
and Manchuria proper. Their papers declared them "tourists on a sightseeing trip." But as their train bowled north through flat fields of millet
and soya bean they turned their cameras and field glasses on every passing
hamlet and pointed out to one another features of the landscape on which
they took written notes.

[2] Trading on the magic of the Constitutionalists' own name, Hamaguchi had
named the new party the *Rikken Minseito* or Democratic Constitutionalists.

[3] Later the "moderate of the Peace Faction" who would become prime minister
under MacArthur in October 1945.

"It is like an ocean," breathed one of the captains in awe.

"Yes," mused the lieutenant colonel in charge, "on such a terrain we may have to adopt naval tactics."

No one asked the lieutenant colonel what he meant by this remark—something fluid, they assumed, something brilliant and dynamic—for this was Lieutenant Colonel Ishiwara Kanji, the most original young strategist in the Japanese Army, the member of the ubiquitous Suzuki's Study Group whom Emperor Hirohito had hand-picked for the planning of the Manchurian venture in late 1928. During the eight months since his arrival in Port Arthur, the leasehold capital, Ishiwara had spent all his time reading books, studying maps, and talking to old hands in the Kwantung Army officer corps. Now he was out for twelve days of personal reconnaissance into Manchurian topography. When the twelve days were up, he and his staff must begin to develop their ideas on paper for the scrutiny of the Emperor.

The light of sunset warmed the drab colors in the railroad coach and softened the perpetual scowl on Lieutenant Colonel Ishiwara's boyish face. The members of his staff did not dream of disturbing his reverie. They adored him personally, treasured him as a military genius of the nation, and also revered him as a religious leader and prophet. At forty, Ishiwara had made a name for himself as the *enfant terrible* of the Army. Few other commanders could be so gentle with subordinates, so acidly blunt with senior officers. He invented pet names for all his superiors which he did not hesitate to use to their faces. He addressed the commander of the Army in Taiwan as "Daddy Raccoon." Colonel Tojo, the later World War II prime minister, he called "Dear Dunderhead." From his father, a spellbinding Buddhist priest, Ishiwara had inherited a huge following in the militant, gong-beating, knight-templar sect of Buddhism, the Nichiren. Returning home in 1925, after three years of service with the cabal's European spy ring in Berlin, Ishiwara had been met at every station platform by welcoming committees of his father's Nichiren devotees. He had ingratiated himself with them by delivering a set platform speech, telling them how he had always worn traditional samurai dress to Reichstag banquets, how he had always kept chopsticks tucked up his kimono sleeve with which to delight his hostesses.

Now, as the young prophet stared out the train window at the rich, unconquered farmlands of southern Manchuria, he was acutely conscious of the trust placed in him. It was his bold idea that Japan might take Manchuria from the inside out, by an action more resembling a coup d'etat than an invasion. Japan's right of way in the South Manchuria Railroad would provide the necessary access and privileges. And infiltration and subversion would be far less expensive and dangerous than outright conquest. Chang Tso-lin's son, Chang Hsueh-liang, had a tremendous numerical superiority in troops. But if the timing were perfect; if privates, officers, diplomats, and politicians were all properly coached; if a Manchurian government of puppets were ready in the wings to present a fair face at once to the League of Nations; then Ishiwara would be able to take Manchuria for Hirohito like a magician in a flash of powder.

If Ishiwara could do all this—and he felt that he could—he would be in a position to advise the Emperor on the policies which the Empire should pursue in years to come. The righteous course for the nation was a theme close to Ishiwara's heart, one on which he was writing a book.[4] In his almost completed manuscript, he foresaw harmony, alliance, and ultimately unification for Japan, Manchuria, and China. This unification of Asia would be followed, perhaps in thirty years, by a "total war" between yellows and whites. If Japan could supply moral leadership, she would gain the support of Asia's masses and the total war would end inevitably in the annihilation of the West.

Lieutenant Colonel Ishiwara knew that his dreams were shared in general terms by most of the young officers in Hirohito's cabal. All of them agreed that the first order of business was military seizure of Manchuria. Beyond that horizon, however, loomed fundamental moral differences of opinion. The visionaries, of whom Lieutenant Colonel Ishiwara was one, felt that with the addition of Manchuria, Japan should perfect herself as a self-sufficient theocratic state. There should be a thoroughgoing domestic reform to make Japan a classless, co-operative, single-family society inspired by filial obedience to the Emperor, the father. Once this uniquely Japanese form of communistic utopia was realized, it would serve as a model for the other nations of Asia. And when the racial Armageddon came, the other nations of Asia would voluntarily side with Japan and trust themselves to Japanese leadership. It was axiomatic that the Armageddon would begin against the largest Western colony in the Orient, belonging to "the natural enemy of the Imperial Throne," namely, the Siberia of Bolshevik Russia.

The pragmatists of the cabal—and Ishiwara was afraid that Hirohito might be one of them—scoffed at the idea of idealism in other Asiatic countries. They foresaw no way to unify the Continent except through conquest. They counted on the raw materials of Southeast Asia as prerequisites for Armageddon. They anticipated that the collective Russian society might be persuaded to remain on the sidelines. They believed that the first enemy would be the "individualistic societies," the democracies with colonies in Southeast Asia: France, Great Britain, the Netherlands, and the United States. Lieutenant Colonel Ishiwara feared that this pragmatist view would lead Japan into a war which would be unjustified from a moral standpoint and would be dangerously premature from a practical one.

Last week Kita Ikki, the ideologist of the visionaries, had accused Lord Privy Seal Count Makino, the patron of the pragmatists, of accepting kick-

---

[4] *Sekai Saishu Senso*, The Ultimate World War.

backs in the handling of imperial estates in the northern Japanese island of Hokkaido. If such accusations were made in the cabal of officers closest to the Emperor, the rift between visionaries and pragmatists might ultimately spread to the ranks and the national program might be jeopardized. As the light went out over the Manchurian plains and as Lieutenant Colonel Ishiwara unbuttoned his Army tunic for a nap before his train arrived in Mukden, he conceded to one of the young officers in his suite that the military problems of the future were minor in comparison to the political ones.

YOUNG NAVY GENIUS

That same evening of July 3, 1929, when Saionji walked in Ueno Park and Lieutenant Colonel Ishiwara began spying out the land of Manchuria, the naval officer who would later plan and execute the 1941 raid on Pearl Harbor emerged from the Tokyo villa of his patron and protégé, the Empress's brother, Prince Asa-akira. Captain Yamamoto Isoroku of the Naval General Staff was a friend of Lieutenant Colonel Ishiwara in Manchuria. Indeed the forty-five-year-old Yamamoto was considered to be Ishiwara's naval counterpart: the most brilliant of the younger generation of naval strategists. But Yamamoto was no pale, irrascible prophet. He was a calm, diffident professional, a muscular athlete, a clown and storyteller. The son of a humble schoolteacher, he had no following except his shipmates, no conviction except his self-confidence.

Captain Yamamoto had called at the villa of Prince Asa-akira in order to sign the guest register in the foyer as a token of condolence for the illness of the Empress's father, Prince Kuni. Old Prince Kuni had severe ulcers and little hope of living out the year. He had championed the development of air power in Japan since before World War I, and Captain Yamamoto had been the brightest of his disciples.

After graduating first in his class at Naval Staff College, Yamamoto had gone on, under Prince Kuni's sponsorship, to two years at Harvard. Already appreciating the problems of the future, he had specialized there in the manufacture of petroleum and aviation gas. He had hitchhiked to Mexico during one of his vacations and spent a summer slumming in the Mexican oil fields. Back in Japan in 1921, he had put in two years as an instructor at the Naval Staff College and at the University Lodging House in the palace. In 1923 he had taken over planning for air development in the Naval General Staff. And in 1924 he had assumed charge of the Navy's top-secret Air Development Station on the banks of Kasumi-go-Ura, the Misty Lagoon, a lake the size of Lake George some 30 miles northeast of Tokyo. There he had worked with Empress Nagako's cousin, young test pilot Prince Yamashina, to develop naval torpedo-bombing techniques superior to any in the West. There, in the mists, preparing for the day when Japan would have task forces of aircraft carriers, Yamamoto had taught a generation of Navy pilots to land on the simulated flight decks of wharves and barges. After brief stints of duty as an attaché in Washington and as a skipper in the fleet, he had returned to the Navy General Staff in 1928 as a full-time planner and proponent of non-conventional weapons.

Now, as he had just confirmed in his brief call on Empress Nagako's brother, Yamamoto was to be offered a new assignment as chief technical advisor to the Japanese delegation at the forthcoming naval disarmament conference in London. If he accepted the appointment, he would be expected to trade on former friendships in the West in order to deceive the other naval powers as much as possible. On the other hand he would have the opportunity to help work out the international diplomatic bargain on which would depend the building of a powerful naval air force.

Outside Prince Asa-akira's villa, Captain Yamamoto broke his usual rules of frugality by hailing a taxicab instead of a ricksha. He gave the driver the address of a teahouse—the equivalent of a nightclub—in Tsukiji near Tokyo's big Western hospital, St. Luke's. There he knew he would find a convivial hostess and a group of fellow officers with whom he could waste the evening while he sorted out his thoughts.

The naval disarmament question was politically complicated. The shipbuilding ratios agreed on in Washington in 1922 were unpopular with many Japanese because they acknowledged in legal form Japan's position of naval inferiority to the United States and Great Britain. At the same time the ratio system had released funds from capital-ship construction and had made possible the secret naval development plan which Japan had pursued since 1922. No one could deny that the secret plan had vastly enhanced the strength of the Japanese fleet relative to the American and British fleets. Japan now had four of those new experimental ships, aircraft carriers, in which Yamamoto saw the future of naval warfare. She was building destroyers superior in speed and armament to anything which Western nations had on their drawing boards. Her new cruisers were in fact the precursors of pocket battleships. Her submarine fleet was the world's third largest. Every year since 1923 the Diet had approved without once demurring the unearmarked "supplementary naval funds" which had made these new weapons possible. And while Japan had been developing novel ships to the limit of her capacity, the United States had not yet even launched her allotted quota of conventional battleships and cruisers.

Japan would soon be equipped, Yamamoto felt, to defend the western Pacific against U.S. fleet attack in any hypothetical war. Continued development of unorthodox weapons, in particular of aircraft, would make it possible, if necessary, for Japan to fight an offensive war. Perhaps Japan must have this threatening capability to gain equality among nations. If so, she must continue to avoid an expensive competition with the United States in the building of battleships. The unpopular ratio system would have to be kept and Yamamoto, at the disarmament conference, would have to take the responsibility for seeing that it was kept.

Yamamoto's taxicab rounded the southernmost salient of the palace walls and sped on southeast towards the fashionable stews of Tsukiji ward. Yamamoto tried to imagine the welcome he would receive at the teahouse to which he was going if he did not have the right introductions. The very thought made him squirm with humiliation. It was not the best of the teahouses but it was on the same block with them. Someday he would graduate to the Sign of the Carp, down the alley, where Emperor Taisho's prime minister, Katsura Taro, and Hirohito's Prime-Minister-Maker Saionji had found their mistresses in years past.

An hour later, in a private room at the teahouse, Captain Yamamoto was drinking saké and gambling money against favors in a card-guessing game with a popular apprentice geisha. As he touched the backs of the cards, he did his best to conceal the fact that two fingers were missing from his left hand. They had been blown off by a Russian shell in one of the naval engagements of the war of 1904–05. It was the challenge of hiding them when they were most exposed which had first drawn him to card games. And now card games were an essential part of his philosophy: bluff or be bluffed; peek as little as necessary; study routine combinations with the utmost care for they were the ones which concealed the greatest opportunities for subtlety and surprise. For Yamamoto card games were a social occasion in which he could gauge the mentality of potential adversaries or quarry. He had learned to play poker while assessing his classmates at Harvard. He had become an enthusiastic bridge player among his fellow naval attachés in Washington.

Having lost money gracefully to his entertainer, he returned with her to the outer room of the teahouse, traded jokes with a carousing circle of fellow naval officers, and had a word with the proprietress. Someday, he promised her, when he became a famous admiral, he would make her hostel famous and bring to it half the officers of the fleet. At the moment, he said apologetically, he could offer her nothing but a Havana sent to him by a friend in America. As predicted by the young geisha, the proprietress admitted that she was inordinately fond of cigars and gave permission for the girl to leave with him. Yamamoto made a triumphant exit with his conquest at his heels. A recently promoted captain from Yamamoto's last fleet command, the aircraft carrier *Akagi,* led the other captains and rear admirals in the room in a rousing banzai to cheer him on his way.

In those days in Japan, a trained entertainer, attached to one of the good teahouses, did not give her favors lightly. To have one for a night was to have her for many nights. And this was possible only for a man with money or with powerful friends to put in the right words for him with the leaders of the entertainment guild in the Black Dragon Society. In his own right Yamamoto had no way to keep such a mistress. It was hard enough for him on his captain's salary to support his wife and his little home. Then again, a mistress was a recognized sign of success, bringing glamor and prestige to a man in his career.

The girl took Yamamoto to an inn where they were expected. She found—so she liked to say in later years—that beneath his façade of rough-and-tumble boyish charm he was shy and serious. A few hours later, in great pleasure, Yamamoto decided that she was indispensable to him. He would accept the assignment offered to him by Prince Asa-akira. He would go to London, play bridge and poker, and negotiate a continuation of the ratio system which would give the Japanese Navy time.

HIROHITO IMPATIENT

The coming negotiations in London caused Hirohito to turn his attention to the Navy and to the long-range objectives of his reign. The Army might conquer Manchuria, but it was the Navy on which he must ultimately rely in the dimly envisaged war with the West.

Hirohito's great-grandfather Emperor Komei had vowed to rid the sacred homeland of infidels and to safeguard it by surrounding it with a buffer zone. The discredited samurai of Choshu had created a small buffer zone by adding Korea to the Empire. The modern Army thought only in terms of deepening this zone by acquiring more miles of dry land on the Continent in which to maneuver regiments and dig trenches.

Since about 1900, the imperial family had taken a more sophisticated view of the national program, based on a growing appreciation of trade and technology. In order to face down any challenge by the barbarians, the Empire had to be a self-sufficient military bloc, including within its borders not only the buffer zones on which to fight invasion but also the raw materials with which to maintain a war machine that would be a standing deterrent. In terms of the physical geography of Asia, this meant that Japan must control the oil of Borneo, the rubber of Malaya, and the rice and metals of Java and Sumatra.

To extend the Empire to the islands off the coasts of Southeast Asia and also to create a buffer zone on the open Pacific side of Japan, a navy was needed capable of meeting the U.S. and British fleets. The Army need be strong enough to handle only the relatively crude and ill-equipped land forces to be found in China and Siberia. The Navy by comparison must meet the most demanding technological standards of the times.

For all Japan's amazing industrial growth during the last seventy years, she was still an underdeveloped nation. If her Navy was to rival the world's finest, it must be given a disproportionate share of the national budget for at least a decade to come. Hirohito had known for years that it would take a long time to build up the Navy to required strength, and also that the nation must be perfectly disciplined in patience and silence while the build-up proceeded. The Army must not become jealous. The Navy must not grow proud. Foreign nations must not be alarmed.

In considering the arduous task ahead, Hirohito in the summer of 1929 felt impatience. He did not see in the widening rift in the cabal, or in the emergence of a second intractable political party, or in the continuing fashion-following, peace-loving, pleasure-seeking frivolity of the masses, any sign of the national dedication which was called for.

"I have always tried to leave domestic politics to my advisors," he told an old school friend, "but I sometimes wonder if they are necessary, or at least if they need be so complicated."

All summer long Hirohito continued to worry his chief vassals with such complaints. Unless domestic politics could show some progress, he said, it would become necessary to tear down the chrysanthemum curtain, step forward onto the apron of the stage, and take personal charge of the state. This was the sort of self-destructive threat which Hirohito had been making to chamberlains ever since he had first thrown a tantrum as a child. But the chamberlains were still impressed. Lord Privy Seal Makino begged him repeatedly to be prudent. Prime-Minister-Maker Saionji, from his seaside villa, sent him a cautionary message:

> Bismarck firmly believed that Germany would expand in the future and although he was strongly determined to realize this belief he was also aware of the fact that it could not be done immediately for lack of power. Therefore Bismarck paid his respects to a seemingly unnecessary extent to Disraeli in London and Napoleon the Third in Paris.

A WIN WITHOUT TRUMPS

Count Makino and other subtle minds at Court advised Hirohito to make the most of the worrisome naval negotiations pending in London by turning them into a noisy national debate which would arouse the martial spirit of the people and might serve also to confuse and soften Western attitudes toward Japan.

On October 10, 1929, Hirohito called together in his presence the Cabinet and his own Navy General Staff and had them agree privately that, if better terms were not negotiable, Japan should accept continuance of the 10:10:6 ratio set at Washington in 1922, which gave Japan 60 per cent of the fleet strength allowed the United States or Great Britain. It being only good statecraft, however, to go to the London Naval Conference asking as much as possible, Prime Minister Hamaguchi emerged from the meeting announcing to reporters that his government wanted a semblance of parity with Western nations and would insist on 10:10:7 or fight.

The venal Japanese press immediately mounted a campaign to show that naval limitations were unpopular in Japan. Out of a drowsy autumn sky readers were given reasons to think that limitations would impose personal hardships on them. Dockyard workers would be idle. There would be no room for young sailors in the Navy. The influential periodical *Nihon oyobi Nihonjin,* Japan and the Japanese—a publication founded by Hirohito's favorite tutor, Sugiura Jugo, and now staffed by Sugiura's disciples—devoted an entire issue to the question of national defense. Some of the most trusted members of Hirohito's cabal contributed articles on "National Mobilization, the Basis for the National Defense," on "Japan and the Air Defense of Her Cities," and on "The Coming War and Our Navy."

On October 24, 1929, the New York stock market collapsed in a heap of ticker tape, and the free economics of the world were plunged into a decade of financial night. Japan had already survived a small depression of her own, and the co-operative measures of control worked out between the government and Japan's handful of banking families now proved adequate to prevent the world panic from affecting the domestic economy.

The Wall Street crash greatly improved Japan's bargaining position at the naval conference because it stripped Western delegates of attentive home audiences. Hirohito personally instructed Japan's delegation, before it left for London in November, to hold out for the 10:10:7 ratio until it received his instructions to accept less. On the eve of its departure Saionji summoned the chief delegates to his home on the seashore to give them his own instructions. He exhorted them to reach an amicable arrangement with the West at all costs.

One of the delegates, Navy Minister Takarabe Takeshi, asked Saionji whether it would not be better to take a straightforward approach to the Emperor, the public, and the world. "How would it be," he inquired, "if we convoked a council in the Imperial Presence in order to unify public opinion and decide, once and for all, on the claims made by the Empire." Saionji told Takarabe that he would consider the suggestion, but as soon as Takarabe had gone, Saionji sent a message to Lord Privy Seal Makino, Hirohito's chief civilian advisor, registering "absolute opposition" to the idea. Saionji still hoped to change Hirohito's expansionist ambitions, and he feared that Hirohito, if pressed to take a stand, might ask Japan to claim half the earth.

The Navy minister, Takarabe, and a former and future prime minister, Wakatsuki Reijiro, led the Japanese delegation to London. Its day-to-day decisions, however, were made by the cabal's Captain Yamamoto, the later hero-villain of Pearl Harbor. En route to London for the formal part of the conference, Yamamoto spent three weeks in Washington negotiating an informal pre-conference agreement with the United States. He dealt at a high level through an old Washington acquaintance, Captain Allen Buchanan, who was the naval aide to President Herbert Hoover.[5] He

---

[5] Buchanan was prematurely retired in 1933 from what seemed to be a brilliant career in the Navy and was not awarded the customary retirement rank of rear admiral. He died in 1940.

learned that the United States was prepared to declare a moratorium on the construction of battleships and aircraft carriers until 1936.

Yamamoto readily agreed that Japan would do the same. Battleships, he felt, cost far more than they were worth and aircraft carriers could be replaced in the western, Japanese half of the Pacific with runways on the permanently anchored flight decks of Japan's mandated islands. The only problem, then, was to establish a United States–Japanese ratio for cruisers, destroyers, and submarines. Japan wanted a 10:7 ratio; the United States wanted a 10:6 ratio. By dint of charm, "sincerity," and hours of bridge playing, Yamamoto wrung from his American contacts an assurance that Japan would get a ratio close to the one she wanted.

On December 18, 1929, the Japanese delegation concluded its feeler negotiations by dining with President and Mrs. Hoover at the White House. The table was laden with pink snapdragons, butterfly roses, and smilax. Captain Yamamoto, who sat far down it with Hoover's aide, Captain Buchanan, was so relaxed that, in the course of the state banquet, he showed his companions a trick with matchsticks and the White House wine goblets.

Four months later, in London, Yamamoto's expectations were fulfilled when the American and British delegations formally acknowledged Japan's right to maintain 6.9945 tons of cruisers and destroyers for every 10 U.S. and British tons. In addition the U.S. delegation agreed to delay the construction of three heavy cruisers for which appropriations had already been allocated in order to give Japan 73 per cent of naval parity with the United States until at least 1936. Best of all, from Yamamoto's point of view, no limitations whatsoever were attached to the building of naval aircraft.

In gaining this dazzling, unexpected diplomatic victory, Yamamoto had made no promises but had successfully convinced his Western counterparts that he and the Emperor and the Japanese Navy were only interested in defending Japan's home waters against Chinese pirates and Soviet fishing fleets. Twelve years later when Yamamoto crept up on Pearl Harbor and sank half the Pacific fleet, his smiling reassurances and parlor tricks were not to be forgotten or forgiven. When an opportunity arose during the war, the U.S. government, by President Roosevelt's own particular order, took an unusual personal vengeance on the Japanese naval commander.[6]

NAVAL SMOKESCREEN

Yamamoto came home from his triumph in London in 1930 with Navy Minister Takarabe, one of the two chief delegates to the "disarmament conference." They took the Trans-Siberian Railroad and, before arriving in Japan, were met secretly in Manchuria by the tall, languid Prince Konoye of the House of Peers—the youngest and most aristocratic of the

[6] The story is told in Chapter 28.

Big Brothers who had taken Hirohito in hand when he was still a toddler. It was Konoye's mission to remind the delegates that they had left the artificial world of international diplomacy and were re-entering the peculiar insular reality of the Japanese ruling class. Konoye gently warned them that their success in London was "unexpected" and constituted a positive embarrassment in Tokyo. It had been assumed that the West would give Japan no more than 6 tons for every 10 tons of British or American capital ships, a ratio which Hirohito had been prepared to accept. When Yamamoto got an official 6.9945 tons for Japan on paper and U.S. word for an actual 7.3 tons afloat, it was more than Japan had demanded. Indeed, said Konoye laughing, it "transcended reality, extended credibility, and confounded sanity." Japan had half the population, a tenth the gross national product, and a twentieth the area of the United States, yet that nation had just accorded Japan the right to better than 70 per cent naval equality with her.

Having congratulated Takarabe and Yamamoto on their fantastic feat, Konoye went on to explain to them, with apologies, that much of the public recognition for their achievement would have to be smothered. Having anticipated a continuance of the 10:6 ratio, the Emperor's cabal had already made arrangements for a great public outcry to be staged, protesting Japan's treatment as an inferior power. It was now too late to cancel the arrangements without much loss of face for the cabal's loyal editors, ward heelers, and gang leaders. Besides, an issue was vitally needed with which to drum the people out of their pacifist lethargy. Technically the 6.9945 tons received were less than the 7 tons demanded, and so the public outcry would go ahead as planned. The figures after the decimal point would be ignored by the Japanese press; the Emperor would delay in ratifying the treaty; and, while he considered it, the people would be treated to a great national debate.

To oppose the treaty the cabal was exploiting a group of conservative admirals, known as the Fleet Faction, who believed in capital ships; Navy Chief of Staff Admiral Kato Kanji was among them. Konoye warned that, except for his Highness Admiral Prince Fushimi, the members of the Fleet Faction were dangerously sincere individualists. They opposed Yamamoto's treaty because they saw in it a blind behind which Japan could prepare in secret to make war with the United States and Great Britain. To impress the Emperor, they spoke like hawks, but in reality they were doves who wished to abandon the national program handed down by Emperor Meiji.

Konoye did not know it at the time but events would prove his analysis correct. The members of the Fleet Faction would all resign their commissions or go into the reserve in the years ahead. By contrast those who spoke like doves in favor of Yamamoto's "disarmament treaty" would turn out to be hawks who would help Yamamoto plan and execute the 1941 attack on Pearl Harbor.

Duly warned by Konoye of the situation at home, Captain Yamamoto and Navy Minister Takarabe disembarked in Japan on May 18, 1930. Crowds turned out, unprompted, to acclaim them as conquerors. The vast majority of the people, knowing only what they had read in the newspapers, welcomed naval limitations as a guarantee against high taxes and as a blow for peace. When the two delegates reported at the palace, Hirohito delivered to each of them his customary noncommittal words of praise, "Thank you for your pains."

The chief civilian delegate to the London Naval Conference, Wakatsuki, a former and future prime minister, arrived home by ship a month later. By then receptions were better organized. The crowds still cheered, but a professional agitator of the Black Dragon Society handed Wakatsuki a ceremonial dagger wrapped in silk—a delicate hint, it was said in the newspapers, that he should commit suicide for having endangered the national defense.

While the great fake debate filled headlines and occupied the public mind, liberals allied with Prime-Minister-Maker Saionji urged Hirohito to sign the naval limitations treaty at once and the conservative Fleet Faction urged him not to sign it at all. Hirohito insisted that, before deciding on the treaty, a co-ordinated national defense plan be prepared, one that would govern military expenditures during the coming decade. The plan was duly drawn up in great secrecy by key men in the Army and Navy bureaucracies. Its text is not extant, but an officer who worked on it recalls that "it agreed pretty well with the actual military development of Japan as far as 1939."

By July 23, 1930, the War and Navy ministers and the Board of Field Marshals and Fleet Admirals, controlled by Hirohito's cousins, accepted the plan and forwarded it to Hirohito. With the plan went a covering memorandum to the effect that the naval limitations treaty would create some "insufficiencies in the national defense" but that the offensive power provided for by the plan would offset any real danger and would assist substantially in "advancing the national program."

The next day Hirohito asked his Privy Council of elders to consider the treaty and advise him on whether or not to sign it. Under the Emperor's benign gaze and with his tacit encouragement, the Privy Councillors refused to recommend the treaty for his sanction because they were not allowed to see the co-ordinated national defense plan which Hirohito, as commander-in-chief, had sponsored, approved, and declared top secret.

The reason for this Gilbert-and-Sullivan impasse was that Hirohito had no intention of signing the naval limitations treaty until the elected government approved a long-range budget for the defense plan—in particular for the naval and naval air development programs which were the most expensive parts of it. At the behest of eighty-year-old Saionji, however, Prime Minister Hamaguchi refused, under one pretext or another, to find funds even for the first year of the plan.

EPIDEMIC OF ABSENTEEISM

In blocking the co-ordinated national defense plan, Saionji counted heavily upon an ally in the Army, one with enough influence to mire section after subsection of the plan in deep red tape on the desks of major generals. This was War Minister Ugaki Kazushige, the bull-necked officer who had served Hirohito, earlier in 1925, by purging the Choshu clan from the Army. Having given his approval in vague, reluctant terms to the defense plan, Ugaki pleaded a middle-ear infection and retired to rest in his country home for the next four months. In so doing he withdrew from Hirohito's support the Ugaki Faction—a majority of the generals and colonels in the Army. These were the military professionals who assessed with realism Japan's strength as a warrior nation. They were eager to add Manchuria to the Empire but they would not support long-term naval preparations for war with the United States and Great Britain.

During Ugaki's absence from Tokyo—his "sick-down strike" as it was called by Hirohito's clever, Oxford-educated brother, Prince Chichibu—Prime-Minister-Maker Saionji caught an extended case of the flu which made it impossible for him, too, to exercise his political influence on behalf of the Throne. From his quarantine, Saionji sent a tongue-in-cheek note to Ugaki begging him not to give in:

> Although I should come to you in person [he wrote], I am, as you know, sick myself. . . . Certain individuals are passing rumors to the effect that you will resign. For the sake of the fatherland, I beg you to be prudent. Leave the cares of your ministry to someone else. Then take all the time you need to rest and recover.

On August 17, 1930, Big Brother Konoye of the House of Peers invited Marquis Kido—the first of the Big Brothers, the son of Hirohito's childhood foster father, the loyal retainer who would go to prison as Hirohito's personal representative in 1945—to a round of golf at the Hodogaya Club near Kido's villa in Yokohama.[7] It was a fine day but hot, and the tall, languid Fujiwara prince stretched himself in the rough near one of the early greens. The dapper, owlish marquis, a rabid golfer, stood over him scolding for a moment and then signaled their companion, the director of the Bank of Japan, to play through.

Marquis Kido had had few opportunities to speak privately to Prince Konoye in more than a year. In early 1929 Kido had gone abroad on an extended sightseeing trip to indicate to the public that he took partial responsibility for the killing of Chang Tso-lin. Kido had made a tour of the United States, hating every minute of it. After a day at Niagara Falls,

---

[7] This account is based on the reconstruction of a third party who talked to Kido and Konoye in the clubhouse that afternoon.

he had written superciliously in his diary, "In this humdrum fashion, I celebrated the 1930 New Year." Returning home from exile in late January, he had plunged back into his work at the Commerce and Industry Ministry. He had been busy ever since drafting memos on industrial mobilization for perusal by the members of the Eleven Club. This was a forum which Kido had founded on the eleventh day of the eleventh month of the eleventh year of the reign of Emperor Taisho—that is, on November 11, 1922. At least once a month, usually on the eleventh, the club met for lunch or dinner in a private room at one or another of Tokyo's best restaurants.[8] Since its founding, its membership had grown from three to more than a score. Under Kido's tactful direction it had become the co-ordinating center of the Big Brotherhood, which was itself the brain of Hirohito's cabal.

Sensing that he was about to hear something which would not be said even at an Eleven Club meeting, Kido sat down in the long grass. Konoye beside him launched into one of his "résumés of the present situation"—a prelude always to some sort of important Konoye proposal. It was time, said Konoye, to break the "sick-down strike" of General Ugaki and old man Saionji. Matters had come to such a pass that Saionji was privately accusing Count Makino, the lord privy seal, of opposing disarmament and advising Hirohito not to sign the naval treaty. On the other hand the Fleet Faction's Admiral Kato, since resigning in June as Navy chief of staff, had been accusing Count Makino of exerting improper influence over the Throne on behalf of the treaty. Specifically Kato complained that Count Makino had sidetracked his privileged reports to the Throne and kept Hirohito from hearing the facts.

In order to refute Saionji's charges against Makino and to mollify Admiral Kato, said Konoye, Hirohito had agreed to let Count Makino's chief secretary retire.[9] It would be noised abroad that he was taking responsibility for certain irregularities in connection with Admiral Kato's efforts to report to the Emperor. The public would then see that Hirohito had gone so far in the cause of disarmament as to condone a breach of Court rules rather than hear the conservative admiral's arguments against the naval treaty.

"It is my feeling," said Konoye, "that the Emperor is disappointed by the attitude of the public." Opinion had not turned against Saionji or against pacifism, and Hirohito was obliged to go on dissimulating, even

---

[8] It would continue to meet until the night of January 11, 1945, when the conspirators agreed that the shriek of air raid sirens made further talk unprofitable.

[9] Okabe Nagakage, the son-in-law of former Prime Minister Kato Taka-aki who had served the Twenty-One Demands on China. Okabe was consoled with the title of viscount and a seat in the House of Peers. As a faithful member of the Eleven Club, he remained an influential figure behind the scenes and would re-emerge into the limelight when he became minister of education in the 1943 Cabinet of World War II Prime Minister Tojo.

before his most loyal subjects. Under the circumstances, said Konoye, it had been decided to "strengthen the Emperor's personal leadership of the nation." Hirohito had just appointed Colonel Nagata Tetsuzan, the first of the Three Crows of Baden-Baden, to the directorship of the sprawling, influential Military Affairs Section in the War Ministry. Now the office of secretary to the lord privy seal was vacant.

"I have been thinking," said Konoye, "that His Majesty might be pleased if you were proposed, Kido, as a candidate for the vacancy. In fact, if you feel that you can give up your career to serve as Count Makino's secretary, I can assure you that the position is almost certainly yours."

Kido was deeply gratified that the Emperor recognized his accomplishments in keeping the Big Brotherhood together. Up to now the principal intermediary between the Throne and the civilian half of the cabal had been Prince Konoye who had the hereditary Court rank to meet Hirohito often at social functions. Now, if Kido moved his files into the palace as secretary to the lord privy seal, he would be bringing papers to the Imperial Study at all hours of the day and night. He would be the reins of the cabal, close at hand for Hirohito whenever he wished to reach for them.

"I accept without any reservations," said Kido, standing up. "Let's play a few more holes."

A day or two later, the aged Field Marshal Prince Kanin, senior member of the imperial family, summoned to his villa his old protégé from the cavalry, Major General Tatekawa Yoshiji, the Peerless Pimp. "The time has come," announced Prince Kanin, "to break the deadlock with War Minister Ugaki." The suave Tatekawa, who had so smoothly handled the Peking end of the killing of the Manchurian war lord Chang Tso-lin, was now director of Army Intelligence. With Prince Kanin's backing Tatekawa began at once to beg, buy, and borrow the allegiance of the officers of the Ugaki Faction in the General Staff. He was assisted in the War Ministry by Colonel Nagata of the Military Affairs Section.

HIROHITO HAS HIS WAY

By September 1930, War Minister Ugaki's Army slowdown had been effectively canceled, and necessary outlines and estimates for the defense plan had begun to move across desks into the hands of the civilians in the Finance Ministry who were trying to draw up budgets. With the co-operation of First Crow Nagata, Intelligence Chief Tatekawa went ahead to devise an intimidation for the bankers, intellectuals, and politicians who made War Minister Ugaki and Saionji formidable forces to be reckoned with.

Tatekawa had his Intelligence experts draw up its annual "Inspection of General Circumstances" in a revolutionary new form. In previous years this cryptic title had always graced the cover of a report in depth on the political, economic and military conditions within a potential enemy nation such as Great Britain or the Philippines. This year, 1930, the adversary scrutinized was Japan itself. And the conclusions were, briefly, that corrupt political parties and cartels were interposing a fogged filter between the pure executive light of the Emperor and his moths of men in the regiments and on the farms. To remove the blemish and "perfect the national structure" a *Showa Isshin* or Hirohito Restoration must be carried out which would convert Japan into a "National Defense State" that would be "mobilized for total war."

The threat implied by the 1930 "Inspection of General Circumstances" was clear: either the politicians and business magnates of Japan would find money for the co-ordinated national defense plan or they would be conscripted in a total mobilization. To make sure that this message was broadcast widely, Intelligence Chief Tatekawa sponsored the organization of a noisy debating society in the ranks of young Army staff officers—one which received so much publicity at the time that some historians have seen in it the fountainhead of Japanese fascism. It was called the *Sakurakai* or Cherry Society, a name rich in murderous historical associations, which meant by implication society of young warriors ready to die.

Veteran politician that he was, Saionji could not help but admire the marksmanship and saturation of the fire being poured upon his faction of liberals. In a self-mocking mood, over his saké cup one night, he acknowledged to his political secretary, Big Brother Baron Harada, that the only satisfaction left in life for Prime Minister Hamaguchi was "like scratching your toes with Western shoes on."

Finally on September 15, 1930, with a sigh of approval from old man Saionji, Prime Minister Hamaguchi gave in. At a meeting of Hirohito's Privy Council of elders he put himself on record promising to assume full responsibility for finding the necessary funds for future secret naval development. The Privy Councillors asked him several waspish questions and finally he replied, "We are all men of the Inner Circle. There is no room for debate." At its next meeting the Privy Council resolved that the Board of Field Marshals and Fleet Admirals could keep its secret co-ordinated national defense plan and that the naval limitations treaty might now be submitted to Hirohito for his sanction. According to the notes of Baron Harada, this abrupt *volte face* on the part of the Privy Council was brought about by one Privy Councillor telling the chairman in private that the treaty debate was beginning to "vex" Hirohito.

LION SLAYING

Trusting Prime Minister Hamaguchi's word that funds would be found, Hirohito signed the naval limitations treaty on October 2, 1930, and gratefully turned his attention from politics to military matters. Lieutenant

Colonel Ishiwara, whom Hirohito had entrusted in late 1928 with the planning for the conquest of Manchuria, had now, in September 1930, submitted his detailed tactical blueprint to Hirohito and the General Staff. Hirohito saw that it was satisfactory and tabled it temporarily while he studied the more important, longer-range naval development program. This had been drawn up, in large part, by Rear Admiral Yamamoto, the future architect of the attack on Pearl Harbor. It contained one imponderable: Yamamoto's enthusiastic belief in the eventual effectiveness of naval air power.

Since the London Naval Conference, Yamamoto had been feverishly drilling his naval pilots in all-weather operations from the decks of Japan's tiny task force of four aircraft carriers. A score of pilots had crashed and died but now Yamamoto was ready to justify the trust which the imperial family had placed in him by staging a demonstration of naval air power at the annual Navy grand maneuvers. In the fourth week of October 1930, Hirohito steamed south to the Inland Sea to watch the maneuvers from the bridge of his battleship.

On October 22, while Hirohito was absent from Tokyo, Prime Minister Hamaguchi presented the national budget to his cabinet. The Navy minister was far from satisfied. Instead of the 500 million yen ($250 million) requested for the naval half of the new national defense scheme, the government was offering some 300 million. Weeks of bargaining lay ahead. Prime-Minister-Maker Saionji cautioned his political secretary, Baron Harada, not to let the Navy's budget exceed 400 million yen because it might "cause popular agitation."

"In Germany," he said threateningly, "the people on the whole possess a martial spirit and they do not engage in agitation. As a result, political control there is no great problem. In Japan, however, matters have come to such a pass that the people could easily turn Communist. My anxiety on this account would be altogether out of place in Germany, but here, unless something is done, the militarists among our leaders will see to it that my worst fears are realized."

On October 26, the Navy's grand maneuvers came to an end in a glorious triumph for Rear Admiral Yamamoto and his flyers. Carrier-borne torpedo planes of "Fleet White" had theoretically sunk the battleships of "Fleet Blue."

On October 27, a young professional hoodlum, Sagoya Tomeo, who belonged to a provincial patriotic club spawned by the Black Dragon Society, came to Tokyo by train with the express purpose of assassinating Prime Minister Hamaguchi. He understood that the prime minister, in offering 300 million yen instead of 500 million for naval development, had broken his word to the Emperor. On the train, however, Sagoya had an "encounter with an imperial prince"—so he later described it to the police —which persuaded him to postpone his deed.[10]

Instead of killing Hamaguchi immediately, cutthroat Sagoya followed the prime minister around the city, posing a silent threat during the conclusion of the budget debate. Saionji's political secretary, Baron Harada, learned from the police that "someone has been stalking the prime minister." Official Tokyo watched the hunt with fascination. Home Minister Adachi Kenzo, who had charge of the police, was himself a member of the Black Dragon who had ingratiated himself with the Throne in the 1890's by contributing to the murder of the queen of Korea. His police shadowed the shadower but made no attempt to arrest him.

Prime Minister Hamaguchi, the Lion, refused to be intimidated. On November 9, he finally persuaded the Navy minister to accept a compromise budget of 374 million yen. It appeared that Hamaguchi had won a great victory, and finding himself still alive, he began to talk bravely of making a thorough overhaul of the machinery of Japanese government. It was his ambition, he said, to subordinate to the supreme authority of the Cabinet all de facto instruments of policy making, even the Emperor's own Privy Council. Prime-Minister-Maker Saionji sympathized with this goal and asked his political secretary to encourage the prime minister. Harada reported Saionji's words at Court.

One evening in the second week of November 1930, Big Brother Prince Konoye received a visit from Iogi Ryozo, the burly, sixty-year-old editor of *Japan and the Japanese,* the periodical that had touched off the naval limitations debate in 1929 with its special issue on national defense. Iogi was a charter member of the Black Dragon; it was he who, in 1921, had notified Konoye in advance of the assassination of Prime Minister Hara. Now, in 1930, he intimated to Prince Konoye that a similar mishap might soon befall Prime Minister Hamaguchi. "Things," he added, "may gradually start to happen from now on. Something big will follow in due course, about February or March."

On the evening of November 13, 1930, Big Brother Baron Harada spent an hour and a half in private with Prime Minister Hamaguchi at his residence. The Emperor was out of town again, this time attending the annual grand maneuvers of the Army. Hamaguchi explained to Harada his government reorganization scheme, the implications of the new budget, the need to curtail the powers of Hirohito's Privy Council and Army and Navy General Staffs. "Take good care of yourself," said Harada meaningfully, as he left the prime minister's residence.

"I hoped there would be no mishap," he added piously to his diary when he had returned home.

[10] The prince was almost certainly Big Brother Higashikuni who took the same train back to Tokyo from the naval maneuvers.

Sagoya, the assassin, spent that night in one of Tokyo's best brothels. His bill was taken care of for him by a patron whose identity the police later kept secret. The next morning, November 14, 1930, at 9:00 A.M., Saionji's secretary, Harada, and Prince Konoye were closeted together when the phone rang. An aide informed them that five minutes earlier Prime Minister Hamaguchi had been shot at Tokyo station as he was about to board a train on his way to join the Emperor at the Army grand maneuvers. Assassin Sagoya had thrust a Mauser-8 from the crowd on the Tokyo platform and sunk a bullet deep in Hamaguchi's vitals.

Two doctors who happened to be on the scene attended him in the stationmaster's office. They found him conscious but in great pain. His pulse fell to 90 and his belly swelled alarmingly. The chubby figure of Baron Harada pushed its way through the circle of bystanders, looked at the body and then withdrew, without speaking, to make some calls on the stationmaster's phone. Harada then took a train to report to Saionji in the town of Okitsu two hours away.

Hamaguchi murmured, "I feel worse." At 11:30 A.M., he was moved to the infirmary at Tokyo Imperial University. There, he was given a partial anaesthetic and X-rayed. He had lost two pints of blood and had eight perforations in his small intestine, plus several more in the adjoining valves. The University chief of surgery,[11] snipped out 20 inches of intestine and sewed together the tract that was left. Exploring from the rear, the surgeon found the bullet lodged deep in the pelvic arch where he felt he could not safely get at it. So he sewed Hamaguchi up and gave him 250 grams of whole blood. He estimated that the prime minister had a 60 to 70 per cent chance of survival but feared he would be too weak to defend his budget at the coming session of the Diet.

At the time of the shooting Hirohito was at his grand-maneuver field headquarters, 300 miles south of Tokyo. When he received word there of Hamaguchi's "mishap," he expressed his regrets and advised the Cabinet to pick an acting prime minister to handle routine administrative affairs while Hamaguchi remained incapacitated. On the afternoon of the shooting, the Cabinet duly met to carry out the Emperor's instructions. The members finally settled on Foreign Minister Shidehara, the sanctimonious moderate of Japanese diplomacy who would become prime minister in his own right under MacArthur in late 1945.

A ghost of a lion, Prime Minister Hamaguchi continued to haunt the fringes of the political forest for nine months to come. He would finally die after a succession of debilitating surgeries on August 26, 1931. His dream, which he shared with Saionji, of constitutional prime ministers who would

---

[11] Eighteen months later, through incompetence or design, this same surgeon, Dr. Shioda Hiroshige, would fail—under extremely suspicious circumstances—to save the life of another prime ministerial assassination victim, Inukai Tsuyoshi. (See Chapter 15.)

run the nation in fact as well as name would die with him. So, too, would his hopes for peace.

The police made a lengthy investigation of the assassination and divulged no relevant details except that the assassin, Sagoya Tomeo, resented Prime Minister Hamaguchi's part in passing the naval limitations treaty. As far as the public was concerned, that ended the matter. Sagoya spent three years out of jail on the recognizance of various police chiefs during his investigation and trial. Then, on November 6, 1933, he was finally condemned to death. Three months later, on the eve of his execution, he was amnestied by Hirohito and set free. Under the name of Sagoya Yoshiaki, he continued, until the late 1960's, to live the life of a national hero, supported by unseen hands, and always ready to contribute a rabble-rousing speech at gatherings of Japanese rightists.

11

MARCH 1931

OLD MAN AT SUNUP

When Baron Harada phoned Prime-Minister-Maker Saionji with the news of Hamaguchi's shooting on the morning of November 14, 1930, the old man seemed momentarily shocked and confused. He demanded querulously that Harada come out from Tokyo immediately with full particulars.

Saionji had celebrated his eighty-first birthday the month before, and like most well-cared-for old men, he thought of his personal health as a matter of some importance. Surely it was inconceivable that anyone would dare to assassinate him. He was the elder of the Fujiwaras, the second family of the nation. He was the last of the noblemen who had brought the restoration to Japan in 1868. In the eyes of Japan's spirit worshippers, he was surrounded by an aura of divinity almost as bright as the Emperor's. And if he should fall by the hand of a political assassin, not even the Emperor would be immune from the vengeance of Saionji's partisans in the clans and in the cartels and political parties. Yet Saionji knew how easy it was to arrange assassinations through the Black Dragon Society. If the mad dogs of Hirohito's cabal would gun down a revered leader of sixty like Prime Minister Hamaguchi, where would they stop? Hamaguchi had politicked with Saionji for thirty years. In paring the naval budget he had only followed Saionji's suggestions.

By the time that Baron Harada arrived at Sit-and-Fish Villa in Okitsu that afternoon, Saionji had regained his composure and was coldly indignant. He gave Harada explicit instructions to all the Cabinet ministers that they must not be intimidated but must carry on with Hamaguchi's program as if nothing had happened. By evening Saionji was on the phone trying to make sure that the Cabinet would appoint a moderate as prime

400

minister pro tem. The next day he was disappointed by the defeat of his own candidate, War Minister Ugaki, but half satisfied with the compromise candidate, Foreign Minister Shidehara.

On the morning of November 16, according to a banker friend who was close to him at that time, the old man could not sleep. He arose at first light, drew the screens of the room where he lived and worked, and stood on the balcony watching the fishermen launch their boats. If ever there had been a time to think, it was now.

A decade ago Saionji had seen in Hirohito's ambitions the callow innocence of youth. But Hirohito, at thirty, had not mellowed. He was unflagging in his attention to duty, always fair-minded in discussion, invariably courteous and intelligent. But he remained deceptive in his openness, hard in his kindness, ruthlessly objective in matters of life and death. Even his warmest partisans acknowledged a cold, mechanical quality in him. They called it a "godlike, awe-inspiring purity," but Saionji sometimes wondered if it were not a form of madness.

All efforts to guide Hirohito had failed. The time had come to oppose him positively. The chiefs of the Army and Navy and police were under the Emperor's control. Only the people could help. But to tell the people the truth would be to make them all republicans, Communists, regicides. They must be kept in ignorance and led. The problem was to give them a leader, a twentieth century shogun to compare with Ieyasu, the first of the Tokugawas. Then Hirohito would have to back down.

Saionji called out in the silent house for someone to help him. His maid appeared, half awake, and assisted him as he put on a lined winter kimono. Since the infidelity of Flower Child in 1924, Saionji had had no regular live-in mistress, and the maid was no more than a servant. Saionji never felt more lonely than on a morning such as this when he wanted a sympathetic listener on whom to try his thoughts. As he passed through his garden gate and started up the hill, the maid roused his gatekeeper and chauffeur so that someone would follow him and be ready to help him if his walk tired him.

Above the streets of the fishing village of Okitsu where he lived, Saionji planted his cane resolutely on each flagstone step along the wooded pathway up the hill. When he reached the gate of the temple at the top he turned to rest and look back over the bay below. Then he turned and contemplated the view inland toward Mount Fuji. A turban of mist had slipped down over the sacred mountain divorcing its perfectly conical, snow-capped summit from any visible connection with the earth. To safeguard this mountain, this land of the gods, this heritage of the difficult young Emperor— these were Saionji's tasks. And he felt inadequate to fulfill them. His sight and hearing were sound, but his diabetes troubled him. He could no longer drink enough to feel drunk. He could no longer remelt his thought processes and pour them into new molds. The art of politics had become for him a stale exercise in tricks which he had learned decades ago.

In the lee of one of the stone lanterns of the temple he struck a match and lighted one of his favorite imported cigarettes, a Pall Mall. The sun peered over Izu Peninsula, the spur of Mount Fuji running down into the sea. The pine trees turned to blood and fire, the waters of the bay to bursts of diamonds. Saionji's mind floated back to the sunrises of his childhood, which he had watched from the courtyard of the palace in Kyoto before the coming of Perry. In those days he had been Emperor Komei's favorite page boy and had felt superior to his junior, the future Emperor Meiji. Now Meiji and Meiji's son were both dead and he alone remained to remember the honorable aspirations of the country at its awakening.

Saionji dropped the butt of his Pall Mall as it began to burn his stained knuckles. His faithful private secretary Nakagawa—not a Court spy like Harada—came up the mountain behind him, breathing heavily. The priest of the temple was approaching from the other direction to offer a cup of hot green tea. In a few minutes Nakagawa would escort him down the hill to his breakfast.

Saionji abruptly made up his mind. He would break with his lifelong public advocacy of civilian government and would join forces openly with the Army faction of War Minister Ugaki. Ugaki might not have the greatness required of a shogun but he had courage and good intentions and his followers in the officer corps were known as moderates.

SAIONJI WARNS HIROHITO

That afternoon when Baron Harada, the secretary-spy assigned him by the Court, came out to Okitsu with a report on the selection of the prime minister pro tem, Saionji conveyed his purposed threat to the Throne in guarded hints. He told Harada that it was a pity War Minister Ugaki had not been made acting prime minister. Didn't the Emperor know that during Ugaki's long convalescence in the country he had been asked separately by representatives of each of the two major political parties to become their president? Didn't the Emperor know that Ugaki might create an opposition by putting together either of the political parties with disaffected elements inside Hirohito's own cabal of military officers?

"Mark my word," concluded Saionji, "if the administration does not make enough of Ugaki, he may well resign and strike out on his own. Then, believe me, the administration's loss of face will be something to see."

Secretary-Spy Harada hurried back to Tokyo and waited impatiently for Hirohito to return from the Army grand maneuvers. Hirohito, on his way home, had had his battleship heave to off the Kii Peninsula so that he could spend a day there with the scientists of a biological institute specializing in bacteriological and chemical warfare studies.[1] When he finally arrived back in the palace on November 21, Harada at once sought an emergency audience with Lord Privy Seal Makino, the Emperor's chief civilian advisor. Baron Harada told Count Makino that Saionji was ready to make common cause with Strike-North visionaries in the Army and also with Baron Hiranuma, the long-faced lawyer who would itemize Hirohito's mistakes before allowing him to surrender in the bunker in 1945.

In reality, Saionji had not even considered an alliance with Hiranuma. He was one of Saionji's oldest and most bitter political enemies. He represented the clan lords of yesteryear and the Black Dragon gang lords of the modern cities. He stood—at least in Saionji's mind—for a return to the eighteenth century police state of the Tokugawas against which Saionji had fought as a young knight in green armor riding for the royalists in 1868.

Nevertheless, in Harada's imagination, War Minister Ugaki was about to be backed by a Saionji-Hiranuma-Strike-North coalition and had become a formidable threat. "General Ugaki's value as a man," he said, "may be vastly overrated, but the charisma seen in him by the public could enable him to wreak havoc. We must try to keep General Ugaki as happy as possible within the present Cabinet."

After duly weighing Harada's warning, Count Makino decided that instead of placating Ugaki it would be better to frame him for high treason and then control him by threat of exposure. Makino turned the matter over to his private political fixer, Dr. Okawa, the ideologist of the Strike-South pragmatists and former headmaster of the palace Lodging-House indoctrination center.

THE MARCH PLOT

Dr. Okawa proceeded to make Ugaki the chief gull of a fantastic scheme for an imperial coup d'etat. The coup was never executed nor was it ever meant to be. It never made the headlines nor, until years later, was it much talked of outside the ruling class. Yet within that tiny insular world the March Plot, as it came to be called, would ruin Ugaki, shackle Saionji and remain a sharp instrument of Hirohito's domestic power for the next seven years.

The March Plot had been first conceived as a way of preparing domestic politics for the conquest of Manchuria. The idea was that a threat of coup d'etat by right-wing elements could be used to persuade the masses that

---

[1] His suite found the scientific talk boring and Grand Chamberlain Suzuki Kantaro, the old Taoist who would be prime minister at the time of the surrender in 1945, inquired, "Are you not tired, My Liege?"

"No, whatever I hear I listen to," said Hirohito. "If you understood, you would find many useful things to be learned here."

"If he were not a god," sighed one of the chamberlains, "he could not do it."

Manchuria would provide a safe spilling space for domestic poisons. As a member of the Black Dragon Society, Dr. Okawa had been recruiting underworld involvement in the scheme since some time in the fall of 1930.[2] Army involvement was being arranged at the same time by Field Marshal Prince Kanin, the Army elder who was also senior member of the imperial family. The combined threat of militarists and street bullies was calculated to intimidate all the many Japanese who had never handled a gun or studied karate.

As stirred by Dr. Okawa's spoon, this diversionary plot quickly thickened as if it were being improvised by a pair of joke writers in a hotel room late at night. While pretending to make General Ugaki and Black Dragon Toyama the leaders of a scheme to dynamite the Diet, why not also implicate the troublesome anti-Soviet Strike-North visionaries in the bosom of Hirohito's own cabal? Why not incriminate the cabal's First Crow, Colonel Nagata, or even the propriety-loving members of Hirohito's Big Brotherhood? From Dr. Okawa's point of view, it was good personal insurance to involve as many important people in the web as possible. So well did he succeed that he was later able to plan murders with impunity and even to slip the noose of MacArthur's justice.[3] Indeed the ghosts of blackmail and counterblackmail which he raised in March 1931 still hang over the moats like will-o'-the-wisps to haunt the palace to this day.

UGAKI'S COYNESS

During the incubation of the March Plot in late December 1930 and early January 1931, General Ugaki, the war minister, asked time to consider Saionji's secret proposal that he join in a coalition against the Throne. He dined almost nightly with representatives of the two major political parties, trying to decide of which one he would accept the presidency.

In those same weeks Acting Prime Minister Shidehara was busy amending the budget forced through by his mortally wounded predecessor and trying to find in it an extra 50 million yen ($25 million) for the Navy. With Hirohito's backing he even asked the Army to curtail its own development schemes. As chief of the Military Affairs Section in the Military Affairs Bureau of the War Ministry, the first of the Three Crows of Baden-Baden, Colonel Nagata, was forced reluctantly to draft an unpopular plan to lay off manpower from every Army division in order to preserve some funds in the Army till for long scheduled increases in tank and mobile units.

---

[2] That was why Editor Iogi—also a member of the Black Dragon—had promised "something big in February or March" when he had advised Prince Konoye of the imminent assassination of Prime Minister Hamaguchi.

[3] The palace made special efforts to help him evade American trial and cross-examination—efforts which were not made for any of the other war criminals after their formal indictment. The story of his escape under guise of feigned insanity is told in the final chapter of this book.

In the second week of January 1931, as War Minister Ugaki was returning to his office from one of his lunches with politicians, he was accosted in the corridors of the War Ministry by Lieutenant Colonel Hashimoto Kingoro, who would go down in American history for ordering the sinking of the U.S.S. *Panay* in the Yangtze River in 1937. Hashimoto had just returned from a tour of duty as an attaché in Turkey. He had interesting theories about fascism for small nations. When he hailed Ugaki as the "Kemal Ataturk of Japan," Ugaki stopped to chat with him. By way of explaining his greeting, Hashimoto persuaded Ugaki to stop by for a moment in the office of Major General Koiso Kuniaki, the over-all chief of the War Ministry's Military Affairs Bureau. Though technically a subordinate of Ugaki, Koiso administered his bureau with great independence, born of his recognized position as an old favorite of Field Marshal Prince Kanin.[4]

With many hooded words, Major General Koiso suggested to General Ugaki that the "Center of the Army"—a euphemism for Hirohito—had a historical mission for him to perform. Koiso then took Ugaki to an unpretentious adjunct of the General Staff Headquarters and ushered him into the office of Major General Tatekawa, the Chief of the Second Department, Intelligence. The ponderous, sleepy-eyed Tatekawa—the "Peerless Pimp" who had masterminded for Prince Kanin the Peking end of Chang Tso-lin's killing in 1928—suavely suggested to Ugaki over a cup of green tea that Emperor Hirohito was tired of Japan's interminable dirty politics; that the time had come to cleanse the nation; that Hirohito was ready to accept an honest shogun like Ugaki if he would lead the Army in an imperial coup d'etat.

The first diary reaction of the enthusiastic General Ugaki was favorable to the proposal, but after a few days' thought and investigation, he grew increasingly cautious and circumspect. He told Koiso and Tatekawa that he wished to see evidence of genuine national support before he committed himself. It was arranged for him on January 29, 1931, to take lunch with members of the Eleven Club, Hirohito's inner civilian circle, presided over that day by Big Brother Marquis Kido, the secretary of Lord Privy Seal Count Makino, and by Big Brother Baron Harada, the secretary-spy of old man Saionji.

Ugaki was visibly gratified by the luncheon but remained evasive about accepting his role in the plot. During the first week of February 1931, he told Major General Koiso that he was waiting to see realistic preparations for the coup. Koiso summoned his principal section chief, First Crow Nagata.

---

[4] Koiso had ridden with the Mongols in their drive on Mukden during Prince Kanin's abortive coup in Manchuria in 1916. It would be Koiso who would act as Japanese prime minister during the black months of the kamikaze in late 1944 and early 1945.

"Nagata-san," he said, "I want you to draft an operations plan for a military coup d'etat which will bring General Ugaki to power as the Emperor's shogun. Unless we have such a plan ready to use, a plan to restore the Emperor to true imperial power, we will never be able to get the politicians to support our program in Manchuria."

"Is it to be a real or a fake plan?" asked Nagata suspiciously.

"Write it as if it were real," ordered Koiso.

"It is a bad South American way to gain power," said Nagata, shaking his head. But a few days later he obediently slapped down a sheaf of papers on Koiso's desk with the contemptuous comment: "Here is the novel you asked me to write."

Nagata's novel called for a mob of 10,000 patriots to surround the Diet on March 20 and hurl smoke bombs at it. Then the 1st Division and the Imperial Guards Division were to proceed, for the sake of public peace, to throw a cordon of troops around the administrative heart of Tokyo. Major General Tatekawa of Intelligence or Major General Koiso of Military Affairs would stride into the Diet and demand a quick vote on the Army program: realization of the National Defense State under Ugaki and dissolution of political parties. Thereafter Ugaki would present himself to the Emperor in the palace to crave sanction for what was done, and an emissary would go to old man Saionji in Okitsu to demand his formal approval of it.

When Ugaki was advised of the plan, he wondered only where the bombs and the mob of 10,000 patriots were to come from. Major General Tatekawa promised that the mobs would be provided by the Black Dragon Society under the direction of Lord Privy Seal Makino's man, Dr. Okawa. As for the bombs, Tatekawa undertook to see to them himself. He wrote a letter to the principal of the Infantry School in Chiba, asking him to deliver to bearer 300 training grenades. The bearer was Lieutenant Colonel Hashimoto, the later *Panay*-sinker. The grenades were large, paper-encased firecrackers designed to create the illusion of battle during maneuvers. Each was guaranteed by the manufacturer to produce a six-foot jet of smoke and as much noise as four simultaneous rifle reports. Lieutenant Colonel Hashimoto brought them back to General Staff Headquarters in Tokyo, stacked them in Intelligence Chief Tatekawa's offices, and there, a day or two later, delivered them to an underling of Dr. Okawa for distribution to his civilian agitators.

Seeing at last that the coup might have some solid foundation in gunpowder, Ugaki sounded out Lieutenant General Mazaki Jinzaburo, the commander of the crack 1st Division which was slated in the coup planning to seize the Diet.[5] To General Ugaki's consternation Mazaki insisted that

---

[5] Mazaki was soon to become the number-two leader of the Strike-North idealists in the Army who would fight a long losing political battle with Hirohito over his

he knew nothing of any plans to seize the Diet and had no intention of participating in "illegal activities" without direct written orders from the Emperor.[6]

UGAKI'S SEDUCTION

War Minister Ugaki was so shaken by Mazaki's advice that the unsavory Dr. Okawa had to begin courting him all over again. On February 11, 1931, Okawa took Ugaki out for an evening of talk and play at the Golden Dragon geisha house in Tsukiji. It was one of Tokyo's most expensive pleasure restaurants, a favorite of Lord Privy Seal Count Makino. Now, however, Ugaki was not easily to be seduced. The political planning for the coup still seemed vague to him, he said, and he was not yet convinced that it had the support of the "Center of the Army." After much drinking of saké, Ugaki went home, pleased with his discretion, to await developments.

On February 13, by Dr. Okawa's arrangement, Ugaki began a social whirl calculated to turn the head of any man born, as he had been, in a farmhouse, and living, as he was, on a salary of $3,000 a year. Not a day passed in which he did not lunch or dine with someone above his own hereditary station who could claim to be close to Hirohito. He started on January 13 with Colonel Okamura Yasuji, the third of the Three Crows of Baden-Baden, who, but for Commodore Perry, would have inherited the command of the Tokyo castle guard. Ugaki went on to lunch on February 14 with Hirohito's trusted go-between to Chiang Kai-shek, the ubiquitous Lieutenant Colonel Suzuki. A few days later Ugaki dined with Suzuki's patron, Big Brother Colonel Marquis Inoue Saburo, the illegitimate son of Emperor Taisho's Prime Minister Katsura. Next it was an invitation to the villa of Prince Konoye, the leader of Hirohito's faction in the House of Peers. And finally, through Konoye, War Minister Ugaki sat down to dinner in the villa of Count Arima, an in-law of the Empress.

Count Arima stated unequivocally that it was time to complete the Restoration of 1868 and place the Emperor at the helm of a National Socialist state.

For further details, Count Arima referred the befuddled, bedazzled Ugaki to the "paymaster of the proposed March incident," Baron Toku-gawa Yoshichika, a scion of the great family of shoguns which had governed Japan from 1600 to 1868. Baron Tokugawa was well-to-do but not truly rich. Nevertheless, for the March Plot, he had at his disposal

---

plans to conquer China. He was a thoroughly blunt and honest officer, and the father of the Mazaki, mentioned in the Foreword, who befriended the author and his fellow inmates at a concentration camp in the Philippines during World War II.

[6] By so saying, Mazaki permanently alienated himself from the Throne. He would be relentlessly persecuted by the princes of the blood for the next five years and finally disgraced by unjust imprisonment and dishonorable discharge.

$100,000, which, as he said himself, was a large sum to disburse in the midst of a world depression.[7] War Minister Ugaki agreed.

On February 26, 1931, after two weeks in high society, Ugaki returned to a second evening of beguilement with Dr. Okawa and the geisha of the Golden Dragon teahouse. Ugaki was far more respectful toward Dr. Okawa than he had been but he continued to ask questions. What had become of the manifesto which Dr. Okawa was drafting? What was being done to enlist the massive popular support which Dr. Okawa had promised? The glib doctor assured Ugaki that the manifesto was being written and that an underground web of conspiracy was spreading through the people like mushroom roots. In the meanwhile it would greatly facilitate preparations if Dr. Okawa could tell his recruits that the great General Ugaki had promised to head the coup d'etat government.

"I have waited to see a concrete political plan for the new government," said Ugaki, "and some evidence of popular support for it. When I see these things, then I will give you my answer."

Ugaki passed the evening drinking saké, enjoying the geisha entertainment, and talking to a group of young Army officers who came to the party late with *Panay*-sinker Lieutenant Colonel Hashimoto. Before dawn, his head in the lap of a geisha, Ugaki was heard to boast: "If our plans go awry and the Emperor refuses to give his approval, I swear to cut open my belly in the Imperial Presence." Drunk though he was, Ugaki had thoroughly incriminated himself before geisha witnesses. He had threatened to embarrass the Throne. He had committed lèse majesté. It was all that the March Plotters needed—enough to keep Ugaki out of politics, enough to blight the rest of his career.

The next day, while Ugaki was recovering from his hangover, some of the members of the cabal who were closest to Hirohito began to spread word among their minions that the plot had served its purpose and would soon be canceled. At the same time Prince Kanin's Army conspirators, who wished to create a genuine national scare in preparation for the seizure of Manchuria, urged Dr. Okawa to stage at least a small public riot before the plot was allowed to grow moribund.

For the next three days Dr. Okawa remained imperturbably drinking saké at the Golden Dragon and signing chits in the name of Baron Toku-

---

[7] Tokugawa was the brother of Hirohito's chamberlain in charge of peerage and heraldry. His hobby was natural history and he was one of a group of amateur biologists who dined regularly with Hirohito in his private quarters. Through business interests in Malaya and Sumatra and through friendship with the rajah of Johore, Tokugawa was also a leading advocate of a policy of Striking South. When the Strike South finally came in 1942, Hirohito made him curator of the Botanical Gardens and Natural History Museum of Singapore. Under his charge this cradle of the theory of evolution would become, in 1943, a front for the master intelligence organization through which Hirohito kept track of his proconsuls in the newly acquired territories of the South Seas.

gawa. Finally, on the evening of March 2, Military Affairs Bureau Chief Koiso invaded the teahouse, dragged Okawa from the arms of Yoshimaru, his geisha mistress, had him immersed in a scalding tub, and then sat him down in a quiet room to dictate notes to Black Dragon leaders instructing them to raise a mob the following afternoon in Hibiya and Ueno parks.

The "show of force" which materialized in the parks the next day was disappointing. Three thousand laborers, vagrants, and drunks, hired at fifty cents apiece, turned out to hear some routine patriotic speeches by ward heelers and shout a few banzais.

Too late, on the morning of March 3, General Ugaki telephoned Military Affairs Chief Koiso and announced, "I see no reason to become a party to this foolish scheme." Three more days passed before Ugaki realized that "this plot was not an ordinary one" and that he had been thoroughly traduced and suborned. On March 7, he went to the palace to declare his innocence of any disloyal intent. Dr. Okawa's patron, Lord Privy Seal Makino, who saw him on behalf of the Emperor, agreed to be lenient and promised Ugaki a face-saving assignment soon, out of the way, in Korea.

DR. OKAWA'S PROFITEERING

For the purposes of state the March Plot ended here, with Ugaki's shamefaced withdrawal from the presence of Lord Privy Seal Count Makino. For the private purposes of Dr. Okawa, however, it did not end until many months had passed. The devious doctor realized that his position was precarious and that he must make the most of his blackmail materials while they were still relevant and in his hands. The lord of the Black Dragon Toyama had lost face and needed to be recompensed. Prince Kanin's minions in the Army were disgusted by Okawa's performance and disposed to be unfriendly. After communicating by letter with his patron Count Makino, Dr. Okawa determined to use the 300 training grenades in his possession to embarrass the Army and to make sure that his bills would be paid to the hustlers of both the Black and Golden Dragon establishments with which he had done his business.

Until the third week of March, Dr. Okawa maintained that he intended to go ahead with the planned bombing of the Diet on March 20. Military Affairs Chief Koiso and General Staff Intelligence Chief Tatekawa became increasingly fearful that the Army's part in supplying the bombs might be made public. Finally, through the mediation of retired Colonel Komoto Daisaku, the Baden-Baden Reliable and bridge-blower who had dynamited Manchurian war lord Chang Tso-lin, Dr. Okawa agreed to give up his attack on the Diet in return for a suitable fee—one million yen ($500,000)! Baron Tokugawa, the March Plot's financier, observed that "these details make me feel unpleasant."

By retired Reliable Komoto's arrangement, Tokugawa met with Dr.

Okawa at the Totaku Building in downtown Tokyo on the afternoon of March 18 and agreed on a greatly reduced but still stiff settlement of 200,000 yen ($100,000). The deal was witnessed by the administrator of Baron Tokugawa's estates and by Dr. Okawa's chief henchman. The administrator undertook to pay the 200,000 yen in four monthly installments and the henchman, "weeping with patriotic disappointment," promised to cancel the attack on the Diet.

It was agreed that Dr. Okawa would keep the Army's bombs for security until the money had been paid. That night Dr. Okawa's henchman moved the bombs secretly from his girl friend's home to a trucker's warehouse in northwestern Tokyo. There they were kept for a year and used as a reminder to the high brass of the Army that the March Plot could be revived at any time. Baron Tokugawa paid the huge blackmail, stayed solvent, and continued to enjoy his intimacy with Hirohito. Dr. Okawa settled with the Black Dragon, paid his bill at the Golden Dragon, and remained at large to carry out many more nefarious commissions for Hirohito's chief advisor, Lord Privy Seal Count Makino.

Late on the afternoon of the settlement, the first of the Big Brothers, Count Makino's secretary, Marquis Kido, took the train out to Prime-Minister-Maker Saionji's villa on the seashore at Okitsu and told the old man about "the coup d'etat of General Ugaki" which had just been successfully "nipped in the bud." Saionji, recognizing defeat, assumed an air of noncommittal indifference. In the course of the evening, however, he allowed some of his bitterness to come out in critical reminiscences about Lord Privy Seal Makino at the Versailles Conference. Years later, writing in prison, Kido was to admire Privy Seal Makino's deftness "in conducting . . . the March Plot . . . out of darkness into darkness."

Both the Strike-North rightists in the Army and the strike-nowhere Constitutionalists around Saionji had been intimidated. General Ugaki had seized the bait and run with it far enough to spoil his chances for a political career. Many important fish knew of the fishing but hardly a bubble had broken through to the surface of Japan's deep political sea. In less than a year Hirohito was to appoint Major General Koiso, the plot-master, to the post of vice war minister.

12

SEIZURE OF MUKDEN

(1931)

CLEARING THE DECKS

Disquieting rumors of the March Plot, dissatisfaction with budget cuts, and alarm at the military's share in the planning for the future made for a stormy spring session of the Diet. At the end of it, in April 1931, the Cabinet resigned and left its prime minister, Hamaguchi, to die of his gunshot wounds in the quiet of private life. Hirohito appointed as the next prime minister Wakatsuki Reijiro, vice president of Hamaguchi's party and former chief delegate to the 1930 London Naval Conference. Ex-War Minister Ugaki, notwithstanding his past services to the Throne, his firm intention of going into politics, and his recent flirtation with high treason, meekly withdrew from the domestic scene to become the governor general in Korea.

Prime Minister Wakatsuki obediently submitted to Hirohito an ordinance requiring all government employees except judges to accept a 10 per cent decrease in salary if they made more than $50 a month. Judges' salaries, by a peculiarity of the administrative code, could not be decreased except by the judges themselves. During the formulative stages of the ordinance there had been bitter complaints from young bureaucrats of good family and even from some of the patriotic but already underpaid officers of the armed forces. Now, however, when Hirohito signed the decree on May 27, 1931, the nation's servants gave an astonishingly Japanese exhibition of self-denial by "tightening their loincloth strings" and submitting in silence. The bar association resolved that the judiciary should follow suit voluntarily and individual judges did so without known exception.

Hirohito was now ready, politically and financially, to launch his imperial program on the Asiatic continent. Throughout the summer of 1931

he devoted his attention to a detailed review of the military plans which
had been made. His objectives differed from those of most of his Army
advisors. He wanted to control Manchurian bases in order to establish a
pattern which would enable him later to control other strategic bases all
down the China coast toward Singapore. He did not set high priority on
outright conquest and colonization of Manchuria. The acquisition of Korea,
under his grandfather, had already demonstrated that Japan's overpopu-
lation problem could not be solved by expansion toward the north. The
mass of Japanese were simply not interested in emigrating to chilly farmlands, no matter how rich. Even Ainu Hokkaido, subjugated centuries
ago, was still sparsely populated. What Japan needed were warm lands
for colonists and resources for industrial development—the oil and rubber and minerals of the East Indies. Only the unsophisticated Army mind
could desire Manchuria as an end in itself.

Hirohito had before him two plans. One called for a cutback in Army
manpower, an increase in mechanization, more divisions stationed in Korea,
and no increase in the Army budget. It would strengthen the Army for
any use to which it might be put. Hirohito approved it formally on July
15, 1931.

The other plan, of greater moment, was the operational blueprint for
the take-over of Manchuria which Hirohito had commissioned in 1928 from
the young, corrosive-tongued military genius, Lieutenant Colonel Ishiwara
Kanji. Ishiwara's completed study was exhaustive and imaginative. It anticipated all military contingencies and gracefully suggested a number of
political strategems which might be used in Japan and abroad to make the
operation seem accidental. Hirohito admired all of it except for a few visionary pages toward the end in which Ishiwara expressed his hopes for
making Manchuria a "paradise."

Officially, in late 1930, Hirohito had had Ishiwara's opus filed away as
"contingency planning, top secret." Unofficially he had told his great-uncle,
Field Marshal Prince Kanin, to see that all necessary military preparations
were made so that the plan would be ready for execution by August 1931.
Secretly with Count Makino, Hirohito was now gnawing over the political
implications and deciding on certain options which he would reserve for
himself, to exercise or not, when the time came.

As soon as Hirohito gave his unofficial nod, operatives of the cabal in
Army Intelligence and in the military secret police began to find and make
provocations for intervention in Manchuria. In June 1931, a Japanese intelligence agent, traveling as an "agricultural expert" in eastern Mongolia,
was apprehended and shot by Chinese soldiers for being a spy. In July the
Kwantung Army sent troops into a border area of Manchuria to protect
the rights of Korean immigrants there who were being harassed by Chinese farmers in the digging of a drainage ditch.

CHOICE OF A COMMANDER

From July 13 to 17, the regimental commanders of the principal division which would be used in Manchuria, the 10th, met for "map exercises" and "tactical studies." Their chief was Lieutenant General Honjo Shigeru, an ideal leader for a controversial operation. At fifty-five he was respected by the rank and file as one of the most capable of the elder generation of nonpolitical Army professionals. Trained in garrison duty in China, long a friend of the murdered Manchurian war lord Chang Tso-lin, he spoke fluent Chinese and was a firm believer in ultimate Sino-Japanese partnership. Now, because of mounting tension with China he was letting his mustache grow to conceal his striking personal resemblance to Chiang Kai-shek.

On July 13, as Lieutenant General Honjo presided over the opening of his division's map exercises, General Ugaki, on his way to Korea as the new governor general, stopped by at the 10th Division base southwest of Osaka to greet Honjo and have a talk with him. Seven years of strict Japanese military seniority separated the two, but Honjo, the junior, was warmly disposed toward Ugaki. He owed Ugaki many past favors, and he knew that Ugaki's new post was not all that the older general had hoped for.

The two men met over tea in a kiosk beside the railroad track. Ugaki circled in slowly to the point of the conversation. It was a part of his penitence to the Throne for high treason—part of the price he was paying for his position of continued honor in the hierarchy—that he persuade his protégé Honjo to lend his name and leadership to the seizure of Manchuria. Without going into details, he suggested to Honjo that a bargain had been made with Chiang Kai-shek, that Japanese occupation of Manchuria was a necessity in view of the growing military strength of Bolshevik Russia. Some day, he piously hoped, Manchuria would be a model Asiatic state which would serve as a bridge and a bond of friendship between China and Japan. Then, abruptly, he told General Honjo that he was "the choice of the Center of the Army" to be the next commander-in-chief of Japan's leasehold presence in Manchuria, the Kwantung Army. Honjo realized that he was being asked a question and replied at once that he would be greatly honored if the majority of the Army, the sensible field officers of the Ugaki Faction, should back him for such a promotion.

Ugaki grunted his appreciation and returned to his train. At the next station, he wired old Prince Kanin's man, Major General Koiso of the Military Affairs Bureau in Tokyo, that Honjo would accept. Two days later Hirohito set his great seal upon Honjo's reassignment papers, and the cabal's ubiquitous Lieutenant Colonel Suzuki Tei-ichi arrived at Honjo's headquarters to inform him, unofficially, of the great confidence which the Emperor placed in him.

Furthermore, continued Colonel Suzuki, the Emperor had approved the appointment of Colonel Doihara Kenji as chief of the Special Service

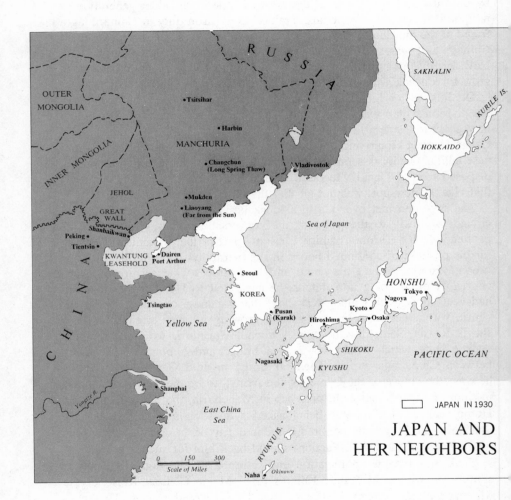

JAPAN IN 1930

JAPAN AND HER NEIGHBORS

Organ in Mukden, the Army's political espionage agency there. General Honjo knew Doihara well—he had worked with him in Peking in 1918. Doihara was one of the Eleven Reliables chosen at Baden-Baden. Having served in China almost continuously since 1913, he had a wide acquaintance with petty war lords, malcontent mandarins, and out-of-power Manchu princes. His understanding of transactions conducted in the irregular currencies of China—women, bombs, opium packets—had gained him a name as the "Lawrence of Manchuria." The Mukden branch of the Special Service Organ had hitherto been run by minor operatives; at the very least, Doihara's appointment to it meant a change in Chang Hsueh-liang's regime in Manchuria.

Finally, Suzuki reported, the Emperor had appointed Colonel Tojo Hideki, the later military strong man of World War II, to be chief of the General Staff's Organization and Mobilization Section. Honjo knew Tojo only slightly; he seemed to be a competent desk man, a stickler for details and efficiency.

Honjo sighed expressively and told Suzuki that he was ready for whatever duty lay ahead. Privately, as revealed in his diary, he had many doubts, suspicions, and second thoughts.

AN EERIE QUIET

In mid-July old Saionji confided to Prime Minister Wakatsuki that he was alarmed by rumors which he heard from many directions about plans for war in China. Wakatsuki took advantage of the recent "incidents" in Korea and China to make a special report to the Throne on the growing tension between Japan and China. Chiang Kai-shek, he said, had correctly accused the Japanese Army in a recent speech of supplying money and guns to anti-Chiang insurgents in the Canton area. A delegation from the Canton faction of the KMT or Kuomintang had now arrived in Tokyo to negotiate official Japanese recognition and support for their regime. The experts in the Foreign Ministry advised a friendly but noncommittal response on Japan's part. Nodding approvingly, Hirohito said that he deplored the deterioration in Sino-Japanese relations. He added, "I may assume, may I not, that you will keep Sino-Japanese goodwill as the cornerstone of our policy?"

Prime Minister Wakatsuki, emerging from the audience chamber, asked Baron Harada if the Emperor meant "Sino-Japanese goodwill or its opposite." Saionji, when the quip had been relayed to him, sent a note to Privy Seal Makino asking him to clarify the Emperor's ambiguity. A vice chamberlain at once arrived in Okitsu by the sea to assure old man Saionji that when the Emperor said "Sino-Japanese goodwill," he meant only that and nothing more.

"Bear in mind," sniped Saionji at his political secretary, his intermediary with the cabal, "that they sent me only an *assistant chamberlain.*" He implied that any higher chamberlain, knowing better, could not have relayed the message without shame of lying.

Everyone in the aristocracy, many in the middle-class bureaucracy, and a few in the masses of the foot soldiers knew that the conquest of Manchuria was in the making, but not a word of their suspicion was printed in the press or discussed at public gatherings. The Emperor's secret was the secret of the nation. Nowhere but in Japan could the plans of the chief be held so privily in the minds of the whole tribe. On small uncivilized islands out in the Pacific American anthropologists had encountered similar secrecy toward outsiders. But in such a large industrial nation as Japan, the thought had to be dismissed as madness. Intelligence officers at the American Embassy in Tokyo warned Washington of tension in the Far East but discounted the possibility of war.

Even the Chinese government showed no unusual signs of alarm. Chiang Kai-shek was waging one of his periodic "bandit suppression campaigns" against the peasant "rabble" of Communist Mao Tse-tung. Chiang had with him the whole of the Manchurian Army as well as its leader, his faithful disciple, young Chang Hsueh-liang. It seemed inconceivable to Western military observers that Chiang and Chang would leave Manchuria defended only by raw levies unless they thought that Japan meant nothing serious. Western observers, however, did not know that Chiang Kai-shek, and Sun Yat-sen before him, had agreed to sacrifice Manchuria with only a token face-saving fight if Japan would promise not to interfere with KMT unification of the rest of China.

By July 22, 1931, it was apparent to American reporters in Manchuria that the Kwantung Army had set up field pieces all along the right of way of the Japanese-owned South Manchuria Railroad. Chiang Kai-shek filed no protest, and Chang Hsueh-liang merely retired to the American Rockefeller Hospital in Peking for one of his recurrent treatments for opium addiction.

READY AND AIMED

On July 25 the last bolt was tightened on the iron floor of the most monstrous of Japan's unseeable war preparations: a pair of 9.5-inch cannon mounted in a shallow silo in the very heart of the Manchurian capital of Mukden. Twenty-five years earlier the Russians had used the cannon to good effect at the siege of Port Arthur. The bold idea of trucking the weapons north and installing them in the Japanese compound in Mukden had occurred to the brash young strategist, Lieutenant Colonel Ishiwara in late 1928. During the summer of 1929, he had prepared an emplacement for them under the unlikely cover story that the Japanese community of attachés and aides in Mukden were building themselves a swimming pool.

Hired Chinese coolies dutifully sank in the earth a concrete pan 33 feet in diameter and 39 inches deep. To keep out the cold and preserve bathing officers from the ogling of Chinese passers-by, the "pool" was surrounded by a large shed covered with a flimsy pretext of a roof that would permit an easy exit for shells. At one end were hung big barnlike doors to permit an easy entrance for heavy aquatic equipment such as diving boards. Late one night in May 1931, however, the doors were opened to admit two heavily guarded vans, containing the cannon. One of the cannon was installed so that it was permanently trained on the main barracks of the Mukden constabulary; the other so that it was aimed at the airfield from which Chang Hsueh-liang flew his fledgling air force. While this incredibly brazen piece of chicanery was under construction, Chinese plainclothesmen stood daily watch across the street from the shed. When the moment to use the guns finally arrived, no countermeasures had been taken to prevent them from hailing down shot on their two targets.

COMPROMISE FOR CONQUEST

Since receiving Hirohito's go-ahead in early June 1931, Ishiwara had worked with a fanatic's zeal to prepare for his scheme of inside-out conquest. As soon as the emplacement of the big guns in Mukden had been completed, he returned to Tokyo, in the last week of July, to answer questions about his efforts from the other military members of the cabal. The young bloods of the Strike-North faction in the General Staff approved his plans enthusiastically. But from older cabalists—like First Crow Nagata and the later World War II prime minister, Tojo Hideki—he received only qualified encouragement, tempered with many political anxieties.

The thorny Ishiwara, knowing his own limitations as a politician, had come to Tokyo forearmed for such objections. He had brought with him from Manchuria Colonel Itagaki Seishiro, one of the Eleven Reliables chosen at Baden-Baden. Itagaki had worked with him in Manchuria since the summer of 1929, supplementing his tactical vinegar with the oil of a consummate politician. Itagaki came of a good family, high among the retainers of the old Nambu clan which had governed the northern extremities of Japan for the Tokugawa shoguns. He had the sleek round-faced neatly mustached look of a seal, and he slapped backs like a veteran tour director. He never gave the impression of being too quick-witted. Indeed, on a later occasion, Emperor Hirohito would tell him to his face, "You are the most stupid man alive." But he had the knack of making other men's ideas socially presentable and politically acceptable. Long after Ishiwara's genius and ideals had been put prematurely to pasture, Itagaki would remain at Hirohito's side, full of bland inoffensive energy. He would lead Japan's best mobile division to the worst defeat of Japan's war with China. He would reign as war minister during Japan's disastrous Nomonhan border war with Russia in 1939. He would command the Korean

Army throughout World War II. He would officiate over the humiliating surrender of Singapore to the British in 1945. Until his hanging in 1948, he would serve in prison as the most relaxed and optimistic of the defendants at the Tokyo war crimes trials. Even his American captors would admire him for his open, bloodthirsty, devil-may-care attitude.

On the morning of August 1, 1931, Lieutenant General Honjo reported at the Summer Palace in Hayama to take lunch and receive his new command officially at the hands of the Emperor. The time had come, under Honjo's aegis, to brief the field commanders of the Army on the confusing pressures which would be exerted on them in the months ahead. Hirohito, as the representative of his high priestly ancestors, could not openly take responsibility for the seizure of Manchuria. The responsibility must be shouldered by the official government of Cabinet and prime minister. The government, however, was unwilling to accept the responsibility. Hirohito and Count Makino planned to use the Army to intimidate the government. At the same time, the government's timidity would serve as an excuse to keep the Army from bulling north across Manchuria into a war with Soviet Russia. In this fashion Hirohito hoped to control both the moderates, who wished to avoid foreign entanglements, and the militarists, who wished to exhaust Japan's empire-building energies in Siberia. Hirohito's personal ambition, the Strike-South into the rich fleshpots of the South Seas, was still so futuristic in terms of national strength that mention of it would only align the militarists and moderates against Hirohito.

The commanders of Japan's seventeen standing divisions and three colonial armies met for briefing on the Manchurian operation on August 3. Hirohito gave an individual audience to each commander, dropping word that he knew and approved of the events scheduled for the near future. During the audiences with the Emperor, General Honjo of the 10th Division was put in another room of the palace to work out secret lines of liaison between the Throne and his future command in Manchuria. Closeted with him were the ubiquitous Lieutenant Colonel Suzuki, to speak for the Throne, and the affable Colonel Itagaki, to speak for strategist Ishiwara and the Kwantung Army's troops in the field.

That night at a secret meeting in the muggy offices of the General Staff just outside the palace walls, Prince Kanin's two minions, Peerless Pimp Tatekawa and March Plotter Koiso, cautioned a select gathering of field commanders not to divulge classified sections of the planning for Manchuria to War Minister General Minami Jiro. Too much knowledge, they agreed, would only compromise Minami and compound the difficulties of the role he had to play as intermediary between the Throne and the Cabinet.

The next day, August 4, General Minami delivered his scheduled address to Japan's commanders before they returned to their divisions. It was the one function of the three-day conference which was to be public and open to the press. Innocently assuming that the conquest of Manchuria was to be a blunt, straightforward, above-board military operation, General Minami added to his speech a patriotic exhortation to the troops.

"Accordingly," he concluded, "those who must render service in military affairs this fall have the obligation to pursue their training and arduous education diligently. It is to be expected that they will be completely prepared to exercise their duty."

War Minister Minami had unwittingly alerted the public to the coming Manchurian campaign, for Japanese newspaper reporters heard in his words the first official admission that Japan was going to war.[1] The big dailies at first printed Minami's remarks without comment, but two days later, *Asahi* (the equivalent of *The New York Times* in Tokyo) noted editorially: "The military seems to be openly disregarding public opinion and defying the government."

This oblique statement was the only reporting of the fact that old Saionji and his fellow liberals were waging a desperate last-ditch struggle behind the scenes to prevent the planned war. Saionji had persuaded the civilian members of the Cabinet to refuse to approve the necessary transfers of funds for the war. Hirohito, for his part, refused to give his official sanction to the war unless the Cabinet would back him by assuming fiscal responsibility. War Minister General Minami took the position that he could not begin the war without properly signed imperial orders.

Unofficially, Hirohito was encouraging the junior officers of his cabal to push forward on their own. On August 25 the spokesman for a group of concerned young men in the Naval General Staff asked Secretary-Spy Harada to warn Saionji that Hirohito was, in effect, planning to move troops in Manchuria even without first giving his sanction.

Saionji was obliged to recognize that the Cabinet's refusal to be involved in the war would avail him nothing. That same day, at his summer villa in the mountain resort of Gotemba, he received a visit from Prime Minister Wakatsuki who urged him to accept a compromise. As he watched the sun sink behind the towering cinder cone of Mount Fuji, Saionji said he would consider Wakatsuki's proposal.

Sometime in the following week, a month before his eighty-second birthday, Saionji sent word to Prime Minister Wakatsuki that he would accept the offered compromise: first a limited operation around Mukden in southern Manchuria, then "a pause for reflection" before further ad-

---

[1] That night Kido, Lord Privy Seal Makino's secretary, wrote in his diary: "A strong wind from Minami made things very damp." In one of his typically discreet private jokes with his diary, Kido was punning on the name Minami, which is also the Japanese word for south. Honjo's diary and the newspaper weather columns for the date of Minami's speech leave no doubt that it was an ordinary hot, overcast, August day without a drop of rain or a breath of wind.

vances. Through Japan's ancient, efficient, uncensorable communications system, the word-of-mouth grapevine, the general public was informed that an adjustment had been made and a consensus reached. During the next week the Tokyo daily papers received several thousand calls from readers asking, "When is the war going to start?" Westerners living in Japan, particularly Western intelligence agents, were given hardly a hint of the excitement in the air.

VEILED ORDERS

On September 14 Saionji summoned War Minister Minami to his villa in Gotemba and gave him a broadly constructed version of the terms which he had accepted. The Emperor, Saionjo said, had decided that the Kwantung Army must proceed with "prudence and caution" and must limit its operations—at least to begin with—to the environs of Mukden and a few other railheads in south central Manchuria. Saionji did not explain how the Army could attack and kill with prudent caution or how it was to seize and hold an enclave without strategic boundaries, in the midst of China.

When War Minister Minami returned to Tokyo the next morning, he summoned an emergency meeting of Army brass and relayed Saionji's strictures. At first the majority of the officers present were in favor of shelving the conquest plans entirely rather than court disaster by starting something that could not be finished. The officers closest to Hirohito, however, assured the others that no such drastic change of course was expected of them. In the end it was agreed that Saionji's orders must be delivered verbatim to the Kwantung Army but must also be explained lest they cause confusion. To tell an obedient, circumspect commander like Lieutenant General Honjo that the Emperor wished him to move with caution would be to tell him not to move at all without further instructions.

The choice of the emissary to Honjo might have been made by War Minister Minami if alert members of the cabal had not pointed out that a commander on war duty was under the jurisdiction of the General Staff and that the courier to General Honjo should be appointed by the Chief of Staff. Minami agreed and the meeting broke up.

Major General Koiso of the Military Affairs Bureau at once telephoned Major General Tatekawa, the Peerless Pimp, Chief of Operations in the General Staff, and Tatekawa quickly arranged to have himself sent to Manchuria with Saionji's message. Then Tatekawa summoned to his office the chiefs of the Russia and China Desks in Army Intelligence, who listened while Tatekawa treated them to a long, musing soliloquy. The scheduled date for the "rising" in Manchuria was September 28, was it not? In view of the mounting dissension in the Army, it would be well to move the date up to the earliest moment possible. The Emperor had taken it upon his own conscience to lead the nation in what must be done. Because of Japan's relative weakness, duplicity was required. It was up to every loyal

Japanese to lighten the Emperor's burden as much as possible and prevent any tarnish from settling on the sacred Throne bequeathed by the ancestors. In this present critical period, there must always be one official plan for foreigners, a second for Japanese, and a third for the Emperor's personal retainers. It should not be necessary for the Throne to issue explicit orders for the drawing up of such covers. They should come into being automatically out of the patriotic desire of every Japanese to preserve the honor of the nation.

Having expressed his thoughts in front of his two subordinates, Tatekawa sat down and drafted an official Army cablegram to General Honjo. Tatekawa announced that he planned to visit Mukden, the Manchurian capital, three days later, arriving by train at 7:05 P.M. on the evening of September 18. The fact that he gave Honjo three days to prepare for his coming and that he wished to meet Honjo in Mukden rather than the Kwantung Army's leasehold headquarters in Port Arthur 250 miles to the south suggested broadly that Honjo should carry out the coup ahead of schedule and be ready as conqueror to receive visitors in the enemy capital by September 18. Tatekawa read the cable aloud, affixed to it his seal, and asked the two desk chiefs, who had been standing by throughout his performance, to see that it was properly encoded and dispatched.

The chief of the China Desk returned to his office and drafted a second telegram of his own to Colonel Itagaki, the politician of the Kwantung Army. In it he repeated the itinerary of Tatekawa's trip to Mukden, and added: HOSPITABLE TREATMENT WILL BE APPRECIATED; HIS MISSION IS TO PREVENT THE INCIDENT. The Russia Desk man, Lieutenant Colonel Hashimoto, who six years later was to order the sinking of the U.S.S. *Panay,* sent off a third telegram. Stamped "top secret, personal," it was addressed to a close friend who was an aide of Ishiwara, the strategist of the Kwantung Army. This telegram said succinctly and dramatically: PLOT EXPOSED. ACT BEFORE TATEKAWA'S ARRIVAL.

While Tatekawa proceeded leisurely by train through Japan and Korea, stretching a one-day journey into three, his cablegrams were causing consternation at Kwantung Army Headquarters in Port Arthur. General Honjo was away inspecting preparations in Mukden, and Itagaki and Ishiwara had been left in charge. Itagaki, the politician, took the cable to mean that the Emperor wished the seizure of Mukden to be executed immediately. Ishiwara, the strategist, was concerned lest his delicately timed plans be spoiled by last-minute haste. Both men feared that General Honjo's reaction to the cables would be to postpone everything until he heard more from Tokyo. Then the glorious enterprise for which they had both worked night and day for over two years might all come to naught. While they discussed what to do, they held up the cable to Honjo and did not forward it. Finally they resolved to ask Honjo to schedule the seizure of Mukden for the night of September 18, a few hours after the anticipated arrival of Peerless Pimp Tatekawa. In this way they would be able to hear from Tatekawa the situation in Tokyo around the Throne and would still have time, if need be, to call all units and cancel the action. While Ishiwara was drafting the necessary orders, Itagaki entrained for Mukden to present the plan to General Honjo.

On September 16, while Ishiwara and Itagaki were agonizing over the contents of the cablegrams, Honjo completed his inspection and went by rail to a place called Liaoyang or Far-from-the-Sun, a junction 40 miles south of Mukden where the Japanese railroad management had a small airfield. There Honjo met old General Suzuki Soroku who had just flown in from Tokyo. Suzuki was the near twin and for forty years the cavalry comrade of Field Marshal Prince Kanin, the gray eminence of the imperial family. He had left Tokyo at about the same time as Tatekawa's cablegrams. Over dinner he and Honjo discussed the situation at home.

Later that evening when Itagaki arrived breathless from Port Arthur, Honjo introduced him curtly to General Suzuki and told him, please, to take some responsibility and handle details himself rather than bothering old generals in their moments of relaxation. Itagaki hastily bowed his way out, consulted with Ishiwara by phone, and then issued the necessary orders for the night after next.

Cover plans were now completed. If the operation went awry, Prince Kanin was ready to take responsibility for Hirohito, Tatekawa for Prince Kanin, Honjo for Tatekawa, and Itagaki for Honjo. If all went well, each would share in the credit, according to his station. Ultimately Ishiwara and Itagaki would take the blame, and Itagaki would be hanged for it by the Allies.[2]

THE GO-AHEAD

On the morning of September 17, 1931, after spending the previous evening with Prince Kanin's emissary from Tokyo, General Honjo went to a park in Far-from-the-Sun. There he reviewed a dress rehearsal by Japanese troops of the "incident" on the railroad which was to serve as provocation for the war of conquest scheduled to start the next night. Early on D-day, September 18, Honjo canceled a scheduled visit to one of the battlefields of the Russo-Japanese War and devoted the morning and early afternoon to a detailed run-through of all plans with his field commanders. At 2:00 P.M. he boarded a Pullman car for a good sleep during the six-hour journey back to his headquarters at Port Arthur.

While his Pullman clattered away from Mukden toward the southwest, the train of Peerless Pimp Tatekawa crossed the Korean border and ap-

---

[2] The multiplicity of cover stories would convince Western historians that junior officers had acted on their own and later shamed senior officers into sanctioning what had been done. The reality, in which every man on the ladder, from lowest to highest, conspired to deceive, knowing exactly what was afoot, is demonstrated by Lieutenant General Honjo's diary.

proached Mukden from the southeast. At 5:18 it stopped to take on water at the village station of Pen-hsi-hu, Lake-at-the-Bottom-of-the-Valley. There it was boarded by the affable politician of the Kwantung Army, Itagaki. He was ushered to the parlor car of the affable Tatekawa, and the two like-minded officers sat down to enjoy an hour and forty-seven minutes of circumspect belly talk while their train completed its run into Mukden. The opening gambits of their conversation, as reconstructed from stories they later told their friends, went like this:

Itagaki: "You are well, sir, I hope."

Tatekawa: "Well, as a matter of fact, I have not slept much on the train and I hear you boisterous youngsters need discipline, but let's leave all that until I have had a good night's rest."

Itagaki: "We young men are also tired by our recent efforts, sir. So have no doubts about us but let me take you to a good inn when we arrive in Mukden and we will discuss business in the morning."

When the train reached Mukden at 7:05 P.M., a staff car was waiting, chauffeured by a young major, the officer who had received *Panay*-sinker Hashimoto's cablegram three days earlier. He drove Tatekawa and Itagaki to the best teahouse in the Japanese quarter, the Literary Chrysanthemum. There the choicest geisha and saké had been laid on for the night. Itagaki drank one toast and then said that he was expecting a very important phone call at the Special Service Organ. With this excuse, he left Tatekawa, to have his bath and drink and eat, in the care of the young major and the geisha.

The Special Service Organ office, a two-story building of reinforced concrete, had been chosen as the communications center for the night's activities. Linesmen of the South Manchuria Railroad had equipped the switchboard with open connections to all the Japanese garrisons along the railroad right of way. A staff of lieutenants and captains stood by to man the phones, armed with maps and synchronized watches. Colonel Doihara Kenji, the "Lawrence of Manchuria," who was in command of the Special Service Organ, was out on the town politicking with Chinese friends to prepare a way for himself to become "Mayor of Mukden" in the morning. In his absence an elaborate pretence was maintained that Colonel Itagaki was merely filling in for him during a routine evening's operation.

When Itagaki arrived from the Literary Chrysanthemum, he put through a call from Doihara's private office in Mukden to a portrait painter in Dairen, the harbor town adjoining Port Arthur. It so happens that, a few moments earlier, at 8:00 P.M., General Honjo had also intruded upon the same portrait painter in Dairen. On his way to Port Arthur, after his exhausting day of reviews and travel, he had decided to stop off and inspect progress on a portrait of himself which the artist was painting. After what must have been a prolonged chat with Itagaki on the phone, Honjo left the painter's home a little after 9:00 P.M., drove to Port Arthur, and retired to restore his flagging energies in a hot Japanese tub.

In Mukden, having finished his phone call, Itagaki emerged from his office all smiles, thereby signifying to his staff that the light was green. Then he lay down ostentatiously on a couch to take a nap in preparation for a long night's work.

At the South Manchuria Railroad track north of Mukden, an operative of the Special Service Organ [3] was wiring up forty-two cubes of yellow blasting powder on the embankment, five feet to the west of the tracks running in from the northern town of Changchun or Long Spring Thaw. He buried the explosives carefully so that they would throw a lot of dirt but would cause no real damage to the strategically important Japanese-owned railroad track. Later the Japanese Foreign Ministry would maintain that Chinese soldiers had set the blast and that it had destroyed over a yard of track, seriously disrupting operation of the line. While making repairs, the Japanese Army would cordon off the area so that no Chinese could go near the damage to inspect it. After an "official investigation" the Army would try to explain how the 10:40 express from Long Spring Thaw had passed over the track a few minutes after the explosion and arrived in Mukden without its passengers feeling a jolt. The Army would produce an "eyewitness" of the should-have-been derailment and quote him as saying: "When the express reached the site of the explosion, it was seen to sway and incline to one side but it recovered and passed on without stopping."

ONE-NIGHT WAR

The plunger for the mock bombing of the tracks was pushed at approximately 10:20 P.M. Japanese railroad guards who had been ready waiting in the area for a week "conducting night maneuvers"—so they had told the Chinese—at once fell upon a Chinese constabulary patrol which had been sent to watch them. Two companies of Japanese regulars from the Kwantung Army, who were billeted nearby, joined instantly in the mopping-up operations.

The Japanese dynamiter at the track phoned the Special Service Organ in Mukden. There Colonel Itagaki had just risen, glanced at his watch, yawned, put on his coat, and announced to his amazed staff that he was going home to sleep in his billet. When the phone call came, however, he calmly told the dynamiter at the other end of the line to begin at once to attack the North Barracks of the Chinese garrison, some 300 yards from the scene of the mock bombing. No sooner had he given this order than the switchboard cut him into a second line, leading to the concealed battery of 9.5-inch Russian cannon. He ordered the gunnery officer there

[3] Lieutenant Komoto Suemori, a member of the same Kobe family of Komotos whose Colonel Komoto Daisaku had blown up Chang Tso-lin under similar circumstances in 1928.

to commence firing. One after another the staffers of the Special Service Organ connected Itagaki with duty officers at Japanese garrisons up and down the right of way of the South Manchuria Railroad. Over and over again Itagaki repeated the order: "This is Itagaki; proceed at once according to plan." Within two hours most of the small junction towns in south central Manchuria were in Japanese hands.

At 9:00 P.M., in the Literary Chrysanthemum, Major General Tatekawa from Tokyo had retired to rest with one of the geisha provided for him. "I have no intention," he told her, "of blocking our patriotic young officers." At about 10:30 when the big guns opened up on the Chinese airport and constabulary barracks, his bedmate shook him awake and said she was frightenend by the explosions. He made his way to the inn lobby, dressed only in sleeping kimono, and found there a group of soldiers who politely assured him, "We have been ordered to guard you and prevent you from going out where it is dangerous."

"Very well then," said Tatekawa, "the girl and I will go back to bed and leave the hard work to you young men." Tatekawa returned to his room, slipped on his clothes, and stole out a back door to be escorted by another group of soldiers to the headquarters of one of the units engaged in the action. Later that night, while his geisha swore he was sleeping like a baby at her side, he was seen with drawn sabre leading an attack on the walled citadel of Mukden.

As the shells of the big guns fell upon the massive gate leading into the Chinese constabulary barracks, the 10,000 Chinese within the compound began an orderly withdrawal through a back gate. They left the lights on in the buildings where they had lived in order to draw Japanese fire and demonstrate to the world that they had been going about their normal evening pursuits, expecting nothing. A force of 500 Japanese soldiers, in full battle dress, occupied the vacant compound inch by inch and secured it without casualties.

At 11:00 P.M., as the "storming of the barracks" began, General Honjo was still steeping in his hot bath at Port Arthur, 250 miles to the south. His chief of staff burst in on him, exclaiming, "Itagaki is on the phone! He has activated the garrisons without your express permission!"

"So that's how it is, is it?" growled Honjo. He arose majestically from the bath water, donned a kimono, and strode into the next room where his staff officers were waiting for him around the phone. Ishiwara, the strategist, spoke for them in terms of supplication. "The odds against us are staggering.[4] The entire countryside may rise. Offense is our only defense. I hope,

---

[4] By later Japanese reckoning 200,000 to 10,000. In reality Honjo had at his disposal about 20,000 men—an augmented division plus five battalions of railroad guards. The 200,000 Chinese arrayed against him consisted of green levies and irregulars, ill-equipped and undisciplined. They were under orders to avoid confrontations and to retreat in order if fighting did erupt.

sir, that you will allow Itagaki to proceed with the contingency plan that has already been prepared."

Lieutenant General Honjo squatted dramatically on the matting by the telephone for a moment of Zen contemplation. "Very well then," he declared, opening his eyes, "let it be done on my own responsiblity." He took the phone, loudly reproved Itagaki for acting without authorization, and then simply listened, interjecting an occasional "Hai! So be it."

Honjo approved Itagaki's plans for attacking the walled city of downtown Mukden at 11:30 P.M. A full regiment, said Itagaki, had already grouped for the attack. Major General Tatekawa, incognito, was assisting the colonel of the regiment in order to give the troops "fighting spirit." By the railroad track north of the city Japanese troops had occupied most of the constabulary barracks. The 9.5-inch cannon trained on Chang Hsueh-liang's airport was reported to be putting shells right on target, demolishing hangars and planes. None of the Chinese airmen had attempted to take off in the dark.

Honjo hung up smiling and ordered his staff to prepare for immediate transfer of Kwantung Army Headquarters north to Mukden. At 1:30 A.M., September 19, he phoned the commander of Japan's Korean Army in Seoul, seeking to share a little of his responsibility. He was assured that Japanese troops in Korea would lend assistance as necessary. A wing of Japan's Korean-based air force would be ready to land at the Mukden airfield as soon as light came. Having notified Colonel Itagaki of these arrangements, Lieutenant General Honjo boarded a train for Mukden at 3:30 A.M.

Ten minutes later Mukden's walled citadel was declared secure and Major General Tatekawa returned to the Literary Chrysanthemum to sleep. About an hour later the Hasebe Brigade occupied the center of Long Spring Thaw, 190 miles north of Mukden. By 5:00 A.M. all the Chinese towns along the South Manchuria Railroad from Port Arthur 500 miles north were in Japanese hands. At first light Japanese bombers from Korea landed at Chang Hsueh-liang's captured airport.

By noon, when General Honjo arrived in Mukden, the war for south Manchuria was virtually over. There was still heavy fighting in Long Spring Thaw but it would be finished by nightfall. By then all Chinese troops would be in full retreat toward the Sungari River which separated south Manchuria from north Manchuria and the thoroughly Chinese business community of Mukden from the White Russian lumbermen, miners, and moneylenders of the northern provincial capital of Harbin. The plans for inside-out conquest which strategist Ishiwara had begun to lay more than two years earlier had fully justified the obsessive patience and attention to detail which he had lavished on them. Only 400 Chinese had been killed—and precisely two Japanese.

SEARCH FOR LEGITIMACY

On the evening of September 19, twenty-four hours after his arrival in Mukden, Major General Tatekawa, the Peerless Pimp, strolled down the pacified streets from his billet at the Literary Chrysanthemum. He savored the long twilight of the northern summer and issued jovial remarks at frightened Chinese shopkeepers who were being forced by the military police to open their shutters for business as usual. At the Special Service Organ he announced himself and climbed the stairs to the command post on the second floor. General Honjo was waiting for him, and now at last Tatekawa officially delivered the message from Prime-Minister-Maker Saionji that the Kwantung Army should proceed "with prudence and caution."

Honjo was impatient with the mock solemnity of Tatekawa's manner. That morning—so Honjo had learned while Tatekawa was sleeping—the Emperor had been awakened before dawn with the news from Manchuria. He had started his palace day by giving audience to Prime Minister Wakatsuki. Wakatsuki, without first feeling out the position of the Throne in the usual manner, had declared precipitantly that it was the government's policy to curb the Army in its unauthorized "adventure" and to insist on "non-enlargement" of the Army's operations. Taken aback, Hirohito had replied cautiously, "The government's position seems altogether appropriate." With this encouragement Wakatsuki had spent the day trying to force the War Minister to ask the General Staff to order all Japanese forces back to the Kwantung Leasehold. The General Staff, of course, had refused and lacking any new orders from Hirohito would continue to do so. But Honjo was frankly worried. Japan's ambassador to the League of Nations had promised on behalf of his government that the Kwantung Army would be recalled to its barracks. How committed, how dedicated was the Emperor?

"Rest easy," replied Tatekawa. "Just restrict operations to south Manchuria for the time being and everything will be all right." Tatekawa went on to explain that Hirohito wanted the people and the Cabinet to support the Army in what had been done before doing more. He wanted to assess the reaction of the world's banks and chancelleries before swallowing the rest of Manchuria. While his political advisors were negotiating domestic and international acceptance, it was Honjo's duty to hold what had been gained and wait patiently. Honjo shook his head dubiously. The present positions were difficult to defend. Hesitation now would allow the enemy to regroup north of the Sungari River. The morale of Japanese troops would sink rapidly if they had to take a defensive stance without any surety that the Emperor approved of their war. In vain Tatekawa lured Honjo out of his command post for a night of victory celebrations. At every saké house, with every wench and geisha, Honjo kept a phone by his side in order to keep track of military and political developments in the field and in Tokyo.

At 6:30 P.M.—about the time that Honjo and Tatekawa had begun their conversation—Prime Minister Wakatsuki summoned to his Tokyo residence the political secretary of Saionji, Baron Harada. He asked Harada to tell Saionji that the civilian members of the Cabinet had decided to appeal directly to the Throne. They would beg Hirohito to order the Army to obey Cabinet instructions and to refrain from enlarging the theater of operations. After dinner at 8:30 P.M.—about the time that Honjo and Tatekawa finished their conversation—Hirohito's principal advisors met in an anteroom of the new concrete Imperial Library in the palace woods to consider the Cabinet's demand. Attending were Lord Privy Seal Count Makino; his level-headed secretary, Big Brother Marquis Kido; Grand Chamberlain Admiral Suzuki Kantaro, the cigar-smoking Taoist philosopher who would preside over Japan's surrender in the bunker under the library fourteen years later; and Imperial Household Minister Ikki Kitokuro, a graduate of the bureaucracy who had been used at Court since Emperor Meiji's day for handling delicate liaison work with the Home Ministry and police forces. These four discussed Prime Minister Wakatsuki's demand until 11:00 P.M. They recognized the fact that the prime minister represented not only the civilian politicians of Japan but also Saionji, the Sumitomo cartel, and a majority of intellectuals, industrialists, and professionals. In vain the four courtiers looked for a compromise, a formula of words which would please all parties. The Army wanted imperial sanction. The Cabinet wanted imperial non-sanction. And Hirohito wanted national unity. He demanded that the Cabinet vote funds and encouragement for the men in the field.

After two and a half hours of brain teasing, Hirohito's three principal chamberlains, together with Marquis Kido, decided to tell the prime minister that it was "displeasing to the Emperor for the prime minister to depend too much on others"; that the Throne sensed "a lack of complete unity in the Cabinet"; and that, therefore, if the prime minister wished to stop unauthorized troop movements, "he must do it on his own responsibility." After Hirohito had approved the message, it was delivered to Prime Minister Wakatsuki the following morning, September 20.

Also that morning the ranking officers of the Army met at the old War Ministry outside the palace walls to consider a request from Lieutenant General Honjo in Manchuria. Honjo asked that reinforcements be sent to him from the Japanese Army in Korea. War Minister Minami pointed out that the policy of the Cabinet—a policy which Hirohito had called "appropriate"—was one of "non-aggravation of the incident."

In essence the reinforcements would make possible an enlargement of the theater of operations. It was up to the officers present, said War

Ministry Minami, to decide whether or not this would constitute an "aggravation of the incident." After debate Minami found that the majority were against him. A group of senior generals who had been to see Emperor Hirohito's chief aide-de-camp, General Nara, earlier that morning sided with the young members of the cabal and spoke in favor of the reinforcements. Finally, with great solemnity, General Minami acknowledged, "I see now that non-aggravation of the situation does not necessarily mean non-enlargement of the theater of operations."

Prince Kanin's man, Major General Koiso of the Military Affairs Bureau, arose with equal solemnity to add that, of course, no reinforcements should be sent from Korea without the consent of the war minister and the entire Cabinet. Constitutionally no such consent was necessary. The right to move troops belonged exclusively to the Emperor, advised by the General Staff. In a matter of such national importance as war, however, it was well for the Emperor to have the unanimous support of all the branches of the government, including bureaucrats and politicians. The gathered generals agreed that such unanimity was worth waiting for. They approved a cable to the commander of the Japanese Army in Korea which stated: IF CONSENT FROM TOKYO CANNOT BE OBTAINED IN TIME . . . [YOU ARE] GIVEN THE AUTHORITY TO TAKE APPROPRIATE MEASURES.

The commander of the Japanese Army in Korea [5] had various telephone connections in Tokyo which enabled him to understand the message. For one full day he waited, studiously avoiding a scheduled liaison conference with General Ugaki, the governor general. Then at noon on September 21, he cabled back to the General Staff that his 39th Mixed Brigade had been ordered to move and would cross the Manchurian border in about twenty-four hours. This leisurely scheduling was meant as a politeness to the Cabinet to allow it time to change its collective mind. Everyone of importance knew that planes of the Japanese Army in Korea had been in action over Manchuria for two days and that the whole of the Korean Army was massed along the Manchurian border ready to cross it in five minutes if General Honjo really needed help.

Prime Minister Wakatsuki might maintain that troop movements were none of the Cabinet's business. Generals were normally inclined to agree. But in the present instance, generals were helping Hirohito prove that the lives of Japanese boys in the field were the business of everyone, particularly of politicians. On September 21, General Honjo sent the Peerless Pimp Tatekawa and Prince Kanin's private emissary General Suzuki both back to Tokyo to add their weight to government councils. At the same time he moved the bulk of his strength north to the Sungari River, leaving Mukden unprotected while it awaited the reinforcements.

On September 22, as popular pressure mounted on behalf of the men

[5] Lieutenant General Hayashi Senjuro, a later war minister and prime minister.

overseas, Hirohito offered the prime minister a face-saving compromise. Let the Cabinet vote funds for the expedition, and Hirohito would personally take responsibility for ordering in Japan's Korean Army. To old man Saionji's disgust, Prime Minister Wakatsuki capitulated. On the morning of September 23, the Cabinet voted to fund the troop movement, and Hirohito signed the orders for the Korean Army to cross the frontier into Manchuria.

Japanese Counterintelligence, as a part of its cover story for the Emperor, later made much of the fact that one battalion of the Japanese Army in Korea crossed the Manchurian border before receiving the imperial sanction. The implication was that Hirohito had bowed to the pressure of a *fait accompli*. The truth was that eager Army officers had such excellent liaison with the Throne Room that they knew when to move even before receiving their formal orders.

During this mummery the world reacted. On the advice of their ambassadors in the Orient, all the Western powers believed that the Kwantung Army had acted without orders and would be brought into line shortly. For months the ambassadors had ignored warnings by Western journalists and businessmen and had heeded reassurances from officials of the Japanese Foreign Ministry. Now the ambassadors had much face at stake and were not prepared to change their professional judgment overnight. Nelson T. Johnson, for instance, the U.S. Minister in Peking, had received a memo from an American advisor of Chiang Kai-shek only twenty-four hours before the seizure of Mukden. The memo had bluntly stated that the Japanese Army was about to occupy Manchuria. Minister Johnson had labeled the memo "incredible, fantastic" and forwarded it to Washington in an ordinary diplomatic pouch which did not reach its destination until Mukden was already in Japanese hands.

In Tokyo, U.S. Ambassador W. Cameron Forbes, the polo-playing grandson of Ralph Waldo Emerson, had thought so little of similar warnings that he had arranged to embark for the United States for a routine re-briefing on the very day of September 19. When news of the Mukden coup broke that morning, he of course called Washington and inquired whether he should not cancel his sailing. Secretary of State Stimson—the same man who would later urge the atomic bombing of Hiroshima on President Truman—advised Ambassador Forbes to come home as planned. Stimson could not believe that all his competent observers overseas had been deceived and that Japanese diplomats, handing out reassurances everywhere, could all be whistling nervously in the dark.

Accordingly, on September 22, 1931, Stimson cabled the chief U.S. observer of the League of Nations in Switzerland: "It is apparent that the Japanese military have initiated a widely extended movement of aggression only after careful preparation. . . . The miltary chiefs and the Foreign Office are evidently sharply at variance as to intention and opinion. Consequently it would be advisable . . . that nationalist feeling not be aroused against the Foreign Office in support of the army." Similar instructions were sent by other Western governments to other representatives at the League. The truth was that no power was prepared, militarily, to oppose Japan. The U.S. Navy, half of it in mothballs, had never been weaker. Stimson was told that it would take five years to prepare for war with Japan.

That same afternoon the Council of the League of Nations voted to ask the "Chinese and Japanese governments to refrain from action that might aggravate" the situation. Coincidentally, a few hours earlier, Great Britain had announced that she was going off the gold standard. The whole of the sterling bloc—half the economies of the world at that time—would no longer redeem their scrip in precious metal. Clearly the West, weak and preoccupied, would send no troops to the Orient. Not even the Soviet Union showed any readiness to intervene.

To Hirohito and his palace advisors, it seemed that Asia could belong to Japan if Japan could take it politely enough. No Japanese could deny that Hirohito had won a great victory. His men in the Kwantung Army had seized south Manchuria against great odds, with negligible casualties. The diffident Japanese public had been given a heady sniff of military glory. The elected government had shouldered a part of the responsibility. The moderates had acquiesced. Hirohito had invoked his true powers without exposing so much as a little finger from behind the sacred chrysanthemum curtain.

Only Hirohito's closest intimates knew how premature victory celebrations would be and how many balls still remained juggled aloft. The most talented members of the cabal in the Army—the visionaries who wished to conquer Russia—had been promised north as well as south Manchuria. Saionji, the business community, and the moderate Army officers of the Ugaki faction had been promised a national pause for thought before the escalation into north Manchuria began.

Abroad the League of Nations had recessed until October 13 to await developments. Then, it might yet impose economic sanctions and boycotts. Even without ships and guns the League still had the power to touch the Japanese pocketbook and weight the domestic Japanese scales against Hirohito and in favor of Saionji. Many Japanese businessmen, in their proud, indirect, belly-talking fashion, said as much to their Western colleagues, but almost no Westerners grasped the urgency of the message.

The day the League voted for "non-aggravation," Hirohito's most loyal vassals turned at once to the problems pending. Means must be found to awaken the West as gradually and painlessly as possible to reality. Face must also be saved for old Prime-Minister-Maker Saionji and the Strike-North idealists in the cabal. To meet these challenges, Prince Konoye, Count Makino, Marquis Kido, and the others devised for the year ahead—for 1932, the unlucky Year of the Monkey—a triple intrigue and a triple assassination. Their efforts, never before described in English, were to be Machiavellian masterpieces of pure witch gossamer.

13

DOLLAR SWINDLE

(1931–1932)

THE SPY SERVICE

One tangled skein of intimidation—of war and threat of war abroad, of assassination and threat of assassination at home, and of bribery and blackmail on both fronts—preoccupied Japan from late September 1931 to late May 1932. Only a few score men starred in this eight-month melodrama: a motley cast of palace advisors, patriotic street toughs, retired China experts, crack naval pilots, and Army Intelligence officers. In Japanese accounts their individual parts are recorded separately, without being fitted into any over-all script. It is always noted, however, that this actor dealt with that actor, and when all these connections are put together, it turns out that a single web was involved, of men who were all friends of friends of one another. They were associated not because they shared the same guilty aims but because they were organized—organized by a brain trust roughly comparable to that of the Central Intelligence Agency in the present United States.

Not much is known about this "Civilian Spy Service" as it is called by one informant. What few written records it kept of its transactions, it destroyed annually. Before the American Occupation in 1945, even its last official code name was successfully forgotten. However, the clues that survive indicate that it was not an authorized institution of the Japanese government but an ad hoc network which had grown up, contact by contact and friendship by friendship, around the person of the Emperor and his well-lined privy purse. All evidence suggests that Hirohito inherited the skeleton of its structure from his grandfather, Emperor Meiji.

The shadowy directors of the spy service acted as nerve center for many different semi-autonomous organs of espionage: Army and Navy Intelligence departments, market research organizations in some of the largest cartels, and civilian clearinghouses for information which were disguised as cultural or scientific foundations. One of the most important of the clearinghouses was the Everyday Meiji Biographical Research Institute in Oarai, a spa in the old loyalist region of Mito some 50 miles northeast of Tokyo. The staff of the institute sent its briefs to Hirohito's advisors through an unpublicized cover agency on the palace grounds, which was known in the 1920's as the Imperial Code Research Institute.

The director of the Everyday Meiji Biographical Research Institute in Oarai was Japan's spy emeritus, Count Tanaka Mitsuaki, sometimes known as the "Spider." This tough old conspirator was eighty-nine and stone deaf, but healthy enough to live to be ninety-six and see the conquest of China. For thirteen years, from 1898 to 1911, he had served as imperial household minister and had been one of the two most trusted chamberlains of Emperor Meiji. It was Spider Tanaka who had arranged the peculiar circumstances of Hirohito's post-mature birth. It would be Spider Tanaka who would now provide terrorists for the intrigues ahead.[1]

In the two decades since the Meiji era, Spider Tanaka had watched the spy service grow until by 1931 it had cast its net over all Asia as far south as Australia, as far west as Iran. By 1941 it would be world-wide, with operatives in every major city of North and South America as well as Europe. When the war with the West broke out, President Roosevelt would appraise its fifth column so highly that he would allow the forcible relocation of all Americans of Japanese parentage on the West Coast to detention camps inland. In the Philippines when the Japanese Army arrived in 1941, U.S. colonials would be surprised to find that Filipino carpenters and masons of Japanese birth stepped immediately into high positions of authority in the Japanese occupation governments. In Baguio (where the author and his family were captured), a chain of command within the Japanese community would spring into being or be activated even before the arrival of the first Japanese occupation forces.

---

[1] Tanaka had been born a provincial samurai of Tosa in 1843, had gone up to the ancient capital of Kyoto in 1863, and had participated there in the complex intrigues which had preceded the restoration of 1868. At twenty-five he had been appointed chief judge in Kobe, the most important of the ports opened to foreigners. In 1871 he had been sent along as secretary-spy when Emperor Komei's murderer, Iwakura, embarked on his fact-finding tour of America and Europe. After coming home in 1874, Tanaka had been made first the auditor, then the treasurer of Japan's new national army. In 1885, when the later-to-be-assassinated Ito took office as Japan's first prime minister, Tanaka was inserted under him as chief Cabinet secretary. In 1889 he was made principal of the Peers' School and supervisor of the education of Emperor Meiji's twelve-year-old son, the future Emperor Taisho. At the end of his thirteen years' service as imperial household minister, Tanaka retired to supervise the writing of Meiji's official biography. It was for this purpose, ostensibly, that he had founded the Everyday Meiji Biographical Research Institute.

A unique glimpse into the leadership of the spy service was given in a book written in 1936 by Amleto Vespa, an expatriate Italian Blackshirt who had made a career in China as a mercenary, a police chief, and an espionage expert. The Japanese were able to dismiss his revelations when they appeared in print as the spiteful fabrications of an adventurer. But Vespa was a professionally trained observer with years of relevant experience. Evidence brought out at the war crimes trials after World War II showed his dates and descriptions to be accurate. His verbatim reports of Japanese boasting and exultation seemed too melodramatic for credence when he published them, but they were later matched many times by speeches made to Allied P.O.W.'s during World War II.[2]

Vespa had worked for Manchurian war lord Chang Hsueh-liang and was impressed into Japan's spy service in February 1932, five months after the seizure of Mukden. Four years later he escaped in disgust and despair to central China and wrote his book. He prepared it frankly and carefully as blackmail to secure the release of his wife and children who were still held hostage by the Japanese in Manchuria. A copy of the manuscript won freedom for his family but not payment of his back wages. And so he broke his blackmail agreement with the Japanese and published his book anyway. He had no other means, he said, of raising enough money to transport himself and his family home to the West.

Vespa was first introduced into the spy service by Colonel Doihara, the Baden-Baden Reliable and so-called Lawrence of Manchuria who had taken over as mayor of Mukden on the morning after its seizure. Having tested Vespa, Doihara turned him over to his "chief"—"a pleasant-looking man," wrote Vespa, "of about forty-five . . . in civilian clothes . . . of unusual intelligence." Vespa continued:

> During the whole of my service under this remarkable man I never discovered his name or his true identity. Never have I met him at any function, at any party, or at anyone else's house. He always had at his disposal an aeroplane which he reached by private car when he went on his mysterious journeys. . . . His English, a rare thing among the Japanese, was almost perfect, leading me to believe that he must have lived many years abroad. . . . I remember almost every word he said.
>
> "Mr. Vespa, . . . if Colonel Doihara has told you anything unpleasant, please pay no attention to it. . . . He delights in showing his greatness by his hectoring manner. He has worked for me for many years. . . . He has done well in many of his undertakings, but . . . he has many failures to his discredit. . . . For instance, do you think that the death of Marshal Chang Tso-lin was a master stroke? . . .
>
> "Remember that I never appear on the scene; I am never in evidence

---

[2] Theatricality was part of the Japanese samurai tradition. It is faithfully reflected in a Japanese movie cliché: the guttural scream, the rush of footfalls in the darkness, then the blade glistening with blood in the moonlight.

except in matters strictly and intimately Japanese. Your main capacity is to act as my intermediary. . . . I do not give you this privilege because I trust you, but because you are a naturalized Chinese citizen, and as such I can have you shot at any time. Besides, we hold your family. . . .

"The Japanese are the only divine people on earth; that is the reason why they never try to mix with other people. Our culture is sacred. . . . The people whom we have conquered or shall conquer . . . will simply disappear. The Koreans will be eaten by vices; the Chinese will be the victims of opium and other narcotics; the Russians will be ruined by vodka. . . . Do not smile. . . . The destiny of Japan has been outlined by the gods. Nothing can stop Japan from becoming the greatest empire on earth. . . .

"No, no, do not speak Japanese, even though you know the language. . . . It sounds sacrilegious. . . . Every time I have to listen to a foreigner speaking Japanese, I feel a strong desire to strangle him. Let us speak English. . . . It is the proper language when speaking of things unpleasant and disagreeable. Whenever I have to swear at anyone I always prefer to do it in English. . . .

"These instructions which I am giving you I have given also to all the other heads of the Japanese Intelligence Service in northern Manchuria. I am the only one who can give you orders, and you have no one to report to but me. . . . Our Intelligence Service must not be anything like a chain. One link must not lead to another link. Rather it must be a succession of points which work in harmony but without any immediate contact."

The speaker of these words, if he and Vespa were telling the truth, must have been a Court noble of the highest rank. No other Japanese in his mid-forties could have spoken as he did about Doihara, a forty-nine-year-old of samurai caste. Elsewhere Vespa distinguishes carefully between his chief, belonging to the Civilian Spy Service, and the chief of the Special Service Organ, the "Military Mission" as he called it, belonging to the Intelligence Department of the Army General Staff. According to his portrayal, the two worked closely together but the military chief was always subordinate to the man in plainclothes. Vespa regularly knew the name of the military chief and correctly identified the three Special Service Organ directors in north Manchuria between 1932 and 1936. He never knew the name of his civilian chief in the same period. The second of his civilian chiefs, however —"a man in his early fifties"—he recognized as the former director of the Special Service Organ in Irkutsk whom he had met in Siberia in 1918. Available Japanese personnel records reveal that this was a young aristocrat named Takeda Nukazo. From 1918 to 1928—when he vanished into the anonymity of the spy service—Takeda had worked his way up through military intelligence in close collaboration with Hirohito's two uncles and with Hirohito's former deckboard sparring partner, Marquis Komatsu Teruhisa. The first of Vespa's "chiefs," who spoke with such impassioned paranoia about Japan's aspirations, was undoubtedly a disguised princeling from the same circle.

DINNER AT KIDO'S

At 6 P.M. on Wednesday, September 23, 1931, five days after the Japanese seizure of Mukden, Marquis Kido, the first of Hirohito's Big Brothers, received the members of the Eleven Club, his fellow Big Brothers, at his town house around the corner from the American Embassy. There he treated them to a modest supper of fried duck and saké, served without benefit of geisha. The occasion was not a social one. The guests were all high-level operatives of the spy service and had come together to consider "arguments" which might be used against Prince Saionji and his supporters, the liberals and banker-industrialists, during the "pause for reflection" which the Emperor had promised before completing the conquest of Manchuria. Specifically, a plan was needed to circumvent the League of Nations and to head off economic sanctions or boycotts that would damage Japan's international trade. Also, a way must be found to silence and control the banker-industrialists so that they would continue to provide funds for military budgets, particularly for the build-up of the Navy. In five hours of brainstorming, the members of the Eleven Club decided that three ideas were worth pursuing. These three were the germs for the three acts of the eight-month drama which followed, the Triple Intrigue.

The first idea, the Dollar Swindle, was concocted by Baron Harada, the secretary-spy from Saionji's own household. He had picked it up that afternoon from banking circles.[3] The second of the ideas, the Fake War to "save the face of the League of Nations," was relayed by Konoye, the tall, languid prince of the ancient Court family of Fujiwara. It was being proposed tentatively, he said, by officers of the Emperor's cabal in the Kwantung Army in Manchuria. The third of the ideas, Threat of Coup d'Etat, was an old one on which Big Brother Uramatsu, in touch with underworld operatives of the spy service, simply gave a progress report.

The Dollar Swindle was to be a speculative peculation of monumental proportions designed to furnish Japan's business community with a massive bribe. Two days earlier, when Great Britain had unexpectedly gone off the gold standard, the value of the pound on the free market had dropped 20 per cent. Japanese bankers calculated that collectively they had lost $22 million by the sudden depreciation of their sterling holdings. Some of them were angry that they had not been forewarned by British colleagues, but others pointed out that British bankers had themselves lost far more. The British government had failed to protect its financiers by privately spreading advance information of the move. If a similar step were contemplated

---

[3] Harada was nominally a banker himself. He drew his salary from a purely titular position at the great Sumitomo bank—a position created for him by the director of the bank, Sumitomo Kinzaemon, who was old Saionji's nephew and grandson-in-law.

in a nation like Japan, said the British apologists, the relatives of the finance minister would have profited handsomely. They would have sold their yen for foreign currencies beforehand, and afterwards they would have bought back their yen at a substantial discount. Forced to admit the truth of this argument, the disgruntled Japanese bankers said that the British must be fools.

The titled young men of the cabal were delighted by the thought that the bourgeois moneybags of the nation—Saionji's staunchest supporters— might be bribed en masse to betray their Western liberal cause. Those in the Eleven Club who understood high finance reckoned that as much as a $100 million profit might be turned if yen were sold discreetly for several months before the gold standard was renounced. Those who knew politics saw in this figure a bribe of sufficient size to rob Prime-Minister-Maker Saionji of his main support. Later it might be possible to take back most of the profits from the cartels by threatening to reveal their speculations to the public. Harada said that Saionji was counting heavily in the forth-coming "pause for reflection" on the backing of the largest of the cartels, the Mitsui combine, which traditionally made up the campaign purses of most of the candidates of the Constitutionalist party. How would it be if Mitsui were promised the appointment of a Constitutionalist Cabinet in three months and the approval of the Emperor in advance for a paper-backed Japanese currency?

When the immediate political crisis with Saionji was over, other cartels could be brought in for a share of the spoils. The government's Yokohama Specie Bank could itself buy dollars. The nation's finance would benefit over all. And Hirohito would be pleased. In July, after President Hoover had proposed a one-year moratorium on all debts payments between nations, Hirohito had had a personal translation made for him of Hoover's statement and had suggested after reading it: "We should be able to find some way of circumventing these unilateral financial pronouncements of the other powers."

The Fake War, item two in the Triple Intrigue, was touched on at the Eleven Club meeting but not discussed in depth. Prince Konoye said only that the Kwantung Army was prepared to stage a diversion in Shanghai that would provide the League of Nations with an opportunity to satisfy its peace-making propensities and so "save the League's face." As it turned out, Konoye's "diversion" became a bloody little brush-fire war, costing 30,000 lives, that would directly jeopardize a billion dollars' worth of Western investment in the Chinese port of Shanghai. In demanding that it be stopped, the nations of the West would be surprised and gratified: Japan would back down, would suppress the wounded honor and aroused passions of many samurai, and would withdraw after breaking open the very door to Nanking, the Chinese capital.

After gaining this public concession, the League's peacemakers might be inclined to ignore the conquest of north Manchuria which would take place during the diversion. To make appearances as flattering as possible for the League, Manchuria would emerge from the gunsmoke as a nominally independent nation. The former boy emperor of China, Henry Pu-Yi, would be restored to the Manchu throne of his forefathers and would rule Manchuria for Japan as a puppet. The thought of Pu-Yi, a pathetically effete and ineffectual young man, posturing as the head of a modern police state in the hands of the Kwantung Army, amused the most knowledgeable of the Big Brothers. At Kido's supper party the wits found enough material in it momentarily to break up serious discussion. Konoye drolly called for order and the meeting resumed.

The Threat of Coup d'Etat, item three on the agenda, had been suggested earlier in 1931 by the aftermath of the March Plot. At that time Lord Privy Seal Makino's henchman, Dr. Okawa, the former headmaster of the cabal's palace indoctrination center, had kept the bombs which the Army had provided for the plot. He had done so simply to make sure that the Army General Staff would help him pay his bills to the Black Dragon Society and to the Golden Dragon geisha house. But as the months had passed, his continuing possession of the bombs had proved a most useful political tool. It had helped silence the Army's moderate faction before the seizure of Mukden, and it was still being used to intimidate vested interests in the business world. With a little twisting, it had convinced Western ambassadors in Tokyo that Japan required delicate handling; that allowances should be made for the difficult domestic problems faced by Hirohito; that unless the West were understanding, the stability of the biggest market in Asia might be swept away by revolution.

According to Big Brother Uramatsu's report to the Eleven Club, Dr. Okawa's services could be used further. Through old Spider Tanaka's Everyday Meiji Biographical Research Institute in Oarai, Dr. Okawa had been put in touch with three bands of loyal activists who were eager to keep the Threat of Coup d'Etat alive—willing, on behalf of the Emperor, to plot coups and if necessary to stage them.

One group from which willing assassins might be recruited was the Native-Land-Loving Society, a commune of philosophic farmers who admired Tolstoy and worked a twelve-acre co-operative about halfway down the ten-mile spur of track connecting Oarai with the prefectural capital of Mito. In 1930, after a poor harvest, Big Brother Konoye of the House of Peers and Hirohito's uncle Prince Higashikuni had arranged an endowment for the Native-Land-Lovers so that they could start a school on their farm and teach their communal philosophy to others.

The second cell of activists was the Blood Brotherhood, a cadre of toughs selected from the ranks of student spies being trained for work in

China. They were all graduates of two schools—one for self-defense, the other for spiritual indoctrination—which had been set up in Oarai as subsidiaries of the Everyday Meiji Biographical Research Institute.

A third "death-defying band" had been recruited from the officers of the Navy flying unit at the Air Development Station on the Misty Lagoon 30 miles south of Oarai. Since ordinary pilots and bombardiers in the Japanese Naval Air Force were noncoms and seamen, these lieutenants and commanders at the lagoon considered themselves an elite, ranking at least two grades above their counterparts, of equal rating, in any of the other branches of the armed forces. They were the students of the brilliant Captain Yamamoto Isoroku who would devise the 1941 attack on Pearl Harbor. They were the protégés of Empress Nagako's father, Prince Kuni, the pioneer of Japanese air power. They were the day-to-day comrades of torpedo-plane test pilot Prince Yamashina, the best of the five aviators in the immediate ranks of the imperial family.

At mention of the Misty Lagoon airmen, some members of the Eleven Club audibly sucked in breath. To expose such men in a political mission showed extreme determination on the part of the imperial family. When the Eleven Club meeting broke up at eleven o'clock that night, its participants were resolved to try to spare the Throne the necessity of a Coup, and if possible of a Fake War as well. Other, political means, such as the Dollar Swindle, must be exhausted before resorting to such extreme measures.

HENRY THE PUPPET

While his Big Brothers were preparing the Triple Intrigue, Hirohito agreed to a period of watchful waiting. It was not easy for him. When the first favorable reports came in from the League of Nations, his cabalists in Manchuria began to agitate at once for an advance across the Sungari River into northern Manchuria. In Manchuria's northern provincial capital of Harbin, the Kwantung Army's local espionage agent—the secret policeman Amakasu who had strangled Socialist Osugi, his wife, and nephew during the aftermath of the 1923 earthquake—hired Chinese toughs to hurl bricks and grenades nightly into Japanese shopfronts. By day he penned plaintive wires to Kwantung Army headquarters begging for troops to come and protect the hapless local Japanese residents. One of Empress Nagako's numerous relatives in the Tokyo General Staff had to go to Harbin and tell Amakasu to be patient. Other imperial messengers dealt equally firmly with provocateurs in other unconquered areas.

At a nod from the palace, the disappointed young officers of the cabal diverted their energies into preparations for the Triple Intrigue. On September 30, 1931, twelve days after the seizure of Mukden, a young Japanese Army interpreter, sent by Colonel Itagaki, the politician of the Kwantung Army, called at the villa of Henry Pu-Yi,[4] the former boy emperor of China. It was a modest home in the outskirts of the Japanese Concession in Tientsin, the second city of north China. The interpreter was shown into the "audience hall," a small Western-style sitting room replete with over-stuffed chairs and antimacassars. The walls were virtually papered with calligraphies, the testimonials penned by Chinese, Japanese, and West-erners who had sought to flatter the boy emperor during his twenty years as pretender to the Manchu throne.

The interpreter looked at the crowded, boastful walls with some con-tempt. This shabby "palace" belonged to the boy emperor only because the Japanese government had for many years paid the light and gas bills. Henry Pu-Yi could pretend to be a king only because he had allowed Japan to keep him, like an ugly concubine, for some conceivable moment of usefulness.

Pu-Yi was a great-nephew of the Chinese empress dowager, the Manchu harpy Yehonala, who from 1861 to 1908 had ruled China by a combina-tion of whimsy, cunning, murder, and depravity. It was largely due to her dissolute methods of statecraft that imperial China had squandered its treasures, its authority and pride, to become the broken confederacy of knaves and paupers which, in Japanese eyes, was the Republican China of 1931.

From his crowning in 1908 at the age of three to his deposing in 1912 at the age of seven, Henry Pu-Yi had grown up among eunuchs and con-cubines who had apprenticed under the salacious tutelage of great-aunt Yehonala. Until he was seventeen, the Chinese Republican government had continued to support him and his entourage in a corner of the old palace in Peking. He had matured to be a weak, vain, bespectacled pervert. He cultivated classical literary pursuits at which he was pathetically incom-petent. He found his sexual pleasure in caning the buttocks of his few remaining eunuchs. In the 1920's during Chang Tso-lin's occupancy of Peking and Chiang Kai-shek's rise to power in south China, the Republic had not always remembered to post him his pension checks. Enticed by Japanese blandishments, he had moved to the Japanese Concession in Tientsin.

Pu-Yi entered his drab little hall of state accompanied by his prime minister. The Japanese envoy snapped to attention with a great show of respect and announced to Pu-Yi that his fellow emperor of the great Japa-nese Empire looked favorably upon him. A messenger had come from Hirohito's army in Manchuria bearing a communication which could be delivered to Pu-Yi only in person and only at the Japanese garrison in

---

[4] This is the form of his name which he used in dealing with the West. In China he was known as the Emperor Hsuan-Tung. In modern Communist China, until his death in 1968, he was addressed as citizen Aisin Gioro.

Tientsin. If His Majesty Pu-Yi would condescend to accompany the humble interpreter in a staff car, he would hear a proposal of great interest. Pu-Yi had been expecting some such approach ever since the seizure of Mukden twelve days previously. With ill-concealed excitement, he turned to his prime minister for an opinion. Fat and impassive, the minister stated that His Majesty was disposed to accede to the highly irregular Japanese request.

Minutes later Pu-Yi was ushered into the commander's office at the Japanese Treaty Forces' barracks in Tientsin. The lieutenant general in charge introduced him to the messenger from Mukden and then excused himself. The messenger said, "If Your Majesty will come to Manchuria, Japan is prepared to restore the Manchu throne there and make you an emperor again." Pu-Yi beamed and promised to consider the proposal. The messenger, a member of the spy service, wired Colonel Itagaki, the Kwantung Army's politician, that the boy emperor could be persuaded to accept the role of Japanese puppet. Itagaki in his turn wired the director of the Special Services Organ in the Japanese Concession in Shanghai, 800 miles to the south, asking him to come to Mukden immediately for rebriefing.

EASTERN JEWEL

The director of the Shanghai Special Service Organ was Major Tanaka Takayoshi, the big man with the huge head and leviathan memory who would later become the star witness for Allied prosecutor Keenan at the Tokyo war crimes trials. When Itagaki's wire arrived, Tanaka was out dancing at Shanghai's Cathay Hotel with the girl spy who would become the provocateuse for the Fake War. She was a distant cousin of the boy emperor and a Manchu princess. Her original given name had been Eastern Jewel. Eastern Peril would have been more appropriate.

Like the boy emperor Pu-Yi, Eastern Jewel was a direct descendant of the roughriding conqueror Nurhachi who had founded the Manchu dynasty in 1616—the death year of Shakespeare and of the first of the Tokugawa shoguns. Unlike the anemic Pu-Yi, Eastern Jewel was a creature of boundless vitality, eternal itch, and catholic taste. Her father, one of the eight "Princes of the Iron Helmet" in the former imperial court in Peking, had inherited the allegiance of the tribes of Inner Mongolia. He had been a rash, extreme Manchu prince of the old school, a close friend of Empress Nagako's great-uncle Prince Kanin, and the rouser of the rabble of Mongol horsemen who had attempted to seize Mukden for Prince Kanin in 1916. Eastern Jewel was only one of his score of daughters; he had given her in 1914, when she was eight, to his Japanese blood brother, a member of the spy service, Kawashima Naniwa. Kawashima had renamed her Kawashima Yoshiko, had moved her from her fourteenth century yurt to a twentieth century home in Tokyo, and had re-educated her as a Japanese. At fifteen,

according to her later boasting, she was seduced by Kawashima's septuagenarian father. At sixteen she slept with Kawashima himself. Before she
was twenty she had begun to seduce in her turn.

Married off during the mid-1920's to the son of a Mongol prince, she
quickly deserted her husband and returned to the Chinese student quarter
in Tokyo where she was known as Yang Kuei Fei, a Chinese imperial concubine of yore who had played Helen of Troy in wrecking an empire. In
late 1930, at the age of twenty-four, Eastern Jewel took a trip to Shanghai
with a Japanese Dietman who rapidly ran out of money in his attempts to
support her. By luck, at a New Year's party there, she met Major Tanaka
of the Shanghai Special Service Organ. She was entranced by the hugeness
of the man and astounded him by recalling a Buddhist funeral service at
which she had seen him in Tokyo twelve years earlier when she herself had
been only twelve. That night she tried to seduce him. He rebuffed her
politely, reminding her that she was a princess and he was a commoner.
The next day she dropped by his office and borrowed the equivalent of
$160 (U.S.) from him. She continued to borrow smaller sums from him
in the weeks that followed. Finally her insistence on being his debtor
destroyed his caste humility. "You are a giant of a man," she said, "and
I am small in every part."

"She was then twenty-five and still exceedingly pretty," wrote Tanaka
in later years. "Our encounter was a mature one of muscle against muscle."

She and Tanaka shared a foot fetish. He loved to wear high black boots
and she insisted that he wear them always. The boots scuffed the polish
on the brightest dance floors of Shanghai and ended each evening dangling
over the end of a bed. To justify the sums he withdrew from the Special
Service Organ's "plot fund," Tanaka in the summer of 1931 sent her to a
Chinese school to learn English so that she could be useful in the future
as a Japanese spy. By the fall of 1931 she had learned her role so well
that her relationship with Tanaka was to blossom into a rather general
affair between herself and the Army officers of Hirohito's cabal. It would
last almost up to her final beheading at the hands of the Chinese in 1948.

On the morning of October 1, 1931, in response to the wire from Colonel
Itagaki of the Kwantung Army, Eastern Jewel's lover Tanaka boarded a
train for Mukden. He expected to be disgraced for his embezzlement of
Special Service Organ funds. He spent the two-day train journey going
over and over in his mind the arguments by which he hoped to represent
Eastern Jewel and her extravagances as a useful investment. When he
arrived in Mukden he was surprised to find Colonel Itagaki concerned with
something else entirely.

"The Japanese government," said Itagaki, "is cowed by the League of
Nations. As a result our plans have been disturbed. At our next push we
want to take Harbin [the northern capital] and make Manchuria independent. We have detailed Colonel Doihara to go and get Pu-Yi [the boy

emperor]. If we are successful, the League of Nations will make a big fuss and the government in Tokyo will be worried. I want you to start something in Shanghai, please, that will serve to distract the attention of the Powers. During your commotion, we will take Manchuria."

Nodding with relief, Major Tanaka assured Colonel Itagaki that he would be able to carry out the assignment. He had in training, he said, the perfect agent to buy Chinese agitators in Shanghai and start the Fake War.

"Yes, I know all about your mistress," interrupted Itagaki. "She is a childhood friend of Pu-Yi's number-one wife. The wife is a dope addict and a bundle of nerves. She is trying to persuade Pu-Yi not to accept our plan. If Doihara has too much trouble with her, I may want to borrow Eastern Jewel from you so that she can go to Pu-Yi's villa in Tientsin and reassure them."

Then Colonel Itagaki gave Major Tanaka the equivalent of $10,000 (U.S.) from the Kwantung Army's coffer of nonaccountable special service funds, and Tanaka returned to Shanghai. With the money he cleared Eastern Jewel of debts and began frugally to arrange provocations for the Fake War.

BALKY OLD MAN

On September 17, the day before the seizure of Mukden, Prime-Minister-Maker Saionji had abruptly decamped from his summer villa in the mountains and gone to Kyoto, the old capital in the south, to pray at the graves of his illustrious forefathers. By removing himself from the Tokyo area and from Hirohito, he silently told the nation that he had been consulted in advance about the Manchurian adventure and did not approve of it. Family unanimity is considered essential in Japan. As long as Prince Saionji absented himself from the Emperor's circle of advisors, no Japanese would feel easy in mind about the nation's new course of conquest.

Less than three days after the meeting of the Eleven Club at Big Brother Marquis Kido's residence, Saionji's private agents began to bring him gossip in Kyoto of the plots being prepared for the Triple Intrigue. Realizing that Hirohito and his advisors were not observing the promised "pause for reflection," the old man mustered his energies to open the eyes of the ruling classes to the machinations in the making.

At the Kyoto villa of his late brother Sumitomo, Saionji was in a position to wield his influence over the managers of the Sumitomo cartel and persuade them to take no part in the Dollar Swindle. Through them and through his other contacts in the nearby business community of Japan's great merchant city, Osaka, he launched a whispering campaign. It was directed not against the Emperor, of course, but against his advisors.

Still more pointedly, Saionji had one of his agents—Takuno Dempu, an artist and bohemian who belonged to the Black Dragon Society—publish a letter in the newspaper *Nippon,* accusing Lord Privy Seal Makino of malfeasance. So well prepared was Saionji to document the charge that when the Special Higher Police—the Thought Police as they were commonly called—arrested Takuno on suspicion of lèse majesté, Saionji simply had a heart-to-heart talk with his secretary-spy, Big Brother Harada. Much shaken, Harada at once went up to Tokyo, spoke to the head of the Thought Police, and had Takuno released without indictment.

Alarmed that Saionji might be reaching a breaking point at which he would betray his heritage and broadcast Court secrets to the masses, Hirohito's three chief chamberlains sent Secretary-Spy Harada back to Kyoto on October 6, 1931, to draw out Saionji further.

Saionji was delighted to have an opportunity to transmit to Hirohito the observations which he had been spreading through the business community. At the "center of the Army," he said, a communistic tendency was at work, militating for state socialism. In this tendency he saw a prelude to revolution and the overthrow of the Throne—a set of symptoms familiar to him from his experience of prerevolutionary Russia and Germany. The Black Dragon Society of the underworld, he said, was splitting into two factions: elders who advised caution and young radicals who agitated for more conquest immediately. The nations of the West, he said, might not be willing to fight Japan or even to impose sanctions against her, but privately the Western Establishment was ready to cut off Japan from raw materials and markets.

Finally, he said, even the masses were restless and suspicious. People were saying—and Saionji was conveying a truth—that imperial princes of the blood like the Emperor's uncle Higashikuni were sponsoring terrorist societies and pricking their fingers at voodoo ceremonies in order to subscribe to the blood compacts of assassination gangs.

Secretary-Spy Harada hastened to Tokyo to report Saionji's veiled threats at the palace. Two days later, on October 8, he was back in Kyoto with a request from the Emperor that Saionji come up to Tokyo at once and preserve the appearance of national unity. In his quick trip north Harada had met with Biggest Brother Kido, with Lord Privy Seal Makino, and with old cigar-smoking Taoist Grand Chamberlain Suzuki Kantaro. He returned to Kyoto with the knowledge that the largest of the cartels, Mitsui, had succumbed to temptation and bought $100 million (U.S.) in anticipation of the Dollar Swindle. With Mitsui committed to a heavy speculation in a dollar that was sagging on the international exchange, the business community in which Saionji had banked his hopes was already subverted. Other cartels were beginning to buy in on the swindle. If they held back, Hirohito was ready to retain the gold standard, ruin Mitsui, and plunge the nation into economic chaos. If they joined in the bribe, they stood to make millions; if they supported Saionji, they stood to lose millions.

Knowing that he was cornered, Saionji nevertheless refused to come up to Tokyo. At the same time he advised the bankers of his late brother Sumitomo's cartel that a financial killing was in the making, and he released them to profit or not to profit by it as they saw fit. To their credit most of the branch directors of Sumitomo remained loyal to Saionji and sustained heavy losses two months later when the yen was devalued.

On orders from Tokyo, Secretary-Spy Harada remained in Kyoto for two days trying to persuade Saionji to return to the capital. In the course of his protracted conversation with the old man, Harada discovered that only one consideration moved Saionji at all: the Emperor's health. According to Empress Nagako, said Harada, Hirohito was suffering great strain in the prolonged crisis. He worried night and day that the League of Nations might impose economic sanctions. When no one was looking, in the private corridors of the imperial apartments, he limped and shuffled again, showing the signs of the inherited infirmity which he had successfully concealed since his boyhood. Sentimental courtier that he was, Saionji melted a little at such pleas. He refused, however, to give in completely. He promised Harada that he might come up to Tokyo on October 21, after he had "observed a little longer the trend of events."

DIVERTING THE LEAGUE

The League of Nations Council had recessed shortly after the seizure of Mukden with an admonition to both China and Japan "to refrain from action that would aggravate" the situation. Now it was to reconvene on October 13. Five days before that date Lieutenant Colonel Ishiwara, the zealous strategist of the Manchurian campaign, acted to foster the impression that the Kwantung Army was a law unto itself and might not be bound by any promises which the League could exact from Tokyo. Ishiwara personally led an eleven-plane air raid that dropped 10,000 leaflets and 75 bombs on the southwestern Manchurian city of Chinchow. The Japanese Foreign Ministry had specifically promised the League that the Army would not attack Chinchow; now it branded the raid as unauthorized. Western newspapers played the incident on their front pages and expressed skepticism as to the good faith of Japan's foreign minister.

To further impress the League Council with the domestic problems faced by the Japanese government and with the impracticality of sanctions against Japan, the Emperor's Big Brothers decided to give the world a glimpse of the Coup d'Etat Threat which they had ready in the wings. Secretary-Spy Harada heard of their scheme as soon as he returned to Tokyo on October 10 and promptly labeled it the October Plot.

Got up on short notice, this October production was a burlesque of the earlier March Plot. "Young militarists in the Army" would be "uncovered," prevented "in the nick of time" from effecting their horrendous plan, and full particulars would be leaked as news to all the foreign correspondents in Tokyo. Dr. Okawa, the master plotter, and the cabal's ubiquitous Lieutenant Colonel Suzuki handled the preparations offstage. On stage were Lieutenant Colonel Hashimoto of the Russia Desk in Army Intelligence— the same who in 1937 would sink the U.S.S. *Panay*—and Major Cho Isamu of the North China Special Service Organ. These two had repaired to the Golden Dragon teahouse in the first week of October and had stayed there ever since, competing to see who could drink the most and who could write the best operational "novel" for the coup.

Major Cho's novel was the one chosen to be publicized. He had a gift for dramatic writing. It was he, in 1937, outside the walls of Nanking, who would draft the orders signed by Prince Asaka saying, "Kill all prisoners." It was he, in 1945, in the caves of Okinawa, who would pen the final command to Japanese soldiers and civilians on the island: "Fight to the last and die." Now, however, he showed some sense of humor. His October plan called for Dr. Okawa, the ideologist of the Strike-South Faction, to man a barricade beside his most bitter intellectual rival, Kita Ikki, the apostle of the Strike North. Cho designated as their support "about ten men of the Navy's fencing unit."

Waxing serious, Cho proposed that the coup be supported by ten infantry companies, one machine-gun company, and thirteen planes from the Misty Lagoon Air Station.

> Our objectives [he wrote] are to attack the prime minister's residence and kill Wakatsuki and his ministers during a Cabinet conference; to seize Metropolitan Police headquarters; to occupy the War Ministry and General Staff Headquarters; to punish various good-for-nothings in the Army and the bureaucracy; to establish a new government with Lieutenant General Araki Sadao [the senior officer of the Strike-North Faction] as prime minister, [*Panay*-sinker] Hashimoto as home minister, [Peerless Pimp] Tatekawa as foreign minister, [master plotter] Okawa as finance minister, [the bloodthirsty Major] Cho Isamu as Metropolitan Police chief, and Rear Admiral Kobayashi Shosaburo [the commander of the Misty Lagoon Air Station] as Navy minister.

Every au courant geisha, party politician, and Army bureaucrat learned of this huge joke between October 10 and October 13. The serious Colonel Tojo, later the World War II prime minister, circulated a memo in the Army Ministry criticizing it as "a foolish action." The newspapers published hints of the plot on October 13 and 14, the first two days of the League of Nations Council meeting in Switzerland.

On the evening of October 15 the most important young generals and colonels of the cabal met in the War Ministry to ring down the curtain. They decided that the senior officer of the Strike-North Faction in the cabal, Lieutenant General Araki Sadao, inspector general of military education, should be given the responsibility, as the might-have-been prime minister of the coup government, to go down to the Golden Dragon and speak to the plotters.

Court advocates of the Strike South may have hoped to gain a small blackmail hold on Araki by making him the supposed strongman of the plot, but Araki was far more sophisticated than General Ugaki, the dupe of the March Plot. Araki was a consummate politician and a golden-tongued orator. With great zest he went down to the Golden Dragon and regaled the geisha there with a sermon on the samurai sword which, he said, "should never be drawn indiscriminately from its scabbard." In conclusion he added, "It is almost inconceivable that I should have to come here in military uniform to a place where you are drinking saké in order to admonish you in this sort of matter."

Having broadcast his integrity to the entire teahouse, Lieutenant General Araki sat down with Hashimoto and Cho to toss off a few thimbles of saké and explain to the two conspirators, in reassuring terms, the disciplinary procedures which would have to be applied to them for form's sake.

More than a day later, in the early hours of October 18, the secret police descended on eleven young officers involved in the October Plot and impounded them wherever they found them. Cho and Hashimoto languished pleasantly under protective house arrest at the Golden Dragon for twenty days. The other nine young officers were held briefly and then released after being delivered lectures. Dr. Okawa and his civilian participants were not troubled at all. Lord Privy Seal Makino told anyone who would listen that the plotters had planned to assassinate him. His protégé, Dr. Okawa, went about town bragging that the October Plot "had inflicted a mortal wound on corrupt Japanese party politics."

When the October Plot was exposed on October 18, Saionji visited an obliging medical friend in Kyoto for a physical examination. On October 20 he told Harada that, on doctor's orders, he was going straight to his seaside villa in Okitsu for a long rest. He could not come up to Tokyo on October 21 as he had hoped, and he wished Harada to convey his regrets to the palace.

On the way from Kyoto to Okitsu on October 21, Saionji's train was boarded by Military Affairs Bureau Chief Koiso Kuniaki, the cavalry crony of Prince Kanin who had arranged the Army's part in the March Plot. Hirohito had just promoted him to the rank of lieutenant general. On the train Koiso sat down beside Saionji and in polite Japanese belly talk warned him that his health would fail utterly if he did not come up soon to see the Emperor in Tokyo. Saionji listened in silence and pretended that his uninvited traveling companion did not exist. On arriving in Okitsu, he withdrew to his seaside villa and waited there, incommunicado, for the decision of the League of Nations.

The League Council disappointed Saionji and reacted to the October Plot exactly as the plot planners had intended. On October 24, after a twelve-day session in which it had taken into account the "delicate situation in Tokyo," the Council recessed without asserting any blunt censure of Japan. Instead it resolved to reconvene on November 16 by which time, it piously hoped, Japan would withdraw her forces from Manchuria. The Japanese representative on the Council deplored the impoliteness of "this ultimatum," and in voting against it, cast his first lonely nay.

ANOTHER HUMILIATION

Through his protégés in the Foreign Ministry, old Saionji had followed the debate in the League hour by hour. As soon as he saw how the vote would go, he capitulated as quickly and gracefully as possible. His surrender was announced at a cabal dinner party on October 23. Saionji neither denied nor confirmed the announcement. He waited until October 30 and then, in response to a humble note from Lord Privy Seal Makino—who said, "I feel inadequate to advise the Emperor at the present juncture"—Saionji agreed to pay his long postponed call at the palace.

Court circles politely spread the face-saving story that Hirohito's nerves were frayed by the prolonged crisis and that Saionji, as a loyal courtier, was coming up to Tokyo to encourage the Emperor and exhort him to take better care of his health. The health of the tired, intimidated, eighty-two-year-old was politely ignored, as Saionji proudly asked that it should be. Nevertheless newspaper men who saw him helped down from the train at Tokyo station on November 1, 1931, remarked on his growing feebleness and the "blue caves" which surrounded his eyes.

On the morning of November 2, 1931, Saionji was driven to the Imperial Household Ministry in the palace to meet his former protégé, his lieutenant at the Paris Peace Conference, Lord Privy Seal Count Makino. As soon as the two were alone, Saionji told Makino in many carefully chosen Japanese words that he had failed his country.

"Your father, Okubo Toshimichi," said Saionji, "was a great man. . . . At a time of crisis, when it was touch and go whether the nation would sink or survive, when the people had been worked up over Korea until they were almost in favor of war, your father turned away from his dearest friend, Saigo, his elder and fellow townsman, and by his opposition succeeded in preventing the attack on Korea. Since it is largely because of Prince Okubo's stand at that time that Japan is what she is today and that the Meiji restoration was a success, he was a minister of state, a so-called great retainer, who was literally worthy of the name. Believe me, a man who wants to accomplish anything lasting in today's world must stand equally firm. . . ."

"Yes," rejoined Count Makino quietly, "it is a fact that Father was a close friend of Saigo and that nevertheless he did what he did." Makino did not need to add that, as his father had destroyed Saigo for the Emperor, so he, Makino, might have to destroy his old mentor Saionji.

From Lord Privy Seal Makino's office Saionji went on, at 2:00 P.M., to visit the Imperial Library. He spent forty-five minutes alone with Hirohito in correctly formal conversation. Afterward he sent a message to Foreign Minister Shidehara advising him to play upon the Emperor's fear of economic sanctions.

"There is no need to exaggerate," said Saionji. "Just speak to the Emperor carefully and fully, in a leisurely, sophisticated, agreeable manner."

Saionji returned to Okitsu in a more hopeful frame of mind. The next day, however, he learned that, while the Emperor had been talking to him, Japanese troops under imperial orders had been crossing the Sungari River into the northern half of Manchuria.

FEINT IN MANCHURIA

Lieutenant General Honjo in Mukden had ordered the invasion of north Manchuria on October 30. The invasion was part of the cabal's master plan for dealing with the League of Nations. The objective was to seize the town of Tsitsihar in far northwestern Manchuria and then withdraw from it ostentatiously as a present to the League of Nations when it reconvened on November 16. Tsitsihar was chosen as the target because, of all the cities of north Manchuria, it was the farthest from Mukden and therefore the most spectacular to capture. In addition, the largest of Chang Hsueh-liang's armies was regrouping in the Tsitsihar area. If it could be smashed now, north Manchuria would remain easy to conquer later in the winter when the League's face had been saved.

To spearhead the invasion, Lieutenant General Honjo dispatched cadres of engineers to repair the railroad bridges leading north across the Sungari. They had orders to clash with the Manchurian troops dug in on the northern bank of the frozen river. The engineers were backed by a hastily assembled puppet army of Manchurian mercenaries—a façade for the fiction that the Kwantung Army acted on behalf of a native Manchurian independence movement. Behind the mercenaries trainloads of Kwantung Army regulars rolled north to do the real fighting.

Warm in their olive-drab suits of blanket cloth, their sleeveless goatskin jackets, their padded stormcoats, their fur-lined helmets with earflaps, the Kwantung Army soldiers expected to break through the ragged, hungry, provincial levies of Chang Hsueh-liang in four days. General Ma, the Chinese commander, however, told his men that, if they could hold Tsitsihar until the League met on November 16, they would cause Japan a great loss of face. With this limited objective in mind—this small revenge—the Chinese fought like dragons and upset the Japanese timetable by two bloodstained weeks. Not until November 18 could the Japanese take Tsitsihar. Not until November 26 could they turn the town over to the Manchurian puppet army which they had hired, and withdraw as promised. By then their gesture of courtesy to the League had become a graceless concession to angry League demands.

HENRY'S ABDUCTION

The same day that Saionji said he would come to Tokyo and that Lieutenant General Honjo launched the invasion of north Manchuria, the collective leadership of Japan's spy service activated their plans to install boy emperor Henry Pu-Yi as the puppet ruler of Manchuria. That morning Colonel Doihara, mayor of Mukden and chief of Special Service Organs in Manchuria, called on the Pu-Yis at their villa, the "Quiet Garden," in Tientsin. He found that the boy emperor had succumbed to the worries of his wife and eunuchs. Pu-Yi still longed to be restored to the throne of his ancestors, but he had been persuaded that it would be too rash to move his court to Mukden until Japan had completed her conquest of Manchuria and settled her differences with the League. In vain Doihara cajoled and argued. Pu-Yi was adamant. Shortly before noon Doihara returned to the Tientsin Special Service Organ and wired Shanghai for the services of the seductive Manchu princess, Eastern Jewel.

When the phone rang and the summons was relayed to her in her Shanghai apartment, Eastern Jewel was still in bed. She called a Japanese pilot of her acquaintance and persuaded him to fly her to Tientsin immediately. Then she got up, tucked her bobbed hair into a skullcap, and put on the loose robes of a Chinese gentleman. In this disguise, she arrived in Tientsin that same evening. She and her pilot friend checked in briefly at a hotel and before midnight she was at Doihara's headquarters in the Tientsin Special Service Organ. With an air of great mystery she told the desk sergeant that she could not reveal her name except to Doihara personally. Doihara, who did not expect her for at least another day, was putting in an evening catching up with his paper work. He kept her waiting while he finished it, then laid his service revolver on the desk before him and had the mysterious visitor ushered into his presence.

"Your name, please?" he said with a curt nod.

"My name is of no importance," she muttered in her deepest voice. "I have come to help you."

"You speak like a eunuch," observed Doihara. "Are you one of Pu-Yi's men?"

She shook her head and laughed at him.

"Very well then," said Doihara, according to the account he later gave friends, "if you will not tell me who you are, let's see what you are." He drew his sword, and with the tip of it, holding it at arm's length, he deftly cut one after another of the string fasteners down the front of her robe. She held her ground unflinching and continued to smile at him provokingly. He flicked open the robe, moved in, and seized her by the shoulder. Then with a guttural samurai yell, he suddenly severed the silk scarf with which she had bound her breasts. "I saw that she was a woman," he liked to say later, "so I conducted a thorough investigation and determined that I had not put even the smallest scratch on any part of her white skin."

The next day Eastern Jewel visited the "Quiet Garden," the villa of boy emperor Pu-Yi. Her tongue tripping with all the latest Shanghai gossip, she spent the afternoon reviving her acquaintance with Pu-Yi's neurasthenic, opium-smoking wife, Elizabeth. That evening Elizabeth ate her dinner without throwing a single tantrum. "The 'Quiet Garden' is quiet again," noted one of Pu-Yi's ministers. Pu-Yi invited Eastern Jewel to consider his home her home as long as she remained in Tientsin.

Much as Elizabeth enjoyed Eastern Jewel's company, no amount of coaxing would make her favor the contemplated move to Mukden. After four days had passed, Colonel Doihara grew impatient and decided to frighten Pu-Yi into going to Mukden alone. He bribed a waiter at a local café to call the villa and warn Pu-Yi that he was about to be assassinated by partisans of the former war lord of Manchuria, Chang Hsueh-liang. Daily thereafter Doihara saw to it that the unhappy boy emperor received a letter of warning from an old friend or a threatening phone call from an old enemy. When Pu-Yi still hesitated, Eastern Jewel arranged to slip two harmless but ugly-looking snakes into his royal bed just before he retired for the night. On November 8, a former Manchu acquaintance sent Pu-Yi a basket of fruit in which Eastern Jewel discovered two bombs. A squad of Japanese military policemen summoned by Eastern Jewel carried the explosives out of the house with a great show of bravado and excitement. Investigation by Japanese criminologists promptly "proved that the two bombs had been manufactured in the arsenal of Chang Hsueh-liang."

That night, November 8, Doihara engineered the first in a series of nightly riots in the Chinese quarter of Tientsin. Using the disturbances as a pretext, the Japanese garrison commander on November 10 declared martial law in the Japanese Concession and isolated the "Quiet Garden" with a cordon of protective troops and armored cars. Now at last the frightened Pu-Yi agreed to flee to Manchuria. Eastern Jewel persuaded him that he would be safest if he went alone that very night and left his wife Elizabeth to follow later.

Pu-Yi was spirited out of the "Quiet Garden" locked in the trunk of his convertible. The Japanese sentries and roadblocks outside the villa made his chauffeur so nervous that he took a wrong turning, backed up, and smashed into a telephone pole. Pu-Yi, in the trunk, received a hard blow on the head and completed his wild ride in a daze. The car pulled up at a restaurant on the darkened outskirts of the Japanese Concession.

Pu-Yi was let out of the trunk and given a Japanese Army overcoat and cap. In this disguise he was whisked off in a Japanese staff car which took him to a dock in the British Concession. There a motor launch was waiting for him.

Stowed in the bilge of the launch—beside a drum of high-octane gas which was meant to incinerate him if anything went wrong—Pu-Yi was piloted down river, past Chinese coastal entrenchments, toward the China Sea. Once, the launch was challenged by Chinese sentries and ordered to put in to the bank for inspection. The helmsman obediently cut his motor and drifted in toward shore. When the sentries on the bank had relaxed and the current of the river had carried the boat a little downstream, the pilot abruptly started the motor and roared away safely to the accompaniment of scattered rifle fire.

At the mouth of the river the merchant ship *Awaji Maru* lay anchored under a full head of steam. Pu-Yi was bundled aboard in a boatswain's chair, and the *Awaji* headed out across the gulf for the Kwantung Leasehold. The following day at the Yingkow docks of Japan's South Manchuria Railroad Company, Pu-Yi was welcomed ashore by a delegation under the leadership of the infamous secret police strangler, Amakasu Masahiko. It was a foretaste of the type of Court which would surround Pu-Yi's puppet throne in the years ahead.

During the next five weeks Pu-Yi was kept a pampered prisoner. He was regally lodged, first at a spa outside Port Arthur and then in the executive suite of the Yamato Hotel in Mukden. At both places, however, he found that he was not allowed to mingle with the other guests. In mid-December, his wife Elizabeth, lulled into her pipes by Eastern Jewel, finally joined him. The two resumed their separate dream lives together in a Mukden villa which had once belonged to Eastern Jewel's father, Prince Su of the Iron Helmet. The following March Pu-Yi was to be proclaimed chief executive—not emperor—of the new puppet state of Manchukuo.

PRE-SWINDLE POLITICS

During these Army preparations to take all of Manchuria and put it under a puppet government, Hirohito's Big Brothers in Tokyo were busy devising a suitable combination of political forces to take responsibility for the Dollar Swindle. The swindle, Act One of the Triple Intrigue, was to raise funds for the Fake War, Act Two, which in turn would distract the League and save its face. The Big Brothers succeeded in putting together a coalition of Strike-North Army officers, Constitutionalist politicians, and the directors of the Mitsui cartel. The arrangements with the Strike-North Faction were handled personally by Prince Chichibu, Hirohito's younger brother.

Since the seizure of Mukden, Prime Minister Wakatsuki had tendered his resignation repeatedly to Hirohito. He and his anti-Constitutionalist party, the Democratic Constitutionalists, were eager to be out of office during the Triple Intrigue. They made no secret of the fact that they hoped to lose at the next elections. The out-of-power Constitutionalists were also reluctant to form a government, but they had no alternative because they had promised their financial backers, the magnates of Mitsui, to take Japan off the gold standard. The Mitsui directors had $100 million stagnating in U.S. banks. They were impatient for a change of government that would allow them to collect their profits and put their money back into use.

Hirohito insisted that Prime Minister Wakatsuki remain in office until the League of Nations delivered its verdict. Days of waiting turned to weeks and the bookkeepers of Mitsui grew increasingly nervous. To give them temporary relief, the president of the Constitutionalists, at a rally on November 11, 1931, promised publicly to take Japan off the gold standard. The announcement caused a drop in the value of the yen on the open market and a rise in the relative value of the dollars being hoarded by Mitsui abroad. It decreased the risk Mitsui was taking and cut the potential profits of Mitsui competitors who were latecomers to the dollar-buying swindle. When old Prime-Minister-Maker Saionji heard of the announcement, he shook his head in puzzlement. "It is like a bank," he muttered, "declaring bankruptcy before it opens its doors."

THE LEAGUE'S DECISION

After the League met in Geneva, Switzerland, on November 16, it remained in session debating the Manchurian problem for a month. In Tokyo Hirohito suffered from the prolonged tension and his courtiers feared for his health. On November 19, as he returned aboard his battleship from the annual Army grand maneuvers, he went on deck after dark and stood at the rail waving his hand at the black empty sea. A chamberlain who had been following him at a discreet distance ran to his side full of solicitude and alarm.

"It's all right," said Hirohito, laughing. "On that headland, beyond the dark, thousands of firefly bonfires have been lit by the peasants in honor of my passing tonight. I am simply acknowledging their homage."

As the League's debate turned increasingly against Japan, the professional politicians in Tokyo expected momentarily the fall of the Wakatsuki government. In speculating on the composition of the Cabinet which would take its place, most of them predicted a coalition which would divide the responsibility for the future among all factions. Black Dragon Lord Toyama opined that only a "darkside cabinet" of his own underworld leaders could be patriotic enough to shoulder the burden. Hirohito and his courtiers kept their own plans to themselves and waited for the League to deliver its verdict.

The League voted on December 10, 1932. It decided neither to condemn Japan's aggression nor to condone it. Instead, in a surrender of principle which the New York *Herald Tribune* called "handsomely staged and impressive, but virtually unconditional," the League opted to send a "commission of inquiry" to the Orient to decide on the spot the rights and wrongs of the case. Though better than a vote of censure, the League's decision to temporize hardly pleased Hirohito and his Court. To have an unsympathetic commission snooping about in the Orient, under a spotlight of publicity, violated every maxim of aristocratic Japanese government. The commission would stir up domestic political problems. It would encourage Chinese belligerence. It would extend indefinitely Japan's crisis with the League.

The day the League voted, Hirohito allowed the home minister, a hireling from the Black Dragon, to topple the Wakatsuki government by refusing for forty-eight hours to attend Cabinet meetings. Hirohito accepted the resignation of the Cabinet en bloc and sent Secretary-Spy Harada to Okitsu to fetch Prime-Minister-Maker Saionji for the ceremony of nominating a new government. Saionji sarcastically asked Harada what choice had already been made by the Eleven Club. Harada mentioned President Inukai of the Constitutionalists. "In that case," sighed Saionji, "Inukai seems inevitable."

Tiny, even by Japanese standards, and rated deep in political cunning, even by Chinese standards, Inukai qualified as a leader for the Fake War, Act Two of the Triple Intrigue, because he was a close friend of Chiang Kai-shek. Together with Black Dragon Toyama and with General Matsui, the future scapegoat Butcher of Nanking, Inukai was one of the three messiahs of Asia for the Asiatics. He had befriended Sun Yat-sen and Chiang Kai-shek many times during their years of exile in Japan. If he told Chiang now that the projected war in Shanghai was a sham, staged for the benefit of the League, Chiang might believe him. If he also told Chiang that the war was a smokescreen behind which Japan meant to prepare for a Strike North into Russia, Chiang might even be willing to co-operate with him in the staging.

At 2:23 P.M. on December 12, the day after Hirohito accepted the resignation of the Wakatsuki Cabinet, Saionji arrived at Shimbashi Station in Tokyo to fulfill his onerous ceremonial duties in selecting the next Cabinet. His Secretary-Spy Harada extricated himself from the crowd of dignitaries which had assembled on the station platform to greet Saionji and ducked into the stationmaster's office to use the telephone. He called Marquis Kido, the favorite Big Brother who was secretary to Lord Privy Seal Makino.

"I can say positively," he told Kido, "that Inukai's is the name which Prince Saionji will submit to the Throne."

"That's fine," said Kido in his usual guarded manner. "There will be no objection to Inukai. The lord privy seal, however, is greatly concerned about financial management—or shall we say foreign relations? Accordingly it would be most appropriate if you would just give a hint to the finance minister, telling him that it will probably be Inukai and that various matters should be taken care of before the resignation of the Cabinet is announced to the public."

CASHING IN ON $$$

That evening, a Saturday, when the bourses of New York, London, and Paris were all closed, Finance Minister Inoue Junnosuke alerted Japanese businessmen abroad to the favorable opportunities in the offing. Various loose ends of complex transactions in "short sale" of currency and "short purchase" of commodities were hastily tied up in a dozen different capitals. In Japan department store clerks worked all weekend long to retag merchandise with new inflated prices reflecting the sudden drop expected in the value of the yen. On Monday morning housewives despaired at food prices which had jumped 30 to 40 per cent since Saturday.

In September 1931, before the Dollar Swindle had been conceived, Japan had had 900 million yen of paper currency in circulation backed by 870 million yen in gold. Each paper yen had been worth half a U.S. dollar. Now the 900 million paper yen were backed by only 370 million yen's worth of gold and the paper yen would soon be quoted at a value of 32 U.S. cents apiece. No less than 500 million yen's worth of gold had been shipped abroad to cover Japan's quiet but enormous speculation in depressed Western currencies. In theory the paper money of Japan should have fallen to 43 per cent of its previous value. In fact the secret of the swindle had been so well kept that the yen fell to only 64 per cent of its pre-swindle value. Because the yen remained inflated, Japanese speculators abroad converted their dollars first to raw materials and then secondarily to yen. Mitsui textile executives, for instance, bought heavily in the bumper 1931 U.S. cotton crop. They shipped it back to Japan, wove it into yard goods on the cheap Japanese labor market, and used it to swamp the bazaars of India and the Middle East. Textile mills in England went bankrupt and Japan acquired a name as a purveyor of cheap goods. Japanese industrialists doubled their swindle money by taking full advantage of the lag between domestic inflation and domestic wages. Collectively the Japanese cartels and the government's own Yokohama Specie Bank had netted an immediate paper profit of $60 million which would be realized finally as a cash profit of almost $200 million.

14

FAKE WAR

(1932)

A PRINCE TAKES COMMAND

The curtain rose on Act Two of the Triple Intrigue with the investiture of the Inukai Cabinet on December 13, 1931. That afternoon, in a frigidly formal audience with Hirohito, Saionji formally recommended Inukai as the nation's next prime minister. The new Cabinet met immediately and voted funds for the final pacification of all Manchuria. In China an envoy of Prime Minister Inukai, who had been ready and waiting in Nanking for several weeks, called on Chiang Kai-shek. Before dusk Chiang Kai-shek had stirred up a tempest in his KMT party and threatened to resign. He carried out his threat two days later and retired to his luxurious villa in the mountains. There he would remain, observing the Fake War, until the time came for him to take credit for ending it.

On December 16, the day after Chiang Kai-shek resigned, so did General Kanaya Hanzo, the chief of the Japanese Army General Staff. For two years he had performed deeds of political heroism above and beyond the normal call of military duty and now he begged to be relieved of the onus of presiding over the Fake War ahead. The triumverate of generals who managed the Army—war minister, chief of staff, and inspector general of military education—agreed to nominate General Minami, the outgoing war minister, as Kanaya's successor. Hirohito, however, had found Minami somewhat obtuse during the seizure of Mukden and suggested, through intermediaries, that the three chiefs reconsider their recommendation. After discreet inquiries the three chiefs discovered that Hirohito's personal choice for chief of staff was Prince Kanin, the gray eminence of the imperial family. Prime-Minister-Maker Saionji and the Strike-North Faction in the General Staff fought the appointment for six days—to no avail. On De-

456

cember 23, Hirohito overrode all objections and confirmed his great-uncle in Japan's highest military office.

Though still only sixty-six years old, Prince Kanin was the last surviving brother of Prince Asahiko who had counseled Emperor Komei at the time of Commodore Perry's opening of Japan seventy-eight years earlier. He alone knew all the secrets of imperial family policy making in the years which had intervened. He alone outranked Prime-Minister-Maker Saionji as a father of the nation. It was his cavalry cronies, Tatekawa and Koiso, who had masterminded the plots leading to the seizure of Mukden. It was his responsibility to enact the rest of the imperial program bequeathed to Hirohito by his grandfather, Emperor Meiji. For the next nine years, until the autumn of 1940, Prince Kanin would fulfill meticulously the trust he had inherited. He would preside over the formulation of all Army staff plans and would present them to Hirohito for his signature. Before his retirement he would oversee the conquest of north Manchuria, Mongolia, China, and northern Indochina. Before his death—of severe hemorrhoids in May 1945—he would see Japan's Armageddon against the West spend itself in rubble and flame.

Kanin's appointment was celebrated by a mass rally of "national thanks" at Tokyo's Meiji Stadium. No less than 18,000 members of veterans' associations, youth groups, women's leagues, and cultural clubs turned out to express their gratitude to the Emperor for appointing a member of his own family to a position of public responsibility. The proceedings were broadcast on radio and beamed overseas to the farthest corners of the Empire. No member of the imperial family had ever before talked on the radio to the common people. To assure them that they might listen without being struck deaf, Black Dragon Toyama, the idolized Robin Hood of the slums, acted as master of ceremonies. After his introduction Prince Kanin arose, ramrod stiff in his field marshal's uniform. Strikingly handsome, his waxed mustache glittering under the lights, he delivered his speech with great dignity. In a few well-chosen words he called for national unity and selfless service to the Throne in the heroic ordeals which Japanese would have to face in the years ahead.

SEDUCTIONS IN SHANGHAI

Having reunited boy emperor Pu-Yi with his number-one wife, the energetic Manchu princess Eastern Jewel returned in mid-December, at the time of the Cabinet change in Tokyo, to the arms of her muscular lover, Major Tanaka of the Special Service Organ in Shanghai. Sun Fo, the son of Sun Yat-sen, was in Shanghai trying to persuade Japan to support his Cantonese faction of the KMT against the faction of Chiang Kai-shek who had just resigned. Major Tanaka had money to spend for arranging provocations for the Fake War. Eastern Jewel was in her element. She seduced

Sun Yat-sen's son and passed on to Major Tanaka an exhaustive account of the rivalries and factions within the KMT party. She slept with a British military attaché in Shanghai and wheedled out of him a realistic estimate of the small commitment which Western nations were willing to make in stopping Japanese aggression in Manchuria. In her spare time she hired Chinese thugs to stand by for street brawls, arsons, and bombings that would serve as tinder for the Fake War. Being a Chinese princess she could move in Chinese circles closed to any other employee of the Shanghai Special Service Organ. Being a Manchu princess she looked down upon the Chinese masses with a fanatic contempt beyond Chinese understanding.

On December 17, 1931, four days after Eastern Jewel's return to Shanghai, a certain I Pong-chang of the Korean Independence Movement in Shanghai took ship for Kobe with a suitcase of hand grenades and a determination to throw one of them at Hirohito. At the Kobe docks he managed mysteriously to slip past Japan's usually efficient immigration officers. On the eight-hour train ride up to Tokyo he somehow escaped the notice of railroad plainclothesmen. In Tokyo he took a room at the Owariya Inn in the lower-class pleasure district of Asakusa. There he spent his time reading newspapers, studying Tokyo street maps, and waiting for his opportunity.

HIROHITO'S EXTRAORDINARY ESCAPE

Throughout the last week of 1931 the Kwantung Army in Manchuria was preparing for a final, full-scale occupation of Manchuria's northern provinces. In the first week of January the plans were executed with an aplomb and celerity that left the League of Nations gaping. On January 5, 1932, the politician of the Kwantung Army, Colonel Itagaki, flew to Tokyo to report to Hirohito and the General Staff that the spine of Chinese resistance was broken and that nothing remained to be done except routine mopping-up operations. Itagaki stayed on in Tokyo to assist in the operational planning for the Fake War.

Japan's renewed aggression in Manchuria, at a time when the League of Nations' Commission of Inquiry had not yet started for the Orient, stung many Western statesmen like a slap in the face. Secretary of State Stimson considered recalling the American ambassador in Tokyo and curtailing U.S.-Japanese trade. He found, however, that he could not muster enough political support in Washington for either measure. He contented himself with sending to Japan the stiffest note up to that time in the history of U.S.-Japanese relations. The note promised that the U.S. government would never recognize a Japanese puppet regime in Manchuria.

If Hirohito's cabal had any lingering doubts about activating its plans for the Fake War in Shanghai, they were dispelled when Stimson's note arrived in Tokyo early on Friday morning, January 8.

That day the Emperor was to attend a military review in the north Tokyo suburb of Yoyogi. Contrary to precedent, a map of the route he would follow had been published in the newspapers five days earlier. Security precautions were unusually strict. Secret policemen from the Kwantung Army in Manchuria had been flown in to assist the various Tokyo police forces. Many teahouses, brothels, and Korean boarding-houses had been raided and searched beforehand. Nevertheless the Korean assassin from Shanghai, I Pong-chang, with a grenade in each pocket, managed to find a place for himself in the front ranks of the spectators outside the Cherry Field Gate of the palace through which Hirohito was to pass on his way home.

Ever since the attempt on Hirohito's life in 1923, the policemen along the margins of an imperial progress had stood with their backs turned to the roadway, their heads respectfully inclined and their eyes staring into the eyes of the crowd. The crowd by ancient tradition was kneeling. From this reverent posture I Pong-chang had an opportunity to study the imperial cortege as it came toward him down the street. There were several carriages in the procession but only one emblazoned with the crest of the imperial chrysanthemum. Nevertheless, according to the account given out later by the police, I Pong-chang became confused. He leapt to his feet, snatched a grenade from his pocket, and hurled it 65 feet—a fair toss even for a trained shot-putter. Under the left rear wheel of the carriage of Imperial Household Minister Ikki Kitokuro, there was a small explosion. No one in the dense throng along the curbs of the roadway was harmed, but three scraps of shrapnel were later exhibited as having been dug from the underside of Household Minister Ikki's carriage. The assassin was seized at once by the police and held entirely incommunicado. Nine months later the secret police announced that he had been sentenced to death.

Big Brother Kido of the Eleven Club noted in his diary before the assassination attempt that he felt something bad would happen that day. Afterwards he characterized the bombing briefly as "a kind of political plot." Imperial Household Minister Ikki, whose coach had been struck, calmly told Secretary-Spy Harada on the phone a few minutes after the bombing that the incident was not important enough to warrant a special report to Prime-Minister-Maker Saionji. Hirohito himself, when told the identity of the assailant, chuckled and said, "He would have to be from the Korean Independence Party." Kinoshita Mikio, one of the palace chamberlains, remarked that afternoon that the attempted assassination would be useful in re-enlisting the sympathy of citizens who had grown disillusioned with Hirohito. Many patriotic Japanese felt that the home minister, who had charge of the police, should make amends for the carelessness of his subordinates by committing hara-kiri. But the home minister merely tendered his resignation to Hirohito as a formality along with the rest of the Cabinet.

Without reading them, Hirohito handed the letters of resignation back to the prime minister and asked the entire Cabinet to remain in office.

That night Secretary-Spy Harada arrived in Okitsu to give Saionji a full briefing on the assassination attempt and the background for it. Harada in his diary reported none of the details of the conversation except one statement by Saionji, a statement which no other Japanese could have made without being arrested by the Thought Police.

"It is generally said," mused Saionji with bitterness, "that the Emperor transcends the Constitution, but where except in the Constitution is his existence justified?"

The day after the bombing, Saturday, January 9, 1932, a Chinese newspaper acquaintance of Eastern Jewel in Shanghai wrote tactlessly in his column that the bomb meant for Hirohito had "unfortunately missed its mark." The story was carried by the *Minkuo Daily News* in Shanghai and by a number of papers in other Chinese cities. Well-disciplined Japanese residents in China rioted in protest and demolished the offices of several Chinese newspapers. Though Chinese editors apologized for their impoliteness, Japanese Special Service Organ agents kept the insult alive and finally, after three weeks of agitation, inflated it into a cause for war.

GHOST HOUSE

No sooner had the *causa belli* been supplied for the second act of the Triple Intrigue, the Fake War, than preparations began for the third act, the Threat of Coup d'Etat.

On the evening of the day after the unsuccessful bombing of Hirohito's entourage, the children of a neighborhood in north Tokyo reported to their parents that the ghosts of "the empty house" were holding a meeting again. The families in the immediate vicinity of the empty house politely drew their rain shutters so that they would not see the eerie lights next door or seem to be prying into the affairs of the spirits.

The empty house belonged to a veteran of the spy service with long experience in China.[1] He had lived on the premises once and had written a book there on agrarian philosophy. But about a year ago he had closed the place up and gone to live elsewhere. Not long after his departure lights began to be seen in the house at night. Whenever the police were called to investigate, the lights went out and the police could find no one inside. The neighbors accepted the fact that spirits had moved in and did their courteous best to ignore the house thereafter.

What the neighbors could not guess and the local police may have been instructed to overlook was that the empty house had been taken over as the secret headquarters of the Blood Brotherhood, one of the

[1] Gondo Nariaki.

three groups of potential terrorists with which Lord Privy Seal Makino's man, Dr. Okawa, had been put in touch through the good offices of old Spider Tanaka, the director emeritus of the spy service.

On the night in question, the empty house was the scene of an initiation ceremony. A burly Buddhist priest in white vestments stood at the end of the entry hall, limned from the rear by flickering candlelight. From time to time a tapping at the front door would stimulate him to chant a sepulchral welcome. A sturdy recruit would enter the foyer and at the priest's direction would put on a white hood from a pile beside the umbrella stand. Then the priest would usher him into the darkness of the room beyond—the "bone-cooling hall"—and tell him to meditate until everyone had arrived.

When a dozen men had assembled to contemplate the darkness of the inner room, the priest joined them with his candle. He chanted the mystic Lotus Sutra from Buddhist scripture and then delivered a solemn sermon of indoctrination. Their time of service was approaching, he said. From now until they were given their assignments, they would live with him here performing the necessary purification rites. When they had purged themselves of all unclean and selfish motives, they would be ready for the final cleansing in blood, the "killing of one man by one man" which would gain them entry into paradise. After the priest's lecture, the recruits pricked their fingers with their daggers and renewed their signatures on a scroll which the priest called "the compact of blood." Then he assigned each of them a small room and a pallet for the remainder of their stay in the empty house.

Like the owner of the empty house, the priest, Friar Inoue, had once been a member of the spy service in China. He had returned to Japan in 1920 with his good friends and former colleagues Dr. Okawa, the ideologist of the Strike South, and Kita Ikki, the ideologist of the Strike North. When Okawa and Kita had fallen out, Friar Inoue had felt his loyalties torn between them. He had retired to meditate in a hermit's cave among the grotesque rock formations along the Pacific coast near the spy-service center of Oarai. One day while fasting—so he later remembered in his autobiography—he fell into a trance and saw a vision of Japan conquering the United States. The vision persuaded him to follow the star of Dr. Okawa and the Strike-South Faction. He emerged from the mountains and announced that he had changed his name from Inoue Akira, Inoue the Radiant, to Inoue Nisho, Inoue Summoned by the Sun Goddess. Along with his new name he assumed the frock of a Buddhist priest of the warrior Nichiren sect.

In the late 1920's, under the sponsorship of old Spider Tanaka of the spy service, Friar Inoue had opened a "school for the defense of the nation" in an abandoned temple in Oarai a few doors from Spider Tanaka's Everyday Meiji Biographical Research Institute. Here he gave advanced courses in espionage to the most promising graduates of Oarai's elementary school for spies, the Purple Mountain Academy.

Now, in the empty house, Friar Inoue had with him the most dedicated of his former students. In a few weeks each of them would be ready to assassinate a sacrificial victim—an industrialist or politician from the "plutocratic classes" which, in Inoue's view, were impeding the fulfillment of Hirohito's mission in life.

Before a dusty mirror Friar Inoue removed his hooded robe. A shaven pate and a hard round face emerged. Two cold humorless eyes peered out through perfectly circular spectacles. Friar Inoue snuffed out his candle and lay down for the night. The ceremony of initiation had gone well. The idea of using stage effects borrowed from Western spiritualism and African voodoo had been a good one. He was much obliged for it to the Emperor's uncle, Prince Higashikuni. In a moment Friar Inoue was asleep.

For the next two months Friar Inoue's Blood Brotherhood was to terrorize Japan's Westernized community of businessmen and politicians. By assassination and threat of assassination it would prevent Japanese liberals from talking frankly to the League of Nations' Commission of Inquiry and would force them to put up money to pay for the Fake War and the development of the new colony of Manchuria. Until the brotherhood's mission was accomplished, it would enjoy a strange immunity from police arrest, an immunity made possible by the high rank of its patrons. Friar Inoue was an intimate of Big Brother Prince Konoye and of Big Brother Prince Higashikuni. Inoue took his orders from Dr. Okawa who relayed them by special messenger directly from Hirohito's chief civilian advisor, Lord Privy Seal Makino, in the palace. In addition Friar Inoue had the support of the naval fliers of the Air Development Station on the Misty Lagoon. The fliers supplied him with guns and ammunition and had set up their own coup-threat headquarters a few blocks from the empty house. This close collaboration was hardly surprising because the fliers were all disciples of Friar Inoue's elder brother, Navy Commander Inoue Fumio. Commander Inoue was the senior flight instructor at the Misty Lagoon. He had taught the imperial family's test pilot, Prince Yamashina, how to fly, and also Captain Yamamoto who would raid Pearl Harbor.

PROVOKING WAR

On January 10, 1932, the day after the initiation ceremony in the empty house, Colonel Itagaki, the visiting political officer from the Kwantung Army, completed his arrangements with the Army General Staff in Tokyo for the Fake War. From his Tokyo hotel room he dispatched the following telegram to Shanghai Special Service Organ Chief Tanaka, the lover of Manchu princess Eastern Jewel:

THE MANCHURIAN INCIDENT HAS DEVELOPED AS EXPECTED, BUT THE OPPOSI-
TION OF THE STRONG COUNTRIES IS STILL GIVING CERTAIN PERSONS AT THE
CENTER DOUBTS. SO PLEASE USE THE CURRENT TENSION BETWEEN CHINA AND
JAPAN TO BRING OFF YOUR INCIDENT AND TURN THE EYES OF THE STRONG
COUNTRIES TOWARD SHANGHAI.

The next morning Itagaki went to the palace and delivered a full report to Hirohito on the "progress being made in establishing the new
nation" of Manchukuo. According to Big Brother Marquis Kido, who
received a résumé of the audience in an anteroom afterwards, Itagaki explained to Hirohito that the new puppet state would preserve a façade of
independence and self-rule. Japanese "advisors," he said, would really
run the state, but they would be given Manchukuoan citizenship and
would be called Manchukuoans. At the same time they would keep their
Japanese citizenship and would remain obedient to orders from Tokyo.
Hirohito inquired whether there were any precedents for such dual na-
tionality, and Itagaki cited several. At this turn in the conversation, the
Emperor's chief aide-de-camp, who had stood in attendance during the
first half of the audience, hastily bowed himself out. It was a Court rule
that he must never listen to discussion of personnel questions. As a result
Hirohito and Itagaki finished their meeting in complete privacy.

On receipt of Colonel Itagaki's telegram from Tokyo, Major Tanaka of
the Shanghai Special Service Organ advanced some $6,000 from organ
funds to his mistress, Eastern Jewel. Disguised as a man, she distributed
half of the money, by her own accounting, to some Chinese laborers at
the Japanese-owned Three Friends bath towel factory. The manager of
the factory was unpopular in the local Japanese community because he
was supposed to have socialistic leanings. The other half of the money,
Eastern Jewel said, she gave to a gang of street toughs who were to assist
the towel weavers.

On the afternoon of January 18 two Nichiren priests and three disciples
of the Myoho Buddhist temple came swaggering along Yinhsiang Creek
near the towel factory, banging gongs and bellowing sutra as was their
offensive wont. Tanaka later explained that he chose them as victims because most Myoho temple men "were only Koreans." The five monks and
novices were set upon by the Chinese towel weavers—and by enough
street toughs to justify Eastern Jewel's expense account—and were brutally
beaten. One of the priests subsequently died on January 24, but long
before he did, on January 19, a scant ten hours after the original skirmish,
thirty-two members of the Japanese Young Men's One-Purpose Society,
led by a secret policeman named Shigeto,[2] made a predawn attack on the
towel factory and burned down one of its buildings. During the fire the

[2] The brother of Colonel Shigeto Chiaki of the Tokyo General Staff who had
played a prominent role in the March Plot a year earlier.

Chinese police appeared on the scene. Two of them were killed and two wounded. Of the One-Purpose Society's goon squad, one was killed and two wounded.

Shortly after daybreak that same morning, the Japanese residents of Shanghai held a mass meeting and at the urging of Major Tanaka resolved to beg the Tokyo government for an expeditionary force to protect them. Tanaka and secret policeman Shigeto took the request to the local representative of the Mitsui cartel and forced him at pistol point to relay it by cable to his head office in Tokyo. The Mitsui management in Tokyo failed to submit the request to the prime minister, as ordered, but the telegram was later used by the cabal as evidence that the Fake War had been launched to protect Mitsui interests—a service for which Mitsui should bear part of the financial burden.

The mayor of Shanghai, Wu Tieh-ching, immediately apologized on behalf of China for the roughness of the Chinese towel weavers who had been hired by Japan. On January 21, he went so far as to promise that he would arrest and punish the towel weavers and would pay medical and consolation expenses to the kin of the termagant Nichiren priests. The Japanese had demanded that he should also make the Chinese citizens of Shanghai stop feeling hostile to Japan. Mayor Wu promised to do his best but pointed out, with polite regrets, that the private feelings of the populace were out of his hands. The Japanese consul general in Shanghai retorted: "In the event that such compliance is refused, we are determined to take such steps as may be necessary." In the days that followed young Japanese bravos in Shanghai and even small Japanese children went out of their way to pick fights with their Chinese counterparts. The carefully manufactured tension grew by the hour.

DOMESTIC EXTORTION

In Tokyo that day Prime Minister Inukai asked Baron Dan Takuma, the top executive of the Mitsui cartel, to contribute 22,000,000 yen—some $8 million—to the government to cover the cost of shipping troops to Shanghai to protect Mitsui interests. Baron Dan protested that Mitsui needed no such protection, could ill afford such a huge sum of money, and would pay it only under compulsion. Prime Minister Inukai reminded Baron Dan that Mitsui had made at least $20 million when Inukai had taken Japan off the gold standard and that one good turn deserved another. If Mitsui would pay for the Fake War, Inukai had an arrangement with Chiang Kai-shek by which the Manchurian problem might be settled and constitutional government in Japan might be preserved.

Inukai did not state his plan but Baron Dan probably knew it already. Inukai hoped to establish Manchuria as a nation independent of both Japan and China. The conversations between Inukai's representative in

Nanking and Chiang Kai-shek indicated that Chiang would recognize such a nation. In return Japan would destroy the Chinese 19th Route Army in Shanghai—the army of the dissident Cantonese faction in the KMT which contested Chiang Kai-shek's absolute authority. Once Chiang Kai-shek recognized the independence of Manchuria, the League of Nations would have no reason to censure Japan. For the sake of international harmony and the domestic co-operation of Japan's business community, Hirohito might be willing to accept such a compromise. He would only have to order the Kwantung Army to return to its garrisons in the South Manchuria Railroad zone and all the rest could be worked out. A token of good faith on the part of the cartels, however, was urgently needed to persuade Hirohito to consider the plan.

Baron Dan promised to think over Prime Minister Inukai's proposal but held out no hope that he could persuade the Mitsui family or the industrialists of the other cartels to back the scheme. Baron Dan suspected that Hirohito was already too committed to military empire-building to change his plans now and that the lines of conflict between the liberal Saionji faction and the imperial faction at Court were too sharply drawn to be erased without a showdown.

That afternoon, January 21, 1932, Hirohito recessed the Diet in preparation for a general election on February 20. In the interim he would have the constitutional right to arrogate the one power which the Diet possessed—that of authorizing additional expenditures which had not been foreseen in the last national budget.

That night Lord Privy Seal Count Makino, Hirohito's chief civilian advisor, warned Saionji, through Secretary-Spy Harada, that continued nonsupport of the Fake War by the cartels would lead to a new imperial coup d'etat on or about February 10. What he meant, as it turned out, was that the Blood Brotherhood of Friar Inoue would then assassinate its first sacrificial victim.

COMMENCEMENT OF HOSTILITIES

Shanghai was an ideal city in which to make the nations of the West appreciate Japan's effort to save the face of the League of Nations. Here were the biggest Western enclaves and the headquarters of the main Western business interests in central China. Here the Western nations had invested more than a billion dollars. Here Japan had a garrison of 2,000 of her crack troops, the Imperial Marines.

On Saturday, January 23, 1932, a Japanese cruiser and four destroyers, all loaded with additional bluejackets, cast anchor in the mouth of the Yangtze, to be followed the next day and the day after by two aircraft carriers. On Sunday, January 24, Chinese civilians held a mass meeting to ask Nanking for military reinforcements. Chiang Kai-shek, however, was sulking in his villa, and the other KMT leaders entrusted the defense of Shanghai to the 19th Route Army of Sun Yat-sen's son, Sun Fo, who was in Shanghai negotiating with the Japanese and sleeping with Eastern Jewel. That night a group of Eastern Jewel's hirelings made an unsuccessful, almost nonexistent attempt to set fire to the Japanese consulate in the French Concession.

On Tuesday, January 26, before a shot had been fired, Hirohito's Supreme War Council, presided over by Chief of Staff Prince Kanin, instructed Admiral Shiozawa in Shanghai to "exercise the right of self-defense." That afternoon Shanghai's Mayor Wu closed the *Minkuo Daily News,* which had offended Japan by regretting the poor aim of Hirohito's Korean would-be murderer. On Wednesday, January 27, Major Wu ordered his police to break up all anti-Japanese societies and demonstrations. The next morning, Thursday—"about eight o'clock," according to the official Japanese account at the time—"a Chinese, seemingly of the anti-Japanese National Salvation Society," threw into the Japanese consulate "what seemed like a bomb, though it failed to explode." Eastern Jewel had successfully laid on her last pathetic straw.

That afternoon at 3:15 Mayor Wu notified the Japanese naval commander, Admiral Shiozawa, that the Chinese municipal government would comply with every Japanese request. Nevertheless at 4:00 P.M. the non-Chinese Municipal Council of the International Settlement, acting under Japanese pressure, proclaimed martial law throughout the concession area, and British, French, and Japanese guard units deployed to defend their assigned sectors against the possibility of attack by Chinese mobs.

At 5:00 P.M. *New York Times* correspondent Hallett Abend visited the Japanese flagship in the harbor for cocktails with Admiral Shiozawa. Over the second Scotch and soda, Shiozawa told Abend that Mayor Wu's acceptance of all Japanese demands was "beside the point."

"At eleven o'clock tonight," said Shiozawa, "I am sending my marines into Chapei to protect our nationals and preserve order." Chapei was the show-piece borough of Chinese Shanghai. It lay just to the north of the Japanese quarter of the International Settlement. The Japanese who lived in Chapei and supposedly needed protection had already been evacuated two days earlier.

As soon as he politely could, Abend hurried ashore and cabled his story to New York. Then he phoned all the Western diplomats of his acquaintance in Shanghai. To a man they told him that he was mongering sensationalism. But Admiral Shiozawa was as good as his word. After eleven o'clock that night, he sent Mayor Wu a note declaring his intentions and before twelve o'clock his bluejackets began crossing the northern boundary of the Japanese defense sector and moving north along the dark streets of Chinese Chapei. Behind them at the border their rear guard unrolled barbed wire and built roadblocks. Westerners in evening dress, who had come across town after their dinner and theatre parties to see if there would be any action, stood about smoking and joking. The only thing worse than a Japanese victory, said the wits, would be a Chinese one.

When the probing patrols had been gone for about half an hour, heavy firing broke out. The Japanese marines had been told not to expect much resistance. They had advanced as if to a picnic, talking and laughing and lighting their way with flaming torches. Now their outing had turned into an immense ambush. On walls and in upstairs windows between the border and the North Station for which they were headed, there had suddenly materialized riflemen and machine gunners of the 19th Route's 78th Division. The marines were caught in cross fire and several hundred of them were mowed down before they could regroup and begin to withdraw.

As the night wore on, every dispensable seaman on the Japanese ships in the harbor was given a gun and sent ashore on the double to join the battle. Despite their efforts, the men of the Chinese 19th Route Army pressed forward. By the first light of day on Friday, January 29, they were threatening to break through the barricades into the Japanese settlement. In desperation Admiral Shiozawa ordered into action the planes of his two aircraft carriers. By 7:00 A.M. they were strafing the advancing Chinese soldiers and strewing little 30-pound terror bombs all over densely populated civilian Chapei. One of their targets was the Commercial Press, the factory for all China's textbooks. It housed a priceless collection of old Chinese scrolls and manuscripts. It was reduced to a gutted shell. The Japanese were frank to explain that anti-Japanese propaganda had been printed on the premises.

Never before had the world witnessed the results of wholesale civilian bombing by airplane. Dynamite dropped from German dirigibles had cut open a few houses in London toward the end of World War I, but casualties had been negligible. Now, in Chapei, the later horrors of Hiroshima might be glimpsed as in a glass darkly. Hundreds of women and children were blown to shreds. Admiral Shiozawa became known in the West as the "baby-killer."

As the bombing and the morning progressed, the 19th Route commander, General Tsai Ting-kai, to the chagrin of his political leaders—especially of Sun Yat-sen's son, Sun Fo, who had taken refuge from the fighting in Eastern Jewel's apartment—announced that the 19th Route would "fight the Japanese to the last man if it has to dye the Whampo River red with its soldiers' blood." That afternoon when Chiang Kai-shek realized that the men of the 19th Route were making heroes of themselves instead of being wiped out, he returned immediately to Nanking and offered his leadership to the KMT "at this time of crisis." The Cantonese faction of the KMT might be his domestic rivals but they were Chinese, and he could ill afford to be out of command when they were sacrificing themselves for the nation.

For Japan's benefit, Chiang continued to negotiate in secret with Prime Minister Inukai's emissary in Nanking, Kayano Chochi. For China's benefit he announced publicly that he had ordered his own personal "guard divisions" to prepare for action. None of Chiang's men, however, arrived at the battle line until over three weeks later. Moreover, Chiang's small navy declared itself neutral and kept out of harm's way well up the Yangtze River. It had ordered a new vessel from a Japanese dockyard in Kobe. The warship was launched while the war still raged and the Chinese minister in Tokyo attended the commissioning ceremony. He drank toasts with the Japanese naval officers present and exchanged sentiments with them of Sino-Japanese friendship and good will.

In later years the valiant 19th Route Army would go over to Chiang's open enemies, the Communists of Mao Tse-tung. In 1932, however, its officers were simply idealistic agrarian reformers. They served the socialist Cantonese faction of the KMT because they believed it to be more in tune with the interests of the Chinese peasantry than were the bankers around Chiang Kai-shek. In their political innocence they felt inspired by Chiang's promise of aid. They dug into the rubble of Chapei and, to the surprise of the Japanese Imperial Marines, held their ground even under a hail of bombs and naval shells. Japanese local civilian reservists— the "mufti army" as they were known in Tokyo—took revenge behind the lines for the losses being suffered by the marines at the front. They raided Chinese shops on the fringes of Chapei, looting, raping, and beheading. The naval deck hands who now held rear posts for the marines spent their days disposing of the bodies of Chinese civilians murdered by Japanese vigilantes.

Altogether the Chinese had some 33,500 men in the Shanghai area compared to a Japanese force which at first numbered less than 5,000. Other foreign armies in the International Settlement and French Concession amounted to over 18,000 men and with their superior equipment and training were thoroughly capable of defending foreign interests against the 19th Route Army. But the Japanese Navy was not disposed to seek Western support. Instead it fought its own desperate defensive battle, bringing in the crews of all the Japanese ships it could muster in the China Sea and finally, in great humiliation, asking the Japanese Army for help. The Imperial Marines were beside themselves with rage to retrieve their laurels.

In Tokyo Hirohito was gravely worried that the wounded honor of his samurai might turn the controlled "incident" into a runaway war which Japan would not be able to afford. Repeatedly he sought assurance from those about him that reinforcements, when landed, would proceed slowly, avoid face-saving confrontations, and remain ready to withdraw at his command. His absorption with the tactical and financial details became so tiresome that Big Brother Marquis Kido of the Eleven Club waxed almost critical of him and expressed a wish that he would shed his pettifogging anxieties and "sit big as a mountain." Hirohito's nervousness was need-less, as it turned out, but he was playing a dangerous game. He was trying to deceive not only the world but also the Japanese electorate and the men who were dying.

As a precaution against uncontrollable escalation Hirohito approved the appointment of his wife's cousin, Prince Fushimi, as chief of the Navy General Staff.[3] In a breach of normal Court protocol, old Prime-Minister-Maker Saionji was not consulted about the appointment beforehand but was simply informed of it afterward when it was a *fait accompli*. Now imperial princes were in charge of the operations of both military services, and absolute, reverent obedience could be expected of the samurai in the ranks.

The Imperial Household Ministry made a special point of announcing that Prince Fushimi's appointment had nothing to do with the fighting in Shanghai. But the nation knew better. An imperial prince would not have been put at the helm unless Hirohito meant to see the Shanghai incident through to an honorable conclusion. To all those wealthy, cosmopolitan, educated Japanese who felt that Japan should not try to deceive the world or risk alienating friends abroad for the sake of Manchuria, the appoint-ment was a clear warning that they would have to reckon with Hirohito.

On this note began Act Three of the Triple Intrigue: Threat of Coup d'Etat. No longer was the threat directed simply at the West; no longer was it intended simply to persuade sympathetic Westerners that the official Japanese government stood powerless and in danger of overthrow. Now the threat was aimed also at internal opponents of imperial policy; now it offered domestic dissenters a hard choice—co-operate or face the pos-sibility of assassination.

---

[3] The previous staff chief, Admiral Taniguchi Naozane, had discovered the involve-ment of the Misty Lagoon Air Development Station with the killers of the Blood Brotherhood. He had pointed out that flight instructor Inoue Fumio, the brother of Friar Inoue of the assassin band, was "a strange man" to have in the Navy. When his request to discharge Commander Inoue was tabled by Hirohito, Admiral Tani-guchi had resigned in protest.

15

GOVERNMENT BY ASSASSINATION

(1932)

BLESSING THE KILLERS

On Saturday, January 30, 1932, the bombs had been bursting in Shanghai for more than twenty-four hours, and the banking houses of Mitsui
and the other cartels had not yet agreed either to give or lend the government enough money to pay for the action.[1] The money itself was important, but the gesture of making it available was symbolically still more
important. By withholding it, the Japanese business community remained
in dissent against the imperial program. The merchants, in effect, were
denying the uniqueness of the Japanese race and the mission handed down
from the sun goddess.

That same Saturday night, therefore, Friar Inoue, the leader for the
Blood Brotherhood, conducted the final rites of purification for the assassins under his charge who were to intimidate the business community.
One by one the young killers filed into the "bone-cooling hall" of the empty
house and to the accompaniment of dedicatory incantations were allowed briefly to handle one or another of the ten pistols which had been
provided by Dr. Okawa and Commander Inoue Fumio's naval group at
the Misty Lagoon. Having blessed the weapons and their wielders, Friar
Inoue returned the guns to their locker for distribution later.

On paper Friar Inoue assigned each of the eleven assassins eleven specific victims to kill at specific times and places. But in practice he later
juggled and postponed the assignments so that only two of the victims
were ever killed. On one occasion he failed to get the assassin his gun

---

[1] In Japan it was and is normal procedure for the government to consult the great
banking families on policies affecting national finance.

on time and on another he sent the killer to a rendezvous where the quarry was not to be expected.

In such fashion great fear was created by only two murders, and it was arranged for many leaders of the cartels and of the Constitutionalist party to be ostentatiously spared. Typically, Lord Privy Seal Makino was one of those who turned out to be not for killing. The assassin assigned to take care of him was a knowledgeable Tokyo University graduate student who had acted as the courier between the Blood Brotherhood and Makino's own man, Dr. Okawa.

STAY OF EXECUTION

The first week of February 1932 was taken up entirely with the outbreak of the Shanghai war. The restless fliers of the Misty Lagoon, who were to supply military support for the Blood Brotherhood, found themselves temporarily distracted from all else by being called to duty for raids and reconnaissance at the front. On Monday, February 1, while their precision bombing was demolishing Chinese structures a stone's throw from Western-owned docks and warehouses, the Japanese foreign minister offered Western diplomats in Tokyo the opportunity of using their good offices to mediate the Sino-Japanese "misunderstanding." That same evening the American, French, and British ambassadors responded to the suggestion informally but favorably.

On the afternoon of the next day, Tuesday, February 2, Lord Privy Seal Makino told Prime Minister Inukai that "resolution of the Manchurian problem is going unexpectedly well" and that "the results may be almost perfect because of the understanding attitude of the United States and Great Britain." Perhaps, after all, the Shanghai affair might not have to be carried through to the end.

"What's done is done, of course," said Makino, "but now we must cooperate as much as possible with the other nations to prevent escalation."

Prime Minister Inukai had just come from a Cabinet meeting at which his ministers had approved the dispatch of regular Army troops to Shanghai. For a few hours he found himself in the awkward position of having approved a war which might not be necessary. That evening, however, it developed that U.S. Secretary of State Stimson would not co-operate in any Shanghai settlement that did not also include some provision for a Manchurian settlement. Neither the Emperor nor the Army would accept such a proviso, and for the next three days the Fake War was held in abeyance while Japan negotiated with the United States.

In the interim, on Thursday, February 4, the war minister was carefully briefed by the finance minister on the reasons why the war must be a brief gesture and nothing more. Japan could not afford a real war, not even if it could be won in six months, not even if it could be waged on a budget of $30 million. The Army, emphasized the finance minister, must be ready and disciplined to obey at any moment a truce arrangement. Army talk of breaking through to Nanking and teaching Chiang Kai-shek a lesson must be stopped.

"We have absolutely no righteous cause," said the finance minister, "to warrant hopes of being able to raise financial assistance in foreign capitals." Then he showed War Minister Araki telegrams demonstrating that Japanese credit in New York had struck rock bottom and that President Hoover had recently written financier Thomas W. Lamont that the U.S. government had now "wholly lost confidence in the Japanese government."

KILL THE BANKER

By February 5, unofficial secret negotiations had made it clear that the United States could not be cajoled out of coupling the Manchurian and Shanghai settlements. Nor would the cartels subsidize the Shanghai war as long as they could hope for a firm Western stand. Accordingly Hirohito directed Prime Minister Inukai to reject the mediation plan of the West as unsatisfactory, and all plotting lights were turned on green again.

On Saturday morning, February 6, Friar Inoue in the empty house received a visit from one of the junior officers of the Misty Lagoon, Second Lieutenant Ito Kijomi. Ito brought with him a Browning automatic which had belonged to his squadron leader, Lieutenant Commander Fujii Hitoshi, who had been shot down and killed on reconnaissance over Chapei the day before. Commander Fujii had been the prize pupil of Friar Inoue's brother, the flight instructor, and also the leader at the fliers' coup headquarters near the empty house a week earlier. Lieutenant Ito begged Friar Inoue to proceed according to plan even without the fliers' support. The Browning automatic, he said, shone with the departed spirit of Lieutenant Commander Fujii whose dying regret it had been that he could not lead the Emperor's coup in person. Friar Inoue accepted the Browning and swore to use it to satisfy the one-day ghost of its former owner. That night after suitable ceremony and dedications he turned over the Browning and forty-six bullets to one of his best assassins, a young man named Konuma Tadashi.

Konuma's assigned victim was the former finance minister, Inoue Junnosuke. He had to be killed for several reasons. He had made the initial arrangements with the Mitsui cartel to buy dollars in preparation for the Dollar Swindle. He was one of the few men in Japan who knew that the idea for the swindle had emanated from the palace. He had not co-operated later in forcing the cartels to turn back a suitable percentage of their profits to the service of the nation. And finally, someone had to be assassinated as an example to the rest of the recalcitrant business community. Assassin Konuma spent two days practicing with his Browning and waiting for final orders.

In the interim on Sunday, February 7, the Japanese Army came to the rescue of the embattled Navy by landing a mixed brigade of 10,000 men in Shanghai. On Monday, February 8, Hirohito gave his personal instructions to the Japanese Diplomat who was going to Shanghai to be ready to negotiate a truce as soon as the Fake War had served its purpose. The negotiator was Matsuoka Yosuke, a University of Oregon graduate who would later become famous for his expansive hobnobbing with Hitler and Mussolini. Since 1925 he had been one of the junior members of the cabal in the Foreign Ministry. His meeting with Hirohito that quiet Monday morning was disguised as a "lecture in the Imperial Study on non-current historical events." At the end of it, however, Hirohito had a few words with Matsuoka on current events.

Matsuoka expressed the opinion that the Fake War should not be stopped until the Japanese forces in Shanghai had taken the offensive and won a decisive victory. China, he said, was Japan's lazy elder brother. The industrious younger brother had the duty of chastising the elder brother when the honor of the whole family was at stake. Appealing to Hirohito's interests as a biologist, Matsuoka cited the "Darwinian principle" that competition is always most fierce between those who are closely related. Hirohito nodded, but Saionji, when he heard of the Matsuoka audience, asked that Army and Navy commanders in Shanghai be warned about Matsuoka's proclivity "for falling into paradoxes."

It followed from Matsuoka's advice that the Fake War must be well staged and that the cartels must be cowed into paying for a handsome production. Early the next afternoon, Tuesday, February 9, Emperor Hirohito invited a most unusual "lecturer" to speak to him in his study at the Imperial Library. This was Lieutenant General Banzai Rihachiro, retired. Banzai for many years had run Japan's espionage network in China and had been the immediate superior of Friar Inoue, the leader of the Blood Brotherhood. In the shadowy directorate of Japan's Civilian Spy Service, Banzai now ranked second to no one except perhaps old Spider Tanaka of the Everyday Meiji Biographical Research Institute in Oarai.

Retired General Banzai emerged from his talk with Hirohito that Tuesday afternoon at two o'clock. Two hours later the Blood Brotherhood's assassin, Konuma, received a messenger from Friar Inoue, telling him to proceed according to plan. At 7:00 P.M. assassin Konuma alighted from a streetcar on a corner a few blocks from Tokyo Imperial University. He took up a loitering vigil at the gate of the Komagome Elementary School where former Finance Minister Inoue Junnosuke was scheduled to deliver an election speech that night. Although Konuma paced back and forth and smoked countless cigarettes, the passers-by paid him no special attention. Twenty-two years old, fifth son of an Ibaraki fisherman, first in his class at junior high, later a baker's assistant and a carpenter's apprentice, he looked like any restless, impoverished university student, waiting for a girl or the results of a crucial examination.

The former finance minister's limousine pulled up to the curb at 8:02 P.M. The candidate for whom he was stumping stepped out and bowed to a political welcoming committee. The sixty-six-year-old financier followed; he advanced five or six steps and was just inclining his head to the crowd when Blood Brother Konuma burst from the ranks of spectators behind him and fired three shots into the old man's back. One bullet lodged in his left buttock, another in his right lung, and the third shattered his spine. Former Finance Minister Inoue Junnosuke died almost immediately. Assassin Konuma let himself be taken to the police station where he was treated with such unusual gentleness that he appeared in criminal court a few months later looking the rosy picture of health.

KILLERS LEFT AT LARGE

On the day of financier Inoue's murder, his namesake, Friar Inoue of the Blood Brotherhood, moved his base of operations from the empty house to the House of Heavenly Action, a student hostel maintained by the Black Dragon Society next door to the home of the Black Dragon himself, Toyama Mitsuru. The hostel was managed by Toyama's son, Hidezo, and by Toyama's secretary, another former spy of the China Service, Honma Kenichiro. Until 1930, Honma had been Friar Inoue's colleague at Oarai and had run the elementary school for spies there, the Purple Mountain Academy.[2]

In his new headquarters Friar Inoue maintained business as usual, pursuing his campaign of escalating terror as if nothing had happened. Messengers shuttled back and forth daily between his House of Heavenly Action and the nearby coup headquarters of the Misty Lagoon flight officers. The pledged assassins of the Blood Brotherhood boarded in private homes nearby and kept in touch. The civil and military police compiled dossiers on the Blood Brotherhood and the Misty Lagoon fliers. The dossiers were handed up through channels to the chief of police and to the supreme commandant of the secret police, and then, after guarded inquiries had been made at the palace, were filed away for reference.

Although nothing was done to prevent further murders, everything was done to advertise their lurking danger. The very day after the assassination, Wednesday, February 10, Count Arima of the imperial family lunched with Big Brother Kido and the gossipy Secretary-Spy Harada at the excellent Known-for-Mulberries Restaurant, the Kuwana. Count Arima asked Kido and Harada to spread the news that a coup d'etat remained

---

[2] Black Dragon Toyama and his son Hidezo later maintained successfully in court that they had known nothing of Friar Inoue's activities and had given him lodging only at the recommendation of Honma.

an imminent likelihood and that a Strike-South millionaire [3] had replaced Baron Tokugawa of the March Plot as the paymaster for cutthroats employed by the Throne.

That same day the Board of Fleet Admirals and Field Marshals met to pledge full Army-Navy co-operation in a "burst of power" to break the back of the Chinese 19th Route Army in Shanghai. Twenty thousand fresh Army troops were landed in Shanghai between February 14 and 16. The joint chiefs of staff, Prince Kanin and Prince Fushimi, hoped that these reinforcements, added to the 10,000 soldiers and 10,000 sailors already fighting, would be able to make the Chinese 19th Route Army give ground.

VOTE FOR NONVIOLENCE

The week of the troop dispatches, February 14 to February 20, was also the last week before elections—the elections which had been called in order to muzzle the Diet at a time when the Emperor wanted to exercise his powers of fiat to authorize the Shanghai war expenses. The anti-Constitutionalist party of former Prime Minister Wakatsuki campaigned on the slogans "Inukai and Dollar-Buy," "Friends of Dollar-Buyers are Enemies of the Masses," "Rising Prices and Declining Loyalty." Prime Minister Inukai's Constitutionalists were somewhat embarrassed by posters that they had put up earlier proclaiming "Finance Minister Takahashi Brings Fortune; Former Finance Minister Inoue Brings Misfortune." Since former Finance Minister Inoue had had the misfortune of being assassinated, the posters did not seem to be in the best of taste. The people, however, understood. The Constitutionalists had inherited the Dollar Swindle and the Fake War from the previous administration and were not held responsible for them.

As election week progressed, it began to look as if the Constitutionalists would win a resounding victory. Hirohito's political advisors were disappointed. A big vote for the Constitutionalists traditionally meant dissatisfaction with imperial policy-making. For a generation the Constitutionalists had stood for economic rather than military expansion of the Empire, for long-term co-operation with China, for low taxes and cheap money, for blustering loudly and carrying a small stick.

[3] Ishiwara Hiroichiro. Baron Tokugawa Yoshichika had introduced Ishiwara as his successor to Dr. Okawa at the Fukuya teahouse in Hamamachi—the eastern terminus of Tokyo's modern airport monorail—on Sunday, January 10, the day after the first initiation of assassins in the empty house. Along with Baron Tokugawa and with Count Ohtani Kozui, a husband of Hirohito's mother's sister, who would later play a vital role in planning the conquest of Singapore, millionaire Ishiwara had been staked by the Throne during World War I to set up a commercial arm of the spy service in the Dutch East Indies. Through his cover, a mining company in Java, Ishiwara had made a fortune of some $5 million and was now one of the most affluent proponents of the Strike South in Japan.

Encouraged by the popular trend, the Japanese business community stiffened its spine and refused to be intimidated by the continuing threat of assassination. The previous October many of the cartel leaders had deserted old Prime-Minister-Maker Saionji for the profits they saw in the Dollar Swindle. Finding himself fighting alone, Saionji had withdrawn in disgust and had quietly watched developments ever since from his seaside villa. Now, however, the great merchant families began once more to court Saionji's favor. They founded a "Constitution Protection Movement" and began to recruit goon squads of their own with which they hoped to be able to meet the Blood Brotherhood on equal terms. Instead of offering to lend the government enough money to pay for the Shanghai war, they sought to bribe the Kwantung Army and so strip Hirohito of his most ardent supporters. General Honjo in Mukden refused the first of many such bribes on election-week Wednesday, February 17. A representative of the second-ranking cartel, Mitsubishi, came to Honjo's office and tried to give him a check for over $100,000 as a "contribution." Honjo refused to touch the check, told the Mitsubishi representative that the sum was far too small, and advised him, when Mitsubishi was ready to be more generous, to present its donation directly to the war minister or chief of staff in Tokyo.

On election-week Friday, February 19, the Big Brothers of the Eleven Club spent the entire day consulting with operatives of the spy service, with leaders of the underworld, and with one another. They were reassured that the cartels could never recruit a formidable following among the dispossessed samurai of the demimonde. In the words of one of the most knowledgeable of their underworld contacts: "No movement either of the Left or the Right can ever succeed unless it is centered around the Emperor."

STAGE MANAGERS' MEETING

That same evening the dapper, owlish Big Brother Marquis Kido from the office of the lord privy seal in the palace and the lanky, languid Big Brother Prince Konoye from the House of Peers met for dinner with their Army counterparts at the elegant villa of Colonel Marquis Inoue Saburo, the son of Emperor Taisho's Prime Minister Katsura. To speak for the military half of the cabal, their host had invited his protégé, the ubiquitous Lieutenant Colonel Suzuki, and the most aristocratic of the Three Crows of Baden-Baden, Colonel Obata Toshiro.[4] The prince, the two marquises, and the two soldier-courtiers drank cocktails, Western style, on Marquis Inoue's screened porch overlooking Yokohama Bay

---

[4] Saionji's Secretary-Spy Harada had been included in Marquis Inoue's original guest list but had been finally excluded because the Army members of the cabal did not trust his wagging tongue.

where Commodore Perry had steamed in with his Black Ships seventy-nine years earlier.

All five men agreed that the Throne faced an acute political crisis. The self-seeking merchants of the realm had won the support of the voters and now threatened to buy the support of the Army. Prime Minister Inukai persisted in negotiating with Chiang Kai-shek in an effort to neutralize Manchuria and make it an autonomous region outside the Empire. He and his government had outlived their usefulness. No other political-party government would be any better. Party politicians had simply become too "corrupted" by money and Western parliamentary ideas to serve the Throne obediently.

The alternative of an imperial coup d'etat, making Hirohito open dictator, was not feasible either. The threat of coup might still be a useful political tool, but a genuine coup was opposed by all Hirohito's senior courtiers as an infringement of the Constitution and an unnecessary exposure of the imperial family.

The only possibility left, then, was a "transcendental," nonpolitical government of recognized national elders—old men who understood the imperial program and could take responsibility for it. Such governments had been tried several times during the years of Emperor Taisho's madness in the early 1920's. The people did not like them but had always put up with them because, in the past, transcendental patriarchs had tended to be cautious and not do much.

Now a transcendental Cabinet was needed that would advance the national program. It must obviously have a strong war minister, for unless the privates in the Army felt adequately represented by their minister, they could, by their letters home, cause more peasant discontent than a rise in taxes, a flood, or a famine.

Present War Minister Araki was known to be well liked in the ranks. Indeed, as Big Brother Kido acknowledged, he was "too popular to be dispensed with." Unfortunately, however, he believed that Japan's true mission was a Strike North into Bolshevik Russia. Since in this he differed with the Throne, the Big Brothers wanted to know how loyal he was. They had invited Colonel Obata to their cocktail party because Obata was himself a Strike-North leader and could speak as an intimate friend about Araki's character.

Obata gave it as his considered opinion that War Minister Araki would serve honestly to unify the nation during the build-up of military strength planned for the next four years. Araki would hope to use the new strength against the Soviet Union but he would bow to the wishes of the Emperor, the Supreme Field Marshal, if his views and the Throne's finally came into conflict. Second Crow Obata, himself, would do the same. Russia was the natural enemy of Japan, but if Hirohito could not be persuaded to lead Japan against Russia, Second Crow Obata and War Minister Araki would be willing to retire gracefully and leave the strategy of Armageddon to others.

The suave, ubiquitous Lieutenant Colonel Suzuki—impeccably tailored as always and looking like a banker costumed in military uniform for a fancy dress ball—pointed out quietly that War Minister Araki would make a difficult ally because he was a man of principle.

Recognizing this danger, Hirohito's political stage managers, when they broke up that night, had nevertheless decided to recommend to Hirohito that Prime Minister Inukai be replaced by a transcendental government built around the popularity of War Minister Araki of the Strike-North Faction. The next morning, Saturday, February 20, the people went to the polls and, as anticipated, gave Inukai's Constitutionalists in the Diet 301 seats to the anti-Constitutionalists' 147. Hirohito's kitchen cabinet of Big Brothers at once launched a campaign of rumor and innuendo by which they hoped to nullify the people's vote and overthrow Inukai.

At the urging of Big Brother Kido, Secretary-Spy Harada that night told Saionji that the Kwantung Army had become completely intractable and had laid definite plans for a coup d'etat to "suppress political parties" and safeguard Manchuria from "exploitation by political party interests." To Harada's astonishment old Saionji simply smiled and shrugged his shoulders.

"Oh well," he said, "if the plot plans are already complete, that's that."

After four months of hibernation and thought, Saionji was a jump ahead of the young men around the Throne. He knew that there would be no genuine coup d'etat. Through intermediaries, he had already reached his own understanding with War Minister Araki. He had determined that Araki was a man of integrity and brains, and in addition a golden-tongued demagogue who knew how to lead the masses. Araki undertook to embroil Hirohito by 1936 in a war with Russia. Better by far for Japan to fight Russia, if fight she must, than to attack the combined powers of America and western Europe. In the great undesirable buffer land of Siberia, Araki might be able to bury Hirohito's samurai ardor in a desert of stalemate and weariness.

INSPECTION EVE

The week following the elections was a hectic one. The League of Nations' Commission of Inquiry was expected to arrive in Japan on leap year's day, February 29. The Japanese forces in Shanghai were still attempting—as yet with little success—to drive out the Chinese 19th Route Army. On March 1, Manchuria was scheduled to be declared an independent sovereign state, Manchukuo, under Chief Executive Pu-Yi, the former boy emperor of China. If all went well, the League's investigative team would be presented on arrival with a cease-fire in Shanghai and a new nation in Manchuria—with every evidence, in short, that the "Far Eastern crisis" had blown over and that the League's investigation had become academic.

Prime Minister Inukai was exchanging flurries of cables with Chiang Kai-shek in an attempt to reach an understanding with him on what both of them would say privately to the League's commissioners. It was Inukai's idea that he and Chiang and the commissioners, acting in concert, could persuade Hirohito to give Manchukuo genuine independence and to order the Kwantung Army back to its leasehold.

Hirohito's Big Brothers were busy undercutting Prime Minister Inukai and solidifying their plans for the regime with which they hoped to replace him. They spread excited gossip about the imminence of an Army coup d'etat and told newspaper reporters that Prime Minister Inukai was negotiating treasonably with Chiang Kai-shek while Japanese boys were dying in Shanghai.

On Wednesday, February 24, Prince Konoye went down to Okitsu by the sea to try to find out why his elder kinsman, Saionji, seemed so smugly unconcerned about the possibility of a coup d'etat. He proposed to Saionji that after the coup a military man like War Minister Araki should be made prime minister and that a member of the imperial family like Prince Higashikuni or Prince Asaka (the Emperor's two uncles in the spy service) should take the post of lord privy seal at Hirohito's side.

Saionji had nothing against Araki as a duly appointed prime minister but much against unconstitutional processes such as coups d'etat. And as for the two imperial uncles, Princes Asaka and Higashikuni, Saionji distrusted them both. At the thought of either one of them taking the position of lord privy seal—the traditional position of Minister on the Left which had been occupied for centuries by the most tried and true elders of Saionji's own Fujiwara family—Saionji blazed up.

"Before I recommend any such appointments," he spat, "I shall resign my post as senior advisor to the Throne. I shall renounce all my ranks and privileges as a prince. And I shall descend to the status of a commoner."

Konoye returned to Tokyo puzzled by Saionji's self-assurance and convinced that the old man had something up his kimono sleeve. He sent Secretary-Spy Harada back to Okitsu to keep a close watch. The old man, however, revealed nothing to Harada except more mysterious good spirits. The next evening, Thursday, February 25, over a bedtime cognac, he said to Harada: "When you youngsters have forced Prime Minister Inukai out of office through some exposure or other, I shall be interested to see how you go about forming this 'Rising Nation Cabinet' you all want."

BETWEEN TWO THREATS

While Saionji still mystified and the League inquiry drew closer, the frenetic activity of the preceding days began coming to a head. On Saturday, February 27—two days before the League commission's scheduled arrival in Tokyo—the morning papers carried a letter—one written to be leaked—from U.S. Secretary of State Stimson to William E. Borah, the chairman of the U.S. Senate's Foreign Relations Committee. The letter warned Japan that any modification or abrogation of the structure of interlocking treaties which was intended to safeguard the peace would release the United States from its obligations under any one of them. That is, if Japan, with impunity, violated the Nine-Power Treaty guaranteeing the "open door" and "territorial integrity" of China, the United States would feel free to build capital ships beyond naval treaty limitations and to strengthen U.S. military establishments in the Philippines, Guam, and Hawaii.

Prime Minister Inukai promptly telephoned the palace and announced that he would recommend sending a special envoy to the United States to clear up Secretary Stimson's misunderstanding of Japan's intentions. The envoy proposed by Inukai was Baron Dan Takuma, head of the Mitsui cartel.

That afternoon Army Chief of Staff Prince Kanin's old cavalry minion, Koiso, the later kamikaze prime minister of 1944, called upon Baron Dan in his office at the Mitsui holding company headquarters. Lieutenant General Koiso, since his leadership of the March Plot, had been elevated by Hirohito to the office of vice war minister. He was patently a man whose patrons would back him to the hilt. He warned Baron Dan bluntly not to accept the mission of good-will ambassador to the United States. Baron Dan knew only too well that he could not protect his family from assassins nor his cartel from loss of Army contracts. At the same time he was too proud to negotiate with Koiso the exact degree of his intimidation. With many stiff smiles and bows, he told Koiso that he had no intention of leaving Japan at the moment. On the contrary, he said, he was engaged in a patriotic struggle for the nation's survival and would not leave his post of duty until he either conquered or died.

Vice Minister of War Koiso returned to the War Ministry and reported to his patron, old Prince Kanin, chief of the Army General Staff. That night Friar Inoue, operating out of the Black Dragon Society's House of Heavenly Action, sent a student messenger to one of his Blood Brotherhood assassins, instructing him to stand ready to kill Baron Dan Takuma of Mitsui. The assassin, a former professional gangster named Hisanuma Goro, began at once a thorough study of Baron Dan's daily movements and work habits.

SAIONJI SHOWS HIS HAND

On the following morning, Sunday, February 28, 1932, old Saionji awoke to a buoyantly crisp winter's day. He looked out at the fairy-story waters of Suruga Bay, dancing with fishing boats and sunbeams, and resolutely put through a call to Tokyo. The time had come to declare himself. He roused Secretary-Spy Harada from sleep and summoned him to come down at once to Okitsu by the sea. Four jolting hours later, having had to take a local express, Harada knelt on Saionji's matting floor and watched the old man stride in, wearing a new kimono, with an air of great purpose.

"I called you," said Saionji, "because the other day the grand chamberlain dropped in, concerned about the Emperor. The Emperor, he says, is not sleeping well. The other night at about eleven o'clock he sent a chamberlain to the grand chamberlain requesting an immediate consultation. Well, the Emperor is undoubtedly worrying, but this old Saionji is worrying even more. . . . So I am planning to go up to Tokyo about March fifth. . . . Tell them Saionji does not have to come out into the open this way, nor does he expect to bring peace. Tell them that he is going out of his way, right or wrong, to take this opportunity to stand up and do his duty. If you are questioned further, I want you to say, 'It is primarily to pay respects to His Majesty that he comes and because, at a time like this, he feels he should meet personally with the people who bear the responsibility.' "

Harada listened to the old man's speech with mounting, ill-suppressed horror. After pleading ill health repeatedly and refusing to pay attendance on the Emperor, Saionji was now coming up to Tokyo in order to make himself available to members of the Lytton Commission who were due to arrive in Tokyo on the morrow. It seemed almost an act of treason. Harada hurried back to Tokyo to have a tap put on Saionji's Tokyo phone and to apologize for lack of foresight to fellow Big Brother Kido.

VICTORY IN SHANGHAI

Late that night, up an estuary in the gaping, mud-yellow mouth of the Yangtze River in China, a division of Japanese soldiers—almost 20,000 men—silently waded ashore, wave after wave, from their assault boats. They, too, were under pressure because of the League commission's arrival in Tokyo the next morning. For two weeks, despite Japanese numerical equality and fire-power superiority,[5] the heroic young provincials of the Chinese 19th Route Army had refused to be driven from the native

[5] At the start of the fighting, the 33,500 men of the 19th Route had only 27,500 rifles, 72 machine guns, and 64 trench mortars and light field pieces.

quarters of Shanghai. They had fought for the borough of Chapei street by street and ruin by ruin, and now they still occupied most of the two remaining boroughs. The Japanese frontal advance, begun nine days before, had been thrown back repeatedly by counterattacks and had gained ground only by inches. Hirohito himself had criticized the commander in Shanghai and now had replaced him.

The pressure, passed down to the men, had forced three privates on February 22 to make a suicide charge against a crucial barbed-wire entanglement, carrying on their shoulders a tube of dynamite. They had blown up themselves and the entanglement and were now immortalized by the Japanese press as the "three human bullets." A Japanese major who felt responsible for their sacrifice had himself been captured by the Chinese in their counterattack. When liberated by the Japanese a few days later, he had gone to the site of the hard-fought roadblock, knelt, and deliberately blown out his brains.

Now on the eve of the League commission's arrival, the Japanese 14th Division had just added some 20,000 fresh troops to the barricades in downtown Shanghai, and the Japanese 11th Division was disembarking under cover of night on the mud flats upriver to turn the Chinese flank. By morning there would be some 70,000 Japanese troops pressing in on three sides against the 20,000-odd survivors of the 19th Route Army.[6]

The early-morning landing of the 11th Division behind his lines took General Tsai Ting-kai of the 19th Route completely by surprise. He had entrusted watch over that particular stretch of coast line to only 100 men with three machine guns. Japanese give the credit for his shortsightedness to the deceptive wiles of Eastern Jewel, the Manchu princess and Japanese girl spy. During the first desperate days of the fighting, when vengeful Japanese vigilantes roamed the streets around her, Eastern Jewel had kept Sun Yat-sen's son safe in her apartment and had extorted from him letters of introduction to all the most important officers of the 19th Route Army. In return she had finally smuggled him aboard a coastal tramp steamer of uncertain registry, which took him out of harm's way to his home port of Canton in southern China.

Her principal lover, the huge Major Tanaka of the Shanghai Special Service Organ, now put her in touch with some of the Navy fliers of the Misty Lagoon Air Station who were flying reconnaissance over the Chinese

---

[6] There were also three of Chiang Kai-shek's guard divisions, numbering 40,000 men, loitering just outside Shanghai. In a spare moment on February 18 or 19, detachments of the 19th Route had turned briefly from the Japanese and had captured a substantial part of one of these guard divisions. The prisoners had been marched to the front and forced at gunpoint to fight the Japanese. Some were later captured by the Japanese, and some died honorably fighting the Japanese, but most were mowed down by their 19th Route countrymen when they panicked and fled before a Japanese advance on February 25.

lines. They took her along on several missions as co-pilot and gave her thorough briefings on the topography of the Chinese city and the command posts of the 19th Route Army. One of them later complained that she was a troublesome co-pilot because she pestered him to arrange some way of making love aloft.

Fully briefed and equipped with her letters of introduction from Sun Yat-sen's son, Eastern Jewel one night in late February put on her favorite spy disguise of a boy and set out on foot to visit 19th Route Commander Tsai Ting-kai. By prearrangement Japanese sentries let her pass without question through their lines and then followed her with a hail of bullets in the air. Hearing her piteous cries for help, uttered in her best approximation of Cantonese dialect, the sentries of the 19th Route let her into their lines. There her letters of introduction passed her up the chain of command until she came to the dugout of Tsai Ting-kai himself. She spent several hours with him and gave him more or less reliable information about Japanese troop dispositions. She undertook to take back to Shanghai a verbal message from him to Sun Yat-sen's son, who she said was still in her apartment. She told of having seen the Japanese 11th and 14th divisions unloading at the Shanghai docks that afternoon. In fact they were still lying out to sea in their transports. Tsai Ting-kai knew from Chinese agents in Japan that the two divisions were on their way. He had taken men from his second line to guard the various harbors on the river where he thought they might make a surprise landing. Now, after Eastern Jewel's departure, he recalled the men to the fighting line and left the possible landing points unguarded.

So it was that on leap year's day, as the League's Commission of Inquiry steamed into Tokyo harbor, the tired men of the 19th Route found themselves outnumbered three to one, outgunned twenty to one, and attacked from the rear as well as the front. For a month they had fought stolidly and shrewdly. Now, in forty-eight hours, their defenses collapsed on all fronts. Tsai Ting-kai ordered them to give up the city. They fell back to the southwest and succeeded in preventing the Japanese from completing their encirclement until most of them had withdrawn with order into the countryside beyond. On March 3 and 4, their rear guard broke up into pockets. The Japanese troops attempted to annihilate them, but many survivors submerged into the civilian populace and succeeded in slipping through the Japanese cordons to rejoin their units upcountry.

LEAGUE'S WELCOME

The Frenchman, German, Italian, American, and Englishman who were to write a judgment on the circumstances of the Manchurian Incident for the League of Nations were given an effusive welcome by the crowds organized to greet them when they disembarked at the Yokohama docks on

February 29. In Tokyo a swirl of social activity had been laid on for them and their first five days in Japan were all banquets, toasts, and speeches.

Emperor Hirohito's special envoy in Shanghai, diplomat Matsuoka Yosuke, opened negotiations with Chiang Kai-shek's representatives on March 1 and concluded them in an armistice agreement on March 5. Less than two weeks later Japan's 70,000-man expeditionary force began to be shipped home, leaving the defense of the Japanese quarter in Shanghai once again to the small garrison of Imperial Marines. Only cynics remarked on the marvelous discipline of the Japanese troop withdrawals. The Japanese militarists who were supposed to be completely out of hand in Manchuria had proved completely tractable in Shanghai. Having opened the door for a drive on the Chinese capital of Nanking, having sustained heavy losses of both life and face at the hands of the 19th Route Army, they nevertheless obeyed orders perfectly in giving back to China the hard-won streets of Chapei. The League's commissioners were supposed to be favorably impressed. They were supposed at the same time to realize that Shanghai was only one half of the bargain and that the other half was the new Japanese puppet state of Manchukuo, which was proclaimed with pomp and ceremony on March 1.

On March 2, an event took place in the United States which deprived the League's commission of all front-page publicity in the West and diverted the attention of many Japanese. The infant son of U.S. aviator Charles Lindbergh was kidnapped.[7] During the partial news blackout which followed, Secretary of State Stimson found to his dismay that most of his fellow statesmen in the West were disposed to accept Pu-Yi in Manchuria for peace in Shanghai. They acknowledged that Japan's play in Shanghai had been tantamount to blackmail, but also that the West had no guns to commit to the Far East. In the public distraction created by the Lindbergh kidnapping they saw an excellent opportunity to let the Far Eastern crisis blow over.

KILL THE BARON

While the Shanghai "incident" was being settled, the state of Manchukuo founded, and the world distracted, the League's Commission of Inquiry

---

[7] Lindbergh had been out in the Orient on a flood relief mission to China seven months earlier. He had greatly annoyed the Japanese authorities by making a forced landing in a sensitive fortified area in Hokkaido. In Tokyo he had been entertained by Japan's leading aeronautical engineer, Wada Koroku, the brother of Marquis Kido, the Emperor's favorite Big Brother. A White Russian menial of the spy service in Harbin would later insist—in a manuscript which he smuggled out of Manchuria before his death at the hands of the Japanese—that the Lindbergh kidnapping had been arranged by Japan through payments of Dollar Swindle money to the American Mafia.

stood by in Tokyo, beholding in mute astonishment the murder of their Japanese League colleague, Baron Dan of the Mitsui cartel.

Dan was the director of the central holding company of Mitsui. He was a member of the League's Investigation Committee, the parent body of the Commission of Inquiry. He was known as a friend of DuPonts and Fords and Rockefellers and as a prominent member of the Japan-American Society. In 1871, at the age of thirteen, he had been one of the fifty-four Japanese children sent to the United States to learn at first hand the ways of Commodore Perry's homeland. Lord Privy Seal Makino, then nine, had also been one of the fifty-four children. Makino had swallowed his eight years in the United States as dutifully and courageously as a pill and had regularly omitted all mention of them from the annual entries which he had since submitted to Japanese biographical dictionaries. Baron Dan, by contrast, looked back with pleasure on his seven years in America and always had a bed ready in his villa for any itinerant graduate of his American alma maters—of Miss Arland's School in Boston or of the Massachusetts Institute of Technology. As director of the holding company of Japan's largest cartel, Baron Dan was the unquestioned leader of Japan's business establishment.

On Wednesday, March 2, 1932, the directors of all the Mitsui companies met as stockholders to hear the annual report of their great cartel's nerve center, the Mitsui Bank. The manager of the bank, elegant in his Saville Row tailoring, gravely recited a story of hard luck. "The general banking business," he reported, had been fairly good that year, "but because of the drop in the market prices of securities" and "the decline of pound holdings," the bank had suffered "a net loss for the term of 12,297,026 yen"—about $4 million. He added that "any criticism for having carried on speculative buying of the dollar is unjustified." He pointed out that there were matters of arbitrage and gold movement to be considered. His easy flow of financial jargon, however, failed to disguise entirely the fact that the stockholders in the room had all received unusually large dividends that year from holdings in other branches of the Mitsui combine, some amounting to 17 and 18 per cent.

Undeterred by the Mitsui Bank's statement of losses, the Japanese Finance Ministry announced the next day, on Thursday, March 3, that to meet debts incurred in the Shanghai fighting, it was floating a 22-million-yen bond issue (roughly $8 million) which it expected to be subscribed by Mitsui and the other cartels. On Baron Dan, as chief of Mitsui, devolved the dangerous duty of replying that the great industrialists of the nation were agreed that for lack of ready cash they could not co-operate.

In the evening Friar Inoue of the Blood Brotherhood had his student go-between deliver a Browning and sixteen bullets to assassin Hisanuma Goro for Dan's killing. Dan himself, in an attempt to assess the amount of support and of publicity he could expect from the United States in the domestic struggle he saw ahead, held a dinner party for all his most influential American friends in Tokyo.

"His home was simple," recalled Wilfred Fleisher, the editor of the *Japan Chronicle,* "but the garden of the Dan mansion was famous for its beauty. The house was built on the edge of a slope which led down to a pond where storks strutted about, and the hillside was covered in spring with azaleas, and in the autumn with the red tint of the maple foliage."

On the following morning, Friday, March 4, Baron Dan was formally introduced to all his colleagues on the League's Commission of Inquiry and sat down with them for their first business meeting. Assassin Hisanuma Goro went out to Funabashi Beach on Tokyo Bay just east of the city to practice firing his Browning. Saionji's secretary-spy, Baron Harada, consulted with other Big Brothers of the Emperor before entraining for Okitsu to bring the Prime-Minister-Maker up to the capital for his announced trip of protest.

In the evening Baron Dan attended a banquet given in honor of the League's commission by the posh Industrial Club of which he and other captains of Japanese enterprise were directors. Knowing that he would be called upon to make a speech, he penciled notes for himself, as he ate, on a piece of paper which is preserved by his family. According to the notes he concluded his welcome to Lord Lytton with the sentence, "Any questions you may feel inclined to make we are pleased to answer frankly." Then in his final act of discretion and personal honor he crossed out the word "frankly" and delivered his remarks without the dubious benefit of the adverb.

At 11 A.M. on Saturday, March 5, Baron Dan had his car draw up at the inconspicuous side entrance of the Mitsui Bank Building. But Hisanuma Goro, the most sophisticated tough in the Blood Brotherhood, had cased well the nervous habits of his victim and was waiting on the curb. He lunged to open the door of the limousine. Finding it locked, he allowed the chauffeur no time to start away but fired once through the glass of the car window. Once was enough. Baron Dan died in twenty minutes, and assassin Hisanuma calmly waited for the police to come and arrest him.

Saionji and Secretary-Spy Harada were then on their way to Tokyo. Their train was immediately stopped and boarded by civil police who placed the old man under guard. In Tokyo Saionji repaired at once to his city house and for the rest of that day and the next refused to see anyone.[8]

---

[8] A classic photograph survives that shows him as he alighted from his car at the porte-cochere of his Tokyo residence. His eyes blaze with indignation out of a gaunt and wasted face. Secretary-Spy Harada stands by, having just opened the car door for him. The photographer's lens has foreshortened Harada's body in its bowing and scraping so that it appears hideously deformed—a gnome of malevolent lickspittle.

SAIONJI'S SETTLEMENT

On the second day after Baron Dan's murder, Monday, March 7, Saionji began to receive official visitors: Prime Minister Inukai in the morning; Hirohito's personal financial advisor, the minister of the imperial household, in the afternoon; Hirohito's personal diplomatic advisor, the cigar-smoking Taoist philosopher, Grand Chamberlain Suzuki, in the evening.

As a son is expected to call on his father when he returns to his home town after a long absence, so by the rules of Court etiquette a chief vassal of the Throne like Saionji was expected to call on the Emperor as soon as possible after his arrival in Tokyo. The Japanese public waited with fascination, but Saionji did not make his mandatory palace visit—not that day, and not the next, and not for six days thereafter. From Baron Dan's killing on March 5 until March 14, the ancient statesman snubbed Hirohito and nursed all his energies for phone calls and interviews with others. He was trying to negotiate a bargain which would put a stop to the assassins' reign of terror and preserve some hope for constitutional parliamentarianism. He intimated that he was in earnest and would call a press conference that would amaze the world if he was not given his way. He said that if anything happened to him the hired goon squads of the Constitution Protection Movement would cause a small civil war in Japan and certain safety deposit boxes in foreign capitals would be opened to the Western press. He accepted no personal guards for his house who had not been approved by his personal cronies in the secret police.

On Tuesday, March 8, Dr. Okawa had his chief henchman—once a bicycle repairman in Shanghai—return the smoke bombs of the March Plot of 1931 to War Minister Araki.

On Wednesday, March 9, Saionji for the first time met Araki face to face. "He has a slight utopian tendency," he said to Secretary-Spy Harada afterwards, "but, my goodness, he really knows how to talk, doesn't he?"

On Thursday, March 10, having judiciously felt out members of the Court circle for permission, the Tokyo Metropolitan Police chief began to make gingerly arrests on the fringes of the Blood Brotherhood.

Finally, on Friday, March 11, six days after Baron Dan's killing and thirty days after banker Inoue's, assassin leader Friar Inoue was deferentially escorted by the police from the Black Dragon's House of Heavenly Action to one of Tokyo's cleanest jails. Friar Inoue's colleague, Dr. Okawa, however, was left at liberty. He was so well known as the henchman of Lord Privy Seal Makino, Hirohito's chief civilian advisor, that Saionji did not insist on his arrest.

Saionji insisted only that the killing cease and that the duly appointed prime minister, Inukai, be allowed to continue in office. In return Saionji persuaded Mitsui and the other cartels to subscribe the $8-million bond issue for the Shanghai war and to advance another $7.5 million as a loan for the development of the new puppet state of Manchukuo.

Saionji spent the weekend of March 12 and 13 working out the financial details of his settlement with the cartels. Finally, on Monday, March 14, he consented to come out, under heavy guard, from his villa and pay his long postponed courtesy call on the Emperor. Contrary to custom, he did not take lunch at the palace but ate it alone before setting out for his audience. At 2 P.M. he met the Emperor and Empress and paid them his formal respects. Then the Empress withdrew and he talked to Hirohito alone for a little over an hour. He told his secretary-spy Harada afterwards that the Emperor had said "nothing special."

Saionji spent three more days in the capital in which he attended to private business and paid a courtesy call on his Fujiwara kinswoman, Hirohito's mother, the Empress Dowager. She was his staunchest ally. At forty-seven, she was still extremely handsome. She had great charm and poise in handling people, and her years taking care of Emperor Taisho had given her a sophisticated understanding of state affairs.

As queen mother she had consultative and veto powers over most of the domestic arrangements in Hirohito's household. She had long disapproved of her son's policies and had frequently remonstrated with him, to no avail. Saionji urged that proper guidance had never been more necessary. Empress Dowager Sadako promised to do her best and to send trustworthy messengers to Saionji who would keep him informed at all times on affairs at Court.

Saionji returned to Okitsu-by-the-sea on March 18, feeling proud of the settlement he had worked out. His kinsman, Prince Konoye, personally escorted him. The younger Fujiwara prince respected the elder's political experience and patriotism, but in his view the settlement that Saionji had accomplished was an unrealistic, stopgap arrangement. For three days Konoye tried to persuade the old man to agree that the continuation of the old, corrupt political parties would only give rise to more intrigue, more assassinations, more haggling and waste of talent. Better by far to declare Japan the totalitarian state that it was, to let Hirohito lead it and to surround him with the smartest, most realistic advisors. Old Prince Saionji stubbornly refused to see any merit in this solution.

Prince Konoye returned to Tokyo convinced that the game of intrigue must continue and that means must be found to circumvent Saionji and his supporters.

On April 3, Lord Privy Seal Count Makino's disciple Dr. Okawa gave a flight lieutenant from the Misty Lagoon $500, five pistols, and 200 rounds of ammunition as a token to show that the coup d'etat was still alive and seriously considered. That night and again at breakfast and lunch on April 4, members of the Eleven Club met in great privacy to decide among themselves who would be the first non-party, all-nation, post-coup prime minister of Japan. Out of courtesy they at first nominated Prince Konoye as their ranking leader. Big Brother Kido, however, who was their effective leader, had already agreed with Prince Konoye that this must be a gesture of courtesy and nothing more. Marquis Kido pointed out that Prince Konoye had as yet no viable policy nor slate of ministers.

For the transcendental prime minister a more realistic choice must be made. After discussion the Big Brothers decided on 73-year-old Admiral Saito Makoto, once a favorite of Emperor Meiji, long a governor general of Korea, a man whom Prince Saionji, Emperor Hirohito, and they, themselves, could all accept.

Chosen by Hirohito's junior clerks on April 4, 1932, Admiral Saito would in fact become prime minister of Japan forty-two days later when all arrangements had been made, Prime Minister Inukai had been murdered, and the long-envisaged coup d'etat had taken place. Admiral Saito himself would be notified of his appointment when Hirohito called him to the palace and made it official. In the interim, Hirohito felt satisfied that his Big Brothers had a workable plan.

LORD LYTTON

The League of Nations' five-man, five-nation Commission of Inquiry was headed by its Englishman, Lord Lytton. He was the son of a viceroy to India and the grandson of the Bulwer-Lytton who wrote *The Last Days of Pompeii*. An Eton-Cambridge man, he had seen service in the Admiralty, the India Office, the governor's mansion of Bengal, and briefly in the Indian statehouse as viceroy. At fifty-six, though somewhat uncomfortable and short-tempered as a result of kidney difficulties, he prided himself both on his statesmanship and his command of lucid, stylish, author's prose. He knew little about Japan but he was a conscientious reader and clear-sighted observer.

In his first five days of banqueting in Japan Lord Lytton had received hints from some of the Japanese he met which convinced him that he must correct the tendency of his aristocratic public school alumni in the British government to excuse Japanese imperialism. After the murder of Baron Dan, his Japanese colleague, he was more than convinced; he was incensed. During old Prince Saionji's settlement-making stay in Tokyo, Lord Lytton and his fellow commissioners all tried to see Saionji. Through emissaries, Saionji excused himself repeatedly because of the delicacy of the situation in which he was involved. The emissaries, however, did their discreet best to tell Lord Lytton that Saionji wanted the League to go as far as possible in condemning Japan's actions on the Continent.

The day that Saionji finally went to the palace to pay his respects to Hirohito, Lord Lytton and his fellow commissioners took ship for Shanghai to begin hearing the Chinese side of the story. They planned to spend five weeks in China, interviewing all the various factions there, and then to proceed on April 21 to Mukden in Manchuria to inspect the source of the trouble.

During the commissioners' stay in China—the first honeymoon weeks of Saionji's settlement in Japan—the Army half of Hirohito's cabal saw to it that they would receive the most favorable possible impression of Japanese-occupied Manchuria. Hirohito assigned the former Japanese ambassador to the Soviet Union to Kwantung Army commander General Honjo to advise him on the diplomatic niceties. One of the Eleven Reliables chosen at Baden-Baden, Colonel Watari Hisao, was detached from his post as chief of the European Section of the Intelligence Department of the General Staff so that he could travel as an advance man for the Lytton Commission and see that suitable arrangements had been made for it wherever it went.

Watari was the America expert of the Eleven Reliables. A Kyoto nobleman of presence and charm, he had specialized in English, put in five years at the Japanese Embassy in Washington, and won a name for himself as a good friend to all the foreign military attachés at the Western embassies in Tokyo. According to British intelligence officer F. S. G. Piggott, he was "a sincere admirer of Anglo-American ideals . . . universally respected."

With all the resources of the Kwantung Army put at his disposal by General Honjo, Watari was determined that whatever the Lytton commissioners wished to see, whenever they wished to see it, would be shown to them in a state of fresh whitewash that would not strike them unfavorably. The political inmates of Manchukuoan prisons and the French- and English-speaking patients in Manchukuoan hospitals were removed from their cells and sick rooms and sent for the duration of Lytton's stay to detention camps in the countryside. They were joined there by all the unsightly beggars and derelicts which the military police could sweep from the streets and by anyone suspected of having enough courage and conviction to stand up and shout anti-Japanese remarks during parades. Literally thousands of potential face-spoilers were put under preventive arrest—1,361 in Harbin alone. Substantial rewards were offered for information leading to the apprehension of anyone who schemed to smuggle a bill of complaints to Lytton's party.

"Petitions" in praise of Japanese rule were drawn up a month in advance at Kwantung Army Headquarters and given to prominent Chinese and Russian citizens who had to sign them and later submit them to Lytton. Crowds were coached in what to shout and how to dress. An enterprising official of the South Manchuria Railroad netted over $100,000 for his firm and for the Army by suggesting that the military police require every inhabitant along Lytton's itinerary to buy for one yen a small

Manchukuoan flag to hang over his doorway and a cheap portrait of Pu-Yi to put in his window. Manchukuoan officials scheduled to be interviewed by the commissioners were carefully rehearsed in what they must say. Every opium den was aired out, cleaned, and hung with a new sign which proclaimed it to be either a "Cultural Center" or a "Social Club." Every Japanese uniform vanished from sight and the man inside it endured the temporary indignity of going about in a span-new Manchukuoan one.

In all the hotels where the commission would be staying, Japanese and White Russian agents of the Manchukuoan State Political Police were given rooms adjoining those to be occupied by the commissioners. Desk clerks, bell boys, waiters, room boys, hall boys, and chambermaids were all replaced by specially coached police agents. Spies were spotted in the staffs of leading stores, theatres, and restaurants. The drain on the police and intelligence personnel pool was heavy. When the pool ran dry, the local chief of the spy service in Harbin distributed 500 Manchukuoan Army uniforms to a native bandit band in the employ of the spy service and stationed its cutthroats as "guards of honor" at the homes of Chinese malcontents who were too prominent in society to rusticate at the detention camps.

Colonel Watari, who arranged this magnificent reception for Lord Lytton, was joined in Manchuria on April 15, a week before Lytton's arrival, by the second of the Three Crows, Obata Toshiro. Obata had attended the Big Brothers' cocktail party at Marquis Inoue's two months earlier, and now Hirohito had just promoted him to the rank of major general. Obata knew that Hirohito was planning a "transcendental government." If Lord Lytton could be persuaded to approve what he saw in Manchuria, the transcendental government might prove to be unnecessary. Obata reviewed with Colonel Watari the preparations made for Lord Lytton and discussed them several times with Kwantung Army commander Honjo. He warned Honjo that if Lytton could not be deceived, a military coup d'etat would have to be staged in Tokyo to overthrow political party government and show the League of Nations that it could achieve no constructive result by condemning Japan as an aggressor. In the event that the coup became necessary, he asked General Honjo to lend him a division and a cavalry brigade.

Second Crow Obata stayed in Mukden long enough to witness the arrival of Lord Lytton on April 21 at the Mukden railroad station. Then he took a train himself to the South Manchuria Railroad's executive airport, south of Mukden, and flew home to report to Hirohito and the Big Brothers. He judged that Lord Lytton was not favorably disposed toward Japan and that his attitude probably would not be changed by the preparations made for him in Manchuria. At the same time Lytton seemed to be approaching his task carefully, like a scholar, and would probably not deliver his judgment of Japan, good or bad, until many months had passed.

POLICY REVIEW

Prompted by Major General Obata's assessment of Lord Lytton's intentions, Hirohito's Big Brothers commissioned the ubiquitous Lieutenant Colonel Suzuki to draft a tough new foreign policy for Japan "in the light of the changed situation in the Far East" and a domestic political plan for "realization of the Hirohito restoration." The gifted Suzuki, whose years as private envoy of the Throne to Chiang Kai-shek had accustomed him to thinking in global terms, completed his assignment in thirty-six hours and presented the results, in the form of two position papers, to Big Brother Kido on Saturday evening, April 23. In the first he advocated that Japan pursue an independent course in the Orient without troubling herself about Western reactions. In the second he urged immediate suppression of political parties and a transcendental caretaker government, backed by General Araki and the Army's Strike-North Faction, which would allow Hirohito to come forth gradually as the absolute master of the Japanese nation.[9] Kido took Suzuki's two papers to the palace the next evening and discussed them with the other Big Brothers on the following Tuesday and Wednesday.

On Thursday, April 28, 1932, Hirohito's personally instructed delegate to the Shanghai truce negotiations, University of Oregon graduate Matsuoka, called at the palace to report to Hirohito on the successful completion of his mission. Hirohito asked him what he thought of the ubiquitous Suzuki's proposal to pursue a tough independent foreign policy in the Far East. Matsuoka responded with enthusiasm. Japan, he said, had nothing to fear from the League. Indeed, if Japan withdrew from the League altogether, she would gain stature and influence in the minds of the most powerful and practical Western statesmen.

After talking to Matsuoka, Hirohito had his Big Brothers discuss the Matsuoka proposal. None of them saw any harm in withdrawing from the League, though some of the Army officers felt that it might not be necessary. In due course old man Saionji heard of the idea. "Wishful thinking," he called it.

"I am truly worried," he told Secretary-Spy Harada. "The Emperor may be smart and may avoid bringing the nation to catastrophe, but plans shown me recently by Lord Privy Seal Makino for dealing with Russia do not look smart."

Nevertheless, Hirohito tentatively accepted Matsuoka's League-withdrawal plan, and a year later he would put Matsuoka in charge of executing it.

---

[9] These summations are based on the recollections of a member of the Army bureaucracy who saw the two position papers some months later. The full texts are not now extant but may perhaps come to light after the publication of this volume.

In his second position paper—"on the realization of Hirohito's restoration"—Lieutenant Colonel Suzuki had dwelt in some detail on the difficulties that might be encountered if an Army coup d'etat were used to improve Hirohito's leadership position. Suzuki warned that many Army officers, particularly those of the idealistic Strike-North Faction, would expect a coup d'etat to make Hirohito overt military dictator of Japan, governing exclusively through staff officers. The problem in establishing a transcendental government by means of a coup, therefore, would be to prevent Army radicals from carrying the coup to extremes and robbing Hirohito of civilian executives—of courtiers, economists, diplomats, gang lords, politicians, and publicists.

ARRANGEMENTS WITH HONJO

On Monday, April 30, 1932, when Suzuki's position papers had been studied for a week, an embassy set out for Manchuria to make arrangements in the Kwantung Army for keeping firm control over the projected coup d'etat. One of the ambassadors was Dr. Okawa, the headmaster of the cabal, the ideologist of the Strike-South Faction and the minion of Lord Privy Seal Count Makino. Having worked for many years under the cover of a research employee of the South Manchuria Railroad, he had a wide acquaintance with the spy service's commercial and secret police agents in the blossoming Japanese underworld in Manchuria. During the next eleven days he made sure that everyone who was to be involved in the coup d'etat could be controlled through some form of blackmail.

The other member of the embassy was Hirohito's personal emissary, Lieutenant General Segawa Akitomo.[10] He had been an intelligence officer in Switzerland in 1919, an aide-de-camp in the palace during the 1920's, and was now the scholarly noncontroversial principal of Japan's military academy. Segawa took with him to Mukden a troop of his mili-

[10] Two years later, in April 1934, Segawa became critically ill with a gall bladder inflammation. When the news arrived in the palace late one evening, the aide-de-camp on duty happened to be Colonel Machijiri Kazumoto, who had helped Prince Higashikuni set up the spy ring in Paris in 1920. Machijiri was the brother-in-law of the Empress's aunt Suzuko and also the husband of the Empress's cousin Yukiko. Presuming on his close ties with the Empress and on his intimate knowledge of the Emperor's affairs, Colonel Machijiri dared to telephone the news of Segawa's illness to the imperial bedchamber. The Emperor at once arose and came in person to the chamberlains' common room. Having heard the particulars, he ordered a present of cheer to be sent immediately to Segawa's sickbed. The civilian chamberlain on night duty with Machijiri ventured to object that there was no precedent for such unusual imperial solicitude. Hirohito said: "I used Segawa as my personal envoy so it is unnecessary to consider precedents." And with that he went back to bed.

tary pupils—the cadets who were to be used as foot soldiers in the coming coup d'etat.

Segawa spent the afternoon of Sunday, May 1, in earnest conversation with his old friend General Honjo, commander of the Kwantung Army. He persuaded Honjo that the projected coup was not intended to establish a military dictatorship, that its purpose was to intimidate the cartels and the Constitutionalist party, and that the plan had the Emperor's backing. Afterward the two generals set out to show the cadets—the young men whose careers were soon to be blighted by their involvement in the coup d'etat—a big night on the town.

Late the next afternoon, Monday, when all the cadets had sufficiently recovered, Honjo personally led them on a short march to the monument erected for Japan's war dead in Manchuria. Before the monument, he delivered to them, in the words of his diary, "an elevating lecture." After the lecture he saw them off on their return to Tokyo.

When Segawa had left, Lieutenant General Honjo began to hear the details of the coup plan which he had told Segawa he would support. He met with Dr. Okawa on Saturday, May 7, and then on Tuesday, May 10, with a second team of underworld operatives from Tokyo: the equerry of Hirohito's spy-service uncle, Prince Higashikuni, and the lawyer who had undertaken to defend Friar Inoue and the Blood Brotherhood.[11] Honjo did not like all the details he heard and sat up most of the night arguing with the lawyer and the equerry. It was one thing, he objected, to support a controlled coup d'etat in the interests of moderation and Hirohito; another thing to sanction the blackmail, deception, and physical intimidation of some of the best families in Japan. Honjo had had long experience with intrigues in China, but he was a stuffy, proper, honorable man in terms of his own Japanese society.

In the morning, convinced against his will, Honjo saw off the equerry, the lawyer, and Dr. Okawa on their departure for Tokyo. With them he dispatched retired Colonel Komoto Daisaku, the Baden-Baden Reliable who had taken responsibility for the killing of Manchurian war lord Chang Tso-lin in 1928 and who had conducted the final financial negotiations in calling off the March Plot in 1931. Having given his reluctant blessing to these four "fixers," Honjo washed his hands in his diary by labeling the projected coup "the business of [War Minister] Araki." He thereby implied that the coup, in its emasculated, controlled form was not the concern of field officers but belonged purely to the political world of the War Ministry where any right-thinking samurai should fear to tread. The next day Honjo remained so full of doubts, questions, and second thoughts that he spent three hours closeted with the Naval Special Service

[11] Yasuda Tetsunosuke and Amano Tatsuo.

Organ chief in Manchuria, Rear Admiral Kobayashi Shosaburo, who until the previous December had been in command of the Misty Lagoon Air Station.

AT A COUNTRY INN

When Dr. Okawa arrived back in Tokyo on Thursday, May 12, he reported to Hirohito's chief civilian advisor, Lord Privy Seal Makino, and then turned over 2,000 yen, or about $700 to one of the Navy fliers of the Misty Lagoon. The next morning, Friday, two of the Misty Lagoon fliers met at Tokyo's Ueno Station with the ranking military academy cadet who had accompanied Hirohito's emissary, Lieutenant General Segawa, to Manchuria. The fliers and the cadet were joined shortly by the Tokyo Imperial University student—unaccountably overlooked by the police in their arrests after the murder of Baron Dan—who had served as Friar Inoue's courier in delivering Blood Brotherhood messages to Dr. Okawa for relay to the palace.

The four young men, student, cadet, and fliers, took a train out through the northeastern suburbs. It had been raining steadily for the last twenty-four hours but now the sun shone fitfully through scudding clouds. Out in the country the train ran through farm villages and paddies. The thatched roofs glistened and steamed, and the pale green shoots of young rice plants protruded from the flooded fields.

The foursome got off the train in Tsuchiura, a garrison town a few miles from the flight school on the Misty Lagoon. A car from the air station drove them out through the farmer's market and the busy district of bars and brothels to the town's best inn. It was a rambling provincial hostelry with a good kitchen and many private eating rooms. For years it had enjoyed the patronage of Chief of Staff Prince Kanin and other princes of the blood as a place where a man could spend a pleasant weekend with a geisha or meet in absolute privacy with a contact from the underworld.

The four conspirators advised the innkeeper that they would require no baths, no kimonos, and no geisha to entertain them and that they expected no one to join them except a "farmer" from the neighborhood. He arrived a few minutes later, and over a pitcher of the cheapest grade of saké the four young men from Tokyo felt out the reliability of their visitor, one Tachibana Kosaburo. Their long conversation that afternoon was eventually recorded in police interrogations and court trials years later.

Tachibana was no ordinary farmer but the leader of the Native-Land-Loving Society, the Tolstoyan farming commune which Prince Konoye and Prince Higashikuni sponsored, near the spy center at Oarai. He and his followers were genuine idealists who wanted a change of regime to improve the lot of Japan's peasants. They were needed in the coup to lend it a smudge of genuine earthy support, and the two flight officers soon found that a share of their 2,000 yen provided by Dr. Okawa was not required—Tachibana was ready to act for ideas alone.

The young men from Tokyo had been assigned the task of planning the assassination of Prime Minister Inukai, who they understood must be killed because he continued to oppose substantial budgets for the military and because he was involved in treasonable negotiations with Chiang Kai-shek and other Chinese leaders. Tachibana agreed to this objective, and toward the end of their five-hour conversation the five conspirators got down to details—to duty assignments and the synchronization of watches.

The youthful shavetail from the military academy, who had just come back from Manchuria, wanted to act at once, on the following day, Saturday. Then, he observed, the famous motion-picture comedian, Charlie Chaplin, was arriving in Yokohama. The secret police would be busy arranging security for him. And in the evening a Cabinet reception was scheduled for him at Prime Minister Inukai's residence. That, surely, would be the perfect time to strike. The murder of Charlie Chaplin along with the Japanese prime minister and the entire Japanese Cabinet could not fail to command international attention.

The two flight officers from the Misty Lagoon hastily interceded to spare the life of Charlie Chaplin. "As a matter of fact," stated the senior of the two, "we have already made sure that the police will be expecting an attack on Chaplin. They will all be out in force Saturday night exhausting themselves. That is why, on Sunday, when we really plan to attack, most of them will be off duty, catching up on their sleep."

According to the final plan agreed upon at the country inn, Tachibana's farmers, armed with sweat towels, axes, and a few grenades, would knock out Tokyo's electric power substations and throw the city into darkness. At the same time the military academy cadets, led by Misty Lagoon flight officers, would blow up several government establishments such as the Bank of Japan. The main body of flight officers would lead a raid on the prime minister's residence and assassinate Prime Minister Inukai.

When times and muster points had all been arranged and written down in notebooks, the five conspirators adjourned. Staff cars took the young men back to the railroad station for Tokyo, and Tachibana boarded a train north to Oarai to organize his farm hands.

KILL INUKAI

Came the dawn of Sunday, May 15, 1932. At 7 A.M., Hirohito's favorite Big Brother Kido, the secretary to the lord privy seal, was just dressing for a day of golf when, according to his guarded, elaborately edited diary, he received a phone call from his boss in the palace, Lord Privy Seal Makino. Never before had Count Makino called so early in the morning—and on a Sunday, too. Kido finished dressing and negotiated the quarter mile around the southern skirts of the palace between his official residence and Makino's in fifteen minutes. Makino told him—according to Kido's diary—that the Emperor had received important information the evening before from the former ambassador to the Soviet Union and that the Emperor wished the Eleven Club to arrange a meeting with the former ambassador as soon as possible in order to hear the information at first hand.[12]

This was all belly talk. The former ambassador to the Soviet Union, for the last month, had been in Manchuria as Hirohito's highest representative, advising Kwantung Army commander Honjo on the handling of Lord Lytton and incidentally watching over the coup preparations which had been made there. In his audience the evening before with Hirohito he had advised the Emperor that Manchukuo would never be a self-sufficient nation without strict Japanese supervision and that the League of Nations could never be persuaded that Manchukuo was independent as long as that strict supervision had to be exercised.

Kido left out of his diary the important news that the Emperor, acting on the former ambassador's advice, had given his final go-ahead to the coup d'etat scheme. But Kido showed by his actions that he understood perfectly that the coup would be staged that day. On leaving the palace he called on Secretary-Spy Harada. Harada phoned members of the Eleven Club to arrange a meeting with the former ambassador to the Soviet Union on the following evening. Then Harada took a train to Shizuoka, not far from Okitsu where old Prime-Minister-Maker Saionji had his seaside villa. He did not notify Saionji of his presence in the area. He registered at a good local inn and told the manager to listen to the radio all day and inform him if any important news was broadcast. Then he retired to his room and spent the afternoon "quietly writing letters."

Kido meanwhile went to his golf club at Hodogaya, outside Yokohama, and, instead of competing in the "Prince Kuni Cup tournament" as he had intended on awakening that morning, took a lesson from the club's golf pro. After a siesta, he played a few holes with club members of no consequence and then, with a great show of insouciance, started home just after five in the afternoon.

At about that same moment, as the sun was growing long shadows, three naval fliers of the Misty Lagoon, five cadets of the Army military academy, and one naval reserve lieutenant, ranging in age from twenty-four to twenty-eight, stepped out of two taxis at the side entrance of Tokyo's Yasukuni Shrine. Here, according to Shinto belief, lived the spirits of

---

[12] The former ambassador was Tanaka Tokichi, a kinsman of Hirohito's cigar-smoking Taoist grand chamberlain, Suzuki Kantaro, Japan's final World War II prime minister.

126,363 heroes who had laid down their lives in the imperial cause since the Meiji restoration.[13] Here, by definition, was the Valhalla of all good soldiers who died in action. Five white stripes running horizontally around the walls, each signifying one of the five Fujiwara families who were supposed to stand around the Throne and protect it, proclaimed the special status and utter holiness of the place. In other shrines encircled by such stripes dwelt exclusively the souls of departed Emperors and princes. Only here—albeit in death—could the subject be honored as the equal of his sovereign. Within the wall, at the center of a spacious park, squatted the shrine building, its round rafters jutting out beyond the green copper roof on both sides of the ridgepole after the fashion of the earliest Japanese tent architecture.

The young officers walked a quarter circle around the park in order to enter the shrine building, which faced toward the sunrise and the goddess of the nation, from the east. Once inside they stood before the altar, caps tucked under their arms, and clapped their hands to invoke the 126,363 ghosts of the "never-opened chamber" within the "inner-inner room." They inclined their heads briefly for a moment of prayerful communion and then bowed profoundly in the direction of the mirror kept in the room "where the spirits of the deities are invited to descend." The mirror had been presented to the shrine by Emperor Meiji as a token, if not a replica, of the sacred one in which he communed with his ancestress.

Turning on their heels like any officers summoned to Manchuria, the assassins started out of the shrine. On the way one of them bought some charms from a priestly attendant and distributed them to his fellows for protection against police bullets. Emerging through the north exit, they passed the military museum, paused at the purifying "hand-washing place," circled around to the "hall where sacred dances are performed," and finally came out again on to the street by the south entrance where an officers' club, a men's club, and a veterans' club crowded up against the outer shrine walls. For the second time that day, they called taxis and squeezed in, four in one vehicle and five in another.

Turning their tailpipes to the gilded dome of the Russian cathedral and the Kanda quarter—the "Boul' Mich' " of students, universities, and second-hand book stores—they motored along the wide boulevard which skirts the immense moated park of the Imperial Palace. At 5:27 P.M. they reached the southern extremity of the Emperor's urban fief where stood, not far from the walls, the prime minister's official residence. Built of volcanic stone like Frank Lloyd Wright's Imperial Hotel, laid out in

[13] Official Japanese casualty figures were always understated. Unless ten of the enemy died for every one Japanese, it was considered an affront to the virtue of the Emperor. At Yasukuni Shrine, however, the roll of honor was kept honestly and, on a year-to-year basis, the number of Army and Navy souls crossing the river may be found graven to a man.

horizontal slabs like Wright's hotel, designed by a Japanese architect after the hotel, it was said by Western wits of the time to be an excrescence created when Wright's structure one ghostly evening took a short walk north and pupped. Disembarking from their cabs the nine young assassins entered the hotel-like lobby of the prime minister's residence.

At that moment on the other side of the city in the port area to the south, a second group of plotters consisting of one naval officer, three military academy cadets, and one civilian had just completed rites at the graves of the Forty-Seven Ronin in Sengaku Temple.[14] Now they, too, had embarked in taxis on their own mission of terror. A third group had mustered at Shinbashi Railway Station eleven blocks south of the prime minister's residence.

The first group of assassins stormed into the prime minister's residence and politely inquired of the receptionist where the Right Honorable Inukai might be on that quiet Sunday afternoon. She replied coolly that she did not know, but if they left their cards, she would give them to Inukai's secretary in the morning. The assassins turned to the policeman on guard and asked him, still politely, to lead them to Inukai's private apartments. The policeman tried to make conversation. A plainclothesman rose from a seat in the corner of the lobby and sauntered toward the front exit. One of the young officers noticed him as he broke for the door and felled him with a bullet. The policeman blanched and refused to utter another word. Leaving a guard to watch the receptionist, the policeman, and the wounded plainclothesman, the young officers set out to search the house. They captured and threatened several servants in the labyrinth of stair-cases and corridors but not one would point out the front door to Inukai's inner quarters.

Then one of the assassins heard the scratch of a key in a lock on the second floor. He called his comrades and broke down the door. Inukai's personal secret police bodyguard stood waiting for them in the prime

---

[14] The Forty-Seven Ronin of Sengaku Temple in Shinagawa quarter are revered by Japanese for an act of heroic adherence to the code of feudal loyalty and vendetta. In 1701 a certain haughty lord, by studied insults and oversights, baited their master into drawing his sword in the shogun's anteroom. The shogun summarily ordered their master to commit suicide in expiation. Left liegeless, the forty-seven then refused all new employment and lulled the police into ill-founded contempt for them by pretend-ing to live as vagrants and wastrels. On the night of December 14, 1702, however, they crept up on the Tokyo mansion of their master's tormentor, took him by surprise, cut off his head, and carried it to Sengaku Temple where they laid it as a peace offering on their master's grave. In recognition of their valor and popularity, the shogun allowed them to take their own lives in a solemn ceremony of collective belly-cutting and then to be buried beside their late lord. Ever since then Japanese youths and maidens have paid a steady stream of tribute at their graves and have relived their romance with death in countless prints, poems, novels, movies, and TV serials.

minister's front parlor. They shot him and rushed over his wounded body to the dining room where Inukai sat smoking in an unlined summer lounging kimono such as a man might wear in the bosom of his family after his evening bath. He had been talking to his daughter-in-law and his personal physician who sat beside him. The assassins saluted him and addressed him politely. Then one of them, Second Flight Lieutenant Mikami, raised a pistol, aimed, and pulled the trigger. The gun clicked harmlessly, for it was not loaded. The seventy-six-year-old Inukai shook his long white goatee emphatically and held up both hands in an authoritative gesture to them to stop and wait a moment. One of the military academy cadets excitedly accused the old man of signing letters and checks which had been found in the safe of Manchurian war lord Chang Hsueh-liang in Mukden.

"All right, wait," said Inukai. "You will understand if you talk with me a while. Let's go over there to my work room." He stood up calmly and walked slowly to the door. Second Flight Lieutenant Mikami was surprised to see that the five-foot Inukai was as tiny as everyone said he was.

"I decided," said Mikami in his later testimony in court, "that it would be only a warrior's mercy to listen to what he had to say in his last testament."

Throwing his left hand over the prime minister's shoulder and prodding him with the pistol in his right, Mikami proceeded to escort the old man from the room. "I didn't have any personal grudge against him," he recalled later, "but I felt a tragic feeling. I tried to convince myself that we were straws in the wind of revolution. And so nothing changed my will to kill."

Mikami's colleagues turned guns on Inukai's maid, daughter-in-law, grandson, and doctor to prevent them from following the master of the household into the next room. The doctor, who had just treated Inukai for a nose condition, later told in court the strange story that he thought the young officers were merely escorting the prime minister from the room to protect him from a mob outside—this despite the shooting of Inukai's bodyguard in the next room.

Out in the corridor, Second Flight Lieutenant Mikami shouted to the lagging members of the death squad from the second taxicab who had entered the house by the back gate: "Here he is! Here he is!"

Prime Minister Inukai retorted, "Not too hasty. Not too hasty."

Mikami and Inukai entered the study, a big room of some thirty feet by thirty feet, and squatted on the *tatami* at either side of the square table at the center of it. Two of the other assassins took places, one at Inukai's side, the other standing cater-cornered from him with gun trained.

Inukai said sternly, "How about taking off your shoes."

Having invaded the sanctity of a home and already defiled the delicate matting of several rooms with their Western boots, the officers replied:

"Worry about that later. You know why we are here. Do you have anything to say before you die?"

Nodding assent, Inukai leaned over the table in a bow, pressed his hands down firmly on it for emphasis, and half rose as if to speak.

"Mondo muyo" ("No use discussion"), cried the Misty Lagoon lieutenant beside him, and a second lieutenant on reserve—the man who had picked up the 2,000 yen from master conspirator Dr. Okawa three days earlier—dashed out of his corner and fired the first shot. Inukai folded forward onto the table, and the talkative Mikami, drawing a bead on the sinking forehead, fired carefully and let a stream of blood from the right temple.

The assassins stood up. Mikami would later have liked to have said, "Wish you a peaceful slumber." But someone cried "Out!" and they tumbled back toward their waiting taxicabs. In the corridors they met a Metropolitan policeman whom they shot twice and wounded gravely. But they got away in their cabs without having yet killed anyone. The secret police bodyguard would die ten days later. The servants and policeman whom they had wounded would all recover.

REFUSAL TO DIE

As for the prime minister, he seemed at first to be merely wounded. "Call them back," he demanded, as his family gathered around him. "I want to talk to them."

One bullet had torn into his left nostril, down through the roof of his mouth and out his right cheek. The other had pierced his right temple, furrowed his forehead, and come to rest just behind the bridge of his nose. His physician, Dr. Ono, did his best to staunch the bleeding of the two head wounds. Then he called Dr. Shioda, the chief of surgery at Tokyo Imperial University, who had operated on Prime Minister Hamaguchi after his shooting in 1930. Shioda sent over two specialists from his university staff to take charge of the case. They found the seventy-six-year-old prime minister not only conscious but still talking coherently and authoritatively. They judged it best not to aggravate the bleeding by moving him. When the amazing old man did not go into shock, they concluded that his condition was not critical.

At 7 P.M., a little more than an hour after the shooting, Inukai called a Cabinet meeting at his bedside and discussed with his ministers the measures which would have to be taken. He learned that his assassins had driven on past the Metropolitan Police Headquarters, firing bullets wildly into the air. They had continued to the Bank of Japan where they had repeated the same performance. Finally they had pulled up at the secret police station in Kojimachi, paid off their cabbies, and given themselves up.

A second death squad had driven from the tomb of the Forty-Seven

Ronin to Lord Privy Seal Makino's residence where they had lobbed a grenade, wounding the policeman on guard at the entrance. They had flung a second grenade outside Metropolitan Police Headquarters, but it had failed to explode. Finally they too had surrendered to the secret police in Kojimachi.

A third death squad, driving in taxis from Shinbashi Railroad Station, had bombed the empty-Sunday-afternoon headquarters of Inukai's Constitutionalist party and had also surrendered after a noisy pass at Metropolitan Police Headquarters.

Finally, the Tolstoyan farmers of the Native-Land-Loving Society had attacked an impressive number of transformers at the city's unguarded power stations. For lack, however, of electrical know-how and of bombs that would explode, they had done no serious damage. A single sub-ward in the slums had suffered a temporary power blackout because one dauntless Land-Lover had severed a high-tension cable with a stroke of his wooden-handled knife.

Relieved that the incident had not been worse, Inukai wearily dismissed his ministers about 8 P.M. The two doctors from Tokyo Imperial University decided to build up his strength with a shot of blood. They took "150 grams" of blood from the arm of Inukai's eldest son, "mixed it with Ringer's solution"—normally a neutral medium for diluting blood—and "injected" it into Inukai. This procedure went unquestioned by the nonmedical bystanders but would have been questioned as idiotic and possibly murderous by any physician interested in preserving Inukai's life. One hundred and fifty "grams" or cubic centimeters of blood amounted to less than a third of a pint—a drop in a desert to a man with a nose-bleed like Inukai's. Such an injection could not possibly do Inukai any good and might do him harm if his son's blood did not match his own. In minutes, however—long before any mismatch effects could have shown themselves—Inukai suddenly lapsed into semiconsciousness and began to twitch and babble as if "confused in his thinking."

From his golf game, instead of going home to his wife in the suburbs as he usually did, Big Brother Marquis Kido drove to his official residence, just outside the palace, and took a bath. The phone rang and he learned from a minor chamberlain that the residence of his superior, Lord Privy Seal Makino, had been bombed. Before rushing over to inquire about the state of Count Makino's health, he phoned to the inn at Shizuoka where Secretary-Spy Harada was standing by to bring old Prime-Minister-Maker Saionji up to Tokyo.

Harada had already heard radio news of the "incident" from his innkeeper and had already phoned Saionji's seaside villa to announce his presence in the vicinity. Saionji, too, had been listening to the broadcast bulletins and tartly observed that Prime Minister Inukai did not seem to be dead as yet. Therefore Saionji, at the moment, was making no preparations to go to Tokyo for the ceremonial chore of advising the Emperor on the selection of a new prime minister. Furthermore, Saionji had many questions in his mind and had no intention of seeing Harada until they could be answered.

Kido advised Harada to stay where he was and make the best possible use of his phone to get answers to the questions which Saionji might ask. Then Kido went to the palace where he reported to Lord Privy Seal Makino. Saionji, he said, was being his usual troublesome self and would muster other malcontents around him if the incident should be unduly protracted.

Standing by in attendance on Hirohito, Kido and Makino waited for Inukai to die and made the necessary ceremonial preparations for the investiture of a temporary prime minister who would take the reins of state until Saionji came up to Tokyo. When Inukai did not die, Hirohito dispatched his own personal physician to Inukai's residence to have a look at the case. Kido, in his diary, took pains to note that Hirohito's physician was dispatched at 8:20 P.M. and that the blood and Ringer's solution had been injected into Inukai at 8:10.

THREAT OF MUTINY

While Inukai lingered on and the palace waited impatiently, a group of young staff officers of the Strike-North Faction gathered at the war minister's residence to demand further action which would "make the coup meaningful." As section, squad, and desk chiefs in the Army bureaucracy, they demanded to know why this coup d'etat, which was to have established Hirohito finally as ruler in his own right, should have been allowed to waste itself in sham and mockery. War Minister Araki, the senior spokesman of the Strike-North Faction, had deliberately gone away to the seashore for the weekend, leaving his lieutenant, General Mazaki, vice chief of staff, to parry criticism for him. Mazaki, in a normal Japanese attempt to share responsibility, had collected a group of other senior officers to stand behind him. They included the Three Crows of Baden-Baden and Vice War Minister Koiso, the later kamikaze prime minister, a proponent of the Strike South.

Since Koiso was known to represent Army Chief of Staff Prince Kanin, the elder of the imperial family, he was allowed to speak first. He explained that the coup had been organized simply to rid the nation of the corruption of political parties. He waxed so eloquent as to the evils of party politicians that War Minister Araki's friend, General Mazaki, interrupted him brusquely. Too much oratory, said Mazaki, was not required in the Army. The pride of the Army was discipline. Every member of the officer corps was pledged to obey the Emperor, not to reason why. And with that, Mazaki stalked from the room.

Five of the young men of the Strike-North Faction ran after Mazaki and caught up with him in the lobby of the war minister's residence. They were led by a lieutenant, War Minister Araki's personal valet, who had lost much face by having helped to recruit the eleven cadets from the military academy who had sacrificed their careers to participate in the pathetic coup. General Mazaki, seeing that his pursuers were angry and carried pistols, ushered them into a waiting room off the foyer where he attempted to reason with them. They refused to sit down, but talk they did—for almost two hours.

"Our comrades," they exclaimed, "are ready all over the country. They expect action. We must rise tonight."

General Mazaki listened to the talk with unusual patience, saying little. Gradually his broad, honest face, concerned and friendly, took its effect. When the young men had talked themselves hoarse, he said simply, "The war minister will not rise, nor should we rise. That is General Araki's opinion as well as mine."

Mazaki stared shrewdly at the young men, waiting to see if any of them would offer now to shoot him. When none of them did, he rang for an aide and summoned the first two of the Three Crows, and three other senior officers waiting outside, to come in and talk to the five young rebels man to man. Second Crow Obata Toshiro, the most dedicated proponent of the Strike North in the triumvirate of the Three Crows, is recorded as having said to his young rebel, "I too feel deep regret over tonight's incident. We were steadily preparing our plans to realize the fruits of national reform with you and the rest, but suddenly everything turned to bubbles."

Even after such expressions of sympathy, the five lieutenants refused to return to their billets in peace. They insisted, instead, that they be arrested by the military police and taken to their regimental lockups. General Mazaki reluctantly humored them. He had them held for several weeks and then released without charges being filed against them. Four years later they would all participate in the military rebellion of 1936, after which two of them would die before a firing squad.

INUKAI SUCCUMBS

The chief aide-de-camp informed Hirohito of the trouble at the War Ministry about 9 P.M. At approximately the same time Lord Privy Seal Makino and the cigar-smoking Grand Chamberlain Suzuki began to hear reports that Saionji was making many phone calls from his seaside villa in Okitsu. Shortly thereafter Big Brother Kido, Makino's secretary, drove from the palace to the prime minister's residence to inquire about Inukai's condition. He had a word with Inukai's secretary, a former district director of the Thought Police, and consulted with the Court physician in attendance at Inukai's sickbed.

The remarkable old Inukai returned to full consciousness at 9:30 P.M., "threw up about 50 cc. of blood"—less than a quarter of a cupful—and said "I feel a little better." These were his last words. One of the doctors gave him a sedative. He lapsed into coma and convulsions but still did not die.

Kido returned to his residence at 11 P.M. and noted in his diary: "The reality of the [Inukai] condition is thought to be less than hopeful." Kido lay down for a nap. Shortly after midnight a chamberlain phoned him to come back to the palace and stand by during the investiture of the new temporary Cabinet. According to the chamberlain, it had been reported to the Emperor that Inukai had died at 11:20.

Having returned to the palace at 1 A.M., Kido learned that the news was premature. Secret police files opened by Allied Intelligence after the war reveal that Inukai was not declared dead by the doctors until 2:36 A.M. Once the news had been reported to the Emperor, the death was, of course, mandatory, but Hirohito, with his usual propriety, postponed the investiture ceremony until the death had become a physical reality. Kido waited about in the palace anterooms for two hours. Finally at 3:15 A.M. on that Monday morning, Finance Minister Takahashi was invested prime minister pro tem, and Hirohito went to bed. Kido remained at the palace, supervising paper work and discussing contingencies with highstrung courtiers until almost 7 A.M.

STERN REPRESSION

At about 8:30 A.M., in Kido's official residence, the phone rang—and rang. Stone-headed after less than two hours of sleep, Kido eventually rolled over on his pallet and reached for the receiver. It was Harada calling from Shizuoka. The secretary-spy had spent most of the night on the phone gathering information for Prime-Minister-Maker Saionji. At first light, when he knew the old man would be stirring, he had presented himself at the seaside villa to deliver his report. But Saionji, with unprecedented rudeness, had refused even to see him. Instead, Saionji had sent out word by a menial that he had no intention as yet of going up to Tokyo and that Harada might as well return to the capital and observe developments until the old man was ready to summon him.

At 9 A.M. Kido was back at the palace with the news that Saionji meant to stage another of his demonstrations of passive resistance. The sixty-nine-year-old Lord Privy Seal Makino, who had had only a few hours of sleep himself, inquired at the imperial bedchamber and learned that Hirohito was already up and dressed. After consulting with him, Makino instructed the cigar-smoking Grand Chamberlain Suzuki to draft a formal summons to Saionji from the Emperor and send it to Okitsu by the hand of an officially designated imperial messenger from the board of chamberlains. By tradition no Japanese nobleman could refuse such a summons except by committing suicide. It was a straightforward hint to Saionji that Hirohito meant to put up with no nonsense.

At 10 A.M., before Kido and Makino could finish their breakfasts, a second crisis broke. Temporary Prime Minister Takahashi arrived at the palace to announce that the Cabinet, after an all-night session, refused to serve under him. He was obliged, therefore, to tender the Cabinet's resignation en bloc. During the next five hours, Hirohito saw each of the Cabinet ministers personally and somehow persuaded every one of them to remain at their posts as caretakers.

In mid-afternoon, Hirohito found time to glance at the missive which had been written to send to Saionji. It struck him as meaningless and old-fashioned. He sat down and dashed off a list of points that he wished the note to make—points so blunt and specific that Count Makino and Grand Chamberlain Suzuki needed the rest of the afternoon to put them into customary veiled Court language. Kido waited about with fascination to see the result, but the text which Hirohito finally approved was considered so full of secret information by the elder courtiers that even Kido was not allowed to see it.

Chagrined and groggy, Kido returned to his residence at 5 P.M. He took a tingling hot bath in his *ofuro*—his "honorable wind on the backbone." And at 6 P.M. he went on to dine at Harada's with the former ambassador to the Soviet Union. Prince Konoye and four other haggard members of the Eleven Club werē present. The ex-ambassador warned them all that Hirohito's temporary alliance with the Strike-North Faction in the Army would be an uneasy one unless something could be done about the administration of Manchukuo. Young Strike-North idealists, who had risked their lives in capturing the new colony, wanted to make it a model state. At the moment, however, influential adventurers, who could claim a semblance of Court backing, were busy milking and looting Manchuria by every shady trick known to man. The new colony could not bear such exploitation. It was undeveloped and underpopulated. Its present products were competitive with Japanese products. Its huge, cold, fertile plains would never attract large numbers of Japanese settlers. To make it a gainful colony, Japan would have to curb the influx of profiteers and send in technical men with slide rules and spirit levels. The administration would have to be put in the hands of more "great spirits like Ishiwara and Itagaki"—the Army strategist and politician whose planning had made the conquest of Manchuria possible. Unless such reforms were carried through, the Strike-North idealists would become a constant source of trouble, threatening discord at home and rebellion or secession abroad.

Kido heard the ex-ambassador's report "with surprise" and went home as soon as he politely could to think it over. Before retiring, he wrote a memo to himself on his conclusions: "Stern measures of repression are required. This is partly because the incident [the assassination of Inukai] happens outwardly, by blind chance, to resemble direct action [the action of rebellious troops acting without orders], but mostly because the incident, if unduly protracted, will shake the very foundations of the national house [the Imperial Throne]."

THE NEW REGIME

The next day, Tuesday, May 17, Hirohito's messenger arrived in Okitsu and delivered to Saionji the threatening imperial summons to come to Tokyo at once. Saionji did not refuse the summons outright, but he politely protested his ignorance of current political events and begged time to study the situation. The imperial messenger returned to Tokyo without being able to say by what train, if any, Saionji would follow.

On the heels of the abashed messenger, a second deputation arrived in Okitsu from the Army bureaucracy. It was led by Prince Kanin's hench-man, the intimidating Vice War Minister Koiso of the Strike-South Faction, and by War Minister Araki's henchman, Vice Chief of Staff Mazaki of the Strike-North Faction. These two opposites were accompanied by the chief of the secret police and by Major General Obata, the second of the Three Crows of Baden-Baden. The four Army men told Saionji that the Strike-North and Strike-South leaders were prepared to co-operate in a transcendental Cabinet but would find it difficult to preserve Army harmony and discipline if Saionji should recommend another political party Cabinet.

Saionji sent the Army delegation back to Tokyo without making any firm commitments to it. Because he liked and trusted War Minister Araki, however, he was visibly mollified by the Strike-South Faction's willingness to include the Strike-North group in future policy making. Within hours, Secretary-Spy Harada was self-confidently setting up appointments with the men whom Saionji would wish to see when he came up to Tokyo. Some of the appointments needed only to be confirmed, for Harada, in an excess of efficiency, had first made them a full week earlier, three days before Prime Minister Inukai's murder.

The following morning, Wednesday, May 18, Saionji continued "to study the situation" from his retreat in Okitsu. Hirohito's two principal Big Brothers, Marquis Kido and Prince Konoye, agreed that the position of the Strike-North Faction was growing stronger by the hour and that Saionji must come to the capital at once or the planned transcendental Cabinet would become a Strike-North Cabinet. The indefatigable train rider, Harada, visited Saionji, offering that Prince Konoye himself should come to Okitsu bringing concessions from Hirohito. Saionji said, "Fine," and Harada phoned Tokyo. Less than half an hour later a palace limousine drew up outside Tokyo Station with a squeal of rubber. Konoye and Kido jumped out and respectively loped and galloped to catch the southward bound 1 P.M. express. Kido rode with Konoye as far as Yokohama, discussing what must be said to Saionji. Four hours later Konoye arrived at Saionji's seaside villa and went in at once for an audience with his venerable kinsman. He promised Saionji that Strike-North leader Araki would be held over into the new Cabinet as war minister and that some lesser portfolios would be given to party parliamentarians. An hour later he emerged with the old man's promise to come up to Tokyo the following day, Thursday, May 19. Konoye and Secretary-Spy Harada retired to the local inn to celebrate their achievement with saké and geisha.

On the morrow, Thursday, May 19, when Inukai had been dead for more than three days, Saionji climbed aboard a special train with Konoye and Harada for a wearisome journey north. Arriving in Tokyo, Saionji moved into the mansion kept for him by the Sumitomo cartel and began the round of political consultations which always preceded the appointment of a new Cabinet.

Prince Konoye reported at the palace. Hirohito agreed to the bargain which had been made, then called his cigar-smoking, philosophizing grand chamberlain, Suzuki Kantaro, and asked him to transmit to Saionji a set of guidelines to follow in picking the members of the transcendental Cabinet:

"Select men who are not real fascists; people who have a relatively mild philosophy and ideology, not too militant; also, they should not have personality problems."

Grand Chamberlain Suzuki honeyed this terse directive with much imperial solicitude for Saionji's health, much protestation of respect for the Constitution, and duly delivered the message to Saionji that same night. Tentatively Saionji had already accepted the transcendental prime minister chosen by Hirohito's Big Brothers six weeks earlier, on April 4. It was to be the biddable, seventy-four-year-old Admiral Saito Makoto, once an aide-de-camp for Emperor Meiji and long governor general of Korea. Nevertheless, Saionji took his time before recommending Admiral Saito officially to the Throne. The young modernists around Hirohito had made all the arrangements as easy for him as possible, but the old man insisted on examining the carefully wrapped package from every angle before putting his seal upon it.

On Friday, May 20, Lord Privy Seal Makino, in his interview with Saionji, asserted that young Army officers in all the main provincial cities were preparing to come up to Tokyo to agitate for an Army dictatorship. "They cannot be arrested," smirked Makino, "because, no matter what you may feel, it is not really a crime to come up to Tokyo." That same afternoon the chief of the Political Investigation Division of the Thought Police warned Saionji that the activities of Saionji's own partisans were fully known to the authorities. Pretending great concern over the possibility of civil war, the Thought Policeman said: "The so-called Constitution Protection Movement, organized by that sector of the economic community which does not yet admit to being intimidated, is mustering to come up and burn the capital."

The next morning, Saturday, May 21, the chief of the Metropolitan Police begged Saionji to see the Emperor soon because "the police are exhausted by their guard duties during the protracted crisis." That evening, when he retired to his private apartments, Saionji was surprised to find waiting for him his former geisha mistress, the mother of his two daughters. He had not seen her since she had left him out of jealousy—not since he had taken up with the wanton Flower Child during World War I. In the sentimental scene which followed, the eighty-two-year-old Saionji resolved to preserve Japan's civil peace at any cost.

On the following day, Sunday, May 22—one week after Inukai's murder—Saionji abruptly capitulated and went to the palace to perform his ceremonial chore. Once again he avoided the customary lunch in the palace and had only the most perfunctory of audiences with the Emperor— lasting from 2 until 2:30 P.M.—but he did what was expected of him and nominated Admiral Saito as the next prime minister.

Old Admiral Saito was summoned to the palace and said to Hirohito, "This is most unexpected. I have had no experience in this sort of thing but I will certainly do my best."

Two days later Admiral Saito was back in the palace with a list of ministers for a "transcendental rising-nation Cabinet." With a few minor exceptions the names on the list were those selected by Hirohito's Big Brothers six weeks earlier. Only one minister in the new Cabinet stood for a group in any way representative of a popular following. This was War Minister Araki, the leader of the schismatic Strike-North Faction which had grown up unwanted in the womb of Hirohito's own cabal—grown too large to be aborted for the moment.

To make sure that War Minister Araki and the Strike-North Faction would not seek to transcend the transcendental Cabinet in which they had been given a place, Hirohito took a small, nepotistic precaution. He raised his wife's cousin, Navy Chief of Staff Prince Fushimi, to the Supreme War Council with the rank of fleet admiral, the naval equivalent of field marshal or five-star general. This meant that the Board of Field Marshals and Fleet Admirals, which was the policy-making nucleus of the Supreme War Council, was now conveniently packed: three imperial princes as against only two subjects of the realm.

HIROHITO'S ACHIEVEMENT

So ended Japan's experiment in government by popular suffrage. The murder of Inukai had effectively silenced his Constitutionalist party.

Throughout the next thirteen years Japanese would continue periodically to go to the polls, but their votes would be meaningless—at best quixotic expressions of opinion on publicized issues of the moment. In the months that followed, while the cartels were allowing themselves to become cogs in a national armaments machine, the only opposition to the military program bequeathed to Hirohito by his grandfather and great-grandfather would come from the "militarists" of the Army.

When the last grenade had fizzled, the last taxicab had screeched to a halt in front of the secret police building, and the last bluff had been laid down by Saionji and called by Hirohito, only four men were dead: Prime Minister Inukai, his bodyguard, Baron Dan, and financier Inoue. Hitler, in seizing power in Germany a year later, would have to assassinate fifty-one political opponents and burn down the Reichstag. Hitler's name would at once become a synonym for monster all over the world. Hirohito, after his great *Putsch,* the Triple Intrigue, would remain as unrecognized as ever— still a mysterious figure wrapped in taboo, and still, to all appearances, a paragon of propriety. It helped to be an emperor. It helped to have a thousand years of experience in intrigue to draw upon. It helped most of all to speak an Oriental language in which no Westerner had the equivalent of a Japanese college education.

Even in Hirohito's cabal, few knew as many details of the putsch as have been recorded in these pages. Even in postwar Japan the story of the plotting has never before been told in sequence. Nevertheless, many and perhaps most Japanese understood at the time that the Throne had conquered and that all the other powers of Japan had been humbled. Hirohito—as will be shown hereinafter—had to go to great lengths to reassure the public of his innocence. Cynics privately dubbed the attack on Prime Minister Inukai "the murder which had to be performed twice." Publicly the putsch was given the noncommittal name of "5–15" or "the May Fifteenth Incident."

In describing their reactions to 5–15, Japanese chose their words carefully and called it "a historic milestone." The peasants, to a man, repeated an age-old formula, *Shikata ga nai* (nothing can be done). An Osaka newspaper editor told an American correspondent, "We are accustomed in times like this to feel that the Emperor and his advisors should make the decisions." At Inukai's funeral on May 19, Western newsmen noted a profusion of expensive orchids on the simple white pine coffin and a totally inexpressive apathy on the faces of some 2,000 onlookers. Kwantung Army commander Honjo, on the day of Inukai's killing, wrote in his diary, "Military men in action under the gaze of their ruler today defied authority with a negative deed of daring."

Recognizing the mixed and apprehensive feelings of his subjects, Hirohito decided to issue a public statement explaining to the people what had been accomplished by the previous six months of concatenated terror.

Two drafts of suitably vague imperial sentiments were drawn up by two separate members of the imperial circle, and both were deemed inappropriate by Hirohito. Finally Big Brother Kido, as secretary to the lord privy seal, took the delicate matter in hand himself and devised a thesis which Hirohito approved of. Kido's draft argued that the two great achievements of Emperor Meiji had been universal conscription of the people in a national army and creation of a native Japanese Constitution which explicitly gave the Emperor absolute power, overriding all other checks and balances. These two great accomplishments and ideals, wrote Kido, had been lost sight of during World War I. Now the assassination of Prime Minister Inukai had brought them once more into view. Hirohito delivered this argument in a formal speech to the new Cabinet three weeks after Inukai's murder. Not a minister, not an editorial writer, ventured to remind Hirohito that Emperor Meiji was most acclaimed for having improved the lot of the masses—for having abolished clans and castes and serfdom, for having created national public education and a measure of equal opportunity for all.

MERRY JUSTICE

After the consummation of the Triple Intrigue, the Throne took good care of all the loyal blackmailers and assassins who had helped to make it a success. A life-long protégé of the eighty-nine-year-old Spider Tanaka of the spy service became home minister in charge of police in the new transcendental regime. Under his auspices, the police moved with marvelous tact in apprehending the law-breakers. About half of Hirohito's Big Brothers were graduates of Tokyo Imperial University Law School, and through their connections they were able to enlist both the judiciary and the police apparatus in Hirohito's cause.

Dr. Okawa, the headmaster of the cabal, turned himself in to the procurator general a few days after Inukai's murder. The procurator questioned him personally on an informal conversational basis for almost a month. Then on the night of June 14, thirty days after Inukai's murder, the procurator phoned the new Cabinet's minister of justice. "There is business to do," he said. To the amazement of the justice minister, Dr. Okawa was suddenly put on the phone. Dr. Okawa was supposed to be wanted by the police, but now he chatted pleasantly with the justice minister. In the course of the phone call, Dr. Okawa revealed conversationally that he expected to be traveling tomorrow to Tsuchiura, the railroad station near the Misty Lagoon. So advised, the justice minister at once notified the home minister that the police, if they were serious in wanting to arrest Dr. Okawa, would be able to pick him up on the train to Tsuchiura.

The next morning, June 15, 1932, detectives mingled with a throng of well-wishers who had come to see Dr. Okawa off on the platform of

Tokyo's Ueno Station. There were so many of the well-wishers that the detectives thought it best to postpone the arrest. They all bought tickets and boarded the train. They sat down in seats near Dr. Okawa, and when the train reached Tsuchiura they arose to arrest him without fuss as he was disembarking.

"You could have arrested me at home," he said, with an air of injured innocence.

A fortnight later, on June 30, Dr. Okawa's secretary was arrested.

On July 10, Baron Tokugawa, who had supplied funds for the preliminaries of the Triple Intrigue, was politely interrogated at the club of the Japan Legal Association.

Native-Land-Loving leader Tachibana, who had organized the inept attacks on Tokyo's power substations during the incident, escaped to Manchuria "to write a book." In the book he called upon the Japanese people to "smash the United States" and "spread the Japanese Imperial Way over the whole world." In another ceremony of exquisitely negotiated courtesy, he turned himself over to the Kwantung Army military police on July 25.

The principal of the spy service's former fencing school in Oarai, Black Dragon Toyama's secretary who had supplied the House of Heavenly Action to the Blood Brotherhood after the empty house had become too hot, negotiated his arrest late in September 1932. Hidezo, the son of Black Dragon Toyama, who had made the House of Heavenly Action available, placed himself in police custody on November 5, 1932, almost six months after the Inukai murder.

Such velvet-gloved methods were hardly characteristic of Japanese police work. On October 30, 1932, sixty policemen in bullet-proof vests stormed a hotel in the seaside resort of Atami where eleven Socialist and Communist leaders were holding a secret meeting. After a prolonged gun battle the subversives were "captured alive." Four days later one of them was announced as having "died of advanced tuberculosis, beriberi, and overexertion while resisting arrest." He was buried in potter's field and all the half-dozen mourners who turned up for his funeral were arrested, interrogated, and tortured. A few days later an aged accessory of the Blood Brotherhood died in the arms of his wife under house arrest. He was given a gangster's funeral, attended by hundreds of rightists including Big Brother Prince Konoye.

After dilatory arrests and kind questioning the killers of 5–15 enjoyed a long year in court in which they made rambling arrogant speeches and told nothing. Their trials did not begin until the second half of 1933, at which point their protestations belonged to a new era of Japanese politics, which will be described in a later chapter. Not one of the murderers, however, was severely punished. Of fifty-four killers and accomplices taken into custody, all but six were free men again by the end of 1935. These six, who had led the death squads and pulled the triggers, were released in 1939 and 1940.

Only token adjustments had to be made after 5–15 by the immediate members of Hirohito's circle. Yamashina, the "Flying Prince," who had incited the airmen of the Misty Lagoon had "a nervous breakdown" and retired from active duty. He is still secluded to this day. His mentor, Commander Inoue, the brother of Friar Inoue, retired to the reserve, where he remained until his professional services as a flight instructor were required again a few years later.

Ancient Spider Tanaka of the spy service converted his Everyday Meiji Biographical Research Institute at Oarai into the Everyday Meiji Memorial Hall, a museum open to the public. To celebrate its debut as a public institution he held a party at it. The Emperor's uncle Prince Higashikuni attended for the imperial family. On his way home to Tokyo afterward Higashikuni caused a scandal by stopping off indiscreetly at the Native-Land-Loving Society to cheer up the disciples of the jailed bombers who had failed to destroy Tokyo's power supply on the evening of May 15. The scandal was hushed up with difficulty, but Higashikuni succeeded in holding the loyalty of the Land-Lovers so that their services could be called upon again in future intrigues.

Lord Privy Seal Makino received many anonymous letters after 5–15 protesting that the bomb run made on his home had been "strange and insincere." He ignored the letters but had the police terrorize the writers of the letters, the civilian disciples of Strike-North ideologist Kita Ikki. For their part the police never interrogated Lord Privy Seal Makino; they only asked his permission, regularly, before making their gingerly arrests.

Dr. Okawa, when he submitted to arrest in June 1932, had on his person a number of useful, personal letters signed by Lord Privy Seal Makino and several other of Hirohito's intimates. When he came out of prison in 1935, Hirohito promptly had him made director of the South Manchuria Railroad's East Asia Economic Research Bureau and dean of Hosei University's "Continental Department."

Black Dragon Toyama, who had been genuinely duped by the Blood Brotherhood in the use of his facilities, turned up a trump by making public a letter in his praise which had been written by Prime Minister Inukai shortly before his death. Toyama had the testimonial read aloud at his seventy-seventh birthday party on June 26, 1932, less than six weeks after Inukai's murder. In it Inukai had written:

I deem it my good fortune that Toyama Mitsuru is one of my most intimate and revered friends. Our friendship has endured for more than forty years, since the days when as a young man I entered the Imperial Diet.

Toyama is Japan's foremost subject. He has never held office, has no Court rank, has no official status whatsoever. But he has remained a sort of inspector and overseer of every government of Japan for half a century. He has made his influence felt whenever a national crisis has appeared. It was his magnetic leadership that caused us to risk our very existence in the wars with China and Russia.

What is the secret of his power? I believe that it stems from his immense loyalty to his Imperial Majesty the Emperor and to the Imperial House; from his complete unselfishness; from [his] patriotism . . .

Friar Inoue of the Blood Brotherhood was well treated in prison but did not emerge from custody until 1940 when he had wasted eight years of his life. Then, however, he moved into Big Brother Prince Konoye's villa in Yokohama, became a regular informant to Bigger Brother Marquis Kido, and enjoyed the lean years of World War II as a fatted prodigal on Prince Konoye's unlimited ration card.

Flight Lieutenant Mikami, who had adroitly shot Prime Minister Inukai through the nose, was also paroled in 1940 and remained comfortably unemployed for the next twenty-one years. On June 5, 1961, however, he was rearrested for plotting a coup d'etat in which he hoped to enlist the modern U.S.-trained Self-Defense Forces of Japan. His unsuccessful coup at this later date was dismissed by the Japanese press as the "Three Nothings Incident"—a quixotic attempt to bring bribery, taxes, and unemployment all to nothing. Mikami was held in jail briefly and released without publicity. By 1965, in his late sixties, he was back in circulation making speeches for patriotic clubs sponsored by Hirohito.

As for Eastern Jewel, the provocative little Manchu princess who had given her favors so unstintingly to incite the Fake War in Shanghai and to create her kinsman, Henry, a puppet emperor, she continued for many years to serve and shock the Japanese Army. After settlement of the Shanghai war, she took up with a branch manager of a Japanese cartel who gave her the use of a villa. She hired a bodyguard with the Special-Service-Organ money of her true love, Major Tanaka. Then she slept with the bodyguard. She engaged a "sing-song girl" from a Shanghai restaurant to solace Major Tanaka. Then she slept with the sing-song girl. Her behavior, observed Tanaka, years later, was "beyond common sense." Consumed by jealousy and ruined by extravagance, Tanaka had her transferred in mid-1932 to Manchuria. There she became the mistress of Major General Tada Hayao who was chief military advisor for puppet emperor Henry Pu-Yi. For a time Tada allowed her to play general over her own detachment of big handsome Manchurian soldiers.

Eastern Jewel went on to other influential lovers in the late 1930's. During World War II, beginning to look a little jaded, she became the *douane* of the Chinese community in Peking. As such, she handled the ransoming of wealthy merchants taken into custody by the Japanese secret police. On the proceeds she bought actors and waitresses for herself in the manner of her Manchu forebear, Yehonala, China's nineteenth century empress dowager. After World War II, in 1948, Eastern Jewel was beheaded by the order of one of Chiang Kai-shek's war crime tribunals. Her judge, in his remarks to the court, condemned her most of all for having ridden in Japanese airplanes and looked down in contempt—she, a woman—on the good earth of China.

16

OUTCAST NATION

(1932–1933)

THE AMERICAN AMBASSADOR

How courteous is the Japanese;
He always says, "Excuse it, please."
He climbs into his neighbor's garden,
And smiles, and says, "I beg your pardon;"
He bows and grins a friendly grin,
And calls his hungry family in;
He grins, and bows a friendly bow;
"So sorry, this my garden now."

So wrote Ogden Nash in 1932, expressing a feeling that was widespread in America at that time. The total variance between Japanese deeds and words in Manchuria made it obvious that Japan was predatory and mendacious. Westerners who knew Japan, however, considered the Ogden Nash view a popular prejudice. It was inconceivable to the experts that Japanese events must speak entirely for themselves and that Japanese words must be entirely discounted as national propaganda. No Westerners appreciated the subtle escape clauses of Japanese belly talk, the little adjectives and adverbs which enabled even the best Japanese to lie patriotically without violating their code of honor. And so the conquest of Manchuria, the Dollar Swindle, the Fake War, the assassinations of Inoue, Dan, and Inukai, and the threatened 5–15 coup were passed off in 1932, as they still are by most Western historians in 1970, as spontaneous outbursts of Japanese energy—hardly more than accidents.

On the day party government was murdered in Japan, a new American ambassador to the Court of Hirohito was just boarding the San Francisco-bound *Overland Limited* in Chicago. On the platform a reporter of

516

Chicago's *Herald Examiner* rushed up to him with a copy of the paper's Sunday evening edition. Its headlines announced: "Japanese Premier Slain; Serious Revolt; Palace in Peril." That evening as the *Overland Limited* sped west through the corn belt toward Omaha, the new ambassador wrote in his journal: "In spite of the press reports, I can't believe the Emperor is threatened, considering the supposedly universal veneration for the throne. There must be something wrong here."

For most of the eight months since the seizure of Mukden, the United States had been represented in Tokyo largely by attachés and consuls who were not privileged to peer into the whole keyhole available to U.S. Intelligence in Japan at that time. The previous ambassador, W. Cameron Forbes, had left Japan on the morning after the Japanese seizure of Mukden, returned in time for the Fake War in Shanghai, and left again two months ago during the assassinations. He had been an outspoken man and not at all popular with the Japanese.

The new ambassador, Joseph C. Grew, was resolved to be more diplomatic than Forbes and at the same time more attentive and narrow-eyed. Like Forbes, Grew was a Harvard man. He had won the admiring patronage of Teddy Roosevelt thirty years earlier when he had shot a charging tiger between the eyes from a fallen position, on his back, in the Malay jungle. Since then he had filled a variety of important posts in Europe and the Middle East. One of his brothers-in-law was J. P. Morgan. His wife, Alice, was a granddaughter of every Japanese child's hobgoblin, Commodore Perry of the Black Ships.

Ambassador Grew was to remain the eyes and ears of the United States in Japan for the next ten years, until he was repatriated on an exchange ship in 1942 after the Japanese attack on Pearl Harbor. Later in the war years, Under Secretary Grew headed the faction in the State Department, which successfully advocated retention of the Emperor as ruler of Japan after she surrendered.

When Grew first arrived in Yokohama on June 6, 1932, the Japanese press gave him a snide reception. The *Japan Times* misquoted him as saying, "I know hardly anything about modern Japan but I hope to get down to serious study." The other great daily, *Asahi,* said, "As regards Japan, which has attained a marvelous development unprecedented the world over, his knowledge may be as imperfect as a fairy tale."

Despite Grew's resolve to remain on his guard, despite his rough reception by the Japanese press, he soon found himself charmed by Hirohito's courtiers and impressed by the skillful illusions they created. A month after his arrival in Japan, on July 13, 1932, he called on Count Makino, Hirohito's lord privy seal and master of intrigues. After the interview he wrote in his journal: "Count Makino impressed me as a really great gentleman. He is close to the Emperor but he doesn't, alas, carry much weight in these days of military domination." Within a year Grew would sometimes give way in his diary to such musings as: "The public guesses but does not *know* today who blew up the *Maine*. The public guesses but does not *know* today who engineered the incidents which led to the Japanese attack [on Mukden] of September 18, 1931."

OPERATION CONCUBINE

One day at about the time Grew arrived in Tokyo, Emperor Hirohito took an unprecedented turn in his afternoon walk through the Palace Gardens. As was his wont, he had strolled south from the Imperial Library, where he worked and lived, to the Biological Research Laboratory where he kept his poisonous fungi and his marine worms. From the lab he had continued south to the old private villa of Emperor Meiji which was used now by the princes of the blood as an occasional overnight lodging house and conference place. There Hirohito turned northeast to the white-pebble courtyard of the Palace Shrine for his brief daily hand-clap and prayer to the ancestral spirits. Continuing north, he entered the best part of the Fukiage Gardens, stopping repeatedly to appreciate the vistas of gnarled pines, rock heaps, and early summer flowers arrayed artfully along his way. Atop a knoll he came to the particularly gratifying outlook over Calabash Pond. He descended, crossed a rainbow bridge, and looked in at the pondside Pavilion of Frosty Brocade where Empress Nagako pursued her hobby of experimental sericulture. With several of her attendants, all dressed in aprons, slacks, and blouses, she was deeply immersed in sorting out the mulberry leaves to be fed to her various colonies of silkworms.

It was on leaving the Empress and the Pavilion of Frosty Brocade that Hirohito departed from his usual itinerary. Instead of following the path northwest from the sericulture laboratory to his Imperial Library, he took the path northeast past the comfortable English-style house of half-timbered brick known by the quaint old name of *Ka-in-tei* or Concubines Pavilion. There he and the Empress did their private entertaining. Beyond it, on the other side of the roadway which bordered the Inner Palace enclosure, he came to the cottage where dwelt his three daughters, aged six, two, and one.[1] Across the rustic dirt track from the Daughters Abode stood the Court Ladies Dormitory. It was not unheard of for him to stop at the Abode for a brief romp with the children, but today he walked purposefully past the Abode to the Court Ladies Dormitory and strode directly into the ladies' common room. There Empress Nagako's personal attendants were gossiping in French and sewing pearls to one of Nagako's Paris gowns.

The Court ladies did their best to conceal their panic and to entertain Hirohito with sophisticated small talk. He gruffly returned their courtesies

[1] Another daughter, the second, had died at birth.

and went about the room looking hard at each one of them. Some of the elder ladies had been beauties in their day but almost all the younger ones were at least as plump as the five-foot, one-hundred-twenty-pound Empress Nagako herself. Hirohito complimented several of them and then nodded his way out to complete his short walk back to the Imperial Library.

The next day the office of chamberlains promulgated a secret directive to the astonished Court ladies reminding, advising, and telling them that, first, the Empress had just passed her twenty-ninth birthday and as yet had borne the Throne no heir; second, the Emperor was considering the taking of a concubine; and third, it was every Court lady's patriotic duty to make herself as available and attractive to Hirohito as possible. The Court ladies professed horror to one another at the waywardness of the Emperor—and still only thirty-two years old!—but collectively they lost more than a thousand pounds and began to wear, as everyday, their finest dresses and perfumes. The ladies' common room, noted one chamberlain, "took on the air of a sultan's harem."

Throughout the early summer of 1932, Hirohito made the common room a regular stop in his afternoon rounds. He listened gravely to each lady's witty anecdotes but always returned to the library without giving any sign as to which lady he fancied. The ladies, for their part, were graduates of Bryn Mawr, Radcliffe, Oxford, and the Sorbonne. They deplored the bad old days of female servitude in Japan, but they began to see advantages in the straightforward customs of the past. They recalled with a certain scholarly nostalgia that, in the Court of thirty years ago, Emperor Meiji had simply dropped a handkerchief before an attendant when he wished her to go to bed with him.

Poor ladies, they were the dupes of a monstrous diversionary public relations scheme propagated by old Spider Tanaka of the spy service. The moderates of Japan were meant to hear of Hirohito's shy advances toward the Court ladies, meant to imagine him a loving husband under pressure from dirty old chamberlains, meant to think that perhaps, after all, Hirohito really was the proper, progressive young man portrayed by palace press releases in the 1920's.

The truth was that Hirohito felt no pressure at all to produce a son, for if one may believe the testimony of two of his courtiers—testimony corroborated by certain broad hints in the documents of the period—Hirohito had already had a son. After the birth of his fourth daughter, in March 1931, he had faced up squarely to the need for an heir and had agreed with his Great Vassals that the time had come for drastic measures. At the same time he did not wish, for personal reasons, to take a concubine. The affection of Empress Nagako and the support of her family—his imperial cousins, the Fushimis—were too important to him to trifle with. If he was to have a son immediately, the child must be a precautionary measure and nothing more, an heir begot impersonally and kept in the background for the time being. Later, if Empress Nagako remained barren of sons, the boy might be brought forth for adoption as crown prince and explained away, with small blemish to the imperial virtue, as the result of a youthful peccadillo. On the other hand, if Nagako should have a son, the stand-by heir would be kept a secret and handsomely provided for.

Sometime in the spring of 1931, therefore, during an afternoon visit to his Biological Research Laboratory, Hirohito had donated a test tube of seminal fluids to the care of one of his personal physicians. The sperm had been incubated, divided, and distributed to an unknown number of noble female recipients. One of them, in early 1932, had duly borne a male child.[2]

Once the succession was safe and Hirohito had proved his manly ability to sire sons, it was only a matter of time until some chamberlain in the imperial confidence would conceive a way to amuse Hirohito and turn his fertility problems to political account. The honor fell to Spider Tanaka who had helped to arrange Hirohito's post-mature birth at the turn of the century. Eighty-nine and still amorous, Spider qualified for the title of senior cupid in the Imperial retinue. After the 5–15 murder of Prime Minister Inukai, Spider had converted his Everyday Meiji Biographical Research Institute into a museum, had taken up residence at the chamberlains' dormitories and had begun to enjoy a freer run of the Inner Palace than at any time since the termination of his decade of service as imperial household minister to Emperor Meiji, twenty years earlier.

Following Hirohito's first call at the Court Ladies Dormitory, Tanaka held almost daily background briefings for reporters on the unprintable story about "the concubine question." Tanaka complained to the reporters that Hirohito was "too staid" and "a firm believer in monogamy." What the Emperor needed was "a nice sturdy woman—a woman who can produce at the touch of the imperial hand."

So widely did the gossip spread on the grapevine that the newspapers in midsummer of 1932 began to allude, without explanation, to "the delicate situation in the palace." Spider Tanaka kept the gossip alive by visiting the ladies' common room himself and telling the Fujiwara girls there that if they could not do their duty he would find more seductive noblewomen outside of the Court.

Ostentatiously Tanaka compiled a list of eligible aristocratic young women and sent out a deputation of photographers and chamberlains "in quest of the glass slipper." A surprising number of well-born modern Cinderellas professed their willingness to serve the Throne as brood mares.

---

[2] The informant who relayed this gossip to the author sidestepped questions as to the identity of the mother and the later life of the baby. Discreet references in Kido's diary, however, suggest that the existence of the test-tube prince was considered a problem at Court until November 1937. Then Kido ceased to worry about it—presumably because the little boy was adopted, in traditional Japanese fashion, by a noble house which lacked heirs.

Old Tanaka and a committee of aging chamberlains enjoyed a gluttony of reminiscence and boastful story-swapping in poring over the photographs. Finally they chose three candidates whom they judged to be the most blythe, bonny, lissome, eligible, and available. Tanaka personally, in his own most elegant brush strokes, inscribed the pedigree of each of the three temptresses on the back of her eight-by-ten glossy. He had the three photographs wrapped in fine rice-paper tissue and placed on top of the state papers in Hirohito's in-basket. The next morning when Hirohito sat down behind his desk in the Imperial Library, he glanced at the three photographs and moved them to the bottom of the stack of papers. He continued to do so every morning throughout the rest of the summer.

On the national grapevine, the concubine question soon overshadowed all other subjects of debate. Women sympathized with Empress Nagako. Men theorized shrewdly on the political implications. It surprised no one when, in August, Tanaka spread the rumor that he had fallen out with his old friend, Empress Nagako's uncle, Prince Higashikuni. On August 4, when Prince Higashikuni was late for a reception, calls to his villa disclosed that he was detained by a confrontation with Tanaka. The old spy supposedly accused the young princely spy of letting his jealousy for the honor of his niece, Empress Nagako, eclipse his concern for the interests of the nation. Days later old Spider Tanaka was reported to be at swords' points with another old friend, Imperial Household Minister Ikki. He accused Ikki of being too timid in pressing concubines on the Emperor.

Tanaka dueled in the gossip columns with Household Minister Ikki and with Prince Higashikuni for the next six months. Both conflicts were nominal, punctuated by hand-claps rather than by real blows. While they raged, Empress Nagako was represented in the gossip as awakening gradually to the awful possibility that her husband might be considering a replacement for her. The Court ladies discovered her several times dabbing at her eyes. She began to tease the youngest and slimmest of her attendants by making anonymous calls to her on the palace telephone and addressing her as "Fatty."

Fatty's uncle was the deputy grand chamberlain. He told Fatty of the photographs on the Emperor's desk. To escape the Empress's jealousy, Fatty passed on her information to the chief lady of the Empress's wardrobe. The chief lady relayed the information to Empress Nagako. According to her Japanese biographer Empress Nagako reacted in a way that fitted perfectly into the schemes of the palace public relation's experts. "I cannot believe you," she said hoarsely. "He would not do that to me and he could not."

A few days later Empress Nagako described to a group of her ladies a most affecting scene which she said had taken place the night before in the "room of the grated gate"—a euphemism for the imperial bedchamber, harking back to bygone days when a guard always stood outside at a peephole to make sure that the Child of Heaven was safe with his bedmate of the night. Finding Hirohito in an affectionate mood, Nagako by her own account had pointed out the sweet smell of hibiscus wafted in from the garden on the September night air. She had reminisced about their first evening together in bed, and then, beginning to weep, she had said, "I know everything. I just want you to tell me yourself. I love you, even if you don't love me anymore."

It had taken Hirohito a moment, related Nagako, to understand what she was talking about, but then he had reassured her with many tender words that he had no intention of taking a mistress.

In February 1933, five months after Nagako's description of the scene in the room of the grated gate, old Spider Tanaka and Imperial Household Minister Ikki settled their duel of hand-claps by both going into retirement. It was advertised to the grapevine that Hirohito was weary of their quarrel and no longer amused by the concubine question. Oddly enough this protestation was interpreted by Japanese with an ear for belly talk to mean that Ikki and Tanaka had compromised and agreed to share the duty of taking public responsibility for the assassinations and the abortive rebellion of 5–15.[3] Lord Privy Seal Makino, who might have assumed the responsibility with greater justice, remained at Hirohito's side for almost three more years.

In March 1933, a month after the settlement, Empress Nagako became pregnant again. The palace midwives assured her that she was going to have a boy. In April, the lady-in-waiting who had borne Hirohito a son by artificial insemination called at the common room to show off her baby to the other ladies-in-waiting. Empress Nagako looked in at the common room during her visit and enticed the toddling illegitimate heir to the Throne back to the private imperial apartments. There Nagako gave the little boy a teddy bear and assured the mother that she and her son would always be well provided for. The Court ladies said that it was a good omen that the little boy had followed the Empress and recognized the leadership of the unborn child in the Empress's womb.

LORD LYTTON INSPECTS

As Grew in his embassy accustomed himself to the subtleties of communication in Japan and Hirohito in his palace created smokescreens to cover the dark deeds of the previous spring, Lord Lytton was scrutinizing Japanese policy in Manchuria.

The heroic Chinese General Ma, who had fought so effectively against

---

[3] Ikki obediently accepted this responsibility despite the fact that he had opposed the murder of Prime Minister Inukai—opposed it so strongly that Big Brother Kido, three days before 5–15, had announced to Secretary-Spy Harada: *"Ikki dja dame"* ("Ikki is no damn good").

the Japanese in November 1931, pretended to sell out to them in February 1932. Chang Hseuh-liang, the ousted Manchurian war lord, had sent Ma a check for almost $2 million (U.S.) with which to pay his troops. The check was drawn on a Japanese-controlled bank. The Japanese allowed Ma to cash it, and in return Ma accepted the puppet post of war minister in the new government of Manchukuo. Six weeks later, however, Ma absconded into the wastes of Manchuria's northwest with most of the $2 million and a truck convoy of Japanese guns and uniforms. By April 14, he was in Hailun, on the Russian frontier, announcing his independence and defiance of the Japanese.

A week later Lord Lytton and the League of Nations' Commission of Inquiry arrived in Mukden. Throughout the six weeks of Lord Lytton's stay, General Ma and his hastily reassembled army caused the Japanese acute embarrassment by taking the offensive in north Manchuria and demonstrating that the spontaneous popular backing which the Japanese claimed for their administration was less than unanimous. General Ma daily broadcast an invitation to Lord Lytton to come north and see for himself the last corner of a genuinely Manchu Manchuria. Lytton, of course, could not respond to the invitation, much less accept it.

But Ma's stand encouraged many Manchurians to defy the Japanese secret police in an attempt to tell Lytton the truth. Messages were sent to Lytton by every undercover contrivance known to man: wrapped in bath towels, written on menus, buried in pastries. In the northern city of Harbin, alone, hirelings of the Japanese spy service pounced on five Chinese, two Russians, and one Korean who tried to communicate with members of the League Commission directly. All eight died in police custody, most of them after prolonged torture. One young Russian student who merely wished to protest the closing of the Harbin Polytechnique, where he had been studying, was caught on the second floor of the Hotel Moderne and killed so quietly that the League's commissioners, preparing for bed and reading reports in nearby rooms, did not hear a sound.

On June 4, 1932, Lord Lytton returned to China with the scent in his nostrils of an insufficiently aired opium den. He retired to the legation quarter of Peking to pull together the material which he and his fellow commissioners had collected and organize it into a formal report to the League in Geneva. The Japanese Army officers who had chaperoned him through Manchuria suspected that they had failed to deceive him. They turned their spite on the shrewd double-dealing General Ma and hunted down his guerrilla forces, band by tattered band.

On July 27, 1932, Japanese troops on the Russian border ambushed a force of 800 Chinese cavalrymen attempting to escape into Russia. After the slaughter, General Ma's horse and saddle bags were found among the corpses on the battlefield. Emperor Hirohito was officially informed that General Ma was dead. A few days later, an irreverent Chinese editorialist in Shanghai inquired rhetorically: "Can God be misinformed?" General Ma had turned up alive and well in Russia. He proceeded to make a triumphant trip around the world, publicizing the cause of the Manchurians and finally returning to the side of his liege lord, Chang Hsuehliang, in Peking.

LESS THAN PARADISE

Ma's escape was used by Hirohito as an excuse for recalling to Japan the conquistador of Manchuria, Kwantung Army Commander Honjo. Honjo and Hirohito were in polite disagreement as to the colonial policy which should be pursued in Manchuria. Honjo wanted to make the latest acquisition of the Empire a model state, "a paradise," which would set an example of Japanese efficiency for the whole of Asia. Being an Army man, however, Honjo was impractical about economic matters. He begged that the new colony be treated as a long-term investment and excused from showing an immediate profit. Hirohito's Big Brothers, on the other hand, felt that the new colony must pay its way from the start. If Honjo and the Strike-North idealists had their way, Japan's surplus energies might be entirely absorbed by Manchuria for a decade or more and the national program might be set back in its timetable.

From the first Honjo had found himself the dupe of hard, bright disciples of *Machtpolitik*—the young officers of Hirohito's cabal who had been placed under him as staff officers. These young men had their own channels to the palace in Tokyo. Some of them, like the religious zealot and strategic genius, Lieutenant Colonel Ishiwara, who had planned the Manchurian campaign, were idealists whom Honjo admired. But after the operational phase of the Manchurian occupation was over, Honjo found that he had other assistants whom he did not admire: operatives of the spy service, sadistic secret policemen, dispossessed samurai who had become "China experts" in their youth and had learned the trades of dope peddler and white slaver in the Japanese gay quarters of Shanghai, Hankow, and Tientsin.

The original plan for Manchuria, as Honjo had understood it, would entail development of the country's mineral and chemical resources, realization of its potential as a manufacturing nation, and settlement along its borders and in its empty areas of Japanese colonists. Following orders from old Prince Kanin, the chief of the General Staff, he had sanctioned the relocation of some 25,000 Chinese and Manchu farm families to make way for their replacement by Japanese settlers. He had had to delegate the relocation project to subordinates of the spy service and Special Service Organ which were both autonomous of his command and directed from Tokyo.

As executed, the relocation scheme turned out to be an eternal blot on Honjo's honor. Chinese bandit bands hired by the spy service rounded up villages of native farmers and set them to work building Japanese-style houses for the settlers who would take their place. The native farmers were promised new lands, new seed, and implements of their own when their building was done. And when it was done, they were turned over to regular units of the Japanese Army for escort to their new homes. The soldiers of these units were told that the native farmers were bandit families who had been sentenced to death and must be herded into stockades and machine-gunned. Some of the farmers were distributed to Japanese infantry companies to be used for bayonet practice by green privates who had arrived in Manchuria too late for the toughening experience of real combat.

A White Russian university student, who had become a minion of the spy service and who later smuggled out of Manchuria an account of his experiences, described this bayonet drill in some detail. He called it not sadistic but masochistic—a school exercise for the training of automatons. The Japanese boys, he said, seemed dazed and foolish. They smiled and laughed and handed out candy to their victims before tying them, apologetically, to stakes driven into the ground. Then the soldiers took turns charging with fixed bayonets at each bound captive until he finally slipped in gobbets out of his ropes.

Oleg Volgins, which was what the White Russian student called himself in his memoirs, had greeted the Japanese motorcycle troops as liberators when they had entered Harbin in February 1932. As refugees from revolutionary Russia in 1920, Oleg and his family considered any anti-Bolshevik an ally. At first Oleg assured his mother that the Japanese were "simple ascetic warriors." Not until he had worked as an agent of the spy service for a year and seen his mother made a hostage and his wife a prostitute did he become a Japanese slave and learn to hate his masters. His account was not published in the West until 1943, when seven years had passed since its writing and it could be assumed that he was dead.

Oleg himself underwent an indoctrination course at the hands of the Japanese secret police which he compared to the indoctrination being given to Japanese soldiers in Manchuria. His secret police instructor, a man named Kato, asked him, "Do you fish? No one is sorry for fish; you must assume the same attitude." A young Manchurian accused of being a Communist was then brought into the interrogation chamber which served as classroom and beaten up with fists. He was burned with cigarettes on cheeks, lips, and eyelids. A mixture of water and red pepper was poured down his nostrils to give him a taste of burning to death and drowning at the same time. He was hung up and whipped. Attendants burned pits in his privates with their cigarettes. He lost consciousness. A Japanese doctor of evident education and contempt for the proceedings entered the room bowing and smiling and resuscitated the victim with an injection. The young leftist's fingernails were torn out, then his toenails.

Strips of flesh were cut from his body with a knife. His teeth were knocked out. Finally Instructor Kato, "using his favorite tool, the cigarette, methodically burned out his eyes."

"Then, thank God," wrote Oleg, "he died."

These methods, practiced by agencies over which he had no control, induced Kwantung Army Commander Honjo, in June 1932, to beg Hirohito, through all the channels at his disposal, to give Manchuria a more enlightened administration. The answer came a month later, when Hirohito approved the dispatch to Manchuria of 166 young technocrats who were all satellites of Big Brother Kido's Eleven Club. The young technical experts brought efficiency to Manchuria but made the latter state of that colony worse than the first.

A Manchukuoan Aviation Company was chartered, funded with Japanese capital, staffed by Japanese pilots, and dedicated to "the development of air routes into China." For the next five years it would act brazenly as a civilian extension of the Japanese Air Forces, conducting thousands of provocative overflights, touching down at Chinese airfields unannounced, paying no ground-crew fees much less runway tolls, and carrying little beside espionage agents and contraband guns, money, and dope, all calculated to catalyze the disintegration of China.

Japan's great South Manchuria Railroad Company, a quasi-governmental institution modeled on the East India and Hudson's Bay companies of British colonialism, extended its tracks over more than a thousand miles of new rights of way. Each fresh tentacle of track had a strategic purpose: one cutting across the Manchurian branch line of the Trans-Siberian Railway, another opening a way into Mongolia, a third pointing a dagger at Vladivostok, a fourth communicating with a new Japanese artificial harbor for naval vessels in North Korea.

A fine new capital, called New Capital or Hsinking, was built to the north of Mukden, in the former Chinese town of Long Spring Thaw. The streets had been surveyed and laid out even before the Manchurian Incident. By the time of Lytton's visit the new city was nearing completion and was ready for occupancy by Henry Pu-Yi and his puppet government a month later, in July 1932.

An oil refinery and a chemical complex for nitrates, phosphates, and sulphates came into being across the bay from Dairen in the old Kwantung Territory Leasehold. Beside one of the largest strip seams in the world—a slab of coal ten miles long, two miles wide, and some 350 feet deep—the Japanese built the model company town of Fushun just east of Mukden. In it the colliers enjoyed free housing, electricity, transportation, and central heat and had nothing to buy with their wages except food and drugs at the company store. The wages were only 40 cents U.S. a day but that was more than four times the national per capita daily average. Native Manchurians supplied all the labor, 1.3 per cent of the clerical help, and none of the engineering and managerial staff.

To pay for these showpieces of material advancement Hirohito's 166 young technocrats instituted a money raising scheme as diabolical as any ever devised by a colonial power. The Italian operative of the spy service in Harbin, Amleto Vespa, called it "the greatest organized squeeze in history." It was first outlined to him one day in the summer of 1932 when his nameless but princely chief announced: "Japan is poor. The Japanese Army in Manchuria costs millions every day."

The Manchurian farmers had too much peasant cunning to make ordinary tax collecting a feasible proposition, and so Japan's spy service, secret police, and Special Service Organ agents set out to milk the country by exploiting the natives' human frailties. Monopolistic opium, heroin, gambling, and prostitution concessions were sold to guilds of vice experts from the various Japanese settlements in China. Of these the most cold-blooded sharks—sharks in a swimming pool of blood—were the dope peddlers. After they moved into Manchuria, mass graves beside the garbage dumps outside all the major cities were kept open for the daily disposal of overdose victims cleared from the streets each morning.

The Japanese themselves had always had a healthy fear of dope addiction and an enviable record in their other colonies of suppressing it. The smoking of the poppy had been introduced to China about 1650 by the Dutch. Until about 1800 it was a luxury practiced mainly by Chinese who were old and rheumatic and rich. Then competition among British, Portuguese, Dutch, and American traders drove the price down and the supply up. In eighteenth century China, aged mandarin addicts had commonly traveled about on official business accompanied by wet nurses who suckled them in their pipe dreams and kept a supply of easily digestible nourishment flowing into their withered guts. The poor who took up the opum pipe after 1800 could not afford such refinements. They used the marvelous anodyne of the pipe to go on working, without food, until they literally dropped dead in their tracks. It was still common, in twentieth century China, for ricksha coolies, who had run twenty miles on a bowl of rice and a pipe of opium, to expire in their traces without a word of complaint.

The Japanese had recognized from the first the danger of the drug which was debasing China. In 1858, before any treaties had been concluded with the outside world on other matters, the shogun's government negotiated an agreement with Great Britain to keep opium out of Japan. When Japan's abstemious samurai conquered the island of Taiwan, in 1895, they found 14 per cent of the Taiwanese natives smoking opium. Forty years later, the cold, efficient, paternalistic efforts of the Japanese police had reduced addiction to less than one half of 1 per cent of the population. The Japanese drug police licensed addicts, issued them three-day supplies of pipe poppy at prices far below the going rate on the illicit market, and saw to it by stringent detective work that no smugglers could compete with the government monopoly and no youngsters could find courage to try the habit. Eventually old addicts died and few new ones emerged to take their places.

By 1926, when Hirohito came to the Throne, Japan had as fine a record of opium control as any nation in the world. At that time approximately one out of every 3,000 Americans was an addict of opium in drug form— a hangover from the days of narcotic patent medicines. By comparison only one out of every 17,000 Japanese was an addict and only one out of every 4,000-odd inhabitants in Japan's most recent colony, Korea. In Manchuria, however, the Japanese pursued a new policy. Throughout the late 1920's Japanese dope peddlers, operating out of the Kwantung Lease-hold, had sought to weaken Manchurian resistance by selling as much dope in Manchuria as possible. When Japan's take-over of Mukden occurred in September 1931, the League of Nations' statistics indicated that about one out of every 120 Manchurians was an opium addict. Seven years later one out of every 40 Manchurians was an addict.

The Japanese opium-selling campaign was simple and direct. Bonuses were paid to farmers who would rotate their soya beans with poppy crops. All opium smokers were registered and issued a weekly ration for which they were expected to pay in much the same fashion that a subscriber is expected to pay for his weekly issue of a magazine. At first, subscriptions came at introductory rates and comfortable dens were provided for those who wished to dream away from their families.

The smoking dens were supplemented by approximately three times as many booths, installed in the downtown streets of major Manchurian cities, where smokers and novices could learn the joys of the hypodermic. At these booths a man, a woman, a boy, or a girl could take a trip on morphine or cocaine, as well as heroin. Special introductory rates of less than the equivalent of a nickel a dose were offered to teen-agers and children. Officially every partaker was a registered addict on whom the opium monopoly could supply a certified medical record. In reality the booths were open to any and all comers who could plunk down a few coppers. The dispensers at the booths were so undiscriminating that they even gave shots to intrepid American newspaper reporters out for an exposé. One of the reporters wrote that he paid twenty coppers to a roustabout, rolled up his sleeve, thrust his arm through a hole in a canvas tent, and got his needle sight unseen.

Beside the opium booths sprang up brothels. No less than 70,000 Japanese and Korean prostitutes were imported into Manchukuo in its first year as a state. And in addition to the whorehouses, the licensed opium-smoking dens, and the unlicensed dope-by-needle booths, the official Japanese crime syndicate organized a dozen other rackets. Enterprising concessionaires, backed by the Japanese secret police, collected charges for the right to hold a wedding, a wake, or a simple feast; for the duty of having a clean sidewalk; for the privilege of having a new compulsory house number; for the once free right to cut ice in the river; for numberless stamps, seals, and countersignatures on every transfer of property, every business contract; for the duty of having each chimney cleaned once every two months; for the privilege of not being constantly dunned with forged IOU's. Every bank transaction ran a gauntlet of special charges which made it impossible to liquidate an asset without a loss of 30 to 40 per cent.

Breakfasting on humble pie, lunching on air, dining on opium, the Manchukuoans paid and paid again. The Japanese and Korean concessionaries who ran the rackets paid, too. They paid initially for their monopolies and then many times again in bribes to secret policemen who backed up their extortion with terror and torture. Emissaries of the Throne in Tokyo collected twice: first, from the concessionaires for their charters; and second, from the secret policemen for their appointments to positions of responsibility in which they could squeeze the concessionaires. The best of the police jobs were auctioned off in Tokyo for as much as ten times their annual worth in terms of salary. The friends of Hirohito, who used his power of appointment to squeeze the squeezers, realized a substantial part of the total profits and plowed it back into the Throne's intrigues and weapons research institutes. Hirohito remained entirely invisible, behind many veils. A single trustworthy chamberlain from his Court took up residence in Manchukuo to keep watch over the rackets as vice imperial household minister to Puppet Henry.[4]

To administer Manchukuo the Japanese set up an elaborate copy of their own system of curtain government. In front of the curtains sat a native Manchurian Cabinet of ministers, each of whom was the puppet for a Japanese vice minister and a staff of Japanese secretaries. Behind the veil sat Puppet Henry, guarded by Japanese secret policemen. Henry was titular commander-in-chief of a Manchukuoan militia which was officered by Japanese and employed as a labor force by the Kwantung Army. The commander of the Kwantung Army reported to Hirohito's great-uncle, Chief of Staff Prince Kanin. The commander of the secret police reported to the Tokyo secret police chief. Prince Kanin and the Tokyo secret police chief both reported to Emperor Hirohito.

As described by a Japanese who grew up in Manchukuo, the puppet nation was organized "like a miniature garden planted according to the strict aesthetic of mimicry." That is, each shrub was carefully selected, pruned, stunted, and tamed to give an illusion of some natural forest beauty. Each office and institution was made to look like a functional enterprise and to hide the fact that its animus was a shadowy Japanese, a wild creature from the world of reality.

All Japanese of any moment in Manchuria were completely and cynically aware of their role as stage managers. The 166 technocrats sent from Tokyo drafted the plan of the puppet state in consultation with the staff officers of the Kwantung Army. Their plan was modified by the chief of Intelli-

[4] Iriye Kanichi

gence in the General Staff, Major General Nagata, the first of the Three Crows chosen at Baden-Baden. Prince Kanin approved Nagata's draft and Hirohito made minor editorial changes in it. The final wording was sent to Manchuria and subscribed to by the staff officers of the Kwantung Army. Mincing no words, it stated that the Manchukuoan government was to strive for "co-prosperity and co-existence with the Japanese economy." In form it was to be "nominally constitutional" but "substantially autocratic." Its "inner leader" was to be the commander of the Kwantung Army working with state ministers "of Japanese lineage."

REPORT TO THE LEAGUE

Kwantung Army Commander Honjo, when he was recalled to Tokyo in July 1932, and Lord Lytton, when he retired to Peking to write his report in June 1932, both visualized the social monster which Hirohito's planners were creating in Manchuria. Honjo went into semiretirement as a member of Hirohito's Supreme War Council and began to lobby for reform in colonial policy. Lord Lytton, whose kidney ailments had been in no way alleviated by entertainments and frequent changes of drinking water, secluded himself in the German Hospital in Peking, surrounded himself with nurses, and began to write his classic report to the League of Nations. He felt that he must criticize Japan strongly and found that he must negotiate every sentence of his criticism with his fellow commissioners.

The Italian commissioner, a count, and the German commissioner, a former colonial governor, both wished to make the report as vague as possible. General Claudel of France threatened to issue his own minority report unless Japan's position was presented in the most flattering light possible. Lord Lytton strove mightily with his pen, conscience, and temper in order to satisfy his fellow Europeans. Being a literary man he tended to write sentences which said directly and intelligibly what they meant.

The American commissioner, Frank R. McCoy, sided with Lytton on the general drift which the report must take. He had none of Lord Lytton's literary gift, but he was a master mediator.[5] He kept the other commissioners from disturbing the quiet of the sickbed where Lytton lay working. And as countless scribbled drafts and redrafts issued from the hospital,

---

[5] McCoy had made a name for himself as a walker in troubled waters at the very outset of his career. In Cuba, during the Spanish-American War, his colonel asked him if the river ahead was fordable. McCoy waded across to the other side and called back, "It is." The colonel remarked, "I shall make that young man my aide." The colonel's general, however, was standing by and said, "Sorry, Colonel, I already made him my own aide when he was halfway across." In later years McCoy would be recalled from retirement to head the Allied Powers' Far Eastern Commission which was supposed to advise MacArthur in his authoritarian Occupation of Japan. Then, once again, McCoy would be responsible for preserving a semblance of unanimity.

McCoy negotiated the softening phrases which were necessary to preserve the commission's unanimity.

In the last fortnight of Lytton's labors, the Japanese did their utmost to coax and distract him. Between August 21 and 25, Japanese marines in Shanghai took up "sightseeing excursions" into the Chinese areas of the city and enjoyed their outings so boisterously that they caused a panic and evacuation of Chapei. On August 27, *New York Times* correspondent Hugh Byas in Tokyo learned from a source close to Japan's foreign minister that the issue came down to this: "whether or not Japan is to be censured in terms that will compel her withdrawal from the League of Nations. . . . If Geneva merely endorses Secretary Stimson's doctrine of non-recognition of any situation brought about in contravention of treaties, Japan will not object." In other words, if the league issued a statement of theory without being so rude as to criticize Japan by name, Japan would condescend to remain in the League of Nations.

The ousted Manchurian war lord, young Chang Hsueh-liang, dramatized the reality of continuing resistance to Japan's puppet regime by mounting a guerrilla attack on Mukden in the early morning hours of August 29. The guerrillas destroyed the airport, set fire to the arsenal, shot up the wireless station, and even penetrated into the walled city. When the "bandits," having made their point, vanished into the countryside before daybreak, frustrated Japanese spokesmen could only leak to Western newspapermen another threat: that any more such raids would force Japan to conquer the next adjoining province of China, the poppy-growing province of Jehol. Part of the U.S. Atlantic fleet joined the Pacific fleet for maneuvers in a move which Japanese decried as menacing. In Japanese movie houses Hollywood's *Hell Divers,* retitled *The Bombing Corps of the Pacific,* played to capacity audiences which believed that the hypothetical targets depicted in the film were the cities of Japan.

In this maelstrom of pressures, by Tuesday, August 30, the last comma of the Lytton report had been haggled, the last *i* dotted, and the 400-odd pages went into their final typing. The members and secretaries of the commission moved into the German Hospital in Peking and turned its antiseptic corridors and lounges into a publishing office. Compromises scribbled in longhand had to be unscrambled, punctuated, and typed. Not until Saturday, after three days' work, was there a clean master copy, plus carbons, of the historic document. Some secretaries and members of the commission sat up all that Saturday night proofreading it so that it would be ready for signing the next day. Minor last-minute changes were arbitrated on Sunday morning, and after lunch Lord Lytton, using a pen made in Japan, and the other commissioners using a pen made in the United States, put their signatures on it. They consigned it to the pouch of a courier who would set out via the Trans-Siberian Railway to carry it the length of Eurasia to the League in Geneva.

The commissioners at once dispersed to leave Peking that very night, some for planes, some for trains, some for steamers—all to reconvene in Geneva three weeks later. Their report was supposed to be entirely secret and was scheduled to be distributed, one copy to the representative of each nation, on September 25, three weeks later. The very next morning, however, Japanese spokesmen in the Tokyo Foreign Office and War Ministry began to attack the Lytton Report, citing exact references by chapter and verse. Japanese military intelligence had succeeded in buying a true carbon of the report from one of the commission's secretaries. It arrived in Tokyo by plane the same Sunday that the commissioners signed the master copy. There the delicate duty of reading it quickly and writing a fair report on its salient features for perusal by the Emperor and his chief vassals devolved upon the chief of the War Ministry's Press Relations' Squad, Colonel Honma Masaharu.

A close friend and perennial aide-de-camp of Hirohito's brother Chichibu, Honma had become fluent in English with the British army of occupation in Cologne in 1919–20, as an assistant attaché in London in 1921–22, and as an attaché to India in 1922–25. So thoroughly had he imbibed British ways that he was known to his fellow officers as "the linguist with the red nose." Subsequently, in 1937, he became director of the Intelligence Department in the Army General Staff, a post which he occupied throughout the rape of Nanking. He was executed by the United States in 1946 as being responsible for the 1942 Bataan Death March in the Philippines.

After an all-night effort, Honma turned the last of Lytton's stylish pages during the gray morning hours of Monday, September 5. Looking at the sheaf of neatly hieroglyphic notes he had taken, he felt some sense of accomplishment. The Foreign Ministry would not complete its own official résumé and rebuttal of the Lytton Report for another four weeks. At the same time, his labors revealed that—as feared—Japanese Army attempts to deceive, impress, and humor Lord Lytton during his tour of Manchuria had failed utterly. The testy peer complained in his report that "the effect of the police measures adopted was to keep away witnesses, and many Chinese were frankly afraid of even meeting members of our staff. . . . Interviews were therefore usually arranged with considerable difficulty and in secrecy. . . . In spite of these difficulties, we were able to arrange private interviews with businessmen, bankers, teachers, doctors, police, tradesmen, and others. . . . We also received over 1,500 written communications; some delivered by hand, the majority sent by post to different addresses."

The Lytton Report went on unequivocally to deny the various claims which Japan had made to the League in her defense: that China was not an organized state; that Manchuria was not Chinese; that China had no sovereignty there; that the Kwantung Army had acted in self-defense; and that Manchukuo sprang from an indigenous independence movement. Lytton concluded: ". . . without declaration of war, a large area of what was indisputably Chinese territory has been forcibly seized and occupied by the armed forces of Japan and has in consequence of this operation been separated from and declared independent of the rest of China."

THE GREAT WALL BREACHED

On the morning after Colonel Honma's heroic translation effort, a Japanese Foreign Office spokesman announced to Western newsmen that Lord Lytton's findings were "less severe than expected." This was a Japanese way of saying that the report was disappointingly persuasive, and too moderate in tone to give Japan much excuse for righteous indignation. The spokesman added, however, that "Japanese recognition of Manchukuo may modify views at Geneva." By recognizing Manchukuo and giving it diplomatic status, the Foreign Ministry hoped to make the puppet nation legally responsible for its own genesis.

The treaty of recognition between Japan and Manchukuo had been under preparation throughout the writing of the Lytton Report. The Foreign Ministry had taken pains to announce that the treaty would contain "no secret clauses" and that its terms would be "less onerous than those . . . in the U.S. agreements with Cuba and Panama." This was a Japanese way of saying that, instead of clauses, there would be whole separate secret protocols and that they would contain all the onerous terms. The most important secret protocol, duly signed by Puppet Henry, stated flatly that Manchukuo "shall entrust the national defense and maintenance of public peace in the future to your country [Japan], all necessary expenditures for which shall be borne by our country [Manchukuo]."

Hirohito approved the Japan-Manchukuo recognition treaty, secret protocols included, at his regular Wednesday morning meeting with the Privy Council on September 7. The following Tuesday, September 13, he made his approval official at a full dress plenary session of the Privy Council held with great mock solemnity in the magnificent Eastern Hall of the Outer Ceremonial Palace. As at all such special plenary sessions, a full set of minutes was kept and Hirohito sat absolutely mute and motionless before a golden screen on a dais at one end of the room. Below him, arrayed according to their Court rank, at three long tables set vertically to his own little altar, sat the highest ranking princes of the blood,[6] the twenty-six members of the Privy Council and the thirteen ministers of the Cabinet.

The meeting had been carefully rehearsed beforehand. Lord Privy Seal

---

[6] His adult brothers, Prince Chichibu and Prince Takamatsu; the two chiefs of staff, Prince Kanin and Prince Fushimi; and the young fascistic Prince Kaya who was Hirohito's near twin. These five were considered senior princes because they headed traditionally important collateral houses of the imperial family. Later in his reign Hirohito would raise ten other members of the family to senior princely status, thereby making them eligible to sit on the Privy Council and pack it if the necessity ever arose.

Count Makino had spoken to each of the Privy Councillors and Cabinet ministers who were to "debate" the treaty. All the questions to be asked and answers to be given had been submitted in advance to Hirohito. One of the Privy Councillors asked War Minister Araki of the Strike-North Faction how long Japan would have to support Manchukuo. Araki answered that Manchukuo would be able to defray part of the cost of maintaining the Kwantung Army on its soil by 1933 and after five years of development would be able to pick up the whole of the tab. The spokesman of the Throne persisted, "Is it not possible to obtain payment before the lapse of five years?" Araki replied that the defense of Manchukuo was the defense of Japan and it was therefore "fair and reasonable that Japan bear part of the cost."

Another Privy Councillor, speaking on behalf of the Throne, inquired: "Our relations with other countries may become increasingly eventful; are our Army and Navy ready?"

"Always," responded Araki—and went on to orate at length on the fighting spirit of the men in the armed services.

Finally the foreign minister, surrounded by a half circle of sleek, reticent aides who attended Big Brother Kido's Eleven Club meetings, presented the clinching arguments. If Japan recognized Manchukuo as a sovereign state, the foreign minister said, it would be entitled to send an observer to the League of Nations and could take responsibility in its own right for having seceded from China. Moreover, said the foreign minister, he wished to put into the palace record copies of historical documents which showed that Manchuria had not been originally a province of China and that it had first come under the rule of Peking as a part of the dowry of an ancient Manchu princess, Ai Chin-lo.

The proceedings had come to an end. The Privy Council voted unanimously for recognition of Manchukuo. Hirohito was satisfied that the amenities had been observed and that others had taken the necessary responsibility. He nodded his approval and withdrew to the Inner Palace. There, in the comfort of his Imperial Library, he formally sanctioned the treaty and its attached protocols by affixing to them his Grand Seal of State.

Japan's recognition of Manchukuo was announced to the world on September 15, 1932. It was coupled with a rumor, leaked to Western embassies in Tokyo by foreign ministry spokesmen, that an Araki war-party resolution for the immediate conquest of China's next province, the poppy province of Jehol, had been narrowly voted down in Hirohito's inner circle of advisors. Although not usually considered part of Manchuria, poppy-growing Jehol was indisputably Manchu, for it was the original tribal land of the Manchu dynasty which had usurped the Dragon Throne of China in 1644. In fact, until the abdication of the Boy Emperor, Puppet Henry, in 1912, a substantial part of the province had been maintained by Henry's family as a hunting preserve to which the Princes of the Iron Helmet, when they felt themselves growing soft in the luxuries of Peking, would periodically withdraw in order to lead again their ancestors' tough life on horseback.

Japan could and would make good on its threat against Jehol, and the League could not and would not offer any effective military opposition. Yet League members, in a fashion incomprehensible to many Japanese, failed utterly to make any concessions because of the threat. The depression-plagued United States, which had bugled the world to take note of Japan's aggression, underwent a general election. On November 8, 1932, Franklin D. Roosevelt won a landslide victory and Hoover's secretary of state, Henry Stimson, who had played a major role in challenging Japan, became a lame duck.

During the American election campaign, the ubiquitous Lieutenant Colonel Suzuki conducted an embassy for Hirohito to Chiang Kai-shek. In a private house in Peking he met with one of Chiang's intimates, a former Chinese foreign minister, Huang Fu. Through Huang, Suzuki informed Chiang that Hirohito was losing patience with him. Chiang's representative in Geneva was doing his utmost to embarrass Japan before the League of Nations, and Chiang's protégé, the former Manchurian war lord, Chang Hsueh-liang, persisted in harassing the Kwantung Army by guerrilla activities. Huang Fu told Suzuki that Chiang had no political option except to put on a good show for the Chinese press at Geneva and that, as for young Chang Hsueh-liang, he was a law unto himself. Suzuki replied, "In that case, if the League vote goes against us, we will feel compelled to eliminate the threat of Chang Hsueh-liang on our flank by conquering the province of Jehol."

Former Foreign Minister Huang pointed out that Jehol lay along the northern side of the Great Wall of China and that if the Great Wall was threatened Chiang might have no political alternative to war. Suzuki knew that the Great Wall was a symbolic barrier of great importance to most Chinese—the oldest Maginot line in the world. South of it sprawled the old classical heartland of China which had spawned and nurtured an exclusively Chinese civilization until Genghis Khan had breached the Wall A.D. 1227. Begun in the third century B.C. the Wall was one of the greatest engineering feats of ancient man, handily dwarfing the pyramids of Egypt, the hanging gardens of Babylon, or the gigantic funeral barrows of the early Japanese emperors. Two stories high, two chariots wide on top, it ran 1500 miles along the ridges of available mountain ranges from the Tibetan plateau in the west to the Liaotung Gulf of the Pacific in the east. There, where it ran into the sea at Shanhaikwan, it had been perforated by a modern railway tunnel which twice daily let through the Peking-Mukden express.

Suzuki gently reminded the former Chinese foreign minister that the half-baked bricks of the Great Wall already lay in reach of Japanese cannon fire. The recognized boundaries of Manchuria included a narrow finger of coast line which crooked south from the main body of the country, nudging Jehol back from the ocean and just touching the Wall at Shanhaikwan, its seaside terminus. Manchukuo's Kwantung Army already occupied most of this corridor, said Suzuki, and could always push on to Shanhaikwan with a few hours' notice.

Nevertheless, said the Chinese former foreign minister, Japanese occupation of Jehol would expose hundreds of miles of the Wall to possible Japanese penetration and would force Chiang Kai-shek, out of honor, to adopt the undesirable course of all-out war.

"The Japanese Army does not shrink from all-out war," said Suzuki, "but no one enjoys fighting with his brother. If Chiang Kai-shek will redouble his efforts to silence anti-Japanese voices in China, exterminating the Communist bandits of Mao Tse-tung and removing the young war lord Chang Hsueh-liang from his councils, then the Emperor of Japan will undertake to prevent Japanese troops from forcing their way through the Great Wall after their conquest of Jehol. This is the Emperor's promise and I can add to it nothing except the renewed hope that Japan and China will someday share as brothers in dominion over Asia."

The former Chinese foreign minister communicated Suzuki's message to Chiang Kai-shek, and Chiang, as noncommittally as possible, conveyed his acquiescence.

After repeated recesses requested by Japan, the League's central Committee of Nineteen—a body resembling the modern United Nations Security Council—reconvened on November 21, 1932, to consider Lord Lytton's findings. By now the Lytton Report had been circulated in all the major languages, had been exploited as a best-seller by an enterprising Tokyo publisher, and had been officially rebutted as a pack of misunderstandings by the Japanese foreign minister.

The Japanese delegation at Geneva was headed by Matsuoka Yosuke, the imperial cabal's University of Oregon graduate. Earlier that year Matsuoka had handled the Shanghai negotiations for Hirohito and had then suggested to him that Japan would have little to lose by withdrawing from the League. Now it was a foregone conclusion that Matsuoka would eventually lead Japan out of the League. As long as the other nations were willing to carry on the debate, however, Matsuoka had instructions from Hirohito to play for time. Having served as old Prime-Minister-Maker Saionji's information officer at Versailles after World War I, Matsuoka had some training in the nice diplomacy of procrastination, but he employed it crudely. In addressing the League when it reconvened, he stated categorically, "We want no more territory."

While the League deliberated, the Kwantung Army packed troops and supplies into the narrow seaside corridor along the southeastern frontier of Jehol and advanced slowly down it toward the Great Wall. On December 8, 1932, just nine years before Pearl Harbor, the Japanese vanguard entered the Manchurian half of the town of Shanhaikwan, in the shadow of the Wall. The Chinese defenders on the battlements fired a few shots and caused a few Japanese casualties. That night Secretary-Spy Harada gave a quaint glimpse into the thought processes of a courtier by noting in his diary, "the precedent for the Shanhaikwan Incident has occurred." On Christmas Day, 1932, War Minister Araki of the Strike-North Faction concurred in the threat being made to China and the League by announcing in a public speech: "Any part of Jehol which the Kwantung Army feels forced to occupy in defense of its flank, it will indubitably keep."

The heralded Shanhaikwan Incident duly occurred on January 3, 1933. A Japanese soldier was supposedly hit by a bullet fired from the top of the Great Wall. A Japanese armored train forced its way through the railway tunnel in the darkness of night. A flood of Japanese infantrymen followed, occupying the Chinese half of Shanhaikwan and butchering several thousand Chinese in their nightshirts. The breach opened in the ancient Wall put the Kwantung Army at the head of a rail line that ran straight west across flat farmland, 180 indefensible miles, into the old northern Chinese capital of Peking.

JAPAN AN OUTLAW

Having demonstrated its ability to ravage the whole of north China if necessary, the Kwantung Army withdrew all but skeletal guard units from Shanhaikwan and left Chiang-Kai-shek to nurse the wound in China's pride. Later that month, as the League in Geneva neared its final vote, Hirohito approved operational orders for the conquest of Jehol and for the elimination of all Chinese forces which might threaten Japan's corridor to Shanhaikwan. Before affixing his Grand Seal to these orders, Hirohito exacted a solemn promise from Strike-North officers in the War Ministry and General Staff that they would abide by his pledge to Chiang Kai-shek, would not allow troops in the field to pursue Chang Hsueh-liang's levies south of the Great Wall, and would absolutely discourage any attacks on China proper until at least a year had passed after the conclusion of the Jehol campaign. Hirohito had heard that some of the Strike-North idealists hoped to incite the League to intervene in defense of China.

To counter the intrigues of the Strike-North faction, Hirohito's Lord Privy Seal, Count Makino, organized for the first time a semipublic alliance of politicans which held as its express ideal a policy of Strike South. The leaders of the new movement were Big Brother Prince Konoye of the House of Peers and Makino's son-in-law, Yoshida Shigeru, the later World War II Peace Faction leader and postwar prime minister. By arguments unknown, at a Mafia-style meeting on January 24, 1933, Konoye and Yoshida established a rapprochement with Baron Hiranuma, the long-faced lawyer of the monied rightist National Foundation Society and with the conservative wing of Black Dragon Toyama's underworld. Their basic sales slogan was: "First south into China, then await developments." Senior admirals pledged the Navy's support of the new movement.

Up to this time few of the men close to Hirohito had privately supported Strike-South aspirations—much less voiced them in public. The military officers of the cabal, trained in the 1922 palace indoctrination center, had pledged themselves only to break the power of clan leadership in the Army and to make the armed forces modern and formidable. The civilian courtiers and bureaucrats of the Big Brotherhood had a better appreciation of Hirohito's ultimate objectives but thought them too secret and too futuristic to require immediate discussion. Like most Japanese, they feared the possible consequences of a policy which might lead to war with the United States. In the new alliance Count Makino was, in effect, launching a trial balloon. When few politicians rushed to board it, Hirohito let it drift away into the clouds and returned to his old slow tiptoeing style of march.

On February 10, 1933, Hirohito called the philosophizing, cigar-smoking Grand Chamberlain Suzuki Kantaro to the library in the palace woods and told him that Japan was compelled to secede from the League of Nations. Hirohito said that he made the decision reluctantly but that he could see no alternative. The League was almost certain to accept the Lytton Report, asking Japan to withdraw her troops and entrust the preservation of peace in Manchuria to an international police force. Since Japan must reject this proposal, she could not remain in the League as a member in good standing. Grand Chamberlain Suzuki nodded and asked whether withdrawal from the League might not invalidate Japan's title to the islands in the Pacific which had been given her to administer under a League mandate after World War I. Hirohito had a phone call put through to the Foreign Ministry and was reassured that membership in the League was not a precondition for continued rule of the islands. Hirohito then gave his sanction for the Japanese delegation at the League to withdraw when necessary.

On Friday, February 17, in Geneva, the League of Nations' Committee of Nineteen recommended adoption of the Lytton Report to the full League Assembly and issued its own 15,000-word summary of the case against Japan. The summary was broadcast to the world at large in a ten-hour shortwave transmission in Morse code. *The New York Times* made journalistic history by transcribing the broadcast and reprinting it in its entirety the next morning.

That same day the Japanese Cabinet met to consider officially the League question. Prime Minister Saito held out against withdrawal and the Cabinet had to make one of its rare non-unanimous reports to the Throne. Hirohito instructed Prime Minister Saito to accept the majority view and to notify Matsuoka in Geneva to lead Japan out of the League as soon as the vote went against him.

On Tuesday, February 24, the full League Assembly met at the Palais des Nations on the shores of Lake Geneva to consider endorsement of the Committee of Nineteen's acceptance of Lord Lytton's judgment against Japan. The Chinese delegate delivered a rambling academic paean in praise of Lytton's objectivity. Matsuoka spoke well and forcefully on the proposition that China was not an organized nation, could not be represented by a delegate from Chiang Kai-shek's Nanking government, and deserved no more real jurisdiction in Manchuria than Egypt enjoyed in Suez or Panama in the Canal Zone.

Finally the issue was put to a vote and the clerk called the roll. The delegates of forty-five of the fifty-five member-nations were present. All were entitled by League rules to have their votes counted except for the two "disputing parties," China and Japan. As the roll proceeded, the morning mist cleared from the lake outside and the sun shone through into the windows. One by one the delegates arose and said, *Oui*—"Yes, we accept Lord Lytton's findings."

"China, disputing party," called the clerk.

"Oui," responded the Chinese delegate.

More ayes followed uninterruptedly until the clerk called, "Japan, disputing party."

Matsuoka arose, turned slowly, sweeping his fellow delegates with a dramatic look of hurt, and shouted, "No!"

The ayes continued to have it unanimously until the clerk called on the delegate of Siam, the only other nation in the Orient which was not in whole or in part a colony of the West. "Siam," said the Thai in a modulated voice, "has been a friend of Japan since the fifteenth century. Siam abstains." The remaining delegates, from Spain to Venezuela, all voted against Japan with a simple aye.

Since abstainers and disputants were not counted, Japan had been condemned forty-two to nothing. The Assembly president noted that Japan had chosen "to follow her own policy into isolation." Matsuoka strode to the rostrum and read a brisk brief statement of farewell. "With profound regret," he said, "the Japanese government are obliged to feel they have now reached the limits of their endeavors to co-operate with the League regarding the Sino-Japanese differences." He added loudly, "I want to thank the League members." Then he walked purposefully down the center aisle, and as he passed his seat, beckoned to his fellow Japanese delegates to follow him. Many of the Japanese in the room had hoped that he would wait for a translation break and make his exit less dramatically, but at his summons they all arose—not only from the official Japanese benches but from the galleries as well. A single member of the Japanese delegation remained in his seat; he was a hired American consultant, a former *New York Times* correspondent and future State Department advisor, Frederick Moore.

In the lobby, staring out through the trees toward the lake, Matsuoka thrust an unlighted cigar into his mouth and talked loudly to assembled newsmen until his car came for him. That afternoon, Japan being absent, the League Assembly voted to implement Lord Lytton's report by asking all member and affiliate nations to refrain from recognizing Manchukuo *"de jure* or *de facto."*

POPPY PROVINCE

As they voted, the members of the League knew that, at that moment, the Japanese were invading Jehol, China's poppy province. The campaign had been in preparation for weeks. Four days before the vote, on Friday, February 20, an American correspondent had reported that the railway between Mukden and the Jehol border was choked with military traffic; that trainloads of motorcycles and American trucks could be seen on every siding; that he was reminded of France in 1918. The attack had been scheduled to begin after the League voted against Japan—if it did. But China's Chang Hsueh-liang and Japan's Strike-North Faction wanted to make sure that the League would not honey its words at the last moment, and so hostilities had been provoked by both sides on February 21, three days early. The Kwantung Army high command overreacted by occupying all the railheads of eastern Jehol overnight. The next morning, Sunday, the invasion made headlines throughout the world. Hirohito was furious.

On Monday, with some loss of face, War Minister Araki of the Strike-North Faction announced, "Actually Japan's campaign is not yet under-way." While Japanese troops sought to guard the railway stations they had taken in eastern Jehol without seeming too conspicuous about being there at all, an ultimatum was served on China demanding instant withdrawal of Chang Hsueh-liang's forces from Jehol because they were "incompatible . . . with the sovereignty of Manchukuo." Nanking rejected the ultimatum early on Tuesday the twenty-fourth, hours before the delegates at Geneva met to cast their ballots. When Matsuoka left his seat in the council hall, Japanese soldiers had already been up for hours, fighting and dying eagerly after their two days of restraint.

Despite the farce of the false start, the Jehol campaign was no laughing matter. Western military attachés who accompanied the Japanese troops were not particularly impressed by the four-to-one numerical superiority of Chang Hsueh-liang's rabble. But they were impressed by the cold rugged terrain of the battleground, and they foresaw a long and arduous campaign for the Japanese invaders. In the event they were confounded and embarrassed in their professional forecasts by the almost inhuman discipline and efficiency of the Japanese in the field. To cut down on the weight they would carry, the Japanese foot soldiers advanced through the cruel February weather without greatcoats and with only nominal supply packs. They kept warm by marching without pause from town to town, twenty-four hours, thirty-six hours, even forty-eight hours at a stretch. It was a *dengeki sakusen* or lightning-strike campaign—what the Germans would later make famous as *Blitzkrieg*.

In nine days Chang Hsueh-liang's forces had been routed and all the strong points of Jehol—a province the size of Pennsylvania, or of Belgium-Holland-Denmark—had been occupied. On the tenth day, March 5—the day that Hitler won a majority in the Reichstag—Japanese waitresses were serving food in Tungliao, the Jehol capital. Most serious from Chiang Kai-shek's point of view, Shanhaikwan had been reoccupied in force and the Great Wall breached at several other points besides. The whole of north China—a million square miles, two hundred million people—lay defenseless and the samurai sword hung over it by a slender thread of restraint.

Western military attachés admired the curt brilliance of Japan's conquest of Jehol and the nations of the League did their best to ignore it. Hirohito followed it up in March by assigning the Special Service Organ's "Lawrence of Manchuria," Major General Doihara, to the task of buying Chinese leaders throughout north China and Mongolia and sponsoring them to found their own regimes autonomous of Nanking. Doihara's assistant, the huge Major Tanaka who had helped girl spy Eastern Jewel provoke the Fake War in Shanghai a year earlier, was sent to Inner Mongolia where he succeeded in establishing an independent government under the chieftainship of the Mongol Prince Teh, known in the yurts of his tribesmen as Demchukdongrub. Eastern Jewel herself was in Jehol in breeches, somewhat disappointed that she had not been allowed to participate in its conquest, but altogether in her element as the "general" of 5,000 Manchu roughriders. Her captains, all selected on the criterion of physique rather than tactical genius, accepted her embarrassing leadership and humored her indefatigable sexuality because she paid them regularly with Kwantung Army gold.

Chiang Kai-shek was left to negotiate the best peace that he could. In April and May, the Kwantung Army twice impugned Hirohito's word to Chiang by sending foraging expeditions beyond the Great Wall to ravage in the north China farmlands. Hirohito angrily dispatched the Strike North's Vice Chief of Staff Mazaki to the front to put a stop to such adventurism. Mazaki accomplished his mission and Araki apologized to the Throne, but Hirohito never forgave either of the Strike-North leaders for their insubordination.

On May 31, 1933, Chiang Kai-shek's representative and Major General Okamura, the third of Hirohito's Baden-Baden Three Crows, signed a document known as the Tangku Truce. By its provisions, Jehol was ceded de facto to Japan and, more shameful, 5,000 square miles of the densely populated triangle south of the Great Wall, vertexed by Shanhaikwan, Peking, and Tientsin, became a "demilitarized zone." In the zone Chinese were left no rights but those of civil drudgery, and the Japanese soldiers were given all rights and no duties or responsibilities.

Hirohito announced his success to the warrior spirits of the dead by a state visit to Tokyo's Yasukuni shrine. To the living he issued a rescript explaining, with many lofty sentiments, that Japan had been forced to withdraw from the comity of nations because the West misunderstood Japan's goal of keeping peace in the Orient. He emphasized in the rescript that Japan would continue to co-operate with the League in technical matters such as international control of health and currencies. Finally, to reassure the people as to the conduct of statecraft in the future, he formed a "diplomatic general staff" in the palace.

When old Prime-Minister-Maker Saionji heard of these measures, he shook his bald head gloomily. Nothing, he said, could disguise the fact that Japan had now become an outcast among nations. The new "diplomatic general staff," he feared, would prove as dangerous as the old military general staffs. As to the hypocrisy of the imperial rescript of explanation, Saionji was scathing.

"The same old cant," he fumed. " 'Peace in the Orient, peace in the Orient!' That's what he keeps repeating, but just by wanting peace in the Orient, how will that further goals such as world peace? Better talk first of wanting things in the style of world peace and the welfare of mankind, and then peace in the East, as an attainable goal, will ultimately follow. Standing up at the start and just braying 'Peace in the East'—will it get us domestic peace or what? It's an awful funny way to talk."

PART FIVE

DISCIPLINING
THE LEGIONS

17

NORTH OR SOUTH?

(1933–1934)

PSHAW!

George Bernard Shaw, a well-known seventy-seven-year-old Anglo-Irish playwright, arrived in the Orient on Sunday, February 22, 1933, at the height of the League-Jehol crisis. At his first press conference in Peking he said, "If all the thirty million Chinese in Manchuria were to become nationalists in the Irish way, the Manchurian problem would be solved." Having thus questioned the sincerity of Chinese patriotism, he turned to Japan: "There is a Japanese soldier pointing a rifle at every Chinese inhabitant, but keeping down nationalism is like sitting on a horse's head—there's no time to do anything else."

A week later G.B.S. arrived in Japan. "I detest all sports," he told a Japanese sports reporter. "They cause bad manners and ill feeling. International sports meetings sow seeds of war." Commenting on the Jehol campaign two days later, he said: "The European war was imperialistic, yet it led to the disappearance of three empires. Have you in Japan ever thought that in your imperialistic aims you may end as a republic, and that that is not at all what your rulers want? European imperialists, or what is left of them, would give their eyes for the return of 1914." He went on to urge Japan to adopt birth control. "There is no reason," he said, "why Japan should continue to expand and demand the right to overthrow other countries which naturally resent an influx of a lower civilization."

For a week Shaw cut a swathe through Japan, inveighing impartially at "the horrors of modern cities of which Japanese are so proud" and at "the futility of war, patriotism, and the League of Nations." Then, on his last day in Tokyo, March 8, Shaw met his match in a two-hour interview with the golden-tongued War Minister Araki of the Strike-North Faction. Araki seized on the occasion to lay a counterintelligence smokescreen for Japan's biological warfare research, sponsored by Hirohito and Empress Nagako's late father, Prince Kuni.

"I understand," said Araki, "that European countries are studying the use of bacteria for warfare."

"I'm not scared of bacteria, Your Excellency, but of bombs," said Shaw. "When bombs are dropped, children have to run away."

"We in Japan," observed Araki, "lack money for advanced weapons so we feel that the most economic way is to fight sixty million strong with bamboo spears."

"I'm lazy and a coward," resumed Shaw, "so lazy I wouldn't even run to a bomb shelter. I tremble at the sound of guns but find it too boring to go to the basement."

"Laziness," declared Araki, "is courage. You have the enlightenment of *Zen*. I regret that you have never seen an earthquake. No one who is not lazy can live in Japan. An earthquake is both a catastrophe and a form of religious enlightenment for the national spirit. There are no sirens blown to warn of earthquakes. We have only to think of an earthquake here in Japan and we are no longer afraid of air raids."

"If you had been born in Russia," rejoined Shaw, at the end of the conversation, "you would have become a politician greater than Stalin. . . . I would like to stay here talking to you until the Chinese land on the Japanese mainland."

THE STRIKE-NORTH LEADER

War Minister Araki was a tiny, agile man with a narrow, sensitive face and a huge handlebar mustache. During 1932 and early 1933, he had emerged as the only Japanese leader who could stand up against Hirohito. Constitutionalist party politicians, Strike-North idealists in the Army officer corps, cosmopolitan aristocrats in the circle of old Prime-Minister-Maker Saionji, and many businessmen and underworld leaders were all willing to bury their differences in support of his droll, well-meaning political genius.

Araki opposed Hirohito's increasingly explicit Strike-South ambitions because he saw in them the possibility of a suicidal war with the United States. To save Japan from this fate he prescribed a different war in which he foresaw less chance of disaster: a war with the Soviet Union. He specifically proposed to begin it in 1936. A mystical notion that 1936 would be a turning point in the history of Japan had entered the prophetic writings of Dr. Okawa and other intellectuals of the spy service as far back as 1918. By 1933 it held a secure place in the apocalyptic dogma of all true rightists. There was a '36 club and a '36 magazine for Army reservists. Araki could expatiate on the importance of '36 for hours at a stretch. His exploitation of the prophecy was not entirely tongue in cheek nor entirely madness. According to the best intelligence projections of comparative military buildup, Japan would have a better chance of defeating Russia in 1936 than in any of the years just before or after.

Araki's hostility to Russia was professional and deep. He had served as a major in Japanese Intelligence in Russia from 1909 to 1913. He had read *Das Kapital* and begun inveighing against the threat of Bolshevism years before the Russian Revolution. He was convinced that Hirohito was blind to the Marxist menace and had tried in many audiences during 1932 to open Hirohito's eyes. Hirohito, however, trusted his favorite economic advisor, Finance Minister Takahashi Korekiyo. Brilliant, unorthodox, and unscrupulous, the seventy-six-year-old Takahashi was years ahead of his times as a Keynesian economist. His suggestions had been largely responsible for bringing Japan through the world depression with money to spare for armaments. He gave it as his expert opinion that Bolshevism in Russia could not survive once Russia had developed heavy industry and a need for capitalistic complexities.

Hirohito was disposed to believe Takahashi. In Hirohito's personal view Bolshevism could not be compared to Shinto as a national religion. It had no stable leadership group like the Japanese aristocracy. It was merely an economic phase in the growth of a nation which Hirohito felt to be fundamentally flawed by racial impurity and a mixed half-Occidental, half-Oriental culture.

In opposing Hirohito, War Minister Araki relied outwardly on his charm and his ability to persuade. Inwardly, however, he relied on a file which he had been keeping on Hirohito since the early 1920's. To his death in 1967, he always kept the file at his side. He hinted that every paper in it had been photostatted and a copy sent in a sealed envelope to a trustworthy friend. In the event of his untimely death the envelopes were to be opened and their contents circulated. The unopened strongbox is still in the keeping of Araki's family. His nephews consider it a talisman which continues to bring them prosperity.

Araki had begun his file in April 1921 when he was made chief of the Europe-America Section in the Intelligence Department of the Army General Staff. In this capacity he had access to the coded cables from all the young military attachés whom Hirohito was meeting at embassies during his crown-princely tour. Araki had continued to add to his file as commandant of the secret police during Hirohito's purge of the Choshu clan from the Army in 1925. In 1928 at the time of the assassination of Manchurian war lord Chang Tso-lin, Araki had first realized that his ideals differed from Hirohito's and had first gathered his papers together in a portable strongbox.

He founded a club and an employment agency for purged Choshu clan veterans and was shunted into various sidings of honor and impotence in the Army bureaucracy. Nevertheless, his following grew. He won the admiration of disaffected Strike-Northists from Hirohito's cabal. He returned from the twilight of a military career to high noon as an Army politician. At the age of fifty-four, in December 1931, he became war minister in the Cabinet of the ill-fated Prime Minister Inukai. Still war minister in 1933— "too popular to be dispensed with," as Hirohito's Big Brothers acknowledged—he had become Hirohito's last domestic adversary.

RED SMEAR

When Araki crossed wits with G.B.S., he had just begun to feel powerful enough to challenge Hirohito in public. It had been his henchmen in the field who had embarrassed Hirohito by crossing the Great Wall during the Jehol campaign. And earlier, in January, during the debate about withdrawing from the League, Araki had mounted a domestic offensive against the Throne—one so thoroughly devious that Japanese politicians suspected in it the cunning stage direction of old Saionji and Western observers completely missed the point. The attack began when a mossbacked old baron, a friend of Araki, announced in the House of Peers that the law faculty of Kyoto Imperial University was riddled with Reds and fellow travelers.

To Westerners the accusation sounded like a typical rightist smear, violating academic freedom of conscience. To Japanese, however, who did not believe in individual conscience, it had a different ring. Kyoto University was the alma mater of Big Brother Prince Konoye, of Big Brother Marquis Kido, and of Secretary-Spy Baron Harada. In their undergraduate days, during World War I, it had been a hotbed of Marxist study and discussion. There, they had first conceived the strange synthetic form of government toward which Hirohito was leading Japan: a parliamentary Marxist theocracy; a monolithic, one-party super-tribe built on racism; a cartel of cartels held together by a gigantic police protection racket. As this misbegotten creature of the intellectual elite, combining all the worst features of East and West, began to take concrete shape, the public had every reason to hold the university responsible.

If mobs had razed the university, Araki and Saionji would have chuckled at the irony of it, for Kyoto's Big-Brother graduates had made academic freedom a mockery. They had made fear of entertaining dangerous thoughts second only to fear of committing lèse majesté. Public peace legislation sponsored by Prince Konoye in the late 1920's had already stripped most universities of their truly independent thinkers. One by one most of the Marxists, trade-unionists, and Fabian socialists, and many even of the apologists for democratic voting procedures had gone quietly into retirement where they were kept under polite police surveillance. Only the faculties of the Kyoto and Tokyo Imperial universities had survived unscathed and that largely because of the personal ties between the professors and Hirohito's courtiers.

To stop Araki's witch hunt before it gained momentum, the police immediately picked up the one subversive thinker at Kyoto University, professor emeritus Kawakami Hajime. Economist Kawakami had translated *Das Kapital* into Japanese and years ago had taught Konoye, Kido, and Harada all they knew about Marxism. Since his forced retirement in 1928, Kawakami had turned increasingly left and professed to be a Communist. Now he was charged with dangerous thoughts and clapped under house arrest. He remained virtually a prisoner until his death in 1946, thirteen years later.

The police followed on February 20, 1933, with their first wholesale roundup of leftists since March 1928. All the pinks and cranks who had been released after earlier mass arrests were reinterrogated and made to reveal the names of any new recruits to leftist movements.

The prompt action of the police convinced Araki and his allies that their attack on Court thinking would have to take a subtler twist. In March, a month after the arrests, one was devised by an Araki partisan at Keio University. The Keio professor began innocently by attacking a Kyoto law professor for holding the unorthodox Tolstoyan view that adultery should be considered a crime. The Kyoto law professor happened to be the leader of a seven-man economic brain trust of Prince Konoye, including the prince's favorite teacher and six of his former school friends.[1] Swallowing the bait, the seven at once banded together to ridicule the Keio professor for his old-fashioned anti-feminism.

When all the old-fashioned men and women of Japan were thoroughly amused and interested, the Keio professor abruptly lobbed toward Kyoto an intellectual shell of larger caliber. He charged that the seven professors in Kyoto were guilty of the heresy of believing the Emperor an "organ or mechanical component of the state."

Whether the Emperor was a part of the state or whether he transcended the state had been argued by scholars of Constitutional law ever since Emperor Taisho's abortive attempt to be dictator in 1912. Hirohito personally had accepted the theory that he was an organ and could delegate all responsibility for his decisions to other, lesser organs. Indeed his publicists maintained that he was hardly more than an automatic rubber stamp. Theologically, however, Hirohito encouraged the idea that he was the Zeus in the Shinto pantheon of great spirits. Araki's learned friend at Keio University implied that it was sacrilege for the Emperor to hide himself as an "organ" and so shirk his true responsibility as a god. Hirohito's spirit, he insisted, was the state, and the spirit of the state was Hirohito. As

[1] Sasaki Soichi, Suekawa Hiroshi, Tsuneto Kyo, Miyamoto Hideo, Tamura Tokuji, Moriguchi Shigeji, and Takikawa Yukitoki.

the living god and the high priest of the dead gods, Hirohito must strive to *be* his nation and not merely to *lead* it.

To make his point crystal clear, the Keio professor coupled his attack on the Kyoto professors with slurs against the two spy-service faithfuls being held by the police, the owner of the Blood Brotherhood's Empty House, whom he termed "disloyal" and "communistic," and Dr. Okawa, the factotum of Hirohito's Lord Privy Seal Makino, whom he termed "impure and Darwinistic in his observance of Shinto." Whatever the other adjectives meant in the peculiar Japanese dialectic of those days, "Darwinistic" clearly referred to the beliefs of the biologist on the Throne.

The Keio professor's charges represented the sort of delicately snide dangerous thinking that all Japanese belly talkers appreciated. At Araki's urging the minister of education, Hatoyama Ichiro, was soon threatening Kyoto University with suspension of its government subsidies unless the seven "organ theorists" were discharged. For two months Hirohito and Konoye encouraged the Kyoto University administration to stand behind the professors, but ultimately, unwilling to come forth from behind their curtains, Hirohito and Konoye sanctioned an accommodation for the seven professors which gave them all new research posts at better salaries in other institutions.

INCREDULOUS EMPEROR

When Araki began his campaign against the Throne in March 1933, Hirohito was at first loath to believe that he was being opposed intentionally. The Eleven Club held a meeting to discuss how best to teach him "the realities of the existing situation." For his part Hirohito decided that he needed an intermediary to deal with Araki. Therefore, on April 6, 1933, he took into the palace a hero of the Strike-North Faction to serve as his chief aide-de-camp. This was Lieutenant General Honjo, the conqueror of Manchuria. He remained at Hirohito's side for exactly three years and sixteen days, and throughout this period he kept an intimate diary record of his conversations with Hirohito.[2] When he arrived in the palace he believed Hirohito to be an innocent young god who needed guidance through the maze of reality. When he left in 1936, he knew Hirohito to be as tough and cynical as any colonel or general of the secret police. From his diary emerges a clear picture of the struggle between Hirohito and the Strike-North Faction which occupied the next three years.

---

[2] Only a carefully censored 13 per cent of the diary has yet been published in Japan. It came out in 1967, in a limited edition, through a tiny publishing house, largely, I believe, as a result of my own personal representations. The remaining 87 per cent of the diary is kept under lock and key in the Historical Section of Japan's modern Self-Defense Forces.

During Lieutenant General Honjo's first week in the palace, Hirohito laid down a book he had been reading on European history and mused pointedly: "The first half of Napoleon's life contributed to the welfare of France, but in the second half of his life Napoleon worked only for his own honor. The result was not good either for France or for the world." By this parable, Hirohito meant to enlist Honjo's help in persuading the Strike-North Faction to leave the direction of Japan's next strike to Hirohito and give Japan a few years of domestic political peace in which to fulfill her ambitious armaments program.

Despite Hirohito's suggestion, the Strike-North Faction continued to embarrass Japan by making raids south of the Great Wall. Hirohito sent the number-two Strike-North leader, Vice Chief of Staff Lieutenant General Mazaki Jinzaburo, personally to the front to restore discipline. While Mazaki was gone, the Big Brothers succeeded in explaining to Hirohito the grim reality of the Strike-North Faction's opposition to him.

As soon as Mazaki returned from the front in late April 1933, Hirohito's scheming uncle, Lieutenant General Prince Higashikuni, accused Mazaki of trying to exercise improper influence on the Throne. According to Higashikuni's own account, Mazaki came to him one day and ordered him, as a subordinate in the Army chain of command, to use his influence with Hirohito in favor of a Strike North.

Higashikuni replied, "I cannot do such a thing. The Emperor has always looked at the whole picture, sanctioning some requests and refusing others. So I cannot obey you even if you issue me orders."

A week later Prince Higashikuni charged that Mazaki was trying to subvert the servants in Higashikuni's own imperial villa. Another week later, in May 1933, Hirohito retired Vice Chief of Staff Mazaki from office, promoted him to general, and moved him up out of harm's way to the Supreme War Council.

On May 21, 1933, before the decision to repost Mazaki had been made public, Hirohito's popular younger brother, Prince Chichibu, came to the palace to plead Mazaki's cause and to ask Hirohito to reconsider his entire domestic program. He urged his elder brother to give up the pretense of being an organ of government, to tear down the veils around the Throne, to assume direct command of the nation, and if need be, to suspend the Constitution. Hirohito refused, and privileged courtiers later reported that the two brothers "had a hot argument." Afterward Hirohito told one of the courtiers: "I will reserve my absolute power in governing the nation for important matters, maintaining constantly a large view for over-all trends. As for suspending the Constitution, that would be to destroy an institution established by Emperor Meiji, which is absolutely unthinkable."

The next day Hirohito sent Big Brothers Kido and Konoye to Chichibu's villa to have a two-and-a-half hour talk with the wayward prince.

ARAKI'S BIG PLAY

In the next few days War Minister Araki made the grand gesture of his career by mounting a carefully planned political blitz calculated to commit Hirohito to war against Russia in 1936.

On Wednesday, May 24, Araki expanded the earlier Red smear by announcing that members of the imperial family were falling under the spell of the red witchcraft at Marxist study seminars held at the Peers' School. The charge was serious because it was true. For generations imperial family members had been expected to inform themselves on all shades of political opinion. The pink of the modern left was no exception, and Empress Nagako's own brother, Prince Higashi-Fushimi, was deeply tinted and tainted by his researches in it.

On Friday, May 26, War Minister Araki persuaded the minister of education to order Kyoto Imperial University to suspend the chief of the seven professors in Konoye's brain trust who subscribed to the Emperor-Organ theory.

On Saturday, May 27, the leading strategists of the Army met at 3d Division Headquarters in Nagoya, on the road between Kyoto and Tokyo, to decide what nation to recommend to Hirohito as "enemy number one."

Surprised by Araki's swift sequence of blows, Hirohito detailed Marquis Kido to study countermeasures against the expanded Red smear and his uncle Higashikuni to watch the proceedings in Nagoya. In the crisis Hirohito left the Kyoto University administration to fend for itself.

ENEMY NUMBER ONE

The meeting of Army brass in Nagoya had been billed as a table-top maneuver, a routine annual—and sometimes semiannual—exercise which did not require the Emperor's express sanction but was merely reported to him. This year it lasted for a week and Lieutenant General Prince Higashi-kuni sat in as the mute representative of the imperial family.

The Nagoya headquarters of the 3d Division lay a few blocks from the shrine which housed the sacred sword, one of the three treasures in Japan's imperial regalia. The offices were as modern as any in Japan. No delicate white matting forced the attending staff officers to take off their boots and remember their heritage. They marched in, sat down at desks, and reached for telephones when they wanted detailed information from their staffs in Tokyo.

The Strike-North position was represented by War Minister Araki and an overwhelming majority of the other officers present. They pushed forward chart after chart showing that Japan would have provocation, international backing, and a reasonable chance of success if it attempted to seize Siberia in 1936. They left most of the presentation of their case to Major General Obata, the second of the Three Crows of Baden-Baden. He had long been "one of the Emperor's men" and few of the junior Army bureaucrats present knew that he and Hirohito were now at odds.

Hirohito's own wishes were represented at the exercises—somewhat half-heartedly—by First Crow Major General Nagata, who was now chief of the General Staff's Intelligence Department. Nagata spoke from memoranda which had been drawn up for him by his disciple and chief assistant at the conference, Major General Tojo, the later World War II prime minister. It was Tojo's strategy to conceal his faction's objective of a Strike South and to plead instead for a policy of "Reorganize China first, then Japan."

Nagata and Tojo argued that Japan could never attack any Western nation, even Russia, without being prepared to confront and face down all the other Western nations. Japan must, therefore, be able to call on the resources of all the yellow race and must be "mobilized for total war." This meant that China and her 500 million inhabitants must stand behind Japan's samurai as a vast work battalion and that Manchuria's resources and Japan's own factories must submit to a complete "industrial rationalization." Such a program, insisted Nagata, could not be completed by 1936. It would take years merely to infiltrate, subvert, and reorganize China. Then would follow the Herculean labor of domestic renovation. During these years of preparation, he said, Japanese should not even talk of attacking the Soviet Union. On the contrary the first order of business was to negotiate a nonaggression pact with the Soviet Union which would keep Russia on the sidelines until China and Japan were both sufficiently "rationalized."

The Strike-North Faction of Araki allowed Nagata, on behalf of the Emperor, to lead the proceedings up to a vote on this nonaggression pact with Russia. Then Araki made one short speech and the pact was voted down. Araki immediately called for a second vote resolving that the assembled staff officers of the Japanese Army should advise Hirohito that the "enemy number one" was not China but Russia. The resolution was passed by an overwhelming majority, and Nagata, Tojo, and one other general were left together talking in a corner.[3]

This juncture of the table-top exercises was reached on the seventh day, June 2. As soon as the vote was cast, the silent observer, Lieutenant General Prince Higashikuni, left the meeting and took a train to Okitsu where he paid a call at the seaside villa of old Prince Saionji who was widely believed to be backing Araki in his intransigence. Emerging from the presence of the venerable statesman, Higashikuni announced to the press that he and Saionji were perfectly agreed that war with Russia, the

---

[3] The ubiquitous Suzuki and other leading Strike-South officers were away in China signing the Tangku Truce which concluded the seizure of Jehol.

United States, or any other nation must be avoided at all costs. Then Higashikuni hastened home to the palace in Tokyo to report to Hirohito and prepare a counterplot against the Army's unwelcome advice.

MUD TO BURY MUD

Hirohito politely tabled the Army's recommendation that Russia be considered enemy number one. In the meantime, in hopes of turning the Red smear against Araki's own hidden patrons, Big Brother Kido, secretary to the lord privy seal, was conducting an exhaustive research into Communist influence on all members of the Japanese aristocracy. On June 3, the day after Prince Higashikuni had left the table-top maneuvers in Nagoya, Kido played a game of golf with one of his son's friends, Saionji Kinkazu, the twenty-seven-year-old grandson of the prime-minister-maker, begot by the daughter of the old man's first and favorite geisha mistress. The ambitious young Saionji was weary of his grandfather's liberalism, disillusioned by his grandfather's defeats, and eager to find new political creeds for Japan. He had come home from Oxford University in 1930 with a degree in politics and economics, and had associated since with a variety of aristocratic intellectuals, most of them left-wing.

Between putts on the greens and again in the club house later in the afternoon, the forty-four-year-old Kido drew out the young nobleman with casual questions. Young Saionji responded freely, taking iconoclastic delight in showing Kido how widely Marxism, individualism, and other dangerous thoughts had spread through the establishment's hereditary leadership.

In the next week, following up the leads which young Saionji had given him, Kido received a liberal education in the political left. He was made to glimpse the world of *To-a Dobun,* the East Asia All-One-Culture University founded by Prince Konoye's father, Atsumaro, in 1901 in Shanghai. There Japan's spy-service intellectuals and aspiring scholars of the Chinese classics had shared desks and lockers and enthusiasms with a motley assortment of nationalists and revolutionaries from other Asian nations—followers of Sun Yat-sen, Gandhi, U Nu, and Mao Tse-tung, the best and brightest, worst and shrewdest outcasts of Western colonialism.

The students at the East Asia All-One-Culture University learned as freshmen to recognize plainclothes operatives of the Western consular police, of the Russian Comintern, of the Japanese Spy Service, and of Chiang Kai-shek's gestapo, the Blue Shirts. Off campus, at the *Zeitgeist* Bookstore, subsidized by the donations of German and Russian Communists, the students fraternized with *apparatchiki* from all over the world who crossed paths there to swap dialectic parables and occasional packets of money and microfilm.

At the *Zeitgeist* Bookstore, the mannish, eccentric, determined Missouri-born journalist Agnes Smedley, one of the earliest apologists for Mao Tse-tung, held court with Indian intellectuals and boys from the Bronx. There a man named Johnson, alias Richard Sorge—now famous as the Russian agent whose Tokyo spy ring would play an influential part (described later in this book) during the final fateful years before Pearl Harbor—widened his journalistic acquaintance with Chinese and Japanese intellectuals. There Ozaki Hotsumi, the only important traitor Japan would ever have to acknowledge, got to know Agnes Smedley and was introduced by her to Richard Sorge of whose spy ring he would later become the main cog.

Kido—though of course he learned little of these prophetic details—sopped up the atmosphere of Shanghai's cosmopolitan spy world with fascination. At the same time, in his usual businesslike fashion, he compiled a roster of aristocrats who were allies of old Saionji or the Strike-North Faction and could be tarred with Araki's own brush. He found that the House of Peers' outspokenly capitalistic Baron Inoue Kiyozumi had a niece who was a fellow traveler. Count Yoshii Isamu, a poet who wrote paeans in praise of individualism, had a wife who collected literary men of extreme opinions and entertained them not only in her salon but also in her bedroom.[4]

Most important, Secretary Kido unearthed political dirt to sling at the conservatively liberal leader of the anti-Konoye faction in the House of Peers, the eighty-year-old Prince Tokugawa Iesato, heir presumptive to the Tokugawa clan, who would have been shogun had it not been for the intervention of Commodore Perry eighty years before. On his last trip to Europe, to attend an international conference of the Red Cross, Prince Tokugawa had taken with him as cabin mate a young female interpreter, Imanishi Keiko, who had a long record of previous associations with leftists.

Months later, when Kido had fully milked his threat to Prince Tokugawa's good name, he leaked his information to the gossip columnists. Then, as he sarcastically noted in his diary, the Tokugawa advisors held "a pigeon-necked" conference—a capsulated Japanese image for a meeting of old men cocking their heads, craning their necks, and pecking all about them in a bootless effort to solve an insoluble problem.

By his researches, Kido laid the ghost of the Red smear against the imperial family. Empress Nagako's younger brother, Count Higashi-Fushimi, who had attended Marxist seminars at the Peers' School, was demoted from prince to count and had to retire to a professorship of literature at Kyoto University. Several old palace retainers, including the mistress of the Empress's wardrobe, had to be pensioned off out of reach of scandal. By dint of Kido's efforts, however, Red infiltration of the aristocracy had

---

[4] The best-known of her lovers was Kawaguchi Matsutaro, the novelist, playwright, and movie producer.

proved too widespread to be used to advantage by the Strike-North Faction. Moreover, in young Saionji, Kido had acquired a valuable contact in the left wing—one which he would later use to influence no less a maker of history than Joseph Stalin.

GO-STOP INCIDENT

On June 17, 1933, two weeks after the table-top maneuvers, an incident took place in Osaka, the big port city near Kyoto, which War Minister Araki, the Strike-North leader, played up at his news conferences as evidence of growing popular resentment against civil government. Second Class Private Nakamura disregarded the gestures of a traffic policeman in Osaka and crossed a street against a red light. The policeman stopped all traffic in order to ask the soldier slowly and distinctly, before bystanders, how a peasant such as he, from the northern provinces, had ever learned enough to pull on a pair of Imperial Army breeches. The soldier, who was not such a peasant after all, haunted the street corner and repeated his offense again and again. When he had crossed against the lights seven times, increasing his audience with each performance, the policeman naturally arrested him and had him booked and fined in septuplicate.

The Go-Stop Incident, as it came to be dubbed by the people in their persevering quest for humor, rapidly escalated in late July and August to become a major confrontation between the civil and military police. At one juncture, flying wedges of both forces, starting from opposite ends of an Osaka street, were narrowly prevented from meeting in head-on battle. The military secret police maintained that Private Nakamura should not pay his seven-fold fine because his honor as a member of the Emperor's Army had been publicly injured. The Osaka municipal police insisted that a traffic violation was a traffic violation and a fine was a fine. The metaphysics of the matter were wrangled out almost daily in the newspapers. Finally Hirohito personally advised War Minister Araki to settle the farce with a compromise. The Army paid Private Nakamura's fine, and the Osaka police sent a written apology to Nakamura's commanding officer for any discourtesy which might have been done to the Army in the manner of his arrest.

PRAYER MEETING PLOT

During its day on the front pages—a day that lasted from July to December of 1933—the Go-Stop Incident applied pressure on the Throne while another, less publicized incident, bruited about only on the grapevine, was applying pressure on Araki. This was the Prayer Meeting Plot of July 10, 1933, a warlock's brew for the universal blackmail of all Hirohito's opponents which Prince Higashikuni had been mixing ever since his return from the table-top maneuvers on June 2. Its many strands of blackmail were so intricately woven that Japanese law courts would not acquit the last of the unwary plotters implicated in it until that final hectic month of unfinished secret business, September 1945, twelve years later, when MacArthur had already landed in Japan and begun the Occupation.

Higashikuni's plot was superficially a simple one. It called for 3,600 stout rightists from the provinces to come to Tokyo disguised as pilgrims. They were to assemble for prayer at the huge park-girt shrine dedicated to Emperor Meiji in western Tokyo, and there receive a blessing as "soldiers of the gods" from the imperial priest on duty. After the prayer meeting they were to disperse and terrorize Tokyo. One death band was to assassinate War Minister Araki, another Prime Minister Saito, and another the leaders of the Constitutionalist party. Civil police headquarters were to be seized and the prisons stormed to let out Friar Inoue and the members of the Blood Brotherhood. Overhead, Commander Yamaguchi Saburo, one of the dozen highest ranking officers in the naval air force, was to be cruising, eagle-eyed, ready to drop bombs on any centers of resistance. When Tokyo had been pacified, Prince Higashikuni or Prince Chichibu was to be made prime minister.

All this grandiose planning was pure humbug. The leaders of the conspiracy were enlisted partly by bribes and partly by assurance that the plot had the backing of the Emperor. The recruiting agent was Colonel Yasuda Tetsunosuke, retired. Yasuda was the son-in-law of General Fukuda who had kept martial law for Hirohito after the 1923 earthquake. Yasuda had served for many years, both at home and in Paris, as Prince Higashikuni's equerry. Yasuda still lived in Prince Higashikuni's villa and received a regular stipend from him. When one of the dupes of the conspiracy doubted his intimacy with Higashikuni, Yasuda posted the dupe across the street, marched up to the front entrance of Higashikuni's villa, and asked the Prince to come out in person to give him an effusive welcome.

By such methods Yasuda collected for Prince Higashikuni a motley band of plot co-sponsors, all representing factions in political life which the Throne needed to blackmail. Commander Yamaguchi, the naval air leader, for instance, had been active in a cell in the Navy which agitated for reconstruction at home as a prerequisite to further conquest abroad. He was the director of the Experimental Weapons' Workshops at Yokosuka, the largest naval yard in the nation. Other co-sponsors included Amano Tatsuo, the lawyer who was representing the Blood Brotherhood assassins of 5–15 in their public trial in law court; Nakajima Katsujiro, a member of the Saionji family's clan of hereditary gatekeepers and in former years a confidential messenger and bodyguard for the old prime-minister-maker; Suzuki Zenichi, the leader of the youth movement of the Black Dragon Society; Fujita Isamu, a publisher and agent of the spy service, who in his undercover work of infiltrating leftist circles had grown too close to the Strike-North Faction; and finally a stock market plunger who represented one of the cartels, the Matsuya department store interests.

This plunger, a fellow called Naito Hikokazu, provided both the money for the plot and the comic relief. Naito had staked a borrowed fortune on Strike-North Army plans for a munitions factory to be built on a piece of property he owned in northern Tokyo. The projected factory had been cut from the national budget in the interests of naval development. Naito tottered on the verge of bankruptcy. Prince Higashikuni's equerry, Yasuda, had promised Naito early warning of an imperial coup d'etat in exchange for financial backing. Naito had borrowed some $200,000 from creditors who hoped to keep him afloat and had raised another $400,000 by the sale of forged stock certificates. He had contributed about $20,000 to equerry Yasuda for the coup and had invested the other $580,000 to buy $3.3 million worth of stock on margin. He sold the stock on margin for promissory cash and waited to buy the stock back at a discount when the coup d'etat had materialized and plunged the market into a panic. By this devious transaction, if the coup succeeded, he stood to gain more than a million dollars.

The coup did not succeed, nor was it ever meant to. Prince Higashikuni's factotum, Colonel Yasuda, laid in a supply of 98 swords, 10 pistols, 700 bullets, and 16 canteens of gasoline. Word spread to the 3,600 gun hands recruited by the Black Dragon Society's youth movement that they would be insufficiently supplied with arms for the seizure of Tokyo. Throughout the first week of July 1933, the young patriots journeyed to Tokyo, looked at the arsenal, and, for the most part, went home in disgust.

July 10, the day scheduled for the Prayer Meeting, dawned fine and clear. One of the morning newspaper gossip columns carried hints that a fake coup d'etat was in the air. A group of creditors called on plunger Naito that morning and found him ashen-faced and shaky. He asked them to come back in two days when he assured them that they would all get their money. They went away unconvinced and some of them instituted legal proceedings against him that afternoon.

That evening the Prayer Meeting at Meiji Shrine drew a total congregation of only thirty-three stalwart sword hands. At the urging of their sponsors—and with the blessing of a priest who was intimate with Prince Higashikuni—they resolved to go ahead with their plan "as a gesture." That night at ten o'clock the police raided the hostel for pilgrims attached to Meiji Shrine. They surprised the thirty-three men who had attended the Prayer Meeting, plus an additional sixteen fresh strong-arm recruits, lighting lanterns and tying on their samurai swords for a midnight attack on War Minister Araki's home. Five hours later, at 3:00 A.M. on July 11, the police intercepted a busload of seventeen fanatic farmhands approaching Tokyo from the former spy service center of Oarai. All seventeen belonged to the Native-Land-Loving Society, the Tolstoyan farming commune, subsidized by Prince Konoye and Prince Higashikuni, whose members had attacked Tokyo's power stations on the evening of 5–15 a year earlier. The police had the bus turned around and driven back whence it had come. Eleven more Native-Land-Lovers were roused from their pallets at a cheap Tokyo inn and returned to Oarai by the morning train. Before noon the police politely searched the headquarters of the Black Dragon Society's youth movement and confiscated a number of headbands, bellybands, cigarette lighters, leaflets, and banners proclaiming, "Establish Government by the Emperor," "Exterminate Communists," "Perfect the National Defense."

Offstage laughter of the gods; a fist covered with velvet, leering jesters' faces emblazoned on the knuckles—that was all the threat that was intended by the Prayer Meeting Plot. The toughs arrested at the shrine were all released on probation by the police and their cases were not even brought to trial—much less disposed of—until almost five years later. Most of the sponsors of the plot were handled with equal caution.

The police compiled a dossier on Prince Higashikuni and turned it over for adjudication to Hirohito's chamberlains. His equerry Yasuda was forced to move out of the Higashikuni villa.

The spy service's Red expert, publisher Fujita, was booked on unspecified charges and released immediately to behave better in the future. For the next three years he acted as an undercover agent for the police and the Throne in the ranks of the Strike-North Faction. In 1935 and early 1936, he provided money, food, and lodging to a fellow antagonist of the Strike-North, a man named Kawai, who became a member of Richard Sorge's Communist spy ring.

The leader of the youth movement in the Black Dragon Society, Suzuki Zenichi, was released on the understanding that he would provide full information on Black Dragon activities. His intelligence enabled the police in the next two years to destroy the Black Dragon as a political force.

Amano Tatsuo, the lawyer for the Blood Brothers who were standing trial for the murders leading up to 5-15, escaped to Manchuria and was given sanctuary there by operatives of the Strike-North Faction. The spy service made an attempt to poison him and when he survived it with nothing more than a severe stomach ache, he submitted to a negotiated arrest and extradition home to Japan. Released on parole, he visited the prison cell of his client, Friar Inoue of the Blood Brotherhood. The trial of the Blood Brothers had begun on June 28, 1933. Now, six weeks later, it was abruptly discontinued. Friar Inoue and his twelve Blood Brethren arose in the dock, accused the presiding judge of inattention, and announced that they would take no further part in the trial. The judge called a recess and went personally to Friar Inoue's comfortable cell to learn what the trouble was. Friar Inoue explained that, as a partisan of Prince Konoye, he must decline to stand trial during the term of the present crisis. The judge, who was forty-seven years old and due for promotion to the District Court, accepted this explanation but resigned his career on the bench. He withdrew, on a comfortable pension, to permanent retirement. The trial was prorogued until March 27, 1934—at which time defense lawyer Amano, himself out on bail, conducted a nice quiet case, a model of harmless patriotic propaganda.

Naval Commander Yamaguchi Saburo, who had rashly offered to provide the Prayer Meeting with tactical air support, never took off to participate in the plot but was treated more harshly than any of the other plot sponsors. For four months he remained at liberty while the police sought to negotiate with him. He proved utterly intractable, however, refusing to abandon his belief that Japan must be reformed internally before expanding further externally. And so, in November 1933, he was arrested, in December interrogated, in January tortured and killed.

As for plunger Naito, he fled his creditors on the day after the Prayer Meeting by getting himself admitted as a patient at Tokyo University Hospital. There, under police guard, a few months later, he died "of stomach cancer"—a police euphemism for the fact that he was finally induced to take the honorable way out of his debts and forgeries by cutting open his belly.

A TRUCE IN THEIR TIME

The grapevine news that samurai with swords had set out from Meiji Shrine to assassinate the leader of Japan's mechanized twentieth century Army touched the sentimental heart of every traditionalist count and baron in Japan. It also touched War Minister Araki, the intended victim. In the weeks that followed, a temporary settlement was negotiated. In effect the Emperor said a *mea culpa* and his antagonists promised to cause no more trouble. The decision whether to Strike North or to Strike South was briefly postponed.

On July 17, six days after the Prayer Meeting, Hirohito sent word to old Saionji that on the one hand Empress Nagako was pregnant again and that on the other he was thinking of abdicating. His place on the Throne, the Emperor suggested, could be filled by the toddling bastard prince engendered by artificial insemination, and the realm could be ruled by one of Hirohito's uncles or brothers acting as regent.

At this same juncture, War Minister Araki and the rest of the Cabinet agreed to a settlement of the Red smear. Professor Takikawa, the leader of Prince Konoye's seven organ theorists at Kyoto University, would resign his post. So would the principal of the Peers' School, which was accused of sponsoring Marxist seminars. And so would the palace chamberlain of peerage and heraldry who was responsible for the Peers' School. The new peerage and heraldry director would be Big Brother Marquis Kido who would continue concurrently in his old post as secretary to Lord Privy Seal Count Makino. Kido duly purged all Marxists from the palace. In addition he instituted a procedure for entering on the Court rolls the mistresses of noblemen. By this device he enlisted for the Throne the help of marchionesses and countesses in all future dealings with refractory marquises and counts.

For his part War Minister Araki acquiesced in a reposting of Strike-North officers from influential positions in the Army bureaucracy to field commands. Their places were taken by officers who were "China experts." In addition Prince Higashikuni was assigned out of Tokyo to command of the 2d Division in the northern Japanese city of Sendai. First Crow Nagata and his opponent, Second Crow Obata, were both removed from the General Staff and reposted as active brigade commanders. Major General Tojo, the later World War II prime minister, organized a new body to study Army discipline and morale, the watchdog Committee for Investigations, which was attached to Araki's own War Ministry.

The settlement in Tokyo, designed to take the Army out of politics, coincided with an unexpected change of command in Manchuria—a sudden death or suicide which robbed Araki of one of the main props of his Army influence. Lieutenant General Honjo, who was now Hirohito's chief aide-de-camp, had been succeeded as commander-in-chief of the Kwantung Army by "Silent General" Muto Nobuyoshi, who had opposed Hirohito in the national policy-making of the Far Eastern Conference before the 1928 murder of Manchurian war lord Chang Tso-lin. Early in July 1933, just after the Prayer Meeting, Silent Muto, now a field marshal, wrote Hirohito a letter pleading for a policy of greater liberality and mercy toward the Manchukuoan citizens under his charge. Hirohito's answer is not on record but on July 21, after receiving it, Silent Muto mailed a thirty-one-syllable poem to his second and favorite daughter Misako in Japan:

> You here and I there—
> understand, please, that we part
> for sake of country.
> Even when we've spent our lives,
> we can meet again beyond.

The next day, July 22, Silent Muto retired to his private quarters and announced that he was ill. Five days later, on July 27, Hirohito was informed that he had died of "a general abdominal ailment." The imperial household minister submitted a formal petition to the Throne suggesting that the title of baron be conferred upon the late field marshal.

Hirohito answered, "Although it is altogether fitting and proper to reward Muto with a barony, how will it sit with his children?"

Big Brother Kido, as secretary to the lord privy seal and now, concurrently, director of peerage and heraldry, researched the question and replied to the Throne a few days later that Silent Muto's heirs would find it a financial burden to support a baron's title.

"Muto's wife," wrote Kido, without having consulted her, "has already reported herself [in her own family name] as mistress of the household.

Therefore it is very clear that she would have no desire to see the title passed on."

Hirohito, accordingly, made Silent Muto, posthumously, a non-hereditary baron and with that the matter was dropped.

In Muto's place as ambassador to Manchukuo and commander-in-chief of the Kwantung Army Hirohito appointed a fire-breathing, sabre-rattling general of the Navy-oriented Satsuma clan named Hishikari Taka. There was poetic justice in the choice because the ideographs in Hishikari Taka's name meant literally "cutting back water-chestnut prosperity." Water chestnuts were known by Japanese as a gourmet's delicacy in China, a symbol of the epicurean degeneracy of China's ruling classes. On meeting the Japanese press after his appointment, Hishikari strode forward in summer kimono wearing an ancient samurai sword handed down in his family. He fanned himself energetically with an antique fan.

"If there is anyone who opposes the Imperial Army," he barked, "I will do this to him."

And with that, according to the accounts published the next day, he drew his *katana,* cut the air with it, and "laughed boisterously."

Hishikari, on his arrival in Manchuria, legitimized and systematized all the malpractices which Hirohito's young experts had introduced the year before in their attempt to make Manchuria pay. Strike-North staff officers in the Kwantung Army prepared a booklet on conditions in Manchuria and had it smuggled home to their former commander, Lieutenant General Honjo, the chief aide-de-camp in the palace. On August 6, 1933, Honjo submitted it to Emperor Hirohito, telling him that it described "the realities of peace preservation in Manchukuo." In his diary, on August 8, Honjo wrote: "I asked the Emperor to read it, adding, 'It has been hot recently, so do it whenever you have a moment.' Today, two days later, he called me and said, 'I have read the passages you marked.' And he gave the booklet back to me. I was surprised at how quickly he had read it—personally I spent a long time on it."

THE KASPÉ KIDNAPPING

Hishikari brought to Manchuria a new form of racket, kidnapping. Many well-to-do Chinese merchants were kidnapped two or three times before they were ascertained to be either dead or bankrupt. Westerners, too, who could claim consular assistance against other forms of extortion, found themselves helpless against the kidnapping routine. In carrying out the abductions, the secret police used agents who were invariably described as bandits: Chinese desperadoes against Chinese victims and White Russian ones against whites. The kidnappers were given the benefit of Japanese secret police protection and were rewarded with a percentage of the ransom money when and if it was paid. In scores of cases it *was* paid and the victims were returned to their homes. They seldom gave their stories to the press because they feared Japanese vengeance.

On August 24, 1933, less than a month after General Hishikari's appointment, the spy service operatives in Harbin struck at the most potentially lucrative kidnap victim in Manchuria, the son of a wealthy Russian Jew named Joseph Kaspé. The elder Kaspé had settled in Harbin after the Russo-Japanese war in 1907. A jeweler by trade, he had started out as a watch repairman and pawnbroker and ended up as one of the richest gem and silver merchants in the Orient. As well as his business, he owned Harbin's main café and Hotel Moderne, and most of the movie houses in North Manchuria. It was said by his detractors that he owed his prosperity to the gratitude of the Soviet Union for his services as a fence for jewels and art objects seized from the homes of White Russian aristocrats during the Russian Revolution. For this alleged traffic in Soviet stolen goods, Kaspé was cordially detested by the White Russians among whom he lived. But so were the rest of Harbin's Jewish community. Anti-Semitism was engrained in White Russian culture, and it had deepened in recent years because many White Russians, being by definition anti-Communists, were also admirers of Adolf Hitler.

The Japanese, too, at this time were beginning to use Jews, along with Masons and Bolsheviks, as bugbears in propaganda. It was a posture which many Westerners thought ludicrous because few Japanese could tell Jew from gentile and there were less than a dozen self-appointed converts to Judaism in all Japan. To the haunted mind of the samurai, however, unfamiliar devils could be as fearful as familiar ones. The Jews of Harbin, most of them virtually stateless and so defenseless, soon learned to their grief that Shinto persecution could be as merciless as Christian. As soon as the Kwantung Army entered Harbin in 1932, it made an agent and collaborator of the local Russian Nazi leader, a hoodlum intellectual by the name of Rodzaevsky who edited a hate sheet called *Nash Put.*

When millionaire Kaspé saw the drift of Japanese political thinking, he put all his properties in the names of his two sons who were both French citizens. From the Japanese point of view it was an insulting gesture and after the make-Manchuria-pay policy came into force in late 1932, the Japanese authorities began to work overtime on schemes for milking Kaspé somehow of his millions. Kaspé himself was not one to be caught unawares. He never left his suite in the Hotel Moderne without a substantial bodyguard.

One of Kaspé's sons, however, was less cautious. He returned to Harbin in the summer of 1933 after graduating from the French Conservatoire de Musique, a talented pianist with high hopes for a concert career. While his father arranged bookings for him in Shanghai and Tokyo he made the most of Harbin night life and often ordered the armed chauffeur, supplied him by his father, to drive down to the gay quarter on the river bank and leave him at the Tatos or Iberia Club where he could find some Chinese sing-song girl, Japanese mama-san, or Russian café chantant.

On the evening of August 24, 1933, when young Semyon Kaspé was escorting home a Miss L. Shapiro, two White Russian fascists in the pay of the Japanese secret police jumped his car, disarmed his chauffeur, and drove the car to the suburbs. There they let out the chauffeur and, after arranging maildrops and phone numbers, released the girl so that she could act as go-between in the ransom negotiations. Her dedicated involvement in the later ins and outs of the case suggest that she either loved young Kaspé deeply or was a paid agent of the secret police. The kidnappers drove Semyon to a hideout in the woods "some 55 versts" or about 36 miles west of Harbin and from there delivered daily phone calls, ransom notes, and ultimatums.

Semyon's father indignantly refused to pay the $100,000 demanded and offered $12,000 instead, to be paid on delivery. After a month of negotia-tion he was delivered a bloody half of one of his son's ears. Either out of obsessive frugality or stubborn courage in the face of intimidation, he still refused to pay. He had interested the French Vice Consul Monsieur Cham-bon in the outrage, and Chambon's agents were working on good leads. Moreover the Japanese secret police commandant himself said that he had all his men at work on the case. Agents stood by at Harbin's central tele-phone exchange to trace ransom calls from the kidnappers, but, according to the Japanese explanation, the artful abductors always put through four calls at once to all four of the monitored numbers, thereby making it im-possible, for technical reasons, to trace the calls.

In October the agents of energetic Vice Consul Chambon captured the youngest of the kidnappers, a teen-age hoodlum called Komisarenko, who confessed the names of his White Russian accomplices. Chambon went to court and pressed charges against the members of the gang. The Japanese secret police seized Komisarenko and took him out of town. They made the mistake of hiding him in an area along the South Manchuria Railway's right of way which fell under the jurisdiction of Japanese railway agents who despised the secret police. Colonel Oi Fukashi in charge of the railway police happened to be a fine unreformed old samurai. Exercising his full powers, he relieved the secret police of Komisarenko and took the young thug into his own custody. The secret police arrested all of Vice Consul Chambon's agents on various trumped-up charges and encouraged fascist Rodzaevsky in his newspaper *Nash Put* to label Frenchman Chambon a Jewish Bolshevik. Colonel Oi brought Komisarenko back to Harbin and had him swear out a formal confession to the native Manchurian police. Foreign newspapers began to take note of the case and cause embarrass-ment.

Kidnapped concert pianist Kaspé was meanwhile dying by inches. His captors starved him, periodically beat him, and began to wrench out the nails from his soft, piano player's hands. At least once the secret police provided vehicles to move the young man and his tormentors to a new hideout. In his last detention place Kaspé lived underground in a pit dug into the half-frozen earth and covered with a lid. Finally on November 28, 1933, Colonel Oi arrested two more of the kidnappers and the gang panicked. One of them made tentative arrangements to return Semyon to his father for $3,000. That same night, in a move modestly described as a "triumphant raid," the secret police descended on the hideout, shot the double dealer, allowed the other guard on duty to escape, and either killed or merely buried the mutilated, gangrenous young pianist. In the days that followed the White Russian members of the gang gave themselves up to the Manchukuoan police.

After several months of questioning and litigation, their trial began before a native Manchukuoan court. It was conducted—with a fine Chinese flair for diplomatic mockery—as a miniature of the trials being conducted in Tokyo for the heroes of 5–15 and the Triple Intrigue. The accused were allowed to make interminable political speeches in their defense. They contended that Kaspé's fist was full of Bolshevik gold and that they had sought to extract it, out of pure selfless patriotism, in order to contribute it to the cause of White Russian partisans operating along the Soviet border.

The Chinese judges listened politely and patiently for two years and then, in 1936, sentenced six of the gang to hang "within three days" and the rest to serve long prison terms. Taken by surprise, the Japanese authorities behind the curtains of Manchukuo's puppet stage were forced to act with awkward abruptness. Two days after the sentence was passed they had both the judge and the lawyers for the prosecution picked up and held for interrogation on suspicion of being "grafters." At the same time, on the appeal of one of the wives of the kidnappers, Kwantung Army Chief of Staff Itagaki ordered a new trial under the political rather than the bandit section of the criminal code—to be conducted by a Japanese court.

In the retrial the Japanese prosecutor spoke eloquently about the extenuating difficulties and pure motives of the "fine young patriots" in the dock and asked lenient sentences for them of no more than ten to fifteen years. The court complied and the prisoners were relieved at their reprieve. Japan, however, was not about to support idle hands in prison which might be useful elsewhere. To the astonishment of the prisoners themselves they were haled back into court a week later and told that they were eligible for amnesty. Ten days later, in consideration of services rendered and promised, they were set free and given jobs with the Special Service Organ in other cities in Manchukuo.

The Harbin *Herald* and the Harbin *Observer* denounced the proceedings as a travesty. Long ailing under oppression, both papers were now closed down and their editors deported. Colonel Oi was recalled to Japan. Vice Consul Chambon was declared *persona non grata* and recalled, to France.[5] As for old man Kaspé, he is said to have gone mad when he saw the exhumed corpse of the son he would not ransom. He lost interest in his financial empire and retired thereafter to oblivion with his French wife. His motion-picture houses were bought up by the Manchuria Motion Picture Association, a monopoly headed by Amakasu Masahiko, the secret police tough who had welcomed Puppet Henry Pu-Yi to Manchuria in 1931 and had, strangled socialist Osugi, his wife, and nephew during the aftermath of the Tokyo Earthquake in 1923.

WAR FOOTING FOR THE NAVY

As the pianist Kaspé lost his fingernails one by one in Manchuria, Hirohito in Tokyo pushed forward with his plans, oblivious of oppression abroad and of opposition at home. He had never felt more buoyant. Midwives and doctors agreed that the child in Empress Nagako's womb was a boy. War Minister Araki had bowed loyally to imperial pressure and for the time being had stilled his partisans' agitation for war with Russia. Hirohito walked Empress Nagako on the beach at the Summer Palace at Hayama and quarreled amiably with chamberlains who protested that walks might not be good for her in her present delicate condition. The Eleven Club held a rousing geisha party for Prince Higashikuni to cheer him on the eve of his departure to the 2d Division in northern Japan.

On August 4, 1933, the Empress's cousin, Navy Chief of Staff Prince Fushimi, began to ask his colleagues in the Navy's bureaucracy to support a change in regulations which would put the Navy on a permanent war footing. Specifically Navy General Staff decisions and orders would no longer have to be cleared with the Navy minister who was a member of the Cabinet but only with the Emperor in the privacy of the Throne Room. The Navy minister, War Minister Araki, and Saionji all protested the change as uncalled for. Hirohito himself asked that a full set of secret position papers be drawn up for his consideration so that he could examine all the implications of the change.

To remind the people that the Army, too, was preparing for emergencies, and that Soviet air bases were not too far away, War Minister Araki had

---

[5] It was French policy at this time to avoid giving any offense to Japan. Ever since the breakdown of the Anglo-Japanese Alliance in the 1920's, the possibility of a Franco-Japanese alliance had seemed attractive to many French statesmen. General Claudel had done his best to emasculate the Lytton Report. And on October 17, 1933, it was a French syndicate, with government blessing, which first broke the League boycott and lent Manchukuo $60 million. The South Manchuria Railroad then spent the money mainly for the development of a port and naval base in Korea. Ultimately, of course, it would be Germany rather than France which Japan would choose as its European ally.

his subordinates institute air raid drills. Starting August 9, announced the military police, Tokyo and other brightly lit cities would observe strict blackout regulations. Everyone was inconvenienced, and the police found themselves both busied and embarrassed by the number of violations. Even from the palace airmen observed a few bright twinkles of defiance. And so, after two gloomy evenings, the drill was dropped without explanation.

On August 16, while still studying the proposed change in naval regulations, Hirohito boarded the battleship *Hiei* for his annual attendance at the Navy's grand maneuvers. His retainers observed his behavior closely for they knew that it would reflect his pleasure or displeasure with the proposed change in the status of the Navy. From the moment he was piped aboard, Hirohito positively beamed. His chief vassals took pains to spread anecdotal evidence of his high spirits. They reported that the next day, during a conversation with the grand chamberlain, the imperial household minister, and the chief aide-de-camp, Hirohito abruptly arose from his deck chair, fell prostrate on a hatch cover, and began to do push-ups. When his courtiers all jumped to their feet, he said, "I am exercising for myself and you three are not, so why don't you continue your conversation without being disturbed?"

Returning to port on August 19, Hirohito entered wholeheartedly into a game of croquet on deck. When his team had won and he was standing by watching the late finishers, he remarked: "My side worked together as a team. We dispersed the enemy's balls. We used billiard techniques. We applied our geometry." It was Hirohito's way of saying that he had liked what he had seen of naval science and discipline. After years of preoccupation with Army matters, the sea breeze and feel of the deck had returned him momentarily to 1921 when he had set out full of youth and adventure for Europe. Plans made then for modernizing the Army and ridding it of feudal clans had been realized. The Army had gone on to put a buffer zone between Japan and the Red menace in the north. Now the time had come to look south and think again in naval terms. Hirohito returned to the grim confines of his moated battlements in Tokyo refreshed and reassured that his reign was going aright.

Hirohito's good spirits were not dampened in the least by Strike-North-Faction attacks against the Navy and against Hirohito's advisors during the weeks that followed. At a meeting with Cabinet ministers on August 30, 1933, he impressed everyone with his "penetrating questions" about the welfare of Japanese colonists in Sakhalien to the north and in Dutch New Guinea far to the south. Chief Aide-de-Camp Honjo, in his diary, expressed "awe that in a mere thirty-three years" Hirohito could have acquired "such a vast store of knowledge and relevant inquiries." What Honjo meant was that he wished Hirohito would think less of Papua and more of his home island, Honshu.

The peasants of Japan, who formed the backbone of the Army, had suffered greatly during the last two years. Villages had lost their best workers to the Army and the munitions factories. Dollar swindle and devaluation had raised the purchase price of all manufactured goods but not the market value of rice and turnips. The depressed American public had almost given up buying Japanese silk. And worst of all, the weather had made for poor harvests for several seasons. Under such circumstances it was difficult for Army politicians like War Minister Araki to preserve discipline in the ranks, much less enthusiasm for naval development.

Day after day Honjo gently, stubbornly sought to dispel the Emperor's euphoria. He observed that Prince Takeda, twenty-four, and Prince Kitashirakawa, twenty-three, had sought honorary memberships in the Tokyo Riding Club and that their applications were being processed slowly instead of being seized upon eagerly. Big Brother Kido, the director of peerage and heraldry, confessed that the "attitude of the other club members" was "bad," and had been bad ever since Prince Higashikuni had joined the club. It was the same way in the club for training Army carrier pigeons which Prince Takeda and Prince Kitashirakawa had already entered.

One day, in his campaign of attrition, Chief Aide-de-Camp Honjo complained to Hirohito that no monument had ever been erected in the palace to commemorate the peasant soldiers who had fallen in the Manchurian campaign and that imperial afternoons away from work, collecting marine biological specimens from a boat on Sagami Bay, were widely regarded in the ranks as callous frivolity. With blithe even temper, Hirohito took Honjo out on the battered old imperial biological yacht, explained to him that there was no money, patriotically speaking, for meaningless monuments, and gave him a lecture on the tides of Sagami Bay. Honjo learned that, if the Emperor had not made his own observations, the hydrographic office of the Navy would not have corrected its charts and some day some Japanese ship would have miscalculated the depth of Sagami Bay. Honjo expressed his admiration for the Emperor's dazzling display of broadmindedness and perception.

On September 21, Hirohito suggested to Chief Aide-de-Camp Honjo that the change in naval staff regulations, which would bring all fleet movements under his exclusive control, had best be kept secret from the reading public except in broad outline. Four days later Hirohito approved the new regulations with the one proviso that they should be set down sharply and simply in writing. He went to some pains to explain his decision to Honjo as follows:

Years ago when Holland was prosperous and strong, the famous Admiral Ruiter defeated the British Navy and was on the point of pursuing the British fleet into the Thames Estuary. But the Dutch Army was in trouble and so, to help the Army, the Navy was called back. Thus Ruiter was frustrated, which led to the decline of the Navy and with it of Holland. So armaments for the

Navy must not be decreased. At the same time an imbalance in national finance must not be created by increasing the mere number of the Navy's sailors. Balanced adjustment is very important.

DECISION TO GO SOUTH

The new status for the Navy was but one part of a package which also included more money for the Navy in the forthcoming budget and official Cabinet sanction for a national Strike-South policy. The Army's tabled recommendation that Russia should be considered enemy number one was entirely forgotten. War Minister Araki fought vainly, through months of subtle but unimportant maneuvering, to have it remembered. By October 1933, however, the rest of the Cabinet had given in to Hirohito's wishes and War Minister Araki was fighting only a delaying action.

At a meeting of the inner Cabinet, on October 11, the foreign minister shrugged hopelessly toward the Army and Navy ministers and declared, "We will expand as far as we can by diplomacy but after that we will have to call on you." Three days later the old man, Prime-Minister-Maker Saionji, expressed a similar feeling of fateful resignation to Big Brother Kido who had come to the seashore in an attempt to improve relations between Saionji and his fellow prince of the ancient Fujiwara clan, Konoye.

"There is no middle way," said Saionji, "between complete military dictatorship and retention of the constitutional system we have. If Konoye is flirting with the former, I shall disappear as a person of the past."

The next day, October 15, Hirohito's Big Brothers—all in their forties now—gathered for a Chinese feast at Konoye's hilltop villa overlooking the ocean in Kamakura and talked for five hours.

Six days later, on October 20, 1933, the ministers of the Cabinet officially put their seals to Hirohito's program. They agreed: "to go as far as possible by diplomacy; . . . to build up as much military strength as possible; . . . to co-operate domestically, ministry with ministry, in order to realize our international goals."

PATRIOTS ON TRIAL

All this had been accomplished while the executioners of Prime Minister Inukai and the 5–15 plot were standing trial and talking reams of newsprint. The trials were potentially explosive because most of the defendants had been partisans of the disgruntled Strike-North Faction. Many of them now distrusted War Minister Araki, the Strike-North leader, however, because they suspected that he had persuaded them to act in the 1932 coup even after he knew it was to be a fake one. Confused by the way in which they had been used, they now allowed themselves to play a role for which they had been perfectly coached by loyal or at least venal police minions of the Throne. Araki could hardly believe it, but the defendants, in their long day in court, incriminated none of their sponsors, neither Lord Privy Seal Makino nor Araki himself. Still more incredible from Araki's point of view, they voiced at tedious length the yearning of the people for domestic reform and Hirohito paid absolutely no attention to it.

The Army court-martial of the eleven military academy cadets who had assisted at the murder of Prime Minister Inukai had opened on July 25, 1933, and closed on September 19. Given every opportunity by the judge to speak their minds, the cadets had strummed on the theme that Japan was a unique society in which the Throne did not exist for the State but the State for the Throne. As one of the shavetails put it: "We demand direct rule by the Emperor. Our focus today is on the imported egotistical notion of popular rights. That is wrong. Manhood suffrage and the grant of social and political rights to the people are a gigantic mistake."

The Navy court-martial for the ten more sophisticated flight officers of the Misty Lagoon had opened on July 24, 1933, and would come to a close on November 9. Their ringleader, Lieutenant Koga, told the court: "The condition of the country is such that it cannot be improved except by shedding blood." His assistant, Ensign Mikami, explained: "Our revolution is intended to bring about . . . harmony between ruler and ruled. . . . As we aim to establish direct imperial rule, we are neither leftists nor rightists." Another of the ensigns asserted: "My life's desire will be fulfilled if a state is established on the principle that the Emperor and his subjects are one." The naval reservist who had fired the first shot at Prime Minister Inukai expressed some slight regret: "I felt sorry but I thought his death unavoidable as he had to be sacrificed at the shrine of national reformation."

The civilian trial of twenty disciples of the Native-Land-Loving Society had commenced on September 26 and would continue until February 3, 1934. Tachibana, the Tolstoyan leader of the Land-Lovers, was allowed to explain himself in a harangue to the court which lasted for six days. "The nation," he said, in the course of his peroration, "must stand on the basis of farming villages. . . . Japan is a debtor nation, yet Tokyo and the cities grow larger year by year. Where does this strength come from? It is clear that if the villages were released from the burden of sustaining the cities, the national power of Japan would increase. At a stroke, we could exclude the influence of the United States from the Pacific, liberate China from the yoke of the war lords, set India free, and enable Germany to rise again. . . . It is necessary to get rid of capitalism in the interests of peace, and the people should oppose capitalism. The defense of Asia must be perfected. . . . The Japanese people must prepare for the day when all the men on the farms will go to the front to fight and the women will take the place of the men."

When the other civilian trial, that of Friar Inoue and his twelve disciples of the Blood Brotherhood, reconvened on March 26, 1934, there was little left to say. "Party politics in Japan," opined Friar Inoue humbly, "are politics of the privileged classes. In Germany, the politics of the right wing are politics of the gods. Party politics should be corrected, and the Emperor should give the final word. . . . I am thinking about the future society but I am not learned and cannot decide such important matters alone."

To these peculiarly Japanese polemics the Japanese people for the most part responded favorably. In particular the ideas of strength emanating from the farms and of religious virtue in direct rule by the Emperor struck responsive chords. A petition asking clemency for the Native-Land-Lovers was signed by 357,000 well-organized patriots. The officers of the various courts received over 110,000 letters in the same vein. Nine men of the town of Niigata chopped off their little fingers and sent them to War Minister Araki in alcohol together with a note saying that the defendants "broke the law but their motives were pure. We are profoundly impressed by their spirit of self-sacrifice." The Osaka Bar Association went so far as to pass a resolution declaring that the assassins, in the deepest sense, had merely acted in self-defense.

At the end of the trials the Army cadets, on September 19, 1933, were given four years in prison and were released for good behavior during the New Year celebrations of 1935. Then they were met at the prison gates by nine limousines and driven to the Double Bridge of the palace to do grateful obeisance. The naval flight officers of the Misty Lagoon, on November 9, 1933, were sentenced to from one to fifteen years, of which only their three ringleaders served more than a few months. The Native-Land-Lovers, sentenced on February 3, 1934, were immediately amnestied and set at liberty by Hirohito on February 17—all but Tachibana, their dangerously articulate leader. The Blood Brothers were sentenced in November 1934 and, except for Friar Inoue and the two who had actually pulled triggers, were amnestied in early 1935.

HOLY BIRTH

By a word from either Araki or Hirohito the trials might have been turned into a spectacle of recrimination between the Strike-North and Strike-South factions. Instead, while Araki watched with amazement, they slid by in months of perfectly disciplined oratory. Araki had hoped that the discontent expressed by the trial defendants over farm and labor conditions might be taken up by editorial writers and street demonstrators and turned into an outcry against Hirohito's policies in general. His hopes were dashed, however, on December 23, 1933, when Empress Nagako gave birth to another child—at long last a son, Crown Prince Akihito.

After the previous accouchement, in 1931, resulting in the birth of Princess Atsuko, Hirohito had grunted and gone out into the garden to collect specimens of moss. Now the cigar-smoking, philosophizing grand chamberlain, Admiral Suzuki Kantaro, burst into Hirohito's modest Western-style study in the Imperial Library and flapped his kimono sleeves like some great bat of good omen.

"It is a boy," he cried. "I saw the honorable signs of manhood myself."

Hirohito arose in rumpled Army uniform from his small, Spartan desk and with a sigh and a smile ordered champagne to flow for the rest of the day for any visiting wellwishers who might need it. Saionji's Secretary-Spy Harada, informed by phone, came over for several glasses and, feeling somewhat tipsy, told Chief Aide-de-Camp Honjo how thankful everyone was that Honjo had made the Army understand and believe in "the Emperor's personal sagacity." The more temperate Kido announced to his diary, "Now, at last, the biggest problem has been solved."

The full significance of the blessed event was admitted two days later on Christmas Day when the Constitutionalist and anti-Constitutionalist parties overcame past differences and held a "purely social" get-together "for the sake of the nation." The birth of the crown prince gave the influence of the Throne a much needed infusion of sentimental popular support, and the two parties amicably agreed, on that December 25, 1933, that there was now no longer any way of standing against the Throne. On December 31 Prince Higashikuni arrived in Tokyo from his command in Sendai, went to the palace to pay his respects to the new-born crown prince, and then let it be known that "it is time for Araki to quit."

Two weeks of bitter infighting followed in which Araki tried at least to appoint his own successor. On January 3, Big Brother Kido and Secretary Harada called on old Saionji and found him exhausted.

Major General Nagata, the first of the Three Crows, at 1st Brigade headquarters in the Tokyo suburbs, collected an unofficial staff and renewed position-paper work on a policy of "first reorganize China, then renovate Japan."

On January 7 Marquis Kido, the ubiquitous Suzuki, and others of the Big Brothers' fraternity gathered by the inconspicuous but slow transportation of private automobile at Prince Konoye's villa in Kamakura. They agreed that, whatever Araki might think, the next war minister had to be an officer who could manipulate the Army-Navy lobby which advocated friendship with China. Specifically they concluded that General Matsui Iwane, the later scapegoat "Butcher of Nanking," could best be led by a certain General Hayashi Senjuro, the man who had loyally sent troops from Korea into Manchuria before receipt of official orders in 1931.

Hirohito made one concession to Araki's sense of morality and personal face. He agreed, both for Araki's and Konoye's political comfort, to proclaim an amnesty for the civilian participants in the carefully aborted 5–15 coup d'etat which had killed Prime Minister Inukai. The amnesty would be given to the nation as a token of imperial magnanimity on the occasion of the birth of the crown prince.

"We will leave out thieves, murderers, and those who have committed lèse majesté," explained Prime Minister Saito to the Throne, "but the amnesty will bring commutation of sentence to the Blood Brotherhood and the men of 5–15."

Hirohito replied, "The dignity of the law must not be tarnished, but I think, within those limits, an amnesty is permissible."

The amnesty enabled Araki to go in peace and honor without toppling the entire Cabinet. It satisfied his private commitment to partisans who had gone to prison for him after the murderous 5–15 coup. And resignation would now satisfy his public commitment to believers in domestic reform and the Strike North.

Accordingly, on the next day, January 16, Araki sequestered himself in the hospital at the Military Medical School and announced himself stricken with pneumonia. He summoned to his bedside the generals, colonels, and majors of his faction and told them one by one that he intended to resign, at his doctor's suggestion, if a suitable replacement could be found for him. For the next five days he struggled to have General Mazaki, his blunt honest henchman, formerly vice chief of staff, put in his place. Hirohito said, however, that Mazaki had personality problems. And Prince Kanin, the sixty-eight-year-old chief of the Army General Staff, the last surviving brother of Prince Asahiko who had counseled Emperor Komei at Perry's coming eighty years earlier, emerged briefly from his veils to take personal responsibility for blackballing Mazaki.

Araki resigned the war ministership on January 22, 1934, and his loyal lieutenant, General Mazaki, was placated with the nominally important but substantially uninfluential post of inspector general of military education. The Prayer Meeting Plot had reached its benedictus. The strategic concept of a Strike North to meet the supposed international crisis of 1936 had passed behind a cloud of imperial frowns. The nation would now lapse into two years of full peace and hectic hard work. The mass of the people might suppress doubts; the peasants and privates might toil in positive resentment; but the majority of the Army's officer corps had retired to their corner to await fresh tocsins and another round before Araki would finally be counted out.

ZERO

Given a free hand to prepare for a Strike South, Hirohito acted first to create a good naval airplane. Up to now the only hot military planes made in Japan had been pieced together one by one, like racing cars, out of components which were largely imported. In January 1934, when Araki's retirement was imminent, the members of the Eleven Club made a personal effort to free the air force from dependence on Western parts and to develop consistent Japanese types of planes, designed domestically to meet specific Japanese requirements. On January 12 and again on February 9 and 13,

Prince Higashikuni, Big Brother Kido, and Secretary-Spy Harada met with executives of aircraft plants and with officers of the two air force head-quarters to found a joint Army-Navy-Tokyo Imperial University Aviation Institute. It came into being a few months later under the direction of Kido's brother, the aeronautic engineer Wada Koroku (who was Colonel Charles Lindbergh's friend), and of seventy-seven-year-old physics professor Tanakadate Aikitsu, lecturer on aviation to the Emperor. The institute at once procured the services of the British Sopwith company's talented designer, Herbert Smith, who was celebrated for his unstable but highly maneuverable Sopwith Camel fighter of World War I fame. In a year, with the help of Smith and a team at Mitsubishi, the experts at the institute had test-flown a superb Japanese fighter plane, the A5M, forerunner of the famous Zero which would terrorize Allied Hawk and Buffalo pilots in the opening months of World War II.

LET THEM EAT CAKE

On February 8, 1934, Chief Aide-de-Camp Honjo tried to tell Emperor Hirohito that the Strike-North Faction was still alive and that there was still much political unrest in the Army. Hirohito asked how it was that Army men, who were pledged to take orders—particularly men of a faction which professed a belief in direct rule by the Emperor—could think to cause unrest or have an interest at all in politics. Honjo replied that some interest in politics was desirable in an officer because it was his duty to inculcate his peasant soldiery with political morals and patriotism.

Hirohito understood at once where the conversation was heading—to another lecture on the plight of the farmers. It had been a disastrous year agriculturally. The northern part of Japan, from which the Army drew its stoutest recruits, was being ravaged by one of the worst famines in history. The old nineteenth century practice of farmers selling their daughters had come back into fashion. In 1932, the number of girls from the farms of the north bound over under contract to Tokyo labor heelers had been 12,108. In 1933 the number had more than quadrupled to 58,173. Of these 19,244 had been indentured as nursemaids; 17,260 as factory hands; 5,952 as bar girls; 5,729 as odd-jobbists; 4,512 as common prostitutes; 3,271 as cabaret hostesses; and only 2,196 of the best looking for relatively honorable service as apprentice geisha. Hirohito had sent chamberlains to inspect the stricken farm areas and offer words of consolation. He had helped to apply pressure to the Mitsui cartel to set up a $10 million philanthropic fund for the re-education of dispossessed peasants. But he had done nothing material on his own behalf or that of the government to alleviate the farmers' lot.

To Honjo, Hirohito said: "It cannot be helped that officers, especially the noncoms who are closest to the men, should feel some concern and sympathy for the miserable conditions in farming villages. On the other hand, if in so doing their interest becomes excessive, it is harmful."

"I do not mean," replied Honjo, "that they should ever engage in political activity or have any taste for it. Indeed they should stop short of feeling any interest beyond what is required of them in the line of duty."

"Although one must naturally sympathize with the troubled condition of the farm villages," persisted the Emperor, "nevertheless the peasants have their own joy in the heaven of the land, and it is not to be said that that a man of noble rank is always invariably happy. I, for instance, in visiting Europe, found the feeling of freedom there a great change for me. As long I was able to enjoy it, it put me in a most pleasant frame of mind. It is presumptuous to speak of the former Emperor, but I recall that when my father was still a prince, he was extremely vigorous and healthy, and on visits to the villas of his aunts he was carefree and agile. Then after he ascended the throne everything became narrow and tight for him. As his physique was by nature frail, he finally fell sick. Believe me, it was an awesome thing to see. Reflecting on his example, the farmers should not talk on and on about the unpleasant aspects of their life but should concentrate rather on the enjoyment of nature around them. In sum, it should be emphasized in the guidance of peasants that a man must rely on moral effort and not dwell purely on the legality or logic of his lot."

"Full of awe and trepidation" at the Emperor's words of wisdom, Honjo, by his own account, then reminded Hirohito that in the case of the extremely poor, some concern for material welfare could not be overlooked in the course of giving the nation moral guidance.

18

ORGAN OR GOD?

(1934–1935)

UNCTION AND CONSOLIDATION

The ouster of the Strike-North Faction's General Araki from the war ministership ushered in a two-year period of quiet domestic struggle in which Hirohito consolidated his position and faced a growing swell of passive mass resistance. On the one hand the people began to feel the heel of police state tyranny and to appreciate that Japan was headed on a dangerous course. On the other hand Hirohito's inner circle of Big-Brother advisors, the friends and classmates of his uncles—now all men in their mid-forties—began to replace the elders of Japan, the carry-overs from Emperor Meiji's time, in positions of public responsibility. Concurrently the armament programs of the late 1920's and early 1930's neared completion and the control of Japan's modernized armed services passed from popular demagogic leaders to professional disciplinarians and technocrats.

A month after Strike-North War Minister Araki had fallen from power, Hirohito held a three-day celebration in the palace in honor of his two-month-old son, Crown Prince Akihito. On the first day, February 23, 1934, imperial princes and princesses, Cabinet ministers and foreign ambassadors in Tokyo all sat down at one big table to a luncheon with the Emperor and Empress. American Ambassador Grew described the occasion as "magnificent." The food and wines were delicious. The servants bowed much lower than in Europe. An orchestra played softly from behind gold screens in front of which were arrayed artful displays of hothouse flowers and stunted pine trees. Mrs. Grew sat between two princes of the blood. Crimson saké cups embossed with the imperial crest in gold and small silver samurai helmets were presented to each guest. In an audience afterwards, Ambassador Grew found the Emperor "exceedingly cordial" and the Empress "beaming."

Not one of the Court diarists who were intimates of Hirohito jotted down any mention of this festivity. Their reality was the Hirohito in Army uniform, hunched over his desk in the Imperial Library. After Araki's ouster they were busy insinuating young men affiliated with the Eleven Club into all the key positions of the Japanese government; busy, too, trying to pacify the Strike-North Faction and keep it quiet. Ambassador Grew shrewdly guessed that there was far more afoot than met his eye and that "the great majority" of Japanese, themselves, were "astonishingly capable of really fooling themselves." Grew judged that the new Japanese foreign minister might be sincere and then again that his "moderation" might be "one of manner and strategy rather than substance." Grew concluded:

We shall sooner or later be seriously concerned as to whether the new generation will acquit itself successfuly of the gigantic task to which the nation seems committed, because American and Japanese policy in the Far East will directly conflict—unless someone puts the helm over hard.

In giving up the war ministership in January 1934, General Araki had succeeded in having the number-two leader of the Strike-North Faction, the blunt, honest General Mazaki, appointed to the post of inspector general of military education. The inspector general, along with the war minister and chief of staff, was considered one of the Big Three of the Army. He was, however, the least powerful of the Big Three and the one who had least personal business with Hirohito.

As a further gesture to save the face of the Strike-North Faction, Hirohito accepted as the new war minister a man who was known to be one of General Mazaki's best friends. This was General Hayashi Senjuro, the obedient commander who had bravely ordered his men to cross the Manchurian frontier without official sanction during the 1931 take-over of Mukden. Now, on assuming office, Hayashi quickly revealed that his loyalty to the Throne was far more important to him than old friendships. He began his term of office by issuing a blanket prohibition against use of the Strike-North slogan "Crisis of 1936" in all Army publications and speeches. He followed by purging Strike-Northists from the staff of the Kwantung Army and from the high command of the secret police.

Hayashi's purge and prohibition brought the secret struggle between Strike-North and Strike-South factions to the attention of the newspaper-reading public for the first time. As usual in that era, the real issues at stake were heavily veiled in the press accounts. The names of the Strike-North and Strike-South factions, in use previously only by top-level strategists and bureaucrats, were changed. The Strike-North Faction, of which the Emperor disapproved, was publicized as the Imperial Way Group. The Strike-South Faction, of which the Emperor was the guiding light, came out as the Control Clique—a name that implied manipulation of the Throne.

It would have been taboo, of course, for either faction to claim the personal backing of the Emperor. Instead the Imperial Way Group and its naval affiliate, the Fleet Faction, associated themselves with conservative samurai ideals, reliance upon force of numbers in the armed services, abhorrence of the regicidal creed of Bolshevism abroad, and a co-operative type of decentralized socialism at home. The Control Clique and its following in the Naval Air Force associated themselves with military mechanization, strict discipline, and a fascistic type of centralized national socialism.

In March 1934 Hirohito gave a hint as to which type of socialism he preferred by dispatching Empress Nagako's senior cousin, his own childhood playmate and near twin, Prince Kaya, on a six-month tour of observation in Europe. Major Kaya and his princess-wife, a niece of Hirohito's mother, scurried through most of the European capitals and then settled down to be wooed for the bulk of their holiday in Hitler's Berlin. There they witnessed one of the early meetings between Hitler and Mussolini, and Prince Kaya told the press, "I was deeply moved to see those two heroes taking a motorboat ride together."

A NOT-SO-MEDIEVAL SCANDAL

Almost immediately after War Minister Hayashi had commenced his regime, Constitutionalist party politicians, working under the tired but approving eyes of old Prince Saionji, began searching for an Achilles' heel in Hirohito's new body politic. They found one in the person of Commerce and Industry Minister Nakajima Kumakichi, a confidant of the Throne who had once been secretary for Emperor Taisho's favorite, Prime Minister Katsura. The Constitutionalists began by accusing Commerce Minister Nakajima of having written an appreciation of the shogun who had deposed the true emperors of the southern dynasty in the fourteenth century. Although Hirohito came of the northern dynasty and occupied the Throne because of this shogun's king-making, it was official doctrine that the shogun had been a traitor. The attack embarrassed Hirohito and brought him out in defense of Commerce Minister Nakajima. To and through his courtiers, Hirohito explained that northern and southern dynasties were both of the same blood and had had equal rights to the Throne.

As soon as Hirohito committed himself in defense of Nakajima, Saionji's cunning political henchmen leveled a more serious charge. They revealed that Nakajima was involved in a major stock swindle and had made millions on the market by manipulating government holdings of the Teikoku Rayon Company. What was more, the swindle had been devised in the geisha house of Child of the Carp, the former mistress of Emperor Taisho's favorite, Katsura. Not only was Katsura's former secretary, Commerce Minister Nakajima, involved in it, but also Katsura's natural son, Big Brother Colonel Marquis Inoue Saburo, who had brought the ubiquitous Suzuki into Hirohito's circle. As a result of the scandal Commerce Minister

Nakajima had to resign his portfolio in April 1934, Saito his prime ministership in July, and Big Brother Marquis Inoue his colonel's commission in August.

As soon as the attack on Commerce Minister Nakajima looked as if it would be effective, old Saionji paid an unexpected visit to Tokyo. On May 9, 1934, he called at the palace to pay his belated respects to the infant crown prince and to meet briefly with Hirohito for the first time in almost two years. The encounter took place over tea and cookies in the crowded chamberlains' common room. A dozen courtiers' ears were bent to catch every nuance of the conversation.

"Your Majesty," observed the eighty-four-year-old Saionji, lighting one of his favorite imported Pall Malls, "does not smoke or drink saké at all."

"That's right," replied Hirohito. "When I was four or five years old, I was made drunk by saké and since then I have never liked the stuff."

"Your Majesty means to set a good example for his subjects in a natural manner without having to say a single word," noted Saionji dryly, before the congregated chamberlains. "But it makes for a subtle relationship with the people. Perhaps it would be better to express the virtues of the Throne in some more expansive way."

Chief Aide-de-Camp Honjo, who stood by, noted in his diary that Saionji's manner, as he delivered his remarks, "seemed full of loyalty and respect."

A SECOND NAVAL CABINET

Two weeks later, on May 23, 1934, Baron Harada, the secretary-spy assigned to Saionji, dined with Big Brother Marquis Kido, the secretary to the lord privy seal. The two young intimates of the Throne admitted to one another that the Nakajima scandal had emasculated the effectiveness of Prime Minister Saito. A new government would have to be organized which paid a nod to old Saionji's prejudices. Kido and Harada agreed that the best next prime minister would be another admiral, Okada Keisuke, a well-spoken former Navy minister with a long career in unconventional weapons development and an old friendship with Saionji. For more than a month after Kido and Harada had reached this understanding, the Saito Cabinet died a lingering death while the ramifications of the Teikoku Rayon case curled over the toes of almost every government minister.

When the Cabinet finally resigned *en bloc* on July 4, 1934, old Saionji, the official prime-minister-maker, had already been persuaded to accept the Big Brothers' choice and recommend Admiral Okada to the Throne as the next head of state. His Secretary-Spy Harada had made it clear to him that the only alternative would be an imperial Cabinet headed by one of Hirohito's uncles or brothers. So sure was Hirohito of the arrangements which had been made that he first summoned his political advisor, the nervous, soft-spoken Lord Privy Seal Count Makino, and said to him, "Okada will

suggest his own Cabinet members and by then it will be impolite to comment on them, so please take care now to keep out people who will cause
problems."

Only then, secondarily, did Hirohito summon Saionji to come to Tokyo
and select a prime minister. The message to Saionji was carried by the
cigar-smoking Taoist, Grand Chamberlain Suzuki. In it Hirohito wrote,
"There is no need to ask you, Prince Saionji, to abide by the Constitution
when you arrange the new Cabinet, but remember also that you must not
achieve an unfavorable result."

Saionji arrived in Tokyo the next day, made a perfunctory investigation
of the political circumstances, and, in a frigid audience with Hirohito that
lasted less than five minutes, rubber-stamped the arrangements which had
already been made. A friend said to Saionji afterwards, "You have covered
a boil with ointment because you are afraid of drastic operations. It may
be all right for the time being, but I am afraid that in the long run the
boil will burst."

As soon as the Okada Cabinet took office, Hirohito required the new
prime minister to reratify the decision passed seven months earlier by the
Inner Cabinet—the prime, foreign, war, navy, and finance ministers—to
expand south as far as possible by diplomacy and then to rely on force of
arms. In asking for this reaffirmation, Hirohito wanted the Navy to agree
specifically to certain goals it must pursue. The naval Strike-North group,
the Fleet Faction, had used the Strike-South decision as an excuse for
demanding more capital ships and an increase in naval manpower. Hirohito wished it clearly understood that naval expenditures should be entirely
dedicated to real aggressive striking power rather than showy dreadnoughts
and masses of samurai in sailor suits.

The officers of the Naval General Staff found themselves in a difficult
position, for in compromising with the Fleet Faction they had already
allowed keels to be laid for ships which did not fit perfectly into the Emperor's plans. Hirohito wished to keep international naval limitations in
force as long as possible as a cover for the building of the Japanese Naval
Air Force. The ships under construction could not all be launched on
schedule in 1937—at least not legally—unless Japan in late 1934 gave a
year's notice to other nations that it would cease to abide by naval limitations after 1936.

To carry out the contemplated Strike South toward the riches of the
Indies, the Naval General Staff officers sincerely believed that they needed
the ships which they had planned. Hirohito suspected them of sympa-
thizing with the Strike-North Fleet Faction and of trying to deceive him.
To disabuse him they wrote a stack of position papers and entrusted them
to Empress Nagako's cousin, Admiral Prince Fushimi, the chief of the
Naval General Staff. Fushimi called at the palace impromptu on July 12,
1934, in order to present the Navy's case. Hirohito had been thinking of
other matters and found the visit an intrusion. He and Fushimi exchanged

hot words. Fushimi slapped down the sheaf of position papers on Hiro-hito's desk, told him to read and consider them, and then stormed from the palace. Hirohito, in anger, sent an aide-de-camp after him to give back the bundle of position papers unopened.

Then, for the next week, Hirohito reconsidered his position, cross-questioned his naval aides, and saw that he had been wrong. On July 17, squirming a little, he sighed to Prime Minister Admiral Okada, "If the treaty must be abrogated, how about handling the negotiations so that France will bear the brunt of the criticism?"

Hirohito had forehandedly appointed the chief Japanese delegate to the 1934 naval disarmament conference eight months earlier, in November 1933. He had chosen fifty-year-old Vice Admiral Yamamoto, the future architect of the daring raid on Pearl Harbor. Yamamoto had been detached full time since February 1934 to study the problems of the forthcoming conference, and it was his opinion that Japan's best weapon in the negotiations would be one he had used earlier, in 1929, during his unofficial bargaining with President Hoover. Why not disarm the disarmament conference by offering, on Japan's part, to abolish all such offensive vessels as aircraft carriers? Since there were few "stationary aircraft carriers"—few islands—in the California half of the Pacific, the proposal might force the United States to take upon herself the responsibility for abrogating the limitations treaty.

On July 21, nine days after his spat with Cousin Fushimi, Hirohito gave an audience to the Japanese ambassador to the United States, who was home for rebriefing. The ambassador told him that the United States took a hostile legalistic position toward Japan's aspirations but could still be managed for several more years by appropriate short-term political gestures. Hirohito asked the ambassador's opinion of Yamamoto's aircraft-carrier stratagem and the ambassador endorsed it enthusiastically.

SHEDDING LIMITATIONS

A month later, on August 24, Hirohito personally dictated to the Navy minister an outline of the instructions which he wished Yamamoto to carry with him to the limitations conference. On September 6, Hirohito approved the instructions as they had been drafted for the Cabinet. On September 11, Hirohito sanctioned the final draft of the instructions passed by the Cabinet.

Yamamoto set out on his mission a week later. The conference, once again, was to be held in London, and once again Yamamoto traveled by way of the United States. Crossing the Pacific he stayed in his cabin and played poker. Crossing the continent, he stayed in a locked compartment on the train. General Billy Mitchell was then making headlines with his demands that the United States equip herself with an air force for ultimate use against Japan. Newsmen pestered Yamamoto's aides for an interview.

Finally Yamamoto held one press conference. "I have never thought of America as a potential enemy," he declared in Japanese, "and the naval plans of Japan have never included the possibility of an American-Japanese war." American editorial writers applauded his calm good sense and branded Mitchell an alarmist. Refusing to say more on the grounds that he could not speak English, Harvard graduate Yamamoto sailed for England on the *Berengaria*. The day he arrived in Southampton he abruptly called a press conference and gave British reporters a frontpage story. "Japan," he said in his best New England accent, "can no longer submit to the ratio system. There is no possibility of compromise by my government on that point."

That same day in Tokyo—October 16, 1934—Hirohito authorized a telegram to be sent to Yamamoto instructing him to break off discussion and announce abrogation of the treaty "at the earliest convenient moment in the negotiations." Time was important because the treaty had to be abrogated by December 31 if Japan was to be allowed legally to launch the ships she was already building. Throughout November, Yamamoto held his carte blanche from the Throne close to his chest and did his utmost to seem earnest and likeable. Admiral Chatfield, the British Lord of the Admiralty, realized that Japan did not want to take responsibility for aborting the conference and brought pressure to bear on U.S. colleagues to be conciliatory. The American delegates complained that they represented a navy which had to be split between two oceans and that they could not, therefore, accept a total fleet strength exactly equal to Japan's. Yamamoto insisted on perfect parity. "I am smaller than you," he said at a dinner party, "but you do not insist that I eat three fifths of the food on my plate. You allow me to eat as much as I need."

Finally in early December, as time ran out, Yamamoto made his dramatic proposal to abolish aircraft carriers. Admiral Chatfield sounded out the U.S. delegates and found that they were willing to discuss absolute parity if all capital ships were abolished. As indication of good faith, the U.S. delegation canceled its bookings home and offered to stay on in London indefinitely for further unscheduled weeks of conversation. The British vied with the Japanese in pacifism by offering to give up a third of their destroyer tonnage. Poker player Yamamoto realized that his bluff was being called and raised. If the Western nations agreed to give up building capital ships, they might begin to spend their naval funds on the unconventional weapons—the one-man submarines and dive and torpedo bombers—in which Yamamoto saw the victories of the future. Much embarrassed, Yamamoto had his palace advisor and traveling companion, the father-in-law of Hirohito's brother Prince Chichibu, cable home for further instructions.

After consulting with Hirohito, Prime Minister Okada penned a long, noncommittal reply to Yamamoto's query, informing him that domestic politics were "extremely well in hand" and that therefore no repercussions at home need be considered in dealing with the British peace offensive. Yamamoto mulled this reply for twenty-four hours, then returned to the conference table with a fresh attitude and a suddenly hard concern for technical details. The American delegates responded in kind by booking passage home on a ship sailing December 29.

The American date of departure was an awkward one. Yamamoto did not wish, after his protestations, to announce abrogation of the limitations treaty while there was still any possibility that he might have to meet face to face with his opposite numbers from the United States. At the same time, abrogation must be announced before December 31. Yamamoto cabled home asking that notification of abrogation be postponed until the last minute. After consultation with the palace and with the Japanese ambassador in Washington, the Navy minister agreed that abrogation should be announced to the U.S. State Department on Saturday, December 29, a few minutes before commencement of the American New Year holiday. The plan worked to split-second perfection. The State Department received the notice of abrogation before it closed its doors, and Yamamoto was just able to see off the American delegation from Southampton before news came from Washington that abrogation had been declared. It was a close call in timing and one that would be re-enacted—unsuccessfully—seven years later when Japan sought to declare war with technical propriety a few seconds before Yamamoto's attack on Pearl Harbor.

DOMESTIC DISCIPLINE

During Yamamoto's abrogation of naval limitations—a challenge, incidentally, which failed to make the complacent United States build even her quota of naval vessels—Emperor Hirohito back in the palace had been seeking fresh ways of controlling the Strike-North-minded ranks of the Japanese Army. He had found a new Army leader in Lieutenant General Count Terauchi Hisaichi, an in-law of Secretary to the Lord Privy Seal Big Brother Marquis Kido. Terauchi was the son of one of Emperor Meiji's oligarch-generals, a dedicated believer in the Strike South, and the future World War II commander-in-chief for all of Southeast Asia.

In the summer of 1934 Terauchi founded a stern disciplinarian faction in the Army officer corps which was known as the Army Purification Movement. It stood for nonintervention in politics and strict obedience to orders. In August 1934, when Yamamoto was getting his instructions for the naval conference in London, Hirohito approved a set of summer repostings which greatly diminished the Strike-North Faction's influence at key desks and garrison outposts. At the same time Hirohito dispatched purification leader Terauchi to organize provisional Strike-South preparations on the island of Taiwan. As Terauchi set out on his mission, he told well-wishers, "The problem of the Army still remains that of having no work to do."

Two months later, from October 1 to October 18, 1934, the senior warrior of the imperial family, Prince Kanin, visited Terauchi's command in Taiwan and approved plans for setting up a top-secret intelligence organization there, recruited largely from civilian sources, which would begin to collect data from Japanese commercial travelers and emigrants about Malaya, Luzon, Java, and other points south. Under the name of the Southward Movement Society, the organization would later be funded publicly with money voted in the Diet. In late 1940, it would provide the maps and facts for the staff officers who drew up the operational plans for the conquest of Malaya and the Philippines.

To Yamamoto's efforts in London and Terauchi's in Taiwan, Hirohito, during September 1934, added a reorganization in Manchuria. This Manchukuo Structure Plan formalized the malpractices already in use in Manchuria by bringing them all under the jurisdiction of a single organization loyal to the Emperor, the secret police. The first of the Three Crows of Baden-Baden, Major General Nagata Tetsuzan, surprised his intimates by coming out with members of the Strike-North Faction in opposition to the structure bill. Nagata insisted—pretense be damned—that Manchuria should be honestly annexed and given a decent administration such as it would enjoy if it were a part of the Empire and not merely a phony autonomous buffer zone. Nagata was defeated in his stand, and other members of Hirohito's cabal suggested in his defense that he had acted under the compulsion of blackmail. Retired War Minister Araki had possession of the plan—the "novel"—which Nagata had drawn up for the March Plot in 1931. Nagata was, therefore, subject to blackmail, but whether he resisted the Manchukuo Structure Plan because of political or conscientious pressure remained a moot point. Hirohito himself was not sure of the truth and thereafter dealt with Nagata cautiously.

No sooner had the Manchukuoan structure bill passed its hurdles than the Army publicity squad completed a project begun by its former director, the ubiquitous Suzuki Tei-ichi, and came out on October 1, 1934, with a booklet entitled "The True Meaning of National Strength and Proposals for Building It." Prepublication copies, containing return postcards for comment and criticism, were sent out to all leaders of the Army bureaucracy including the aides-de-camp at Court. Hirohito had glanced through the text and passed on it even earlier.

The booklet began with the words: "War is the father of creation and the mother of culture." It was a phrase brought back from Mussolini's Italy by a former attaché in Rome and aide-de-camp in the palace. The booklet went on in detail to explain what the slogan, "National Defense for Total War," would mean as distinct from Araki's slogan, "Crisis of 1936." Japan was a small backward nation in a commanding position. If she were to dominate Asia, every aspect of national life from the lowliest newspaper article to the mightiest industrial enterprise would have to come under "national defense discipline." The whole people must purge itself of Western individualism and work together for the glorious Armageddon ahead.

Business leaders were naturally alarmed by this pronouncement, and War Minister Hayashi at a get-together on November 14 had to assure them in person that construction of the defense state would be gradual and that their vested interests would not be disregarded.

REBUFF ON MANEUVERS

On November 10, 1934, Hirohito went off into the rugged Gunma alps to attend the Army's annual grand maneuvers. All seemed well. The purge of the Army and building program of the Navy seemed settled. Hirohito did honor to the Imperial Guards Division by bivouacking with their commander, his uncle, Lieutenant General Prince Asaka, who would later rape Nanking.

However, the Strike-North Faction had an unpleasant surprise in store. The maneuvers were meant to demonstrate how Japanese forces would deal with a hypothetical attack by Soviet forces in Manchuria. This they failed to do because the "Army of the West," commanded by the former war minister, General Araki, and staff-officered by the second of the Three Crows, the brilliant, dissident Major General Obata, entirely rearranged itself on the opening night of the big show and by dint of forced marches surprised the "Army of the East" at the outset. In the two days that followed, the aristocratic "Eastern" General, Abe Nobuyuki, continued to be outwitted and outmaneuvered by the mock-Russian forces of Araki and Obata. At the close of the exercise Abe's "Eastern Army" had been reduced to scattered pockets. The Strike-North Faction had won a battle where it most counted—on the battlefield. Hirohito could see what the advice of aristocratic generals might lead to, and the men in the ranks had tangible evidence that preparations against Russia must not be suspended.

On November 15, the day after the Strike-North Faction's triumph at the maneuvers, several young officers broke into War Minister Hayashi's residence, seized one of his aides, and warned that if national policy were not redirected there would be, finally, a genuine Army coup d'etat in Japan. The young troublemakers belonged to a sub-faction of Araki's Strike-North following which believed that domestic reform must take precedence over foreign involvements, whether to the north or the south. Some of them had been parties to the earlier break-in at the war minister's residence, when, after the assassination of Prime Minister Inukai in May 1932, they had sought to prevent War Minister Araki from aborting the planned 5–15 coup d'etat. Now, in 1934, they once again returned to their billets in peace. No disciplinary action was taken against them because they knew far more than could be told publicly about the Army-palace plots of 1931 and 1932.

The tension generated by these latest Strike-North stratagems was indirectly revealed the next day, November 16, 1934, in "an unpleasant incident" which occurred during an official inspection by Hirohito of two schools in Nagano prefecture near the alpine site of the just completed maneuvers. First Hirohito was to visit Nagano Middle School, then the Nagano Higher Technical High School. On the way the security policeman who led the imperial cavalcade took the wrong road by accident and brought the Emperor to the technical school first. Being caught unprepared, the school faculty was embarrassed and Minister of Education Matsuda was not there to greet the Emperor. Hirohito was visibly put out by the delay, and a few minutes later the policeman in charge of guidance committed suicide. Then the Emperor hastily said, in a voice which could be heard by all around him: "Did you change the schedule? It is all right but it may disturb the school."

"Such a generous mind!" concluded Chief Aide-de-Camp Honjo in his diary account.[1]

THE MILITARY ACADEMY PLOT

On November 20, 1934, shortly after Hirohito's return from the maneuvers to Tokyo, a plot came to light at the military academy which discredited the Strike-North Faction in general and in particular the young domestic reformers who had broken in to the war minister's residence five days earlier.

The plot was reported to the palace by Major General Yamashita Tomoyuki, the strategic genius and "Tiger of Malaya" who would later, in 1942, capture the supposedly impregnable British fortress of Singapore. Yamashita had been assigned since August by one of Hirohito's aides-de-camp to establish an undercover network in Araki's Strike-North circles. One of Yamashita's agents was a thirty-one-year-old captain named Tsuji Masanobu who would later serve as Yamashita's chief staff officer during the Singapore campaign. Brilliant, fanatic, colorful, and intensely puritanic, Tsuji would become famous during the war with China for going out at night in the streets of Shanghai with a lighted faggot in hand and burning down brothels which were supposed to be off-limits to Japanese troops. At war's end in 1945 he donned the clothes of a Buddhist priest and walked home "underground" from Burma. He resurfaced in Tokyo as an author in 1949, was elected to the Diet in 1952, and in 1958, when he was fifty-five and the United States had become involved in Vietnam, disappeared without trace in Hanoi.

Major General Tiger Yamashita had insinuated Captain Tsuji into the military academy as the morals instructor for a dissident company of cadets there. In line of duty Tsuji had learned that some of his cadets were

[1] A few days later, on November 23, 1934, Honjo wrote: "Today the Emperor officiated at the Harvest Festival. Last night he changed his underraiment and did not go to the Imperial bedchamber but slept instead on a couch outside his office. He is always extremely careful, I am told, on this particular point. About dawn he arose and sat down, solemn and motionless, for two hours of meditation."

in touch with the group of young domestic reformers in the officer corps who perennially broke into the war minister's residence. The young reformers, in fact, had asked the cadets to take part in an armed uprising intended to open Hirohito's eyes and persuade him to "renovate the nation." Morals instructor Captain Tsuji persuaded his charges to take no part in the plan. He warned them that they were being incited by mere talkers who had been involved in several fake coups already and would never carry out anything.

In the course of his counseling Tsuji learned that one of the officers who had tempted his cadets was a special student at the Army Staff College who had assisted Major General Obata, the second of the Three Crows, in drafting the brilliant plan which had confounded all at the Army grand maneuvers. This was information of value, for it implicated the top brass of the Strike-North Faction with the sedition at the military academy. At the request of Major General Yamashita, Tsuji reported it to his friendly neighborhood secret police contact, who happened to be Captain Tsukamoto Makoto, the later watchdog of the fake coup in the palace on the night of August 14, 1945.

At 2 A.M. on November 20, 1934, morals instructor Tsuji and secret policeman Tsukamoto called at the official residence of the vice minister of war and roused him from bed to tell him their story. The vice minister, Lieutenant General Hashimoto Toranosuke, was one of the few partisans of the Strike-North Faction who was venal enough to make a deal with. He had been secret police commandant in Manchuria from August 1932 to August 1933 and was known to love money. Tsuji and Tsukamoto showed him an operations plan for the seizure of Tokyo which they told him had been proposed to the innocent cadets at the academy by the eager young reformers in General Araki's following of staff officers. After several hours of talk, Vice War Minister Hashimoto agreed to have three of the ringleading troublemakers kept under arrest in their quarters for the next three months.

During the three months in which the activists were detained, the reputed Strike-North plan for rebellion was bruited about Tokyo and used effectively to divide the Strike-North Faction and prevent it from exercising the influence it had won at the grand maneuvers. At least in part the plan was a forgery, put on paper by Tsuji and Tsukamoto. But having been forced to take the blame for it, the young Strike-North reformers finally adopted it as their own. And when they rose in insurrection over a year later they took with them, regiment by regiment and company by company, the units stipulated in the plan.

The plan included an excellent little list of a dozen palace advisors who were deemed worthy of assassination. In the event, fifteen months later, the most culpable villains on the list would escape unharmed, but during the interval, from November 1934 to February 1936, all men of influence in Japan walked a gossamer span of mounting tension and intrigue.

BETRAYING CHIANG KAI-SHEK

While the inciters of the Military Academy Plot were restricted to quarters, Hirohito pressed forward, ignoring all opposition. On December 7, 1934—seven years before Pearl Harbor and seven years after Chiang Kai-shek's last visit to Tokyo—Hirohito decided to turn his back on Chiang, to stand by no longer while Chiang attempted to unify classical China, and finally to take for Japan more than the outer Chinese provinces of Manchuria and Mongolia which had been stipulated in Japan's early bargains with Chiang and Sun Yat-sen. Specifically, on that fine winter Friday, Hirohito approved a resolution of the Inner Cabinet: "For the time being it is desirable to reduce to a minimum the influence of the Nanking government on the regimes in north China." A few days later the foreign minister informed Prime-Minister-Maker Saionji that a power play could be expected in north China the following spring.

Japanese moderates registered their disapproval of Hirohito's decision in their usual discreet ways. For instance, on December 30, 1934, the Supreme Court judge who was conducting the preliminary hearings in chambers for the pilgrims who had met at Meiji Shrine a year and a half earlier for Prince Higashikuni's Prayer Meeting Plot came in some bemusement to old Saionji's Secretary-Spy Harada and protested that it would be absolutely impossible ever to stage a public trial of the case. "Why!" he exclaimed, "names of the imperial family appear constantly . . . not only Prince Higashikuni's but Prince Chichibu's and Prince Fushimi's as well."

The most effective opposition to Hirohito's latest step forward was put up by the politicians of the Constitutionalist party in the Diet, and from December 1934 to February 1935, Hirohito's political agents fought the most protracted budgetary battle of their careers. The Constitutionalists and Strike-Northists tried to bleed the naval development program by drawing off from it funds for domestic famine and hurricane relief. Even when Lord Privy Seal Makino's henchmen had bought or bludgeoned all the venal Constitutionalist politicians they could, there still remained a majority which would not settle. Finally, when the Constitutionalist party had been split by inducements, its two halves met on separate floors of the same restaurant, both armed to the teeth with swords and pistols. In the course of a saké-steeped evening the two factions, upstairs and down, climbed back and forth and compromised without firing any shots. Once again a budget was passed containing not a drop of relief for the victims of drought and typhoon in the rice-root farming areas.

NATIONAL PRINCIPLE

During the budget battle and the continuing house arrest of the reform-minded staff officers, fellow dissidents in the Army organized themselves as a National Principle Group. On February 5, 1935, they published a catechism of questions and answers entitled "Two Basic Movements for the Renovation of the Nation, the Fascistic Group and the National Principle Group."

> The fascists [warned the pamphlet] are the National Socialists who wish to carry out a reformation under the slogan, so they say, of "National Defense." The National Principle Group, however, believes that our national defense is inadequate because the nation as a whole is not under the control of the true national principle. . . . If the people close their eyes to the national principle and dance to the flute of fascism, there will be a critical day for Imperial Japan. That is what you must be most concerned about.

During the two weeks after publication of this blunt manifesto, Lord Privy Seal Makino's secretary, the original Big Brother Marquis Kido, undertook a comprehensive research into the feelings and factions of the Army. He concluded that "the main trunk" of the Emperor's Strike-South following was still sound. Lieutenant General Tatekawa, who had stayed abed at the Literary Chrysanthemum during the seizure of Mukden in 1931, seemed faithful still to his patron, Prince Kanin, the chief of staff. So did Lieutenant General Koiso who had masterminded the March Plot paving the way for the Mukden Incident. Even War Minister Hayashi, despite years of friendship with the leaders of the Strike-North Faction, could now be considered dependable.

On the other hand First Crow Nagata, the original center of the Emperor's cabal in the Army, was under extreme pressure because Inspector General of Military Education Mazaki, the number-two leader of the Strike North, was threatening to make "disclosures about half a million past incidents." The ubiquitous Colonel Suzuki Tei-ichi was also in difficulties. Many of the young officers whom he had recruited for the imperial cabal in days gone by were weary of waiting for reform, indignant about peasant suffering, and fast becoming downright dangerous.

Kido cited several names and by way of illustration expatiated briefly on the feelings of a Lieutenant Colonel Mitsui Sakichi, a devout young Shintoist who the year before had pushed his way into the home of a namesake, the senior Mitsui of the Mitsui cartel, and had delivered a long sermon there. Such firebrands disliked the fact that at the Big Brothers' Eleven Club meetings Colonel Suzuki and Major General Nagata talked and bargained with politicians and industrialists—with corrupt and corrupting "plutocrats."

Big Brother Kido submitted his evaluation of Army loyalty to Hirohito and to a number of elder chamberlains close to Hirohito, including old Prime-Minister-Maker Saionji. With it, as documentation, he circulated a compendium of secret police intelligence briefs which he had collected from his sources in the bureaucracy. The briefs reported that the National Prin-

ciple Group "believes only in righteousness," that it "has leagued itself"
with Baron Hiranuma, the horse-faced lawyer of the Aristocratic National
Foundation Society who would sit in judgment at the surrender scene in
Hirohito's bunker in 1945, and that "with unusually grim determination,
they have resolved to take political power."

THE ORGAN CONTROVERSY

All the various opposition groups which were springing up against Hirohito's increasingly explicit Strike-South policy were unified in early 1935
by an ingenious issue devised by one of Saionji's elderly cronies. It was an
issue which police state methods could not combat, yet one that struck
at the very root of Hirohito's power. Old Saionji received word of it on
February 18, 1935, in a radiogram from his bohemian underworld agent,
the artist Takuno Dempu. Takuno advised Saionji that now even the
elders of the Black Dragon Society wished to reprimand Hirohito and embarrass the Throne. To this end they were planning to launch an attack
on one of Hirohito's most loyal elder retainers: Ikki, the former minister
of the imperial household and present president of the Privy Council. The
charge against Ikki would be that in his youth he had advocated ideas
"against the Constitution of the nation" and specifically that he had subscribed to "the theory that the Emperor is merely an organ of the state."

The attack was duly opened the next day, February 19, 1935, in the
upper chamber of the Diet, the House of Peers. The speaker was Baron
Kikuchi Takeo, the scion of a brilliant family of physicians, lawyers, and
scientists, and the same man who had engineered the slur on Konoye's
friends in the Kyoto Law School faculty two years earlier. Baron Kikuchi
began his defamation quietly and obliquely by noting that Privy Council
President Ikki was a follower of a certain Professor Minobe.

The accusation sounded harmless enough for Dr. Minobe was himself a
member of the House of Peers, the Dean of Law at Tokyo Imperial University, and one of the most respected scholars in the land. He had
delivered educational lectures frequently to Hirohito and his family in the
Imperial Study. Only the year before he had written two magazine articles
in support of the Throne. In one of them, which he had been asked to write
by Secretary-Spy Harada, he had speculated on the role which political
parties might play in a truly imperial Japan, united behind the Throne
under a "whole-nation" prime minister such as Fujiwara Prince Konoye
or one of the princes of the blood. In the second article, published later
in 1934, Dr. Minobe had deplored the oversimplifications of militaristic
thinking and had warned against the staff-officer approach to politics and
economics.

Having asserted that Privy Council President Ikki was a disciple of
Professor Minobe and having then established that Professor Minobe was
a pedagogue of stature, valued highly by Hirohito, the cunning Baron

Kikuchi began gradually and insidiously to explain to the House of Peers Professor Minobe's theories of constitutional law. He introduced quotation after quotation from Minobe's own writings demonstrating that, in Minobe's view, the Emperor did not transcend the state or comprehend the state but was merely an organ of the state. Finally, in a crescendo of passion, Baron Kikuchi accused Professor Minobe and Privy Council President Ikki of heresy, sacrilege, and lèse majesté.

Professor Minobe did not appreciate the grave religious implications of the charges leveled against him. On February 25, 1935, when he arose in the House of Peers to answer, he spoke slowly, quietly, almost disdainfully, and carefully explained fundamental theories of constitutional law as set forth by learned men of many nations. When he had concluded, the applause was scattered. Neither his hearers nor the masses really cared about the academic fine points of constitutional law. The issue was the Emperor's leadership. Would Hirohito hide behind the Constitution as "an organ of state" and continue to manipulate the nation or would he come out into the open and take responsibility for his rule?

Popular clamor in opposition to the organ theory of the Emperor and in favor of "a clarification of the national structure" pre-empted headlines daily for six months and was not completely stilled until the shame of insurrection, exactly a year later, had dropped a stained mask over the nation's much prized "face." Hirohito did everything in his personal power to end the controversy without bloodshed. He compromised again and again with General Araki's Strike-North Faction and taxed his brain to find arguments which would impugn the motives of his metaphysical tormentors. But the Strike-North Faction had struck on an issue of devilish ingenuity, which united both patriots and pacifists. The great mass of the people, accustomed to shouting slogans on order, did not realize that they were crossing the Emperor's personal wishes. They were urged on by the same military officers and underworld labor leaders who had previously organized them in the Emperor's service. And the Emperor, of course—even if he had been willing to come so far out into the open—could hardly explain his own position without damaging the simple religious faith in which his power consisted. As for the rich and the educated who opposed imperial policy, they found themselves in a uniquely enjoyable position. By agreeing that it was sacrilege to call the living god an organ they could snipe at the Throne and at the same time utter sentiments that were impeccable.

As soon as Minobe had made his chilly answer to the House of Peers, retired Major General Eto Genkuro—one of those Choshu officers who had been purged from the Army in the 1920's—lodged a formal charge against Minobe for the capital offense of lèse majesté. Out of realism the charge was later reduced to one of press code violation, but nevertheless the case against Minobe was dragged through the courts for the next nine months. Moreover, similar charges were brought against eighteen other public figures who were alleged to have subscribed to Minobe's theories. Only two of the accused were professors; the other sixteen were bureaucrats and politicians who had been used by the Throne in the past as covert messengers or manipulators. They included even Okada, the prime minister.

The lawyers enjoyed a field day turning the phraseology of recent peace preservation and censorship laws against the pillars of propriety who had drafted them. The people participated in the controversy with back-street discussions. Now if ever was the time to remind Hirohito that he was "above the clouds" and that his "Voice of the Crane" should only be heard on earth infrequently as a kind of miracle. Poor Professor Minobe, who was a deluded academician rather than a deliberate villain, fought blindly for his status, his "face," and his means of livelihood.

GOD DEMURS

The Emperor's first reaction to the attack on Minobe verged on petulance. On February 18, the day before Baron Kikuchi's speech to the Peers, Hirohito had agreed that when Manchukuo's puppet emperor, Henry Pu-Yi, came to Tokyo on a ceremonial visit in April the soldiers on review would be excused from paying him the customary international courtesy of dipping their colors. As soon as Baron Kikuchi made his speech, however, Hirohito called in Chief Aide-de-Camp Honjo and abruptly attacked him about the non-dipping of the colors to which he had given routine consent the day before.

"I return the salute even of one soldier," he announced without prologue. "If the Army flag cannot be dipped in acknowledgment of my generosity to Henry Pu-Yi, then the Army flag is more respected by the soldiers than I am."

Honjo replied: "In general it is ruled that an officer must return the salute of a junior officer, but there is no rule like that for the Emperor. As I understand it, when the Emperor returns a salute he does so as a voluntary gesture, out of his infinite sympathy for the people. The Army's flag which is given to the Army by the Emperor is dipped only to the Emperor in person—not to the Empress, not even to the crown prince. In peace and war the flag is a symbol of the Emperor to which all men of all services give their full belief. Where it goes, they go, even to the water and the fire. The faith and courage of the national Army depend upon this severe respect for the flag."

"The Emperor," in Honjo's words, "nodded his silent understanding." Men could more easily die for a god who was a figurehead than for one who functioned materially as an organ of government. Hirohito summoned War Minister Hayashi to a private audience, and a few days later Hayashi gave a soothing speech to the Diet explaining that the doctrine of the Emperor as an organ of the state was merely a national convenience for dealing with other nations. Western states, he pointed out, could not conceive the true nature of the Emperor and, preferred to contract treaties with a whole people rather than a deified individual.

On March 9, after reading the shorthand notes of Hayashi's remarks to the Diet, Hirohito called Chief Aide-de-Camp Honjo and said: "Of course my ranking is different but physically I am no different from you or anyone else. . . . Therefore, this is a most vexatious problem for me because the Army's attack on the organ theory may restrict my future movements, both physical and spiritual."

Honjo carefully dodged the obvious question—how anyone's freedom could be curtailed by being acknowledged absolute decision maker for the nation—and answered noncommittally: "The Army, Sire, intends no restriction on your movements." And with this Honjo backed his way out of Hirohito's workroom.

Up to this point Hirohito's Big Brothers had treated the organ-or-god controversy lightly. Prince Konoye's group in the House of Peers had prepared a resolution condemning anti-organ ideas as old-fashioned and reactionary. Now, however, after some canvassing, Konoye decided that the resolution could not safely be brought to a vote.

In March 1935 the Black Dragon Society launched a League for the Extermination of the Organ Theory and in co-operation with a lower-class religious sect, Omoto-kyo, a Movement for Modification of the National Structure. The Shinto fundamentalists of Omoto-kyo collected 400,000 signatures on a petition to the Emperor asking him to come out into the open, take responsibility for what was being done, and appoint a Cabinet composed of princes of the blood. Hirohito asked Lord Privy Seal Count Makino how to handle the petition if it were ever presented. Count Makino assured him that it would not be presented. The police and secret police began a vigorous persecution of the "heretical" Omoto-kyo sect and of the Black Dragon Society itself. No less than 515 Black Dragon hoodlums were arrested for crimes which had been previously overlooked. Two hundred of them were even brought to trial and sentenced.

On March 22, 1935, the lower house of the Diet resolved for "renovation of national thought" and "clarification of the nation's fundamental moral principle." Saionji's Secretary-Spy Harada observed to his diary that "the Diet should be burned to the ground." [2] The next day Privy Council President Ikki was set upon and beaten at his wife's funeral. The police, according to their files, determined that the thugs had been hired by a relative of Baron Kikuchi Takeo who had begun the accusations against the heretic Minobe in the House of Peers the month before.

Original Big Brother Marquis Kido, secretary to the lord, privy seal, tried

---

[2] Big Brother Harada, in fear of assassination at the hands of the Black Dragon Society or of the Strike-North Faction, had just moved to a villa in the country, near Saionji's home, and announced that temporarily, on doctor's orders, he would be performing his duties from retirement.

to persuade Professor Minobe to resign his chair at Tokyo Imperial University and apologize for the misunderstandings which his academic theories had caused. In vain Kido enlisted Minobe's brother and one of his richest friends in this endeavor. Professor Minobe offered to withdraw his works from print and even to rephrase the most misunderstood statements in them but refused to resign or recant utterly. Privy Council President Ikki offered to resign in his stead, but courtiers agreed that this would seem too much of a personal concession on the part of Hirohito.

GOD ARGUES

On April 4, 1935, the commanders of Japan's seventeen divisions gathered at the palace for individual briefings from Hirohito on the objectives of Japan's forthcoming push through the Great Wall into north China. Now had arrived the moment of decision on which all the organ-theory controversy was predicated. The number-two leader of the Strike-North Faction, Inspector General of Military Education Mazaki, tried to subvert the proceedings by circulating in advance among the divisional commanders a memorandum which asked them to endorse flatly the statement: "The organ theory is incompatible with the fundamental principles of the nation."

Hirohito heard of the memo from one of the assistant aides-de-camp. He at once summoned Chief Aide Honjo. "Does the Army hope," he asked, "that I will sanction this statement?"

"No, never," said Honjo. "I have simply had it reported to the Throne. It is wholly Mazaki's responsibility."

In the five days that followed Hirohito saw the divisional commanders individually and impressed upon each of them the need to disregard Mazaki as a hothead and to serve loyally in the approaching north China crisis. At the same time Hirohito officiated over Manchukuoan Emperor Henry Pu-Yi's state visit to Tokyo.[3]

When the ceremonies were over on April 9 Hirohito called Honjo into his study and concluded their unfinished business by taxing him with semantic fine points. "In his statement," said Hirohito, "Mazaki calls me the *shutai* of the nation [the main constituent or grammatical subject of the national sentence]. . . . This is absolutely no different in fundamental interpretation from Professor Minobe's *kikan* [organ]. It is only unfortunate that Minobe improperly used the *kikan* meaning 'mechanical organ' instead of the *kikan* meaning 'body organ.' . . . In short, if we regard the Emperor as a brain in charge of the nation's life and if we regard the rest as hands, feet and so on which are activated by order of the master brain, then there is no dispute at all with Minobe's ideas. . . . On the

---

[3] He was both shocked and amused by Henry's servility to him. He told intimates that, on one reviewing stand, Henry had gone so far as to thank him effusively for making the sky clear and the sun shine that day.

other hand, if sovereignty is to reside exclusively in the Emperor rather than the nation as a whole, it will raise the suspicion of tyranny and make for all sorts of difficulties in international treaty and credit arrangements."

Hirohito felt that the farce of the organ-theory attack against him had now gone far enough. Through his Big Brothers he approached Lieutenant General Terauchi, the loyal martinet who had charge of early Strike-South preparations in Taiwan, and asked him for his help in discipling the Army. Terauchi at first shook his head and said, "It is a difficult problem." But on April 12, 1935, he informed Hirohito's envoys that he had negotiated with War Minister Hayashi and that the war minister was now committed to a total purge of the Strike-North Faction from the Army, including the retirement of his friend, the number-two Strike-North leader Mazaki from his post as inspector general of military education.

In preparation for the showdown with the Strike-North Faction, Hirohito, on April 18, 1935, summoned his wife's cousin Prince Fushimi, the chief of the Navy General Staff, to the palace and demanded that the Navy must have a determination, unwritten but agreed upon, as to how far it was committed to go. Hirohito asked that it be a secret *hara* policy, or policy "in the guts." Prince Fushimi at first tried to equivocate but finally pledged that the Navy would go all the way with the Emperor, abandoning dreadnoughts, large crews, and political strength in preparation for aggressive war. Chief Aide-de-Camp Honjo, representing the Army, tried to find out what the Navy had agreed to. He was met with a blank look of ignorance by the Navy minister and by a security-conscious "no comment" from his friends on the Navy General Staff.

At about this same time, in mid-April 1935, the veterans clubs of retired Choshu-clan officers, organized by Strike-North leader Araki after the great purge of 1924, began to circulate a petition explaining the evils of the organ theory and begging Hirohito to renounce it. On April 19, having just read the pamphlet, Hirohito asked Honjo playfully: "Will it be all right if I take this theory about the absolute sovereignty of the Emperor in earnest instead of as a mere theory on paper? During the Manchurian Incident when I tried to make the Cabinet conduct an appropriate investigation, Army officers frequented the aides-de-camp office and made all sorts of demands. They did not listen and try to understand."

Honjo recorded in his diary, "When I checked these assertions with aides-de-camp from General Nara's era, I could find no facts such as the Emperor mentioned." He returned to the Imperial Presence and said, "If someone believes that the Emperor could be wrong in a way that would injure his virtue, he is obliged to rebuke the Emperor with utmost virtue. Since the Army never did what you just told me, it will harm your virtue if I do not rebuke you."

For the first time since childhood, Hirohito had been called a liar to his face. He dismissed Honjo without a word and for six days mused or sulked behind a mask of formality. Then on April 25 he said very simply to Honjo, "The Army, in attacking the organ theory, is acting against my will. In so doing they are treating me as an organ. Is that not true?"

"Not absolutely," squirmed Honjo. "The reservists are merely circulating a small pamphlet and trying to unify their own thinking on the matter."

"If science is suppressed by emotion and conviction," declared Hirohito darkly, "the progress of the world will be retarded and the theory of evolution will be upset."

After further reflection, Hirohito called Honjo on April 27 and itemized his objections to the veterans' arguments in a veritable blizzard of learned hailstones. He spoke extremely tersely, without any attempt to explain his nuggets of thought. In the process, however, he gave the most complete and personal statement of his beliefs on record, and exposed in himself the young sheltered intellectual, sure of his unlimited power and convinced that scientific rationalism could be applied to statecraft for the betterment of Japan and all Asia. He said:

> In the first place the theory that a nation's sovereignty resides in the nation itself is not necessarily the same as the theory of democracy and it is utterly indefensible to argue that it is.
>
> In the second place, it is a mistake to regard the trend in the world at large as a trend toward individualism. It is correct to say that democracy in Europe and the United States is an outgrowth of individualism in the past. But how do you regard the enactment of the prohibition law in the United States? As individualistic? How do you account for the fact that men in England died for their nation in great herds during the last world war?
>
> In the third place your Army theorists in their discussion of constitutional theory speak much of the constitutions of England, France, and other democracies but do not seem to have studied the German constitution [of Bismarck] which was the model for the drafting of the Imperial Constitution of Japan.
>
> In the fourth place, though natural science is susceptible to proof and though matters pertaining to life are not susceptible to proof, it is impossible to point to the line of demarcation and say that thus and so is outside the realm of scientific proof. For instance, there is no distinction which can be made between physiology and philosophy.
>
> In the fifth place, these veterans in their discussion of purely academic theories occasionally mention individual names like [Privy Council President] Ikki's in a most personal way. In so doing, they run the risk of inciting unexpected incidents.
>
> Finally, in the sixth place, it is true that the Emperor of Japan is the center of everything—of art, literature, and of the whole national life as well as politics. But it is not correct to say, on the other hand, that the kings of Europe are involved only in politics. I happen to know for a fact that the king of England makes great contributions in cultural areas.

Hirohito had turned his biggest intellectual guns on Chief Aide-de-Camp Honjo, and Honjo was somewhat impressed. "Thus the Emperor," he wrote in his diary, "gave his honorable explanation and aired his views in detail. I felt particularly awed as to point number five and cautioned the Army about it," that is, cautioned the Army lest its theorists, by mentioning individual names, cause untoward incidents such as individual assassinations.

Three weeks later Chief Aide-de-Camp Honjo was still trying to maintain that anti-organ agitation was honest philosophical debate and not mere heckling of the Throne. On May 18 he went so far as to say that the controversy was sharpening and strengthening the people to resist insidious "Anglo-Saxon propaganda" of the type which had "speeded Germany's collapse during World War I."

Ignoring the silliness of the statement, Hirohito retorted tartly: "The prime reason for the fall of Germany was that, of all the German states, only Prussia gave full obedience and perfect trust to the kaiser." Hirohito added as an afterthought that the kaiser had compounded the disaster by his cowardice in retiring to Holland after the war instead of remaining in Berlin to see out his destiny. Then Hirohito reiterated his contention that the trend of the world in 1935 was not toward individualism but toward non-individualistic nationalism.

GOD SNARLS

Four days later, on May 22, 1935, Hirohito was shocked to discover that even some of his trusted Navy minions were joining the opposition to him. Navy Minister Osumi, who had been an attaché in Paris during Hirohito's visit in 1921 and had assisted the Throne faithfully during the conspiratorial military reorganizations of the 1920's, gave open notice of his disaffection by asking that Strike-North Admiral Kato Kanji be made governor general of Taiwan. In the context of government gossip at the time, it was like saying that Taiwan Commander Terauchi needed watching; that preparations were afoot in Taiwan that would not bear scrutiny by light of day.

Court officials dismissed the request summarily as an impractical one, and Hirohito that same morning summoned Chief Naval Aide-de-Camp Rear Admiral Idemitsu Mambei. "Men in the Navy," he declared, "are insisting on a non-organ theory of the Throne. This is a contradiction in terms, for in so doing they are disregarding my wishes."

Idemitsu replied recklessly: "Where affairs touching the position of the Emperor are concerned, the Navy may sometimes fail to respond to the hints of the Honorable All-including Mind. Nevertheless it is a mistake to confuse the main point by overregard for trivia. In routine business, the Navy may sometimes follow badly, but this does not mean, as you imply, that there is any disobedience in the Navy or any contradiction in our faith that the Emperor is supreme. If you continue to speak this way about a matter as important as the national structure, it is a confusion on your part of major and minor issues. I, Idemitsu, in genuine humility, think that the Emperor should wait, should survey the arguments of his subjects from a vantage point, and should, for the time being, direct his mind to other matters than these theoretical ones."

That afternoon Hirohito had Aide Idemitsu reposted, at fifty-one, to the headmastership of the naval academy. Three years later Idemitsu would go further into exile and while away the last years of his blighted career as commander of a port arsenal. In his anger Hirohito did not even accept the Navy Personnel Bureau's first recommendation as to Idemitsu's successor. Confronted suddenly with the demand for a replacement, the bureau listed two names, one a brilliant man whom Honjo identifies only as Rear Admiral So-and-So, and the other a loyal plodder, Rear Admiral Hirata Noburo. Hirata was the son of the lord privy seal to Emperor Taisho during his mad declining years of 1922–1925. In his own right Hirata recommended himself by having long served as aide-de-camp for the Misty Lagoon's "Flying Prince" Yamashina.[4]

Navy Minister Osumi and Chief of the Naval General Staff Prince Fushimi both questioned Hirohito about his acceptance of Hirata as naval aide and pointed out that there was no precedent for demanding the second candidate. Hirohito refused to change his choice. Navy Minister Osumi withdrew from the Imperial Presence remarking, "There is nothing more to be said. It is the Emperor's decision."

THROUGH THE GREAT WALL

The emotional explosive which lobbed these metaphysical shells from room to room in the palace had been kindled by Hirohito's new tough policy toward Chiang Kai-shek. Instead of alliance with China, Hirohito was now demanding outright seizure of the Chinese facilities needed for a Strike South.

For two months, since March 1935, one of the Eleven Reliables chosen at Baden-Baden, Major General Isogai Rensuke, had been negotiating with Chiang in Nanking for what amounted to Japanese sovereignty over the whole of north China. Major General Isogai asked Chiang "to neutralize" north China. Japan, he said, had no territorial aims in the area, of course, but felt obliged to silence the anti-Japanese agitation there and deal once and for all with the Communist bandits of Mao Tse-tung with whom Chiang's forces had been fighting inconclusively for five years. Would

---

[4] Yamashina, who was still ill from the "nervous breakdown" he had suffered after Prime Minister Inukai's murder in 1932, was troubling chamberlains at this time by having an affair with his nurse, a certain plebeian Miss Murayama.

Chiang please, therefore, withdraw all officials of the Nanking government from north China and leave administration of the area to local mayors and police subservient to Japan. It was as if a trusted major general of a victorious Kaiser Wilhelm had arrived in Philadelphia a few years after World War I and demanded that the area of the thirteen original states be neutralized by withdrawal of federal troops, tax agents, and party politicians to the west of the Appalachians.

Chiang Kai-shek still had no military power to set against Japan. And he owed many debts of kindness to the Japanese. He agreed with them, basically, that the Orient must someday stand united, on its own feet, as a single bloc of self-interests in the international arena. But he had made great strides since 1930 in uniting his shattered land. He had rid it partially of opium addiction and almost entirely of local war lords. He had driven the Communist armies of Mao Tse-tung into the badlands of the northwest.

Moreover, Chiang had found new sources of political strength in the coolie classes of his land. At the urging of Protestant missionaries from the West, he and Madame Chiang had launched a mass movement for spiritual and moral reform called The New Life. It was a simple, personal, evangelistic program emphasizing self-help and brotherhood. It drew its inspiration partly from Confucius and partly from the Oxford Group, the New Church, Seventh-Day Adventism, and other manifestations of the Second Protestantism in the West. It was intended, frankly, as a constructive supplement to Chiang's interminable "bandit suppression campaigns" against the Communists. In spite of the suspect Western influences and political motives behind it, the Chinese masses were taking to The New Life movement with surprising fervor.

Full of hope for his program, Chiang Kai-shek offered Japan nothing more, after six weeks of negotiation, than a pact of mutual nonaggression and friendship. Accordingly, in late April 1935, Hirohito set in motion the machinery for a show of strength. Because of the delicate situation domestically in his own army, he monitored the operation through a personal respresentative. On May 1, Prince Kaya, fresh from his recent holiday in Berlin with heroes Mussolini and Hitler, set off on a tour of north China and Manchukuo with a group of military academy cadets. Major Prince Kaya was their tactics instructor and proceeded to give them a routine demonstration of Japanese tactical intrigue. On his way to Manchukuo he stopped in Tientsin and visited with the Strike-South lieutenant general who was in command of the garrison there.

While feasting Prince Kaya, the staff officers of the Tientsin garrison accused a Chinese weekly magazine, *The New Life,* of committing lèse majesté against the Japanese Emperor. In consequence—by whose hand is not clear—two Chinese newspapermen who had been writing pro-Japanese propaganda were assassinated inside the Japanese concession in Tientsin. The Japanese staff officers blamed the murders on Chiang Kai-shek's counterespionage force, the Blue Shirts. And the Tientsin commander, as he left the city to accompany Prince Kaya to Manchuria, told his chief of staff that it might be well, in his absence, to issue the Chinese a stern warning. The chief of staff then visited the governor of Hopei, the province in which Peking is situated, and told him that his territory would be occupied by Japanese troops unless all KMT party organs and security agents were promptly expelled from it.

Lest the governor of Hopei and his master, Chiang Kai-shek, take the warning lightly, Prince Kaya was joined in Manchukuo by everyone of importance in the Japanese Army—War Minister Hayashi, Chief of Staff Prince Kanin, and the commanders of the Korean and Formosan armies. The pretext was the dedication ceremony of a shrine in Long Spring Thaw, the Manchukuoan capital, to Amaterasu, the Japanese sun goddess. But the conclave was meant to appear, as indeed it was, a high-level consultation of the most ominous gravity. So much top brass was there that Secretary-Spy Harada complained to his diary that there was no one left in the Tokyo bureaucracy to gossip with and consult about Army matters.

Japanese noncommissioned officers on weekend passes swaggered through the streets of Tientsin and Peking looking for any pretext to start an "incident." On May 24, Prince Kaya and his class of tactics students from the military academy returned home from Long Spring Thaw, followed a week later by War Minister Hayashi and Army Chief of Staff Prince Kanin. When Chiang Kai-shek continued to seek face-saving terms, Prince Kanin and Hirohito, on June 6, 1935, signed combat orders and dispatched them to the Kwantung Army and the Tientsin garrison. On June 10, as anticipated, Chiang Kai-shek capitulated short of battle. His representative, General Ho, met with the Tientsin garrison commander, Lieutenant General Umezu Yoshijiro, and signed a document known to this day only as the Ho-Umezu Pact.

By the terms of the Ho-Umezu Pact, China promised to prevent her citizens from "scowling" at Japanese soldiers and to cede all but civil police powers in the bulk of north China to representatives approved by Tokyo. Hirohito's inner circle of Big Brothers hoped to use the pact to split north China into several autonomous regions, each governed by a puppet regime responsive to Tokyo. Then, through infiltration of Japanese economic and military advisors, north Chinese labor, raw materials, and railroads were to be integrated into the over-all "defensive structure of the Japanese Empire." Finally, said Japanese visionaries, the example of mutually beneficial Sino-Japanese co-operation in the area would make the rest of China sympathetic to Japan and would prepare the way for a Sino-Japanese alliance against the West.

Emperor Hirohito had long ceased to expect much of Sino-Japanese friendship. He was already preparing for a full-scale war with China and would launch it two years later, in July 1937. In the interim his advisors' dreams for north China would vanish like smoke, and officers of the Japanese Army opposed to war with China would stage a mutiny. On February 26, 1936, elements of Japan's two crack divisions would seize the center of Tokyo and lay siege to the palace in an effort to change Hirohito's mind. All Western writers up to now have ascribed the rebellion to Army extremists who wished to make Hirohito more rather than less militaristic. The story of the rebellion, however, and of the events leading up to it has become available in Japan only in the last few years.

19

PURGES OF 1935

THE ARMY GROWS DESPERATE

Neutralization of north China marked a chapter's end in the imperial program. Autonomous and under Japanese influence, the region would offer as much buffer zone against the West as Hirohito's great-grandfather Komei and his advisors had ever envisaged when they sought means of preserving Japan's security in the nineteenth century. North China could be used as a staging area for the Japanese Army to go north, or south, or even west into Mongolia and Tibet. For the majority of Japanese Army officers it was enough. To some of them it seemed more than enough—an overextension of Japanese capabilities which would only lead to disillusion, demoralization, and greed. Old-fashioned samurai were well aware that base, profit-conscious merchants—the traditional scum of the nation in samurai eyes—would exploit the area and see it as a steppingstone to the rice and oil fields of the East Indies.

A few days after the signing of the Ho-Umezu Pact in June 1935, Colonel Ishiwara Kanji, the zealous religious fanatic who had drafted the military planning for the conquest of Manchuria before 1931, submitted a hurried memo to Hirohito and the General Staff in which he stated categorically: "There is only one course for us: to consolidate and perfect our gains. If we do a fine job of reconstruction even only in Manchukuo, then the rest of China will follow us as a matter of course."

The time to attack Russia which staff planners had long calculated as optimum—namely, 1936—was fast approaching and no preparations were being made for it. The Strike-North Faction cast about for new forms of pressure to apply which might be more effective than organ-theory agitation. Two of the young antifascists who had been arrested after the Military

602

Academy Plot and then released in late February 1935 circulated a pamphlet, which they had completed on May 11, entitled, "A Written Opinion on Purging the Army." In it they accused by name a number of Crows and Reliables, who were known to be close to the Emperor, of having officiated over such outrageously illegal activities as the March and October Plots of 1931.

In a more general way the authors held that factional strife could never be stilled until the Army was given a strong, upright, imperial leadership under popular, trustworthy figures. Count Terauchi's proposed policy of "purification" by straightforward discipline and outright dismissal of all troublemakers might be a cure but would effectively kill the patient and rid the officer corps of its best men. The other policy of constant manipulations and plots pursued by the ruling Control Clique would lead nowhere except to more vicious manipulations and plots. The members of the Control Faction—of Suzuki Tei-ichi's 1927 Study Group, of the Baden-Baden Reliables, and of the Three Crows—were all too deep in guilt and blackmail to supply honest leadership. Mazaki and Araki of the Strike-North Faction, by contrast, had played no part in plots, said the authors, except to prevent their fulfillment. It followed, then, that if respect for discipline and regulations was to be brought back to the Army, only Mazaki and Araki could set an honest example for younger officers and lead a genuinely sincere reform movement.

It was the first time that such revelations had been made in writing, and by June 1935 a privately printed edition of the pamphlet was being read avidly by everyone who could lay hands on a copy. The pamphlet seemed particularly timely because of the impending struggle in the Army over the August repostings. The rumor had reached the grapevine that War Minister Hayashi had promised to force out his friend Mazaki from the inspector generalship of education and rid the Army brass of its last tarnish of Strike-Northists.

The supporters of Araki and Mazaki sent out letters to all their sympathizers in the officer corps appealing for help in the forthcoming power struggle. By late June, on the basis of response to these letters, it was widely rumored that the Strike-North Faction would be able to call out at least a thousand officers in open insurrection if Mazaki's dismissal were forced through. A slim majority of the old-line generals who sat on the Supreme War Council advised Hirohito, Army Chief of Staff Prince Kanin, and War Minister Hayashi that such gross insubordination should be disregarded and the purge carried out as planned. At the end of June, Hayashi and Prince Kanin flew to Manchuria to explain the purge to the proconsuls of the Kwantung Army and remind them of their oaths of fealty to the Emperor. The two returned to Tokyo reassured that most of the men in the field could still be counted on to obey orders.

THE FIRING OF MAZAKI

On July 10 War Minister Hayashi called on Inspector General of Military Education Mazaki in his office on the edge of the palace woods and handed him the list of the August repostings. Almost all remaining Strike-North partisans in the bureaucracy were to be sent to the reserve or transferred to field commands. Mazaki himself was to be replaced as inspector general and moved up to the honorary position of supreme war councillor. Mazaki looked up from the list and stared at Hayashi accusingly.

Hayashi quickly said: "His Imperial Highness Prince Kanin wanted to have you removed from active service altogether, but I reported to His Highness that this would be impossible. However, if you cannot agree to this personnel shift, I must ask you for the sake of discipline in the Army to resign your commission."

"Very well," replied Mazaki, "if you publicly require it, I will resign. But personnel shifts are customarily approved by a joint meeting of all of the three chiefs [war minister, inspector general of military education, and chief of the Army General Staff]. If you should be allowed to force through this decision alone, you would damage the office of inspector general. Therefore I cannot give my consent on a purely personal basis; it must be done officially."

In demanding a full-dress confrontation with War Minister Hayashi and Chief of Staff Prince Kanin, Mazaki was requiring, in effect, that Prince Kanin, as the elder of the imperial family, take public responsibility for the decision to purge the Strike-North Faction from the Army. Implied in acceptance of this responsibility would be the larger one of having decided on the Strike South—of having done so, in secret, without consulting the councils of the other great families of Japan, the collective feudal leadership which still underlay the structure of the modern government.

The autocratic Prince Kanin accepted the challenge and the next day, July 11, told War Minister Hayashi to go ahead and schedule a conference of the three chiefs for the twelfth. When Hayashi phoned Mazaki with the news, Mazaki begged for a postponement. War Minister Hayashi refused. it.

"All right," said Mazaki, "I shall come but I cannot prepare for a conference I know nothing about. I will merely be there without speaking." [1]

On the following morning when the conference of the three chiefs con-

---

[1] That afternoon, by no coincidence, retired Major General Eto Genkuro, who had helped to lead the attack on organ theorist Professor Minobe in the House of Peers, presented a formal petition at the palace asking that the Emperor declare himself an absolute sovereign rather than an organ of the government. On the advice of Privy Seal Secretary Kido, Hirohito decided to thank Major General Eto and promise him that the petition would be formally filed with the papers of the lord privy seal for the future reference of the Throne.

vened, Mazaki went straight to the attack. "Since I have not had time to study what these repostings are all about," he announced, "I would like to move for a recess."

The last surviving brother of Prince Asahiko—of Emperor Komei's chief counselor at Perry's coming eighty-two years earlier—nodded his head almost imperceptibly. At sixty-nine Prince Kanin was still one of the most handsome men in Japan. Now he stood up deliberately, ramrod straight, his mustache bristling, his luxuriant eyebrows slightly raised, and his square-cut, almost Occidental features set in cold hauteur. "How long do you need to prepare?" he asked.

"Please give me three or four days," begged Mazaki, jumping to his feet.

"I have my own convenience to consider," stated Kanin, "so we will set the fifteenth as the date." He nodded again and Mazaki and War Minister Hayashi instantly backed from the office, bowing waist deep.

Mazaki drove directly to the home of retired War Minister Araki across the street from Meiji Shrine on the other side of the palace. After hearing his report on the meeting, Araki accompanied him back to the General Staff offices, beneath the southwest walls of the palace, and sought an immediate private audience with Chief of Staff Prince Kanin. Once admitted to Kanin's presence, Araki proceeded to deliver one of the casual, articulate monologues for which he was famous in his dealings with the monosyllabic members of the imperial family. War Minister Hayashi, he suggested, had made too much of an issue out of the August repostings and his attitude was considered by many of his colleagues to be "off the beaten track."

Araki continued somewhat threateningly: "If Mazaki's transfer is mandatory, I will persuade him to accept it, but I beg of Your Highness not to involve yourself directly, for that will only enlarge the strife and injure your cause."

"Then how," inquired Prince Kanin, "would you have me act at the three chiefs' conference?"

"Why, simply instruct Hayashi and Mazaki to confer together earnestly and bring you a plan for the repostings which they both agree upon."

"You think it sensible to try to achieve results through the consultation of only two men?" mused Kanin. "Well, all right, I will think about it."

In the ensuing three-day quest for compromise, War Minister Hayashi demonstrated repeatedly that he was pliable and that it was Prince Kanin who was adamant. Kanin would make only two concessions. He had wanted to put Lieutenant General Koiso, the March Plotter, in charge of Army Air Force headquarters and make Lieutenant General Tatekawa of the Literary Chrysanthemum vice chief of staff. At the urging of Araki, he finally agreed to postpone these moves and to leave Tatekawa and Koiso, who were his old cavalry cronies, in field commands.

Concerning the two most controversial transfers on the list, however,

Prince Kanin remained absolutely inflexible. Mazaki, who pretended to greater righteousness than the Emperor, must go to the Supreme War Council, and former Secret Police Commandant Hata Shinji, who had been supplying Mazaki with information to use in making accusations, must resign his commission and retire to civilian life. It was rare for a member of the imperial family to show such personal animosity. In an effort to excuse Prince Kanin and so shield the Throne, War Minister Hayashi spread the report that it was really First Crow Nagata and other subordinates in the War Ministry who had insisted on Mazaki's dismissal.

At noon on July 15, an hour before the fateful three chiefs' conference was to commence, Araki made a final, unavailing attempt to break the deadlock. He called on War Minister Hayashi and warned him that it was unpatriotic to embroil a member of the imperial family in a matter of discipline for which Hayashi alone as war minister should be accountable; that historically any minister of the Emperor who sought to hide behind the Throne was automatically condemned by the Japanese people.

At one o'clock, after a hasty bowl of Japanese noodles, it was a worried War Minister Hayashi who convoked the three chiefs' conference. The Strike-North Inspector General of Military Education Mazaki once again leapt to the offensive. "Behind this conference," he declared, "I can see only impure motives." He drew from his uniform a document and laid it on the table. War Minister Hayashi and Prince Kanin saw at a glance that it was the "novel" which First Crow Nagata had drawn up for the government of Japan in the event that the March Plot had succeeded in 1931.

"This present plot, too," continued Mazaki, "has been created by the men of the March incident. It is the Control Clique which has destroyed discipline and caused unrest in the Army. Our pledge to the gods to purge the Army of vicious elements must be accomplished. And the first item on the agenda is to get rid of the Control Faction."

Prince Kanin's handsome face flushed and he interrupted: "Are you presuming to interfere in the duties of the war minister?"

"I have no place to hide," muttered Mazaki. "I may be a man of no ability but I am the duly invested inspector general of military education for the Emperor of Japan. I feel that the work of rebuilding the Imperial Army is of utmost importance and I also feel small when I find myself opposed by the words of Prince Kanin." Headlong, with words tumbling, Mazaki delivered his prepared thoughts on the realities of emotion in the ranks, of the institution of inspector generalship which he represented, and of the alien, unworthy motives which he saw behind this suicidal South-Striking purge of the Emperor's best samurai.

When Mazaki's outburst was over and he had spent his last blunt sentiment, Prince Kanin quietly declared: "I understand the inspector general's thoughts, but right now the Army is looking forward to the inspector general's resignation. You would prefer not to resign. Violence may come out of this meeting, but if so, the war minister is empowered to deal with it."

Once again Chief of Staff Prince Kanin arose and nodded, and Hayashi and Mazaki backed from the room, bowing.

RIPPLES AND THEIR CONTROL

War Minister Hayashi waited at the curb until the mortified Mazaki had driven away. A few moments later Prince Kanin emerged from General Staff Headquarters, all spit and polish in full dress, and climbed into the staff car which War Minister Hayashi had waiting. The two drove together with police escort to the Summer Palace at Hayama on the shore. Hirohito had arranged forehandedly not to be absent that afternoon on the imperial biological yacht. When the pair arrived at three o'clock, Hirohito saw Prince Kanin briefly in private, after which the chief of staff retired to a nearby inn. War Minister Hayashi meanwhile was held in conversation by Chief Aide-de-Camp Honjo and his assistants.

"I sensed that the situation was out of the ordinary and an emergency," noted Honjo in his diary. "So I had Aide Ishida listen to what War Minister Hayashi planned to report to the Throne. For myself I phoned Personnel Bureau Chief Imai and learned that the issue was indeed Inspector General of Education Mazaki, and that Field Marshal Prince Kanin had already committed himself to a stand. Therefore, after taking deep and sour consideration within myself, I officially reported to the Emperor the purpose of War Minister Hayashi's visit."

Emerging from Hirohito's presence, Honjo learned that now Mazaki, too, had arrived at the Summer Palace and was being entertained by one of the aides in a separate anteroom. Honjo went to greet him and learned that he wished to present a written protest to the Throne. Honjo returned to the Emperor and asked him if he would see Mazaki before War Minister Hayashi. Hirohito replied with a firm negative. And so at five o'clock Honjo reluctantly ushered War Minister Hayashi into the Imperial Presence. Honjo himself drank a whisky with Mazaki, advised him that his cause was hopeless, and sent him back to Tokyo with his protest still in his pocket.

In his tiny summer study, overlooking his beloved Sagami Bay, the well-briefed Hirohito was meanwhile putting War Minister Hayashi through an inquisition to make sure that what had happened would not be considered the responsibility of the Throne.

"As far as the main issue is concerned, the control of the Army," said Hirohito, "I am concerned that this appointment [of Mazaki to the Supreme War Council] may create a circular ripple. Do you accept responsibility for seeing that it will not spread?" Hayashi acknowledged that he would.

"And will you see to it that this does not affect the established regulations and process of law in regard to conferences of the three army chiefs?" Again Hayashi promised that he would.

"And War Minister Hayashi, if you find that men opposed to the principles of the inspector general of military education, such as Koiso, Tatekawa, and Nagata, have dealt unfairly with him, are you prepared to punish them in their turn?"

In view of the role played in the ouster by Prince Kanin, it was an unfair question, but the bland Hayashi scarcely blinked. "If I investigate," he said, "and find any unfairness I will deal with it severely."

Emerging much compromised from the Imperial Presence, War Minister Hayashi was cornered by Chief Aide-de-Camp Honjo and plied for a full report on the audience. He told Honjo of the Emperor's concern about causing circular waves but neglected to mention the Emperor's requirement that any unfairness must be punished.

After a restless, thoughtful night Honjo arose early the next morning and before breakfast called on three retired generals, three former aides of the Emperor, for advice. At 9:30 A.M. he begged audience with Hirohito and told him that he feared grave repercussions; that the imperial family had assumed an unprecedented amount of open responsibility; that it would be well for Field Marshal Prince Kanin and Field Marshal Prince Nashimoto [2] to take a conciliatory attitude toward the Strike-North Faction and do all they could "to smooth things over." Hirohito said that he felt it was too late for that but agreed to invite the two field marshals for lunch.

Hirohito went on to itemize in detail his personal grievances against the ousted Mazaki. He was constantly stirring up debate and criticism. He "acted against my will during the Jehol operation" of 1933 and had to be sent to the front to repair his error.[3] "I expected him to tender his resignation but he did not." Mazaki "has never shown much common sense." For instance, he recently sent an Army position paper to civilian advisor Count Makino, the lord privy seal, when everyone in the palace knew that it was utterly forbidden to mix civil and military business. "For some time now we have grappled with the need to take a firm stand toward China, yet it is said that Mazaki and Araki have recently tried to force War Minister Hayashi into adopting their views on the matter." Finally, "War Minister Hayashi says that the Military Academy Incident of last October was a plot engineered by Mazaki." In regard to this last accusation Honjo noted parenthetically in his diary: "Possibly Mazaki did mean to cause an incident which would be difficult to settle by court-martial but he surely did not mean the Military Academy Cadets' Incident in earnest."

---

[2] Nashimoto, the hostage imprisoned by MacArthur in 1945–46, was then the second oldest member of the imperial family.

[3] In which officers of Mazaki's Strike-North Faction had violated Hirohito's pledge to Chiang Kai-shek by breaching the Great Wall and penetrating China proper.

That noon, while Hirohito was lunching in strict privacy with the two field marshals, Prince Kanin and Prince Nashimoto, the principal topic of conversation in other rooms of the palace was Major General Nagata, the first of the Three Crows of Baden-Baden. As chief of the Military Affairs Bureau, Nagata had concurred in the purge of Mazaki. Yet it was his written March Plot plan in the hands of Mazaki and Araki which now compromised the Throne. It was said that he had carelessly left the document lying about the War Ministry in a strongbox. There it had been found in 1932 and passed upward through channels to the then War Minister Araki, who had kept it. As if this were not reprehensible enough, Nagata had recently come out with two position papers, both of which hued closely to opinions held by Mazaki: that there would be no peace and stability in the Far East without Sino-Japanese friendship and that there could be no discipline within the Japanese Army unless a stop were put to the "unjust" practice of using the Army for political purposes. In short Nagata had become a liability, and Araki and Mazaki must be discredited.

After lunch Prince Kanin and Prince Nashimoto left the Summer Palace to return to Tokyo; Chief Aide-de-Camp Honjo was warned by the cigar-smoking grand chamberlain, Suzuki Kantaro, that it displeased the Emperor to hear excuses made in defense of ousted Mazaki; and Hirohito himself returned to duty by performing the ceremony of investiture for a new, more obedient inspector general of military education.

ARAKI'S REVELATIONS

Later that afternoon—July 16, 1935—a certain Lieutenant Colonel Aizawa Saburo called on First Crow Major General Nagata at the War Ministry and advised him to resign his post. Nagata knew the man as a master of *kendo,* the Japanese art of fencing, who had taught swordsmanship years ago at the military academy. Nagata also knew him to be a familiar of Hirohito's uncle, Prince Higashikuni, and of Prince Higashikuni's general factotum, retired Lieutenant Colonel Yasuda Tetsunosuke who had arranged the Prayer Meeting Plot. Back in the teens of the century when Prince Higashikuni had been the captain of a company, Yasuda had been one of his lieutenants and swordsman Aizawa one of his second lieutenants. Now, as Nagata knew, Aizawa was attached to the command of the 41st Regiment in Fukuyama on the Inland Sea some twelve hours away by train. How was it that he was here in Nagata's office full of indignation about Mazaki's dismissal? The dismissal had been announced on the radio only that morning less than ten hours ago.

As such thoughts flashed through First Crow Nagata's quick, filing-cabinet mind, swordsman Aizawa came to the end of his indignant tirade. Nagata thanked him for his interest in the nation's welfare and explained to him that Mazaki had been dismissed for the sake of discipline in the

Army as a whole. Nagata added that he personally had no plans for resigning at present, and with that, pleading business, he saw Aizawa to the door in the comradely brusque manner for which he was renowned. As soon as he was alone, he called for Aizawa's dossier. It confirmed his recollections. Without more ado Nagata put through orders for Aizawa's transfer to the Japanese Territorial Army in Taiwan.

On July 18, before Aizawa received his new orders, the Supreme War Council met to put its stamp of approval on the August repostings already decided. Prince Kanin wisely sheathed the imperial power which he had brandished so autocratically at the three chiefs' conference three days earlier and did not attend. In his absence Araki and Mazaki put on a performance which confirmed the darkest fears at Court. Mazaki the day before had announced to all his friends who would listen that his dismissal had been "an intrusion on the supreme command" and had sought legal advice of the horse-faced Baron Hiranuma, president of the influential conservative National Foundation Society. Now, at the Supreme War Council, Mazaki and Araki turned a routine meeting into "four hours of anger," which, as one participant remarked, was "a rare thing to see in a group of old men."

The minutes of the meeting have not been preserved but according to the secret police sleuth assigned to inform himself on the proceedings, War Minister Hayashi opened with a monotone report on the sequence of events which had led up to Mazaki's resignation. Then four other generals, including Mazaki himself, stood up in turn to announce that they had no comment. Finally the articulate chieftain of the Strike-North Faction, former War Minister Araki, arose to his feet, beetled his brows at War Minister Hayashi, and said:

"When I left the war ministership what I asked was that you, Hayashi, and you, Mazaki, should get along, and reorganize and re-equip the army. I never suspected your integrity," he said, glaring at Hayashi, "but I never dreamed either that the friendship between Hayashi and Mazaki could be so weak. What happened? It must have been some major castastrophe to break the bond between you two."

Hayashi disregarded the sarcasm and stared unblinking back at Araki. "I am not aware that there has been any break in our friendship," he said.

"Oh," said Araki, "then you and Mazaki agree. No change in your friendship. What beautiful control of the Army! I can't understand this word 'control.' What does it mean?"

Hayashi responded by trying to sniffle in the sleeve of the dragon. "Actually," he said, "someone did say that Mazaki was disturbing the Army and so I was obliged to do what I did."

"This other fellow, was he inside the Army or outside?"

"Inside."

"On active duty?"

"Not exactly."

"How many of him were there?"

Hayashi then muttered the names of three retired generals who were known as cronies of Prince Kanin and also of Araki himself. Two of them were classmates of Mazaki and Araki.

"These men," said Araki, "are excellent people but they are all on the reserve list and remote from present conditions in the Army. They have no right to opinions on personnel matters. If it is true that these outsiders helped you to make your decision, it is indeed an outrage. By and large, the whole proceeding strikes me as rash and hasty. Any responsible war minister would have discussed matters at a conference of the three chiefs of the Army, not taken precipitous action on the basis of outside advice. But aren't there any other men involved?"

"No, only these three came to me," said Hayashi miserably.

"Just three outsiders? What were you doing as war minister to let yourself be pushed around by three outsiders? I put it to you that you made this decision yourself. And I ask you now, will you change your mind when ten more powerful men come out on the other side of the question?"

Hayashi did not answer. Having made it apparent that Hayashi was too weak to serve as a responsible shield for the Throne, Araki took advantage of the dramatic silence to lay three items in evidence on the table: First Crow Nagata's incriminating "novel," one of the March Plot smoke bombs, and a certificate written by the officers of the Chiba Infantry School attesting to the authenticity and purpose of the bomb.[4]

"These proofs," thundered Araki in the shocked silence of the Supreme War Council, "need no explanation here. Let us only consider for a moment whether this March Plot was wrong or right. Or is it possible that one of the anti-plotters like Mazaki was right? What on earth happened in these personnel shifts? Do you gentlemen think by such shifts we can control young officers who have already been led to ignore their superiors? I cannot permit the war minister to behave in such a double-dealing fashion. I feel ashamed of having recommended him."

General Watanabe Jotaro, the new inspector general of military education, was the first to find his tongue: "It is you who have upbraided us with these proofs of the ancient March Plot. Why have you had them so long in your own keeping? It is an insult—one I would like you to explain."

Araki said: "Now that it is too late, why add further to the blood-stained confusion? Such papers are never public papers. These, in particular, were discovered by accident in the belongings of a certain bureaucrat. Suppose these proofs were to be seen by all. What would happen? To keep

---

[4] The bombs had been kept in storerooms at the infantry school until 1933 when a fire had called attention to their presence. Araki, as war minister at the time, had been shown one of the bombs which had survived the fire and had kept it. He had ordered the rest to be destroyed.

them from the prying eyes of potential conspirators I have kept them personally as my private responsibility. I once considered burning them but slander is so popular nowadays and a man's name is so easily changed from white to black overnight that I just thought I might need them some time."

The meeting was effectively over though there was more argument. General Watanabe, the new inspector general, sought to establish the fact that Nagata's "novel" was a private plan written years ago in an excess of youth.

Araki replied: "Nagata was the chief of the Military Affairs Section in the War Ministry when he wrote this plan. He left it among his official papers. His superiors never asked him to explain it. It demonstrates a pure and utter corruption of discipline."

War Minister Hayashi promised that he would make it his own responsibility to "discipline Nagata." The meeting broke up after a bootless but lengthy argument as to whether Araki had any right to possess the papers he had produced and as to whether they were public or private papers.

Little sickly General Matsui Iwane, later branded the Butcher of Nanking, professed after the meeting that he was completely astonished by Araki's revelations. After pondering them for a few days, he requested—in a voluntary gesture almost without precedent—that he be retired from active service and put on the reserve list. At a meeting of the Eleven Club on July 26, Hirohito's inner circle of Big Brotherly advisors resolved that Matsui's resignation was "most regrettable." Awakening to the fact that plots and murders of the previous years had been planned at the highest levels of government, Matsui felt that he personally must do something to save China. In his retirement he went directly to Peking and spent the rest of the fall there, in a private capacity, attempting to set up a native Chinese equivalent of the Greater East Asia Society which he had helped to found in Japan in 1933. The Chinese with whom he talked were understandably suspicious. As one of them later put it, "We thought Matsui's slogan 'Asia for the Asiatics' sounded like 'Asia for the Japanese.' "

On July 20, two days after the dramatic confrontation in the Supreme War Council, the ousted Mazaki came to the Summer Palace in Hayama to relinquish formally his staff of office. Beforehand Chief Aide-de-Camp Honjo begged the Emperor to be gracious with him and to accord him the customary words: "Thank you for your pains." Hirohito objected that once before when he had given such words to a military man dismissed in disgrace the fellow had gone about Tokyo citing the conventional courtesy as evidence that the Emperor had been on his side all along and had approved of the official stand he had taken.

"Mazaki," answered Honjo hotly, "may not be able to bend his principles but he is a faithful vassal and not such a man as would exploit the Emperor's words for his own private face."

A few minutes later, on his way to the audience chamber, Mazaki asked

Honjo if it would be all right for him, when he saw the Emperor, to explain briefly the position he had taken. Honjo strictly enjoined him against doing anything so rash and irregular. And so Mazaki was given the bleak imperial thanks and retired permanently from the Emperor's presence. Chamberlains who witnessed his withdrawal described his open honest face as "smudged by tears."

NAGATA'S MURDER

News of the stormy session at the Supreme War Council, though censored from the newspapers, spread widely by word of mouth. With it traveled rumors that Araki was contemplating hara-kiri as a final protest and that the overwrought Mazaki elements might attack the War Ministry and burn it to the ground. In such an atmosphere, Lieutenant Colonel Aizawa, the fencing master who had warned First Crow Nagata to resign, received notification of his reposting to Taiwan. He at once traveled to Osaka, 300 miles away, and was received in audience by his old company commander, the Emperor's fork-tongued uncle, Prince Higashikuni.

What was said is unknown, but Higashikuni later volunteered the following account to Saionji's Secretary-Spy Harada: "Aizawa is an even simpler fellow than [my factotum] Yasuda. . . . When I was resting in Osaka after the recent maneuvers, Aizawa asked to see me. I at first declined, being exhausted, but when he said he was going to Taiwan I did see him. Apparently he really intended to go to Taiwan at that point and only got violent ideas after he went back up to Tokyo. Mazaki at that time was speaking slander of Nagata . . . and possibly he spoke in the same vein to Aizawa."

After talking to Higashikuni, instead of going on toward Hiroshima and Fukuyama, where his division was stationed—instead, that is, of going to pack for his transfer to Taiwan—Aizawa traveled in the other direction to Tokyo. There he did see Mazaki. According to Mazaki's own story, a story which the secret police failed to break down when they interrogated Mazaki for more than a year in 1936 and 1937, he advised Aizawa to obey orders and avoid violence. He added in jest, "If you want to kill anyone, take a stab at General Ugaki who began all this mess with the March Plot in 1931."

No longer sure of the resolve which had brought him to Tokyo, Aizawa went next to see Prince Asaka, Higashikuni's brother, who would later superintend at the rape of Nanking. According to the humorous story which Prince Asaka afterward told his best friends: "Aizawa said to me, 'I would like you to introduce me to General Ugaki,' and it appeared that if I had arranged the introduction, he would have assassinated Ugaki."

Prince Asaka declined to give the introduction. Instead, he did better. He went to the palace and told the chamberlain in charge of ceremonials that it was a matter of some urgency that he see the Emperor in private without attracting public attention. This was difficult because the Emperor was away at the Summer Palace in Hayama and no one could pay him a call without the journey being noticed. Therefore, Prince Asaka requested that when the Emperor came up to Tokyo on July 29 to attend the annual service for his grandfather at Meiji Shrine, Prince Asaka alone be allowed to serve as the member of the imperial family detailed to welcome him at the Tokyo railroad station. Somehow young Prince Kitashirakawa, twenty-four, failed to be informed of the arrangement and went to the station to ask his revered cousin a petty favor. Prince Asaka at once called the lord privy seal's secretary, Marquis Kido, and told him to make absolutely sure that, when Hirohito returned to Hayama, Asaka and the Emperor would have a few moments of complete privacy together. Kido promised to do what he could and found that the Emperor himself had already issued the necessary instructions. Imperial Household Minister Yuasa had cross-checked with the Emperor to be certain that the imperial wishes had not been misunderstood. Now Yuasa was "taking thought for the effect upon public opinion and doing his best to arrange matters." Kido was at pains to set forth in full in his diary his own part in these transactions and noted gravely at the end of his entry, "If the Emperor has already given the order it must be done as specified according to the unquestionable holy will."

When Hirohito returned to Hayama, Prince Asaka saw him off and all was settled. On August 5 War Minister Hayashi sent the vice war minister to plead with First Crow Nagata to accept a leave of absence and go on a trip abroad. Nagata steadfastly refused. Having served for fourteen years as Hirohito's principal implement within the Army, having engineered the fall of the Choshu clan in the 1920's, having recruited all the young faithfuls who had participated in the plots to take Manchuria and suppress industrial and political dissent at home, he perhaps did not believe what was about to happen to him. Or perhaps he had reached a point in life where he felt required to stand on principle. Or perhaps he genuinely believed that the sacrifice of his life would help the imperial cause which he had so long served.

In any event Prince Higashikuni's former subordinate, Lieutenant Colonel Aizawa Saburo, arrived at the War Ministry on the morning of August 12, 1935, resolved to murder First Crow Nagata. At the reception desk he gave the name of Major General Yamaoka Shigeatsu whom he had known as an instructor at the Staff College when he himself had been a fencing master at the military academy. He was duly ushered into the office of Yamaoka who was now director of the War Ministry's Equipment and Supplies Bureau. Yamaoka was one of the Eleven Reliables chosen at Baden-Baden. He had sided with the Strike-North group during the faction fight but would survive the rebellion ahead and continue to hold field commands until his retirement in 1939. He was known to fellow officers as a religious fanatic who worshipped the ghosts in old samurai swords. He had a personal collection of over one hundred historic blades and was responsible for the regulation that all members of the Japanese officer corps should own a sword and wear it at all public ceremonies. When the overwrought Aizawa appeared in his presence, Yamaoka calmly chatted with him and then, eschewing the telephone, sent a messenger boy to the Bureau of Military Affairs to make sure that its director, First Crow Nagata, was in. When the messenger returned with an affirmative answer, Yamaoka gave Aizawa directions as to how to find his way.

Moments later Aizawa rushed through the outlying offices of the sprawling Military Affairs Bureau, the largest in the Army, and burst in on Nagata unannounced. Nagata was closeted with the commandant of the Tokyo secret police.

"What is it?" he barked, without looking up.

Aizawa drew his sword with an audible swish. The secret police commandant gasped. Nagata sprang up, dodged a blow, and dashed for the door. Aizawa slashed at him and striped his back with blood. The secret police commandant tried to intervene and was pinked in the shoulder. Nagata, on his knees, struggled to open the door. Aizawa finished him off with a clean stroke that ran him through from back to front.

Leaving Nagata to die some minutes later, Aizawa ran to the office of Nemoto Hiroshi, a member of the 1927 Suzuki Study Group who was now in charge of the Army's Press Relations Squad.

"Ah soka yattanai!" ("So you really did do it!") exclaimed Nemoto.

Aizawa's finger was bleeding. He was sent under escort to the infirmary to have it bound up. On the way he crossed paths with Nagata's stretcher, which dripped blood. "I then remembered," he later testified in court, "that I had failed to kill Nagata with one blow and, as a fencing master I felt deeply ashamed."

Having received first aid for his finger, Aizawa announced that he must return at once to his regiment in Fukuyama in order to pack his gear for the trip to Taiwan. He was, as Prince Higashikuni said, a simple fellow. He had committed a holy murder. He had been encouraged by the Emperor's two uncles. Prince Asaka had gone to see the Emperor in private to make sure that it would be all right. To Aizawa's "surprise," however, as he later testified, the secret police took him into custody and held him for trial.

When the secretary to the lord privy seal, Big Brother Marquis Kido, heard the news of First Crow Nagata's assassination, he failed in his diary to express his customary regrets. When Hirohito was informed of the murder by Chief Aide-de-Camp Honjo, he said, "It is extremely regrettable that such an incident has occurred in the Army. Please investigate and report the full details to me. Do you think it will be all right if I take my ordinary daily swim today?"

Honjo replied, "I, Shigeru, think this is an inexcusable incident but I do not think there will be any special succession of breaking waves as a result of it. And I will take pains to see that there are none. As for the honorable daily exercise, please go ahead with it."

PERIOD OF MOURNING

Nagata, once first among the Three Crows, had been murdered because he had allowed the evidence implicating the Emperor and his circle in the March Plot to come into the hands of the Strike-North Faction. He had also given indication that he parted with the Emperor over plans for war with China. Like most thoughtful Japanese he had considered friendship with China a prerequisite to the Pax Japonica which had been the national aspiration.

Nevertheless there was a certain meaningless malice about the sacrifice of Nagata. And it troubled members of the imperial circle who knew how deeply Hirohito was involved. Old Prince Saionji, when he heard Secretary-Spy Harada's report of the affair on August 16, muttered, "I thought that Japan could avoid it, but if these things happen often, perhaps Japan after all will have to take the course [of overthrowing monarchs] followed by France, Germany, and Russia." Harada noted that Saionji sighed "as if talking to himself."

For the next seven months all three Court diaries are eloquently gloomy. Chief Aide-de-Camp Honjo felt that the Emperor "mistrusts my attitude in regard to the recent imperial family incident." Saionji's Secretary Harada found himself increasingly out of things, and talking mostly to Foreign Office people. Kido became, if possible, more circumspect than usual in his jottings. Hardly anyone, in the Army or out of it, believed that Mazaki had engineered the killing of First Crow Nagata. Colonel Niimi of the secret police, who had been with Nagata when he died, was transferred to Kyoto; and Major General Yamaoka Shigeatsu, who had told Aizawa how to find Nagata's office, was reposted to a field command. War Minister Hayashi, who had stayed at home "with a cold" on the sultry August morning of Nagata's murder, was widely criticized: first for having foisted the responsibility of Mazaki's ouster on to Nagata's shoulders, then for having done nothing to protect Nagata. People called Hayashi "a silly man riding a good horse," "a fool in bed with a beautiful woman."

At Nagata's funeral there were two masters of ceremonies, one representing the Strike-North Faction, the other—Third Crow Okamura Yasuji —representing the Strike-South Faction. The walls at the wake were banked with flowers from the palace. Chief of the Army General Staff Prince Kanin sent a message of condolence which called Nagata "a man of surpassing genius [who] . . . always took the lead both in Japan and foreign lands."

One of the mourners was Nagata's best friend, Major General Tojo Hideki, the later World War II prime minister. Ever since Baden-Baden he had served Nagata with a respectful devotion that amounted, in the eyes of his fellow officers, almost to servility. As soon as Nagata died Tojo had been granted leave from his command of the 24th Infantry Brigade in the southern island of Kyushu so that he could come to Tokyo for the obsequies. Now he stayed in Tokyo for a month settling Nagata's affairs and conferring with Field Marshal Prince Nashimoto, a friend of his late father, Lieutenant General Tojo Hidenori. Thereafter, until his own hanging in 1948, Tojo sent Nagata's widow a small but regular monthly allowance which he said came from his own pocket. At that time he made $1500 a year and had a wife and seven children.

When Tojo returned to duty in September he was entrusted with the extremely lucrative post of commandant of the Kwantung Army's secret police. Six months later when rebellion broke out in Tokyo, his secret police displayed uncanny efficiency in picking up all Kwantung Army sympathizers of the rebels and clapping them into preventive custody. From that time onward his career was meteoric: chief of staff, Kwantung Army, 1937; vice war minister, 1938; war minister 1940; prime minister and executive dictator in 1941. Throughout this rise he would be shown special marks of confidence by the Throne. And finally, during the war, he would be closer to Hirohito than anyone else except Big Brother Marquis Kido.

Under pressures generated by the Nagata murder, War Minister Hayashi on September 3, 1935, "saved the Cabinet" by resigning. The Cabinet itself was made to survive because its dissolution would have meant a general election, and a general election, unless carefully prepared, would almost certainly strengthen opposition to present policies. In War Minister Hayashi's place Hirohito was obliged to accept girl spy Eastern Jewel's adoptive kinsman, General Kawashima Yoshiyuki, a much compromised nonentity who stood politically in Erehwon.

Hirohito took an instant dislike to the new war minister but resolved to make the best of a bad situation. He took pains to have Kawashima carefully instructed from the outset: "The Army must be the Emperor's Army and all must unite and exert their efforts to make it a magnificent one. The Emperor personally wishes to supervise all diplomatic and military affairs so please inform him prior to making decisions on all matters."

Hirohito now found that one concession led to another. On September 16, news of the Prayer Meeting Plot of 1933 was finally allowed to be published in the newspaper. Prince Higashikuni's name, however, was not mentioned, and the trials of the guilty were to be postponed for another two years. On September 18 Professor Minobe, under great inducements, resigned from the House of Peers. In return, the various legal cases against him were dropped. On October 1, the Okada Cabinet, in a much negotiated statement designed to "clarify the national policy," promised "to stamp out the organ theory," to investigate the ideas and books of all professors, and to ban all injurious ones. On October 21 it was spread on the bureaucratic grapevine, and attested by Privy Seal Secretary Kido to be a matter of fact, that Prince Higashikuni was still paying his factotum, Lieutenant Colonel Yasuda, $86 a month for his help in past plots.

"SPIRIT OF POSITIVE FORCE"

By making concessions Hirohito was buying time while trying to consolidate Japan's new position south of the Great Wall. China's compliance with the terms of the Ho-Umezu Pact remained purely formal, superficial, and unhelpful. The Chinese smiled, as requested, at Japanese troops but made polite excuses not to assist them in any other way. Japanese plans for autonomous regions throughout north China were foundering for lack of influential Chinese who would serve as puppets.

On September 20, 1935, Foreign Minister Hirota—the only civilian to be hanged as a war criminal by the Allies in 1948—enunciated to Chiang Kai-shek "three principles of Japanese foreign policy": Nanking must help control anti-Japanese movements in North China, she must sign a cultural agreement with Manchukuo and Japan, and she must join Japan in fighting the Bolshevik menace in north China. In a fourth "principle," which Foreign Minister Hirota transmitted verbally and in secret, Chiang Kai-shek was informed that "centralization of power in China in the city of Nanking is neither necessary nor desirable." It was almost an exact repetition of the statement which Hirohito had approved as secret Japanese policy a year earlier.

In his "principles" Foreign Minister Hirota was making a last effort to realize Hirohito's desire that north China be made an independent puppet state without resort to arms. The "principles" were made explicit to Chiang Kai-shek because it was becoming apparent that, without his co-operation, pressure alone would never make north China independent. As Third Crow Major General Okamura had just informed Prince Kanin: "It is predictable that Chiang Kai-shek will persist in his negative attitude until he is driven to the wall. . . . For the time being Japan must maintain a policy based on the spirit of positive force."

In due course Chiang Kai-shek rejected Hirota's "principles" and Emperor Hirohito accepted the need for positive force. On October 1, 1935, Finance Minister Takahashi sent word to Saionji, who was celebrating his eighty-sixth birthday: "Several days ago the foreign minister came to me and explained our plans in north China. Now it seems that preparations for war are being made in secret."

The preparations were spurred on two days later when Mussolini set a precedent and created a distraction by invading Ethiopia. Japan's underworld leader, "Darkside Emperor" Toyama, promptly called a mass meeting to express sympathy for the fellow "colored people" of Ethiopia. The police used the meeting as an excuse for a final crackdown on Toyama's

Black Dragon Society and on its affiliated lower-class religious sect, Omoto-kyo. Thereafter the society held no more mass meetings and its once powerful mafia-style leadership dwindled to a few score superannuated rabble-rousers who maintained the society's dread name on the door of a dusty one-room walk-up office on the periphery of Tokyo's downtown business district.

World sympathy for the Ethiopians and failure of the Italians to achieve a blitzkrieg conquest caused the Japanese General Staff to refine its plans for China. On October 25, the chief of staff of the Kwantung Army, a Strike-South lieutenant general named Nishio Toshizo, cabled the vice minister of war, another Strike-South lieutenant general, Furusho Mikio, advising him that propaganda must be carefully supervised and centralized in the planned war with China. "It must be made clear," he explained, "that when we do send our military forces to China some time in the future, we do it for the purpose of punishing the Chinese military clique and not the Chinese people at large."

The two princely chiefs of staff dealt sternly with Strike-North partisans who were still in a position to hamper the war preparations. In November Admiral Kato Kanji, the leader of the Navy's Strike-North Faction and a onetime friend of Navy Chief of Staff Prince Fushimi, was retired from active service. Remaining Strike-North admirals and generals were assigned watchdogs from the loyal ranks of Prince Kanin's Control Clique. In both Army and Navy a drastic reshuffle of the top brass was planned for December in order to remove Strike-North advocates from their last positions of power.

TENSION AT COURT

Prophets and supporters of the Strike-North policy were now faced by a loss of face. The "Crisis of 1936" was about to pass in peace. Chamberlains at Court waited tensely for the last day of 1935. The published plans of the Military Academy Plot of the year before made it abundantly clear that young dissidents might try to kill all the statesmen around the Throne. Kido, Harada, Makino, and the rest had been assigned plainclothes guards since First Crow Nagata's murder. But no one felt much reassured when, on October 30, an angry young man looked up organ theorist Minobe's name in the telephone directory and was narrowly apprehended at Minobe's door as he sought to break in with intent to kill.

Lord Privy Seal Makino, receiving anonymous letters and hearing constant gossip to the effect that he was "the originator of all past incidents," grew haggard with insomnia. His long-time cohort in the palace, Privy Council President Ikki, complained of intestinal bleeding. Even Chief of Staff Prince Kanin, a member of the Emperor's family, was not immune from attack. Prince Higashikuni, up to Tokyo on a visit from his command in Osaka, told Secretary-Spy Harada on October 18, 1935, that there was agitation in the ranks for Prince Kanin to resign because of "his lack of sympathy for Mazaki and Araki." It was a "strange" idea, said Higashikuni with indignation, because "princes never express their sympathies." Harada nodded and then observed sanctimoniously that, of course, the impartiality of princes "should not extend to the distinction between right and wrong."

On November 27, 1935, Lord Privy Seal Count Makino begged leave of the Throne to go into retirement. Privy Council President Ikki followed suit a few hours later. Both pleaded neuralgia, decrepitude, and general ill health. Hirohito was loath to break in new senior advisors and said that he would need time to consider their requests. For once old Prime-Minister-Maker Saionji, when consulted, was pleased to agree with the Emperor. "Ikki and Makino," he said, "are still capable of discharging their duties as assistants to the Throne. I am eighty-six, with a bad memory and bad eyes. It would be more natural to allow me to resign first." [5]

Nevertheless on December 11, Lord Privy Seal Makino submitted his formal resignation verbally to the Throne. Hirohito, expressing regret, promised to find a replacement for him as soon as possible. Hirohito wished to make former Prime Minister Saito the next lord privy seal but found that many chamberlains feared Saito would be controversial because it was Saito's cabinet, in 1933, which had first endorsed the decision to try for a Strike South. On December 20, while chamberlains were still endeavoring to change Hirohito's mind, Count Makino forced the issue by submitting his resignation in writing. Hirohito accepted it and duly appointed Saito to take his place.

Privy Council President Ikki was persuaded to remain in office. Hirohito personally recommended a new type of therapeutic belt which he had read about as remedy for Ikki's sagging guts. At the same time, as a sop to the Strike-North Faction, Hirohito made General Araki a baron; as a prop for the Throne, he brought back martinet General Terauchi from his preparations in Taiwan to stand by close to the Throne in the troubled months ahead.

[5] Ikki was then sixty-eight and would live to be seventy-eight; Makino was seventy-three and would live to be eighty-seven.

20

FEBRUARY MUTINY

(1936)

TEASING A SHOWDOWN

The venal old loyalists on the steps of the Throne had good reason to worry about their health. In effect, Hirohito had set them up as targets and was encouraging a group of would-be assassins to start shooting. The silent three-year struggle with the Strike-North Faction had gone on long enough. It was time for a confrontation. Hirohito and his kinsmen had decided that only an outright rebellion would shame the nation and provide justification for a thoroughgoing purge of disaffection. By the same token Generals Araki and Mazaki of the Strike-North Faction, along with many samurai of the old school, felt that a mutiny in the ranks, if large and protracted enough, would win popular support and force Hirohito to reflect.

The chosen assassin-dupes for the coming confrontation were the young antifascistic captains and lieutenants of the National Principle Group who had started the Military Academy Incident of the year before. They qualified as sacrificial moderators in the feud because, though nominally aligned with the Strike-North Faction, they were not really interested in any strategic concept abroad but only in reform and frankness at home.

The young men of the National Principle Group began meeting at bars and cheap geisha houses to consider the possibility of insurrection in November 1935. Their ringleaders were two former Army comrades, Muranaka and Isobe, who had written the seditious pamphlet in May which had called attention to First Crow Nagata's involvement in the 1931 March Plot. Their pamphlet had been pointed out to Chief of Staff Prince Kanin during his struggle in July to fire General Mazaki. It had angered him. On July 30 he had sent War Minister Hayashi on a special trip to the Summer Palace in Hayama to ask Hirohito to approve the expulsion of the

621

two pamphleteers from the Army. To retire men from active to reserve status was not an uncommon form of punishment for Army dissidents but to expel them from the Army altogether was most unusual. Former messmates gave the two disgruntled new civilians much sympathy.

Emperor Hirohito's brother Prince Chichibu personally kept abreast of the plans of the National Principle Group through four of its members who had been his classmates in military academy. These four he regularly invited up to his villa for chats. And these four, when they later faced firing squads, protested in vain that Prince Chichibu had encouraged them. One of them left his family a note lamenting: "Prince Chichibu told me, 'When the coup d'etat comes, I want you to head a company and invite me to see you off as you march from your barracks.'" Another left a bundle of poems, written in prison, which the secret police impounded and turned over to Chichibu's equerry. Having gone through them, Prince Chichibu returned most of them to the young man's family. The bereaved parents felt greatly honored that Princess Chichibu had selected several of them with her own hand and had had them beautifully mounted and framed.

Prince Higashikuni and Prince Asaka, the Emperor's two uncles, also talked frequently with the young plotters and sympathized with their complaints. The rebels' greatest encouragement, however, came from Major General Tiger Yamashita who had charge of the palace effort to infiltrate the Strike-North movement with spies. Yamashita made a practice of meeting the young rebels at bars and having a drink with them. He introduced them to Third Crow Major General Okamura, who was now chief of Intelligence in the General Staff, and also to Colonel Nemoto of the War Ministry Press Relations Squad, who had grunted congratulations at swordsman Aizawa after the murder of First Crow Nagata. Tiger Yamashita and his companions all reported their observations to Chief of Staff Prince Kanin.

The young men of the National Principle Group were flattered by all the attention they were receiving from intimates of the Throne but knew enough to be wary. Their friends warned them against being exploited and told them, jokingly, that they were "natural leftists trying to dress on the right." The young men sent a deputation to the home of former War Minister Araki, the leader of the Strike-North Faction. Araki smiled at them encouragingly but carefully avoided saying anything by which he would commit himself. They went back to Major General Tiger Yamashita, the spy of the Strike-South Faction, and were advised by him "not to act without careful preparation." They set Christmas Day 1935, when Western military attachés would be out wassailing, as their tentative deadline for revolution.

On December 20 they sent an embassy to the second ranking leader of the Strike North, General Mazaki. He told them that they were fools to consider rebellion and doubly fools to consult him about their plans when they knew he was already discredited and under constant police surveillance. They accosted a third Strike-North general and got even more explicit advice: "The gods, the Emperor, and the good earth are all against you. The members of the Control Clique [Strike-South Faction] are just waiting for a half-prepared outbreak to give them an opportunity for a house cleaning." [1]

On December 22 Tiger Yamashita, the infiltrator from the ranks of the Strike-Southists, agreed to meet the young idealists at the Honored Parlor Restaurant in northern Tokyo. He did not keep the appointment, and when the conspirators had waited in vain for him all evening, they agreed to give up their plan for an outbreak on Christmas Day. On their way home a group of them stopped at a police station and voluntarily swore out a complete report on their own activities.

Still at large, the conspirators, on Christmas Eve, stopped for a few consoling thimbles of saké at the home of the ideologist of the Strike-North Faction, the tough old radical writer Kita Ikki, who had first split the Emperor's cabal in 1922 by refusing to participate in Hirohito's palace indoctrination center, the University Lodging House. Schooled by years of experience with the secret police, Kita advised the young men to be patient and await their opportunity. In the meantime he proposed that they participate in a small public rally to protest the appointment of former Prime Minister Saito as lord privy seal. He convinced the young officers that Saito had taken bribes in connection with the Teikoku Rayon Company stock swindle of 1934. The protest meeting was duly held on December 30, 1935, and was duly broken up by the police. Several of the young officers were taken into custody but all were released a few days later to ripen their plans.

At year's end Big Brother Marquis Kido, secretary to the lord privy seal, leafed into his diary the police report on the conspirators' latest insurrection plan: 1st Infantry, 1st Company, to take the home minister's residence; 3d Infantry, 3d Company, to kill the prime minister; 1st Infantry, 2d Company, to hunt down Lord Privy Seal Saito—and so on. Except for a few details it was substantially the Military Academy Plan of 1934 and also the plan that would be executed two months later. By the time that fateful New Year of 1936 had arrived, the chamberlains in the palace knew it almost by heart.

If any complacent courtiers retained a doubt as to the depth of disenchantment in the ranks of the Army, it was dispelled a few days later in January, when an entire company of Japanese infantry, together with their commissioned and noncommissioned officers, crossed the border from

[1] The speaker was Lieutenant General Yanagawa Heisuke, who had been vice war minister under Strike-North leader Araki. He was known to Hirohito as a moderate of the Strike-North Faction and a close friend of the ubiquitous Colonel Suzuki. At this moment he was on his way to Taiwan to replace martinet Terauchi as commander-in-chief of Japan's territorial army there. Later, in 1937, he would clear himself of Strike-North guilt in Hirohito's eyes by devising the Hangchow Bay landing which enabled the Japanese Army to take Nanking.

Manchukuo into Russia and surrendered to the Red Army. The officers hoped to create an incident which would redirect policy toward the Strike North. The men were simply glad to escape the Manchukuoan hell of torture and murder in which they were obliged to officiate. No body of Japanese soldiers had ever defected before to a foreign power, and everyone in authority realized that only desperation could have driven them to it now.

THE TALKING GODDESS

To prepare for the ill-conceived insurrection in the offing, Hirohito's double-dealing uncle, Prince Higashikuni, devised an ingenious religious fraud to blackmail and gag aristocrats who had criticized Hirohito most outspokenly in the past. On November 22, 1935, Prince Higashikuni had invited a religious confidence man, the ventriloquist, Ohara Tatsuo, alias Ohara Ryukai or Dragon-Sea, to a room in the old unused private quarters of Emperor Meiji in the southern extremities of the palace's gardens. There he gave Dragon-Sea a set of ceremonial imperial robes and other tokens of imperial favor including a pair of Hirohito's gloves and a cigarette case embossed with the chrysanthemum crest. To these props Dragon-Sea added a statue of the goddess of mercy which could talk—at least he could make her seem to talk—and thereupon he set himself up in business as an oracle in the little temple of Iribune in the Tokyo suburb of Shiina.

By Higashikuni's introduction Dragon-Sea acquired the patronage of former chief Court Lady Shimazu Haruko, who had been eased out of the palace in 1933 for her involvement in the Red Scandal and the concubine controversy. Lady Shimazu loved nothing better than an uplifting, shiver-filled seance. So did many of her best friends, and she was ideally well connected. As a cousin of Empress Nagako's mother and an intimate of Hirohito's own mother, the Empress Dowager, she was on fervent spiritual terms with almost every kindly body in the elder generation of the aristocracy—almost everyone who took a high-toned moralistic approach to matters of state. In addition to counts and countesses, the circle of her acquaintance included retired admirals, retired generals, leaders of veterans' organizations, and anti-organ theorists by the score. One of her dearest friends was Shinto priest Hata Shinji, the former commandant of the Tokyo secret police who had supplied damaging material against the Strike-South Faction during the struggle before Mazaki's ouster.

By mid-January Lady Shimazu was bringing her friends by droves to hear the ventriloquistic prophesies of Dragon-Sea's statue and to attend spiritualistic manifestations and materializations. Outside the walls of Dragon-Sea's fashionable little temple, trustworthy police agents stood nightly guard to take notes on attendance. In later police reports aged Admiral Yamamoto Eisuke figured prominently as a regular participant in the "services." He was one of the first choices for prime minister in the cabinet which the young insurgents of the National Principle Group hoped to bring to power. Many other prominent members of Tokyo's high society, particularly wives, also attended. All were thereby induced to hold their peace in the months ahead.

At the seances the congregations of aristocrats heard a combination of filth and philosophy which was provided Dragon-Sea by Prince Higashi-kuni. The gossip amused them and compromised them. According to former Court Lady Shimazu Haruko's confession, preserved in police files after she had been committed to a sanatorium in December 1936, spirits of people alive and dead appeared before the audiences and traded in all sorts of blasphemous gossip about the imperial family:

> The dead spirit of Namba Daisaku [Hirohito's 1923 assassin, who missed] appeared with the living spirit of Prince Chichibu [Hirohito's brother]. Chichibu's spirit says that Namba steals the virginity of his fiancee.[2]
>
> Prince Takamatsu [Hirohito's second brother] appears in spirit and says that his real mother, Lady Blank Blank, was one of Emperor Taisho's serving girls. . . .
>
> The chamberlain [General Nogi] appeared who served the crown prince [Hirohito] and then committed hara-kiri. His ghost, dressed like an imperial prince himself, said, "I was defeated for saying that Prince Chichibu should be the one proclaimed Crown Prince. . . ."
>
> The ghost of Emperor Taisho's chamberlain appears and says that he has been a lover of the Empress Dowager [Hirohito's mother]. . . .
>
> Questions were put by the Kujos [the Empress Dowager's brother and sister-in-law]. . . .
>
> Prince Chichibu's living ghost appears and speaks of his affair with Princess Noriko [Ito Noriko, who had been implicated in the Red Scandal at the Peers' School]. . . .
>
> There is a front face and a back face to every mirror. On our front face it is inscribed officially that if we worship the gods they will protect us. On the back face we believe that the Imperial Purpose will ultimately make itself clear and light the road toward restoration of the Throne. The back face is pregnant with such meanings and the front face is kept to convince ordinary men so that they may someday see around to the back. Faithful souls can approach the back of the mirror only gradually. And even beyond the back of the mirror there are further stages of enlightenment such as *himarogi* and so on which bring full revelation. Only men of the highest consciousness can attain them and it is very rare. . . .
>
> On July 17 there will be a meeting of all the spirits of the world. It will be the first meeting of the Five Lights. . . . The honorable soul of the Emperor Meiji will not attend, being temporarily detained by the work of the Empress Dowager.[3] Then the way to clarification of the national structure

[2] There may be a confusion of brothers here. Empress Nagako's brother, Asa-akira, in 1924, broke off his engagement with a girl because it was discovered that she was having an affair with a kinsman of the Namba clan.

[3] The Empress Dowager was then involved in petty palace intrigues against her son Hirohito. The identity of the Five Lights is mysterious. According to one well-

and to restoration will be revealed—the way to divine government and to the world of a just god.

The work of the Five Lights is to decide on a regent and select an assistant for the time of minority of the crown prince [Akihito, who is still crown prince in 1970]. In the world of spirits the crown prince possesses the soul of Emperor Meiji and at the same time has a greatness of his own self. This has been revealed to us. Therefore Prince Chichibu [Hirohito's brother] will withdraw in favor of Prince Takamatsu [Hirohito's second brother], and Takamatsu will become the assistant and regent. The Emperor himself will die after fifteen years [1951]. . . . The Emperor has a karma [inherited guilt] to expiate and so cannot realize revelation and restoration. He cannot escape an early death. We have to achieve enlightenment and a supreme offering to the gods of our own soil in order to restore our gods and clarify the national structure. It is like opening up the rocks that they may speak but we have the key to do it. . . . The Five Lights will become ten, twenty, forty lights. . . . We must have faith and expand.

Wild words they were as Lady Shimazu recalled them to the police. But even the smut was enough, wild though it might be, to convict anyone of lèse majesté who listened to it without protest. The mysticism was worse, for it showed a definite longing to be rid of Hirohito and it imputed to him a fatal guilt for the many murders done during his reign.

FINAL INCITEMENTS

On January 27, 1936, Prince Higashikuni sprang another trapdoor in his Pandora's box of blackmail when the police released some 500 sturdy sword arms who had been jailed on suspicion of complicity in the 1933 Prayer Meeting Plot. Under the supervision of Higashikuni's faithful factotum, retired Lieutenant Colonel Yasuda, the paroled convicts opened a headquarters and remained ready at hand as a riot squad—"all picked men"—who could be thrown into the breach if the forthcoming rebellion in any way misfired. Higashikuni's man Yasuda kept the prince informed of their doings by messages delivered by courier to the bodyguard at the gates of Hagashikuni's villa.[4] In the event, the riot squad never had to be used but the men in it won freedom from prosecution by their stand-by service.

On January 28, 1936, the court-martial proceedings began against First Crow Nagata's killer, Prince Higashikuni's former second lieutenant,

educated Japanese guess, the first four may have been noted loyalists who died for the Throne in centuries past and the fifth may have been the recently sacrificed martyr, First Crow Nagata.

[4] The chief of Higashikuni's bodyguard was Captain Kiyoura Sueo, the eighth son of former Prime Minister Kiyoura whom Hirohito had recalled from oblivion to lead the government during the Choshu purge of 1924.

Aizawa. They were held in the most emotionally flammable surroundings possible: the barracks of the 1st Division. It was this division, one of the two stationed in Tokyo, which contained most of the young officers of the antifascist National Principle Group. It was this division which, on the papers of past plot plans, was expected to supply a majority of the forces for any rebellion. Court-martial defendant Aizawa had served as a captain and major in the division from 1926 to 1931, and the men of the division had just been notified in December that they were all to be transferred imminently to garrison duty in Manchuria. The 1st Division had never before been sent overseas except for action in time of war.

The advocate assigned to defend assassin Aizawa was Lieutenant Colonel Mitsui Sakichi, the young man who had forced his way into the home of the Mitsui cartel magnate two years earlier and who for several months had been working closely with the Strike-South Faction's spy in Strike-North ranks, Major General Tiger Yamashita. In 1937, Mitsui would be given three years' suspended sentence for his part in the 1936 rebellion. In 1942, during the war, he would be elected to the Diet.

At Aizawa's trial Mitsui played to packed houses. "If an error is made at this trial," he orated, "it will have serious consequences. . . . If the court fails to understand the spirit which guided Aizawa, a second and even a third Aizawa will arise. . . . A large majority of the junior officers are determined to purge the Army of outside influence, and the nation sincerely desires that the Army will prove itself to be the Army of the Emperor."

Assassin Aizawa himself was put on the stand and cross-questioned sympathetically. He breathed not a word of his meetings with Prince Higashikuni and Prince Asaka. He testified, however, that on his first journey to Tokyo, when he warned Nagata instead of killing him, "I could not sleep on the train and in the morning I heard a voice, as if from on high, telling me not to act too rashly. . . . Only later did I come to realize that Nagata was the headquarters of all the evil. If he would not resign there was only one thing to do. I determined to make myself a demon and finish his life with one stroke. . . . When on the Emperor's authority the inspector general of military education was transferred to the honorable post of a Supreme War Councillor, it seemed to me like converting the Imperial Army into a private concern."

Big Brother Kido, secretary to the lord privy seal, kept close track of the proceedings at the Aizawa trial and worried about them. On February 2, after careful research, however, he decided that everything would be all right. He compared defense lawyer Lieutenant Colonel Mitsui with Colonel Ishiwara Kanji, who had planned the conquest of Manchuria, and with Colonel Hashimoto Kingoro, the firebrand who would later sink the U.S. gunboat *Panay*. All three felt the need for domestic reform and sympathized with the National Principle Group. "But when it comes to the point," Kido concluded, "they will all present a united front to outsiders."

While the Aizawa trial was in progress, the Diet was dissolved and the nation was treated to its first election campaign since 1932. The Strike-North group in the Army sided with the Constitutionalists on a platform of traditional samurai bravado. The Anti-Constitutionalists, Hirohito's Control Clique, and the Army Purification Movement backed incumbent Prime Minister Okada. Although fascistically inclined themselves, they campaigned under the slogan, "What shall it be, parliamentary government or fascism?" The people responded to the slogan by giving them a landslide victory: 205 Diet seats to 174 for the Constitutionalists. It was a clear triumph for Hirohito's public sentiments, and a rebuff to the fascist ideas he toyed with privately.

COURAGE AT STICKING POINT

During January the dissident young officers of the National Principle Group had paid calls on Prince Chichibu, on War Minister Kawashima, and on General Mazaki of the Strike-North Faction. They found everyone of importance friendly but evasive, not willing to support them nor yet to discourage them. General Mazaki, for instance, offered to lend them money but added, "If anything happens, don't say I gave it to you."

On the evening of January 28, the conspirators met with a sympathetic company commander, Captain Yamaguchi Ichitaro, who was the son-in-law of General Honjo, Hirohito's chief aide-de-camp. On February 10 they met again with Yamaguchi in the staff room of the 1st Regiment, 1st Division, where he was duty officer. There for the first time they discussed plans for a rebellion in concrete operational terms. The next day they sent a deputation to the home of the Strike-North ideologist, Kita Ikki, to see his disciple and servant, Nishida Chikara. Like themselves, Nishida was a friend and former classmate of Prince Chichibu. It was he who had first mimeographed and distributed intellectual Ikki's radical writings for Prince Chichibu in 1921. Now Nishida welcomed the rebels and promised to muster popular backing for them.

On February 15 the reluctant rebels finally revisited Major General Tiger Yamashita, their watchdog from the palace. The next morning the young officers took steps to see that they would have access to weapons from their divisional arsenal. Three days later Captain Ando Teruzo, the ringleader of the conspiracy who was closest to General Yamashita, threw a fresh crimp into the planning by admitting frankly at a cell meeting, "Now that it is decided, I do not dare to do it." [5]

The best that the other conspirators could agree to, after Ando's admis-

---

[5] At Yamashita's order, after the assassination of Prime Minister Inukai in 1932, Ando had, for several days, given refuge in his personal quarters to the Tokyo University student, Yotsumoto Yoshitaka, who had served as messenger boy between the Blood Brotherhood and Lord Privy Seal Count Makino.

sion, was a tentative zero hour "about the middle of next week." On the following day, February 19, another meeting of the conspirators was heartened to hear that kindred spirits at the military school in Toyohashi down the coast had agreed to join in their plans by assassinating the venerable Prince Saionji.

On February 21, Isobe and Muranaka, the two pamphleteers who had been drummed out of the Army the year before, sought reassurance by meeting again with Chief Aide-de-Camp Honjo's son-in-law Yamaguchi. As duty officer of the 1st Regiment Yamaguchi promised that no one in the regiment who did not join the rebellion would ever receive orders to suppress it. That evening duty officer Yamaguchi invited to his home mimeographer Nishida, the number-two ideologist of the Strike-North Faction, and advised him to tell his master, old revolutionary Kita, that Plot Day had been set tentatively for February 26.

The next morning, P-day minus four, the young officers met, admitted to one another that they were frightened, and adjourned after writing the first draft of a manifesto which they meant to post on walls and broadcast over the radio when and if they ever captured the center of Tokyo.

On February 23, P-day minus three, they took out a supply of 2,000 rounds of ammunition from their division's arsenal and recruited several new captains and lieutenants. The plan to assassinate Prince Saionji sat ill with some of the more politically sophisticated backers of the plot. And that same day, February 23, Chief Aide-de-Camp Honjo's son-in-law Yamaguchi consulted the discredited Strike-North General Mazaki about it. On Mazaki's advice Yamaguchi went on to see a professional information peddler, Kamegawa Tetsuya, who had been acting as go-between to bring financial support to the plotters from a branch of the Constitutionalist Party.[6]

The next morning, February 24, P-day minus two, informer Kamegawa visited the civilian lawyer for the defense at the Aizawa trial, told him of the entire conspiracy, and begged his aid in persuading old Prince Saionji to recommend ousted General Mazaki as the next prime minister. The lawyer, a friend of Saionji named Usawa Fusa-aki, promised to do what he could and then warned Saionji that he was about to be assassinated.[7] The warning arrived in Okitsu through a typically complex chain of intermediaries including Saionji's steward, a Dietman named Tsugumo Kunitoshi, and Saionji's sometime private secretary, the industrialist Nakagawa Kojuro.

---

[6] Specifically from Kuhara Fusanosuke, the founder of the Hitachi industrial empire. He was an ardent apostle of American-style capitalism resting on common stock and a broad basis of ownership of capital goods.

[7] At a clandestine court-martial in the home of the minister of justice a year later, the secret police sought to press charges against Defense Counsel Usawa as an accomplice in the plot. Usawa's timely warning to Saionji then saved him from prison, for after several hearings, when it became apparent that Usawa could not be tried without implicating Saionji, the proceedings against him were dropped.

Saionji had no doubt as to the importance of the warning and acted on it without delay. He arranged to have what Secretary-Spy Harada called "an infallible line of liaison" kept open between Okitsu and the palace in Tokyo. He gave instructions to his servants to answer the phone naturally, as if they knew nothing and as if their aged master were still peacefully in residence. Then he had himself secretly carried away in a sedan chair over the hills behind his home. On the other side he was picked up on a deserted stretch of road by an official car which whisked him away to the well-guarded mansion of the governor of Shizuoka prefecture.

Meanwhile, on P-day minus two, Captain Nonaka, who was the senior officer of the plotters and the closest of them to Prince Chichibu, took the draft manifesto to the home of Strike-North ideologist Kita Ikki and asked his help in polishing it. Kita obliged by adding to the blunt sentiments of the soldiers much fiery rhetoric and difficult Chinese syntax to produce a contemporary classic—one which would be read aloud a few days later to Emperor Hirohito. After its composition Captain Nonaka sat down in Kita's parlor with Kita's henchman Nishida and made a fair copy on a scroll of fine rice paper for presentation to the Throne.

That evening Captain Yamaguchi, the son-in-law of Chief Aide-de-Camp Honjo, met with the conspirators in the duty room of the 1st Regiment, went over their plans in detail, and gave them 200 mimeographed copies of police maps of the war minister's residence, the War Ministry, and the Headquarters of the General Staff. The next morning, P-day minus one, the conspirators were delighted by a letter from one of their wives saying that old plotter Makino, the former lord privy seal, had been found finally, living quietly at a rural inn in Ugawara two hours away. On the basis of this intelligence one of the young officers set out by car to Yugawara to be ready to strike at the same time as his comrades in Tokyo.

That same morning, P-day minus one, ousted General Mazaki of the Strike North was called as a witness for the defense at the Aizawa trial. He refused to answer questions put to him in Aizawa's behalf on the grounds that anyone who had been a high official in the palace might not divulge, without the Emperor's express permission, matters which he had learned in the course of his official duties. After fifty taciturn minutes in court Mazaki also refused to answer the questions of newspaper reporters. In the afternoon Aizawa's military counsel for the defense, Lieutenant Colonel Mitsui Sakichi, delivered his summation. He spoke eloquently but brought out no facts, only feelings.

In the 1st Division barracks where the trial was being held, it was apparent to all that Aizawa would go silent to the gallows, that Mazaki would remain mute in retirement, that the Strike-South Faction had won. Out of religious hope, the young officers of the 1st Division felt that perhaps the Emperor, their contemporary, did not fully understand the realities. Through Tiger Yamashita, through Chief Aide-de-Camp Honjo's son-in-

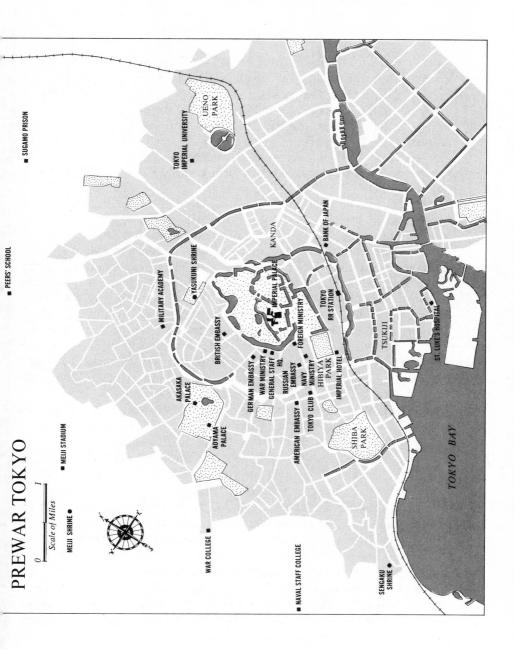

PREWAR TOKYO

Scale of Miles

0   1

MEIJI SHRINE ●

MEIJI STADIUM ■

■ PEERS' SCHOOL

■ SUGAMO PRISON

WAR COLLEGE ■

■ NAVAL STAFF COLLEGE

SENGAKU
SHRINE ●

UENO
PARK

TOKYO
IMPERIAL UNIVERSITY ■

MILITARY ACADEMY ■

YASUKUNI SHRINE ■

AKASAKA
PALACE

BRITISH EMBASSY ◆

KANDA

● BANK OF JAPAN

IMPERIAL PALACE

AOYAMA
PALACE

GERMAN EMBASSY ■

WAR MINISTRY ■

GENERAL STAFF
HQ.

FOREIGN MINISTRY

TOKYO
RR STATION

RUSSIAN
EMBASSY

NAVY
MINISTRY

HIBIYA
PARK

TSUKIJI

AMERICAN EMBASSY ◆

TOKYO CLUB ■

IMPERIAL HOTEL

ST. LUKE'S HOSPITAL

SHIBA
PARK

TOKYO BAY

law Captain Yamaguchi, and through Prince Chichibu, they thought they might be able to show Hirohito the truth.

BLOODSHED AT LAST

After more than three months of high-level encouragement, the rebels were finally committed, in all good face, to make their move. All that evening the nineteen lieutenants and captains who were already parties to the conspiracy sounded out fellow officers of the 1st and 3d Regiments. Prince Chichibu had been a member of the 3d Regiment from 1922 until August 1935, but his name, which they used freely, won over only two new converts, both of them second lieutenants. The best that the conspirators could exact from most of their colleagues was a pledge not to interfere.

At 2:00 A.M. on February 26, without any pretense of secrecy, reveille was bugled in the 1st and 3d Regiment barracks in Azabu some twenty blocks from the palace. For the next hour the sleepy soldiers were treated to harangues from the conspirators and also to some words of warning from anti-conspirators. Nevertheless the soldiers responded with some enthusiasm and by about 3:30 A.M. 1,359 of them, together with 91 noncommissioned officers, had elected to follow the two captains, eight lieutenants, and eleven second lieutenants who were already committed. By 4:00 A.M. kits were packed and the insurgents began to move out. They left behind some 8,500 men in the barracks and in nearby officer quarters a number of sedulously snoring majors and colonels. They also left behind Chief Aide-de-Camp Honjo's son-in-law Captain Yamaguchi to make sure that the pledge of noninterference was kept.

Outside in the bitter February morning the rebels were joined by the 7th company of the 3d Regiment of the elite Imperial Guards Division, barracked within the holy precincts of the palace. Unlike the others, these men did not know that they were rebelling. Their leader, Chichibu's friend Lieutenant Nakahashi Motoaki, had told them that they were marching to a religious ceremony at Emperor Meiji's Shrine. Thirteen trucks were waiting to transport the advance guard. Three medical trainees were on hand to care for the wounded in case anyone got hurt.

Tokyo lay blanketed in snow. The flakes were still falling. The boots of the men crunched softly up the dark empty streets. It was less than a mile and a half march from their bunks to the walls of the palace. By 4:30 the scouts of the silent columns had taken up watch outside all the main nerve centers of bureaucratic Tokyo short of the forbidding walls of the palace itself: the Diet, the War Ministry, the General Staff offices, Police Headquarters, the Land Survey office, the Home Ministry, the Overseas Ministry, and even the Navy Ministry and Staff offices. Within the cordon of rebel pickets lay the residences of Prince Kanin, Prince Takamatsu, the lord privy seal, the war minister, the vice war minister, the foreign minister, the vice foreign minister, the home minister, and the prime minister.

Before 5:00 A.M. the rebels had occupied their primary objectives. At the Sanno Hotel, which they intended to make their field headquarters, they roused guests from their beds—including two or three Westerners—and courteously manned the hotel switchboard to find fresh accommodations for them in inns and hotels elsewhere in the city. At the war minister's official residence they apprised War Minister Kawashima of their presence, and then, because he pleaded a bad cold and a need to sleep, left him undisturbed until 7:00 A.M. when he rose to parley with them. At Metropolitan Police Headquarters they simply mixed with the sergeants on night duty and doubled the guard outside.

In the offices of the General Staff lights were burning because Colonel Ishiwara Kanji, the strategist of the Manchuria campaign, now chief of the Operations Section of the General Staff, had received belated warning of the rising and was in conference with some of his staff. At about 5:00 A.M. Colonel Ishiwara stormed from his office, shot a rebel guard on duty outside, and screeched away in his official car to see what he could do. He could do nothing; he was too late.

The death squads had already gone out to be ready at the stroke of five to kill "the evil men about the Throne." At 5:05 the first squad struck. A hundred soldiers under the command of Chichibu's friend Lieutenant Nakahashi Motoaki of the Imperial Guards Division surrounded the home of the unkempt, bushy-bearded Santa Claus of Japanese finance, the brilliant, heterodox economist, Finance Minister Takahashi Korekiyo, eighty-one years old. After wounding the policeman on guard outside, Lieutenant Nakahashi burst into the house, ran to the old finance minister's bedroom, ripped the covers from him and cried *"Tenchu!"* ("Heaven's punishment!") When Takahashi opened his eyes, Nakahashi shot him thrice and then for good measure stabbed him twice. He died instantly.

At the same moment a second squad of 200 soldiers, a lieutenant, and three second lieutenants surrounded the home of the new lord privy seal and former prime minister, Admiral Viscount Saito Makoto, seventy-seven. The suave, good-natured old courtier was sleeping heavily after a late night at the American Embassy where he had viewed a private showing of the Jeanette MacDonald-Nelson Eddy movie *Naughty Marietta* with Ambassador and Mrs. Grew.

Hearing the young officers running into the house, Viscountess Saito rose from her husband's side in time to slam the bedroom door in their faces. "Please wait a moment," she cried.

By the time the young officers had forced the door, Admiral Saito had awakened and was standing behind his wife in his sleeping kimono. Three officers shot him almost simultaneously. Viscountess Saito fell on the body and clung to it tenaciously, weeping. Unable to drag her off, the young officers thrust in their weapons underneath her and pumped more bullets hysterically into the corpse. They later testified that they wanted to cut the old man's throat as well but could not because the woman was in the way.

In all forty-seven bullets were lodged in the admiral's body and his wife was wounded in both arms and a shoulder. On the way out the murderers paused at the front door to give three lusty "Banzai!" for the Emperor.

A third company of assassins under the command of Tiger Yamashita's minion, Captain Ando Teruzo, had attacked the home of Grand Chamberlain Admiral Suzuki Kantaro. They had been delayed for ten minutes by a skirmish at the gate in which they had wounded the policeman on guard. Grand Chamberlain Suzuki, too, had been at the Grews the night before. Ando found him in bed with the baroness and tarried to discuss national policy with him. The grand chamberlain was no mean juggler with words and he regaled Captain Ando for almost ten minutes.

Finally at 5:10 A.M., according to the official story, Ando invoked cloture with his pistol and fired three bullets into the sixty-eight-year-old chamberlain. "I can still feel a pulse," he announced to Baroness Suzuki, who stood by. "I shall dispatch him finally with my sword."

The baroness, with Spartan presence of mind, responded, "If you consider that necessary, let me do it." And so Ando "felt ashamed" and retired from the room.

For the next two days, while his comrades patrolled in the snow, Ando whiled away his hours in a nearby restaurant, the Koraku. Then, when the rebellion had collapsed, he made an unsuccessful attempt to commit suicide. Apparently he had made a deal with his wily old victim. Grand Chamberlain Suzuki was off the critical list four days later and lived to be Japan's last World War II prime minister.

Suzuki made a virtue of his "embarrassing" survival, as he called it, by a story which he loved to tell thereafter. It seems that one of the bullets fired into him lodged in a most tender part and the surgeon who treated him wrote a riddling, mock-heroic stanza celebrating his deft extraction of "the leaden ball from the honorable golden one."

While Grand Chamberlain Suzuki lay in agony, a fourth death squad of 300 men and five officers went for the third Strike-South admiral of the night, Prime Minister Okada Keisuke. His official residence was that same architectural monstrosity—a parody of Frank Lloyd Wright's Imperial Hotel—in which Prime Minister Inukai had been shot by the airmen of the Misty Lagoon four years before. Despite the earlier tragedy and the manifold warnings on the grapevine, there were only four policemen on guard. The attacking troops shot all four of them, and the five officers began a systematic search of the maze of rooms and corridors in the residence.

The seventy-three-year-old prime minister had spent the previous evening with his mistress, a famous geisha, and was in no mood to save himself. "It's all up," he said miserably. "Why get all excited?"

His maids and his brother-in-law secretary, Colonel Matsuo Denzo, however, dragged him from his bed and hurried him out of his own suite into the servants' quarters. Hearing the approaching footfalls of a search party, they shoved Okada unceremoniously into one of the toilets there and told him to draw the wooden cleat which would lock it from the inside. Then Colonel Matsuo, in a signal act of heroism, ran out into a courtyard nearby shouting, "Long live the Emperor." He fell instantly in a hail of machine-gun bullets, his face disfigured almost beyond recognition.

The soldiers who had shot him carried his corpse back to Okada's bedroom and laid it out. They compared the face with photographs and decided, with the help of prompting from the maids, that they had killed the prime minister.

In the morning secret-police officers infiltrated the area along the wall of the palace occupied by the rebel troops and fraternized with the soldiers. In the course of their investigations they learned from the maids at the prime minister's residence that Admiral Okada was still alive. Okada's son-in-law and another of his secretaries were called in through the rebel lines to perform obsequies over the corpse of Matsuo, the prime minister's stand-in. The now all-too-sober Okada was moved to a closet where he would be more comfortable. His mourners won the sympathies and relaxed the surveillance of the rebel guards.

On the following morning his surviving secretary, Fukuda Ko, brought a score of elderly secret-police pallbearers in frock coats to the Prime Ministry, together with a flu mask and horn-rimmed glasses. Disguised in these, the hungry, weary Okada joined the mourners at the coffin of his brother-in-law. As the bier was borne from the house, one of the aged pallbearers imported by the secret police fell to the ground in a mock heart attack and was carried off on a stretcher. In the confusion the shaken Prime Minister Okada was bundled into a car and escaped.

The killings in Tokyo were well co-ordinated with more attacks in the provinces. During the night of the rising, groups of soldiers, reservists, and cadet officers converging on Okitsu to assassinate aged Prince Saionji were met and dispersed by police. At Yugawara hot springs, where former Lord Privy Seal Makino was hiding at an inn with his twenty-year-old granddaughter Kazuko, the child of postwar Prime Minister Yoshida Shigeru, no precautions had been taken. At 5:40 A.M. a group of rebels who had set out on their mission at midnight arrived at the inn, set up a machine gun before the entrance, hailed the innkeeper, and demanded Makino. A moment later Makino's bodyguard appeared, blazing away with a gun. He wounded the leader of the squad, Captain Kono Hisashi, but was himself riddled with machine-gun bullets. The spray of lead tore through the fragile façade of the Japanese inn and wounded Makino's nurse and one of his servants.

During the brief battle old plotter Makino and his granddaughter, together with other guests and members of the staff, stole out the back of the inn and climbed the hillside behind it. The wounded Captain Kono, who subsequently died under arrest, ordered his men to set fire to the place. While the building blazed, the soldiers trained their machine gun on the figures which could be seen scuttling away up the slope.

According to the story told later by Makino and oft repeated in after years by Makino's prime ministerial son-in-law, Yoshida Shigeru, the former lord privy seal reached a point on the hillside at which he found his breath too short and the ascent too precipitous for him to go farther. He slumped to a squat and faced the would-be executioners below. His granddaughter Kazuko stepped in front of him and spread her kimono to shield him. Both felt that they were picked out by the flames and would surely die. They could see the soldiers all too vividly against the bright background of the fire, but the soldiers could see little of them against the dark hillside.

The machine gunners did not shoot, and forty minutes after the attack had started Makino was safely away in the hills. As firemen arrived to hose down the blaze, the young rebels packed up their machine gun and started back for the provincial garrisons from which they had come.

Back in Tokyo, having gained their primary objectives, the rebel troops went on to secondary ones. At 6:00 A.M. a part of the same bloodthirsty group which had pumped forty-seven bullets into Lord Privy Seal Saito jumped from a truck outside the home of General Watanabe Jotaro, who had taken Mazaki's place the previous summer as inspector general of military education. One of the young officers blew the lock on the front door with machine-gun fire and then he and his comrades poured into the house. Mrs. Watanabe confronted them at the end of the entryway and demanded the name of their unit. They threw her aside and dashed into the living quarters where General Watanabe stood waiting for them. Before he could bark out the order "Halt!" he had taken his first bullet and then went down in a fusillade. A second lieutenant completed the attack by cutting the throat of the corpse with his samurai sword.

A HAND OF POKER

The violence was over. The rebels went on to occupy the offices of the five major newspapers later that morning and to wreck the presses at one of them, the conservative *Asahi,* but there were to be no more killings. In a fashion that astonished Western residents, the drama of the insurrection suddenly turned cerebral, and while it was being played out the 1,483 mutineers [8] were left in undisputed occupation of the heart of Tokyo. For three full days the rebels held the nerve centers of the Japanese Empire, and Hirohito engaged all officials dissatisfied with his rule in a silent test of strength. Personally, almost singlehandedly, he fought and won three major

---

[8] 1359 soldiers, 91 noncoms, 21 officers, 3 medical corps trainees, 8 civilians, and one reservist.

political battles. He refused, until the rebels had surrendered, to make any concessions as to the policy or personnel of the next government. He insisted that the Army take full public responsibility not only for the suppressing of the rebels but also for their rising, and that it do so, moreover, on its own authority, without invoking Hirohito's personal power as god-king. Finally he took a firm hand with the elders of his own Court and family and overruled a substantial bloc of them who rose in dissent.

When the rebellion had been suppressed, Hirohito's courtiers spread an account of events in the palace during those three days which their own diaries expose as false.[9] By so doing they meant to protect the Throne against reaction in case the coming gamble of war should turn out badly. Thus they suggested that Hirohito was forced by the rebellion to seek employment for his soldiers' idle hands and to consent in the preparations for war against China. The true situation is aptly illustrated by Chief Aide-de-Camp Honjo's diary. On February 25, the day before the rebellion, Honjo notes that the Emperor approved an enlargement of the command structure for the Tientsin garrison army in north China to put it on a war footing. He asked Honjo to see that the enlargement be made in such a way as "not to excite foreign suspicion" and "not to make control inconvenient as was the case when we reorganized the Kwantung Army" [before the conquest of Manchuria].

"The problem," Hirohito had explained to Honjo, "is not what we do but world reaction to what we do."

[9] Until recently historians have had to accept it for lack of documentary evidence.

21

SUPPRESSION

(1936)

RISING TO A REBEL DAWN

The record of Hirohito's great victory over the mutineers and their sympathizers commences a few minutes before the first of the early morning killings. At 5:00 A.M. Chief Aide-de-Camp Honjo was shaken awake in his home in northwestern Tokyo by a second lieutenant from the 1st Regiment who brought a note from his son-in-law Captain Yamaguchi informing him that 500 officers and men of the regiment had already left their barracks as insurgents and that more were going out every minute. Honjo was on his feet instantly ordering the second lieutenant to go back to son-in-law Yamaguchi and have him stop the rebellion and call the men back.

"It is too late," said the second lieutenant.

"Do your best," commanded Honjo. Turning to the phone he called the commander-in-chief of the secret police and the aide-de-camp on night duty a few steps from the imperial bedchamber in the palace. Both men were calm and noncommittal. Honjo summoned a car and set out for the palace. On the way he encountered almost a company of soldiers near the British Embassy just west of the palace. He deduced from their uniforms that they were not Imperial Guardsmen of the elite Konoye Division and that therefore they must be rebels from his son-in-law's 1st Division. He did not stop his car to parley with them.

Arriving at the Inner Palace at 6:00 A.M., Honjo learned that Hirohito was already up and at work at his desk. When he was received in audience a few minutes later, the Emperor said to him, "Make this incident end quickly and so turn calamity into good fortune." Then Hirohito added accusingly, "Only you, Chief Aide-de-Camp, worried beforehand that there might be such an outbreak."

Thinking of his son-in-law, Honjo said, "The young officers only mean to find a place for their sense of righteousness as individuals in the all-encompassing righteousness of the Emperor. They wish a little fresh air for their ideas to bloom in."

Marquis Kido Koichi, the secretary to the lord privy seal—secretary until two months ago of Count Makino and until fifteen minutes ago of Admiral Viscount Saito—was awakened at 5:20 A.M. by a phone call from the palace which told him of the attack on Saito. Kido at once "sensed an incident of great magnitude." He called Metropolitan Police Headquarters and found that no one there, being surrounded by rebels, could speak without constraint. So he called the official car pool and asked for immediate transportation to the palace. While waiting for it, he phoned Prince Konoye and Saionji's Secretary-Spy Harada to give them the news. When his driver arrived, he shrewdly directed the man to take a long way around the area which he imagined would be occupied by the rebels.

At six o'clock Kido was at his desk in the Imperial Household Ministry within the outer precincts of the holy palace walls. He made numerous phone calls to evaluate the situation including one, at 6:40, to Prince Saionji's residence in Okitsu. The maids there assured him that the venerable old man and the rest of his household were soundly asleep in bed. Kido has never revealed whether or not he knew that Saionji was really asleep miles away in the home of the governor of Shizuoka. In his diary Kido wrote only: "I felt greatly relieved."

After making his phone calls and becoming as knowledgeable as he could, Kido waited at the Household Ministry for Saionji's Secretary-Spy Harada. On foot, with his Imperial Household pass in his hand ready to show to any rebel who stopped him, Harada arrived shortly before 7:00 A.M. and was given instructions by Kido. After receiving them, instead of going to one of the north gates of the palace and proceeding to Okitsu to be with Saionji as duty demanded, Harada returned to his home in rebel territory and spent the next two days doing phone business as usual from a hideout in the house of a neighbor. Though he may not have known it, he was on the "shoot-at-sight" list of the rebel officers as "that meddlesome little baron." In going back to his neighborhood he played the part of heroic intelligence agent. He kept in constant telephonic touch with Kido and ventured out in the evening to observe the rebel camp.

After issuing instructions to Harada, Kido walked across the palace park and through the inner wall to Hirohito's own residence and offices. He found the aides-de-camp, Imperial Household Minister Yuasa, and Vice Grand Chamberlain Hirohata already in attendance outside Hirohito's study. They gave him more up-to-date intelligence than he had been able to elicit from his own informants on the phone: the grand chamberlain, the prime minister, and the finance minister had all been attacked, along with the lord privy seal. Like other trusted minions of the Throne, Kido was not to leave the palace for a week. He was given a temporary cubicle down the corridor from Hirohito's study in the Imperial Library. He bunked down on open stretches of matting floor in the rooms of chamberlains. He was on call to the Emperor twenty-four hours a day.

REBEL TERMS

Also at 7:00 A.M. that February 26—that *ni-ni-roku* or 2–26 as it is called by Japanese—War Minister Kwashima condescended at length to come down from his bedroom and parley with the rebel officers who occupied the ground floor of his residence. They gave him the original of the manifesto, of which they had plastered copies on all the walls of the occupied area, and demanded that he present it to the Emperor. They also stipulated that the government must announce a full restoration of the Emperor to power; that the Army must rid itself of factionalism; that the "arch traitors" of previous plots, including Generals Minami, Koiso, Tatekawa, and Ugaki, must be arrested; that some other officers of Hirohito's original cabal must be dismissed from the service; that General Araki must be made commander of the Kwantung Army in order to "coerce Russia"; and finally that the war minister should consult with Strike-North leader Mazaki before stating their demands to the Emperor. They recommended that he talk also to Lieutenant General Furusho Mikio, the vice minister of war, an aviation expert whom the Emperor trusted, and to Major General Tiger Yamashita who was—unknown to them—a palace undercover agent. War Minister Kawashima listened gravely to their requests and, promised to do what he could.

At 8:00 A.M. Prince Fushimi, the chief of the Naval General Staff, arrived at the palace and went straight into Hirohito's presence. Units of the fleet, he reported, were being brought around from Yokosuka Naval Base into Tokyo Bay and could be ready, at a word from the Emperor, to shell the rebel positions. At the same time, he felt, it would be advisable to form a new Cabinet quickly and to compromise a little with the rebels. Since some of the rebels were close friends of Prince Chichibu, it would be wrong to deal with them too severely. Did not the Emperor agree?

Hirohito, who had had many disagreements in the past with Fushimi and knew that he was disposed to argument, replied only: "I asked for your report on the situation in the Navy. As to my opinions in regard to the present incident, I have given them already to Imperial Household Minister Yuasa."

"Have I your permission, Sire, to ask them then of Yuasa?"

"I would like to reserve judgment on that petition," snapped Hirohito, and waved Prince Fushimi from the room. Full of indignation Fushimi went directly to Big Brother Kido, the president of the Bureau of Peerage and Heraldry, and ordered him to circulate an account of the spat to all princes of the blood.

At 9:00 A.M. War Minister Kawashima, fresh from his parley with the rebels, arrived at the palace and was given audience by the Emperor. He produced the rebels' manifesto scroll and solemnly read it in the Imperial Presence.[1]

A PROSPECTUS FOR DIRECT ACTION TO PROTECT THE ESSENCE OF THE NATION

After humble reflection as children of the land of the gods we submit these grievances to the one eternal god, the Emperor, under whose high command we serve. The essence of our country consists first in accomplishing the evolutionary formation of a single nation that is one body and then in comprehending the entire earth under our roof. The superior excellence and dignity of our national essence has grown systematically, and by careful nurture, from the founding of the nation by Emperor Jimmu, to the transformation of society by the Meiji Restoration. Now once again we are reaching the autumn of an epoch in which we confront many outside lands and must make visible progress toward a new enlightenment.

Despite the critical period ahead of us, gangs of effeminate sadists spring up in our midst like toadstools; we indulge our selfish desires and interests; we allow superficial formalism to arrogate the absolute sanctity of the Throne; we obstruct the creative evolution of all the people, causing them to groan in anguish and misery. Increasingly Japan is pursued by foreign troubles, and riding at the mercy of the waves, becomes the butt of foreign ridicule. The elder statesmen, the leaders of Army factions, the bureaucrats, the political parties, and so on have all contributed as leaders to this destruction of the national essence. . . . The March Incident and the special interests of false scholars, false Communists, treasonable religious groups and the like are all woven together in a dark plot which, though unrealized, has set a most conspicuously bad example. The crimes are smeared so gory across the heavens that we have reached a juncture at which bloodshed is a mere figure of speech to express indignation. The pioneering self-sacrifice of the Blood Brothers . . . ; the volcanic spouting of the 5–15 Incident; the flashing out of Colonel Aizawa's sword—truly these men had reasons for what they did, reasons which have made them weep.

How many times must lifeblood water the earth to produce a bit of introspection and penitence even now at this late hour? As of old we continue to play for time and look the other way out of private greed and status seeking. Russia, China, England, and the United States are within a

---

[1] I quote at length from the original. Its deep and alien feelings defy summary. And the only previously available translation, which may be found in one form or another in half a dozen textbooks of modern Japanese history, is an independent composition prepared in 1936 by a Japanese interpreter for the Tokyo office of *The New York Times*. It includes some ideas from the original but rearranges them and smothers all their fire and brimstone.

hair's breadth, at this present outbreak, of ensnaring our land of the gods and of destroying our culture, our bequest from the ancestors. Is this not clear? Is there not light in fire?

Indeed there is, and grave uneasiness at home and abroad. The false counsels of false vassals sap the national essence, shade the divine radiance of the Throne, and retard the Restoration. . . . At this moment when the First Division has just heard its imperial order of dispatch overseas . . . we cannot help but look back on conditions at home. . . . In so far as we can, we and our kindred spirits must make it our responsibility to crumble the inner doors and strike off the heads of the treacherous army traitors in the palace. Though mere retainers, we now take a positive road as if we were the trusted lieutenants of the Throne. Even if our actions cost us our lives and our honor, vacillation now has no meaning for us.

We here who share the same grief and the same aspirations take this opportunity to rise as one man. To make the traitors perish, to make the supreme righteousness righteous, to protect the national essence and make it manifest, we dedicate our own true hearts as children of the sacred land, thereby giving our livers and brains to be consumed in the fire.

We humbly pray the sun goddess and the ancestors, riding on spirit wings, to lend us their dark assistance and second sight in our undertaking.

Eleventh year of Showa, second month, twenty-sixth day.

Hirohito listened in silence to the manifesto. Behind its impassioned words and its brave show of martial spirit, he could see a complete repudiation of all his warlike policies. In their veiled, belly-talking fashion, the rebels were begging him to shrink from the danger of further foreign entanglements and devote his energies to domestic reform and the preservation of Japan's traditional homespun virtues.

"Whatever their excuses," said Hirohito icily, "I am displeased. They have put a blot on the nation. I call on you, War Minister, to suppress them quickly."

Kawashima sought to find some small token of conciliation to give the men who occupied his home. But Hirohito forbade him to convey to them any message of sympathy and understanding from the Throne—merely that the Throne had been informed of their intentions.

FIRST DAY OF SIEGE

As soon as War Minister Kawashima had withdrawn to think over his predicament, Hirohito began to interview, one by one, all the generals who sat on the Supreme War Council. Confident that they would not be molested en route by their own Army's insurgents and eager to show their loyalty and give their advice to the Throne, they had all come to the palace early in the morning when Cabinet ministers and admirals were still conspicuous by their absence. Hirohito impressed on them one point: the Army must take the responsibility for suppressing "these violent rioters."

If it did not, he would call in the Navy or go down to the barricades himself.

While the Emperor was personally reminding the elders of the Army of their duty, the six young rebel officers in command at War Minister Kawashima's residence waited for a reply to their demands and held court for a steady stream of senior officers who came to remonstrate with them or wish them well. Indeed, though it seems incredible, business at the residence, and at the nearby War Ministry and General Staff offices, went on much as usual despite the rebel pickets who stood guard at the doors.

The incongruity of the situation was demonstrated at 10 A.M. when Major Katakura Tadashi, the nephew of the Manchurian Incident's War Minister General Minami, came to Kawashima's residence on a routine staff errand. Major Katakura had helped to expose the Military Academy Plot in 1934 and had thereby betrayed most of the young men who were now insurgents. Not surprisingly, one of them, the pamphleteer Isobe who had been dishonorably discharged, greeted Katakura with a bullet in the head. Unfortunately for later Allied war prisoners in Burma, whom he worked and killed in 1944, it was only a flesh wound and Katakura recovered. Many of his fellow officers felt that he had received no more than he deserved, and the coming and going of callers at the war minister's residence continued unabated.

At noon, when the last Supreme War Councillor had emerged from the Imperial Presence, War Minister Kawashima dispatched Major General Tiger Yamashita to go from the aides' office in the palace out to the rebels and give them their answer. It was in brief: "The Emperor has been told your intentions; the war minister recognizes the sincerity of your motives; the Supreme War Council has met and decided to uphold the national prestige."

The message could not have had a more fateful ring. The blood-stained young rebels could sense in it the Emperor's icy attitude toward them. They were lost. If they were to die in vain, they promised Tiger Yamashita that they would do so on their barricades fighting to the last man.

Yamashita phoned the palace. He was told to keep talking and was promised reinforcements. Shortly afterwards he was joined at the negotiating table by the ubiquitous Colonel Suzuki Tei-ichi, who was known to be close to the Emperor, and by the commander of the 1st Regiment, Colonel Kofuji Satoshi, who could be held responsible for the young officers as members of his command.

While the negotiators slogged on through a mire of patriotic metaphysics, Hirohito convoked the highest consultative bodies of the land and spent the afternoon with them. In one palace room the Privy Council sat in the Imperial Presence; in another met those members of the Cabinet who had finally dared to come to the palace; in a third conferred the Supreme War Council, including Strike-North leaders Araki and Mazaki. The Cabinet had been asked by the Emperor to see to continuance of civil gov-

ernment in the absence of Prime Minister Okada who still hid in a closet
at his residence. The Supreme War Councillors had been asked by the
Emperor to suppress the incident as quickly as possible with a minimum of
bloodshed.

It was a long afternoon. The Emperor was unwilling to appoint a new
prime minister because any change in the government might be construed
as a step toward reform and a victory for the rebels.[2] Nor was he willing
to ease the task of the War Councillors by even a token gesture of conciliation. When the rebels had returned to their barracks he would resume
constructive government. Until then he took the position that he would
sign nothing and would preside over the realm as a displeased Presence
and nothing more.

The Cabinet finally chose Home Minister Goto Fumio as their de facto
administrator. And the Supreme War Council finally agreed to issue the
rebels "a persuasion paper" and "an order." The persuasion paper stated
in brief: "You wished to attract the Emperor's attention and you have
succeeded; your sincere desire to see the essence of the nation realized has
been noted." The orders stated in brief: "In accordance with the National
Defense Plan of fiscal 1935, you are to take up your prearranged positions
for the defense of Tokyo alongside the other units of your division."

The Privy Council, meanwhile, which sat in the Imperial Presence, debated whether it would be better to make the rebels disband by sending
them a direct order from the Emperor or to declare martial law and leave
the responsibility for suppression to the Army. Hirohito, as was required
in order to preserve an appearance of free debate, listened attentively but
said nothing. He caused the second course of action to be taken, however,
by a simple expedient: every twenty or thirty minues he would have
Chief Aide-de-Camp Honjo summoned and would say to him, as if asking
for news, "Has the Army succeeded in suppressing the crazy violent
rioters yet?" The Privy Council finally agreed to recommend that the
reluctant Army should impose martial law.

At 3:00 in the afternoon 1st Division soldiers took up defensive positions
according to the contingency plans of fiscal 1935 and were not joined by
their rebellious comrades. At 5:00, after half a day of empty talk, Tiger
Yamashita returned to the Palace to report. Three cf the rebel officers
tried to follow him into the holy precincts and had to be stopped by the
Palace Guard.

After hearing Yamashita's disappointing news, Imperial Household Minister Yuasa relayed a request from Hirohito that all trusty vassals sleep in
the palace that night and that martial law, as decided, earlier by the War

---

[2] It may be assumed that the secret police had informed Hirohito early that afternoon that Prime Minister Okada was still alive. Not until the following afternoon,
however, when Okada had been safely smuggled out of rebel territory, was the
news of his survival given to the courtiers around Hirohito.

Council, be imposed on Tokyo from midnight onwards. War Minister Kawashima promised to comply but doubted that martial law would be effective. He asked Household Minister Yuasa if he might submit to the Throne a list of names which the Army would like to see in the next Cabinet. Yuasa rejected the request angrily and called it an attempted infringement of imperial rights. War Minister Kawashima "looked surprised" and went to see about setting up a martial law headquarters. Navy Minister Osumi was granted audience at 6:30 and implored the Emperor to ease the nation's tension by appointing a provisional Cabinet and a prime minister pro tem.

The Emperor refused. "If the Army had wished to avoid this confrontation," he said, "it might have given me a gently worded reproof." That evening the five rebel officers in the war minister's residence parleyed with no less than seven full generals, including Hayashi, Mazaki, Araki, and Terauchi. The dazzling display of brass failed to break the deadlock. The rebels repeated their earlier demands and added further that they must not be called traitors.

That evening the Cabinet resigned—not once but twice. The first time, at 9 o'clock, de facto Prime Minister Goto submitted a cabinet resignation *en bloc*. It was a routine gesture expected of a cabinet after a national disaster, and the Emperor routinely dismissed it. "Retain your posts with sincerity," he said, "until peace and order have been restored."

This was not enough, however. The ministers withdrew and returned to the anteroom where they had been in debate all afternoon. Intimidated by the assassinations that morning and to some extent sympathetic with War Minister Kawashima, they resolved to submit individual written resignations. They did so at 1:00 A.M. Hirohito had no choice but to accept them, but he ordered each minister to "remain in charge of political affairs until the realization of a new Cabinet." He was obviously put out. It had been an exhausting day.

Even members of Hirohito's own family felt that he was taking a dangerously uncompromising position. Prince Fushimi and Prince Asaka had asked for a meeting of the Imperial Family Council, and Hirohito's brother Chichibu, who sided with them, had been summoned from the country to attend it. The Lord Privy Seal's Secretary Kido had spent the evening feeling out the positions of Prince Asaka and Prince Higashikuni and had reported reassuringly of their loyalty.

But Hirohito was in no mood for reassurances. Still wearing the rumpled Army uniform that he had put on early that morning, he sat down shortly before 2:00 A.M. to read the resignation papers submitted by the Cabinet. At 2:00 he phoned Chief Aide-de-Camp Honjo, rousing him from bed: "War Minister Kawashima has submitted a resignation which is identical to all the others. Does he think that his responsibility is identical? With such a mentality he is not fit to be war minister."

"I suppose," sighed Honjo to his diary when the Emperor had hung up, "that he passed through the honorable latticed door [to bed] sometime after that."

THE SECOND DAY

When dawn came on February 27, P-day plus one, the snow had ceased but it was still cloudy. Martial law had been officially proclaimed at 2:50 that morning. At 5:00 A.M. Chief Aide-de-Camp Honjo was roused bleary-eyed from his makeshift pallet in the palace by a personal visit from Prince Fushimi. Fushimi reported to Honjo that young Army officers had called at the Fushimi villa during the night to ask him to take the post of lord privy seal as a means of settling the incident. He had, of course, refused to commit himself. At 7:00 A.M. the Emperor's uncle Prince Asaka called on the Emperor's brother Prince Takamatsu at the Naval Staff College to seek his support in urging Hirohito to appoint a new cabinet as soon as possible. Takamatsu declined.

In the palace the chamberlains' common room looked like a refugee camp. Elderly Cabinet ministers, generals, princes, and marquises sat about in their sleeping kimonos eating rice, drinking tea, and exchanging short guttural comments after an uncomfortable night. Just outside the palace gates, the rebel sentries still paced up and down on the snow. Service on the Center line of the subway was suspended, and commuters on their way to the business district and docks in southern Tokyo had to change many times in order to circle the stricken area around the palace. Hirohito slept late. After his usual hearty breakfast of oatmeal and eggs he did not reach his desk until some time between eight and nine o'clock.

When Chief Aide-de-Camp Honjo went to pay his good morning greetings to the Emperor, he was met with a barrage of gruff high spirits: "If the rioting mobsters do not begin soon to respect the orders of the Army high command, I can see that I will have to go down in person to the barricades."

Honjo replied: "The officers of the direct action group called out the Emperor's troops arbitrarily without orders. In so doing they intruded on Your Majesty's right of supreme command. Naturally this is impermissible but the spirit in which they acted deserves some consideration. They were moved entirely by patriotic convictions and thought they were acting on behalf of the nation. In their psychology there is no room to think of exerting pressure on you, Sire, or of abusing your prerogatives."

A little later Hirohito called Honjo and said: "They killed my right-hand elder vassals. Those crazy violent officers may not be excused in any way—not even in terms of their psychological motivation. To fell my most trusted vassals is a way of trying to strangle me with a silken cord and smother my own head in soft cotton."

"There is no question," admitted Honjo, "that it is the blackest possible crime to have killed and wounded the elder vassals. But though these young officers are confused and do not understand, they believe that they acted for the sake of the nation. That was their idea."

Honjo noted in his diary, "I repeated this to the Emperor in several different ways."

Hirohito shook his head and said, "Can't you admit, Chief Aide-de-Camp, that their action stemmed simply from their own passions and selfish ambitions?"

Having no adequate rejoinder to make, Honjo wrote in his diary: "On this day also the Emperor was very agitated by the fact that the Army's efforts to suppress the action group are not getting anywhere. He told me, 'I, *Chin,* would like to take command of the Konoye Guards and crush the insurgents personally.' " [3]

All day long the nation was held in suspense. In the course of it the stubborn Emperor called Honjo no less than thirteen times to ask him if the Army had acted yet. War Minister Kawashima and most of the other full generals busied themselves with the logistics of establishing a martial law headquarters in the secret police building a few blocks north of the palace perimeter. At 10:30 A.M. the Konoye Imperial Guards took up positions facing the northwestern edge of the rebel lines—and then sat tight. Loyal units of the 1st Division did the same along the southwestern and southeastern edges. Along the northeast edge ran the massive wall of the palace. During the afternoon the rebels broke into the Peers' Club, searched everyone they found there, and held an assortment of some sixteen marquises, counts, viscounts, and barons at pistol point until evening.

Saionji's Secretary-Spy Harada passed through the rebel lines, talked to some of the detained peers, and was stopped on his way home by a rebel officer who recognized him. The officer later testified, "If he had not shown fear or if he had attempted to lie to me or run away, I would have killed him. But he spoke to me in such a small voice that I let him go with a warning."

During the afternoon lull, everyone was waiting for the arrival in Tokyo of Prince Chichibu, Hirohito's brother, the personal friend of the rebel leaders. Chichibu was expected to confront Hirohito that night at the scheduled meeting of the Imperial Family Council. Privy Seal Secretary Kido spent most of the day in conference with Prince Asaka and Prince Higashikuni discussing "remedial measures." It was rumored that the rebels or the Army meant to kidnap Prince Chichibu, and so at 5:17 P.M. when his train drew in to Ueno Station, he was met by a chamberlain and a strong police escort. Driven at full speed, sirens blaring, his cavalcade negotiated some four miles of city streets to arrive at the Inner Palace

---

[3] *Chin* is the old imperial "we" used by Chinese emperors. Its ideograph represents the moon speaking into the ears of heaven.

thirteen minutes later. He was ushered at once into the Imperial Presence and went on to dine with the Emperor in private.

At about 7:00 P.M. the royal brothers joined other princes of the blood in the Imperial Family Council Chamber.[4] According to chamberlains' gossip, voices were modulated and the atmosphere was urbane. Hirohito questioned each of the princes in turn and heard short prepared speeches that touched on a variety of topics including China, long-range military planning, and domestic reform. The main concern, however, was that the spirit of rebellion might spread to the provinces unless a new Cabinet was appointed promptly and a compromise worked out with the Army. Hirohito thanked his kinsmen, promised to think over their ideas, and at 8:30 the meeting adjourned on a note of noncommittal anticlimax. Prince Chichibu went on to a half-hour conference with Big Brother Kido.

Only two concrete results emerged from the family conference. Army Chief of Staff Prince Kanin, who was indisposed at his villa in Odawara on the shore, was asked to come to Tokyo and stand behind Hirohito "even if it is inconvenient." Kanin obeyed the next day but was given no reason to meet with his monarch for a week. Also that night Prince Chichibu penned a personal note to his friend Captain Nonaka, the highest-ranking rebel officer, asking him as a favor to withdraw his troops. Nonaka responded, after a day's thought, by putting a pistol in his mouth and pulling the trigger. Chamberlains were relieved to see that the princes of the blood, embarrassed though they might be by their many friendships and commitments in the ranks of junior officers, nevertheless chose to stand by Hirohito when it came to a confrontation. Chichibu left the palace that night at 9:10 P.M., accompanied once again by an army of police.

The next morning Hirohito sent his own impressions of the council meeting to Big Brother Kido, the president of the Bureau of Heraldry and Peerage, for inscription in the palace rolls: "Prince Takamatsu [my brother] is the best. Prince Chichibu [my brother] has improved greatly since the time of the 5–15 Incident. Prince Nashimoto was moved to tears when he

---

[4] According to the Imperial House Law "the members of the imperial family shall be under the control of the Emperor" and the family council "shall be composed of the male members of the imperial family who have reached the age of majority." In addition the Emperor was expected to require the presence of an outside witness, specifically the privy seal, household minister, minister of justice, or president of the Supreme Court. In 1936 there were sixteen princes eligible to sit on the family council, six of the higher rank called *Shinno* and ten of the lower rank called *O*. The six *Shinno* were Hirohito's three brothers plus three princes of the less immediate family who had been created *Shinno* by Imperial election: Prince Kanin, the Army chief of staff; Prince Fushimi, the Navy chief of staff; and the fascistic Prince Kaya who had visited Hitler in 1934. The princes who took part in the February 27 meeting of the Council were brother Chichibu, brother Takamatsu, and cousin Fushimi, all *Shinno;* and uncle Higashikuni, uncle Asaka, cousin Nashimoto, and Prince Kanin's son, Haruhito, all *O*.

asked my pardon [for this rebellion]. I appreciate him greatly. Haruhito [Prince Kanin's son] is fine. Prince Asaka talks of the individual's sense of righteousness and of its place in the over-all righteousness of the Throne, but being under radical influence, he is not blameless. As for Prince Higashikuni, he is showing good sense."

Hirohito, as family disciplinarian, had just been required to read police dossiers on Prince Higashikuni's recent blackmail plots and religious humbuggeries. The Emperor evaluated his kinsmen in terms of loyalty and disloyalty rather than by ordinary Japanese moral standards. At the quiet family conference he had proved himself above influence even by his own kinsmen.

Shortly after the council adjourned, Generals Mazaki, Abe, and Nishi called at the war minister's residence and told the five young rebel officers in command of the ground floor there that they must give up hope and submit to the Imperial Will. If they did not, Strike-North leader Mazaki promised that he personally would lead the detachments sent to destroy them. Weary and heartsore the young men agreed to capitulate. At 11:30 P.M. the three generals reported back to the palace, and orders were issued to the sentries of the Imperial Guard and 1st Divisions to be generous that night toward common soldiers who sought to escape from the rebel-occupied area.

All was not over, however. The rebels, throughout their sad outing, had maintained radio contact with the radical Strike-North ideologist Kita Ikki in his hideout in the Tokyo suburbs. Heretofore in his long career as a professional revolutionary, Kita had always avoided overt participation in coup d'etat plots. Now, however, he realized that he was deeply implicated and would probably be executed if the rebellion failed. For the last two days he had stood by his radio transmitter encouraging the rebels at every turn, advising them on political subtleties and relaying to them heartening prophecies from his wife who had some reputation as a woman of occult powers.

After the generals had left the war minister's residence that night of February 27, P-day plus one, Kita about midnight talked to two of the rebel officers and told them that they should not yet give up: the pressure on the palace was mounting; if they lacked wind for the long run they would find themselves put to death summarily without a hearing. Kita added that his wife had dreamed an apocalypse in which the young officers ruled triumphant in a Japanese paradise where there were no poor. The rebels listened and agreed.

THE THIRD DAY

February 28, P-day plus two, was once again cloudy. Chief Aide-de-Camp Honjo was informed of the rebels' change of heart at 7 A.M. It meant that the rebels would have to be destroyed. It meant that Honjo's son-in-law Captain Yamaguchi Ichitaro would have to go to prison for giving aid to men who were now, clearly, traitors. It meant that Honjo himself after his long and loyal career was disgraced. Men who knew him said later that he aged sixteen years that day.

At about eleven in the morning Yamaguchi, the son-in-law, went to martial law headquarters and pleaded eloquently for almost an hour against issuance of orders to use force against the rebels. Generals and colonels listened to him in complete sympathy and said nothing. Finally a little before noon the martial law chief of staff, Colonel Ishiwara Kanji— that brilliant religious zealot who had planned the Manchuria campaign and had ever since preached peace with China—arose from one end of the long staff table and said, "We shall attack as soon as possible." He walked from the room and gave the couriers outside written orders to deliver.

The 1st and Konoye Divisions grouped for attack and planes revved up to bomb the rebel barricades. The rebel officers were told by radio, "Surrender or be attacked." The rebels replied that they would "not obey orders formulated by organ theorists who perverted imperial intentions."

At this point a "hold" was sent to the waiting attack forces because Prince Chichibu's message was being delivered to Captain Nonaka, and Tiger Yamashita had one last idea for a compromise. After a parley at the barricades, Yamashita came to the palace aide-de-camp office at one in the afternoon, accompanied by War Minister Kawashima. He gave Chief Aide-de-Camp Honjo a pledge from the rebel officers that they would all commit hara-kiri provided that a chamberlain would come out from the walls to witness their act with all due ceremony and report it to the Throne. Honjo reported the proposal at once to Hirohito.

Hirohito said, "If they wish to commit suicide let them do it at their own pleasure. To send an imperial witness to such men is altogether unthinkable."

Honjo muttered miserably that the 1st Division, in which his son-in-law was the duty officer, was loath to go into action against former messmates.

A nasal edge came into Hirohito's voice. "If the chief of the 1st Division," he said, "does not think he can act effectively, he does not understand his own responsibility."

Honjo noted, "I have never seen such severity and anger in the Emperor before."

Army leaders were stunned by Hirohito's rejection of the suicide proposal. Desperate and incredulous, son-in-law Yamaguchi phoned Honjo begging him to talk to the Emperor again. Honjo explained to him repeatedly that the Emperor had already expressed his will beyond any ambiguity and that there was nothing more to be said. When the son-in-law persisted, Honjo sadly hung up on him.

At 3 P.M. the droll Vice Chief of Staff Sugiyama—whose face was said to be as "noncommittal as a toilet door"—requested audience to make Hirohito a further explanation. There had been a misunderstanding, he said. The rebels did not expect an imperial witness at their suicides. They had merely hoped that a chamberlain might take a look at their bodies afterward and report to the Throne whether or not they had carried out their rites of disembowelment in a correct fashion. Hirohito dismissed the new face-saving formula with rekindled anger. When so informed, one of the rebel officers lamented, "But even airplane accidents are reported to the Throne."

Vice Chief of Staff Sugiyama returned to Hirohito and for almost an hour used all his jester wiles in an effort to make Hirohito more lenient. Finally he lay down in a doorway and told the Emperor to trample on him. The Emperor merely stepped over him and went to await developments in another room. Finally at 4:30 P.M. Sugiyama and the commander of the martial law force,[5] Lieutenant General Kashii Kohei, reported to the Emperor that it was too late in the day for an attack but promised him religiously that one would be launched first thing in the morning. Hirohito dismissed them curtly, summoned Chief Aide-de-Camp Honjo, and accused the Army leadership of gross insubordination.

"There is a rumor," said Hirohito, "that the Army belongs to the Emperor. There is another rumor that the Army is intentionally stalling in order to increase the significance of the incident."

"In the last few hours," replied Honjo, "people have been saying that in the present situation the Army is being evasive about following the Imperial Will in an intentional attempt to establish a military government. This sort of comment is extremely insulting to the Army of the Emperor and ignores the Army's honest effort to resolve the incident quickly and peacefully." Honjo later wrote in his diary:

> Thus I appealed to the Emperor, saying that the public atmosphere of misunderstanding directed against the Army was cruel and hard for the men to bear. At that moment, without controlling my emotions, I wept and could not speak. The Emperor walked from the room without saying a word.
>
> After a while, he called me and said: "You, Chief Aide-de-Camp, appealed to me on the grounds that unjust criticisms are being leveled against the Army and you did so with tears. But I say to you that if this incident is not resolved quickly an uneasy situation will follow. Three days have passed and the seat of government has not yet been recovered. Foreign exchange has almost stopped and soon there may be a run on the banks. Unrest is spreading outside the capital and there is a danger of rebellion. The loyal elements of the First Division might even join their comrades who killed my hands and feet and did the most brutal things to old men. I

[5] No less than 23,491 men and 350 officers had been mustered to deal with the 1,483 mutineers.

therefore permit you, Chief Aide-de-Camp, to deliver your own dissenting comments and feelings officially to the Supreme War Council, and then I require you to bring this situation to an immediate resolution."

Honjo was supposed to take official responsibility for all the Emperor's opinions regarding military matters. In the past when the two men had differed, Hirohito had either coaxed the old general into line or compromised a little himself. Now Hirohito had specifically released Honjo from responsibility and asked him to go on record, officially, as dissenting. In one and the same breath Hirohito was saying that he had great respect for Honjo and that he would no longer require Honjo's services as a confidant.

> Accordingly [wrote Honjo in his diary] I requested of the War Council that it send a representative to my office to speak to me. General Araki [the Strike-North leader] came and I delivered to him on the one hand my own sentiments and on the other the Imperial Will. General Araki said, "I suppose that ever since the imperial order was issued there has been no way except the exercise of military force."

The two generals, Araki fifty-nine and Honjo sixty, stared at one another bleakly. They had graduated together from the military academy in 1898 and had worked together in a dozen different assignments for the General Staff since then. They both knew that Hirohito had often chosen in the past between the opinions of disagreeing advisors. They both knew that Hirohito had sometimes gone out of his way to find an advisor who would propose the course of action which he personally wished to follow. But Hirohito had never before ignored the advice of all his military councillors. Now the thirty-five-year-old god-king had emerged from the chrysanthemum curtain and was taking full autocratic responsibility. As the two elderly generals bowed curtly to one another, they bowed also to the Imperial Will. Thereafter all elders of the Japanese Army would behave as if they had no responsibility of their own but merely followed orders. It was a historic moment, and the two generals acknowledged it, in parting, by nothing more than a slight raising of the eyebrows.

The supreme military councillors made one last effort to prevent Hirohito from putting the Throne in a dangerously exposed position. At 7:30 P.M. a delegation of them, including former War Minister General Araki, former War Minister General Hayashi, and Vice Chief of Staff Lieutenant General Sugiyama, met Prince Kanin as he arrived by train from Odawara and tried to persuade him to change Hirohito's mind. Prince Kanin refused to interfere and drove on to his villa. The delegation of Army elders proceeded to martial law headquarters, convoked a meeting of the staff there, explained the situation, and gave it as a united opinion that "we must at all costs avoid an armed clash that will destroy Army morale."

Chief of staff of the martial law forces, Colonel Ishiwara Kanji, planner of the Manchurian campaign, had seen his orders held up since noon. Never known for his tact, he now rose, stared at General Araki, the spokesman of the delegation, and said: "This is a violation of the supreme command. Please state your name and rank, sir."

"You know perfectly well that I am General Araki. And I know that you are trying to insult a superior officer. I would advise you to hold your tongue."

"I cannot," said Ishiwara. "It is absolutely impermissible for soldiers to use the arms of the Throne against the Throne. That would be beyond common sense and has nothing to do with Army morale. You call yourself a general but I cannot believe anyone so silly can be a general in Japan."

For this devout outburst Ishiwara remained in the Army after the great purge of the months ahead. He was to be known in later years as "the last of the Strike-Northists." When he had stamped out of the staff room, Araki and the other generals had no way to prevent the attack planned for the morning. But they did persuade Martial Law Commander Kashii to do his utmost to persuade the rebels by means short of force. All night long sound trucks and radios along the rebel periphery repeated the refrain, "Surrender or be destroyed." Bombers flew over and dropped pamphlets promising forgiveness to noncoms and privates. Advertising balloons went up at dawn begging the troops to surrender for the sake of their wives and children.

Also that night Chief Aide-de-Camp Honjo's son-in-law Captain Yamaguchi was arrested by the secret police and held on suspicion of high treason.

HIROHITO'S SETTLEMENT

At eight-thirty on the morning of February 29, P-day plus three, units of the 1st Division moved through undefended segments of the rebel perimeter and began to evacuate civilians from the prospective battlefield. The rebels gradually drew back into the main buildings which they had occupied. At 9:00 Martial Law Commander Kashii went on the air to announce to the nation, "The young officers have finally come to the point of being considered rebels." At ten, as troops and barbed wire closed in on them, rebel enlisted men in twos and threes began to drift across the snow-covered lawns and parking lots around their strong points and give themselves up. At noon Prince Chichibu's intimate, Captain Nonaka, killed himself. By a little after two all the troops had surrendered and their officers were in secret-police custody.

Hirohito remained stubbornly suspicious until the last. When it was first apparent, at eight-thirty that morning, that the Army had given in, Privy Seal Secretary Kido advised him "to soothe people by appointing a new Cabinet." Hirohito replied that he would "wait until pacification is complete." Then when it was complete, he was all impatience. At two o'clock he had the conventional request to Prince Saionji—that he come up to Tokyo and recommend a prime minister—transmitted to Okitsu by telephone instead of the customary imperial messenger. Pleading lumbago, Saionji asked for a little time to prepare for the journey. At four o'clock Hirohito had him called again and told that Cabinet formation was urgent and that he must come as quickly as possible.

While Saionji collected himself a day passed, March 1. It was a Sunday, and for once on Sunday official Tokyo enjoyed not only the weekly official Western-style day off but a day of genuine exhaustion and rest. Hirohito was the exception. He was up early in Army uniform and remained at his desk until late in the evening. It was a regimen which he would insist on for weeks to come. He gave up his daily hour of exercise and paid no attention even when a delegation of his chief vassals came to him on March 18 and begged him to take better care of his honorable body. He knew well the military dictum that victory can be deceptive unless it is pursued inexorably to the last surrender of the last foot soldier.

On March 2, when the venerable Saionji did arrive in Tokyo, arrangements had been made by Hirohito's Big Brothers which would enable their leader, Prince Konoye, to refuse power in the manner of Julius Caesar— first the crown of prime minister, then the crown of lord privy seal. It was an elaborate gesture staged to prepare the way for a Konoye prime ministership when the war began with China. Konoye had never served in any public office but was known merely as a leader in the aristocratic House of Peers. The people needed exposure to the idea that he was prime ministerial timber. And though the docile people might accept him now, he did not wish to be in charge at a time when the Army was about to be ruthlessly purged. It would have made his leadership over the Army difficult in time of war.

Saionji made an attempt to expose the insincerity of Konoye's candidacy. When he found the Konoye name pushed at him from every direction by well-primed politicians, he spoke to Konoye and found him unwilling. When Konoye's modesty was admired in the newspapers, Saionji went ahead, over Konoye's objections, and insisted on proposing him officially to the Throne. Hirohito himself broke precedent by objecting that Konoye's health might not be good enough. Saionji declared that it was and repeated his recommendation. Hirohito had no choice, as a matter of protocol, but to summon Konoye on March 4 and ask him to form a Cabinet.

Emerging from his audience, Konoye confided to Lord Privy Seal Secretary Kido, "I am in real trouble." After a night's sleep Konoye returned to Saionji and begged for mercy. He brought with him a certificate from his doctor stating that his health would not be up to the responsibilities of office for at least another three months, that is, until the purge of the Army would be completed.

Saionji could then have ruined his young kinsman's career by announcing that, at a time of crisis, Konoye had refused to obey the imperial order to form a government. Instead, after long discussion, the old man softened. He let reporters know that he had a low opinion of political aspirants who could not sacrifice their health for the sake of the nation. Then, however, he returned to the Throne Room and announced that he was extremely embarrassed but would have to change his recommendation. This time he recommended a lesser member of Hirohito's middle-aged inner circle, Foreign Minister Hirota Koki.[6]

Hirota was commanded by Hirohito to form a Cabinet on March 5 but was not finally invested prime minister until March 9. In the four-day interim military and political circles made mutually insatiable demands on him as to both the policies and personnel of his Cabinet.[7] While Hirota's difficulties pre-empted headlines and left Japan without an official government, Hirohito quietly pushed through a number of stern disciplinary measures on his own.

On March 4 the Privy Council, sitting in Hirohito's presence, agreed to advise him to decree that the young officers of the rebellion be tried by court-martial in secret, that they be given no rights of appeal, and that their sentences be executed as swiftly as possible. On March 2 all full generals in the Army had offered to resign their commissions as a token of regret to the Throne for "the recent unforgivable incident." Now on March 6 Hirohito accepted the mass resignation as no mere gesture but a matter of earnest, effective April 23. Moreover, he saw fit to stipulate by name three exceptions to the general rule. General Terauchi, the leader of the Army Purification Movement, together with his cohorts General Nishi and General Ueda, would not resign. Terauchi would become war minister, Nishi inspector general of military education, and Ueda commander of the Kwantung Army.

When the cries of protest and the scurrying of feet in palace corridors had subsided, Chief Aide-de-Camp Honjo, waiting out a painful fortnight of face-saving delay before his own obligatory retirement, noted in his diary that the exceptions were "part of the Emperor's supreme right." In a similar vein on March 9, Hirohito ruled that the only members of the Supreme War Council and Army high command who did not need to submit their resignations were Field Marshal Prince Kanin, Lieutenant General Prince Asaka, and Lieutenant General Prince Higashikuni.

When the Hirota Cabinet finally established a workable milieu for itself and took office on March 9, Hirohito continued in uniform, at his desk

---

[6] A career diplomat, Hirota had started his career as a personal protégé of gang lord Toyama. He had made the acquaintance of Prince Konoye in 1921 and become one of Konoye's informants inside the Black Dragon Society.

[7] At Army insistence Count Makino's son-in-law Yoshida Shigeru, who would be prime minister five times between 1946 and 1954, was denied the powerful police portfolio of the home ministry.

from morn to midnight, giving his opponents an object lesson in non-organ imperatives. He changed his official signature on state documents from "Supreme Sovereign of the Great Land of Japan" to "Heavenly Emperor of the Great Land of Japan." [8] He considered abolishing the four regiments which had contributed men to the mutiny and then, in a gesture of magnanimity to the loyal majority, allowed them to keep their colors and remain a part of the armed services.

At the same time he approved tentatively a new draft plan for national defense which was drawn up in four parts by many different offices in the defense establishment: a financial section which "in accordance with the Constitution" might be shown to the Diet; an over-all policy and strategy section which might be reported to the Cabinet; a section on mobilization and manpower which might be revealed to the prime minister; and a section of detailed operational plans which might be seen in its entirety only by the Emperor and a handful of officers in the General Staff. One of its subsections, formulated that very month of March 1936, was a plan for night maneuvers near Peking which could be used—and would be used sixteen months later—to trigger the full-scale war with China.

The bulk of the new defense plan was devoted less to specific preparations against China than to an over-all buildup of national military strength. Japan had to be ready not only to win against the Chinese but also to discourage Western intervention. The Hirota Cabinet instituted a program of regimentation which was known, even at the time, as "the quasi-wartime economy." Military expenditures more than trebled in the next twelve-month. Deficit financing, which had been held to a minimum by the late, clever Finance Minister Takahashi, murdered in the mutiny, now became the order of the day. Every aspect of economic life from factory norms to foreign exchange was made the thrall to cheap printing-press money and rigorous government control.

At the same time secret arrangements were made in minute detail for increasing the size of the Army from seventeen to twenty-four divisions. The seven new divisions were to be drawn from the reserve. So thoroughly were supplies, officers, and retraining facilities prepared for them in advance that when they were needed in the opening weeks of the war with China, they became fighting realities overnight. Thus, if we are to believe official records, the 114th Division was created in October 1937 and in less than a month was in China driving on Nanking.

While this dramatic 41 per cent increase was being planned in the over-all size of the Army, the angry Hirohito demanded a drastic purge of the men who would command it, a purge which would lead to a critical shortage of trained officers in the two years ahead. The need for the purge was undeniable, however, and was eloquently explained by Prince Kanin in a

[8] It was a step he had been considering since late January.

conversation with Saionji's Secretary-Spy Harada on March 3: "As we cannot get along without the cause of this latest outbreak—namely, our principle of keeping an excessively tight lid, no matter what, on our own stinking fish—we are forced to do a thorough job this time, even to the point of ruthlessness, in cleaning up the Army."

The unpopular task of carrying out the house cleaning was shouldered by the new war minister, the Purification Movement's General Terauchi. Between March and August of 1936 he sent to pasture more than 2,000 of the 8,000-odd commissioned officers in the Army. The Strike-North contingent was almost wiped out and with it went the better half of the Army's strategic brain power. By way of compensation, the purge struck most heavily in the upper echelons and thereby cleared a way for the eventual promotion of fresh young talent.

To counter the resentment and the new politician-veteran coalitions which would inevitably spring up in the wake of the Throne's latest authoritarian measures, the Big Brothers of the Eleven Club devised a plan by which Hirohito could veto any Cabinet not of his choice and do so secretly without seeming to have played any part in the matter. Every Cabinet had to have a War and a Navy minister. The law, as revised in 1913, allowed these two posts to be filled from either the active or reserve lists of generals and admirals. As only active officers were bound by imperial orders, it was possible in theory for a prime ministerial candidate recommended by Saionji to fill a complete slate of Cabinet ministers without first obtaining the Emperor's approval. The Emperor, of course, could refuse to sanction such a Cabinet, but not gracefully, not without revealing his partisanship. And so in early May the Privy Council, sitting in the Imperial Presence, recommended to the Hirota Cabinet that the law be changed and that only officers on active service be eligible for the War and Navy ministerships. The Cabinet agreed to the change and Hirohito quickly signed it into law. Only when it was a fait accompli, on May 18, was it announced to press and public. Hirohito and his inner circle used it regularly thereafter to block the formation of undesirable cabinets or to topple cabinets which had served their purpose. That vague beast "The Army" was always held publicly responsible, and the fearful, reverent, taboo-stricken people politely ignored the reality—that Hirohito, since the mutiny, was in fact as well as name the Army's commander-in-chief.[9]

While such momentous changes were being made in the fabric of Japan, the protagonists of the February Mutiny quietly disappeared. Chief Aide-de-Camp Honjo was at first encouraged by War Minister Terauchi to keep

---

[9] No reserve officer had ever been made a service minister during the twenty-three years from 1913 to 1936 while such an appointment was legal. In 1944, however, when it was technically illegal, Hirohito would make a retired admiral Navy minister by simply calling the Navy Personnel Bureau and having the man's name—Yonai—reinstated on the active list.

his post. "I too am in a position of many troubles," he told Honjo on March 8, "so please do not think of resigning."

But on March 16 Honjo wrote in his diary: "Terauchi came to see me and told me the details of my son-in-law Yamaguchi's guilt and said that he was sorry for me. . . . On that day Yamaguchi's family moved into my home. Their furniture was put in the home of the elder Yamaguchi [a lieutenant general]. It is at the request of the Yamaguchi family that my daughter and her children have been sent to live in my house."

The next day, March 17, Honjo communicated his intention to resign to the Emperor. "The Emperor asked me, 'To what extent is your relative involved?'

"I said, 'It is not certain to what extent, but under present conditions the first consideration is the cleansing of the Army and I feel obligated to resign if only to set an example.'

"The Emperor replied, 'That may be right; I shall consider it well.' "

By March 28, the resignation was accepted. Honjo received a number of presents from the Emperor including money, art objects, and a pair of paperweights from the imperial desk. "I give you those," Hirohito said, "because I have used them for a long time." The Empress Dowager gave Honjo platinum cuff links, fresh fish, and *omochi*—a type of holiday rice cake—which she had prepared with her own hands. On April 22 Honjo was ordered into the First Reserve with General Minami who had served over him as war minister during the Manchurian Incident.

"I cannot help feeling a kind of sticky sentimentality," he wrote.

Other suspects were dealt with more harshly. The blunt, honest number-two Strike-North leader, General Mazaki, was held by the secret police for a year and a half. In the final weeks of 1936, still stubbornly unrepentant, he went on a month-long hunger strike at the end of which he refused even to drink water. Restored to health by brute force of medicine in the hospital, he was finally acquitted by a verdict which his friend General Araki, the articulate number-one Strike-North leader, later called "one of the strangest legal documents in history." It cited all Mazaki's treasonable involvements in minute detail and then abruptly exculpated him in one brief declarative sentence. His pardon was widely attributed to the efforts of Prince Konoye who wished to heal the wounds of factionalism and unite the nation behind the war effort.

Major General Tiger Yamashita, who had spied for the palace in the ranks of the Strike-North Faction and who had served as go-between in negotiating with the young rebels, found himself reposted to the command of a brigade in Korea. For months he worried that he had interpreted his instructions from the palace too broadly, that he had gone too far in inciting the rebellion or too far in attempting to mediate it. He sank into dejection and, according to his wife, began to look about for civilian employment. Then, in December 1936, his palace contact, former Aide-de-Camp

Lieutenant General Kawagishi Bunzaburo, came to Korea as his commanding officer. Kawagishi brought Yamashita a personal note of encouragement and appreciation from Hirohito. After reading it, Yamashita took heart. He went on to rise steadily in Hirohito's esteem until he conquered Malaya for the Empire in 1942.

As for the young officers who had resorted to violence, they were shot. Lieutenant Colonel Aizawa who had assassinated First Crow Nagata returned after the mutiny to a court-martial which was no longer open to the public. He was sentenced to death on May 7 and executed on July 3. Nine days later thirteen of the surviving nineteen officers who had led the mutiny followed him to the firing squad. All had hoped for a chance in court to explain their aspirations and grievances. Each had been given a single hour before a panel of Army judiciary officers in a hearing that was entirely secret.

At the moment of death most of them gave a last "banzai" wishing the Emperor ten thousand years of life. Some of them added a sardonic banzai for their disappointing friend Prince Chichibu. Several of them called out, "I leave my corpse to your discretion." One of them shouted, "I entreat those of the privileged classes to reflect deeply." Another said quietly, "It seems that we all cry ten thousand years for the Emperor on the steps of Heaven, so I, too, repeat banzai for the Emperor and add a banzai for my Imperial country."

Yet another sought to communicate a more difficult technical Army message: "In as much as the Japanese put absolute trust in their Imperial Army, their trust has been betrayed. Russia cannot be defeated in central Asia. That would bring Japan to destruction." The Strike-North group had wanted to attack Russia only at her eastern extremity, the Vladivostok region. After the occupation of China's main cities and agricultural valleys, Hirohito would attempt to strike at Russia in her soft underbelly, across the Mongolian deserts, in central Asia. The attempt would fail.

When it came time for the civilians of the February Mutiny to face their firing squad, Kita Ikki, the veteran ideologist of the Strike-North Faction, looked down the muzzles of the rifles and said, "Is it to be sitting or is this way all right?" When forced to squat, he shouted: "Hah! so the standing position of Jesus Christ and Sakura Sogo [a patriot crucified in 1645] is no longer allowed, eh?" His irony fell on deaf ears and his execution stirred little interest in the press, for it took place on August 19, 1937. By then the Japanese people shared his spirit of bitter cynical fatalism. By then they had allowed themselves to be marshaled and marched forward. By then they were at war with China and had been for the last month.

PART SIX

TRIUMVIR OF ASIA

22

NEUTRALIZING RUSSIA

(1936–1939)

DROWNING A RADIO

At seven o'clock on a May morning in 1936, two months after Hirohito's suppression of the Army Mutiny, Japanese commuters on the platform of the Shinjuku station in Tokyo eyed curiously two European hikers, bowed under what were obviously very heavy rucksacks. The commuters were all going toward downtown Tokyo. The two foreigners with their packs boarded a train in the opposite direction, out toward Mount Fuji. One of them was Max Klausen, a Red Army signal corps graduate, born to poverty on an island off the north German coast. His companion, Branko de Vou-kelitch, was a Yugoslavian photographic technician. Klausen had been in Japan only a few months and was ostensibly trying to set up a blueprint shop for copying the plans of architects and contractors. Voukelitch had operated for over two years in Japan as a correspondent for the French news agency Havas. Both men were Soviet agents. The weights in their rucksacks were transformers from a clandestine radio transmitter.

The two spies rode out into the glistening rice paddies of the countryside, changed to a trolley-car branch line, and completed the final leg of their journey by taxi over a dirt road to the resort hotel on Lake Yamanaka at the foot of Mount Fuji. The hotel servants who relieved them of their rucksacks remarked at once on the great loads they were carrying.

"We brought along half a dozen bottles of beer," explained Klausen hastily.

"We have plenty of beer here," said the hotel manager in injured tones.

As soon as possible that evening the two hikers hired one of the boats at the hotel waterfront and took their two rucksacks of beer out for a few hours of fishing and moon viewing. Away from the lights ashore, under

663

the evening shadow of Japan's sacred volcano, they dropped the contents of their packs into the profound waters of the lake: three transformers, a knotted mass of copper wire, and a dozen gassy triodes. They breathed a relieved sigh of requiescat, for they had put to rest the last telltale remains of a bulky, badly engineered, Russian radio transmitter which had been smuggled into Japan two years earlier and had consistently failed to get out messages to Vladivostok.

In place of the scuttled transmitter one of the two hikers, the German, Max Klausen, had put together a more compact, more powerful, more easily dismantled sending set out of components bought in the already sophisticated hi-fi stores on Tokyo's shopping street, the Ginza. Over the new set, for the next five years, Klausen would transmit to Vladivostok the reports of one of the most successful intelligence operations in history, the Sorge Spy Ring.

The Sorge ring was successful not because it revealed Japanese secrets to the Kremlin but because it maintained a kind of liaison between the Kremlin and the Imperial Palace in Tokyo. Its reports helped to expose an anti-Stalinist "Strike-South faction" in the Soviet high command in Siberia —one which wished to attack fascist Japan and one which Stalin ruthlessly purged. Still more to the point, its reports repeatedly assured Stalin that the Strike-North activists in the Japanese Army would never be allowed to act. As a result Stalin left his long frontier with Japan lightly guarded, and Hirohito found it so much the easier to restrain his eager Strike-North myrmidons and use them elsewhere. In sum the Sorge ring helped to keep peace between Japan and Russia in the critical years, 1936–1941. The delicate understanding it established between Stalin and Hirohito enabled the one to prepare a defense against Germany and the other an attack upon the United States.

SORGE, THE MASTER SPY

Agents of most Western nations considered Tokyo the one information center in the world which, for reasons of language difficulty and native patriotism, could not be tapped. The "impossible" Soviet ring was founded in Tokyo by Richard Sorge, a middle-class German intellectual, with a Russian mother, who had conceived an idealistic hate for war while serving with the German Army on the western front in World War I. Brilliant as a journalist, beloved by all sorts of women, comrade to all sorts of men, Sorge was a spy's spy, so much the loner and double-dealer that not even his own superiors in the Fourth, or Intelligence, Bureau of the Red Army completely trusted him. Not until 1964, twenty years after his execution by the Japanese, was he acknowledged a Hero of the Soviet Union. During his hour of service in Japan, he hazarded his life for Russia and sent Moscow all his best information. But at the same time he also supplied information to German Intelligence and allowed himself to be used as a planting ground for information which Hirohito's intimates wished transmitted to Moscow.

Sorge had joined the Communist party in 1920, at the age of twenty-four, in Hamburg. He had gone to Moscow in 1924 and become a professional agent for the Comintern. Until 1928 he operated as such in Scandinavia. In 1929 he was reassigned to Red Army Intelligence and sent to Shanghai where he established himself as a specialist in Chinese agricultural problems for the German newspaper *Frankfurter Zeitung*. Between 1929 and 1932, in Shanghai, he made the acquaintance of two native-born Japanese who would later serve him as agents in Tokyo. Both of them were liaison men, closely associated with the Japanese Spy Service, who built their careers on the making of friends in leftist circles.

In June 1931 the questioning of a Malayan Communist by British police in Singapore led to the arrest of the paymaster of all Communist activities in Shanghai and the seizure of all his codes and account books. Thereafter the British, French, and Japanese police in Shanghai followed Sorge's trail closely. Sorge studiously refused to panic and remained in Shanghai writing his articles on Chinese agriculture for nineteen more months. Then he returned to Moscow for rebriefing and reassignment.

Sorge personally suggested that he should operate next in Japan. On consideration, the brass of the Red Army accepted his proposal and gave him a single, specific mission: to try to warn Moscow in advance of any Japanese plans to invade Siberia. To prepare himself for this task, Sorge went home to Germany for a few months. He applied for membership in the Nazi party. He worked out free-lance contracts with fresh German newspapers. He begged letters of introduction from German notables to Japanese notables. Finally in September 1933 he arrived in Yokohama.

In his first year and a half in Japan, Sorge did little but make contacts and establish himself as a journalist. As was their wont with unknown Westerners, the Japanese police shadowed him closely but did nothing to check his activities. He drank heavily and wenched promiscuously with Japanese girls who duly reported to the police that he was a silent man and a good lover. He spoke no Japanese and associated mainly with other Europeans. He became a familiar figure talking to other Germans or other journalists at the bar in the Tokyo Club. He cultivated the staff of the German Embassy in Tokyo and made himself a valuable informant and good companion to the attachés there.

At the same time he was attempting slowly and secretly to acquire a ring of Japanese agents. Moscow naïvely sent him an Okinawan-born American Japanese from the Communist party in California to assist him as an intermediary. The Californian, an artist named Miyagi, was watched by the police as closely as Sorge himself. Nevertheless Miyagi arranged a number of secret meetings for Sorge with Japanese liberals and leftists. Most of

them agreed to provide Sorge with information in order—so they understood—"to prevent a Russo-Japanese War." As a pacifist and an intellectual, Sorge astutely realized that in this common concern all the ideological
slogans of East and West could be laid aside and that on this one objective
the Kremlin could agree with many of the most patriotic Japanese. Sorge
probably did not realize that one of the patriotic Japanese to whom his
proposition appealed most was Emperor Hirohito or that the Japanese
agents with whom he dealt were loyal to Hirohito.

Late in the summer of 1935 Sorge returned briefly to Moscow to tell
his chiefs that the Tokyo ring was ready to begin serious work and was
only hampered by the incompetence of its radioman and the consequent
difficulty of sending home reports. Moscow promptly recalled the radio
operator previously assigned to Sorge and gave him an old Shanghai friend
as a replacement. This was the hiker Max Klausen. He had been consigned
to corrective proletarian labor in the Volga Republic because he refused
to give up an anti-Communist White Russian mistress whom he had
brought back with him from Shanghai. Sorge's admiration for Klausen's
technical ability, however, carried enough weight to get the man restored to
favor. Klausen's gratitude for the good turn rendered made him personally
loyal to Sorge in a way that a doctrinaire Communist would have found
impossible during the ideologically confusing years which followed.

In November 1935 when Sorge returned to Tokyo, Klausen followed
him. On arrival Klausen set to work immediately building a radio transmitter of his own design, from locally available components, which he could
assemble in ten minutes and take apart in five. During March 1936 he
began to test it. In April he established contact with "Wiesbaden," the
Russian station in Siberia set up to monitor his dispatches. In May he and
the ring's photographic technician, Voukelitch, disposed of the old transmitter in Lake Yamanaka. Now the ring was ready to operate.

JAPAN'S LOYAL JUDAS

Three months after the drowning of the radio, the Russian spy ring
gained a further sense of security on the banks of a second scenic body
of water, this time the Merced River in California's Yosemite National
Park. There, on August 15–29, 1936, the Institute of Pacific Relations, an
organization backed by U.S. philanthropists, held a meeting of scholars to
thrash out the questions at issue between China and Japan. The Japanese
delegation to the meeting was chaperoned by the executive director of
Japan's own shadowy spy service, retired Lieutenant General Banzai
Rihachiro—the same man who had conferred with Hirohito just before the
first of the three political assassinations of 1932.

Banzai shepherded a prepossessing flock of intellectuals who had been
chosen to present Japan's most liberal face to the world. One of them was

the Prime-Minister-Maker's grandson, thirty-year-old Saionji Kinkazu, whom Hirohito's favorite Big Brother Marquis Kido had regularly consulted on all Communist problems since the 1933 Red scandal at the Peers' School. Saionji had with him a new friend and protégé, the thirty-five-year-old Ozaki Hotsumi who was the chief of the two Japanese "leftists" whom Sorge had cultivated since 1930. Ozaki was to be hanged as a traitor by the Tokyo secret police in 1944 but is remembered by knowledgeable Japanese aristocrats as one of the supreme patriots of his time.

Ozaki had been born—just a year after Hirohito, on May 1, 1901—in a special compound of Strike-South-minded Japanese adventurers on the island of Taiwan. The compound had been organized by Emperor Taisho's prime minister, Katsura Taro, and by Big Brother Marquis Kido's father-in-law, the Meiji oligarch, General Kodama Gentaro. With such men as sponsors, Ozaki's father, an impecunious journalist, was able to send young Ozaki to the finest schools in the Empire. The boy attended a preparatory school in Taipei especially founded for twenty-six gifted children of the local Strike-South elite. He went on to the First Higher School in Tokyo, the best of the academies which placed young patriots at Tokyo Imperial University, Japan's Harvard.

Ozaki matriculated at the university at eighteen and began to specialize in German. Two of his best friends there were Ushiba Tomohiko, later a private secretary to Prince Konoye, and Matsumoto Shigeharu, also a future member of Konoye's "kitchen cabinet." [1] The three young men were all known as protégés of Prince Konoye's father, the founder of the Great Asia All-One-Culture Society.

At graduation Ozaki went on to a year of further training, in psychology and sociology, which was paid for by an old Taiwan friend, the influential doctor-administrator Goto Shimpei, who had recommended himself to Emperor Meiji in 1891 by poisoning a leading critic of the plans for the first war with China.

At twenty-five, after remaining as long as possible in the academic world, Ozaki put in two years learning the craft of journalist on Tokyo's big daily *Asahi*. He proved to be a tortuous writer and an unaggressive reporter, and so, after a brief tryout as an essayist on the *Asahi* magazine, he was sent overseas in 1928 to Shanghai. There he came into his own, not as a journalist but as a friend to Marxists of many nations. He began to read Marx himself and to learn the necessary dialectic jargon.

In 1929 Ozaki made friends with Agnes Smedley, an aggressive, mannish political malcontent from Missouri. She too was a journalist. She had taken

---

[1] Today Matsumoto runs International House in Tokyo, a hostelry where young visiting scholars from abroad are accommodated and watched at minimal expense to all concerned. Ushiba was responsible during the war for putting in final form the "memorials" and "diaries" that Prince Konoye dictated for the Peace Faction as cover stories for the Emperor.

upon herself the task of befriending the downtrodden of the Orient. For eight years in the 1920's she had been the common-law wife of an Indian revolutionary in Berlin. Now she took Ozaki into her cell of Asian nationalists and, according to her own boast, made him her lover.

In late 1930 Agnes Smedley introduced Ozaki to "an American sympathizer named Johnson," who was in reality Richard Sorge, Ozaki's later spy chief. Ozaki and "Johnson" took an immediate liking for one another and formed a masculine intellectual friendship which transcended and overrode both their personal ideologies. To judge from the sum total of evidence about these two suave, gregarious, close-mouthed men, Sorge believed in Russia as the fatherland of a world organization which would bring equality and peace to all people. Ozaki was more parochial but equally idealistic. He believed that Japan was the Messianic nation which would lead all Asia up out of its poverty and its servitude to Western exploitation. In Russia he saw only the best of many potential Western allies, and in communism he saw only a community creed of sharing which had been preached as an imperial ideal in Japan for centuries.

Neither Sorge nor Ozaki ever pried into the private life and thoughts of the other, yet the two were destined to die together fourteen years later, still loyal friends, in the chambers of the Tokyo Thought Police. For the first six years of the friendship, Ozaki knew Sorge only as "Johnson" and never tried to find out whether he took his orders from Russia's Red Army or from the guiding body of the international socialist movement, the Comintern. Sorge, in his turn, never asked why Ozaki was a socialist or whether he, too, took orders from some non-visionary agency of his own government.

In February 1932, when Soviet espionage in Shanghai was on the run, Ozaki was recalled by his newspaper, *Asahi,* to Japan. It was nineteen months later that Sorge arrived in Japan. In the spring of 1934 he sent his American-Okinawan intermediary to Ozaki and asked to meet him secretly in the deer park attached to one of the Buddhist temples in the old eighth century Japanese capital of Nara, twenty-five miles south of Kyoto. Ozaki kept the appointment and, in his own words, "readily agreed" to give Sorge whatever information was available to him as a reader of Japanese and a rising journalist. For the next two years the reports which Sorge smuggled out of Japan by courier through Shanghai were almost entirely based on Ozaki's journalistic insights. Because of Sorge's ability as a writer, the reports satisfied the Red Army's Bureau Four but they penetrated few veils of secrecy. The Sorge report on the 1936 Army Mutiny, as an instance, exhibited total ignorance of the factions, motives, and high-level palace participation which had been involved in the affair.

Ozaki could have written far more realistically about the mutiny, for his friend and former fellow leftist in Shanghai, Kawai Teikichi, a future member of the Sorge Spy Ring, had been in on its preparation. Kawai had gone on from Shanghai in 1932 to infiltrate Chinese Communist circles in Tientsin in north China in 1933. He lodged in Tientsin across the street from the Japanese Special Service Organ there, and it is difficult to tell from his results whether he was infiltrating Japanese circles for the Chinese Communists or Chinese Communist circles for the spy service. In 1935 he returned to Japan and lived in the home of Fujita Isamu, an operative of the Japanese spy service who had assisted in the 1928 murder of Chang Tso-lin, the 1931 March Plot, and the 1931 take-over of Mukden in Manchuria. Throughout 1935 Kawai served Fujita by making friends with the young idealistic domestic reformers who would participate in the Army Mutiny. Ozaki failed to communicate to Sorge any of this complicated background when Sorge filed his much applauded analysis of the Army Mutiny with Russian Intelligence, German Intelligence, and several European newspapers.

In 1936, after the February Mutiny, Ozaki's position in the inner world of Japan suddenly skyrocketed. Because of his old connections with the coterie of Prince Konoye's father and because of his knowledge of China and Chinese, he was recruited by a group of young men around Prince Konoye who hoped to rationalize and temper Hirohito's military ambitions in China. First, Ozaki was made a member of a China-study committee organized by his newspaper, *Asahi;* then he was sent to Yosemite with young Saionji and Lieutenant General Banzai of the spy service to present the merits of Japan's position in China to the world at large.

At Yosemite Ozaki delivered a well-reasoned defense of Japan's activities in China and thereby improved greatly his reputation among Japanese rightists. After the Yosemite meeting he was taken into the Eleven-Club circle of Hirohito's Big Brothers and at the same time, as a fully fledged agent, into Sorge's Spy Ring. In September 1936, at a tea party for the returning Yosemite delegation, held amid the Aztec Gothic of Frank Lloyd Wright's Imperial Hotel in Tokyo, Ozaki was officially introduced to "Johnson" and told that his old "American" friend was in reality a German named Sorge. Two months later Ozaki was recruited as one of the original members of the Showa Research Society, a body organized in advance to write position papers and slogans for Prince Konoye to use if, as anticipated, he should become the China-war prime minister in 1937.

Thereafter, as many writers have observed, Ozaki served as Soviet agent Sorge's chief source of high-level Japanese government information. For lack of access to the full texts of certain important diaries, however, Western scholars have failed to note that for the next three years, whenever a crisis threatened between Japan and the Soviet Union, Hirohito's favorite Big Brother Marquis Kido invariably consulted with Saionji Kinkazu. Saionji, in turn, transmitted his impressions to Ozaki and Ozaki to Sorge. Through this intelligence chain Hirohito repeatedly used the Sorge Spy Ring to allay the suspicions of the suspicious Joseph Stalin and keep Japan out of war with Russia.

INNER MONGOLIA

At the moment that Ozaki, the new link with Russia, was admitted into Hirohito's circle, the Japanese Kwantung Army in Manchuria made a tentative probe into Inner Mongolia along the southern borders of Siberia.

It was November 1936. Sleet collected on the wings of the observation plane and its movements, especially when it flew low, seemed dangerously sluggish. Lieutenant Colonel Tanaka Takayoshi, the lover of Japan's girl spy, Eastern Jewel, hugged his huge knees nervously in the skirts of his Chinese robe—his civilian disguise—and peered out the cockpit window at the specks on the snow-covered plain below. Tanaka watched the specks with humiliation. They were Mongol horsemen who had been under his command since the start of the offensive nine days earlier on November 10. Now the offensive was over and the horsemen were retreating to the east, back toward Japanese-controlled territory on the edge of Manchukuo. Throughout the last week Tanaka had directed their movements from the air, keeping in touch with other Japanese spotter planes by radio and occasionally swooping down to drop a bamboo cylinder of instructions.

Despite Japanese equipment and leadership, the Mongol roughriders had failed in their mission—failed to take Inner Mongolia from China and make it once again an independent Tartar state. At Pailingmiao, the Shrine of a Hundred Spirits, they had fought and lost a week-long battle against the KMT forces of Chang Hsueh-liang, the former Manchurian war lord. Colonel Tanaka writhed inwardly because his orders forced him to fly back to Mukden instead of sharing the hardships of his retreating men on the ground. His fellow staff officers in the Kwantung Army would make fun of him. Eastern Jewel would be disappointed, angry, and scathing.[2] Worst of all, his face with the Mongols would now be lost. Years of work would blow away into the steppes—and all for lack of a few battalions of Japanese regulars to support the brave but undisciplined Mongol cavalry.

The Mongol Prince Teh, a kinsman of Eastern Jewel, had first agreed to work with Tanaka in March 1933. Ever since then, at the Shrine of a Hundred Spirits, Prince Teh had headed a Mongol government secretly in league with Japan. Little by little it had won the allegiance of fifty-nine of Inner Mongolia's seventy-seven tribes or "banners." In January 1936

---

[2] At this period Eastern Jewel's principal lover and main source of support was a highly successful Osaka confidence man named Matsuo Masanao, alias Ito Hanni. Through her introductions to Japanese Intelligence officers in China, Matsuo had established himself as a liaison man, running guns and carrying bribes from the Japanese Army to the dissident Canton faction of the KMT. He worked directly for Major General Tojo and other leading Kwantung Army staff officers and had handled about $8 million (U.S.) worth of Special Service funds. In kickbacks and commissions he had pocketed almost $2 million for himself which Eastern Jewel had done her best to help him spend. Now that Matsuo was falling under suspicion, however, she had returned to Manchuria in search of fresh patrons and pastures.

the Plot Section of the Kwantung Army—euphemistically translated as the Strategic Planning Section by most Western scholars—had detailed Tanaka to bring all Inner Mongolia, openly, into Prince Teh's fold. Hirohito and the Tokyo General Staff had approved the scheme on one condition: that it cost no more than a few million yen.

From Tokyo's vantage point an independent Mongolian nation, stretching across the north of China, would be moderately useful. It would cut the ancient caravan routes leading in to China from Russia and would help to isolate Chiang Kai-shek during Japan's planned war against the central KMT regime in Nanking. For Tanaka, who did not know the over-all war plan and had specialized in Mongol affairs since military academy, a "wedge between China and Russia" had become a premise for living. It would halt the spread of communism in China. It would facilitate a Strike North against Russia when the proper time came. And most important, it would rehabilitate the Mongols who Tanaka mystically believed to be a lost tribe of the Japanese nation itself.

In vain Tanaka had asked for more Tokyo support. When he had seen it was not forthcoming, he had undertaken to make do with contributions he could raise in Manchuria. The "Independent Volunteers' Squadron" of the Manchurian Aviation Company had provided him with thirteen light planes for air support. Manchukuoan Electric had fitted them out with two-way radios. The South Manchuria Railway Company had furnished 150 cars and trucks. The Kwantung Army had given the services of three fellow staff officers and $1.8 million in gold.

Now all was lost. Tanaka's plane dipped low so that he could drop his last cylinder of orders. Then he made for home. That night in Mukden he began a two-day drunken spree of protest against the stinginess of his superiors. He succeeded in making them offer the Mongol Prince Teh more money, on the strength of which one of Prince Teh's generals succeeded briefly in recapturing the Shrine of a Hundred Spirits. Thereafter all the Mongol horsemen made good their retreat through the snow. A few of them enlisted in one or another of Japan's puppet constabulary forces in Manchukuo. One group of them, on December 10, found constabulary duty so distasteful that they massacred the Japanese officers in charge of them and fled into the steppes. Most of the Mongols, however, followed Prince Teh when, on December 12, he forsook Japan and proclaimed his renewed loyalty to Chiang Kai-shek.

THE GENERALISSIMO KIDNAPPED

On November 18, 1936, when the battle at the Shrine of a Hundred Spirits had first turned against Tanaka's cavalry rabble, Chiang Kai-shek himself had arrived by plane behind the front to inspect operations. Having lost Manchuria and the other northeastern provinces to Japan, Chiang was glad to associate himself with a Chinese victory over Japan. Since late in the spring of 1936, when his intelligence reports indicated that the Army mutiny in Tokyo had not in any way set back Japanese plans for the conquest of China, he had been busy fortifying the railroad lines which might be used by the Japanese in an attempt to move against him out of north China. At the same time he had announced his sixth bandit suppression campaign against the Communists of Mao Tse-tung in the northwest.

Not since 1925 had Chiang been so beleaguered by enemies. His power was secure only in central China along the valleys of the Yangtze River and its tributaries. Tibet, under the Dalai Lama, was virtually a fief now of British India. Outer Mongolia and the huge western province of Sinkiang had become economic dependencies of Russia. Manchuria and the Peking area were controlled by Japan. The Communist faction of Mao Tse-tung collected taxes in the northwest. In the southeast the perennially dissident generals of the KMT's Canton faction threatened rebellion. Sun Yat-sen's dream of a united China had lost its flush of youth, and Chiang, in Sun Yat-sen's mantle, was in danger of being regarded as just another war lord.

In going to the front, Chiang hoped to make sure of the allegiance of Chang Hsueh-liang and of his expatriate Manchurians. He had given Chang an important assignment in the sixth campaign against the Communists. But instead of attacking the Communists vigorously, Chang had entrenched his forces and diverted all the men he could spare to fight the Inner Mongolian battle on his extreme right flank. It was rumored in Nanking that Chang and the Communists had agreed to fight Japan first and settle their own differences later.

Chiang Kai-shek took with him on his inspection tour 200,000 words of important state papers, including his own diary for the years in which he had ruled the KMT. He needed the papers to persuade Chang Hsueh-liang that he had been acting in the best interests of China and buying valuable time by his repeated concessions to Japan. In return Chang, too, must show a statesmanly spirit and realize that alliance with the Communists might be more dangerous in the long run than temporary surrenders to the Japanese. Chang Hsueh-liang stubbornly refused to be persuaded, and he and Chiang negotiated for three weeks. Then on December 12, 1936, in an attempt either to coerce Chiang or to save Chiang's face before the inevitable settlement, Chang Hsueh-liang had his leader kidnapped.

It was five o'clock in the morning and Chiang Kai-shek was in his nightshirt. At the sound of shots he jumped from his pallet, ran to the rear of the temple in which he was camped, and scaled a ten-foot wall. Dropping to the other side he twisted his back and had to scramble painfully on hands and knees up the hillside beyond. Two white hares, he later recounted, guided him to a rocky overhang under which he could hide and rest. There, when it was almost noon, he confronted a group of the rebellious soldiers who were beating the bushes for him and courageously demanded that they either shoot him or provide him with a suitable escort back to his quarters. One of the dissidents, a battalion commander, respectfully offered his broad shoulders and carried Chiang in his nightshirt down the mountain piggyback. Chang Hsueh-liang and Chiang's own local bandit-suppression commissioner had him put to bed comfortably under guard, and negotiations were resumed.

That night in Shanghai Madame Chiang Kai-shek, her brother, her brother-in-law, and Chiang's Australian advisor W. H. Donald gave the news of Chiang's kidnapping as an exclusive to Hallett Abend of *The New York Times*. They thereby made sure that the story would first reach Japan from an authoritative Western source rather than from a suspect Chinese one. In China, where news was always well controlled, it was an odd maneuver, savoring more of publicity for an event which they had foreseen than of concern for public knowledge about an uncertain situation which had taken them by surprise.

Meanwhile in Sian, the town in the northwest where Chiang was detained, Chang Hsueh-liang was beginning to read the 200,000 pages of state documents which Chiang demanded that he study before they resume their conversations. In the next three days Chang read, and Chiang Kai-shek stayed in bed, refusing to eat and threatening, by suicide, to leave China without a leader. Chang called in Chou En-lai, the later foreign minister of Communist China, to plead the cause of Mao Tse-tung. By the end of the third day, Chiang Kai-shek had agreed "in principle" to present a united front of all patriotic Chinese factions against the Japanese. Then for another ten days he remained in bed lecturing eloquently on the republican principles of Sun Yat-sen and negotiating an elaborate save of face for himself in any future dealings he might have with the Japanese.

Chiang's Australian secretary, W. H. Donald, flew into Sian, the rebel stronghold, on December 14, 1936. Chiang's brother-in-law T. V. Soong joined the negotiations four days later. And Madame Chiang arrived in Sian to add her authority on December 21. While his minions made secret promises, Chiang continued to lie abed, saving face, daring his abductors to assassinate him, and maintaining, with stubborn courage and indignation, the rectitude of all his past decisions of state.

On Christmas Day 1936, Chiang and his spokesmen were allowed to fly back to Nanking. With them went Chang Hsueh-liang to surrender himself as a voluntary hostage to Chiang's brutal secret police. It was Chang's way of demonstrating to the Chinese people the sincerity of his patriotism. And Chiang Kai-shek appreciated it. The police touched not a hair on the hostage's head but simply put him under house arrest in one of the most comfortable mansions in Nanking. While he accustomed himself to a life of leisure, his captor Chiang fulfilled the unspoken pledges he had made during his own captivity. He called off the sixth bandit-suppression campaign against the Communists and began a succession of conferences at his country villa in the mountains with all the generals and war lords who owed him allegiance. He asked them one by one to stand by him in a long ordeal, a full-scale war with Japan—and to each of them he assigned commands and duties.

Chang Hsueh-liang remained under detention for the rest of his life. He never relapsed into the opium-smoking of his youth but instead cultivated the polite recreations of bridge, golf, books, fine food and wines, paintings, and handsome mistresses. In 1940 he was permitted a trip abroad and impressed all his fellow passengers on shipboard with his charming air of resignation and his excellence at the card table. After World War II, in 1949, he was brought to Taiwan under guard by Chiang Kai-shek, and there he remains a pampered prisoner at the age of seventy-two in 1970. He and his final mistress, Miss Chao, who is said to grow more seductive with each passing year, are still seen sometimes in Taipei attending the theater. At secret conclaves of the KMT leaders, it is reported that Chang still acts the part of a conscience for his eighty-three-year-old mentor, Generalissimo Chiang.

ALLIANCE WITH HITLER

On November 20, 1936, as Chiang Kai-shek began to negotiate the stiffening of backbone which his partisans required of him; as the Kwantung Army's gigantic Lieutenant Colonel Tanaka nursed his recent humiliation on the snowy wastes of Inner Mongolia; and as the new Soviet spy, Ozaki, was accustoming himself to the rarefied atmosphere of Konoye's inner circle, Hirohito at a Privy Council meeting approved Japan's first tentative alliance with Nazi Germany. The alliance was formalized five days later when Hitler's super-diplomat, Joachim von Ribbentrop, sat down at a table in Berlin with one of Hirohito's courtiers and signed a document known as the Anti-Comintern Pact. This instrument pledged Japan to act in concert with Germany in resisting the spread of communism. Secret protocols attached to it bound each nation to assist the other economically and diplomatically in the event that the other should make war on the Soviet Union.

Hitler and Ribbentrop had first begun to suggest such a pact to prominent Japanese visitors in 1933. The pact went against Hitler's early Aryan principles, as enunciated in *Mein Kampf,* but agreed well with his political objectives. At his direction the German propaganda apparatus under Goebbels had begun in 1934 to call the Japanese "the Prussians of the East." His Bureau of Race Investigation had decided that German-Japanese marriages were permissible because "the blood of Dai Nippon [Japan] contains within itself virtues closely akin to the pure Nordic strain." From Hitler's point of view the pact would help to neutralize Russia when the time came for the *Wehrmacht* to overrun France and the Low Countries. Hirohito's 1934 envoy to Berlin, Prince Kaya, had come home pointing out that the pact would help to neutralize Russia when the time came for the Japanese Army to overrun China.

Throughout 1934 Japanese representatives in Berlin had remained coy and noncommittal to the German overtures. But in the spring of 1935, when Hirohito decided on the war with China, negotiations had begun in earnest. They were conducted for Japan in Berlin not by the Japanese ambassador there but by Major General Oshima Hiroshi, the military attaché at the Japanese Embassy. Similarly in Tokyo they were conducted on behalf of Germany by Colonel Eugen Ott, the military attaché at Tokyo's German Embassy. In the summer of 1936, when the pact was finally ready for signing, Ott had returned home briefly to explain all its unwritten ramifications personally to Hitler and Oshima had done the same for Hirohito in Tokyo.

Ott had qualified for his mission in Hitler's eyes by useful service on the personal staff of General Kurt Schleicher, the last pre-Hitler chancellor of Germany. In Hirohito's eyes he was recommended by understandings he had reached in 1933 as liaison officer to Prince Higashikuni, Hirohito's uncle, at 5th Brigade Headquarters in Nagoya.

Oshima, the principal Japanese negotiator of the pact, was also an old friend of Prince Higashikuni, and he was sent to Berlin as military attaché in March 1934, shortly after the conclusion of the preliminary conversations between Higashikuni and Ott. It was understood by Ribbentrop and Hitler that Oshima could speak for the Emperor and for the chief of the Japanese Army General Staff, Prince Kanin. And so he could. As an assistant attaché in Germany in 1921, at the age of thirty-five, Oshima had been privy to all the plans of the Crows and Reliables of Hirohito's original cabal in the Army. He was not then designated as a recruit of the cabal because he was already a member of the Big Brothers' Inner Circle. His father, General Oshima Kenichi, had studied with Prince Kanin in France in the 1880's, had gone along with Prince Kanin on a tour of the front during the Boer War in South Africa in 1899, had assisted as war minister in Prince Kanin's abortive Mukden coup of 1916, and finally had accompanied Kanin and the crown prince—to help "make arrangements"— during Hirohito's European tour of 1921.

SORGE'S FIRST EXCLUSIVE

At first the Japanese accepted the Anti-Comintern Pact without much comment. They had long needed an ally in Europe, and even having Nazi Germany for a friend seemed better than fighting the preventive war with Russia advocated by the Strike-North Faction. In the West, however, the pact was decried as a dangerous fascist alliance, unfriendly to the democracies. France, the Netherlands, England, and the United States all released evidence to show that the pact contained secret military clauses in addition to the overt diplomatic ones acknowledged in its published text.

The Soviet Union, being the nation most directly threatened by the pact, had begun to spread rumors about the secret protocols more than a year before the pact was signed. Stalin, however, was less concerned by the protocols than other antifascist leaders because he knew what was in them. Germany and Japan had not committed themselves to assist one another militarily against the Soviet Union. In the event that either of the two contracting parties became involved in war with Russia, the other was simply pledged to provide diplomatic support and to "consult" with its ally on the joint military measures which might be taken. In short, neither Japan nor Germany had promised the other much of anything except friendly words.

Stalin knew this because Sorge had read the secret papers about the pact which had passed through the German Embassy in Tokyo and because Ozaki had kept abreast of the interpretation being placed upon them by men around Hirohito.

Eugen Ott, the German attaché in Tokyo, who had helped to negotiate the Anti-Comintern Pact, was one of Richard Sorge's prime contacts in Japan. When Sorge arrived in Tokyo in September 1933, he carried a letter to Ott from the chief editorial writer of *Tägliche Rundschau,* a liberal German newspaper. Sorge delivered his note of introduction in a visit to Nagoya where Ott had just concluded his preliminary conversations with the commander of the Nagoya Brigade, Hirohito's uncle Prince Higashikuni. Ott and Sorge had served in the same German division during World War I and soon became boon companions.

Through Ott, Sorge learned what few details of Kwantung Army strength in Manchuria the Japanese had divulged to the Germans in the course of the pact negotiations. In Sorge's opinion, which he swiftly conveyed to Moscow over Max Klausen's radio transmitter, the posture of the Kwantung Army constituted no threat to the Soviet Union and indicated no immediate intention of carrying out a Strike North. As a result, although Moscow made much propaganda out of the pact's secret protocols, the Red Army did not reinforce its garrisons in the Far East. Moreover, the day before the pact was made public, the Soviet government delivered Japan a calculated slap in the face by refusing to renew the Russo-Japanese treaty regulating quotas and privileges on the fishing banks off Siberia.

By his report on the Anti-Comintern Pact, Sorge proved to his superiors in Moscow that the two painstaking years he had spent in organizing his ring had not been wasted. His further reports, over the next five years, were to play an increasingly important part in enabling Russia and Japan to stand off from one another and prepare for their respective wars with Germany and the United States.

BLOCKING UGAKI

Although the Anti-Comintern Pact sailed smoothly, unopposed, through the Cabinet and the Emperor's Privy Council, it aroused noisy misgivings when the public realized what it meant to the West. The decrepit Saionji

called it a fool's bargain which "will only result in Germany exploiting us."
The leading Tokyo dailies joined Saionji editorially in pointing out that one
untrustworthy ally had been bought at the cost of many true friends.

At Saionji's behest, the Constitutionalist party began sniping at the
Cabinet from the floor of the Diet. One intrepid representative, the former
speaker of the lower House, Hamada Kunimatsu, demanded that War
Minister Terauchi—who was Hirohito's Army strong man of the moment—
submit to a trial of courage. If the Diet voted that Terauchi was sincere,
Representative Hamada promised to disembowel himself; on the other
hand if the Diet voted that Representative Hamada was sincere, Terauchi
would have to cut his belly. War Minister Terauchi declined to accept the
challenge because the Constitutionalists had a majority in the Diet and
would surely enjoy watching him commit hara-kiri. The next day, however,
on January 22, 1937, Terauchi submitted his resignation in writing to
Prime Minister Hirota. Hirota followed, late in the afternoon of Saturday,
January 23, by offering the mass resignation of his Cabinet to Emperor
Hirohito.

As always Hirohito insisted that old Saionji take the responsibility for
recommending the next prime minister. When so informed by Lord Privy
Seal Yuasa on the phone, Saionji asked to be excused, protesting that he
was too frail to come to Tokyo to investigate the political situation properly before making a selection. Hirohito replied, through Lord Privy Seal
Yuasa, that Saionji could do his research by telephone and then report his
choice to an imperial envoy who would call on him in Okitsu.

"In that case, without further deliberation," said Saionji, "I warn you
that I will recommend Ugaki."

General Ugaki was the bull-necked loyalist who had cleansed the Army
of its Choshu leadership for Hirohito in 1925 and had then allowed
himself to be duped and defamed by the March Plot of 1931. Since then,
as governor general of Korea, he had made himself the leader of the
many Army officers who took a moderate position between the Strike-
North and Strike-South Factions. He had the support of the political
parties and of the cartels. Most important, he was outspoken in his opposition to the planned war of aggression in China.

First on the phone and then in a face-to-face discussion the next day,
Sunday, with Saionji in Okitsu, Lord Privy Seal Yuasa tried in vain to
change the eighty-seven-year-old's mind. Returning discouraged to Tokyo
that night, Yuasa went in directly to a two-hour audience with Hirohito.
He persuaded Hirohito that, to avoid a public scene with Saionji, it would
be best to let Ugaki try to form a Cabinet. At 10 P.M. Ugaki was phoned
at the hot spring where he was waiting fifty miles outside of Tokyo and
told to come to the palace immediately.

Ugaki had his limousine waiting and set off at once. Outside the entrance to the palace, the car was stopped by an unexpected roadblock

set up by the secret police. As Ugaki blustered that the policemen were delaying a general on the Emperor's business, the barrier was opened and a figure stepped out of the night into the back seat and sat down beside Ugaki. It was Lieutenant General Nakajima Kesago, the chief of the secret police—the sadist who later that year would bring special oils from Peking to assist Prince Asaka in burning the bodies at Nanking.

Nakajima had been working closely with the palace on the maintenance of public peace since the February Mutiny the year before. Now he advised Ugaki to decline the mandate to form a Cabinet. A general like Ugaki, who had been involved in such previous Army plots as the March Incident, could not become prime minister, Nakajima said, without setting back seriously the program of Army discipline which had been imposed since the February Mutiny. General Ugaki thanked the sinister secret police chief for his advice and let him off at the next checkpoint, at the entrance to the Inner Palace enclosure. Then Ugaki drove on alone through the moonlit woods of the Fukiage Gardens. By the time he arrived at the Imperial Library he was doubly determined "to save Japan."

Hirohito admitted Ugaki to audience at 1:00 A.M.

"You may as well know," said the Emperor, "that Prime Minister Hirota has begged leave to resign, so I am asking you to form a Cabinet. I understand, however, that there is a movement against you in the Army. Do you think you can cope with it?"

"The situation is a complicated one," replied Ugaki with unusual modesty. "Please give me a few days, Sire, and I will see what I can do."

Hirohito nodded and dismissed him.

Two hours later, at 3:00 A.M., Marquis Kido, the first and favorite of the Big Brothers who had taken Hirohito in hand when he was a little boy, received a phone call from one of Lord Privy Seal Yuasa's protégés [3] telling him that the "right wing in the Army" was prepared to block Ugaki's prime ministership.

After daybreak Marquis Kido went to the palace and conferred with Lord Privy Seal Yuasa. Kido himself no longer had much of an official position in the palace. As a part of the change in palace window dressing after the February Mutiny, he had resigned from the secretariat of the lord privy seal and retained only his minor Court post as director of the Peerage and Heraldry Bureau. Nevertheless, he now consulted at length with Privy Seal Yuasa, with Yuasa's secretary,[4] and with one of Hirohito's

---

[3] Goto Fumio, a former home minister and leader of Strike-South colonials in Taiwan. He would survive MacArthur's purge after World War II to return to the Diet and become an elder statesman at Hirohito's Court in the 1960's.

[4] Matsudaira Yasumasa, who would succeed Kido as chief civilian advisor to the Emperor in 1945 and would handle liaison for Hirohito with American Prosecutor Keenan and with Keenan's star witness, the elephantine lover with the elephantine memory, retired Major General Tanaka Takayoshi.

military aides-de-camp.[5] On returning home, Kido at once began cogitating in his diary over the best man for the Emperor to appoint when Ugaki failed to form a Cabinet.

While Kido and other courtiers were working against him, Prime Minister-elect Ugaki set about routinely to form a Cabinet. At four o'clock that Monday afternoon he called on outgoing War Minister Terauchi and asked him politely to recommend a successor to himself. Terauchi shook his head gravely and warned Ugaki that officers willing and eligible to serve as war minister might be difficult to find. An hour later, after consulting other Army chiefs. Terauchi informed Ugaki that the three most appropriate candidates for the war ministership all declined the honor. Ugaki responded angrily that in that case he would hunt up his own war minister.

Late that night, at one o'clock, the vice minister of war called an emergency meeting of his section chiefs and, in a ten-minute briefing, advised them that Ugaki's search must be frustrated.

On Tuesday morning Ugaki took to the telephone. He knew most of the 200-odd generals on the active list and had done favors for many of them. Now, however, they squirmed evasively and pleaded personal reasons for being unable to accept the war ministership.

In the afternoon, having consulted an authority on constitutional law, Ugaki tried a fresh approach. He himself was a general, and if reactivated from the reserve list to the active list would be eligible to take the portfolio of war minister in addition to that of prime minister. On inquiry he found that there were a number of other retired generals who would also be willing to take the war minister portfolio. By early the next morning, Wednesday he had queues of reserve officers waiting outside the doors of War Minister Terauchi and of Chief of Staff Prince Kanin, pleading their candidacies. Some of them were such obscure field commanders that chamberlains at Court were kept busy looking up their personnel records in case the Emperor should ask questions about them.

The Emperor had the power to order any officer on active service to take the war ministership. It was, however, a power which the Emperor had never exercised. On the other hand, the Emperor had frequently reactivated reservists to fill unpleasant commands during the conquest of Manchuria. Saionji had suggested to Ugaki that in the present crisis the Emperor could be called out into the open by being forced publicly to refuse to reactivate Ugaki or any of his cronies.

All that Wednesday morning Marquis Kido, Lord Privy Seal Yuasa, and other chamberlains consulted on what countermeasures to take against the ingenious new Saionji-Ugaki strategy. They decided finally to rely on a metaphysical argument. If the Emperor, they reasoned, should agree to

---

[5] Major General Nakajima Tetsuzo, who in some Japanese accounts has been identified as the Nakajima who jumped into Ugaki's car the night before.

see Ugaki a second time to consider his reactivation request, it would be tantamount to giving him a second order to form a Cabinet. In effect it would be asking the god to issue the same orders twice—a clear sacrilege. If a vassal failed to perform the Emperor's bidding, that was a fault in the vassal's virtue, but if, on failing, he tried to enlist imperial support for a second try, that would call in question the Emperor's potence and could not be permitted.

Ugaki arrived at the palace in the forenoon and was given this answer after being kept waiting for several hours. In vain he argued that he had the right of direct access to the Throne. Ancient precedents were adduced to show that he did not. Finally Ugaki stamped from the outer ceremonial palace, threatening that he would never again wear the uniform of the Imperial Army. The next morning, Thursday, he formally tendered the resignation of his commission in the reserve.

On Friday, January 29, Hirohito called Ugaki to the palace to deliver his official report on the failure of his attempt to form a Cabinet. When Ugaki had finished reading and had begun stiffly to bow his way out of the Throne Room, Hirohito came forward, all solicitude, and apologized for having put Ugaki to so much trouble. The Throne, explained Hirohito, could never swim against the current of the times. Then he pressed back into Ugaki's hand his letter of resignation from the reserve and begged him to keep his salary and "to continue to do your utmost for the nation." Entrapped in the coils of patriotism and self-interest, Ugaki wavered for a few weeks and finally agreed to keep his commission and to accept the post of foreign minister in the Cabinet after next—a Cabinet which was to materialize three months later.

On that same Friday that Ugaki abandoned his attempt to form a government, a journalist, who was later tracked down and tortured and executed by the secret police, sent anonymous letters, beautifully penned and framed in black, to all the units which had been involved in the February Mutiny of 1936. He advised them that Prince Kanin, the senior member of the imperial family and chief of the Army General Staff, was the principal villain of the times and should be assassinated.

SAIONJI DROPS OUT

With the rejection of his protégé, the tragic old man Saionji—the knight in green armor of the restoration of 1868—gave up his futile, fifteen-year struggle to steer Hirohito from the shoals he saw ahead. After Ugaki's failure to form a Cabinet, Saionji was offered the alternative of nominating as prime minister either his old enemy, the far-right lawyer of the National Foundation Society, Baron Hiranuma, or General Hayashi, the former war minister who had eased the Strike-North Faction out of the Army bureaucracy before the 1936 mutiny. Muttering protests and dire predictions, Saionji allowed his name to be given to the choice of Hayashi.

Saionji reflected on this, his latest, capitulation for several days. He admitted to friends that he was approaching senility and that he spent most of his time living in the past. He complained that his secretary-spy, Harada, was constantly feeding him twisted or irrelevant information in order to distract him from concentrating on "the main trends of the time." Nevertheless he still had days of energy and complete lucidity in which he phoned old friends and understood completely the iron grip which Hirohito's middle-aged Big-Brother statists were taking on Japan. He felt personally responsible for them, for he had overseen their political educations. He also felt personally responsible for what they were doing. As long as he remained prime-minister-maker, the cartels and political parties of Japan would continue to look up to him as the leader of the young men at Court. And for the hundredth time he had just proved that he was not the leader. Perhaps if he resigned some other more forceful aristocrat of good sense would spring up in his place; perhaps his kinsman Prince Konoye and even Emperor Hirohito would begin to take their responsibilities more level-headedly.

Accordingly, in the week after Ugaki's humiliation, Saionji formally petitioned the Throne, asking that he be consulted no longer on changes of government. Hirohito refused to release him from his post of prime-minister-maker but allowed it to be inscribed officially on the Court rolls that Saionji would not have to come again to Tokyo for a Cabinet crisis. From now on the lord privy seal would relieve him of the duty of consulting with other elder statesmen on the nominee who should be recommended to the Throne as the next prime minister. In effect the lord privy seal would conduct all the business involved in the choice of a prime minister and simply inform Saionji of what he had done before carrying his advice to Hirohito.

Saionji welcomed this relief from responsibility and lived on for another three years and nine months as a sideline critic, sometimes crackling with sarcastic fire and sometimes remaining mute or ignorant.

The prospect of war with China dismayed the old man. What dismayed him still more was the prospect of direct involvement in enterprises which he considered rash and hazardous by members of the imperial family. On March 15, in an argument about China policy with Secretary-Spy Harada, he learned that Prince Higashikuni was slated to command the Army Air Force when it would begin to bomb China and that Prince Asaka, the Emperor's other uncle, was expected later to lead the Japanese troops who would occupy the Chinese capital of Nanking.

"The devil you say!" piped the old man testily. "I tell you that this business of installing imperial family members in military posts is for the sake of making the Army act as the Emperor's army in the time of emergency. It is understood that the members of the imperial family are usually the Emperor's allies. Therefore it would seem that the main point in having allies in military posts is to persuade the military, as the Emperor's own army, to conduct operations even to the ends of the earth."

LAST WORDS OF THE PEOPLE

When Saionji had already given up, the Japanese people themselves made one last bootless effort to escape from going to war. Hirohito's courtiers realized that the pacifism of the masses needed some form of satisfaction and had shrewdly set up General Hayashi, the new prime minister, as a straw man of militarism for the people to destroy.

Misunderstanding something said to him by Hirohito at his investiture ceremony, Hayashi launched his regime by asking everyone "to honor the Emperor and the spirits of the forefathers and to realize the identity of government administration and religious ceremony." In other words, the people from now on should participate in government only by worshipping and Hirohito should officiate absolutely as high priest. Westernized liberals were quick to point out that Emperor Meiji had promised separation of church and state, and Hirohito hastily disassociated himself from Prime Minister Hayashi's sentiments.

On the floor of the Diet the antimilitary sniping which had toppled the previous Hirota Cabinet swelled to a chorus. Rumors of war planning against China was discussed in every corridor. On March 18, Hirohito's brother Prince Chichibu left Japan with a suite of fifteen of the great vassals to attend the coronation of George VI in London. He had a secret mission—of which nothing is known from Western documentation—to persuade George VI to renew an unwritten understanding as to Japan's privileged position in China which Hirohito felt that he had had with George VI's brother, the recently abdicated Edward VIII. On the eve of Prince Chichibu's departure, his equerry told friends that if the mission were not successful war with China could be expected in early July.[6]

On March 31, 1937, two weeks after Prince Chichibu's sailing, Hirohito finally dissolved the carping Diet and called for a general election. During the following month, while the politicians were out stumping, he made full use of his edict powers to find funds for fully manning the seven new Army divisions which he had created in skeletal form after the February Mutiny the year before.

When the masses convened at the polls at the end of April, they delivered a resounding vote of non-confidence in the militaristic, archaically devout Prime Minister Hayashi. Both of the major parties, the Con-

---

[6] The equerry was Major General Honma Masaharu who would later be executed for his titular responsibility in the Bataan Death March. He was already well known and respected in Japan as "the linguist with the red nose" who had sat up all one night in 1932 translating into Japanese the Lytton Report on Manchuria.

stitutionalists and their traditional opponents, had asked for a vote for peace, and only the minority rightist party, the *Kokumin Domei* or People's League, had supported Hayashi. In the returns the Hayashi party won exactly eighteen seats in a House of 408.

A month later Hayashi resigned. He had served his purpose. The people had made their gesture. The seven new divisions were already established. Army men who wished to interfere in politics had been given a graphic demonstration of the Army's unpopularity and political incompetence. Now the way was clear to disregard the mandate of the voters and to appoint a popular civilian prince, a consummate politician, who could lead the people to war.

KONOYE

Prince Konoye, heir to the first of the five houses of the ancient Court family of Fujiwara, had been groomed as a national leader ever since his birth in October 1891. As a teen-ager he had been the youngest of the aristocratic Big Brothers who attached themselves to the person of young Hirohito when he was still a toddler living in the foster care of Marquis Kido's father. Since 1921 Konoye had led Hirohito's forces in the House of Peers and had mediated for Hirohito with all sorts of troublemakers: with Konoye's kinsman, Saionji; with the tong of the Black Dragon; with the dissident Strike-Northists in Hirohito's Army cabal.

The tall, languid, elegant prince was a sybarite in private life, but in public he was a politician down to the tips of his gloved fingers. Hirohito's ambition to aggrandize Japan territorially and technologically before the eyes of the West interested Konoye hardly at all. He responded first to the challenge of domestic Japanese government and second to the challenge of leading the Buddhists of Asia. Systems of government—of people-manipulation and propaganda—fascinated him; deployment of military forces caught his fancy only sporadically as a tool of politics.

Since the 1935 imperial decision to prepare for war on China, Prince Konoye had begun to appreciate the gulf between his concerns and those of the Emperor. It mattered little to Konoye whether Japan fought Russia or the colonial democracies. Konoye wished only to unify Japan—to make it the most perfectly governed anthill in the community of nations. After the Army Mutiny of February 1936 he had lobbied tirelessly in the palace to prevent the number-two Strike-North leader, General Mazaki, from being harshly punished. In his fascination with the problem of creating a super-state, he dismissed Hirohito's territorial aspirations as narrow and irrelevant.

For these reasons Prince Konoye at first refused when emissaries from Court asked him to assume the prime ministership in 1937. Over a period of weeks, however, in the declining days of the Hayashi Cabinet, he made a deal with Hirohito: a free hand to reorganize the state domestically in exchange for giving his name to military consolidation of the Japanese position in China. Saionji encouraged Konoye to assume the responsibility, for Konoye was, after all, a Fujiwara and the old prime-minister-maker knew no other leader influential enough to obviate national disaster.

Prince Konoye submitted a list of Cabinet ministers to Hirohito and accepted Hirohito's command to form a Cabinet on June 4, 1937. For the first time in twenty years Saionji had not been consulted officially—only unofficially. The well-primed gentlemen of the press greeted Konoye with editorial enthusiasm, comparing him with Prime Minister Okuma, "the professor," who had taken office in 1914 and had kept Japan from becoming deeply embroiled in World War I. Konoye at once went on the radio to announce an administration of national unification and conciliation in which the military, the cartels, the bureaucrats, and the political parties would all have a place. He looked forward, he said, to the time when Imperial Japan would be governed by a monolithic single party of patriots. He established a council of advisors which included representatives of all dissident factions and at the same time a fuel board to ration and control Japan's most scarce military commodity: oil and gasoline.

MARCO POLO'S BRIDGE

On June 9, 1937, five days after the investiture of the Konoye Cabinet, the porcine uncle of the Empress, Prince Nashimoto, who would later be held as imperial-family hostage by MacArthur, attended a banquet in his honor given by the brass of the Kwantung Army in the Manchukuoan capital of Long Spring Thaw. Nashimoto had left Japan in late May when Prime Minister Hayashi had announced his intention of resigning and had since conducted a leisurely inspection tour of Japanese garrisons in Korea and Manchuria. This particular Wednesday night he sat beside the new chief of staff of the Kwantung Army, Lieutenant General Tojo, Hirohito's future World War II shogun, and savored a succession of Chinese delicacies, including bird's nest soup, Shansi dumplings, Peking duck, and Peking dancing girls.

In the midst of the banquet Tojo withdrew briefly to his office to draft a telegram. He returned to table with it, showed it to Prince Nashimoto, and consigned it to an aide for coding and dispatch. It was addressed to the vice chief of the general staff and the vice minister of war in Tokyo, both loyal opportunists.[7] It told them in indirect Japanese fashion that the imperial family had reached an understanding with the Strike-North officers in the Kwantung Army. It promised that the Army would be given a chance to fight Russia after the ports and railheads of eastern China were in Japanese hands. Specifically the Tojo-Nashimoto cable stated:

---

[7] Lieutenant Generals Imai Kiyoshi and Umezu Yoshijiro.

FROM THE STANDPOINT OF OUR STRATEGIC PREPARATIONS AGAINST RUSSIA, WHEN VIEWED AGAINST THE PRESENT STATE OF AFFAIRS IN CHINA, WE DEEM IT MOST IMPORTANT AND DESIRABLE, IN ORDER TO ELIMINATE THE THREAT IN OUR REAR, TO STRIKE A DIRECT BLOW AGAINST AND INTO THE NANKING REGIME—PROVIDED, OF COURSE, THAT IN OUR OPINION AT THE TIME WE HAVE SUFFICIENT ARMED STRENGTH FOR IT.

The next morning, when the saké cups had been cleared away, pro-consul Tojo accompanied Prince Nashimoto in his plane back home to the nearest of the main Japanese islands, Kyushu. There, having worked out all the details of their agreement, the general and the prince parted, the one to fly back to his command in Manchuria, the other to fly on to report at the square mile of moat-girt palace in the center of downtown Tokyo.

Having secured the support of Tojo and the Kwantung Army, Hirohito pressed ahead with the final phase of war preparations. His uncle Prince Higashikuni flew to Taiwan to review the air units and some of the in-fantry units which had been trained for the invasion of central China. Prince Asaka, the other uncle, inspected the 11th Division which was to be used for the attack on Shanghai. Prince Mikasa, Hirohito's youngest brother, flew home from London with a pessimistic progress report on Prince Chichibu's conversations with the new king of England, George VI. From the palace the twenty-one-year-old Mikasa proceeded to Yokosuka, the great naval base on Tokyo Bay, and told the officers there that the Emperor expected every man to do his duty.

On the last day of June 1937, the Army sought to attach a condition to its willingness to fight: namely, imperial approval for preparation of a foray across the Korean border into Russia in late 1938, fifteen months hence. Hirohito was ready to call a full-scale conference in the Imperial Presence with Army leaders in order to thrash out the question. Instead his courtiers arranged a meeting for him and for Chief of Staff Prince Kanin with War Minister Sugiyama. At the meeting Hirohito agreed to sanction staff studies of the possibilities in an aggressive probe of Russia but re-fused absolutely to make any promises. Two weeks later, at a social break-fast on July 13, Big Brother Marquis Kido dropped word of the Em-peror's stand to Saionji Kinkazu, the imperial link with the Sorge Spy Ring.

War Minister Sugiyama was able to use the Emperor's small concession to quiet rebellious underlings, and on July 6 Hirohito received his final go-ahead from Prince Chichibu in London. Through a member of his suite, Chichibu reported the futility of his conversations with King George in a previously agreed-upon voice code: "Prince Higashikuni's problem with the lady in France has not yet been solved." Since Prince Higashikuni had left France more than ten years ago, it was a message that amused Japanese courtiers and successfully titillated and bemused its monitors in British Intelligence.

The next night, July 7, the war with China began on schedule at the Marco Polo Bridge. As described in Chapter 1, a Japanese soldier left his patrol briefly in order to urinate and his commander shelled a nearby Chinese garrison which was supposed to have abducted him. Local Chinese and Japanese diplomats quickly negotiated half a dozen settlements of the affair, but neither Hirohito nor Chiang would give the negotiators more than polite encouragement. Chiang secretly moved troops north and Hirohito had transports loaded with reinforcements in Japan. Chinese and Japanese soldiers picked quarrels in several fresh localities. Native constabulary in the autonomous regions founded by Japan two years earlier grew rebellious and in one town massacred 230 of their Japanese masters. Kwantung Army Chief of Staff Tojo, in the one combat experience of his career, led an expedition into Inner Mongolia and, after an efficient blitz-krieg, subjugated the areas which had eluded Japan's grasp the year before. The Japanese Tientsin garrison occupied Peking. With many protestations of peaceful intent, Prime Minister Prince Konoye dispatched three of the divisions of reinforcements lying at anchor in Japanese ports, and by the end of July they had landed and seized the key railheads throughout northeastern China.

PREVENTING PEACE

The Japanese Special Service Organ in Shanghai, the gateway to central China, at once staged a second incident. On August 9 a Japanese naval officer and a seaman tried to force their way into the Chinese military airport in Shanghai. They shot a Chinese guard who challenged them and were both shot in their turn. Within a week Hirohito had commanded the little tubercular general, Matsui, to lead an expeditionary force to central China and Prince Higashikuni to take charge of the Army Air Force in Taiwan and initiate a program of civilian bombing in Shanghai.

Two and a half months of street fighting followed, against Chiang Kai-shek's best divisions, and then the Japanese began their drive on Nanking. In December, Prince Asaka, the Emperor's limping uncle, relieved Matsui of command at the front and put Nanking to its month and a half of unspeakable torture.

During the genocidal debauch, that tall, tolerant, loose-jointed experimentalist, Prime Minister Prince Konoye, wrung his hands cynically. He told intimates that he did not approve of Hirohito's reliance on military force. He had tried first, he said, to restrict the war to north China, then to Shanghai in central China. Now the sinking of the U.S.S. *Panay* by one of his minions successfully deterred Hirohito from spreading the war at once down the coast to the environs of British Hong Kong in south China.

Konoye had expressed his unhappiness as early as October by threatening to resign the prime ministership. To stiffen his spine, Hirohito had put favorite Big Brother Marquis Kido into the Cabinet as minister of education in charge of propaganda. In November, when Hirohito took personal charge of the war by opening Imperial Headquarters, superior to the General Staff, on the very grounds of the palace, Prince Konoye had once more tried to resign—this time so sincerely that Education Minister Kido had warned him that his career would be over permanently if he bowed out now in a time of emergency.

Japan's allies, the Germans, did their utmost to mediate the war and find terms on which it could be settled. Ribbentrop pointed out from Berlin that miring down in the paddies of China would emasculate Japan as a German ally against Russia, and that the Third Reich was not in any way committed by the Anti-Comintern Pact to help Japan fight Bolshevism south of the Russian border. The German ambassador attached to Chiang Kai-shek's refugee regime in Hankow communicated daily with the German ambassador in Tokyo on new formulas for making peace. Backed by Hirohito, however, the soft-spoken gentlemen of the Japanese Foreign Ministry repeatedly increased the severity of their demands on China. The much maligned "militarists" on the Tokyo General Staff begged the civilian Cabinet to offer realistic terms which Chiang might possibly accept, but Hirohito, behind the scenes, remained obdurately hard of heart. No settlement would do short of complete Japanese mastery and the reduction of China to the status of a puppet dependency.

In late December when the rape of Nanking first began to look as if it would fail to unseat Chiang Kai-shek, Hirohito took up a suggestion, made earlier by Konoye, for threatening Chiang politically. Unless he would accept Japanese terms, Japan would no longer recognize him as China's chief of state and would find a rival to deal with in the KMT—one amenable to leading a puppet government in China. The majority of officers in the Army General Staff opposed this new ultimatum as unrealistic and fought it as they had earlier fought the preparations for the rape of Nanking. Chief of Staff Prince Kanin, the seventy-two-year-old elder of the imperial family, interviewed each of his subordinates individually and suppressed their opposition. On January 16, 1938, after a fortnight of hesitation, in a speech which he regretted for the rest of his life, Prince Konoye announced and explained his non-recognition policy to the people.

The sated Japanese troops in Nanking at once gave up their weary efforts to raise new hackles of terror among the numbed and starving survivors of the great rape. Chiang Kai-shek, in his temporary capital up-river in Hankow, broadcast an appeal to all Chinese to fight to the death. He ignored the Japanese ultimatum and continued to rule free China. Hirohito was forced to acknowledge that the mass murders and rapes of Nanking had all gone for nought. He excused himself by blaming War Minister Sugiyama Hajime, the Strike-South stalwart who always looked "as blank as a bathroom door." Sugiyama, explained the playful Hirohito, had assured him six months earlier that the Japanese Army could "crush China in a month."

Although Hirohito is nowhere on record as saying so explicitly, his actions make it plain that he did not want to end the war with China. As long as the war lasted he had an excuse not to honor his vague secret pledge to the Army to turn north against Russia. Moreover, the Chinese hinterland provided an excellent training ground for recruits. There eager young samurai could learn to handle modern weapons with minimal casualties and at minimal cost. There the troops could live off the land and maintain themselves as combat-ready veterans for the more demanding campaigns against Western armies in the years ahead.

In effect the war with China kept the troublesome Army distracted but ready. The elite service, the Navy, had for fifteen years received the bulk of appropriations earmarked for weapons' development. The Navy alone had the technological knowhow to challenge the West. In the first eight months of the China War it was the Navy's air force which provided the Army with dive bombing at the front and with long-range strategic bombing of China's inland cities. The Army's own air force was fit only for transport duty and for short-haul dumpings of dynamite. Yet the patrician technocrats of the Navy insisted that they needed another four or five years to perfect their sophisticated seagoing systems before launching a full-scale Strike South. Until then Japan must only nibble at Southeast Asia and keep the Army from wasting itself in futile expeditions against Siberia.

THE NANKING HANGOVER

When reports of the feckless incontinence of Nanking trickled home along the grapevine from soldiers in the field, Japanese began referring sarcastically to Hirohito's "holy war"—so proclaimed by propagandists— as the "unholy war." Education Minister Big Brother Kido made a mighty effort, through carefully worded editorials planted in the leading newspapers, to reassure the people that Nanking was an unfortunate accident. War Minister Sugiyama imposed heavy penalties on returning veterans who violated security by talking too freely about their combat experiences. Hirohito and Prince Kanin placated the General Staff by showing renewed interest in contingency planning against Russia. General Araki, the popular Strike-North leader, was brought back from oblivion as education minister in charge of propaganda.[8] Big Brother Marquis Kido moved on to found a new ministry, Welfare. His mission was to correct the deplorable state

[8] Only a year earlier Araki had been calling Japan "a disagreeable society in which I cannot bear to live." He had vowed that if Mazaki, his lieutenant, was ever let out of prison, he and Mazaki would become mendicant Buddhist priests, traveling in rags and praying for the nation. Now Mazaki was indeed released from prison, and Araki, in return, had rejoined the Establishment.

of national health and physical fitness revealed in the draft call-ups of the previous autumn.

What to do with the conquests in China, that was the question pending. And Hirohito promised that he would give serious attention to the Soviet Union only when the gains in China had been consolidated. The Tientsin-Peking area in north China and the Shanghai-Nanking area in central China must be tied together by Japanese control of the north-south railroads connecting Tientsin with Shanghai and Peking with Chiang Kai-shek's new temporary capital of Hankow, up the Yangtze River from Nanking.

Athwart the north-south railroads, between the northern and southern areas of Japanese occupation, Chiang Kai-shek still had one of his best generals and armies. In February 1938, Hirohito directed his crack mobile division, the 5th, led by Lieutenant General Itagaki, the politician of the Itagaki-Ishiwara partnership which had conquered Manchuria in 1931, to drive down the Tientsin-Shanghai rail link. Itagaki's men teamed up with the 10th Division and drove two thirds of the way required of them. Then at Tai-er-chuang, or Dynastic-Child-Manor, in the first week of April 1938, the 10th Division marched into a Chinese ambush and was temporarily surrounded. Itagaki's mobile 5th came to the rescue with tanks and big railroad guns and succeeded barely in extricating their beleaguered comrades. Six thousand Japanese dead, however, littered the battlefield, and some thirty thousand Japanese casualties hobbled or were carried from it. Chinese journalists, long despondent, made much of the victory.

In mid-April Prince Higashikuni, the Emperor's uncle, and Viscount Machijiri, the Emperor's in-law and aide-de-camp who had accompanied Higashikuni to Paris in 1920, took personal charge as commander-in-chief and chief of staff of the Japanese 2d Army in north China which was detailed to avenge the defeat at Dynastic-Child-Manor. All of the ten Japanese divisions in north China converged on the Dynastic-Child-Manor area in May, hoping to surround and capture the shrewd Chinese general who had humiliated the forces of the Emperor.

In the last two weeks of May, however, the Chinese general—Li Tsung-jen, a southerner who had backed Chang Hsueh-liang in his kidnapping of Chiang Kai-shek eighteen months earlier—skillfully retreated to the west, getting out not only his men but even his heavy artillery pieces from the closing Japanese pincer. When he had made good his escape his rear guard dynamited the levees which controlled the wayward second river of China, the Hwang Ho or Yellow. An entire flat province of dry river beds, where the Yellow River had formerly wandered in centuries gone by, was suddenly inundated in muddy water. Approximately 45,000 square miles of fertile farmland—an area as large and populous as New York State—was flooded. Tens of thousands of Chinese peasants perished. Japanese trucks, tanks, and field guns bogged down in mud. Chiang Kai-shek made relatives of the flood victims feel like patriots by announcing that China would go all out in her resistance to the Japanese and from now on would fight superior fire power with a "scorched earth" policy—a massive westward migration of peasants, moving like locusts and leaving nothing to eat behind them.

Despite flooded fields, Prince Higashikuni's men pressed on down the raised embankment of the railroad and joined up with comrades moving north from Shanghai. One of the two north-south railroads was secure. Prince Higashikuni asked leave to open the second one as well. The majority in the General Staff in Tokyo objected that the primary objectives of the war with China had been won. The principal cities and rail lines were in Japanese hands and it was time to stand pat and face back toward Russia. Hirohito's admirals, however, wanted to move on up the Yangtze River, 150 miles beyond Nanking, to the Anking airport which was within flying range of Hong Kong and the coveted harbors of the south China coast. Hirohito agreed with the Navy and ordered the Army to proceed up the Yangtze first to Anking and then another 200 miles to Hankow which was the seat of Chiang's refugee government and also the terminus of the second of the north-south railroads.

The advance on Hankow began in May 1938 and ended in October. Prince Higashikuni personally took command of four divisions which fought their way overland to the north and west of the Yangtze in order to approach Hankow from the rear. Four more divisions, under Lieutenant General Okamura Yasuji—the only one of the Three Crows of Baden-Baden who remained alive and in Hirohito's good graces—moved up the banks of the Yangtze to attack Hankow frontally. Okamura took the strategic air base of Anking on June 12, 1938, and pressed on upriver toward Hankow. Chiang Kai-shek began to move the lower echelons of his bureaucracy still farther upriver to Chungking, above the easily defended gorges of the Yangtze, more than 900 miles by air from the coast and the Japanese ports of supply.

Above Anking Third Crow Okamura's men encountered the boom and the forts of Matang, which had been designed for Chiang Kai-shek by his German advisors three years earlier. They were formidable obstacles. Okamura surmounted them by first calling Tokyo and paying a bribe of over $100,000 (U.S.) to the local Chinese commander. Chiang Kai-shek heard of the transaction and shortly afterwards had the commander summarily executed.

It cost Chiang far more than $100,000 to repair the damage done by the Japanese bribe. He desperately needed time to remove valuable men and materials from the rich valley of the middle Yangtze. In an all-out effort he succeeded in raising and equipping provincial levies to fight a holding action around the sacred mountain of Lushan, 80 miles above Anking. All summer Okamura's men pounded a rubbery wall of resistance which sagged by day and sprang back by night. Few of the Chinese peasants in the area survived the months of village-burning battles except the children who, on parents' orders, marched west alone in sad Pied-

Piper columns. Finally in September Okamura's men broke through the Lushan impasse and moved ahead quickly up the next 120 miles of Yangtze river bank to capture Hankow in October.

A SOVIET DEFECTOR

On June 11, 1938, when Okamura was still blasting his way into Anking, a Soviet general, G. S. Lyushkov, crossed the Russo-Manchurian border and gave himself up to the Kwantung Army. He described to Kwantung Army staff officers the disposition, organization, and armament of the twenty-five Soviet divisions in Siberia. He also stated that the Red soldiers in the Far East were demoralized by shoddy equipment and a growing difference of opinion with the Kremlin. The Russian commander in Siberia was General Vasili Blücher, a former advisor to Sun Yat-sen. He wanted Russia to give military assistance to China, particularly to the Chinese Communists, in an effort to stop "fascist" Japan. Stalin on the other hand felt that Russia could not afford to become entangled in the Sino-Japanese war while Hitler's power was growing menacingly in the West. Stalin's secret police chief, Lavrenti Beria, had infiltrated the Siberian command with agents and turned it against itself.

The staff officers of the Kwantung Army transmitted defector Lyushkov's intelligence to Tokyo. They reminded Chief of Staff Prince Kanin that the Army had been promised action against the Soviet Union as recompense for its unpleasant service in central China. They pointed out that if Lyushkov's intelligence was correct, now would be the ideal time for a full-scale Strike North, or at least for a limited probe of Red Army strengths and weaknesses.[9]

Chief of Staff Prince Kanin acknowledged the Kwantung Army's request but asked that defector Lyushkov be sent on to Tokyo for further questioning. It was possible that Lyushkov might be an agent for General Blücher, the Siberian commander, and might be enticing Japan to strike north in order to force Stalin into the Far Eastern conflict against his will. In Tokyo the interrogators of the Special Higher Police, who ordinarily dealt with "dangerous thoughts" only in the upper levels of domestic Japanese society, reported that they had insufficient knowledge of European affairs to make sure of Lyushkov's veracity. They asked that an expert be sent to help them from Himmler's Gestapo apparatus in Berlin. While the

---

[9] In making their plea, the tacticians of the Kwantung Army counted heavily, but unrealistically, on the fact that two of their former representatives were now highly placed in Hirohito's councils. Lieutenant General Itagaki, the politician of the team which had led the Kwantung Army in its 1931 conquest of Manchuria, had been recalled from command of Japan's panzer division in north China to take the post of war minister in the Konoye Cabinet. At the same time, at the end of April 1938, Kwantung Army chief of staff, Lieutenant General Tojo, had gone home to serve under Itagaki as vice war minister.

German intelligence agent was on his way, Hirohito and Prince Kanin ordered the Kwantung Army to wait in patience.

AN UNAUTHORIZED INCIDENT

The Kwantung Army obeyed Hirohito's wishes but the territorial army in Korea did not. Vice Chief of the Army General Staff Tada, who had opposed both the rape of Nanking and Konoye's non-recognition of Chiang Kai-shek, plotted with the commander of the 19th Division in Korea to start an incident on the Russian border. On July 3, 1938, three weeks after Lyushkov's defection, Soviet troops stationed at Lake Khasan, near the point where the borders of Siberia, Manchuria, and Korea all meet, observed two companies of Japanese troops taking up positions on the far side of the hill overlooking the lake. Three days later the Red soldiers noted with alarm that the Japanese were evacuating the civilian Manchu population from the area across the border.

The strip of land between the shores of Lake Khasan and the watershed to the west of it had previously been handled as Soviet territory in name and as an unfortified buffer zone in practice. The spot was beautiful and wild, but also important strategically, for it lay only 70-odd miles southwest of the Russian naval base of Vladivostok and only 15-odd miles northeast of the Japanese naval base of Rashin in Korea. On July 11, just a month after Lyushkov's defection, the Soviet forces at Lake Khasan moved into no man's land and began digging trenches on it.

On Wednesday, July 13, Korean Army H.Q. belatedly informed Tokyo officially of the Russian trench digging and asked permission to take countermeasures. The next day Vice Chief of Staff Tada warned the commander of the 19th Division at the front that he must improve liaison with Korean Army H.Q. in order to prevent it from sending any more cables which would excite the suspicions of the home authorities. At the moment, Tada pointed out, the Japanese government could only promise that the Foreign Ministry would protest strongly in Moscow.

On Friday, July 15, Vice War Minister Tojo scented Tada's plot and personally cabled the commander of the 19th Division:

RE RUSSIAN BORDER CROSSING OUR POLICY TO SETTLE BY DIPLOMATIC MEANS. IF RUSSIANS DO NOT ACCEPT OUR TERMS AND WITHDRAW, THEN AND THEN ONLY SHOULD WE CONSIDER PRUDENTLY THE POSSIBILITY OF PUSHING THEM BACK BY FORCE.

Tojo's word carried great weight. The day of his telegram, five Japanese secret policemen had crossed to the Soviet side of the border to take photographs of the fresh Russian foxholes on the hillside above the lake. The Russian border guards had shot and killed one of the photographers and captured his film. Yet for the next two weeks, the Japanese 19th Division fired not so much as a shot at the Russians. Instead it brought up all its strength, as quietly as possible, and entrenched itself on the Japanese side of the watershed.

HIROHITO'S ANGER

For five days, from the Friday of Tojo's cable until the Wednesday of July 20, Prime Minister Konoye and the members of his Cabinet could not find out what was happening. The officers on the Tokyo General Staff were not communicating with their opposite numbers in the War Ministry. Chief of the General Staff Prince Kanin was out of town at his summer villa and War Minister Itagaki deliberately sequestered himself. Vice War Minister Tojo used all his influence to get information and to summon Prince Kanin and War Minister Itagaki back to Tokyo.

Since the Lake Khasan incident had not been planned, Hirohito, at his summer villa, remained for several days entirely in the dark about it. Then on July 20, Prince Kanin and War Minister Itagaki returned to Tokyo. Tojo saw Itagaki. Kanin saw Itagaki. Kanin phoned the Emperor. Through his courtiers Hirohito immediately took steps to suppress the incident without unduly shaming the rebellious officers in the 19th Division and the General Staff.

The next day, July 21, Prince Kanin arranged that War Minister Itagaki be granted an audience by Hirohito at the seaside Summer Palace of Hayama at 11 A.M. sharp. Kanin met with Itagaki beforehand at his own villa down the coast to discuss all the background facets of the case. At about 10 A.M. a chamberlain called at Prince Kanin's villa to say that the Emperor hoped the audience would take place on time because he was eager to be out on the water for an afternoon excursion aboard his battered marine biological yacht. In the next hour War Minister Itagaki nervously suggested again and again to Prince Kanin that perhaps they should be starting for the palace. Prince Kanin kept asking Itagaki detailed questions about the men involved in the Lake Khasan incident with Russia. Finally at about 11 A.M., the scheduled time of the audience with Hirohito, Prince Kanin and Itagaki set out to drive to the palace. Itagaki was dismayed that it took a full hour. When he arrived in the Imperial Presence, an hour late, he was all nervousness.

"The foreign and Navy ministers," blurted Itagaki, "have both agreed to our use of force in the recent border incident with Russia."

"You!" exclaimed Hirohito. "You helped to bungle the Mukden incident in 1931 and the Marco Polo Bridge incident last year in China. You are undoubtedly one of the most stupid men in the entire world. From now on, unless it has orders from me, the Army is not to move so much as a single soldier."

Itagaki retired, covered with confusion. The next day he submitted his resignation and Hirohito refused it, apologizing for his impatience at being kept waiting and exhorting Itagaki to solve the unauthorized incident as quickly as possible.

Two days later, on July 23, Hirohito's favorite Big Brother, Marquis Kido, who was now minister of welfare in the Konoye Cabinet, met with young Saionji Kinkazu, for the first time in three months, to relate to him the Emperor's words with Itagaki. A day or two later, young Saionji's protégé, Ozaki, reported to Soviet spy Sorge that "Japan" had no intention of allowing the Lake Khasan incident to develop into a war. Even as an agent of the Soviet Union, Ozaki could not bring himself to say, "The Emperor has no intention . . ." Instead when Sorge pressed him to give solidity to his vague word, "Japan," Ozaki offered only theoretical arguments. He pointed out that the Japanese Army was fully engaged in its drive on Hankow and that the Kwantung Army had already detached several divisions to the south and was in no state to mount an attack on Russia.

THE MASTER SPY, DRUNK

Three months earlier, at the time of Marquis Kido's last meeting with young Saionji, the Japanese Foreign Ministry had just learned that Major General Eugen Ott, the German military attaché in Tokyo—the one who had negotiated the prior understandings for the Anti-Comintern Pact with Prince Higashikuni in 1933 and had made friends with Soviet spy Sorge in 1934—would be Germany's next ambassador to Japan. Ott did indeed become ambassador on April 28, 1938. He promptly elevated Sorge to an unofficial position as a consultant, with an office of his own, inside the German Embassy.

Sorge immediately ran a mission for Ott, and incidentally for himself. He delivered a packet of intelligence for Ott to a German agent in Manila and then another of his own to a Soviet agent in Hong Kong. On the evening of his return to Japan, in early May, he celebrated his infiltration of the German Embassy with a spree at his favorite Tokyo bar, *Das Rheingold*. When the bar closed at 2:00 A.M., he went on to drink an entire bottle of Scotch in a friend's room at the Imperial Hotel. Some time later, annoyed that his drinking companion would not ride on with him to further adventures on the back of his motorcycle, Sorge set off for home alone. He roared east down Hibiya Park and then north up Sotobori-dori, or Outside the Moat Boulevard.

At the next intersection, with a growing sense of exhilaration and acceleration, he cornered left into the curving dirt road behind the Manchuria Railway Building and up the hill toward the American Embassy. Dirt, curve, and hillside were too much for his numbed navigational faculties, and his motorcycle skidded into the solid, whitewashed embassy wall. He knocked out his front teeth, broke his jaw, and scarred his cheeks for life. Through the good offices of the Japanese police, he saw Max

Klausen, his radio operator, before being wheeled into surgery. Klausen barely managed to burglarize Sorge's home and remove from it all incriminating papers before its contents were catalogued and put under seal by an efficient representative of the German News Service.

General Lyushkov defected while Sorge was still recovering in Tokyo's most up-to-date hospital, St. Luke's (an instituton of the U.S. Protestant Episcopal Church). German Ambassador Ott and his wife took care of Sorge in his convalescence and briefed him fully on the Lyushkov case as it developed. Throughout late June and early July Sorge was able to keep the Red Army's Fourth, or Intelligence, Bureau well informed on the case in so far as it was being revealed to the Germans. In the last week of July, Sorge relayed his intelligence from Ozaki, from Saionji, from Kido, and indirectly, at fourth hand, from Emperor Hirohito, that "Japan" would suppress the Lake Khasan incident short of war.

THE LAKE KHASAN MUTINY

Never would Sorge's credibility at the Kremlin be taxed more sorely. In flagrant disregard for Hirohito's wishes the Japanese troops at Lake Khasan caused the incident to escalate. On July 29, in the only known Army defiance of imperial orders on record, the 19th Division launched a full-scale attack on the Russian positions at Lake Khasan. All through the night Japanese artillery pounded away at the heights above the lake and the Russian border guards huddled in their holes. During the days which followed, the Japanese at first advanced a few hundred meters down the hillside and then were pushed back again by Soviet tanks and heavy aerial bombardment. Japanese flyers in Korea obeyed imperial orders and provided no air cover. They remained grounded even after August 8, when the Soviet Air Fleet began to bomb Korean bases behind the front lines.

The Foreign Ministry sought to save the Army's face by demanding concessions in its negotiations in Moscow. While the negotiations continued, the misguided men of the 19th Division suffered a terrible beating. Through the machinations of Vice War Minister Tojo, two of the division's four regimental commanders were replaced on August 1 by a pair of colonels who could be counted on to obey a cease-fire. One of them was Colonel Tanaka Takayoshi, girl-spy Eastern Jewel's huge lover, who would later become U.S. Prosecutor Keenan's star witness at the Tokyo war crimes trials. The other of them was Colonel Cho Isamu, Prince Asaka's former staff officer, who had promulgated the order to kill all prisoners just before the rape of Nanking, and who, in years to come, would be the last holdout in the caves of Okinawa. These two mad dogs of the Emperor won the confidence of their men by urging them to make suicide rushes against the Russian tanks. At one desperate juncture in the fighting they both took

down their pants and stood exposed on a sandbag parapet to show the
flagging captains and lieutenants of their command how loosely and courageously a Japanese officer should hang in the face of fire.

The battle raged on the scale of full war from July 29 to August 10.
Japan's 19th Division suffered almost 10,000 casualties and the Russians
fared not much better. But the Russians, aided by their tanks and planes,
were advancing when the Foreign Ministery, on August 11, made a truce
and agreed to return to the status quo ante.

The Japanese back-down vindicated Sorge's judgment and encouraged
Stalin to adopt Sorge's view that war with Japan not only must be but
could be avoided. In September 1938, a month after the cease-fire, Beria's
secret police spirited away the Siberian commander, General Blücher, who
had been a patron of defector Lyushkov and had wished to fight Japan. A
month later, in October, Sorge borrowed from a German Embassy attaché
the final report of the Himmler agent sent from Berlin to assist in the interrogation of Lyushkov. Early the next morning in his embassy office, from
six o'clock to ten, when he was usually preparing a digest and interpretation
of the day's Japanese news for Ambassador Ott, Sorge read the 100-odd
pages of the report and, with his Leica, photographed most of them for
transmission to Moscow. Siberian commander Blücher is reported to have
died in Beria's dungeons a few months later.

THE VICTORIOUS STALEMATE

The Japanese Army was chagrined by its defeat at Lake Khasan and
Hirohito made immediate concessions to save its face. In August, when
the ink on the cease-fire was scarcely dry, he approved a General Staff
proposal to plan a better staged, fully sanctioned workout against the Red
Army, to take place the following year in the remote fastnesses of Mongolia. One aviation colonel was immediately given maps of the exact area
in which the war would occur and instructed to devise air-to-ground communications suitable to the terrain and type of operations which might be
expected there.

Seven weeks after the Lake Khasan cease-fire, on September 30, 1938,
British Prime Minister Neville Chamberlain, wielding his much caricatured
umbrella at the famous "peace-in-our-time" conference in Munich, conceded to Hitler the right to take back for Germany the German-speaking
region of Czechoslovakia known as the Sudetenland. As Hitler's storm
troopers poured into Czechoslovakia to realize Chamberlain's concession,
Hirohito reimplemented the operational plan for the seizure of the south
China coast which had been canceled after the sinking of the U.S.S. *Panay*
a year earlier. On October 21, 1938, from a landing at the old pirate cove
of Byas Bay, Japanese troops pushed into Canton, the principal city of
south China.

Four days later, on October 25, 1938, the Japanese forces of the third of the Three Crows of Baden-Baden, Lieutenant General Okamura Yasuji, ended their six-month drive up the Yangtze River, past the sacred mountain of Lushan, and occupied Hankow, the principal city of central China. With Peking and Tientsin in the north, and Shanghai on the coast in the east, Canton and Hankow completed the roster of China's five most populous cities. All of them now lay in Japanese hands. Hirohito had no other ambitions in China except to keep open the railways between the five principal cities and make full use of the docks and harbors attached to them.

The Privy Council, Cabinet, and General Staff all agreed with Hirohito that from now on the war with China would be a holding operation. No offensives would be mounted except to gain limited tactical objectives or to serve as training maneuvers for green troops. Six new divisions, manned by 120,000 fresh recruits, had been created in April 1938 when this planned stalemate in China first received Hirohito's approval. Now the six new divisions were deployed for garrison duty in China. As the men in them gained experience, they would be transferred to other, more active commands in the years ahead. Until 1945, however, the China front would remain, in Japanese strategic thinking, only a schoolyard.

On December 16, 1938, Prime Minister Konoye founded an Asian Development Board to co-ordinate the economic exploitation of China. Having masterminded the looting of Nanking, the ubiquitous Suzuki Tei-ichi—now at last a major general—took charge of the Political Affairs Branch of the board.[10] He made it his economic mission to develop a native Chinese puppet government with enough influence to replace Chiang Kai-shek in the Japanese-occupied areas of China.

Two days later, on December 18, 1938, months of underground negotiation came to fruition when Wang Ching-wei, the vice chairman of the KMT party and a trusted lieutenant of Chiang Kai-shek, surreptitiously boarded a plane at the Chungking airport and flew to Hanoi in the north of French Indochina. From Hanoi he exchanged telegrams with Chiang, begging him to join Japan in the cause of Asia. At the same time he exchanged countless cables with Tokyo, asking assurance that he be given authority to govern in eastern China if he agreed to establish a regime there which would settle Sino-Japanese differences.

Wang's telegraphic communications were cut short a few weeks later when an assassin, variously reported to have been a Chinese secret agent and a hireling of the Japanese spy service, shot dead the man sleeping in Wang Ching-wei's bed. Frightened by the death of his bodyguard, Wang took to sea in a small coastal steamer made available to him by Japanese Army Intelligence. He was overhauled by a storm at sea, and having lost his

[10] The presidency of the board was given to Yanagawa Heisuke, the retired Strike-North general who had rehabilitated himself by leading the flanking movement and breakthrough of the advance on Nanking.

way, was rescued from the gale by a large, conspicuously Japanese cruiser. Taken to Japanese-occupied Shanghai, he was housed and hidden first in one then another of three lavishly appointed, elaborately guarded villas. For fifteen months he continued to exchange communications with Chiang Kai-shek and then, in March 1940, he would agree to become the Japanese puppet in China.

On December 22, 1938,[11] Prime Minister Konoye, counting heavily on the arrival of Wang Ching-wei in Hanoi two days earlier, announced publicly that Japan sponsored a New Order in East Asia which would enable Asian peoples, under Japanese leadership, to realize their native aspirations and throw off the shackles of Western colonialism.

At the same time Konoye announced a New Structure politically for Japan. The people, he said, must unite monolithically behind the Emperor and co-operate in unselfish effort to wage a "holy war" of liberation for all Asian peoples. Konoye had in mind a plan for a single mass party which would rule Japan as effectively as the Communist party ruled Russia or the Nazi party ruled Germany. His announcement was received so coolly that he did not, in fact, launch the new mass party until October 1940, almost two years later.

The draft of the New Structure plan had been written for Konoye by Ozaki Hotsumi, the member of the Konoye brain trust who served as liaison link between young Saionji Kinkazu and Soviet spy Sorge. Sorge himself asked Ozaki what he thought he was doing in suggesting the plan, and Ozaki replied that he was looking forward to the time when Japan would become a socialist nation. He did not add that he meant a nation of communal share-and-share-alike, under the Emperor. Sorge would not have understood such a Japanese concept.

At the same tidying-up time in December 1938, Hirohito reposted two of his sharpest military thinkers: Major General Ishiwara Kanji, the religious zealot who had planned the conquest of Manchuria for him seven years ago, and Lieutenant General Tojo Hideki who had prevented the February Mutiny of 1936 from spreading into the ranks of the Kwantung Army. In the fall of 1938, Tojo had advocated a two-front army capable of waging war to the north or south as occasion might demand. Ishiwara had begged for a no-front army, trained to consolidate previous Japanese gains and to make peace with the natives in the occupied areas. When the dispute between the two men had crept onto the pages of the newspapers, Hirohito made a Solomon's decision by pretending to fire both of them. He banished Ishiwara, the vice chief of staff of the Kwantung Army, to the command of a provincial arsenal. But he gave Tojo, the vice war minister, a challenging opportunity as head of the new office

---

[11] The occasion was a victory parade for Prince Higashikuni on his return from eight months of successful leadership of the 2d Army in the campaign to take Hankow.

of Inspector General of Army Aviation. Tojo solaced and aggrandized himself by filling posts on no less than nineteen of the new boards and committees which had been founded as a part of Prime Minister Konoye's New Structure.

Just to list Tojo's memberships reveals how far Konoye had brought Japan along the road to totalitarianism. Tojo belonged to: the Japan-Manchukuo Economic Committee; the Central Air Defense Commission; the Manchukuoan Affairs Board; the Cabinet Information and Cabinet Planning Boards; the Scientific Council; the Central Price Committee; the Ship Control, Electric Power, City Planning, Home Industry, and Motor Car Manufacturing Committees; the Valuation Commission for Iron Manufacturers; the Disabled Soldiers' Protection Trust; the Naval Council; the Air Enterprises Investigation Committee; the National General Mobilization Committee; the Education Control Council; and the Liquefied Fuel Committee.

FIRST SPAT WITH HITLER

As soon as the old year's loose ends had been tied up, Prince Konoye greeted the new, on January 4, 1939, by resigning the prime ministership. He felt tired and hypochondriacal after his eighteen months at the helm, and he wanted to devote his full energies to negotiating the compromises, the reconciliations, and the outright purchases of loyalty which would enable him to form the single mass party he planned for the future.

Hirohito appointed in his place Baron Hiranuma, the long-faced lawyer-president of the staidly rightist National Foundation Society—the man who would act as Hirohito's spokesman and tormentor at the surrender deliberations in the Imperial Bunker six and a half years later. Being well known for his extreme anti-Bolshevism, Hiranuma might be able to quiet the resurgent Strike-North Faction which was disgruntled by Hirohito's continued postponement of the promised military probe into Russia. Moreover, if the probe had to be staged and should turn out unsuccessfully, Hiranuma could be easily saddled with the responsibility for instigating it.

Domestically Hiranuma made no changes in the programs and slogans announced by his predecessor. The "defense state" mobilized for "total war" continued to grow apace as cartel after cartel fell into cogwheel place in it. The New Structure for the bureaucracy continued to materialize committee by committee and board by board. Konoye in retirement continued his masterful management of the political world.

Under Hiranuma's aegis, the Navy pressed forward with preparations for the eventual Strike South by seizing two strategic bases in the South China Sea. On February 10, 1939, Prince Takamatsu, the Emperor's second brother, personally looked on from the bridge of a battleship while the Imperial Marines poured ashore onto the mud flats of Hainan, an island larger than Maryland and Delaware combined, lying off the

southernmost point of the south China coast.[12] In the next three days Prince
Takamatsu flew reconnaissance in a naval plane overhead while the conquest of the big island was completed.

A month later, in March 1939, the Japanese Navy quietly occupied the
seven French-claimed but uninhabited Spratly Islands, strategically placed
at a point in the South China Sea almost exactly equidistant from the
Philippines, Indochina, and Borneo. Japan used the islands immediately
as a base for seaplanes running cartographic missions down the ill-charted
Borneo coast and carrying radios and technicians to spy rings in Mindanao
and Vietnam. The existence of the islands had come to Hirohito's attention
when one of his wife's in-laws had conducted an ornithological expedition
there a few years earlier to study the island birds.

While Hirohito nibbled at Southeast Asia, Hitler swallowed the remaining Moravian and Bohemian scraps of Czechoslovakia. Then, in late March
1939, he paused briefly to survey the German position. He planned soon
to turn west against France and England but first he had to secure his
rear against Russia. He meant to seize half of Poland as a buffer zone
against Russia and give the other half of Poland to Russia as a bribe.
In return for the bribe, he hoped to negotiate a nonaggression pact with
Stalin. Stalin, however, could not be trusted, and so, as further insurance
against being nipped in the rear by the Russian bear, Hitler wished to commit Japan definitely to fight on the side of the Third Reich. Through Rib-
bontrop he pressed Japan to sign a tripartite pact with the Reich and Italy
pledging all three nations to war if any of them should become involved in
hostilities with Russia or the democracies of Western Europe.

Because of his prejudice against a Strike North, Hirohito had long
refused Germany a promise of all-out military help even against Russia.
As for promising to fight France and England as well, that, for the moment,
was unthinkable. The Navy was not prepared to challenge Western naval
supremacy in the Pacific until at least 1941, and preferably 1942. The
naval development program which Hirohito had tenderly nurtured since
1922 still depended on Western imports of raw materials and machine tools.
If Japan could once gain, even briefly, the naval edge in the Pacific, she
might take the rubber of Malaya and the oil of Borneo and render herself
independent of Western imports. Then and then only would she be ready
to challenge the democracies to open warfare.

Hitler's demand for an immediate Berlin-Tokyo-Rome alliance of the
fascist states against the rest of the world did not fit into the timetable which
Japan, as an underdeveloped nation, had been patiently following for years.
On the other hand, Hirohito had long stationed trusted emissaries in Berlin
and was well informed on the might of the *Wehrmacht*. If, as seemed

---

[12] Hirohito, at a conference in the Imperial Presence three months earlier on
November 30, 1938, had had the seizure of Hainan brought up and appended to
his approval of the Army's plans for Wang Ching-wei's escape from Chungking.

possible, Hitler would soon conquer the Netherlands and France, then Hitler would be a friend or enemy who could either give or refuse Japan the Dutch East Indies and French Indochina.

In a quandary as to whether to jeopardize the carefully worked out National Program by siding now with Hitler or to alienate Japan's potentially best friend by refusing to side with him, Hirohito squirmed in anguish. In early April 1939 he confided to Marquis Kido that the decision facing him was the most fateful of his reign. If he decided wrongly, he foresaw that he might someday find himself "left alone and stripped of my closest retainers and elder statesmen." He complained that he could not sleep, weighing the alternatives.

The Army pressed Hirohito to sign the pact with Hitler, and the Foreign Ministry advised him to protract negotiations with Hitler as long as possible. Navy Minister Yonai, one of those who would later sit with Hirohito in the bunker on the night of the decision to surrender, tipped the scales by stating flatly that the Navy, in its present state of development, could not hope to win in the Pacific even against the British fleet alone.

On Monday, April 24, 1939, Ribbentrop darkly hinted to Japanese Ambassador Lieutenant General Oshima in Berlin that if Japan could not reach a clear-cut decision as to which side she was on, Germany would be forced to improve her relations with the Soviet Union. That same evening, having consulted with his closest advisors, Hirohito made a final firm decision as to how far Japan was prepared to commit herself. He agreed to a full military alliance with Hitler—but on two provisos: that the clauses of the alliance directed against the democracies should be kept secret and that Japan's entry into World War II should not necessarily follow at once upon Germany's but should be made, in all good faith, as soon afterward as Japan's strength warranted.

On Tuesday, April 25, the five ministers of the Japanese Inner Cabinet met and approved Hirohito's decision. It was agreed by all that if Hitler would not accept the Emperor's provisos, the negotiations with Germany might have to be broken off and Japan might have to wait, perhaps even for decades, before being strong enough to act on her own. Wistfully, a Cabinet secretary observed that Germany, by her "loud talk," had caused the democracies to start rearming and so had spoiled everything.

Ott, the German ambassador in Tokyo, was informed of the Emperor's decision by Prince Higashikuni's former assistant of Parisian days, Lieutenant General Machijiri, now director of the powerful Military Affairs Bureau in the War Ministry. Knowing that Machijiri had been close to the Emperor for years as a palace aide-de-camp, Ambassador Ott, on Wednesday, April 26, nine days before he would be officially informed of the Emperor's stand by the Foreign Ministry, cabled his understanding of it to Berlin. At the same time he discussed the situation with his journalist-advisor, Soviet spy Sorge.

Hitler was enraged by Ott's news and rejected Hirohito's provisos out of hand. He ordered Ribbentrop to proceed at once with the conclusion of a nonaggression pact with Russia. Much talk continued to be exchanged between Tokyo and Berlin for another four months but the Führer scorned all Japanese attempts to hedge, and Hirohito stood firm by his decision not to join Hitler yet.

Reports of Hitler's anger and of Ribbentrop's negotiations with Russia filtered through to Tokyo, and Hirohito resolved to test Germany's trustworthiness. The Anti-Comintern Pact obligated Hitler to render Hirohito all means of assistance short of troops in the event that Japan became involved in hostilities with the Soviet Union. If Germany so much as swapped a stein of beer for a glass of vodka while such hostilities were in progress, it would constitute a monumental breach of faith. All those who advocated a German-Japanese alliance for the sake of promoting a Strike North would be eternally shamed and silenced. Accordingly, on or about the Russian holiday of May 1, Hirohito instructed old Chief of Staff Prince Kanin to activate the plans for a limited border war with Russia in Outer Mongolia. Ambassador Oshima in Berlin was advised to represent the incident to Ribbentrop as a pro-German act which would tie up Soviet troops in central Asia while the *Wehrmacht* was making sure of its half of Poland.

NOMONHAN (1)

On May 11, 1939, two hundred Bargut horsemen under the banner of an Inner Mongolian chieftain controlled by the Japanese, crossed the frontier into the Soviet protectorate of Outer Mongolia, at a point 500 miles northwest of Mukden, near the junction of the border lines of Manchukuo, Inner Mongolia, and Outer Mongolia. The Barguts were accompanied by patrols and advisors from the Japanese 23d Division, a unit of the Kwantung Army. The invaders rode some 15 miles into Soviet territory until they came to the scattered yurts and sheep pens of the village of Nomonhan, belonging to the Outer Mongolian Tsirik tribe. The villagers at once warned their kinsmen who manned a constabulary outpost for the Soviet government on the west bank of the Khalka River, some 5 miles farther into the hinterland beyond Nomonhan. The next day the Tsirik troops from the log fort on the river sortied and drove the Barguts back to the border.

On May 14, the Inner Mongolian tribesmen reinvaded in force, backed by two companies of Japanese regulars. They swept the Tsiriks from the 20-mile strip between the border and the river and camped at nightfall just opposite the outpost of the Tsirik constabulary.

That night the Tsiriks alerted the local Russian advisor, Major Bykov. When Bykov drove up in his armored car to the fort the next morning he found it a shambles. It had just been bombed and strafed by five Japanese planes. Bykov at once phoned Ulan Bator, calling in the 6th Mongolian cavalry division and a detachment of Red Army regulars. By May 18, he had massed his forces on the west side of the river. The Barguts and Japanese on the east bank broke camp and vanished.

HITLER'S COLD SHOULDER

Hearing of the clash in central Asia, Hitler realized that Hirohito was brandishing the Anti-Comintern Pact at him and trying to shame him out of making a deal with Russia. Not one to be ashamed easily, Hitler saw a way of turning the Japanese move to his advantage. Stalin had responded warily to the German feelers for a nonaggression pact and was simultaneously talking with London about the possibility of an Anglo-Russian alliance. Only the threat of the Anti-Comintern Pact and of war on two fronts with Germany and Japan might persuade Stalin to refuse the British overtures.

Accordingly, Hitler had an icy message delivered to Japanese Ambassador Lieutenant General Oshima telling him that Japanese Army efforts to tie up Soviet forces in central Asia would be most welcome if indeed the Japanese Army was capable of tying up any Western troops anywhere. Hitler proceeded to salt this wound to samurai pride by turning toward Japan a calculated cold shoulder. On May 22, he ostentatiously signed a full military alliance with Mussolini and so cemented the much heralded Rome-Berlin Axis without benefit of Japanese inclusion. The next day he informed his fourteen most trusted generals and admirals that they must be ready for war with England before year's end and that they must not count too heavily on Russia remaining neutral because German relations with Japan had now become "cool and unreliable."

The subtle minds at Hirohito's Court were not taken in by these histrionics or disposed to ignore them either. If Japan helped to neutralize Russia by pursuing the probe into the Mongolian underbelly of Siberia, no harm would be done and Hitler would owe Japan a favor.

NOMONHAN (2)

On the night of May 22, when speeches about the new military alliance between Hitler and Mussolini were running on interminably at the Reich Chancellery in Berlin, Major Bykov, the local Russian commander in the Nomonhan area, moved a substantial force across the Khalka River to reconnoiter. It picked its way cautiously east through the night as far as the pastures of Nomonhan and there was suddenly set upon by Barguts and Japanese. After a desperate hand-to-hand tussle in the darkness, Bykov's force broke out of encirclement and escaped to the river bank.

On May 25 Bykov threw in all his forces in a counterattack and reoccupied Nomonhan. By May 27, having established over 10,000 Mongolian constabulary on the east bank, plus two Russian machine-gun companies and a battery of 45-millimeter cannon, he moved his command post into one of the Nomonhan yurts.

The area seemed clear of Japanese and Bykov thought that the border incident was over. It was not. Hirohito had sent some of his most trusted minions to the fastnesses of Outer Mongolia to enlarge the incident and manipulate it delicately as an instrument of high state policy. At 3 A.M. on May 28 a regiment and a battalion of Japanese regulars, some 5,000 men assisted by a horde of Bargut horsemen, attacked the Russian encampment. The cautious Major Bykov had fortified his flanks by the book and was able to fall back gradually toward the river. He took a Japanese prisoner in the course of his retreat and learned that his assailants were commanded by Colonel Yamagata Tsuyuki and Lieutenant Colonel Azuma Otohiko.

At his testimony before the International Military Tribunal for the Far East, seven years later, Bykov did not indicate that he saw any special significance in these names. The fact was, however, that Yamagata and Azuma had been the last two aides-de-camp of Prince Asaka, Hirohito's limping uncle who had raped Nanking. Moreover, they had in their charge, as a lieutenant of artillery, Higashikuni Morihiro, the son of Prince Higashikuni and the intended of one of Hirohito's daughters.

The participation of a member of the imperial family under the tutelage of Prince Asaka's aides-de-camp persuaded the Strike-North elements in the Kwantung Army that Hirohito was finally fulfilling his vague promise that Japan would attack Russia when the proper opportunity arrived. Well-prepared staff plans emanating from Tokyo reassured even skeptics that the moment had come. The commander of the 23d Division and then the commander of the 6th Army, both veteran proponents of the Strike North, were soon committed wholeheartedly to the battle which had been started for the yurts of Nomonhan. Never would Japanese troops fight harder, against greater odds, for a more worthless piece of territory. Theoretically they had the Emperor's mandate to take Outer Mongolia and so control the Trans-Siberian Railway connecting Moscow with Vladivostok. In practice, however, Hirohito would commit only three divisions or about 60,000 men to the action and the battle would never progress beyond the 20-mile-deep strip of pastureland between the Outer Mongolian border and the Khalka River.

BELLY TALK WITH STALIN

While the 23d Division and then the rest of the 6th Army were being moved to the front in June of 1939, Hitler closeted himself with his generals at Berchtesgaden, planning the blitzkrieg of Poland. Stalin continued negotiations with both Ribbentrop and Great Britain's Neville Chamberlain. And in Tokyo Hirohito and the spy service made every effort to improve their channels of liaison with Stalin, the common unknown in the international equation.

On June 1, Ozaki Hotsumi, the Japanese patriot or traitor who belonged to Prince Konoye's brain trust and supplied Soviet spy Sorge with his best inside-Tokyo intelligence, took a new job as a direct advisor of the Japanese spy service. Since the fall of the Konoye Cabinet five months earlier, Ozaki had had no outlet for his talents except his none-too-competent journalism for *Asahi*. Now, through Konoye, he became a consultant of the research branch of the South Manchuria Railway, one of the oldest and most important clearinghouses of the spy service. It was run by Dr. Okawa Shumei, the multilingual scholar of Sanskrit and of the Koran, who had organized the Lodging House indoctrination center in the palace for Hirohito in 1922 and had gone to prison for Hirohito in 1934–35 for his managerial role in the 1932 assassinations.

On June 9, a week after Ozaki had begun work for Dr. Okawa, Big Brother Marquis Kido, now home minister in charge of police, met with his Red contact, Saionji Kinkazu, the grandson of the aged, impotent prime-minister-maker. Kido and Saionji talked alone for the first time since the outbreak of the Lake Khasan incident a year earlier. The next week Soviet spy Sorge filed a detailed intelligence report to Moscow, assuring Stalin that the Japanese buildup at Nomonhan portended no war but only a military exercise and a limited probe of Russian strength. Sorge was able to substantiate his assertions by giving evidence that new Japanese divisions were being shipped out, not battle-ready to Manchuria but green and ill-equipped for garrison duty in central China.

Stalin was understandably suspicious of the intelligence coming from Sorge in Tokyo, and in early July he appointed one of his most trustworthy and brilliant generals to command the Russian forces on the Mongolian frontier, opposite the continuing Japanese troop buildup. This was Lieutenant General Georgi Zhukov, a specialist in tanks and armor who would later become a field marshal and would share with Eisenhower in the laurels for the conquest of Germany. On reviewing the situation in the Nomonhan area, Zhukov asked the Kremlin for full support in repulsing what might well be an all-out Japanese attack. Stalin responded by giving Zhukov all the troops and equipment that could be spared and by suggesting to Hitler, on July 18, that after all Russia might be willing to conclude a nonaggression pact.

NOMONHAN (3)

On assuming his command, Lieutenant General Zhukov organized a classic of positional defense. He beat off half a dozen Japanese attempts to cross the Khalka River in the second and third weeks of July and began to build up gradually a reserve force behind his lines with which to take the offensive.

On July 19, in a night of fire, Zhukov's men withstood the best offensive which the Japanese forces in the area could muster. By July 24, Zhukov's first probing counterattacks had become so blistering that Lieutenant Higashikuni, the twenty-three-year-old son of Prince Higashikuni, decamped without orders from the field of battle. He waited in a town behind the lines for a reposting to a quieter theater. His new orders came through a week later and his equerry took full responsibility for having advised him to desert. His comrades in the field muttered over his exemption from normal discipline, but the story was suppressed by the censors and few of his tentmates lived to carry it home to Japan.[18] The commander of the 23d Division took the imperial desertion as an ill omen, but being committed fatalistically to the Strike-North concept, he only drove on his men so much the harder.

Soviet commander Zhukov knew precisely from Sorge's intelligence what forces the Japanese had committed to the war, and all through July and early August he methodically assembled behind his lines an absolute superiority over them—a superiority of three to two in manpower, two to one in planes and artillery, and four to one in armor.

HITLER'S TREACHERY

During Zhukov's preparations, Hitler and Stalin negotiated and, on August 19, 1939, agreed to sign their mutual Non-Aggression Pact. It pledged both Germany and Russia to refrain from making war on one another no matter what their respective commitments to other nations individually.

The next morning at 5:45 Zhukov launched his offensive. He had ready 500 tanks, 500 planes, 346 armored cars, and almost 80,000 men. He threw them all into the strip of territory 40 miles wide and 20 miles deep which the Japanese had occupied between the Khalka River and the Mongolian-Manchurian border. Heavy flame-throwing Russian tanks led the way, spewing before them burning petroleum with a prodigality that the oil-poor Japanese could scarcely imagine. Never until the Pacific War would the samurai be given such a lesson in technology. And never at any time would they fight back more fanatically. It took Zhukov's tanks eleven days to roll the twenty miles to the border and 20,000 of the 60,000 Japanese defenders died in front of them. More than 50,000 of the 60,000 were counted afterward as wounded, dead, or missing in action.

---

[18] Associated Press correspondent Relman Morin, who got wind of the story a few months later, was told by an Army Press Relations officer that the young prince had not really deserted but had been captured and held as a hostage by the Russians—which explained why Japan had been forced to make peace!

Six years later, talking to Eisenhower's Chief of Staff Bedell Smith, Zhukov described the Russian triumph with low-keyed but callous braggadocio: "The Japanese are not good against armor. It took about ten days to beat them."

At the time of Zhukov's breakthrough, on August 23, Hitler summoned a meeting of his generals to explain his Non-Aggression Pact with Russia and his disregard for the Anti-Comintern Pact with Japan. "The [Japanese] Emperor," he shouted, "is a companion piece for the late czars of Russia. He is weak, cowardly, and irresolute and may be easily toppled by revolution. . . . Let us think of ourselves as masters and consider these people at best as lacquered half-monkeys, who need to feel the knout."

Hirohito did not hear these words until he read them in a book in 1957. Had he heard them at the time, it would have made little difference, for he had already determined through Nomonhan and Hitler's Non-Aggression Pact with Russia that he must exploit Hitler's strength if he could and must trust it never.

On August 31, after their ten-day offensive, the Russian tanks in central Asia drew up and stopped at the Manchurian border. Their guns were pointed east toward Tokyo. The Kwantung Army was rushing all its reserves to the front to contest their further advance. Zhukov paused, fearing a trap. And before morning he had received orders to release his heaviest armor and send it scurrying back toward the nearest railheads for express transportation west toward Poland.

On September 1, Hitler's *Wehrmacht* poured into western Poland to begin the rape of Warsaw. Bound by treaty and ashamed of the concessions made at Munich seventeen months earlier, Great Britain and the nations of the British Commonwealth at once declared war on Germany. The Red Army began the next week to occupy eastern Poland. In a back street outside the Kremlin in Moscow, Soviet and Japanese foreign officers began serious negotiations for settlement of the Nomonhan incident.

THE HITLER-HIROHITO STANDOFF

News of the Soviet-German Non-Aggression Pact, turning the *Wehrmacht* loose on the democratic world, had reached Tokyo on August 22, 1939, the night before Zhukov's breakthrough at Nomonhan and Hitler's contemptuous speech about Japan to his generals. Big Brother Kido, the home minister, wrote in his diary: "However we consider the Anti-Comintern Pact and its attached secret protocols, we are startled that there has been this breach of faith." Prime Minister Hiranuma, who had lent qualified support to the strengthening of Japan's pact with Germany, considered the sudden turn in German diplomacy "intricate and baffling." He promptly tendered Hirohito his resignation and Hirohito accepted it.

Now, at last, the problems of many months had been solved. Hitler might be angry, but he owed Japan a favor and had implicitly set Japan free to abide by her own timetable in the Far East. Japan had suffered a great loss of face at Nomonhan, but the Strike-North Faction in the Army had suffered a decisive defeat at the hands of the Russians and had learned that promises of alliance made by Hitler were worth nothing.

Hirohito had sent the vice chief of staff, his former aide-de-camp, Lieutenant General Nakajima Tetsuzo, to the Nomonhan front on September 1 to bring about an end to hostilities. The officers of the Kwantung Army had begged to be allowed to mount one more counteroffensive on September 10 if only to save Japan's face. Nakajima had flown back to Japan, talked to the Emperor, flown again to Nomonhan, and suppressed the plans for the counteroffensive. Hirohito replaced the commander-in-chief of the Kwantung Army in Manchuria, and on September 16 the Russian and Japanese diplomats meeting in Moscow agreed to settle the war by a return to the border lines of the status quo ante.

Lieutenant General Komatsubara Michitaro, the Strike-North commander of Japan's 23d Division, which had suffered 99 per cent casualties at Nomonhan, returned to Japan to die of an "abdominal ailment." Several officers of lesser rank blew their brains out or committed hara-kiri on the edge of the field of battle.

The Strike-North Faction which had troubled Hirohito since 1930 was dead at last. And for the next year Hirohito would be able to develop his private national plans in peace and quiet. The factories would hum with armament business. The quixotic liberals of Japan would continue to murmur, making it necessary to change the Cabinet occasionally. But the secret police would ably nullify all serious attempts at protest. And Prince Konoye, in retirement, would arrange to replace all previous political parties with a single mass party called the Imperial Rule Assistance Association. Germany in the meanwhile would march, and when the time was ripe Prince Konoye would resume office to lead Japan once again to war.

23

JOINING THE AXIS

(1940)

HURRIED BY HITLER

Between August 1939 and August 1940, patriotic Japanese almost forgot their favorite hobby of domestic political intrigue while they worked feverishly to prepare the country for World War II before Germany should fight and win it. Starts were made on over a thousand new military airplanes and over a million and a quarter tons of new or converted naval vessels. Twelve new divisions and a quarter of a million men were added to the Army.[1]

Domestic tabloids harped on what they considered the hypocrisy, self-interest, and overbearing of the Americans and British in their support of Chiang Kai-shek. But while the tabloids played upon inferiority feelings and old racial grievances, the official policy toward the United States, voiced by diplomats and English-language editorials, was conciliatory. The Army and Navy were stockpiling war commodities unavailable in Japan. Handsome prices were being paid U.S. businessmen for oil, scrap iron, and machine tools. U.S. Ambassador Grew was encouraged to make a speech "straight from the horse's mouth" about U.S. business grievances in China and was given to understand afterward that the speech had been privately applauded by men close to the Emperor.

The lawyer, Baron Hiranuma, had been succeeded as prime minister on August 30, 1939, by the "Army moderate" General Abe Nobuyuki. General Abe was, in fact, the least talented and most aristocratic of three officers who had played the part of "Crows" to Emperor Taisho.[2] In November 1939 Hirohito's Big Brothers saw that a Navy Cabinet would

---

[1] The 24th, 25th, and 32d through 41st divisions. This buildup has not been noted previously by Western historians.

[2] The other two were Araki, the Strike-North leader, and Honjo, Hirohito's former chief aide-de-camp.

better please the United States and would better inspire the domestic armament effort. And so in January 1940, General Abe was succeeded by Admiral Yonai, the former Navy minister who had tipped the scales for Hirohito against accepting a premature alliance with Hitler.

Great events were afoot abroad which riveted Japanese attention. Stalin, after taking his proffered half of Poland, fought a war with Finland from November 1939 to March 1940 and won it without much dispatch or glory. Hitler, after securing his half of Poland, dug in for the winter behind his Siegfried line on the western border of Germany and kept the French waiting behind their Maginot line, just opposite, along the eastern border of France.

On March 25, 1940, one hundred members of the Diet, recruited by Prince Konoye but representing all parties, buried their difficulties and formed a League for Waging the Holy War. They agreed to support Prince Konoye, to collaborate with Germany and Italy, to rid Japan of laissez-faire, communism, liberalism, and utilitarianism, and to dedicate themselves to a New Order in East Asia.

The next month, April, Hitler conquered Denmark and Norway. In early May he ordered his panzers and paratroops to blitz Belgium and the Netherlands and so outflank the Maginot line.

LORD PRIVY SEAL KIDO

On May 8, 1940, the day that news of Hitler's order for the attack on the Low Countries arrived at the palace in Tokyo, Hirohito sent an emissary [3] to the first of his Big Brothers, the son of his foster father, Marquis Kido Koichi. He asked Kido to take the post of chief civilian advisor to the Throne, that of lord privy seal. Kido had been out of public office for nine months advising Prince Konoye in behind-the-scene preparations for a new totalitarian state structure to be dominated by a single mass party, the Imperial Rule Assistance Association or I.R.A.A. Kido protested that he must first complete these political chores and that even then he could not consider the post in the palace until it had first been offered to Prince Konoye. Two days later he acknowledged to his diary that the way had been cleared for him and that he intended to give up his plans for becoming vice president of the new mass party.

During the next fortnight Kido exerted all his considerable powers of persuasion and blackmail to hurry Japan's politicians into line with the so-called New Structure. On May 26 he dined with Konoye and Count Arima of the imperial family to tell them that his arrangements were nearly complete. The three men agreed that the old political parties should

---

[3] Matsudaira Yasumasa who would later succeed Kido as the Emperor's chief advisor, in November 1945.

be given a little time in which to save face before dissolving themselves and merging, and that the actual announcement of the New Structure should not be made until Prince Konoye became prime minister again. On this understanding Kido wound up his political mission three days later by securing the signatures of Japan's most important professional politicians on a contract which bound them all to co-operate in the New Structure and to dedicate themselves to "fulfillment of the national defense" and "an expansion in foreign affairs." The signatories further agreed that "politicians who do not join the new [I.R.A.A.] party shall not be cared for."

Marquis Kido turned over the finished plans for the New Structure to Prince Konoye at a last lunch on June 1, 1940. Then, from Konoye's Hate-China Villa in Yokohama, the dapper marquis drove straight to the palace where he was invested lord privy seal by Hirohito in a simple ceremony at 3 P.M.[4]

THE FALL OF FRANCE

It was a critical month in which Kido, after years of apprenticeship, finally took his public place at the Emperor's side. The German Army invaded France from the ill-defended Belgian border and swiftly threw back a hastily organized stopgap British expeditionary force to the beaches of Dunkirk. The remnants of the British rear guard evacuated the beaches on June 4. Mussolini declared war on the Allies on June 10 and invaded southern France. The government of the dismembered French nation, reorganized in defeat under Prince Kanin's old friend Maréchal Pétain, capitulated to the Axis on June 22.

The collapse of France and the Low Countries orphaned French Indochina and the Dutch East Indies, the richest colonies in Southeast Asia. It also sapped British power in the Far East by pulling back fleet units from Singapore to the defense of England's white cliffs. The pearls of Asia lay exposed on the half shell and Hirohito's councillors feared that if they were not grabbed quickly they would be appropriated either by Germany or the United States. If Japan offered to co-operate in the European struggle against Great Britain, a bargain could probably be worked out with Hitler. The United States, however, remained a great imponderable. It might stir from its pacifist lethargy and block Japanese seizure of the Indies. As yet the Japanese Navy was still two to three years from acquiring the strength needed to challenge the United States.

Through his aides-de-camp Hirohito received and studied scores of

---

[4] The former Lord Privy Seal Yuasa, who had occupied the post since March 1936—and before that, since 1933, the post of imperial household minister—was at last allowed to retire and nurse the gastric ailments of which he had begun to complain in 1934.

position papers drawn up by young officers in the Army and Navy ministries. Some described Japan's position as a "fateful juncture" and some as "a moment of golden opportunity." Some dwelt on the impossibility of matching economic sinews with the United States. Others envisaged a Japanese Empire extending to Australia, to India, and even to a territory of Alaska which would include western Canada and the state of Washington.

In an anguish of indecision in the face of so many possibilities, Hirohito made a spur-of-the-moment progress to the tombs of his ancestors in the old Japanese heartland of Yamato. He was accompanied by the new Lord Privy Seal Marquis Kido. According to the official chronology of the imperial house, invented during Emperor Meiji's reign, Japan's first emperor, Jimmu, had founded the Throne on February 11, 660 B.C. Therefore February 11, 1940, had been the 2600th birthday of the nation. Now Hirohito belatedly used the anniversary as an excuse to visit the old capital, Kyoto.

As the first stop on his pilgrimage, on June 10, he went to pray at the antique shrine of the sun goddess on the wooded slopes of Ise Peninsula overlooking the sea from which the imperial dynasty had come. There Kido stood by under the trees watching as Hirohito disappeared into a little hut of unvarnished white wood, the Holy of Holies, wherein reposed the fragments of the ancient sacred mirror in which every duly anointed emperor was supposed to be able to communicate with the mother of the Japanese race. Kido admitted to his diary: "My feelings were profoundly stirred and I wept. I prayed for the future fortune of the imperial family and reflected with awe on the importance of my new position. Before the imperial shrine of Japan, my mind widened and I felt large and fearless."

The heralded state visit of Hirohito to the tomb of Jimmu, the first emperor, which took place the next day, was perfunctory by comparison. At every intermission in the ceremonies, Kido was kept busy answering sotto-voce questions from the Emperor as to the significance of Italy's entry into the war.

The following day, June 12, after bathing at his Kyoto inn, Kido was honored to dine in privacy with the Emperor in the Kyoto Palace of the imperial forebears. He agreed with Hirohito that Hitler's overwhelming victory in Europe made it mandatory for Japan to take control of French and Dutch colonies in the Orient before they should fall into other hands.

That same day the foreign minister had signed a nonaggression pact with Thailand, the one other nation in the Orient besides Japan which could be considered its own master. Thailand had ceded large areas of Laos and Cambodia to French Indochina in 1893, 1904, and 1907. On the pretext of mediating Thailand's just claims for the return of these territories, Japan planned to introduce military observer teams into French Indochina and finally to take over the colony by a police action which could be represented to the United States as a temporary intervention. By befriending Thailand in this manner, diplomatic brains in the Foreign Ministry hoped to win the trust of natives throughout Southeast Asia and so recruit them in movements to oust Western colonialism and replace it with Japanese colonialism.

At his private dinner with Marquis Kido in the dark and draughty paper-screened halls of the old Kyoto Palace, Hirohito acknowledged that Japan would soon need the discipline of Prince Konoye's contemplated one-party government if the nation was to take advantage of the Strike-South opportunities opened by the fall of France. On returning to Tokyo the next day, June 13, Kido set to work at once translating the Emperor's words into action. He advised the ministers of Admiral Yonai's Cabinet to stand ready to resign and make way for Konoye. He urged the vice minister of foreign affairs, Big Brother Tani Masayuki,[5] to press home negotiations with France, Great Britain, and the semiautonomous Dutch government of the East Indies. Tani embarked at once on conversations with Monsieur Charles Arsenne-Henry, the French ambassador in Tokyo.

The sudden "low" position of France enabled Tani to demand that Arsenne-Henry stop the flow of war supplies through Indochina into the "free China" of Chiang Kai-shek. By June 20 Arsenne-Henry and his Vichy masters had capitulated. They agreed to "recognize . . . Japanese . . . special requirements" and to let Japanese observers into Indochina to supervise the make-up of all trains running north from Hanoi. As a result, Chiang Kai-shek lost 80 per cent of his trade with the West. Another clause in the Franco-Japanese agreement forced the French settlement in Shanghai, on June 23, to turn over its defense sector to Japanese troops and to open the whole of the French Concession in Shanghai to Japanese police search and extradition.

The next day, June 24, an aide-de-camp reported to Hirohito that Chiang Kai-shek would soon meet with the Chinese puppet president, Wang Ching-wei, and with the Japanese vice chief of staff, to settle the China War before the Strike South should begin. The meeting eventually did take place, weeks later, with a trusted lieutenant standing in for Chiang, at the city of Changsha in the half-conquered lake country south of Hankow. Chiang, through his representative, refused to accept Japanese conditions for a "complete settlement of the China incident," but he did discuss, in great detail, a limited, unofficial truce with Japan in areas where there were no Chinese Communists. Though little known and almost entirely undocumented in the West, this unsigned truce was in reality ob-

---

[5] Tani had run the China Desk in the Foreign Ministry from 1930 to 1933 during the conquest of Manchuria. Then Hirohito had been forced to rusticate him to Manchuria for three years in order to disassociate the Throne from his aggressive enthusiasm for leaving the League of Nations and prosecuting the Strike South.

served rather strictly in the field until Japan's defeat five years later. The Japanese Army fought Mao Tse-tung almost exclusively. Its probes into areas held by Chiang Kai-shek's forces were mostly arranged in advance with Chungking and amounted to little more than political gestures.

On yet another diplomatic front, the Foreign Ministry held talks with the British ambassador in Tokyo, Sir Robert Craigie. While they were in progress, the British and Australian governments inquired in Washington whether it might not be best to present Japan either with clear-cut concessions or challenges. The British Empire was ready on the one hand to join the United States in recognizing Japanese claims to China or on the other hand to assist the United States in an all-out trade embargo against Japan. U.S. oil and steel companies, however, were doing a land-office business with Japan and their lobbies in Washington argued ably against accepting either of the extreme alternatives recommended by the British. With considerable justice, President Roosevelt contended that he had no right to give away China for the Chinese and no mandate from Americans to provoke Japan to war. Appeasement of Japan would be craven and unjust; restraint of Japan would be politically unwarranted. Better to give Japan rope and let her prove to herself and the world that she was doing wrong. Then and only then would it be time to crush her back into her place.

Engaged in the Battle of Britain, England had no hope of protecting her interests in the Pacific except through the United States. On July 15, 1940, British Ambassador Craigie in Tokyo agreed to close for three months the Burma Road which brought Chiang Kai-shek supplies from the ports of India.

The fourth prong of the Japanese diplomatic offensive, against the Dutch East Indies, had seemed initially as if it should be the easiest to push home, but in the event it turned its point on a wall of stolid, stubborn Dutch charm. The Indonesian colony had announced its continuing loyalty to the Dutch queen who was an exile in London. In early July Vice Foreign Minister Tani demanded a renewal of defunct trade negotiations with the Dutch East Indies. The colonial government in Java complied by giving months of handsome entertainment to a high-powered trade delegation from Tokyo consisting of twenty-six oil and intelligence experts and the Japanese minister of commerce. In the end, however, the Dutchmen produced an abundance of sound technical reasons to show that they were unable to supply Japan with more aviation gasoline.

Throughout these predatory overtures to the French, Chinese, British, and Dutch, the war for air superiority known as the Battle of Britain continued to rage indecisively over southern England. As early as June 21, Prince Asaka, the Emperor's uncle and conquistador of Nanking, assured Hirohito that the British were losing and that, incidentally, Japan would do well to unify her Army and Navy air forces in emulation of the Luft-waffe. Hirohito shook his head and told his uncle that evidence as yet indicated no British defeat.

PRINCE KONOYE'S RETURN

On June 24, 1940, Prince Konoye resigned as president of Hirohito's Privy Council in order to devote himself full time to the final preparations for his second prime ministership. Four days later he showed Hirohito his provisional list of Cabinet ministers. Hirohito approved it in general but questioned whether the proposed war minister, Lieutenant General Tojo, had had enough combat experience to lead the Army in a time of antici-pated warfare. In his years in Manchuria Tojo had secured a strong hold on the secret police and lately, by indefatigable membership on committees, had made himself the most powerful individual in the Army bureaucracy. Then again, in his current post as inspector general of military aviation, he had worked closely and well with the Emperor. Hirohito liked him and shared with him a concern for practicality and detail.

Lord Privy Seal Kido suggested that if the Emperor had any doubts about Tojo's popularity with the field commanders, why not let Lieutenant General Anami—the man who had treated the young officers of the cabal to drinks on the night of Hirohito's accession to the Throne in 1926 and the man who would commit hara-kiri during the fake coup d'etat on the night of Japan's surrender in 1945—stay on in his present post of vice war minister as a foil and watchdog for Tojo? Anami was popular with field commanders and, having long served as a palace aide-de-camp, he could be trusted implicitly to act in the interests of the Throne. Hirohito accepted the suggestion appreciatively.

Eighteen days later, on July 16, 1940, the Yonai Cabinet tendered its resignation en bloc and the first of Japan's major political parties liquidated itself and waited, in a state of *nolo contendere* and suspended animation, for further orders. The last of the parties, the Anti-Constitutionalists, would follow suit a month later. In the meanwhile, on July 17, Lord Privy Seal Kido, after a perfunctory thirty-minute meeting with all Japan's living ex-prime ministers, recommended Konoye to the Throne as the next head of state. Lieutenant General Tojo learned that he was Konoye's choice as war minister the next day when he arrived back in Tokyo from an inspection of air bases in Manchuria.

On July 19, Tojo, Konoye, and Konoye's candidates for foreign and navy ministers met and agreed that they could all work together to "per-fect a high-degree defense state." Three days later, on July 22, Hirohito accepted Konoye's slate and invested the neurasthenic Fujiwara prince once more prime minister. In the bitter opinion of old Prince Saionji, de-livered months earlier when the subject had first come up, Konoye's reappointment was "like inviting a robber back to investigate his crime because no one else could be such an authority on it."

THE NEW ORDER

The languid Prince Konoye resumed office with two of the most energetic members of Hirohito's cabal at his back. One was Lieutenant General Tojo, former inspector general of aviation, former vice war minister, former Kwantung Army chief of staff, former Kwantung Army secret police chief, and before that, until the murder of First Crow Nagata in 1935, the Fourth Crow of Baden-Baden who had fulfilled a score of difficult assignments in the bureaucracy as Nagata's factotum.

The other activist of Konoye's Cabinet was the foreign minister, Matsuoka Yosuke, a long-time hanger-on of the Big Brothers. He had attended the 1926 meeting in Hangkow at which the Big Brothers' "China experts" had first formulated Japanese plans for using Chiang Kai-shek. Later, in 1932, he had negotiated settlement of the Fake War in Shanghai. In 1933 he had led Japan's delegation out of the League of Nations.

Matsuoka commanded the curiosity and respect of Hirohito's inner circle because he knew how to talk big and independent—like an American. Indeed, Matsuoka was as much American as he was Japanese. The son of an impoverished samurai of Choshu, he had been singled out as a potential talent at his coming-of-age ceremony in 1893 and had been sent the next year, at the age of fourteen, to live with an uncle who had emigrated to Portland, Oregon. Taken in by a mission school there he had lived up to all his early indications of precocity by graduating from high school and the University of Oregon, with a law degree, before his twenty-first birthday.

On becoming foreign minister, Matsuoka at once saw U.S. Ambassador Grew. He confessed to Grew that he was not an old-school diplomat but a blunt, honest sort of man. If war ever came between the United States and Japan while he remained in office, he hoped to see to it that both sides would know why. War, he said, "should not develop, as in so many other cases in history, through misunderstanding." Then he gave Grew an oral message to relay to President Roosevelt. In it he protested Japan's love for peace but asked the United States to give up its defense "of the status quo" and recognize the fact that "a New Order" was taking shape in the world.

That same day, July 26, 1940, the new Cabinet formally adopted its program, a document entitled "Main Principles of Fundamental Japanese National Policy," which had been drawn up by civilians under the direction of Prince Konoye. With considerable rhetoric and bombast, it declared Japan's intention "to capitalize on the inevitable trend in the development of world history" by "building a new order in Greater East Asia." For this purpose the Cabinet agreed to bring the China "incident" to a successful conclusion and to make Japan strong and self-sufficient in order to fulfill the national program. In the dialectic of the time this meant that Japan intended, one way or another, to gain control of the oil of the Indies. On the domestic front the Konoye government called for creation of a new form of government, economy, and culture in Japan. The people would be asked to give their complete devotion to the state, ridding themselves of all "selfish thoughts" and—in a phrase beloved by Hirohito—"cultivating a scientific spirit."

Hirohito took the Cabinet's decision as an approval for war and promptly that same afternoon activated a standing plan for removing the members of his family from positions of responsibility before the war should break out. He had the Army and Navy ministers informed that the two imperial princes, Kanin and Fushimi, who were chiefs of the Army and Navy General Staffs, might soon have to retire. War Minister Tojo replied that the Army would regret the loss of Prince Kanin as its leader but agreed that the Army could take a stand in the world more freely if its actions did not directly implicate the Throne. On the other hand Navy Minister Yoshida Zengo insisted that Navy Chief of Staff Prince Fushimi be left in office for at least nine more months as insurance against involvement in war before the Navy was ready for it. Hirohito listened to the Navy's point of view and for the moment suspended judgment on it.

The next day, July 27, the most important ministers of the Cabinet met with the chiefs of staff and some of the officers from palace Imperial Headquarters to ratify the program passed by the Cabinet and to discuss its military implementation. This was the first "liaison conference" between domestic policy makers and the field strategists of headquarters since the month after the rape of Nanking more than two years earlier. The officers from headquarters brought with them a plan entitled "Main Japanese Policy Principles for Coping with the Situation Which Has Developed in the World." It specified the measures which would be taken for cutting off Western aid to Chiang Kai-shek via Burma and Indochina. It called for stronger ties with Germany and renewed diplomatic efforts to neutralize Russia. And finally it committed all present to press for Japanese expansion into Southeast Asia and Indonesia.

"Positive arrangements," it declared, "will be undertaken in order to include the English, French, Dutch, and Portuguese islands of the Orient within the substance of the New Order." If possible the goals of the expansion were to be achieved by diplomacy and trade treaties; if possible the China incident was to be settled first before demands on the Dutch East Indies were made too stridently; if possible resort to force would only be made against Great Britain. But if necessary war with the United States would not be shunned and preparations for such a war must be completed by August 1941.

Navy representatives at the liaison conference refused to give their whole-hearted backing to the outlined program. They insisted that every effort must be made to settle the China incident before any exploits farther afield and that war with the United States must be avoided at all costs.

In the next two days heated arguments about the respective Army and Navy positions almost tore the new Konoye government asunder. Army underlings accused Navy underlings of being frightened of war with the United States. Navy underlings accused Army underlings of stupidity in engaging the nation in actions like the China incident which could not be won. Civilian expansionists accused both services of being militarily in-competent and politically boastful. Prime Minister Konoye sought vainly to pour oil on the troubled waters. War Minister Tojo grew so impatient with the back-room bickering that he protested to Lord Privy Seal Kido that Konoye was a puppet for every faction and that unless Army-Navy and Court-bureaucracy relations could be improved, nothing would ever be accomplished.

The day after the conference ended, July 30, 1940, Hirohito personally analyzed the Cabinet's difficulties out loud and in so doing enforced, if not harmony, at least a truce. He ventured the opinion that Prince Konoye was trying to cut losses and shorten battle lines in China in order to release forces and divert public opinion in preparation for the nation's historic mission, the Strike South. The Navy, he said gently, wanted an absolute solution to the China incident before venturing farther. The Army, he said sternly, wanted an immediate entanglement in the south in order to cover up its failure in China. He added mildly that both points of view were ultimately based on a laudable sense of pride and a fear of failure. How-ever, he concluded, the services must work together in co-operation with domestic politics and international diplomacy.

Bowing to Hirohito's wishes, the Cabinet smothered its internal dif-ferences and on August 1 subscribed to a vaguely worded declaration an-nouncing that it was the "fundamental policy" of the new government to "found a Co-Prosperity Sphere in Greater East Asia." The adjective "greater" had a special significance which was missed by Western observers. It meant that Japan intended to embrace in her sphere not only China and the new Buddhism but also India and the old Buddhism. It meant, in short, that "co-prosperity" was to extend from Teheran to Honolulu and from Harbin to Port Moresby.

FRUGALITY AND HATE

"No nation," announced the epicurean Prince Konoye in a radio address on July 23, "ever became powerful by devoting itself to luxury and pleas-ure." And so, in the first weeks of the Konoye Cabinet, while the prime minister himself continued to take days off with professional male and female entertainers, the nation at large tasted the bitterness of police-state discipline and glimpsed the drabness of the toiling years ahead. At last the fun-loving populace, who had survived previous gestures at efficient totalitarianism with cynical jokes, was to march in clogs on a treadmill of overtime labor, keeping step with a steady blare of martial music.

Soon Ambassador Grew was noting in his journal, with astonishment and amusement, that concubines would no longer be allowed to have telephones. Soon Hirohito would make wives and geisha put away their bright kimonos by ordaining a new national dress, first for men, then for women, too: a dingy mustard-green schoolboy uniform of pants and high-collar jackets.

No Japanese was allowed to work for a foreigner except as a police spy. Indeed, no Japanese was allowed to work at all unless in dedicated service to the new total-war defense state. Many proprietors of small factories discovered overnight that they were producing "nonessential materials" and that they must return to operating lathes and drill presses for others as they had done when getting their starts in life a generation earlier. If they protested, they were beaten up by thugs.[6]

The gentlemen of the Japanese press, according to Prime-Minister-Maker Saionji, who was now in his ninety-first and last year of life, had begun to write "like drunkards." They spewed out adjectives in defense of Japan's "just cause" and buried news under mountains of mystical philosophizing in an attempt to beautify the underlying opportunism of Hirohito's national program. For the most part they played upon Japanese racial sensibilities in order to inspire hate of all white men except Germans and Italians.

THE COX CASE

As soon as France had fallen, on June 19, Japan's ambassador in Berlin [7] had told the German Foreign Office that Hirohito was ready to reconsider the Ribbentrop idea, turned down a year earlier, of joining Hitler and Mussolini in a firm tripartite military alliance. Flushed with victory, the Germans had replied with studied indifference. Possibly, they said, if Japan could offer Germany tangible advantages, such as supplies of raw materials, an agreement might be worked out. Japan, however, would have to aban-

---

[6] After the dissolution of the Black Dragon Society, underworld boss Toyama Mitsuru had, in 1936, made a truce with the Throne, negotiated by the Emperor's uncle Prince Higashikuni. As a result Toyama continued to rule the slums and the imperial entourage continued to use him for work considered too illegal for the police. Lord Privy Seal Kido, in late 1940 and early 1941, communicated regularly with Toyama through ex-convict Friar Inoue, the former leader of the Blood Brotherhood which had assassinated Baron Dan and financier Inoue in 1932.

[7] Kurusu Saburo, later one of the two special envoys sent to conduct smokescreen negotiations in Washington while the Japanese fleet was stealing up on Pearl Harbor.

don her traditional sympathies for that other island-nation, Great Britain. In particular the pro-British sentiments expressed by the English-language newspapers in Japan—most of which were edited by Englishmen—would have to be suppressed.

The moment Prince Konoye came to power, he and his Cabinet ministers agreed, on July 19, 1940, that they would satisfy the Germans by launching a campaign of vilification to turn Japanese against the British. Accordingly, on Saturday, July 27, while the Konoye government was still wrestling internally to reconcile Army and Navy fears of war, the secret police arrested fifteen British residents in the Tokyo area and accused them of being espionage agents. Most of them were typical British colonial businessmen of whom their own house servants could report nothing more damaging than a somewhat superior attitude of kindliness toward Japan. It was necessary to show, however, that they were polished spies and subtle double-dealers. The demonstration was difficult to stage but the accomplished Japanese secret police, drawing on years of experience in Manchuria, found a way.

On Monday, July 29, one of the fifteen British prisoners, a Reuters correspondent named Melville Cox, hurtled from an upper-story window of Tokyo secret police headquarters and crashed to his death on the pavements below. When attachés from the British Embassy were summoned to pick up his broken body, they counted no less than thirty-five needle punctures in his arms.

The other fourteen "spies" were released to be deported as personae non gratae. Some of them testified that they too had been given depressant and hallucinatory drugs. One of them recalled coming to his senses, between interrogations, before an open window through which he felt a powerful urge to jump. Out of a deeply suspicious animal shrewdness, he had resisted the urge. The British attachés who investigated Cox's case reached the conclusion that he had been similarly tempted and had succumbed.

The Japanese secret police produced a "suicide note" in Cox's own handwriting which they said he had written to his wife before his fall.

> See Reuters re rents
> See Cowley re deeds and insurance
> See Hkg * re balance and shares in London
> I know what is best
> Always my only love
> I have been quite well treated
> but there is no doubt how matters are going.

The note looked as if it had been written with more than one pen, one line at one interrogation, another at the next. Mrs. Cox was convinced that

* Hongkong Bank.

it expressed nothing which her husband might have wished to say. The British ambassador took her into the protection of his own home until he could get her out of the country, as quickly as possible, on a ship bound for England. The "suicide note" was advertised in the Japanese press as proof that Britain was spying on Japan and that Englishmen were enemies. The vast majority of Japanese were incensed.

THE BATTLE OF BRITAIN

Throughout August 1940, as U.S. Ambassador Grew noted in his diary, the new Konoye government concentrated on "building up the 'new structure' in Japan" and "marking time in foreign affairs while awaiting the result of the 'Battle of Britain.' " With less charity but greater accuracy, Grew could have said that Hirohito was waiting for an opportunity to throw Japan's weight into the war when it might tip the scales of history. Hirohito had much personal feeling, pro and con, for the British, but in his official capacity as Emperor he cared not who won the war in Europe as long as Japan could gain postwar influence which would enable her to achieve the national goal of domination over Asia. By mid-August it seemed clear that Japan's moment had arrived. Great Britain still staggered on the brink of defeat and the Germans had begun to admit that they needed help in delivering the conclusive shove.

On August 13, after weeks of coolness toward Japan, Ribbentrop sent his Far Eastern specialist, Heinrich Stahmer, to the Japanese Embassy in Berlin to say that Ribbentrop was ready to resume negotiations for strengthening the Japanese-German alliance. Foreign Minister Matsuoka responded by inviting Stahmer to Tokyo and by taking steps to create a pleasant atmosphere before Stahmer's arrival. On August 20 he asked and received the Emperor's permission to replace thirty-nine pro-Western diplomats abroad, including almost all chiefs of mission in North and South America. The purge was duly executed over the next three months, putting young men, close to the spy service, in charge of all key embassies and consulates.[8]

Also that day Matsuoka consummated weeks of secret negotiations by signing a new treaty with Vichy France on the future status of Indochina. After the arrival in Indochina of Japanese observers to prevent routing of war supplies through Hanoi to Chiang Kai-shek two months earlier, the Japanese had escalated their demands. Now they required that the French not only stop helping China but start helping Japan. They wanted air bases in northern Indochina from which to bomb the Burma

---

[8] For instance, the new ambassador to the Soviet Union, recommended by his years of diplomatic experience with geisha and bomb throwers, was retired Lieutenant General Tatekawa Yoshiji, the Peerless Pimp who had slept so soundly at the Literary Chrysanthemum on the night of the seizure of Mukden in 1931.

Road and also staging areas and rights of transit which would enable Japanese armies to attack Chiang Kai-shek's southern flank across the Indochina border. Finally they even asked to station a few garrisons of "observers" in south Indochina within striking distance of British Malaya.

When Arsenne-Henry, on instructions from Vichy, gave in to these demands on August 20, he warned Matsuoka that the French colonials in Indochina might not feel bound by the arrangements made for them in Vichy and might, as a matter of pride, resist further Japanese encroachments. Matsuoka reported these possible complications back to the palace, and Hirohito promptly reassigned two trusted members of his Army cabal to the Indochina area to make a show of strength and stage a genuine battle with which to satisfy the French sense of military honor.[9]

As the move into Indochina was being mounted, Ribbentrop's Far Eastern expert Stahmer, on August 23, accepted Matsuoka's invitation and set out with plenipotentiary powers for Tokyo. The Battle of Britain was not going well. In dogfight after dogfight, the German fighter pilots had failed, even with numerical superiority, to clear the skies of southern England, or to inactivate the airstrips from which British night bombers were making devastating sorties against the invasion fleets which Hitler was trying to collect in the French channel ports. The Luftwaffe was planning to resort to the desperate measure of massive indiscriminate terror bombing.

On September 2, while Stahmer was still on the high seas, old Saionji heard of the plans for a military alliance with Hitler and guardedly observed: "By our present policies the Emperor's aura of sanctity will be made invisible and the assertion that His Majesty is wise and sagacious will become an untruth. . . . In the end, I believe, Great Britain will be victorious."

The next day Navy Minister Yoshida Zengo, a charter member of Hirohito's cabal, resigned in protest against the pact plan and the hastening of naval preparations which would inevitably follow from it. Hirohito replaced him with Admiral Oikawa Koshiro, a former imperial aide-de-camp whom he described as "easy to talk to." [10]

---

[9] Lieutenant General Tominaga Kyoji, chief of the all powerful Operations Department of the General Staff, stepped down to an advisory position in the command of the South China Army to mastermind the face-saving operation. Colonel Cho Isamu, the veteran intriguer who had helped rig the October Plot for the benefit of the League of Nations in 1931, who had issued the kill-all-prisoners order for Prince Asaka before the walls of Nanking, who had taken down his pants before the Russians at Lake Khassan, and who would eventually have himself decapitated at the mouth of a cave on Okinawa, was appointed by Hirohito to take command of the Army observer team in Hanoi.

[10] Oikawa would in turn resign from a position of trust, as Navy chief of staff, to protest Hirohito's studied deafness to U.S. peace feelers when kamikaze pilots were throwing their lives away in May 1945.

On September 4, Prince Konoye was received privately at the Imperial Library in the palace woods and submitted to Hirohito three "points of revision" which he said must be written in to the basic policy of the nation before his prime ministership could progress farther. First, the Emperor and his chief ministers must resolve to be willing to fight a war with the United States. Second, Japan must conclude a military alliance with Germany. Third, Japan and Germany must publish a joint statement announcing their intention to found a New Order in the world. Konoye told Hirohito that the war and foreign ministers had agreed to the three points on August 17 but that the Navy held out in opposition to them. With evident nervousness, Hirohito authorized Prince Konoye to bring the Navy into line if he could.

Three days later, on September 7, Luftwaffe commander Goering launched 625 of his bombers against London in the first of World War II's great fire raids. It was that night when flames engulfed miles of cockney slums that a charlady approached a fireman who was battling with his hose and reportedly said: "Spare a few drops for my pot, luv, and I'll make you a nice cup of tea."

Japanese observers at the embassy in London remembered the wood-and-paper structures of their own capital and sent home to Tokyo thoughtful descriptions of the holocaust which they had witnessed. Having read their reports three days later, Hirohito suffered a moment of trepidation and doubt. He told Lord Privy Seal Kido that the German bombs had damaged the British Museum, endangering some of the manuscripts of Charles Darwin. Then he asked rhetorically whether Japan could not somehow use her influence with the Germans to mediate the European War and stop the headlong rush of world events. Kido made no reply. He knew that the Emperor was only indulging a mood, yearning wistfully for a return to Japan's old cautious war schedule and an escape from the pressure of opportunities offered by Hitler.

The previous morning, on September 9, Hirohito had already cast his lot. He had dropped in unexpectedly at a liaison conference of the Cabinet and General Staff in the Imperial Headquarters building on the palace grounds. There Foreign Minister Matsuoka was trying vainly to persuade the Navy's representatives to subscribe to alliance with Germany and to its implied accompaniment, war with the United States. The Navy was stubbornly contending that only disaster could result. Hirohito's arrival converted the proceedings into a Conference in the Imperial Presence. No record has been preserved of what words, if any, Hirohito uttered before the conferees. But the Navy representatives ceased to argue in broad terms against the pact with Germany and began, stiffly and professionally, to answer questions about their capabilities against the United States under optimum conditions at the end of a year's preparation. Hirohito seemed pleased by their answers. When the conference adjourned that afternoon no conclusions had been reached explicitly, but Prime Minister Konoye felt that the Navy, implicitly, had capitulated.

That evening of September 9, Foreign Minister Matsuoka welcomed Hitler's envoy Stahmer to Japan with a small reception in the lantern-lit garden of his residence—the setting which would later be remembered as the garden of atomic sunshine. Stahmer had arrived in Japan two days earlier and was eager to start doing business. Before the evening was over, he and Matsuoka, conversing in their common language, English, had agreed on the main purposes of the Tripartite Pact. Japan wanted a free hand in Southeast Asia. She should have it. Germany wanted pressure put upon the British fleet which still maintained naval supremacy in the Strait of Dover. Matsuoka undertook to supply it by having the Japanese Navy prepare to attack the British Far Eastern bastion of Singapore.

The next day, September 10, Matsuoka and Stahmer sat down together for a long day's haggle while they penned the original English draft of the pact which was to ally Nippon and the Reich militarily against the West. At every step in the talks Matsuoka cross-checked his concessions and reservations with the palace. Japanese and German texts of the pact were compared on September 11 and on September 12 the final text was ready for Hirohito's consideration.

On September 13, an unlucky Friday, Hirohito studied the text of the pact word by word for four and a half hours. He understood full well that he had a fateful decision to make which would almost certainly lead to war with the United States. He expected that many of even his closest advisors would be opposed to the pact. He knew, on reflection and meditation, that the institution of the Throne, representing his forefathers, must be cleansed in advance of responsibility for the pact. Nevertheless, when he had wrestled with all his misgivings, he approved the text of the alliance with one minor editorial change. He struck out five words, "openly or in concealed form," from a description of the kind of attack which might launch Japan's participation in World War II. They were too explicit, too suggestive of the actual event as it was envisaged by his naval planners.

Having approved the text of the pact with Hitler, Hirohito the next morning sought to allay the fears of the Navy by promising that Prince Fushimi, the chief of staff, would be allowed to remain in office, as requested, until at least April 1941. This was Hirohito's way of telling the Navy that the war would not break out immediately but that it would break out and that preparations for it must be hastened. At an unofficial liaison conference at Imperial Headquarters later that day, the Navy bowed to Hirohito's wishes and agreed to accept without protest the pact with Hitler and the accelerated national program.

For the benefit of the masses, the information officers of the Foreign Ministry had the newspapers whip up an outcry against the "Anglo-Saxon conspiracy" which was said to be strangling Japan's legitimate aspirations abroad. The pact decision happened to coincide with the arrival in Java of the trade-and-spy delegation which had been sent there in quest of aviation gasoline. The importance and righteousness of the oil mission filled the front pages. At the same time Japanese demands for bases throughout Indochina were masked by an agitation for reduction of Indo-china's tariff barriers.

Finally, on that same Saturday of September 14, Hirohito requested that an official Conference in the Imperial Presence be convoked so that his ministers could second the pact decision and take responsibility for it. Hirohito warned Lord Privy Seal Kido to exclude from the conference all elder statesmen and former prime ministers who might cause time-consuming difficulties.

TRIPARTITE PACT

The historic Conference in the Imperial Presence, which allied Hirohito with Hitler and Mussolini, was duly held in the Paulonia Hall of the Outer Ceremonial Palace from three to six o'clock on the afternoon of Thursday, September 19. As always on such occasions the entire agenda had been carefully negotiated and rehearsed in advance so that every position—every agreement to take or refuse responsibility—would be clearly etched on the record. Hirohito sat motionless before a golden screen at one end of the audience chamber and said nothing. The other eleven participants sat at two long tables down the walls of the chamber and delivered their set speeches to one another back and forth across the Emperor's line of sight. The important policy statements were made by six of the participants.

On behalf of the Navy General Staff, Prince Fushimi inquired, "It is quite likely that a Japanese-American war will be a protracted one. What are the prospects for maintaining our national strength?"

In replying Prince Konoye, on behalf of the Cabinet, admitted that Japan depended heavily "on Britain and the United States for her principal war materials" but concluded that by stringent civilian rationing and careful use of stockpiles "we should be able, in the event of a war with the United States, to supply military needs and thus withstand a rather prolonged war."

After a detailed discussion of war materials and their procurement, Navy Chief of Staff Prince Fushimi observed: "In the end, we will need to get oil from the Dutch East Indies. There are two ways of getting it—by peaceful means and by the use of force. The Navy very much prefers peaceful means."

In regard to the provisions in the Tripartite Pact which might pledge Japan to make war on the United States if the United States made war on Germany, Prince Fushimi went on to say: "We must be able to determine independently when we should commence hostilities. What has been done about this?"

Foreign Minister Matsuoka replied: "The question of whether or not the United States has really entered the war will be decided by consultation among the three pact countries. . . . Since our government will make the final decision, it will be made independently."

Hara Yoshimichi, who had recently been appointed president of Hirohito's Privy Council of advisors, noted that the questions he had been asked to put by the Throne were already being voiced by Navy Chief of Staff Prince Fushimi. Then, as a professional politician of liberal but compromised views, he inserted a hesitant opinion on his own behalf: "I think it will be impossible to obtain oil from the Dutch East Indies by peaceful means. I would like to hear the government's views on this."

Foreign Minister Matsuoka replied: "Since Germany is now in control of the Netherlands, she can help us greatly in putting pressure on the Dutch East Indies. In international relations, it is often possible to work behind the scenes. . . . When Japan withdrew from the League of Nations some years ago, so many people wanted to sell us munitions that one had difficulty turning them down. If Japan would abandon all, or at least half, of China, it might be possible for the time being to shake hands with the United States, but still pressure on Japan would not cease—not in the foreseeable future."

The discussion returned to details of oil consumption and procurement. War Minister Tojo cut in impatiently: "In the end I think this question comes down to the matter of the Dutch East Indies. The liaison conference between the government and Imperial Headquarters held shortly after the formation of the present Cabinet . . . agreed that we should settle the China incident quickly and at the same time cope with the Southern Question, taking advantage of favorable opportunities. As for the Dutch East Indies, it was decided that we would try to obtain vital materials by diplomatic means, and that we might use force, depending on the circumstances."

Privy Council President Hara, on behalf of Japan's sane but silent cosmopolitan minority, asked several waspish but ineffectual questions about the degree of Japan's commitment if she signed the Tripartite Pact.

Foreign Minister Matsuoka stated simply: "The object of this pact is to prevent the United States from encircling us."

In conclusion Army Chief of Staff Prince Kanin, the elder of the imperial family, three days short of his seventy-fifth birthday, declared: "On the basis of our studies to date, the Army section of the Imperial Headquarters agrees with the government's proposal for a stronger Axis Pact with Germany and Italy. Furthermore, since the improvement of relations with the Soviet Union is extremely important both for the settlement of the China incident and for future defense policies, we would strongly urge that the government redouble its efforts in this area."

Summing up for the Navy, the other staff chief and imperial family elder, Prince Fushimi, said: "The Navy section of Imperial Headquarters agrees with the government's proposal that we conclude a military alliance with Germany and Italy. However, on this occasion we present the following desiderata: firstly, that every conceivable measure will be taken, even after the conclusion of this alliance, to avoid war with the United States; secondly, that the Strike South will be attempted in so far as possible by peaceful means, and that bootless friction with third parties will be avoided; and thirdly, that the guidance and control of speech and the press will be strengthened, that unrestrained discussion of the conclusion of this pact will not be permitted, and that harmful anti-British and anti-American statements and behavior will be restrained. Although it is recognized that the government and the Navy Supreme Command agree on the need to speed up the strengthening of naval power and preparedness, nevertheless we would ask the government now, in view of the great urgency of the time, to give us unstinting co-operation."

Finally Privy Council President Hara made a prepared statement on behalf of the Throne: "Even though a Japanese-American clash may be unavoidable in the end, I hope that sufficient care will be exercised to make sure that it will not come in the near future, and that there will be no miscalculations. I give my approval on this basis."

INDOCHINA

At the end of the conference in his presence, Hirohito arose with a stiff nod of approval and returned to the Inner Palace in his Mercedes limousine. Foreign Minister Matsuoka drove in the opposite direction to put in a full evening's work at his office. He at once cabled an ultimatum to Hanoi, the capital of French Indochina, giving the governor-general there three days to accede to the agreement which had been worked out between Matsuoka and the Vichy-French ambassador in Tokyo. The alternative, he implied, would be a full-scale Japanese invasion. Matsuoka spent the next several hours receiving the congratulations of cronies and approving messages of explanation to Japanese embassies in Western capitals.

At 3:00 P.M. on September 22, just seven hours short of the Japanese deadline, the French governor-general in Hanoi replied to Matsuoka's note, saying that he was obliged to accept the terms offered. He had tried to bargain. He had tried to hedge. He had even begged Vichy for help and guidance. Now, having found no other recourse, he capitulated.

That night, about eleven o'clock, Major General Tominaga Kyoji, the high-ranking emissary from the General Staff whom Hirohito had dispatched to the South China command for this purpose three weeks earlier, persuaded Japanese units to invade northern Indochina without official orders and in advance of the timetable agreed upon with the French. Colonial garrisons in the Japanese line of march resisted and fought stoutly for three days. Then, when French military face had been saved and Tokyo had apologized for the impetuosity of its myrmidons, the occupation of northern Indochina was completed peacefully. Western newspapers said that the French had made a valiant stand. Japanese newspapers said that the soft French troops had proved no match for Japan's combat-tested veterans.

War Minister Tojo made a great disciplinary show after the unauthorized border crossing by recalling the commander of Japan's South China Army, Lieutenant General Ando Rikichi, and placing him on the inactive list. Hirohito at once reassigned the compliant general, secretly, to Strike-South preparations with the spy service in Taiwan. A year later, just before the attack on Pearl Harbor, Hirohito would reactivate Ando as the commander of the Japanese Army in Taiwan. The true instigators of the border crossing—Hirohito's emissaries—went on, unreprimanded, to delicate new assignments. Their ringleader, Major General Tominaga Kyoji, for instance, was put in charge of the Army Personnel Bureau in Tokyo to choose the commanders who would mount and lead the Strike South in the year ahead.[11]

The United States responded immediately to the Japanese move on Indochina by loaning $25 million to Chiang Kai-shek. The next day, September 26, President Roosevelt ordered a complete embargo on the sale of scrap iron and steel to nations outside the British Commonwealth and the Western Hemisphere.

On September 27, the Tripartite Pact was signed, with pomp and circumstance, in Hitler's presence at the Reich Chancellery in Berlin. By its first article Japan recognized "the leadership of Germany and Italy in the establishment of a new order in Europe." By its second article Germany and Italy extended the same recognition to Japan's predatory rights in Asia. Articles III–VI pledged the Axis partners, for a ten-year period, "to assist one another with all political, economic, and military means" if any one of them should be attacked by the United States. An addendum of secret protocols, on which Hirohito had insisted, left Japan free to decide for herself what would constitute such an American attack.

On the day that the pact was signed, *Asahi,* the largest of the Tokyo dailies, in which the imperial household owned stock, declared editorially: "It seems inevitable that a collision should occur between Japan, deter-

---

[11] The other three principals were the outgoing chief of the Japanese observer team in Hanoi, Major General Nishihara Issaku; the incoming chief of the same mission, Colonel Kill-All-Prisoners Cho Isamu; and the South China Army's vice chief of staff, Colonel Sato Kenryo.

mined to establish a sphere of influence in East Asia, including the Southwest Pacific, and the United States, which is determined to meddle in affairs on the other side of a vast ocean by every means short of war."

During the weeks which followed, Japan's presence in Indochina was steadily strengthened. Hirohito confessed to Lord Privy Seal Kido that in his Indochina policy he felt a little as if he were looting a store during a fire. When Thailand, in mid-winter, pressed her claims on French-held areas in Laos and Cambodia, Japan interceded on Thailand's behalf. A lazy little border war was fought in which the most active participants were Japanese volunteers flying for the Thai air force and reinforced Japanese observer teams at the French rear, led by Hirohito's emissary to Hanoi, Colonel Kill-All-Prisoners Cho Isamu. The French colonial government again bowed to Japanese pressure and gave Thailand the territory she demanded. The ceded areas, covered with luxuriant rain forest, were then occupied quietly by Japanese troops and used for intensive training exercises in jungle warfare.

CLEARING THE DECKS

Realizing that the Tripartite Pact and the seizure of northern Indochina had committed Japan, almost certainly, to a premature and desperate war with the West, Hirohito's Court, in October 1940, activated its back-up plan for safeguarding the Throne in case the war should end in defeat. The first step was to withdraw the members of the imperial family from positions of responsibility; the second step was to create a cover story for them so that they would seem to have played no part in the events leading to war.

The withdrawal behind the chrysanthemum curtain was begun on October 3 when the seventy-five-year-old Prince Kanin, the last surviving brother of the prince who had counseled Hirohito's great-grandfather during the opening of Japan eighty years earlier, finally resigned his office of Army chief of staff. He was replaced by his minion, General Sugiyama Hajime, the man with "a face as noncommittal as a bathroom door." Although Kanin's retirement had first been suggested by Hirohito three months earlier, the wily old prince pretended that he was resigning in disgust at the recent unauthorized activities of his subordinates in Indochina. Speaking "confidentially," he told a Western correspondent, "not even I can any longer control the troops in the field."

Another member of the imperial family went further and actually sent word to U.S. Ambassador Grew that Hirohito had approved the Tripartite Pact out of fear of assassination by Army extremists.

Behind the scenes, a certain Captain Takagi Sokichi of the Navy began to consult regularly with Lord Privy Seal Kido and Secretary-Spy Harada. Captain Takagi had been assigned by Hirohito in 1939 to the Naval Staff

College to study "postwar problems." He would remain at his task until 1946. Before the outbreak of war it would be he who would arrange to send naval listening teams to Europe to pick up and transmit any Western peace feelers to Japan. During the war it would be he who would organize the Navy's part in the Peace Faction which finally staged the reception for General MacArthur in 1945.

Secretary-Spy Harada made his contribution to the imperial cover story by producing a document now known as the Saionji-Harada Memoirs. He had been writing the memoirs for ten years as a part of his job of managing and distracting old Prince Saionji. In them he had regularly included all possible justifications for the Emperor's conduct and all possible gossip and ceremonial detail which might occupy Saionji's attention. Once a week he had taken the latest installment of the manuscript, neatly transcribed from dictation by Prince Konoye's sister-in-law, to Saionji for marginal comments and editing. Saionji had understood that the journal was being kept for Hirohito's perusal—to show the young Emperor the day-to-day complexities of politics. Harada was a good writer with a flair for color and personalities, and Saionji had enjoyed his role as editor. In Harada's pages the old man had often found it possible to look at trees and ignore the forest.

By October 1940, Harada's manuscript had grown to 10,000 pages, and now he showed it to Prince Takamatsu, Hirohito's favorite brother, a lieutenant commander attached to the Navy General Staff. Prince Takamatsu agreed that it would be a most valuable document in the event that the Emperor ever needed whitewashing. Arrangements were made to move the manuscript from the vaults of the Sumitomo Bank, where Harada held a nominal vice presidency, to the sanctity of Prince Takamatsu's villa, where Army secret policemen would not be tempted to destroy it in the interests of patriotism and the war effort.

These private preparations for the possibility of failure were made behind a façade of great public bustle and bluster. On October 8, the Japanese ambassador in Washington handed U.S. Secretary of State Cordell Hull a note warning that "future relations between Japan and the United States" would become "unpredictable" if Roosevelt persisted in curtailing U.S.-Japanese trade.

On October 12, Prime Minister Prince Konoye formally inaugurated his monolithic totalitarian party, the I.R.A.A. or Imperial Rule Assistance Association.

On October 16, sixteen million Americans registered for military duty under the new Selective Training and Service Act, the cornerstone for later U.S. war preparations. In the fortnight that followed, U.S. military representatives in Washington, London, and Java began conversations with their British and Dutch counterparts on joint defense planning for the Western colonies in Southeast Asia.

On October 17, Hirohito held a special ceremony at the Palace Shrine to invoke "the protection of the gods and a happy outcome to the treaty" with Germany.

On October 24, by Court arrangement, a delegation of Japanese naval officers traveled to Osaka, Japan's mercantile center, for a three-day conference with Japanese bankers. For the Navy's samurai to set foot in Osaka was a concession. In Osaka the traditional greeting was not "hello" or "good morning" but "are you making money?" True samurai so despised such materialism that during the three centuries of Tokugawa rule merchants had been ranked below artisans and farmers in the caste structure. Now, however, the aristocratic samurai needed help.

The naval delegation was led by Vice Admiral Yamamoto Isoroku, commander-in-chief of the Combined Fleet, the suave opportunist who had negotiated naval limitations in London in 1929 and 1934 and who would shortly devise and lead the attack on Pearl Harbor. Yamamoto told the bankers that unless the number of ships and aircraft in the fleet could be doubled in a year, he would be forced to retire to the Inland Sea and harass the enemy like a pirate while U.S. carrier planes were strafing Tokyo. The cunning elders of Japanese finance were pleased by Yamamoto's frank and unassuming approach and put their grizzled heads together to fund a crash effort for completing the Japanese naval building program a year and a half ahead of schedule.

During the naval finance negotiations in Osaka, Hirohito succumbed to worry and overwork and retired for two weeks with a severe case of flu. As soon as he had recovered, on November 9, he requested that a secret conference of staff chiefs and inspector generals be held in his presence two days later to review the progress which had been made in military preparations.

The next day, November 10, Hirohito presided at an official celebration of the nation's "2600th birthday." He impressed all foreign ambassadors and correspondents by the clarity and force with which he delivered a set speech in favor of peace and science. He was introduced by his brother Lieutenant Commander Prince Takamatsu. Takamatsu's voice was broadcast on the radio as a sign to all Japanese that the decision to fight on the side of Germany had been approved by both the imperial family and the Navy.

DEATH OF SAIONJI

On November 12, 1940, when he had just turned ninety-one, and when all that he had lived for had just been thrown away, old Prince Saionji was reported at Court to be ill with a kidney inflammation. Secretary-Spy Harada hastened to the Sit-and-Fish Villa in Okitsu to have a few last words with the old man. "I told him," wrote Harada, "of the magnificence of the 2600th anniversary of the founding of the Empire and of Konoye's latest efforts to negotiate with Chiang Kai-shek."

"No matter what is done right from now on," murmured Saionji, "I don't think Chiang Kai-shek will ever agree to what Japan says."

"The interview," wrote Harada, "was like that, and so I withdrew after five or six minutes."

Six days later Saionji delivered his last bon mot when he said to his doctor, "Never mind these details about the local parts of my body. Please endeavor more to see to the recovery of the strength of the whole body."

On November 24, weak but clearheaded to the last, the sad old man of Japanese liberalism finally expired, leaving the Throne without check or balance. Hirohito had sent fresh milk and flowers to his bedside during his sickness. Now, on November 25, Lord Privy Seal Kido went personally to Okitsu to express the imperial regrets.

At the obsequies Kido met, for the first time since the Nomonhan War in 1939, his former contact with the Sorge spy ring, Saionji Kinkazu, the grandson of the deceased. Kido had left young Saionji uninformed during the recent pact negotiations with Germany, and Soviet spy Sorge had had to rely for news entirely on his sources in the German Embassy. Kido's reason for neglecting his young protégé was not personal: Ribbentrop's pact negotiator, Stahmer, had simply brought word from Berlin that Sorge was finally suspected of being a Soviet agent.

A routine Gestapo security check in June 1940 had uncovered Sorge's early affiliations with the Communist party in Germany. The head of the Gestapo's foreign intelligence section, Walter Schellenberg, on reviewing the evidence, had decided that Sorge's dispatches to the Nazi Party Press Department were too valuable to dispense with as yet. And so instead of exposing Sorge, Schellenberg had sent a Gestapo colonel to Japan with the Stahmer Tripartite-Pact mission to keep an eye on Sorge. The Gestapo colonel, Josef Meisinger, was a dull-eyed robot who had made himself odious even in Berlin by his officious sadism at the rape of Warsaw in 1939. In Tokyo Meisinger quickly and clumsily revealed German suspicions about Sorge to colleagues in the Japanese secret police. The aristocrats around Hirohito learned of Meisinger's indiscretion and at once wrote off their links with the Sorge spy ring as too dangerous, politically, for further use.

Less than a week after Meisinger's arrival in Tokyo, Prime Minister Prince Konoye had offered young Saionji Kinkazu the post of ambassador to Australia in an effort to get him out of harm's way. Young Saionji, however, had refused the appointment, saying that he did not wish to be expatriated at an exciting juncture in Japanese history. Konoye warned him that the nation was swinging toward the right and that Saionji, as a leftist, might find himself in a difficult position. Young Saionji hastily manufactured a camouflage for himself by becoming the leader of a rightist cell which included Mikami Taku, one of the young naval lieutenants, recently released from prison, who had led the deadly attack on Prime Minister Inoue in 1932.

Now, two months later, at Saionji's funeral in November 1940, Lord Privy Seal Kido adopted a noncommittal correctness in his dealings with the young Saionji heir. He would have further use for young Saionji in the months ahead, but for the moment he was turning his back on the ashes of old Saionji and on the muddled humane liberalism which they represented.

UNCANNY FORESIGHTS

On December 3, 1940, the day after Saionji's state funeral, Hirohito suffered one of his recurrent attacks of self-doubt and fear. Calling in Lord Privy Seal Kido, he complained that relations with the Soviet Union still gave no assurance of safety in the rear when Japan turned south. Negotiations for a new Russo-Japanese fishing treaty were going poorly. A special effort must be made to neutralize the colossus in the north. Kido was himself in a dark mood that day and struggled to find his usual words of comfort. In an astonishing display of long-range realism he admitted to the Emperor:

After this world war, the United States and the U.S.S.R. may unquestionably emerge unhurt when all other nations are devastated. I can imagine, therefore, that our country, which is placed between these two giants, may face great hardships. However, there is no need for despair. When these two lose the competition of other countries in their respective vicinities, they will grow careless and corrupt. We will simply have to sleep in the woodshed and eat bitter fruits for a few decades. Then when we have refurbished our manliness inside and out, we may still achieve a favorable result.

In so many words, Hirohito was reassured, in December 1940, that his purposed attack on the United States was a calculated gamble which could be recouped even if it lost. Kido's encouragement was bleak but still far more cheerful than the predictions of most of Japan's professional military strategists. For instance, Fleet Commander Yamamoto Isoroku, who would have to plan the attack on the United States, viewed the future with unrelieved fatalism. On October 14, he had dined with Secretary-Spy Harada, and staring gloomily into his saké cup, had conjured up a vision of apocalypse:

It is my opinion that in order to fight the United States we must be ready to challenge almost the entire world. . . . I shall exert myself to the utmost but I expect to die on the deck of my flagship, the battleship *Nagato*. In those evil days you will see Tokyo burnt to the ground at least three times.

The result will be prolonged suffering for the people. And you and Konoye and the others, pitiful as it may be to contemplate, will probably be torn limb from limb by the masses. It is indeed a perplexing situation. We have come to such a pass that our fate is inescapable.

The national program had reached its point of benedictus and no return. The gods had spoken. Hirohito had committed himself. And well-informed Japanese like Vice Admiral Yamamoto might pray hopefully for miracles but realistically they could only prepare themselves proudly to do and die as samurai.

24

PASSIVE RESISTANCE

(1940–1941)

YAMAMOTO'S DUTY

Hirohito never reversed his decision of September 1940—to strike south even at the cost of war with the United States—but in the twelve months before Pearl Harbor he had to withstand constant pressure from those about him who still hoped for a national reprieve. Only Lord Privy Seal Kido and War Minister Tojo stood by him wholeheartedly and refused to question the Imperial Will. Surrounded by subtle, gentle opponents, Hirohito succeeded, nevertheless, in sponsoring and co-ordinating a secret war plan which surprised the world. It involved hundreds of thousands of men and millions of tons of valuable state property, yet neither its foreign nor domestic opponents appreciated its effectiveness until it was already well on its way to success. In realizing this astonishing feat, Hirohito made free use of the brains of officers in the Army and Navy—the only brains left in Japan which still dared to oppose the war openly and frankly.

One of the stoutest and most influential opponents of a war with the United States was its chief strategic expediter and implementer: Admiral Yamamoto Isoroku, the commander in chief of Japan's *Rengo Kantai* or Combined Fleet. Since his feats in negotiating increases in Japanese naval strength at the international disarmament conferences of 1930 and 1934, he had risen meteorically in his service. His flying protégés of the Misty Lagoon had proven themselves in the Navy's long-range bombing missions in China. His unorthodox weapons systems were now acknowledged to be the most efficient in the armed forces. He was the darling of every armchair strategist and the most popular commander in the fleet. No longer did he need imperial family patronage to find entertainment in the stews of Tsukiji. He now enjoyed the exclusive favors of Chrysanthemum Path, one of the seven most sought-after geisha in Tokyo.

Yamamoto had observed to his chief of staff after a successful exercise with torpedo bombers in May 1940 that a "crushing blow can be struck against an unsuspecting enemy fleet by mass torpedo attack." Detail by detail, throughout the summer of 1940, he privately worked out his daring plan for a surprise attack on Pearl Harbor—and nightly he brooded on the slips which could spill all his cup in a dark pool of blood and shame. He realized, as an experienced intelligence officer, that the Achilles' heel of his plan was security. How could he push such a gambling, controversial scheme through the wordy decision mill of Japan's family government without hints leaking out to the enemy through the innumerable middlemen and double agents who were part of the political system? How could he assemble an armada and move it two thirds of the way across the Pacific without alerting the U.S. radio picket ships which prowled the shores of Asia monitoring Japanese fleet messages?

Yamamoto answered the second question first. Throughout the summer of 1940 he taunted naval code experts with excoriating comments on the conventionality of the fleet's best communications disguises. As a result he was rewarded in October with a new Admirals' Code, a cryptographic system so complex and so novel in principle that Japanese signalmen had trouble using it and U.S. cryptanalysts failed to delve its mysteries until almost the end of World War II. Yamamoto began to use the new code for all top-secret fleet dispatches on November 1, 1940. The fact that it remained uncracked was to be one of the principal reasons for the success of Admiral Yamamoto's Pearl Harbor plan.

Yamamoto solved his other security problem by going directly to the summit of the Japanese pyramid. Late in November 1940, through his friend Prince Takamatsu, a commander in the Navy General Staff, he communicated the Pearl Harbor plan to Commander Takamatsu's brother, Emperor Hirohito. Hirohito was interested in it and after a few days' thought instructed Takamatsu to have it turned over for independent evaluation to a top-security circle of naval officers in the imperial cabal. On the advice of Takamatsu's close friend Rear Admiral Onishi Takajiro, who later conceived and commanded the kamikaze corps of suicide pilots, the study of Yamamoto's plan was turned over to one of the Navy's most brilliant flight officers, Commander Genda Minoru. Genda, during the first two weeks of February 1941, locked himself in his quarters on the aircraft carrier *Kaga,* at anchor in Ariake Bay on the southern island of Kyushu, and arrived at a minutely critical but favorable verdict. Agreeing with Yamamoto, he concluded—so he later wrote when he had become the commander of Japan's postwar American-equipped Self-Defense Air Force—"that the attack would be extremely hazardous but would have a reasonable chance of success."

On this assurance, while orthodox admirals wracked their brains for other, less desperate solutions to the problem of Japan's imperial ambition, Yamamoto went ahead and began training his most trustworthy fleet officers for the parts they would have to play in his scheme.[1] Late in the spring of 1941 he selected the harbor of Kagoshima, the old capital of the seagoing Satsuma clan, as the site for carrier-pilot exercises in dive bombing and low-level torpedo-dropping runs. Aside from its historic associations as the sixteenth century womb of the Japanese Navy, Kagoshima harbor was suitable because its topography closely resembled that of Pearl Harbor.

UNIT 82

Yamamoto's dutiful war planning for the Navy was matched in the Army by a research team, known as Unit 82, set up in Taiwan. It came under the command of General Itagaki, the Baden-Baden Reliable who had expedited the planning for the conquest of Manchuria in 1929 and 1930. The real brains behind the unit, however, were those of Lieutenant General Yamashita Tomoyuki, the later "Tiger of Malaya." It was Yamashita in 1934 and 1935 who had led on the young officers of the National Principle Group to mount the February Mutiny and so discredit the Strike-North Faction.

Before Tiger Yamashita could see his proposals for Unit 82 enacted, he was dispatched by Hirohito, in November 1940, to make a first-hand study of the *Wehrmacht*'s preparations for the invasion of England. In Yamashita's absence, an unsavory colonel from Army Intelligence, Hayashi Yoshihide, was put in charge of the unit.[2] Hayashi, however, was given as assistant Yamashita's most trusted minion in the intrigues of 1934 and 1935, Tsuji Masanobu, the former military academy instructor, now a lieutenant colonel. Tsuji had made a name for himself in dispatches by his ruthlessly puritanic zeal as a field commander in China and at Nomon-

---

[1] The details of this previously untold story come from verbal sources, but the crucial point is recorded in the most unimpeachable of all primary sources, a memorandum written later that same year, in October, by Army Chief of Staff General Sugiyama: "In January 1941, in answer to Commander of Great Fleet Yamamoto, Emperor ordered Rear Admiral Onishi to research Hawaii attack."
It is an eloquent commentary on Japanese historical research that when this piece of primary documentary evidence—directly contradicting all the secondary accounts previously printed—was published (together with other memoranda by Sugiyama) in Japan in 1967, it appears that not a single Japanese much less Western newspaper carried an item on it.

[2] Hayashi had masterminded the Nonni Bridge Incident which had served as pretext for the Japanese invasion of northern Manchuria in November 1931. Later in 1942 and 1943 he would make himself feared and hated as the director general of Japanese Military Administration in the Philippines.

han. He was especially admired at Court for having taken a torch one night in Shanghai and having personally burned down forty Chinese brothels which he felt were sapping the fighting spirit of troops on their way to the front.

Tsuji joined Unit 82 on January 1, 1941 and was given charge of the planning for what was expected to be the most difficult part of the Strike South: the capture of Singapore. Junior officers were assigned to study the subsidiary strikes against the Philippines and the Dutch East Indies. The unit's first task was to cull and collate the roomfuls of intelligence about Southeast Asia which civilian agents of the spy service had been amassing in Taiwan since 1900, and more intensively since 1934 when Hirohito had first privately announced his decision to look south.

To open the doors for Tsuji and his colleagues in Taiwan and to show them around the archives, Emperor Hirohito delegated his mother's brother-in-law, Count Ohtani Kozui. Ohtani was the renegade abbot of Kyoto's *Nishi Hongan-ji,* or West Fundamental Temple of Buddha. In 1912 Count Ohtani had been discovered selling temple treasures and spending temple monies for his personal gratifications. He had resigned as chief abbot of his sect, which was and is one of the most popular and powerful in Japan, and had taken to missionary work, founding branch temples throughout China and Southeast Asia. In the mid-twenties he had been expelled from Java for nonpayment of the mortgage interest on a large temple property, a sacred mountain, which he had bought there. In some of the sultanates of Borneo and Malaya his missionary temples were closed as subversive organizations by the local rulers. He was, however, a good friend of the sultan of Johore, the wealthy potentate who owned the best rubber plantations in British Malaya. And in Japan he retained a position of great influence, at the center of the Strike-South circle at Court. After 1930 he divided his attention between Strike-South politicians in the Diet in Tokyo and Strike-South business colonials centered in Taiwan.

Under Count Ohtani's imperial tutelage, Lieutenant Colonel Tsuji and the other officers of Unit 82 were able to review all the geographic, ethnic, and political information on Southeast Asia stored by Japanese business and religious organizations in Taiwan. The young Army officers, trained in modern German techniques of blitzkrieg, found many gaps in the data which had been collected. In March Tsuji and his colleagues began to go along on overflights with Japanese commercial pilots and Japanese naval shore patrols to fill in the lacunae in the maps on hand. At the same time, at Tiger Yamashita's insistence, select shock troops were assembling on the island of Hainan and in the forests of northwestern Indochina for practice in techniques of jungle infiltration and for training in amphibious operations against reef-girt islands.

Yamamoto's Navy had meanwhile sent fresh spies to the Hawaiian Islands to watch with binoculars the comings and goings of ships through the entrance of Pearl Harbor. A monitor service was established for all radio messages in the Pearl Harbor area. The monitors got to know the call signals of the various ships in the U.S. Pacific fleet and the tastes of the various supply officers. After a few months of listening the monitors could tell which ships were in port by the orders for groceries delivered at various Pearl Harbor piers.

Farther to the east in Mexico, Japanese naval intelligence established a listening post in Baja California to keep track of U.S. Navy ship movements from West Coast ports and also an office in Mexico City to eavesdrop on the movements of the U.S. Atlantic fleet.

NATIONAL HALFHEARTEDNESS

Even while they presided over war preparations Admiral Yamamoto and his Army colleagues took every opportunity to plead with their political leaders "not to be dragged into war." Again and again Yamamoto recited a refrain which he had first delivered to Prime Minister Prince Konoye in August 1940: "In the first six to twelve months of a war with the United States and Great Britain I will run wild and win victory upon victory. But then, if the war continues after that, I have no expectation of success."

As the architect of the naval development program, Yamamoto was idolized in the ranks of the fleet and his views carried immense weight. His Army friend and counterpart, the strategic genius Lieutenant General Ishiwara Kanji, who had planned the conquest of Manchuria, agreed with Yamamoto and spread his gospel of caution to hundreds of junior officers in the Army.

By the end of January 1941 persistent failure to meet new, unrealistic ship and plane building schedules had persuaded many Japanese naval officers that haste was making waste and that the crash program inaugurated in September 1940 was actually retarding naval preparations. One of the few war plants which had met its norms was the mint which was printing paper money for use in the territories Japan hoped to conquer. There were pesos to spend in Manila, rupees to spend in Calcutta, pounds to spend in Brisbane, even dollars to spend in Honolulu—if and when enough ships could be built to transport the spenders. The worthless paper money became a joke in informed circles, and it was said that the crisp new bills "made ideal spills for lighting dream pipes."

Army procurement officers knew the difficulties of their opposite numbers in the Navy and helped to spread dissatisfaction with war planning to the Army rank and file. After years of steady growth, the Army was not budgeted in 1941 to add so much as a single new division. Before the war with China there had been seventeen divisions. Seven new ones had been mustered in 1937, ten in 1938, thirteen in 1939, and eleven in 1940. Now, on the eve of war, because of the taxing demands on the economy made by the Navy's crash program, the accumulated fifty-eight divisions, manned by over a million men, marked time in China with holding operations and elsewhere with training exercises.

In business and economic circles, too, the planning for war was meeting powerful opposition. The professional politicians of the Diet, brandishing their one weapon, the power to veto budget increases, cut appropriations for the new national mass party, the I.R.A.A., to which they were all supposed to belong, from 100 million yen (about $23 million) to a niggardly eight million yen (about $1.8 million). Prince Konoye persuaded Hirohito to have the Army bolster the sagging New Structure by instructing all reservists to join the I.R.A.A. Diet opposition persisted nonetheless, and Prime Minister Konoye was obliged to let the I.R.A.A. subside as "an educational and spiritual association" rather than a true totalitarian party. Count Arima, Hirohito's in-law, resigned as I.R.A.A. leader and his place was taken by the popular, retired General Yanagawa Heisuke, the one-time Strike-Northist who had redeemed himself in Hirohito's eyes by commanding the amphibious flanking operation which had made possible the drive on Nanking in 1937.

Bankers and industrialists fought Konoye's totalitarian structure by refusing to co-operate with the "New Bureaucrats" whom Kido had trained years earlier, from his desk in the Commerce Ministry, to take over the national economy and "rationalize" it for war. Since Hirohito and the Army and Navy were asking for a national budget amounting to two thirds of the national income—a budget of which 75 per cent would have to be met by deficit financing—the moneybags of the nation had their way. For a time it seemed that all war planning would have to be abandoned. But the most talented member of Hirohito's cabal somehow negotiated a compromise. This was the ubiquitous Suzuki Tei-ichi, now a lieutenant general. Since handling the looting of Nanking in 1937 he had had charge of the economic exploitation of China as the acting director of the Prosperous Asia Institute or Asia Development Board. In April 1941, by agreement with the old men of Japan's family cartels, he resigned his Army commission and assumed command of the Cabinet Planning Board as a minister of state in Konoye's government. In this capacity he undertook to organize the Japanese economy by working within the framework of the family alliances which had controlled high finance theretofore. So well did he succeed in his difficult post that he remained at it, co-ordinating Japan's industrial war effort, until July 1944.

DIPLOMATIC OFFENSIVES

In early 1941, as second thoughts trickled down to the subordinate motor centers of Japan's military mind and as general dissatisfaction mounted with the perils and paucities foreseen in the proposed war with the United States, Hirohito pressed for the accomplishment of two diplomatic missions which had been promised to him at the time of the Tripartite Pact decision: negotiation of understandings with the Soviet Union and with the United States. In his straightforward way Hirohito wanted the Soviet Union to agree not to attack Japan from the rear when she began to strike south in pursuit of the wealth of the Indies. In return he was willing to relinquish Japanese oil and coal rights in the upper, Russian half of the northern island of Sakhalin, lying between Hokkaido and Kamchatka, and to promise Stalin that Japan would not aid Germany in any future war against the U.S.S.R.

The purpose of negotiating with the United States was more subtle. Hirohito thought that the U.S. government, in view of its probable commitment soon to join England in the war against Hitler, might be willing to advise Chiang Kai-shek to cede Manchuria and adjacent provinces to Japan in return for Japanese withdrawal from most of central and southern China. In addition, to keep the samurai sword sheathed, the United States might agree to special trade and oil exploitation rights for Japan in Southeast Asia and the Indies. By consolidating and expanding such footholds, Japan might be able to gain the objectives of the Strike South without having to fight for them. If the United States stood on principle and refused to make the necessary concessions, a second function would be served by the Washington negotiations: they would gain time for the Navy and lull the Americans into a false sense of security while Yamamoto was preparing his attack plans. Most important, the negotiations, if skillfully reported in the Japanese press, would unite the nation behind the war effort, persuading pro-American Japanese that everything had been tried and that the United States still remained intractable.

Hirohito entrusted the American half of his diplomatic offensive to a sixty-four-year-old admiral, a genial six-foot tower of a man with a broad shoulder for responsibility, Nomura Kichisaburo. A Court emissary approached Nomura and asked him to accept the post of ambassador in Washington immediately after the Tripartite Pact decision in September 1940. At first, however, Nomura refused the appointment. He knew that he was being selected because, as a naval attaché in Washington during World War I, he had struck up a personal acquaintance with Franklin D. Roosevelt, then Assistant Secretary of the Navy. Nomura was pessimistic about exacting concessions from the United States, and he was aware that he might be used as a blind while Japan was training her guns. Throughout October 1940 he continued to refuse the Washington post, explaining candidly that he wanted no part in an "act which might disgrace the nation." Finally in November Hirohito summoned Nomura to a private audience and assured him that the U.S. negotiations would be carried out in a spirit of realistic sincerity. Then and only then did Nomura capitulate and agree to serve.

Hirohito assigned the Russian half of his diplomatic program to Foreign Minister Matsuoka Yosuke. Matsuoka could not be trusted to handle the American half because ever since coming to office in July he had shown a persistent inability to form a policy for dealing with America. Hirohito had commented on this inability many times but he was inclined to be tolerant of the foreign minister's peculiarities. After all Matsuoka was a Christian and had grown up in Seattle. Since 1926 he had served faithfully with Hirohito's Big Brothers in a multitude of assignments. He had shown great craft in negotiating the settlement of the Fake War in Shanghai in 1932. He had then predicted correctly that the West would take no reprisals if Japan walked out of the League of Nations over the Lytton Commission Report on Manchuria. A year later, in 1933, he had commanded much grudging Western admiration by his blunt and honest style in actually conducting the League withdrawal. Since then he had consistently pleased the Emperor with his straightforward cynicism and logic in regard to diplomacy.

In January 1941, when Nomura was packing his trunks to go to Washington, Hirohito pressed Foreign Minister Matsuoka to begin negotiating the desired pact of mutual non-aggression with Stalin. The Japanese ambassador in Moscow, Peerless Pimp Tatekawa Yoshiji, the retired lieutenant general who had slept out the seizure of Mukden with the geisha of the Literary Chrysanthemum in 1931, had been conducting preliminary conversations with Soviet Foreign Minister Molotov throughout the last quarter of 1940.

Japanese Foreign Minister Matsuoka insisted that, before Ambassador Tatekawa committed himself too deeply, Matsuoka should personally reconnoiter the European situation. Prime Minister Konoye, who had observed his foreign minister closely for fifteen years, at once warned Hirohito to look with suspicion on Matsuoka's proposed trip to Berlin. Konoye pointed out that throughout the mid-Thirties Matsuoka had shown signs of sympathy with the Strike-North Faction which advocated Russia as a safer opponent than the United States. Moreover Matsuoka, despite much threatening talk, did apparently harbor a feeling of obligation to the United States. It was known that, in 1933, without fanfare and out of his own pocket, he had erected a fine marble monument over the grave of the American woman in Seattle who had taken him in and raised him as a child. It was also known that he spoke mysteriously to American friends in Tokyo about his mission to prevent war between the United States and Japan. Finally, almost alone in Hirohito's entourage of intimates, he had remained on good terms with old Prince Saionji until his dying day.

Hirohito tended to dismiss the insinuations of Prince Konoye. After all, Matsuoka had negotiated the Tripartite Pact which gave Japan a semblance of claim to the Southeast Asia colonies of the nations which Germany had conquered in Europe. Also, Matsuoka had from the first upstaged Prime

Minister Konoye and War Minister Tojo. He clearly had the fault of vanity. He loved the limelight and moved everywhere with a troupe of newsmen at his heels. Hirohito suspected that the shy and furtive Konoye was merely jealous of Matsuoka.

And so, in early 1941, Hirohito disregarded Konoye's doubts and gave Matsuoka leave to spend a month in Russia, Germany, and Italy, satisfying his stated need for first-hand knowledge of "world realities." In so doing, Hirohito made a mistake. He enabled Matsuoka to gain a position of importance in the eyes of the public and from that position to launch a six-month campaign of subversive procrastination against the imperial program.[3]

Matsuoka did not want Japan to sign a pact of neutrality with the U.S.S.R. because he hoped secretly that Japan would soon join Germany in war with the U.S.S.R. He knew from the reports of the Japanese Embassy in Berlin that, unless Ukrainian wheat and Caucasian oil were made available in desired quantities to the Reich's purchasing agents, Hitler might soon abrogate his nonaggression pact with Stalin and attack the Soviet Union. Matsuoka anticipated that Germany might win such a war quickly, in which case Japan would be unsafe from German aggression unless she held, as buffer zone, the eastern third of the Soviet Union. Then again Germany might bog down in Russia in a war that would last for decades. In that case Great Britain, supported by the United States, would ultimately win and Japan would be judged least harshly if she had attacked only communism. For the moment Matsuoka placed prime importance, for both personal and patriotic reasons, on the avoidance of war with the United States.

MATSUOKA'S GRAND TOUR

On February 3, 1941, Prime Minister Konoye and the chiefs of the Army and Navy met in liaison conference to consider Matsuoka's proposed trip to Berlin. They agreed that he was "voluble and unconventional" and recommended that his powers and objectives be carefully explained to him before he set out. In particular they requested that Matsuoka make no promises to Hitler about an immediate Japanese attack on Singapore.

Since the signing of the Tripartite Pact the German military attachés in Tokyo had had a sand table set up at their embassy to show Japanese visitors how easy it would be to take Singapore. Naval members of Imperial Headquarters had witnessed the table-top demonstrations and had returned

---

[3] The type of devious passive resistance in which Matsuoka was indulging was common in Japan at that time. U.S. Ambassador Grew reported several examples in the spring of 1941. In a translation of a speech by Hitler run in one of the English-language newspapers, for instance, a mischievous Japanese typesetter had changed *"Herrenvolk,* the master race," to "hairy horde, the monster ape."

tight-lipped to their own charts of Japanese military capacity. Matsuoka had seen the table-top maneuvers and had ever since taunted War Minister Tojo with questions as to why Japan should not seize Singapore at once. Tojo had responded by asking Foreign Minister Matsuoka why he had not yet forged the classic Eurasian alliance of Germany, Russia, and Japan which geopoliticians had been saying for decades could someday dominate the earth.

As a result of the liaison conference of February 3, Hirohito made his own personal study of recent diplomatic dispatches and of Japan's foreign-policy posture. On February 7 he called in Lord Privy Seal Kido and complained that the latest cables from Ambassador Kurusu Saburo in Berlin indicated a strong likelihood that Germany would soon betray previous understandings with Japan by attacking Russia. In such an eventuality, Hirohito asked, was Japan obligated to give up the Strike South and assist Germany by a Strike North?

Kido did his best to soothe the Emperor by assuring him that a German-Russian war would not break out immediately. Kido acknowledged, however, that the Tripartite Pact with Germany might create a serious problem if Japan, having already embarked upon the Strike South, should be asked by Germany to "turn around and go north again." Kido concluded that "we must therefore be extremely cautious in developing our Strike-South policy" and that "we must use the opportunity of Matsuoka's impending visit to Germany and Italy in order to get to the bottom of Hitler's and Mussolini's intentions."

Hirohito gave the problem several weeks' thought and then issued Foreign Minister Matsuoka strict instructions. In Italy and Germany he was to act purely in a private capacity and to find out as much as he could. In Moscow, however, he was to act officially and, if possible, conclude a neutrality pact with Stalin which would serve as an excuse for Japan not to join Germany in a war against Russia.

On March 3, the day Hirohito made clear to Matsuoka that these were his imperial wishes, Lord Privy Seal Kido met in another room of the palace with young Saionji Kinkazu, informing him that he was to accompany Matsuoka on his mission to Moscow and was to use all his left-wing connections to create a favorable atmosphere for talks between Matsuoka and Molotov, or between Matsuoka and Stalin. Saionji reported back to Ozaki, the Japanese agent who worked both with Soviet spy Sorge at the German Embassy and with Dr. Okawa of the spy service at the South Manchuria Railroad Research Institute. Ozaki duly briefed Sorge on the full background of Foreign Minister Matsuoka's trip abroad. Sorge then relayed his information to the Red Army's Fourth Bureau.

Sorge had always believed that the main purpose of his intelligence work in Tokyo was to prevent a Japanese attack on the Soviet Union. Now, in his radio dispatch to Siberia, he made it clear that Japan wished to strike south and needed only some assurance of Soviet neutrality in rear areas before doing so. The alternative, he stressed, might be Japanese participation in a German invasion of the Soviet Union.

After a parting audience with Hirohito on March 11,[4] Foreign Minister Matsuoka set out on March 12 with Saionji Kinkazu and other technicians to ride the long tracks of the Trans-Siberian Railway. He arrived in Moscow on March 15 and spent ten days there talking in a desultory way about the possibility of a Soviet-Japanese neutrality pact. Since he wanted Japan to fight Russia as a preventive to the ills of fighting the United States, he did not throw himself wholeheartedly into his task. With nothing accomplished, he went on to Berlin, where he arrived on March 26.

That night Hitler was preoccupied with an unforeseen political coup in Yugoslavia which forced him to invade that country. He postponed his state reception of Matsuoka until the next day, March 27. He had already, three weeks earlier, written and circulated a memo to his officers explaining German objectives in dealing with the Japanese foreign minister:

> It must be the aim of the collaboration based upon the Tripartite Pact to induce Japan as soon as possible to take active measures in the Far East. . . . Operation Barbarossa [the scheduled attack on Russia] will create most favorable political and military prerequisites. . . . The seizure of Singapore as the key British position in the Far East would mean a decisive success for the entire war conduct of the Three Powers. . . . The Japanese must not be given any intimation of the Barbarossa operation.

The state secretary of the German Foreign Office, Ernst Weizsacker, and the German naval commander in chief, Erich Raeder, both disagreed with Hitler's desire to keep secrets from the Japanese and asked that Matsuoka be told about the planned invasion of Russia.

On March 27, as soon as Hitler had delivered orders to deal with the little problem of Yugoslavia, Matsuoka was given a Wagnerian stage reception of black boots in goose step and of dinner in full dress at the *Reichskanzlerei*. That night and for the next week, Matsuoka remained closeted with the highest officials of the Third Reich, spending the best part of four days with Ribbentrop and of four hours, on two occasions, with Hitler. He learned that for the time being Hitler had definitely suspended Operation Sea Lion, the invasion of England. Nevertheless, Ribbentrop pressed him to agree to an immediate Japanese attack on British Malaya. Hitler told him that "never in the human imagination" had a nation been presented with such favorable opportunities. "The moment will never return. It is unique in history." For once in his life Matsuoka

---

[4] At which he proudly reported the conclusion of Japan's successful, self-interested mediation of the border dispute between Thailand and French Indochina. He made much of the fact that this was the first time that Japan had ever played the part of a Big-Power arbitrator.

listened and said little. "He sat there inscrutably," wrote Ribbentrop's official secretary-translator, Dr. Paul Schmidt, "in no way revealing how these curious remarks affected him."

As to Russia, Ribbentrop told Matsuoka that German-Soviet relations had become "correct but unfriendly." Hitler pointed out that the Reich had over 160 divisions massed on the Soviet frontier. Matsuoka and his aides had noticed the signs of preparations for war when they had passed through the Russian frontier the previous week. Ribbentrop admitted that a German war with Russia was "in the realm of possibilities" and assured Matsuoka that, if it broke out, the Reich would "crush the Soviet Union within a matter of months."

For his own part Matsuoka lied outrageously. He promised that he would work personally for a Japanese attack upon Singapore but would have to advocate such a move only "in hypothetical terms" for the moment because many influential "intellectuals" in Japan were still afraid of the Anglo-American partnership which had won the last world war. More forthrightly, Matsuoka revealed to the Germans that he was commissioned to seek an understanding with Russia which might free Japanese hands and make the contemplated attack on Singapore more attractive in terms of practical domestic politics. Ribbentrop warned him "not to get too close to Russia," assured him that Germany stood ready to attack Russia if Russia ever endangered Japan's rear, and finally agreed that a Russo-Japanese understanding would do no harm.

When Matsuoka had "sat inscrutably" for a week, eager to hear ever more and more of Ribbentrop's boastful persuasions, Ribbentrop's translator Dr. Schmidt noted that the proceedings were beginning to tax the "Gilbert-and-Sullivan" talents of the Third Reich's protocol officers. The dapper, energetic Matsuoka was a dwarf beside the sleek and bloated Ribbentrop. Cartoonists figured a shrewd sparrow beside a large pouter pigeon.

On April 1 Matsuoka sensed that his entertainment was growing wearisome to his hosts and gave them a brief respite by taking a two-day side-journey to Rome to talk with Mussolini. After enjoying Il Duce's most hospitable pomp he returned to Berlin for further soundings of German intentions. Hitler again granted him private audience and voluntarily committed himself to an assurance which Japan had not asked for: "If Japan gets into a conflict with the United States, Germany on her part will take the necessary steps at once. . . . Germany will participate in case of a conflict between Japan and America."

HUGGING THE BEAR

Matsuoka began his return to the East on April 6. Deceits were buzzing in his ears but he traveled with a light heart for he had revealed less truth than anybody else. Hitler demanded vehemently that Japan play her part as an ally by attacking Singapore. But Hitler was obviously planning a war soon with the Soviet Union and would no doubt be satisfied if Japan waited a while and attacked Siberia instead. Hirohito favored the attack on Singapore but was not yet ready for the concomitant of war with the United States. He wanted Matsuoka to safeguard the Japanese rear in Manchuria by concluding a pact of mutual neutrality with Russia. If necessary Matsuoka would have to obey his instructions. But later, when the German-Soviet war broke out, he could tell Hirohito that the totalitarian diplomats of the New Order regarded such scraps of paper lightly. The Japanese Army General Staff had wanted for decades to fight Russia. The *Wehrmacht*'s drive on Moscow would provide the perfect opportunity. To spurn it would be politically difficult for Hirohito. It looked as if, after all, Matsuoka might be able to save Japan from war with the United States and fulfill all his promises to friends in the West.

Arriving in Moscow on April 8, Matsuoka paid his first call not on Foreign Commissar Molotov but on American Ambassador Laurence Steinhardt. Over lunch he resumed with Steinhardt a belly talk on the world situation which he had started fifteen days earlier on his way to Berlin. In the course of these two conversations Matsuoka revealed much about his own motives. He wanted Japan to avoid war with the United States, he said, because he felt grateful for his boyhood years in Seattle. At the same time, he warned, Japan might be obliged by the Tripartite Pact to fight the United States if Roosevelt insisted on siding with Great Britain against Germany. Matsuoka made it clear that his friendly feelings did not extend to the British and that he regarded them as the despoilers and enslavers of the Orient. The sooner Hitler conquered Great Britain, he said, the better. And he protested that U.S. aid to Chiang Kai-shek and Churchill was prolonging war and misery on two continents.

In his outward-bound conversation with Steinhardt, Matsuoka had suggested that Japan was weary of war with China and might be willing to withdraw most of her forces from China if the United States would help by persuading Chiang Kai-shek to co-operate in saving the face of the Japanese Army. Matsuoka had added that U.S. leaders were naturally suspicious of him because of his action in leading Japan out of the League of Nations in 1933 but that they would find him a good friend if they would give him a chance. President Roosevelt, he said, was known as a shrewd poker player. Would he not gamble on Matsuoka's sincerity and assist him in the delicate task of handling anti-American elements in Tokyo? Finally Matsuoka stated that it was to the Soviet Union's advantage to encourage war between Japan and the United States.

Now, at his second meeting with Steinhardt, on April 8, Matsuoka was disappointed to learn that Steinhardt had cabled Washington the gist of his March twenty-fourth remarks but had not as yet received any response to the suggestion that Roosevelt should mediate the Sino-Japanese war. Matsuoka did not know that Steinhardt in his report home had discounted the possibility that the Japanese foreign minister could be sincere and had dwelt instead on his brash and boastful manners. So Matsuoka pressed ahead optimistically trying to persuade Steinhardt to plead his cause in Washington. He told Steinhardt that Hitler and Ribbentrop—he really meant Hirohito—were urging him to sign a neutrality pact with the Soviet Union and that he might have to comply. As yet, however, Foreign Commissar Molotov was asking Japanese concessions which Matsuoka thought he could represent at home as too high a price to pay.

Leaving Steinhardt to ruminate on these subtle considerations, Matsuoka went on, buoyantly, to see Foreign Commissar Molotov. Having piqued Molotov's curiosity by an apparent disinterest in advocating the proposed Soviet-Japanese pact, he at once left town for a sightseeing jaunt to the Hermitage art collection in Leningrad. Back in Moscow on April 12, after exerting his diplomatic charm as little as possible, he wired Tokyo that Molotov seemed unsympathetic and that the chance of concluding a pact with Russia was almost nil. The dour, pedantic Molotov that day would have been inclined to agree. Matsuoka had larded the conversations thus far with a liberal smear of insult and German propaganda. Molotov, however, did not know the full background as it was known to his master, Stalin.

Red Army Intelligence had received the cipher from Soviet spy Sorge in Tokyo explaining that the Konoye circle wanted the neutrality pact in order to free Japan to strike south. Young Saionji Kinkazu was in Moscow with Matsuoka, fully instructed by Lord Privy Seal Kido. He was telling all commissars to whom he had introductions that Japan wished to avoid joining in the German attack which well-informed Russians knew to be imminent. One justifying scrap of paper to weigh against the Tripartite Pact—that was all that Japan needed to remain on the sidelines.

From Lavrenti Beria's secret police apparatus and from the Red Army's Fourth Department, Stalin had access to the full particulars of the Saionji and Sorge representations. On the morning after Matsuoka's radiogram on the breakdown of negotiations, Stalin had a secretary phone Matsuoka and summon him at once to a private audience in the bed-sitting room where Stalin did most of his work.

Matsuoka took the offensive in the interview by lecturing Stalin on the meaning of the Japanese slogan *Hakko Ichiu,* Eight Corners Under One Canopy, which the first emperor, Jimmu, in the seventh century B.C. was supposed by mythologists to have proclaimed as the goal of the nation he was about to found. Matsuoka explained that the slogan did not mean that Japan hoped to conquer the earth but that Japan hoped to bring together all the peoples of the earth under one tent of mutual respect and comfort. Stalin fidgeted and listened impatiently for ten minutes and then interjected a single *da,* "Yes."

Then the conversation at once came down to business. Stalin urged that Japan sell him the southern Japanese half of Sakhalin, the island between Hokkaido and Kamchatka, which had been partitioned after the Russo-Japanese War of 1904–1905. Matsuoka replied that he was empowered to give away some Japanese coal and oil rights in the northern Russian half of Sakhalin but that the southern half of the island was now settled with Japanese and that Russia would be well advised to look for territorial expansion in the direction of Arabia and Iran rather than in islands near the Japanese homeland.

Stalin crinkled his mouth in a smile and said, "I agree." He pushed forward the proposed Japanese text of the Soviet-Japanese non-aggression pact and said, "Let's initial it." So they did and Matsuoka withdrew from the Kremlin greatly impressed and astonished.

The next day, April 14, less than forty-eight hours after his pessimistic cable home, an unexceptionable draft of the required pact lay before Matsuoka in his hotel suite, and Commissar Molotov was waiting to escort him to a celebration in the Kremlin. Stalin was again on hand and personally arranged the chairs for the speech making and vodka drinking which followed. When Matsuoka worried about missing his train home, Stalin called the commissar of transportation and told him to hold the Trans-Siberian express that night until whatever hour Matsuoka and his party might arrive at the station to board it.

At the end of the formal speeches, teetotaler Stalin raised a glass of red juice and boomed: "Banzai for the Emperor!"

In response Matsuoka raised his own glass and said: "The treaty has been made. I do not lie. If I lie, my head shall be yours. If you lie, rest assured that I will come for your head."

Stalin winced slightly and then said, with great seriousness, "My head is important to my country. So is yours to your country. Let's take care to keep both our heads on our shoulders."

Then Stalin toasted the Japanese delegation, taking special care to praise the contribution of its military members and of the Japanese ambassador, retired Lieutenant General "Peerless Pimp" Tatekawa.

"These military and naval men have concluded the neutrality pact from the standpoint of the general situation," replied Matsuoka mirthlessly, "but they are really always thinking of how to defeat the Soviet Union."

Stalin refused to be distracted by Matsuoka's surliness.

"The Japanese Army," he said, "is very strong. The United States may build a large navy but it will never have the spiritual strength of the Japanese Navy. Then again, I wish to remind all Japanese military men that Soviet Russia today is not the corrupt czarist imperial Russia which you once defeated."

After more toasts, Stalin said to Matsuoka, "You are an Asiatic and so am I."

Matsuoka raised his glass: "We're all Asiatics. Let's drink to Asiatics."

From the reception Stalin insisted on accompanying Matsuoka to the railroad station. On the platform he embraced the Japanese foreign minister and said, "The European problem can be solved naturally if Japan and the Soviet Union co-operate."

"Not only the European problem," echoed Matsuoka. "Even Asia can be solved."

"The whole world can be settled," said Stalin.

After enduring one final embrace, the diminutive Matsuoka boarded the waiting Trans-Siberian express and escaped from Stalin's hug.

KONOYE'S PEACE PLOT

On his way home from Moscow, Matsuoka dallied for five days of politicking in Manchukuo where he had spent the years 1935 to 1939 as president of the South Manchuria Railroad Company. There he explained his pact with Stalin to the leaders of the Kwantung Army and learned that he could still count on much Army support if he succeeded in turning Japan's war preparations from the south to the north. On April 20, when he was still in the Kwantung Leasehold port of Dairen, he received a telephone call from Prime Minister Prince Konoye, asking him to come home at once for an important conference.

In Matsuoka's absence, Konoye had secretly developed a plan of his own for starting the diversionary conversations in Washington which were called for as a part of the preparations for war. The previous fall two American Maryknoll Fathers had come to Tokyo to negotiate for the retention of Roman Catholic mission properties in Japan, Korea, and Manchuria which were in danger of government expropriation.[5] A few days before Christmas, 1940, having had no luck in their mission, they were suddenly surprised by being allowed to see Foreign Minister Matsuoka in person. Matsuoka promised to do what he could for them if they would deliver a message for him to President Roosevelt. Matsuoka explained that he wanted to get in touch directly with the President, through a line

[5] The Konoye government, in a program reminiscent of 1601, was in process of de-emphasizing Christianity by organizing it into two denominations, one Catholic and one Protestant, both under the control of patriotic Japanese clerics.

The two Maryknoll Fathers were Bishop James Edward Walsh and Father James M. Drought. Father Drought appears to have been the most active of the two. He died before the preparation of this book, but his part in the affair has been documented by Ladislas Farago, formerly of U.S. Naval Intelligence. Bishop Walsh was later imprisoned by the Chinese Communists and made headlines when he was released in 1970. His recollections differ in some slight details from Farago's account. For the most part Farago is followed here because his version fits best with Japanese sources.

that would be clear of tapping by the usual censors, code-breakers, and timid diplomatic officials, so that he and President Roosevelt could do something man to man about resolving the growing war tensions.

Word of Matsuoka's essay in private diplomacy leaked from his staff to Prime Minister Konoye. Konoye had the two Maryknoll Fathers summoned to his official residence and told that their efforts would be greatly enhanced if backed by the Army. The fathers agreed and, to their surprise, were sent on to interviews with Rear Admiral Oka Takasumi, chief of the Naval Affairs Bureau in the Navy Ministry and Major General Muto Akira, chief of the Military Affairs Bureau in the War Ministry. These two veterans in Hirohito's cabal persuaded the fathers that the military, in whom all real power in Japan was thought to reside, genuinely wanted to avoid war and had a concrete proposal to offer Roosevelt. Oka and Muto outlined the main points of the proposal and entrusted the working out of the final wording to the fathers themselves and to a well-connected fixer and go-between of the financial world, Ikawa Tadao, who had been acting as their guide.

The salient points of the proposal were these: Japan would withdraw her troops from all but the northeastern corner of China in return for Chinese recognition of Manchukuo and a new Chinese government formed by merger of the Chiang Kai-shek and Wang Ching-wei regimes. The United States would help Japan procure oil, rubber, tin, and nickel in return for a promise that "Japanese activities in the southwestern Pacific area shall be carried on by peaceful means." The United States and Japan would act jointly to prevent the transfer of existing colonies in the Far East from one European master to another, to guarantee the independence of the Philippines, and to persuade Great Britain to give up her Far Eastern "doorways" of Hong Kong and Singapore. Finally the United States would give "amicable consideration" to easing Japanese immigration to America and the southwestern Pacific area.

The two Maryknoll Fathers embarked for the United States on December 28, 1940, enthusiastic about the importance and realism of their mission. On arriving in San Francisco one of them telephoned a friend, financier Lewis Strauss, the later Atomic Energy Commission chairman, and asked him how best to proceed. Strauss provided an introduction to former President Hoover who was living in Palo Alto. Hoover suggested that the Fathers proceed at once to Washington and see Postmaster General Frank Walker, who was a Roman Catholic. On January 23, 1941, Postmaster Walker took the two peacemakers to the White House where they sat down in the Oval Study and explained the whole background of the Japanese proposal in a three-hour tête-à-tête with Roosevelt. The President was impressed by their story and by a memo which they left with him, stating in part:

The Japanese government cannot admit, through official channels . . . that the Japanese would now welcome an opportunity to change their international, and modify their China, positions. . . . If the conservative authorities . . . can win, by diplomacy, a safe economic and international position, public opinion in Japan would restore the conservatives to complete control.

President Roosevelt welcomed the Japanese feeler. Like Prime Minister Konoye he felt that he needed time, politically as well as militarily, to prepare for entry into World War II. Over Secretary of State Cordell Hull's objections, he appointed Postmaster General Walker a "presidential agent," with a budget from the President's unvouchered funds, to run down the sincerity of the Japanese overture. Walker gave a go-ahead to the Maryknoll Fathers. On February 14, financier Ikawa, the guide who had led them through the bureaucratic labyrinths of Tokyo seven weeks earlier, arrived in San Francisco on the same ship with Admiral Nomura, Hirohito's new ambassador to Washington.

Ikawa, who had many friends on Wall Street and an American wife, quickly vouched for the authenticity of the proposal which the Fathers had brought home from Tokyo. To satisfy Postmaster General Walker that the proposal also had the backing of Japan's "militarists," Ikawa summoned from Tokyo Colonel Iwakuro Hideo, the chief of the Military Affairs Section of the War Ministry, a henchman of Military Affairs Bureau Chief Muto and a trusted subordinate of War Minister Tojo.[6] Colonel Iwakuro arrived in New York on March 21 and two weeks later, on April 5, a "draft understanding" which he and Ikawa had approved was submitted to President Roosevelt. The President was satisfied that it followed both the spirit and letter of the Fathers' original understanding and instructed Secretary of State Cordell Hull to present it to Ambassador Nomura as a basis for official U.S.–Japanese negotiations.

Hull's brilliant assistant on Oriental matters, Dr. Stanley Hornbeck, warned Postmaster General Walker: "Nothing that might be agreed upon between the American and the Japanese governments within the next few days or weeks will substantially alter the world situation in its material aspects. . . . The decision of Japanese leaders whether or not to move southward will be made in the light of the physical situation in Europe as they view it and the physical situation in the Pacific as they view it."

Nevertheless Hull presented the "draft proposal," as it was being called,

---

[6] Iwakuro, after the ubiquitous Suzuki Tei-ichi, was the Army's leading economic wizard. He had been responsible for inviting the cartel of Ayukawa Gisuke, a U.S.-oriented believer in common stock and public ownership, to take over the muddled development of Manchukuo in 1936. After World War II Iwakuro would become the chief purchasing agent of U.S. arms for Japan's modern Self-Defense Forces.

to Ambassador Nomura for official transmission to Tokyo. Nomura cabled it on to Prime Minister Konoye on April 17, admitting knowledge of its background, stating its official U.S. government support, and asking for speedy action on it.

Konoye at once called the palace and explained all that had developed to Hirohito. The next morning Hirohito gave an audience to Ambassador Kurusu Saburo, the diplomat who had recently returned from Germany where he had signed the Tripartite Pact on behalf of Japan. Kurusu was to be sent later in the year to assist Ambassador Nomura in dragging out the negotiations in Washington. After consulting Ambassador Kurusu, Hirohito summoned Prime Minister Konoye and told him to pursue the tack of the "draft proposal" as far as he wished but to remember that Japan must "keep faith with Hitler" and "must not jeopardize realization of the Greater East Asia Co-Prosperity Sphere."

The next day Konoye cleared the "draft proposal," as a basis for the U.S. negotiations, with the War and Navy ministers and with the two chiefs of staff, General Sugiyama and Admiral Nagano Osami.[7] It was then that Konoye phoned Matsuoka and asked him to cut short his triumphant progress through Manchuria and come home at once.

MATSUOKA'S STALL

Matsuoka deplaned at Tachikawa Air Base outside Tokyo on the morning of April 22. In his limousine, on the way to the palace to greet the Emperor, he was told by his vice minister about the Bishop Walsh negotiations in Washington. He pretended to be greatly put out that, during his magnificent accomplishments in Berlin and Moscow, others had usurped his office at home and begun making foreign policy without him. He knew that his government colleagues, as a matter of automatic Japanese etiquette, would defer to him if he seemed to feel that he had lost face. He had hoped to use the Bishop Walsh pipeline to draw Roosevelt into his private plan to embroil Japan in war with Russia. He was dismayed that his pipe had been uncovered and made into an official conduit. But now, as his future actions would show, he was resolved to subvert the Washington talks and break them off as quickly as possible. He saw that they were unrealistic. He knew that Hirohito and the Army and Navy would never concede enough to make possible a genuine settlement with the United States. He realized that formal diplomatic negotiations would be used by both sides to gain time for their own purposes. He could imagine that

---

[7] Nagano had replaced Prince Fushimi as Navy chief of staff ten days earlier, thereby completing the imperial family's withdrawal from public posts of military responsibility. Prince Kanin had retired in favor of General Sugiyama as Army chief of staff the previous October.

negotiations conducted in that spirit would only exacerbate ill will when they were broken off.

When Matsuoka's limousine drew up in the palace at 7:30 P.M., he was received in audience immediately by Hirohito. He delivered a hurried report on his hobnobbing with the dictators of the world and gratefully accepted an invitation to take lunch with the Emperor four days later in order to reveal the full particulars. Then Matsuoka rushed on to the prime minister's official residence to attend a liaison conference with Konoye, the inner Cabinet, and the chiefs of staff.

At this conference Matsuoka gave an enthusiastic and boastful description of his dealings with Hitler and Stalin and then, when the negotiations with Roosevelt came up, dismissed them as just another feeler. Complaining of weariness after his long journeys, he excused himself at 11:00 P.M. and left his colleagues to deliberate alone on the Japanese response to the "draft proposal" forwarded by Ambassador Nomura. The military men stayed on with Prince Konoye for another eighty minutes and agreed to pursue the Washington negotiations "regardless of the foreign minister's attitude."

For the next ten days Matsuoka basked in attention, "recovered from fatigue," and refused to do anything about the note awaiting his reply from Ambassador Nomura. Finally on May 3 he dispatched an "interim reply," telling Nomura that the "draft proposal" was being studied and asking him to look into the possibility of concluding a full-scale neutrality pact with the United States which would obligate both countries to stay out of the war. When Chief of Staff Sugiyama pointed out to him that this posturing and procrastination would only succeed in making the United States distrustful of the negotiations, Matsuoka replied with an irrelevant taunt. If the Army had followed his advice and seized Singapore the previous autumn, he said, this whole difficult situation would never have come up.

On May 8 another liaison conference was called between Cabinet and Supreme Command to put pressure on Matsuoka and force him to authorize Ambassador Nomura to proceed with negotiations on the basis of the "draft proposal." Matsuoka continued to play for time. "It is my intention," he said, "to prevent the United States from entering the war, and to make her withdraw from China. So please don't rush me."

Navy Minister Oikawa replied that in his opinion the United States did not want to enter the war; that she had everything to gain and nothing to lose by measures short of war; and that the time would never be riper than now for Japan to make a negotiated advance into Southeast Asia while the United States was preoccupied with helping Britain.

On the contrary, countered Matsuoka, the likelihood that the U.S. would not enter the war had recently decreased from 70 per cent to 60 per cent. His colleagues looked at one another in amusement at his

American habit of bolstering arguments by quotation of exact but unfounded percentages. Then they listened seriously to his next statement.

"If the United States participates in the war, it will last a long time, and world civilization will be destroyed. If the war lasts ten years, Germany will fight the Soviet Union to secure war materials and food, and will then advance into Asia. What do you think would be the proper position of Japan at that time?"

The answer was implicit. Japan should side with the United States to secure Siberia and safeguard the western Pacific against German predation. No one at the liaison conference ventured to answer Matsuoka's question. As soon as the meeting had broken up, Matsuoka presented himself at the palace, asking for an audience. Hirohito had just returned to his desk in the Imperial Library after his usual light Japanese lunch of rice, fish, and vegetables. He summoned Lord Privy Seal Kido and kept Matsuoka waiting for forty minutes while he questioned Kido on "how to fathom Matsuoka and how to deal with him." Matsuoka was then admitted to Hirohito's presence at 2 P.M. and said, in the course of a long speech, "Unless we keep faith with Germany and Italy, I will have to resign."

Hirohito was only somewhat impressed by Matsuoka's protestations. After the audience, Lord Privy Seal Kido told Prime Minister Prince Konoye, who was waiting in an anteroom, "Matsuoka today has lost the imperial confidence."

The next day Prime Minister Konoye called a secret liaison conference between himself and the Army and Navy chiefs. Matsuoka was not invited or informed and the subject discussed was "how to deal with Matsuoka." Everyone present recognized that he had become a dangerous man, who could seriously disrupt the unity of the nation on the eve of war. The conclusion was reached, however, that Matsuoka must be given more rope before he could be eliminated.

By the following day, May 10, Hirohito himself was aware of the game Matsuoka was playing. To Konoye Hirohito complained: "Matsuoka says that an attack on Singapore will bring the United States into the war, and that that, in turn, will protract the world war and will force Germany, sooner or later, to invade the Soviet Union for war materials. Then Japan, he says, will have to denounce her neutrality pact with the Soviet Union and occupy Siberia as far as Irkutsk."

"It seems to me," concluded Hirohito, "that Matsuoka has been flighty ever since his return from Europe and that you should start considering a replacement for him."

MATSUOKA'S TREASON

If Hirohito had known the full extent of Matsuoka's "flightiness" he might have commanded the foreign minister to disembowel himself. On

May 2 Dr. Heinrich Stahmer, the chief of Japanese-Reich relations in the German Foreign Ministry, had called Ambassador Oshima in Berlin to tell him, with icy hysteria: "It has been established that the U.S. government is reading Ambassador Nomura's coded messages." Oshima cabled this appalling news to Matsuoka on May 3. Matsuoka considered it for two days and then cabled Nomura in Washington: "It appears almost certain that the U.S. government is reading your code messages." At the same time Matsuoka urgently requested further particulars from Oshima.

In Berlin Oshima could learn only that his clearance for briefings on German preparations for war with Russia had been revoked, effective April 30, and that his earlier reports home on German war preparations had somehow got into the hands of the U.S. government which had made them available to the Soviet government. Since these reports had been sent to Tokyo and then relayed to Nomura in Washington in Japan's highest-security code, it was apparent that either the Americans could read the code or a high official in the Japanese Foreign Service was a traitor. Matsuoka at once ordered a complete security investigation of the Japanese Embassy in Washington, of Oshima's staff in Berlin, and of his own Foreign Ministry Telegraphic Section in Tokyo.

In Washington the U.S. Army's Signal Intelligence Service and the U.S. Navy's Op-20-G, the two cryptanalytic units in the intelligence sections of the armed services, ordered their own outraged investigations. Decoded intercepts of the frenzied Matsuoka-Oshima-Nomura exchange revealed that the U.S. ability to read Japan's top-secret messages was now, itself, an exposed secret. This meant that one of the handful of U.S. officials cleared to read *Magic*—as the decoded intercepts were called—had talked too much. Worse, it meant that the Japanese would probably change their codes—change them on the eve of war when there might not be time to break any new codes.

U.S. cryptanalysis of Japanese government messages had begun in 1922 during the post-World War I Washington Naval Limitations Conference. It had continued more or less regularly ever since, first in the State Department, then in the office of Naval Intelligence, then in the offices of both Naval and Army Intelligence. In 1928 the original genius of this eavesdropping effort, Herbert O. Yardley, had grown so disgruntled by lack of appreciation for his head-splitting efforts that he had turned traitor and sold the secret of his work to the Japanese for $7,000.[8] As a result the Japanese had learned early of American cryptanalytic ingenuity and had taken pains ever since to change and improve their codes frequently.

---

[8] Because of extenuating circumstances and the amount of undivulged information which Yardley still possessed, he was not tried for treason. Instead he returned to U.S. government payrolls during World War II and was buried with military honors at Arlington Cemetery in 1958.

In Yardley's day the Japanese codes had been manually contrived jumblings of the seventy possible syllables used in the difficult Japanese language. Then in 1931 the Japanese had begun to use mechanical encoding and decoding devices which jumbled the syllables many more times and in many more ways than could be readily worked out with pencil and paper. With the help of mathematical analysis, call girls, fake power failures, and outright safecracking, U.S. Naval Intelligence finally built its own replicas of these first-generation Japanese coding machines in 1935, when they had been in use for four years.

Without realizing that their first machine, known to U.S. experts as the Red machine, had been compromised, Japanese cryptographers went on in 1937 from a mechanical coding device to one of the world's first electronic coding devices. Entirely Japanese in conception, it remained entirely baffling to U.S. cryptanalysts for twenty months of brainstorming. Then, in the twentieth month, August–September 1940, a young Army cryptologist, Harry Lawrence Clark, re-conceived the type of circuitry which the Japanese were using. The operatives of the Signal Intelligence Service built a generalized machine embodying Clark's principle, and by trial and error, plugging in its various possible interconnections on a sort of telephone switchboard, they finally managed to duplicate the actual circuits of the Japanese original. The U.S. Purple machine began to produce fully intelligible texts of Japanese cables and telegrams on September 25, 1940, the day before the signing of the Tripartite Pact in Berlin.

It was this monumental decipherment of Code Purple, the highest code of the Japanese government, that seemed suddenly wasted eight months later when Code-Purple messages from Matsuoka, Oshima, and Nomura revealed that the Japanese no longer had confidence in the code's security. Specially cleared agents of the F.B.I. investigated the offices of every one of the dozen or so U.S. statesmen who had access to translations of Purple messages. The investigation revealed that President Roosevelt's personal aides were sometimes lax and had left at least one copy of a decoded Japanese telegram crumpled up in an ordinary White House wastepaper basket.[9]

In the end, however, the F.B.I.'s investigators traced the security leak which had caused the damage not to the White House but to the State Department. In early April 1941, when Ambassador Oshima in Berlin had first started cabling sure warning to Tokyo of the German attack on Russia, one of his intercepted cables had been shown to Under Secretary of State Sumner Welles. Welles was not on the regular distribution list of officials who saw every item circulated by *Magic* but on a subsidiary list of

---

[9] As a consequence, from May to November 1941, F.D.R. was no longer allowed to handle *Magic* messages personally. Instead he was briefed on them by his naval aide, Captain John Beardall, who was permitted to read them, without taking notes, in the presence of a duly cleared pouch carrier at the Office of Naval Intelligence.

officials who were given a glimpse of *Magic* messages when they were judged to have "a need to know." As a result Welles did not appreciate the full importance of *Magic* nor the years of intellectual labor which had made *Magic* possible. His "need to know" was determined by a project he was working on: to bring the Soviet Union out of the spell of Hitler's strength to the side of the Anglo-American alliance. For this purpose he had shown a *Magic* translation of one of Ambassador Oshima's Purple-Code dispatches on the forthcoming Russo-German war to the Soviet ambassador in Washington, Constantin Oumansky. Oumansky had then confronted the German ambassador in Washington, Dr. Hans Thomsen, with it, and Thomsen had warned Ribbentrop in Berlin that Japanese security was not secure.

While U.S. intelligence officers waited in misery for a completely new departure in Japanese coding techniques, Foreign Minister Matsuoka and one of his old cronies from Manchuria, the chief of the Telegraphic Section in the Foreign Ministry, conducted their investigation of everyone connected with the codes at home and abroad. Originally Japanese naval officers had invented the Purple Code and had built the Purple-Code machines with Foreign Ministry funds. Now, however, the highest-security naval communications were all being dispatched in the new Admirals' Code, developed at the insistence of Yamamoto and sure to remain uncracked for many months to come. Army codes, too, were not in question and Ambassador Oshima in Berlin was an Army man, a lieutenant general. For these reasons Matsuoka and the Telegraphic Section chief in the Foreign Ministry were able to conclude their investigation with a whitewash.

On May 19, Matsuoka submitted a report on his investigation to the Cabinet and to the palace stating that no traitors had been uncovered, that the machine codes of both Red and Purple remained unbreakable, and that the security leaks alleged by the Germans were the results of routine American cryptanalysis of messages sent in the old-fashioned, paper-and-pencil, subsidiary codes of Japan. These lesser codes would now be revised, but Code Purple and Code Red would continue to be used and could be considered fail-safe.

Matsuoka and a number of the clerks under him knew that Oshima's intelligence regarding German war with Russia had never been entrusted to one of the subsidiary pencil-and-paper codes. Yet Matsuoka succeeded ostensibly in persuading Hirohito and the Navy General Staff that Code Purple was still secure. For the remaining six months before Pearl Harbor, all top-secret Japanese diplomatic messages went on being sent in Code Purple and being read by U.S. intelligence officers in Army S.I.S. and Navy Op-20-G.

The American beneficiaries of Matsuoka's generosity could not at first believe their own good fortune. They warned that future Purple messages might all be intentional obfuscations and distractions. But as time wore on, they became convinced that Matsuoka had blundered and left unguarded the innermost citadels of Japanese deceit.

Perhaps Matsuoka meant to leave the United States with access to Japanese secrets or perhaps he wished to save the Foreign Ministry from disgrace at a time when it needed all its influence. Perhaps Admiral Yamamoto and others, sophisticated in intelligence work, knew of Matsuoka's whitewash and used it later to give U.S. eavesdroppers an unwarranted sense of complacency. Then, again, perhaps the naval liaison officers attached to the telegraphic section of the Foreign Ministry were bribed and blackmailed by Matsuoka's men to hold their tongues. In the lack of documentary evidence, it may be assumed that both Japanese and American intelligence experts acted with professional competence and tried to allow for all possibilities.

MATSUOKA'S MADNESS

Having hushed up the Code-Purple scandal at the Foreign Ministry in mid-May 1941, Matsuoka went on throughout late May and all of June to wage an extraordinary campaign of double talk within the councils of the Japanese government—a campaign which sounded patriotically belligerent and anti-American but which, at the same time, delayed Strike-South preparations and vitiated the negotiations in Washington. He had many silent allies in his efforts who joined him because they recognized that a desperate breakdown in faith threatened between the will of the people and the will of Hirohito, the people's god.

At noon on May 12 Matsuoka gave in after three weeks of urging from Prime Minister Konoye and the Army and Navy leaders and cabled Ambassador Nomura a revised version of the Maryknoll fathers' "draft proposal" for improving U.S.–Japanese relations. U.S. Secretary of State Cordell Hull noticed at once that Matsuoka's revised draft omitted the previous Japanese pledge to use only peaceful, nonmilitary means in advancing Japan's position in the southwestern Pacific.

To make absolutely sure that the United States would not feel conciliatory, Matsuoka two days later called on Ambassador Grew and told him "that the 'manly, decent and reasonable' thing for the United States to do would be to declare war openly on Germany." Grew considered Matsuoka's harangue, though delivered off the cuff in an unofficial chat, "bellicose both in tone and substance." Lord Privy Seal Kido heard of Matsuoka's rudeness and promptly sent Grew a message begging him not to feel too put out. Prime Minister Konoye and Navy Minister Oikawa both let Grew know that they would prevent any hasty action by the foreign minister. At liaison conferences on May 12 and 15, Matsuoka's government colleagues did indeed question the soundness of his diplomatic technique. Matsuoka, however, insisted that he knew best how to handle Americans and how to make Roosevelt back down.

Nothing that happened in the following week tended to vindicate Matsuoka in his claims. Nomura reported pessimistically on U.S. reactions. Oshima cabled from Berlin that he had had to soothe Ribbentrop by telling him that the purpose of the Washington negotiations was to give "the pro-American groups among the Japanese people the impression that reconciliation between Japan and the United States is impossible." In Java the Dutch colonial government was so unintimidated by Matsuoka's big talk that the head of the Japanese negotiating team there reported deadlock and demanded that he be recalled to Japan so that he could spend his time in some more useful service.

Prime Minister Prince Konoye called a liaison conference of the Cabinet and General Staff chiefs on May 22 to talk over these negative results. Hirohito sent his thirty-six-year-old brother Prince Takamatsu to sit in on the proceedings as a member of the Navy General Staff.[10] Nothing daunted, Matsuoka put in one of his better performances, conjuring up bewildering geopolitical contingencies on almost every continent. Finally the level-headed Prince Takamatsu intervened personally in an effort to pin Matsuoka down:

MATSUOKA: I would like to discontinue negotiations with the Netherlands East Indies and recall Yoshizawa. I would also like to have the timing left up to me.

A CERTAIN PERSON [PRINCE TAKAMATSU]: I can well understand that the present attitude of the Netherlands East Indies brings us to the point of recalling Yoshizawa; but it is British and American support that allows the East Indies to assume this sort of stance. If we take this final step against the East Indies [of ceasing to negotiate], it means pushing forward with military operations for Malaya and even for the Philippines. It is therefore a grave decision, by which the nation will sink or swim, and such matters as scheduling and implementation must be given sufficient thought.

MATSUOKA: If we do not make up our minds, won't Germany, Britain, the United States, and the Soviet Union be united in the end and bring pressure to bear on Japan? It is possible that Germany and the Soviet Union may form an alliance and turn against Japan, and also possible that the United States may begin a war with Japan. I would like to know how the Army and Navy chiefs of staff intend to deal with such eventualities.

[10] Army Chief of Staff Sugiyama, who took the only available minutes of the liaison conferences, complies with the imperial taboo by calling Prince Takamatsu simply *Bo,* a Certain Person. Gossip alone identifies *Bo* as the prince, and men in a position to know do not deny the identification. Moreover, at the eight important liaison conferences in which he took part—those of May 22 and 29, June 12, 16 and 25, August 16 and September 20 and 25—*Bo* cut short generals and grilled ministers of state with an incisive authority unimaginable in anyone of lesser rank.

ARMY CHIEF OF STAFF SUGIYAMA: This is a serious matter. For the Malayan part of this decision alone, we must first lay a foundation in Thailand and French Indochina from which to mount our operations. I fully explained this point at one of the previous Liaison Conferences. The Foreign Minister has not yet done anything [about negotiating bases for us in Thailand and south Indochina], and I would like to be told why.

MATSUOKA: Before we proceed against Thailand and French Indochina, we must decide what to do about Britain and the United States. We cannot enter into negotiations without having our minds made up on this point. I will go ahead as soon as we have made up our minds.

NAVY MINISTER OIKAWA: What about Matsuoka's mind? Hasn't he gone queer in the head? [11]

And so it went for two hours. Leaving the Dutch East Indies question undecided, Matsuoka skipped on over the China problem and the German alliance problem. The other conferees did not hesitate to echo Oikawa's doubt about Matsuoka's sanity but they did hesitate to make the brilliant, famous foreign minister lose face by overruling him. Near the end of his performance Matsuoka gave a hint of the hope on which he was banking in his madness—the hope that Germany would soon suck Japan into a sensible, safe war with Russia. He introduced into the record a quote from one of the recent telegrams sent from Berlin by the Japanese ambassador there, Lieutenant General Oshima:

> I [Oshima] said [to Ribbentrop] . . . in regard to the Japanese attitude in case of a war between Germany and the Soviet Union, I daresay the attitude of the Imperial Government will not be easily decided. Finally it will be up to the Emperor to decide.

LAST STRIKE-NORTH PLOT

Playing for time, refusing to facilitate the spurious negotiations with the United States, refusing also to start negotiations for Strike-South bases in Indochina and Thailand, Matsuoka weathered another liaison conference on May 29. He maintained plausibly that most Americans shared his own anti-British, anti-Chinese, anti-Communist bias and that they would soon force Roosevelt to accommodate himself to Japan's leadership position in Asia and need for *Lebensraum*. Home Minister Hiranuma, the long-faced lawyer of the conservative business community's National Foundation Society, sided with Matsuoka. Long a proponent of war with Russia, he was waiting, like Matsuoka, for the outbreak of war between Germany and the Soviet Union. In vain Prince Takamatsu sought to saddle

---

[11] *Matsuoka wa atama ga hen de wa nai ka?*

Matsuoka with some responsibility for having originated the unfortunate conversations with the United States.

"Didn't you get an American priest," he asked, "to start things off?"

"No," said Matsuoka. "I did not. I know who did, but please do not press me now to tell you who it was."

Prince Takamatsu fell silent, knowing that it had been Prime Minister Prince Konoye.

Finally, on June 5, the long-awaited cable arrived from General Oshima in Berlin saying that Hitler had officially informed him that the Third Reich would soon open war on Russia. Oshima advised Tokyo that, if an attack could not yet be mounted against Great Britain in Singapore, it would be well to co-operate with Hitler by striking at the Soviet rear in Siberia.

The next day, June 6, a brief liaison conference was held which was so secret that Chief of Staff Sugiyama kept no notes on it. Lord Privy Seal Kido's diary suggests that the Emperor may have attended it personally for twenty-five minutes. According to Hirohito's report to Kido later in the day, Matsuoka was insisting that there was still a 60 per cent chance of a German-Russian reconciliation but that until the outcome was clear all Japanese negotiations and decisions should be postponed. Certainly the Foreign Ministry should not now antagonize the United States by asking the French colonial government of Indochina for bases within striking distance of Singapore.

The next day, on June 7, at still another liaison conference, Matsuoka greatly enlarged the areas for doubt by musing, "I wonder whether Hitler's intention to wage war is actually based on his reported intentions to smash communism. I wonder if instead he does not intend to attack [Russia] because the war is going to last for twenty or thirty years."

"I think," added Chief of Staff Sugiyama, in a parenthesis in the notes that he was taking, "that we will have to be alert to the possibility of a reconciliation between Britain and Germany." In short a Japanese move on Singapore was rapidly losing its most attractive aspects. Germany might begin to prefer a Japanese move against Russia and Great Britain might feel free to send back adequate defense forces to Singapore. In the days that followed urgent messages went out from the officials of the War Ministry to the military aides at the embassies in Berlin and Rome asking for immediate warning of any signs of slackening in Anglo-German hostility.

In the impending Russo-German war, Matsuoka had at last found a good issue which brought him allies. The officers of the General Staff who had grown up with the mission of fighting a continental war against Russia began to smile at him during conferences and listen to his arguments. Even some members of the imperial family—notably Prince Higashikuni and Prince Fushimi—began to show sympathy for his views. If Hitler would only do what he promised this time, Hirohito might be induced to postpone his inherited crusade against the land of Perry and to capitalize on this golden opportunity by stealing through Russia's back door and seizing half the empire of the czars.

Hirohito and Prince Takamatsu, however, were not easily diverted. In the second week of June Hirohito read and approved a General Staff document entitled "Acceleration of the Policy Concerning the South." It called for immediate negotiations with the French in Indochina to allow Japanese troops to move into Saigon and the Mekong Delta and establish airfields and training centers. It resolved that French refusal would be countered by armed force and that in case of British, U.S., and Dutch intervention, Japan would "not refuse to risk a war with Britain and the United States." At a liaison conference on June 12, Matsuoka voiced innumerable objections both to the negotiations and to the posture of military threat envisaged in this plan. Finally that Certain Person, Prince Takamatsu, asked him, "Do you agree to using military force? Or do you disagree?"

"I do not disagree," said Matsuoka. But then he introduced a number of editorial quibbles which he wished to see embodied in the text of the accelerated program under consideration.

"How about the following arrangement?" cut in Prince Takamatsu. "Keep everything secret, adopt the present draft, and add the following clauses as understandings: first, we agree that we will finally execute the plan as it stands; second, since we will need time anyway to prepare troop movements, we will negotiate in two separate escalating stages; third, when the first-stage negotiations are complete, we will go on at once to the second-stage negotiations."

Matsuoka said that he agreed and was given time to consider matters of wording.

At the next liaison conference, on June 16, it quickly emerged that he had not agreed. He complained that previous agreements with Indochina would be invalidated by the new plan and that the Japanese presence in northern Indochina would become illegal. He warned that Japan would suffer reprisals and would probably lose her present supply of rubber, tin, and rice from the Dutch East Indies.

"If Vichy," he said, "does not agree to the occupation, it would be bad faith to force it on her. The previously signed treaty has not yet been ratified. Occupation by force is an act of bad faith. Japan is said internationally to lack integrity. I will fight for our international reputation, even if I have to fight all by myself."

Finally, Matsuoka, in so many words, threatened to expose the Emperor before the press. "Frankly," he said, "as the nation's foreign minister, I will have to report to the Emperor that this is an act of bad faith."

Chief of Staff Sugiyama tried politely to draw attention away from the threat by explaining the need to equip airfields in Indochina before the typhoon season in November. Navy Minister Oikawa chimed in with a remark to the effect that the Navy had never considered one of the possibilities raised by Matsuoka—that of an Anglo-Russian alliance—and would like time to investigate it.

Prince Takamatsu, however, was not to be put off. Looking blackly at Matsuoka, he said, "Can't you change your mind?"

"No," replied Matsuoka bravely, "I cannot."

Tojo intervened to emphasize the need for "finishing the job" in Indochina before the end of the year.

Matsuoka refused to budge from his threatening stance. "It is necessary, is it not," he said, "to make an official report to His Majesty about these preparations. . . . All this has happened because you didn't take Singapore last year as I suggested. When are we going to report officially on this matter to His Majesty? I would like you to give some thought as to how we may report to His Majesty."

"Thus," wrote Chief of Staff Sugiyama, "the meeting was adjourned so that the matter could be studied for two or three days."

HITLER'S INVASION OF RUSSIA

On June 21, after forty days of consideration, U.S. Secretary of State Cordell Hull gave Ambassador Nomura in Washington an American revision of the Japanese revision of the "draft proposal" for friendlier relations with the United States. What had once been a trenchant clarification of the two nations' mutual interests and disagreements had become, in the latest version, a pleasant but wordy expression of U.S. philosophy regarding treaties, trade, and the rule of free enterprise under law. Hull had, of course, been reading the uninterrupted flow of telegrams from Berlin to Tokyo and from Tokyo to Washington in the Purple Code which Matsuoka had kept in use after he knew it had been broken. As a result Hull indicated that—like Matsuoka—he did not expect his conversations with Nomura to succeed. Their function was only to gain time. To make sure of this point, he took another page from Matsuoka's book by accompanying his note with an Oral Statement. In it, pointing an insulting finger at the insulting Matsuoka, he said: "Some Japanese leaders in influential positions are definitely committed to . . . support of Nazi Germany. . . . So long as such leaders . . . seek to influence public opinion in Japan, . . . is it not illusory to expect . . . results along the desired lines?"

Hull dispatched this dishearteningly realistic missive to Tokyo at a time when he knew it would receive scant attention. A few hours later, as he and other well-informed statesmen had expected for several days, 160 divisions of highly mechanized German troops, protected overhead by the best squadrons of the *Luftwaffe,* poured into Russia. The world had never seen such a powerful army of invasion but no one in the chancelleries of the world was surprised. Japanese observers were particularly well informed on the war because they had been passing through the Russo-German frontier repeatedly in the preceding weeks, their binoculars focused, their cameras snapping. They had seen the flatcars of war materials and the crowds of uniforms on the German side and the placid farmlands on the Russian side. They knew that the Red Army High Command had brought back 150,000 of its best troops to European Russia from Siberia but they saw no signs of Russian fortifications between Warsaw and Moscow. Despite the lesson taught to Napoleon more than a century earlier, they did not appreciate Russia's reliance on sheer width of territory. They could not understand Stalin's confidence in the dependability of the Russian peasant at a time of sacrifice. They could not credit Stalin's ruthlessly realistic strategy of letting his land swallow Hitler's shiny host. They could only believe that the Third Reich would win in a matter of months.

As soon as the news of the German attack was fully confirmed, Japanese Foreign Minister Matsuoka called at the palace and asked Hirohito for an immediate Japanese invasion of Siberia. When Hirohito inquired what was to be done with the carefully prepared plans for the Strike South, Matsuoka recklessly spoke of fighting first Russia, then Great Britain, then the United States, and finally all three together. Hirohito ordered Prime Minister Prince Konoye and Lord Privy Seal Kido to investigate the foreign minister's "true intentions." On June 24, they reported back to the Throne that as far as they could tell, Matsuoka really did propose a two-front war on the north as well as the south. Hirohito postponed the liaison conference scheduled for that day so that he could review the military situation with the Army Chief of Staff Sugiyama. Matsuoka had gained in political strength from Hitler's move, and Hirohito needed to assure himself of the Army's determination to proceed according to plan.

He gave audience to Army Chief of Staff Sugiyama early on the afternoon of June 25. Sugiyama reiterated the arguments for the approved imperial policy of striking south. The ABCD powers—American, British, Chinese, and Dutch—said Sugiyama, were daily strengthening their "encirclement" of Japan. If the nation was to move forward toward the Co-Prosperity Sphere in Asia, Japan would have to secure bases at once in southern Indochina. Sugiyama emphasized the need for carrying out the occupation of southern Indochina by diplomacy if possible, but conceded that Japan should be ready to use force. Hirohito assented and asked specific questions about the dispatch of troops. How much would it cost? Which divisions would be used? Where precisely would the South Indochina bases and airstrips be built? At the end of the briefing, Hirohito said, "I am greatly worried about international repercussions, but let it pass."

Army Chief of Staff Sugiyama left with Hirohito six detailed position papers: the first, an explanation of the strategic reasons for securing bases in south Indochina; the second, a list of U.S. and British preparations and provocations in 1941; the third, an intelligence assessment of ABCD military strength; the fourth, a count of ABCD aircraft in the entire area of the southwestern Pacific; the fifth, an evaluation of ABCD economic strategy for the containment of Japan; the sixth, an evaluation of enemy political strategy.

The postponed liaison conference was held later that afternoon. The original purpose of the meeting had been to get Matsuoka's approval of a revised version of the "Acceleration of the Policy Concerning the South"— a version which left out the assertion that Japan was ready to risk war with Great Britain and the United States. Matsuoka gave an airy token acquiescence to the Indochina acceleration plan in the opening minutes of the conference and then went on to fascinate all present by discussing the implications of the Russo-German war. Navy Minister Oikawa stated the Navy's firm opposition to a two-front war and then begged Matsuoka: "In any case please don't talk so much about the future."

Matsuoka said: "When Germany wins and disposes of the Soviet Union, we can't share in the spoils of victory without having done something. We have either to shed blood or engage in diplomacy. It's best to shed blood. The question is what Japan should want when the Soviet Union is disposed of. Germany is probably wondering what Japan is going to do. Aren't we going to war when the enemy forces in Siberia have gone westward? Shouldn't we at least make a diversionary move? Whatever we do, I hope we will hurry up and decide what it is."

The Certain Person, Prince Takamatsu, said, "Yes, but whatever we do, we must not do it prematurely."

Having adjourned on this inconclusive note, the conferees met again the next day, and the day after, and again on June 28, June 30, and July 1. Throughout this almost continuous liaison conference between the highest potentates of the Japanese state, Matsuoka filibustered and squirmed, made concessions and promptly retracted them.

On June 26 he ended the conference by saying, "I agree . . . but I won't put my agreement in writing."

On June 27 he protested: "I would like a decision to attack the Soviet Union. . . . You tell me to engage in diplomacy, but I don't think our negotiations with the United States will last much longer."

On June 28 he said: "To strike south is like playing with fire; and if we strike south we will probably go to war against Britain and the United States and the Soviet Union too. . . . I don't believe that now is the best time to enter the war, given the general situation. . . . The Navy has expressed the view that it is absolutely opposed to entering the war but it will not say so openly. . . . I would be pleased if our operations toward French Indochina were suspended."

On June 30, Matsuoka proposed a six-month postponement of the occupation of southern French Indochina. Navy Minister Oikawa whispered wistfully to Army Chief of Staff Sugiyama, "How about postponing it for six months?" The Navy's vice chief of staff echoed to the Army's vice chief of staff, Lieutenant General Tsukada Osamu, "Yes, let's think about postponing it for six months." However, Lieutenant General Tsukada—a charter member of the cabal, a life-long friend of Prince Asaka, and the chief of staff inserted under poor little General Matsui before the rape of Nanking—pointed out that the occupation of southern Indochina had already been sanctioned by the Emperor and "must be carried out."

Matsuoka made his last stand by predicting disaster in a Strike South and by challenging Chief of Staff Sugiyama to see any other outcome. Matsuoka concluded by saying, "If we occupy southern Indochina it will become difficult to secure oil, rubber, tin, and rice. Great men should be able to change their minds."

This implied slur on the greatness of the Emperor lost Matsuoka his staunchest supporter in the debate. The long-faced rightist lawyer Hiranuma, home minister and president of the conservative businessmen's National Foundation Society, responded coldly: "I, too, think we should go north. The question is whether we can. And in this we must follow the thinking of the military."

The leaders of the Army had already explained, on several occasions, that they could not mount an offensive ground war against Siberia as long as three quarters of the Army's available divisions were tied down in China. On behalf of the Navy, Chief of Staff Nagano now concurred. "If we get involved in the north," he said, "we will have to switch around all the preparations we are now making from south to north. This would take at least fifty days."

And so ended Matsuoka's desperate struggle to reverse imperial policy. Army, Navy, and right-wing politicians and businessmen had all supported him in his last-minute promotion of a Strike-North policy but none of them had been willing to go as far as he had in making noisy speeches and in laying down careers for principle.

At a meeting of the Supreme War Council later that night, the members of the imperial family went out of their way to inscribe in the record their own openmindedness toward the possibility of a Strike North. General Prince Asaka, the imperial uncle who had overseen the rape of Nanking, said, "It appears that we are sitting on the fence. Which is first, North or South? Personally, I think North might be best first."

Hirohito's other uncle, Prince Higashikuni, who was also a full general now, inquired archly, "What is the goal of going south?"

In replying, Army Chief of Staff Sugiyama chose his words carefully, for he knew that he was taking full responsibility for the decision which had been made. "There are," he said, "several possible timetables and methods for moving south, but for the purpose of survival and self-defense, we are thinking of going as far as the Netherlands East Indies—"

"From what the Navy tells me," interjected Prime Minister Prince

Konoye, "we are not going all the way in one stroke. For the moment we will go as far as French Indochina. After that we will proceed step by step."

"Compared with the way Germany does things," laughed General Prince Asaka, "we are being pretty cautious, aren't we?"

"That's true," said Konoye, "but this is a matter of grave concern to our national fate. It is not hypothetical; it cannot be treated lightly."

The next day, July 1, 1941, Matsuoka surrendered as gracefully as he could. It was agreed at a liaison conference to proceed with the occupation of southern Indochina and with preparations for the Strike South. At the same time it was agreed that the Kwantung Army in Manchuria should be reinforced against the possible contingency of war with Russia. In regard to Manchuria, however, Army Vice Chief of Staff Tsukada said: "We are making preparations all right, but our intention is to get the minimum number of troops ready for action. We have no idea of preparing an unnecessarily large number of troops."

At the end of the conference, having surrendered unconditionally, Foreign Minister Matsuoka sought to maintain his future influence by declaring: "Things have turned out pretty well. That's because I listened to the opinions of all of you."

MATSUOKA'S OUSTER

On the day of Matsuoka's surrender, July 1, 1941, President Roosevelt in Washington sent a letter to Secretary of the Interior Harold Ickes, who was also petroleum administrator for national defense. He wished to persuade Ickes that the time had not yet come to force Japan into a corner by cutting off her oil supplies. "The Japs," wrote the President, "are having a real drag-down and knock-out fight among themselves and have been for the past week—trying to decide which way they are going to jump—attack Russia, attack the South Seas (thus throwing in their lot definitely with the Germans) or whether they will sit on the fence and be more friendly with us. No one knows what the decision will be but, as you know, it is terribly important for the control of the Atlantic for us to help keep peace in the Pacific. I simply have not got enough Navy to go round. . . ."

Unknown to the President, Hirohito had already opted to jump south and—at least to his own satisfaction—had settled the knockdown, dragout fight. That is, he had settled the fight in policy-making circles. In Army and Navy staff-officer circles it would rage on for another fortnight.

On July 2, the day after Roosevelt penned his letter, Hirohito and all his responsible ministers convened to approve the go-ahead into south Indochina and to reject the golden opportunity offered by a distracted Russia and an ill-defended Siberia. At this full-dress palace conference in the Imperial Presence, the conferees considered and adopted a long position paper entitled "Outline of National Policies in View of the Changing Situation." The key passages were only three:

> Our Empire is determined to follow a program which will result in the establishment of the Greater East Asia Co-Prosperity Sphere. . . .
>
> Preparations for war with Great Britain and the United States will be made. . . .
>
> Our attitude in regard to the German-Soviet war will be based on the spirit of the Tripartite Pact. We will not enter the conflict for the time being. We will secretly strengthen our military preparedness against the Soviet Union. . . . If the German-Soviet war should develop to the advantage of our Empire, we will, by resorting to armed force settle the Northern Question.

Prime Minister Konoye, Army Chief of Staff Sugiyama, and Navy Chief of Staff Nagano all entered statements in favor of this program. Foreign Minister Matsuoka filed a lone dissent, pleading for a re-evaluation of national policy in light of the "new situation arising out of the outbreak of war between Germany and the Soviet Union." He predicted that Japan would never get what she wanted in the south by negotiating in Washington and would finally be forced into the dreadful alternative of war. In conclusion he stated glumly: "I believe that our Empire is confronted literally with a danger that has no precedent."

When Matsuoka had lapsed silent, his struggle was carried on by the cosmopolitan Hara Yoshimichi, once head of the Constitutionalist party and now president of Hirohito's Privy Council. Ordinarily at conferences in the Imperial Presence, the president of the Privy Council was supposed to ask questions on behalf of the Throne. Before this conference, however, Hirohito had requested a free debate and had positively ordered Privy Council President Hara to speak for himself. By letting everyone have his say, by allowing all objections to be officially set down in the palace records, Hirohito could release dissenters from responsibility and could get on with what had to be done.

"I do not think," stated Privy Council President Hara, "that the scheduled movement of our military forces into French Indochina is consistent with the assurances we gave last year to Indochina when we said that we would respect her territorial integrity."

Hirohito nodded and smiled.

"I believe all of you would agree," said Hara, "that the war between Germany and the Soviet Union really represents the chance of a lifetime for Japan. Since the Soviet Union is promoting communism all over the world, we will have to attack her sooner or later. Since we are still engaged in the China Incident, I see that we cannot attack the Soviet Union as freely as we would wish. Nevertheless, I believe that we should attack the Soviet Union when it seems opportune. . . . The Soviet Union is notorious for her habitual acts of betrayal. If we were to attack the Soviet Union, no one would regard it as treachery. . . . I would ask the government and the Supreme Command to attack the Soviet Union as soon as possible."

Hirohito, who had spent half his adult life fighting the Strike-North sentiments of the Army, nodded emphatically. Hara's objections were now inscribed in the palace rolls where they could be interpreted ambiguously as representing either Hara's private views or his official views on behalf of the Throne. Chief of Staff Sugiyama noted in his minutes: "The questions put by the President of the Privy Council Hara were relevant and pointed. The Emperor seemed to be extremely satisfied."

On emerging from the council, Hirohito returned to his desk in the Imperial Library to stamp his approval on a number of military orders for which the way had now been cleared. One was a call-up of the reserve so that it could man vacant military barracks in Japan and be ready to supply casualty replacements for the divisions of the standing army which would now be in the field. Another was a peculiar little order which created a new command in Manchuria, the Kwantung Special Maneuver, a Strike-South training exercise to which were reassigned most of the veteran troops of the Kwantung Army. A third was a posting of fifteen of the divisions left in Japan to Manchuria where they would bring up the strength of the Kwantung Army and Special Maneuver forces from 400,000 to 700,000 men. A fourth was an alert to units in Taiwan, Hainan, and South China to be prepared for new uniforms, new combat rations, and new amphibious landing manuals. A fifth was an authorization for the complete rebuilding of the Imperial Headquarters shed to the north of the Fukiage Gardens in the palace grounds. It was to be greatly enlarged and sheathed entirely in armor plate. Whereas formerly it had served as a handy private place for Cabinet ministers and staff chiefs to meet occasionally, it would now become a full-time liaison office with its own staff officers, maps, and records.

Having secured the acquiescence of his ministers in a formal decision to go South on July 2, Hirohito was chagrined to find that his nod, for once, had not settled the matter. The dispatch of troops to Manchuria worried the Sorge spy ring for a while—until Sorge's agents discovered that Army purchasing agents in Osaka were ordering mosquito nets instead of fur caps—but it failed to placate the field officers of the Army. All their lives long they had trained to fight and die if necessary in war against the Russians. Now they were called upon to mount a feint against the Soviet Union and at the same time, in the Kwantung Special Maneuver, to start practicing support operations for the Navy's Strike South.

It was more than most colonels could bear, and from July 2 to July 16, Japan's domestic atmosphere crackled with tension. Intelligent men of affairs encouraged the Army in its discontent because they knew that the alternative to attacking Russia would be a fearful and perhaps suicidal war with the United States. The murmuring against imperial policy reached such a pitch that the Home Ministry turned out all its police on twenty-four-hour alert and the Education Ministry closed all high schools and state universities.

During these two weeks of simmering revolution, Foreign Minister Matsuoka persisted in his devious efforts to sabotage the sham negotiations in Washington. U.S. Secretary of State Hull, he maintained, had personally attacked him in the American Oral Statement of June 21 and had, in effect, meddled in Japanese domestic affairs by trying to get him fired. Matsuoka made the most of this negative compliment and the press supported him in his lament. The right-wing forces of former Black Dragon lord Toyama held sympathy demonstrations in his behalf. Osaka businessmen raised the price of cotton for tropical khaki uniforms and lowered the price of wool for northern winter uniforms.

In the inner councils of state, however, Matsuoka was looked upon with increasingly hard eyes and listened to with increasingly deaf ears. At his final appearance before a liaison conference on July 12, Matsuoka gave voice to the last distracting insight which he would put forward as an American expert. "The American President," he stated, "is trying to head his country into the war. There is, however, one thread of hope, which is that the American people might not follow. . . . Japanese-American accord has been my cherished wish ever since I was very young."

War Minister Tojo said, "Even if there is no hope, I would like to persist to the very end. I know it is difficult, but it will be intolerable if we cannot establish the Greater East Asia Co-Prosperity Sphere and settle the China incident. . . ."

Navy Minister Oikawa said, "According to Navy reports, it appears that Secretary of State Hull and others are not prepared to provoke a Pacific war. Since Japan does not wish to engage in a Pacific war, isn't there some room for negotiation?"

Matsuoka countered, "Is there room? What will they accept?"

Oikawa suggested, "Something minor."

Matsuoka replied, "If we say we will not use force in the south, they will probably listen. Is there anything else they will accept?"

Oikawa said, "Won't they accept the security of the Pacific? The Open Door Policy in China?"

"Well," answered Matsuoka, after some further discussion, "I'll think about it." These were his last words in argument before his peers. On July 13 he took to his bed with a feigned illness and at first refused to read a revision of the revised revision of the Draft Proposal for friendly American-Japanese relations. A parade of Army and Navy visitors on July 14 persuaded him to promise to send the revision to Ambassador Nomura. That evening, however, when he felt more courageous, he withheld the new Japanese draft and cabled Nomura only the news that Hull's latest version was inacceptable to Japan.

On the following day, July 15, Matsuoka still kept to his sickbed and the rest of the Cabinet met without him. They decided to ask to resign in protest against his non-co-operation. That afternoon at three, Prince Konoye arrived at the Imperial Summer Palace in Hayama on the beach to discuss the situation. He found Hirohito somewhat hurt and suspicious. Hirohito had made Konoye swear when he had formed his second Cabinet in 1940 "to share joys and sorrows with the Throne all the way." It now appeared that the weak Konoye might be trying to drop his burden of prime ministerial responsibilities before seeing "his mission" through to the end.

"Why should the whole Cabinet resign?" demanded Hirohito. "Why not simply replace Matsuoka?"

Konoye explained that it would disturb the unity of the nation to be rude to Matsuoka and that it would be better to save Matsuoka from any semblance of disgrace by letting the entire Cabinet resign together. Then if necessary, said Konoye with a sigh, he would accept a fresh imperial mandate and would form a new Cabinet with a different foreign minister. After making absolutely sure that Konoye was sincere in his willingness to form a third Konoye Cabinet, Hirohito agreed to permit the second Konoye Cabinet to resign.

That evening, July 15, an imperial messenger called at Matsuoka's residence requesting him, since he was sick and could not attend Cabinet meetings, to lend his signature seal to Konoye so that it might be used to stamp urgent papers of state. As a loyal subject, Matsuoka had no choice but to comply. He knew, however, that his proxy would be used for a resignation of the whole Cabinet and he took to the phone the next morning to muster his Army and business supporters. Konoye, at his phone, was equally busy assuring other Cabinet ministers that if they resigned they would be promptly reappointed to office.

In the afternoon, at 2 P.M. July 16, Hirohito took a moment out from the gathering Cabinet crisis to give audience to Lieutenant General Tiger Yamashita. Having suggested the Unit 82 Strike-South research group in Taiwan the previous fall, Yamashita had just returned from seven months of reconnaissance in Germany. He had submitted a report on his trip in which he warned that Japan's Army lagged far behind European armies and was woefully deficient in paratroops, medium tanks, and long-range bombers.

Yamashita had gone as far as the French coast and had seen at first hand the growing air superiority of the British Royal Air Force. He had schemed with his aides to pay an unscheduled inspection visit at a German radar factory and had come away with the knowledge that radar in the West was already a formidable tool of war while in Japan it still remained a crude toy of research. On the basis of such findings, Yamashita advised a two-year moratorium on all Japanese war plans and an all-out modernization of the Japanese Army. His recommendation was being used as a political weapon by junior members of the General Staff who wished to prevent Japan from committing herself to war in the south.

In the course of his audience with Hirohito, Yamashita redirected his thinking so that he derived new conclusions from his German field trip. On June 30 the General Staff had received a provisional Strike-South plan from Unit 82 in Taiwan. It revealed astonishing weaknesses in the British defenses for Malaya, grave inadequacies in the American position in the Philippines, and a negligible capacity for resistance in the Dutch East Indies. Presented with this assessment from his own minion, Lieutenant Colonel Tsuji of Unit 82, Yamashita was obliged to concede that the Japanese Army might be able to win victories in the south even if it could not vie with continental European arms in the north. He advised that the Army should not be used for offensive purposes at all if possible, but that if war was inevitable, employment in the south would be better than in the north.

Yamashita withdrew from the Imperial Presence to silence Strike-North proponents in the General Staff and to lead hesitant field officers toward the Strike South. Hirohito at once dispatched him to Manchuria to command the Kwantung Special Maneuver and four months later would put him in charge of the march on Singapore.

After talking to Yamashita, Hirohito accepted the resignation of the Cabinet *en bloc* and immediately issued the mandate to Prince Konoye to form a new Cabinet. The next afternoon, July 17, Konoye brought his proposed list of ministers to the Hayama villa and the following afternoon, July 18, Hirohito presided over the new Cabinet's ceremony of investiture. Foreign Minister Matsuoka was still on the phone. His portfolio of foreign affairs had been taken in the new Cabinet by Admiral Toyoda Soemu, a trusted member of the cabal who had attended Hirohito in 1921 in England. At the same time Baron Hiranuma, Matsuoka's chief ally in the final attempt to make Hirohito face north, was replaced as home minister by a nonentity, Tanabe Harumichi.

Gently as it had been expressed, Matsuoka's rejection by the Throne was pointed enough to lose the famous foreign minister his right-wing backing almost overnight. He retired to his small private home in the Mount Fuji foothills to contemplate in silence the sources of true political power. Five years later he was unearthed by Allied war criminal investigators, put in prison, and made to stand a few days' trial as the arch-villain of Japanese diplomacy. In the month after the beginning of the International Military Tribunal he was excused from further appearances in the dock and released into the custody of doctors. Two months later, in the fall of 1946, he died of cancer. In his final days he said not a word about his one-man attempt to deceive Hirohito and redirect the imperial program by his big talk as an "American expert." He left behind him a family which had to live in Japan.

25

KONOYE'S LAST CHANCE

(1941)

THE OIL CRISIS

The same day, July 18, on which Hirohito invested the new Japanese Cabinet, Roosevelt's American Cabinet met in Washington to approve an act of reprisal. The broken Purple Code, which Matsuoka had saved from being scrapped, informed U.S. leaders that Japan was about to occupy south Indochina and build bases with which to threaten Singapore. The U.S. Cabinet therefore approved a proposal to freeze all Japanese assets in the United States. All Japanese vessels in U.S. ports were to be prevented from sailing. All Japanese balances in U.S. banks were to be impounded. All Japanese business transactions were to be suspended in mid-air. The flow of oil, scrap iron, and machine tools from the continental United States would cease forthwith.

Before these economic sanctions were announced, and before Japanese troops began their move into south Indochina, the new Japanese Cabinet at its second liaison conference, held in the refurbished Imperial Headquarters in the palace on July 24, heard its new Foreign Minister Admiral Toyoda announce that the American government would probably take exactly these measures of reprisal which it had in fact already taken. "The United States," said Toyoda, "will adopt a policy of putting an embargo on vital materials, freezing Japanese funds, prohibiting the purchase of gold, detaining Japanese vessels, etc."

At the first liaison conference of the new Cabinet, on July 21, Navy Chief of Staff Nagano had explained that "in a war with the United States, there is now a chance of achieving victory. But the chance will diminish as time goes on. By the latter half of next year it will be difficult for us to cope with the United States. After that the situation will become pro-

774

gressively worse. The United States will probably drag things out until her defenses are built up and then will try to settle. As time goes by, therefore, the Empire will be put at a disadvantage. If we could settle matters without war, there would be nothing better. But if we conclude that conflict cannot ultimately be avoided, then I would like you to understand that time is not on our side. Furthermore, if we occupy the Philippines, it will be easier, from the standpoint of the Navy, to have prosecuted the war fully from the start."

As the Japanese fleet lived on oil, the Navy's need to fight—to fight now or not at all—would become compelling if the United States imposed an oil embargo. Everyone knew this, both in Tokyo and in Washington, yet the machinery of provocation and reprisal ground on remorselessly. Right on schedule Japanese Army tanks arrived in Saigon on July 24, and in the words of a contemporary press release "subjugated the city peacefully." The next evening F.D.R. duly announced the U.S. decision to freeze Japanese assets. Japan responded in kind and froze American assets. Japanese nationals in the United States were allowed to withdraw up to $500 a month from their frozen bank accounts. U.S. nationals in Japan were allowed to withdraw from theirs 500 yen a month—approximately one quarter as much.

The drawing of battle lines had a subtle effect on the feeling of the Japanese masses. They began to accept the inevitability of the war in store for them. The Tokyo stock exchange slumped to its lowest point since 1931. The Yokohama silk exchange shut down entirely. In their editorials the leading newspapers agreed that Japan had been challenged and would not back down. One tabloid called the U.S. reprisal an "insolent and outrageous challenge." *Nichi Nichi,* the third of the great dailies, said: "There is no greater misconception than to think that Japan will grow conciliatory because the United States strengthens her economic sanctions."

The acute Hirohito sensed the danger of fatalism among his advisors even before its rigor mortis had begun to take hold on the masses. He had no intention of going to war if he could possibly get what he wanted for Japan by means short of war. On July 22, he warned Army Chief of Staff Sugiyama that he must not fall prey to war psychology and that use of armed force must be considered only as a last resort because "our national power is small and our economic resources are scarce."

Sugiyama noted in his daybook of memoranda: "This must be kept absolutely secret but to judge from His Imperial Majesty's questions today, he is obsessed by the hope of using nonmilitary means. Therefore, I will in future try to change his feelings. I think it will be necessary to guide him step by step."

On July 29 the Navy Chief of Staff Nagano Osami tried to impress on Hirohito the need for making a firm decision to declare war on Great Britain when it became necessary to seize Malaya. Hirohito evinced "extreme dissatisfaction" and warned Nagano against assuming "the inevitability of war with Great Britain and the United States." He instructed Nagano to confer with former Navy Chief of Staff Prince Fushimi, who was his patron. At the same time the Cabinet and staff chiefs were meeting in liaison conference to discuss the problems posed by the national morale.

The next day, July 30, Navy Chief of Staff Nagano reported back to the palace that he and Prince Fushimi were agreed that they would like to avoid war if possible. Assuming hypothetically the possibility of a war, Hirohito asked, "Is it certain that we will win?"

Nagano replied, "No, it is not certain that we will win."

Hirohito said, "Then I fear that our entry into the war might mean fighting in despair."

After the audience Lord Privy Seal Kido assured Hirohito that Nagano took too extreme a stance. Between an immediate decision for war, fraught with the possibility of disaster, and a decision to accept a steady diminution of national strength for lack of oil, there were, said Kido, still many alternatives. The diplomatic offensive might be pressed in Washington by a summit conference of Prime Minister Konoye and President Roosevelt. And if that failed, Japan could swallow her pride and adopt a ten-year plan "pinned on ultimate penetration of the South."

Hirohito realized that the Strike South could indeed be postponed for a few years and that it would be foolhardy to jeopardize seventy years of effort by striking prematurely. He therefore asked Kido to determine whether, by waiting, Japan really could improve her relative position. That is, before drafting a ten-year plan for Japan, Kido should make a projection of normal U.S. growth. Unless Japan could reasonably expect to surpass the United States in absolute enlargement of her synthetic oil production, of her heavy industrial and machine tool capacity, and of her merchant marine, ten years of crash effort would avail her nothing.

Then Hirohito summoned Navy Minister Oikawa, his former personal aide, and asked his views. Oikawa said that a majority of naval officers were opposed to war with the West. The Emperor nodded and Army Chief of Staff Sugiyama, who was standing by, wrote in his notes: "I could not help thinking that we as a nation have not yet come to a point at which we can reach a decision to make war against England and America."

On July 28, the Netherlands East Indies had followed the United States and Great Britain in cutting off all oil shipments to Japan. On July 31 the U.S. oil embargo, announced earlier, went into effect. After that date Japan's ability to fight against superior odds could only ebb.

A CHOICE OF EVILS

During that last bleak week in July 1941, when all Japan realized that a decision must be made either to back down or to stake everything on a desperate war with the West, an enterprising Japanese reporter bulled his way into the villa of the discredited former Foreign Minister Matsuoka, at the foot of Mount Fuji, and extracted from him a statement. Waving a hand at the summit of the sacred volcano, Matsuoka confessed: "As viewed from the top of the mountain, the international situation may present a variety of different vistas."

Hirohito alone stood at the top of the mountain. He alone had full access to Army planning, Navy planning, Foreign Ministry planning, and the policy-making thoughts of all his intimate advisors. He fully understood the need to decide soon on war or peace. He may have genuinely hoped that by negotiation and threat he could wring a foothold in the East Indies from the British, Dutch, and Americans without having to fight for it. At the same time he was planning for the contingency of war, and in so doing he was preoccupied with considerations beyond the ken of his chiefs of staff.

He felt, for instance, that if the people were to support the war, they must first live with anxiety for a while and come to believe sincerely that the nation was being bled to death. As Prime Minister Konoye pointed out to Lord Privy Seal Kido on August 5, after an audience with the Emperor on the peace negotiations in Washington: "Suppose it turns out that Chamberlain was betrayed by Hitler. Still you cannot dismiss the fact that Chamberlain met many times with Hitler and so helped to prepare England for war."

On the other side of the equation Hirohito juggled military factors. If the Americans were to be taken by surprise and beaten, utmost security must shroud Japan's attack plans; they must be worked out and practiced down to the last detail; and Japanese officials—even the chiefs of staff—must be kept in ignorance of them until the last possible moment. Officials who had to deal with newsmen and ambassadors would stand a far better chance of lulling Western suspicions if they knew nothing of the attack plans than they would if they knew everything and tried to conceal their knowledge.

The available documents indicate that, in July and early August when Hirohito was pleading with his chiefs of staff to avoid if at all possible the use of military force, neither of the staff chiefs yet knew of the plan for Pearl Harbor. The fact that Hirohito had ordered the plan submitted to Vice Admiral Onishi in January, for an independent appraisal, first came to Navy Chief of Staff Nagano's attention in a memorandum headed "August 22, 1941," and this memorandum was not entered in the notebook of Army Chief of Staff Sugiyama—"the bathroom door"—until October 30, 1941.

"Keeping in mind," as he liked to say, "the whole situation," Hirohito in early August turned down a request from the commander of the truncated Kwantung Army in Manchuria for discretionary power in dealing with possible aggressive moves by the Red Army in Siberia. In the same week Hirohito encouraged Prime Minister Konoye to arrange a peace meeting, if possible, with President Roosevelt in Hawaii; he asked Lord Privy Seal Kido to draw up a ten-year contingency plan for peaceful economic infiltration of the East Indies; and in another compartment of his security-conscious, protocol-observing existence, he reviewed the preparations which the Army and Navy were separately making for the possibility of war.

The Army plans were the first ones presented. Lieutenant Colonel Tsuji Masanobu, the brains of Unit 82 in Taiwan, outlined them to Hirohito's aides and to the officers of the Operations Department of the General Staff in a three-day briefing, July 24–26, 1941. Afterwards Chief of Staff Sugiyama congratulated Tsuji on a brilliant presentation and asked him, "What is your estimate of the rate at which the operations you have demonstrated can be carried out?"

"If we commence on Emperor Meiji day [November 3]," replied Tsuji, "we should be able to capture Manila by New Year, Singapore by National Foundation Day [February 11], Java by Army Commemoration Day [March 10], and Rangoon by the Emperor's birthday [April 19]." [1]

In support of Tsuji's plans Hirohito authorized massive troop movements to Manchuria in the first week of August 1941. There, the reinforcements gave the impression that Japan was about to strike at the Soviet Union. In reality, however, the reinforcements relieved the combat-tested veterans of the Kwantung Army from guard duty so that they could be trained for the Strike South. Starting in late July, General Yamashita, the Tiger, began two months of intensive exercises in which he selected and rehearsed the best units in the Japanese Army, some for the occupation of the Philippines, some for the campaign in Malaya, and some for the conquest of Java, Sumatra, and Borneo.

Soviet spy Sorge was radioed by his center in Siberia to turn all his attention to evaluating the intentions behind this latest build-up in Manchuria. Sorge responded at once with a message protesting that, as far as he could determine, no Japanese attack on Siberia was contemplated. He bolstered his contention at the end of July by reporting that the Japanese Army was in process of requisitioning a million tons of merchant marine for transport to destinations which could hardly be continental. In early August he had Klausen radio the center that there was a "possibility of [Japanese] operations against the Dutch East Indies." On August 15, Sorge reported that his friends in the German Embassy in Tokyo had despaired of Japanese help against Russia. In late August, through his Ozaki-Saionji-Kido link to the Emperor, he learned that Hirohito had already decided against a Strike North at the conference in the Imperial Presence on July 2. Not

---

[1] In the event the attack would start more than a month late—on December 8— but the schedule would still be met. Manila would be captured January 2, Singapore February 15, Java March 10, and Rangoon March 8.

until early October, however, could Sorge radio Moscow that Japan contemplated "no attack [on Russia] until the spring of next year at the earliest"; and that "there will be war with the United States this month or next month."

U.S. intelligence officers in Washington, working from afar with decoded intercepts of Japanese diplomatic messages, correctly assessed Hirohito's July 2 decision long before the Soviet ring in Tokyo. In memos GZ-1 and GZ-4, dated August 4 and 9, Lieutenant Commander Alwin D. Kramer of Naval Intelligence greatly impressed the men around Secretary of State Hull by extracting the following salient points from intercepts:

> Japan will not go to war against the U.S.S.R. in the north.
> She will intensify preparations for "the southward move."
> She will immediately begin to "arm for all-out war against Britain and the United States to break the British-American encirclement."

In the second week of August, Hirohito commenced his review of the Navy's war planning. Combined Fleet commander Admiral Yamamoto had spent the spring and early summer of 1941 conducting exercises, in the guise of routine training, to make sure that his men and ships and planes were physically capable of the attack which he imagined for them. Off the Kyushu ports of Kagoshima, Kanoya, and Saiki and the Shikoku port of Sukumo, his dive-bomber and torpedo-plane pilots had proved their ability to follow maps and briefings and carry out difficult mock missions over unfamiliar mountainous terrains with a high degree of pinpoint success. Now in early August Yamamoto and a handful of his most trusted staff officers arrived in Tokyo to explain their military convictions to a select cadre of Hirohito's personal naval representatives.

Yamamoto still protested that war with the United States should be avoided if possible, but he insisted that if war was necessary he must first knock out the Pearl Harbor fleet or Japan would have no chance at all. Since his ideas were as yet known only to Hirohito, to Prince Takamatsu, and to a few fully reliable staff officers in the fleet, he gave his sales presentation not at the offices of the Navy General Staff but at the Naval Staff College, which was presided over by its dean, Rear Admiral Marquis Komatsu Teruhisa, the imperial family member who had run Hirohito's physical education program on the deck of the battleship *Katori* in 1921.

In the staff college Yamamoto's staff officers mingled with the students— the experienced fleet commanders and captains who were intent upon bettering themselves with instruction in the technical and strategic postgraduate aspects of modern naval warfare. Yamamoto worried that any serious-looking member of the college might walk by accident into one of his seminars and take out of it the rumor that Japan meant to attack Pearl Harbor. In the event, however, Yamamoto's table-top demonstration went off without interruption and convinced Marquis Komatsu and Prince Takamatsu that the Pearl Harbor plan was well thought out and had a real chance of success.

DEADLINE FOR WAR

Immediately after Yamamoto's table-top maneuvers, on August 16, Navy General Staff officers who had been present at the demonstration in the staff college presented to their opposite numbers in the Army General Staff and War Ministry a timetable of necessary political preparations for war. Their proposition was that the Cabinet, meeting in the presence of the Emperor early in September, should make up its mind to approve final preparations by the armed forces, starting in early October, unless the United States showed signs of giving in to Japanese demands earlier. The section chiefs of the War Ministry and Army General Staff agreed to the plan and began to circulate it for approval throughout the military bureaucracy. Although it had the backing of imperial henchmen like Marquis Komatsu, and was presumed to have the backing of Hirohito, it was considered only a position-paper project and was not shown to the chiefs of staff until late in the month, August 28.

Also on August 16, when the Navy's junior officers first broached this plan, Prince Takamatsu, as the "Someone" at liaison conferences, made a special request of the ministers present. "In the past," he said, "we have had cases in which secrets have been leaked out because they were discussed in the Cabinet. Therefore, except in matters of a grave political nature which must be submitted to the Cabinet, it is best if the full Cabinet should not be consulted."

Roosevelt and Churchill had just met in mid-Atlantic to sign their historic affirmation of democratic ideals, the Atlantic Charter. On August 17, as soon as Roosevelt had returned to Washington, Ambassador Nomura obtained a few minutes with him to beg that he meet personally with Prime Minister Konoye somewhere in the middle of the Pacific. F.D.R. at first seemed to respond favorably to the suggestion, but after consultation with the State Department he informed Ambassador Nomura that an American-Japanese summit conference would serve no purpose unless adequate spadework had been done in advance to make possible a meeting on level ground. By the end of August Konoye and Hirohito knew that the free-wheeling American president was not likely to be seduced even if the mid-Pacific conference could be arranged.

On September 2, Admiral Yamamoto and his staff officers gathered once more at Marquis Komatsu's staff college on the edge of the Shiragane imperial woods three and a half miles south of the main palace. This time the college was the rehearsal stage for all the naval operations required by the Army's Unit-82 Strike-South plan. Yamamoto's scheme was only a sideshow which might or might not be used on opening night. The main event was a demonstration of the Navy's tactical plans for supporting co-ordinated troop landings in Malaya, the Philippines, Wake, Guam, Borneo, and Java. Thirty-nine of Yamamoto's peers—the most gifted and technically-minded admirals, captains, and commanders in the Navy General Staff and Navy Ministry—had charge of the production. And until they were sure that the main event was feasible, they could not even consider diverting ships and planes for Yamamoto's hazardous enterprise. For six days Yamamoto watched and criticized their presentations, paring from their task forces all fatty margins of safety and gaining for his own ends a destroyer or tanker here and an air squadron or carrier there.

While Yamamoto fretted, the Army-Navy deadline for giving up negotiations and deciding on war was considered, on September 3, by a liaison conference. Navy Chief of Staff Nagano opened the debate by explaining: "We are growing weaker while the enemy is growing stronger. . . . When there is no hope for diplomacy and war cannot be avoided, we must be ready to make up our minds quickly." Seven hours later the conferees agreed that if the United States "does not meet our demands" by October 10 "we will then at once decide to commence hostilities against the United States, Britain, and the Netherlands."

When the conference closed at 6 P.M., the policy statement on which it had passed—"Essentials for Carrying out the Empire's Program"—was sent on for reference to the Imperial Library. Hirohito was expected to read it that evening or the next morning. Foreign Minister Toyoda and Prime Minister Konoye were both troubled by it because it seemed to emphasize the preparations for war more than the negotiations with Washington which were supposed to achieve Japan's goals without war. And so the next afternoon Foreign Minister Toyoda called at the Imperial Library to report on the deadlocked Washington negotiations and see how Hirohito was reacting. The Emperor had nothing special to say. On the following afternoon, September 5, therefore, Prime Minister Konoye called on Hirohito and pointed out to him that the first paragraph of the "Essentials" was devoted exclusively to military preparations and that diplomacy was relegated to the second paragraph. Hirohito agreed that this was a misplaced emphasis and promised to speak about it to the chiefs of staff on the morrow. Konoye begged him to summon the chiefs of staff at once and speak about it right away. Hirohito consulted with Lord Privy Seal Kido and decided to accede to Konoye's request.

The two chiefs of staff arrived out of breath at the library at 6 P.M. According to Army Chief of Staff Sugiyama's memorandum written immediately afterwards, Hirohito greeted them abruptly with an imperative:

"Do use diplomacy and peace as much as possible. Do not use diplomacy and war preparations as equals at the same time. Give diplomacy precedence."

The two staff chiefs stammered apologetic explanations of the order of paragraphs in the "Essentials" and Hirohito continued:

"Do you think the southern operations can be carried out as planned?"

Sugiyama gave a detailed defense of the Unit-82 proposals for operations in the Philippines and Malaya. The Emperor cut him short:

"There must be things which will not go according to plan. You say five months, but isn't it possible it can't all be done in five months?"

"Since both the Army and Navy have studied it several times," said Sugiyama stoutly, "it should be carried out almost exactly as planned."

Hirohito objected that amphibious operations were always fraught with unexpected difficulties and pointed out that in one mock landing exercise on the coasts of Kyushu recently the attacking force had theoretically lost half its men before they had reached the beach.

"That happened," said Sugiyama, "because our convoy started to move before the opposing air cover had been destroyed. I don't think the blunder will ever be repeated."

"Well then," asked Hirohito, "how about adverse weather?"

"That," replied Sugiyama, "is an obstacle which we must overcome."

"But you do think," said Hirohito, "that you can do what you plan? Remember that when you were war minister [in 1937] you said that Chiang Kai-shek would surrender immediately. But you still haven't made him do it."

In his memorandum Sugiyama then continued his narrative in indirect dialogue. "I took this opportunity," he wrote, "to elaborate and to explain to the Emperor the need to improve the outlook of the nation while it still has elasticity. Before all national power is spent, we must face obstacles in order to open up the national destiny."

According to a version of the same conversation written by Prince Konoye for the Peace Faction three years later, Sugiyama excused his mistaken forecast of prospects in China by admitting that he had underestimated the resilience and sheer size of the Chinese nation.[2]

Then, according to Konoye, Hirohito said acidly, "If you call the interior of China broad, isn't the Pacific Ocean even broader? How can you confidently say [this time that it will take only] three months?"[3]

---

[2] The Konoye account of this scene is the only one which has previously been published in English. Despite the fact that it was written years after Sugiyama's account and written for a public relations purpose, I have introduced a portion of it here on the chance that Sugiyama, even in his private memoranda set down in the presence of the spirit ancestors, may have suppressed a part of Hirohito's wounding words to him.

[3] Sugiyama, as his memoranda state, had undoubtedly said "five months" rather than "three." The Unit-82 schedule did indeed call for five months: November 1941 to April 1942. But Konoye years later, recalling the breathtaking speed of Japan's actual advance, put "three months" into the Emperor's mouth by mistake.

According to Sugiyama's own account the Emperor merely said "in a loud voice":

"Are you absolutely sure this time that we can win?"

"I hesitate," replied Sugiyama, "to say I am absolutely sure, but I can say that there is a good possibility of winning. I cannot say that I am absolutely sure but I know that, for the price of a short-term peace of six months or a year, we cannot afford a long-term national catastrophe. We must think in terms of a lasting peace of twenty or fifty years."

"Oh, I see," said Hirohito, and once again he spoke "in a loud voice."

"We are not happy to wage this war," insisted Sugiyama. "We are thinking of war only in case all peaceful efforts fail."

Navy Chief of Staff Nagano interceded to remind the Emperor of the winter of 1614 when the first of the Tokugawa shoguns had invested the Osaka castle of the son of Hideyoshi, the great plebeian general who had invaded Korea in the 1580's and 1590's. Nagano pointed out that the shogun had finally taken the castle only by first making peace and persuading Hideyoshi's son to fill in the outer moats of the castle. Then by stealth the shogun had filled in the second line of moats as well and succeded in crossing the third and final line to storm the walls and take the keep. According to Nagano's analysis Japan should beware of a settlement with the United States which might fill her outer moat and should not be contented with one which failed to fill the outer moat of the enemy. "Hirohito listened with interest."

Finally Prime Minister Konoye said: "As both staff chiefs have acknowledged we shall try to use peaceful diplomatic means up to the end. I am in complete accord with the chiefs that after that and only after that will we go to war as specified."

The two military men bowed themselves from the room and Konoye thanked Hirohito for his support. Then Hirohito went to supper.

The next morning, from 10 A.M. to noon, September 6, Hirohito presided over a historic conference in the Imperial Presence which tied the next-to-last knot on Japan's neatly packed war bomb. As always at such conferences the important matters under consideration were circulated beforehand in written form, were read by all participants including Hirohito, but were alluded to rather than discussed. The speeches made were all set pieces, rehearsed beforehand and delivered out loud solely for the purpose of the record—for the assignment of responsibility on the sacred palace rolls.

At the beginning of the conference, all the Cabinet ministers and staff chiefs who were present emulated Hirohito as he sat at his little altar at one end of the room silently shuffling through the position papers before him to indicate that he found them familiar and all in order. One of the papers stated: "The purposes of war with the United States, Great Britain, and the Netherlands are to expel the influence of these three countries from East Asia, to establish a sphere for the self-defense and self-preservation of our Empire, and to build a New Order in Greater East Asia."

A second item stated: "A war with the United States and Great Britain will be long, and will become a war of endurance. It is very difficult to predict the termination of war, and it would be well-nigh impossible to expect the surrender of the United States. However, we cannot exclude the possibility that the war may end because of a great change in American public opinion, which may result from such factors as the remarkable success of our military operations in the south or the capitulation of Great Britain [to Germany]. At any rate, we should be able to establish an invincible position: by building up a strategically advantageous position through the occupation of important areas in the south; by creating an economy that will be self-sufficient in the long run through the development of rich resources in the Southern Regions, as well as through the use of the economic power of the East Asian continent; and by linking Asia and Europe in destroying the Anglo-American coalition through our co-operation with Germany and Italy. Meanwhile, we may hope that we will be able to influence the trend of affairs and bring the war to an end."

A third of the position papers on the tables explained: "We must carry out military preparations as secretly as possible, conceal our intentions, and refrain from sending additional forces to southern French Indo-china. . . . Diplomatic negotiations during this period should be conducted with a view toward facilitating the switch-over from political to military methods."

A fourth document under consideration concerned the "minimum conditions" and "maximum concessions" which Japan would accept from the United States as the price for peace. It stipulated that if "we promise not to use military force in the south, we must put China under the complete control of our Empire. To do that, it is absolutely essential to station the necessary forces there. . . . If they [the Americans] do not accede to the conditions that we propose, we must regard it as disclosing their true intention, which is to bring Japan to her knees."

In regard to the withdrawal of Japanese troops from China which the United States had persistently demanded as a prerequisite for serious negotiation of peace in the Far East, a codicil suggested: "We have no objection to affirming that we are in principle prepared to withdraw our troops [from China] following the settlement of the incident, except for those that are dispatched to carry out the purposes of the incident."

When these support papers had been leafed through and the imperial conference of September 6 opened, no one present pointed out the utter hopelessness and insincerity of Japan's negotiating position vis-à-vis the United States. Instead a parade of ministers took the floor one by one to take responsibility for advising simultaneous negotiations and war preparations until October 10, after which date war preparations should be finalized and negotiations continued only in the hope of a miracle or as a form of subterfuge. Prime Minister Prince Konoye, Navy Chief of Staff Nagano, and Army Chief of Staff Sugiyama all spoke in favor of the motion. Foreign Minister Admiral Toyoda gave a straightforward, factual description of the entire course of the Japanese-American negotiations theretofore. The ubiquitous Suzuki, now a retired lieutenant general in charge of the Cabinet Planning Board which ran the Japanese economy, described the condition of the nation's strategic stockpiles and strongly urged immediate acquisition of new sources of supply in the Dutch East Indies.

Finally Privy Council President Hara arose. On this occasion he had been enjoined strictly by Lord Privy Seal Kido to speak only on behalf of the Throne and to make absolutely clear in the record what Hirohito had said to the chiefs of staff the day before. Accordingly, the Privy Council president said in part:

"I take it that starting now, we will prepare for war at the same time that diplomatic measures are being used; that is, everywhere we will try to break the deadlock through diplomacy, but if this should fail, we will have to go to war. The draft seems to suggest that the war comes first, and diplomacy second; but I interpret it to mean that we will spare no efforts in diplomacy and we will go to war only when we can find no other way."

When Hara had made his point on behalf of the Throne, Navy Minister Oikawa hastened to reassure the Emperor that all present understood his wishes and would respect them. Then Hara continued, "When the prime minister visits the United States in the near future, he must be determined to improve relations by using all conceivable diplomatic measures, even though we will be making preparations for war as a matter of policy. If the proposals under consideration are given imperial assent, I ask all of you to co-operate in promoting the aims of the prime minister's U.S. visit."

Hara went on to ask Chief of Staff Sugiyama some technical questions about Soviet diplomatic and military strength. Then Hara said:

"I have been told that this war decision will be subject to careful deliberation and so I will not ask any further questions. I shall be satisfied if the diplomatic negotiations can be carried out under the conditions indicated in the attached papers, and so I give my complete consent to this proposal."

Since the conditions indicated in the attached papers were known to be completely inacceptable to the United States and had been inacceptable ever since Japan's invasion of China four years earlier, Hara's last statement on behalf of the Throne clearly settled the issue of war and peace. Hara went on to deliver a page of comment on the state of the nation's

morale, asking everyone present to suppress dissidents and to encourage
the people to pull as a team. Finally he concluded, "I would like to see
courageous and drastic action taken, so that the decisions of the imperial
conference can be carried out even if worse comes to worst."

Home Minister Tanabe Harumichi, who had succeeded Hiranuma at
the time of Matsuoka's ouster from the Cabinet in July, proceeded to
deliver a detailed explanation of the measures which would be taken by
the police to keep the people in line. Then the decision to negotiate for
five weeks while completing war planning—together with all the position
papers which had been silently presented in its support—was unanimously
recommended to the Throne.

Hirohito arose and, instead of nodding and making his exit as he usually
did on such occasions, dramatically drew a slip of paper from his pocket
and read a noncommittal little poem composed by Emperor Meiji, his
grandfather, on the eve of the war with Russia four decades earlier:

> In as much as all   *Yomo no umi*
> the seas in all directions   *mina harakara to*
> seem twins of one birth,   *omou yo ni,*
> how often must the winds and   *nando namikaze no*
> the waves clash in noisiness?   *tachisawaguramu.*

Having spoken in this dubious fashion on the side of the angels and
philosophers, Hirohito withdrew, leaving his responsible vassals to contemplate, for a few silent moments of "awe and trepidation," the depth
of his still waters. As events would soon show, he had just belly-talked
Japan into war.

PRINCE KONOYE BOWS OUT

Prime Minister Konoye, immediately after the fateful conference in the
Imperial Presence adjourned, had one of his secretaries phone the American
Embassy and arrange a clandestine meeting for him with Ambassador Grew.
The two men were driven to their tryst in specially provided unofficial cars,
with plain license plates, which would not be noticed by reporters or policemen. They met at the home of Baron Ito Bunkichi, the adopted son of
Prime Minister Ito Hirobumi who had died by assassin's bullet in Manchuria in 1909. All the servants in the house had been given the night off
and Baron Ito's daughter personally served the conferees with food and
drink. Konoye had with him his secretary, Ushiba Tomohiko, and Ambassador Grew his embassy counsellor, Eugene H. Dooman. The four men
dined and talked together for three hours and, in Grew's words, "presented
with entire frankness the fundamental views of our two countries."

In an effort to enlist Grew's help in arranging a Konoye-Roosevelt summit meeting, Konoye went to the length of assuring Grew that "we conclusively and wholeheartedly agree with the four principles enunciated by the secretary of state." These called on Japan to promise: "Respect for the territorial integrity and the sovereignty of each and all nations; support of the principle of non-interference in the internal affairs of other countries; support of the principle of equality, including equality of commercial opportunity; and non-disturbance of the status quo in the Pacific except as the status quo may be altered by peaceful means."

In his diary Grew continued:

> Prince Konoye recognizes that the responsibility is his for the present regrettable state of relations between our two countries but, with appropriate modesty as to his personal capabilities, he likewise recognizes that only he can cause the desired rehabilitation to come about. In the event of failure on his part, no succeeding Prime Minister at least during his own lifetime, could achieve the results desired. . . . Prince Konoye told me that from the inception of the informal talks in Washington he had received the strongest concurrence from the responsible chiefs of both the Army and the Navy. Only today he had conferred with the Minister of War [Tojo], who had promised to send a full general to accompany the Prime Minister to the meeting with the President. . . . Prince Konoye repeatedly stressed the view that time is of the essence. . . . He could not guarantee to put into effect any such programme of settlement six months or a year from now. He does, however, guarantee that at the present time he can carry with him the Japanese people to the goal which he has selected. . . . He expressed the earnest hope that in view of the present internal situation in Japan the projected meeting with the President could be arranged with the least possible delay.

Konoye's desperate bid to involve Grew and Roosevelt in his own domestic political struggles continued for a month and ultimately came to naught. The State Department dissuaded Roosevelt from meeting with Konoye until the "Japanese government" could promise specific reforms in its international conduct. The position-paper writers and the responsible ministers of the Japanese government refused to let Konoye make the official assurances that were needed. Hirohito refrained from exercising his immense influence on Konoye's behalf.

The crux of the impasse was China. The United States insisted that Japan promise to withdraw her troops from China if and when a general Pacific settlement could be reached. Japan refused to make such a pledge except in the most vague and futuristic terms. On the other hand Japan insisted that she be given access once more to supplies of oil while the diplomatic settlement was being negotiated. The United States refused to comply unless Japan would make an equivalent gesture of solid, material good faith.

As the circular logic of the situation exhausted all the negotiators, both in Tokyo and in Washington, the Japanese Army and Navy were pressing forward with their war planning. At the Naval Staff College in southern Tokyo, the general table-top maneuvers neared an end on September 8 with a decision by the elder staff admirals, who acted as umpires, to let Yamamoto explain the strategic value of his Pearl Harbor plan and the tactical means by which he proposed to execute it. The admirals agreed that Yamamoto might hold a special top-secret map exercise from September 10 to September 12. He would be judged by twelve top-brass strategists in relation to his performance against five officers of an E-team (for England) and seven admirals, captains, and commanders of an A-team (for America).

That night, September 8, when Yamamoto had just won this chance to present his case, Marquis Komatsu, the dean of the staff college, held a banquet of celebration for members and intimates of the imperial family. Lord Privy Seal Kido attended with his mother, once a minor princess, now an old lady in her seventies.

The next morning, September 9, Yamamoto gave his over-all presentation to the umpires, explaining the forces he would need, the results he hoped to achieve, and finally the absolute strategic necessity for an early debilitating blow at the U.S. Pacific fleet. The umpires were impressed but reserved in their praise. If Yamamoto could demonstrate the technical feasibility of his plan in the "special maneuvers" scheduled for the next three days, the plan should certainly be incorporated, tentatively, in the over-all war strategy.

That afternoon, right after lunch, the two chiefs of staff reported on the progress of the war games to the Imperial Library. According to Army Chief of Staff Sugiyama, Hirohito greeted them buoyantly:

"Now I fully understand our operational plans. But what if there is pressure from the north while we are doing the south?"

"Once we start in the Southern Regions," replied Sugiyama, "we must look neither to left nor right until we have accomplished our purpose. We must concentrate on it to the exclusion of all else. I beg Your Majesty to assent to this proposition. If an incident occurs in the north, we can divert forces from China. We must not, however, stop our operations in the south half way."

"It pleases me to hear that," said Hirohito. "Diverting forces from China must be difficult for you."

Sugiyama replied that it would be difficult but not impossible.

The next day, September 10, Hirohito gave the staff chiefs permission for a full-scale national call-up of the reserve. "You may mobilize," he said, "but if the Konoye-Roosevelt talks should become successful, you will stop, correct?"

"Absolutely correct," replied Sugiyama.

Meanwhile, Yamamoto's map exercise had opened at the Naval Staff College. His forces, hypothetically, had rendezvoused, under complete radio silence, in the extreme north of Japan, the Kurile Islands, and begun a quiet voyage across the northern Pacific, far from trade routes. As they made their approach on paper to Hawaii, a yeoman stood by in the small crowded room where Yamamoto was playing his tactical game and calculated the fuel consumption of the various ships in the fleet on an abacus.[4] Despite the shrewdest moves which the opposing admirals in adjoining rooms could make on the basis of their knowledge of Yamamoto and of the false intelligence which the umpires thought fair for Yamamoto to throw in their direction, the Pearl Harbor fleet arrived unexpected at its destination and did great damage. In its retreat the umpires calculated that it might lose almost a third of its ships but that the loss which it had inflicted might be worth the price.

After this verdict, Yamamoto returned triumphant, on Saturday, September 13, to his Combined Fleet flagship, the *Nagato*. His staff officers spent a day going over the papers he had brought back from Tokyo and discussing the moves they must make next. Then, on the following day, Monday, September 15, Yamamoto and a few of his aides went ashore to reveal the Pearl Harbor plan for the first time to a representative of the Army.

At the headquarters of the Iwakuni Air Group, Yamamoto met with Count Terauchi Hisaichi, the general of the former Army Purification Movement who had reorganized civilian espionage for the Strike South in Taiwan in 1934; who had assisted the Court in overseeing arrangements in 1935 for the 1936 Army mutiny; who as war minister in 1936 and 1937 had carried out the Army's purge of the Strike-North Faction. Now, at sixty-two, Terauchi had been promised by Hirohito the post of Supreme Commander for the Southern Regions.[5] He and his protégé, Lieutenant General Tiger Yamashita—who had been specially flown in for the occasion from Manchuria—digested Admiral Yamamoto's plan and promised their support and co-operation in it. At the same time, they both agreed with Yamamoto that war would be a desperate gamble and should be avoided if at all possible.

A few days later, on September 21, Yamamoto and his staff began work on Order Number One, a comprehensive war plan so detailed that it would take an expert typesetter, cleared for top secrets, three days to set and print 300 copies of it. This was the order which, when stamped and signed by Hirohito, would launch World War II in the Pacific.

Unnerved by the speed with which war preparations were being pushed

---

[4] The yeoman was later captured on Saipan where he gave American intelligence officers their first knowledge of the September 2–13 table-top maneuvers. He was interrogated by a friend of the author, Otis Cary, now a member of the faculty of Doshisha University in Kyoto and the administrator of Amherst House there.

[5] The Strike-South Faction's inclusive term for all the land between India and Australia.

ahead and unwilling to take responsibility for them, Prime Minister Konoye began to think of ways of resigning. He had promised to share joys and sorrows with Hirohito to the end but he did not wish to go down in history as a complete fool and villain. He did not share Hirohito's interest and expertise in military matters and he could not believe that Japan's armed forces would have any success against the United States. On the other hand he understood diplomacy. Hirohito expected him to get what Japan wanted through negotiation and the threat of force, but Konoye felt that this would be impossible. Hirohito had inherited from his ancestors the sacred duty of cleansing Japanese soil of barbarians. Konoye had inherited from his ancestors a simpler mission: to guard the institution of the Throne and preserve it for posterity. He now began to think that he might be more effective in salvaging the institution of the Throne from the ruins of defeat than in saving Hirohito, personally, from the fate he seemed driven to pursue.

On September 18 four toughs jumped on the running board of Konoye's car as it was leaving his Kamakura villa and brandished daggers and pistols at him. The incident was kept out of the newspapers but widely publicized on the bureaucratic grapevine. It was even said, erroneously, that one of the thugs fired a bullet which missed Konoye's head by eighteen inches. The would-be assassins were arrested and kept in jail for a few months. All four of them belonged to a previously nonviolent faction of right-wing socialists who had long enjoyed Konoye's patronage. As a result the story was current at Court that Konoye had staged the attack himself in order to gain public sympathy and provide the first of several excuses for resigning the prime ministership. The alternative explanation had it that the war party was trying to intimidate him.

Two days after the attack, on September 20, Konoye attended a liaison conference of the Cabinet and General Staffs at which, under protest, he accepted October 15 as the final deadline for diplomacy with the United States. After that date negotiations might continue but mostly as a façade while war plans were being pursued in earnest. On September 26 Konoye told Lord Privy Seal Kido that the third Konoye Cabinet would have to resign unless the October 15 deadline could be further relaxed. Kido replied that Konoye was "behaving irresponsibly."

The next day, September 27, Konoye retired to his Kamakura villa for a rest and remained there until the first of the month, refusing to converse with anyone on public affairs.

Hirohito hardly noticed Konoye's unco-operative attitude, for he was immersed in the pros and cons of war. Thus, on September 29, he asked Lord Privy Seal Kido to investigate the amount of rubber the United States had stockpiled and to determine the quantity and quality of rubber which the United States could obtain from South America if Malayan and Indonesian sources were shut off. He was gratified to learn that the United States, under such circumstances, would have to depend almost entirely on synthetic rubber.

From October 1 to October 5 Hirohito was taken up with table-top maneuvers being held at the Army's War College. The exercises were to determine how long the Army would need to proceed "from Phase One of preparedness to Phase Two." Phase One called for some 400,000 troops to be mustered and ready near ports with adequate shipping in the heart of the Empire. Phase Two called for first-wave invasion forces to be waiting aboard transports on the southern frontiers of the Empire: Taiwan, Hainan, and Indochina. Hirohito had insisted earlier that Phase Two must be delayed as long as possible so as not to prejudice diplomatic negotiations. The Army had insisted that it would need three weeks to move from Phase One into Phase Two. The War College maneuvers demonstrated that the difficult and dangerous transition period could be abridged to two weeks.

The sulking Prime Minister Konoye finally returned from his tent to duty on October 1. The next day U.S. Secretary of State Hull, in an oral statement to Ambassador Nomura in Washington, reaffirmed the hard U.S. line that Japanese forces must withdraw from China as part of any lasting American-Japanese settlement in the Far East. A fortnight of frenzied political activity ensued in Tokyo. Influential Japanese pulled strings to get messages to the Emperor that war with the United States would be a disaster. Hirohito's closest advisors pinched themselves and told one another that they must be living through a bad dream. Navy Minister Oikawa suggested to Generals Tojo and Sugiyama that the Navy could not enter the war with any hope of success. Prime Minister Konoye alternately begged Ambassador Grew and Emperor Hirohito for help and comfort but was turned down by both. In Washington Ambassador Nomura began spending less time in secret negotiation with Secretary of State Hull—in a suite at the Wardman Park apartment hotel—and more time driving about the Virginia and Maryland countryside in sad meditation. Books have been filled with the comings and goings of that tragic fortnight, but nothing really happened, nothing changed.

Even Lord Privy Seal Kido had moments in which his dedication to the national program wavered. On October 9 he admitted to Prime Minister Konoye that the world situation was too complex for a clear-cut preference as to war or peace. Perhaps it would be best to live with U.S. economic sanctions, to be satisfied with a few of the provinces of China, and to ask the people to practice frugality and industry and build up the national strength for another ten years before seeking further expansion. If Konoye, he said, believed that this would be the best course for the nation, he should act on his own responsibility in favor of peace. If he had the conviction to pursue a policy of retrenchment, the Emperor, said Kido, could be persuaded to cancel the war decision of the imperial conference of September 6. Konoye promised to give the possibility serious thought.

The next day, October 10, Hirohito called in his cousin, former Navy Chief of Staff Prince Fushimi, and asked his opinion as to whether or not the Navy was prepared to fight. Fushimi replied that the Navy, despite pessimists like Navy Minister Oikawa, was not only ready to fight but to win. That same day Hirohito approved a combined Army-Navy command for operations in the Southern Regions and asked that the government reach a firm determination before the rapidly approaching deadline of October 15.

When the Cabinet met on October 12, War Minister Tojo expressed disgust with the continuing negotiations in Washington which were only wasting time and improving the relative position of the United States. Navy Minister Oikawa agreed that war was a possibility but asked that diplomacy be considered as an alternative. Moreover, said Oikawa, the decision should be made now for one or the other, for if diplomacy was continued much longer it would become a dishonorable smokescreen for war.

The next day, October 13, Hirohito indirectly admitted to Lord Privy Seal Kido that he saw no hope in further diplomacy. "The day after the war begins," he said, "we will have to issue an Imperial Declaration of War. Please see to it." He went on to disclaim all responsibility for the warlike sentiments of his people, observing that he had stressed his love for peace in the rescripts he had issued at the time of Japan's withdrawal from the League of Nations in 1933 and the signing of the Tripartite Pact in 1940. Finally, he asked Kido to make sure that lines of communication would be kept open for negotiating with the United States after war began. He suggested that a special envoy be sent to the Vatican so that the Pope could be used as a mediator.

On October 14, Prime Minister Konoye sent a last desperate message to President Roosevelt by the hand of Bishop Walsh, the Maryknoll Father who had first presented the basis for peace talks in Washington ten months earlier. He told Walsh to tell F.D.R. that unless a dramatic peace gesture was made immediately, the third Konoye Cabinet would have to resign and chances for a peaceful settlement would go aglimmering. Bishop Walsh accepted the assignment reluctantly for by now he was convinced that the United States was even less willing to patch up a peace settlement than Japan was. Nevertheless, as a matter of Christian duty, he accepted a place on a plane to Hong Kong, provided for him by Konoye, so that he could catch the next trans-Pacific Clipper.

As Bishop Walsh was embarking, Lord Privy Seal Kido and War Minister Tojo reached an agreement in the palace that the Konoye Cabinet must be replaced. Kido noted in his diary that Tojo was willing to take the responsibility for a last postponement of military operations and a last try at diplomacy. Tojo reported as follows on the conversation to Chief of Staff Sugiyama:

> Kido: The next Cabinet will be difficult. The Army says we can fight on the strength of the September 6 decision in the Imperial Presence, but the Navy is worried. I think that is why Prime Minister Konoye can't make up his mind. He has to think as a politician.

TOJO: I asked the Navy Minister, "Has there been any change in the Navy's resolve since September 6? If there has been we will adjust plans accordingly." But he said, "No, there has been no change." . . . It seems to me that we have to stop trying to assign responsibility for the past and face up squarely to the question as to whether or not we can pursue the national program as decided.

To Sugiyama, Tojo added, "The Navy minister [Oikawa] won't say he has no confidence in victory but he continues, nevertheless, to talk that way. We can't make a decision because he won't commit himself. If the Navy can't make up its mind, we will have to look around for other solutions."

Sugiyama and Tojo agreed, after further chat, that one solution might be a new Cabinet with a new Navy minister.

By the next morning, October 15, everyone at Court was agreed that a Cabinet change seemed inevitable. Konoye reported that Tojo by now was so disgusted with procrastination that he would no longer talk to Konoye at Cabinet meetings. Hirohito was disappointed that Konoye should break his 1940 pledge "to share joys and sorrows with me to the very end." Nevertheless Hirohito approved the Cabinet change without demur, and all day Konoye's secretaries and the ubiquitous retired lieutenant general, Cabinet Planning Board Director Suzuki Tei-ichi, shuttled in and out of the palace as go-betweens in the quest for a suitable new government.

To accept the responsibility for the past and unify the Army and Navy for the future, War Minister Tojo and Prime Minister Konoye agreed on one point: that the best prime ministerial candidate would be Hirohito's scheming uncle, Prince Higashikuni, who had originally recruited Tojo and the rest of Hirohito's Army cabal in 1920. Lord Privy Seal Kido and other courtiers all expressed horror at the thought of putting a member of the family in front of the chrysanthemum curtain at a time when Japan might enter a hazardous war with the United States. Hirohito said that a Higashikuni Cabinet presented certain problems but "might be all right."

After an afternoon and evening of scurrying conversations, Konoye went late at night to Prince Higashikuni's villa to "feel him out." Higashikuni asked for a few days to consider the proposal. While Konoye was absent from the palace, Hirohito and Lord Privy Seal Kido interviewed War Minister Tojo and persuaded him to take the responsibility for forming the next Cabinet and for shouldering in it, simultaneously, the portfolios of prime minister, war minister, and home minister.

The next afternoon Hirohito gave Tojo a private audience asking him if he would be willing to set aside the war decision of September 6 and take responsibility for holding the armed forces in check while the final orders for war were postponed for another month. Tojo noted that this additional time for negotiations would be bought at the cost of a steady deterioration in

Japanese strength relative to U.S. strength, but he cheerfully acknowledged that he felt strong enough politically to bear the responsibility. A little over an hour later, at 5 P.M., Prince Konoye officially presented the mass resignation of his Cabinet.

The following day, October 17, Lord Privy Seal Kido solemnly consulted seven of the living former prime ministers of Japan: the *Jushin* or Elder Statesmen. The eighth, Baron Hiranuma, who had supported Foreign Minister Matsuoka in his quixotic diversionary schemes earlier that year, was conspicuously absent.[6] So were several others who might have been present if they had not been assassinated. Wakatsuki, the disgruntled dupe of the Manchurian Incident, suggested that General Ugaki might make a good prime minister. Hayashi, the dupe of the 1935 faction fight, sought to settle responsibility on Prince Higashikuni. Then Lord Privy Seal Kido interrupted to propose Tojo. General Abe and diplomat Hirota both approved the choice. Admirals Okada and Yonai and the antediluvian Kiyoura all agreed to go along with it. Kido reported unanimity to the Emperor.

After confirming Tojo in his new triple responsibilities as prime, war, and home minister, Hirohito, about 6 P.M., called in outgoing Navy Minister Oikawa. From 1915 to 1922 Oikawa had been attached to Hirohito's person as naval adjutant and in 1921 he had gone along with Hirohito aboard the battleship *Katori* on the trip to Europe. In 1940 Oikawa had forced the Navy to accept the Tripartite Pact. Now Oikawa had taken more responsibility than he could, in conscience, bear. Hirohito gently told him that he would be replaced by Admiral Shimada Shigetaro who had also been close to Hirohito in the cabal in the early 1920's and who was a close personal friend of Tojo. It would be Shimada's responsibility, along with Tojo, to force the elder admirals of the Navy, against their better judgment, to embark on war with the United States. Hirohito thanked Oikawa for his long and painful service. Later, in 1944, as events turned out, he would make Oikawa the Navy chief of staff.

So it was that Tojo became prime minister of Japan and, in American eyes, the arch-villain of Japan's eighty years of planning for war with the West. On assuming office Tojo actually undertook to postpone the outbreak of war for a month, giving the eager myrmidons of the armed forces more time to ripen and rehearse their operations, giving the people more time to accept Japan's absolute rejection by the United States, and giving the

---

[6] The seventy-five-year-old Hiranuma was recovering from a bullet which had grazed his neck and nicked his jaw on August 14. Since the toughs who had set upon him were some of Prince Higashikuni's Prayer-Meeting Plotters—still out on bail because of Prince Higashikuni's influence with the police—Hiranuma was understandably vexed. The fact that the Emperor had offered him the services of one of the Court physicians and had sent him a basket of fruit had failed to placate him. Since the accident, he had, however, given up his outspoken criticism of the alliance with Germany.

diplomats one last impossible chance to negotiate Japan's inacceptable demands in Washington.

On October 18, Hirohito agreed to catapult Tojo, years ahead of normal schedule, from the rank of lieutenant general to that of full general. In the afternoon Hirohito and Kido went together to Yasukuni Shrine to worship the spirits of the dead warriors who had served the national program in the last century.

On October 20, in a routine conversation with Hirohito, Lord Privy Seal Kido took the opportunity to explain that he had suggested Tojo as prime minister in order to give Japan a moment's breathing space, for careful consideration, before leaping into a hasty war. Hirohito gazed at his favorite advisor and said, "You cannot catch a tiger cub unless you dare to enter the tiger's cave." It was the Japanese equivalent of "nothing ventured, nothing gained."

RUSSIA

Lake Baikal

MANCHURIA
1932

SAKH.

OUTER MONGOLIA

1932

1931

Vladivostok

HOKKA
c. I

MONGOLIA
1935

JEHOL
1933

KWANTUNG
LEASEHOLD
1905

Mukden

SEA OF
JAPAN

HONSHU

INNER
1937

Peking
Tientsin

KOREA
1910

Seoul

Tokyo
Kyoto

C H I N A

Tsingtao

YELLOW
SEA

SHIKOKU

EASTERN
CHINA
1937-38

Nanking

Shanghai

KYUSHU

SOUTH
JAPAN
c. A.D. 50

Chungking

Hankow

Yangtze R.

RYUKYU IS.

APR. 1, 1945

Canton

Hong Kong

TAIWAN
1895

Okinawa
1609

OGASAW

INDIA

BURMA
1942

HAINAN
1939

Hanoi
1940

SOUTH
CHINA
SEA

Apparri

Vigan

Luzon

F

Rangoon

THAILAND
(by alliance)
1941

Baguio
Manila

PHILIPPINES
1941-42

Bangkok

INDOCHINA

ANDAMANS

Saigon
1941

Leyte

OCT. 20
1944

Yap

NICOBARS

Patani
Kota Bharu

Jesselton

Sandakan

Mindanao

Palau

SEPT. 15

Singora

MALAYA
1941-42

BRITISH
BORNEO

Morotai

SEPT. 15, 1944

Singapore

DUTCH
BORNEO

MAY 2

Biak

SUMATRA

Balikpapan

Celebes

DUTCH
NEW GUIN.

D U T C H

E A S T   I N D I E S

Batavia

Surabaya

JAVA

1942

Djakarta

TIMOR
(Dutch/Portuguese)

Darwin

AUSTRALIA

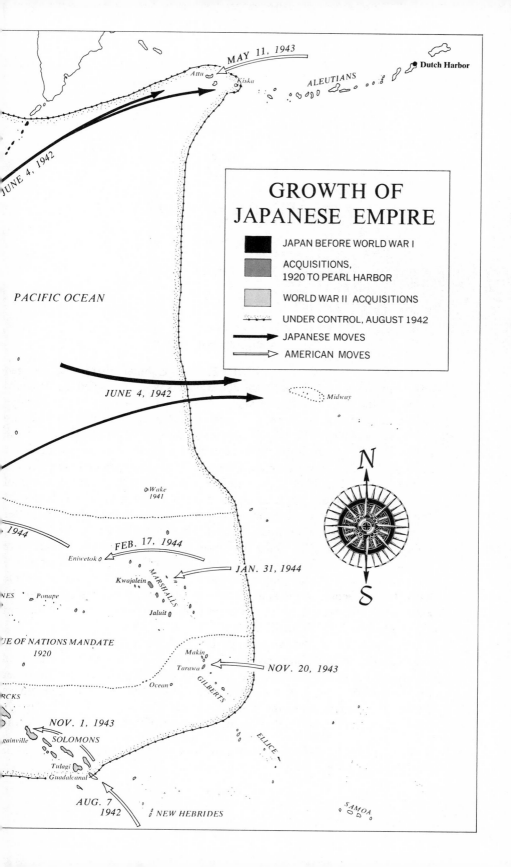

GROWTH OF JAPANESE EMPIRE

- JAPAN BEFORE WORLD WAR I
- ACQUISITIONS, 1920 TO PEARL HARBOR
- WORLD WAR II ACQUISITIONS
- UNDER CONTROL, AUGUST 1942
- JAPANESE MOVES
- AMERICAN MOVES

MAY 11, 1943

Attu
Kiska
ALEUTIANS
Dutch Harbor

JUNE 4, 1942

PACIFIC OCEAN

JUNE 4, 1942

Midway

N

S

Wake
1941

1944

FEB. 17, 1944

Eniwetok

JAN. 31, 1944

Kwajalein
MARSHALLS

NES   Ponape

Jaluit

UE OF NATIONS MANDATE
1920

Makin
Tarawa

NOV. 20, 1943

Ocean
GILBERTS

RCKS

NOV. 1, 1943

gainville   SOLOMONS

ELLICE

Tulagi
Guadalcanal

AUG. 7
1942   NEW HEBRIDES

SAMOA

26

PEARL HARBOR

(1941)

During the last two weeks of the Konoye Cabinet, the police arreste
and imprisoned the members of the Soviet spy ring headed by Richai
Sorge. At the time, German Gestapo observers ascribed the fall of Konoy
to his embarrassingly close relations with Ozaki Hotsumi, the leadii
Japanese member of the ring. Western scholars, however, on review of th
police files, have concluded that the arrests and the government turnov
had little bearing on one another. Certainly, if Konoye was embarrassed, t
"militarists" had nothing to do with it, for the arrests and interrogations
the spies were handled entirely by the civilian Thought Police of the Hon
Ministry. The military secret police were deeply chagrined that, in a matt
of military security, they had not been able to strike first. The Thoug
Police, who had been watching the Sorge ring closely for over a year, we
connected at a much higher level with state policy. They were probab
directed to clean up the ring as a routine preparation for war at a tin
when the ring could serve state policy no further. Home Minister Tana
Harumichi had served as the vice president and manipulator of pupp
Henry Pu-yi's Privy Council in Manchukuo from 1932 to 1938.

The roundup of the ring began on September 29, 1941, when t
Thought Police took into custody Ito Tadasu.[1] After earlier arrests a
interrogations as a subversive, Ito had been broken and made an inform
for the police. They had then found him a job at the South Manchur
Railroad Research Institute, the spy-service center run by Dr. Oka
Shumei who had served as liaison man between palace and assassins duri

---

[1] In English he has previously been known by an alternate reading of his na
characters, Ito Ritsu.

798

the terror of 1932. At the institute it was Ito's assignment to watch his fellow worker, the China expert Ozaki Hotsumi, who, as a member of the Sorge ring, had transmitted earlier messages from Lord Privy Seal Kido and young Saionji to Sorge for relay to the Soviet Union.

Now the Thought Police questioned informer Ito for eleven days before they felt that they had picked his brains clean. To the Thought Police, it seemed difficult to believe that Sorge could operate as he did within the German Embassy unless some larger conspiracy than his spy ring was involved. Finally, however, the interrogators were satisfied that Ito was concealing nothing and they moved on to their next arrest.

On September 11 they picked up Miyagi Yatoku, the Okinawa-born artist who had been sent to assist Sorge by the American Communist party in 1933. Miyagi alone in the Sorge ring behaved with unsophisticated heroics and refused to admit anything. In the first week of his interrogation he jumped or was pushed from an upstairs window of the Thought Police building, was caught by a tree, and only broke a leg.[2] He finally died in prison in August 1943.

Ozaki Hotsumi, the confidant of Prince Konoye and most valuable Japanese member of the ring, learned of Miyagi's arrest and waited stoically for his own. On October 14, he was supposed to eat dinner with Sorge at the Asia Restaurant in the South Manchuria Railroad Building. Leaving Sorge waiting in vain for him, he chose instead to spend a last evening with his wife and daughter. The next morning a single Thought Policeman came for him. He parleyed a moment with the man, made sure that his daughter had left for school, and then without a further word to his wife left his home for the final three years of his life.

At the police station Ozaki authoritatively and successfully asked to see the chief prosecutor who would be assigned to his case by the Justice Ministry. The ordinary procedure of interrogation by detectives would not, he made clear, be required in his case because he was privy to state secrets for which detectives were not cleared and because he was already persuaded to tell the full truth. He was transferred at once to the detention section of Sugamo Prison where he began a three-year conversation with procurator Tamazawa Mitsusaburo who would present Japan's case against the Sorge ring in court. At the outset Ozaki revealed the names of all the agents in the ring and pleaded that both he and Sorge had been intermediaries in international negotiations rather than spies in the accepted sense. Months later, after countless interrogations, he would begin to confess that he was at fault in having always believed in a single socialist government for the

---

[2] Being an American, Miyagi was suspected of being not only a Communist spy but also a U.S. spy. His continued existence, during the first year of anti-American war hysteria, greatly complicated negotiations for the rest of the Sorge spy ring and may have prevented the Thought Police from disposing of the ring as charitably as they might otherwise have done.

entire world. Despite much time for thought and several written "changes of heart" he never succeeded in demonstrating a sincere rejection of his youthful idealisms. His interrogators all sympathized with him, but finally, after the fall of Tojo in 1944, when Peace Faction and kamikaze enthusiasts were delicately balanced on the scales of state, he was to be executed for the good and sufficient reason of political convenience.

After Ozaki's failure to keep his appointment and after learning that Miyagi, too, had disappeared, Richard Sorge spent two days waiting in fear. He admitted both to himself and to the other European members of his ring that the game was probably up. He drafted a halfhearted request to Moscow for reassignment, tried to book passage on a ship to Shanghai, and spent much time in bed, moping and dozing. Early in the evening of October 17, Max Klausen, the radio technician of the ring, called on him and found him finishing a case of saké with Branko de Voukelitch, the Yugoslavian photographic technician. Klausen was so depressed at the sight of Sorge lounging about fatalistically in his pajamas with a glass in his hand that he asked the news, contributed a fresh bottle of saké to the wake, and left it after ten minutes.

The next morning at 5 A.M. several Thought Policemen from the Home Ministry and an assistant procurator from the Justice Ministry waited outside Sorge's home for a German official car to go away from the curb out front. The head of the German News Agency was inside having a maddeningly mysterious conversation with Sorge which the police were never able to explain to their satisfaction. Sorge later insisted, throughout his interrogation, that the German had stopped by, at 5 A.M., simply to pick his brain on the recent change of Cabinet.

As soon as the German had left, the police presented themselves at Sorge's door and asked him to come with them for questioning in regard to his 1938 motorcycle accident. Sorge objected, as a foreign national, but was forced into a car and bundled off, still in his pajamas. The police noted that he had left behind him, open beside his bed, an arcane volume of sixteenth century Japanese poetry. That he might want to read it and understand it was set down in his favor.

Six days later, under severe and painful questioning, Sorge admitted that he was a Soviet agent and was handed over by the Thought Police to the assistant procurator from the Justice Ministry who had stood by at his arrest. This procurator, Yoshizawa Mitsusada, would become a familiar figure to American audiences at the 1951 Sorge hearings of the House Un-American Activities Committee. Alternately befriending Sorge and leaving him to the mercy of brutal guards, Yoshizawa would lead the broken spy question by question, revelation by revelation, process by due process through three years of examination, trial, judgment, and appeal. Finally Sorge would mount the gallows, forty-seven minutes after Ozaki Hotsumi, on the morning of November 7, 1944.

TOJO'S RESPONSIBILITY

In appointing Tojo simultaneously prime, war, and home minister, Hirohito gave him enough power to act as a shogun, a wartime dictator. Hirohito showed no uneasiness at delegating this immense power, for he was really delegating only responsibility and he trusted Tojo implicitly. Events would prove that his trust was not misplaced. Tojo and the Emperor had much in common: a quick appreciation of technical realities, a meticulous attention to detail, an impatience with too much indirection and belly talk, a charm which extended only to immediate personal relationships, and a blind pride in the righteousness of Japan's cause. Both men shared a conviction that "the Japanese race" had been persecuted by the white race. Both men had succeeded in cloistering themselves from the realities of Japan's own barbarous racism in dealing with fellow Asiatics.

In accepting the Emperor's mandate to be "shogun," Tojo promised to postpone war for a month, to discipline the noisy strategists who demanded war now or not at all, and to conduct a thorough, rational review of all the past policies and present exigencies which seemed to make war necessary. Hirohito does not appear, from his actions and comments, to have expected any change in policy from this review; rather, he seems to have wanted every argument and statistic, which had been working in his own mind, to be set forth sharply and clearly in black and white so that the fuzzy-minded politicians of his realm like Konoye would be made to see the need for war and so that posterity would understand his point of view. Accordingly, for a fortnight, from October 19 to November 1, shogun Tojo held the leaders of Japan in continual conference in order to make clear to them and their cohorts the rationale for the desperate gamble ahead.

At his first liaison conference of the Cabinet and General Staffs on October 23, 1941, Tojo expressed the Emperor's wishes firmly. Navy Chief of Staff Nagano said, "The Navy is consuming 400 tons of oil an hour. The situation is urgent. We want it decided one way or the other quickly." Army Chief of Staff Sugiyama said, "Things have already been delayed for a month. We can't devote four or five days to study. Hurry up and go ahead."

Tojo replied, "I well understand why the Supreme Command emphasizes the need to hurry. The government, however, would prefer to give the matter careful study and do it in a responsible way. There are now new ministers of the Navy, finance, and foreign affairs. I would like to have us decide whether the government can assume responsibility for the September 6 decision as it stands, or whether we must reconsider it from a new point of view. Does the Supreme Command have any objections?"

The two chiefs of staff both admitted that they could have no objections. For the next week, at daily liaison conferences, they watched Tojo parade experts, representing all factions in the Japanese state, and build up an irrefutable case for war. The presentations were long and complex. Little by little they brought out all the objections to war and contrasted them to the enormity of the retrenchment which Japan would have to make if she did not go to war while her oil and other stockpiles made war a feasible proposition. In the process the "experts" revealed a clear and bleak appreciation of the probable realities of the future.

The two chiefs of staff and their assistants argued convincingly with statistics that Japan could now seize Southeast Asia, with all its oil, rubber, tin, tungsten and rice, but that if she did not act now her ability to take the offensive would gradually wane until by mid-1942 U.S. defenses in the south would be too strong to breach. Thereafter Japan's military position would deteriorate progressively until a time would come only three or four years hence in which the United States could demand that Japan withdraw to her 1890 boundaries and she would have no rational alternative but to bow and comply.

The ubiquitous Suzuki, of the Cabinet Planning Board, backed the two chiefs of staff, but in the most pessimistic terms. If everything went perfectly and all norms could be met, Japan would just have enough steel, oil and ship producing capacity to tide herself over until the Dutch East Indies could be exploited and the Co-Prosperity Sphere could be made a self-sufficient economic bloc. Suzuki volunteered the information that accidents of weather or underestimates of the damage done by U.S. submarines could tip the scales and turn a slim margin of hope into a certainty of despair. Nevertheless, Suzuki insisted that this desperate gamble was preferable to the alternative of capitulation without a struggle. He predicted that Japan would lose little more by fighting and being defeated than by standing pat and being overpowered by economic pressure.

Finance Minister Kaya Okinori, a protégé of Prince Konoye, disagreed. He felt that the people might be willing to starve in order to meet military requirements but that, still, the military requirements would probably not be met. Runaway inflation might be prevented at home, but the conquered areas would have to be bled white. Japan might be able to take from Indonesia the war materials which she needed but would not be able to supply the manufactured goods which Indonesia now imported from Europe. Finally, Kaya refused to concede that the United States would necessarily take advantage of her strength in order to force Japan to her knees.

New Foreign Minister Togo Shigenori, the same who would later handle Japan's surrender notes in 1945, agreed with Kaya. He and Kaya failed to change the determination for war but they helped to lengthen Tojo's policy review until it became almost unbearable for the edgy military strategists participating in it. Finally, on October 30, a liaison conference adjourned with a firm pledge to sit again on November 1 and to remain sitting all day and all night, if necessary, until a conclusive recommendation could be made to the Emperor.

The next day, Friday October 31, Lord Privy Seal Kido met with Yoshida Shigeru, the postwar prime minister of Japan and son-in-law of Hirohito's former Lord Privy Seal Makino, and began conversations with him for the formation of the Peace Faction which would ultimately prepare for the contingency of Japan's surrender. Kido consummated his understanding with Yoshida at two further meetings on November 1 and 2.

Also on November 1 Admiral Yamamoto Isoroku and his staff gained Hirohito's editorial approval for their final draft of Order Number One, the comprehensive plan of Army and Navy operations which would be carried out in the months ahead. With Prince Takamatsu's blessing the top-secret plan went to a printer who would turn out three hundred numbered copies of it in the three days which followed.

THE CABINET CAPITULATES

Meanwhile, on November 1, shogun Tojo presided over the historic liaison conference which would decide on war. The conference of October 30 had adjourned noncommittally with an agreement to restrict future choice to one of three plans: 1) suspend war preparations and "sleep on logs and drink gall" for ten or twenty years while attempting to make Japan the industrial equal of the United States; 2) decide at once on war and forget diplomacy; and 3) continue war preparations with a firm decision to embark on war in early December while still conducting diplomatic negotiations "at a slow pace." Before the liaison conference of November 1, between 7:30 and 8:30 in the morning, shogun Tojo met for breakfast with Army Chief of Staff Sugiyama and asked him to support plan number three. Sugiyama made no promises but nodded occasionally at Tojo as he ate his rice and sipped his tea.

The liaison conference convened at the Imperial Headquarters building just north of the Fukiage Gardens in the palace at 9 A.M. It was to last for sixteen and a half hours, until 1:30 A.M. the next morning. The reason for this wearisome argument was not that anything new came up for discussion or even that there were many points of disagreement. To be sure, Navy Chief of Staff Nagano and Army Vice Chief of Staff Tsukada would both have preferred to forget diplomacy altogether but they acquiesced without much struggle to the continuance of negotiations until the last minute. Tsukada, in particular, wanted an early deadline of November 13 put on the negotiations so that he would not have to rescind operation orders after that date in case the United States suddenly showed a willingness to compromise.

The training and mustering of some 400,000 men in the heart of the Empire a thousand miles from the future fields of battle had taxed both the logistic and the psychological resources of the Army's officer corps. "I tell you," exclaimed Tsukada, "airplanes, surface vessels, and submarines

are soon going to start colliding with one another." Navy Chief of Staff
Nagano, however, observed wryly, "small collisions are incidents, not wars."
Without much argument, he and Tsukada agreed that war would be called
off if negotiations promised a settlement up to as late as midnight, November 30.

What protracted the proceedings for sixteen and a half hours was the
stubborn refusal of Foreign Minister Togo and Finance Minister Kaya
to make the recommendation to the Emperor unanimous. And what
prompted their recalcitrance was their desire not just to avert war but to
avert a war commenced in a dishonorable fashion. Nothing in the record
of what was said at the conference states clearly that Japan was deciding
to deceive the United States, but there was probably something to that
effect in the position papers which were laid before the conferees because,
early in the proceedings, Army Chief of Staff Sugiyama, in his minutes,
recorded the following exchange.

[FINANCE MINISTER] KAYA: If there were hope of victory in the third year
of the war, it would be all right to commence hostilities, but according to
[Navy Chief of Staff] Nagano's explanation, this is not certain. Moreover, I
would judge that the chances of the United States making war upon us are
slight, so my conclusion must be that it would not be a good idea to declare
war now.

[FOREIGN MINISTER] TOGO: I, too, cannot believe that the American fleet
would come and attack us. I am not convinced that there is any need to start
war now.

[NAVY CHIEF OF STAFF] NAGANO: There is a saying, "Don't rely on what may
not happen." The future is uncertain; we can't take anything for granted. In
three years enemy defenses in the south will be strong, and the number of
enemy warships will also increase.

[FINANCE MINISTER] KAYA: Well, then, when can we go to war and win?

[NAVY CHIEF OF STAFF] NAGANO: Now! The time for war will not come
later. . . .

KAYA and TOGO [sic]: Before we decide on this, we would like somehow to
make a last attempt at diplomatic negotiations. This is a great turning point
in the history of our country, which goes back 2,600 years; and on it hangs
the fate of the nation. It's outrageous to ask us to resort to diplomatic trickery.
We can't do it.

At 1:30 the next morning, Kaya and Togo still held out. The proposal to
continue sincere negotiations up to midnight November 30 and then to start
war a week later still had only majority support. The conferees adjourned
with a vote to recommend the proposal to Hirohito even on this non-
unanimous basis. Togo and Kaya, however, asked Prime Minister Tojo to
give them until eleven o'clock in the morning before reporting their dissent

officially to the Emperor. Finance Minister Kaya phoned the indefatigable Tojo shortly after daybreak to concede that he would add his vote to the majority. The bristling, correct Foreign Minister Togo held out to the dot of 11 A.M. and then, before perfecting the unanimity, succeeded in exacting from Tojo promises of support on two minor points which would give him some legitimate room to bargain in his dealings with the United States.

At 5 P.M. the tired Tojo reported the sweat-stained unanimity that had been exacted of the vassals to Emperor Hirohito. When Hirohito sought to go over the course of the debate in some detail, Tojo broke down and wept in the Imperial Presence. Much time, he said, had already been wasted in study. The deadline requested by the best strategists of the Army and Navy had already been missed by a month. The Supreme Command needed orders from the Emperor to begin the final training exercises for Army and Navy pilots who, being enlisted men, could not expect to prepare without orders. Finally Tojo begged Hirohito to call a conference in the Imperial Presence to formalize the war decision. Also, said Tojo, he hoped that the Emperor himself would support the decision.

Having seen many such protestations in his time Hirohito persisted in asking some questions.

"What ideas do you have," he said, "as to our justification for what we will do, so that we can uphold our honor?"

"We are still studying that matter," replied Tojo wearily, "and will report to you soon."

"I suggest," said Hirohito, "that we send a special envoy to the Pope so that we can use him as a mediator to save the situation if worse comes to worst."

Then the Emperor went on to ask several shrewd questions as to the reliability of Army-Navy estimates of iron and steel production and of shipping losses during the first year of war. Finally, he gave Tojo his approval for what had been transacted.

ORDER NUMBER ONE

The following day, November 3, Navy Chief of Staff Nagano received his bound, numbered copy of Admiral Yamamoto's Order Number One which incorporated the Pearl Harbor attack plan as a salient feature in a comprehensive blueprint for the whole Strike South. Order Number One began with a preamble which attempted to give the justification for war which Hirohito wished to have explained:

Despite the fact that the Empire has always maintained a friendly attitude toward the United States, the United States has interfered in all the measures which we have taken out of self-preservation and self-defense for the protec-

tion of our interests in East Asia. Recently she has blocked our speedy settlement of the China Incident by aiding the government of Chiang Kai-shek and
has even resorted to the final outrage of breaking off economic relations with
us. . . .

After the preamble, Yamamoto quickly got to the main point: "The
Japanese Empire will declare war on the United States, Great Britain, and
the Netherlands. War will be declared on X-day. The order will become
effective on Y-day." Yamamoto's order went on to prescribe in detail the
units to be employed in the various operations and even the voice codes
which would be used by his own Pearl Harbor forces. "The cherry blossoms are all in their glory," meaning warriors are about to fall, would
signify, "There are no warships in Pearl Harbor; the American fleet has
escaped." The message "Climb Mount Fuji" would mean "weather and
other conditions suitable for attack." "Five hundred twenty is the depth of
the moat at Honno Temple" (where the Great Musketeer Oda Nobunaga
was betrayed and assassinated) would mean "Attack scheduled for 0520."
    Some of the admirals who had attended the Yamamoto special maneuver
in the Naval Staff College two months earlier still disapproved of the Pearl
Harbor plan as a poor gamble tactically and as a mere gesture strategically
—one which might temporarily knock out the U.S. Pacific fleet but one
also, which would affront the United States and make it difficult to negotiate a peace later when Japan had occupied the Philippines, Malaya, and
the Dutch East Indies and could bargain from a position of strength.
    Few in the Army knew of Yamamoto's plan. The over-all commander
for Army operations in the south, General Count Terauchi, had been let in
on it only six weeks previously. Army Chief of Staff Sugiyama, by the evidence of his own memoranda, had been informed of it a scant four days
before. Shogun Tojo was probably still in the dark about it.[3] Civilians like
Foreign Minister Togo simply knew that the Navy had a plan for "ambush-
ing" the U.S. fleet. They assumed—and it was one of the assumptions on
which they based their disapproval of war—that the "ambush" would
take place only if the U.S. Navy was foolish enough to steam west in order
to relieve the Philippines after it had been attacked. Only Hirohito, a few
members of his family, the staff chiefs, and some of Yamamoto's own
trusted naval colleagues yet knew of the Pearl Harbor plan.
    As soon as Navy Chief of Staff Nagano received his copy of Order Num-
ber One on the morning of November 3, he took it to the palace. There
he was joined by his opposite number, Army Chief of Staff Sugiyama, and
together with Sugiyama he was ushered into the Imperial Presence. Hiro

---

[3] Professor Robert J. C. Butow, who has made Tojo's various postwar statements
one of his specialties, has written, "It would appear that Tojo did not learn of the
navy's decision to adopt the [Pearl Harbor] plan until a day or two before the imperial conference of December 1."

hito had his own copy of Order Number One before him and began at once to ask questions about points which seemed unclear in it. The Western concession areas in China would be occupied *after* the attack began on Hong Kong, would they not? Sugiyama promised to look into the matter. The monsoon season, continued Hirohito, would adversely affect air operations over Malaya, would it not? Sugiyama gave the Emperor a sheaf of meteorological statistics and said:

"We had planned to overwhelm the enemy [in Malaya] by initial air attacks, but since it rains there now three or four times a day we will concentrate on surprise in the landing of troops. I think the Philippines will go all right. We are studying the two operations together and will decide appropriately."

Hirohito said, "Tojo is much concerned about rapid issuance of orders to the air forces."

Sugiyama answered, "The airmen and their support units are waiting in Dairen, Tsingtao, Shanghai, and other points, ready for take-off. We have studied all the disadvantages in delaying their flight orders and have found countermeasures. We now think that we can overcome all obstacles even if the imperial orders are not issued until after the final conference in the Imperial Presence. I, personally, think that this is the most proper way."

"Yes," said Hirohito, "it's best to keep everything proper." Then, darting on, he said, "I suppose that from the point of view of national justification, it would be best to negotiate as soon as possible with Thailand [for permission to march across Thai territory into Malaya]. But from the point of view of military surprise, it might be better to postpone the Thai negotiations as long as possible. What do you think?"

"His Imperial Majesty," replied Sugiyama, "is absolutely correct. However, if we don't decide [how to continue the negotiations already in progress] we may betray our plans. Now as never before, the situation is urgent and we must be extremely cautious. I will study the matter, talk to the Foreign Ministry, and report to you again."

"What is the Navy's target date?" asked Hirohito.

Navy Chief of Staff Nagano, who had been standing silently by, replied briefly: "December 8 is the target date."

"Isn't that a Monday?" asked Hirohito.[4]

"We chose it," said Nagano, "because everyone will be tired after a holiday."

"Will the same date apply for all the other regions?" asked Hirohito.

[4] Monday, December 8, Japanese time, or Sunday, December 7, U.S. time, was, of course, to be the date of Pearl Harbor. Previous American historians have reported that this date was chosen by Admiral Yamamoto himself in mid-November, and that Hirohito did not know of it or of the Pearl Harbor plan at all until December 2. General Sugiyama's memoranda, published in 1967, have set the record straight and made it credible.

"Well, since there is a great difference in distances [from our various mustering points]," replied Chief of Staff Sugiyama, "I doubt that we can co-ordinate all our attacks on precisely the same date."

Hirohito nodded. With his aides-de-camp he had pored over the charts of Southeast Asia for years. He knew well the distances involved and the difficulties of tides and winds and reefs. With his acquiescence, Navy Chief of Staff Nagano returned to the Naval Staff Headquarters on the edge of Hibiya Park just outside the palace gates. There Rear Admiral Kuroshima Kumahito, who had brought Nagano his copy of Order Number One from Yamamoto's flagship in the Inland Sea, was tensely waiting for him. "I just talked to Yamamoto on the phone," announced Kuroshima. "He says that if you do not agree to his plan, he will have to resign from the service."

Nagano beamed, wrapped an arm around Kuroshima's shoulder, and said, "I fully understand how Yamamoto feels. If he has that much confidence in his scheme, he must be allowed to carry on with it. It has been approved."

Kuroshima had a plane standing by and flew immediately south to give Yamamoto the news. That night aboard the flagship *Nagato,* there was a solemn ceremonial drinking of saké. With the support of Hirohito, Prince Takamatsu, and Marquis Komatsu, Yamamoto and his men felt that they had given Japan a fighting chance.

THE WAR COUNCIL ASSENTS

Before affixing his seal of state to Yamamoto's Order Number One and converting it officially into a *Taimei* or Great Order, Hirohito summoned a meeting of the Supreme War Council to sit in his presence and approve on the following day, November 4. In addition to the Army and Navy ministers, the chiefs of staff, the commanders of the Kure and Yokosuka naval bases, two former Navy ministers, and a former commander at Kure, the meeting was attended by General Terauchi who was to command the Strike South, by General Doihara and Vice Admiral Shinozuka Yoshio of the spy service, and by Princes Kanin, Fushimi, Asaka, and Higashikuni. Hirohito sat silent at one end of the room while old Prince Kanin, just in front of him at a lower altar, presided and moderated. On the two tables running down the sides of the room, before the rest of the conferees, reposed copies of a single brief paper declaring the business of the meeting. It said:

> To break open the present crisis, to fulfill the nation's inner life and self-defense, and to establish a New Order in Greater East Asia, the Empire on this occasion, decides to make war on the United States, England, and Holland.

For this purpose the time to activate our military forces is set for early December.

Navy Chief of Staff Nagano opened the meeting by explaining that the purpose of going to war was to prevent Japan from being strangled by an alliance of the United States, Great Britain, and the Netherlands. "The Empire," he said, "is now facing the most critical situation of its entire history." Going on to describe the expectations of the Navy, he said: "If we start in early December with the strength we now possess, we have a very great chance of victory in phase one of the war. By phase one I mean the defeat of enemy forces in the Far East and the reduction of enemy strongholds throughout the southwestern Pacific. Our degree of success in this first phase may determine the outcome of the war." The recommendation to strike immediately, he continued, was based on careful study of three factors: "the present strength of our forces compared to the enemy's, the need to attack before being attacked, and meteorological considerations." He concluded his presentation with an oblique reference to the secret Pearl Harbor plan, which no one present, except the Emperor, knew much about, and with a plea for secrecy. "As mentioned above, the outcome of the war depends greatly on the outcome of phase one, and the outcome of phase one depends on the outcome of our surprise attack. We must conceal our war intentions at all costs."

Army Chief of Staff Sugiyama continued with a brief résumé of the forces on both sides which might be thrown into the battle. There were, he said, 60,000 to 70,000 men and 320 planes in Malaya; 42,000 men and 170 planes in the Philippines, 85,000 men and 300 planes in the Dutch East Indies, and 35,000 men and 60 planes in Burma. In addition, 300,-000 men and about 200 planes in India, 250,000 men and about 300 planes in Australia, and 70,000 men and about 150 planes in New Zealand might be brought into play by the enemy as reinforcements. In practical terms he anticipated that Japan would have to contend with about 200,000 troops, 70 per cent of them "natives" who had the advantage of being "used to tropical climates" and the disadvantage of "inadequate training and a generally low fighting ability." However, some of the enemy planes, he cautioned, were "high-performance craft with relatively well-trained pilots."

Against the total 850,000-man strength of the enemy's front-line and reserve forces, Sugiyama pointed out that Japan could draw on 51 active divisions with "manpower of about 2 million soldiers." Against the roughly 200,000 men which the Army might realistically meet on the field, Sugiyama expected to use 11 Japanese divisions or about 220,000 men. He reported that "one division is already in Indochina, five are waiting and training in Japan and Taiwan, and five more will be transferred from the China theater. . . . They are all ready to move the moment the Emperor's Great Order is issued."

Sugiyama went on to explain that the enemy was increasing its air power at the rate of 10 per cent every two months and its ground strength at the rate of over 4,000 men a month, making it absolutely essential to attack soon. "The enemy forces, however, are scattered," he said. "Being able to attack with surprise and with our strength concentrated, we will be able to defeat the enemy units one at a time. Once we land successfully, we are quite sure we will win."

After Sugiyama's presentation the floor was thrown open for a perfunctory debate. Prince Asaka, the imperial uncle who had raped Nanking, set the tone by declaring impatiently: "This activation date of early December is about a month and a half later than the one decided upon during the time of the Konoye government. According to the explanation of the two chiefs of staff, it seemed then that the earlier we attacked the better. I fully agreed. What is the reason that early December has been chosen? Does it have something to do with these diplomatic negotiations?"

Prince Asaka was answered by his elder kinsman, the seventy-six-year-old former chief of staff, Prince Kanin: ". . . In international affairs it is necessary to co-ordinate military strategy with diplomatic strategy."

Prince Asaka next asked why the chiefs of staff were planning to fight a long war when it was apparent that only a short war—in view of national resources—would be advantageous. Prince Kanin, Navy Chief of Staff Nagano, and Prime Minister Tojo all responded to this question. In the course of their answers a number of pertinent observations were made. Prince Kanin saw only a 30 per cent chance of concluding a settlement with the United States but opined, also, that the United States was only bargaining at all because it had its own weaknesses: a navy divided between two oceans and a dependence upon Asiatic tin, rubber, and tungsten.

Navy Chief of Staff Nagano regretted that a short war seemed impossible, because he could promise that Japan would win a one- or two-year war but would face countless uncertainties in a three- or four-year war. The United States, he pointed out, was simply too big to be invaded, occupied, and defeated absolutely. Still, there was hope, he asserted, that Germany would conquer England and so make the United States receptive to a negotiated peace.

Prime Minister Tojo observed that he too would have liked to begin the war earlier but that diplomatic negotiations had gained time for military preparations. Army Chief of Staff Sugiyama reviewed the co-ordinated planning of the Navy and the 25th Army for the seizure of Malaya and expressed the conviction that military operations in the south would go according to plan.

The other imperial uncle, the devious Prince Higashikuni, then said: "It seems to me necessary to clarify our reasons for resort to force. What do you all think of explaining our justification and declaring the purpose of our holy war to the nation and the world? Then the people could set their minds on self-sacrifice at a time of national crisis."

Shogun Tojo replied: "I, too, think it imperative to clarify our national justification before we go to war. I am now studying the problem of a clear statement of our war purposes. As yet, however, I am not in a position to make such a clarifying statement in the presence of His Imperial Majesty."

Prince Higashikuni, disregarding Tojo's barbed words, plunged on blandly: "It goes without saying that we must anticipate a long war. Also, however, we must start thinking right now about concluding the war at an appropriate time. Indeed we must consider the possibility of using our commanding position under His Imperial Majesty to settle not only the differences between the United States and Japan but also those which disturb the world at large."

Tojo answered: "It is certainly desirable to end the war in a short period. We've studied the problem from many angles but as yet we have not come up with any really illuminating ideas. I regret that we have no means of controlling the life or death of the enemy. The possibility of a long war is 80 per cent. A short war is conceivable, however, under the following circumstances: destruction of most of the U.S. fleet—a distinct possibility, especially if the United States tries to retake the Philippines after we have occupied it; loss in America of the will to fight—a result which might follow a German declaration of war on the United States and German landings in England; control of England's lifeline—control, that is, of the shipping lanes which keep her from starving; finally, occupation and closing of the sources in the Far East of many of the military raw materials of the United States."

Later in the meeting, when pressed too far to accept all the responsibility for the war, the military members of the Supreme War Council who were not part of the imperial family began to protest a little. At one point Chief of Staff Sugiyama said: "Yes, when the monsoon blows [we may indeed encounter adverse meteorological conditions]. Our early studies showed clearly that it would have been best to finish our preparations in October and conduct our advance south now in November."

A few minutes later Field Marshal Prince Kanin asked that the meeting endorse unanimously the war decision. No one objected. Kanin turned to the Emperor and reported that the decision was recommended. Hirohito nodded, rose, and "withdrew into the Inner Palace."

When he had gone, the various members of the Supreme War Council individually approved for the record certain questions which they had submitted in writing to the General Staff before the meeting and which had been answered—also in writing, beforehand—by the responsible officers in the General Staff. These written questions and answers had been reviewed by the Emperor and were now formally entered as "source materials" on the palace rolls. Although not deemed worthy of live discussion at the conference, they included several surprisingly candid statements. They opened with a question by Prince Asaka requesting that the Army and Navy unify their command functions and co-operate thoroughly in the months ahead. The answer from the General Staffs was reassuring. After Asaka's questions, General Terauchi, the Supreme Commander for the Southern Regions was represented as asking, "Isn't there really any way to avoid a prolonged war?" The answer was, "There are no good ideas on that point but . . ." Again the hope was voiced that England would be occupied by Germany and the United States would grow tired of fighting.

Terauchi's next written question was: "What are the most important points to remember in our administration of the occupied areas?"

The answer was: "First, secure raw materials; second, insure freedom of transport for war materials and personnel; third, in accomplishing these two objectives, we must not hesitate, as we did in China, to oppress the natives. On the other hand, we will not interfere in the details of government, as we did in China, but will make use of existing organizations and show respect for native customs."

A moment later the reading came to the questions of General Doihara, the aging espionage expert known as the "Lawrence of Manchuria." Doihara's second question was: "What is the official excuse for this war against America, Britain, and the Dutch?"

The answer was: "This is a clash between nations which have different world philosophies. The basic purpose of the war is to make the Americans do obeisance to us against their will—that and the establishment of the Co-Prosperity Sphere to make us self-sufficient. Before we achieve these ends we must be prepared for a long war. Our immediate short-term ends are to break out of encirclement, undermine the morale of Chiang Kai-shek, seize the raw materials of the south, expel the Anglo-Saxon race from Asia, make the Chinese and the peoples of the Southern Regions depend on us rather than on the United States and England, open a southern route for closer ties between Asia and continental Europe, and get a monopolistic corner on the rubber, tin, and other raw materials which the United States needs for military purposes."

Having considered such frank questions and answers and having taken responsibility for the war, the Supreme War Councillors adjourned without ever seeing Yamamoto's Order Number One on which they were implicitly passing.

THE FORMAL WAR DECISION

The next day Hirohito presented the same responsibility in still more disguised, security-conscious form to the assembled civilians of the Cabinet. Together with the most trustworthy bureaucrats, both civil and military, the Cabinet ministers met in full conclave for the conclusive conference in the Imperial Presence which finally passed upon the tactical plans that had been incubating for months and the strategic plans which had been incubating for decades. At these proceedings, on November 5, as a result of careful staging, all the right things were said to prepare the people and the palace records for the hazardous gamble on which Hirohito and his family had embarked.

The written motion presented to the conferees for them to pass was almost the same as the one laid before the Supreme War Council the day before: hostilities against the United States, Great Britain, and The Netherlands, beginning in early December. It added: "Negotiations with the United States will be carried out in accord with the attached document. . . . If negotiations with the United States are successful by the beginning of December, the use of force will be called off."

The attached document described two diplomatic offers which would be made to the United States. The first, Proposal A, was intended as an over-all long-range settlement of U.S.–Japanese differences. It promised:

> Withdrawal . . . of the Japanese troops sent to China during the China Incident; those in designated sections of North China and Inner Mongolia, and those on Hainan Island, will remain for a necessary period of time after the establishment of peace between Japan and China. The remainder of the troops will begin withdrawal simultaneously with the establishment of peace in accordance with arrangements to be made between Japan and China, and the withdrawal will be completed within two years.
> Note: In case the United States asks what the "necessary period of time" will be, we will respond that we have in mind twenty-five years. . . .
> Japanese troops currently stationed in French Indochina will be immediately withdrawn after the settlement of the China Incident or the establishment of a just peace in the Far East. . . .
> The Japanese government will recognize the application of the principle of nondiscrimination in the entire Pacific region, including China, if this principle is applied throughout the world. . . .
> Regarding the interpretation and execution of the Tripartite Pact, the Japanese government, as it has stated on previous occasions, will act independently [without regard for Germany's interpretation]. . . .
> Regarding the so-called Four Principles put forward by the United States [respect for other nations' sovereignty, for the right of self-determination, for their right to equal treatment, and in general for the status quo], we will make every effort to avoid their inclusion in official agreements between Japan and the United States—and this includes "understandings" and other communiques.

If this Proposal A failed to gain U.S. acceptance, Proposal B should be offered. This was to be a temporary settlement, a modus vivendi, based on a return to the position the previous June before Japan had occupied southern Indochina and the United States had frozen Japanese assets and interdicted Japan's oil supplies. As the price paid for it, in order to purchase time, both sides were to make promises:

> Both Japan and the United States will pledge not to make an armed advance into Southeast Asia and the South Pacific area. . . .
> The Japanese and American governments will co-operate with each other so that the procurement of necessary materials from the Dutch East Indies will be assured.

When everyone had had a chance to read the decision for war and the two diplomatic proposals by which war might still be averted, Hirohito entered the large ceremonial eastern audience chamber in the Outer Palace and the conference began. Foreign Minister Togo pleaded for help in laying Proposal A and Proposal B as sincerely as possible before the United States. The ubiquitous retired lieutenant general, Suzuki, who was president of the Planning Board, gave a summary of national strength and advocated war in case the United States should turn down the two diplomatic proposals. He spoke with a transparent optimism about increasing steel production, decreasing its civilian consumption and supplementing the merchant marine available for routine trade by the use of "presently idle sailing vessels provided with auxiliary engines."

"Since the probability of victory in the initial stages of the war is sufficiently high," he said, "I am convinced that we should take advantage of our assured victory and turn the heightened morale of the people, who are determined to overcome the national crisis even at the cost of their lives, toward production as well as toward [reduced] consumption. . . . This would be better than just sitting tight and waiting for the enemy to put pressure on us."

Finance Minister Kaya spoke next. He pointed out that the national budget had doubled since 1936 and that only the enforced contributions of the people through bond buying and high taxes had as yet saved the economy from runaway inflation. "The people," he said, "will continue to make every effort and endure sacrifices because they are the subjects of our Empire." He judged, therefore, that it would be possible to keep the country from financial collapse until the people began to die in large numbers from starvation. He warned, however, that "if we cannot supply the materials necessary to carry on military activities and maintain the people's livelihood, the national economy must collapse no matter how perfect the government's financial and monetary policy."

He further warned: "The areas in the south that are to become the object of military operations have been importing materials of all kinds in large quantities. If these areas are occupied by our forces, their imports will cease. Accordingly, to make their economies run smoothly, we will have to supply them with materials. However, since our country does not have sufficient surpluses for that purpose, we will not be able, for some time, to give much consideration to the living conditions of the people in these areas, and for a while we will have to pursue a policy of so-called exploitation."

Navy Chief of Staff Nagano followed with a reiteration of all the arguments for war made on the day before.

Then Foreign Minister Togo gave a résumé of the position in the talks in Washington:

The two parties have virtually agreed upon the matter of preventing the expansion of the war. On this question, what the United States wants is to exert military power against Germany as a right of self-defense, while Japan promises not to exert military force in the Pacific region.

With regard to peace between Japan and China: the two parties have not agreed upon the question of stationing and withdrawing troops. Japan must station troops in necessary places for a necessary period of time. . . . Nevertheless, the United States demands that we proclaim the withdrawal of all troops, but we cannot accept the demand. . . .

Both parties have agreed not to solve political problems in the Pacific region by military force. Concerning this, the withdrawal of troops from French Indochina is a problem we have not agreed on.

There was a discussion of the diplomatic impasse in which, at one point, Prime Minister General Tojo frankly stated, "We can expect an expansion of our country only by stationing troops [in China.]"

Finally Privy Council President Hara delivered a lengthy and carefully prepared statement on behalf of the Throne. It was a statement which Hirohito had personally requested and reviewed in advance and which still bore the imprint of his own turns of phrase and simplifying abstractions.

At the last Imperial Conference it was decided that we would go to war if the negotiations failed to lead to agreement. According to the briefings given today, the present American attitude is not just the same as the previous one, but is even more unreasonable. Therefore I regret very much that the negotiations have little prospect of success.

. . . We cannot let the present situation continue. If we miss the present opportunity to go to war, we will have to submit to American dictation. Therefore, I recognize that it is inevitable that we must decide to start a war against the United States. I will put my trust in what I have been told: namely, that things will go well in the early part of the war; and that although we will experience increasing difficulties as the war progresses, there is some prospect of success.

. . . I do not believe that the present situation would have developed out of the China Incident alone. We have come to where we are because of the war between Germany and Great Britain. What we should always keep in mind here is what would happen to relations between Germany and Great Britain and Germany and the United States—all of them being countries whose population belongs to the white race—if Japan should enter the war. Hitler has said that the Japanese are a second-class race, and Germany has not yet declared war against the United States. . . .

We must give serious consideration to race relations. . . . Don't let hatred of Japan become stronger than hatred of Hitler so that everybody will in name as well as fact gang up on Japan. . . .

[If we do not enter the war] two years from now we will have no petroleum for military use. Ships will stop moving. When I think about the strengthening of American defenses in the Southwest Pacific, the expansion of the American fleet, the unfinished China Incident, and so on, I see no end to difficulties. We can talk about austerity and suffering, but can our people endure such a life for a long time? . . . I fear, that if we sit tight, we may become a third-class nation after only two or three years. . . .

As to what our moral basis for going to war should be, there is some merit in making it clear that Great Britain and the United States represent a strong threat to Japan's self-preservation. Also, if we are fair in governing occupied areas, attitudes toward us would probably relax. America may be enraged for a while, but later she will come to understand. No matter what happens, I wish to be sure that the war does not become a racial war.

Do you have any other comments? If not, I will rule that the proposals have been approved in their original form.

No one said a word. Hirohito nodded his satisfaction and made his recessional. The war had been decided.

HIROHITO INCOGNITO

From that moment, until the Pearl Harbor attack a month and three days later, Hirohito worked night and day to review every detail of war planning. At the same time he impressed on his intimates the importance of gaining the full support of the people; of upholding a façade of propriety and due deliberation for the sake of posterity; and of deceiving the enemy.

As soon as the November 5 meeting had adjourned, Hirohito approved the dispatch of a special envoy to Washington to assist Ambassador Nomura. The envoy selected was Kurusu Saburo, a career diplomat who, as ambassador in Berlin in 1940, had consummated the Tripartite Pact with Hitler. His mission was a delicate one. He must suggest to President Roosevelt, without seeming to threaten him, that Japan was not bluffing this time in attaching a deadline to negotiations. Then, if the United States remained intractable and the deadline passed, he must overcome Ambassador Nomura's sense of honor in order to keep up the negotiations as a subterfuge. Finally, without endangering security, he must make everyone at the Japanese Embassy in Washington aware of the decision which had been reached in Tokyo.

A Pan American Clipper, on State Department instructions, was kept waiting for forty-eight hours in Hong Kong so that Mr. Kurusu could board it. The new ambassador finally arrived in Washington November 16.

During Kurusu's eleven-day departure and journey, Hirohito repaired to his seaside villa in Hayama and there assumed incognito in order to assist personally at two final, three-day reviews of all war planning. So secret were these *gozen heigo,* these "soldier chess games in the Imperial Presence" as Chief of Staff Sugiyama called them, that not even the places at which they were held has ever been divulged. Some of them were probably conducted at sea aboard the flagship of the Pearl Harbor task force, the *Akagi,* and the rest at the Army base near Numazu about forty miles down the coast from Hayama by air, or about one hundred miles by sea.

The published record concerning these *gozen heigo* exemplifies the extreme circumspection of Japanese belly talk. Since late October Hirohito had been talking to his civilian chamberlains about the possibility of going down to Hayama for a brief "vacation." Since it was a bleak season of the year for such an outing, those who knew Hirohito's character assumed that he would be going to Hayama to disarm foreign observers by a show of unconcern before Japan's blitzkrieg.

Even with his military chiefs Hirohito disguised his reasons for wanting to attend the war games. It was his prerogative and his traditional duty to have a few private words with all generals and admirals when they left Japan on important missions. Now, when a great number of commanders were about to leave Japan all at once, a steady stream of military visitors calling at the palace might come to the attention of foreign observers and excite suspicion. Therefore Hirohito had asked the Army and Navy chiefs of staff to devise means by which he could hold his audiences with the commanders in secrecy. It was understood that in this fashion, under the pretext of a ceremonial farewell to his warriors, he could review all war plans without officially sanctioning any of them—without, that is, encumbering the Throne with responsibility for plans that might fail.

With these understandings and covers in mind, Hirohito called the two chiefs of staff into his presence immediately after the Imperial Conference on November 5.

"From the security standpoint," he asked, "when will we dispatch the commanders and the others to their posts in the field?"

"The Supreme Command," replied Sugiyama, "will talk over military plans for three days on the seventh, eighth, and ninth. After that the forces attached to their commands will have similar co-ordinating meetings. I do not think it advisable to dispatch the commanders too early to their posts lest our secret plans leak out."

The Emperor, noted Sugiyama, "seemed to understand well, made his decision at once, and asked several questions."

Hirohito left for Hayama at 10 A.M. November 7. At the seaside villa he was free of most of the protocol and security which beset him in the moats and walls of his Tokyo residence. His imperial marine biological yacht was recognized as a sacrosanct hideaway by both reporters and security police. It was equipped with ship-to-shore radiotelephone and running lights for night voyages.

Kido, who accompanied Hirohito to Hayama and took care of all state business for him during the "vacation," did not see his master from the morning of the seventh until the morning of the tenth. Then, after the general Army-Navy co-ordinating sessions, Hirohito appeared for a forty-five-minute chat with his chief advisor. He at once vanished again until the unit-co-ordinating studies had been completed on November 13. During this second disappearance, he is said to have been aboard the carrier *Akagi*, reviewing the co-ordination of the Pearl Harbor attack fleet.

On November 14, Hirohito resurfaced at Hayama to catch up on civilian developments and to receive briefings from Prime Minister Tojo, Foreign Minister Togo, and Finance Minister Kaya. On the fifteenth he returned to Tokyo.

As soon as he had "re-entered the palace gate" he gave audience to Army Chief of Staff Sugiyama. In his memoranda Sugiyama had eloquently filled the days of Hirohito's absence from Tokyo with eighty-three pages of compressed numerical tables on Japan's present and projected military-industrial strength in comparison with that of the enemy. Now, "on November 15, after the chess game with soldiers in the Imperial Presence," Sugiyama recorded Hirohito's afterthoughts.

"Where," asked the Emperor, "is the Strike-South commander going to set up his headquarters?"

"In Saigon," replied Sugiyama.

"Is there a possibility of our spoiling the Malayan rubber plantations?"

"I don't know," said Sugiyama. "There may be some damage. But since, except for the Kedah area, the roads are narrow, we think the best procedure is to advance in small units of a single regiment led by a few tanks. That way there should be little danger of damaging the rubber forests."

Hirohito nodded and asked Sugiyama for renewed assurance that military operations could be called off at any moment if the United States showed signs of agreeing to Japan's diplomatic demands. Sugiyama went so far as to swear that even if the enemy attacked Japan before Japan attacked the enemy, the Army and Navy had orders to contain the conflict as much as possible until the Emperor personally gave the word for war.

"I have explained to Terauchi and the other commanding officers," said

Sugiyama, "that if diplomatic negotiations suddenly succeed through military backing, it will prove the strength of the military forces and make it possible for them to withdraw with honor."

FLEET DISPATCH

On November 7, the day of the Emperor's arrival in Hayama, Combined Fleet Commander Admiral Yamamoto had revealed to his most trusted staff officers that December 8 would be the day of attack. On November 10, after the first three co-ordinating days of the "war games in the Imperial Presence," Yamamoto had had Admiral Nagumo Chu-ichi, who would personally lead the Pearl Harbor attack force, order all the ship captains in his fleet to "complete battle preparations by November 20." That same day the first of twenty-seven of Japan's largest submarines—320-foot I-class boats with a cruising range of 12,000 miles at fourteen knots—slipped out of the fleet to thread its way between American reconnaissance areas and to take up a watch three weeks later outside the mouth of Pearl Harbor.

On November 11, having thoroughly committed himself and the Emperor to his Pearl Harbor plan, Admiral Yamamoto wrote to one of his mentors, a retired admiral and family friend, "I leave my family to your guidance. . . . What a strange position it is in which I find myself. I am having to lead in a decision diametrically opposed to my personal beliefs. And I have no choice but full speed ahead."

By November 14, most of the Pearl Harbor task force had gathered around Yamamoto's flagship in Saiki Bay, off the northeast corner of Kyushu, so that its captains could have a last word with the commander before they sailed. Admiral Nagumo Chu-ichi's flagship, the carrier *Akagi,* was still in the Tokyo area, at Yokosuka Naval Base, picking up the last of a consignment of special torpedoes which would be used for the attack on Hawaii. They were rigged for shallow running with wooden fins devised in September during trials at Kagoshima Bay. Ordinary torpedoes, it had been determined, would bury and waste themselves in the mud under Pearl Harbor's confined waters.

The other five carriers of the Pearl Harbor attack force now began detaching themselves one by one, and night by night, from Yamamoto's fleet to make their way around Japan to Hitokappu Bay, sometimes called Tankan Bay, a harbor of rendezvous in the northern extremities of the Empire, at Etorofu Island in the Kuriles. There, under the gaze of seals and walruses rubbing up their winter coats on the hard beaches, they were to load drums of oil which Yamamoto had received imperial sanction to cache months earlier in a shed beside a small concrete wharf. The drums would fill the tanks of the carriers and be stacked on their decks for the long dash across the north Pacific.

The last of the advance force of twenty-seven submarines, which were to gather as a wolf pack outside the mouth of Pearl Harbor two days before the attack, left the Inland Sea on November 18. They were accompanied by a tender and a cruiser which were to see them part way to their destination. Eight of them carried two-men "midget submarines" slung on their bellies. The midgets were detailed to slip through the boom and the nets at the mouth of Pearl Harbor and compound confusion by firing torpedoes and diverting fire when the crucial moment came. Their design and development had been sponsored since 1933 by Prince Fushimi of the imperial family. Their crews had been trained for one-way suicide missions but had not been allowed by Yamamoto to join the fleet until adequate provisions had been taken for their recovery by their mother submarines.

As the carriers and submarines involved in Yamamoto's grand design slipped from their anchorages, they kept radio silence—a silence which they would maintain until December 8. Yamamoto, from his flagship, would send them orders in the new Admirals' Code which U.S. cryptographers had not yet been able to decipher. Even if decoded, his messages contained the "voice code" signals—many obscure allusions to Japanese history—which had been agreed upon before the ships sailed. As a final security measure all the attack ships had new signal officers. The old ones, using their own recognizable touch on the radio-telegraph key, were ashore in Japan sending out call signals and bogus messages to one another as if they were still in their ships waiting for war in harbors off the southern Japanese coasts.

JAPAN'S WAR GOALS

Yamamoto's fleet would not sail from Hitokappu Bay until November 26. In the meantime, on November 16, special envoy Kurusu submitted his credentials in Washington and at once began to present Proposal A, Japan's final offer for an over-all settlement with the United States. When it was turned down out of hand, he proceeded to Proposal B for a modus vivendi and a return to the position prior to Japan's occupation of southern Indochina and America's freezing of assets. This proposal was formally tendered on November 20, turned down on November 22, and formally turned down in a U.S. counterproposal of general principles on November 26.

Except to a student of the period, the verbiage of the diplomatic notes might veil the reasons for the unyielding line taken by the U.S. government. They were succinctly stated in a memo to Secretary of State Hull from his advisor Joseph W. Ballantine on November 22: "You might say [to the Japanese] that in the minds of the American people the purposes underlying our aid to China are the same as the purposes underlying our aid to Great Britain and that the American people believe that there is a partnership between Hitler and Japan aimed at dividing the world between them."

Ballantine was correct in his assessment—up to a point. The position papers being written that month by junior members of the imperial cabal and duly forwarded to Hirohito's Office of Aides-de-Camp show that dividing the world with Hitler was the goal only of World War II. After that, there must eventually come another war in which Hitler and his half would be dealt with in their turn.

In World War II, it was planned that Japan would take most of India and everything east of India up to Central America and the Caribbean. "The future of Trinidad, British and Dutch Guiana, and British and French possessions in the Leeward Islands [however] is to be decided by agreement between Japan and Germany after the war." The rest of the Americas were to be handled according to their co-operativeness. "Mexico, in the event that she declares war on Japan, shall cede us her territory east of Longitude 95°30' [Chiapas and Yucatan]. Should Peru join in the war against Japan, she shall cede territory north of Latitude 10° [half the country]. If Chile enters the war, she shall cede the nitre zone north of Latitude 24° [a populous seventh of the country]."

As for the United States, she would remain nominally independent after her surrender and would retain sovereignty east of the Rockies, but the Alaska Government-General of Japan's Co-Prosperity Sphere would "include Alberta, British Columbia, and the state of Washington." There would be other "governments-general" for southern India and the offshore African islands; for Hong Kong and the Philippines; for Oceania; for Melanesia; for Hawaii and the eastern Pacific; for Australia; for New Zealand and Antarctica. The East Indies, Burma, Malaya, Thailand, Cambodia and south Indochina, and Laos and north Indochina were each to be established ultimately as independent "kingdoms."

These were the objectives of World War II and some of them, it was recognized, might have to be deferred until after the war when they could be gained by further infiltrations and encroachments. Finally, however, would come World War III, the last war, the war with Germany, which was supposed to end in a single Japanese world state dedicated to the pursuit of the Japanese aesthetic of harmonious people and appreciation of nature. Ecologically the vision was perfect; practically it meant the elimination of all lower cultures which could not think in the politically sophisticated, technologically awkward terms of the Japanese.

A liaison conference of November 20 considered the "Essentials of Policy Regarding Administration of the Occupied Areas in the Southern Regions." In so doing, it approved this long-range vision, which was embodied in a bushel basket of supporting position papers. At the same time, specifically, it recommended to the Emperor a division of Army and Navy responsibilities in the areas which Japan expected to occupy immediately. Hirohito approved the recommendation six days later, on November 26. It was thus agreed that the Navy would administer Dutch Borneo and all the spoils of conquest to the east of it, and that the Army would administer British Borneo, Java, Sumatra, the Philippines, and everything to the west.

AMERICA STANDS PAT

On November 22 General Terauchi of the Strike-South forces paid his respects to Lord Privy Seal Kido before moving his headquarters from Tokyo to Taiwan, and Foreign Minister Togo gave Nomura and Kurusu in Washington an additional four days' leeway for bargaining. "There are reasons," he cabled, "beyond your ability to guess why we wanted to settle Japanese-American relations by the 25th [of November], but if, within the following three or four days, you can conclude your conversations with the Americans, if the signing [of some sort of agreement] can be completed by the 29th . . . we have decided that we can wait until that date. This time, however, we mean it. The deadline absolutely cannot be changed again. After that things are automatically going to happen. . . . For the present, this is for the information of you two ambassadors alone."

Foreign Minister Togo's warning that things would automatically happen if the United States did not agree to Proposal B before November 29 was monitored by U.S. military intelligence, decoded, translated, and handed to President Roosevelt within twenty-four hours of its dispatch. The mountain of evidence collected by the Roberts Commission and the Congressional Pearl Harbor hearings make it clear that the President and his chief advisors correctly understood the cable as a war ultimatum. They agreed, without dissent, to let Japan do her worst. For months they had been buying time by showing an interest in Japan's contention that she needed *Lebensraum* and deserved to have a privileged position in Asia. Now, although they knew that defenses in the Philippines were far from complete, they realized that Japan could not honestly be stalled much longer.

They encouraged Secretary of State Hull to draft a maddeningly moral statement of the position of the United States and to present it to Nomura and Kurusu as soon as possible. They fully expected that this statement might goad Japan into an attack on the United States. But according to Winston Churchill, who knew them all personally, they "regarded the actual form of the attack, or even its scale, as incomparably less important than the fact that the whole American nation would be united for its own safety in a righteous cause as never before."

On Tuesday, November 25, Roosevelt looked over Secretary of State Cordell Hull's draft of the rejection note to the Japanese and called a meeting of his inner Cabinet. In addition to Hull, those present included Secretary of War Henry L. Stimson, Secretary of the Navy Frank Knox, Army Chief of Staff General George C. Marshall, and Chief of Naval Operations Admiral Harold R. Stark. The six men had before them a memo from Colonel Rufus Bratton of Army G-2 predicting that war with Japan could be expected on or about Saturday, November 29. Everyone at the meeting knew that Colonel Bratton was one of the Army-Navy *Magic* group which routinely intercepted and rendered into English the highest-security diplomatic messages being sent out from Tokyo to Japanese ambassadors. No one present fully appreciated the unadvertised fact that the Japanese Navy had the Admirals' Code which had so far withstood all the efforts of the *Magic* group at decipherment.

Roosevelt opened the meeting by bringing up the approaching break-down in negotiations with the Japanese. Hull added that the Japanese were "poised for attack." According to Stimson's diary, the President then said "that we were likely to be attacked perhaps (as soon as) next Monday, for the Japanese are notorious for making an attack without warning, and the question was what we should do. The question was how we should maneuver them into the position of firing the first shot without allowing too much danger to ourselves. It was a difficult proposition."

The President's inner Cabinet meeting broke up agreeing that Secretary of State Hull should indeed present his reassertion of general moral principles, turning down all Japanese proposals and rubbing Japanese sensibilities the wrong way. That afternoon War Secretary Stimson learned from intelligence sources in Shanghai that approximately 25,000 Japanese troops were embarking on thirty to fifty transports in the Yangtze River roadstead. The report indicated that they were bound for Indochina, Thailand, Burma, or the Philippines. Unknown to Washington, this was one of the eleven divisions selected for Japan's Strike South. Its conspicuous embarkation in Shanghai was intentional—a trial balloon to attract American attention during the sailing of Japan's other attack fleets. When Stimson called Roosevelt with the news, the President "fairly blew up—jumped into the air, so to speak" because he saw in it clear indication "of bad faith on the part of the Japanese" in their negotiations.

A few hours after Stimson got his intelligence from Shanghai—the evening of November 25 in Washington, the morning of November 26 in Tokyo—Hirohito learned that the Foreign Ministry momentarily expected an unfavorable U.S. note. Although it had not yet been presented, Kurusu and Nomura reported that the note would deny all Japanese requests and ultimatums and would, in essence, retract all the tentative U.S. proposals for a settlement which had been advanced since the previous April. Hirohito at once called in Lord Privy Seal Kido and said:

"Although it is with deep regret and anxiety, I am forced to admit that we have reached the point of no return. Before making our final irrevocable decision, however, I am wondering if we should not solicit the opinion of the Elder Statesmen [the ex-prime ministers of Japan] in one last wide-ranging discussion."

Kido agreed with the Emperor's suggestion because, as he pointed out, what was about to be done could "never be undone" if it turned out badly. Prime Minister Tojo, when consulted, objected strenuously that the Elder Statesmen should not be made to share in the responsibility for a decision in which they had taken no part. Overruling Tojo, Hirohito invited the Elder Statesmen to have lunch in the palace three days later, on November 29.

At about the hour that Hirohito was talking to Tojo the advance force of submarines, on their way to the mouth of Pearl Harbor, received a radio message in the Admirals' Code informing them that the Washington negotiations had passed the point of rupture. Still later in the day, at sundown in the Kuriles and before dawn in Washington, the Pearl Harbor fleet began to sail carrier by carrier from Hitokappu Bay. By the time that Hull had officially handed his note to Ambassador Nomura, at 5 P.M. Washington time, the fleet had vanished into the fogs of the north Pacific. Proceeding under radio silence, it steered a narrow course between the southern fringes of U.S. air reconnaissance from the Aleutians and the northern fringes of reconnaissance from Guam and Midway.

When he handed his note to Nomura and Kurusu, Secretary of State Hull was left in no doubt as to what the reaction of the Japanese government would be. As the two envoys wired to Tokyo that evening: "We were both dumbfounded. . . . We argued back furiously but Hull remained solid as a rock." Getting nowhere with Hull, they then asked to see the President. Hull made an appointment for them at the White House for two o'clock the following afternoon.

PEARL HARBOR PRECAUTIONS

The next morning, November 27, was the traditional American Thanksgiving Thursday. Secretary of State Hull called on the President early to inform him of the Japanese envoys' reactions to his note. Then Hull spoke on the phone with Secretary of War Stimson and told him, "I have washed my hands of it and it is now in the hands of you and Knox—the Army and the Navy." For the rest of the morning, guided by numerous telephone calls to and from the White House, the leaders of the Army and Navy were busy deciding what if any measures they should take. Two actions emerged from the phone conferences: all the aircraft carriers and half the Army airplanes were ordered out of Pearl Harbor and all the U.S. commanders in the Pacific were sent a war warning.

When Secretary of War Stimson telephoned the President to authorize the war warning, Roosevelt replied that he not only authorized but positively ordered Stimson to give "the final alert." Stimson and Chief of Naval Operations Stark—"Betty" as he was always called by the President—promptly sent urgent messages to Panama, San Diego, Honolulu, and

Manila. The stronger of the two, Stark's, said in part: "This dispatch is to be considered a war warning. . . . An aggressive move by Japan is expected within the next few days."

The warning went on to say that the move would probably be an "amphibious expedition against either the Philippines, Thai or Kra Peninsula [in Malaya], or possibly Borneo."

When the war warning arrived in Hawaii, Admiral Husband E. Kimmel and the Army commander there, Lieutenant General Walter C. Short, were already negotiating with one another as to how to comply with the instructions they had just received to send away all their aircraft carriers and half their Army airplanes. They finally agreed to activate a plan to send the planes and carriers on as reinforcements to Wake and Midway. The agreement was difficult to reach because it meant not only emasculating their commands but also putting Army planes under Navy jurisdiction. Nevertheless, Vice Admiral William F. Halsey was ordered to depart the next morning for Wake with the carrier *Enterprise,* three heavy cruisers, nine destroyers, twelve Marine Grumman Wildcat fighters, and some Army bombers from General Short's command. Vice Admiral J. H. Newton would depart for Midway with the carrier *Lexington,* three cruisers, five destroyers, and eighteen more of the Marine fighters on December 5. The third of Kimmel's aircraft carriers, the *Saratoga,* was in San Diego and could be left there for an overhaul.[5]

Admiral Kimmel later testified that he understood the Navy Department's "explicit suggestion" that he divest himself of all his fastest ships and his fleet air cover to mean that Hawaii was in no danger of attack. It was in this frame of mind, and in a negative spirit of caution, that he and General Short reacted to the war warning when it arrived in Hawaii later that day. On behalf of both of them, General Short at once wired Washington the full official extent of their response to the warning:

REPORT DEPARTMENT ALERTED TO PREVENT SABOTAGE. LIAISON WITH NAVY.

This meant that, after consultation with the Navy, General Short had ordered the lowest form of alert and preparedness for the forces under his

[5] These dispatches of valuable fleet elements—first Halsey's with the most useful ships of the U.S. Pacific fleet, then Newton's with the next most useful ships—were both made just before weekends when it was most likely that the Japanese might try a surprise raid. As a further precaution the battleships remaining in Pearl Harbor were moored in pairs, with less valuable older ships to seaward, where they would be vulnerable to torpedo attack, and new valuable ships inboard where they would be shielded from torpedoes by land on one side and by additional layers of armor plate on the other, outward side.

Notwithstanding these shrewd safety measures, Admiral Kimmel, who had charge of Pearl Harbor, was later held responsible for the disaster which took place there. He was relieved of command along with Admiral Stark, the Chief of Naval Operations in Washington.

command: a close lookout for signs of subversives and bombs in suitcases. Chief of Staff General Marshall, apparently in an absent moment, indicated that he had read General Short's report on the precautions taken by initialing the copy of it presented to him.

President Roosevelt's military advisors ordered the carriers and planes out of Pearl Harbor because these weapons were valuable and mobile. The war in Europe had conclusively demonstrated the importance of air power. Carriers, being defended by planes instead of big guns and heavy armor plate, could travel and maneuver almost twice as fast as most U.S. battleships at that time. Eight old, slow battleships and eight old cruisers were left in Pearl Harbor because little better use could be seen for them. They were already obsolescent weapons. They could neither escape nor defend themselves at sea.

Despite the precautions taken to save the carriers in the Pacific, and with them the best planes, cruisers, and destroyers, it appears from the record that no one in Washington really expected Pearl Harbor to be attacked. The Japanese Army was known to be moving transports down the China coast toward Malaya or the Philippines. It was already axiomatic, because of the careful publicity work of Hirohito's advisors, that the Japanese Army ruled supreme in Japan and had long ago encased official Tokyo thinking in a wooden suit of samurai armor. That the Army would allow the Navy to divert a strong force from the Strike-South operations and stage a daring raid on Pearl Harbor, four thousand miles off to one side, seemed highly improbable.

Not that a Pearl Harbor raid was thought to be unfeasible; on the contrary, Admiral Harry E. Yarnell had theoretically surprised and sunk the U.S. Pacific fleet with only two carriers during the U.S. naval maneuvers of 1932. As late as June 1940 the U.S. Army in Hawaii had been ordered: "Immediately alert complete defensive organization to deal with possible trans-Pacific raid." Still later, after the successful British torpedo plane attack on the Italian fleet at Taranto in November 1940, Navy Secretary Knox had advised War Secretary Stimson: "The success of the British . . . suggests that precautionary measures be taken immediately to protect Pearl Harbor against a surprise attack in the event of war between the United States and Japan." Stimson had responded by giving Pearl Harbor special priority in the allotment of antiaircraft guns and of new radar equipment. Still later, in March 1941, Major General Frederick L. Martin, who commanded the Army air forces in Hawaii, supervised a study of the attack possibilities and concluded, as Yamamoto was doing at about the same time, that a carrier task force might best approach Pearl Harbor from the north and launch its planes for an attack at dawn.

All these studies and orders to take precautions were apparently made without conviction. They were contingency planning and nothing more. On

January 27, 1941, Ambassador Grew had warned Washington of intelligence from the Peruvian Embassy in Tokyo that "in the event of trouble breaking out between the United States and Japan, the Japanese intend to make a surprise attack against Pearl Harbor with all their strength and employing all their equipment." U.S. Naval Intelligence forwarded Grew's note to Admiral Kimmel in Hawaii with the comment that "no move against Pearl Harbor appears imminent or planned for the foreseeable future."

U.S. naval strategists discounted the possibility of a Pearl Harbor attack for the same reason that a majority of the best Japanese naval strategists had opposed Yamamoto when he had presented his plan at table-top maneuvers in September 1941. The venture seemed to them then, and still appears to many of them even now, as a flamboyant gesture profiting Japan nothing. Tactically a few U.S. ships would be put out of commission for a while but strategically the Pearl Harbor base would remain undestroyed. And politically the United States would be galled at the very time when Japan wished to make a few quick seizures and then negotiate a truce. "It was," says one retired Japanese naval officer, "like sticking a spear into a sleeping hippopotamus while you were building a dam to take away half his pond."

Hirohito had known better than to think that U.S. leaders were genuinely asleep, and so he had intervened to force through Yamamoto's plan over the objections of most of the top brass in the Japanese Navy General Staff. Knowing nothing of Hirohito's power, the U.S. Office of Naval Operations had wrongly concluded, by majority vote, that a majority of their opposite numbers in Tokyo would have vetoed any plan to raid Pearl Harbor.

DIPLOMATIC DECEIT

That Thanksgiving Thursday, as soon as the orders that seemed necessary had been sent to Pearl Harbor and to the other U.S. command posts in the Pacific, President Roosevelt met on schedule, at 2 P.M., with the Japanese envoys in Washington, Nomura and Kurusu. Although he spoke with more charm and friendliness than Cordell Hull, Roosevelt backed his subordinate by refusing to hold out any hope of U.S. concessions.

That evening Kurusu was telephoned for a report on the conversation by an underling in the Foreign Ministry in Tokyo. The underling's name happened to be Yamamoto Kumaichi, but he was no relative of Admiral Yamamoto. It was already noon the next day in Tokyo and Yamamoto, wide awake, employed a previously agreed-upon voice code which the tired Kurusu found difficult to handle. U.S. naval monitors of the trans-Pacific cable chuckled at what they heard:

YAMAMOTO: How did the matrimonial question [the negotiations] get along today?

KURUSU: Oh, haven't you got our telegram yet? It was sent—let me see— at about six, no seven o'clock. Seven o'clock. About three hours ago. There wasn't much that was different from what Miss Umeko [Cordell Hull] inti- mated yesterday.

YAMAMOTO: Really? not much different?

KURUSU: No, not much. As before that southward matter, that south, south, southward matter [the movement of the Japanese transports down the China coast], is having considerable effect. You know? southward matter?

YAMAMOTO: Ah so! the south matter? It's having an effect?

KURUSU: Yes, and at one time the matrimonial question seemed as if it would be settled. But well, of course, there are other matters involved too. However that was it; that was the monkey wrench. Details are included in the telegram which should arrive very shortly. . . . How do things look there? Does it seem as if a child might be born?

YAMAMOTO (in a very definite tone): Yes, the birth of the child seems im- minent.

KURUSU: Oh it does? It does seem as if the birth is going to take place? (pause) In which direction? (pause, with confusion). I mean, is it to be a boy or a girl? [war or peace]

YAMAMOTO (after laughter and hesitation): It seems as if it will be a strong healthy boy.

KURUSU: Oh, it's to be a strong healthy boy?

YAMAMOTO: Yes. Did you make any statement [to the press] regarding your talk with Miss Kimiko [President Roosevelt] today?

KURUSU: No, nothing. Nothing except the mere fact that we met.

YAMAMOTO: Regarding the matter contained in the telegram of the other day [the sending of a personal peace plea from Roosevelt to Hirohito], no definite decision has yet been reached but please be advised that effecting it will be difficult. . . .

KURUSU: Well, I guess there's nothing more that can be done then.

YAMAMOTO: Well, yes. (pause) Then today.

KURUSU: Today?

YAMAMOTO: The matrimonial question, that is. The matter pertaining to arranging a marriage—don't break them off.

KURUSU: Not break them? You mean talks? (helpless pause) Oh, my! (pause with resigned laughter) Well, I'll do what I can. Please read carefully what Miss Kimiko [Roosevelt] had to say as contained in today's tele- gram. . . .

So it was that the Japanese envoys and their eavesdroppers in Washing- ton learned that the response to Hull's note would be war, that a message to Hirohito would not help matters, and that from now on diplomatic negotiations must be continued only as a façade to conceal Japan's last-minute preparations.

Knowing of the Kurusu-Yamamoto conversation, President Roosevelt met with his War Cabinet—Hull, Stimson, Knox, Marshall, and Stark—at noon the next day, Friday, November 28. They discussed the likelihood of war that weekend without ever mentioning Pearl Harbor once. Roosevelt was still preoccupied with the possibility of sending—if only "for the record" now—a personal appeal to Emperor Hirohito. His advisors were more concerned—for the record—about Congress. They urged F.D.R. to deliver a message to the nation's legislators, warning them that war with Japan might break out at any moment.

As Stimson wrote in his diary, the President "had better send his letter to the Emperor separate as one thing and a secret thing, and then make his speech to the Congress as a separate and more understandable thing to the people of the United States. This was the final decision at that time, and the President asked Hull and Knox and myself to try to draft such papers."

Later that day the President and his advisors received intercepts of Japanese messages to consulates and embassies in South America ordering the destruction of all codes and secret papers.

On Saturday November 29 Secretary of State Hull told Kurusu and Nomura that he was willing to continue negotiations as long as Japan wished to negotiate. Privately he told friends that he was doing so, if not for the record, then at least "for the purpose of making a record."

Roosevelt retired for the weekend to await developments in his retreat at Warm Springs in the north Georgia hills where he had established a sanitorium for fellow polio victims. Nothing, however, happened. The Japanese division sailing down the China coast disembarked in Indochina and waited there for final orders. As General Marshall later described the anticlimax: "We entered into December without anything happening other than the continuation of these movements, which we could follow fairly well, down the China coast. . . ."

In Tokyo Hirohito was running, unhurried but with clockwork precision, on the schedule which he had approved weeks earlier. At noon on Saturday, November 29, over Tojo's objections, he lunched with the ex-prime ministers of Japan and encouraged them to express their views at the formal Elder Statesmen's Conference which was to follow dessert. Eight former prime ministers were present, four military men and four civilians. Seven of them either objected that there was no need for war or maintained sullenly that they had been given insufficient information of late on which to base an opinion. Only one of the eight, the civilian diplomat Hirota, approved the war, and he did so, he said, because he felt that Japan could not better her negotiating position with the United States unless she demonstrated her readiness and ability to seize ground held by U.S. military forces. On behalf of the Throne, Lord Privy Seal Kido thanked them all for their opinions, indicated to them that war, regardless, was about to break out, and asked them all as patriots to help unify Japan in this time of unprecedented crisis.

As soon as the elder statesmen had left the palace, Prime Minister Tojo convened a liaison conference of Cabinet and Supreme Command. It was attended by no less than three "Unidentified Persons" who spoke with authority, as if they were members of the imperial family. They considered the value of continuing the negotiations in Washington and decided that considerations of secrecy and surprise far outweighed those of deceit and dishonor. As one of the unidentified persons stated, probably Prince Kanin: "I would like to see our diplomacy executed in such a way as to win us the war."

The next afternoon at 1:30 Lord Privy Seal Kido was called to the residence of Prince Takamatsu, the second of the Emperor's three brothers. In the presence of Prince Mikasa, the youngest of the brothers, Takamatsu told Kido that the officers of the Navy General Staff had agreed to appeal to the Emperor, saying that they had no confidence in the Navy's ability to win the war. Kido returned to the palace at 2:30 and after an hour's wait secured an audience with his master.

Hirohito, after hearing the message from Takamatsu, said, "As the Navy is having great trouble reaching unanimity of opinion, I feel as if I should avoid a U.S.–Japanese war, if that is at all possible, but just how, realistically, can I manage it?"

Kido replied: "I don't think it proper, even after long deliberation, for the Throne to take a step if there is still any shadow of doubt in the imperial mind. This is especially true on the present occasion because the decision is a unique one of great gravity. Accordingly I advise the Emperor to summon at once the Navy minister and the Navy chief of staff and ascertain what is the true feeling in the guts of the Navy. I also suggest that it would not do to alienate the prime minister at this juncture and that I would like the Emperor to consult with him also."

At 3:30 Prime Minister Tojo was received in audience by Hirohito, with Kido standing by. After that Navy Minister Shimada and Navy Chief of Staff Nagano conferred with the Emperor for about two hours. Kido waited restlessly outside the Imperial Study talking with the chief aide-de-camp at 4:00 and with the grand chamberlain at 6:00. Finally at 6:35 Kido was summoned into the Imperial Presence. Hirohito said:

"Instruct Prime Minister Tojo to proceed according to plan. The Navy minister and the Navy chief of staff have both given affirmative answers to my question regarding our war chances."

Kido wrote in his diary. "I immediately phoned the prime minister to inform him of the above: After stopping for supper with the Suos, I returned home about midnight."

This was the midnight of the deadline set earlier, after which war would become automatic and negotiations would become a sham.

A WEEK OF STRANGE QUIET

Fourteen hours later, at midnight Sunday, November 30, Washington time, the undecided Battle of Moscow continued to absorb Western attention and the critical weekend in Japanese-American relations seemed to be passing uneventfully into a new working week. Allied intelligence had observed that Axis nations seldom attacked except on weekends or holidays. There might yet be time for Christmas shopping. Perhaps, after all, Japan had been bluffing.

At that very moment, however—2 P.M., Monday, December 1, Tokyo time—Hirohito was bringing to order the conference in his Presence at which he would give the final go-ahead for war. The conference was only a ceremony, but in the course of it several revealing statements were made. Foreign Minister Togo reviewed the unhappy eight months of negotiations with the United States. Navy Chief of Staff Nagano reaffirmed his pledge of the day before that the Navy had confidence. Prime Minister Tojo spoke at length on the morale of the nation.

"To stabilize the views held by the people," Tojo acknowledged, "it will be necessary to guide public opinion and at the same time to exercise rather strict controls over it."

Finance Minister Kaya delivered an exhaustive report on "Our Long-term Financial and Monetary Capacity." In it he promised that the government would underwrite the indebtedness of all banks, of all essential industries, and of all war-damage victims. He undertook to shore up the stock market by a policy of "unlimited buying on the part of the Japan Joint Securities Corporation."

Agriculture Minister Ino Tetsuya presented an equally detailed, equally visionary, and equally pessimistic report on the possibility of feeding the nation during a long war.

Finally, Privy Council President Hara stood up to speak on behalf of the Throne. He scolded the ubiquitous Suzuki of the Cabinet Planning Board for inadequate preparations against the contingency of enemy incendiary raids. Having registered the desire of the Throne for adequate fire-fighting equipment, he went on to explain in broad terms why Hirohito felt justified in deciding on war:

> In negotiating with the United States, our Empire hoped to maintain peace by making one concession after another. But to our surprise, the American position from beginning to end was to say what Chiang Kai-shek wanted her to say, and to emphasize those ideals that she had stated in the past. The United States is being utterly conceited, obstinate, and disrespectful. It is regrettable indeed. We simply cannot tolerate such an attitude.
>
> If we were to give in, we would surrender at a stroke not only our benefits from the Manchurian Incident but also our gains in the Sino-Japanese and Russo-Japanese wars [of 1895 and 1905]. This we cannot do. . . .

We cannot avoid a long-term war this time, but I believe that we must somehow get around it and bring about an early settlement. In order to do this, we will need to start thinking now about how to end the war. Our nation, governed by our magnificent national structure, is, from a spiritual point of view, certainly unsurpassed in all the world. But in the course of a long war . . . it is particularly important to pay attention to our psychological solidarity. . . . Be sure you make no mistakes in handling the inner turmoil of the people.

I believe that the proposal before us cannot be avoided in the light of present circumstances, and I put my trust in my officers and men whose loyalty is supreme. I urge you to make every effort to keep the people in a tranquil state of mind, in order to prosecute a long-term war.

In replying to the Throne, Prime Minister General Tojo said:

At this moment our Empire stands at the threshold of glory or oblivion. We tremble with fear in the Presence of His Majesty. We subjects are keenly aware of the great responsibilities we must assume from this point on. Now that His Majesty has reached a decision to commence hostilities, we must all strive to repay our obligations to him, bring the Government and the military ever closer together, resolve that the nation united will go on to victory, make an all-out effort to achieve our war aims, and set His Majesty's mind at ease. I now adjourn the meeting.

The bleak and hollow ring of these proceedings made no impression on Hirohito. According to Chief of Staff Sugiyama's minutes: "His Majesty nodded in agreement with the statements being made during today's conference, and displayed no signs of uneasiness. He seemed to be in excellent spirits, and we were all filled with awe."

Later in the day when Sugiyama reported to the Throne on the orders which had just been sent out to Saigon "concerning the responsibility of the forces in the Southern Regions," Hirohito said, "We couldn't have avoided this situation. I beg that the Army and Navy will co-operate."

Sugiyama expressed himself deeply moved by the Emperor's graciousness, and Hirohito asked, "Has there been any change in the disposition of U.S. forces?"

"Since my report to His Majesty this morning," replied Sugiyama, "we have heard that two troops of American Marines, each about 400 strong, have arrived [as reinforcements] in Manila."

Hirohito nodded and "seemed extremely satisfied."

That night all the ships of the Japanese Navy changed their call signals.

The next morning, Tuesday, December 2, Hirohito gave permission to Navy Chief of Staff Nagano to send out Great Navy Order Number 12 which told the various Japanese fleet commanders that the day of attack was December 8. This message, in Admirals' Code, was not deciphered by U.S. intelligence. Yamamoto relayed his own personal version of the message to the fleet steaming toward Pearl Harbor: "Climb Mount Niitaka 1208." Niitaka was the Empire's highest mountain.

That night, Tokyo time—Tuesday morning, Pearl Harbor time— Admiral Kimmel in Hawaii received a call from the Naval Intelligence officer in charge of monitoring Japanese fleet signals. He learned that analysis of Japanese ship movements had been confused by the change in call signals the previous day. The confusion was compounded by a shrewd suspicion on the part of the analysts that many of the signals coming in were phoney ones being sent by land-based operators. In conclusion, Naval Intelligence suspected that it had not heard a genuine signal from any Japanese aircraft carrier in the last week. The carriers, in effect, "were lost."

"Do you mean to say," asked Admiral Kimmel, incredulously, "that they could be rounding Diamond Head and you wouldn't know it?"

"I hope," replied Lieutenant Commander Edwin T. Layton, the intelligence officer, "they would be sighted before now."

On Wednesday, December 3, the Japanese Pearl Harbor fleet rendezvoused at 42 degrees north latitude, 170 degrees east longitude—a point in the empty north Pacific about 2,300 miles northwest of Pearl Harbor. There, in a light swell amidst fog, the carriers took on oil from the tankers which had accompanied them this far on their historic voyage. Then the tankers and their escort of short-range destroyers turned back toward Japan and left the fast light carriers to make their lightning run on Hawaii.

During the refueling, before the carriers started their dash, Hirohito confirmed their orders by giving an unprecedented secret and private audience to the commander of the Combined Fleet. Admiral Yamamoto had been left restless in home waters to co-ordinate the actions of all his scattered fleet elements. He now repeated to Hirohito his fears that Japan would be defeated in a long war. Hirohito repeated his reasons for believing the war justified and inevitable. Yamamoto promised, to the best of his ability, to fight like a man possessed. After the audience, by telephone, radio, and Admirals' Code, Yamamoto sent the carriers on their way.

Also that day, Japanese envoys in Berlin and Rome felt out the positions which would be taken by Japan's Axis partners in the event of an American-Japanese war. Ambassador Oshima in Berlin did not tell Ribbentrop what was about to happen but exacted from him a pledge that Germany would declare war on the United States as soon as Japan did and would not stop fighting until both Japan and Germany were satisfied with the peace terms. The Japanese ambassador in Rome, Horikiri Zenbei, was somewhat more straightforward, and Count Galeazzo Ciano, Mussolini's foreign secretary, noted in his diary that evening:

> Sensational move by Japan. The ambassador asks for an audience with Il Duce and reads him a long statement on the progress of the negotiations with America, concluding with the assertion that they have reached a dead

end. Then, invoking the appropriate clause in the Tripartite Pact, he asks that Italy declare war on America immediately after the outbreak of hostilities and proposes the signature of an agreement not to conclude a separate peace. The interpreter translating this request was trembling like a leaf. Il Duce gave fullest assurances, reserving the right to confer with Berlin before giving a reply. Il Duce was pleased with the communication and said: "We are now on the brink of the inter-continental war which I predicted as early as September 1939." What does this new event mean? In any case, it means that Roosevelt has succeeded in his maneuver. Since he could not enter the war immediately and directly, he has entered it indirectly by letting himself be attacked by Japan.[6]

By Thursday, December 4, the unannounced but de facto state of war between Japan and the United States was so clearly understood by both parties that Walter Foote, the American consul in Batavia, Java, found himself out in his backyard burning code books while his opposite number from Japan, who lived next door, was doing likewise with his secret papers just over the garden fence.

That night the Japanese Navy changed its fleet code, making the routine signals of its vessels not only scrambled but temporarily unintelligible. U.S. naval cryptographers interrupted their work on the unbroken Admirals' Code and succeeded in recovering the new fleet code in a matter of days— but not until after Pearl Harbor.

On Friday morning, December 5, Tokyo time, the Japanese task force of Tiger Yamashita and his long-time helper, Colonel Tsuji, cast anchor from Samah harbor, Hainan, and began their obvious advance against the beaches of Malaya. Later in the day, in Tokyo, Hirohito approved a Navy schedule for handing the final note to Cordell Hull. He understood that it would inform the United States of a rupture in diplomatic relations a scant half-hour before the appointed hour for the attack on Pearl Harbor.

Still later in terms of absolute time, the Friday morning papers in the

---

[6] Ciano's catty but shrewd diary continues:

"December 4. Thursday. Berlin's reaction to the Japanese move is extremely cautious. Perhaps they will accept because they cannot get out of it, but the idea of provoking America's intervention pleases the Germans less and less. Mussolini, on the other hand, is pleased about it.

"December 5. Friday. A night interrupted by Ribbentrop's restlessness. After delaying two days, now he cannot wait a minute to answer the Japanese and at three in the morning he sent Mackensen to my house to submit a plan for a triple agreement relative to Japanese intervention and the pledge not to make a separate peace. He wanted me to awaken the Duce, but I did not do so, and the latter was very glad I hadn't.

"December 8. Monday. A night telephone call from Ribbentrop; he is overjoyed about the Japanese attack on America. He is so happy about it that I am happy with him, though I am not too sure about the final advantages of what has happened. . . ."

United States headlined a Hearst exclusive: "Roosevelt War Plan." Isolationist military men, who have not yet been identified, had leaked from the office of the General Staff a number of authentic contingency planning papers for mobilizing the nation in the event of war. The political accusations and counter-accusations which followed helped to distract Americans for the next two days.

That night Washington time, the next morning, Saturday, December 6 in Tokyo, the Japanese General Staffs and Cabinet met in a liaison conference to assume formal responsibility for the timing of the final note which was to be served on the United States. Without much debate the conferees agreed that the note should be "dispatched at 4 A.M., Japanese time, on December 7"—twenty-three and a half hours before the scheduled time of attack—and should be "handed to the President at 3 A.M. December 8, Japanese time": that is, at 1 P.M. December 7, Washington time, or at 7:30 A.M. December 7, Pearl Harbor time.

LAST DAY OF PEACE

As Saturday, December 6, dawned in Washington, the British high command in Singapore learned from aerial reconnaissance that two Japanese convoys had moved into the Gulf of Siam, off the southern tip of Cambodia, between Indochina and Malaya. They were moving at a leisurely pace westward as if to land troops on the eastern shore of the Kra Isthmus, the narrow point in the Malayan Peninsula where British territory abutted on Thailand. When Roosevelt heard this news between 10 and 11 A.M. that Saturday, it appeared that the Japanese would storm the Malayan beaches in about fourteen hours, or early on Sunday morning.

At noon, when Roosevelt was preparing to eat his modest lunch from a tray on his lap in the White House Oval Study where he worked, Naval Intelligence decoded a message from the Foreign Ministry in Tokyo advising envoys Nomura and Kurusu that the long-awaited reply to Hull's November 26 rejection of Japanese demands would be on the wires shortly. The reply to the rejection, said this "pilot message," would come in fourteen parts which must be presented to Secretary of State Hull at an hour which would be specified in later communications. Naval Intelligence realized that a declaration of Japanese hostility was in the offing and promptly informed the President.

Roosevelt gave the clerical help in the White House the afternoon off, so that they could have the last minutes of peace to themselves. For his own part he consulted privately with Secretary of State Hull, with Lord Halifax, the British ambassador, and with the Australian minister in Washington, Robert G. Casey. At the same time he rewrote the latest State Department version of the personal appeal which he had been agitating for ten days to send directly to the Emperor of Japan.

No records were kept of the activities in the White House that afternoon, but War Secretary Stimson noted in his diary that everyone was worried about the Japanese fleets converging on the Gulf of Siam. "That was what we were at work on our papers about. . . . The British were very excited. . . . Our effort this morning in drawing our papers was to see whether or not we should act together. . . . We all thought that we must fight if the British fought."

At 5:30 in the afternoon Roosevelt recalled his secretary, Miss Tully, from a cocktail party at the Mayflower Hotel and mixed a martini for himself and his old friend Vincent Astor who had dropped by at the White House to see if he could do anything to help. Miss Tully arrived breathless a few minutes later and took down the President's personal message to Hirohito.

It began with the words, "Almost a century ago the President of the United States addressed to the Emperor of Japan a message extending an offer of friendship. . . . That offer was accepted. . . ." Apparently Roosevelt did not fully realize that "that offer" had been accepted by Japan most reluctantly; that Hirohito's great-grandfather, Emperor Komei, had elected to be martyred, after thirteen years of domestic strife, rather than accept it. From this beginning Roosevelt went on to plead for justice and freedom from fear for all the peoples of Southeast Asia. He pledged that "there is absolutely no thought on the part of the United States of invading Indochina." After planting these prickers in Hirohito's pride, President Roosevelt drove them home with unction:

> I address myself to Your Majesty at this moment in the fervent hope that Your Majesty may, as I am doing, give thought in this definite emergency to ways of dispelling the dark clouds. I am confident that both of us, for the sake of the peoples not only of our own countries but for the sake of humanity in neighboring territories have a sacred duty to restore traditional amity and prevent further death and destruction in the world.

Without fervor, without confidence, Roosevelt sent this missive on to Secretary of State Hull. "Dear Cordell," he memoed, "shoot this to Grew— I think can go in gray code—saves time—I don't mind if it gets picked up. F.D.R." Hull had some editorial reservations which were negotiated over the phone by dinner time. By 7:40 P.M. the White House had informed the Washington press corps of the President's dramatic gesture. At 8 P.M. Hull cabled Ambassador Grew that a message from Roosevelt to Hirohito was on its way. At 9 P.M. the message was sent, triple priority.

While Roosevelt had been drafting and arranging to send his message to Hirohito, the particularly able lieutenant commander in the Office of Naval Intelligence, Alwin D. Kramer, had been supervising the decipherment of the first thirteen parts of the final fourteen-part Japanese rejection notice.

The President's personal naval aide, Captain John R. Beardall, had gone off duty that afternoon leaving Kramer in direct contact with the President through a junior White House naval aide, Lieutenant Robert Lester Schulz. Now, at 9:30 P.M., half an hour after the President's message had been dispatched to Hirohito, Lieutenant Commander Kramer brought to the White House the first thirteen parts of the Japanese rejection notice. The fourteenth part, Kramer reported, had not yet been received and was apparently being saved as a final exclamation point to cap the epithets being hurled in the first thirteen parts.

Lieutenant Schulz at once delivered the thirteen intercepts from the pouch to the Oval Study where Roosevelt was waiting expectantly for them in the company of his favorite advisor, Harry Hopkins. Roosevelt spent ten minutes reading the 2500-word note, then handed it to Hopkins. Hopkins read it and handed it back to the President. As Roosevelt returned the top-secret document to Lieutenant Schulz for safe filing, he said in effect, "Harry, this means war." Hopkins agreed. Schulz stood at the door waiting to be dismissed while Hopkins and Roosevelt discussed the implications in some detail. Hopkins regretted "that since war was undoubtedly going to come at the convenience of the Japanese, it was too bad that we could not strike the first blow and prevent any sort of surprise."

"No, we can't do that," replied Roosevelt. "We are a democracy and a peaceful people." And then, raising his voice as Lieutenant Schulz later recalled, the President said, "But we do have a good record."

Roosevelt tried to call "Betty" Stark, Chief of Naval Operations, but found him out for the evening at the National Theatre. Rather than excite the theater audience by having Stark leave his box in the middle of the third act, Roosevelt told the White House operator to try the Stark residence in about half an hour by which time the admiral should have returned home. Then Roosevelt dismissed Lieutenant Schulz and the historical curtain fell on the scene in the White House Oval Study.

It was now the morning of Sunday, December 7, in Tokyo. The I-class submarines of the advance force had been waiting for more than a day outside Pearl Harbor watching the comings and goings of vessels through the harbor mouth. In the north the carriers of the task force were beginning to increase speed and veer south for their final approach. Admiral Nagumo, who commanded the flagship *Akagi,* was sitting in his wardroom listening to jazz and news reports from the local Hawaiian stations. He had run up the actual flag which Admiral Togo, Hirohito's former tutor, had flown at the battle of Tsushima straits, when he had crossed the T of the Russian fleet and sunk it in 1905.

At noon Tokyo censors intercepted the cable from President Roosevelt to Ambassador Grew, enclosing Roosevelt's personal message to Hirohito. While making inquiries, the censors held the cable and kept it from being presented to Grew. Through channels to Imperial Headquarters the censors determined that the cable would only be an inconvenience to the Emperor at this moment. Without anyone having to take much responsibility, the cable was at once packaged in all the permissible red tape of Japan's many police regulations and was unwrapped tape by tape so that it would not finally be presented to Ambassador Grew until late that evening. At 3 P.M. U.S. overseas broadcasts began to announce that the message had been sent, but Japanese police surveillance of shortwave radios was so efficient that few outside top palace and government circles heard the American broadcasts. At 5:30 P.M. the Pearl Harbor fleet turned full south and began its final dash at full speed, 26 knots. At 6:00 P.M. copies of Roosevelt's telegram were circulated by the censors to all officials who had reason to study its text.

At 6:15 P.M., when it was still 4:15 A.M. in Washington, Hirohito presided over a solemn feast. For security reasons it was held at Omiya Gosho, the palace of his mother, west of the main palace, on the estate where he had grown up. The Empress Dowager was not present. She had retired to a villa in the country, vowing with embarrassing frankness that she meant to get as far away as possible from the bombs which her son's policies would certainly bring on Japan. Lord Privy Seal Kido and other Big Brothers of the Emperor's aristocratic circle of intimates attended the party to toast the spirits of the commanders in the field and hear a prayer of supplication and benediction by Hirohito, the nation's high priest. The gathering broke up after less than two hours because Hirohito wished everyone to take a rest before the important events of the evening began after midnight.

A SUNDAY MORNING

While official Tokyo napped in preparation for the long night ahead, official Washington began to wake up to a tense Sunday morning. At 7 P.M. Tokyo time, 5 A.M. Washington time, the final fourteenth part of Japan's rejection notice started coming in to the skeleton staff on duty at the code machines in the Office of Naval Intelligence in Washington. The first thirteen parts had reviewed Japanese propaganda claims that the United States was an aggressive colonial interloper in the Orient, trying to strangle Japan in her normal growth processes. The fourteenth part announced that Japan was breaking off negotiations with the United States.

The alert Lieutenant Commander Kramer, who had distributed the first thirteen parts of the note to Roosevelt and his advisors late the night before, was back at his desk by 7:30 A.M. supervising the preparation of the fourteenth part. At the same time in the Japanese Embassy in Washington neither the last nor the first part of the note had yet been typed. There had been a final party the night before and Embassy staffers had gone to bed without realizing that the note must be ready for delivery by 1 P.M. the next day. Now an Embassy duty officer had just received the presentation instructions from Tokyo and was frantically telephoning his colleagues to summon them back to work. Not only must the note be ready by one, it must be typed by someone cleared for top secret. A muster of the officials who had the requisite clearance revealed that only one of them could type. While this individual struggled manfully, key by key, to prepare a fair copy for Nomura to hand Hull, Kramer's staff completed its own copy and Kramer delivered it to the White House and the Departments of State, War, and Navy by about 10 A.M.

Returning to his office, Kramer was now handed the American intercept of the presentation instructions. His eye fixed on the one o'clock deadline and he checked with his assistants to make sure that 1 P.M. would be dawn in Hawaii and two hours after midnight in Manila. Then, at 10:30 A.M., having phoned the news to Admiral Stark at Naval Operations, Kramer hurried over to the White House to deliver a copy of the presentation instructions to the President. Shortly afterward Ambassador Nomura underscored the importance of the one o'clock deadline by calling Secretary of State Hull and apologizing that, despite its being Sunday, he must see Hull at one that afternoon. Even without benefit of *Magic* intercepts, this unusual request, in the context of that crisis-conscious week, would have sufficed to make Hull and Roosevelt expect the worst.

Fully realizing, then, that Japan meant to start war on or about one o'clock, Roosevelt consulted his advisors and decided simply to wait. It was policy that the United States should not react until after Japan had struck. That was the way to keep an unblemished democratic record. What was more, the majority of the President's military advisors felt that Japan would gain only a small temporary advantage by striking first. There was a tendency on the part of U.S. admirals and generals to underestimate the fighting qualities of the Japanese soldier and the originality and daring of the Japanese strategist. Coincidentally many Japanese admirals and generals suffered from the same dangerous complacency in regard to American genius.

The White House switchboard had access to a direct line—the "scrambler phone"—which could put the President through in a minute to any one of the major U.S. command posts in the Pacific. If Roosevelt had realized that the Pearl Harbor base in Hawaii was on "third alert," looking out only for sabotage, it is inconceivable that he would not have picked up the phone and ordered all men to battle stations. Like every other fully informed leader, however, the President believed that the Japanese were moving against Malaya and that they lacked strength to strike in many directions at once.

Several of the President's advisors did suggest that a final warning be sent to commanders in the Pacific, but since a war warning had already gone out ten days earlier, no one considered such a message to be vitally important. At noon Chief of Staff General Marshall cabled Lieutenant General Short in Hawaii that Japan's envoys were going to break off negotiations at 1 P.M. Marshall's cable reached Short—by bicycle from the telegraph office—nine hours later, when the antiquated battleships of the U.S. Pacific fleet had already become graveyards.

During the busy morning of waiting in Washington, there was a last moment of doubt in Tokyo. About the time that Hirohito retired to nap, the Navy General Staff received a last intelligence broadcast from the Japanese consul in Honolulu. It reported that Pearl Harbor was full of battleships but contained not so much as one aircraft carrier. The Japanese naval planners knew that the U.S. Pacific fleet included at least six carriers. They did not know that three of them were currently on loan to the Atlantic fleet, or that the other three, as a precaution, were being kept out of Pearl Harbor as much as possible. The unknown whereabouts of the carriers represented a grave hazard to Admiral Nagumo's fleet; their absence from the target to be ambushed was a bitter disappointment

When Admiral Yamamoto heard the news aboard his flagship in the Inland Sea, he considered the possibility of radioing Nagumo to conduct an air search for the missing carriers. On consideration, however, he decided to let Nagumo make his own decision. He dispatched to Nagumo only the following message: NO CARRIERS REPEAT NO CARRIERS IN PEARL HARBOR. Nagumo, when he received the message, flung it down with disgust on his chart table. He saw no option, however, but to proceed according to plan and try at least to sink the U.S. battleships.

At about this same moment—10:30 P.M. Tokyo, 8:30 A.M. Washington—Grew finally received Roosevelt's cable of appeal to Hirohito. For an hour and a half he struggled to make arrangements to deliver it. Finally at midnight he drove to the foreign minister's residence where he saw Togo fifteen minutes later. He demanded to see Hirohito personally. Togo replied that it would be impossible for the Emperor to entertain a foreign envoy at this hour of night but that he would undertake to disturb the Emperor and deliver the message if Grew wished to leave it. Grew handed Togo a copy of the message and drove home.

Ten minutes later, at 12:40 A.M., Togo telephoned Lord Privy Seal Kido at his official residence. Kido agreed that, for the sake of the record, the Emperor should certainly see Roosevelt's message at once. Moreover, Kido assured Togo that the Emperor would not mind at all being disturbed after midnight on this particular night. Kido promised to join Togo at the palace.

When Kido hung up and started leisurely to dress, it was 12:45. At that precise moment Japanese bluejackets in Shanghai began silently crossing over from the Japanese Concession into the downtown banking district of the International Settlement along the riverfront. British police observers did not attempt to contest this first conquest of the Pacific War but simply watched while the Japanese Marines seized customs sheds, set up road blocks, and trained field pieces on Western ships in the harbor. They took such swift control of the communications lines leading out of Shanghai that apparently no word of the take-over reached Western capitals for several hours.

At 1:30 A.M. Lord Privy Seal Kido drove from his official residence to the Imperial Library in the palace woods to assist Hirohito in the reception of the note from Roosevelt. At that moment on the deck of Admiral Nagumo's flagship, the aircraft carrier *Akagi,* some 230 miles north of Pearl Harbor, the first planes were preparing for take-off. It was 6 A.M. local time. The night was still black and the seas were wild. On the heaving flight deck, mechanics clung to the planes as they wheeled them from the lifts. Feet slipped on spray as the towering swell lapped over the ship's sides.

The pilot who was to lead the attack, Commander Fuchida Mitsuo, lurched toward his plane. As he came, he bound around his flight helmet a symbolic white headband such as samurai had always worn when they wished to indicate that they were dueling *à outrance*—fighting to the death. His plane, painted with red and yellow stripes, looked unearthly under the hooded blue lights on the flight deck. A 1,600-pound projectile was slung on the undercarriage—not an ordinary bomb but a fifteen-inch armor-piercing naval shell specially fitted with fins to make it fall true.

Fuchida and his crew climbed into their bomber, the *Akagi* swung around into the north wind, and the first of the Pearl Harbor raiders took to the air. In the next fifteen minutes another 182 planes—50 more bombers and dive-bombers, 89 torpedo planes, and 43 Zero fighters—would join Fuchida as he circled above the fleet. Then, with a dip of his wings, he would lead the way south.

Lord Privy Seal Kido found Hirohito in the study of his library in the palace woods listening to pops of static and incomprehensibly terse ejaculations which emanated from a high-powered short-wave set. At that moment, 1:40 A.M. in Tokyo, a Japanese task force was beginning to shell the dark, forested shores of Kota Bharu, the beachhead on the Kra Isthmus in northern Malaya where Japanese forces meant to land in order to start their overland drive on Singapore.

Knowing better than to disturb his master at such a moment, Kido silently took a seat. From time to time Hirohito gave a few words of commentary on the action in progress. From time to time the telephone jangled on Hirohito's desk and he received a confirmed bulletin from one of his aides-de-camp in the chart room of the Imperial Headquarters building a few hundred yards to the north of the library.

While Kido listened impassively in the Imperial Library in Tokyo, President Roosevelt in Washington was receiving his usual lunch on a tray in the Oval Study in the White House. His Scottish terrier, Fala, begged tidbits from the tray. His friend Harry Hopkins, in a V-necked sweater and slacks, lounged nearby on a couch commenting on the political scene.

At 2:05 A.M. Kido heard the actual short-wave transmissions from the assault boats of the Malayan invasion force as they hit the Kota Bharu beaches. In the next half hour the Japanese troops overran Anglo-Indian barbed wire entanglements and secured their foothold. Lieutenant General A. E. Percival, the British commander in Singapore, called in the news to the War Office in London. It was then 5:40 P.M. in England and 12:40 P.M. in Washington.

In the Imperial Library in Tokyo excitement had slackened enough so that Kido could explain to Hirohito that Foreign Minister Togo was waiting in an anteroom to discuss the message from President Roosevelt. Hirohito had Togo admitted, listened to him read the note from Roosevelt, voiced admiration for its sentiments, but regretted that it had come too late. Then Hirohito approved the wording of a rejection of the note which Togo had thoughtfully drafted in advance.

At 3 A.M., while Togo was in audience, Ambassador Nomura in Washington was supposed to be delivering the fourteen-part note to Hull which was meant to serve in lieu of a formal declaration of war. Instead, at that moment, 1 P.M. Washington time, Nomura was phoning the State Department to apologize about his staff's difficulties in decoding and typing the note. Would it be all right if he postponed his meeting with Hull until 1:45? Hull, since he already knew the contents of the note, nursed his wrath and declared that he was ready to wait as long as necessary until the representatives of Japan were prepared to show themselves.

At 3:15 A.M. Togo left the Imperial Library and hurried over to the Foreign Ministry to stand by at his own short-wave set. Kido lingered on in the company of Hirohito for another fifteen minutes—the fateful minutes that were to decide the opening round of the war.

TIGER, TIGER

Commander Fuchida of the Pearl Harbor attack squadron had sighted the coast of Oahu Island at about 3:05 A.M.—7:35 A.M. Hawaiian time, 1:05 P.M. Washington time. Flying at 9,000 feet, above broken clouds, Fuchida saw the white line of surf and the green mountains beyond through a "pink-stained morning mist." He was coming in with his planes on the north side of the island. Pearl Harbor and Honolulu lay on the south side. He therefore banked to his right and led his planes out to sea down the west side of the island so that his torpedo bombers could start their run on Pearl Harbor from the south—over water—low.

Running ahead of his pack, Fuchida rounded the southwestern corner of the island, Barbers Point, and surveyed the prospects. If his approach had been detected, there would be fighters in the air and his Zeros, which flew 5,000 feet above him, would have to fall upon them and win air superiority over the target area before the bombing could begin. He would then have to shoot off two smoke rockets—"two black dragons"—to indicate that total surprise had not been achieved.

Though Fuchida did not know it, total surprise should not have been achieved. A radar station, manned by two noncommissioned officers, had watched the approach of his air fleet for forty minutes. No one whom the two noncoms had been able to raise at headquarters by telephone would take the reported threat seriously. In another sector of communications and command, a Japanese midget submarine had been reported sighted, then shelled, depth-charged, and sunk by U.S. destroyer *Ward* outside the mouth of Pearl Harbor. But these reports, too, for the last hour, had gone unheeded.

Fuchida saw below him a scene so peaceful and unprepared that he could scarcely believe his eyes. "I have seen all German ships assembled in Kiel Harbor," he later wrote. "I have also seen the French battleships in Brest. And finally I have often seen our own warships in review before the Emperor, but never, even in deepest peace, have I seen ships anchored 500 to a thousand yards from one another. . . . Had these Americans never heard of Port Arthur [where the czar's Asiatic fleet was sunk in 1905]?"

At 7:40 A.M.—3:10 A.M. in Tokyo—Fuchida fired one black dragon. His dive-bombers responded by climbing toward an altitude of 12,000 feet. His torpedo bombers spiraled down to the level of the wave crests. His own plane with its accompaniment of horizontal bombers descended to 3,500 feet. But the Zeros far above had apparently failed to see his rocket. They were supposed to come down and support the bombers with strafing attacks. Once more Fuchida fired a single black smoke rocket. Now the fighters began tumbling. But so did the dive-bombers. The dive-bomber flight leader had misinterpreted the second rocket as meaning "incomplete surprise." After one black dragon he was supposed to follow the torpedo planes over the target. After two black dragons he was supposed to precede them in an effort to knock out anti-aircraft batteries.

Fuchida had a few split seconds in which to make a decision. The dive-bomber attacks would obscure targets for the torpedo bombers. The two types of planes might even collide. But the wing leaders were all veterans of the China War. The pilots had all learned by heart the topography of Pearl Harbor with a huge sand model constructed on the northern coast of Japan in October. Fuchida could count on his men to adapt themselves to the battle as it developed and keep in mind the objective of destroying the U.S. fleet. Breaking radio silence, he signaled *To-to-to,* "Attack, attack, attack." All his planes responded. It was 7:49 A.M.—3:19 in Tokyo.

Four minutes later all of Fuchida's 182 planes were converging on their targets from different angles and directions for their attack. On the Army runways of Wheeler and Hickam fields, the Marine runways at Ewa, the Navy runways on Ford Island, the Catalina flying-boat basin at Kaneohe, the planes were all parked neatly in compact clusters—a dream almost too good to be true. They had been placed this way so that they could be easily guarded from pedestrian saboteurs who might try to steal up on them and hurl bombs by hand.

In the harbor or on patrol at its mouth lay at least 90 vessels of the U.S. Pacific fleet: eight old battleships, an ex-battleship used as a target hulk, two modern heavy cruisers, six light cruisers, thirty destroyers, five submarines, nine minelayers, ten minesweepers, two repair ships, two cargo ships, three destroyer tenders, one submarine tender, one hospital ship, six seaplane tenders, two oilers, and two gunboats.[7] Not a puff of flak nor the glint of a rising wing tip suggested that any of them were aware of the death hurtling in on them.

So confident was Commander Fuchida of success that at that moment, 7:53 Hawaiian time, 3:23 A.M. Tokyo time, he sent out the radio message, *Tora, tora, tora,* "Tiger, tiger, tiger." It was a prearranged signal of triumph based on an old Chinese saying: a tiger may roam two thousand miles but he will always return home.

Through a freak of atmospherics, Fuchida's tiger-tiger signal was picked up directly in Tokyo. That Hirohito heard it personally on his own short-wave set is doubtful, but it was relayed to him in a matter of seconds by phone. Seven minutes after Fuchida had sent it, at 3:30 A.M., Hirohito dismissed Lord Privy Seal Kido so that he could return to his residence and catch a few hours of sleep before the busy ceremonials scheduled for the morrow. Hirohito showed the steel of his own nerves by retiring to do likewise.

Now, as the Emperor prepared for bed, America's nightmare, Pearl Harbor, played itself out in a chaos of smoke and fire. The first bombs and machine-gun bullets began splattering runways and decks at 3:25 A.M. —7:55 A.M. Hawaiian time. Japanese torpedo bombers ran in low from all directions on the eight battleships lined up along the eastern shore of Ford Island in the center of the harbor. Within five minutes four of the battlewagons had been pierced by one or more of the 1,000-pound explosive fishes. At the same time dive-bombers were swooping down to nest their eggs on decks, turrets, and bridges. The horizontal bombers, of which Fuchida's was one, dropped their armor-piercing shells with deadly accuracy. Some of them failed to explode but killed men literally

---

[7] *California, Pennsylvania, Maryland, Oklahoma, West Virginia, Arizona, Nevada,* and *Tennessee; Utah; San Francisco* and *New Orleans; Raleigh, Detroit, Phoenix, Honolulu, Helena,* and *St. Louis; Monaghan, Farragut, Dale, Alwyn, Henley, Patterson, Ralph Talbot, Coyngham, Reid, Tucker, Case, Selfridge, Blue, Allen, Chew, Cassin, Downes, Jarvis, Mugford, Bagley, Hull, Dewey, Worden, MacDonough, Phelps, Shaw, Cummings, Schley, McFarland,* and *Ward; Narwhal, Dolphin, Tautog, Cachalot,* and *Cuttlefish; Gamble, Montgomery, Breese, Ramsey, Preble, Tracy, Pruitt, Sicard,* and *Oglala; Grebe, Tern, Bobolink, Vireo, Turkey, Rail, Crossbill, Candor, Cockatoo,* and *Reedbird; Medusa* and *Vestal; Castor* and *Antares; Whitney, Dobbin* and *Rigel; Pelias; Solace; Curtiss, Tangier, Thornton, Avocet, Swan,* and *Harlburt; Neosho* and *Ramapa; Sacramento* and *Taney.*

by hitting them on the head. Some of them pierced too well and made their way right through the armored decks of the warships and out their hulls to bury themselves in the mud below. Still others blew up on the second or third decks of the battleships creating carnage in mess rooms, sick bays, and recreation areas.

Within the first twenty-five minutes of the attack, the 32,600-ton *Arizona,* commissioned in 1916, took a hit from a dive-bomber directly down her stack. The boilers blew up, touching off her forward magazine. With a great roar she broke in two and went down almost immediately, taking with her 1,104 lives.

The 29,000-ton *Oklahoma,* also commissioned in 1916, lost her trim from three torpedo hits and capsized before all the surviving members of her crew could climb topside to escape. Thirty-two of the captives were later released through holes cut with torches in her bottom plates.

When the eighteen-year-old, 31,800-ton *West Virginia* went down with one bomb and four torpedo hits, some of the men trapped in her compartments were not so lucky. The salvage crews who later raised her found a diary scrawled on a bulkhead by three men who had not died until sixteen days after her sinking.

On the 32,600-ton *California,* commissioned in 1921, fires reached the fuel tanks. She burned for three days before she finally foundered.

One of the battleships, the 29,000-ton *Nevada* commissioned in 1916, succeeded in getting up steam in an effort to escape. Japanese bombers at once converged on her and sought to sink her in the entrance of the harbor. Her skipper managed, however, with the help of two courageous tugboat crews, to beach her in sinking condition on a mud flat at one side of the harbor mouth.

Two of the most valuable battleships were protected from torpedoes and saved from being sunk because they had been moored on the landward side of *Oklahoma* and *West Virginia* which shielded them. The 31,500-ton *Maryland,* commissioned in 1921, sustained only bomb damage. The 32,600-ton *Tennessee,* commissioned in 1920, came off equally well but was so securely wedged between the sunken *West Virginia* and a concrete dock that she could not be towed away for repairs until more than a week later when the dock itself had been delicately dynamited.

One other big ship was sunk: the ex-battleship *Utah,* 21,825 tons, commissioned in 1911. Before the attack she was in process of being retired from the Navy and stripped of all fittings of any value. As a result she had lost part of her superstructure and was sheathed in planks and scaffolds. From the air she looked like a flattop. Delighted Japanese pilots squandered torpedoes on her with prodigal fury. It took them exactly eleven minutes of concerted attack to capsize and sink her. Fifty-eight members of her skeleton crew went down with her and their bones remain in their rusted steel casket to this day.

Of all the battleships, the fleet flagship *Pennsylvania*—33,100 tons, vintage 1916—came through with least damage. One reason was that she lay in dry dock, out of reach of torpedoes. Another reason was a gunner's mate who had been aboard the gunboat *Panay* in 1937. At the sight of the first Japanese plane he grabbed a sledge hammer, smashed the locks on the *Pennsylvania*'s magazine, and began, unauthorized, to pass out ammunition. His determination not to be caught again by the Japanese enabled the *Pennsylvania* to start putting up a withering defensive fire even before the Japanese pilots had cleared their first run. Dive-bombers tried to penetrate the barrage again and again but succeeded in striking the *Pennsylvania* only one glancing blow. Five days after the attack her repairs had been completed and she returned to service.

The frustrated pilots who could not get through to the *Pennsylvania* vented their rage on two destroyers in the dry dock in front of her. The *Downes* took a bomb in her torpedo magazine and blew up, bathing her neighbor *Cassin* in burning oil. Another destroyer, the *Shaw,* in floating dry dock, lost her entire bow.

Pieces of machinery from *Cassin* and *Downes* were later incorporated in new hulls so that these two destroyers would float again to taunt Japan and haunt her. The battleships *California, West Virginia,* and *Nevada* were all raised and completely rebuilt at great expense. Efforts to salvage *Oklahoma* only ended when she sank, under tow, on her way to a West Coast dockyard after the war was over. The Navy's determination to belie Japanese Pearl Harbor claims even extended to the sunken minelayer *Oglala,* which had been converted from an ancient Fall River steamer in 1917, but emerged from World War II as yare as a commodore's pinnace. Only *Arizona* and *Utah* remained unsalvaged and they were left where they sank as national shrines.[8]

At the same time that the ships were sinking in the harbor, the neatly parked airplanes were being destroyed on the runways ashore. Of the Marine Corps' eleven Wildcats, thirty-two scout bombers and six utility planes at Ewa, only two Wildcats and fourteen scout bombers could still be flown when the Japanese had left. Twenty-seven of the thirty-six Catalina flying boats at Kaneohe were demolished beyond repair. Six more were severely damaged. The remaining three were out on patrol and missed the action. Although no reliable statistics have ever been released on over-all air losses, at least 112 out of 148 good Navy combat planes were destroyed and 52 out of 129 serviceable Army fighters and bombers. Only 38 U.S. planes were able to get into the air and ten of these were shot down.

Almost all of this damage was done in the first twenty-five minutes of the attack. After that the Zeros continued to spray burning decks and

---

[8] Other victims of the attack were the 1924 light cruiser *Raleigh,* heavy damage; the 1939 light cruiser *Helena,* heavy damage; the 1938 light cruiser *Honolulu,* moderate damage; repair ship *Vestal* and seaplane tender *Curtiss,* both moderate damage.

runways with machine-gun bullets but the bombers had spent their loads. As they returned to their carriers, Commander Fuchida remained circling to observe the results of the second attack wave. It flew in at 8:45: 78 more bombers, 54 more torpedo planes, and 35 more Zeros. By now, however, the counterfire from the ships and shore batteries was well organized and covered the harbor in an umbrella of flak. Twenty-seven destroyers, five cruisers, and three battleships remained in fighting condition, and even the beached *Nevada,* though technically sunk, was still pouring shells into the sky. Of his first wave Fuchida had lost only nine planes: one dive-bomber, three Zeros, and five torpedo planes. The second wave, which attacked from 8:15 to 9:45, lost six Zeros and 14 dive-bombers and accomplished almost nothing. Ships that were already mortally wounded were finished off and hangars were bombed at the various airstrips, but no important new targets were attacked. The Submarine Base, the Naval Shipyard, the Naval Supply Center, and the fuel oil "tank farm" which held almost as much petroleum as Japan's entire stockpile were all overlooked through ignorance.

After watching the performance of the second wave, Fuchida, shortly before 10 A.M., followed it home to the carriers of Nagumo's task force. He wanted to lead a third sortie to attack permanent installations. Nagumo overruled him. A third attack might reveal the whereabouts of the fleet and jeopardize it. At the cost of 29 planes and 55 men it had knocked out five battleships, three destroyers, a minelayer, a possible aircraft carrier, and almost 200 of the enemy's planes. It had killed 2,008 U.S. sailors, 109 Marines, 218 soldiers, and 68 civilians—in all 2,403 Americans. Admiral Nagumo saw no reason to risk such a record.[9] He turned his fleet back into the fogs of the north Pacific and slipped away to make an uneventful return voyage to Japan.

WAR

Three minutes after the first bomb fell at Pearl Harbor, Rear Admiral P. N. L. ("Pat") Bellinger got off an urgent all-points fleet signal: "From Cincpac to all ships Hawaii area: air raid on Pearl Harbor. This is no drill."

Unlike Army Chief of Staff Marshall's earlier message from Washington to Hawaii, Bellinger's signal crossed the gap to Washington almost instan-

[9] The Japanese advance force of twenty submarines had not fared as well as Nagumo's main fleet of six carriers. One of the I-class submarines was bombed and sunk on December 10 and all five of the two-man midget submarines were lost without doing a trace of damage. One of them ran aground on a reef and was captured together with its captain, Ensign Sakamaki Kazuo. The other nine midget submariners are worshipped today at a special shrine in the old naval academy at Etajima. Survivor Sakamaki lives on, undeified but content, as a mechanic in Nagoya.

taneously. The Office of Naval Operations at once transmitted it to Admiral Stark. "Betty" Stark called Navy Secretary Knox. Knox, after a moment of incredulity and argument—"They must mean the Philippines"—phoned the White House. President Roosevelt was eating an apple and sorting some new specimens for his stamp collection. He at once instructed Knox to obtain all possible details of the attack and to place the entire Navy on a war footing. When Roosevelt hung up, the brass ship's clock on his desk registered 1:47 P.M. or 8:17 A.M. Hawaiian time.

Eighteen minutes later Japanese Ambassador Nomura and Special Envoy Kurusu arrived at Secretary of State Hull's large, shabby, impersonal office to deliver notice of the rupture in Japanese-American relations.[10] Hull kept them waiting for fifteen minutes, then gave them ample opportunity to study the American flag and secretarial standard behind him while he affixed his pince-nez and pretended to read the 2,500-word note. As he cast his eye down the paragraphs which he had already perused in *Magic* versions, he composed a little speech. Ten minutes later he looked up and delivered it, using his Tennessee mountain drawl to good advantage:

"In all my fifty years of public service, I have never seen a document that was more crowded with infamous falsehoods and distortions— infamous falsehoods and distortions on a scale so huge that I never imagined until today that any government on this planet was capable of uttering them."

Ambassador Nomura—a man whom Hull liked personally and affectionately called the "old codger"—opened his mouth to say something. Hull pointed a finger at the door and said, "Good day, gentlemen."

An hour and a half later, at 4 P.M. Washington time, 6 A.M. Tokyo time and 9 P.M. London time, Prime Minister Winston Churchill found himself closeted with Averell Harriman, a special envoy from Roosevelt, and with

---

[10] The incompetence of the Foreign Ministry in failing to deliver the note on time later angered Hirohito greatly. In quest of justification he had Togo commission "A Study Concerning Hostilities on the Outbreak of War" from Tokyo's International Law Society. The lawyers submitted their findings on December 27, 1941. They began by saying: "Suppose that we declared war at 8:00 A.M. in Tokyo and what we wanted to assert with nominal time as the standard—that is, nominal as opposed to practical—is that we did not violate Hague Treaty Number Three." Then, concluded the lawyers, time zones could provide no defense, for though the attack on Pearl Harbor took place later in the day Washington or Hawaiian time than the hour of note delivery Tokyo time, still the attack on Malaya as per Malayan time preceded note delivery no matter what the frame of temporal reference.

The best that the lawyers could do was to find that the Hague Treaty was logically absurd. "It is not a violation of the treaty," they wrote, "to open hostilities in a far-off land only some 20 or 30 minutes after the delivery of the declaration of war to the diplomatic representative of the other country in one's own capital. Hence it is not impossible to say that the Hague Treaty Number Three is nothing but a bluff or simulacrum and that there is no need to respect such a childish treaty at the outbreak of a war in which the fate of a nation is at stake."

John G. Winant, the American ambassador at the Court of St. James's. Japanese troops had been advancing into British territory in Malaya for almost four hours. Churchill switched on the nine o'clock news and heard of the Pearl Harbor attack. At the urging of Harriman and Winant he promptly put through a call to Roosevelt and said, "This certainly simplifies things. God be with you."

At 7 A.M. Japanese time, some fifty minutes thereafter, Tokyo radio announced tersely that the Imperial Navy had opened hostilities on the United States with an attack on Hawaii. At the same moment Ambassador Grew was called by the Foreign Ministry to come at once to Togo's residence. At 7:30 Togo told Grew that the Emperor had rejected President Roosevelt's plea. Togo then handed Grew a copy of the fourteen-part note delivered in Washington. Grew went home to read it, to listen to the radio, and to await internment as an enemy national with diplomatic privileges. At 8:05 Japanese planes raided Guam, at 9:00 Hong Kong, and at 9:05 the northern part of the Philippines.

At 11:40, after several fanfares, the radio finally broadcast the Emperor's rescript proclaiming war. It ended with the words:

> The hallowed spirits of Our Imperial Ancestors guarding Us from above, We rely upon the loyalty and courage of Our subjects in Our confident expectation that the task bequeathed by Our Forefathers will be carried forward, and that the source of evil will be speedily eradicated and an enduring peace immutably established in East Asia, preserving thereby the glory of Our Empire.

A day later Vice Admiral Halsey, returning to Hawaii with the carrier *Enterprise,* surveyed the damage at Pearl Harbor, and, as a barbarian, issued his blunt counter to Hirohito's high-priestly invocation of the shades. "Before we're through with them," said Halsey, "the Japanese language will be spoken only in hell."

Roosevelt that day delivered a special message to Congress and received an almost unanimous vote for war. Senator George Norris of Nebraska, who had voted against war in 1917, had now changed his mind. Only Representative Jeannette Rankin of Montana, who had also voted against war in 1917, still opted for isolationism. Never had the nation been more unified. More than a hundred thousand Americans were to die in the effort to subdue "Japanese militarism." And more than a million Japanese, who distrusted militarism but honored the Emperor, died to defend whatever it was that the Americans opposed. The two cultures clashed tragically, with a hate that fed on ignorance, but the clash enabled the United States to make war on Hitler.

PART SEVEN

ARMAGEDDON

27

THE STRIKE SOUTH

(1941–1942)

CONTROL OF THE AIR

When Hirohito's most intimate civilian advisor, Lord Privy Seal Marquis Kido, returned to the palace at 7:15 A.M. on the morning of December 8, he paused for a moment outside the private postern, by which he would enter the western half of the palace woods, and watched the dawn break. Afterward he wrote in his diary:

Turning up Miyake slope as I climbed the Akasaka approach [to the palace], I saw the brilliance of the sunrise, in a clap, over the [palace] buildings before me, and I worshipped. I was reminded that today is the day in which we have embarked upon a great war against the two powerful nations, America and England. Earlier this morning our naval air force launched a large-scale attack upon Hawaii. Knowing this and worrying about the success or failure of the attack, I bowed involuntarily to the sun and closed my eyes and prayed in silence. At 7:30 A.M. I met with the prime minister [Tojo] and with the two chiefs of staff [General Sugiyama and Admiral Nagano] and heard the good news of our tremendous success in the surprise attack on Hawaii. I felt deep gratitude for the assistance of the gods. I was received in audience by His Majesty from 11:40 to 12. I was struck to observe, if I may say so, that at this time when the nation has staked its future upon war, His Majesty seems completely self-assured and shows no trace of inner turmoil.

While Kido talked to the chiefs of staff at 7:30, dawn was just breaking farther west on the rocky little beach at Basco, the chief village on Batan Island, 140 miles north of Luzon, the principal and northernmost island of the Philippine archipelago. Five hundred Japanese soldiers sloshed ashore through the pearly surf and occupied the village without resistance. It was the beginning of the Japanese conquest of the Philippines.

An hour and a half later Japanese planes descended on the island of Hong Kong and destroyed its air force of three torpedo bombers and two Walrus amphibians. At the same time the regiments of Japan's 38th Division, stationed in Canton, crossed the border from China, the Sham Chun River, and began to fight their way east across the mainland dependencies of Hong Kong, the New Territories and Kowloon.

At about the same moment, in southern Thailand, Lieutenant General Tiger Yamashita opened his 25th Army Headquarters in a house in the town of Singora. He had come ashore with the second wave of his 5th Division less than half an hour earlier. Unexpected Thai police resistance had been swiftly silenced after an unopposed landing. With him he had most of the best division in the Japanese Army, the highly mobile, mechanized 5th which had had years of experience in China. It was assisted by the cream of Japan's tank corps, artillery battalions, and Army air squadrons. One of its four regiments had landed successfully at a second Thai town, Patani, some 20 miles down the coast to the south.

A third branch of Yamashita's army, the augmented 56th Regiment of the 23d Brigade, 18th Division, had landed 69 miles south in Malaya proper, at Kota Bharu. It was this landing on which Hirohito had eavesdropped over his palace shortwave set seven hours earlier. Fire from a prepared line of pillboxes in the trees just back of the beach had held down the attackers until daybreak, and British planes, flying in darkness, had sunk one and severely mauled another of the Japanese transports lying offshore. But shortly after first light a Japanese sapper had risen from the sand, stuffed himself into a gun port of one of the pillboxes, and while he was being shot to pieces enabled his comrades to lob in grenades, overwhelm the position, and attack the remaining pillboxes from the rear.

Yamashita's army was securely ashore at all three of its landing points. His main strength, the 5th Division, began immediately, while the day was yet young, to advance down the main highway of the peninsula connecting Thailand and Bangkok with Malaya and Singapore.

As Yamashita opened his drive that morning, fog hung over the Japanese air bases in Taiwan far away to the northeast. At both Army and Navy fields, pilots stood beside their planes waiting nervously for it to lift. The United States had thirty-five B-17 bombers or Flying Fortresses in the Philippines—a formidable striking force if it could attack the Japanese bases before Japanese bombers destroyed U.S. bases. About 7:30 A.M. Tokyo time, or about 6:30 A.M. Manila time, the Japanese Army pilots took off despite the fog and less than two hours later bombed Baguio, the summer seat of the Philippines' Commonwealth government. The raid severely damaged the golf greens around Baguio's Camp John Hay, demolished several outbuildings, and took nine lives. Lieutenant Colonel John Horan, the U.S. commander in Baguio, phoned in his losses to

MacArthur's headquarters in Manila but somehow failed to get through to MacArthur's ear the fact that the Japanese were attacking the Philippines.

MacArthur had been awakened five hours earlier with the news of the raid on Pearl Harbor. He knew that Japan and the United States were at war, but he was pledged by both President Roosevelt and by Filipino political leaders to make absolutely sure that the Philippines would be included in Japan's theater of operations before he authorized counteraction.

Having retired from the U.S. Army in 1935 and taken a field marshal's rank in the Philippine Army, the sixty-one-year-old MacArthur had returned to active service only five months previously. In those months he had welcomed some 4,000 American and 82,000 Filipino green recruits into his command and had issued countless reassuring statements to the effect that the Philippines could be defended. Now at 5 A.M. and again at 7:15 and 10 when his air commander, Major General Lewis Brereton, urged him to authorize immediate take-off of all B-17's in the Philippines for a raid on the harbors and fields of Taiwan, MacArthur shook his head and said that such a raid must wait for clearer signs of Japanese intentions.

At his air headquarters Brereton kept his men on alert for defensive action. They had early models of radar and 107 good P-40 fighters with which to anticipate and jump enemy bombers. The most up-to-date planes in the Philippines, the B-17's, however, were difficult to protect. They could not stay in the air indefinitely and they could not perch, at least in Luzon, except on Clark Field, a wide-open plain of runways and flimsy hangars, some 50 miles north of Manila. The inadequate force of fighters on hand, none of which could hope to match a Japanese Zero in a dogfight, had to land periodically and refuel.

Despite MacArthur's six years in the Philippines, personnel were trained for peace, not war. Communications were dependent upon the Philippine telephone system and were undependable. Normal wartime safeguards and procedures were ill defined and inadequately rehearsed. The radar of Air Intelligence in Manila was new gear and easily misunderstood whenever a flock of pigeons flapped their wings in front of it.

All morning long fighters and bombers scrambled in response to false alarms. At 10 A.M., in Taiwan, the fog lifted and the Japanese naval air armada of forty-five Zero fighters and fifty-three Mitsubishi Betty bombers began to take off for their strike south against the U.S. air force in the Philippines. An hour later MacArthur decided that the best use for the ill-protected B-17's might be an attack after all, and he belatedly authorized Brereton to send them on a raid against the fields in Taiwan. At that moment the B-17's were flying defensive patterns in the sky, nursing fuel and staying out of harm's way. Brereton ordered them to land and fuel and arm themselves with bombs. They did so and most of the pilots seized the opportunity to go to the mess for lunch.

At about 12:30 the first Japanese Zeros arrived over Clark Field and began circling leisurely at 22,000 feet. Below them at 15,000 feet they saw a small patrol of U.S. P-40's on its way back to the nearby fighter field at Iba. One of the few Japanese air aces who survived the war remembered the scene as "ludicrous." For ten minutes he and his wing mates cruised, awaiting the arrival of the Betty bombers for which they were the scouts. Below him, parked on the runways, glistened sixty-odd aircraft, including twenty-one of the thirty-five B-17 Fortresses in which rested the entire offensive punch of U.S. forces in the Philippines. A communications breakdown had prevented the U.S. radar center in Manila from warning Clark Field of the vultures gathering overhead. At about 12:45 the Japanese air ace, Sakai Saburo, saw his bombers approaching from the north. They moved directly into their bombing runs.

> The attack [wrote Sakai] was perfect. Long strings of bombs tumbled from the bays and dropped toward the targets the bombardiers had studied in detail for so long. Their accuracy was phenomenal—it was, in fact, the most accurate bombing I ever witnessed by our own planes throughout the war. The entire air base seemed to be rising into the air with the explosions. Pieces of airplanes, hangars, and other ground installations scattered wildly. Great fires erupted and smoke boiled upward.

The marksmanship of the high-level Japanese bombardiers was only matched by the performance of the Japanese fighter pilots who strafed Clark Field and shot down U.S. fighters which attempted to take off after the bombing was over. For an hour—a single hour, ten hours after the Pearl Harbor disaster—the Japanese planes continued to ravage the field. Other planes did the same at the two fighter bases in the area, Iba and Nichols Fields. When the raid was over, eighteen of the twenty-one B-17's in Luzon, fifty-three of the 107 U.S. fighters in Luzon, and twenty-five to thirty other U.S. aircraft had been destroyed. Fourteen of MacArthur's thirty-five B-17's escaped attack because they were based at Del Monte Field on the southern Philippine island of Mindanao, 600 miles farther south. These fourteen later plagued Sakai and his fellow Japanese airmen over the Netherlands East Indies. Forty-six days later, over Borneo, Sakai paid eloquent tribute to what the Japanese had accomplished and what MacArthur had lost at Clark Field:

> Again. Dive, roll, concentrate on one bomber! This time I caught one! I saw the shells exploding, a series of red and black eruptions moving across the fuselage. Surely he would go down now! Chunks of metal—big chunks— exploded outward from the B-17 and flashed away in the slipstream. The waist and top guns were silent as the shells hammered home.
>
> Nothing! No fire, no telltale sign of smoke trailing back. The B-17 continued on in formation.

For the eighteen B-17's destroyed on the ground at Clark Field that first day of the war, and for the seventy-eight other U.S. planes destroyed in the Clark Field area, the Japanese paid the price of not a single bomber and only seven Zeros. It seemed inconsiderable. On their return to Taiwan the Japanese pilots modestly claimed only forty-four kills and four probables. They were feasted that night as heroes. Yet the seven Zeros which they had lost represented value which neither they nor Americans could then appreciate. All seven downed Zeros had been piloted by flyers with years of experience in China. The Zero was a hot plane. It could dance mazurkas around U.S. fighters of heavier plate and firepower. But the Zero needed a thoroughly trained acrobat at its stick. And the seven Zero aces lost over Clark Field on December 8 began an attrition in trained men which Japan would ultimately come to realize as more important than patriotism.

Later that same afternoon, at 4 p.m. Singapore time, 5:30 p.m. Tokyo time, the Anglo-Indian troops in northern Malaya withdrew from Kota Bharu airfield. Japanese planes began using it immediately—first Navy Zero fighters and staff planes, then by morning Army Betty bombers. Theretofore all the Japanese planes had been flying at the limits of their range from fields in Indochina and strips on islands off the Indochina coast. Now they were ferried in to Kota Bharu via Thai airfields and could remain in the air for hours over the fighting lines before they had to return to their bases for fuel. By the dawn of the next day, December 9, they had captured air superiority over northern Malaya.

The first day of the war had ended with complete success for Hirohito. The American battleships had been sunk at Pearl Harbor. The long-range American bombers had been burned on the ground outside Manila. And the head of the roadway to the British bastion of Singapore had been occupied in force by the best troops in the Japanese Army. The foreign concessions in Shanghai had all peacefully capitulated. The nearest barbarian stronghold in the Far East, Hong Kong, almost 2,000 miles to the southwest and without hope of reinforcement, was under strong attack. It seemed that the cry of Emperor Komei, Hirohito's great-grandfather, was about to be answered. The barbarians had not yet been expelled from the Orient but all except Axis nationals would soon be prisoners.

Only a cloud the size of a man's hand marred that fine cold December evening in Tokyo: the British in northern Borneo, knowing themselves indefensible, had destroyed their runway at Lutong, demolished their refinery at Miri, and set a torch to their oil field at Seria. It was the first of many earth-scorching blazes which would damage the resources for which Japan had gone to war. Nevertheless Hirohito, after a long day of proclamations and meetings, retired well satisfied to his bedchamber behind the "grated gate" in his palace. Few of his footsore infantrymen slept more soundly than he did.

Early the next morning, December 9, as high priest at a special ceremony in the white-pebbled courtyard of the Palace Shrine, Hirohito reported the successful outbreak of the war to his ancestors. Throughout the Empire it was a day for prayer and rejoicing; for bowing to bad weather and contemplating the fall of rain; for digesting the victories of the day before and preparing more great deeds for the morrow.

At about 1 A.M., December 10, Tokyo time, 400 Japanese marines from a task force of nine transports landed on the beaches of the American island of Guam in the Mariana Islands, a Pan American Clipper stop about a third of the way east on the route between Manila and Hawaii. After three and a half hours of fighting, the 430 U.S. Marines and naval personnel on the island, together with 180 Guamanian Insular Guards, surrendered.

Shortly thereafter, as day lightened off the northern coast of Luzon in the Philippines, a picked force of about 4,000 men from the 2d Taiwan Regiment of the Japanese 48th Division waded ashore at Aparri, a town on the north coast which had an airstrip. The U.S. lieutenant who had charge of the 200 Filipino recruits in the town sensibly packed up his machine guns and withdrew at once into the hills toward the south.

At the same time, around the northwestern tip of Luzon, on the beaches of the town of Vigan which faced toward China, another detachment of the Japanese 48th Division landed unopposed to take a second airstrip in northern Luzon. Five of the formidable B-17's, the Flying Fortresses which had been in Mindanao two days earlier and had escaped the holocaust at Clark Field, were sent to bomb the Vigan task force. They serenely ignored anti-aircraft fire and fought off the attacks of Japanese fighter cover but were unable, due to the inexperience of their crews, to do much damage with their bombs. They left three transports burning and returned to their base.

CONTROL OF THE OCEAN

While Japan was taking control of the air and seizing strategic airfields, a tense game of cat and mouse was playing itself out along the coast of Malaya. The importance of the game was symbolic, for the winner might claim the long unchallenged title of Great Britain as Mistress of the Seven Seas. The latest-model British battleship, the 35,000-ton *Prince of Wales,* had sortied from Singapore on the evening of December 8 in a daring attempt to make a surprise raid on the Japanese transports landing troops in northern Malaya. She boasted a ninety-five-barrel battery of the most up-to-date machine cannon for use against hostile aircraft, plus thirty-two pom-pom muzzles and an assortment of standard anti-aircraft guns. All her armament firing together was said to be able to loft 60,000 projectiles a minute. Her 14-inch cannon could lob one-ton shells farther than the 18-inch guns of the biggest Japanese battleships. She was the pride of the British fleet.

Churchill and Roosevelt had signed the Atlantic Charter aboard the *Prince of Wales* the previous summer, and Churchill, over British Admiralty objections, had personally dispatched her to the Orient in November to quash Japanese belligerence. The new carrier *Indomitable* was to have accompanied her, but *Indomitable* had run aground on her shakedown cruise and Churchill had insisted that *Prince of Wales* go ahead into Far Eastern waters alone. He hoped that she would "exercise that kind of vague menace which capital ships of the highest quality whose whereabouts are unknown can impose on all hostile naval calculations." He envisaged her mission as that of an impregnable raider—of a presence that "appears and disappears, causing immediate reactions and perturbations on the other side." He told Stalin enthusiastically: she "can catch and kill any Japanese ship."

Sensing that they were to play knight errant, the crew of the *Prince of Wales* had irreverently dubbed her "Churchill's yacht." Despite the Battle of Britain, their beloved sixty-seven-year-old prime minister had learned to appreciate the sting of the airplane no better than had General MacArthur. Churchill had apparently forgotten the oldest and least romantic rule of chivalry: that the most heavily armored knight can be overthrown by grooms and bowmen if he does not have good grooms and bowmen of his own.

The men of the *Prince of Wales* were not downhearted, however, for in place of an aircraft carrier they had an escort of four destroyers and the formidable 32,000-ton battle cruiser *Repulse*. Though old in hull, *Repulse* had been completely rebuilt in the late 1930's and was now the equivalent of a pocket battleship. She boasted 15-inch guns, a speed of 29 knots, and an anti-aircraft battery hardly less fearsome than that of the *Prince of Wales* herself. Indeed, *Repulse* was 55 feet longer than *Prince of Wales,* slimmer and somewhat more maneuverable.

Hirohito and his naval brother, Prince Takamatsu, shared Churchill's romantic interest in the *Prince of Wales.* They, too, identified themselves with spectacular pieces of naval hardware and felt personally engaged in oceanic jousting. Ever since *Prince of Wales* had arrived in Singapore from Africa a week earlier, the young naval staff officers at Imperial Headquarters had wracked their brains for schemes either to lure her to sea or to destroy her at her berth within the heavily gunned Singapore harbor perimeter. When she took to sea of her own accord and was observed by Japanese spies in Singapore slipping out of the harbor into the cloudy gray twilight of December 8, Imperial Headquarters heard of her sailing almost immediately. The naval air aides in the palace were overjoyed. On Hirohito's authority they at once ordered an all-out effort to waylay and destroy the British dreadnoughts. A hundred of the best pilots in the Navy air force—the most gifted graduates of the Misty Lagoon Air Development Station—were told to stand by at airports in southern Indochina. All submarines were alerted in the lower half of the Gulf of Siam. Reconnaissance planes were sent out from Saigon to fly search patterns over the most probable avenues of approach which the *Prince of Wales* and *Repulse* might take toward the north Malayan beachheads.

Admiral Sir Thomas ("Tom Thumb") Phillips stood personally on the bridge of the *Prince of Wales.* He was the commander of all British naval forces in the Far East and had previously served as assistant chief of staff in the British Admiralty. Small, pugnacious, and brilliant, he had long played an unpopular role in the Admiralty as a champion of air power and a detractor of all capital ships except aircraft carriers. Now he found that the conservative fates had taken their revenge upon him by putting him in command of two beautiful capital ships which had no air support.

Tom Thumb Phillips had taken every precaution to slip out of Singapore unnoticed. He had succeeded in impressing even upon the overconfident, peace-minded public relations office of the British Navy in Singapore the need for secrecy about his foray. As a result half a dozen correspondents in Singapore had been offered a "four-to-five-day" blind press junket with no explanation except that it would be "exciting and important." Most of them—including the representatives of *The New York Times* and the Associated Press—naturally turned the offer down. O. D. Gallagher of the London *Daily Express,* however, sensed that it would involve the great new British battleship in the harbor and persuaded his American friend Cecil Brown of the Columbia Broadcasting System to gamble and come with him. The two correspondents promptly found themselves assigned, with misgivings, to a cramped and stuffy cabin on the battle cruiser *Repulse.*

Taking no chances on Singapore security, Admiral Phillips steamed at top speed due east toward Borneo throughout the night of December 8–9. By dawn he had reached the Anambas Islands which he rightly calculated would be beyond the range of the air search which Japanese staff officers would order if they had heard of his departure. December 9 dawned in accordance with meteorological predictions, for once. The sky was overcast and rain squalls could be seen both visually and by radar spotted all over the Gulf of Siam, offering welcome shelter from detection.

Having rounded the Anambas Islands, Phillips lunged north, directly toward the airfields in Indochina from which he knew that Japanese planes would be taking off to look for him. It was a well-considered plan. Japanese planes were looking for him, but closer to shore, on a more direct route between Singapore and the beachheads where the Japanese had landed.

After coming about into the teeth of the Japanese threat, Phillips had a message posted on all ships' bulletin boards telling the crews that "we are off to look for trouble." He explained that he intended "to carry out a sweep to the northward," to run up the coast under cover of bad weather, and then if not detected by sunset to turn shoreward and make an overnight dash toward the beachheads in southern Thailand where Tiger Yamashita was disembarking his main strength. "At dawn," he wrote, "we shall be to the seaward of Singora and Patani, where the Japanese landing is taking place. . . . I think it is most probable that only submarines and enemy aircraft are likely to be sighted."

A brave word, "only." It meant that Admiral Phillips expected to be intercepted by Japanese aircraft. To anyone who had read his unpopular arguments for many years previously, it meant that the *Prince of Wales* and the *Repulse* would almost certainly be sunk.

Nevertheless, until an hour before sunset on December 9, Admiral Phillips was confounded by good luck. Japanese air crews searched for him in vain to the west of his true course. At 2:10 P.M. a Japanese submarine compounded the confusion by reporting that it had sighted him less than 100 miles off the southern tip of Indochina. At that time he was, in fact, some 140 miles farther to the south and east. He had just changed direction slightly to bring himself still farther to the east, so that he was steering straight for Saigon.

Just after 5 P.M., about an hour before sunset, Phillips's luck ran out. The weather cleared and three Japanese reconnaissance planes on the horizon indicated to the admiral that he had been spotted. He was at that moment closer to the Japanese airfields in Indochina than were the beaches of Kota Bharu. He knew that his two great ships were in mortal danger. Before dark, while he could be sure that the reconnaissance planes were still watching, he turned west and began a high-speed feint straight toward the Japanese beachheads in Thailand which lay about eleven top-speed hours distant.

True to his expectations the Japanese reconnaissance planes had seen him, and on the fields near Saigon, Japanese naval bombers, armed for a dawn raid on Singapore, were hastily rearmed with torpedoes for an attack on capital ships. Four Japanese reconnaissance planes took off at dusk in hopes of following Phillips through the night, and forty-five minutes later eighteen Japanese bombers and fifteen torpedo planes followed the reconnaissance craft south to make a night attack.

Phillips meanwhile had conferred with some of his staff and was scheming not only to deceive the Japanese but also to calm the junior ratings on his own vessels. At 5:58 P.M. when it still seemed to casual observers that he might be attacked at any moment, he knew from radar that no large flight of Japanese planes was yet approaching and he stood down his tense gun crews from first-degree to third-degree alert. At the same time he detached his oldest destroyer, *Tenedos,* to retrace the course of the fleet back to Singapore. Officially the *Tenedos* had engine trouble and "needed oil." Actually the commander of the *Tenedos* was entrusted with the delicate role of decoy: he was to move away from the main fleet and then start sending radio messages to Singapore "as from Phillips." So well did he play his part that the antiquated *Tenedos* succeeded in drawing the fire of a Japanese submarine during the night and then the next morning of nine Japanese bombers.[1]

Shortly after 8 P.M., when it was completely dark and he had maintained his high-speed feint toward Thailand for more than an hour, Phillips abruptly broke off the feint and doubled back toward the southeast. The Japanese night reconnaissance and bombing planes dispatched from Saigon looked for him in vain along his projected course toward the Thai beaches and at about midnight they returned disappointed to their bases. On the other side of Phillips, some 50 miles to the east, the decoy *Tenedos* began breaking radio silence and quacking discreetly.

Phillips told his crews nothing of the dangerous game of blindman's buff and bluff that he was playing. At 9:05 P.M. he had his captains announce to all hands that the fleet had been discovered, that its mission must be aborted, and that he was running for home. A little later, at about 12:45 A.M. on December 10, he again changed course. At that moment he was about 200 miles or less from the Japanese beachhead at Kota Bharu in Malaya. At that moment, fortuitously, his radio room received a message from Singapore stating that the Kota Bharu airfield had been in Japanese hands for more than twenty-four hours and had been in use by Japanese planes for at least twelve hours. Possibly this message came in response to a query broadcast by the decoy destroyer, *Tenedos,* a little earlier.

Hunted from the north, Phillips now knew that his pursuers had a resting and refueling point directly to the west. If he ran for Singapore at top speed, he might make port by noon the next day. He rightly feared that the Japanese naval air force, expecting him to do just that, would catch him short of the mark and sink him. If on the other hand he turned toward Kota Bharu at maximum speed, he might appear off the Japanese beachhead there with the sunrise at his back and shell the newly established Japanese shore positions for half an hour or more before the planes out looking for him converged to attack. For both these alternatives, he knew, his Japanese hunters must be fully prepared. And so, to make the most

---

[1] The submarine squandered five torpedoes from a distance under the misapprehension that *Tenedos* was the much larger and therefore much closer *Prince of Wales.* The air group spent their bombs on her out of sheer frustration because they had not been able to find the rest of the British fleet. Having survived both attacks, the *Tenedos* would go on to assist in the evacuation of Singapore and in the final naval holding actions in the Dutch East Indies, after which she would retire to a well-deserved overhaul in Ceylon.

of the sacrifice of the two magnificent but unsuitable war machines at his disposal, he decided to take a third course which would extend the game and the gamble a little further and might even enable him to achieve what he was looking for as a raider: the element of surprise.

Phillips turned his ships slightly south and made for Kuantan, a harbor halfway up the Malayan coast between Singapore and Kota Bharu. At dawn, when he was about 60 miles offshore, he had his crews told that the Japanese were reportedly landing at Kuantan and that he was going in to shore with hope of shooting up a Japanese convoy of transports. Such a report of a rumor had, in fact, been sent to him during the night, along with many other pieces of confused intelligence, and it is possible though not likely that he believed it.

At 8 A.M. the *Prince of Wales* and the *Repulse* arrived off Kuantan, and Admiral Phillips sent the destroyer *Express* into the harbor to make sure that everything inside appeared as tranquil as it did outside. With the excuse that he had seen barges under tow to the north, he then turned in that direction to investigate. He crept up the Japanese coast apparently still hoping to sneak through and give his big guns to the battle being waged in the Kota Bharu area. By this time, however, more than a hundred Japanese planes were out looking for him, and the Kota Bharu airfield in front of him buzzed on his radar like a hornet's nest. He would have his best chance against the planes to the south which had been looking for him for hours and must be running short of fuel.

At 10 A.M., hearing that his decoy, *Tenedos,* was under attack by bombers to the southeast, Phillips gave up his sneak approach to Kota Bharu and moved out to sea where his ships would have maximum room to maneuver in the encounter which by now seemed inevitable. For forty-one hours he had played mouse. The moment had now come for him to run out his claws. On the basis of past fleet actions against aircraft, he could hope to hold off the Japanese planes until they were forced to return to their bases for fuel. Then he would have about seven hours before they returned—time enough to escape into the darkness of the next night. To harass him during those seven hours, the Japanese would have to divert planes urgently needed on the front in north Malaya. All such expectations—reasonable as they might be on the basis of past experience—were to be confounded in the next three hours by a single unforseen circumstance: the Japanese pilots out hunting Phillips were better than any Western pilots previously encountered by the British fleet.

At 10:15 A.M. one of the 100-odd Japanese bombers spread out in search patterns over the lower half of the Gulf of Siam spotted Phillips's ships and at once notified the rest. In a moment twenty-seven Mitsubishi Betties armed for high-level bombing and sixty-one Betties armed for torpedo attack all turned their props toward the sighting point. They were piloted by the best airmen of the Misty Lagoon.

The first run on the British fleet was made at 11:17 A.M. by a nine-plane group which had won the Yamamoto Combined Fleet Prize for high-level precision bombing the year before. The nine prize winners selected the longer of the two capital ships below as their target and came in at an altitude of between 10,000 and 12,000 feet over the battle cruiser *Repulse* Many of the men on the *Repulse* had seen the German and Italian effort at high-level bombing of fleet units in the Mediterranean and were no concerned by the Japanese approach. Thousand-foot misses were customary in such cases and the anti-aircraft crews of the *Repulse* directed their fire at two low-flying Japanese planes which looked as if they might make a torpedo attack.

No Western bombardier—German, British, or Italian—had ever gone through the training and selection process of his prewar Japanese naval counterparts. At the Misty Lagoon Air Development Station the Japanese teaching technique of practice makes perfect, which is of great help in making the writing of Chinese characters an automatic hand-felt understanding rather than an intellectual exercise, had been carried to great lengths. At a time when bombsights were still in a crude state of development, the Combined Fleet Prize winners had developed an uncanny split-second feel for co-ordinating hand, eye, wind, height, and speed.

Nine bombs from nine planes fell at least 10,000 feet toward the moving target of the *Repulse,* and the British crewmen below had time to watch them fall and to comment before they struck that they were falling remarkably true. All nine landed within 100 feet of the moving vessel, bathing her with spray and a moment of panic. Only one, however, landed directly on the decks of the vessel. It fell amidships on the catapult equipment which was designed to launch the *Repulse*'s four observation flying boats. The bomb disappeared through the struts of the catapult and exploded on the plates of the hangar deck below. There it destroyed the reconnaissance potential of the *Repulse,* started a distracting conflagration, and killed or disabled fifty of the ship's 1,309-man complement.

That first bomb augured truly of what was yet to come. British officers, who had been telling C.B.S. correspondent Cecil Brown only a few hours earlier that Japanese pilots were hampered by constitutionally faulty vision and by ineptly designed, inadequately serviced aircraft, now revised their estimates. Brown heard a gunner mutter, "Bloody good shooting for those blokes." The other correspondent, O. D. Gallagher of London's *Daily Express,* learned from officers with experience in the North Sea and Mediterranean that they had never seen such bombing either by the Luftwaffe or the R.A.F. The Japanese pilots themselves later said that they had never dropped a better bomb pattern even in practice.

While the crew of the *Repulse* fought flames and jettisoned debris, five torpedo planes from a second group of Japanese bombers attacked the

Prince of Wales, launching five well-aimed, true-running torpedoes from five different directions. The officer at the helm succeeded in evading only three of them. One struck aft, disabling the battleship's rudders and reducing her speed from 30 to 15 knots. Another flooded her communications room, rendering her mute throughout the rest of the action and forcing Admiral Phillips to fall back on the slow, undependable sign language of heliograph, semaphore, and mast signals.

Listing and doomed to go around and around in a predictable circle— "an enchanted maiden in a waltz with death," as one poetic crewman later said—the pride of the British fleet had become an easy mark for any Japanese pilot who cared to test the marksmanship of her gunners. All her batteries of cannon and pom-poms continued to blaze away, making her sinking a dangerous undertaking. The Japanese flight leader, Lieutenant Iki Haruki, with his own and three other planes' torpedoes unexpended, circled and studied the situation.

After fifteen minutes, at noon, when he had been joined by eighteen more planes, Lieutenant Iki launched a torpedo attack on the *Repulse.* Four minutes later the skipper of the *Repulse,* Captain William G. Tennant, proudly signaled his crippled flagship, the *Prince of Wales,* that *Repulse* was not yet seriously wounded and had successfully dodged the wakes of no less than nineteen torpedoes.

Lieutenant Iki called off his planes and again studied the situation. Twenty-four of the available sixty-one Japanese torpedo planes in the air had already spent their fish. Neither of the British dreadnoughts was yet sunk, although one was now an easy target. While Iki waited, the *Repulse* and the four destroyers drew in around the stricken *Prince of Wales,* making their curtain of defensive fire more dense but also giving the *Repulse* less room to maneuver.

At 12:20, after a sixteen-minute lull, Lieutenant Iki personally led fourteen torpedo bombers into the barrage to get the *Repulse.* Each of the fifteen planes attacked simultaneously from a different direction making it impossible for skipper Tennant to "comb the wakes" and twist his broadside away from the oncoming furlers of white water. According to Japanese accounts, no less than fourteen of the fifteen torpedoes found their mark. Captain Tennant dodged one of them, his twentieth, and then was hit by the rest. Five minutes after the attack started Tennant ordered abandon ship. Eight minutes later the ship sank. In those eight minutes, with a shocked, disbelieving calmness and order, 796 officers and men succeeded in jumping overboard and surviving in the oil-filmed waters. Another 513 ratings were carried under by the hull or drowned while waiting to be picked up by the attendant destroyers.

Captain Tennant himself was thrown into the water when *Repulse* capsized as she went under. He was sucked deep but bobbed to the the surface and was rescued. One of the men in the control tower, at the top of the main mast, dived 170 feet and lived to swim away. A companion who followed him failed to clear the deck. Another companion plummeted into the ship's funnel. Twelve Royal Marines leapt for safety too far aft and were chopped up by the still turning propellors. Forty-two men from the engine room climbed up to the mouth of the dummy smokestack and were last seen trying vainly to cut their way through a wire screen which stoppered it.

When the *Repulse* went down, the score or more Japanese planes which remained armed turned their attention to the lame *Prince of Wales*. Five more torpedoes were driven into her and at least two bombs registered hits on her. She sank at 1:15 P.M., forty-two minutes after the *Repulse*. Because of the leisurely nature of her last minutes, only 327 of her complement of 1,612 failed to jump overboard and remain afloat until rescued.

Admiral Phillips chose not to be one of the survivors. He refused even to be manhandled to the rails and pushed. Fighting to the last, he pushed others and returned to the bridge to go down with his ship. For two days he had exercised the best half of the Japanese naval air force and had come within an hour, twice, of achieving surprise off the Japanese beachheads. On his own responsibility, deceiving even his fellow officers, he had made a supreme effort to make capital ships count for something in a world which had passed them by. Having failed, he wanted no part in the inquest; he did not wish to serve as the scapegoat for the follies of senior admirals and politicians. He may have taken bitter satisfaction in having proved, as he had often maintained in debate, that capital ships were no match for airplanes.

According to one of the two news correspondents who were now sick with oil and clinging to flotsam in the water, one of the Japanese planes dropped a message onto the screen destroyer, *H.M.S. Vampire:* "We have completed our task; you may carry on." It was the high-water mark of Japanese *noblesse oblige,* registered by one of the flower of Hirohito's Misty Lagoon air elite. Only three of the Japanese pilots had been shot down by the two great ships' vaunted anti-aircraft firepower but the like of those pilots would never be seen again. They had carried the skill of manual flying and fighting to a point of refinement which would never be exceeded but which would shortly be superseded by electronic bombsights, radar, and computerized fire control.

The Japanese planes flew away without bombs or torpedoes left for the destroyers and without even machine-gun bullets left to strafe the survivors being picked up by the destroyers. A few minutes later a belated flight of slow, American-made Buffaloes from Singapore arrived to survey the wreckage and fly air cover over the rescue operations.

The Japanese pilots, winging home to the northeast, radioed news of their incredible victory ahead of them. It reached Hirohito at 3 P.M. Tokyo time, 1:30 P.M. Malaya time, exactly fifteen minutes after the *Prince of*

Wales had disappeared beneath the sea. Lord Privy Seal Marquis Kido was talking to a diplomat when the news was relayed to him by phone. Into the mouthpiece of the phone, in his best approximation of a British accent, he shouted, "Hup, hup, hooray!"

Japan had lost three planes and pilots. Great Britain had lost two ships and 840 crewmen and officers. More important, the Allies, having lost control of the air on December 8, had now, on December 10, lost all hope of keeping control of the sea in Southeast Asia. Allied land forces in the area could, from now on, expect that the Japanese would dispatch bombing raids and invasion convoys at will. There would be no hope of protection from above or of reinforcement from behind.

Churchill heard the news of the sinking of the *Prince of Wales* less than an hour after Hirohito heard it. It was then not yet 7 A.M. in London and the British prime minister was in bed opening his dispatch boxes. He later wrote: "In all the war, I never received a more direct shock. . . . As I turned over and over in bed the full horror of the news sank in upon me."

CONTROL OF THE LAND

After three days of war, the power of the Allies to retaliate by air had been smashed at Clark Field and by sea at Pearl and Kuantan Harbors. There remained, however, Allied land power, and on paper it looked impressive. In Malaya Lieutenant General A. E. Percival commanded 100,000 men: three Indian divisions, one British division, and one Australian division. During the course of the campaign his army would be reinforced by an additional 30,000 British and 7,000 Indian troops. His total force of 137,000 men would lack air support and tanks but would have plenty of trucks, armored cars, artillery, and ammunition.

In the Philippines MacArthur had about 112,500 men: 82,000 recently called-up Filipino reservists, 12,000 well-trained Filipino Scouts, 11,000 U.S. regulars, some 4,000 green U.S. reinforcements, and about 3,500 Marines and naval personnel.

In the Netherlands East Indies the Dutch fielded an inconsequential force of about 20,000 soldiers and 40,000 volunteers split up into a score of small garrisons sprinkled over a vast expanse of territory.

The Japanese were to destroy all these colonial armies in a matter of weeks: the "impregnable bastion of Singapore" in ten weeks, the Dutch power in thirteen weeks, and MacArthur's "Filamerican" army in twenty-one weeks. According to postwar Japanese accounts each of these triumphs was gained with a one-to-two inferiority in troops—a claim which may be doubted. Military textbooks all prescribed at least a two-to-one superiority for landings on hostile shores, and Japanese commanders knew their books.

Inconsistencies in the published Japanese record suggest that the units used in the Strike South were not at full strength but at double and even triple strength. For instance, at one point during the Malayan campaign the 114th Regiment in the 18th Division—a unit which is claimed to have had a strength of 5,000 men—required no less than 550 trucks, loaded "to breaking point," to transport itself to the front. Anyone who has ever seen a Japanese truckful of soldiers must conclude that, at that moment, the 114th Regiment included from 11,000 to 16,500 men and that it was overstrength by a factor of two to three.

It profits not at this late date to play the military numbers game, but Japanese historians appear to have counted only front-line troops and to have ignored roughly equal numbers of men waiting in reserve or playing service roles in the rear. Without discredit to Japanese military prowess it may be said that, on all fronts, approximately one Japanese soldier was pitted against one Allied soldier in the early campaigns of the war and that the Japanese, despite the fact that they were landing on beaches and advancing into prepared positions, everywhere emerged victorious. They were veterans, the best troops in the Japanese Army, and they had air cover.

In Malaya, the first, largest, and most important of the encounters, three Japanese divisions—the 5th, 18th, and the 2d Imperial Guards, with a front-line strength of about 60,000 men—marched 600 miles down a two-lane road through the jungle and repeatedly threw back the combatants from a British force of 137,000 men. At the end of the road they crossed a mile-wide strait and captured Singapore, one of the half dozen major naval bases in the world.

The credit for this remarkable military achievement belongs largely to its planner, Lieutenant Colonel Tsuji Masanobu of Unit 82 which had worked out the Strike South on Taiwan the previous summer. Tsuji had pushed his plans through the roadblocks of other General Staff officers during his brief visit to Tokyo in August 1941. He was, as his fellow officers said, "a personage of great and mysterious influence." They compared his career with that of the ubiquitous Suzuki Tei-ichi who, as a retired lieutenant general, was now director of the Cabinet Planning Board and virtual dictator of the Japanese economy. Like Suzuki, Tsuji came of uncertain parentage; he had always exercised extraordinary authority over senior officers, possessed real ability, and was well connected at Court.

After graduation with highest honors from the military academy and then the staff college, Tsuji had become, in 1934, a tutor for the youngest and brightest of Hirohito's brothers, Prince Mikasa. Still barely twenty-six at the time of Pearl Harbor, Prince Mikasa had been consulted and had cast his lot with Hirohito in the final decision to go to war on November 30, 1941. On the night of August 14, 1945, Mikasa's closest friends and possibly Mikasa himself were to participate in the abortive but effective palace revolution which persuaded Allied intelligence officers that Hirohito had been an intimidated puppet of military strongmen.

Already in 1934, with Prince Mikasa's patronage, Captain Tsuji had recommended himself to Hirohito by his deft handling of the Military Academy Plot, the framing of Strike-North partisans which had smoothed the way for the strange face-saving rebellion of the Army in 1936 and for the capitulation of the Army to Hirohito's personal rule. Since that time, as a major and a lieutenant colonel, Tsuji had become an unpopular but effective missionary in the Japanese Army for Hirohito's gospel of Asia for the Asiatics. If anyone doubted his imperial mandate, he had only to show his credentials: a set of cuff links from Prince Mikasa, embossed with the fourteen-petal chrysanthemum of imperial princes, and a saké cup from Hirohito, embossed with the sixteen-petal chrysanthemum reserved for the Emperor himself.

Tsuji's plan for the conquest of Singapore was a good one, but it would not have succeeded without unusual co-operation from other Japanese Army commanders and from the Navy and the naval air force. Hirohito had made the co-operation possible by sending to the final Strike-South co-ordinating sessions in Saigon during November 1941 his eldest first cousin, the thirty-two-year-old Prince Takeda Tsuneyoshi.[2]

Through Prince Takeda and Prince Mikasa, and from Emperor Hirohito, Lieutenant Colonel Tsuji derived the power to borrow choice troops from other divisions and to make the five divisions assigned to the Malayan and Philippine campaigns stronger than any Japanese divisions which had ever before taken the field. For his own Malayan theater, in particular, Tsuji succeeded in recruiting most of the Japanese Army's tank forces, the best artillery, mortar and machine-gun units, and a host of auxiliaries including small-boat and jungle commandos, bicycle troops, all sorts of bridge and railroad engineers, communication linesmen, and field medics. When Tsuji had finished outfitting the Strike-South forces, the other fifty-three Japanese divisions—sixteen left in Japan, thirteen in Manchuria and Korea, nineteen in China, and five in Indochina and Taiwan—had been stripped clean of offensive power. Their veterans and their ancillary units had both been expropriated by the divisions at the front. Straw-stuffed scarecrow units remained, fit only for marching police beats against

---

[2] Takeda was the son of Emperor Meiji's sixth daughter, Masako, and of Tsunehisa, one of the four young scions of the blood whom Emperor Meiji had selected as dinner companions during the last decade of his reign. Takeda's uncle was Prince Kitashirakawa who had died at the wheel of the powerful touring car in France in 1923. Kitashirakawa's son, Nagahisa, who was the same age as Takeda, had followed in his father's footsteps by crashing in a take-off from a Manchurian airfield while on a mission of the spy service in 1940. The three other surviving blood cousins of Hirohito were younger: Takahiko and Tadahiko, the boys of Prince Asaka, the Nanking rape commander, and Morihiro, the son of Hirohito's other uncle, the devious Prince Higashikuni.

guerrilla activity.[3] Disgruntled Strike-North partisans in the officer corps
bowed without protest to this raiding of their forces because they respected General Yamashita, the "Tiger," who had been given charge of
the Singapore campaign.

As well as armor and experts, the Japanese Strike-South forces had a
professional zeal which verged on fanaticism. Japan was the underdog
and every Japanese infantryman knew it. Before he sailed he was issued a
manual which bore the encouraging title, *Just Read This and the War
Is Won*. It concluded with realisms which would have terrified any but
toughened veterans:

> When you encounter the enemy after landing, regard yourself as an
> avenger come at last face to face with his father's murderer. The discomfort
> of the long sea voyage and the rigors of the sweltering march have been but
> months of watching and waiting for the moment when you may slay this
> enemy. Here before you is the man whose death will lighten your heart of
> its burden of brooding anger. If you fail to destroy him utterly you can never
> rest at peace. And the first blow is the vital blow.
>
> Westerners—being very superior people, very effeminate, and very cowardly
> —have an intense dislike of fighting in the rain or the mist or at night. . .
>
> By jungle is meant dense forest in which a large variety of trees, grasses
> and thorny plants are all closely entangled together. Such places are the
> haunts of dangerous animals, poisonous snakes, and harmful insects, and
> since this is extremely difficult terrain for the passage of troops, it will be
> necessary to form special operation units for the task.
>
> This type of terrain is regarded by the weak-spirited Westerners as im-
> penetrable, and for this reason—in order to outmaneuver them—we must
> from time to time force our way through it. With proper preparation and
> determination it can be done. Maintenance of direction and good supplies of
> water are the supremely important factors. . . .
>
> You must demonstrate to the world the true worth of Japanese manhood.
> The implementation of the task of the Showa Restoration [the Reign of
> Hirohito], which is to realize His Imperial Majesty's desire for peace in the
> Far East, and to set Asia free, rests squarely on our shoulders.
>> Corpses drifting swollen in the sea-depths,
>> Corpses rotting in the mountain-grass—
>> We shall die. By the side of our lord we shall die.
>> We shall not look back.

[3] In Japan the 4th and 39th divisions were being held in reserve ready to move
anywhere at any time. The 7th, 19th, 20th, 52d, 53d, 54th, and old Imperial Guard
divisions were still in barracks. The 40th and 50th divisions were in training. And
the experienced 101st, 106th, 108th, 109th, and 114th were on call-up status. In
Manchuria and Korea remained the depleted 1st, 8th, 9th, 10th, 11th, 12th, 14th,
23d, 24th, 25th, 28th, 29th, and 57th divisions. In China were the despoiled 3d, 6th,
13th, 15th, 17th, 22d, 26th, 27th, 32d, 34th, 35th, 36th, 37th, 38th, 41st, 51st, 104th,
110th, and 116th divisions. In Indochina and Taiwan the 2d, 21st, 33d, 55th, and 56th
divisions stood ready at full strength for assignments in the Dutch East Indies, Burma,
and Australasia.

The ancestor-haunted Japanese, who went into battle with this cheerless poetry burned on their minds, thought and fought like demons. They marched great distances with little food or sleep and then hurled themselves at surprised Allied entrenchments without regard for life. Though famished, groggy, and decimated, they attacked until they broke through. They took few prisoners in mopping up because they were encouraged to think that it would be a slur on the Emperor's virtue if they did not take more lives than they had lost.

Allied troops, by comparison—particularly the British in Malaya—fought under the misapprehension that they were innately superior. When they began to suffer more casualties than they inflicted, they were tormented by feelings of individual inadequacy and their group morale fell accordingly.

In the postmortem of later years Allied commanders were largely held responsible for this complacency. They underestimated the Japanese Army because it had failed to achieve any final victory over the ill-trained hordes of Chiang Kai-shek. They discounted the Japanese air forces and Navy because they thought that Japan during her war with China had had no money to build good planes and ships. They encouraged journalists to exude baseless optimism and noncoms to spread foolish tales about Japanese nearsightedness, imitativeness, and lack of individual initiative. As a result much genuinely sound staff planning was vitiated by troops who were not prepared psychologically for a hard fight.

MALAYA'S JITRA LINE

Colonel Tsuji personally accompanied the vanguard of General Yamashita's 5th Division forces when they crossed the Thai frontier and began their southward advance down the long paved road connecting Bangkok with Singapore. After minor skirmishes with Anglo-Indian companies which had been sent belatedly to fight a delaying action in southern Thailand, the Japanese advance units, about thirteen miles south of the border ran into the forward posts of the only prepared defense position in Malaya, the Jitra line.

With about 500 men and thirty light and medium tanks, Tsuji pushed ahead through the line. At 4 P.M. December 11, the third day of the war, he surprised the first Gurkha outpost while its men were away from their guns, taking shelter from the usual afternoon rainstorm under the rubber trees beside the road. The Japanese troops captured the guns and armored cars of the Gurkhas and pushed on south until a bridge blew up in front of them. Tsuji had his men wade the stream and fight defensively while the bridge was being repaired. Then his tanks rushed through both the Japanese and British infantry lines and succeeded in capturing the next bridge before it could be blown. Now the Jitra line, manned by more than 20,000 British and Indian troops, had been broken at its center, and all night long Allied troops from the flanks moved in to break off the point of the Japanese needle. Tusji's 500 men held their salient until, on the morning of December 12, they were relieved by an augmented regiment of some 10,000 men with more tanks.

That evening, after numerous telephone calls between the British front lines and the British command in Singapore 600 miles to the south, the Jitra line was abandoned; its minefields, entanglements and trenches, its caches of food and ammunition, and many of its guns, trucks, and armored cars were allowed to fall into Japanese hands. Half its defenders had been Indians who had never before seen a tank. All its armored cars were sturdy Rolls-Royce products left over from World War I. Nevertheless, there was no other prepared defense line to compare with it in the rest of Malaya. At rivers farther south, the Anglo-Indian-Australian forces would give a better account of themselves, but by then the Japanese infantrymen would be unbeatable. They would have lost their fear of the strange tropical surroundings and their awe of white soldiers. Their strength would have fattened on captured food, gasoline, trucks, and ammunition. Indian prisoners of war would have told all they knew about the positions ahead. And the triphammer sequence—advance, breakthrough, pursuit, consolidation—would have become routine.

Colonel Tsuji felt that at the Jitra line he had demonstrated the only tactics which would be needed throughout the campaign. Foot soldiers would ford rivers and infiltrate, enabling engineers to repair blown bridges; then tanks would lunge through and dash forward until stopped by another unbridged river. To keep pace with the tanks and to extend their salients even beyond the next river, the Japanese infantry would employ collapsible bicycles which they could carry on their backs across streams. By pedaling fast enough these bicycle troops could maintain a steady pressure on the rear of the retreating British troops and give them no time to regroup even when they had just left a blown bridge behind them. When disabled Japanese or British armor piled up at hard-fought roadblocks, impeding further advance, the bicycle troops would be at hand to heave the derelict armor off the road into the jungle. The concept of the bicycle troops was a pet of Hirohito himself. Japan was the world's leading manufacturer of inexpensive bicycles, and the thought of using them to chase Rolls-Royce machines appealed powerfully to the imperial imagination.

By a straightforward battering-ram approach, Tsuji believed that the Japanese Army could go all the way down the main road to Singapore. General Yamashita insisted that this main drive must be supplemented by flanking movements. Troops indoctrinated for jungle fighting must creep through swamps and turn British lines by passing through terrain considered impassable. "Small-boat parties" must compound the terror by running down the jungle-girt west coast of Malaya and creating pockets of infiltration deep behind the British lines.

Colonel Tsuji saw heavy losses in such adventures. General Yamashita refused to abandon any means which might keep the British off balance. Possibly Tsuji was right and lives could have been saved by leaving these peculiarly Japanese forms of blitzkrieg untried. General Yamashita had his way, however, and Prime Minister Churchill later gave much credit for the Japanese success in Malaya to the unnerving flanking movements, by boat and jungle, which made British forces pull back repeatedly, for fear of encirclement, from the hammering down the main road.

The minor tactical differences of opinion between Colonel Tsuji and his former patron, General Yamashita, grew into a major falling-out which would have important consequences of state. Yamashita first caused Tsuji to lose face before fellow staff officers by overriding him on the issue of the small-boat parties and outflanking movements down the west coast. Then Tsuji took the part of some Japanese troops who had committed unauthorized atrocities on the west coast island of Penang and was again overridden. Tsuji sulked and offered to resign. Yamashita refused to accept his resignation but failed to heal the breach.

Before the Malayan campaign was half over, Tsuji had begun a campaign of vilification against his commander which was jealously pursued in Tokyo by the politically-minded general, Prime Minister Tojo, and sympathetically represented at Court by Hirohito's brother, young Prince Mikasa who was Tsuji's patron and protégé. As a result, when Singapore fell, two months later, Hirohito would turn his back on his ablest general, would deny Yamashita a triumphal return to Tokyo, and would repost him directly back to his old command in Manchuria. Most important, Hirohito would turn a deaf ear to an audacious plan, advocated by Yamashita, which might have changed the course of the war. It was a plan for the immediate invasion of Australia.

WAKE

During the opening skirmishes of the battle for the Jitra line in Malaya, Allied forces won their only victory of the first month of the war. At dawn on December 11, a Japanese cruiser, six destroyers, and two transports hove to off the tiny two-and-a-half-square-mile coral atoll of Wake, an air Clipper stop about two thirds of the way from Manila to Hawaii. For forty minutes the Japanese ships shelled the atoll and then, having roused no answering fire, they moved in to land troops. When they were 4,500 yards from shore, Major James Devereux, who commanded the 450 U.S. Marines on the island, finally allowed his 5-inch gun crews to go into action.

Taken by surprise, the Japanese ships turned tail to get out of range.

The Marines' four Wildcat fighter planes were wheeled from hiding places in the scrub which covered the island and managed to take off from the pockmarked coral airstrip which had been bombed repeatedly in the previous two days. As the Japanese task force retreated, the Marines' shore batteries sank one of the destroyers. The four Wildcats continued the attack beyond the range of the shore guns and sank a second destroyer. Most of the Japanese ships had been damaged and over 500 Japanese had been killed, with the loss of one U.S. Marine. The Japanese commander, Rear Admiral Kajioka Sadamichi, sailed back to his base on the Japanese mandated island of Kwajalein for refitting.

Kajioka would return twelve days later to complete his mission with six heavy cruisers, two aircraft carriers, fifty-four planes, and over 1,000 landing troops. Again the defenders of Wake would give a good account of themselves, killing over 800 Japanese and losing only forty-nine Marines, three sailors, and seventy civilians. At the end of a twelve-hour battle, however, 470 U.S. Marines, sailors, and airmen, together with 1,146 construction workers and other civilians attached to the air base, would become Japanese prisoners. A third of them would not live to be liberated.

HONG KONG

The retreat of Japan's fleet from its initial repulse at Wake was a unique movement. Everywhere else Japanese forces were advancing. Yamashita's tanks were capitalizing on their breakthrough of the Jitra line in Malaya and taking a heavy toll of ill-trained Anglo-Indian forces as they attempted to fall back upon a new defense position. In Thailand, on December 11, the support forces of the Malayan expedition reached an agreement with the Thai government, declared Bangkok secure, and moved on west into southern Burma to occupy a British aerodrome there, Victoria Point.

The next day, December 12, the U.S. Navy withdrew its remaining planes from the Philippines to Java, leaving the U.S. Army in the Philippines with a total cover of thirty-three Army fighters.

Allied commanders looked on askance and swore that Japan was violating every principle of offensive warfare by scattering her forces in all directions. In all directions, however, the Japanese buckshot continued to drill through. Small Japanese convoys were observed converging on British North Borneo. On December 15 and 16 they hit the beaches of Sarawak and Brunei and captured these two British protectorates almost immediately. In so doing they gained possession of wells which at that time produced more than one per cent of the world's petroleum. British demolition experts, however, had been busy for a week and had done their work conscientiously. The subterranean fires they had started would burn for a month, and when the pall of smoke had cleared, the wellheads would gush less richly.

Outside of Malaya, the main Japanese Army offensive in these days was aimed at the conquest of Hong Kong. The Japanese 229th and 230th regiments, 38th Division, with untold and unknown assistance from elements of the 18th, 51st, and 104th divisions, took five days to sweep down through the mainland dependencies of the British crown colony. On December 13 Major General C. M. Maltby completed the withdrawal of his forces to Hong Kong island, the showplace of colonialism, where some twenty-four square miles of handsome bungalows and gardens crowded up the slopes of a beautiful little mountain range encircled by a sunny blue sea.

For five days, December 13 to 18, General Maltby's 14,500 defenders—a quarter of them British troops, a quarter Canadian, a quarter Indian, and a quarter civilian, naval, and air volunteers—awaited the onslaught of the 20,000 to 30,000 Japanese soldiers gathering at embarkation points across the mile-wide waters of Kowloon Bay. All the while some of the best artillerymen in the Japanese Army rained shells upon Hong Kong's beaches and docks.

On December 18, under cover of dusk and the smoke of the great oil tanks which had been ignited by the Japanese shelling on the northeastern point of the island, some 10,000 Japanese troops from three regiments crossed the bay in barges and sampans and established themselves on a broad beachhead. They then surprised the British defenders by driving toward the least populous area of the island, the mountain peaks. For two days British forces waited to defend the valuable installations on the shore beside the Japanese beachhead while the Japanese troops stormed the difficult heights of the interior which were defended by small but well-entrenched groups of Canadian soldiers who had recently arrived from the plains of Manitoba.

The purpose of the strange Japanese tactic was quickly realized when the three invading regiments converged on the reservoir in the mountains which supplied the entire island with drinking water. Hirohito had taken a special interest in the reservoir during his visit to the island as crown prince in 1921 and had insisted upon being driven up off the beaten track of tourists to take a look at it. Now his men concentrated their first efforts on seizing it, and Major General Maltby, grasping the implications, committed all his reserves to the defense of the ridges and passes around the reservoir.

Several thousand of the best Allied and Japanese troops died around the reservoir in a five-day battle which the British ultimately lost. On December 23 the Japanese finally gained control of the chief pumping stations and reduced the main body of Hong Kong's defenders to the two-day supply of water which was left in the storage tanks in the city of Victoria.

While the reservoir was being defended and lost, Hirohito's men made a lateral strike against the Hong Kong power station. It was defended by a group of wounded soldiers and a force of puffy-faced, middle-aged businessmen. These civilian volunteers were representative of the "colonialists" who had made Hong Kong a model colony and the most crowded enclave of peace, police, and opportunity in the Far East. True to the last to their "white man's burden," they defended the power station until they saw that their position was untenable. Then they sortied in a last brave gesture and were all killed. Many of them had learned to handle guns only in the week before. All of them could have remained noncombatants and could have chosen less certain death as civilian prisoners in a Japanese internment camp.

From December 23 to December 25, while other Japanese units were landing in force on Luzon, bombing Rangoon in Burma, and moving into Dutch Borneo, the Hong Kong attackers advanced steadily down from the captured reservoir in the mountains into the thirsty thoroughfares of Victoria, Hong Kong's chief city. Major General Maltby, at the insistence of the diehard civilian governor of the colony, Mark Young, had already rejected out of hand two Japanese recommendations of surrender, delivered under flag of truce.

On Christmas eve Japanese officers were instructed by their commander, Lieutenant General Sakai Takashi, to let the British know that if they did not surrender soon they would have to abandon hope of being taken prisoner at all. During Christmas morning lone survivors from overrun British outposts were released to bring this message to Maltby's attention and to tell how their comrades had all been killed. By afternoon Maltby could see that his forces were breaking up into pockets which the Japanese would be able to annihilate at leisure. Feeling that there was no use in fighting on when his men could no longer take a life for a life, Maltby got Governor Mark Young's approval to capitulate.

British troops and civilian volunteers in the western half of the island, who had been cut off and ignored after the Japanese seizure of the heights, refused to believe that the rest of the island had surrendered and continued fighting. They held a strong position at Fort Stanley, on a highly defensible peninsula at the southeastern corner of the island. Heavy bombardment from land and sea had failed to silence their batteries and their shells were inflicting high casualties on the Japanese. To hasten their surrender the Japanese, all through Christmas day and night, staged a gruesome display of escalating reprisal and terror. Early in the morning, the Japanese had captured St. Stephen's College outside the walls of Fort Stanley. On its premises they had found installed a field hospital. Obedient to General

Sakai's orders they had begun their occupation of the hospital by bayoneting some sixty of the ninety-odd patients.

Later, when word of the surrender had been received and Fort Stanley still held out, they put four Chinese and seven British nurses in one room and about a hundred orderlies, doctors, and stretcher-bearers in another room. During the afternoon they took out the male captives, two or three at a time, and one by one, limb by limb, dismembered them. They chopped off fingers, sliced off ears, cut out tongues, and stabbed out eyes, before they killed. A few of the victims were allowed to escape to tell the Fort Stanley defenders what was happening. In the other room the nurses were made to scream. Beds of corpses were built for them on which they were tied down for raping.

At some time in the evening the four Chinese nurses and then the three youngest and prettiest of the English nurses were put to death by bayonet. About then negotiations with the defenders at Fort Stanley began to progress, and the last four elder British nurses were locked in a room and left alone. During the night Fort Stanley surrendered, and in the morning British prisoners were brought in to the hospital to clean up. They released the four surviving, gibbering nurses. They literally waded in blood as they gathered corpses for burial from the execution room. They carried away a hysterical British lieutenant who was the husband of one of the three British nurses who had been abused and then bayoneted. For the first Allied war captives, the years of imprisonment had begun.

LUZON

In the Philippines the main body of the Japanese invasion force, some 40,000 strong,[4] had begun landing from a convoy of seventy-three transports, plus auxiliary and escort vessels, on the beaches of Lingayen Gulf, on the western shore of northern Luzon, on December 22. They quickly joined up with the two detachments of about 4,000 men each which had landed twelve days earlier at Aparri and Vigan still farther north.[5] "Filamerican" troops under the over-all command of U.S. Major General Jonathan M. Wainwright, who had the responsibility for guarding the

[4] My estimate. I saw the invasion fleet through field glasses from the mountains and have talked to Japanese generals about it. MacArthur, on the basis of aerial reconnaissance, claimed that 80,000 Japanese came ashore. Japanese commanders, in postwar prison interrogations, have claimed that only about 15,000 troops landed, those of the 16th Division's 20th Regiment and of the 48th Division's 47th and First Taiwan Regiments. I give other estimates in what follows about the strength of other Japanese landings. Official Japanese figures are noted in the footnotes.

[5] At Aparri a battalion and a half of the 2d Taiwan Regiment of the 48th Division with a claimed strength of about 2,200 men; at Vigan the other, "'nuclear" half (i.e., including commanding officer and his staff) of the same regiment with a claimed strength of approximately 3,000 men.

500-mile-long coasts of northern Luzon, offered light resistance at the beaches and then fell back.

Wainwright used green Filipino reservists to contest the Japanese landings. He held a few thousand seasoned troops in reserve at important roadheads to the south of the Japanese beachheads. It was his duty, as gracefully as possible, with a maximum show of force and a minimum loss of life, to abandon northern Luzon and fall back to the south.

For political reasons MacArthur had promised Filipinos that he would defend all 115,00 square miles of the 2,000 islands in the Philippine archipelago. In reality he had no intention of squandering his little army of 26,500 trained fighters and 86,000 green recruits on any such impossible task. He had about 80,000 of his men, including almost all his professionals, with him on the large northern island of Luzon. There he intended to use them where they would give the best account of themselves.

Since December 15 he had been moving stockpiles of ammunition and food into 400 square miles at the tip of Bataan, a small peninsula which jutted south from the middle of the western coast of Luzon and crooked its appendix across the northern half of Manila Bay. On Bataan he would be able to wedge his green troops between his experienced soldiers and fight a positional battle which would take the maximum toll of Japanese lives. Bataan controlled the landward approaches to Corregidor, an island fortress of concrete tunnels, artesian wells, and heavy guns which had been built at great expense to defend the entrance of Manila harbor.

The fall-back of General Wainwright's forces toward Bataan in the south left the northern half of Luzon undefended, including the summer capital of the Philippines, Baguio, which nestled in the pine-clad Benguet mountains some 30 miles east of the palmy shore where the Japanese had landed. The Japanese seized the approaches to the tortuous paved road which led up the mountainsides on December 23. That evening the U.S. commander in Baguio, Lieutenant Colonel Horan, drove his armored cars over a clay embankment to destroy them and began marching his men away into the hills to become a guerrilla chieftain.

On Christmas eve, American residents in Baguio anticipated by a few hours the fighting colonials of Hong Kong by establishing the Pacific War's first internment camp for Allied civilians. They gathered voluntarily at a local school in order to turn themselves over in a well-organized body, giving as little excuse as possible for rape or murder and retaining as much as possible of self-government. At the same time local Japanese fifth columnists took over Baguio's municipal government.

The advance troops of the Japanese Army, when they arrived in Baguio more than a day later, were presented with a peaceable, submissive city. They suspiciously wasted the opportunity, however, and proved the slogan "Asia for the Asiatics" to be propaganda. Within a week of their entry, the Baguio market place was empty; sentries stood at every street corner;

the homes of the Hispano-Filamerican rich had all been sealed with Japanese-Army-property stickers and their furnishings removed to Japanese-Army bodegas; the native poor, who joined as scavengers in the looting, were being shot on sight. A semblance of good government would not be restored for a month. The substance—including adequate opportunities to earn and eat and hope for betterment—would not return until after the end of the war in 1946 and 1947.

The Japanese commander in the Philippines, Lieutenant General Honma Masaharu, climbed the ramp of one of his landing barges and came ashore at the Lingayen beachhead on the morning of December 24. As he did so, another 18,000-odd Japanese soldiers from twenty-four deep-sea freighters were landing east and south of Manila on the shores of Lamon Bay at the other side of Luzon.[6] They quickly joined up with about 8,000 more soldiers who had landed at the town of Legaspi, farther south on the same coast, on December 12.[7] In all, General Honma had at his disposal, converging on Manila, some 74,000 of the most brutal troops in the Empire.[8] Roughly 26,000 of them were advancing from the south. He had the other 48,000 with him as he advanced from the north. A further force of 12,000 to 15,000 retired veterans, the 65th Brigade, was on the high seas behind him, sent to provide reliable occupation troops for his rear.[9]

General Honma's landing at Lingayen Gulf and General Wainwright's quick withdrawal in the face of it compelled MacArthur to reveal to Filipino leaders his intention of standing to fight only in Bataan. His chief staff officers had all known that he could not fulfill his oft-reiterated public pledge to defend the whole island of Luzon, but no civilians had been let in on the staff secret and only sensibly discreet pessimists had guessed it. During the autumn of 1941, he had even gone so far as to discourage—"for the sake of Filipino morale"—the evacuation home to the United States of the wives and children of American civilians in the Philippines. The dissimulation was necessary because, without it, he would never have been able to bring over 80,000 Filipino reservists into his army in the final two months before the war broke out. The men called up hoped to defend their *barrios* or home villages. Had they known that they would serve hopelessly on Bataan, in order to gain time for a global

---

[6] A battalion of the 33d Regiment of the 16th Division and all of the Division's 9th Regiment. Total claimed strength: 6,510 men.

[7] Two battalions of the 33d Regiment, 16th Division, with a claimed strength of 3,254.

[8] Honma's 16th Division was the force which had been left in Nanking after Christmas 1937 to carry out the last five disciplined weeks of the rape there. His 48th Division was the permanent garrison force on Taiwan; two of its three regiments were recruited from the old Strike-South community of Japanese colonists in Taiwan.

[9] The 122d, 141st, and 142d regiments looted from the 17th and other divisions in China, a claimed strength of 6,659 men which landed on December 28, 1941.

U.S. strategy in which the Philippines counted for little, they would have thought twice before offering to sacrifice themselves.

MacArthur announced his decision to the president of the Commonwealth of the Philippines, Manuel Quezon, on the evening of December 23. By then most of the Filipino reservists were already organized in units, enjoying good pay, reliant upon their American officers, and indoctrinated with the belief that they could win. The Japanese landing at Lingayen Gulf was only twenty-four hours old. It had been expected for a fortnight and predicted in contingency planning for years, yet efforts to contain it had already been abandoned. Quezon felt deceived, for it was apparent to him that MacArthur had always secretly expected to fall back on Bataan. MacArthur himself was not as cordial as usual with his old crony, for an American policeman had been apprehended the week before trying to pass through the lines north of Lingayen with a message from Quezon to the colonel of the Japanese force which had landed on December 10 at Vigan.

Something like an abduction took place in the presidential Malacanan Palace that evening. Quezon agreed to become virtually a prisoner of MacArthur's staff officers and MacArthur made political promises in return. In later years, after the tubercular Quezon had died in a U.S. hospital, MacArthur honored the promises even to the extent of excusing from trial certain members of Quezon's staff who, in the meanwhile, had succumbed to Japanese blandishments and become quislings.

During the night of December 23–24, the most recent draft of Filipino inductees—a force of 9,000 men which MacArthur had hoped to add to his troop strength of 112,500—deserted in a body from their boot camp.

The next morning President Quezon met with his Cabinet ministers and, by his own account, "revealed the agreement with General MacArthur." As Quezon later explained it: "To avoid the destruction of the city and save the civilian population from the horrors of indiscriminate bombardment from Japanese planes and siege-guns, Manila was to be declared an open city."

Satisfied with the political cogency of this excuse, most of Quezon's Cabinet accompanied the president and a U.S. Marine guard of honor to Corregidor that afternoon. In the tunnels of the island fortress, at the tip of Bataan Peninsula, barely forty-eight hours after the Japanese had landed in strength on Luzon, the Philippine government established itself in refugee status, under U.S. protection. It would soon go on to Washington where its exile would be extended for more than three years.

Having waited for the emergency to provide him with a propitious moment for the settlement of his difficult political problems, MacArthur now faced a still more difficult military problem. Some 80,000 dispersed and mostly ill-trained men had to be withdrawn into Bataan over a single two-lane paved road before 48,000 well-collected, highly mobile Japanese veterans could advance 120 miles to his northern flank and turn the retreat into a rout. Some of MacArthur's best units, fighting the other 26,000 Japanese invaders on the southeast coast, would have to drive more than 200 miles before they could reach the entrance to Bataan. What was worst, MacArthur, for fear of lowering Filipino morale, had stockpiled little food or ammunition in Bataan. These prerequisites for a defense had to be brought into the peninsula now, along with the great crowd of troops.

To carry off his fall-back on Bataan, MacArthur needed an act of Providence. Orderly withdrawal had always been difficult even for seasoned soldiers. In the twentieth century it had become more difficult because of the absolute dominance of mobile firepower which, in the tropics, could only travel on roads and railroads. Without air cover to protect his trucks and without broad thoroughfares to expedite their movements, MacArthur's withdrawal to Bataan was a desperate venture. After nine days, however, by January 1, 1942, most of MacArthur's men would be in Bataan, and after fourteen days, by January 6, even his brave and battered rear-guard units would pull back successfully into the Bataan perimeter, blowing their bridges behind them.

Some of the credit for this miracle belonged to the able officers and men who held off the Japanese during the retreat; the rest belonged to Lieutenant General Honma, MacArthur's opposite number. If MacArthur had faced a general of the caliber of Tiger Yamashita in Malaya, the withdrawal to Bataan might have turned into a disaster. Honma, however —"the linguist with the red nose"—had qualified for his command by seven years as a liaison and intelligence officer with the British Army, by six years as aide-de-camp to Hirohito's brother Prince Chichibu, and by sitting up all night in 1932 to give the Emperor a quick translation of the Lytton Report to the League of Nations. He had gained his only experience as a combat commander during the brief Japanese drive up the Yangtze against Hankow in the fall of 1938.

Honma had been put in charge of the Japanese expedition to the Philippines only after the plans for it had already been drawn up by the staff officers around Colonel Tsuji in Unit 82. Then, Chief of Staff Sugiyama had simply summoned Honma and handed him the plans as orders. Honma had demurred at this unusual treatment and had asked time for personal research and appraisal of the Philippine situation. "If you don't like your assignment," Sugiyama had barked, "we can give it to someone else." Honma had bowed quickly but stiffly and ever since that moment had followed his orders like an automaton.

The plans called for Honma to occupy Manila by mid-January. He went about his task without looking to left or to right. On his left guerrillas stole away to learn their trade in the mountains. On his right the "battling bastards of Bataan" cursed their drivers and kicked stragglers in noisy traffic jams which extended for a dozen miles on both sides of each of the two major bridges along the highway leading into Bataan.

Japanese pilots flew over the long lines of desperately impatient motorists and reported what they saw. But Honma ignored the scraps of firsthand intelligence which filtered up to him. He knew that MacArthur commanded only 20,000 to 30,000 properly trained troops, and he saw no great danger in letting such a small force dig in on Bataan. Even at its narrowest point, the peninsula was 14 miles wide and no 23,000 men could hold a 14-mile front against concentrated bombardment, determined bayonet charges, and amphibious outflanking movements. Given time to suffer the hunger and frustration of being beseiged, the Americans would make easy marks. It was Honma's plan to occupy the uncontested streets of Manila and then turn at leisure to pluck the thorn from his side. As a former palace aide-de-camp, Honma should have known better. His error was to ruin his career and cost Japan at least 15,000 of her best troops.

MANILA

On December 27, when MacArthur began to feel that the retreat into Bataan might succeed, he made public his decision not to defend Manila and to declare it an open city. A few hours later, in Tokyo, Lord Privy Seal Marquis Kido, on behalf of the Emperor, interviewed Lieutenant General Tanaka Shizuichi, a former commandant of the secret police.[10] Out of the interview came an appointment for Tanaka as military governor and commander in chief of Japanese forces in the Philippines, effective as soon as General Honma should complete mopping-up operations there. As events turned out Tanaka would not be able to occupy his post until August 1942.

Hirohito took MacArthur's open-city declaration to mean that the campaign in the Philippines was nearing a successful conclusion. He urged Chief of Staff Sugiyama, therefore, to abbreviate the Strike-South timetable by six weeks and proceed at once with the invasion of the Dutch East Indies. According to the plans of the previous summer, the number of islands and sheer size of the Indies would require an expeditionary force of three augmented divisions of front-line troops, plus a corps of veterans

---

[10] Tanaka had headed the secret police from August 1938 to August 1939 and again from September 1940 to October 1941. An Oxford graduate, with a fine Hindenburg mustache, he was a partisan of Konoye, a "moderate," a fence-sitter, an opportunist. He would re-emerge as the general of the Eastern Area Army who, at dawn on August 15, 1945, would enter the palace grounds to put down the gesture of revolt there against surrender.

for rear-area police and guard duty. The crack 2d Division from Sendai in northern Japan would be assisted by the 38th Division which had just taken Hong Kong, and by the 48th Division which Honma, supposedly, had no further use for in the Philippines.

Honma's staff officers, even in the strategy sessions months earlier, had protested that they must keep the 48th Division until after the reduction of the U.S. fortress of Corregidor. They were promised, instead, that they would not have to reduce Corregidor by assault but would be allowed to starve it into submission. Through an oversight Hirohito had not been informed of this understanding. If he had been, he would have disapproved it. An isolated Allied force, left in the rear of Japan's advance, might have no great military importance, but its continued resistance and its uncensored radio broadcasts would be of incalculable propaganda value to the enemy, affecting the attitude of conquered natives and the eagerness of the United States and Great Britain to accept Japanese peace terms.

When General Honma learned in late December that he was to give up the 48th Division even earlier than originally planned, he at once filed a protest with General Count Terauchi, the aged martinet of the Army Purification Movement, who presided in Saigon as the over-all field commander and arbiter of the various armies engaged in the Strike South. After making inquiries, Terauchi informed Honma that he would indeed have to give up the 48th Division but that perhaps, for the moment, the U.S. forces on Bataan could be considered part of the Corregidor defense forces and could be represented at Court as "a carp in a pond," unable to escape and easy to catch at any time, especially when hungry.

Terauchi sent this message to Honma verbally through the assistant chief of staff in Saigon, the commander of the 40th Division, Lieutenant General Aoki Sei-ichi. Aoki was used as messenger because he was flying to the Philippines anyway as Terauchi's representative at the official entry of Japanese forces into Manila—a victory parade scheduled for January 5. Hirohito also sent a representative to this ceremony: his cousin Prince Takeda, who had attended the final Strike-South co-ordinating conferences held in Saigon the previous November. Lieutenant General Aoki and Prince Takeda both arrived in Manila the day before the festivities, January 4. Aoki reported at once to General Honma. Prince Takeda conferred with a number of officers and learned the "real situation in the Philippines." That same night he communicated the results of his inquiries—by telephone or telegraph—to Hirohito.

The next morning, to the boom of guns and blare of trumpets, as General Honma, in full dress, was guiding his charger past the presidential Malacanan Palace of the Philippines, an aide discreetly handed him a telegram. It was signed Sugiyama, Chief of the Japanese Imperial General Staff. It curtly commanded him:

REPORT AT ONCE ON HOW YOU EXPECT TO PROCEED WITH THE BATAAN
OPERATION. THIS INFORMATION IS NEEDED IN ORDER TO REPLY TO A QUERY
PUT BY THE THRONE.

General Honma hurriedly pocketed the dispatch, but at a reception
after the parade he closeted himself with Prince Takeda and learned the
full extent of the bad news. In the opinion of the Emperor he had bungled
the occupation of the Philippines. Corregidor might have been left to grow
hungry and to be ridiculed as a "carp in a pond" if the main strength of
U.S. forces in the Philippines had been destroyed first. As matters stood,
however, Bataan could not be ignored, nor could the 48th Division be
spared to help Honma repair his blunder.

Honma bowed silently to the Imperial Will but showed his resentment
by assigning the vanguard for the attack on Bataan to the 65th Brigade
under the command of Lieutenant General Nara Akira. Nara was a
kinsman of former Chief Aide-de-Camp Nara Takeji, who had guided
Hirohito in Army affairs from 1921 to 1933. The 12,000-odd men of
Nara's 65th Brigade were middle-aged reservist veterans who had expected
to play sedentary roles as rear-area occupation troops. They were eager,
however, to prove themselves still worthy as front-line warriors, and Nara
was happy to give them their opportunity, for he considered General
Honma a timorous worrywart.

THE DEFENSE OF BATAAN

Starting with a night attack at 11 P.M. on January 11, 1942, Lieutenant
General Nara flung his veterans against the forward U.S. position on
Bataan, the Abucay line. After fourteen days of unremitting assault, he
succeeded in forcing the Filamerican troops back ten miles to their second
position, the Bagac-Orion line. There, in an all-out effort to break through
General Honma reinforced Nara with the 9th and 20th regiments of the
brutal 16th Division which had raped Nanking. Almost half the men of
the two fresh regiments were infiltrated by boat behind the U.S. lines and
for the next week fought a desperate "battle of points and pockets" with
the Filipino Scouts and U.S. pilots and Marines who backed up the
Filamerican trenches. When the battle was over only one of the infiltrators
had been captured; all the rest had died.

The Bagac-Orion line held firm, and on February 2 General Honma
was forced to acknowledge that he had suffered a humiliating defeat. He
committed his sixth and last regiment, the 16th Division's 33d, to cover
the withdrawal of the rest of his men. They stumbled back to rear-area
field hospitals in appalling condition. Of one of the five regiments, the
20th, only 34 per cent of the men and none of the three battalion
commanders still lived.

More than a third of all the combat troops under Honma's command had been killed in action [11] and two thirds of the remainder were incapacitated by sickness, wounds, or exhaustion. According to Honma's own postwar statement he had left "only 3,000 effectives." [12] The troops standing against him, including even the green Filipino recruits who were still learning how to fire a rifle, had made the most of their entrenchment and suffered far less grievously.

Having taken stock, General Honma felt forced to acknowledge his defeat in dispatches. A delegation of staff officers promptly descended upon him from Tokyo. It was led by Colonel Hattori Takushiro, the soft-spoken chief of the Operations Section, Operations Department, General Staff. It included a new chief of staff for Honma: Major General Wachi Takaji, a tough fanatic who had been chief of staff of the colonial Taiwan Army. The group met with General Honma on a sweltering afternoon, February 8, at his headquarters in San Fernando, 115 miles behind the battle line.

Operations Chief Hattori brought with him an official message from Imperial Headquarters, stamped with a palace seal which showed that Hirohito had read and approved its contents. It stated, in a sentence which burned itself on General Honma's vision: "The Emperor is acutely worried about Bataan." Honma cradled his head in his arms and wept. The visitors from Tokyo were embarrassed to see him so fatigued and emotional and they did their best in the weeks ahead to save his face. At the same time they effectively relieved him of his command, placed operations in the Philippines under the direct leadership of the Emperor, and relegated Honma to a titular capacity. They reported home that Honma acknowledged officially a need for reinforcements.

Colonel Hattori had brought with him from Tokyo a number of psychological warfare experts. It was through the efforts of these men that the "battling bastards of Bataan" first noticed that the Japanese command in the Philippines had taken a new tack. The Japanese psychologists were all surprised by the fact that the Filipino soldiers in Bataan, despite Japanese Pan-Asian propaganda, were standing and dying by their "colonialist American masters." On-the-spot inquiries revealed that the Filipinos in general were far more antagonistic to Japanese than to U.S. colonialism. As a result, efforts to woo Filipino soldiers away from their American officers were de-emphasized and a more basic psychological strategy was

[11] Officially 5,852 out of a total of 14,610. According to various unofficial sources, Honma also had—even after the 48th Division had been taken away from him—some 35,000 support troops. Used as replacements, these, too, had suffered heavy losses in the fighting, perhaps as many as 8,000 dead.

[12] Again he meant picked combat troops, for I know from personal observation that there were more than 3,000 able-bodied Japanese in Army uniforms in Baguio, 150 miles behind the front, strolling about the streets and buying bananas and papayas.

adopted. That is, the leaflets dropped on Bataan would no longer make ideological claims but would portray the simple joys of living: Philippine scenery, tables groaning with food, pretty girls in bed.

Before the next attack, Bataan must be softened up by privation and hunger. The Japanese knew from their own experience on Bataan that the jungle and the mosquitoes could take more lives than gunpowder. They knew, too, that the "battling bastards" had been living on half rations since New Year's Day. Time, therefore, would tell. In the phrase of the day, "an old carp in a large pond must be fished patiently."

For two months, February and March 1942, action on the Bataan front remained suspended while hunger and disease did their work. By March a thousand Filamericans a week were dropping out of the lines on sick call. By the end of March the U.S. field hospitals in southern Bataan contained 12,500 patients and could handle no more. In the meanwhile, Operations Chief Hattori had written a new plan of attack and was waiting for the troops who would execute it to be released from Japanese campaigns elsewhere.

MacArthur cabled home plea after plea for reinforcements, ammunition, or at least food. He could not believe that the Pacific fleet was now too weak to escort a few convoys through to the Philippines. He could not believe that Washington would dare to write off his entire force of 112,500 men. That was 6,000 men more than the number of U.S. servicemen who had died in the whole course of World War I. It seemed incredible to him that President Roosevelt could afford politically to begin World War II with such a loss—not while sending military aid across the Atlantic to England.

MacArthur had sworn publicly that the United States would defend the Philippines. He had buoyed up Filipino morale and loyalty with a flood of false promises. Now he found himself as utterly humiliated as General Honma. One of his former staff officers, Brigadier General Dwight D. Eisenhower, had the ear of Chief of Staff General George C. Marshall in Washington. Eisenhower, by his own account, had "studied dramatics under MacArthur for five years in Washington and four in the Philippines." He did not admire MacArthur's political methods of generalship and he took a cool East-Coast view of American commitments in Asia. The menace of the Swastika impressed him far more than that of the Rising Sun.

In the opening days of the war Eisenhower conducted a staff study for General Marshall, assessing over-all U.S. war objectives and priorities. In his report Eisenhower concluded that it was too late to help the men on Bataan and that, if Germany were to be defeated swiftly, no effective U.S. military pressure could be applied in Southeast Asia until at least 1943. The best that could be done immediately was to hold Australia. U.S. Navy staff officers concurred. They could send a few submarine loads of medical supplies to Bataan and Corregidor but no surface vessels: no convoys of troops, bullets, or food.

So it was that "the battling bastards of Bataan" were left to die. Only a sentimentalist, who saw the curses some of them later wrote against their native America on the walls of death cells in Japanese prisons, could question the logic of the decision made to sacrifice them. On the other hand it would be difficult for anyone to maintain that their lives might not have been sold more dearly on some other, better supplied defense line closer to Australia.

RETREAT FROM MALAYA

While the defenders of Bataan were winning the battle of bullets and beginning to lose the war against ill health and hunger, Hirohito's forces elsewhere gained steady ground by assault alone. On January 23, a Japanese amphibious force landed at Balikpapan on the southeastern coast of Borneo and captured the last of Borneo's oil fields. As at Tarakan, Kuching, Lutong, Miri, and Seria in previous weeks, the wells were burning and the derricks had been dynamited. It would take months to put out the fires and start pumping oil again. With the taking of Balikpapan, however, the major ports of Borneo and Celebes were all in Japanese hands, and a huge wedge had been driven down the center of Indonesia, reaching more than half the way from the southern Philippines to Australia, and separating Java and Sumatra in the west from New Guinea in the east.

That same day, January 23, a force of Japanese marines backed by carriers from Admiral Nagumo's Pearl Harbor task force landed on the Pacific side of New Guinea, in Australian territory, and seized the strategic harbor of Rabaul at the eastern tip of the big Taiwan-sized island of New Britain. From Rabaul southeast stretched a dagger of islands—the Solomons, the New Hebrides, and New Zealand—through which all U.S. convoys to Australia would have to pass. Control of the air in the Rabaul area might make it possible to establish forward fields in the Solomons and New Hebrides and so isolate Australia. Indeed, only the lack of a long-range bomber like the Flying Fortress prevented Japan from cutting the sea-lanes to Australia immediately. The landing at Rabaul was contested by a handful of Australians, and soon Japanese workmen were busy extending the Rabaul airstrip. In the weeks ahead they were to make Rabaul such a fortress that U.S. offensives later bypassed it, leaving it behind, a starving enclave which marked the high-water of imperial fortunes.

On that same fateful day, January 23, British Lieutenant General

Percival decided that he must abandon Malaya and retreat to the island of Singapore. Ever since Colonel Tsuji, his panzers, and his bicycle troops had pierced the Jitra line in northern Malaya six weeks earlier, withdrawal to new lines had become a dispiriting weekly routine for the British forces. In the course of the backward march, 20,000 of Percival's Indian troops, who had manned the front lines in northern Malaya, had been left behind in pockets and had surrendered. In southern Malaya Percival had shored up the lines by throwing in his Australian division.

The Australians had fought well. They had taken the offensive, infiltrated, ambushed, and dispelled the growing notion that the Japanese were peculiarly, demonically, at home in the jungle. In the last ten days the Australians had inflicted heavier losses on Yamashita's men than they had suffered earlier or would suffer later. With another division as good as the Australians, Percival might have held the line, for by now the Japanese attackers were themselves hungry, footsore, and sick. But gaps in the Australian position were plugged with Indian troops who had already been chased south for 400 miles. The plugs broke and Percival had no choice but to fall back on Singapore.

The Australian troops, for the most part, were disappointed, because they were still fresh and had so far outfought the Japanese. Nevertheless they pulled back and with the help of English and Scots companies succeeded in re-establishing a final line across the southern tip of the Malayan peninsula. Some of the British companies had been used repeatedly to stiffen resistance upcountry; others were now brought up to the front for the first time. Behind the new holding line, the spent Indian forces were withdrawn across a stone causeway onto Singapore Island. The Australians, fighting from rubber tree to rubber tree, followed. The honor of bringing up the rear was accorded to the ninety survivors of a battered Scots regiment, the Argylls, who backed into Singapore at dawn on February 1 with their bagpipes intoning "Highlan' Laddie" and "Jeannie with the Light Brown Hair." At 8 A.M., the landward end of the massive 70-foot-wide stone causeway connecting Singapore with Malaya was hurled into the air by dynamite.

The British naval base was now supposed to be a self-sufficient fortress. Only 300 feet of broken causeway and open water, however, separated it from the Malayan shore. Nothing but trenches and barbed wire defended the beaches across from that shore, and the big guns of the fortress, as Winston Churchill would later complain ruefully, were all pointed south, out to sea, in the opposite direction to that from which the Japanese were attacking.

On the beleaguered island the British still had over 100,000 troops, including recently arrived reinforcements, and enough fuel oil and ammunition to supply both the Japanese Army and Navy for months. In addition the island was packed with native residents and refugees. Theoretically

General Percival still had more than enough power to beat back the Japanese invaders. In practice he would find his force of numbers an encumbrance.

General Yamashita, by comparison, still had only 60,000 troops in his front line and not enough heavy artillery and shells to subdue Singapore by bombardment. Unless he struck quickly, British morale might revive and remaining British strength begin to realize its potential. The brilliant Japanese campaign might turn into a costly, protracted positional battle.

Yamashita extracted a herculean effort from his engineering and logistics officers. Every capable soldier and every working gun left behind in the jungles was brought down the shell-pocked roads and over the half-blown, half-repaired bridges to the shore of the Johore Strait between Malaya and Singapore. Only four days after the British withdrawal across the causeway, Yamashita had assembled enough cannon and ammunition in the tip of Malaya to begin a softening-up bombardment. Necessary shells and even a few large-caliber railway guns were brought in over the quickly repaired tracks of the Bangkok-Singapore line. The Japanese naval air force, flying in close support from freshly captured airstrips only a dozen miles behind the new front, bombed and strafed Singapore without let or check.

General Yamashita personally directed the withering fire upon the streets of his objective from a glass-domed tower where he could see the effect of every explosion through his binoculars. The tower stood conspicuously on the northern side of the strait and might have been easily demolished by British gunners on the south side. The tower belonged, however, to the sultan of Johore. It was the private observatory attached to the sultan's palace. The sultan was one of the wealthiest men in the world. He dressed and spoke like an Englishman and had been most generous in helping British field hospitals in the weeks which had just passed. No British officer even considered the possibility of shelling his palace. No British officer knew that he was a close friend of Count Ohtani, Hirohito's mother's brother-in-law, or of Baron Tokugawa, the paymaster for Hirohito's lethal political plots in the early 1930's. General Yamashita and his staff made the exposed palace their headquarters at the insistence of Colonel Tsuji who had worked with Count Ohtani during the final planning for the Strike South on Taiwan the previous summer.

In effect, Yamashita had a third-hand invitation to use the palace from the sultan himself. The Japanese staff officers took care not to reveal their presence by lighting any fires in the palace stoves. Cold boiled rice was brought in to them from the rubber groves out back. There shell fragments flew and latex flowed, but on the palace lawns the British fire was conspicuously accurate in that it disturbed not so much as a divot.

Haunting the glass-domed observatory and subsisting on cold food, General Yamashita was able to know more about what was happening on the Malayan side of Singapore Island than his British opposite numbers at their headquarters on the seaward side. By telephone he and Tsuji directed Japanese gunfire not so much at British entrenchments as at the geometric lines of communications wire which connected them. By February 8 many British units were already isolated and many British officers and engineers were working desperately to maintain touch with General Percival's headquarters.

On the night of February 8, shortly after dark, Japanese troops in small boats began crossing Johore Strait. General Percival might have flooded the strait with burning oil, but he had not expected the Japanese attack so soon and his engineers were not ready. By dawn several thousand Japanese were ashore on the island, overrunning positions and taking prisoners.

Having landed, the Japanese troops drove through the Australian defense sector and made for Bukit Timah heights and the life-blood reservoirs of Singapore which Hirohito had inspected twenty years earlier. The story of Hong Kong was about to be repeated, but on a larger scale.

SINGAPORE'S AGONY

First light on February 9 discovered the men of the Japanese 5th and 18th divisions inching forward through Australian entanglements on the northwest coast of Singapore Island. In the armor-plated Imperial Headquarters shed on the north edge of the palace woods in Tokyo it was already 7:30 A.M., and sleep-deprived staff officers were anxiously preparing themselves to deliver the morning operations briefing to the Emperor. Information from the Singapore beachhead was fragmentary and confused. To make matters worse Operations Section Chief Hattori, who ordinarily fielded the most difficult of the Emperor's questions, was away in the Philippines, conveying the imperial reprimand to General Honma and writing a new plan for the reduction of Bataan and Corregidor. Hirohito, who remembered every ridge and promontory along the north coast of Singapore from his circumnavigation of the island by yacht in 1921, was sure to be full of detailed queries. In addition he would be looking forward and asking whether the Army and Navy had yet written their position papers about the future.

On February 4, five days earlier, Hirohito had emphasized to a liaison conference between the government and high command that he wanted to follow the military success of the Strike South with a two-fold effort: militarily, to "expand the perimeter of Japanese occupation" and to "prepare for a long-term aggressive war of victory"; and diplomatically, to be ready for any Allied peace feelers which would make possible a quick peace settlement on Japanese terms. The staff officers in the headquarters shed were not united in their interpretation of the imperial wishes. The naval officers wanted to push on to an invasion of Australia. The Army officers preferred a quick peace but were ready to commit themselves to the conquest of Burma and the invasion of New Guinea.

As anticipated Hirohito called for his briefing early that morning and protracted it with question after question for many hours. In the course of the morning he approved the next day, February 10, as sailing date for Japan's Sumatra invasion fleet; he authorized the Army to proceed with the conquest of Burma and to start planning the conquest of New Guinea; he asked the Navy to pursue plans for the final destruction of the U.S. Pacific Fleet and the interdiction of U.S.-Australian supply routes.

When the staff officers' ordeal was at last over, in the post meridiem, Hirohito held Chief of Staff Sugiyama for a final tête-à-tête. Curiously enough, this private conversation was the only one in the entire day of which an official record has survived and been published. In it the ebullient Hirohito indulged in some ominous belly-talk by referring to a Chinese warlord named Yen Hsi-shan.

General Yen—who would ultimately die in Taiwan with the title of "senior advisor" to Chiang Kai-shek—was known in the late 1920's and early 1930's as "the model governor of Shansi." He had graduated from military academy in Tokyo in 1909 and had long been considered by Japanese leaders as a protégé who might be used as a rival to Chiang Kai-shek. In 1928, when Chiang had first kicked at his Japanese traces, Hirohito's advisors had briefly contemplated abandoning Chiang and raising up Yen in his stead. It had been partly to impress Yen and give him time to reconsider his allegiances that Hirohito's troops had delayed the "northern march" of Chiang Kai-shek in 1928 by intervening from the Tsingtao Leasehold and massacring 7,000 KMT partisans in the town of Tsinan.

Yen, in 1928, had served the peaceful interests of his Shansi peasants by insisting on remaining neutral. He had again made much the same decision in the fall of 1937 when the Japanese Army entered Shansi. Mao Tse-tung's troops contested the entry and inflicted a temporary but bloody check to the Japanese forces at the battle of Ping-hsing-kuan Pass. After the battle, Yen refused to attack the retreating columns of Mao's army from the rear and persisted, once again, in maintaining his neutrality. In reprisal on November 7, 1937, elements of Japan's 5th Division, under the command of Captain Tsuji Masanobu—the same who was now the master planner of the Singapore campaign—massacred the inhabitants of Yen's home stronghold in the Shansi mountains. Yen, who was elsewhere with his troops, had then replied by affirming that the men of Shansi would stand with Chiang Kai-shek and the cause of China.

Ever since 1937 Japan had continued off and on to negotiate for Yen's support. A clerk in the offices of the General Staff kept a Yen file. At one time or another a dozen aspiring Japanese captains and majors in the

Intelligence Department had proposed use of Yen for "settling the China Incident." The puppet governor of Japanese-occupied China, Wang Ching-wei, had written uncounted letters to Yen, asking him as an old school friend to reconsider his position—all to no avail.

By 1941 Japanese hopes for Yen had become a bad joke and his name, in World War II planning, had become a code word for certain acts of terror, butchery, and reprisal which were seen as possible necessities in the "pacification" of Southeast Asia. This new meaning had first attached it-self to Yen's name in a General Staff discussion of the problem of the overseas Chinese. The expatriate Chinese merchants of Singapore, Manila, Batavia, and Surabaja had long contributed money and influence to Chiang Kai-shek's cause and it was foreseen that they would continue to play a subversive role in the conquered Co-Prosperity Sphere. An anonymous staff officer had suggested "the Yen Hsi-shan treatment" for them, and by extension Yen's name had come to cover all reprisals which were visualized in connection with the Strike South. It was inevitable that, here and there, an example would have to be made of Western colonials, so as to destroy their face in the eyes of the natives. It was inevitable, too, that the natives themselves might sometimes have to be intimidated.

Against this semantic background, on February 9, 1942, when Hiro-hito detained Chief of Staff Sugiyama after the exhausting morning briefing, the Emperor's in-camera remarks struck Sugiyama as particu-larly noteworthy.

"The Chungking government," said Hirohito, "seems to be weakening. Isn't it about time that Yen Hsi-shan came over to our side? What's happened to that operation since last time?"

Not for nothing was Chief of Staff Sugiyama called "the bathroom door." He was proud of his reputation for noncommittal belly-talk and now he chose his words carefully, punctuating them with grunts and ex-pressive pauses.

"The Yen Hsi-shan operation," he said, "is a continuing and repeated thing. Looking back on its history, one sees that a Yen, in Chinese fashion, seeks to stretch time, look for fair weather, and gain the best possible terms from us. I'm afraid that, on the whole, such an operation may be too hastily planned from the beginning. That was why Yen could take ad-vantage of us and give the impression that he had improved his position. From now on, however, since the over-all picture is expected to go on brightening for our side, the Yen side cannot be expected to initiate the moves. We are planning our handling of Yen Hsi-shan operations on that basis." [13]

"I see," said the Emperor—and went on to ask about operations in

---

[13] For lack of pronouns, singular-plural distinctions, and strong tenses, Sugiyama's Japanese was even more ambiguous than my English representation of it. I have tried to reproduce the flavor and sequence rather than a one-to-one word equivalence.

Kyongju, a town in Korea where there had been a massacre in the Chinese quarter during the months leading up to the Manchurian Incident. Sugiyama made it clear that he followed what the Emperor was getting at by replying that the "Kyongju operation" was being taken care of by the Japanese Army stationed in south China. An eavesdropper might have thought he understood the conversation but would have detected nothing irregular in it. Sugiyama, however, interleafed an unusual note to himself in his memoranda: "Since His Majesty is quick to see ahead of things and ask questions in detail, I would like to be better prepared to give impromptu answers to questions about secondary developments."

The guarded but suggestive imperial question about Yen Hsi-shan operations disturbed Sugiyama, troubled staff officers in the field, and finally brought pain and horror to thousands of Chinese, Indians, Englishmen, Australians, Filipinos, and Americans. The Emperor's remarks reflected his dissatisfaction with the repulse on Bataan and implied that, to keep the war on schedule, he wished extreme measures to be taken. In early planning the Army had promised to take Singapore by *Kigensetsu,* National Foundation Day, February 11. It was important to Hirohito's pride as high priest to have something to offer his ancestors that day, but with *Kigensetsu* only two days away and with the Japanese troops moving forward by inches out of their Singapore beachhead it was unlikely that the British fortress would fall on time.

Sugiyama withdrew from the Imperial Presence to discuss the situation that evening with his aides. The next morning, February 10, he dispatched a staff officer by plane to Saigon to explain the Emperor's state of mind to General Count Terauchi, the over-all Strike-South commander. Terauchi consulted with General Yamashita by phone and then reported back to Tokyo that the Emperor could celebrate *Kigensetsu* by announcing to the gods the capture of Bukit Timah, the central high point of Singapore which overlooked and commanded one of the weak points in the island's defenses, spotted by Hirohito twenty years earlier: namely, its reservoirs. The next morning Hirohito duly went to the white-pebbled courtyard of the ancestors in the palace woods and formally announced to them that the capture of Singapore was assured.

A few hours earlier, only just on time, Japanese troops had consummated an all-night offensive by storming the rain-forested summit of Bukit Timah heights. Spotters swarmed up into the high trees to direct fire against British positions around the three Singapore reservoirs beyond. On the far side of the reservoirs wound the paths of the Botanical Gardens where Hirohito had walked twenty years before and where A. R. Wallace, eighty years before, had launched the theory of evolution.

During the day the Japanese forces occupied the western shores of the reservoirs, and General Yamashita had twenty-nine boxes of leaflets dropped on Singapore declaring that further resistance, no matter how heroic, would be useless. General Percival ordered a counterattack. Both he and Yamashita committed their best remaining troops to a desperate hand-to-hand combat which raged around the reservoirs for the next thirty-six hours. The reiterated shock of shell-burst and demolitions kept ears deaf and minds numb. Hot humid weather left uniforms limp and dark. Only the pungency of cordite and sweet rot of corpses masked the pervading sour smell of sweat. A pall of smoke from burning oil tanks hung between the island and the sky.

After dark on February 12, while the issue of the battle for the reservoirs still remained in doubt, Japanese divisional staff officers met with General Yamashita at his advanced headquarters a few hundred yards behind the lines. All had heard of the Emperor's impatience and all were exhausted by their efforts to give the Emperor better satisfaction. Some were wounded and some nodded and dozed in spite of themselves. The planner of the campaign, Colonel Tsuji, however, remained as demonically on edge as ever. He urged all to expend themselves utterly and hinted that he was relaying his exhortations directly from Prince Mikasa, Hirohito's brother. Tsuji later described in a book the situation as he then saw it:

> Our Army was now deployed over the whole front and the strategic position seemed to reach a climax when we received a signal from General Headquarters. "On 15 February an officer attached to the Court of the Emperor will be dispatched to the battlefield. We can postpone the visit if the progress of your Army's operations makes it desirable to do so. We wish to hear your opinion."
>
> There were some who said, "Let us welcome him," and others who argued "We must postpone the visit of the Emperor's envoy for a little while"; and so opinions were divided into two camps.
>
> Once previously during the China Incident I had been in a similar position when conducting military operations in Shansi together with the Itagaki group. During a bitterly contested battle for the reduction of Taiyuan Sheng on 7 November, Shidei, the aide-de-camp to the Emperor, arrived on the battlefield. I immediately began to think of the reduction of the mountain stronghold of Yen Hsi-shan.
>
> After a general discussion we unanimously resolved: "On the fifteenth day of February the enemy will positively surrender to the power of the august Emperor." We drafted these words as a telegram of welcome to the Emperor's envoy.

The next morning, February 13, Colonel Tsuji began a sixty-hour day of sleepless activity. At daylight a fresh note was dropped on General Percival's Fort Canning headquarters, couched in effusive, uncertain English, demanding surrender, promising leniency, threatening reprisals. In the afternoon, when Percival failed to respond, Tsuji made his shell-spattered way to the forward headquarters of the 18th Division, commanded by Lieutenant General Mudaguchi Renya, a loyal and sympathetic officer who as a colonel four years earlier had commanded the Japanese forces at Marco Polo Bridge and had touched off the war with China. The understanding General Mudaguchi put Tsuji in the hands of a dependable combat team which could take him beyond the front. A few hours later this team emerged from the trees behind the Alexandra Barracks Hospital, one of the two functioning medical units left in Singapore, and bayoneted to death 323 of the hospital personnel including 230 of the patients, many of them in their beds or on operating tables.

By the morning of February 14, Tsuji had seen to it that survivors of the Alexandra Barracks Hospital massacre were returning to British lines to explain what might happen to everyone in Singapore if General Percival did not surrender soon. Percival had over 100,000 fighting men and more than a million civilians under his charge. He got the message that afternoon, slept on it that night, attended an Anglican communion service early the next morning, Sunday, and then called a meeting of his unit commanders to discuss hopes and chances. Only five days earlier Percival had relayed to these same men a stern and inspiring Order of the Day:

> It is certain that our troops on Singapore Island greatly outnumber any Japanese that have crossed the straits. We must defeat them. Our whole fighting reputation is at stake and the honour of the British Empire. The Americans have held out in the Bataan Peninsula against far greater odds, the Russians are turning back the picked strength of the Germans, the Chinese with almost complete lack of modern equipment have held the Japanese for 4½ years. It will be disgraceful if we yield our boasted fortress of Singapore to inferior enemy forces.
>
> There must be no thought of sparing the troops or the civilian population. . . .

Since this order had been issued, the Japanese had continued to advance despite their numbers. General Percival's commanders now knew that neither they nor their men could match the uncanny performance of the canny veterans flung against them. In discipline, morale, initiative, co-ordination, weapons handling, and determination, Yamashita's picked troops had shown themselves superior. In a week all the defenders of Singapore, military and civilian, would die of thirst or bayonet wounds if they did not surrender now.

Fatigue, decimation, and shortage of ammunition might temporarily check the Japanese if the British forces could all resolve to die fighting, but experience had shown that badly mauled Japanese units always sprang back to life with an infusion of well-trained replacements. There were some Japanese units which had stormed position after position yet had remained at full strength, with unimpaired efficiency, throughout the whole 700-mile course of the Japanese advance from Thailand. By comparison, the quality of British units had steadily deteriorated. Another day or two of attrition would leave only the born fighters and survivors who could escape as individuals, fugitives, guerrillas, outlaws.

Percival's officers agreed to give up. That afternoon General Percival himself carried the white flag to the slope of Bukit Timah, where, in a Ford factory chosen by General Yamashita for the occasion, Great Britain surrendered her Far Eastern naval base. Percival in shirt and shorts and Yamashita in Kwantung Army tunic, leggings, and boots sat down at a table. Percival pleaded for conditions. Yamashita barked that there would be no conditions. Percival bowed his head and whispered the word unconditional. The oft-described scene came to an end at 7:50 P.M. Forty minutes later the guns stopped firing. Nature lovers noted that the silence was unearthly in its completeness. Singapore's rich bird fauna had flown the battleground and did not bring back so much as a twitter to the island until two dawns later. Historians have said that during the birds' absence the Western colonialism of Alexander, Richard the Lion-Hearted, Vasco da Gama, Columbus, Magellan, Tasman, Cooke, Raleigh, Clive, and Raffles found its quietus.

On Singapore and in Malaya, about 60,000 Japanese front-line troops took prisoner over 130,000 British troops: some 15,000 Australians, 35,000 Scots and Englishmen, 65,000 Indians, and 15,000 assorted local reservists, most of them Malays. The captives were herded into camps and prisons to endure more than three years of scornful abuse, brutality, slavery, and starvation. As soon as they were behind barbed wire the rest of the Yen Hsi-shan operation was carried out. The Japanese secret police screened the entire overseas Chinese population in Singapore and after a massive but cursory investigation, which lasted less than a month, selected between 5,000 and 7,000 undesirables to serve as an example for the rest. The most important of the hostages were killed by the secret police themselves through every graduated form of humiliation, terror and torture known to man. The less important were turned over to Army execution squads for use in bayonet practice, sword demonstrations, or the amusement of the troops.

SWEET SMELL OF THE INDIES

As soon as the "Chinese Massacres" were well in hand in Singapore Hirohito's favored staff officer, Colonel Tsuji, was to accompany a regiment of the 5th Division to the Philippines where he would carry on with the Yen Hsi-shan operation, this time against Americans. In the meanwhile however, Tokyo and the Imperial Court were celebrating the capture of Singapore.

Lord Privy Seal Kido, who understood well the imperial temperament had warned Hirohito as early as February 5, ten days before the fall of

Singapore, not to fall prey to a mood of exultation. "The Great East Asia War," he said, "will not end this easily. In the final analysis there is only one road to peace and that is to fight the war so thoroughly that we include in it the process of reconstruction after the battles are over." The Emperor was impressed by Kido's caution and, according to Kido's diary, "leaked his heart on the matter to the Empress."

Five days later, on February 10, the eve of his National Foundation Day report to the ancestors, Hirohito had relayed his awakened doubts to Prime Minister Tojo:

> I presume that you have given due consideration not to lose any opportunity for ending this conflict. It would be undesirable to prolong the war without purpose for that would only increase the suffering of commoners. I want you to keep this in mind and do everything possible for peace. I want you to take into account the present and future sensibilities of the Anglo-Americans, whom we cannot ignore. It will also be necessary for you to ascertain the Russo-German relationship and look forward to its outcome. At the same time we must not fail to obtain, to the fullest extent possible, the resources of the South. I fear that the quality of our troops will deteriorate if the war is prolonged.

The day Singapore finally fell, February 15, 1942, the cautious Kido was not summoned by the Emperor. Instead Prime Minister Tojo phoned during the evening to read Kido the telegram of victory from General Yamashita. The next morning, however, in a brief audience which lasted from 10:50 to 11, Hirohito informed Kido that, to end the war, Prime Minister Tojo was recommending an envoy to the Vatican. Hirohito explained the religious and other qualifications which such an envoy should have and asked Kido to find a man who would fit them. Kido promised to do his best and then "extended congratulations to the Emperor regarding the Singapore victory."

Hirohito, according to Kido's diary, was "very well pleased and said, 'You may think, Kido, that I harp on this tune, but I tell you again that it is my sincere belief that the excellent war results with which we are repeatedly favored, although they may seem to stem from divine providence, are really the results of our own providence and of the thorough research with which we did our planning.' "

Kido wept with gratitude at the compliment and bowed his way, snuffling theatrically, from the Imperial Presence.

The days which followed were stuffed with "excellent war results"—enough to turn a lesser conqueror's head. Only long training and sage advisors kept Hirohito's feet on the ground.

On February 7, Hirohito had watched newsreels showing the use of a recently formed paratroop corps in the invasion of the sparsely populated, little-defended Dutch island of Celebes. After seeing the film, he had approved the use of parachutists in large numbers for the capture of densely populated Sumatra. Now on February 16, the paratroopers had scored a success. Two days before they had dropped in regimental strength behind Dutch lines near Palembang in southern Sumatra and now all Dutch and British forces in Sumatra were evacuating the huge island and crossing the Sunda Strait to the central island and administrative center of the Dutch East Indies, Java. Sumatra was larger than California and twice as populous. It had been captured by 10,000 troops.

While the Army mopped up in Sumatra, the Navy extended to the north coast of Australia the wedge it had been driving through central Indonesia. On February 19, Marines landed almost unopposed on the lovely, lazy tropic isle of Bali, off the east end of Java. Nearby, over the eastern Javanese city of Surabaja, twenty-three Zero aces of the Misty Lagoon were winning air superiority over the Dutch East Indies in a spectacular dogfight with about fifty P-40's, P-36's, and other outmoded Allied pursuit planes. Seven hundred miles farther east, other naval forces were establishing a beachhead on the Connecticut-and-Massachusetts-sized, half-Dutch, half-Portuguese island of Timor which lay only 300 miles off the Australian shore.

Also, on that same day, February 19, Admiral Nagumo's Pearl Harbor task force, standing off Timor, launched a devastating air strike on the northern Australian city of Darwin. Flying at the limit of their range, 189 of the crack bomb crews trained at the Misty Lagoon Air Station succeeded in sinking a U.S. destroyer, four U.S. transports, one British tanker, and four Australian freighters in Darwin harbor; in knocking out twenty-three Allied planes, ten of them beyond repair; and in demolishing several of Darwin's finest buildings, killing 238 Australians and wounding about 300 more. In exchange only five of the Japanese aces were lost. The other 184 crews returned from their mission, having posted a record for efficient use of gasoline and explosives.

In the fearful week which followed, Australians braced themselves for invasion. The Australian army was already committed in England, Africa, India, and the crumbling fortresses of the British Empire in the Far East. At home only 7,000 Australian regulars remained to fight—less than half the number which had just surrendered in Singapore. Man, woman, and child, the entire Australian population, dispersed over an area five sixths that of the United States, outnumbered the trained men of the Japanese Army by only five to one.

Admiral Yamamoto, the hero of Pearl Harbor, wanted to land an expeditionary force on the undefended north coast of Australia and at least terrorize the subcontinent with a division or two. General Yamashita, the hero of Singapore, seconded Yamamoto and offered to lead the invasion himself. Despite the vastness of Australian distances, he felt that it would be feasible to land a division almost immediately at Darwin and thrust half-

and fast down the north-south railroad and road links toward Adelaide and Melbourne on the south coast. Later, he supposed, a second division could be put ashore on the east coast to leapfrog its way from port to port down toward Sydney. Tough as they might be, not even Australian civilians, he felt, would be any match for disciplined troops. Moreover, he thought that the clean, hygiene-conscious Japanese soldier would perform far better in the antiseptic wastes of Australia than in the septic jungles of Burma and New Guinea.

General Tojo, the prime minister, and most of the elders in the General Staff spoke against the Yamamoto-Yamashita plan. Admiral Nagumo's air raid on Darwin had been a successfully improvised spectacular, but full-scale invasion was another matter. The General Staff had no well-considered contingency plans for such an operation. In the Australian barrens, a Japanese force would have to depend entirely on supplies from the rear. The Japanese merchant fleet was already taxed to the utmost without taking on new assignments. Also, if the United States became alarmed and poured Flying Fortresses into Sydney, it would be difficult to maintain air superiority. On the Australian badlands Japanese columns would be fearfully vulnerable to long-range, high-level air attack.

On reviewing the arguments of both sides, Hirohito decided that the invasion of Australia could be postponed until after the conquest of Burma. In terms of global strategy and of dividing the world with Hitler, an advance toward India and the Middle East took precedence over the capture of the Australasian land's end.

Hirohito announced his decision with characteristic obliqueness at a liaison conference in the Imperial Headquarters shed on February 23. He probably knew, through Japanese monitoring of Corregidor's radio traffic, that President Roosevelt, the day before, had directed MacArthur to leave Corregidor and assume command of Allied forces in Australia. He certainly knew that almost 20,000 British troops in Burma had just surrendered or been surrounded after the Battle of Sittang Bridge on the road to Rangoon. As he had done with increasing frequency of late, Hirohito attended the liaison conference impromptu, embarrassing his deputies and forcing them, without preparation, to deliberate in the Imperial Presence. Instead of listening to the discussion, however, as he sometimes did, he pointedly ignored the burning issue of an expedition to Australia and manifested his disinterest in it by asking two explicit questions about unimportant side issues.

His first question concerned relations with the neutral Portuguese in eastern Timor. It suggested that he wanted Portugal kept friendly so that she might act as a channel of mediation in Japan's efforts to seek a peace settlement. His second question had to do with the stabilization of currencies in Japan's rapidly multiplying conquered territories. It indicated a desire to consolidate gains already made before embarking on new conquests. The liaison conference responded by promising to find ways of staying on good terms with the Portuguese in Timor and of saving Filipinos, Malays, and Indonesians from runaway inflation.[14]

After the liaison conference of February 23, Hirohito did not meet again with his ministers for twelve days. In those twelve days all the scattered Japanese landings in the islands off southeastern Asia were fused to form a single massive addition to the Empire. Japan's new perimeter reached to within easy flying range of Australia and except for the U.S. forces on Bataan and Corregidor, 1,600 miles behind the front lines, it contained only guerrilla pockets of resistance. The keystone to the vast addition was Java, the densely populous administrative center of Indonesia.

On February 25, Field Marshal Sir Archibald Wavell of Britain, who had been given charge of combined British, U.S., and Dutch forces in Indonesia, dissolved his command as hopeless and withdrew his headquarters to India. Most British and some U.S. forces proceeded to withdraw with him. The Dutch, who had contributed several of their ships and planes to the defense of Singapore, fought on, embittered and almost alone. On the sea they were allowed to keep command of the U.S. heavy cruiser *Houston,* the British heavy cruiser *Exeter,* the Australian light cruiser *Perth,* three British destroyers, and four old U.S. four-stack destroyers. These they combined with two light cruisers and two destroyers of their own in a fourteen-ship fleet for the defense of Java. Two Japanese invasion armadas, of forty-one and fifty-six transports, plus escort vessels, were approaching the island from the north across the Java Sea.

The Dutch admiral, Rear Admiral Karel Doorman, sallied out with his squadron to attack the smaller of the two Japanese fleets. He engaged it on February 27 and in a seven-hour action lost two of his cruisers, three of his destroyers, and his own life. Next day the remnants of his fleet tried to escape to Australia through the Lombok and Sunda Straits at the east and west ends of Java. Shadowed by Japanese aircraft and pursued by Japanese surface vessels, all three of the remaining Allied cruisers and two of the destroyers were ambushed and sunk. Only the U.S. quartet of antiquated four-stack destroyers succeeded in getting away. The ill-conceived Battle of the Java Sea, the largest fleet action since Jutland, was over. The Allies had sacrificed five cruisers, five destroyers, and about 3,000 lives. None of the Japanese warships had sustained more than minor damage, which could be repaired at sea.

Following the battle, elements of the Japanese 2d and 38th divisions

---

[14] The financial solution was curious and ingenious. It was resolved that the paper scrip of Japanese occupation currencies would be convertible into yen but that, henceforth, there would secretly be two kinds of paper yen with separate sets of serial numbers: one redeemable in precious metals and circulated only in Japan; the other worth nothing except as a promissory note against the future of the Japanese Empire.

landed in western Java, and elements of the 48th Division and 56th Brigade in eastern Java. They made short work of the 15,000 Allied regulars and 40,000-odd reservists and volunteers in the Java defense force. After a week of confused skirmishing, the Dutch governor general of the Indies, on March 8, agreed to capitulate to the Japanese 16th Army commander, Lieutenant General Imamura Hitoshi. The formal instrument of surrender was signed by the Dutch four days later.

Also on March 8 fell Rangoon, the capital of Burma. The last trainload of dispirited refugees pulled out toward Mandalay in the north even as the first Japanese soldiers were entering the city, unopposed from the south. Since Rangoon was the only port of any consequence in Burma, the 50,000-odd Anglo-Indians of the British Army there were now effectively cut off from help except from China. Chiang Kai-shek sent three divisions to their rescue, and over the next two and a half months, the "Burma Corps" fought its way backwards along jungle tracks and river banks to the Indian and Chinese frontiers. Thirteen thousand men of the British Army were lost along the way. The Japanese 15th Army, of two divisions and about 35,000 front-line fighters, lost 5,000 men.

On March 7, the day before the Dutch surrender and the fall of Rangoon, a liaison conference in Tokyo formally adopted a plan called "Basic Principles of Future Operations." This plan responded to Hirohito's feelings that the war must continue to be prosecuted aggressively but that Japan must not overextend herself or neglect the consolidation of the immense territories which she had already conquered. Specifically the plan called for further Army advances in the Burma theater, with a view to the possible conquest of India; further Army-Navy probes in the New Guinea-Solomons area, in order to cut Pacific supply lines and isolate Australia; and further action by Admiral Yamamoto against the U.S. fleet in the central Pacific.

During the morning of March 9, the day after the Dutch surrender and the fall of Rangoon, Hirohito realized that, for the last forty-eight hours, he had been neglecting his civilian advisors. He at once telephoned Lord Privy Seal Kido at his office in the Imperial Household Ministry in the Outer Palace and asked him to come on over to the Imperial Library in the palace woods for a chat. Kido hurried to respond and later wrote in his diary:

> The Emperor was beaming like a child. "The fruits of war," he said, "are tumbling into our mouth almost too quickly. The enemy at Bandung on the Java front announced their surrender on the seventh and now our Army is negotiating for the surrender of all forces in the Netherlands East Indies. The enemy has surrendered at Surabaja and also, on the Burma front, has given up Rangoon." He was so pleased that I hardly knew how to give him a congratulatory answer.

Hirohito had a right to feel complacent. More than a month ahead of schedule his myrmidons had accomplished all that they had promised to accomplish and more than he had been sure they ever could accomplish. A month short of his forty-second birthday, he found the goals of his youth suddenly realized. It would take weeks of buoyant weariness and happiness before he set his feet again upon the ground and acknowledged that the ancestors still required more of him.

FALL OF BATAAN

On March 11, two days after Hirohito had expressed his military euphoria to Kido, General and Mrs. MacArthur, with their four-year-old son Arthur, boarded a PT boat under cover of darkness and escaped from the besieged enclave of Bataan and Corregidor.[15] Before embarking MacArthur had taken pains to tell all who remained behind that he went with reluctance, at presidential orders. "I shall return," he said—an assurance which was to become his slogan for the next three years.

The accommodations provided for MacArthur in his escape were not the safest available. He might have gone by submarine as did a group of Army nurses from Corregidor almost two months later. Some say that he chose the PT boat himself for theatrical reasons; others that there was someone in logistics who hoped he would perish en route. In any case the spray-soaked dash through enemy lines was a genuine adventure for a man of sixty-two. It lasted thirty-six hours and took MacArthur and his family 600 miles: from Luzon in the northern Philippines to Del Monte on Mindanao in the southern Philippines. Most of the way lay along enemy-controlled shores, over enemy-controlled seas, under enemy-controlled skies. The PT boat had to crash through squalls and fifteen-foot waves. It passed within sight of a Japanese cruiser. Its skipper had to navigate most of the way in the dark.

[15] Hirohito that day added an odd footnote to history by having the liaison conference formulate an explicit policy for dealing with the large numbers of Jews who had been brought into the Empire with the acquisition of Singapore and Java. "With special exceptions," no Jews would be allowed to immigrate into the Empire in the future. Those already present would "be treated as nationals of the areas in which they reside, except that, due to their special racial characteristics, surveillance of their homes and businesses will be intensive and all pro-enemy activity on their part will be suppressed and eliminated." In other words, an Amsterdam Jew captured in Batavia would—despite his Dutch passport—be treated as an Indonesian rather than a Hollander. On the one hand he would be exempt from internment as an enemy national; on the other he could claim no protection under the rules of war. The object of the decision was "not to persecute the Jews" as that "would make propaganda for the United States" but to "select carefully those Jews who can be used for the Empire and give them appropriate treatment."

When MacArthur landed, exhausted, in Mindanao, he learned that he must wait a day for the four B-17 Flying Fortresses which had been sent for him from Australia. Only one of them arrived. Two of the others had turned back with engine trouble and the fourth had crashed into the ocean. The survivor, a battered veteran of three months of bombing missions, suffered from faulty brakes and inoperative turbosuperchargers. MacArthur refused to fly in it. He fired off angry messages to Washington and Sydney and waited for another two days while a more fitting fleet of three span-new B-17's were being flown up from Australia for him. In these on the night of March 16–17, he and his family and staff traversed the 1,400 miles of Japanese-controlled air to northern Australia.

Shortly after his arrival MacArthur asked for a press conference and told reporters:

> I am glad indeed to be in immediate co-operation with the Australian soldier. I know him well from World War days and admire him greatly. . . . I have every confidence in the ultimate success of our joint cause, but success in modern war requires something more than courage and willingness to die. It requires careful preparation. This means furnishing sufficient troops and sufficient materiel to meet the known strength of the potential enemy. No general can make something from nothing. My success or failure will depend primarily upon the resources which our respective governments place at my disposal. My faith in them is complete. In any event I shall do my best. I shall keep the soldier's faith.

In this statement—one of the most clear and honest of his career—the chastened MacArthur apologized for past mistakes to the men he had left behind and promised them vengeance. Theirs, however, would be the hunger, humiliations, filth, fever, torture, and despair of imprisonment, and theirs the curses against MacArthur and Roosevelt which would be found scribbled on death-cell walls when Japanese concentration camps were liberated three years later.[16]

On March 10, a few hours before MacArthur began his personal anabasis from Corregidor, British Foreign Secretary Right Honorable

---

[16] As a sixteen-year-old, suffering from dengue fever and malnutrition, I spent the first week of February 1945, after the U.S. liberation of Manila, in one of those cells in old Bilibid Prison. It was a room about 12 by 20 feet, solidly walled on the short sides and open to the air through iron gratings on the long sides. It was then a hospital ward for American civilian internees who had passed their first thirty-six months of Japanese imprisonment outside Baguio in the mountains to the north. I shared the room with five other fellow internee patients. A year earlier it had been stuffed with fifty to a hundred veterans of Corregidor with bashed limbs, malaria, and dysentery. I long studied a graffito on the wall above me reviling Roosevelt and MacArthur in obscene terms. The author, I was told, had died in the cell of hunger, thirst, and a general septicemia.

Anthony Eden delivered a speech in the House of Commons revealing and protesting to all the world that Japan had committed abominable atrocities on a wide scale in Hong Kong. Eden was probably moved to speak by Chiang Kai-shek's secret service agents who were reporting to Chungking that Japanese rapine was continuing at Singapore. Five thousand Chinese had been executed there as examples. Women and children evacuated from Singapore in small boats at the last minute had been strafed by Japanese planes and torpedoed by Japanese naval launches and submarines. A shipful of wounded men accompanied by sixty-four Australian nursing sisters had been sunk off Banka Island on the Sumatra coast. The wounded men who managed to get ashore were almost all bayoneted on the beach. Twenty-two of the nurses with them, landing in a lifeboat, were waded out into the surf and machine-gunned. A single survivor of the massacre, Sister Vivian Bullwinkel, was now in a prison camp in Sumatra.

On March 13, Lord Privy Seal Kido spoke to Hirohito about Eden's Hong Kong disclosures. Hirohito refrained from doing anything to prevent recurrences. It was the position of his uncles and some of his other Army advisors that the commission of atrocities fortified Japanese troops for the role they had to play and persuaded them that they must never surrender because, if they did, what they had done unto others would be done unto them.

On March 27, Chief of Staff General Sugiyama flew to Sumatra to "inspect the front" and unofficially to assess the prisoner-of-war situation there and in Singapore. Almost a quarter of a million civilian and military captives had fallen into Japanese hands. It was Sugiyama's mission to convey to all commanders Hirohito's feelings about prisoner treatment. To satisfy the outcry in the West and prevent Japan from seeming uncivilized, the prisoners must be put in regular camps and must be dealt with in an organized fashion. They must not, however, be pampered, any more than the common Japanese soldier. Nor must they, insofar as possible, become a financial burden upon the Empire. They must work for their board and lodging and must not be allowed to aid the Allied cause by escaping and becoming propagandists on Allied shortwave radio stations.

On April 3, Chief of Staff Sugiyama completed his inspection of the newly conquered Dutch East Indies and went on to the Philippines. There the time had come to fish out the carp in the pond and silence the subversive "Voice of Freedom" being broadcast every evening from transmitters on Bataan and Corregidor. The Filamerican defenders of the U.S. enclave in the heart of the Co-Prosperity Sphere had sat in foxholes for two months licking their wounds, subsisting on half rations and contracting malaria and bacillary dysentery.

While the U.S. forces had deteriorated, General Honma's command had been strengthened to make impossible any second miscalculation. His battered 16th Division and 65th Brigade had been restored to full strength in February with fresh replacement troops who were by now trained and integrated into the skeletal veteran units which had survived the January offensive. In addition some 15,000 men had been brought in from the crack 4th Division stationed at Osaka in Japan. The reserve force in Indochina had contributed about 11,000 men from the 21st Division. Colonel Tsuji, the planner of the Malayan campaign, had brought from Singapore an augmented regiment of his 5th Division veterans and another augmented regiment of volunteers from his 18th Division—in all about 20,000 troops of the highest quality.

In sum total Honma's 14th Army now numbered about 110,000 of the best front-line troops, supported by enough artillery to blast a breach in the Maginot Line. U.S. Major General Edward King's Bataan command, by comparison, consisted of just over 70,000 gaunt, listless, fever-wracked, dysentery-ridden gun-bearers. Only a quarter of them had ever considered themselves soldiers and of these less than half were still classified as "effectives." Even in this small fraction of fractions on whom General King most relied, morale was low. The men felt that they had already held out longer than any other Allied troops in the Far East. They had been abandoned and adjudged expendable. They wanted food and rest and they yearned for decent capture and imprisonment.

April 3, the day that Chief of Staff Sugiyama arrived in Manila, was Good Friday 1942. It was that day that the overwhelming Japanese forces gathered in northern Bataan began their offensive. The "Good Friday attack" ran ahead of its timetable and overachieved its objectives almost from the moment of its launching. The eastern half of the Filamerican line collapsed in the first twenty-four hours of fighting. A handful of relatively well-fed U.S. officers repeatedly halted routs and reformed lines by brandishing pistols. The men on the western half of the Filamerican line were ordered to make a counterattack on the Japanese flank. Only a few of the front-line troops even tried to obey the order. The rest felt themselves too weak from hunger and disease to drag themselves over the tops of their trenches.

On April 9, six days after the beginning of the Japanese offensive, Major General King was forced to acknowledge that the men on Bataan were no longer a fighting force and would soon be annihilated company by company. General Wainwright, whom MacArthur had left in over-all command on Corregidor, ordered him to go on fighting to the death. King could see no prospect of inflicting much damage on the enemy by sacrificing the 70,000 men under his command and so decided to disobey Wainwright's orders.

Under flag of truce King drove through the Japanese lines and sat down with General Honma's senior operations officer at a table set out in the open before the Lamao Experimental Farm Station. King asked that U.S. trucks, which were fueled and ready for the task, be allowed to move his men to the detention camps where the Japanese wished to imprison them.

"Surrender must be unconditional," said the interpreter.

"Will our troops be well treated?"

"We are not barbarians," snapped the interpreter.

On this slender reassurance, King handed over his pistol in token of Bataan's unconditional surrender.

THE DEATH MARCH

For the next twelve days the no-longer "battling bastards" were herded out of their foxholes and prodded forward, without benefit of transportation, toward the town of San Fernando, 60 miles away. Many of them staggered with weakness from the outset of the march. Before the march was over all of them staggered—all, that is, who still lived.

The word had gone out on the Japanese Army grapevine that General Wainwright, who still held out on Corregidor, must be shown what would happen to his men if he did not surrender quickly: that the Filipino people must be made to appreciate the toughness of their new masters and the utter humiliation of their old ones.

Some of the Japanese officers on Bataan protested that their men did not follow belly talk and suggestions and did not cause prisoners to die without explicit orders. Underlings of Colonel Tsuji telephoned several of these recalcitrant commanders and told them that the order to get rid of American prisoners stemmed from Imperial General H.Q. in the palace. A few commanders refused to be bullied by Colonel Tsuji's "influence" and insisted that they see the Emperor's order in writing. Tsuji never produced the written order, but the careers of officers who decided to ignore his directions did not prosper, and the career of Colonel Tsuji prospered exceedingly. Within the year he was back in the General Staff in Tokyo, meeting frequently with Hirohito as one of his closest advisors on military operations.

The responsibility for the Death March was later taken by General Honma and he was executed for it by MacArthur. At the time of the Death March, however, Honma was virtually a captive himself—of the staff officers who had been sent in from Tokyo to assist him and to repair the blunder he had made initially in letting the Bataan forces entrench themselves. Knowledgeable former members of the Japanese General Staff place the entire responsibility for the Death March on these unwanted helpers: on "Tsuji and the China gang," on "staff officers from Imperial

Headquarters," on "experts in Yen Hsi-shan operations." [17] After the war Hirohito's Army minions gave Honma the role of scapegoat and he accepted it because of his failure in Bataan before the Death March, not because of his titular authority during it. In effect, MacArthur, by an ironic twist which pleased his Japanese misinformants, had Honma sentenced to death for having been an inefficient enemy.

When the Death March began at Mariveles on the southern tip of Bataan, many Japanese officers who realized and opposed what was about to happen made a point of showing their disapproval in front of the common soldiers who were to be the executioners. Some of these dissident officers offered canteens of water and packs of cigarettes to marchers. Others stopped prisoners to ask if personal effects had been stolen from them, then slapped the faces of noncommissioned Japanese pilferers in order to return to the prisoners their wedding bands and watches. Still other Japanese officers went to the length of seeking out and publicly embracing tottering Americans whom they had known before the war at U.S. colleges. None of the Westernized Japanese officers, including General Honma, however, tried to countermand the secret orders which had been spread by Colonel Tsuji and his fellow staff officers. The orders seemed to be backed by imperial authority brought to Manila by the hand of Chief of Staff Sugiyama on April 3.

The guards assigned to escort the U.S. prisoners over the 60-mile course of the Death March were hardened veterans of the 16th Division. Almost all of them had been wounded in the first attacks on Bataan in January and early February. Many of their sergeants had officiated under Prince Asaka and Nakajima Kesago at the rape of Nanking in December–January 1937–38.

The whole concept of the Death March was infused with peculiarly Japanese notions of excuse, justification, and legality. None of the U.S. prisoners were taken out forthrightly and butchered as the Chinese captives had been at Nanking. Instead the sick and weary who fell out of step,

---

[17] Japanese officers tell no tales on one another but the membership of the "China gang" is well known from other sources and contexts. It consisted of General Staff intelligence officers who emerged from the plots of the early 1930's as protégés of Prince Higashikuni and Prince Asaka, and who went on to play important roles in the Marco Polo Bridge Incident and the rape of Nanking. Three of the most important of them involved in the Bataan Death March were: Major General Wachi Takaji, who in March 1942 was forced on Honma as his new chief of staff and who, in 1937, as chief of the Special Service Organ in Peking had arranged the Marco Polo Bridge Incident; Lieutenant General Mudaguchi Renya, who brought Honma his 18th Division reinforcements from Malaya, and who, in 1937, had commanded the Japanese regiment at Marco Polo Bridge; and finally "Kill-all-prisoners" Cho Isamu of the October Plot, the Nanking rape, the Lake Khasan Incident, and the 1945 last stand on Okinawa. In April 1942 Cho was a major general handling liaison between the headquarters of General Terauchi in Saigon and of General Honma in Manila.

either to relieve themselves or to catch a moment's rest, were cuffed with a fist or rifle butt. Once dazed and down, they were shouted orders in Japanese to resume their place in line and if they did not respond immediately they were stabbed with bayonets or shot in the head for desertion and disobedience. To encourage desertion the marchers were given little food and no water and led past farmyards and wells. When they broke for clean water they were shot. When they lapped at the polluted waters of carabao wallows and privy overflows they were allowed to drink their fill. Most of those who succumbed to such temptations died a few days later of severe, untreated intestinal infections.

Japanese witnesses at the trial of General Honma after the war insisted —without justification—that the rigors of the Death March were no different from those endured routinely by any Japanese soldiers in boot camp.[18] Western witnesses protested that the prisoners of Bataan before they began their 60-mile march were already sick men. In rebuttal the Japanese witnesses said smugly that, yes, everyone had been surprised by the weakness and malnutrition of the American captives. The American prosecutors at the trial correctly maintained that Honma's officers had known the American troops would be starving and had counted on that factor to make the Death March effective.

From San Fernando, the terminus of the Death March, the men of Bataan were transported another 40 miles north by rail to Camp O'Donnell, a swampy field of huts and tents surrounded by barbed wire, where most of the survivors were to spend their first six months of imprisonment. On the train ride to O'Donnell each boxcar was packed with over a hundred men—as tightly as Tokyo subway cars in rush hour. The steel doors were closed and there was no ventilation system. Sick men suffocated and died in the stench. Strong men rode standing on the bodies of their dead comrades.

Of the 70,000 "battling bastards" who had surrendered on April 9 only 54,000 arrived in Japanese custody at Camp O'Donnell. Between 2,000 and 3,000 of the 12,000 Americans who surrendered are known to have died during the march, and about 8,000 of the 58,000 Filipinos. Another 6,000 Filipinos, more or less, are believed to have dropped out of the Death March columns and survived. Some were allowed to escape in return for bribes. Some melted into the crowds of spectators at Lubao and San Fernando near the end of the march. Some dropped into roadside paddies and cane fields, played dead, and were spirited away by the peas-

[18] As an unnoticed boy, taking care of the trash and garbage at the Japanese guard house of Camp Holmes Internment Camp in the Philippines during the war, formed the impression that Japanese garrison life, except for Taiwanese and Korean in work battalions, was no harder than garrison life in the U.S. Army. The Japanese guards were better fed than their civilian counterparts at home and, through official Army brothels, better serviced sexually than their American counterparts in the field.

ants. A handful of American airmen and officers did the same and lived to lead guerrilla bands of fellow drop-outs in the years ahead.

The full horror of the Death March was best appreciated by those who brought up the rear. They saw the results of deeds which Japanese had never done to Japanese, which Germans had never done so publicly to Jews, which Western troops had not experienced since Khartoum or the Black Hole of Calcutta. Corpses and faded purple intestines were draped by the yard on Filipino farm fences. Open-mouthed bodies lay in puddles along the roadside ditches. Beheaded torsos leaned against walls, squatting frozen in their last act of toilet.

News of the great reprisal spread quickly from the Filipino barrios in northern Bataan. In the last stretches of the march, the streets of Lubao and San Fernando soon became lined with Filipino women bearing food, water, herbals, and bandages which were passed to the marchers despite the sternest efforts of their guards. Behind the peasant women wealthy Filipinos from Manila stood looking for their sons. In shops and cantinas deals were made with Japanese captains and sergeants which saved the lives of some of the Philippines' most prominent scions. The same deals greatly strengthened Japan's puppet government in the Philippines during the three years ahead.

Through Chief of Staff Sugiyama and through daily reading of secret police reports, Hirohito was at least indirectly responsible for the Death March and aware of its magnitude.[19] Japanese attuned to such delicate matters point to certain episodic sidelights in the Court records which suggest that Hirohito, at the time of the march, was feeling no regrets. On the contrary he was busy preparing fresh brutalities for other occupied areas and silencing objections from softhearted women in his Court circle.

On April 5, Hirohito approved the appointment of a certain Korematsu Junichi as chief secretary and effective regent for the civil administrator of the entire eastern half of the Co-Prosperity Sphere. It was an incredible choice. Korematsu was a mobster from the slums, one of those who organized shape-up bosses and controlled Japanese coolie labor. Lord Privy Seal Kido knew the man well and had long used him as a personal go-between and informant in dealings with the ultranationalistic gangs of the underworld. Now Korematsu would dispense his rough-and-ready street justice over the extended exurban neighborhood of Celebes, New Guinea, the Bismarcks, the Marianas, the Carolines, the Marshalls, and the Gilbert Islands.

[19] If Hirohito did not issue secret orders for the Death March in advance, he should, at the least, have known of it in time to save most of its 10,000 victims. Even assuming that somehow, during the twelve days of the march, he shirked his reading chores and cut himself off from his usual sources of information, then he would still have to be held accountable, because a year later when the U.S. government allowed the Death March to be publicized throughout the world, Hirohito ordered no investigation, no courts-martial, and no punishment of the executioners.

Under Korematsu's administration villages and sub-tribes of inarticulate or uninfluential island "cannibals" would disappear without trace. They would be replaced by Japanese colonists who, later in the war, held banquets at which were served, literally, the barbecued limbs of shot-down American fliers. Little is known of this dark chapter in Japanese oppression, and Korematsu, its chief architect, went down with a torpedoed ship on his way home for a palace briefing in 1945.

On April 17, as the Death March neared its conclusion, Lord Privy Seal Kido was summoned to the seaside villa in Numazu at which Hirohito's handsome fifty-seven-year-old mother, the Empress Dowager Sadako, had lived in self-imposed, disapproving exile since three days before Pearl Harbor. She subjected Kido to a two-and-a-half-hour grilling on "the steps which had led to the war and subsequent expressions of brute military strength." Afterward Kido joined Hirohito who was in the neighborhood attending a fleet exercise. Lord and vassal, they went mushroom-picking together on the grounds of the Hayama imperial villa. In the course of the botanical ramble, Kido reported at length and in privacy on his conversation with the Queen Mother. Having heard him out, Hirohito abruptly left the pathway, entered the underbrush, and with his own hand plucked up a specimen of *Siler divaricatum* (or *Ledebouriella seserioides Wolff* as it is now classified). The root of this little herb, related to parsley and carrots, and called *bofu,* was much prized by old peasant ladies as a cure for the rheums and stiffnesses of their old men. Hirohito ceremoniously presented his specimen of it to Kido and delivered a brief factual disquisition on the pharmaceutical folklore surrounding it. Kido listened, laughed, abandoned his recital of the fears and compunctions of Hirohito's mother, and turned the conversation into more manly channels.

WHAT DOOLITTLE DID

The next morning at dawn, April 18, 668 miles to the east of Tokyo, a small U.S. task force of two carriers and a cruiser was discovered by the Japanese picket boat *Nitto Maru No. 23.* Twenty-nine minutes and 925 shells later, the *Nitto Maru* sank under the fire of the U.S. cruiser *Nashville.* Vice Admiral William Halsey, aboard the carrier *Enterprise,* advised his other carrier, *Hornet,* that Tokyo had almost certainly been alerted. A few minutes later Colonel James Doolittle of the U.S. Army led sixteen B-25's from the *Hornet*'s deck to begin—from a launching point 150 miles farther out than planned—the first air raid on Tokyo.

Flying individually, each plane for itself, Doolittle's raiders came in over Japan at tree-level altitude shortly before noon. They crossed the coast at sixteen different points, dispersed over almost 200 miles of shoreline. Japanese defenses were not ready for them because staff officers had calculated that the two approaching U.S. carriers would not be able to launch a threat with standard-issue short-range Navy bombers for many hours yet. Ten of Doolittle's planes zeroed in on Tokyo minutes apart and from several directions in a diabolical random fashion which confused and terrified the most brilliant tacticians at Imperial General Headquarters. Doolittle's own plane, the first to arrive on target, flew directly over the Imperial Palace, which he had been told to spare, and dumped his 2,000 pounds of incendiary clusters in downtown Tokyo, in the Shinbashi station area. The other nine Tokyo raiders hit steel plants and oil refineries in north Tokyo and along the dockfront in south Tokyo. Some of the latecomers were hounded by Japanese fighters and jettisoned their bomb loads haphazardly in order to lighten ship, gain speed, and escape. They hit a middle school, a hospital, and several purely residential streets. By chance they also ignited a large, camouflaged oil-storage farm which burned black and heavy for many hours after the raid was over.

Three more of Doolittle's raiders struck factories and oil tanks in Yokohama; two hit the industrial town of Nagoya on the way to Kyoto; one struck Kobe on the Inland Sea and caused a remarkable amount of damage to the Kawasaki aircraft factory.

By one o'clock in the afternoon the raid was over. Fifty Japanese were dead, 252 wounded, and ninety factory buildings gutted. A fuel farm and six large gas tanks had been subtracted from Japan's most precious stockpile, her liquid fuel.

One of Doolittle's raiders, short on gas, turned north to Russia and landed near Vladivostok. After a three-hour feast of celebration and toast drinking with the staff of the local Russian commander, the plane's five-man crew was flown to central Russia where it was interned for over a year before being allowed, diplomatically, to escape into Iran.

Doolittle's other fifteen marauders made for Chuchow, a railway town in south central China, about 200 miles south of the Yangtze, in an area which the Japanese had never taken the trouble to occupy. All of the planes ran out of fuel short of their mark. Three of the crews crash-landed in the ocean south of Shanghai, a few yards from the shore; one pancaked on the still waters of a rice paddy; the other twelve, over mountainous terrain farther inland, set their planes on automatic pilot and bailed out. It was a rainy night. The planes crashed against mountain tops. The parachutists—except for one whose chute did not open—sprained ankles and cracked ribs against wet mountainsides all over the Chinese province of Chekiang. The men of one crew floated to earth just south of Japanese-held Nanchang and were taken captive immediately.

The crews of two of the planes which crash-landed in the surf off the shore both suffered debilitating injuries. One of them, due to the efforts of a single uninjured nineteen-year-old corporal, David J. Thatcher, was smuggled out of Japanese eastern China on stretchers by hardy peasants in the employ of Chiang Kai-shek's resistance fighters. Along the way, the pilot, Lieutenant Ted Lawson, had to have his gangrenous leg amputated, under Novocain, at a missionary infirmary in Lishui. The crew of the other plane which crash-landed was not so lucky. Two of its men had drowned, with severe internal injuries, on their way to the beach. The other three crewmen made contact with Chinese partisans but were shortly afterward betrayed by a double agent and captured by the Japanese.

In the end, five of Doolittle's eighty men were detained in the Soviet Union, three died in crash landings in China, sixty-four found their way to Chungking, the capital of unoccupied China, and eight suffered the terrors of Japanese vengeance.

The eight captured airmen were assembled in Nanking and Shanghai and after a day of gentle routine field interrogation were flown to Tokyo for torture by the secret police. Hirohito was consulted a week later, on April 28, as to his wishes in disposing of them. He refused to commit himself directly but through his intimate, Chief of Staff Sugiyama, he suggested that all eight of them be tried and executed for crimes against the civilian populace of Tokyo who had died in the raids.

For six months the newspapers controlled by the imperial family inveighed against the airmen and denounced them as mass murderers of school children and hospital patients. Prime Minister General Tojo, who knew the facts of the raid and also the facts of Prince Higashikuni's mass bombings of Chinese civilians in 1937, waged a one-man campaign of legal rectitude on behalf of the airmen. He pointed out that there was no statute on the books which made it a capital crime for an enemy flier to bomb Tokyo.

Finally in October Tojo succeeded in persuading Hirohito to commute the sentence of five of the prisoners to life and to execute only three of them. The condemned were flown back to Shanghai. One of them, Lieutenant Dean Hallmark, the pilot of Doolittle's plane number 6, was no longer sane enough to appreciate what was happening to him. On the afternoon of October 15 he and the pilot and gunner of plane number 16, Lieutenant William Farrow and Sergeant Harold Spatz, were taken to a cemetery outside Shanghai and shot. One of the remaining five captive Doolittle raiders died in solitary confinement in a Japanese prison in 1944; the other four lived to be liberated by American parachutists who dropped into the Peking area on August 20, 1945.

Hirohito's wrath against the American raiders was as nothing compared to his wrath against the Chinese peasants who had helped most of them escape. On April 20, two days after the Doolittle raid, he instructed the third and last of the Three Crows, General Okamura Yasuji, the senior commander in China, to prepare for a reprisal expedition against the Chinese province of Chekiang where Doolittle's pilots had found refuge. A few days later Hirohito stamped orders for a punitive sweep through

Chekiang and adjoining areas south of the Yangtze "to destroy the air bases from which the enemy might conduct aerial raids on the Japanese Homeland."

Hirohito's orders were unusually specific on this occasion:

The captured areas will be occupied for a period estimated at approximately one month. Airfields, military installations, and important lines of communication will be totally destroyed.

Separate instructions will be issued in regard to matters pertaining to the moment of withdrawal. . . .

The commander in chief of the China Expeditionary Army will begin the operation as soon as possible. He will concentrate on the annihilation of the enemy and the destruction of key enemy air bases in the Chekiang area.

A hundred thousand Japanese troops were called from garrison duty to break the uneasy truce with Chiang Kai-shek. They began to descend on Chekiang only a fortnight after the last American plane had crashed. They continued to ravage the entire Pennsylvania-sized area of Chekiang and adjoining Kiangsi for three months. When they finally withdrew in mid-August 1942, they had killed 250,000 Chinese, most of them civilians. The villages at which the American fliers had been entertained on their way west to Chungking were reduced to cinder heaps, every man, woman, and babe in them put to the sword. In the whole of Japan's brutal eight-year war with China, the vengeance on Chekiang would go down unrivaled except by the ferocious march on Nanking in 1937.

It was not the damage caused by Doolittle or his sacrilege in violating the sacred air space of Japan which angered Hirohito. The raid was clearly a propaganda spectacular staged to hearten U.S. servicemen and civilians who were tired of defeats. It had cost more than it had gained and was not likely to be repeated. Moreover, it had reminded Japanese that their islands were vulnerable to air attack from the empty oceans toward the sunrise; it would help the government in getting the people to take air-raid drills and civilian defense seriously.

What most disturbed Hirohito was the answer implicit in the raid to the peace feelers which he had put out through Lisbon and Geneva after the fall of Singapore. He had offered then to halt Japan's advance at any moment and stop the massacre of hopelessly beleaguered Allied garrisons. Until the Doolittle raid, he had hoped that his diplomatic feelers might still elicit a response. Doolittle's incendiaries, however, clearly stated that the United States was not yet ready to settle, that the terms had not changed since the Hull-Nomura conversation of 1941, that Roosevelt still insisted on "self-determination" and "freedom of opportunity" throughout Asia before he would consider any Japanese claim to a "special position" there.

It would be a long war and the butchery in Chekiang, to prevent

U.S. planes from flying off the airfields there, was but one of the preparations which Hirohito approved in an effort to increase Japan's staying power. First the Co-Prosperity Sphere would be "completed and perfected" by eliminating the last Western enclave in Asia: Corregidor. Then—so the plan stated—the Navy would advance into the Coral Sea between New Guinea and Australia in order to capture New Caledonia and cut U.S.–Australian shipping lanes. Finally an armada would be dispatched to occupy Midway Island on the way to Hawaii and force the remnants of the U.S. Pacific Fleet to fight a decisive last battle.

THE DEATH OF CORREGIDOR

All through April 1942 heavy Japanese artillery on the newly won peninsula of Bataan dueled with heavy American artillery on Corregidor, the island rock off the tip of the peninsula. The U.S. guns had been emplaced scientifically at great expense before the war. The rock was honeycombed with tunnels filled with ammunition and impervious to bombardment. At first the Corregidor guns had the best of the shoot-outs simply by virtue of caliber. But gradually the Japanese ability to look down and report hits from airplanes gave the mobile field pieces on Bataan an advantage. One by one the great 10-ton mortars of Corregidor were silenced by direct hits which first smashed the steel gun ports and finally stopped the U.S. muzzles with rubble. By May 3 only two of the big guns were still firing and the whole of Corregidor's "topside" looked like a newly excavated quarry. That day and the next the Japanese batteries redoubled their barrage in what was obviously intended as a final softening up.

Between 11 P.M. and midnight on May 5, some 600 Japanese out of an amphibious assault force of over 2,000 survived the two-mile crossing from Bataan and succeeded in digging in on Corregidor's blasted shingle. All through the night the 6,500-odd Filamerican defenders filed from their tunnels and attempted with rifles and bayonets to drive the invaders back into the bay. Honma poured all the men and assault craft he could muster into maintaining the beachhead. Despite his reinforcement by some 50,000 men six weeks earlier, he was desperately short of combat troops. Simply being in Bataan had given most of his men dysentery or malaria.

When the sun rose, General Wainwright had sent out from the tunnels his last infantrymen: the "4th Provisional Battalion," a pick-up team of trained paint scrapers and deck swabbers left in Manila harbor by merchant and naval vessels. They, too, had failed to dislodge the Japanese foothold. One more night or one more amphibious assault, Wainwright calculated, would leave Corregidor a disorganized, demoralized invitation to total butchery. And so at 10:15 A.M., as Honma was considering asking for more reinforcements, Wainwright radioed him for free passage through the lines under flag of truce.

In his first interview with General Honma, General Wainwright tried to capitulate in the name of Corregidor alone. He was, however, the titular commander of all U.S. troops in the Philippines: the 50,000 who still clung to life in Japanese prison camps, and the 20,000 who still marched free in Mindanao, Panay, Leyte, Samar, Mindoro, and North Luzon, as well as the 6,500 deafened, shell-shocked members of his personal command in Corregidor.

Honma gave Wainwright twelve hours to think over his offer and suggested that, if he did not strike the colors for all U.S. forces in the Philippines, those who were already in Japanese clutches might suffer dearly for it. When Wainwright returned from Honma's command post on Bataan, he found that, during the cease-fire, Japanese troops had swarmed ashore on Corregidor and occupied even the entrance to the central Malinta tunnel which housed the rock's hospital and kitchens.

After a sleepless night Wainwright had no choice but to order the U.S. troops in the southern islands of the Philippines to submit themselves, undefeated, to Japanese captivity. Since Wainwright commanded only 6,500 men and Major General William Sharp in Mindanao commanded more than twice that number, it was a difficult order to enforce. In what was, for the United States, the most humiliating moment of World War II, Wainwright on the next day, May 7, broadcast his decision from the Japanese radio station in Manila. MacArthur in Australia ordered Major General Sharp to pay no attention to the broadcast since it was obviously made under duress. Wainwright, however, followed up his radio speech by sending members of his staff to carry letters from him, under Japanese escort, to Sharp and his other subordinate commanders.

Sharp, for one, acknowledged that the American lives which the Japanese already held in their hands counted for more than anything which he and his men could accomplish militarily. He surrendered most of his scattered troops and forced his satellite commanders in other southern islands to do likewise. At the same time he encouraged those few Filamericans who knew the terrain and had the individualistic talents for it to take to guerrilla warfare. General Honma was satisfied. The men of Corregidor were moved to the starving, disease-ridden Japanese concentration camps without special reprisal. And those U.S. soldiers in the south and far north who were willing to sacrifice prisoner-of-war status for the precarious and totally unprivileged status of guerrilla-spy fought on. Some of them succeeded so well as irregulars that, in the mountains of Mindanao, they maintained throughout the war a prison camp in which the inmates were Japanese.

During the final bombardment of Corregidor and the days of General Wainwright's humiliation, Prince Higashikuni's twenty-five-year-old son, Morihiro, the classmate, companion, and near twin of Hirohito's Army brother, Prince Mikasa, represented the imperial family in a triumphant

tour through the conquered southern areas. In Bali, on May 4, he gave
audience to air and naval commanders who were supposed, in the weeks
ahead, to occupy or isolate Australia. On May 8, he was in Manila to witness a bedraggled procession of U.S. troops from Corregidor being walked
through the downtown streets on their way to concentration camp. Because of General Wainwright's co-operation, it was not a death but merely
a humiliation march.

THE CORAL SEA

On that same day, May 8, Japan's scientifically planned and predictably
successful Strike South suddenly jerked to a halt. It had been moving
ahead of schedule because of a long run of good luck: the right rain and
the right shine whenever needed and many a hole-in-one bomb drop.
Now abruptly the laws of chance reasserted their arbitrary authority in
one of the most impartially accident-ridden encounters which has ever
changed the course of history. It was as if ships and planes were momentarily forgotten while Amaterasu the Sun Goddess squatted down with
the Statue of Liberty to shoot crap.

This event, which has been charitably remembered as a battle, the
Battle of the Coral Sea, took place in the amethystine, reef-girdled waters
which separate eastern New Guinea, the Louisades, the Solomons, the
New Hebrides, and New Caledonia from the northeastern coast of Aus-
tralia. Nowhere on earth basks a balmier or more beautiful sea basin.
There it was that the weirds went wild and improvised.

Scientific cryptanalysis gave the U.S. Navy an initial advantage by telling Rear Admiral Chester Nimitz, the post Pearl Harbor commander of
the Pacific Fleet, that the Japanese were going to send an invasion force
around the high mountainous barrier of New Guinea to seize Port
Moresby. This was the main Australian base on the south shore of New
Guinea and commanded the approaches to Australia's populous east coast.
In his advance information, Nimitz saw a fine opportunity to lay an am-
buscade. The carriers *Enterprise* and *Hornet,* however, were still on their
way back to Pearl Harbor from launching Doolittle's raiders. Consequently
Nimitz could arm his trap with only the heavy carrier *Lexington* and the
medium carrier *Yorktown.* The Japanese Port Moresby task force included
two heavy carriers, *Zuikaku* and *Shokaku,* and one light carrier, *Shoho.*

On route to the battleground the Japanese forces stopped off to land a
garrison on the little island of Tulagi, just north of Guadalcanal in the
Solomons. Nimitz's carrier commander, Rear Admiral Frank Jack
Fletcher, revealed his presence prematurely by sending his carrier planes
on May 4 to attack the Japanese beachhead on Tulagi. In three waves
and 105 missions, his pilots expended twenty-two torpedoes, seventy-six
1,000-pound bombs, and over 80,000 rounds of machine-gun bullets and

succeeded in forcing one Japanese destroyer to beach, in killing the skipper of another with a machine-gun bullet, and in sinking five seaplanes, four landing barges, and three minesweepers. "Disappointing," Admiral Nimitz later termed the results and urged more target practice for all hands.

Having given himself away, Admiral Fletcher first fled south, then turned abruptly west with hopes of intercepting the separate Japanese fleet of Port-Moresby-bound troop transports which he calculated would be rounding the eastern tip of New Guinea at any moment. Japanese Admiral Inouye Shigeyoshi, with his main striking force of heavy carriers and superior planes and pilots, steamed south in hot pursuit of Fletcher. On the night of May 6, heading south, Inouye passed 60 miles from Fletcher, heading west. Both were desperately looking for one another but it was the closest they would ever come to seeing one another. At daylight on May 7, Inouye's search pilots sighted an eastward-sailing destroyer and a flattish-topped oiler, the *Neosho,* which had been detached from Fletcher's fleet after refueling the previous day. Mistaking them for a cruiser and a carrier, the Japanese reconnaissance pilots called in fifty-two bombers which administered a massive dose of overkill, sinking the destroyer and leaving oiler *Neosho* a derelict which had to be scuttled.

Meanwhile Admiral Fletcher had learned from his scout planes that two carriers and four heavy cruisers were steaming toward him from the northwest. In reality the only force which might have answered to this description was that of the ships which had passed in the night and were now in exactly the opposite direction. The squadron seen by Fletcher's scouts consisted of two elderly light cruisers and some gunboats which were tagging along as reinforcements for the escort of the Port Moresby invasion transports. Admiral Fletcher, however, could not afford to wait for confirmation of the scouting report, because he felt he must strike first or be stricken. Accordingly, he launched an all-out attack on the phantom force with ninety-three of his best planes and pilots.

Admiral Inouye at that moment was receiving accurate reports of Fletcher's position but regarded them with a wait-and-see attitude because some of his fliers already claimed to have sunk one U.S. carrier that morning—the oiler *Neosho*—and were now reporting another U.S. carrier force far to the west. This last was an eager Australian-led detachment of cruisers and destroyers which had steamed on ahead of Fletcher's main strength in order to look for the Port Moresby invasion transports.

Admiral Inouye decided to do nothing while waiting for clarification of the conflicting intelligence being passed along to him. He knew that the United States could not possibly have more than five carriers in the entire Pacific; that two of these had just accompanied the Doolittle raiders and could not yet have reached the New Guinea area without wings; and that, therefore, some of the four carriers being reported to him by his reconnaissance pilots must represent either misidentifications or a diabolical American plot.

While the prudent Inouye waited for enlightenment, the Statue of Liberty made a lucky throw. En route to target, Fletcher's hastily dispatched planes happened to notice off to starboard another covering force for the Port Moresby invasion, a hitherto unsuspected quantity, the Japanese light carrier *Shoho* steaming along independently with a light screen of cruisers and destroyers. The U.S. dive-bomber flight leader, Lieutenant Commander William L. Hamilton, knew a bird in hand when he saw one. He led in his ninety-two torpedo and dive-bombers to the attack and, despite indifferent marksmanship, succeeded in sinking *Shoho* in twenty-six minutes. Some 500 Japanese sailors and pilots went down with their ship. According to a few captured survivors, their vessel sank because the last of the attacking American planes, frustrated by *Shoho*'s obstinate buoyancy, crash-dived into her and blew her up with unexpected suddenness. According to U.S. records, only three of the American planes failed to return to their flight decks.

Later that same afternoon three of Fletcher's cruisers and five of his destroyers crossed the exit from the passage through the Louisades by which the Port Moresby invasion transports were supposed to enter the Coral Sea. Admiral Inouye at once instructed the invasion fleet to hang back and tread water while his carrier planes disposed of the threat. Forty-two Japanese bombers attacked in three waves but Rear Admiral John Crace, the Australian commander of the squadron, succeeded in dodging the bombs without a scratch. No sooner had the Japanese bombers disappeared over the horizon than Crace was set upon by U.S. land-based B-26's from Australia. By skillful maneuvering he succeeded in surviving this "friendly" attack also and lodged a protest which MacArthur's public relations officers succeeded in suppressing and disregarding.

As dusk fell on May 7, the *Lexington* and *Yorktown,* which were equipped with radar, and *Zuikaku* and *Shokaku,* which possessed superior search auxiliaries, had still failed to locate and hit one another directly. Admiral Fletcher decided to postpone future battle until morning, and Admiral Inouye sent out twenty-seven bombers and torpedo bombers to make, if possible, a night attack. In one of the few well-informed decisions of the battle, Fletcher learned of their approach from radar and sent up interceptors in time to jump them in the twilight. For the first time in World War II, the American pilots had the best of a dogfight and shot down nine planes for three losses. The surviving eighteen Japanese pilots became confused on their way home and six of them tried to land on the *Yorktown*. Communications officers aboard the American carrier did all they could to copy blinker signals and bring the Japanese pilots into range of the *Yorktown*'s guns, but only one of the enemy planes could be blown out of the sky before the rest of them were spooked and ran away to look for friendlier decks. Eleven of the remaining seventeen ran out of fuel while still searching and "splashed" in the ocean.

The next morning at sunup, May 8, the two carrier fleets finally learned one another's position from their scout planes. *Lexington* and *Yorktown* promptly launched all their available aircraft to attack the Japanese fleet. Equally promptly *Zuikaku* and *Shokaku* launched all their available aircraft to attack the American fleet. Compared with earlier performances against Pearl Harbor or Tom Thumb Phillips, the Misty Lagoon bombardiers were distinctly below par. The *Yorktown* evaded their blows entirely except for a single bomb which penetrated four decks and killed sixty-four men below. The *Lexington* was hit by at least two torpedoes and two bombs but maintained full steam and 25 knots. An early list was corrected by counterflooding. It looked as if the "Old Lady," which still included in her crew a few veteran hands who had been with her ever since her commissioning in 1928, might yet survive. Then at thirteen minutes to one in the afternoon her smothered fires somehow met a seepage of high-octane gas, touching off a succession of fires and explosions which ultimately, more than seven hours later, sent her settling, fully trimmed and right side up, to the bottom. All but a few of her crew, who had been killed in the fight, swam away and were rescued.

While *Lexington* sank, her planes and *Yorktown*'s had caused Admiral Inouye to retire. *Zuikaku* had waited out the American attack under the cover of a tropical ocean cloud burst. *Shokaku,* caught in the open, had suffered as much deck damage as *Lexington* and had been counted sunk by U.S. planes. But below decks *Shokaku* was still sound. U.S. torpedoes at that time in the war were almost as difficult to work with as the lumbering, heavily armored flying machines which American pilots had to use as launching platforms. As Japanese Zero pilots could be sure of shooting down unmaneuverable U.S. fighters, so Japanese ship skippers could be sure of seeing the wakes of approaching U.S. torpedoes, of turning in time to avoid them or, if necessary, laying on steam and simply outrunning them.

So it was that *Lexington* sank after the battle from an explosion deep in her vitals while *Shokaku,* her decks mangled and smoking, sailed away from the action and returned to Japan for extensive repairs. *Zuikaku* went with her and had to wait in port for months before new pilots could be found to replace those whom she had lost.

Yorktown, the surviving U.S. carrier, also limped for home and for what should have been, under ordinary circumstances, months of refitting, liberty, and dry dock. Having recovered many orphans from the *Lexington,* however, she had aboard a full complement of fliers and planes. And it turned out, as a matter of necessity, that her repairs could be greatly abbreviated and that she could be sent to sea again after only a few days.

The tactical score for the Battle of the Coral Sea stood at one Japanese light carrier sunk and one U.S. heavy carrier sunk. The strategic score, from the Japanese point of view, was one invasion temporarily postponed. Hirohito was irked and impatient, but not concerned. He expected to resume the southeasterly advance in July and drive it home to the shores of New Zealand. On May 26, eighteen days after Coral Sea, he asked his chief aide-de-camp, General Hasunuma Shigeru, to have someone look into the handling of a touchy diplomatic question: the sovereignty of New Caledonia. This Massachusetts-sized island north of New Zealand belonged to the French, but whether to De Gaulle or Pétain remained a moot point. Would Vichy or Berlin be offended when Japan annexed it?

From the U.S. point of view the stand-off at the Coral Sea represented a month or more of time in which U.S. manufacturers might yet make good their boast of technological pre-eminence. The reckoning was to come only a month later at Midway. The manufacturers were not ready for it and by all rights the United States might then have lost the war. But the Statue of Liberty was now throwing sevens.

MIDWAY

Two square miles of barren briny scrub were at issue. Midway's two islets, Sand and Eastern, together with an undeveloped, uninhabited rock named Kure a hundred miles to the west, lay all alone in the northwestern quadrant of the Pacific Ocean. Midway's airstrip, a third of the way on a direct line from Pearl Harbor to Tokyo, served as the salient point in the U.S. air-search-and-patrol triangle maintained between Midway, Pearl Harbor, and the Aleutians. Without Midway, U.S. intelligence would have no relay station through which to radio-eavesdrop on the Co-Prosperity Sphere and no early warning line of air reconnaissance with which to detect incoming Japanese invasion fleets.

On the battle for Midway's unprepossessing acres rode more than President Roosevelt and his chiefs of staff cared to admit at the time. Indeed, few battles since Thermopylae have been fought more desperately and for better reason. If the Japanese had won the battle they would have been in a position to carry out their plan for taking Hawaii in August 1942. They intended to go on to seize the Panama Canal and terrorize California, forcing the United States to abandon Australia, cancel plans for an expeditionary force to the European theater, and concentrate all resources on the defense of the U.S. West Coast. Under these conditions, Japanese strategists thought that the Anglo-American alliance would break down; that combined German-Japanese pressure would make American business interests turn against President Roosevelt; that perhaps the leading American families, assumed to be politically conservative, would bring the United States over to the Axis side. Fortunately for the inner peace of Washington, American strategists never had to evaluate, even contingently, the realism of these Japanese hopes. U.S. forces at Midway had incredibly good luck and made the most of it.

Admiral Yamamoto advanced on Midway with the most formidable fleet ever assembled up to that time: ten battleships, eight aircraft carriers, twenty-four cruisers, seventy destroyers, fifteen large I-boat submarines, eighteen tankers, and forty auxiliary vessels and transports—in all 185 vessels. His carriers, two heavy, three medium, and three light, together with his four small seaplane carriers, could put up 352 of the lethal Zero fighters, 105 dive-bombers, 162 torpedo bombers, fifty-six reconnaissance craft, and ten land bombers—a total of 685 airplanes.

Part of Yamamoto's forces were to open the battle with diversionary landings at Attu, Kiska, and Adak at the western end of the Aleutian Islands arc. These were expected to bring the U.S. Pacific Fleet out of Pearl Harbor and start it steaming north. Then Yamamoto's advance force—the heavy carriers of Admiral Nagumo—were to begin softening up Midway 1,500 miles to the south. Landings on Midway would follow from heavily escorted transports. The U.S. fleet would naturally turn west to counterattack. Admiral Nagumo's carriers would retreat. The U.S. fleet would pursue and find themselves ambushed by Yamamoto's main force lurking to the west of Midway. There, Yamamoto, on the bridge of his gigantic 64,000-ton flagship, the *Yamato,* would supervise personally while the immense long-range guns of his battleships blew the U.S. fleet out of the water.[20]

This was the imperial plan for the Battle of Midway. To frustrate it Admiral Nimitz, the over-all commander of the Pacific fleet, could call upon exactly three aircraft carriers, no battleships, eight cruisers, fourteen destroyers, and twenty-five submarines. By any criterion—number of ships, tonnage, firepower, or carrier planes—he was outnumbered almost three to one. What was more, on the basis of past performance, Nimitz had no reason to think that his men or his machines would be any match, individually, for their Japanese counterparts. He had to fight, however, because Japanese seizure of Hawaii and of West Coast ports must be delayed until the superior manpower and industrial capacity of the United States began to make themselves felt. Two or three more unexpectedly brilliant Japanese victories would begin to sap American strength at its wellhead.

Nimitz had one major advantage over Yamamoto: he knew enemy intentions beforehand. U.S. Naval Intelligence had warned him even before

[20] Most of the Japanese battleships weighed far more than they had been registered as weighing with the prewar naval limitations committee in Geneva. *Yamato*'s "special-type 16-inch guns" actually had a caliber of 18.1 inches and could carry 25 miles. Similarly the heavy Japanese carriers *Kaga* and *Akagi,* registered at 27,000 tons, actually weighed in at 36,000 tons, and the "light" 10,000-ton carriers *Hiryu* and *Soryu* really weighed over 17,000 tons.

the Battle of the Coral Sea that the Japanese were planning something big in the central Pacific in early June. Even without full access to Yamamoto's Admirals' Code, U.S. cryptographers had made enough sense out of monitored Japanese fleet messages to learn the gist of Yamamoto's plan and to know that it was directed against a point in the Pacific called AF for "American Forces." Nimitz's own analysts thought this point was Midway; analysts in Washington, who thought more globally, believed AF stood for Hawaii. Nimitz had the garrison on Midway send out a bogus radio message complaining that their water distillation plant had broken down. A few days later U.S. Navy monitors picked up a Japanese message informing Yamamoto that AF was short of fresh water.

On his own responsibility, Nimitz had already set in motion the U.S. plan for the Battle of Midway. It was simply to get into Midway as many men, guns, and airplanes as the islets would hold and to move as secretly as possible into Midway waters every available fighting ship.

On May 26, nine days before the battle, the U.S. carriers *Enterprise* and *Hornet* pulled into Pearl Harbor from a vain dash toward the action in the Coral Sea after their successful sneak approach on Tokyo with the Doolittle raiders. Their tired, liberty-hungry crews were set to work at once preparing the ships to sail again in less than forty-eight hours. The navigator of the *Enterprise,* Commander Richard Ruble, listened to the briefing for key officers on the forthcoming Midway mission, and said, "That man of ours in Tokyo is worth every cent we pay him."

The next day, May 27, the carrier *Yorktown* limped into Pearl Harbor from her drubbing nineteen days earlier in the Coral Sea. She had made the 4,500-mile voyage under her own steam but at ten knots attended by a swarm of fretfully solicitous destroyers. She leaked badly from near misses, and the one bomb which had hit her had penetrated four decks and touched off fuel and ammunition fires which had made a shambles of her interior. The Japanese counted her sunk. Admiral Nimitz gave his shipyard commanders three days to repair her. American welders and fitters moved aboard at once and wrought wonders which could not be matched at that time by any Japanese shipyard. Some of them worked on her without sleep for the next forty-eight hours. Some of them were still aboard her and returned ashore in tugs when she cleared Diamond Head on May 30 and hied herself after the *Enterprise* and *Hornet* which had left for Midway on May 28.

The sailing of the American carriers, with their screens of cruisers and destroyers, was entirely unknown to Admiral Yamamoto. In operational planning he had assigned the task of keeping watch on Pearl Harbor to his advance force of submarines, commanded by Big Brother Vice Admiral Marquis Komatsu Teruhisa, the cousin of the Empress who had presided at the Naval Staff College during the Pearl Harbor planning in 1941. Marquis Komatsu exercised his submarine command at Midway from Kwajalein in the Marshall Islands, 2,000 miles from the scene of action. His flagship was the *Katori*, a vessel registered as a light cruiser of 6,000 tons. She was the namesake of the battleship on which Marquis Komatsu and Hirohito had wrestled and played croquet during the crown prince's world tour in 1921.

Marquis Komatsu had great confidence in the Midway operation and a belief that the immense superiority of Japanese naval forces would inevitably tell in Japan's favor. He was preoccupied with planning the details of an envisaged raid on the Panama Canal after the battle. His submarines were supposed to take up their advance scouting stations outside Pearl Harbor and in two cordons between Pearl Harbor and Midway eight days before the battle. In the event none of them reached their stations until four days before the battle. During those four days of tardiness *Enterprise, Hornet,* and *Yorktown,* too, slipped through the Japanese early warning zone and took up a vigil in the cloudiest available stretches of ocean northeast of Midway.

Despite his preoccupation with future victories, the bookish Admiral Komatsu realized that his submarines had failed to provide any knowledge of the whereabouts of the U.S. fleet. His picket submarines had arrived on station too late to detect advance movements of the U.S. fleet, and his snooper submarines had encountered too many patrols in the Hawaiian area to launch scout planes for a look at the berths in Pearl Harbor itself. On or about June 3, Komatsu notified Admiral Yamamoto of his failure to make sure that the U.S. fleet was still in Pearl Harbor. Apparently, however, he did not call to Yamamoto's attention the late arrival of his picket submarines between Pearl Harbor and Midway. It was a serious lapse, but because of Komatsu's membership in the imperial family, Japanese historians in later years would allude to it only obliquely, and American historians, in their exhaustive postmortems, would follow the lead of the Japanese.[21]

When Admiral Yamamoto sailed out from Hashirajima anchorage off Hiroshima in the Inland Sea on May 27, he had ample evidence to know that Admiral Nimitz in Hawaii was expecting him. Yamamoto's radio monitors for several days had reported unusual message activity between U.S. ships and command posts. From his first day out of port his lookouts spotted the periscopes of U.S. submarines shadowing his great fleet. Nevertheless, he had no reason for concern. Now that his ships had sailed, it mattered not what U.S. admirals knew. Knowledge would do them no

---

[21] Despite his blunder, Marquis Komatsu, who had been one of the Big Brothers of Hirohito's youth, remained in command of Japan's submarine fleet and rose to the rank of full admiral. After the war he was elected to the House of Councillors, the successor to the House of Peers. At this writing he is eighty-two years old and lives near former Lord Privy Seal Kido within an old man's stroll of the western postern of the palace. His daughter is married to Kido's son.

good unless they could act upon it, and they could not act upon it without moving their ships through the cordons of surveillance which Yamamoto believed to be strung across the northern Pacific by Marquis Komatsu's submarine wolf pack.

A week later, at dawn on June 3, Yamamoto's northern force began operations by launching twenty-two bombers and twelve fighters for a raid on Dutch Harbor, the main U.S. base in the Aleutians. To the puzzlement of the attackers no U.S. planes were caught on the ground and the only targets were oil tanks and a radio shack. On their way back to their flight decks, the raiders spotted some U.S. destroyers offshore, but the weather closed in and for the next three days the northern force milled about in it waiting on events to the south.

By that evening the forces for the Battle of Midway were in position. Yamamoto's four advance carriers, under Admiral Nagumo, were steaming in on Midway through a front of bad weather from the northwest. Since the attack on Pearl Harbor, Nagumo's task force had fared proudly, raiding Darwin in February and sinking the British carrier *Hermes,* plus a cruiser and a destroyer, off Ceylon in April. Admiral Nimitz's three carriers, which as yet had no boastworthy record, were steaming about surreptitiously northeast of Midway, hiding in squalls and awaiting their chance. The Americans knew that the Japanese were in the vicinity; the Japanese thought that the Americans were at least 1,200 miles to the east beyond the Japanese submarine picket lines.

At 4:20 on the morning of June 4 Admiral Nagumo's carriers began to launch thirty-six bombers, thirty-six dive-bombers, and thirty-six Zeros for a strike against the airstrip and Marine garrison at Midway. Half an hour later when the planes had all reached their formations and were winging on their way, Nagumo had routine precautions taken against the unlikely possibility that there might be a U.S. fleet in the area. Reconnaissance planes took off belatedly to execute a lackadaisical search pattern over the surrounding ocean. Seventy-two of the bombers and thirty-six of the fighters remaining on board Nagumo's carriers were armed with suitable weapons for attack, if necessary, on hostile surface vessels.

On Midway the Marine garrison, which had been greatly reinforced with men and machines during the previous fortnight, knew from aerial reconnaissance that a convoy of Japanese troop transports was approaching from the southwest. The men had been told to assume that Japanese carriers were simultaneously descending from the northwest. And so at 5:53 A.M., when the incoming Japanese planes appeared as bogeys on a radar screen, U.S. pilots were ready and waiting. Fifteen B-17 Flying Fortresses had already taken off to bomb the convoy of transports to the southwest. They were redirected toward the carriers in the northwest. The other sixty-two pilots on Midway scrambled. Thirty-seven of them turned their bombers toward the carriers; twenty-five of them spiraled up for altitude so that their fighters—their obsolescent Buffaloes and their seven untried Wild-cats, span-new from the production line—could fall upon the approaching Japanese planes.

The U.S. bombers passed their Japanese opposite numbers coming the other way and the pilots thumbed noses at one another without fighting. The twenty-five Marine fighters tangled with the thirty-six Japanese Zeros. In a ten-minute dogfight two of the Zeros and twenty-two of the new Marine F4F Wildcats and old F2A-3 Buffaloes had been put out of action. Ten of the U.S. crews and three of the planes survived but the men were bitter. "Any commander," reported one of them, "that orders pilots out for combat in an F2A-3 should consider the pilot as lost before leaving the ground."

Having disposed of Midway's fighter cover, the remaining 106 Japanese planes strafed and bombed every target on the ground which they could see. They destroyed the hospital and fuel tanks on Sand Island, demolished the powerhouse, mess hall, and PX on Eastern Island, ruptured the fuel lines to the airport gas pumps there, and pockmarked the runways. They were surprised at the amount of anti-aircraft fire they encountered, for they had been told that there were only a few hundred Americans on the islands when in fact the garrison had been built up to over 5,000. The American defenders were so well prepared with trenches and sandbag emplacements that only eleven of them were killed and few of their guns put out of action.

When the Japanese fliers had spent their bombs and bullets, they felt disappointed. They had caught no U.S. planes on the ground and it was obvious that they had not destroyed Midway's firepower. Four of the Japanese bombers had been shot down or were so badly mauled that they would splash on the way back to their flight decks. At 7 A.M. flight leader Lieutenant Tomonaga Joichi, the scion of a great Nagasaki textile family, turned for home and radioed Admiral Nagumo: "There is need for a second strike."

The fifty-two Midway-based U.S. bombers were now converging on Nagumo's carrier force. They had been indoctrinated in the previous week with a full understanding of the importance of their mission. Either they sank the Japanese carriers or the Battle of Midway and perhaps the war would be lost by the United States. It is commonly said that the concept of suicide pilots was invented by the fanatic, fatalistic Japanese. On the contrary it was first put into practice by American pilots at Midway.

From 7:05 to 10:20 on that morning of June 4, seventy-eight U.S. crews hurled themselves at low altitude against the Japanese carriers.[22] Few of them expected to survive. Most of them knew that, even if they did

[22] The high-level bombing by fifteen B-17's from Midway is excluded from these figures as a tactically different species of attack.

survive, they had not enough fuel to make it home. Forty-four out of the seventy-eight crews perished according to their expectations. Worst of all they did not manage in their dying to register a single hit on any of the Japanese ships. The apparent futility of their sacrifice, the inferiority of their weapons, and the superior professionalism of their antagonists frustrated them as they died, but by a stroke of luck their lives were not wasted. Their insistent, ill-co-ordinated attacks finally drove Admiral Nagumo to make a fatal error of judgment which cost Japan her hope of winning the war.

In brief detail what happened was this. At 7:05 A.M. six U.S. Avenger torpedo bombers bore in on the Japanese fleet. They launched their fish while trying to evade the bullets of Zeros which were on their tails. Their slow, ill-finned, ill-fused torpedoes were all dodged successfully by the helmsmen of the Japanese carriers. Only one of the six Avengers flew away from that bomb run. Next at 7:11 A.M. came four Army B-26 Marauders, also armed with torpedoes. The Zeros got one of them, the anti-aircraft guns got another, and the other two skipped away over the spume for home. Their torpedoes, adroitly avoided by the Japanese helmsmen, ran away toward the empty horizon. At 7:55 sixteen of the newest Marine dive-bombers descended on the Japanese fleet in a long, gentle glide attack, which was all that the flight commander felt his green pilots were capable of executing. Six of them were shot down by Zeros, two more by flak. Two of the remaining eight planes survived and all eight of the crews. Again, there were no hits.

At 8:14 A.M. the fifteen B-17's from Midway dropped 127,500 pounds of bombs on the Japanese ships from 20,000 feet. None of the bombs killed anything but fish. The B-17 crews all survived because they were flying too high for the carriers' anti-aircraft guns.

Three minutes later eleven antiquated Marine Vindicator dive-bombers, known irreverently by their crews as "Vibrators," arrived belatedly over the Japanese fleet and swooped down at the battleship *Haruna*. Nine of the crews came through the curtain of fire and fled. The *Haruna* steamed on unscathed.

For over an hour Admiral Nagumo and his ship captains had been fully occupied with excitement and maneuvering as they dealt with these five ineffective U.S. air raids. At 7:15, after the first two, Nagumo had been convinced that the Midway airfield would need a second drubbing, and had ordered the 108 planes of his second-wave force disarmed of torpedoes for fleet attack and rearmed with bombs for land-installation attack. Then at 7:28 A.M. a Japanese search plane had reported an enemy fleet of indefinite numbers and composition over the horizon to the northeast. Nagumo requested confirmation and clarification and while waiting for it, at 7:45, ordered his sailors to suspend rearming of the second-wave force and stand by.

Nagumo's staff officers realized belatedly that they had committed a tactical error in using planes from all four carriers for the first strike and in retaining half the planes of each carrier for the second strike. If, instead, they had dispatched all the planes from two carriers against Midway and retained all the planes from the other two carriers for action against surface vessels, they would now have been in a position to send out the planes of one reserve carrier against the reported American fleet, ready the planes of the other reserve carrier for a second strike at Midway, and keep the decks of the two empty carriers clear for the retrieval of the planes which had already been committed As matters stood, the four carriers were all disconcerted by the various demands which might be made on them. They had to be ready to recover planes from Midway, to send out planes armed with bombs, and to send out planes armed with torpedoes. As a result the hangar-deck-to-flight-deck elevators were stuffed with contradictions and countermanded orders. Planes were being moved up. Planes were being moved down. And bombs and torpedoes were being stacked, exposed, on the flight decks.

The minutes from 7:55 to 8:35 were taken up with the third, fourth, and fifth Midway-based American air strikes. In the midst of them, at 8:20, the exasperatingly vague pilot of the Japanese search plane to the northeast reluctantly and incredulously reported that the U.S. fleet elements he was glimpsing through breaks in the clouds included "what appears to be a carrier." Nagumo at once ordered any and all stand-by planes which had been rearmed with bombs to be slung once again with torpedoes for fleet attack. He might then have begun to launch an air strike except that the returning planes from the raid on Midway were now circling and asking permission to land. For the next fifty minutes their reception fully occupied Nagumo's flight decks.

The U.S. carriers *Enterprise, Hornet,* and *Yorktown* had long ago received reports as to the approximate position of the Japanese carriers. Rear Admiral Fletcher of the battered, half-repaired *Yorktown* and Rear Admiral Raymond Spruance of the *Enterprise* and *Hornet* had also, however, their own delicate decision to ponder. In order to make the most of their secret existence and of their inferior numbers, planes and pilots, they had to achieve success with their first fly-off or their decks would never be in a condition to send off a second wave. All planes had to be committed once and for all on the first strike.

After consultation Fletcher, who was in over-all charge, agreed with Spruance that the *Hornet*'s and *Enterprise*'s planes should take off immediately to make the most of the element of surprise and that the *Yorktown* would hover in the rear and add to the enemy's discomfiture as soon as the exact location of the enemy was established and stabilized by the first attacks. Accordingly, between 7 and 8 A.M., while the Midway bombers were spending themselves against Nagumo's fleet, the *Enterprise* had launched thirty-three dive-bombers, fourteen torpedo planes, and ten fighters, and the *Hornet* had launched thirty-five dive-bombers, fifteen torpedo planes, and ten fighters. Since the range to target was at least 150 miles, the fighters would have almost no chance of returning unless they spent little gas in dogfighting. The torpedo planes would have a slightly better chance if they found their quarry at once and did not have to hunt for it. The dive-bombers would have the best chance and might reasonably be expected to return home unless the search for the Japanese fleet was a long one. As it turned out only the dive-bombers did not fly a one-way mission; survivors from the fighter and torpedo-plane groups, such few as there would be of them, were almost all going out to spend hours in the ocean swimming about in life jackets. The rest of them were going to their deaths.

The *Hornet*'s thirty-five dive-bombers and ten fighters flew to the reported position of the Japanese fleet, then flew a little farther, then turned south to search for the Japanese ships in the direction of Midway. The *Hornet*'s ten fighters ran out of gas and splashed near Midway where their crews were mostly rescued. The thirty-five dive-bombers landed on Midway, refueled, and remained a viable reserve force which finally returned to their ship after the battle was over.

The thirty-three dive-bombers from the *Enterprise* also proceeded to the reported position of Nagumo's carriers and, finding it vacant, turned north to search the waters away from Midway. They continued to search after most of their pilots had any hope of eking out the fuel left in their tanks for the return home.

Meanwhile the fifteen torpedo planes from the *Hornet* and the fourteen torpedo planes from the *Enterprise,* escorted by the ten *Enterprise* pursuit planes, succeeded in finding the Japanese fleet. Lieutenant Commander John C. Waldron, the flight leader of the *Hornet*'s torpedo planes, had had a brief conference with his skipper before taking off and had led his planes to the north of the anticipated Japanese position. He was loved by his men as an eccentric from South Dakota who boasted of his Sioux ancestry, prided himself on his instincts, and insisted that they all carry hunting knives for use in possible crash landings near Robinson-Crusoe islands. He told his men that he had a hunch that the Japanese admiral would make a sudden change of direction to the north. Waldron's hunch, which may have been suggested to him by his skipper, proved correct. In case it did not, the fourteen torpedo planes from the *Enterprise* were flying off to his left, bisecting the angle between his flight and that of the two dive-bomber groups.

At 9:20 A.M., when Nagumo had just finished recovering his Midway raiders, Commander Waldron arrived overhead with his knife-girt crews from the *Hornet*. The directness of his flight from deck to target would have done credit to a honeybee on route to its hive. The night before

Waldron had memoed his men: "If there is only one plane left to make a final run in, I want that man to go in and get a hit." Now Waldron's followers, in their lumbering Devastator torpedo bombers, clung to his tail through the Zeros and the flak. They last saw Waldron standing up through the blasted dome of his cockpit as his flaming plane disintegrated and spattered into the sea. All fifteen of the Devastators launched their torpedoes, missed with them, and were blown from the sky. A single one of the thirty crewmen, Ensign George Gay, the pilot of the fifteenth plane, survived to watch the rest of the battle from the ocean. There he alternately supported and concealed himself with a buoyant black cushion which he had retrieved from the flotsam of his plane.

No sooner had Waldron's men fallen than the group of fourteen torpedo bombers from the *Enterprise,* which had been following him off to the south, veered in to make their own suicide runs. Four of them launched short, banked away, and survived. The other ten dropped their torpedoes inside the flashing white cloud above Nagumo's ships. None of them came out of it and none of their torpedoes found a mark.

By the superb flying of his Zero pilots and the sharpshooting of his gunners, Nagumo had now survived the attacks of eighty-one U.S. planes in seven separate attacks. The last two attacks had been executed by twenty-nine planes which clearly came from U.S. carrier decks. Up to that moment Nagumo had received news of only one U.S. carrier in the area— obviously a small one or it could not have slipped through the submarine cordon outside of Pearl Harbor or escaped immediate and exact identification by his reconnaissance aircraft. Twenty-nine torpedo planes were about all the attack that might be feared from one small carrier.

After a few minutes of waiting, Admiral Nagumo made his fateful decision. He ordered his ready-armed torpedo planes brought up to his flight decks for take-off against the troublesome American fleet. He knew, of course, that any of his carriers, with planes and fuel lines exposed on their top decks, would be highly vulnerable to bombs from above. He had just repelled two flights of torpedo planes, which obviously came from the mysterious American carrier. There should also be dive-bombers from the carrier, arriving at approximately the same time as the torpedo planes, or slightly earlier. More than an hour earlier, he had, indeed, survived the attacks of two waves of dive-bombers. Had these come from Midway or from the carrier? It was anyone's guess whether he had already coped with the U.S. carrier's dive-bombers or whether they were still out looking for him. Nagumo decided to gamble on the probability that they no longer existed, had never existed, or had long since returned home without finding him.

At 10:15 A.M., the 108 planes of Nagumo's second strike were finally on deck, armed with torpedoes and ready for take-off. At that moment, in a most improbable development, twelve more U.S. carrier torpedo planes appeared above. It seemed incredible that any American commander would have sent out three waves of planes all armed with such ineffective weapons as the slow, untrue American torpedoes. Admiral Nagumo did not know it, but he was now under attack by the torpedo planes of the third American carrier, the late-launching *Yorktown,* which was supposed to have been sunk in the Coral Sea. His men coped with the attack as efficiently as they had coped with the torpedo planes of the *Hornet* and *Enterprise.* His tired Zero pilots splashed seven of the *Yorktown*'s planes; three more were knocked down by gunfire; two disappeared damaged, limping for home. Again Nagumo's skippers, by skillful steering, combed the white hairs of the torpedo wakes and let them pass.

The four Japanese carriers turned into the wind and prepared to launch the 108 planes of their second strike. The 108 planes of the first strike, which had bombed Midway, were below decks, waiting rearmed, by the elevators, to follow them out in an overwhelming blow against the U.S. fleet. At that moment the destiny of the United States hung by the slender thread of half an hour's launching time. If the Japanese second strike had taken off, all of the U.S. carriers would almost certainly have been sunk and the Japanese carriers would have been in a condition, once more, to survive.

Instead, at that moment, 10:22 A.M. June 4, the last available U.S. planes, the last hope of the U.S. fleet, happened to converge at once upon the Japanese carriers. The *Yorktown*'s complement of seventeen dive-bombers came in from the southeast after a relatively businesslike flight from deck to target. Out of the southwest, however, came a miracle: the thirty-two dive-bombers of the *Enterprise* which had been wandering about the Pacific for more than three hours. The *Enterprise* pilots had abandoned their original "interception course" and turned to search north more than an hour earlier. They had long since gone beyond the halfway point in their gas supply, and their flight leader, Lieutenant Commander C. Wade McClusky, had accepted the probability that they were all on a one-way mission. McClusky had sighted a Japanese destroyer twenty-five minutes earlier which was returning from chasing down a reported U.S. submarine. Assuming that the destroyer was heading toward the rest of the Japanese fleet, McClusky had made a sharp turn and adopted the destroyer's course. Now he was rewarded by the sight of Nagumo's whole task force spread out below him.

Nagumo's Zero pilots were all at lower altitudes where they had just finished off the torpedo planes of the last American attack, which had begun only seven minutes earlier. Nagumo's sailors were absorbed by the maneuver of turning the carriers into the wind for launching planes. Nagumo's decks were piled high with flammables and explosives. Coming from opposite directions, Lieutenant Commander Maxwell Leslie's dive-bombers from *Yorktown* and McClusky's from *Enterprise* had achieved perfect surprise and now made the most of a perfect target.

McClusky and most of his pilots screamed down upon the 36,800-ton Japanese carrier *Kaga*. The rest ran the gauntlet of the 36,000-ton carrier *Akagi*. The seventeen *Yorktown* dive-bombers released over the 17,500-ton carrier *Soryu*.

Most of the planes emerged intact from the fire of the unprepared Japanese gunners. Fourteen of the thirty-two *Enterprise* dive-bomber crews even managed to nurse their planes and their fuel supplies home to the U.S. fleet. McClusky landed with five gallons left in his tanks. Some of his pilots came in dead stick. All but two of Leslie's *Yorktown* dive-bombers flew home.

The twenty U.S. dive-bomber crews which perished had sold their lives dearly. In six minutes they and the twenty-nine surviving crews had crippled a Japanese fleet which, in the previous three and a quarter hours, had repelled ninety-three [23] other American planes and destroyed forty-four of them without suffering a scratch.

Four U.S. bombs scored direct hits on the decks of *Kaga*, two on *Akagi*, and three on *Soryu*. All three flattops were at once turned into high-octane infernos. The Japanese carriers' damage control compared unfavorably with their gunnery. Their sailors were samurai, not smiths. And later that day, when fires had licked into magazines, when bulkheads were popping everywhere like firecrackers, when engine-room crews had been gassed, and when lists had increased to the capsize point, all three carriers were finally abandoned.

The undamaged 17,500-ton carrier *Hiryu* launched a tiny reprisal raid at five minutes after noon when it was apparent that the rest of the carriers were burning out of control and doomed. Only eighteen of *Hiryu*'s sixty-three planes, her dive-bombers, took part in the raid, yet they succeeded. They found the *Yorktown,* and the seven of them which penetrated *Yorktown*'s fighter cover scored three direct hits. Five of the *Hiryu*'s planes flew home and the *Yorktown* was left a pillar of fire. Skilled American mechanics, however, quenched the fires and made *Yorktown* outwardly battleworthy again in two hours. Then a second pathetically small flight from the *Hiryu*—this time of only five planes—found her again and sunk two torpedoes into her ravaged guts. All five of the Japanese planes survived her gunfire and flew home. Again the mechanical geniuses of the American fleet kept *Yorktown* afloat. They had her under tow and might have brought her ghost back to Pearl Harbor again, if, the

---

[23] Fifteen high-level Flying Fortresses, none of which had been destroyed; thirty-seven torpedo and dive-bombers from Midway, twenty-three of which had been destroyed; and forty-one torpedo planes from the U.S. carriers, twenty-one of which had been destroyed.

next day, she had not been finished off, once and for all, by two more torpedoes, this time from the Japanese submarine I-168.

In the aftermath of the battle, as both sides began to retreat, *Enterprise* pilots and orphaned *Yorktown* pilots hunted down the *Hiryu* and took their revenge. They left her so dead in the water that, at 5:10 A.M. on June 9, Admiral Nagumo ordered the destroyers attending her to sink her.

Before Coral Sea and Midway, Japan had had ten carriers, rated *in toto* at 215,100 tons.[24] After Midway she had left five carriers with a displacement of only 96,100 tons. She had lost 55 per cent of her striking power. During the remainder of the war her shipyards would launch another five carriers, displacing 142,800 tons. By then, however, these replacements for the vessels lost at Midway would seem hopelessly inadequate next to the carriers which were sliding by the dozen down U.S. ways.

Worse still for Japan was the loss of skilled pilots. Only six had perished in the dawn raid on Midway, only twelve in the defensive morning dogfights against U.S. raiders, only twenty-four in the attempts to find and then to sink the *Yorktown*. But in the pyres of the flight decks and in the ocean later were lost more than half the crew members of the 280-odd planes which went down, caged, in the hulks of the four sinking Japanese carriers. All the early morning flush had been taken from the mists of the Misty Lagoon. Japan had lost almost half her aces. Their years of experience, and of cool hand-eye co-ordination, gained over China, Luzon, Malaya, and Java would never be reproduced in the hectic Japanese manufacturing effort of the next three years.

With the carriers and the pilots Japan had lost all hope of fighting an aggressive war and winning it. There remained only a process of attrition and a hope that by stout defense the United States could be induced to pay a fair price for peace.

The six minutes of stubborn heroism and good luck which had finally enabled the United States, with its superior radio monitoring and code breaking and analysis, to win the Battle of Midway could not, at first, be believed by Admiral Yamamoto, in his 64,000-ton battleship to the rear. Until almost midnight of June 4, 1942, he continued to order countermeasures—even an artillery duel between his ships and the shore batteries on Midway. Shortly after midnight, however, when two of his carriers had sunk and two more were fit only to be scuttled, he gave up and called for a general retreat. Earlier in the afternoon one of his staff officers had asked: "How can we apologize to His Majesty for this defeat?" Yamamoto had replied, "Leave that to me. I am the only one who must apologize to His Majesty."

---

[24] There were also a half dozen Japanese merchant vessels rigged with flight decks. Such improvised carriers came to dominate the Japanese carrier fleet toward the end of the war. For lack of prestige, morale, and armament, none of them ever accomplished much.

No one in the Navy General Staff screwed up courage enough to tell Hirohito of the Midway debacle until some time after 3 P.M. on June 5, when it was 6 P.M. June 4 Midway time.[25] In Tokyo terms, "Abandon ship" had been ordered on the heavy carrier *Kaya* at 1:40 P.M., and the medium carrier *Soryu* had sunk at 4:13 P.M. *Akagi* and *Hiryu* were both derelicts already and would have to be abandoned later that night. Hirohito had spent the early afternoon in routine scheduled audiences and had only begun to ask how the Battle of Midway was going about 3 P.M. Thereafter, for the next twenty hours, he remained incommunicado to all but naval staff officers.

Lord Privy Seal Marquis Kido was officially told of the Midway disaster the next afternoon, June 6, at 1 P.M., by a naval aide-de-camp. Kido did not see the Emperor that day or the next. Instead he passed his time with his brother, Wada Koroku, the nation's leading aeronautical engineer, and with other leaders of the aircraft industry who might suggest balms for the sudden painful wound which had been inflicted in Japan's air arm. Finally at 10:40 A.M., June 8, Kido was summoned into the Imperial Presence. In his diary he wrote afterward:

> We talked about the Midway battle. I had supposed that news of our terrible losses would have caused him untold anguish. However, his countenance showed no trace of change. He said that the setback received had been severe and regrettable, but that notwithstanding he had told Navy Chief of Staff Nagano to carry on and to make sure that naval morale did not deteriorate. He emphasized that he did not wish the future policy of the Navy to become inactive and passive. I was very much impressed by the courage displayed by His Majesty today and I was thankful that our country is blessed with such a good sovereign.

Hirohito had lost. Kido knew that he knew it. But, on Kido's advice, he would not admit it for another three years.

---

[25] Tokyo's clocks ran three hours earlier by the sun than Midway's but by the calendar one day later.

28

CRUMBLING EMPIRE

(1942–1944)

MIDWAY DISMAY

To adopt a sumo-wrestling image used by an admiral in a letter to Lord Privy Seal Kido after the Battle of Midway, Japan had fancied herself a fencer in beginning the war—a small, deft, light-footed samurai. Through the protection of the gods, she wielded a fairy foil, an Excalibur of gossamer and lightning which had been kept for her, imbedded in the rock of ages, ready to be pulled out at the moment of her destiny. The terrifying U.S. monster, brandishing a battle-ax, must be dodged and pinked and slashed until it sighed from loss of blood and sank to its sluggish knees. Hirohito had given modern shape to Japan's holy sword in his naval air arm and its fast, light Zero fighter plane. At the Battle of Midway, the sword had broken off at its hilt.

Outside of Hirohito and his top courtiers, almost no civilians in Japan were allowed to know the fearful news of what had happened at Midway. On June 9, the day after Hirohito emerged from complete despair and resumed contact with his advisors, he called from the shadows General Ando Kisaburo, a trusted sixty-two-year-old partisan of the Strike South who had been one of the early patrons of Prime Minister Tojo. Hirohito appointed Ando czar of propaganda, serving in the Cabinet as a minister without portfolio.

The next day, June 10, Tokyo radio broke its five-day silence on the subject to announce that Japan had won a great victory, sinking two American carriers at Midway and destroying 120 U.S. planes for the loss of one Japanese carrier and thirty-five planes. Previously the Japanese news media had ignored some setbacks in China but never before had they had to tell such an utterly outrageous lie. On the following morning, June 11,

Hirohito asked Chief Aide-de-Camp Hasunuma whether it might not be well to reinforce popular acceptance of the false news by issuing an imperial rescript in praise of the Japanese commanders at Midway. Hasunuma consulted Lord Privy Seal Kido, and Kido, being less committed to war logic than Hirohito, saw the Emperor at once and persuaded him that the Throne was not yet so desperate as to make sacred rescripts into vehicles of propaganda.

Through the Navy General Staff Hirohito issued instructions that the wounded from Midway be brought back to Japan under tight security and impounded in tightly packed wards at Yokosuka Naval Hospital outside Yokohama. There they were to be held incommunicado until they could be healed, heartened, hushed, and reassigned.

Also on June 11, Kido received a visit from former Lord Privy Seal Count Makino's son-in-law Yoshida Shigeru. The versatile and accommodating Yoshida, who had led the first public political Strike-South movement as a trial balloon for Hirohito in the early 1930's and who would become for Hirohito the perennial prime minister of U.S.-dominated postwar Japan, was now charged with the difficult duty of organizing a Peace Faction for the possible political contingency of defeat. At a time when all but victorious thoughts were considered treasonable by the Thought Police, Yoshida's assignment was delicate and dangerous.

Even before Midway, Yoshida's Peace Faction had already established itself as a viable enterprise, subversive but countenanced. The initial task had been to enlist the services of Prince Konoye and of his right-wing partisans in the business community, in the rackets, and in the underworld of labor leaders. Here were the traditionalists and the practical patriots who could be relied upon to see future Japanese interests even through the purple filters of war propaganda.

The first difficulty had been in harnessing Prince Konoye himself. The Fujiwara prince felt keenly his failure in averting the war and was bitter about the downfall of the third Konoye Cabinet. In the second week of December 1941, when other Japanese were celebrating the Pearl Harbor victory, Konoye had gone about Tokyo making himself unpopular with dire predictions as to the future. Prime Minister Tojo, on December 17, asked Hirohito to muzzle him. On December 16, Kido had already moved in that direction by having a long heart-to-heart talk with Konoye. He had impressed upon the former prime minister that Japan was at war now, that the Emperor was deadly serious about prosecuting it, that loose pessimistic talk would not be condoned, and that, if Konoye expected defeat for Japan, he must serve the nation by preparing for it constructively.

Konoye took hard to his new role. Plotting peace quietly in back rooms did not suit his talents. He was more at home under the lights, leading mass rallies. Kido, however, held an ax over his head: exposure as a spy for treasonable association with Saionji Kinkazu, Ozaki Hotsumi, and

Soviet agent Sorge who were now under investigation or interrogation by the police. Prime Minister Tojo, who believed in seeing the war through, would be happy to prosecute Konoye if given a nod to do so. Konoye bowed to this argument, and a month later, on January 20, 1942, he met again with Kido, secretly, in one of the detached garden pavilions of the Kinsui Restaurant, where the rice at that time of year came in a little cold but the talk could be entirely private. There he reported to Kido on his first tentative efforts. He was in touch with Prince Higashikuni and with Count Makino's son-in-law Yoshida, also with Army and Navy staff officers who had been handling the contingency planning for defeat since 1938, and he was working on drafts of memoirs about his first, second, and third prime ministerships which would help to absolve the Emperor of his responsibility if and when they ever fell into enemy hands.

Meanwhile the ailing gossip Baron Harada, formerly secretary-spy in the household of the late Prime-Minister-Maker Saionji, was handling liaison with the police on the Sorge case. He reported to Kido on January 24, 1942, that Saionji Kinkazu, the grandson of the Constitution-framing patriarch, was severely condemned by police investigators for his part in mediating with the Soviet Union through Sorge during the years 1938–41. Kido had the secret police take an opinion poll of the leaders of various Japanese tongs, factions, and interests. The poll found that, when informed of the particulars of the Sorge case, the leaders were almost unanimously indignant against the "upper-class intellectuals" who had brought Red spies to the very portals of the Throne Room. A retired admiral, speaking for a naval veterans' group, succinctly voiced the consensus: "I take it for granted that Konoye has been put in custody, and that the announcement is being withheld in view of its international repercussions."

With this poll in pocket to use in managing Konoye, Kido advised Hirohito that it would be all right to spare Konoye embarrassment in the Sorge scandal. Hirohito called in the home minister, Yuzawa Michio, on February 19, 1942, and discussed the Sorge case with him in detail. On March 17, Saionji Kinkazu, Konoye's former intimate and the Sorge ring's contact, was taken into custody. He was tactfully interrogated for two months and then given two years in prison, sentence suspended.

Kido had the Imperial Court evince an attitude of strictly correct, wait-and-see impartiality about the Saionji case. Viscount Musha-no-koji Kintomo, director of the Peerage and Heraldry Bureau, was deeply concerned that his close association with the young Saionji might trouble the Throne. After consulting Hirohito, Kido assured Musha-no-koji that there was no cause for alarm: Hirohito himself would protect the Court from guilt by association and would see to it that young Saionji was fairly treated. In public token of the fact that the Saionji case must not be judged too hastily, Kido himself ostentatiously undertook the ceremonial duty of go-between in arranging the fashionable wedding of Saionji Fujio, a grandnephew of the late prime-minister-maker, with Aikawa Haruko, the daughter of Aikawa Yoshisuke, who had brought common-stock financing to Japan in the 1920's and had managed the industrial development of Manchukuo for the Army in the 1930's.

The marriage of Fujio and Haruko was celebrated at Frank Lloyd Wright's Imperial Hotel on the afternoon of April 3, 1942. The guest list included enough titled courtiers and beribboned admirals and generals to impress upon even the most zealous military secret policeman that the Saionji name was not to be dragged in the mud lightly. At the same time it was noted that Prince Konoye had begun to speak politely, almost meekly, of Prime Minister Tojo. This was because Kido had had a brutally frank conversation in private with Konoye before the wedding, on March 20, and had, in Kido's own words, "strongly and persistently impressed upon Konoye the need for prudence."

After the wedding, on April 12, the chastened Konoye, who despite his years as prime minister remained the youngest and most easily teased of Hirohito's Big Brothers, called on Kido and obediently "submitted for an opinion" a draft of a memoir on the course of the Japanese-American pre-war peace negotiations. Kido curtly urged him to take it home and rewrite it; it did not yet go far enough as a document of state in exculpating the Emperor.

This was the background against which Peace Faction leader Yoshida Shigeru called on Kido at his room in the Outer Palace on June 11, 1942, six days after the Battle of Midway. Yoshida knew that all chance of winning the war had been lost and felt that the Peace Faction must take diplomatic action at once to salvage as much as possible of Japan's empire before attrition set in. He proposed to Kido that Prince Konoye be sent immediately to Europe—with himself, Yoshida, in attendance as guardian-secretary—and there make a serious effort to see Allied diplomats and work out the terms of a peace settlement.

Yoshida submitted his proposal in the form of a letter written on paper suitable for presentation to the Throne. In this remarkable document—previously untranslated—the sixty-three-year-old Yoshida showed scant respect for the fifty-year-old Konoye, acute solicitude for Hirohito's personal pride, and a total lack of appreciation for the swiftness of events in a world at war:

> Mr. Konoye's primary purpose at the present pass is to do his utmost for the completion of the war and the establishment of a lasting peace. He might well take with him an ambassador or other emissary and a staff of Foreign Ministry experts. Under the guise of an inspection trip to Europe, he would travel west and on the way, whenever invited, he would talk to the heads of states and to various local leaders. He should proceed through the Soviet Union and other nations and on the way, in his informal capacity, should

stop for a while in some such neutral state as Switzerland which is strategically situated between the belligerent camps. There he would be able to
watch the development of political affairs and at the same time his suite
would be able to induce influential men of various nations to approach him.

If Germany then seemed to be winning, U.S. and British representatives
might come to him, looking for a way out. If otherwise, Germany might turn
to him with similar purpose. His background leads me [Yoshida] to think that
both the United States and Germany would consider him their ally. If I
[Yoshida] take due advantage of that fact, I could become the vanguard
leader of the peace.

If after several seasons in Europe, there does not seem to be any ray of
hope, Konoye should start for home as if nothing had happened. On the
other hand, if there is hope, I [Yoshida] will invite suitable cultural and
military officials, scholars, and business leaders—always when possible men
with good connections in Europe or America—to join us and help us prepare
a draft of a peace treaty which may be submitted to His Majesty as an
initial position paper. At the same time we shall try to enlighten the nation
as to where our true interests lie. Once the time comes ripe for world peace,
Konoye will thus be enabled, at the request of the imperial government, to
attend the peace conference as a plenipotentiary, taking with him all the responsible members of his suite. I, as a member, will be in charge of the
peace-making business at his plenipotentiary headquarters.

Not too surprisingly Kido pocketed Yoshida's letter and told the prime-
minister-to-be of postwar Japan that, before he and Konoye could go on a
peace junket to Europe, there was "much to be considered." No doubt
Konoye and Yoshida might get better terms than Japan would be able to
get if she fought on. But Kido, as a civilian, was not sure enough of his
assessment of the military situation to be positive that this was so. And he
knew that the people, after all the sacrifices they had made, the triumphs
they had gained, and the propaganda they had swallowed, would never
accept a realistic peace settlement now when they seemed to own all Asia.
Hirohito himself had not yet given up the war. He might be persuaded
personally that he had lost his gamble and that it would be best to give back
the Indies, the Philippines, Malaya, and China in return for Manchuria
and oil concessions in Borneo, but publicly the institution of the Throne
could not afford to seem so cowardly and sell so short.

Konoye's proposed trip abroad might be of use later in the war if Japan's
empire began to prove costly for the Americans to recapture. Now, after
the Battle of Midway, it could only impress the West as an admission of
weakness. It could serve no purpose which could not be served as well by
the tentative informal conversations which were taking place and getting
nowhere between Japanese and Allied spokesmen in Rome, Lisbon, Teheran, Bern, Buenos Aires, Madrid, Moscow, Stockholm, and Bangkok.
Later in the war, perhaps, when the democracies began to appreciate the
immense military strength of Russia and the Japanese people began to feel

weariness, hunger, and fear, it might be possible to negotiate a peace acceptable politically to both sides.

Kido was bound by his oath of office to tell Hirohito of Yoshida's proposal. Being a loyal vassal he presumably performed his bounden duty, but if so, he did not record the particulars in his diary. Instead Japan maintained a greedy appearance before the world and let slip her last chance of negotiating an advantageous peace.

"WHAT CAN THESE SHIPS BE?"

Before sending any special plenipotentiaries abroad, Hirohito hoped to recoup the Midway disaster and regain a bargaining position for the various peace emissaries he had posted to neutral capitals. In this endeavor the Japanese Army undertook to do by land what the Navy, at the Battle of the Coral Sea, had failed to do by sea: break in the door of northeastern Australia.

On July 21, 1942, an augmented Japanese regiment of about 8,000 men landed at Buna on the northeast coast of the island of New Guinea. Without opposition they established a beachhead and began to move inland toward the 7,000-foot passes of the Owen Stanley Range which lay athwart the overland route to Port Moresby. Australian scouts watched their advance and MacArthur began hurriedly to organize forces which would contest their passage through the mountains.

Hirohito and his staff at Imperial Headquarters expected that the Army thrust across New Guinea would be the focus of war activity in the months ahead. The day after the New Guinea landing, however, on July 22, 1942, the U.S. 1st Marine Division set out from Wellington, New Zealand, to create an altogether different theater of war which the Tokyo General Staffs had not contemplated. The Marines held a dress rehearsal in the New Hebrides north of New Zealand and went on, on August 7, to land 11,000 strong on an island still farther north, in the nominally Japanese-occupied Solomon Islands. Their selected target was the second most southern island in the chain, one that they would make famous, a Delaware-sized mound of coral, rain forest, and inactive volcano: Guadalcanal.

Guadalcanal was held by 2,500 Japanese of whom 400 were soldiers and the rest laborers and engineers. They were at work building an advance airstrip there. They made no effort to contest the U.S. landing but sent off a plaintive radio message to the Japanese stronghold of Rabaul 650 miles to the north, asking, "What can these ships be?" Then when the ships began disgorging, they hurriedly abandoned their half-built airstrip and retreated into the jungles of the interior.

The Japanese lack of fight disappointed some Marines, but most found their hands full enough without having to contend with hostile enemy fire. The jungle alone prevented the men of the first wave from reaching the

positions which they were supposed to occupy on their first night ashore
Behind them, the beaches were piled high with unsorted, unmoved supplie
—a logistic nightmare. Beyond, in the surf, landing barges milled about ir
confusion, vying with one another for empty stretches of beach where mor
cargo could be dumped and left as quickly as possible.

Hirohito and Combined Fleet commander Admiral Yamamoto wer
both informed of the American landing promptly, and in less than four hour
forty-five Japanese planes out of Rabaul were diverted from a raid on Nev
Guinea to an attack on the nascent American beachhead. An Australia
coast-watcher, left behind months earlier on the Japanese-held island o
Bougainville, saw the Betties and Zeros pass overhead and gave forty-fiv
minutes' warning of their coming on his jungle radio. As a result, severa
hundred American airmen from carriers *Saratoga, Wasp,* and *Enterpris*
were ready and waiting over the U.S. beachhead when the Japanese plane
came in. Avoiding the eighteen Zeros, they dived on the twenty-seve
Betties and wrought such havoc that the Japanese bombardiers scored bu
one direct hit, on the destroyer *Mugford.*

Less than half the Betties survived and started for home. The Zero
stayed on, looking for revenge. The Grumman Wildcat pilots obliged wit
a dogfight—but cautiously. They held together in six-plane clusters an
made the most of their superior numbers. Even so they lost several plane
and splashed only one Zero. They took, however, something of greate
importance to the morale of the Misty Lagoon virtuosos: the right eye o
one of the greatest air aces of World War II, Sakai Saburo.

Sakai had been dogfighting since 1937 and had sixty planes to his credit
plus a score or more probables. He came up from the rear on the bellie
of eight planes, in a group, which he thought to be Wildcats. Too late, a
he closed with them, he realized that they were bigger than Wildcats, som
of the new Avenger-class torpedo bombers. They looked like Wildcat
from the rear and they had lured him in by feigning fear and tightening u
their formation. Realizing that he had been trapped, he put his engine o
overboost and tried to jump through them with his guns blazing. He hi
two of them and was riddled by all sixteen of their tail guns. A burs
shattered his windshield and caught him in the head.

Moments later Sakai regained consciousness in the full freshness of th
slipstream which poured into his perforated cockpit. He did not know i
at the time but his right eye had been destroyed and his left was lidde
with dried blood from head wounds. Spitting on his scarf to wipe away th
blindness, flying sometimes right-side up and then again repeatedly up
side down, regaining consciousness again and again off on a tangent or jus
above the water, he somehow managed to fly a devious route home t
Rabaul. Over the empty ocean and the occasional green islets, his moment
of sober compass study and recollection served him miraculously. Wit
the little vision left in his left eye he landed his plane that evening, empt

of gas and two hours after the other stragglers of his flight had already
come in. The best eye surgeon in Tokyo enabled him to keep the sight of
his left eye, to become a flight instructor and test pilot, and even to go
back into action in a Zero against the next generation of U.S. planes over
Iwo Jima in 1944. Again he would survive and would emerge from the
war credited with sixty-four Chinese, British, Dutch, and U.S. combat
aircraft, a record unexcelled by any other living ace of the war in the
Pacific.[1]

THE SALVOS OF SAVO

During the hours of Sakai's flight home to Rabaul, Hirohito was considering the threat of the American landing on Guadalcanal. He was
vacationing at the time in Nikko, the magnificent mausoleum city of the
Tokugawas, some 75 miles north of Tokyo. As an expert geographer, he
did not need to be told that Guadalcanal lay 650 miles south of the Japanese advance air base of Rabaul and over 780 miles north of the advance
U.S. air base on Efate in the New Hebrides. How many American troops
had come ashore was unclear to him, but evidently they planned to stay
because they were reported to have laden the beaches with supplies and to
have set up anti-aircraft guns. If left to their own devices they would
complete the airstrip begun by Hirohito's own engineers and from this
unsinkable platform would be in a position to seize control of both air and
sea in the southern Solomons area.

There were two ways of countering the American threat: land men on
Guadalcanal in an attempt to drive out the Americans, or try to neutralize
the new American base by building in haste and in secret rival airfields on
other islands of the southern Solomons like San Cristobal or Malaita. Since
Japanese air routes to Rabaul were shorter than U.S. supply routes to New
Zealand and the New Hebrides, even one Japanese airstrip in the southern
Solomons would have an advantage over the field which the Americans
were preparing.

Nevertheless, on the advice of his military aides, Hirohito decided to
launch a counterinvasion of Guadalcanal. It was a questionable decision—
if only because top Army generals, who would have to supply the troops
for the effort, considered Guadalcanal a Navy problem and refused to
appreciate its strategic importance. Adroit commanders of the dissident
Strike-North group, who were charged with the defense of Manchuria

[1] Two other Japanese, who died, ran up higher scores: Nishizawa Hiroyoshi, 104,
and Sugita Shoichi, eighty. In Europe, however, Sakai's mark was topped by two
Finnish aces and over a score of Germans, led by the "Black Devil of the Ukraine,"
Erich Hartmann, who accounted for no less than 352 Allied planes. The top Allied
ace, excluding Russians, was Richard Bong of the U.S. Air Force, with forty kills, all
made in the Pacific Theater.

against the Russians, had only recently recovered the crack units which they had lent to the Strike South in 1941. To the best of their bureaucratic abilities they did not mean to lend again. General Yamashita had returned to their midst embittered, his plan for invading Australia vetoed. On his way back from Singapore to Mukden, he had not been given a victory parade in Tokyo. Indeed he had not been allowed to land in Japan at all, not even to see his family.

Because of the sulky attitude of General Yamashita and his partisans in the Kwantung Army, Chief of Staff Sugiyama planned to use only the troops available in the eastern part of the Empire to repel the American invaders. These, he assured Hirohito, would be more than sufficient. The 28th Regiment, formerly of the 17th Division but now in process of being built up to a division in its own right, was awaiting orders in Guam where it had gone for the aborted invasion of Midway. The 35th Brigade, 18th Division, could be detached from occupation forces in the Philippines and in the Palau Islands east of the Philippines. The 2d Division and, if necessary, most of the 38th Division could be spared from garrison duty in the East Indies. In all 60,000 well-trained troops could be thrown at the Americans without drawing at all from the continental forces in General Yamashita's sphere of influence. The problem would be to provide transports and naval escorts which could move the men for the counterinvasion to Guadalcanal.

The Rabaul commander, Vice Admiral Mikawa Gunichi, began immediately to test the difficulty of the transport problem. On the very night of the American landing, as soon as Hirohito had made his decision, Mikawa embarked all spare sailors and soldiers in Rabaul on six small transports and sent them on their way toward Guadalcanal. The next afternoon, August 8, U.S. submarine S-38 waylaid the little convoy and sank the largest of the transports with two well-placed torpedoes. More than 300 of the troops drowned and Mikawa recalled the other five transports to Rabaul.

That night the last of some 500 Japanese troops on two islets, Tulagi and Gavutu, off the north coast of Guadalcanal died fighting. They took with them more than 200 U.S. Marines. This small, violent action, in which no quarter was asked or given, put a seal of blood and pride on Hirohito's decision. The right to possess the 2,500 square miles of jungle on Guadalcanal would be contested bitterly for the next five and a half months.

A few hours later, at 1 A.M. August 9, Admiral Mikawa arrived in person off Guadalcanal with five heavy cruisers, two light cruisers, and a destroyer. His crews were in perfect prewar trim, unthinned by replacements and undaunted by the process of attrition which had already overtaken the crews and pilots of Japanese carriers. Mikawa's men had long specialized in night engagements and had trained for this moment for years: the first artillery duel between Japanese and U.S. surface fleets.

Mikawa surprised an equal force of U.S. cruisers and destroyers, equipped with radar, and sank it. In this Battle of Savo Island four Allied cruisers and a destroyer went to the bottom. Another cruiser and two destroyers were crippled and had to be sent home to dry dock. About 1,600 Allied sailors, most of them Americans, perished in the action—an action for which the exact casualties remain to this day officially untabulated in the U.S. Navy Department. Admiral Mikawa lost no ships and only fifty-eight men killed and fifty-three wounded. He later attributed his victory to the carelessness of U.S. commanders, the poor marksmanship of U.S. gunners, and the excellence of the Japanese oxygen-powered torpedo.

Despite his victory, or perhaps because of it, Admiral Mikawa returned to Rabaul without landing more than a few hundred troops as reinforcements for the tiny body of Japanese hiding in the Guadalcanal jungle.

Hirohito cut short his vacation at Nikko and on August 12 returned to Tokyo.

So began a routine of survival which became increasingly familiar and lethal to both sides. Every afternoon, a little before dusk, when U.S. planes had started home for their airstrip on Guadalcanal, a Japanese surface fleet—of destroyers usually—would break south from the area of Japanese Rabaul-based air superiority. At close to thirty knots, heading down "the Slot"—the channel between New Georgia and Santa Isabel islands—the Japanese raiders would arrive off Guadalcanal shortly after midnight. There they would have an hour to shell the U.S. airstrip, now named Henderson Field, and to land reinforcements on Cape Esperance at the Japanese end of the island. At about 1:30 A.M. they would turn and run for home, just in time to be taken under wing by Japanese early-morning patrols from Rabaul before being overtaken by planes launched at dawn from Henderson Field.

By day the tables would be turned. Holes in Henderson Field would be bulldozed over; damaged U.S. planes would be dragged from the underbrush, patched up, and put in the air with amazing celerity. Until the next sunset the U.S. dry-land air base would reassert unassailable authority over 100 miles of sea in every direction. Japanese ships would shun the area and marching Japanese soldiers on their end of Guadalcanal would prudently skirt clearings.

U.S. strategists sought repeatedly to break Japan's reign over the night. Theoretically, U.S. skippers had a great advantage because radar, which had not yet been installed in Japanese vessels, made it possible to "see in the dark" and take a bead on approaching Japanese vessels before their crews had been called to quarters. Vigilant Japanese crews, however, slept by their guns and responded instantly when fired upon. U.S. guns, as yet, were not powered by flashless explosives. Given one spurt of flame in the night, one target, and the Japanese gunners and torpedo men were always ready to demonstrate their expert marksmanship. As a result, the nightly "Tokyo Express" of Japanese destroyers repeatedly emerged from U.S. traps claiming correctly that they had ambushed their ambushers.

Japanese strategists, for their part, kept trying to break the U.S. hold over the daylight hours. Again and again large flights of Zeros and Betties seized control of the air over Guadalcanal for a few hours, shot up U.S. air facilities, and returned home after suffering heavy losses and achieving nothing permanent. The next morning there were always planes again to take off from Henderson Field and resist the next Japanese air raid.

Japan did not possess the thousands of planes flying in waves from Rabaul which would have been needed to keep uninterrupted daytime air superiority over Guadalcanal. Consequently U.S. pilots always had time to land and refuel between Japanese raids. In addition, since they fought near home, they could often bail out and survive after their planes had been technically shot down. A day or two later they would be back in action with a new plane or one put together from a dozen wrecks by Henderson Field's uncanny mechanics. As the days passed these U.S. advantages told heavily on the thinning ranks of the Misty Lagoon airmen. New Japanese pilots, arriving daily in Rabaul from accelerated flight courses, proved increasingly incompetent. The mighty Zero, when flown too often without adequate overhaul, proved increasingly treacherous. By the end of August Japanese pilots were flying mostly one-way missions and were saving these supremely patriotic efforts for occasions when they could do something valuable to further the objectives of the next night's Tokyo Express.

TOJO'S THIRD HAT

The deteriorating Guadalcanal situation made Hirohito edgy and precipitated a crisis in the Cabinet. Foreign Minister Togo persisted in looking upon the conquests of the Strike South as temporary acquisitions made solely for the purpose of striking a better bargain with the United States. Hirohito acknowledged that the territories Japan had seized might have to be given back if the war went wrong, but he refused to think of them as poker chips and nothing more. He had liberated them from Western colonialism. He had added their strength to the Empire. At the very least, they represented distances and battlegrounds which would cost the barbarian dear and keep him out of the homeland for many years.

Buffered by the conquered territories, Hirohito thought he could look forward to a long, slow war. After Midway he had ordered Japan's next generation of airplanes and other weapons to be ready for mass production by the end of 1944. He had encouraged Army commanders to build monuments to Japanese war dead in Singapore and Manila, to establish schools for teaching the Japanese language to the natives, and to select local leaders to head puppet governments—José Laurel in the Philippines, Sukarno in Indonesia, Ba Maw and U Nu in Burma.

Foreign Minister Togo refused to take seriously the Co-Prosperity Sphere and the New Order in East Asia. He assigned lowly Foreign Ministry clerks to handle relations with the various quisling governments. He kept all his skilled diplomats at work on the peace problem: on relations with Hitler and Mussolini, the possible victors, and on dealings with neutral nations, the possible mediators.

At the urging of the retired ubiquitous Lieutenant General Suzuki Teichi, chief of the Cabinet Planning Board for wartime legislation, Hirohito had decided to create a Greater East Asia Ministry which would relieve Togo of responsibility for intramural Co-Prosperity Sphere diplomacy. Togo at first had acquiesced in the new ministry as a piece of unimportant imperial finery, but on second thought he had realized that he might be hampered in peace negotiations with the West unless he could speak knowledgeably for the native political leaders in the former Asiatic colonies of the West.

In particular Togo saw that he must keep the right to negotiate with Chiang Kai-shek. If all diplomacy in Asia came under the authority of the proposed new ministry, the only channel to Chiang would be through the puppet Chinese government of Wang Ching-wei. Wang would muddy the waters and prevent the making of the sort of realistic settlement with China which Togo saw as a necessary preliminary to peace with the West. China was beaten. Japan was in process of being beaten. Asia must salvage itself from the wreckage. Hirohito had agreed in principle that all Japanese troops should be withdrawn from China. On this pledge Togo had high hopes of constructing a mutually face-saving treaty with China. Without such a treaty, Togo saw no prospect of making a bargain with the United States. And without a free hand for himself, unrestricted by the proposed Greater East Asia Ministry, Togo feared that he would be unable to negotiate fruitfully with Chiang Kai-shek.

Togo felt fortified in his convictions after talking to Nomura, Kurusu, and other members of the former Japanese Embassy in Washington who returned to Yokohama on a diplomatic exchange ship on August 20, 1942. Lord Privy Seal Kido's daughter and his son-in-law, Tsuru Shigeto, a lawyer and member of the spy service, were also among those repatriated. The homecomers told of the incredible unity which had been wrought in the United States by Pearl Harbor and of the fearsome all-out mobilization of U.S. industry. Hirohito gave lunch to Nomura and Kurusu on August 21 and on August 25 received a briefing from repatriated Navy Captain Yokoyama Ichiro—also of the former Washington staff—who had had charge of Japanese espionage in the United States.

Also on August 25, Foreign Minister Togo came to the palace to speak against the proposed Greater East Asia Ministry and to urge Hirohito to pursue negotiations with Chiang Kai-shek as expeditiously and sincerely as possible. Hirohito listened noncommittally, spoke irrelevantly of his chats with the repatriates from Washington, and obliquely reminded Togo of the Foreign Ministry's failure to declare war on time the previous December. The thorny Togo felt rebuked and left the palace looking even more stiffly correct than usual.

A week later, on September 1, the establishment of the Greater East Asia Ministry came formally before the Cabinet for a vote. Foreign Minister Togo refused to make the vote unanimous and insisted that, if the new ministry was established, he would have to resign. Prime Minister-War Minister Tojo reported to the palace that he, too, would have to resign unless Togo could be brought around. Hirohito asked why Togo could not simply be replaced with a different foreign minister. He was told that no qualified diplomat was willing to set himself up as an opponent of the upright Togo by stepping immediately into Togo's shoes. Hirohito suggested that, in that case, Prime Minister Tojo could hold the portfolio of foreign minister along with those of war and prime minister which he already held.

Tojo demurred. He had already taken responsibility for representing both military and civilian factions in the government. If he also undertook to represent both the war and peace factions in it, his political position would become untenably broad.

Hirohito was "surprised" by General Tojo's modesty and called in Navy Minister Shimada to do something quickly to find a way out of the impasse. Shimada went directly from the Throne Room to an hour and a half tête-à-tête with Prime Minister Tojo. At 5 P.M. September 1, when the conversation had been going on for an hour, Shimada phoned Lord Privy Seal Kido and asked that a further, more complete clarification of Tojo's position be made to the Throne. Twenty-five minutes later, when Hirohito had promised to understand all the fine points of Tojo's scruples, Tojo relented, agreed to fire Togo, and undertook to wear, for himself, all three hats of prime minister, war minister, and foreign minister.

Two weeks later, when the crusty Togo had retired and diplomatic passions had been calmed, a pair of minor members of the Eleven Club, Tani Masayuki and Aoki Kazuo, agreed respectively to shoulder the positions of foreign minister and Greater East Asia minister in the resuscitated Tojo Cabinet. In that interim, on September 7, Baron Hiranuma, the long-faced lawyer who was the leader of Japan's most respectable conservatives, saw the Emperor in private audience about the "Chungking Operation." The next day, September 8, a special envoy was dispatched to China, with Hirohito's instructions, to renew peace negotiations with Chiang Kai-shek. The negotiations would continue, off and on, at the same high, secret, official level throughout the rest of the war. They would accom plish nothing but exchange of ideas until Japan finally admitted defeat. Then, however, they would contribute to the Japanese Army's efficient turn-over of eastern China to the forces of Chiang Kai-shek rather than to those of Mao Tse-tung.

SEESAW STRUGGLE OF SUPPLY

In Washington, too, the costly insolubles of the Guadalcanal situation caused much political anguish. Officially the U.S. government was com-mitted to total support of Great Britain against Germany and minimal at-tention to the Japanese threat against Australia. President Roosevelt, how-ever, had appointed Admiral Ernest J. King to over-all command of the two U.S. fleets, and King was well known to be far more interested in the Pacific than in the Atlantic. On taking office, he had single-handedly com-mitted several important U.S. officials, one by one, to the Guadalcanal gamble. Now, with President Roosevelt's assistance, he was repeatedly finding new planes and ships which could be subtracted from the "crusade in Europe" and stuffed into the breaches being blown in Japan's stubborn defense of Guadalcanal.

For the sake of Guadalcanal's pestiferous swamps and solemn, empty forests, no less than seven major fleet engagements were fought and no less than four major Japanese land offensives were repulsed. Only after these actions could U.S. forces call the tiny Guadalcanal beachhead their own and go on to occupy and investigate the other 2,400 square miles of the island.

The Savo Island engagement, first of several U.S. naval disasters, was followed, on August 18, by the landing on Guadalcanal of the Japanese augmented 28th Regiment, which had been standing by on Guam since the Midway rebuff. This regiment was led by Colonel Ikki Kiyonao (or Ichiki Kiyonao as he is usually but incorrectly called), a kinsman of Hirohito's pre-1933 Imperial Household Minister Ikki Kitokuro. Colonel Ikki led his men against U.S. positions in one of the first large banzai charges of the war. The well-entrenched Marines stood by their machine guns and re-pulsed the attack with dreadful slaughter, killing more than 800 Japanese and losing only fifty Marines.

Another naval battle ensued for the right to land more Japanese rein-forcements on Guadalcanal. It is remembered as the Battle of the Eastern Solomons. It was an air engagement, fought on August 24–25 between Japanese and U.S. carrier pilots. It ended in a numerical victory for the United States. The 10,000-ton light carrier *Ryujo* and destroyer *Mutsuki* were lost by Japan, while the U.S. carrier *Enterprise* was forced to with-draw after three direct bomb hits and a heavy loss of life.

Despite the American victory, the Japanese were able to land on Guadal-canal most of the 35th Brigade, 18th Division, from the Philippines and Palau: another 10,000 or more men to add to the 8,000–9,000 survivors of Ikki's 28th Regiment. The newcomers were commanded by Major General Hyakutake Seikichi,[2] the younger brother of Hirohito's Grand Chamberlain Admiral Hyakutake Saburo.

While Hyakutake's men marched to their positions through the jungle, the Japanese Navy forced some late adjustments on the balance sheet left by the Battle of the Eastern Solomons. On August 28 Marine dive-bombers caught the Tokyo Express at sunset and lit a fire in *Asagiri* which blew the Japanese destroyer out of the water. During the breakfast hour on August 31, submarine I–26 torpedoed the U.S. aircraft carrier *Saratoga,* forcing her to withdraw from the theater of operations for over three months. On September 3 and 5 were sunk three old U.S. destroyers on transport duty, *Colhoun* by bombing, *Little* and *Gregory* by shellfire from the "Express."

Hyakutake's fresh troops mounted full-scale bayonet charges against Marine trenches on the nights of September 12 and 13. A recorded fifty-nine Marines and 708 Japanese died. On September 16 Hirohito personally informed Lord Privy Seal Kido that the Japanese counterattack had failed

Hyakutake had his men withdraw and regroup by dint of long treks through the jungle. They lacked food. They lacked medicine. They found no farms to pillage. The barks and herbs of the rain forest provided bitter sustenance. By the time they had complied with orders, they had lost far more men to malaria and hunger than they had ever lost to bullets.

On September 14, during Hyakutake's retreat, the submarines of Big Brother Marquis Komatsu's wolf pack enjoyed a run of luck. They heavily damaged the U.S. battleship *North Carolina,* standing off Guadalcanal fatally damaged the destroyer *O'Brien;* and sank on the spot the carrier *Wasp.* Only two U.S. carriers remained seaworthy in the Pacific: *Hornet* and *Enterprise.* Despite the U.S. defeat and while Tokyo celebrated it American Admiral Fletcher, on September 18, ran an unexpected convoy up to Guadalcanal and succeeded in landing the whole of the U.S. 7th Marine Division and all its supplies before Japanese airmen at Rabaul were aware of what had happened.

For the first time the U.S. troops on Guadalcanal had adequate supplies of chewing gum, cigarettes, earth-moving equipment, and ammunition. Some of the supplies, to be sure, were not strictly essential. White shoe polish, for instance, soon glutted the Marines' barter market. On the other hand, some useless items possessed great morale-building potential, and a few days after the 7th Marines' landing every man jack on the island was issued, with breakfast, three condoms. The shouts of delight could be heard almost to Rabaul. Visionaries spoke of the day when

[2] Also known as Hyakutake Haruyoshi and Hyakutake Harukichi. He himself used Seikichi, the Chinese-ified form of his given name, for prewar *Who's Who* entries. His parents preferred Haruyoshi, the Japanese reading. Harukichi, found in previous English-language accounts, is a mixed reading coined by a SCAP interpreter

nurses and W.A.C.'s would arrive on the island. Realists wrote letters home describing the new general-issue containers that would keep candy fresh in the swamps. On September 23, Marine commander Brigadier General Alexander Vandegrift mounted his first serious offensive against Japanese positions on the east end of the island. He gave it up quickly when sixty-seven Marines were mowed down from well-placed, well-entrenched Japanese gun positions.

Ten days later, over Prime Minister Tojo's objections, Hirohito publicly upheld the sentence of death passed on three of the captured American fliers who had bombed Tokyo with Doolittle. He thereby impressed upon the Japanese masses that they were in a war to the death.

On the night of October 11–12, the U.S. fleet again ambushed the Tokyo Express, this time successfully. For U.S. destroyer *Duncan,* which was sunk, the Japanese skippers parted with heavy cruiser *Furutaka* and destroyers *Fubuki, Muragumo,* and *Natsugumo,* also sunk. At last U.S. surface vessels could claim a victory. It was marred only slightly by the fact that the Japanese ships before they sank had made a major supply drop to Hyakutake's troops on the island. This small Japanese accomplishment was immediately nullified, on October 13, when advance groups of the 164th Regiment of the U.S. Army began landing on the island. That night, however, two Japanese battleships came down the Slot with the usual Tokyo Express of destroyers and turned big guns on Henderson Field for seventy minutes. Thirty-four of the thirty-nine U.S. dive-bombers on the field and sixteen of the forty Wildcat fighters were destroyed beyond repair.

The Japanese naval sacrifice was followed by the largest offensive yet on the part of the gradually built up Japanese land forces. In addition to the remnants of Ikki's men and Hyakutake's men, most of the Japanese 2d Division from the East Indies was now stealing about through the jungle. The combined Japanese force of some 30,000 men was led by a new commander, Lieutenant General Maruyama Masao, a former military-academy classmate of Hirohito's two uncles and a late (1923) recruit of Hirohito's early spy ring in Europe. Being a fully professional soldier and not merely a nepotistic adjunct of the Imperial Court like Ikki and Hyakutake before him, Maruyama promised sure results. He marshaled his men for a three-pronged attack which was to be co-ordinated with a major Japanese fleet effort.

Due to breakdowns in communications and delays imposed by the jungle, the big Japanese effort dissipated itself over a four-day period like a string of wet firecrackers. The tank attack took place a day early, on October 23, because the tank commander had failed to hear of a twenty-four-hour postponement. Nine tanks and 600 infantrymen perished as a result. On October 24 Maruyama's main effort piled 2,000 corpses before Marine entrenchments but failed, at bayonet point, to overrun them. Two nights later a Japanese regiment, which had been detained by the jungle, burst from the trees in one last banzai fizzle. More than 2,000 Japanese soldiers had been killed and had taken with them less than 200 of their well-entrenched Marine adversaries. In the words of a Marine commander, Maruyama's men had fallen prey to "impetuosity, arrogance, and tactical inflexibility."

During the land action on October 25, the U.S. and Japanese carrier fleets closed to within striking distance of one another in an effort—the Santa Cruz Islands battle—to provide air cover for the men ashore. The Japanese task force withdrew after carriers *Zuiho* and *Shokaku* and heavy cruiser *Chikuma* had been severely damaged and light cruiser *Yura* had been sunk. The U.S. force, however, had lost permanently the services of destroyer *Porter* and carrier *Hornet*. Only one U.S. carrier in the whole Pacific, the *Enterprise,* remained operative, and once again the redoubtable *Enterprise* had sustained much damage, including the loss of forty-four crewmen killed.

HUNGRY AND MAROONED

Hirohito bleakly admitted to Kido on October 27: "The second attack has failed. We will make another." Kido had spent the week encouraging the Peace Faction to perfect its undercover organization and to pursue its preparation of cover stories against the contingency of defeat. He had met with Konoye in Tokyo University Detached Hospital on October 21 and had arranged since then for a clandestine meeting of all important peace proponents early in November at which they could be briefed on the political problems of peace and assigned specific missions. On October 28, after acknowledging the failure of the "second attack," Hirohito gave his personal instructions to a new Japanese ambassador to Rome, Hidaka Shunrokuro, empowering him to assure the Vatican that Japanese armies were ready to withdraw from China and that Japanese claims to a priv-ileged-nation status in Southeast Asia would be minimal if peace could be restored.

President Franklin D. Roosevelt, too, was nervous. As a nautical en-thusiast and former Assistant Secretary of the Navy, he was alarmed by the disappearance of U.S. carriers from Guadalcanal waters and fearful lest the Marine heroes, on the eve of the 1942 Congressional elections, be cut off from air support. Minutes after the sinking of carrier *Hornet* at the Santa Cruz Islands battle, he memoed the chiefs of staff "to make sure that every possible weapon gets into that area to hold Guadalcanal."

In response to Roosevelt's pressure, the Marines on October 30 mounted their second offensive against the Japanese end of Guadalcanal and were again repulsed after seventy-one Marines had been killed. The Japanese positions attacked were those of General Hyakutake's men. General Maru-yama and General Ikki were both lost in the interior of the island, sti retreating, starving, and trying to regroup after their disastrous repulse a week earlier.

During the Marines' election-eve attack, General Hyakutake wired urgently for relief on behalf of his debilitated forces. In the first week of November two battalions of the Japanese 38th Division from the East Indies—some 5,000 men—were duly landed by the Tokyo Express to be added to the hungry mouths already present.

On November 8, with the elections over, Vice Admiral William Halsey, U.S. Navy Commander South Pacific, called personally at Guadalcanal to take a firsthand look at the situation. He was regaled on his first night by a shelling from the Tokyo Express and a bombing from "Washing-Machine Charley," the one extraordinary Japanese night pilot who regularly marked Henderson Field for the offshore destroyers by dropping flares and a 250-pound bomb on it. After a night behind rotting sandbags, Halsey held a press conference in which he delivered a famous prescription for the winning of the war: "Kill Japs. Kill Japs. Keep on killing Japs."

The Japanese effort to supply Halsey with the most necessary ingredient for his formula—cannon fodder—reached its high point a week later when eleven Japanese transports carrying the remaining 17,000-odd men of the 38th Division set sail from Rabaul with suitable naval escort. There followed the naval Battle of Guadalcanal in which, once again, Japanese fleet units overcame U.S. radar advantages of foreknowledge and night vision with superior gunnery and ship management. The battle was rejoined on three successive evenings. When it was over the U.S. Navy had lost seven destroyers, plus three salvageable derelicts; two cruisers sunk and two heavily damaged; and one badly mauled battleship. The Japanese had lost only two battleships and two destroyers from the fleet but with them eleven transports and more than a tenth of the reinforcement troops of the 38th Division. Some of the surviving foot soldiers were dumped in the waters off Cape Esperance to make their way ashore and join the Japanese Guadalcanal expeditionary force; most were returned as salvage to Rabaul aboard Japanese destroyers.

The U.S. Navy had suffered another humiliating defeat, but the Japanese Navy had failed in its purpose of landing a fully equipped Japanese division on Guadalcanal. The United States already had two of its divisions on "the Canal," each equal in firepower and together equal in manpower to a Japanese division. The Japanese still had more than a division's worth of men on the island but not nearly enough ammunition, food, and medicine to make them able-bodied troops.

The news of the Navy's latest victorious failure reached Tokyo in the early morning hours of November 16. Prime Minister Tojo promptly called off a scheduled visit to Manila and points south. Hirohito ordered his former athletics director, Big Brother Admiral Komatsu, to devise means of using his wolf pack of submarines for supply purposes to keep the men

on Guadalcanal from starving. Lord Privy Seal Kido belatedly digeste⟨
news of the battle the next evening, November 17, while listening t⟨
orchestral extracts from *Götterdämmerung* at a farewell concert conducte⟨
by the great German maestro Felix Weingartner. Two days later, on th
nineteenth, Hirohito asked Kido to make necessary arrangements for
state visit to be paid soon to the tombs of the imperial ancestors in Kyot⟨
so that Hirohito could go to pray at the shrine of Amaterasu, the su
goddess, on Ise Peninsula.

Admiral Komatsu's submarine fleet experimented for several weeks wit
methods of using torpedo tubes to launch watertight drums of rice. Whi⟨
the tests were in progress, the 30,000 Japanese on Guadalcanal lived o
root soups and ancient, mildewed packets of dried fish. By the end ⟨
November a minority of the front-line troops, manning the Japane⟨
trenches, were fully ambulatory. The others waddled about on ankl⟨
plump with the fluids of beriberi. The destroyers of the Tokyo Expre⟨
continued nightly to drop drums of supplies off Cape Esperance, but U.
torpedo boats prevented the drops from being made close to shore an
early morning U.S. strafing planes, plus fickle tides and currents, prevente
many of the drums from ever being picked up by the hungry Japanese ⟨
the beaches.

By the end of the month, the Japanese had been goaded into piling th
decks of the Tokyo Express with food containers and stuffing even som
of the destroyers' torpedo tubes with rice and soya sauce. In the sma
hours of November 30 Halsey's men lay in wait for one of these supply ru⟨
with six destroyers and four heavy cruisers. Rear Admiral Tanaka Raizo–
or as he was known to the Marines on 'Canal, "Tenacious Tanaka of th
Tokyo Express"—had with him that night only eight destroyers of whi⟨
six had been modified for transport duty and partially stripped of arm⟨
ment. Tanaka steamed unwarned into the American trap and emerged fro⟨
the other side of it with all his sharpshooting gun crews blazing away
their best and luckiest. The fiasco which followed has never been ful⟨
explained, but some of the U.S. ships were certainly fired upon by o⟨
another as well as by the Japanese. Tanaka dropped no supplies that nig⟨
but his squadron expended all its torpedoes and returned to Bougainvi⟨
with the loss of one destroyer. Behind him he left chaos. Heavy cruis⟨
Northampton sank. Heavy cruiser *Minneapolis* had taken two Japane⟨
torpedoes. Heavy cruiser *New Orleans* remained incredibly afloat a⟨
wallowed off for home under her own steam at five knots despite the lo⟨
of 120 feet of bow, more than a fifth of the ship. In the after engine roo⟨
of heavy cruiser *Pensacola* a fire raged out of control for twelve hou⟨
The bushwhackers had been whacked, and it was evident to U.S. captai⟨
that they had much to learn about the use of radar in night actions befo⟨
they could depend on it.

Tanaka's brilliant victory did nothing to ease Hirohito's concern for t⟨

hunger of the 30,000-odd Japanese troops on Guadalcanal. Somewhat tartly he ordered Big Brother Admiral Komatsu, whose carelessness had contributed so importantly to the defeat at Midway, to spare not his elite submarine corps in running the U.S. blockade. Over the grumbling of his skippers, Komatsu put eleven submarines on immediate Guadalcanal duty and a number more into dry dock for modification as underwater transports. By early January a score of I-boats had been fitted to carry "freight tubes." These were rafts, powered by two torpedoes and steered by a big rudder and a crewman in a loincloth. After the contraption was released from periscope depth, it bobbed to the surface and would carry two tons of food to a beach as much as two and a half miles away. By late January the underwater sleds and their valiant helmsmen were bringing ten ounces of rice a day to every one of the 30,000 famished defenders of Guadalcanal. In the supply operation, Admiral Komatsu, however, lost two of the veteran wolves of his pack: I–3 on December 9 and I–1 on January 29.

WAR'S FIRST BIRTHDAY

On the Guadalcanal beachhead, U.S. commanders waited for hunger and malaria to do their work in the Japanese ranks. The U.S. force now included elements of four Army divisions as well as of two Marine divisions. On December 7, the American anniversary of Pearl Harbor, Marine General Vandegrift turned over his command to the Army's Major General Alexander Patch and accompanied the sick and tired remnants of his 1st Marine Division to Australia for rest and rejuvenation. Less than two thirds of the men were still fit to sit in a trench. Many of them, on the happy day of embarkation, found themselves too weak to swarm up the cargo nets and had to be hauled aboard the transports in slings. No Marine was too weak, however, to mutter a last contented four-letter word at the sight of Guadalcanal dropping below the horizon.

Hirohito celebrated the end of the first year of war the next day, December 8, by exchanging empty telegrams of congratulations with Hitler and Mussolini. The Japanese carrier fleet had been lost at Midway. The rest of the aces of the Misty Lagoon had fallen one by one over Henderson Field. The Army's infantrymen had not been able to demonstrate their long-vaunted spiritual superiority over the U.S. foot soldier. Only in the obsolescent art of surface fleet actions, which had brought Japan to the fore as a military power in the days of Emperor Meiji, had the hand of the samurai kept its cunning.

Hirohito's cup of misery was topped off to overflowing by his mother, Empress Dowager Sadako. Three days before Pearl Harbor Sadako had withdrawn from Tokyo to her villa in Numazu where she had sequestered herself with cronies of the late Prince Saionji in visible demonstration of her antiwar sentiments. Hirohito had complained of her lack of patriotism;

finally, on September 18, in a gesture of extraordinary humility and sincerity, he had sent Empress Nagako personally to Numazu to remonstrate with her. Unable to refuse Nagako's pleas, the lovely fifty-eight-year-old queen mother had agreed to return to Tokyo on December 5 when she would have completed a full year of self-imposed exile. She had kept her promise. Now, on December 8, she was back in her Tokyo palace where she ceremonially belonged. But Hirohito almost wished that he had let her stay in Numazu. He understood that no sooner had she resumed residence than she had begun telling her friends that she had come home to share the suffering of the people of Tokyo in the months ahead.

On December 9, 1942, the first day of the second year of the war, Hirohito arose with hearty gruffness to make a new start. At 10:30, observing a quaint old Court custom, he bestowed articles of his apparel and other souvenirs on his most trusted courtiers and brusquely went on, at 10:35, to have an hour-long talk with Lord Privy Seal Kido. Kido adjured him to do nothing rashly logical, but to nurse the nation's resources, fight as long a war as possible, and give his political advisors maximum opportunity to salvage some sort of favorable settlement.

Hirohito went on to a liaison conference with the chiefs of staff and principal Cabinet ministers at which was debated at length and finally recommended to him for approval a most curious act of state. From now on, it was resolved, the Emperor would continue freely to attend liaison conferences as he had been doing for the last fifteen months, but his attendance would no longer convert the proceedings automatically into a Conference in the Imperial Presence. Instead such meetings would now be officially designated as Political-Military Liaison Conferences Which Happen To Take Place Before His Majesty.[3] The minutes of them would no longer have to be entered on the palace rolls. Observations made at them would no longer be officially binding reports to the Throne, on which a man staked his honor and his life, but simply thoughts and nothing more.

Prime Minister Tojo personally arose in the presence of Hirohito, who was present only unofficially, and promised to explain officially to Hirohito in the Throne Room the object of the resolution. It would enable Hirohito to communicate "frequently to his ministers his decisions regarding national imperial affairs and war guidance"; it would allow him to satisfy his need "to make sure of the decisive willingness of the members of the government and of the supreme command, as his duty-bound assistants, to carry out the war to its end"; and finally it would inaugurate the first of "frequent conferences with His Majesty undertaken without complex procedural arrangements and limitations."

Hirohito withdrew, nodding approvingly, to his Throne Room in the Outer Palace to receive Prime Minister Tojo's official report on the meeting

---

[3] *Gozen ni Okeru Diahonei Seifu Renraku Kaigi.*

which had just been held at Imperial Headquarters in the Imperial Palace. At last, in this moment of national emergency, Hirohito had been freed to exercise his authority openly without being held responsible, as a sacred institution, liable before the ancestors and the sun goddess, for every notion which tripped across his tongue. The mummery had ended and from now on appearances would have to be kept up only for the sake of the masses and of the Americans if they conquered.

Thirty-six hours later, at 7:50 A.M., Friday, December 11, 1942, Hirohito emerged in state from the *Niju-bashi* or Double-bridge Gate of the palace and with police sirens shrilling and tires screaming arrived at Tokyo station in time to pull out with his own chrysanthemum-emblazoned special train precisely at 8 A.M. The train stopped at Kyoto station at 4:10 P.M. Fifteen minutes later Hirohito stepped down from his Rolls-Royce in the palace grounds of his ancestors.[4]

The next day, with equal dispatch and security, Hirohito traveled along the branch line from Kyoto south to Ise Peninsula and the shrine of the sun goddess, Amaterasu. From Ise station, in an amphitheater of wooded hills, his cavalcade drove to the holy Isuza River, through the great wooden π-shaped arch marking the entrance to the sacred precincts, and across the open park where pilgrims camped. He stopped at the "cleansing brook" for a traditional sip of water. On foot now, Hirohito and his retinue entered the forest of giant cryptomerias which surrounded the holy of holies. They paused at the fence, beyond which commoners could not go, then entered the hallowed enclosure of the shrine buildings. At the outer shrine belonging to the goddess of grain Hirohito officiated at a service for the continued fertility and prosperity of his people.

Then the Emperor of Japan left his worldly attendants behind him and went on alone, deeper into the forest, to the inner shrine of Amaterasu. It was a severely simple hut, preserving the architectural styles used by Hirohito's forebears when they still lived somewhere in southeastern Asia two thousand years earlier. It was built of unfinished ground cypress or *hinoki,* the tree of the sun, and thatched with bark of *hinoki.* The gable rafters from the interior crossed through lashings and protruded from the thatch in a pair of horns at either end of the roof. The eaves and doorposts were wrapped in ornaments of bright brass. White silk curtains stirred in the breeze before the entrance and on either side stood fresh branches of *sakaki,* the tree of the gods, *Cleyera ochnacea,* the Shinto equivalent of the mistletoe used by the ancient Druids of Britain.

Outside the inner shrine Hirohito was served a light midday repast by the chief priestess of Ise, a distant cousin. He was by now well versed in the

---

[4] In the interval he had nodded at dignitaries gathered to greet him in the station and had completed, at rush hour, through the narrow, crowded streets of the old capital, a drive for which modern "kamikaze" cabbies usually require fifteen minutes even in the early morning hours before sunup.

Ise mysteries and no longer felt embarrassed by his high-priestly role in them. He had paid his first visit to the shrine a few days before leaving Japan in 1921 for his European tour. He had returned to it to report on his marriage in 1924, on his official enthronement in 1928, and again, on conquests, several times thereafter. He had now made his pilgrimage more often than any other Emperor before him, including even his devout grandfather, that deft master of the appropriate gesture, Emperor Meiji.

Hirohito munched the garnished rice slowly and gazed at the tall cryptomerias. Then he dismissed the priestess and passed alone into the holy of holies which housed the remains of Amaterasu's sacred mirror of wisdom. He spent almost an hour of prayer within while his retainers fidgeted in pious silence a stone's throw away at the outer shrine.

Kido wrote in his diary:

> Since this was an unprecedented occasion, I did not dare to guess the depths of his feelings. It was enough to be one of his retainers and to assume the burden of honor in being able to attend him at such a momentous ceremony.

ADVANCING BACKWARD

Fortified by communion with the wellsprings of his race and his power, Hirohito returned to Tokyo the next day greatly relieved and ready at the same time to retrench and to fight on. During the next two weeks his grand chamberlain's brother, General Hyakutake, repulsed the third U.S. offensive on Guadalcanal with little difficulty. One entrenched Japanese veteran and five of the recently arrived U.S. Army G.I.'s died for every few feet of ground which changed hands. After suffering several hundred casualties, the G.I.'s withdrew. General Hyakutake, however, celebrated no triumph, for behind his lines men continued to die ignominiously of disease and malnutrition. Staff officers at palace headquarters clamored for a Japanese offensive, but Hyakutake advised that his men were too debilitated to mount one. In accordance with the sober realization he had reached at Ise, Hirohito decided to swallow his pride and the Army's and save as many men from the Guadalcanal debacle as possible.

The imperial decision to evacuate Guadalcanal was officially handed down by Hirohito at a meeting in the ironclad headquarters shed in the palace woods on the morning of December 31. After the meeting Hirohito said to Chief of Staff Sugiyama:

> 'Our withdrawal from Guadalcanal is regrettable. From now on the Army and Navy must co-operate better to accomplish our war objectives. I was thinking of issuing an imperial rescript of congratulations if we had taken Guadalcanal. What do you think of issuing one anyway? The men fought hard up to today, so I would like to issue such a rescript. When would be a suitable time?'

'At once would be best,' said Sugiyama thoughtfully. 'But the rescript cannot be issued publicly. It must be given to the commanders secretly.'

Hyakutake and the other Japanese commanders on Guadalcanal duly received the Emperor's words of praise a week later. Some of them murmured that they would have preferred an order to crawl forward and die fighting. Some of them journeyed to the front to see if they could not lead a banzai charge in which to end all the suffering. But the men in the trenches were too sick to move and their officers lacked enough lasting energy to organize them for any concerted action.

In a masterpiece of tact and deception a fresh battalion from the 38th Division in the East Indies was landed on Guadalcanal by the Tokyo Express on January 15 with the avowed purpose of spearheading a new Japanese offensive. Front-line Japanese troops were pried from their foxholes and heavily timbered rain-forest bunkers with the reassuring promise that they were being redeployed for a final victorious battle. The Japanese fleet sortied in strength from its main base at Truk in the Carolines north of the Solomons and began to sail south.

Expecting suicidal attacks from both land and sea, U.S. commanders tightened their stomach muscles to preside over a great slaughter. Instead a small sea battle took place off Rennell Island to the south, and while it was being fought the Tokyo Express, from February 1 to February 7, 1943, evacuated from 1,000 to 3,000 Japanese from Guadalcanal every night. When the eight-day exodus had been completed at least 11,000 able-bodied Japanese soldiers had escaped; another 21,000 were found and counted as corpses by the U.S. forces; almost 10,000 more vanished from the books into the catch-all category of the missing.

Tokyo propagandists boasted of the evacuation as a great victory—a difficult tactical maneuver which they termed "an advance by turning." Japanese civilians were not deceived, however, and archly circulated many jokes about the virtues of "advancing backward." Nor were U.S. commanders unduly elated, for they had been cheated of living prey and left to destroy a charnel house. Moreover the U.S. Navy had had the worst of its engagement with the Japanese decoy fleet in the waters off Rennell Island. After days of maneuvering, the Japanese vessels sailed home with only a few buckled plates while U.S. destroyers picked up crewmen from a sunken U.S. heavy cruiser, the *Chicago*.

In all, in the seven naval engagements associated with Guadalcanal—Savo Island, Eastern Solomons, Cape Esperance, Santa Cruz Islands, naval Battle of Guadalcanal, Tassafaronga, and Rennell Island—the U.S. Navy had lost eleven to six in destroyers, six to three in heavy ships of the line, and two to one in carriers. U.S. submarines and planes, however, had equalized the total by preying upon damaged Japanese war ships in their long, half-speed voyages back to base. In sum the U.S. fleet had lost to the sea two large carriers, six heavy cruisers, two light cruisers, fifteen destroyers, and one big passenger-liner transport, the S.S. *President Coolidge*. It had lost to the repair dock a large carrier, two battleships, three heavy cruisers, three light cruisers, and eight destroyers.

Admiral Yamamoto, by comparison, had lost a small carrier, two battleships, three heavy cruisers, one light cruiser, eleven destroyers, sixteen small and large troop transports, and five submarines.[5] None of his seriously damaged vessels had succeeded in returning to port, but he had on his hands two large carriers, four heavy cruisers, a light cruiser, and a destroyer which had sustained enough damage to merit a return to shipyards on the home islands.

Japan could claim a naval victory at Guadalcanal and even a small tactical plus for having successfully evacuated the island. On the ground and in the air, however, Japan had suffered disastrously. She had killed about 5,000 American sailors for a loss of only about 3,000 Japanese sailors.[6] But she had lost about 2,000 Japanese airmen for a toll of less than 600 U.S. airmen. And in ground troops she had lost more than ten to one: more than 20,000 Japanese soldiers as against less than 2,000 U.S. Marines and Army G.I.'s. From the American point of view Guadalcanal had been a naval campaign and a naval debacle. From Hirohito's point of view it had been a great naval and aristocratic success, attended by appalling loss of life for the commoners of the Army and the expensively trained noncommissioned officers of the Misty Lagoon flight cadre.

NO WORK, NO FOOD

Never again after the desperate six-month campaign for Guadalcanal would Japanese and U.S. fighting men meet on equal terms. The Japanese would be gradually outnumbered on the sea and in the air until, in the final stages of the war, U.S. skippers regularly enjoyed a ten-to-one superiority in ships and U.S. pilots about a fifty-to-one superiority in planes. Through control of sea and air, U.S. ground commanders were able to choose battle-

[5] This count of twenty-five U.S. to twenty-three Japanese fleet vessels differs from the oft-quoted twenty-four-to-twenty-four score given by naval historian Samuel Eliot Morison. To itemize, then, the Allies lost carriers *Wasp* and *Hornet;* heavy cruisers *Canberra, Vincennes, Quincy, Astoria, Northampton,* and *Chicago;* light cruisers *Atlanta* and *Juneau;* destroyers *Jarvis, Colhoun, Little, Gregory, O'Brien, Duncan, Meredith, Porter, Barton, Laffey, Cushing, Monssen, Walke, Preston,* and *Benham.* The Japanese Combined Fleet lost light carrier *Ryujo;* battleships *Hiei* and *Kirishima;* heavy cruisers *Kako, Furutaka,* and *Kinugasa;* light cruiser *Yura;* destroyers *Mutsuki, Asagiri, Akatsuki, Yudachi, Fubuki, Ayanami, Takanami, Teruzuki, Makigumo, Muragumo,* and *Natsugumo;* and submarines *I–123, I–172, I–15, I–3,* and *I–1.*

[6] These are my own totals of ship-by-ship estimates based on casualty reports or descriptions of ship damages. Official figures, as former Marine officer Samuel Griffith wryly observes in his *The Battle of Guadalcanal,* have never been "tabulated."

fields where the numerical strength of the Japanese Army could not be called into play and where U.S. soldiers could be sure of an overwhelming advantage in firepower.

As a trained strategist, Hirohito could foresee these inexorable developments after the Battle of Midway and be certain of them after the vain banzai charges of Guadalcanal. Nevertheless he insisted that Japan fight on, and he continued so to insist while Japan's war dead mounted from less than 100,000 to more than a million.

Hirohito exacted this fearsome sacrifice of his people partly because he found it unbearable to see his life's vision shattered. He could not bring himself to admit failure in his mission of conquering, unifying, and "enlightening" Asia. He could not report to the gods that the pernicious Western creeds of cosmopolitanism and of individual conscience, soul, and salvation were still at large on Japanese soil. Most important, however, Hirohito felt that he could fight on because his advisors advised him to.

Paradoxically, Lord Privy Seal Kido urged that the war must be continued on account of the people. If defeat came prematurely, he feared popular resentment against the Throne. After the 1905 war with Russia, mobs had rioted in the major cities to protest the paltry monetary and territorial gains which Emperor Meiji had accepted in exchange for the Japanese corpses piled outside Port Arthur and Mukden. This time there would be no gain at all for the men lost in China, Malaya, Luzon, Java, or the faraway exotic islands of the Pacific. The Japanese public must be carefully prepared for the bad bargain. In 1943, when any offal carter or radish farmer could look at a newspaper map and see the rays of the rising sun spreading across a third of the earth, no statesman could with impunity sign away the new conquests and restrict Japan again to her tiny home islands.

The people must lose their bloodstained booty by their own failures before they would accept the loss. And more subtly they must be committed to the enterprise of empire before they could agree to abandon it. The conquests had come so easily, and so few Japanese had participated in them, that a majority of the people had only an intellectual interest in them. If they were given away, the village schoolmasters would cry treason and the people would resent the blood spilled for nothing. But if each mile of foreign shore was fought for, the people would come to identify the distant coral strands with dead village boys. They would feel keenly each retreat and would begin to appreciate the glory of the empire which Hirohito had planned for them. Eventually the mothers of the land would cry, "Enough." Only then could come a time when it would be safe to give back the conquests.

Most subtly of all, there was the question of guilt sharing. A part of every Japanese wanted to dominate the earth and accept tribute from once-proud Chinese, Europeans, and Americans, but few Japanese had ever aspired to burn out Chinese eyes, to castrate Englishmen, or to eat the flesh of Americans. By issuing discreet orders which would induce large num-bers of Japanese to participate literally in such bestialities, Hirohito's secret police experts planned to give the entire nation such a guilty conscience that it would never dare to make any one man—least of all Hirohito—respon-sible for Japan's wrongdoing. Through sharing guilt the whole populace could be prepared to accept gratefully any peace which did not exact of it an eye-for-an-eye, tooth-for-a-tooth vengeance.

It was these darkly delicate considerations of people-control that led to the horrors of the Japanese concentration camps. No one scapegoat suffered in them. Hirohito's secret police and camp wardens dispensed death without prejudice as to race, religion, color, or sex. And they did so, fortunately, without benefit of scientific ovens and gas chambers. Nevertheless, for any-one who was not Jewish, the Japanese camps were more deadly than the German. Of 235,473 British and American troops captured by the soldiers of the Third Reich, 9,348—or 4 per cent—died in the Nazi camps. Of 95,134 British, Australian, American, Canadian, and New Zealand troops captured by the Japanese, 27,256—or 28.65 per cent—died in the Japa-nese camps.[7]

Civilians interned by the Japanese were issued the same rations as mili-tary prisoners but fared far better. Indeed, in some civilian camps the death rate ran lower than normal actuarial expectations for communities of like size in the United States. There were no overweight problems and no under-exercise problems; no stimulants and few excitements. As residents in the Orient, the civilians knew the Japanese and local hygiene; they had native friends on the outside who got food to them; they had wives, children, and doctors interned with or near them, keeping up their standards of cleanliness, cheerfulness, and community feeling. They coped with the same captors, the same latent brutality and smouldering hate, but they were not despised by the Japanese for being soldiers who had surrendered. Nor were they used by the Japanese for slave labor.

Differences in worm's-eye view, as revealed in hundreds of books pub-lished after the war by former captives of the Japanese, have persuaded many historians that Japanese brutality was unorganized, individual, hap-hazard. This was not the opinion of most of the writers of these books, nor is it borne out by available Japanese records. On the contrary, surviving

---

[7] Of 21,726 captured Australians, 7,412 men or 34 per cent; of 21,580 captured U.S. soldiers and sailors, 7,107 or 33 per cent; of 121 captured New Zealanders, thirty-one or 26 per cent; of 50,016 captured Britishers, 12,433 or 25 per cent; of 1,691 captured Canadians, 273 or 16 per cent. The differences in death rates re-flected partly a difference in Japanese feeling about the nationalities involved and partly cultural differences in the tractability and adaptability of the various national groups. Complete figures for captured Dutch and Indian troops are not available. Partial figures, however, suggest that the Dutch suffered about the same gross and percentage loss as the U.S. troops and the Indians about the same as the British troops.

directives of the Prisoner of War Information Bureau and Prisoner of War Management Section suggest that it was imperial policy, gradually, patiently, plausibly, and almost legally to exterminate the prisoners to the last man. Locally, Japanese camp commanders and guards construed instructions from Tokyo in order to be humane but never did they have to stretch their instructions in order to be brutal. Moreover, in every camp, whether a good one or a hellhole, each new set of instructions from Tokyo brought about at least a temporary increase in severity.

Japan's policy in regard to the political use and physical abuse of prisoners was enunciated by Hirohito at the very start of the war on December 24, 1941, sixteen days after Pearl Harbor. That morning, a Wednesday, at his usual weekly meeting with the Privy Council, sitting in plenary session, he pushed through an executive motion for the establishment of a Prisoner of War Information Bureau under the War Ministry. The motion was passed without comment or debate, and the "attached papers," of which copies lay before each privy councillor, became law of the land.

The attached papers were couched in judicious belly talk. They declared that the Privy Council, in 1912, had already ratified a convention of the Powers, agreed to at The Hague in 1907, calling upon governments at war to establish bureaus to deal with information and affairs pertaining to war prisoners. With this preamble, Hirohito's Privy Council agreed that Japan's prisoner-of-war bureau would report to the vice war minister, would be directed by Army officers below the rank of colonel and Navy officers below the rank of captain, and would be staffed by clerks of *heimin* or lower-class status. It would engage in research and information about prisoners of war. It would "make and revise a file card for every prisoner." It would "hold in trust and remit to families the belongings and testaments of dead prisoners." It would "handle the monetary affairs of prisoners" and "notification of the bereaved." It would assist enemy governments in telling next of kin about enemy nationals in Japanese hands. In effect the attached documents subscribed to by the Privy Council left little hope that prisoners taken by Japan would ever return to their homelands alive.

The Prisoner of War Information Bureau quickly became a thriving branch of the Tokyo bureaucracy, and the efficient secret police did indeed provide it with file cards on almost all Allied captives. Pilots taken on Bataan, missionaries captured in Baguio after a lifetime of work in China, businessmen who had fled Hong Kong only to be apprehended in Surabaja, prostitutes evacuated from Shanghai and caught on a ship in Manila harbor— all were astonished, when they were interrogated and screened, at the completeness of the dossiers which the Japanese had already compiled on them.

By April 1942, after the fall of Singapore, Rangoon, Java, and Bataan, the Prisoner of War Information Bureau and its subsidiary, the Prisoner of War Management Section, had almost 300,000 charges, about a quarter of them Allied civilians and the rest white and native troops of the British, Dutch, and U.S. armed forces. No matter how it could be manipulated—squeezed out of natives, paid from frozen Allied assets, or reduced by murder—the budget for administering, guarding, and feeding these captives could not be calculated at less than about $10 million a year or $30 a man per annum. This was one six-hundredth of the national revenue and more than Hirohito's frugal economists, during Japan's great gamble, cared to spend.

On April 28, 1942, ten days after the Doolittle raid on Tokyo, Prime Minister Tojo, in his capacity as war minister, called a conference of his bureau chiefs in the War Ministry building outside the palace walls. Chief of Staff Sugiyama had just told him that it was the policy of Imperial General Headquarters to make an example of the captured Doolittle fliers by executing them. Tojo intended to fight against the executions, which he considered hypocritical and barbaric. But he wanted something to offer Hirohito in their place. After a brief discussion with his subordinates, he proposed that, in accordance with the imperial slogan of "no work, no food," the 300,000 war prisoners in the Empire should be made to earn their keep. The chief of the P.O.W. Information Bureau, Lieutenant General Uemura Seitaro, objected that, according to the Hague conventions, prisoners of war should not be required to perform labor useful to their captors. They might raise food and cut wood for their own maintenance but they were not supposed to have to sweat on the docks or in the war plants of the nation which held them. In addition, any work they did outside of their camps was supposed to be recompensed. Finally, their officers—the most highly educated P.O.W.'s—were specifically exempted from all work, even in their own maintenance.

Tojo dismissed the objections of P.O.W. Chief Uemura as impractical. The Foreign Ministry had already informed the West in January, through Buenos Aires, that Japan did not subscribe to the antique Hague conventions but would respect their humanitarian spirit. This meant, in Tojo's view, that the sooner all war prisoners were put to work, for their own support, the longer they would survive.

What seemed right to Tojo in the political circumstances in which he operated in Tokyo turned out to be only partly right for the scattered war prisoners who had been taken all over the new empire to the south. Ratified by the section chiefs at the War Ministry and duly approved by Hirohito at Imperial General Headquarters, the decision to use war prisoners as laborers spared the lives of many Americans who had been marked out for extinction and cost the lives of many other captives who had theretofore enjoyed tolerable conditions of imprisonment.

Up to that time Allied troops who had surrendered easily to Japan had not been treated too badly and Allied troops who had held out tenaciously against Japan had been treated abominably. The U.S. defenders of Guam, for instance, having bowed quickly to the inevitability of defeat, were now being adequately fed and housed at concentration camps in Japan and China to which they had been transported without mishap. On the other hand the U.S. defenders of Wake, who had repulsed one Japanese task force and taken heavy casualties before surrendering to another, had been starved, beaten, and decimated by ceremonial executions.

The contrasting treatment given to the Wake and Guam garrisons had been meted out on a much larger scale to the prisoners taken at Singapore and at Bataan. The Battling Bastards who had caused the Japanese such pain on Bataan had already suffered the horrors of the Death March. Now the 9,500-odd Americans and 44,500-odd Filipinos who had survived the march were continuing to die by the tumbrel at their detention point half-way between Manila and Lingayen Gulf, Camp O'Donnell. Here was a soggy potter's field, strewn with rotting palm-thatched barracks and pup tents, served with only a score of running-water faucets, subdivided by barbed-wire fences, and surrounded by stockades, searchlights, and machine guns. Here, before the end of 1942, 1,500 of the American and over 20,000 of the Filipino Death-March survivors would succumb to floggings, bayonetings, shootings, diphtheria, dengue fever, malaria, infected wounds, beriberi, scurvy, or simple starvation, debility and hopelessness.

Because of Tojo's decision 6,000 of the Americans at Camp O'Donnell would be moved out in June 1942 to join some 2,000 fresh American captives from Corregidor at the all-white Camp Cabanatuan in the more healthy foothills to the east. The diseased veterans of Camp O'Donnell brought with them a rich stew of intestinal parasites which killed 2,000 of the 8,000 inmates at the Cabanatuan Camp in the next three months. The remaining 6,000 plus fellow survivors at Camp O'Donnell and various camps in the southern islands of the Philippines—in all about 12,000 men— were hardy specimens. They had lived out of an original total of about 18,000 American military captives in the Philippines. Another 3,000 U.S. soldiers and sailors had been captured elsewhere in the Pacific and Orient. They had suffered a few hundred deaths in imprisonment. All told almost 15,000 American P.O.W.'s still remained alive in Japanese hands and of these over 14,000 would survive to be liberated three years later.

Tojo's excuse for them—"Let them eat as long as they work"—proved sufficient to save the lives of most of them. In the months ahead they made their way as miners in the Kyushu coal pits, stevedores on the Yokohama docks, yardmen in Osaka station, machinists in Kobe factories, trench diggers in Manchuria, railroad builders in Thailand, and even as script writers and announcers for Tokyo radio.

P.O.W. slave laborers, who received, depending on rank, a take-"home" pay of between three and thirty cents a day, began arriving in Japan about a month after Tojo had handed down his decision to call for them. On

May 30, 1942, when the Combined Fleet had set out for Midway, Tojo personally inspected one of the first P.O.W. shipments at Zentsuji, in Shikoku, across the Inland Sea from the port of Osaka. It included both Americans from Bataan and Englishmen from Hong Kong and Singapore. Tojo told the Zentsuji camp commandant:

> Prisoners of war must be placed under strict discipline insofar as that doe not contravene the laws of humanity. It is necessary, however, not to be obsessed with mistaken humanitarian notions or swayed by personal feelings which may develop in time through long association with prisoners of war. The present situation in this country does not permit of anyone lying about idle while eating freely. Keeping these sentiments in mind, I hope that you will see to it that your war prisoners are gainfully employed.

On June 25, after the defeat at Midway, Tojo addressed a Tokyo conclave of all P.O.W. camp commandants from Taiwan, Korea, Manchuria and Japan:

> You are especially requested to take into account the characteristic view point at your places of posting and so treat the prisoners of war entrusted to your charge as to make the local populace there appreciative of Japanese superior qualities and cognizant of the unique privilege and honor which they enjoy in being subjects during the reign of His Gracious Majesty.

On July 7 Tojo spoke to a similar gathering of concentration camp commandants from the Philippines and Southeast Asia. He exhorted them "Insofar as you can, short of becoming inhuman yourselves, supervise your charges rigidly and permit no idleness."

On August 13, after the American landing on Guadalcanal, the Japanese secret police in Korea reported on a well-advertised parade of P.O.W.'s from Singapore who were landed at the Pusan docks and then marched through the Pusan city streets:

> The arrival of 998 prisoners captured in Malaya had a great effect on the public at large—especially on the Koreans. About 120,000 Koreans and about 57,000 Japanese bystanders lined the streets of downtown Pusan to see the prisoners pass by. Many of the onlookers sneered at the bad manners and indifference displayed openly by the captured British troops and thought it quite natural that an army so lacking in national spirit should be defeated. They realized afresh the magnitude of the victory gained by the Imperial Army. . . . Worthy of special mention is the fact that the Koreans, when they saw the Korean guards accompanying the prisoners, realized that they are directly participating in the war for Great East Asia.

The secret police report went on to quote bystanders who had been asked for their impressions. One common Korean response was: "It's easy o see they lack patriotism by the way they go along whistling indifferently. They are absolutely slovenly." Another was: "When we saw their frail unsteady appearance, we thought 'No wonder they lost to the Japanese forces.'" The most common Japanese reaction quoted by the secret police was one of sober anxiety: "The appearance of the prisoners made me realize that we can never afford to be defeated." Or, as another Japanese said: "They have no shame, but some arrogance still, so they must be treated firmly. Also we must not lose the war."

The Japanese secret police did not have enough presentable Bataan captives to put in a parade. The fittest thousand P.O.W.'s from the Philippines would have wrung tears of pity from a meeting of the Black Dragon Society. Consequently the first American prisoners selected as laborers were brought in small groups to special convalescence camps in Japan proper and there given a few weeks' fattening up before being sent to work at rail yards, docks, and coal mines.

The "frail, whistling" British troops deemed fit for display in Korea had been lucky in their treatment up to now. So had their fellows who remained in Singapore. So had most of 20,000-odd Dutch troops taken on Java. It was on these Britishers and Hollanders that Tojo's "no-work-no-food" decision—favorable to U.S. P.O.W.'s—fell most heavily.

In Java the Dutch soldiers, on the battlefield or in the process of being recognized as prisoners, had been almost decimated. Thereafter, however, they had been assembled in camps where they were loosely guarded and allowed, for the most part, to fend and forage for themselves. On an island of easy agriculture, plentiful food, and a three-hundred-year tradition of Dutch rule, they managed well to keep up their health and good spirits.

The 35,000-odd Britishers, 15,000-odd Australians, and 14,000-odd Anglo-Malay volunteers captured at Singapore had been more strictly but even less harshly used. General Yamashita, the Tiger of Malaya and level-headed student of the German *Wehrmacht,* had given them the run of the whole northeastern tip of Singapore Island, the Changi area, where the British Army had been quartered before the war. Here were airy three-story barracks built by the British, surrounded by lawns, tennis courts, and arbors of bougainvillea. The accommodations were more crowded than they had been before the war but far less crowded than the encampments from which the British troops had been fighting since Pearl Harbor. The official Japanese ration of a pound of dry rice, a tenth of a pound of meat, and a quarter of a pound of vegetables, dairy products, and condiments per man per day was more than enough to keep the prisoners in lean good health. When it failed to meet specifications due to the inefficiency or graft of a Japanese supply sergeant, its shortcomings could be repaired by black-market traffic with natives "outside the fence."

The relative comforts, however, of British P.O.W.'s began to deteriorate rapidly after Tojo had issued the executive order that prisoners must work to be fed. At first General Yamashita merely subtracted from the British camp area a few lawns and golf courses. Then he built fences around the immediate area of the barracks and installed guard garrisons and block houses. Finally, in July 1942, after his unsuccesful plea to Hirohito to let him lead an invasion of Australia, he was posted back to Manchuria.

His successor required all inmates of Changi to sign a statement: "I the undersigned, hereby solemnly swear on my honour that I will not, un der any circumstances, attempt to escape." British officers citing the Hague conventions, refused to order their men to sign. On September 2, 17,300 of the most high-spirited British and Australian prisoners were marched into the eight acres of prewar Selarang Barrack Square so that they could watch the execution—by Sikh firing squad—of four of their number who had escaped three and a half months earlier and had just been recaptured and brought back for punishment. After the execution, the 17,300 interested witnesses were held at attention waiting for their officers to tell them to sign the Japanese oath. They continued to stand under the tropic sun and moon for three days, surrounded by machine-gun emplacements. They had in their midst two water faucets and were allowed three times a day to stand at ease in order to eat rice handed in to them in pails. They were told they had been put on a third of their regular rations. On the third day their British officers advised them that they had "proved compulsion" and could sign the Japanese oath without any sense of responsibility. Even so the enormous phalanx of men took another day to disperse, and some two or three score men of hardened puritan principles remained standing and insisted upon being taken away for final breaking by the torturers of the Japanese secret police.

Thereafter the administration of British P.O.W.'s in Singapore began to approximate that of the newly reformed camps for military prisoners in the Philippines.

THE RAILROAD OF DEATH

Shortly after the first levies of Allied slave labor began to be exhibited in Korea, Hirohito approved in principle a General Staff plan for linking the rail systems of Thailand and Burma. A Japanese soldier could travel by train from Pusan in Korea to Mukden, Peking, Hankow, Canton, Saigon, and Bangkok. Forty miles beyond Bangkok, however, at the Thai town of Bampong, the overland transportation system ended against a wall of some of the thickest, most unhealthy jungle in the world. West of Bampong, swamps and ridges and gullies succeeded one another so closely that there was almost no pleasant forest land for over 200 miles. In the thickets, however, there were enough monkeys and human outcasts to support a rich fauna of malarial mosquitoes and other primate parasites. A single track led through the dense tangle. It had been cut by a British geological survey more than a decade earlier and subsequently abandoned by British and Indian forestry service men as being beyond upkeep.

On the other side of this wilderness, at the eastern Burmese frontier town of Thanbyuzayat, began the Anglo-Burmese rail system which extended to the western frontier of Burma. There gaped another two-hundred-mile gap which, when bridged, would lead to the Anglo-Indian rail system. Beyond the western camel towns of India lay another gap, Baluchistan, after which it was clear rolling, along well-laid lines, all the way to Calais and the English Channel.

Not for naught had the courtiers of Hirohito's great-grandfather, Emperor Komei, sacrificed their dignity to ride, with robes flowing, on the donkey-sized steam engine shown off by Commodore Perry at Uraga. Japan's domestic railroads rivaled the world's best, and all Japan's conquests up to 1941 had been posited and pushed forward on the rail lines of Manchuria and China. Other armies might march on their bellies; the Japanese Army glided like a snake—and went hungry between railroad stations.

After the capture of Rangoon in March 1942, the possibility of converting Japan's probe of Burma into a full-scale invasion of India began to seem attractive to Hirohito. In June the Navy's repulse at Midway, and the decision not to invade Australia, made the Army's presence in Burma positively indispensable. Nowhere else could the Army exert its numerical strength to Japan's advantage and put real pressure on the Allies. The sea-lanes between Singapore and Rangoon, however, were beset by Allied submarines. The overland portage along jungle trails between Bangkok and Rangoon was slow and expensive. If the divisions in Burma were to threaten India seriously, they would need at their back a supply route along railroad tracks. As soon, therefore, as the Americans took the amphibious offensive at Guadalcanal, Hirohito ordered an all-out effort to lay track along the abandoned Burma-Thai geological cut. Japanese engineers resurveyed it and estimated the earth which would have to be moved, and the embankments, trestles, and bridges which would have to be constructed.

Some 3,000 Australian P.O.W.'s from Singapore, recruited under the new slave-labor system, had spent the summer repairing airfields for Japan along the western coast of the Malayan Peninsula in the southern extremities of Burma. Now, in late September, they were disembarked from sweltering ship holds at Moulmein and Ye, the southernmost ports on the Burmese rail network. The first of them arrived at Thanbyuzayat, at the northern end of the unbuilt Burma-Thai railroad, a few days later on October 1, 1942. Most of them were young men, bronzed, lean and fit after months of hard work in the sun and of adequate feeding and foraging at the airfields where they had been employed. In a few months they would all be either dead or walking caricatures of death.

By November the Australians had been augmented by unhardened Britishers from Changi in Singapore and by Hollanders from Java who were already sick and starving after long sea voyages under hot, tight bulkheads. Before the end of the year, almost 10,000 prisoners would be clearing jungle, heaping dirt by the basketful on embankments, and chiseling through hillsides at the Burmese end of the railroad. A like number of captives, mostly British, would be at work in Thailand at the other end of the envisaged line.

The workers in Thailand, if comparisons are possible, had the harder lot. Theirs were the longest segments of line to build, the highest hills, deepest gorges, and most pestiferous swamplands. Both groups, however, suffered from much the same delusions and heartbreaks. They had left Singapore under the impression that they were going to "Shangri-la," an undisclosed location in a more congenial climate to the north where their care would be supervised by representatives of the International Red Cross. Instead they emerged hungry and heat-exhausted from packed holds and cattle cars and found themselves put in the care of Korean menials from work battalions—some of the most abused, ignorant, and corrupt peasants who ever wore the uniform of an army.

Prodded on by these Korean guards, the cheated P.O.W.'s set out at once on forced marches through the jungle. Some of them walked 20 miles, some 150. At the end of their treks they found that Shangri-la was an unimproved jungle clearing where Japanese soldiers had built a few sodden lean-tos out of saplings and palm-leaf thatch. The camp sites were evenly spaced out along the route of the projected railroad and chosen with an eye more to geometric regularity than to geographic suitability. Many of them happened to fall in swamp bottoms where swarmed malarial mosquitoes even in dry season.

Armed only with axes, picks, and shovels, the prisoners began work in the midst of the monsoon or wet season. Ditch as they might, their camps turned quickly into morasses. From dawn to dusk they cut and hauled trees, shoveled dirt, and picked at rock. By night they washed and cooked and tried to live. They had little to eat but sacks of the lowest grade of polished rice wherein the most vitamin-rich content crawled in the form of weevils and maggots. Most of them were soon afflicted by the grotesquely bloated ankles and testicles of "wet beriberi" or by the flaking shins and falling dandruff of "dry beriberi." Their malnutrition was increased by dysentery and their despondency by almost universal diarrhea.

By November no one was healthy but no one who took a sane view of his own psychological condition cared to report himself sick. The sodden palm-thatched long houses known as "hospitals" flowed with such fecal stench and despair that a man indisposed could lie down and die of disgust in any one of them. Dedicated doctors and orderlies worked without sleep to do some good, but they had no medicines, and Japanese medical inspectors refused consistently to make any available. Boiled water, salt, and soda were the main drugs at hand and men who suffered from tropical ulcers, dysentery, and malaria needed at least one more important pharmaceutical: hope. This the doctors and orderlies could not dispense and they had to watch thousands of young men die of combinations of minor ailments, which could have been easily cured by food, rest, and sanitation.

The end of the 1942 rainy season in December brought a temporary improvement in rations and work conditions which lasted for about six weeks. Then in February 1943, after the Japanese withdrawal from Guadalcanal, Hirohito approved a speed-up in the construction schedule, requiring that the railroad be finished, not by December 1943 as originally planned, but by August. All able-bodied Allied P.O.W.'s in Singapore, Sumatra, and Java were moved north to hasten the work. When 60,000 of them had been put in harness, the project still progressed too slowly and the Japanese marched in no less than 270,000 indentured Malays, Burmese, Thais, and Javanese. These hordes of native conscripts lacked discipline, leadership, medical personnel, interpreters, and the resourcefulness conferred by even elementary school education. As a result they suffered horribly and a third of them died.

Hirohito's call for haste lengthened the work shifts of P.O.W.'s from eight to twelve to sixteen hours. During the final frenetic months of railroad construction, the columns of sick white coolies were often driven from their camps at daybreak and not returned to them until 2 A.M. The night work was done by electric lights which glimmered dim and bright as the men who turned the handles of small manual generators wearied, collapsed, and were replaced in a never-ending nightmare cycle.

In the mornings when work parties had set out from camps, Japanese engineers regularly sent Korean guards into the hospital shacks to rout out additional laborers. At one of the larger camps men too weak to stand were forced to sit in rows and tug at ropes to help in log hauling. Men who collapsed were sometimes left to die and sometimes killed by thrashings with bamboo poles or lashings with wire whips. The malingerer who prolonged a squat in the bushes to take a brief nap or smoke a scavenged cigarette butt was commonly punished by being made to lift his eyes toward the sun and stand for an hour holding over his head a boulder or a bucket of earth. Those few men who attempted to escape either died quickly in the jungle or were triumphantly recaptured and publicly tortured to death as examples. Some were gibbeted; others simply tied to trees to die of thirst or ant bite.

In executing these abominations, the Japanese relied heavily upon their brutalized Korean menials and upon a handful of crazily violent noncommissioned officers. The regular Japanese troops in the area mostly averted their eyes or made sporadic efforts to ease the prisoners' lot. Japanese railroad engineers and doctors on the other hand—men who should have represented enlightened Japanese civilian opinion—actively encouraged the killing of the prisoners. Instead of demanding better equipment and food for their slaves, the engineers insisted on turning them out in numbers sufficient to meet work quotas. The doctors were still more knowingly inhuman in that they regularly certified sick men fit for work. Men dehydrated by dysentery they sent to sweat in the sun. Men dizzy with 104-degree fevers they sent to teeter atop high bridge trestles. Many lost their balance and fell to their deaths on the rocky bottoms of ravines far below.[8]

As it took a coldly intellectual Japanese or a miserably sadistic one to supervise the building of the railroad, so it took a coolly resourceful prisoner or a magnificently animal one to survive the conditions of the labor. Then in June of 1943 another protagonist entered the drama: *Vibrio comma,* a bacterium which took its toll impartially of strong or cunning prisoners and of cold or cruel Japanese. The epidemic of Asiatic cholera began in an encampment of impressed Tamil laborers from Burma and swiftly spread, like the plague it was, to Allied P.O.W. camps and Japanese guardhouses. All work on the railroad ceased. The Japanese donned face masks of white gauze and barred the gates of their blockhouses. The rank and file of P.O.W.'s withdrew in final despair to their mouldering huts. Many of the strongest of them, who had heretofore held off the amoebas and bacilli of dysentery and the plasmodia of malaria, were taken by convulsions and died in hours, grinning like wolves.

Only the P.O.W.s' own medical teams, traveling from camp to camp with the reassurance of knowledge and a few simple hints on the boiling of water and on the quarantine and care of the stricken, managed to prevent panic and wholesale death. The Japanese themselves were frightened into demanding air shipments of cholera serum from Japan. Nevertheless, before the epidemic had been brought under control, some British P.O.W. camps had been decimated and some of the Asiatic coolie camps had been entirely wiped out. Crews of Allied P.O.W.'s sent to clean up the Asiatic camps, which were the centers of infection, found tabloids of death which surpassed belief: rat-ravaged fields of corpses flooded with liquids from latrines which had burst their embankments. Fire and lime brought hygiene back to the jungle, but the stench and the horror never left the nostrils and minds of the clean-up details as long as the men in them lived.

After the great epidemic of June and July 1943, cholera never left the

[8] The most cruel Japanese secret policemen were regularly those who had lived abroad, who nursed grievances for slights suffered in the West, and who felt a special need to prove their patriotism to fellow Japanese. Most doctors and engineers, having attended Western Universities, shared to some extent in this pariah outlook. In addition the doctors had no squeamishness about physical suffering or the sight of blood. Many of them assisted at tortures or personally wielded swords at beheadings. One of them, in western Burma in 1944, encountered an African in a group of British captives, tied him to a tree, and cut his heart out to demonstrate to orderlies that it was as red as any other.

railroad of death. Later cholera outbreaks, however, were quickly suppressed with doses of Japanese serum and full Japanese co-operation. The pathetically proud Allied prisoners also co-operated more fully after the epidemic and completed the railroad by November. Some of them were kept on after November, as maintenance crews, to rebuild and replace embankments which, a year earlier, they had purposely underpinned with rotten logs and adulterated with vegetable fill which they had known would cause cave-ins. Some of the maintenance crews even lived to become obsessed by their handiwork and to curse British planes which began bombing the rickety timber bridges late in the war.

Most of the jungle construction camps were abandoned early in 1944. Surviving P.O.W.'s were returned to Changi concentration camp in Singapore and the native laborers to scores of small villages in Burma, Thailand, and Malaya.

Not until after the war was a full reckoning made of the cost of the railroad. It had taken 331,000 men to build: 61,000 Allied P.O.W.'s and roughly 270,000 natives. Of these some 72,000 to 92,000 of the Asiatics—between 25 and 30 per cent—had died, having done less than half of the work. Of the 61,000 Allied P.O.W.'s 20.6 per cent or 12,568 had died: 6,318 Britishers, 2,815 Australians, 2,490 Hollanders, 356 Americans, and 589 whose nationalities were never determined. In laying down their lives they had constructed a 250-mile railroad which would have to be abandoned after the war and given back to the wilderness. They had built nine miles of bridges and moved 150 million cubic feet of earth, about as much as they would have moved if they had dug fifteen decent graves for each corpse they had left behind them. Together with the Asiatic laborers, they had left one dead body for every thirteen feet of completed track. If Japan had lifted a finger of her managerial genius, the idiotic waste of life could have been avoided and the railroad built more quickly, cheaply, and lastingly. As handled by Imperial Headquarters, the project had only one virtue: it was a way of killing prisoners that could be justified to Prime Minister Tojo and other responsible officials in the Tokyo government.

FELLING JAPAN'S ANGEL

While Hirohito's disappointments were being vented on Allied war prisoners, President Roosevelt took a small vengeance of his own: he sanctioned the assassination of Japan's great naval hero and air angel, Admiral Yamamoto Isoroku, the author of the sneak attack upon Pearl Harbor. The chance came for the assassination when Yamamoto's Navy signalmen, in a low-security code, five days in advance, broadcast to the whole Pacific area the itinerary of an inspection tour which Yamamoto planned to make of the front lines on April 18, 1943.

Since the previous April 18, when Doolittle had raided Tokyo, every thing had gone badly for Yamamoto. As the caretaker of Japanese ai power, he had taken personal responsibility for Doolittle's violation o sacred air space over the Imperial Palace. Because of the need for a counterstroke, he had hastened his plans for a decisive blow at the U.S fleet and had lost the Battle of Midway. Again he had taken all the respon sibility upon himself. Then, at Guadalcanal, his vaunted eagles of th Misty Lagoon had proved incapable of overcoming improved U.S. aeria tactics and superior numbers of U.S. planes. There were no longer word, with which to express his regret to Hirohito. Since Guadalcanal nothin Yamamoto could think of had been able to check the run of America success.

In the final six weeks of 1942 the first U.S. fighter planes capable o dealing with the Zero had begun to arrive in the Southwest Pacific: Lock heed Lightnings. These P-38's could not "turn square corners" with th Zero in a dogfight, but they did not need to for they were far bigger heavier, and faster. No longer did U.S. pilots have to attack only ir groups for a single downward pass at diving speed. The Lightning coulc run away from a Zero in level flight, could turn at leisure, and come back with guns blazing.

The mighty Zero, over Singapore, had flown circles around the British Spitfire, had shot down seventeen out of twenty-seven veteran dogfighters of the Battle of Britain with the loss of only two Zeros. Earlier the Spit- fires had demonstrated a similar superiority over the *Luftwaffe*'s best fighter, the Messerschmidt 109E. The Zero, then, could lay just claim to being the world's best fighter plane. Now, however, it had met its match. In the big twin-fuselage Lightning, the U.S. pilot no longer needed to fear individual man-to-man combat. Like the Zero, moreover, the Lightning had range. It could accompany bombers to a target 600 miles away and return with gas to spare.

Having spent his entire career as an apostle of air power and of tech- nical excellence, Admiral Yamamoto needed only a glance at intelligence reports on the Lightning's capabilities to realize the fateful significance of the new American plane. Yamamoto knew that the next generation of Japanese fighter planes—the *Shiden*s and *Raiden*s, or Lightningbolts and Thunderclaps, planes which would make a limited appearance in 1945— were still on the drawing boards.

In 1941, in agreeing to lead the Navy prematurely against the United States, Yamamoto had pinned his hopes on the Zero and on his belief that Americans had no deep interest in Asia and would be eager to ac- cept a negotiated peace with Japan. Now the Lightning nullified the Zero, and in mid-January 1943 President Roosevelt, meeting with British Prime Minister Churchill at Casablanca in North Africa, blasted Yamamoto's other hope.

"The elimination of German, Japanese and Italian war power," Roosevelt announced to reporters after the conference, "means the unconditional surrender of Germany, Italy and Japan."

Yamamoto knew that neither Hirohito nor Japan could surrender unconditionally. Hirohito could not do so because of sacred oaths to his ancestors; the Japanese people could not do so out of pride and out of fear of unconditional American vengeance.

In his despair, Yamamoto was called upon to regain air superiority for Japan over the battlefields in the Southwest Pacific where Japanese soldiers and Marines were dying. After the decision had been reached to evacuate Guadalcanal, the next concern was New Guinea. There U.S. and Australian troops had crossed the Owen Stanley Range from Port Moresby in late October 1942 and in December 1942 and January 1943 had pinched out the three Japanese beachheads of Gona, Buna, and Sanananda on the other side. The Australians had lost over 5,000 men in the action, the Americans over 2,500, and the Japanese about 12,000. At Buna, in particular, the Allied troops had inched forward—through kunai grass against coconut log blockhouses—in one of the most desperate struggles of the war. Had it not been for a dozen tanks floated around New Guinea from Port Moresby on rafts, the Japanese troops might have held out indefinitely.

The fall of Buna had distressed Hirohito. Expressing himself mildly so that no one in the General Staff would resign or commit suicide, he nevertheless reproved Chief of Staff Sugiyama in an audience on January 9:

> Our men fought well but the loss of Buna is regrettable. I understand the enemy used twelve or more tanks. Don't we have any tanks in that area? Now I assume that we will send adequate reinforcements, will we not, to Lae [Japan's next stronghold on the north shore of New Guinea, about 150 miles northwest of Buna]?

In response to Hirohito's suggestion, on February 28, 1943, 6,912 Japanese troops in eight small transports, accompanied by eight destroyers, set out from Rabaul to reinforce the New Guinea enclaves. Yamamoto undertook to provide the convoy with air cover. But between March 2 and March 4, in the Battle of the Bismarck Sea, U.S. planes from Guadalcanal and New Guinea destroyed all of the convoy's transports, four of its eight destroyers, and 4,000 of its troops. Most of the men lost were left swimming in the water where they were systematically massacred by machine-gun fire from U.S. aircraft and torpedo boats.

At the Battle of the Bismarck Sea sixteen P-38 Lightnings engaged forty Zeros, kept them occupied at altitudes ranging from 10,000 to 30,000 feet, and swapped "kills" with them on an equal basis. Far below, U.S. bomber pilots were employing, to good effect, a new technique called skip-bombing, which made the most of their ability to score near misses. B-25's and A-20's roared in low over the wave tops, where the gunners on Japanese ships had the least chance of hitting them. The U.S. bombs were fused to explode five seconds after release when the drop-plane had got clear. It mattered not if the bombs fell in the water: they would still explode and, in sufficient quantities, they would eventually spring a ship's seams and literally shake her to death.

The fast, high-level interception work of the thundering P-38 Lightnings, coupled with the low-level skip-drops of the U.S. bombers, struck Yamamoto's aerial samurai, trained for machine-gun sharpshooting and precision bombing, as crude and unsporting. No one, however, could gainsay the effectiveness of the new American tactics. Long after the Zeros, their gas spent in vain pursuit of the evasive Lightnings, had returned to their bases, the skip-bombers hammered away at the Japanese fleet. When most of the fleet had foundered, the Battle of the Bismarck Sea had been won undeniably by the Americans.

Hirohito was quick now to find fault. He saw at once that, having been discovered by U.S. pilots, the convoy should have made for the nearest Japanese port, Madang, far up the New Guinea coast out of range of the U.S. planes. There it could have regrouped and doubled back at its leisure down the coast toward Lae—where its troops were needed. It could have moved stealthily at night, ship by ship, and creek mouth to creek mouth.

On March 3, even before the Battle of the Bismarck Sea had ended, Hirohito upbraided General Staff Chief Sugiyama for this stupid exhibition of inflexibility:

> Why ever didn't you make a change in plans and land the troops at once on Madang? We have suffered what can only be described as a disaster. I hope we can learn a bitter lesson from it and make it a basis for more successful operations. Please act in future so as to relieve my anxiety. Strengthen our aerial forces where they will be needed. Prepare reinforcement routes through safe areas. Move step by step with careful deliberation. Proceed so that Lae and Salamaua won't turn into another Guadalcanal. After all, our withdrawal there was caused, was it not, by a certain laxity on the part of our forces on the island, a complacency from too many easy victories earlier? All right. So much for that. Now how are we going to make best use of the forces remaining to us?

> Since the enemy is strong in the air [replied Sugiyama, abashed], we plan to reorganize our airfields around Madang, and our air defenses, and our transport routes, and we hope to follow His Imperial Majesty's guidance.

The Emperor's displeasure over the Battle of the Bismarck Sea was quickly communicated to Admiral Yamamoto at his great fleet base on Truk atoll in the Carolines. Without much hope he came to Rabaul personally on April 3, with some 300 of his best remaining Zero pilots, to see what he could do to regain Japan's initiative in the air. He proceeded to launch his aces in a series of 100-to-200-plane attacks against Guadalcanal and U.S. bases in New Guinea. By striking such massive blows he hoped to outnumber U.S. planes locally and so achieve a favorable kill-to-loss ratio. U.S. pilots, however, felt no shame in fighting briefly and running away to rear-area fields where the Zeros could not follow for lack of gas. When the raids were over, the U.S. planes returned to their bases, alive to fight again.

The Japanese pilots vented their spleen by shooting up ships and ground facilities in the target areas but failed to cause any damage that was commensurate with their own normal operational losses in such long-range flights. Another forty-two of Yamamoto's prized naval aviators perished in the raids from enemy fire and mechanical failures. They succeeded in sinking half a dozen Allied ships and in shooting down several dozen U.S. planes—twenty-five by U.S. count, 134 by Japanese—but they failed to take a toll which gave any promise of reversing the course of the war.

After the third of the four big air strikes—a 174-plane assault on General MacArthur's headquarters at Port Moresby—Yamamoto could already see that his new strategy had failed. On the afternoon of April 13, when the last stragglers from the raid could be accounted definitely lost, a message went out in an ordinary fleet code known to U.S. monitors as JN 25. It announced that Yamamoto intended to pay a visit to forward bases in the northern Solomons on April 18, the anniversary of the Doolittle raid. It gave his itinerary precisely: take-off from Rabaul 8 A.M.; arrival Shortland Island 10:40; departure Shortland 11:45; arrival Buin, Bougainville, for lunch, 1:10; departure Buin 6:00; return to Rabaul 7:40. The message was signed by Vice Admiral Samejima Tomoshige, the local air commander, Yamamoto's subordinate. Until five months earlier, Samejima had been Hirohito's chief naval aide-de-camp. He had been posted to Rabaul as an expression of Hirohito's concern for the course of the air war there.

As soon as Samejima's message had been broadcast, Yamamoto armed himself with two bottles of Johnny Walker Scotch and looked in uninvited on a gloomy party that was being held by a group of his flight officers. Not for them that night was the gaudy splendor of Rabaul's "Naval Consolation Unit," or brothel, staffed by 600 Japanese and Korean girls. The airmen were drinking in a spirit of chaste samurai masculinity to toast the departed souls of comrades who had perished in the recent raids. Yamamoto, who had a notoriously weak head for liquor, broke his usual rules of temperance and threw himself into the anesthetizing mood of the wake. Before long, waxing sentimental, he had penned a letter to all dead and living members of the naval academy class of 1904 which he forced his cupmates to sign.

The letter is not extant but something about Yamamoto's manner that night caused his fellow officers to express great concern, in the four days which followed, about their commander's proposed trip to forward bases. On April 17, the day before the trip, Yamamoto lunched with Lieutenant General Imamura Hitoshi, the conquistador of the Dutch East Indies and now the commander of the Rabaul Army Group. Imamura warned him of the dangers of U.S. air ambush and told him of a narrow escape which he had had himself over Bougainville. Yamamoto promised Imamura that he would fly south with an adequate escort of six Zeros. That afternoon Rear Admiral Joshima Takaji, one of Yamamoto's best friends, flew into Rabaul from Bougainville to plead that the inspection trip be canceled.

"When I saw that foolish message," he said, "I told my staff, 'This is madness.' It is an open invitation to the enemy."

Yamamoto smiled gratefully at his concerned friend but refused to change his plans.

In courting death, Admiral Yamamoto sought to end his career at its height before the decline which he saw as inevitable. Because of the indiscreet Fleet message of Hirohito's former naval aide-de-camp, he had, in effect, imperial sanction to secure for himself the most honorable place in the samurai's Valhalla, that of a battle casualty. Other high-ranking Japanese officers might have to take the painful second-best course open to a man of honor, hara-kiri; Yamamoto, with the Emperor's blessing, would die swiftly, if he could, by an enemy bullet.

Not being aware of these subtleties, President Roosevelt was glad to be of service and to help Yamamoto shuffle off his mortal coils. The itinerary of Yamamoto's front-line inspection was picked up by U.S. monitors at 5:55 P.M., April 13, 1943, local time, at two separate listening posts: Wahiawa on Oahu and Dutch Harbor in the Aleutians. Decoded transcripts of the message were in the hands of high-ranking members of the Office of Naval Intelligence in both Washington and Hawaii about five hours later. It was then 5 A.M. in Washington and 11 P.M. in Honolulu. Admiral Nimitz in Honolulu was just going to bed and President Roosevelt in Washington was about to rise.

Roosevelt ordinarily read his pouches right after breakfast and should then have seen the decoded message about Admiral Yamamoto's trip. Whether he did or not is a moot point which several diligent researchers have failed to resolve. The ambush or assassination of an enemy leader is a delicate matter. It invites retaliation in kind. Few statesmen have ever been willing to authorize it because assassination is a relatively easy mission for the espionage service of a major nation to accomplish.

Captain Ellis Zacharias, the deputy director of the Office of Naval Intelligence, an officer with ready access to Roosevelt, showed himself in the days which followed a determined advocate of the Yamamoto assassination attempt. Six hours after Roosevelt's breakfast, at 8:02 A.M. Hawaiian time, when Pacific Fleet Commander Nimitz had finished his own breakfast, Zacharias's man in Hawaii, Commander Edwin Layton, kept an appointment to see Nimitz on a matter of great urgency. Ushered into the admiral's office, he laid down a copy of the intercept and said, "Our old friend Yamamoto."

Nimitz nodded, scanned the intercept, and replied, "Well, what do you say? Do we try to get him?"

"Assuming that we have planes able to intercept him," replied Layton.

"What would be gained by killing him?" asked Nimitz.

"He's the one Jap," said Layton, "who thinks in bold strategic terms. . . . Aside from the Emperor, probably no man in Japan is so important to civilian morale."

Nimitz nodded and asked two questions: were there any better, younger admirals who might replace Yamamoto as the commander of Japan's Combined Fleet; was there any effective retaliation Japan could take? Layton answered in the negative on both counts. Nimitz at once wrote an order to Admiral Halsey, in charge of Southwest Pacific, to determine whether or not his fliers might have a good chance of intercepting Yamamoto on his tour and shooting him down. That same evening, when Halsey's staff had queried the squadron leaders on Guadalcanal, Nimitz got a positive answer. It was relayed to Washington.

A few hours later when Washington awakened, Deputy Chief of Naval Intelligence Zacharias discovered that only one man in the U.S. Navy's high command, Frank Knox, the Secretary of the Navy, had any qualms about the assassination. Knox insisted on getting an opinion from the Navy advocate general as to the legality of the operation, from churchmen as to the Christianity of the operation, and from Air Force General Hap Arnold as to the feasibility of the operation. All his consultants agreed with President Roosevelt that the operation should be carried out. O.N.I. man Zacharias had his staff collect an in-basketful of precedents for international assassinations, kidnappings, and intimidations. Frank Knox gave in, and by the evening of April 15 the best fliers on Guadalcanal were busy preparing to satisfy Yamamoto's "immortal longings."

The go-ahead to Guadalcanal went out coded as Operation Vengeance with a top-secret security rating and a unique "presidential" priority rating. The air commander on Guadalcanal assigned a squadron of P-38 Lightnings to the task and ordered special long-range belly tanks for them from MacArthur's stores in New Guinea. A pinpoint interception was called for, at a distance of 450 miles from home base, and it would have to be flown at the lowest possible, most radar-avoiding, fuel-consuming altitude. The pilots would have to be warned to fly by the horizon and pay no heed to the sparkling waves just below them: otherwise they might become bemused by the splashing sunlight and trip themselves up on rushing walls of water.

It was an improbable mission, but every pilot on Guadalcanal who heard of it volunteered to go along. Only a select eighteen, under the command of Major John Mitchell, received invitations: fourteen of them to fly cover and four to execute the kill. One of the killer planes piled up in take-off. The other seventeen P-38 Lightnings flew north at an altitude of 30 feet by a devious route which kept them out of sight of all islands along the way.

The Lightning pilots climbed out of the west, up from the sea, on Bougainville at 9:33 A.M., exactly two minutes before Yamamoto was expected from the north. As the U.S. airmen stared at the peaks of the island rising out of a tenuous overcast, what had seemed optimistic in planning took on a wildly visionary hue. Even if Yamamoto's planes arrived on schedule the chance of seeing them and gunning them down before they landed began to seem remote.

Then one of the pilots of the cover group, Captain Doug Canning, glimpsed a glint of sunlight on a wing tip against the dark mountains three miles away. He broke radio silence in a husky voice that was almost a whisper: "Bogeys eleven o'clock. High."

In the sudden confused melee which followed, the three killer Lightnings came out of dives at high speed to streak past startled Zero pilots and quickly overtake the the two staff bombers. So brief was the encounter— less than five minutes—that the U.S. cover planes watched from above and never had a need to engage. At the first hint of danger, the two bombers dove for speed and made off in different directions just above the canopy of the rain forest. Both were the new model of Mitsubishi Betty stripped of armor and loaded with engines and gasoline for flights of up to 4,600 miles. So big were they and so well could they burn that their crews called them *kamaki,* flying cigars.

The killer Lightnings were on their tails immediately, followed by swarms of desperate but lagging Zero pilots. Admiral Yamamoto was killed almost instantly—sooner, perhaps, than he had expected—by a machine-gun bullet through the base of his skull. His plane, with its dozen or more passengers and crewmen, plummeted into the jungle and burned. There were no survivors. The other bomber was splashed in the ocean just off the coast. Three of its occupants miraculously survived: the pilot; Yamamoto's paymaster; and his chief of staff, Vice Admiral Ugaki Matome, the brother of General Ugaki who had purged the Army for Hirohito in the 1920's and then in the 1930's had been disgraced through the March Plot. Of Yamamoto's staff intimates, Ugaki alone remained to tell of the Fleet god's death.

The U.S. Lightning pilots flew back to Guadalcanal to wrangle over who had shot down what. They were reprimanded for talking too much and for endangering the U.S. code-breaking program. Then they were given medals shipped home, and silenced. Only after the war, more than three years later, was their story finally given to the public. Even then full documentation of White House participation in the affair remained classified as it still does today. Because of a minor infraction of the international chivalric code, official Washington would keep a secret, keep it well, and keep it more or less indefinitely.

Unprodded by any press release from Washington, Tokyo withheld the news of Yamamoto's death for thirty-four days while soldiers cut their way through the jungle to his wrecked plane and positively identified his charred remains. No one doubted that he had died, however, and Hirohito was so informed immediately. Lord Privy Seal Kido heard the unnerving news from the Emperor's own lips the very morning after the ambush. He wrote in his diary, "I felt shock and bitter grief."

A party of reformed Bougainville headhunters, drafted for the purpose, bore Yamamoto's body to the Japanese base at Buin. There his limbs were ceremoniously cremated and carried in a small white box onto the battleship *Musashi* for transport back to Japan. When the *Musashi* steamed into Yokohama on May 21, Tokyo radio announced that Yamamoto had "met gallant death in a war plane." For the next two days naval officers from all over Japan trooped aboard *Musashi* to pay their last respects. On May 23 the ashes were moved ashore to a funeral train which was greeted at Tokyo railroad station by a crowd of thousands, including all Cabinet ministers and leading bureaucrats and palace officials.

For the next thirteen days rites were performed over the ashes at Yasukuni, the shrine for warriors outside the north gate of the palace. A packet of ashes was given to Yamamoto's wife for interment at his home town of Nagaoka on Honshu's northwest coast. Another packet was given to his mistress, the geisha Kawai Chioko, for her prayer shelf. A third packet was prepared for Yamamoto's official Tokyo funeral.

Since Emperor Meiji's restoration, the Throne had sanctioned only eleven state funerals, ten of them for noblemen and members of the imperial family. Only one had been accorded a commoner, Admiral Togo Heihachiro, the victor over the Russian fleet in 1905 and later the chief of Hirohito's faculty of tutors. Admiral Yamamoto's was to be the second state funeral for a commoner in Japanese history.

Beforehand Yamamoto's last minutes were thoroughly scrutinized to make sure that he was deserving of the honor. Investigators learned that just before boarding the plane for his final flight, the hero of Pearl Harbor had handed an aide a scroll of fine rice paper on which he had inscribed in his own bold calligraphy a copy of a poem written by Emperor Meiji forty years earlier. He asked that the scroll be given to Samejima, the admiral who had sent out the fateful broadcast of his itinerary, the admiral who, until the previous October, had been the Emperor's chief naval aide-de-camp. The copied poem said:

> Now has come the time
> For those of us who were born
> Here in warrior land—
> Now has come the time for us
> To make ourselves truly known.

Another poem, composed in Yamamoto's own words, was found in hi
cabin on the vast 64,000-ton battleship *Yamato,* where he had had hi
headquarters. It was a long, imperfect free-verse effort which had neve
been reduced to the discipline of a proper thirty-one syllable *tanka:* [9]

> So many are dead.
> I cannot face the Emperor.
> No words for the families.
> But I will drive deep
> Into the enemy camp.
> Wait, young dead soldiers.
> I will fight farewell
> And follow you soon.

Having passed muster, even in his poetic sentiments, commoner Yama
moto was duly accorded a state funeral with full honors on June 5, 1943
The date had meaning, for it was the anniversary of the day on whicl
Yamamoto had withdrawn defeated from Midway. Fifteen hundred officia
mourners and a throng estimated at a million gathered in or near Hibiy
Park, south of the palace, to hear the funeral oration and accompany th
small white box of ashes to its final resting place. Along the way nava
bands played Yamamoto's own chosen Western anthem, the famou
marche funèbre from Chopin's second piano sonata. The cortege woun
its way through the crowded streets out to Tama River Funeral Park i
western Tokyo and there, in a newly consecrated Yamamoto shrine, th
nation's share of the ashes was buried beside the shrine to Admiral Togc
the other honored commoner who had become a Fleet god.

Hirohito was not allowed to attend funerals because they would mak
him unclean as national high priest and would force him to perform intri
cate ceremonies of ablution. However, Lord Privy Seal Kido attende
Yamamoto's funeral on behalf of the Throne and reported feeling "

[9] Yamamoto's screed was not shown at once to the Emperor lest it upset hin
Instead it was entrusted for presentation to the Throne to Baron Harada, the forme
secretary-spy who had been attached to the late Prince Saionji. Harada kept it for ove
two months and then gave it to the Empress's steward, Marquis Hirohata Tadatak
Hirohata brought it to Lord Privy Seal Kido on August 18 and discussed with hir
whether or not the Emperor should see it. Kido noted only the subject of the dis
cussion in his diary and did not mention what conclusion was reached. Presumabl
he voted for showing the scroll to Hirohito, otherwise he would have omitted th
matter from his diary altogether.

profound sense of nothingness." Hirohito promptly asked to pay a visit to the Fleet to improve naval morale. The next day, June 9, however, an accident took place in the magazine of the 38,900-ton battleship *Mutsu*, at anchor in Hiroshima harbor. The gigantic warship, larger than any yet sunk in combat, blew up and sank immediately. So few sailors remained aboard to perish in the catastrophe that the naval military police and civilian Special Higher Police investigated the incident as a possible example of espionage or Fleet protest. Nothing could be proved, however, and after a two-week delay, on June 24, Hirohito duly paid his visit to the Fleet and commiserated with wounded men brought back from the war front.

HOPE FISHING

Admirals might wait for decisive fleet engagements; generals might talk of tactical withdrawals; industrialists might explain temporary industrial bottlenecks; but many knowledgeable civilians called continuance of the war "fishing for hope." Sympathetic to Yamamoto's quick grab at immortality, but lonelier by the loss of one of his sturdiest vassals, Hirohito had to go on living and fighting. He had no advisor to compare with Yamamoto for long-range military thinking. The sixty-three-year-old Chief of Staff Sugiyama was an agreeable pachyderm who could accept scoldings and countermanded orders without taking offense. The fifty-eight-year-old Prime Minister Tojo was a correct military politician who could stand up to fellow officers, suppress civilian troublemaking, and resist cartel bribes. The once ubiquitous Suzuki Tei-ichi, now the staid fifty-four-year-old chief of the Cabinet Planning Board, had specialized increasingly in economic matters and had come to talk like a banker. Lord Privy Seal Kido, fifty-three, was a civilian, adept in civilian arts such as image making, police work, and espionage. Moreover Kido was now exerting much of his cold and awesome hysteria, and his meticulous cunning, to advance planning for peace.

In Yamashita, the Tiger of Malaya, Hirohito might have found the type of popular military leader who could make the most of Japan's dwindling opportunities. But the outspoken Yamashita, who had frowned on the Yen Tsi-shan massacres and had urged immediate invasion of Australia, was now in an I-told-you-so position. Hirohito left him in Manchuria.

Instead of Yamashita, Hirohito took into his private councils Yamashita's former staff officer, the brilliant young zealot, Colonel Tsuji Masanobu, who was eighteen months Hirohito's junior.[10] After propagating the verbal orders for the Death March in the Philippines, Tsuji had accompanied General Hyakutake Seikichi to Guadalcanal where he had masterminded the last two abortive Japanese attempts to throw the Marines back

[10] Some Japanese biographical dictionaries give Tsuji's birth year as 1903, but according to his own account he was born on October 11, 1901.

into the sea. Following the second failure, Tsuji had returned to Tokyo to admit candidly his errors in judgment and to urge the evacuation of Guadalcanal, which had turned out successfully. Long known to Hirohito and ardently sponsored by Prince Mikasa, Hirohito's youngest brother Colonel Tsuji had impressed Hirohito by his frankness. As 1943 wore on however, Hirohito saw that Tsuji was too young, fanatical, and provincial ever to replace Yamamoto as an easy-going, informal stimulant in the processes of strategic decision making. In August 1943, without hard feeling, Hirohito sent Tsuji back to China to play the role he loved best that of staff-officer intermediary between the palace and its Army procon suls abroad.

In the early months of 1943, during the retreat from Guadalcanal and the northeastern coast of New Guinea, the desperation which had driven Yamamoto to invite death had oppressed Hirohito as well. Shortly after his January scolding of Staff Chief Sugiyama for having no tanks at Buna Hirohito had tongue-lashed Prime Minister Tojo for lagging industrial efforts. Taking a page from the book of his predecessor, Prince Konoye Tojo had retaliated by falling sick and indulging in absenteeism. Lord Privy Seal Kido had promptly begun a list of possible new prime minister and had, at the same time, written in his diary, "However, I respect Tojo."

Tojo's health quickly improved; he received kind words from the Throne; he agreed to stagger on with Japan's burden. He brought into the government, as his assistant, a new vice war minister, Lieutenant General Tominaga Kyoji, whom Hirohito had long recognized as an authentic Army expert on air power. At the same time Tojo invited into his Cabinet half a dozen industrialists to serve as ministers without portfolio and advise on war production.

While Tojo was encouraged to fortify his government for prosecution of the war, Lord Privy Seal Kido went on making contingency preparation for the chance that Japan might have to surrender and be occupied by enemy troops. On February 4, 1943, at the home of his secretary and post war successor, Matsudaira Yasumasa, Kido met secretly with former Prime Minister Konoye to review Peace Faction planning. They agreed to explo to the fullest U.S. fears of communism and to promote the idea that the Japanese people, in the dark hours of defeat, might turn Communist they were stripped of their god-emperor.

On March 18 Kido reassured Yoshida Shigeru, the postwar prime minister of Japan, that he was the real leader of the Peace Faction and that Prince Konoye, due to ill health and American distrust, could never be more than the faction's figurehead.

On April 7 Hirohito ordered Kido to have two diplomats of the imperial coterie change places: Ambassador Shigemitsu Mamoru to return from the Embassy in Nanking and take the portfolio of foreign minister; Foreign Minister Tani Masayuki to go to Nanking to handle relations with the

Chinese puppet government there.[11] Shigemitsu had for some time been agitating for a quick peace with Chiang Kai-shek: a withdrawal of Japanese troops from China in return for a break in diplomatic relations between Chiang and the Anglo-American Alliance. Both Shigemitsu and Tani believed that such a peace could be made and that they had the necessary contacts with Chungking to negotiate it. The pipeline was to run through Sun Fo, the son of Sun Yat-sen and former lover of Japan's girl spy Eastern Jewel.[12] Sun Fo would communicate Japanese proposals to his mother, Madame Sun Yat-sen. She, being a Communist on the one hand and the sister-in-law of Chiang Kai-shek on the other, would then negotiate the necessary understandings with both Chiang and Mao Tse-tung, the two fighting leaders of China.

Hirohito invested Shigemitsu as foreign minister on April 23. At the same time Hirohito brought back into public office another Big Brother, Viscount Okabe Nagakage, whom he invested as education minister in charge of propaganda. Like Shigemitsu, Okabe had lost some favor with the Throne by inclining toward the Strike-North Faction in the early 1930's. Other sympathizers with the Fight-Russia group would ride in on the two men's coattails. By bringing them back into office Hirohito not only made a bid for the support of the disaffected Strike-North partisans on the domestic scene but also indicated to foreign analysts that Japan was again worried by the threat of communism and was re-enlisting the services of leading anti-Communists.

Two days after the Cabinet shuffle, on April 25, Lord Privy Seal Kido was told by Prince Konoye that contacts in Chungking reported favorably on prospects for an over-all peace settlement that would include the West as well as China. Madame Chiang Kai-shek, said Konoye's informants, had recently learned on a trip to Washington that "U.S. war leaders are surprised by the power of the Soviet Union and have decided, as a result, not to defeat Japan and Germany too utterly."

In early May Shigemitsu, the new foreign minister, pressed forward with his Chungking negotiations. On May 13 he reported to Kido that the greatest obstacle in the talks was a Chinese feeling that the Japanese military would override any agreement which could be drawn up and would remain in China fighting no matter what treaty was signed by the Foreign Ministry. Kido told Shigemitsu to tell Chiang Kai-shek that Japan would honor her diplomatic commitments and that, if necessary to control the

[11] Much later, in 1956–57, Tani was made ambassador to Washington.

[12] Debauched and corpulent, Eastern Jewel was now a "soul broker" for the Chinese community in Peking. She brought to the attention of the Japanese secret police Chinese merchants who still possessed hidden gold, and when they were arrested, she arranged and took a percentage of the ransoms which they paid for their release. She needed the money because she now had to hire professional actors and sing-song girls to satisfy her various sexual appetites.

Army, Hirohito was prepared to appoint an imperial prince as prime minister.

The next day, May 14, Kido asked for an audience with Captain Prince Takamatsu, Hirohito's brother in the offices of the Navy General Staff, and having explained to him what was afoot, asked for his and the Navy' fullest co-operation.

Prime Minister Tojo was quick to see the virtues of a peace offensive and to propose to Hirohito that it be broadened to cover not only China but also other occupied territories. Why not promise independence, at one time or another, to all the lands Japan had conquered? Why not promise to withdraw troops from them at an appropriate moment and leave them with their own duly constituted, independent, anticolonial governments Why not call a conference of Greater East Asian puppet leaders later in 1943, in November, to make public and ratify these magnanimous Japanese goals? Hirohito broached Tojo's idea to Lord Privy Seal Kido on May 19. Kido agreed that it was an excellent suggestion which would fi well into other peace planning. So encouraged, Hirohito telephoned Kido a few minutes later to ask for his opinion on what to do with Hong Kong leave it British, return it to China, or declare it an independent protectorat of Japan?

While participating in these peace arrangements, Hirohito had indirectl admitted that the war was lost but he had not neglected its prosecution He had lunched or dined several times a week with industrialists in a effort to alleviate Japan's growing shortages of airplanes, transport ships machine tools, alloys, petroleum products, and rice. Before anything coul grow out of the understandings reached at these meetings, the America industrial monster struck again with a new invasion, this time to the nort in Arctic waters.

ATTU

Admiral Yamamoto's hunger for death had communicated itself rapidl to all ranks in all theaters. Even the guards in concentration camps fa behind the front lines had begun to talk of the impossibility of winning th war and the inevitability of dying. The numbing new fatalism first expresse itself in action on the desolate island of Attu in the Aleutians.

Attu had been occupied by Japanese troops as a consequence of th Midway debacle. Initially the advance on Attu had been meant as a fein to distract American forces from the main thrust of the Midway operatio across the Pacific toward Hawaii. However, when Midway turned to dis aster, Attu had been occupied by a few hundred Japanese troops, unre sisted, in order to save face and report something successful to the Japanes home front. Attu was the closest to Japan of the islands which stretche across the North Pacific from Alaska. Less than a thousand miles separate

Attu from the northernmost of Japan's own seasonally inhabited Kurile islands which arced north from Hokkaido toward Siberia's Kamchatka Peninsula.

By May 1943, a few weeks after Yamamoto's death, the Attu garrison had grown to 2,630 men. A still larger number of Japanese troops had garrisoned little Kiska, 170 miles farther east toward the American mainland. To U.S. troops these distant Alaskan outposts meant little. Their bonestrewn seal beaches and mushy interiors of muskeg bottomland and tundra plateau were hardly worth fighting for. Their only inhabitants were Russian fur traders and a few hundred native Aleut Eskimos. They had no trees at all and no shrubs higher than a man's knee except for a solitary fir on Umnak, the advance listening post for Dutch Harbor off the Alaskan coast. This one conifer had been flown in, potted, from Seattle, 2,400 miles away. It had been surrounded by a wooden stockade and posted with a sign which declared it the "Umnak National Forest."

On May 11, 1943, defying fogs and the unpredictable Arctic island winds known as williwaws, an American fleet stood off Attu and began to put ashore 11,000 U.S. troops. The 2,630 Japanese defenders of the island, softened up by a naval barrage, knew what to expect and bottled themselves up in the most defensible valley on the island. Eighteen days after the cautious U.S. invaders reached the valley from both ends and began to move in on it. The Japanese were by now hungry and spent from waiting, and their commander, who had been informed by Tokyo that he could expect no reinforcements, called together his staff officers. He told them that it was time for the entire garrison to die. Only by dying could Japanese express the sincerity of their purposes to Americans and at the same time abide by their oaths as soldiers to the Emperor.

The result of this resolve made a deep impression upon the U.S. troops on the island. The last 1,000 of Attu's garrison sortied that night from the old Russian seal station of Chichagof in a banzai charge. They broke through U.S. night picket lines to annihilate an American field hospital and a quartermaster depot. Half of them were shot down in the attack. The other half, at least 500 men, pulled the pins from the grenades tucked into their belts and blew themselves up. Neither Hirohito nor the U.S. troops could understand their bootless sacrifice, for neither had ever known their depths of hunger and hopelessness. U.S. observers were appalled by the piteous waste of life and by the peculiar way in which the cuddled grenades could clean men of their brains and insides while leaving outer shells of bone and skin intact. No G.I. philosophers, however, shed tears for the suicides. Before dying the Japanese garrison had taken 1,800 U.S. casualties, including 600 dead.

Imperial Headquarters had lost radio contact with the Attu garrison on May 27, two days before the suicide charge. As a result, the first news of what had happened on the dark cold hillsides of the island reached Tokyo through American broadcasts. Most Japanese who heard the bulletins applauded the suicidal courage of the defenders. Even Lord Privy Seal Kido was impressed. He noted in his diary: "I sincerely bowed to Colonel Yamazaki Yasushiro and to his men. I felt a sad and limitless rage."

Hirohito, however, was displeased. Suicides might become necessary in the latter stages of the war to evoke American pity and guilt; they might become necessary in the mid-stages of the war to complete the people's sense of participation; but now, in Hirohito's view, was still the first stage of the war, and suicides were wasteful.

By June 6, 1943—the day after Yamamoto's state funeral—Hirohito had had a week in which to weigh the consequences of the Attu debacle. He had seen that Japan would now have to garrison and fortify her northern islands, the Kuriles. This effort would take ship tonnage that was already fully engaged in provisioning Japanese expeditionary forces elsewhere and in bringing back raw materials to Japanese factories. The improvident frugality which had been exercised in the arming and supplying of the Attu outpost would now exact a heavy price. Hirohito called Chief of Staff Sugiyama and complained:

> It is regrettable that we have had to follow this kind of strategy. In future please look ahead before making troop commitments. . . . I wonder if the Army and Navy are really co-operating. . . . We have now suffered frequently from a break in communications, caused by the enemy, between ourselves and the front. Please keep that in mind in future operational planning.

The next day Prime Minister Tojo saw the Emperor and announced ominously to Lord Privy Seal Kido after the audience: "The war has reached a decisive stage. The attitude of Germany will bear watching. Over there, too, the situation has changed."

It had indeed changed. On May 12 the last German troops had been driven from North Africa, and now the Allies were preparing to invade Sicily. For Tojo, who had championed alliance with Germany and Italy the German retreat was personally humiliating. As a matter of honesty and self-punishment in the presence of the Throne, he had warned Hirohito that Japan now fought alone and that Hitler, if possible, would make his own separate peace.

On June 8, the day after Tojo's confession, Hirohito completed his study of the Attu Island tragedy. To Chief of Staff Sugiyama he was now scathing:

> You foresaw this contingency [of Attu being cut off] yet for a full week after the enemy landed on May 12 you took no remedial countermeasures. You apologize that the fog was heavy but you surely knew in advance about the fogs at that latitude. You must have foreseen fogs. Are you sure that

the Army and Navy are really communicating with one another frankly? It seems to me that one service makes a brave boast and the other promises irresponsibly to back up that boast. You must be sure that you can accomplish what you agree upon. To make a fine agreement and break it is worse than to reach no agreement at all. We will never achieve any success in this war unless the Army and Navy can consider their conflicts honestly and frankly.

If fog inhibited our movements, it was surely a mistake to invest ships and airplanes in that theater, for ships and airplanes consume a lot of oil. If we go on fighting this way we will only make China rejoice, confuse neutrals, dismay our allies, and weaken the Co-Prosperity Sphere. Isn't there any way somehow, somewhere, of meeting U.S. force squarely and of destroying it?

The Army is doing fine in Burma. Maybe in its own element the Army will not be defeated, but on the islands in the ocean the full strength of the Army cannot be brought to bear. . . . You have said, Sugiyama, that the Navy's ability to fight a decisive battle "covers" us against disaster in this way, but I am afraid that this ability no longer exists.

The bland and genial Sugiyama, usually so optimistic, had no reply to make. As cheerfully as he could, he reminded the Emperor that a joint Army-Navy air strike was planned for the morrow against the Flying Tigers, the American volunteer air corps in China. The next day, June 9, Hirohito was pleased to be able to commend Sugiyama upon the success of the raid. Sugiyama took the opportunity to beg the Emperor for full support of the Army's campaign to hold what was left of New Guinea. He gave it as his opinion that New Guinea and other outposts which Japan held in the southwestern Pacific, although they might seem remote, represented the "last-ditch chance to defend the nation."

READINGS FROM TOLSTOY

In order to follow his master's thoughts, Lord Privy Seal Kido found it necessary at this juncture of the war to read one of Hirohito's favorite books, *War and Peace*. He found in it "ideas of great interest for current affairs." It was Tolstoy's thesis, in his saga of Russia's struggle against Napoleon, that the war fever of a people, when once aroused, must run its course; that a kind of redemption by bloodshed must take place before a nation could make a fresh start. Also, Tolstoy felt that it was sentimental hypocrisy to wage war by rules as if it were a game. To be of any cathartic value, war should be total and fought to the death. Tolstoy's ideas fitted well into the fanatic spiritualism of Japan and helped to explain to Kido why Japan must follow the course that she did.

Kido's excursion into Russian literature was prompted by a new American move in the Solomon Islands. Throughout early June 1943, aerial reconnaissance told of an invasion fleet gathering off Guadalcanal. Hirohito fretted because costly Japanese air strikes and submarine attacks failed even to hamper the U.S. buildup. On the night of June 20 an advance force for the U.S. thrust—two companies of the 4th Marine Raiders—landed unopposed at Segi Point on New Georgia, more than a third of the way from Guadalcanal to Rabaul, and there began to build an airstrip. For lack of air support Japanese ground forces in the area failed to dent the little enclave and the Marines in it methodically developed it as a reception center for much larger American landings ten days later.

Hirohito was dismayed by the brazen self-confidence of the American invaders and angered by lack of co-ordinated Army-Navy thinking on how to deal with them. The Navy General Staff improvised plans for strengthening fleet and air units in the area. The Army General Staff wrote recipes for reinforcement which smacked of the same stale tactics that had failed in the Guadalcanal campaign. Both chiefs of staff spoke evasively when Hirohito asked them if they could hold New Georgia. For someone who would speak frankly to him out of firsthand knowledge, Hirohito sent to Truk in the Carolines and summoned home his cousin, his one-time sparring partner, Admiral Marquis Komatsu of the submarine fleet. Arriving in Tokyo early on June 29, Komatsu confirmed Hirohito's worst fears: the Solomons could not be held.

Prime Minister Tojo was scheduled to set out the next day on a long-postponed inspection tour of the "Southern Areas." After a stormy morning of consultation at the ironclad Imperial Headquarters shed, Hirohito called Tojo and entrusted him with an imperial message to all commanders in the Solomons. It asked them to fight a tenacious holding action, giving and taking no quarter and selling their lives as dearly as possible.

Tojo sought to cheer up Hirohito with brave reassurances, but he only succeeded in making Hirohito blaze up in a rare exhibition of temper:

> You keep saying the Imperial Army is indomitable but whenever the enemy lands, you lose the battle. You have never been able to repulse an enemy landing. If we do not find somewhere to stop them, where, I ask you, is this war going to end?

Tojo flew to Rabaul the next day, June 30. His arrival coincided with the main U.S. landings in New Georgia which put more than 10,000 troops ashore on five different beachheads. Tojo found most of the front-line commanders assembled to greet him. With some severity he told them that due to the Italian-German collapse in North Africa, the Allies would soon have major forces to spare for offensives in the Pacific. Japan desperately needed to build up reserve strength in rear areas with which to stem the Allied onslaught. Consequently forward garrisons, for the time being, would have to live on their own resources without hope of reinforcement or supply. If they fought well, they would gain time for Japan to make up the losses of her recent bad-luck streak and marshal a counteroffensive.

Back in Tokyo every patrician was mobilized for the total war effort. Only by showing herself ready to fight with every sinew could Japan hope to keep a bargaining position at the peace table. Empress Nagako herself rolled bandages and helped to wrap comfort packages for the men at the front. Lord Privy Seal Kido, for his part, joined his engineer brother, Wada Koroku, in proselytizing indefatigably for complete devotion to the construction of airplanes. Even Hirohito's eldest brother, Prince Chichibu, who had often differed with the Throne, now set up his personal aide-de-camp at a suite in Tokyo's Sanno Hotel to co-ordinate all peace dealings with Chiang Kai-shek.

While Tojo was still in Rabaul explaining total war and the new policy of abandonment for the beleaguered garrisons in the Solomons, the Allies on July 10 staged an awesome exhibition of their might in the European theater. One hundred and sixty thousand Allied troops stormed ashore from 2,000 ships onto the beaches of Sicily. As in New Georgia the Axis defenders found themselves hopelessly outnumbered in every medium: land, sea, and air. A stage in the war that had seemed "decisive" a month earlier now seemed all too clearly decided.

On July 25 the King of Italy and the Italian Grand Council deposed Mussolini, put him in protective custody, and gave the rule of the Italian realm to Marshal Pietro Badoglio and a caretaker Cabinet which was charged with the delicate duty of surrendering. The next day Lord Privy Seal Kido warned Hirohito that one Axis partner would drop from the Tripartite Alliance at any moment and that the other, Germany, could no longer be trusted to help Japan. Soon Japan would fight alone. Kido told Hirohito, "We must prepare for the worst."

Three days later, on July 29, Kido received a visit from Major General Matsumoto Kenji, the personal aide-de-camp of Prince Higashikuni, Hirohito's devious uncle. The secret police, said Matsumoto, were beginning to look into the peace plots of Prince Konoye and Prince Higashikuni. In translation from belly talk this meant that the secret police, with the connivance of Peace-Faction leaders, had put Peace-Faction members under surveillance as subversives and had begun to compile dossiers on them which would tend to clear them of war guilt in American eyes.

During August, while the Allied army conquered Sicily, while Badoglio and southern Italy waited to surrender, and while Hitler studied what countermeasures to take in northern Italy, Hirohito assimilated statistics and understood what Kido meant by "preparing for the worst." U.S. submarines that month took a dreadful toll of Japanese shipping. Almost half the prewar merchant fleet—3,000,000 tons—had gone to the bottom since Pearl Harbor and, despite heroic efforts, Japanese shipyards had replaced only two thirds of the losses. In the air, too, Japan was losing more fighting and transport craft than her factories could produce.

On August 5 Chief of Staff Sugiyama submitted to Hirohito a detailed
report on the hopeless situation facing the Lae and Salamaua garrisons on
the north coast of New Guinea and the Munda-Kolombangara garrisons
in northwestern New Georgia. Hirohito was so distressed by the report that
he dropped his usual mask of moderation and self-control and exchanged
words with Sugiyama that would have made a less hardened counselor
resign.

> HIROHITO: It's not good in any area. Can't we hit the U.S. forces hard
> anywhere?
> SUGIYAMA: No, in all areas it's only a matter of time. We're doing our best
> at the front lines. I'm extremely sorry.
> HIROHITO: You may well be. If we are forced to retreat gradually like this,
> the uplift for our enemies, and the effect even on neutrals, will be great.
> Where in the world are you going to dig in? Where do you propose to fight
> a decisive battle? I don't think that we can afford to keep being pushed back
> like this, bit by bit, do you?

Three days later, in another audience with Sugiyama, Hirohito repeated his plaintive refrain again and again: "Can't we take the offensive
somewhere? . . . Isn't there any way to strengthen the air force
quickly? . . . Isn't there any possibility of slapping the Americans one
sharp blow?"

By way of answer Sugiyama submitted to Hirohito the preliminary findings of a top-secret study of counteroffensive possibilities which had just
been drawn up by the leading department chiefs of the General Staff. The
study began by comparing the two threats confronting Japan: that of the
British thrusting east out of India and that of the Americans and Australian
thrusting north from Guadalcanal. Of the two, said the study, the American threat demanded the more urgent attention. To check it would require
that strength for a major counteroffensive be built up in some rear area like
Taiwan or the Philippines. Transports, planes, guns, supplies, and men
would have to be held back and saved up from current operational expenditures. The study demonstrated in cold figures that present military
commitments left no slack for such a buildup.

Suppose then that Japan reduced her commitments by pulling back her
legions into a smaller defense perimeter and cutting civilian expense to
subsistence level. The study examined what could be gained by cutting off
all imports of rice to Japan, by sending no more supplies to Japanese
forces in the Solomons and in the Marshall Islands, and finally by abandoning to hunger the forces in New Guinea, Rabaul, and the Caroline
Islands. The study concluded that all three of these drastic measures would
have to be taken in order to prolong the war and that even then "we will
not be able to accumulate enough strength in rear areas" or "to mount an
adequate counterattack against the enemy."

By the end of Sugiyama's recital, the mask had fallen again over Hirohito's features. Mechanically he asked time to consider the study. Somewhat later by telephone, he instructed Sugiyama and then Navy Chief of Staff Nagano to have exhaustive, independent studies prepared of war prospects by the Operations and Intelligence departments of both the Army and Navy General Staffs. The operational studies—described earlier [13]—were completed by the end of the year and were both more bleak than Sugiyama's preliminary findings. The studies prepared by the Intelligence departments of the two services are not extant but are said to have prescribed subterfuges closely resembling the events, described in Chapter 2, which would actually take place in and around the palace at war's end a year and a half later.

While hungry Japanese soldiers continued to hurl themselves against the U.S. beachhead on New Georgia in the Solomons, Hirohito received ample confirmation of Staff Chief Sugiyama's chilling conclusions. On August 11, Vice Admiral Nomura Naokuni, a former chief of Naval Intelligence, returned by submarine from Germany, went straight to the palace, and told Hirohito that the condition of the Third Reich was parlous. On September 2, Foreign Minister Shigemitsu reported to the Throne a continuing lack of progress in peace negotiations with Chiang Kai-shek and with U.S. operatives in Europe.[14] Shigemitsu recommended, and Hirohito approved, the sending of a special envoy to the Japanese Embassy in Moscow to see what could be done to enlist Soviet help in negotiating a peace settlement. The scheme later foundered in bogs of bureaucratic Soviet disinterest.

On September 2 the Allies landed in Italy. On September 8 the Badoglio government surrendered in the name of the king. Admiral Carlo Bergamini, the commander in chief of the Italian Navy, with eighty-five warships from the bases at La Spezia, Taranto, and Trieste, attempted to dash south to Malta and give himself up to the Allies. Along the way, however, he was overtaken by German dive-bombers and sent to the bottom in his flagship, the *Roma*.

On September 9, Hirohito attended a liaison conference at which it was decided to close Italian embassies, freeze Italian assets, and intern Italian nationals. On September 10 the Nazis seized Rome, and a select cadre of German paratroopers began briefing for a special mission. Two days later they dropped behind Italian lines, extricated Mussolini from house arrest at one of his villas, and brought him back to Rome to serve as a German puppet.

---

[13] See Chapter 2, page 62.

[14] One of the latest Japanese peace feelers had been extended through a presumed U.S. agent in Sofia, Bulgaria. Such repeated Japanese overtures were either too subtly worded to excite American interest or U.S. documentation on them remains classified. Most of the files of the wartime Office of Strategic Services were taken over by the C.I.A. after the war and have not been opened to public inspection.

Hirohito that day of September 10 approved in principle the transfer o
seventeen of the thirty-four under-strength divisions left in China, Man
churia, and Korea to Taiwan and the Philippines. The Army opposed th
decision because it left the Continent inadequately defended against Rus
sian and Chinese Communist forces, and even against Chiang Kai-shek
Moreover, U.S. submarines prowling the China Sea made the operatio
hazardous. Hirohito, however, argued that, if U.S. submarines made i
dangerous now to ship 300,000 men across the China Sea, they woul
make it doubly so when the men were needed to repulse U.S. landing
in the Philippines. Conversely, if Russia threatened to attack, U.S. sub
marines might not be too zealous in interfering with troop shipments i
the opposite direction, from the Philippines back to the mainland.

The Navy had asked that some of the troops from the Continent be ser
beyond Taiwan out to forward posts in the Marshall Islands. Hirohito
however, sided with the Army in this one particular. Already the garrison
in the Marshalls could not be adequately supplied with rice and bullets. I
would be a waste and a hardship for the Empire to send them more mer
In justification of his sentiments Hirohito gravely quoted a favorite prover
of his father, Emperor Taisho: "Affection between father and son, fairnes
between ruler and ruled."

During the last half of September 1943, Chiang Kai-shek rebuffed th
peace proposals extended through Madame Sun Yat-sen by saying that h
did not trust the sincerity or authority of either the Japanese Army or th
Japanese Foreign Ministry. Anything but direct dealings with Emperc
Hirohito, he suggested, would be a bootless conversational exercise. As
token of his readiness for such dealings, Hirohito, on September 22, gav
an unprecedented private audience to Wang Ching-wei, formerly a KM
lieutenant of Chiang Kai-shek and now the puppet president of Japanes
occupied China. Wang was unwell and would die of cancer in a Japanes
hospital fourteen months later. After explaining to him Japanese hopes fc
a peace settlement, Hirohito said, "I pray for your health and that yc
may establish peace in the Far East."

Afterward, to Kido, Hirohito shook his head and added with a ha
puzzled, half mocking smile: "Wang kept asking, 'How can I manifest ar
incorporate in my own vile body Your Majesty's sacred virtues.' He spol
as if he thought he were a Japanese!"

Despite Hirohito's great condescension and show of favor, Wang w
unable to persuade Chiang Kai-shek to accept Japanese peace terms. T
break with Roosevelt and Churchill in exchange for a Japanese troop wit
drawal from China would have left Chiang alone to cope with Mao Ts
tung and Stalin. Since he feared his wartime ally Mao more than anyor
else, Chiang opted to be patient and to leave Japanese troops in easte
China as long as possible.

On September 25 the ideologist of the Strike South, Doctor Okav humei, re-entered Court records after several years of absence. Having masterminded the plots of 1931 and the assassinations of 1932 he had passed under a cloud of polite police surveillance until 1935. Then, officially released "from prison," he had rejoined the spy service and had held a position of authority in the South Manchuria Railroad Research Institute over Soviet spy Sorge's Japanese accomplice, Ozaki Hotsumi. During the war, while Ozaki languished in prison, Okawa had remained top spy-service operative and maintained close touch with his former chief assassin, priest Inoue Nisho, who now lived in the home of Peace Faction figurehead Prince Konoye. Because of his many services, Dr. Okawa had only to speak in order to be heard. He now sent a message to Lord Privy Seal Kido suggesting to him that the final Prince Higashikuni Cabinet, projected for the end of the war, should include as an advisor or minister without portfolio retired Lieutenant General Ishiwara Kanji, the blunt, irascible strategist who had engineered the conquest of Manchuria in 1931.

Kido dismissed Okawa's suggestion as "sincere but naïve." At the same time he noted in his diary that Okawa wanted the matter discussed with Count Makino, the eighty-two-year-old former lord privy seal who had masterminded Court liaison with all the plotters, assassins, and coup d'etat artists of the early 1930's. Kido had a healthy respect for his charming, nervous, soft-voiced predecessor and did not seek out his company. Perhaps he felt it enough that he met frequently with Makino's son-in-law, the projected postwar prime minister, Yoshida Shigeru. On this occasion, however, when Kido did not immediately consult with Makino, Makino finally came to Kido. The result was that Makino took an increasingly active part in Peace Faction planning, and Manchurian conquistador Ishiwara—"sincere but naïve" though the idea might seem—did in fact become an advisor to Japan's surrender Cabinet. In that capacity twenty-three months later, he would tour the country telling the people that his old rival Tojo was alone responsible for the mistake of having gone to war with the United States.

On October 5, ten days after the reappearance at Court of Strike-South ideologist Okawa, Hirohito began to allow leading war-criminal suspects to retire from possibly incriminating public offices. The first to go was the ubiquitous retired general, Suzuki Tei-ichi. In relieving him of his onerous duties as Japan's war-production czar, Hirohito honored him with permanent ministerial rank at Court [15] and a full-time assignment to peace planning.

Meanwhile Hirohito's Army brother, Major Prince Mikasa, had been trying to find out why Chiang Kai-shek would not accept the favorable peace terms which Japan had offered through Madame Sun Yat-sen.

---

[15] Without such rank he would have been ineligible under Court rules to see and advise the Emperor in private.

Chiang's wartime ally, Mao Tse-tung, seemed to be to blame, but Mikas could learn nothing for sure. He expressed his frustration to Kido c October 8 by observing contemptuously that China had hedged all h⋅ bets. She had a Wang Chiang-wei government to deal with Japan if Hir⋅ hito won the war, a Chiang Kai-shek government to deal with the Unit⋅ States if Roosevelt won the war, and a Mao Tse-tung government to de⋅ with the Soviet Union if the real winner turned out to be Stalin. "The⋅ are three heads in China," said Mikasa, "but only one body. As yet t⋅ Yenan [Mao Tse-tung] government has not been fully appreciated."

In early October Japan's leading fascist publicist and pro-German f⋅ natic, Nakano Seigo, heard of secret peace planning at Court and in t⋅ Cabinet and swiftly recruited a conspiratorial band of right-wing lab⋅ heelers and Army veterans to assassinate Prime Minister Tojo, Lord Pri⋅ Seal Kido, and others. The plot came to light when one of its least r⋅ sponsible recruits, a disabled veteran named Terai who made a livi⋅ by showing his wounds to a dozen different sympathetic widows, a⋅ ducted an aristocratic priestess from one of Tokyo's shrines and to⋅ her on a ten-day spree to the fleshpots of Atami. When the authoriti⋅ caught up with Terai, he revealed the assassination attempt and t⋅ Thought Police moved in on fascist Nakano.

A few days later, on October 27, Nakano committed ritual suici⋅ in prison. The story was put out on the grapevine that he had been order⋅ to do so by Tojo because he refused to divulge the names of certain i⋅ perial princes who were associated with his plot. No knowledgeable p⋅ son believed this carefully leaked rumor. Hirohito alone could expect be obeyed in ordering a man to commit suicide. And all adult princes the realm were closely associated with Kido, one of Nakano's intend⋅ victims. Consequently the double-talk of the official rumor was reduced a single inescapable conclusion: Nakano had threatened, in his enthusias for the war, to expose Court plotting for peace. When told in prison th the Emperor was displeased, he agreed to show Hirohito the sincerity his aims by taking his own life.

END OF THE PUPPET SHOW

The Allied thrust up the Solomons continued. On November 1, U troops landed unopposed on the northernmost island of the archipela⋅ Bougainville. In easy striking distance of Rabaul, they bulldozed an a⋅ strip and held it well against numerous Japanese counterstrokes. Prin Mikasa and Lieutenant General Anami—the former imperial aide-de-car⋅ who was to commit suicide as war minister in 1945—flew south on N vember 4 to bolster the morale of the men in the field. Anami stayed to take command of the faltering Japanese defense of western New Guin⋅

The renewed American advance detracted somewhat from a proud n⋅

ment in the life of Prime Minister Tojo when, on November 5, he presided over the convocation of a Greater East Asia Conference of all Japanese puppet leaders from the occupied territories. The meeting was held in the chilly auditorium of the Diet Building, just behind the prime minister's residence outside the south wall of the palace. Blue woolen cloths covered the U-shaped string of conference tables. At the head of the U, where braziers of hot coals filled the cloths with warmth, sat Tojo and the Japanese delegation. Down the legs of the U, where there were no braziers, sat the representatives of the conquered territories: on Tojo's right, Ba Maw of Burma, Prime Minister Chang Chung-hui of Manchukuo, and Wang Ching-wei of eastern China; on Tojo's left, Prince Wan Wai-thya-kon of Thailand, President José Laurel of the Philippines, and Chandra Bose, the ward of Black Dragon Toyama, who had been groomed for twenty-seven years in Tokyo and Berlin to become the leader of Japan's "government in exile" for India. Sukarno and other Indonesian leaders had not been invited to the conference because Japan needed the raw materials of their land and was not prepared to grant Indonesia independence.

To the other puppet leaders Tojo orated on a text of "Asia for Asiatics." He promised them all "self-determination" as soon as possible. Thailand would remain independent—with Japanese advisors. Burma would be turned loose in 1944 and the Philippines in late 1944 or early 1945. Mukden and Nanking would both have new liberalized treaties with Japan. Chandra Bose would rule India as soon as the Japanese Army could conquer it.

The puppet leaders professed to be greatly moved. "One billion Orientals, one billion people of Greater East Asia!" cried Laurel of the Philippines. Laurel had been entrusted by MacArthur's captive, the prewar Philippine president Quezon, with the task of dealing with the Japanese. Now he distrusted Japan even more than he distrusted America.

"All the nations of East Asia should love their own countries," declared China's noncommittal Wang Ching-wei, "and should love their neighbors and love East Asia."

"I have heard the voice of Asia calling to her children," mused Burma's Ba Maw, "but this time it is not in a dream."

"It is undeniable," said Tojo in his usual short, positive manner, "that the nations of Greater East Asia are bound by indissoluble ties of blood.[16] I therefore believe firmly that it is our common goal to secure stability in the Greater East Asian area and to create the new order on a basis of wealth and happiness for all."

Tojo was at least half sincere. Having given his life to Japan's imperial conspiracy; having permitted the murder of his patron, the first of

16 This was roughly equivalent to saying that Birmingham Afro-Americans, Boston Brahmins, Hungarian Magyars, Spanish Basques, and Orange Irishmen were all blood kin to Romans because all professed to Christianity.

the Three Crows, Nagata Tetsuzan, in 1935; having, in short, seen the
dreams of his youth burn into the ash of old men's cigars, he was con
vinced that the one justification for all that Japan had done must be, his
torically, the liberation of Asia from Western colonialism. Most aged
Japanese generals in postwar Japan would hold to this slender thread o
self-excuse.

During the Greater East Asia Conference, Hirohito himself gave lunch
in the palace to the delegates and spoke a few kind words to each o
them. Then, after a last tea ceremony in the Shinjuku Palace gardens and
a last banquet at Tojo's official residence, the puppets set out to retur
to the harsh realities of Japanese rule in their homelands: printing-press
money which Japanese quartermasters gave for what they took; a spy
hostage system by which Japanese secret police controlled influentia
native families and institutions; levies of conscript labor for the road
railroads, and fortifications demanded by Japanese tacticians; countles
"rationalization schemes" devised by Japanese economists to make sur
of crops and products useful to Japan; and finally the relentless cant an
mass meetings exacted by Japanese propagandists.

On November 19, 1943, as soon as the Co-Prosperity Sphere buntin
had been taken down, Lord Privy Seal Kido received a secret briefing a
his official residence from Rear Admiral Takagi Sokichi, the strategist wh
had been called upon by Hirohito's directive earlier in August to asse
war prospects for the Navy. With a few well-chosen graphs and deduction
Takagi told Kido that Japan had no hope and would have to give bac
everything. His opposite number in the Army, Colonel Matsutani Makot
he said, was even more pessimistic and feared that Japan might have
be decimated before the enemy wearied of killing and allowed Japan
survive at all as a nation.

Prince Higashikuni had a lunch to recruit noblemen for the Pea
Faction the next day, November 20, at the Kasumigaseki imperial vil
near the Diet Building. After dessert Kido drove out to Hongo, a sub-wa
north of the palace, to meet Konoye at a private hospital where he w
recovering from minor surgery. The Emperor was busy for the next thr
days with military concerns arising from the U.S. landings on Tarawa a
Makin in the Gilbert Islands, on November 21. Kido did not confer wi
him on Rear Admiral Takagi's black assessment of prospects until N
vember 24. Then, after a week of consultations, Hirohito appointed
panel of civilian economic experts, headed by the ubiquitous Suzuki T
ichi, retired head of the Cabinet Planning Board, to check Admi
Takagi's conclusions. The next day, December 3, Kido learned that n
gotiations between Wang Ching-wei and Chiang Kai-shek had brok
down once and for all in personal recriminations between the two.

Hirohito celebrated the second anniversary of the war, in somber moo
by making a state pilgrimage to the tomb of Fleet god Yamamoto. Kid

or his part, visited the grave of the unheeded prime-minister-maker, Prince Saionji. Neither the advice nor the forgiveness of the dead, however, could go far toward relieving the fearful ordeal for Japan which loomed ahead.

By mid-December 1943, complete intelligence returns had come in from the Allied summit conferences of November: a meeting in Cairo of Roosevelt and Churchill with Chiang Kai-shek and then a meeting in Teheran with Stalin. The analysts reported that Chiang Kai-shek would never now jeopardize his alliance with Roosevelt for the sake of an early peace with Japan and that Stalin was prepared—notwithstanding the Russo-Japanese neutrality pact—to join in the spoiling of Japan as soon as Germany was laid low.

Three days before Christmas, Kido received one of his rare visits from Count Makino, the knowledgeable, eighty-two-year-old former lord privy seal. Makino asked Kido to see Count Kabayama Aisuke, a seventy-nine-year-old operative emeritus of the spy service who had news of interest to communicate. Kido obediently gave an hour of his busy day that very afternoon to Kabayama. The old count gave him an evaluation of U.S. public feeling based on the reports of Japanese students—Ambassador Bancroft Scholarship winners—who had just returned from New York in an exchange ship. According to the students, most Americans had little hostility toward Japan and little interest in the war in the Pacific. The Pacific war, said the students, was widely considered a private enterprise of "Roosevelt and his henchmen."

Kido thanked Count Kabayama for his intelligence and wrote in his diary, "We must be determined to have ready a secret plan for the conclusion of the war."

During the next two weeks Hirohito took advantage of the holiday season at year's end to make his own over-all appraisal of war prospects. He had the underlings of Imperial General Headquarters to lunch. He then read a letter from Saionji's old Black Dragon informant, Takuno Sempu. Finally, on January 4, 1944, he transmitted his conclusions briefly to Kido. On the one hand, for the sake of the nation's pride, he wished to prosecute the war fully. On the other hand, for the sake of the nation's survival, he wished to have a sound plan ready for defeat. Kido, writing in the first person, set down the gist of his understanding of the Emperor's feelings, in a memorandum attached to his diary entry for January 6, 1944. This memorandum, mentioned earlier in these pages, became the blueprint for postwar Japan.

Kido began by observing that, if Germany could somehow resume the initiative, prospects would brighten for Japan and the rest of the memorandum could be disregarded. If, however, Germany succumbed, Japan must not fall prey to undisciplined pacifists and traitors like Badoglio. There must be a planned approach to peace in which the government at all times remained responsive to imperial bidding. After the Tojo Cabinet fell, as fall it must when "its continuance becomes quite difficult." [17] the next Cabinet should probably be instructed by the Emperor in advance as to the specific opinion-forming mission it was expected to fulfill along the way to peace. So too with the next Cabinet, if a next Cabinet should prove necessary.

In regard to the nation's pride of face, Kido pointed out: "It is clear in the imperial proclamation of war that the Greater East Asian conflict was aimed at breaking down what were called the 'siege lines' of American-British-Chinese-Dutch encirclement. For the time being, therefore, we can consider it as a satisfactory conclusion of the war if we have accomplished this objective."

As to peace terms, Kido concluded that "only considerable concession on our part will be acceptable to the enemy"—self-determination for all Pacific nations with the possible exception of Manchuria.

Kido acknowledged that his assessment might seem to some "weak kneed and conciliatory," but he went on to explain that he was surrendering not in spirit and not forever but only to the brute force of American technology. In a paraphrase of Hirohito's own lordly sentiments, he wrote

> Looking over the future trend of the world, I believe that we must preserve and cultivate our real power in the state for about one hundred years. Through our experience in the Sino-Japanese conflict, the Soviet-German war, and the development of aircraft, we have gained insight into the real strengths of the U.S.A. and U.S.S.R. We have also suffered a terrible attrition of our own national strength. Accordingly, assuming that these assessments are correct, we should avoid at all costs being isolated and attacked by the other nations of the world as a colored race. With this goal in mind I believe that the best course for us is to retain the effective power in the state secretly and to co-operate with the Soviet Union and China. Those nations are essentially Oriental in their thinking. Through them we can maintain our stand against the Anglo-Saxon powers of the United States and Great Britain while we watch developments.

[17] This state of affairs did come to pass six months later, in July 1944.

29

FALL OF THE HOMELAND

(1944–1945)

THINNING THE GARDEN

Not Tolstoy, not even Machiavelli, ever dreamed in their historical ilosophies of an entire nation embracing agony with such eager and un- cessary self-sacrifice as that of the Japanese in the next eighteen months. ne out of every seventy Japanese stoically threw away his life for Em- ror Hirohito—and this after Hirohito had admitted to his closest ad- or, Kido, that the war was lost.

Hirohito could have surrendered in January 1944. The police, to be re, would have had to deal with some diehards, but if the military alities had been explained to the people at large they would certainly ve accepted defeat. Indeed many of them would have welcomed it. By olonging the slaughter for another year and a half, Hirohito gained no tter terms from the Allies, but he did preserve the unity of his people: eir sense of persecution, their commitment to being Japanese, and their ¦ling of participation in his own imperial dream.

No doubt in acting as he did Hirohito was moved partly by wishful nking and by pride and fear of humiliation. The fragmentary docu- ¦ntation, however, which in this period records mostly imperial acts her than imperial conversations, suggests that considerations of state errode Hirohito's complex personal emotions. In the hour of crisis the ¦encerian biologist and the national high priest took charge of the im- rial personality, leaving even less scope than usual for the man.

If Hirohito had stopped the war in January 1944, initial acceptance of ¦ decision might have given way later to grumbling. When death and ¦ioning had ceased, and when the nation's huge war plant had been ¦mantled and taken away by the Allies for reparations, many would in- ¦tably say that he had sold out too cheaply. Millions of unemployed factory workers might find time to look back critically over the last quarter century and perceive the imperial conspiracy. On the other hand if the war were fought out to the brink of national ruin, the same millions would be too busy, as bombed-out refugees scratching a living from the rubble, to think of anything but their own survival.

Then, too, if Japan surrendered in the pink of health and productivity, the Allies would be far more likely to take revenge than if she surrendered hungry, sick, and decimated. By having to kill defenseless Japanese, the white soldiers would be moved to feel pity or guilt. By seeing Japanese give their lives away, the Americans would be forced to wonder if, after all, Japan had not fought sincerely for a cause.

Also, the Allies needed to be given time to fall out with one another. The American-Russian partnership had been formed in a moment of desperation. It could be expected to flaw and crack as soon as victory began to cool war enthusiasms. If Japan could hold out for a year or two, either the Americans or the Russians would grow eager to enlist Japanese support against the other.

Finally, Hirohito, both for scientific and high-priestly reasons, believed firmly in the value of death. The population of crowded Japan needed to be thinned before it would fit back into the narrow confines of the home islands to which the Allies promised to restrict it. Better for the nation to be thinned by enemy bullets than by fratricidal competition for enough to eat.

The killing could ease the Japanese conscience. When it was over, no Japanese would need to feel any further debt to the outside world. Japan would have paid for her predations limb for limb and eye for eye. She would not need to say, *"Sumimasen,"* the conventional equivalent for "Sorry," which literally means, "We are not yet equal; I owe you something." By balancing the moral books with a program of death, Hirohito could hope to enable Japan to start again after defeat with a renewed sense of pride and righteous resentment.

In letting die the myrmidons who had failed him, Hirohito meant no special malice. As archbishop of Japan's spiritualistic religion, he believed—apparently sincerely—that warriors cut down in battle were fortunate. The shades of most men, who died complacently like oxen in the stalls, tended to fade in the afterlife and were soon forgotten by the living but the souls of unavenged heroes were strong and lived long. They were given a warm home at Tokyo's Yasukuni Shrine and there, in that Valhalla, they fed daily on the prayers, offerings, and admiration of pilgrims.

GILBERTS TO MARSHALLS

Hirohito had been moved to consider the dark subtleties of national death and rebirth primarily by the U.S. invasion of the Gilbert Islands

November 1943. Earlier Allied offensives in New Guinea and the Solomons had demonstrated U.S. material superiority, but Japanese forces had not been so outnumbered as to lack a fighting chance. In the Gilberts, however, U.S. strength was overwhelming; there was no contest. This U.S. ability to mount a crushing onslaught in mid-Pacific while also supporting MacArthur's endeavors in Australasia and Eisenhower's vast enterprises in Europe had first convinced Hirohito—at least in the bookkeeping compartment of his mind—that Japan must be ready to abandon her gains and minimize her losses.

The U.S. invasion fleet for the Gilberts included twice as many aircraft carriers as Japan had ever owned: eleven fast fleet carriers and eight escort carriers. In addition there were no less than twelve battleships, fourteen cruisers, and sixty-six destroyers. This armada landed 6,472 American soldiers on Makin, where there was an 800-man Japanese garrison, and 18,600 veteran Marines on Tarawa, where there was a Japanese garrison of 2,000 laborers and 2,500 soldiers. Behind the total U.S. assault force of 25,000 stood a reserve of 10,000 more front-line fighters and an auxiliary of 73,000 with 6,000 vehicles and 117,000 tons of cargo. Six days after the landings, the Gilberts were secure. A thousand U.S. fighters had died and almost all the 5,300 Japanese-Korean defenders.

Seventeen Japanese and 129 Koreans had been taken prisoner. The Japanese were all unconscious or immobilized by wounds at the time of their capture. When they regained their senses they protested that they should have died and that they could never return to their families in Japan. On the other hand, having admitted themselves dead to their own society, they were eager to be helpful to their captors and to find, if possible, a new life.

The great steel press which Admiral Nimitz was using to crush Japan's scattered outposts clamped next upon the Marshall Islands. The 8,675 Japanese manning Kwajalein were assaulted by 41,000 U.S. troops on January 31, 1944, and a week later, with the sacrifice of 372 U.S. lives, all but 805 of the defenders had been buried and accounted for. Eleven days later 8,000 U.S. Marines and soldiers took on the 3,000-man Japanese garrison of Eniwetok. By February 22 the island was secure with a loss of 339 U.S. dead and 2,677 known Japanese dead. Sixty-four Japanese were taken prisoner.

AIR NAVY

When Eniwetok was given up for lost on February 21, the Tokyo daily *Mainichi* ran an unauthorized editorial voicing a suppressed popular sentiment: "WARS CANNOT BE WON WITH BAMBOO SPEARS." The Thought Police investigated but preferred no charges, for it turned out that *Mainichi*'s editors were not traitors but patriots supporting Hirohito's brother Prince Takamatsu in a campaign for increased aircraft production and improved use of aircraft.

The *Mainichi* indiscretion gave the public its only hint of a difference in strategic opinion which had been argued on the steps of the Throne for over a month. On January 24, when the U.S. fleet was just staging for its advance on the Marshalls, Prince Takamatsu petitioned Hirohito to adopt a new aerial strategy proposed by air enthusiasts in the Navy General Staff. The Army and Navy were bickering over their allotment of aircraft output. It would be better, said Takamatsu, if neither service got a share and if all new planes were given to a new service, an air force. Alternatively the traditional Navy might be scrapped completely and replaced by an air force. The point was that scarce planes were being wasted by traditionalists in support of ineffectual conventional troop and fleet movements. Instead, if Japan was to survive, planes must be employed, in their own right, by men who understood their capabilities. They must be expended for one purpose only: to sink the aircraft carriers by which the United States was extending her air superiority into Japanese waters.

In the circles of senior fleet officers, observed Prince Takamatsu, the ideas of the late Admiral Yamamoto were only beginning to be accepted. Yamamoto had developed Japan's air power as an arm of the fleet. Now his ideas were already outmoded. As he himself would have been the first to perceive, the arm had outgrown the body. Fleets now needed airplanes for protection but airplanes did not need fleets except as floating gun batteries, around floating air fields, in offensive actions, far out to sea. In defensive actions, close to landing fields ashore, airplanes did not need fleets at all.

It had been the dying hope of Yamamoto to use Japan's 64,000-ton super-dreadnoughts, the *Yamato* and *Musashi,* in a "decisive" shootout with the smaller-gunned battleships of the U.S. fleet. Now this proposal which Yamamoto had considered a desperate expedient even in 1943, had been seized upon by other senior admirals and made an article of fatalistic faith. Almost complacently they told their juniors: Wait until the American fleet comes to us; then we will meet it in a great surface action which will decide everything.

In the opinion of Prince Takamatsu's iconoclasts the traditionalists' "decisive battle" was a dream which would never be realized. Even if the surface fleets ever came within range of one another, aircraft would still deliver the telling blows. And at sea, from now on, U.S. airmen would always enjoy numerical superiority because their country was producing more aircraft carriers each month than Japan could build in a year.

Japan's only hope was to capitalize immediately on her unsinkable immobile aircraft carriers, the countless islands which crowded her half of the Pacific. If all the Navy's technical competence were immediately rechanneled into air operations and if all the money being spent on war

ips could be diverted to aircraft manufacture, it might be possible
ickly to patrol Japan's island outposts with a highly mobile air fleet.
en thousand planes—less than five months' factory output—would be
ough to overwhelm all the planes which U.S. carriers could bring into
panese waters. If such a force could be hurled from island airfields at the
xt U.S. invasion armada, a dozen or two U.S. carriers would be sunk.
arriers took longer to build than airframes. Japan would gain time to im-
ove her defensive position.

Prince Takamatsu's proposals were too rational to dismiss and too
dical to adopt—at least not without a major political upheaval. And so
irohito promised only to study them. He had long believed in air power,
t so he had in all naval technical innovations, over the sea, on it, or
der it. To junk Japan's big ships would be to antagonize all senior salt-
ater skippers and many of the great vassal families to which they be-
nged. To allocate the cream of Japan's aircraft production to the new
ir Navy would be to antagonize the more plebeian Army as well. At best
e proposed air strategy would only buy time, for it was apparent that the
nited States could eventually build a bigger plane than the B-29, capable
striking the homeland from bases as far away as Australia or Hawaii.
hen Japan's cities would be burned down without a U.S. task force ever
tering Japanese waters. Nevertheless, after ten days of consideration in
hich he heard arguments on every side of the issue, Hirohito made up
s mind that Takamatsu was right.

On February 2 Hirohito summoned Lord Privy Seal Kido and gave him
military briefing of unprecedented fullness. Then he asked Kido whether,
his opinion, the military advantages to be gained from an Air Navy
ould outweigh the disadvantages of a dictatorial imperial decision over-
ding the advice of both chiefs of staff. In listening to the Emperor's stra-
gic disquisition, Kido had particularly noted that the proposed Air Navy
ould not assure Japan of victory. He, therefore, advised Hirohito that, at
is juncture in national life, it would be most unwise to act in any fashion
at might be construed as tyrannical. Hirohito nodded and somewhat
rtly asked Kido to discuss the matter directly with Prince Takamatsu.
his was Hirohito's method of telling Kido that he meant to have his way
d that it was up to Kido to remove the political obstacles.

In his work with the Peace Faction, Kido was already having trouble
ough finding postwar witnesses to excuse, disguise, or shoulder Hiro-
to's responsibility in the authoritarian decisions of the past. Now Kido
as expected somehow to conceal another dictatorial act, a war decision
palatable to all Hirohito's senior military advisors. It was a hopeless
signment but Kido, without murmuring, set about it as if it were a
allenge. He found, to his relief, that he had an ally in the loyal prime
inister, General Tojo. If worse came to worst, Tojo would take responsi-
ity for advising Hirohito to dismiss the two chiefs of staff. It would
better, of course, if the two chiefs would change their views. And fail-

ing that, perhaps they could be induced, by promises, to resign quietly f
reasons of health.

THE "CHUNGKING MANEUVER"

During the complex political process which ensued—an imbroglio whi
lasted for eighteen days and involved all the great lords of back-roo
Tokyo politics—Kido noted in his diary a single imperial diversion. C
February 14 Prime Minister Tojo came to the palace to give Hirohito
progress report on the efforts of Colonel Tsuji Masanobu, the execution
of Singapore and Bataan, to negotiate peace or at least postwar unde
standings with Chiang Kai-shek.

According to Tsuji's latest communication he had made good conta(
in Shanghai with the Chinese underground and with Chiang Kai-shek's s
cret police apparatus, the Blueshirts. Soon, during a "special inspectio
of forward areas, he would meet with direct emissaries from Chiang K
shek. He had hopes that they would take him to Chungking so that
could talk face to face with General Tai Li, the commander of the Blu
shirts, and with Generalissimo Chiang Kai-shek himself.

Hirohito was pleased with the news. His brother Prince Mikasa h
made Tsuji's negotiations possible. During a visit to occupied China t
previous November, Mikasa had suggested and authorized a two-we
memorial celebration for Chiang Kai-shek's mother on the eightieth a
niversary of her birth at Chiang's home town, Fenghwa, in occupi
Chekiang province. Colonel Tsuji had overseen the festivities there a
afterwards, through the Blueshirts, had sent Chiang Kai-shek a memor
album containing photographs of the affair and inscriptions conveying
Chiang the good wishes of Wang Ching-wei, Prince Mikasa, and Hirohi

Although Hirohito had great hopes for this essay in personal diploma(
Colonel Tsuji would fail in his "special inspection" trip to negotiate s
passage for himself to Chungking. Chiang Kai-shek's emissaries want
further assurance that Tsuji could speak for Hirohito. As a result Ts
would make arrangements for one of his best Blueshirt contacts, a dout
agent named Miao Pin, to go to Tokyo and engage in direct conversatio
with Hirohito's uncle Prince Higashikuni. The reciprocal arrangements f
Tsuji to go to Chungking and deal with an intimate of Chiang Kai-sh
were not realized. Instead, five months later, Hirohito would send Ts
on a temporary assignment of greater urgency in Burma, one from whi
he would not finally escape to make his long postponed Chungking p
grimage until the war was already over.

SACKING THE STAFF

Though lightened briefly by Tsuji's "Chungking maneuver," the gloc
of the political crisis in Tokyo was deepening daily. Then, on February 1

944, a devastating U.S. carrier-based air raid on Truk Island in the Caro-
nes, the Pearl Harbor of Japan's surface fleet, persuaded Hirohito that
e could wait no longer for Kido and Prince Takamatsu to work out a
mooth political settlement. Japan must have an Air Navy immediately.

On February 18, the day after the Truk raid, Hirohito summoned his
lunt, broad-shouldered, many-hatted "shogun," General Tojo, and au-
10rized him to request the resignations of both chiefs of staff: Navy Chief
Jagano, who had taken responsibility for Pearl Harbor planning, and long-
uffering, bland, "Bathroom Door" Sugiyama, who had stood close by
Iirohito's side ever since the Army mutiny of February 1936. Neither
Jagano nor Sugiyama thought to oppose Hirohito personally or even to
isagree explicitly with his strategic thinking. That was not the Japanese
vay. Rather, both men felt bound by leadership promises which they had
nade to subordinates whose careers and livings would be adversely af-
ected by Hirohito's decision.

Sugiyama, in particular, felt obliged to reject Tojo's request to resign.[1]
Ie felt that a protest had to be inscribed in the record on behalf of the
army. Kido and Tojo had not been able to find a single suitably qualified
nd willing replacement for him. To enforce the Air Navy decision Hiro-
ito would have to appoint Tojo, who was already prime minister and war
1inister, as chief of staff as well. This would be a clear violation of na-
onal custom. As Sugiyama told Tojo's go-between, the vice minister of
var, on the afternoon of February 19:

> I cannot accept this demand. Supreme military command and civilian
> government cannot be combined. Their separation is an ironclad tradition
> of our form of government. If the war minister and the Army chief of
> staff are one and the same person, political considerations will find their
> way into military decision making, and the entire system of discipline by
> which orders are accepted in the field may well break down.

That evening Tojo called a meeting of himself, Sugiyama, and the
hird of the Army's Big Three, the inspector general of military education,
Jeneral Yamada Otozo. A quiet man who had long preoccupied himself
vith the administration of Hirohito's experimental germ warfare program,
Yamada was present not to say anything but to vote with Tojo.

During the course of the meeting Sugiyama blamed Hitler's interference
vith staff matters for the "mistake made at Leningrad." Tojo shot back:
Hitler was originally a common soldier and I detest the thought of being
ssociated with him. I am a Japanese general. All that I have done as

---

[1] Nagano simply awaited the outcome of the power struggle and then retired to
rivate life. He returned to the headlines briefly in January 1947 when he died of a
omplex combination of infirmities during his trial as a Class A war-crime suspect by
1e Allied International Military Tribunal for the Far East.

prime minister, I have done with due consideration for military implica tions."

A tense debate followed, but in the end, when Sugiyama saw that Yamad sided with Tojo, he bowed to majority opinion. He added, however, tha before resigning he would submit his protest for the record to Hirohitc He did so on the morning of February 21. Hirohito accepted the writte protest gracefully, saying:

> I too felt uneasy about the combining of political and military leadershi but I talked the matter over with Tojo and he has promised to keep it i mind. That satisfies me. It is, as you say, an extraordinary breach wit tradition, and for that reason I ask you to be discreet and co-operativ about it so that we may have success with it for the war effort.

Sugiyama could say no more and the heroic Tojo bravely shoul9dere the triple responsibility for civil prime ministerial politics, for war mir isterial bureaucratic management, and for General Staff planning of wa strategy.

INDIA, THE LAST OFFENSIVE

On being invested executive dictator of Japan, Tojo's first act was t move all government meetings into the palace: those of the Cabinet an War Ministry as well as those of the General Staffs. Although studiousl ignored and obscured after the war, the fact was that all these meeting were now open to informal attendance by Hirohito and that Hirohito ofte took advantage of Tojo's arrangements to attend. The Japanese press a the time acknowledged that the Emperor had imposed "direct imperia guidance."

Under the aegis of Tojo's long-time naval crony, Admiral Shimada, wh was now Navy chief of staff as well as Navy minister, strenuous effort were made to realize Prince Takamatsu's Air-Navy dream. Every promis ing naval recruit was tried out for flight training. Construction of hundred of small airstrips began on scores of small islands. Naval aircraft produc tion rose above 2,000 planes a month and goals were set at 50,000 air frames and engines in the fiscal year ahead. Rather than scrap the existin, surface Navy, which still contained many valuable vessels and officers Shimada and Tojo, at the end of February, moved it from its home an chorage in the Inland Sea to a roadstead in the Lingga Isles, off Sumatra a hundred miles south of Singapore. The aim was to cut back the main tenance costs of the fleet while its remaining strength was being expended At Lingga Roads it would have easy access to the Indonesian fuel oil i burned and would be in easy steaming distance of the anticipated battle grounds off the Philippine Islands where its obsolescent ships were to b sacrificed.

Next Tojo ordered the Army to mount a counteroffensive at the one
point where it was strong and the enemy was weak: the frontier between
Burma and India. This frontier was guarded by a hundred-mile-wide cor-
dor of trackless jungle and mountains. Since the collapse of British resistance in Burma two years earlier, various Allied commando units had
made raids through it from India. Now Tojo ordered an army of 155,000
men—three Japanese divisions and one puppet Indian division recruited
from the ranks of Singapore war prisoners by Chandra Bose and his Indian government in exile—to march through the terrain barrier from east
to west and invade India. The Japanese columns dutifully set out on
March 8, 1944. They had no proper means of supply and no hope of living off the wild, almost uninhabited countryside. Yet to the consternation
of British Lieutenant General William Slim, who had charge of India's
defense, they crossed the frontier and in a month had taken up positions
in eastern India from which they threatened the important railheads of
Imphal and Kohima.

Throughout late April and early May General Slim brought up to the
front every available reserve. At one point the British garrison in Kohima
was reduced to last-ditch defense of two hills. Then, however, attrition
began to tell on the enfeebled, dispirited Japanese soldiers. They failed
to press home their attacks. The monsoon season intervened. In the wet,
an unprecedented breakdown in discipline took possession of the Japanese
army. It retreated despite orders from Tokyo to advance and despite the
orders of its commanders on the scene to hold firm. In the Japanese withdrawal 65,000 died, a few hundred by British bullets, the rest by disease,
hunger, suicide with grenades, drowning in rivers and quagmires, and
finally by fratricidal strife and murder. When the remaining half of the
expedition got back to the plowed fields of Burma in late June and early
July of 1944, reports quickly filtered back to Japan that the samurai
escutcheon had been smirched beyond cleaning and that the Army had
lost its stomach.

To still the wagging tongues and to discourage the possibility of U.S.
landings in loosely held areas along the south China coast, the Army in
China, early in June, broke its truce with Chiang Kai-shek to mount a
major thrust south from Hankow along the branch railroads to Canton
and the borders of Indochina, Thailand, and eastern Burma. To resurrect
Burma Army morale, Colonel Tsuji Masanobu, the great samurai apologist, the great believer in the Japanese Army's spiritual purity, the great
executioner of death-march vengeance, was taken from his negotiations
with Chungking and reposted to Rangoon. There he rallied the retreating
remnants of Japan's India expedition and succeeded in making them once
more an effective fighting force—adequate in the dark months ahead to
fight a delaying action against a major British advance out of India.

DECISIVE BATTLE

Far to the south and west of India, Rabaul had been cut off in the earl
months of 1944 and 30,000 Navy plus 70,000 Army personnel had bee
abandoned there to survive as best they could beside their own swee
potato patches. The 15,000 men remaining of the once crack 6th Divisio
on Bougainville attempted an all-out offensive against the U.S. Marin
"perimeter" from March 9 to March 17 and killed 263 Americans for
loss of 5,469 Japanese dead. The starving Japanese survivors retreate
into the hills to become guerrilla farmers. In New Guinea, too, the Jap
anese retreated and starved. On May 27 MacArthur's leapfrogging ac
vance up the New Guinea coast bypassed the last Japanese strongpoint
at the northwestern tip of New Guinea and struck at the offshore island c
Biak. The local Japanese commander withdrew into the caves at one en
of the island and continued to resist for a month. When the caves of Bia
had been incinerated, 460 U.S. servicemen had died and 10,000 Japanes
On the nearby island of Noemfoor another 1,714 Japanese and sixty-si
U.S. troops were killed. The G.I.'s rescued on Noemfoor 403 emaciate
survivors of a 3,000-man Indonesian coolie gang which had been tran
ported thither as slaves to work on the fortifications.

The capture of Biak brought MacArthur's troops into easy reach of an
number of lightly defended small islands in eastern Indonesia which coul
be used as final stepping-stones for the reconquest of the Philippines. O
June 15, however, nine days after the Normandy D-day in Europe, Ac
miral Nimitz's naval armada stole a march on MacArthur by advancin
into the Mariana island chain and landing Marines on Saipan from whic
U.S. long-range bombers, the new B-29's, could raid Tokyo.

The very day of the Saipan landing, B-29's from bases deep in Chin
gave a small demonstration of what lay in store by striking a glancing blo
at factories in Kyushu, the southernmost of Japan's home islands. Th
raid marked the beginning of the bombing of Japan, and Hirohito wa
quick to realize that, if Saipan fell, bombing of Japan would becom
routine.

Nimitz employed no less than fourteen battleships, fourteen cruiser
twenty-six carriers, and eighty-two destroyers in the Marianas campaig
Hirohito sent out from the Philippines, to seek a "decisive battle," almo
all the expendable remnants of the Japanese fleet: four battleships, nin
carriers, seven cruisers, and thirty-four destroyers. In the Battle of th
Philippine Sea on June 19–20, three out of five of Japan's heavy carrie
were sunk and almost 400 of her 473 carrier planes were shot dow
Nimitz lost about 100 of his 956 airplanes and none of his ships.

The "decisive battle," on which surface fleet commanders for sever
years had based their hopes and their assurances, had now been fough
It had come to an appallingly decisive end. The big guns of Japan's supe

readnoughts had never been brought to bear. The issue, once again, had een settled at long range by air power. Prince Takamatsu's predictions ad been borne out. But Prince Takamatsu's Air Navy, because of the luggishness of the home front, was not yet a force in being. Hirohito was ncensed that a substantial part of it—400 planes—had been lost in sup-ort of the no-longer-needed Japanese carriers. From now on planes would perate from the decks of carriers only in coastal waters whence they ould, if necessary, find quick refuge on airfields ashore.

WANTED: A DIVINE WIND

After the Philippine Sea engagement had been broken off, one of Prince 'akamatsu's partisans, Captain Jo Ei-ichiro, looked aft at the smouldering avoc on the flight deck of his light carrier *Chiyoda* and sat down in his abin to pen a radiogram. Having been recurrently a naval aide-de-camp ₒ His Majesty, and having been second man in naval intelligence at the apanese Embassy in Washington during most of the 1930's, he expected ₁at his missive would be given personal attention by Hirohito. He sent it ₒ Vice Admiral Onishi Takijiro in the Ministry of Munitions, the friend of 'rince Takamatsu who in January 1941 had arranged for the Throne a ₂cret independent evaluation of Yamamoto's Pearl Harbor plan.

Captain Jo's radiogram reached Onishi on June 21 and was reported to lirohito by Prince Takamatsu on June 22. It was couched in bluntly lucid ₂rms such as few Japanese appreciated better than Hirohito:

NO LONGER CAN WE HOPE TO SINK THE NUMERICALLY SUPERIOR ENEMY AIRCRAFT CARRIERS BY CONVENTIONAL ATTACK METHODS. I URGE THE IM-MEDIATE ORGANIZATION OF SPECIAL ATTACK UNITS TO CARRY OUT CRASH-DIVE TACTICS.

Hirohito, too, had digested the fearful lessons of the "decisive battle." lanes had been wasted in a conventional fleet operation. Tojo's naval artner, the Navy Minister and Navy Staff Chief Shimada, was to blame. [e had promised to support the concept of the Air Navy and then, for the ake of old fleet friendships, had allowed planes to be thrown away in this sinine "decisive" debacle.

Prince Takamatsu found Hirohito determined that Shimada must soon ₂ removed from the government and that, because of Shimada's stupidity nd the great loss of planes in the Philippine Sea, the use of crash-dive ₂ctics should indeed be given serious consideration.

The idea of the suicide pilot had been implicit in Prince Takamatsu's ir Navy proposals from the beginning. Staff studies conducted in 1943 ad shown, incontrovertibly, that crash divers could sink more enemy ₁ipping, per man lost, than could pilots using conventional bombing and ₒrpedoing techniques.

From a popular propaganda viewpoint, the airplane was an ideal suicid vehicle. The pilot alone in his cockpit could be compared with the ind vidual samurai swordsman who, in a thousand Japanese romances, cut spectacular dying swathe through the ranks of his enemies. As yet no ant aircraft batteries invented stood more than half a chance of exploding plane hurtling down from the sky in a full-throttle dive. And with on well-aimed crash a plane could sink a vessel costing thousands of time its own worth. By comparison, the banzai charge of massed infantry too real courage and discipline. It offered no satisfaction to the samurai sens of individual heroism. It cost many lives. And because of the astonishin firepower of the enemy's bazookas, flamethrowers, and automatic rifles, offered little hope of gain.

Japan's simple, functional, inexpensive aircraft, too, were admirab suited to throw-away use. Indeed, the quantity production methods of wa time had rendered many of them good for little else. Defective aircraft wer pouring from the assembly lines and could not be relied upon to give ser ice over a protracted period of time. Maintenance crews in combat area were not up to correcting the flaws left by the factories. More planes wer being lost in ordinary operational use or during ferrying flights to forwar areas than were being downed in combat. Those which arrived intact the front were expended cheaply by hastily trained pilots who lacked th skills to fight off enemy interception and to place bombs and torpedoes o target.

A one-way flight by a resolute patriot determined to crash into a maj U.S. warship would multiply by at least a factor of ten the effectiveness every plane which Japan could manufacture. The plane itself would hav to be good enough only to get to the theater of operations and fly a singl mission. The pilot would have to be good enough only to take off, follo a leader, and then steer straight toward a target. A single plane loaded wit gasoline and a 500-pound bomb could wreak more mayhem by a cras dive onto the deck of a carrier than two well-placed torpedoes or a doze conventionally delivered bombs.

Finally, Japan had the patriots who were willing to die. Western indi vidualism—the Christian doctrine of soul and conscience, against whic Hirohito had inveighed a decade earlier in his conversations with Chie Aide-de-Camp Honjo—did not permit U.S. pilots to expend themselve suicidally except in moments of combat stress such as they had experience at Midway. Japanese youths, by comparison, had been brought up to be lieve in themselves as junior members in a national family. The survival the family and of the elders of the family seemed infinitely more importa to them than their own physical survival. In frugal, realistic Japan th rearing of a child was considered an investment in the future. While still his twenties and thirties a man was held a debtor to the society which ha fed, clothed, and educated him. He did not reach decision-making maturit until he passed the symbolic age of forty-one. If he died of natural causes before that age, his spirit would live on in the afterworld but would never attain much influence there for lack of achievements in life. If, however, he died in battle, his spirit would have accomplished something; it would be promoted one rank by the Emperor; it would be given a permanent abode at the warriors' ghostly rest home, Yasukuni Shrine.

Despite all these irrefutable reasons, Hirohito knew that his political advisors, including Kido and even General Tojo, were opposed to any regular, officially sponsored use of pilots for suicide missions. It was one thing to order a half-literate farm boy to charge to sure death in the heat of battle; another thing to keep a corps of semiskilled pilots on permanent suicide call, taking lessons in the most effective techniques of self-destruction. The morale of such a corps could be sustained only by religious fervor and formal imperial blessing. At a time when Hirohito's most sane and cosmopolitan advisors were all racking their brains for ways to refurbish the Emperor's public image after the war, the use of suicide pilots seemed lunacy unless it could absolutely guarantee victory. And that not even its staunchest proponents could promise.

In the educated classes there was also a feeling of embarrassment about combining the traditional Japanese code of the swordsman with the Western technology of the airplane. Well-traveled Japanese sensed that use of suicide pilots would shock Westerners, would be branded fanaticism, and would be remembered with suspicion long after other war passions had cooled.

In talking to Prince Takamatsu about Captain Jo's proposal at the Imperial Library in the palace woods on June 22, 1944, Hirohito alluded briefly to these pros and cons and pointed out that the public-relations side of the question needed much study. Takamatsu was forearmed for this objection. Captain Jo's suggestion, he said, was not an isolated phenomenon. On June 19, three days earlier, Captain Okamura Motoharu of the 341st Air Group, during an inspection of the Tateyama base, on the peninsula due south of Tokyo, had presented a similar petition for "turning the tide of war" to Vice Admiral Fukudome Shigeru of the Second Air Fleet. Fukudome had shown the petition to the vice chief of the Navy General Staff, Vice Admiral Ito Sei-ichi, and Ito was now a proponent of the suicide-pilot idea. So were many of the pilots in the ranks, for they were sick and tired of suffering 50 per cent casualties in mission after mission without achieving results.

Hirohito admitted that, if the idea were presented as a popular ground swell coming up from the ranks, it might be possible to allay the fears of Kido, Tojo, and other advisors. Certainly some such *kamikaze,* divine wind, was needed if the enemy armadas were to be wrecked short of the sacred Japanese shore. For the moment, however, Hirohito would authorize Takamatsu only to pursue design studies for an easy-to-produce piloted bomb which would take maximum economical advantage of kamikaze talents if they were ever harnessed.

SAIPAN AND TOJO'S FALL

By the time Hirohito took this new responsibility on his sacerdotal conscience, the week-old U.S. invasion of the Marianas had put some 70,000 Americans ashore on the island of Saipan. Like the monster in some postwar Japanese science fiction film, the invaders had systematically destroyed the ingeniously prepared positions, traps, and strongpoints of the 30,000 man Japanese garrison.

Saipan was the first of Japan's prewar possessions to be attacked by the enemy. It was the largest of the islands which Japan had seized from Germany during World War I and held under League of Nations mandate. It was a beautiful place and Japan had colonized it heavily, studding its green hills with sawmills and sugarcane fields. In addition to the 30,000 soldiers on Saipan, there dwelled at least 25,000 civilians.

As the battle turned against the Saipan garrison, a question arose: how to instruct the civilian inhabitants. Previously, except for a few prostitutes and bureaucrats, no Japanese civilians had come within U.S. reach. Now an entire Japanese community, including many of low caste, who had emigrated for lack of opportunity at home, was about to fall prisoner. There was a danger that the civilians would be captured alive; that they would be surprised and pleased by U.S. treatment; that they would be used in U.S. propaganda broadcasts to subvert the fighting spirit of the rest of Japan. A Japanese civilian prisoner encampment was, indeed, erected behind Marine lines on June 23 and soon had more than a thousand inmates. It had electric lights which were left conspicuously blazing at night. Thrice daily its mess tents exhaled a sweet savor of cooking rice and meat and were queued by long lines of evidently happy, expectant Japanese.

Hirohito found the defection of the Japanese civilians on Saipan disturbing, and at the end of the month an imperial order went out encouraging civilians who were still at large to commit suicide.[2] The order did not demand suicide; it empowered the commander on Saipan to promise civilians who died there an equal spiritual status in the afterlife with that of soldiers perishing in combat. On June 30 the prime minister, war minister and chief of staff, namely General Tojo, intercepted this order and delayed its sending. It went out anyway, the next day, after Tojo had brought it to the attention of Kido and other civilian advisors in the palace.

[2] Some apologists for Hirohito have asserted that this and other deadly orders issued at other times under the imperial imprimatur were all actually sent by someone at Imperial Headquarters who dared to abuse the seals with which Hirohito stamped state papers. The impious scofflaw has never been identified. Half the staff of the palace, beginning with Lord Privy Seal Kido, would have felt obliged to cut open their bellies if the sacred seals of the Throne had ever been misapplied.

Five days later, on July 6, organized resistance on Saipan collapsed, and ·dmiral Nagumo, the former Pearl Harbor task force commander who had harge of naval forces on the island, squatted at the mouth of a cave, slit pen his abdomen, and then had an aide standing behind him dispatch him ·ith a bullet into the back of his head. That night the starving remnants f the main Japanese garrison on Saipan charged U.S. Marine lines. Those ·ho failed to be killed by U.S. machine guns took their own lives with ·renades, revolvers, mines, swords, knives, and sharp stones.

On July 8 the Marines moved unhindered through the stench of bodies ·ward the north tip of the island. There over 10,000 Japanese civilians ·ere destroying themselves: dashing their babes against rocks, hurling their ·hildren and wives into the sea, jumping from the high cliffs. Before the ·farines could stop the slaughter, on July 12, most of the civilians had ·ccepted Hirohito's offer of a privileged place in ghosts' paradise. Marine ·eterans looked down into the surf, awash with the bodies of children, and ·irned away with troubled minds and queasy stomachs.

Over-all there fell on bloody Saipan some 15,000 Japanese civilians and ·bout 30,000 Japanese soldiers and sailors. Even so, the Marines took their ·rst major bag of prisoners: 921 Japanese troops and 10,258 civilians. Of 7,451 U.S. combat troops 3,426 died.

As soon as Saipan had been secured, the Marines, on July 21, invaded ·uam. This was the largest of the Marianas—209 square miles as com- ·ared with Saipan's 70 square miles—and the one island of the archipelago ·hich had belonged to the United States rather than to Japan before the ·ar. Between July 21 and August 10, some 55,000 U.S. troops fought ·ere against about 20,000 defenders. Some 10,000 Japanese were killed in ·e campaign and another 8,500, who hid in the hills, were killed in the ·ear which followed. Only 1,435 U.S. troops died and only 1,250 Japanese ·ere taken captive.

The third island of the Marianas, 40-square-mile Tinian, was invaded ·y 15,614 Marines on July 24. After three days of blistering pre-invasion ·ounding, in which the first use was made of napalm, a mixture of explo- ·ives and petroleum jellies, the 9,000 men of the Japanese garrison put ·p a ragged resistance. In a week 5,000 of them could be counted dead and ·e rest permanently missing. The Marines had lost 389 killed in action ·nd had taken 252 prisoners. The Japanese airstrip was quickly improved ·o become the finest runway for long-range bombers in the Pacific. From it, · year later, would take off the *Enola Gay* with the bomb for Hiroshima.

During the slaughter on Guam and Tinian, Hirohito was forced by his ·earest and dearest to give up the war, give up his direct participation in ·abinet and staff meetings, and inaugurate the programed succession of de- scalations in war spirit which had been planned by the Peace Faction. ·Iirohito was reluctant to accept this final turning point in his life but he ·owed to it—after a week of vacillation—under pressure rather than coercion. He admitted to his closest advisors that he was beaten and had been wrong; he did not abdicate his place as spiritual war leader.

The moment of Hirohito's resignation was probably July 7, the day after the collapse of organized resistance on Saipan. That day Prince Takamatsu asked Lord Privy Seal Kido to arrange more athletic exercise for Hirohito and more clerical help for him. On July 11, as the horrible suicide of Japanese civilians on Saipan neared its end, the senior generals of the Army and admirals of the Navy, including some of the Strike-North Faction which had opposed Hirohito in the 1930's, met without fanfare at the Army Club north of the palace walls and agreed quietly that the time had come to bury factional differences, to draw in protectively around the Throne, and to make a symbolic change in leadership by ousting the war "shogun," General Tojo.

Accepting the verdict of his senior officers, Tojo immediately tendered his resignation to the Throne. Hirohito at first rejected it and encouraged Tojo to shore up his political position for a while longer. Hirohito did not believe that Peace Faction planners could really whitewash him and felt that it would be cowardly for him even to let them try. He and Tojo might sometimes differ but Tojo, he said, was still the strongest war leader in Japan. Tojo took two days to consider the Emperor's request.

The planning to use suicide pilots disturbed Tojo; if only for the quiet of his soul in the afterlife, he did not want to take responsibility for sending thousands of Japanese young men to certain death when he knew that their sacrifice could not win the war. In addition Tojo owed loyalty to Admiral Shimada, his Navy minister and Navy staff chief; Hirohito wished to make Shimada the public scapegoat for the Marianas debacle. If Shimada were jettisoned from the government it might be possible, thought Hirohito's political advisor Kido, to leave Tojo in office. The main complaint of the critics was the "part-time strategy" of war leaders who had to run the civilian bureaucracy as well as the General Staff offices. Since the U.S. island-hopping campaign made the war mainly naval now, it would be enough for the moment to dismiss the part-time naval strategist and to leave General Tojo in office.

After discussing the situation with his patrons, with his partisans, and with Admiral Shimada, Tojo promised Hirohito on July 13 that he would make an effort to stagger on with the burden of government. During the next five days, however, in trying to give his Cabinet a face-lifting and fresh lease on life, he encountered so much hostility and vilification that he saw he had no sound basis of co-operation with which to work.

On July 18 Tojo submitted his resignation unequivocally to Hirohito, and two days later, Hirohito broke with tradition by investing two men at once with the prime ministerial responsibility. The wizened General Koiso Kuniaki, whose March Plot had paved the way for the invasion of Manchuria in 1931, was to head the partnership; he was to be assisted by the ig, hearty Admiral Yonai Mitsumasa, as Navy minister and assistant prime minister. Since Yonai had been a full prime minister earlier, in the first alf of 1940, he was no longer on the active list of naval commanders. He as, therefore, ineligible by law to serve as Navy minister. Hirohito solved is small difficulty by a stroke of his seal as commander in chief: he simply einstated Yonai to the active list.

DESPERATE SHO

Early in August 1944, not long after the Koiso-Yonai partnership had emoved Cabinet meetings once again to a discreet distance from the alace, Hirohito approved production of the Ohka missile, a 4,000-pound omb, equipped with wooden wings, a cockpit for a pilot, elementary ight controls, and five small rockets which could propel it for a distance of 9 to 20 miles from its point of release by a "mother" bomber. Production models of the Ohka would not be ready for use until the very end of the amikaze effort and then would give poor results. The building of them, owever, involved civilian workers in the kamikaze program, making it all o clearly official.

The Ohka scheme dismayed those of Hirohito's advisors who had the care f his public image. They redoubled their efforts on behalf of the Peace action. At 2:23 P.M. on August 25, still a full year before the Americans ould set foot in Japan, Lord Privy Seal Kido emerged from an hour-long udience with the Emperor at the concrete library in the palace woods and rove to his official residence outside the palace walls. There he spent the ist half of the afternoon, from 3 P.M., getting to know an officer he had sked to see who was reputed to have the most formidable memory in the apanese Army. The officer was retired Major Tanaka Takayoshi and this as the first of several interviews with Kido which would ultimately launch anaka on his second career, that of star witness at the American war rimes trials: witness for the prosecution, witness for the defense, guide to J.S. prosecutor Keenan, informer, double agent, and patriot *par excellence.*

Meanwhile Allied strategists had been fiercely debating the course to ollow in reaching Tokyo and ending the war. General MacArthur main-iained that the United States was committed primarily to the lifting of apan's yoke from the Philippines. To this political pledge, which Mac-Arthur considered a matter of national and personal honor, the reduction f Japan should be considered secondary. Some British and Dutch states-nen went further, advocating step-by-step reconquest of all the islands in he South Pacific so that they could be put back under stable colonial ad-iinistration before Japan fell, and before Allied war zeal fell from fever itch, and before the inevitable postwar peace conference bickering began. he most narrowly efficient and technologically minded commanders in the J.S. Armed Forces, especially admirals, saw no valid military reason for shedding blood and spending bullets in the East Indies, Malaya, or the Philippines. They instead advocated the quickest possible seizure of Japan by the throat: landings on Taiwan and in friendly areas on the south China coast, or possibly landings in the Bonins and Ryukyus, followed by a direct assault on the home island of Kyushu.

A week after the investment of the Koiso-Yonai Cabinet in Tokyo President Roosevelt paid a state visit to Hawaii and resolved these strategic issues in a meeting, on July 27, with MacArthur and Nimitz at the home of an old crony, Chris Holmes, on Kalaukau Avenue in the Waikiki suburb of Honolulu. MacArthur spoke eloquently of the political advantages to be gained by reconquering the Philippines before assaulting Japan. Roosevelt nodded his sympathy with MacArthur's arguments. Nimitz agreed, somewhat reluctantly, that he would as soon destroy the remnants of the Japanese fleet and naval air arm in Philippine waters as in the China Sea, the Bonin Trench, or the Okinawan Deep. And so was decided Final Strategy Japan. The chiefs of staff in Washington would continue to debate it for another ten weeks before it would be made official.

On September 15 MacArthur's Army forces advancing north from Australia and Nimitz's Navy forces sailing west from Pearl Harbor pinched in on the Philippines with co-ordinated landings at Morotai in the Molucca or Spice Islands, halfway between New Guinea and Mindanao, and a Peleliu in the Palau Islands off the eastern shores of the Philippines, two thirds of the way from Guam to Mindanao. At Morotai MacArthur's men quickly overran a garrison of 500 with the loss of only thirty-one dead. At Peleliu the Marines encountered a stout garrison of over 10,000. The desired airstrip and local air superiority were gained in a week but heavy fighting continued for two months.

Improving on the lessons learned in the caves of Biak, the Japanese commander on Peleliu, Colonel Nakagawa Kunio, assisted by an envoy from the palace Office of Aides-de-Camp, made best possible use of the hollows in the coral underlying the main ridge of Peleliu's hills. Drilling had interconnected the vacancies left by prehistoric marine organisms and cement had been added within their gossamer-gothic architecture. Neither shells nor bombs could pierce their galleries from above and Marines equipped with the most long-spurt flamethrowers had to move with extreme caution whenever they came to a turning in a tunnel.

Colonel Nakagawa and his imperial adviser, Major General Murai Kenjiro, held out in their well-stocked subterranean command center for seventy days and finally committed ritual suicide together on the night of November 24–25. Other Japanese, still deeper in the coral Hades, held out longer. Thirty Japanese from an inner cave burst out to kill a number of careless G.I. souvenir hunters in December. And the last five Japanese did not dig out from the labyrinth and surrender until February 1, 1945.

Assured by the landings on Morotai and Peleliu that the Philippines were ndeed, the next U.S. objective, Hirohito affixed his seal to a General Staff efense plan called SHO.[3] The name stood for "victory" but the delibera- ions surrounding the inception of SHO reveal that it was considered a lan for one last glorious *Götterdämmerung* gesture before defeat. In effect coolly prescribed the sacrifice—self-destruction was the term used by the lanners—of almost 250,000 soldiers and 50,000 sailors. They were not xpected to win any victories, unless "by a miracle," but they were expected) sell their lives dearly and so prove to the enemy Japan's will to resist— er "sincerity."

The most total SHO sacrifice was expected of the Navy. Its big ships rere no longer of much value. They did not have oil with which to oper- te. They must not be captured by the enemy. It was the duty of their aptains to shoot up the U.S. armada as much as possible and get sunk.

The Air Navy, on the other hand, was expected to preserve itself insofar s possible for defense of Japan's home shores. Most of it was still in train- ng in Japan and would be kept there, uncommitted. The rest, about 2,000 lanes which were already operating from bases in Taiwan and Luzon, vould strike only if they could do so to advantage, by sinking U.S. carriers. f they could not do so with reasonable expectation of success, they were) exploit the fact that they were land based and had hundreds of safe .elds to fly to. That is, they were to run away and live for the day when he Air Navy was ready for battle.

The Army's part in SHO was more conventional. The 250,000 soldiers vho had been shipped to the Philippines early in the year were to fight to he death for every island, every mountain range, every hill and rill.

The long-range value of the suicidal SHO operation as a means of exact- ng improved surrender terms from the enemy escaped most Japanese Army fficers. About September 20 a group of them who had been sympathetic o the Strike-North Faction in the 1930's conceived a political plot to over- hrow the Koiso Cabinet and replace it with a more talented and realistic 'war prosecution government" headed by General Yamashita, the Tiger of Malaya who had been exiled to Manchuria. Members of the conspiracy pproached Prince Asaka and Prince Takeda asking for their support. Asaka and Takeda, through Hirohito, promptly reported to the lord privy eal. Kido was not about to have an unknown step thrown into his carefully rogramed staircase of governments leading down to surrender. At Kido's uggestion, Tiger Yamashita was recalled to Tokyo, given a week of brief- ngs, and then reposted to an assignment which would fully occupy his enius: the command of the 250,000 fated soldiers in the Philippines. Yamashita obediently reported at Fort McKinley outside Manila on Octo-)er 6. From a platform in a blacked-out hall that evening he explained to lis assembled commanders: "I have been told by our Emperor that the

---

[3] Hirohito had temporarily withdrawn from overt political activity, but he was still ommander in chief.

crisis will first develop on this battlefield. This gives us all a heavy respon sibility." [4]

On October 10, the growing monster of Admiral Halsey's fast carrie task force—nine heavy attack carriers, eight light attack carriers, six battle ships, fourteen cruisers, and fifty-eight destroyers—forayed into Japan' home waters and launched air raids against Okinawa and the other island of the Ryukyu chain connecting Kyushu with Taiwan. The raids caugh few planes on the ground but smashed up many of the stopover field needed by the Air Navy if it was to strike back in the Philippine area. Th next day Halsey's planes temporarily decommissioned many of the landin fields in northern Luzon.

Finally, on October 12 and for three days thereafter, the 1,068 plane from the U.S. task force, supported by B-29's from China,[5] took on th thousand-odd planes which Japan had stationed in Taiwan. More than 50 of the Japanese planes—about a twentieth of the projected Air Navy, abou a tenth of the Air Navy already in being—were destroyed either in the ai or on the ground. In addition, on the third day of the strikes, the U.S pilots uncovered and bombed some fifteen new airfields on Taiwan wit which Air Navy officers had hoped to achieve a measure of surprise whe the time came for full deployment of their forces. For these gains Halse paid a modest price: less than 100 planes lost and two cruisers out c action but successfully towed away.

Having destroyed *in utero* the morale of the recently conceived Air Navy the U.S. forces turned to their main task, the reconquest of a beachhead i the Philippines. There were 840 ships in the converging U.S. armadas, in cluding forty-seven aircraft carriers, ten battleships, thirty-one cruisers, an 176 destroyers. About 1,600 planes based on the carriers were supple mented by an equal number of bombers and long-range fighters flying fro China, Tinian, Morotai, and Peleliu.

The deft elimination of Japanese air power from Taiwan was recognize by the Tokyo General Staffs as a major disaster calling for desperate cour termeasures—one of them being a complete withholding of the news fro the Japanese public. For the sake of morale the Navy concealed the fu extent of its losses from the Army, and the Army the full extent of its losse

[4] Three days later, on October 9, Hirohito dispatched a special envoy to Mosco —an inveterate critic of Matsuoka diplomacy, Morishima Goro—with a letter fro Lord Privy Seal Kido to Ambassador Sato Naotake. The letter was meant fo showing to Russian Foreign Ministry officials as evidence that Sato was empowere to seek Stalin's help as a mediator in ending the war. No detailed account of Mor shima's mission or of Sato's dealings with Molotov has yet been released, but, suggested in Chapter 2, the seed fell on ground frozen by the cold of a Russi diplomatic winter.

[5] The first 500 of the gleaming Superfortresses, each capable of carrying four to of bombs for 3,500 miles, had begun to arrive at bases in China and the Pacific on that summer.

from the Navy. Only Hirohito and a few of the highest officers in the General Staffs were told the whole truth. Hirohito promptly issued a rescript congratulating his airmen on a great victory and commiserating with Taiwanese who had suffered from the U.S. raids. At the same time, privately, he overrode the last objections of his political advisors and ordered that the remaining planes of the Air Navy be used, as needed, for suicide attacks.

On October 17 Hirohito dispatched Vice Admiral Onishi Takijiro, Prince Takamatsu's go-between in Pearl Harbor and kamikaze planning, to take charge of the air remnants in the Philippines. On October 18 Hirohito gave his final approval to the naval part of operation SHO: the sacrifice of Japan's remaining oil-eating carriers and battleships. On October 19, having discovered that there were only some sixty planes in condition to fly left in the Philippines, air envoy Onishi drove out to the Air Command center at Mabalacat, north of Manila, and personally informed the flight leaders there of what was expected of them:

> In my opinion there is only one way of assuring that our meager strength will be effective to a maximum degree. That is to organize suicide attack units composed of Zero fighters armed with 250-kilogram bombs, with each plane to crash-dive into an enemy carrier. . . . What do you think?

Long silence greeted Onishi's words. Many Japanese flight leaders had long advocated *tai-atari* or body-crashing tactics. Frustrated pilots had often collided deliberately with Flying Fortresses in a last angry effort to destroy them. Only four days earlier, when the U.S. Leyte invasion armada had first been sighted steaming in from the east, Rear Admiral Arima Masafumi, a scion of the imperial family, had reportedly taken personal charge of a ninety-nine-plane attack group and had shown the way by crash-diving into a U.S. carrier. The assembled flight leaders had no way of knowing that, according to U.S. records, there had been no suicide attack on any U.S. ship that day or on any of the four days since. To them it seemed only that now, pursuant to Arima's example, Admiral Onishi had arrived from the Emperor, asking them to make good their boasts and give their lives.

At length one of the fliers said soberly, "The chances of scoring a hit will be much greater than by conventional bombing. It will probably take several days to repair the damage one of us can cause on a flight deck."

With this self-deprecating stoicism the *Kamikaze* Corps was officially formed, and in a few hours Admiral Onishi had recruited more willing suicide pilots than he could find room for in serviceable planes.

LEYTE AND LEYTE GULF

The next morning, sunup October 20, 1944, the 420 transports and 157 warships of MacArthur's assault force—about two thirds of all the 840

U.S. ships involved in the invasion—began putting ashore the first 145,000 men of the vast 200,000-man expeditionary force which was to recapture the island of Leyte in the central Philippines. The Japanese had only 20,000 men on the island, later to be reinforced by 50,000 more. A typhoon of naval fire swept inland from the beaches, curtaining a massive ship-to-shore movement of men in landing craft. By noon such a deep beachhead had been established that General MacArthur himself landed, with representatives of the Philippine government in exile. In an historic address to the Filipino peoples, he reinaugurated the Voice of Freedom broadcasts which had been suspended at the fall of Corregidor two and a half years earlier.

As the U.S. Army blasted inland, paving its way with Japanese corpses, the remnants of the Japanese Combined Fleet sortied to execute its part in the SHO plan, the battle for Leyte Gulf. This last and largest of history's naval surface engagements, involving 218 Allied warships with 143,668 crewmen and 64 Japanese ships with about 42,800 crewmen, was fought over a six-day period, October 23 to October 29. Its Japanese planners had little hope for it beforehand, but looked on it as a quick and glorious way to dispose of vessels and crews which would otherwise have to be deactivated for lack of fuel oil. They had admitted this frankly to Hirohito before he gave his final approval to the operation. The scene was a joint Army-Navy meeting in the ironclad Imperial Headquarters shed on October 18. There Rear Admiral Nakasawa Yu-u, Naval Operations Section chief, called the Philippines "a fitting place to die," and pleaded: "Give us of the Combined Fleet a chance to bloom as flowers of death. This is the Navy's earnest request."

Hirohito granted the request but restricted the Navy to a modest, practical, inglorious objective: to attack, if possible, the U.S. troop transports lying off the Leyte beaches. The Navy General Staff drew up a plan which divided the available Japanese ships into three forces, Northern, Center, and Southern, each of which was to approach Leyte Gulf from a different direction by a different passage.

Center Force, the mightiest Japanese fleet to seek action since Midway, consisted of two 64,000-ton super-dreadnoughts, *Yamato* and *Musashi,* plus three ordinary battleships, ten heavy cruisers, two light cruisers, and fifteen destroyers. It advanced from the west, making for San Bernardino Strait, which opened, between the southern tip of Luzon and the island of Samar, on the waters to the north of the Leyte beachheads. Before he set forth from Lingga Roads the commander of Center Force, Vice Admiral Kurita Takeo, had to deal with the murmuring of officers who resented the senselessness of the sacrifice ahead. He called them together on the deck of his flagship, the heavy cruiser *Atago,* and told them:

> It would be shameful to have the fleet remain intact while our nation perishes. I believe that Imperial Headquarters is giving us a glorious op-

portunity. You must remember that such things as miracles do happen. Who can say that we have no chance to turn the tide?

So hopeless was Kurita of any success except by miracles that in steaming toward the Philippines he did not even take the routine precaution of posting destroyers ahead of him as picket ships to guard against submarine attack. Consequently, at dawn on October 23, two boats of the U.S. wolf pack, *Dace* and *Darter,* welcomed him in Palawan Passage, just north of Borneo, with two workmanly spreads of torpedoes. In twenty minutes two of Kurita's heavy cruisers, his flagship the 13,400-ton *Atago* and her sister ship the *Maya,* both went to the bottom. Almost 2,000 sailors drowned. Another thousand survivors, including Kurita himself, were picked up by destroyers to continue their desperate foray. They had to leave behind *Takao,* a third 13,400-ton cruiser, which had taken a torpedo in her engine room.[6]

All that day the remaining twenty-nine vessels of Center Force plunged on toward Leyte, tracked intermittently by U.S. submarines and scout planes. At the same time Japanese air reinforcements were arriving at the airfields north of Manila. By the scheming of General Yamashita's faction in the General Staff, all 350 of the fresh planes were assigned to the Second Air Fleet of Vice Admiral Fukudome Shigeru rather than to the First Air Fleet of the kamikaze enthusiast, Vice Admiral Onishi. Fukudome was a sympathizer but not yet a convert of the kamikaze creed. That evening Onishi pleaded in vain with Fukudome to release some of the planes to him for use in suicide attacks. Onishi, in his entire First Air Fleet, had only thirteen planes which could fly. Fukudome, however, insisted that before he would give Onishi any planes he meant to mount one last massive conventional air attack on the U.S. fleet: a 250-plane raid scheduled for the next morning.

About 150 of Fukudome's planes, in three waves, did arrive successfully over Admiral Halsey's fast carrier task force during the following day. They were driven off with more than 50 per cent losses. One of them, however, diving alone, out of a cloud, planted a lucky bomb on the 11,000-ton light carrier *Princeton,* starting fires below which ultimately crept into fuel tanks and magazines. After most of *Princeton*'s crew had been taken off, her after half erupted in a series of spectacular explosions which bombarded nearby ships with massive pieces of debris. On cruiser *Birmingham,* which stood by alongside helping to fight the fires, the rain of fall-out, which included whole jeeps, took 200 lives, twice as many as were lost on *Princeton* herself. By late afternoon the last fire fighters were withdrawn from *Prince-*

---

[6] She was towed back to Borneo by destroyers. In efforts to get a second shot at her the U.S. submarine *Darter* ran aground on a reef and had to be evacuated and destroyed by her companion vessel *Dace.*

ton's forward decks and U.S. escorts dispatched the blazing derelict wit torpedoes.

During Fukudome's conventional air attack on Halsey, 259 of the 1,06 planes in Halsey's task force were off in the Sibuyan Sea on the other si of Leyte—the "backside" as it was called by the Americans—hammerin away relentlessly at Kurita's oncoming Center Force. All day the U.S. pilo bombed, strafed, and torpedoed, inflicting some damage on every ship i the Japanese fleet. They gave special attention, however, to one of the tw super-dreadnoughts, the 64,000-ton *Musashi*. No ship afloat could la better claim to being unsinkable. Her huge hull was honeycombed wit watertight compartments. By midafternoon it had successfully absorbe nine torpedoes and five bomb hits. Then at 3:20 P.M. the planes of thre U.S. carriers came in on *Musashi* to deliver a death blow. In the course c the attack she took ten more torpedo and twelve more bomb hits. He "special-caliber 16-inch guns"—a naval limitations euphemism for 18.1 inch guns—had never been fired in action. Now in desperation they wer loaded with a type of grapeshot called *sanshiki-dan* which would scar th insides of their barrels. Not even thundering bursts of grapeshot, howeve could deter the intent American pilots. One by one the great guns jamme and the torpedoes struck home. At 7:35 P.M. the leviathan *Musashi* stoo on end and slid under. With her drowned 1,023 of her understrengt 2,399-man crew. Survivors were picked up by Japanese destroyers an taken to Manila.

On *Musashi*'s sister dreadnought *Yamato,* Admiral Kurita had bee vainly sending out pleas for land-based air support. At 4 P.M. he decide that he must at least pretend to retreat. He radioed Imperial Headquarters

. . . . CONCLUDE IT BEST TO RETIRE TEMPORARILY BEYOND RANGE OF HOSTIL PLANES UNTIL FRIENDLY AIR UNITS CAN ENABLE US TO RESUME ADVANCE

So it was that U.S. pilots, when they broke off their attack late in th afternoon, reported to Halsey that Kurita was fleeing west with half his ship smoking. At 5:14 P.M., however, when the American planes had disap peared over the horizon, Kurita again reversed course and bent *Yamat* and her screen of damaged battleships and cruisers back toward San Be nardino Strait at the fair speed of 20 knots. An hour later, when he wa already on his way, he received a message from headquarters which strongl confirmed his decision:

ALL FORCES WILL PROCEED FULL SPEED TO THE ATTACK AND TRUST IN D. VINE GUIDANCE.

As Kurita resumed his advance, Admiral Onishi in Manila was prevail ing upon his fellow air fleet commander, Admiral Fukudome, to use th remaining Japanese planes in the Philippines for suicide missions. In th

.S. fleet standing off the eastern coast of Leyte, American commanders ere hastily preparing receptions for the other two prongs of the Japanese ttack: the Southern Force which Halsey's pilots had sighted at 9:18 that norning 250 miles to the southwest, and the Northern Force which task rce fliers had belatedly discovered at 3:40 that afternoon 400 miles to e north.

The Southern Force was a small one of two battleships, a heavy cruiser, nd four destroyers. It was obviously making for Surigao Strait, the south-rn entrance to Leyte Gulf, between Leyte and the northern tip of Minda-ao. There, since noon, preparations had been underway to give it a robust elcome. In the strait it would run a gauntlet of U.S. motor torpedo boats nd at the exit from the strait it would encounter the broadsides of six U.S. attleships, eight cruisers, and twenty-eight destroyers. Admiral Halsey had o fear that it would break through into Leyte Gulf, a confidence that was Illy justified by the event. Between 11 P.M. and 5 A.M. the whole of outhern Force was blown out of the water except for one destroyer. A einforcement squadron of three Japanese cruisers and four destroyers, hich had come all the way from Japan rather than from Lingga Roads, rrived in Surigao Strait too late for the main action but in time to pick p some survivors. Nevertheless over 4,000 Japanese sailors perished.

Convinced that Center Force had been turned back and confident that outhern Force was being annihilated, Admiral Halsey, at 8:22 P.M. on)ctober 24, steamed off through the night with his task force to attack Northern Force which lay off Cape Engaño on the northeast coast of Luzon. he appearance of Northern Force had surprised him and reports that it ncluded a number of aircraft carriers excited him.

Northern Force had sortied from the supposedly abandoned Combined 'leet anchorage in Japan's own Inland Sea. U.S. submarine skippers had vatched the exit from the Inland Sea, the Bungo Strait, throughout Halsey's arlier attacks on Taiwan. They had concluded, from seeing only a one-way currying of small vessels into the Inland Sea, that all major Japanese fleet nits had, as described by Intelligence, left the Inland Sea months earlier for .ingga Roads. Accordingly they had given up their watch and returned to neir proper business of sinking Japan-bound tankers and merchant vessels.

On October 20, two days after the withdrawal of the U.S. wolf pack, Northern Force had emerged from Bungo Straits undetected. Its com-nander, Vice Admiral Ozawa Jisaburo, was at first relieved and then ositively embarrassed by the lack of attention given to him in his dash outh. His was a decoy force of one heavy aircraft carrier, three light car-iers, two modified battleships with small flight decks, three light cruisers, nd eight destroyers. All were ships which had been half mothballed during he previous four months. They had lain at their berths, forbidden to expend uel and obliged to give away their technicians, one by one, to the Manpower Resources Board. They were considered expendable because now Japan was defending home waters in reach of land airfields and had no further use for carriers.

In the forthcoming engagement, it was the explicit assignment of Admiral Ozawa's Northern Force to lure Admiral Halsey away from Leyte waters and to get sunk by Halsey while Admiral Kurita's Center Force was breaking through. Because of the nature of their mission, the Japanese carriers were manned by skeleton crews and carried less than half their complement of planes: altogether 108 aircraft of all types. The planes were not intended to take part in the battle. They were only aboard the carriers in order to hop a ride to the Philippines where they were being sent as reinforcements for the shattered air wings at Mabalacat.

Arriving undetected off Luzon, Northern Force commander Ozawa saw that he would have to call attention to himself. Early on October 24, therefore, when he dispatched his planes to their bases in the Philippines, he asked the pilots, en route, to strike a glancing blow at Halsey's task force. The scheme worked to perfection: the Japanese planes attacked Halsey from safe heights and distances and most of them succeeded in landing at their assigned fields in Luzon. Halsey's radar technicians noted the direction of attack; search planes were sent out; Ozawa was discovered; and now Halsey was speeding north with his fleet of flattops, leaving behind him an opening for Kurita's battered Center Force when it emerged from San Bernardino Strait.

At 5:40 A.M. on October 25, 1944, Halsey, with twelve of the sixteen fast carriers remaining to him since *Princeton*'s sinking the previous afternoon, had reached a point halfway up the eastern Luzon coast. There and then he began to launch his first air strike against Ozawa's Northern Force 150 miles farther north, which was steaming a box pattern waiting to be sunk. Far to the south the few survivors of Southern Force were backing out of Surigao Strait aboard the reinforcement flotilla which had rescued them. Not so far to the south Admiral Kurita of Center Force had emerged from San Bernardino Strait shortly after midnight, and passing Halsey's rear guard going in the opposite direction, was heading down the east coast of Samar toward Leyte Gulf.

At that moment, in a shack beside a field outside Davao on the big southern Philippine Island of Mindanao, Japan's first six successful kamikaze pilots were receiving their final briefing. The place was one that inspired patriotism for here Japan had had a colony since the fourteenth century. Admiral Onishi had spread the kamikaze gospel widely in the last six days. Volunteers for suicide flights had come forward at every air base in the Philippines. Onishi himself had organized official Special Attack Units at Mabalacat on Luzon and at Cebu City on Cebu in the central islands. The Mindanao unit was unofficial but it had received authorization the evening before to commence operations. Onishi extended to it the same promise he had made to the units he had visited:

You are now all gods, without earthly desires. One thing you will want to know is that your own crash dive is not in vain. Regrettably, we will not be able to tell you the results. But I shall watch your efforts to the end and report your deeds to the Throne. You may all rest assured on that point. I ask you all to do your best.

Each of the six young pilots had volunteered for suicide duty because all the other pilots had. They had been selected because they were the least skillful and most expendable aviators at their base. They had accepted their selection because they were not outstandingly successful young men in other ways and felt themselves suitably unworthy, indebted, and deserving of their fate.

Each of them drank a little saké and then a cup of pure water. Each wound a ghostly white cloth around his forehead. This was the symbolic *hachimaki* worn by the samurai of old when they wished to show that they were entering battle resolved to die. Over their white sweat bands the fledgling crash divers pulled on their tight flight helmets. Then, as nonchalantly as they could, they swaggered to their planes and took off in the first light of dawn.

Out in Leyte Gulf the forces on which Halsey relied to guard his rear were going about routine business. The six battleships, eight cruisers, and twenty-eight destroyers which had destroyed the Southern Force at the exit of Surigao Strait were standing at ease, catching up on sleep and looking up ammunition ships from which to replenish their stores of armor-piercing shells. Farther north between the Leyte beachheads and Kurita's Center Force cruised three flotillas of light, slow escort carriers or "baby flattops." The southernmost of these forces, Taffy One, included four escort carriers with a complement of 118 planes. The northernmost, Taffy Two and Taffy Three, included fourteen escort carriers with a complement of 336 planes. Each baby flattop mounted a single 5-inch gun and carried a flight deck for about twenty-eight planes. Each was protected by the thinnest of armor plate. Three of them were converted 11,400-ton tankers; the rest were 7,800-ton items mass-produced by the Kaiser Corporation.

As dawn broke on October 25 all three of the Taffy escort carrier groups were launching workaday flights to provide cover for the fleet and support for the infantry ashore. Admiral Kurita's Center Force was assumed to be hundreds of miles away, a fleet of cripples wallowing their way home. However, at 6:40 A.M., Kurita's masthead lookouts spied Taffy Three on the horizon. Three minutes later a pilot from the escort carrier *Kadashan Bay,* on routine antisubmarine patrol, reported incredulously that he was flying over what looked like four Japanese battleships, eight cruisers, and any number of destroyers. A moment later bright flashes of anti-aircraft fire persuaded him as well as the distant onlookers of Taffy Three that he was suffering no illusion.

Consternation reigned on both sides. Admiral Kurita assumed that he was encountering Halsey's fast carriers and that Ozawa's decoy mission had failed. Rear Admiral Clifton Sprague of Taffy Three realized that his little squadron of four 7,800-ton escort carriers, three destroyers, and four destroyer escorts was only 20 miles from the biggest guns in the Japanese fleet, the biggest guns afloat anywhere.

Admiral Sprague immediately launched or recalled all the 168 planes under his own command and urgently requested assistance from the 168 planes of Taffy Two and the 118 planes of Taffy One. He ordered his carriers to run away at full speed, which was 18 knots as compared to the 20 knots of which even the most battered of the Japanese vessels were still capable. He had his ships belch the thickest possible screen of smoke.

At 6:59 A.M., only twelve minutes after the sounding of general quarters, 14-inch and 18-inch shells from the Japanese cruisers and battleships began to splash in lurid geysers of orange and purple dye-marking beside the U.S. escort carriers. At first the Japanese aim seemed good. Several ships were straddled with shots and took violent evasive action, trying to hide themselves in the spray from explosions where the skippers knew the next salvo would not fall.

At 7:01 Admiral Sprague threw his code book and security regulations overboard and sent out a plain-language May Day to all U.S. units in hearing. At 7:06 he acknowledged that he had reached "the ultimate in desperate circumstances" and estimated that all his carriers would be sunk in five minutes. He ordered his three destroyers and four destroyer escorts to charge the Japanese array of three battleships, seven heavy cruisers, two light cruisers, and nineteen destroyers advancing against him.

In one of the proudest moments of U.S. naval history, Sprague's destroyers and destroyer escorts not only obeyed his order but seriously disturbed the Japanese formation. Destroyers exchanged broadsides at close range with battleships and destroyer escorts with heavy cruisers. By a combination of luck and good ship handling none of the U.S. small fry were immediately sunk in their desperate attack, and the fifty-odd torpedoes which they launched gave Sprague's carriers a moment's respite. Only one of the torpedoes made a sure hit—on the heavy cruiser *Kumano*— but the rest forced the Japanese ships into strenuous evasive turns which threw them into disarray. Kurita's flagship, the super-dreadnought *Yamato*, found herself chased by two spreads of torpedoes, port and starboard, which threatened to run up her stern garbage chutes. She succeeded, at full steam ahead, in outdistancing them, but by the time their propulsion was expended, she had removed herself so far from the running battle that she never succeeded thereafter in catching up with it.

During the wild melee of the U.S. destroyers' banzai charge, Admiral Sprague and his little thin-skinned carriers took refuge in a providential rain squall. He abruptly changed course in it and came out of it on the side where the Japanese fleet was not. He thereby gained more than fifteen minutes of time and opened the range between himself and the Japanese big guns by several miles. By 7:45 his own hundred-odd planes plus an equal number from Taffy Two were raining the Japanese fleet with torpedoes, bombs, and bullets. When they ran out of projectiles they landed for more on the decks of Taffy Two or on Tacloban Field ashore on Leyte. When concerted strikes were not yet near at hand, pilots without bullets kept Japanese gunners busy by weaving "dry runs" through the flak. "The air attacks," said one of the Japanese officers afterwards, "were almost incessant."

In this incredible battle, in which the Japanese surface vessels had more than a forty-to-one superiority in firepower, the U.S. planes made up the difference. During the first forty-five minutes of action they had created mayhem on the decks of all the Japanese ships and had crippled three of the seven Japanese heavy cruisers. The amazing American victory would have been still more devastating if all U.S. planes in the area could have come to the aid of Taffy Three. But at 7:40, Taffy One, the southernmost of the three U.S. escort carrier groups, was prevented from rendering any substantial assistance by the first blowing of the divine wind, the kamikaze.

The six pilots who had dedicated themselves to suicide at Davao air base two hours earlier bore in on Taffy One from the south after a 250-mile flight. At least two of them were exploded in mid-air as they dived on escort carriers *Suwanee* and *Petrof Bay.* A third broke through to carrier *Santee,* crashed on the flight deck, and penetrated it to blow a 15-by-30-foot hole in the hangar deck below. Sixteen of *Santee*'s crew had been killed and twenty-seven wounded. A gasoline fire roared beside a stack of 1,000-pound bombs. It was put out in eleven minutes and *Santee*'s crew began emergency repairs which would enable her once more, in a matter of hours, to receive aircraft. The three remaining fliers from Davao took notes on what had happened. One of them, about fifteen minutes later, dove out of a cloud on carrier *Suwanee,* tearing through her flight deck and exploding against her hangar deck with much carnage. The two last kamikaze pilots flew home to Davao to report that none of the crash divers had succeeded in sinking their targets.

Failure of the kamikaze-stricken Taffy One to send out her air strike enabled Kurita's fleet to close again on the fragile fleeing carriers of Taffy Three. In the desperate action which followed, the U.S. destroyers, having no more torpedoes, engaged the Japanese battleships and cruisers with machine-gun fire. Two of the three destroyers and one of the four destroyer escorts were sunk with a loss of more than half their heroic crewmen. Kurita's ships broke through to the escort carriers and should have sunk them all. But the Japanese marksmanship was poor. And aging Admiral Kurita, who had not slept for seventy-two hours and who still suffered from the swim he had taken the day before in the Sibuyan Sea after the torpedoing of his first flagship, was issuing orders erratically and inconsequentially.

Kurita commanded the cream of the Japanese fleet, but it did not have the morale of 1941. Its officers knew and resented the fact that they had been sent on a silly suicide mission. They were more preoccupied with the state of their souls and the manner of their final gesture than they were with the conduct of the battle.

U.S. morale, by contrast, was superb. When the Japanese heavy cruisers closed with *Fanshaw Bay,* the Taffy Three flagship, between 8:30 and 9, Admiral Sprague directed the gunner of his single 5-inch cannon: "Open fire with the peashooter as soon as the range is clear." At about 8:50, when escort carrier *White Plains* drew abreast of heavy cruiser *Chokai,* the U.S. gunnery officer pleaded with his men, "Hold out a little longer, boys, we're sucking them into 40-millimeter range." The U.S. carriers were being hit and hit repeatedly, but by armor-piercing shells which passed right through them without exploding. *Fanshaw Bay* was punctured by four 8-inch shells and *Kalinin Bay* by thirteen. The escort carriers' handymen were scalded with steam from burst pipes and drenched with inrushing sea water, but in the elation of battle they somehow welded patches on hulls and stopped the holes.

At 9:07 one of Taffy Three's six baby flattops, *Gambier Bay,* took a hole too many and sank. Destroyer *Hoel* had sunk twelve minutes earlier. Destroyer *Johnston* and destroyer escort *Roberts* were in process of sinking. So were the Japanese heavy cruisers *Chokai, Chikuma,* and *Suzuya.* The lost Japanese ships totaled 34,400 tons; the lost U.S. ships 15,450 tons. At 9:11 Admiral Kurita ordered his vessels to break off action, regroup and survey losses. "Goddammit," shouted the signalman on *Fanshaw Bay* to Admiral Sprague, "they're getting away." Observed Admiral Sprague, with a sigh of relief in his report, "I had expected to be swimming by this time."

The dazed Admiral Kurita drew back and wandered about aimlessly in the Philippine Sea for the next nine hours while he argued with his staff officers. He was still convinced that he had encountered Halsey's task force. He contended that he had inflicted heavy damage on it and that he had made his gesture and was justified in retreating. Most of his staff officers knew better. Under continued air harassment, however, they finally allowed Kurita to send the necessary radiograms to Tokyo and then to withdraw, that night, through San Bernardino Strait toward safer waters.

Taffy Three, as soon as Admiral Sprague could believe that the Japanese fleet was really retreating, sent half its planes in pursuit, sent the other half out to search for survivors of sunken U.S. ships, and then generally relaxed. While most hands were in their wardrooms, toasting one another in coffee, at 10:50 A.M., five more kamikaze flew in, this time from Admiral Onishi's original group of devotees at Mabalacat in Luzon. They approached over the wave crests, below radar range, then soared to 5,000 feet and dived. One missed the bridge of *Kitkun Bay,* tripped over the port catwalk, and tumbled exploding into the sea. Two others went for *Fanshaw Bay,* the Taffy Three flagship, and were blown up before they struck. Another pair started for *White Plains* but pulled up short, riddled with 40-millimeter bullets. One of them came on to explode near *White Plains,* causing eleven casualties. The other veered off to strike *St. Lo* unexpectedly amidships. Flaming debris ignited torpedoes and bombs stacked on the hangar deck. Seven quick explosions followed and at 11:25, thirty minutes later, *St. Lo* foundered. The Kamikaze Corps had made its first kill.

As *St. Lo* sank, Admiral Halsey off Luzon was sending out his third and most telling air strike of the day against Ozawa's Northern Force. By the time its 200 planes returned to their decks all four of Japan's decoy carriers, including the big 27,000-ton Zuikaku which had participated in the Pearl Harbor attack, were in sinking condition. By the end of the day all four had sunk. By the end of the Japanese withdrawal, two days later, a crippled heavy cruiser and two wounded light cruisers were finally dispatched by the far-ranging and tenacious U.S. airmen. Other derelicts of the battle were shadowed relentlessly and finally hunted down in various Philippine harbors within the next month: heavy cruiser *Nachi* on November 5, light cruiser *Kiso* on November 13, battleship *Kongo* on November 21, and heavy cruiser *Kumano* on November 25.

In all, including these after-actions, Japan lost by the Battle of Leyte Gulf four battleships, four attack carriers, eight heavy cruisers, five light cruisers, and seven destroyers. With the ships perished about 15,000 sailors. The U.S. Navy lost a light cruiser, two escort carriers, three destroyers, and less than 2,000 sailors. For a mind like Hirohito's, only one bright statistic emerged from the quixotic venture: nine Japanese kamikaze pilots and their planes had been spent in exchange for over 100 American lives lost, three U.S. escort carriers grievously hurt, and one sunk. A new hope shone on the edge of the dark clouds surrounding Japan. If means could be found to make every Japanese die as effectively as the kamikaze pilots, there would be no Americans left to take possession of Japan after the dying. This vain hope was to see several more hundreds of thousands of Japanese to their deaths.

After the two successful kamikaze attacks on U.S. ships in Leyte Gulf, Imperial Headquarters sent the new commander of the Special Attack Corps, Vice Admiral Onishi, a message of personal congratulations from Hirohito which Onishi was authorized to read to the kamikaze volunteers under his tutelage. Its wording had been carefully considered by Lord Privy Seal Kido and other palace advisors for some time:

When told of the special attack, His Majesty said, "Was it necessary to go to this extreme? The men certainly did a magnificent job."

At the front in the Philippines, Onishi added, "His Majesty's words suggest that His Majesty is greatly concerned. We must redouble our efforts to relieve His Majesty of this concern."

THE GREAT DYING

In subduing Leyte after the Battle of Leyte Gulf about 4,000 U.S. soldiers and sailors died in process of killing some 65,000 Japanese.

The immense U.S. expeditionary force went on in early 1945 to invade Luzon and the other islands of the Philippines. At the cost of 10,400 American lives, another 256,000 Japanese were destroyed.

Iwo Jima came next, a volcanic mountaintop protruding from the sea halfway between Guam and Honshu. It was needed as a way station for the escorts of B-29's flying against Tokyo. On Iwo between February 19 and March 27, 1945, about 21,000 Japanese and 6,812 Americans perished.

The capture of Iwo enabled fleets of 200 to 300 B-29's to range at will over Japan's home islands. On the night of March 9 the first massive incendiary raid on Tokyo burned to death 80,000. Over the next twenty weeks fire raids on five other major urban centers, plus return visits to Tokyo, and at length a systematic burning of fifty-eight secondary Japanese cities cut short an additional 150,000 civilian lives.

At the same time, from April 1 to June 22 1945, U.S. forces conquered Japan's sixteenth century acquisition, the island of Okinawa, where Commodore Perry had put in on his way from Taiwan to Tokyo Bay in 1853. The Okinawa campaign killed 12,500 U.S. servicemen, 110,000 Japanese troops, and about 75,000 Okinawan civilians.

Then, at last, the war ended with the climactic slaughter of 140,000 at Hiroshima and Nagasaki.

Half this fearsome tragedy—the tentative, time-consuming efforts of the Japanese to achieve a war settlement and the hasty impatience of the Allies—has been recounted already in Chapter 2. The other half, the dying, has been described in moving detail by many writers but will never be done full justice, for death is personal and so many deaths cannot be personalized.

The cold, cold statistic is that, in all, 897,000 or one of every seventy-eight of the proud, emotional Japanese people died in those last nine months of the war. They died with animal ferocity and despair, buried in caves and trapped between infernos. They died full of hate and hungry craving: famished, thirsty, and febrile; broken, twisted, and maimed; soiled, suppurating, and loathsome to their own nostrils. Their American executioners—of whom 32,000 also died, and bravely—did only what the Japanese themselves seemed to demand before they would surrender.

Patriotically overwrought after fifteen years of indoctrination, prickly proud after four years of strutting Asian overlordship, genuinely fearful for the sacred homeland under American vengeance, few Japanese could contemplate defeat without writhing inwardly. At the same time few Japanese had accepted propaganda at face value; they were too literate and cynical, too close to the frugal, industrious struggle of Japanese life. Many knew at heart that their defiance of death for the sake of honor was a romantic posture, the stylized grimace of the samurai with his blade flashing in the moonlight.

If the Japanese masses had been told that the bulk of their Navy and a fifth of their Air Navy had been destroyed in the Leyte action, and that the United States had three times as many ships and planes in the Pacific as Japan had ever produced, popular sentiment in favor of surrender would have swelled mightily.[7] The masses were not told, however—neither by Hirohito on domestic radio nor by President Roosevelt in short-wave broadcasts.

As a nation predicated upon a moral code and a belief in self-government by indigenous peoples, the United States, after the capture of Saipan, should have mounted an all-out campaign to tell Japanese of U.S. war grievances, accomplishments, goals, and international commitments. At best such a campaign would have shortened the war; at the least it would have strengthened the U.S. position in postwar Asia. If U.S. planes had dropped leaflets and shortwave sets on Japan as well as bombs, and if the taped voices of Roosevelt and Churchill had been put on the air each night projecting the humanity of Allied convictions, Hirohito might have felt compelled by public opinion to accept defeat before the worst of the blood bath. Even if he had used the fall of Germany on May 7 as an excuse to capitulate, he would still have saved about half a million lives.

Unfortunately Roosevelt and Churchill were concerned mainly with American and European politics. Their constituents labored under profound ignorance and distrust of the Japanese masses. Psychological warfare experts were unsure of the best arguments to use in approaching the Japanese. Writer-translators who could wield a mighty pen in Japanese

---

[7] After the war U.S. Strategic Bombing Survey teams conducted a poll to find out when the misinformed Japanese public began to realize that its side had lost. They discovered, as might be expected, that every reverse which could not be concealed from the people increased the number of pessimists. Two per cent of the population despaired of winning in June 1944 before the fall of Saipan, 10 per cent in December after the first heavy B-29 attacks, 19 per cent by March 1945 when the fire raids began, 46 per cent by June after the collapse of Germany, and 68 per cent by August when the atomic bombs fell. The will to fight decreased proportionately, and by the time of surrender 64 per cent of the people had reached a point at which they felt they were personally unable to go on with the war.

were as scarce in the West as sumo wrestlers. An all-out information war had never been waged before. It would be expensive. It could not win as surely as killing. Consequently no leaflets were regularly dropped with the bombs on Japan until mid-May 1945. And warnings to evacuate specific cities, before they were burned out by massive incendiary attacks, did not begin to be issued until July 27, only ten days before Hiroshima.

So it was that Allied leaders did little to subvert the plans of the Peace Faction. The people of Japan were allowed to reach a state of political disinterest and preoccupation with survival, a state of mind beyond recrimination, before being told that their war sacrifices had been in vain. Hirohito did his utmost to keep them in hope—facing death optimistically—until he was personally ready to surrender. In the last months of the war he repeatedly abused his power of imperial rescript to announce victories in place of defeats. Even at the end, in his historic surrender broadcast of August 15, he personally added the phrase "not necessarily to our advantage" in describing recent war developments.

No one knew better than Hirohito that Japan was defeated; no one could explain why with more logic and candor; but no one clung more tenaciously to straws of unrealistic hope. The shame at having to admit to the ancestors, the people, and the enemy that he had committed Japan prematurely to war with the West was more than he could bear. He saw no alternative for himself in surrender but suicide or retirement in disgrace. He knew that Kido and Konoye had already discussed temples in which he might live in priestly penance after his abdication. And so, although he approved the stand-by measures of the Peace Faction for the sake of the Throne, he remained, for his own sake, addictively engrossed in every desperate effort to salvage some sense of accomplishment from his reign.

THE WILL TO KILL

The reckless do-or-die of Japan in her final throes at first frightened U.S. combat troops, then puzzled them, then disgusted them, and finally moved many to genuine compassion. The brute misery of the Japanese soldiers in their caves and the forlorn desperation of their banzai charges made it increasingly difficult to "Remember Pearl Harbor." And as Japanese prisoners began to be taken in large numbers, their co-operative, industrious, affable ways belied the other wartime maxim: "No good Jap but a dead one."

G.I. hatred for the Japanese probably crested and began to ebb in February 1945 during the battle for Manila. After the U.S. landings along Luzon's Lingayen Gulf, on January 9, MacArthur's troops moved on the Philippine capital cautiously, entering its northern suburbs on February 3. Yamashita had pulled back the bulk of his army into defensive positions in the mountains around Baguio. He had planned to give up the Manila area without a fight and so spare its million-odd Filipinos from the hardships of siege, bombardment, and street fighting.

Hirohito's Imperial General Headquarters had other ideas. At the last minute, over Yamashita's objections, Tokyo Headquarters sent into Manila a naval landing party of some 15,000 sailors and marines under Rear Admiral Iwabuchi Sanji, a former imperial aide-de-camp. Together with 4,000 to 5,000 soldiers, whom Yamashita had left in the city to demolish Army stores and munitions dumps, Iwabuchi and his men contested the city street by street, house by house, and sewer by sewer. A month later when the last sailor had been blasted from his hole, the finest sections of Manila had been turned to rubble.

Iwabuchi made his last stand in Intramuros, the old Spanish walled town in the south of the city. Having themselves decided to die, Iwabuchi's men showed no mercy to the Filipino civilians whom they had entrapped with them. They raped the women and machine-gunned the men. When the battle was done, 1,000 Americans had died, 16,000 Japanese, and 100,000 Filipinos.

The desperate Japanese tactics combined with another circumstance in Manila to feed G.I. hatred. In the northern outskirts, on their first two nights in the city, February 3 and February 4, the U.S. troops liberated some 5,000 Western internees and prisoners of war who had endured three or more years of Japanese captivity. The emaciated *libérés,* who weighed in at between eighty and a hundred and twenty pounds apiece, told chilling stories of starvation, medical negligence, beating, torture, and capital punishment for trivial offenses. Worse, the captured records of concentration camp commandants revealed that Japan had not intended any of these wretched prisoners to return alive into American hands. Only a last-minute dash into Manila by MacArthur's armored flying columns had prevented Japanese guards for complying, reluctantly, with orders from Tokyo to get rid of their charges.

The first discretionary hints to kill prisoners rather than let them fall into the propaganda-making hands of the enemy had been issued in stages by Imperial General Headquarters during the latter half of 1944. In Borneo Japanese commandants had obeyed instantly by instituting a series of death marches and impossible jungle construction details which killed all but six of 2,000 Australian prisoners of war there.

On Palawan, the most southwestern of the large islands of the Philippines, the local commandant decided to dispose of his P.O.W. work force on December 14, 1944, when lookouts reported a large U.S. convoy steaming past the Palawan coast. He ordered the 150 U.S. prisoners under his charge—men captured in the fall of the Philippines in 1942—to take cover in three air-raid shelters. Then, quickly, he had his own soldiers pour buckets of kerosene into the shelter entrances and throw in lighted torches. As burning prisoners came rushing out through the curtain of flame, they were swept with machine-gun fire and bayoneted. Nevertheless some broke through to leap off a fifty-foot bluff into the sea. While the Japanese soldiers were busy shooting at heads bobbing up in the surf a group of prisoners from one of the shelters broke out of an escape tunnel they had been digging which opened on the cliff face. They too dropped into the surf and hid in the rocks at the base of the cliff.

Japanese landing barges patrolled the edge of the bay hunting down the escapees until well after dark. Five, however, survived. At nine that night they swam the bay together and got away into the jungle. Days later they reached a guerrilla encampment where they were sheltered until U.S. forces reoccupied Palawan in March 1945, three months later. Then they led their liberators back to the bluff by the sea and directed the disinterment of the charred bones of their comrades.

Executions cheated the G.I.'s of only some of the prisoners they had hoped to liberate; many more had been spirited away to Japan. In late 1944, when Japanese troops and nurses were still being brought to die in the Philippines, and when more than half of Japanese shipping between the colonies and the home islands was being sunk by U.S. submarines, Tokyo ordered all troop transports returning empty to Japan to take on as many P.O.W.'s as possible. The prisoners might be of service as slave labor; their presence in Japan, subject to Japan's pleasure, might count for something in later peace bargaining.

The wasted transportees were huddled into the hulks so sick and close that on some vessels a quarter of them died at sea in the course of what should have been a three- or four-day voyage. Some fell dizzily and drowned from outboard toilet scaffolds. Others lay down in the excrement of the holds and expired of thirst and hunger. On most of the vessels, at the first indication of U.S. submarine attack, the hatches were battened down. If a torpedo struck, the inmates were left to break out or go down as best they might after Japanese crews had already abandoned ship. A surprising number of practiced survival experts did succeed in swimming away from such sinking prisons and in living to tell about it.[8]

---

[8] I had a heartwarming encounter with one of these survivors on the night of February 5, 1945. Old Bilibid Prison in Manila, where internees from Baguio had been subsisting for the last two months, had been liberated the day before and was now surrounded by fires spreading from demolished Japanese ammunition dumps. The U.S. Army was evacuating us all to the Ang Tibay Shoe Factory about two miles north beyond the flames. There were only enough trucks for the sick and debilitated, and so I and another sixteen-year-old set off down the burning street with our parcels of cherished belongings—our coconut-shell dishes and spare loin cloths—slung between us on a carrying pole. Filipinos, who were also fleeing from the fire, cheered us on with shouts of *"Mabuhay":* banzai, hurrah, victory. In the garish tumult, a half-filled U.S. Army truck stopped to offer us a lift. It came from a separate compound in Old Bilibid which had housed 800 military prisoners of war.

I sat down in the truck next to a shriveled Englishman, a London cockney. He had worked on the Burma-Thai railroad. He had survived to be shipped out of Singapore

U.S. publicists made much of the privations described by liberated U.S. prisoners. As a result, the War Ministry in Tokyo felt obliged to clarify previous hints and make sure that no more captives would be recovered by the enemy. The new instructions, couched in the least subtle belly talk possible, went out to prison camp commandants in a secret telegram under signature of Vice War Minister Shibayama Kaneshiro on March 17, 1945:

PRISONERS OF WAR MUST BE PREVENTED BY ALL MEANS AVAILABLE FROM FALLING INTO ENEMY HANDS.

THEY SHOULD EITHER BE RELOCATED AWAY FROM THE FRONT OR COLLECTED AT SUITABLE POINTS AND TIMES WITH AN EYE TO ENEMY AIR RAIDS, SHORE BOMBARDMENTS, ETC.

THEY SHOULD BE KEPT ALIVE TO THE LAST WHEREVER THEIR LABOR IS NEEDED.

IN DESPERATE CIRCUMSTANCES, WHEN THERE IS NO TIME TO MOVE THEM, THEY MAY, AS A LAST RESORT, BE SET FREE. THEN EMERGENCY MEASURES SHOULD BE CARRIED OUT AGAINST THOSE WITH AN ANTAGONISTIC ATTITUDE AND UTMOST PRECAUTIONS SHOULD BE TAKEN SO THAT NO HARM IS DONE TO THE PUBLIC.

IN EXECUTING EMERGENCY MEASURES CARE SHOULD BE HAD NOT TO PROVOKE ENEMY PROPAGANDA OR RETALIATION.

PRISONERS SHOULD BE FED AT THE END.

Perhaps this stipulation that every prisoner be given a last meal proved too difficult to fulfill; in any case, camp commandants generally disregarded the directive from Tokyo and in the final five months of the war killed far fewer than they might have of the Allied prisoners still in custody on bypassed islands and in Japan proper.

Among the foot soldiers, enthusiasm for killing and being killed was running out on both sides. At the beginning of the Luzon campaign, U.S. troops took almost no prisoners. By the end of March, they were taking prisoners in lots of a hundred. Ultimately over 50,000 starving Japanese soldiers would give themselves up in the Philippines and would be nursed back to health in U.S. pens and field hospitals.

Even Kamikaze Corps pilots began to suffer from loss of fighting spirit. Theirs was the highest morale in the Japanese armed services because they alone were taking more lives than they were losing. Between the Battle

or Japan on a prison hulk. Coast-running up the western side of the Borneo-Philippine archipelago, his ship had been torpedoed by a U.S. submarine off Mindoro. He had swum ashore and joined the Mindoro guerrillas, been recaptured, and finally reduced to his present straits in Manila. Having outlined all this, he began to chant for me his favorite poem, stanza after stanza: Kipling's paean to the common soldier, "Tommy Atkins." The truck lurched across yawning gaps in the pavement. The flames leapt high on both sides of the street. Manila burned and my companion was wracked by dysentery. But he rose to heights of bitter eloquence and ecstasy as he drove home to me: "It's 'Thank you, Mr. Atkins,' when the guns begin to roll."

of Leyte Gulf and the beginning of the battle for Manila two months later
they expended 378 suicide-plane and 102 escort-plane crews but sank
sixteen U.S. ships and damaged eighty-seven more. In the process they
lost about 600 men and killed about 2,000 U.S. sailors. U.S. skippers
feared and hated their wild attacks, but the kamikazes themselves knew
that they were not killing massively enough to change the course of the
war.

Kamikaze commanders agonized over mission assignments. By the end
of January 1945 new suicide pilots were being drawn mainly from the
ranks of bookish university boys, capable of learning the rudiments of
flying in a few weeks but not of arousing excessive sympathy in the minds
of the veteran air officers who had to send them to their deaths.

Sakai Saburo, the ace who had lost an eye over Guadalcanal in 1942,
expressed the feeling of most professional Japanese fighters toward suicide
tactics when he was required to fly a one-way mission against Saipan early
in the battle for Iwo Jima.

He resented the assignment from the start, calling it "a death without
meaning, without purpose." He later wrote:

> I appreciated better than most the wisdom of relying upon my own
> strength and my own skill to escape the death which in a dogfight was never
> more than a split second away. I could count only upon myself and my
> wingmen. . . . A samurai lives in such a way that he will always be pre-
> pared to die. . . . However, . . . there is a great gulf between deliberately
> taking one's life and entering battle with a willingness to accept all its
> risks. . . . Man lives with his head held high; he can die in the same fashion.

Acting on such sentiments Sakai led his two wingmen to within 50
miles of Saipan. He saw seven of the eight bombers and five of the eight
fighters accompanying him shot out of the air by U.S. Hellcats. By superb
flying he led his wingmen out of the ambush and continued to search for
the U.S. fleet. Then the weather closed in and he turned back to Iwo
bringing both his wingmen home with him.

Only two other pilots survived the flight. On alighting, Sakai stumbled
over one of them, lying in shame in the darkness beside the runway. He
picked the man off the ground and arm in arm with him marched to the
office of their commander. There, with a mounting sense of anger, Sakai
reported the total and predictable failure of the mission. No one said anything. He was reposted home to Japan to live out the war as a flight instructor.

FIRE BOMBING

The war-weary sense of perspective which had begun to touch the one-
eyed Sakai after seven years of air combat in China and the Pacific was

novelty among airmen, for they seldom had to see the results of their handiwork at close range. It had not begun to affect Sakai's opposite numbers from the United States, who now, with the fall of Iwo Jima, were called on to deliver the final telling blows on Japan. Newly graduated from accelerated mass flight-training programs, they questioned no orders but killed innocently, on a scale which would horrify a generation of commentators.

The air massacre of Japan opened with the devastating March 9 fire raid on Tokyo. In the days which followed it, Allied moralists missed their supreme opportunity to uphold, elucidate, or repudiate the rules of civilized warfare which Western diplomats had written into the treaties and protocols of international law in previous decades.[9]

The March 9 attack was ordered by Major General Curtis LeMay on his own discretionary authority as B-29 commander in the Marianas. LeMay, however, had recently been appointed to his post as a result of President Roosevelt's dissatisfaction with previous failure of the B-29 program to hasten the end of the Pacific war. On the day before the March 9 raid, LeMay gave a verbal briefing to Major General Lauris Norstad, an emissary from Air Force commander General Hap Arnold's staff. Then LeMay wired General Arnold in Washington to prepare "for an outstanding show."

The raid marked a sudden change in U.S. bombing tactics. Previously the B-29's had struck at industrial targets from high altitude in an effort to cripple Japanese war plants by precision bombing with ordinary explosives. Incendiaries and anti-personnel bombs had been used only sparingly and experimentally. On March 9–10, however, under cover of midnight, the B-29's came in over Tokyo low, at from 5,000 to 8,000 feet, dropping exclusively incendiaries and on the densely populated poor districts in the southeastern sections of the city. In these wards the Japanese were caught unprepared. They had hardly begun to carry out the anti-incendiary programs which were underway in other urban areas: the tearing down of houses to create firebreaks and the evacuation of all non-essential women and children to the countryside. The weather, too, played its part, for Tokyo that night was a center of air turbulence. Strong shifting winds fanned the flames and drove them in first one direction and then another.

The B-29's started the raid by dropping two strings of incendiaries which marked the center of the sixteen-square-mile target area with a blazing cross. Succeeding waves of B-29's drew a circle around the cross and then

[9] Some of them later protested against the atomic bomb because it seemed new and fearful or because—to paraphrase Hilaire Belloc—it was a weapon which the United States had got and the Soviet Union had not. They would have stood on firmer ground, with less suspect political motives, if they had protested the equally lethal use earlier of the "conventional" incendiaries.

filled in the dark quadrants. Through the target wound Tokyo's Sumida River, fed by hundreds of sewage canals which crosshatched the entire area. The flames leapt the canals, destroyed bridges and trapped hysterical mobs of refugees on burning islands. Discipline and etiquette broke down. Many of the weak were trampled; the strong survived briefly and then burned or suffocated. The wind fed the flames and the heat fed the wind. Thermal tornadoes known as fire storms or dragon tails howled back and forth through the fire fronts, leaping into the sky and touching down again on cool ground with blazing fingerprints. The rising drafts from the fires severely buffeted the B-29's more than a mile overhead and the smoke blackened their bright fuselages with soot.

When the fires had been put out four days later the Japanese government admitted an official toll of 78,650 dead—500 more than the official toll it would admit after Hiroshima five months later. As in the case of Hiroshima, the official count was determined in after years to be a conservative estimate. To this day no one knows for sure, but students of the available records generally conclude that the March 9 raid on Tokyo was more lethal than the atomic bombing of Hiroshima.

After the fire raid, a handful of U.S. divines rose in their pulpits to protest indiscriminate bombing of enemy civilians, but no one paid much attention. The United States, in numerous treaties regarding the conventions of war, was on record as condemning civilian bombing. The Roosevelt Administration, however, considered itself unbound by rules of war which the enemy had already flouted.[10] Both Germany and Japan, to the best of their capabilities, had indiscriminately bombed the civilians of Allied nations. Now, therefore, it was thought just for the enemy to reap the tares which it had sown. No distinction was made between the poor of Hamburg and Berlin, who had played some part in allowing Hitler to rise to power, and the poor of Tokyo who had simply inherited Hirohito, without passing upon him.

Emperor Hirohito was quick to appreciate the injustice which would be felt by the impoverished victims of the fire raid. Since mid-December 1944, after the first heavy conventional raids on Tokyo, he had been living, for the most part, in the complex of tunnels and shelters which had been constructed in 1942 under his prewar work place, the Imperial Library *Obunko*. When the first B-29 pathfinders began dropping their incendiary sticks, shortly before midnight on March 9, he was still at duty in his

[10] On the other hand Roosevelt was careful to honor commitments from which he had not been released by enemy action. During the Iwo Jima campaign, when Japanese soldiers were taking many U.S. lives from hot, sulfurous tunnels dug into the slopes and inner craters of the volcanic cones there, a serious proposal was made by the U.S. General Staffs to resort to poison gas. The proposal reached President Roosevelt's desk and was returned marked: "All prior endorsements denied—Franklin D. Roosevelt, Commander-in-Chief."

underground command post, half napping and half waiting up for two important phone calls concerning expected developments. One would tell him about a final Japanese Army take-over from French puppets in Saigon, the other about the birth of his first grandchild, the offspring of Princess Shigeko and Prince Higashikuni's son Morihiro. After midnight both labors were successfully concluded and he would have retired except that he had begun to hear of the horrifying raid then in progress.

During the night, either by accident or invention, sparks from fires in southeast Tokyo three miles away supposedly alighted in the Fukiage Gardens and were beaten out on the very porch of the Imperial Library. It was even said that a U.S. pilot had dropped a single incendiary within the sacrosanct palace enclosure. But LeMay had issued explicit instructions to all B-29 pilots to spare the Imperial Palace because "the Emperor of Japan is not at present a liability and may later become an asset." Earlier precision bombing by B-29's had been disappointingly imprecise but not to the extent of three-mile misses.

In the morning, on arising and coming to the surface, Hirohito surveyed from afar the damage to the Tokyo slums and asked to visit the devastated areas in person so that he could extend his condolences to the bereaved and homeless. Three days later, having given the matter judicious thought, Lord Privy Seal Kido opined that it would be most unwise, politically, for the Emperor to pay an ordinary state visit to the ruins, attended by the usual armies of policemen and prepared through the usual infiltration of the populace by secret police agents. If the visit was to be paid at all it must be arranged to look like an informal, spur-of-the-moment imperial whim. Hirohito insisted that, even on these difficult terms, he owed it to his people. And so, six days later, on March 18, after elaborate preparations, Hirohito walked informally, as if impromptu, through the burned-out shacks along the banks of the Sumida River and shook his head, with a sad countenance, at the heaps of ash and charred bodies still in evidence there.

The fire convinced the Japanese lower classes, as no propaganda ever could, that surrender was, indeed, out of the question and that Americans really were demons bent on exterminating all Japanese.[11] After the raid it took the atomic bomb to persuade them that anything could be worse than the imagined cruelty of U.S. occupation troops. Japanese who had traveled or associated with Westerners in prewar Japan knew better, but they were in a minority. Moreover, even they felt apprehensive. It was clear from plain-language transmissions of the U.S. fleet that racial hostilities had deepened alarmingly since Pearl Harbor and that few Americans any longer looked upon "Japs" as human beings.

---

[11] According to the later U.S. Strategic Bombing Survey's poll, belief in victory at this point in the war fell off far more sharply than will to fight. In short, the Japanese masses took the fire raids stoically as meaning that they must die.

LAST BATTLE

Desperately the Foreign Ministry officers who had supported Hirohito in going to war looked toward Stalin as a sane, humane, neutral mediator. As peace feelers were vainly pursued in Moscow, the monster of the U.S. armada and expeditionary force clawed its way ashore on Okinawa and proceeded, with 183,000 soldiers, to exterminate the well dug-in 110,000 Japanese defenders.

Nine hundred and thirty kamikaze pilots hurled themselves to death against the U.S. invasion fleet, sinking ten destroyers, an escort carrier, and six lesser ships, and heavily damaging 198 vessels including twelve carriers, ten battleships, five cruisers, and 63 destroyers, and killing over 3,000 U.S. sailors.

On April 6, five days after the American landings on Okinawa, Japan's surviving 64,000-ton super-dreadnought, *Yamato,* which had once been Admiral Yamamoto's flagship, made a suicide sortie from the Inland Sea toward Okinawa. She was accompanied by other activated remnants of the Japanese fleet, including a cruiser and eight destroyers. She never had a chance—not even to train her vaunted 18.1-inch guns on a worthy target. She was shadowed from the start by U.S. submarines. And she went down short of her mark under U.S. air attack. With her sank her escort cruiser, four of her destroyers, and about 3,000 hands. Her crewmen perished to little purpose. They demonstrated discipline to "Great Orders," stamped by Hirohito. They kept their great floating coffin from ever falling into enemy hands.

On the night of June 21 when the last trench lines on the southern tip of Okinawa had been breached and the remaining defenders were waiting in caves to be killed, Lieutenant General Ushijima Mitsuru and his Chief of Staff Lieutenant General Cho Isamu held a last feast with other officers in their command cave. They drank up the last cases of Scotch whisky which they had carried with them in their retreat and then made ready to commit hara-kiri. Commander Ushijima, an old-fashioned samurai, told self-deprecating jokes in a soft voice and impressed all who heard him with his fatherly manner. Chief of Staff Cho, however, who had issued the "kill-all-prisoners" order for Prince Asaka outside of Nanking in 1937, had been living on whisky for several days and marred the final rites by "boisterous talk." Earlier he had issued an official suggestion to all Japanese civilians on Okinawa to kill themselves. Now he wrote last messages to friends in Japan. One of them, sent to Prince Asaka's villa for transmission to Hirohito, had a sober ring: "We fought as valiantly as we could with the best strategy, tactics, and technical aids available but our efforts counted for little against the material might of the enemy."

Cho and Ushijima had a white cloth spread at the mouth of their cave and having nostalgically watched the set of the moon, knelt down upon it at 4:10 A.M. on June 22, to face north toward the palace and perform their final act of service. Commander Ushijima had calmly cut open his belly when nearby American troops, hearing sounds in the dark, flung grenades toward the cave entrance. The hard-drinking Chief of Staff Cho half rose as if to order another attack. His second, standing behind him to dispatch him in case his death throes proved too painful, promptly scythed downward with a drawn sword and cut off his head. So it was, according to Army gossip, that butcher Cho died: not by his own hand with honor, having first laid down his guts upon the ground, but by beheading, at the hands of another, like any common thief in Tokugawa times.

HEAD ABOVE SHAME

Japan was beaten as thoroughly as any nation had ever been beaten in history. The average intake of food for every citizen had fallen to less than 1,700 calories a day.[12] Most storage tanks for fuel oil and aviation gasoline had been pumped dry. All ships but a few wooden coastal vessels had ceased to ply even the Inland Sea. Ferries to smaller home islands were being sunk daily. Railroads were running on a catch-as-catch-can basis. The Continent was cut off. A million Japanese soldiers, from Seoul to Singapore, had no way of coming home to join in the final fight.

Sharpened staves of bamboo were handed out as spears to the villagers along likely invasion beaches in southern Japan. And then the U.S. B-29's proceeded to drop the sophisticated atomic bomb.

Hirohito had been expecting to negotiate a surrender in September or October after the loss of perhaps another million of his loyal subjects. The bomb, as he later told MacArthur, gave Japan an excuse to surrender earlier. That is, it forced Hirohito to "bear the unbearable" humiliation of surrender immediately. He realized, correctly,[13] that it would be only a matter of time until an atomic bomb was dropped on Tokyo. Then the entire imperial family would be wiped out and Japan, from Hirohito's point of view, would cease to exist.

Having accepted the irrefutable logic of the bomb, Hirohito acted on it with great decisiveness. As detailed earlier, he overrode the quibbles and vacillations of his chief vassals at the historic meeting in his air raid shelter at midnight on August 9, 1945. Again, on the morning of August 14,

[12] Captives of the Japanese at that time enjoyed 800 to 1,300 calories a day. After the captives had been liberated, however, ordinary Japanese citizens remained on short rations for many months. They suffered little from acute forms of malnutrition like beriberi but they suffered greatly from hunger-aggravated diseases like tuberculosis.

[13] General Carl A. Spaatz, the commander of the U.S. Strategic Air Forces, had already urged strongly that the next atomic bomb be dropped on Tokyo. Two more of the bombs were on their way to Tinian ready for assembly and delivery in the next few weeks. If Hirohito had rejected the Hiroshima-Nagasaki ultimatums, his underground bunker would almost certainly have been crushed forthwith.

when his ministers had debated the Allied reply to Japan's surrender note for two days, he cut off their deliberations and ordered them to accept the U.S. terms without further ado.

In these his final acts as absolute god-king, Hirohito reportedly carried himself well, and for the most part, exuded a serenity and readiness to face death which inspired his retainers. At 9:15 on the morning of August 12, when the Allied reply to Japan's surrender note had just been received and studied by the Foreign Ministry, Lord Privy Seal Kido privately pointed out to Hirohito that the Americans insisted on an eventual form of government in Japan dictated by the will of the Japanese people. This insistence on democracy, said Kido, was the issue which most troubled the imperial advisors.

"If the people didn't want an emperor," said Hirohito with conviction, "all would be futile. I think I can trust the people."

Kido found Hirohito's high-priestly self-confidence a little breathtaking. It turned out, however, to be justified. According to a careful polling of Japanese opinion by the U.S. Strategic Bombing Survey months later: "The Emperor largely escaped the criticism which was directed at other leaders and retained the people's faith in him. It is probable that most Japanese would have passively faced death in a continuation of the hopeless struggle had the Emperor so ordered."

The sublime detachment of Hirohito was shared, to an extent, by other members of the family. On the afternoon of August 12, from 3 to 5:20 P.M. Hirohito had all the adult princes of the blood attend him in the Imperial Library. He asked their support in his decision to accept the Allied note received that morning. The corpulent, seventy-one-year-old Prince Nashimoto—patron of Tojo, go-between with the Kwantung Army before the China War, and since then lord custodian of national shrines and chief priest to the sun goddess at Ise—arose as senior prince and pledged Hirohito the full co-operation of all present. For the next two hours the princes talked over the roles assigned to them by the Peace Faction in the days ahead. No detailed record of their deliberations is extant but the central issue was clear and simple. Hirohito's Navy brother, Captain Takamatsu, who was one of those present, had stated it succinctly to a General Staff gathering nine months earlier: "How to be defeated gracefully."

That evening, as soon as the Imperial Family Council had adjourned, War Minister General Anami, who had been explicitly charged by Hirohito with the task of controlling the Army in defeat, was given an audience by Hirohito's Army brother, Lieutenant Colonel Mikasa. The two met in Mikasa's palace air-raid shelter which adjoined Hirohito's. Anami complained that the Army was being made to take all the blame for the war and pleaded with Prince Mikasa to intercede with his brother for a fairer distribution of war responsibility. With remarkable sangfroid, Mikasa refused. He pointed out that the Army bureaucracy had taken a leading role in advising the Throne since the Manchurian Incident in 1931. Not only had the generals advised but on occasion they had "acted not perfectly in accordance with imperial wishes."

Princess Mikasa, in the next room of the princely shelter, noticed that the prince and the war minister were speaking loudly to one another.[14] She had the impression that Anami was arguing against surrender plans and that Prince Mikasa was insisting upon them. Later that night, when Anami had left, a group of staff officers also called at the Mikasa bunker. One of them, noted the princess, had been a classmate of the prince in military academy. Again voices were raised and the prince took his guests up into the moonlit gardens so that they could talk without disturbing the family.

Two nights later it was a mysterious Lieutenant Colonel X, fitting the description of Prince Mikasa, who led a group of Mikasa's military academy classmates in the elaborate palace coup, previously described in detail, which was billed as an attempt to prevent Hirohito from surrendering. The commander of the palace guard was assassinated in the presence of Lieutenant Colonel X. War Minister Anami retired to his villa to commit suicide. Most of the young officers of the rebellion followed Anami's example except Lieutenant Colonel X, who vanished.

While the Army was taking responsibility for the war in this peculiar fashion, Hirohito, by his own account, lay awake in his bed in the Imperial Library, above ground, until the alarmed whispers of chamberlains in his anteroom told him that the abortive insurrection had been staged as planned. Then he rolled over and went to sleep. He had not needed to worry about the behavior of his people. Almost a million of them had died in the last year. Their deaths had been more painful to them than to him, but they remained his obedient children. Tomorrow noon, when his voice would go out on the radio, acknowledging to them the fact of defeat, they would weep loyally. They would sympathize with him in his humiliation. They would be grateful to him for his final mercy. Now, the next concern was the behavior of the conquerors.

In the morning, after the minions of Colonel X had withdrawn from the offices of Japan Broadcasting Company and Tokyo radio had gone back on the air to announce the impending imperial broadcast, Grand Chamberlain Admiral Fujita Hisanori reported at the Imperial Library for work as usual. He was called in for his first audience at 8:10 A.M. As he straightened up from his deep bow of morning felicitation, he first noticed

---

[14] Princess Mikasa Yuriko was the eldest daughter of Viscount Takagi Masanori. She was cousin to Big Brother Baron Takagi Yoshihiro and kin to Rear Admiral Takagi Sokichi who, since 1939, had had charge of contingency planning for defeat in the Navy General Staff.

how tired the Emperor looked, and then, in spite of himself, he smiled appreciatively. On the shelf for ornaments, recessed in the wall behind Hirohito's back, had stood for years the busts of Darwin and Napoleon; now Napoleon's had been quietly replaced by Abraham Lincoln's. The Emperor had spoken without saying a word.

EPILOGUE

NEW CLOTHES

TO SPOIL THE SPOILS

In the bright darkness of the flamethrowers and burning cities, in the dark darkness of the destroyed palaces and rifled archives were gestated not only a new Japan also a new Asia. The Far East of Western colonialism would never be the same comfortable place again. In the final months of the war Japanese commanders in China, Indochina, Malaya, and Indonesia worked around the clock trying to negotiate lasting understandings with local puppet political leaders. After the surrender, the younger princes of the imperial family were sent out to the legions overseas to make sure that they would surrender peacefully—Prince Kanin Haruhito, the son of the long-time chief of staff, to Singapore; Prince Asaka Takahiko, the son of the rape commander, to Nanking; and Prince Takeda Tsuneyoshi, Hirohito's principal wartime go-between with the legions, to Manchuria. As a result, before French, British, and Dutch troops returned to Indochina, Malaya, and Indonesia, sizable Japanese arsenals had been turned over to native patriots and many Japanese advisors had gone underground to assist local independence movements.

The Japanese advisors were not treated with much gratitude and many of them were subsequently betrayed to Allied justice. Throughout Southeast Asia, however, the Japanese arms handouts fortified native opposition to reimposition of Western colonial rule. Particularly in Malaya, Indonesia, and Indochina, bands of irregulars benefited from the Japanese largesse and figured prominently in guerrilla activity against the British, Dutch, and French during the first year after the war. Later these resistance movements became increasingly Communist-dominated. In Malaya the British fought the guerrillas to a standstill and managed a settlement on favorable terms.

1045

In Indonesia a former Japanese puppet, Sukarno, finally emerged trium
phant over the Dutch and proceeded to make his country, which was natur
ally the richest in Asia, into one of the least solvent. In Indochina, where the
Ho Chi Minh faction gained control of the independence movement, the
little brush fire on which the Japanese had poured fuel grew into a majo
conflagration which burned for more than a quarter of a century.

The great Japanese proponent of these last-ditch, cheat-the-enemy tactics
which did little good for Japan or for Asia but which did severely embar
rass the West, was Colonel Tsuji Masanobu. This angry young messiah o
Asia for the Asiatics, who had worked during the war with credentials from
Hirohito and Prince Mikasa and had directed the slaughter of thousands o
English and Chinese captives on Singapore and of Americans on Bataan
now got himself to a Thai monastery outside Bangkok. Disguised in the
saffron robes of a Buddhist priest, he sought to make his temple hideou
the headquarters for underground movements throughout Southeast Asia
His lines of communication, however, were poor from the start. They were
made worse when the British Army, which had just chased fleeing Japanese
units across Burma, went on to occupy "neutral" Thailand. In Octobe
1945, when British agents began to sniff the incense around Tsuji's monas
tic cell, Tsuji threw himself upon the mercy of Chiang Kai-shek's Blueshir
agents who were also operating in the Bangkok area. The Blueshirts smug
gled him away to Indochina and thence to Chungking where he finall
achieved his wartime ambition of talking to Chiang Kai-shek about the
future of Asia.

As a calling card to Chiang, Tsuji reproduced, annotated, or translate
a decade's worth of Japanese strategic planning against communism is
Manchuria and north China. Out of gratitude Chiang Kai-shek release
from prison a number of Japanese war criminal suspects and took on hal
a dozen of them to serve as advisors in his postwar struggle against Ma
Tse-tung. The chief of them, who became for a while one of Chiang'
intimates, was former General Okamura Yasuji, the third of the Three
Crows of Baden-Baden, on whom Hirohito had first relied as a nucleus fo
conspiracy in the 1920's.[1]

Tsuji remained in China with Chiang Kai-shek until February 1948 whe
it became clear that Mao Tse-tung and his Communist armies would win the
Chinese civil war. Then Chiang began to see less of his Japanese military

---

[1] Lieutenant General Nemoto Hiroshi, another veteran member of Hirohito's Arm
cabal, became a recruiting agent for Chiang on Taiwan. Still another, Lieutenan
General Sumita Raishiro, was made assistant to his fellow Tokyo military academ
graduate, the much abused governor of China's Shansi province, General Yen Hsi
shan. Some of those who fought for Chiang later went on to serve Emperor Hail
Selassie in Ethiopia. They were led from 1953 to 1962 by former Lieutenant Genera
Ikeda Sumihisa who, as Cabinet Planning Board member, had attended the histori
surrender meeting in Hirohito's bunker on the night of August 9, 1945.

advisors and his soldiers massacred many unrepatriated Japanese colonists on Taiwan. Taking these hints, Tsuji, in March, returned secretly to Japan. For the next four years he lived in a state of negotiated hiding, politely ignored by U.S. Allied Occupation forces, and supporting himself with books and articles about his checkered career. In 1952, as soon as the Occupation had ended, he was elected to the Diet where he made laws and continued to write books until 1961.

Then, at a time when Japanese news correspondents were first beginning to cover the war in Indochina and to look for exposés of Western military excesses, Dietman Tsuji visited Ho Chi Minh's capital of Hanoi as a feature writer for *Asahi*. While there he vanished. Ho's Viet Minh government could not explain his disappearance and never produced a body to show that he had died. Japanese veterans' associations, which had proved themselves diligent in bringing home ashes or bones of dead Japanese soldiers from islands in the Pacific, made no effort to recover Tsuji's remains.

Popular rumor in Japan has it that Tsuji did not die but continues his spectacular career in Hanoi. Some say he works there as an agent for the U.S. Central Intelligence Agency; others, that he is an assistant minister of propaganda, helping Japanese correspondents turn out tales of U.S. atrocities; still others, that he remains a stalwart of the prewar Japanese spy service directing Pan-Asian, anti-Western movements in Southeast Asia.

VENGEANCE OF THE VICTORS

Before Japan's surrender, Allied troops killed thousands of Japanese soldiers who, with a little trouble and risk, might have been taken prisoner. In a few isolated areas of reconquest, the killings continued even after the surrender. One of the largest butcheries took place under the aegis of Australian commanders in British North Borneo. There, 6,000 Japanese soldiers who had surrendered were told to stack their arms at Pensiangan and march 150 miles to Beaufort for internment. The previous year these same troops had wiped out many native villages on the Borneo coast suspected of having traffic with U.S. submarines. Now, therefore, vengeful surviving tribesmen were turned loose on the disarmed Japanese columns to enjoy a headhunt in which all but a few hundred of the 6,000 Japanese perished. Some of the Australians who stood by were ashamed of their complicity in the crime and later exposed it for the death march it was.

The atrocities committed by Allied infantrymen on the surrender battlefields could be half excused as products of war passion. More outrageous acts of injustice took place thereafter in courts of law where thinkers should have had time to think. Out of ignorance and lack of appreciation for Japanese politics, MacArthur's war-crime prosecutors sedulously ignored leaders like Tsuji, Prince Mikasa, and Emperor Hirohito and zealously tried, defamed, and hanged military officers who knew no morality but obedience to orders.

Immediately the war had ended, many of the pathetic psychopaths and syphilitic madmen who had been used in the administration of Japan's prisoner-of-war program were tracked down by Allied military policemen, identified by former Allied captives of Japan, and given rough-and-ready justice. Some were beaten during interrogation. Some were identified by face alone and tried under names which were not their own. Some were summarily put to death after hearings lasting less than an hour. By their own private admission, however, none of them was murdered in his cell and none of them was executed without cause.[2] Few tears were shed for them even in Japan, for they had been misfits in their own tolerant familial society.

Altogether about 5,000 Japanese were arrested for the calculated reprisal of state and individual acts of brutality which had taken the lives of over half a million Asiatics and Westerns. Most of those apprehended had committed their crimes against Western nationals who represented less than a tenth of the victims. About 4,000 of the suspects were brought to trial before U.S., British, Australian, and Chinese military tribunals which sat in scattered courtrooms from Guam to Rangoon and from Timor to Tokyo. Of the 4,000 some 800 were acquitted, some 2,400 were sentenced to three years or more of imprisonment, and 809 were put to death.[3] In addition several thousand Japanese captured by Russian troops in Manchuria died in Siberian labor camps.

[2] A committee of nine convicts in Tokyo's Sugamo Prison collected from fellow inmates all the complaints they could about Allied war-crime trial procedures throughout the Empire. They wrote up their findings in a mimeographed volume called *Sen pan Saiban no Jisso,* The Real Facts of the War-Crime Trials. It makes pallid reading beside the affidavits of former Allied P.O.W.'s written at about the same time. In Hong Kong former Japanese secret policemen were struck with rulers, threatened with their own torture tools, knocked down in the course of unwanted boxing lessons, and forced as punishment for food riots to walk barefoot on broken glass. In Singapore former concentration camp guards grew thin on two meals a day, each of which had to be eaten in five minutes. In Tokyo a U.S. interrogator named Dyer, attended by a Nisei interpreter, sometimes brandished a gun and sometimes massaged throats threateningly in efforts to make suspects sign confessions. No Japanese claimed that he had been hung by the thumbs, or filled with water and jumped on, or touched with lighted cigarettes at penis tip, or kept awake with drugs while fine slices of flesh were being cut from his hams, delicately sautéed and eaten before his eyes. These were charges which could be made and authenticated only by liberated Allied prisoners of war—prisoners, moreover, who had simply fought the Japanese, not tormented them in concentration camps.

[3] This figure, which includes 802 minor and seven major war criminals, is the Japanese count. I have had no luck in attempts to declassify complete war-criminal statistics in Washington, and I am told that complete figures for war-criminal processes held by the Nationalist Government in China are not available in any case.

HANGING THE TIGER

Although there was some inhumanity in the Allied handling of lesser
panese war criminals, it was not such as to excite much comment even
the Japanese vernacular press. What did arouse the censure and derision
f Japan was the ignorance which the West displayed in its initial handling
f so-called major war criminals.

The first "major" trials were held in Manila in late 1945 and early 1946.
hey began with the prosecution of General Yamashita. The Tiger of
Ialaya had drilled the Special Maneuver forces for the Strike South in
Ianchuria in 1941. He had bested General Percival in Malaya in 1942.
Ie had embarrassed General MacArthur by his skillful defense of Luzon,
ith pitifully equipped forces, in 1945.[4] These achievements were still fresh
the minds of the Japanese public when, on October 29, 1945, General
amashita was put on trial for his life as a war criminal. To many outside
bservers in the West as well as in Japan, it seemed that MacArthur was
dulging in petty vengeance. In reality MacArthur was simply playing
olitics. The Philippines, he felt, were his constituency. On arriving in
okyo, he had decided to spare Japan and rebuild it as a bulwark against
ommunism. If he did not treat Japan harshly, his Filipino constituents
ould feel cheated, and so he picked on General Yamashita to serve as a
capegoat whose trial would distract Filipinos during the early months of
e lenient Allied Occupation of Tokyo.

The Yamashita trial served its political purpose admirably. For over a
onth Filipino survivors of Japanese atrocities paraded themselves before
ve U.S. generals who sat in court-martial over Yamashita. Little girls
ulled up their frocks to show the court their multiple bayonet wounds.
lder girls testified to the circumstances of their rapes. No attempt was
ade by MacArthur's uniformed prosecutors to show that any of these
rutalities had been ordered by Yamashita. On the contrary the trial brought
ut clearly that the orders authorizing latitude in discipline for such acts had
manated from Tokyo and that Yamashita, locally, had tried in vain to
ountermand the hints of Imperial General Headquarters. The trial defi-
itely established that most of the atrocities of which the Filipinos com-
lained had been committed by the aristocratic Naval Special Landing Force

---

[4] If MacArthur's tactics in the Philippines in 1941–42 had been brilliant, Yama-
ita's in 1944–45 had been inspired. On the same terrain, against similar odds,
IacArthur had held out on Corregidor with a small fraction of his command for six
onths; Yamashita, with most of his starving troops, had held out in the Luzon
ountains for eight months and had only surrendered when ordered to do so by
irohito. Five thousand of Yamashita's soldiers had defended Corregidor, the island
astion at the mouth of Manila Bay, for eleven days in 1945 after the first landings
the island by U.S. forces. Four thousand of MacArthur's men had surrendered the
me island in 1942 less than twelve hours after the first Japanese had set foot on it.

which had intervened belatedly to fight for Manila in direct contraventio
of General Yamashita's orders. All Japanese witnesses agreed that Yama
shita, off in the hills, had no means even of communicating with the despe
ate sailors in Manila, much less of directing them.

During the Yamashita trial, half the Allied correspondents attached t
MacArthur's suite were in Manila, away from Tokyo. In their absence Ma
Arthur was having his first meetings with Hirohito and attempting, in th
words of his political staff chief, Brigadier General Courtney Whitney, t
"blackmail Japan" into acceptance of Occupation reforms. MacArthur pa
for this arrangement by receiving a poor press at the trial in Manila.

The New York Times's Robert Trumbull wrote: "All precedents in la
have been thrown out the window. . . . There are no regulations governin
the American War Crimes Commission, except those it makes for itse
and it has made very few."

Newsweek described spectators as "scandalized by the break with Angl
Saxon justice" and observed that "even third-hand hearsay is admitted a
evidence."

Henry Keyes of London's *Daily Express* at one point reported: "Yama
shita's trial continued today—but it isn't a trial. I doubt if it is even a hea
ing. Yesterday his name was mentioned once. Today it was not brought u
at all."

No doubt, as a seasoned Japanese commander, Yamashita could hav
been faulted for moral turpitude on a number of counts—though perhar
not in a court of law. He had, after all, assisted Hirohito in betraying th
Strike-North movement and in bringing about the February Mutiny in 193
which had enabled Hirohito to insist upon a Strike South. In 1938–39 h
had been chief of staff of the tough North China Army Group at a tim
when it had carried out more than one reprisal massacre of Chinese village
In his 1940 trip to Germany, he had stolen radar secrets from Hitler. B
training Strike-South forces in Manchuria in 1941, he had conspired wit
Hirohito in plans for aggressive war. During his term as commander i
Malaya he had failed to check the secret police in their killing of 5,000 c
Singapore's Chinese merchants.

The one offense for which Yamashita could not be faulted was inhuman
treatment of Westerners. In the non-Asiatic, Junker-trained half of hi
mind—the half he used in dealing with the West—he was a stickler fc
correct war conduct. He had incurred the displeasure of Tsuji and Hirohit
by disciplining officers of his command who permitted battlefield atrocitie
against British troops in the Malayan campaign of 1941–42. In Decembe
1944 he had taken pains—and expended gasoline—to take all U.S. wa
prisoners and internees out of the mountainous areas of Luzon aroun
Baguio where he planned to make his own last desperate stand. His restrain
ing influence had helped to prevent commandants of prison camps in th

hilippines from acting on suggestions from Tokyo Imperial Headquarters
> kill all U.S. prisoners rather than let them be liberated.

Nevertheless, MacArthur, in his studied ignorance of Japanese history
nd his desire to please and exploit the Emperor, chose to prosecute Yama-
hita for crimes of which he was far more innocent than most Japanese
ommanders. What followed put a lasting stain on the American escutcheon
nd created an embarrassing precedent which would be remembered by
.merican lawyers and jurists later after the My Lai incident during the Viet
[am war.[5]

As well as the rape of Manila, of which he was innocent, Yamashita was
harged with the command responsibility for the incineration of 150 Amer-
:an P.O.W.'s on Palawan Island in December 1944 and for a series of
prisal massacres against Filipino villages in the province of Batangas in
ne early months of 1945. The facts were, as brought out in the trial, that
'alawan was under command of the Tokyo-directed Air Navy at the time
f the atrocity, and that the Batangas reprisal raids were also ordered from
'okyo rather than from Yamashita's command post in the mountains. In
ddition, even Filipino witnesses admitted that the Batangas villages had
een centers of guerrilla activity. It was a recognized rule of civilized war-
are that guerrillas had no rights. To the American mind, however, this rule
id not justify the machine-gunning, burning, and bayoneting of women and
mall children, a crime against humanity which had indubitably been com-
itted several thousand times in Batangas under Yamashita's nominal
uthority.

The Batangas massacres supplied the one instance of possible criminal
egligence on Yamashita's part which might have justified singling him out
s an example from the whole hardened corps of Japanese Army officers.
Vhen the time came, however, for Yamashita to speak in his own defense,
e half closed his eyes under the bright lights of the courtroom and delivered
imself with simple eloquence:

> I did not hear at once of the events which took place nor did I have
> prior knowledge that they might take place. . . . I was under pressure
> night and day to plan, study and execute counterstrokes against superior
> American forces. . . . Nine days after my arrival in the Philippines I faced
> an overwhelming American tide moving on Leyte. . . . I was forced to
> confront superior U.S. forces with subordinates whom I did not know and

[5] In January 1971 Columbia University Professor Telford Taylor, a retired briga-
ier general who was U.S. chief counsel for the prosecution at the Nuremberg trials,
as reported by *The New York Times* as saying that, under the rule of the case of
eneral Yamashita, U.S. General William C. Westmoreland, former commander in
'iet Nam, "could be found guilty" of war crimes. Yamashita's former defense at-
orney, A. Frank Reel, protested to the *Times:* "Under the Yamashita rule as set down
y the United States Supreme Court, Westmoreland would be convicted."

with whose character and ability I was unfamiliar. As a result of the inefficiency of the Japanese army system, I could not unify my command; my duties were extremely complicated. The troops were scattered and Japanese communications were very poor. . . . I became gradually cut off from the situation and found myself out of touch. I believe under these conditions did the best job I could have done. . . . I did not order [any] massacres. . . . I put forth my best efforts to control my troops. If this was not enough, then I agree that somehow I should have done more. Some men might have been able to do more. However, I feel I did my best.

Despite the evidence at hand, and despite Yamashita's maverick position in domestic Japanese politics—a position which could have been explained to the court by any reasonably articulate Tokyo ward heeler—Yamashita's judges decided that a military commander, even when uninformed and countermanded by higher authority, should still remain responsible for the acts of his troops. It was a blithely irresponsible postwar decision which would later cause much distress to U.S. Army lawyers. It meant in effect that every senior, from general up to president or prime minister, was responsible for the orders obeyed by every junior. It meant that legal responsibility for war crimes could be adjudged, by reductio ad absurdum, to anyone in a chain of command regardless of his character, motives, and state of knowledge.

Yamashita's sentence of death was handed down in Manila on December 7, 1945, the fourth anniversary of Pearl Harbor. Yamashita's able defense lawyers, who were all volunteers from the legal section of MacArthur's own U.S. Army, appealed the sentence up to the U.S. Supreme Court. In January 1946 the court chose to hear the appeal but after a month of study declined to overrule the military tribunal which had sat in Manila. By a vote of five-to-two the U.S. Supreme Court justices avowed that a military commander did indeed have criminal responsibility for the misdeeds of his underlings, no matter how extenuating the circumstances. Justices Harlan Stone, Hugo Black, Felix Frankfurter, William Douglas, and Harold Burton assented in this argument. Justices Frank Murphy and Wiley Rutledge dissented. Murphy who penned the thirty-two-page dissent, in which Rutledge concurred, wrote with a special authority because he had some knowledge of the Orient, having once been U.S. High Commissioner in the Philippines:

. . . Never before have we tried and convicted an enemy general for actions taken during hostilities or otherwise in the course of military operations or duty—much less have we condemned one for failing to take action. . .

This petitioner was rushed to trial under an improper charge, given insufficient time to prepare an adequate defense, deprived of the benefits of some of the most elementary rules of evidence, and summarily sentenced to be hanged. In all this needless and unseemly haste there was no serious attempt to prove that he committed a recognized violation of the laws of war.

He was not charged with personally participating in acts of atrocity or with ordering or condoning their commission. Not even knowledge of the crimes was attributed to him. It was simply alleged that he unlawfully disregarded and failed to discharge his duty as commander to control the operations of the members of his command, permitting them to commit acts of atrocity. The recorded annals of warfare and the established principles of international law form not the slightest precedent for such a charge.

This indictment, in effect, permitted the Military Commission to make the crime whatever it willed, dependent upon its biased view as to the petitioner's duties and his disregard thereof. . . .

In our opinion such a procedure is unworthy of the traditions of our people or of the immense sacrifices they have made to advance the ideals of mankind. The high feelings of the moment will doubtless be satisfied but, in the sober afterglow, will come the realization of the boundless and dangerous implications of the procedure sanctioned today.

No one in a position of command in any army, from sergeant to general, can escape these implications. Indeed the fate of some future President of the United States and his Chiefs of Staff and military advisors may well have been sealed by this decision. . . .

That there were brutal atrocities inflicted upon the helpless Filipino people, to whom tyranny is no stranger, is undeniable. That just punishment should be meted out to all those responsible is also beyond dispute. But these factors do not justify the abandonment of our devotion to justice in dealing with a fallen enemy commander. . . .

Today the life of General Yamashita, a leader of enemy forces vanquished in the field of battle, is to be taken without regard to the due processes of law. There will be few to protest. But tomorrow the precedent here established can be turned against others.

A procession of judicial lynchings without due process of law may now follow. . . . A nation must not perish because, in its natural frenzy of the aftermath of war, it abandoned its central theme of the dignity of the human personality and due process of law.

When the text of Justice Murphy's dissent arrived in Tokyo in February, eneral MacArthur issued his own counterstatement on the Yamashita se:

I have reviewed the proceedings in vain search for some mitigating circumstances on his behalf. I can find none. . . . The soldier, be he friend or foe, is charged with the protection of the weak and unarmed. It is the very essence and reason for his being. When he violates this sacred trust, he not only profanes his entire cult but he threatens the very fabric of international society. . . . The transgressions . . . revealed by the trial are a blot upon the military profession, a stain upon civilization. . . . Particularly callous and purposeless was the sack of the ancient city of Manila, with its Christian population and countless historic shrines and monuments of culture and civilization which, with campaign conditions reversed, had previously been spared. . . .

No new or retroactive principles of law, either national or international are involved. The case is founded upon basic fundamentals and practice as immutable and as standardized as the most natural and irrefragable of social codes. The proceedings were guided by that primary rationale of all judicial purposes—to ascertain the full truth, unshackled by any artificial ties of narrow method or technical arbitrariness. The results are beyond challenge.

I approve the findings and sentence of the Commission and direct the Commanding General, Army Forces in the Western Pacific, to execute the judgment upon the defendant, stripped of uniform, decorations and other appurtenances signifying membership in the military profession.

The vehemence of MacArthur's assertions and the richness of his prose betrayed an ill-informed anxiety. However, his fears were needless. Yamashita's American lawyers appealed to the court of last resort, the White House, but the fledgling president, Harry Truman, declined to meddle in MacArthur's business. And so Yamashita was given a last meal of asparagus, bread, and beer. It was almost the tenth anniversary of the 1936 February Mutiny in which he had helped Hirohito to assert absolute power over the Japanese Army and point it south. After a brief nap, at 3:27 A.M. on February 23, 1946, General Yamashita climbed the scaffold of New Bilibid Prison, outside Manila. He bowed curtly north toward the far-away palace of the god-king. The trap sprang and he was hanged until he was dead.

CUTTING OFF THE NOSE

As soon as sentence had been passed on General Yamashita on December 7, 1945, the military court in Manila began proceedings against General Honma, the "linguist with the red nose" who had translated the first pirated copy of the Lytton Report on Manchuria in 1932. Honma was tried for having been over-all commander in the Philippines when the Bataan Death March took place in 1942. Somewhat guardedly Japanese witnesses at the trial brought out the true state of Honma's command during the Death March, revealing that it had been pre-empted by higher authority vested in staff officers from Tokyo and Singapore. The U.S. generals who sat as judges discounted this testimony as a weak excuse. From their own experience in the U.S. Army they could not imagine how colonels like Tsuji could usurp the command of a lieutenant general like Honma.

Honma's American defense lawyers themselves did not appreciate the intervention of imperial influence in Honma's command business. As a result they relied in their presentation on an ill-informed argument that really was an excuse; an argument which they could substantiate only through the opinions of some Japanese journalists and civilian bureaucrats; an argument to the effect that no orders had been issued for the Death March and that it had developed as an unpremeditated act of passion on the part of vengeful

Japanese soldiers. The five U.S. military judges could see only evasion and prevarication in such an argument, for they knew that the Death March had continued for a week, that verbal orders had been issued for it, and that at one point its stumbling columns had passed within a mile of General Honma's headquarters. And so, as rational men, they sentenced Honma to execution before a firing squad.

Honma's American lawyers exerted themselves to postpone execution of sentence for three months and to appeal the case, once again, to the U.S. Supreme Court. Honma's chief counsel, John H. Skeen, Jr., pleaded that it had been "a highly irregular trial, conducted in an atmosphere that left no doubt as to what the ultimate outcome would be." As before, however, the court decided to let the Manila verdict stand, and Associate Justice Frank Murphy saw fit again to file a powerful dissent. "This nation's very honor," he wrote, "as well as its hope for the future, is at stake. Either we conduct such a trial as this in the noble spirit and atmosphere of our Constitution or we abandon all pretense to justice, let the ages slip away, and descend to the level of revengeful blood purges."

Justice Murphy's persistent and eloquent objections stung MacArthur. When Honma's lawyers appealed to him for clemency after the Supreme Court decision, MacArthur, on March 21, 1945, issued a lengthy explanation of his reasons for executing the verdict:

> I am again confronted with the repugnant duty of passing final judgment on a former adversary in a major military campaign. The proceedings show the defendant lacked the basic firmness of character and moral fortitude essential to officers charged with the high command of military forces in the field. No nation can safely trust its martial honor to leaders who do not maintain the universal code which distinguishes between those things that are right and those things which are wrong.
>
> [Here MacArthur interpolated a fine tribute to the fighting achievements of the Battling Bastards of Bataan. He continued:]
>
> No trial could have been fairer than this one. . . . Insofar as was humanly possible the actual facts were fully presented to the commission. There were no artifices of technicality which might have precluded the introduction of full truth in favor of half-truth, or caused the slanting of half-truth to produce the effect of non-truth, thereby warping and confusing the tribunal into an insecure verdict. . . . Those who oppose such honest method can only be a minority who either advocate arbitrariness of process above factual realism, or who inherently shrink from the stern rigidity of capital punishment. . . .
>
> If the defendant does not deserve his judicial fate, none in jurisdictional history ever did. There can be no greater, more heinous or more dangerous crime than the mass destruction, under guise of military authority or military necessity, of helpless men, incapable of further contribution to war effort. A failure of law process to punish such acts of criminal enormity would threaten the very fabric of world society. . . .

On final appeal President Truman again did not presume to stand in the way of MacArthur, and on April 3, 1946, General Honma fell before a U.S. firing squad. In his final letter to his children he exhorted them to look for the "right direction" in life rather than to follow the customary direction of bringing flowers to his grave. "Do not miss the right course," he wrote. "This is my very last letter."

Since "our forces were being demobilized in the Philippines," explained MacArthur later, "the remaining United States cases of this kind were tried by the International Tribunal in Tokyo."

TOKYO TRIAL DEFENDANTS

In the Manila trials MacArthur unwittingly rid Hirohito of two subjects who had differed with Imperial General Headquarters in 1942. Yamashita had insisted upon decent treatment of British war prisoners in Singapore and then had predicted dire results unless Japan followed up her initial triumphs with an invasion of Australia. It was Honma's sin that he had seen no need for haste in taking Bataan and then that he had pleaded for an enlightened and humane administration of the Philippines.[6] MacArthur, of course, knew only that Yamashita and Honma had caused the Supreme Commander Allied Powers (SCAP) much unfavorable publicity during the war and after it; and that the State Department wanted future trials of Class A Japanese war criminals to be conducted with more care. For the Tokyo trials of Japan's wartime government leaders, therefore, MacArthur spared neither time nor expense.

Since, by the custom of their society, Japanese leaders always solicited the advice of subordinates and sought out supporters who would be willing to share responsibility for decisions which might go wrong, it was no mean task for MacArthur's war-crime investigators to compile a roster of major war criminals. In Hirohito's retinue there were few foolhardy blusterers who could stand beside Hitler's gang in Germany and be called most blameworthy for leading Japan to war. Selection of Class A war criminals was made doubly difficult by the restriction that neither the Emperor, nor members of his family, nor anyone who would implicate them should be indicted. Finally, as pointed out in Chapter 3, defendants for the trials were selected only after much consultation and negotiation with the palace.

Given the peculiar circumstances, MacArthur's prosecutors performed

---

[6] His efforts at leniency were regularly countermanded by Imperial General Headquarters. To cite an instance, he had Western missionaries in Baguio released from internment camp on January 29, 1942. A day later fresh orders arrived from Tokyo and all but a dozen of the 170-odd libérés were reinterned. I was fortunate in that my family was among those left at liberty, on a technicality, for eight months, as a gesture to save General Honma's face.

as well as they could. They produced a list of defendants which included several of the commoners who had participated most actively in Hirohito's imperial conspiracy. It excluded all but two of a number of suggested candidates who had been at odds with the Throne. These two were little General Matsui, the scapegoat of the Nanking rape, and Matsuoka, the noisy American-bred diplomat who had put on a lonely wheeling-dealing show with Hitler in 1941 in a last vain attempt to make Hirohito consummate the plans of the Strike-North faction. The list even contained the name of one man, Dr. Okawa Shumei, the spy-propagandist, whom palace chamberlains were anxious to keep out of the witness box. It would have brought to court two more of the same sort except that Prince Konoye and Hirohito's former chief aide-de-camp, the Strike-North General Honjo, chose to disbar themselves on the eve of their arrests by committing suicide. The remaining defendants could be counted upon to keep the secrets of Japan's ruling inner circle.

In all, twenty-eight defendants were chosen for the Tokyo trials. The oldest of them was Baron Hiranuma, the seventy-nine-year-old lawyer for right-wing interests who had returned to Hirohito's side in the final agony of the bunker and the surrender. Hiranuma was a member of Emperor Meiji's generation and a crony of old Chief of Staff Prince Kanin who had reportedly died in hospital "of hemorrhoids" on May 21, 1945.

Ten of the twenty-eight defendants ranged in age from seventy-two down to sixty-four and belonged to the in-between generation of Emperor Taisho. They had been brought into the palace circle by Taisho's contemporaries, Field Marshal Prince Nashimoto and Fleet Admiral Prince Fushimi.[7] The remaining seventeen defendants were all either members or satellites of Hirohito's own Big Brotherhood. They broke roughly into three groups: Army officers who were contemporaries and close associates of Hirohito's fifty-eight-year-old uncles, Prince Higashikuni and Prince Asaka;[8] bureau-

---

[7] The Taisho group included General Matsui and diplomat Matsuoka. Its other members were General Minami Jiro, seventy-two, the war minister at the time of the Manchurian Incident; General Araki Sadao, sixty-nine, the canny, compromising, golden-tongued leader of the Strike-North faction; Admiral Nagano Osami, sixty-nine, the Pearl Harbor chief of the Navy General Staff; former Prime Minister Hirota Koki, sixty-eight, the Black Dragon Society graduate who had headed the government for Hirohito after the 1936 mutiny; Field Marshal Hata Shunroku, sixty-seven, a stalwart of the Throne, who complained that he could not hear to answer questions because he had been the "Western Army" commander, headquartered in Hiroshima, when the bomb clapped over his air-raid shelter; General Koiso Kuniaki, sixty-six, the March Plotter and post-Tojo prime minister in 1944; General Umezuo Yoshijiro, sixty-four, the chief of the General Staff at the time of surrender; and finally Togo Shigenori, also sixty-four, who had been foreign minister both at the time of surrender and of declaration of war.

[8] The military men included Tojo's Navy Minister Shimada Shigetaro, sixty-three; Baden-Baden Reliable Doihara Kenji, the "Lawrence of Manchuria," also sixty-three;

crats who had gone to school with Hirohito's fifty-six-year-old foster
brother Marquis Kido; [9] and political thugs and polemicists from the coterie
of the late fifty-four-year-old Prince Konoye.[10]

The care which had gone into the selection of these defendants—these
twenty-eight men who were to bear the whole guilt of Japan's pride, greed,
and cruelty—was justified by their conduct in court. They lived in Sugamo
Prison, wearing G.I. cast-off clothing and eating G.I. rations throughout the
two and a half years of the trial. Their families on the outside were shunned
by neighbors and suffered poverty, hunger, and cold. Nevertheless they went
into court each day and submitted patiently to the alien intricacies of the
quasi-judicial, quasi-political process which had been arranged for them.
They hid the violence and arrogance which had characterized them in years
gone by. They read books of philosophy and religion in their cells and listened attentively to the translated, fragmentary half-truths brought out
against them.

The defeated Tojo, who had failed in his attempt to commit suicide at the
time of his arrest, regained popular Japanese respect by setting his fellow
defendants an example. He listened to every word of his accusers and caught
American prosecution lawyers in a thousand ideological contradictions,
political hypocrisies, and outright errors of fact. He did so with such spirit
and back-biting wit that even chief prosecutor Keenan developed a grudging respect for him. He might be the bureaucratic accomplice in much
rapine but he was undeniably a man of self-respect and presence of mind.
When his patriotic burden as scapegoat became too heavy for his family to
bear, he even had the freedom of spirit to suggest—as described in Chapter
3—that he had ordered no crimes without Hirohito's authorization. As soon
as Hirohito saw to it that the Tojo family was better provided for, Tojo
retracted his hint, resumed his difficult duty, and carried it on to the gallows.

sixty-two-year-old General Tojo, the self-proclaimed villain of the war, who as combined prime minister, war minister, and chief of staff had finally shouldered all the
responsibility; Baden-Baden Reliable Itagaki Seishiro, conquistador of Manchuria,
sixty-one; the Strike-South ideologist and former Army spy, Okawa Shumei, sixty;
wartime ambassador to Berlin Lieutenant General Oshima Hiroshi, also sixty; Tojo's
vice minister of war, Kimura Heitaro, fifty-eight; the Army's ubiquitous economic
expert, Suzuki Tei-ichi, fifty-seven; one of Suzuki's henchmen, Muto Akira, who had
ended the war as Yamashita's chief of staff in the Philippines, fifty-four; and finally
Tojo's wartime Military Affairs Bureau chief, Sato Kenryo, only fifty.

[9] In addition to Kido himself the only men tried from this group were wartime
Finance Minister Kaya Okinori, fifty-seven, and two fifty-eight-year-old diplomats,
Shigemitsu Mamoru of the Peace and Strike-South factions, and Shiratori Toshio,
one-time Big Brother who had gone astray by espousing the cause of the Strike North.

[10] After Prince Konoye took poison, his contribution to the conspiracy was recognized by the indictment of just two of his men: Hoshino Naoki, the chief of his prewar Cabinet Planning Board, fifty-four, and retired Colonel Hashimoto Kingoro,
fifty-six, who had sunk the U.S.S. *Panay* and gone on to head the youth movement
in Konoye's mass party, the Imperial Rule Assistance Association.

Sturdy vassals though they might be, the twenty-eight defendants at the Tokyo trials caused palace chamberlains many restless nights. Diplomat Matsuoka and General Matsui, in particular, had no reason to feel beholden to the Throne. Fortunately Matsuoka, who professed Christianity, died of tuberculosis at the start of the trial, and the half-senile, inarticulate General Matsui never publicly wavered in his devout loyalty. Potentially more dangerous was the undisciplined, unprincipled intellectual Okawa Shumei, headmaster of the palace indoctrination school in the 1920's, geopolitical apologist for the Strike South, and go-between in a dozen plots and assassinations. Prime ministers and commanders of armies might be trusted to go to their deaths quietly, but Okawa, the scrivener, even with the best of intentions, might say more than he should.

So it was that Okawa, alone of the defendants, was helped to cop a plea. Whether American complicity or gullibility most figured in his escape from justice has not been established, but the extraordinary facts of his case are on record and have not been disputed. In May 1946, during the reading of the indictment at the beginning of the International Military Tribunal for the Far East, Okawa fixed a foolish smile on his face, unbuttoned his shirt, and gradually caught the tittering attention of the gallery by scratching his chest. When the shirt slipped off one shoulder, Chief Justice Webb ordered the sentries guarding the dock to see that the prisoner kept himself presentable. Okawa humbly promised to behave, but a few minutes later he began again to undress. An American M.P. was stationed behind him to restrain his arms and preserve decorum. He fell quiet for a few hours. Then, abruptly, when the M.P. had relaxed his vigilance, Okawa rolled up his copy of the charges made against him, leaned forward, and resoundingly slapped the shaven pate of Tojo who sat in front of him. Hauled from the courtroom, he told reporters:

> Tojo is a fool. I'm for democracy. . . . America is not democracy. . . . She is Demo crazy [which in Japanese meant demonstration crazy]. . . . I am a doctor of law and medicine. I haven't eaten in seventy days. You see, I eat air. . . . I am the next emperor of Japan. . . . I killed Tojo. . . . I killed him to save the reputation of his respectable family.

It was Okawa's last day in court. For weeks thereafter he regaled American and Japanese doctors at Tokyo University Hospital with accounts of visitations he had from such as Emperor Meiji, Edward VII of England, and President Woodrow Wilson. Mohammed the Prophet, he said, was a particularly helpful familiar as he and Mohammed were collaborating on a new Japanese version of the Koran.

With coaching from Japanese doctors and some help from Japanese laboratory technicians, Okawa succeeded in persuading the American doctors who examined him that he was suffering from tertiary syphilis, or according to the official diagnosis, "psychosis with syphilitic meningo-encephalitis (general paresis)." This was an irreversible condition leading usually to insane incompetence and swift death. After consultation with chief prosecutor Keenan, the American doctors allowed the court to be advised that Okawa could not "differentiate between right and wrong" and lacked "the ability to understand the nature of the proceedings against him." He was remanded to the care and comfort of a Japanese sanatorium. There he sat out the rest of the war crimes trials writing a 400-page "introduction to religion." When the judicial proceedings were over, he was released to die. Instead he promptly recovered, published several lucid books, and convinced all his friends that his syphilitic insanity had been a hoax. He finally did die of a stroke in December 1957 at the age of seventy-one.

TOKYO TRIAL RESULTS

Doctor Okawa was widely known to have been the rogue mediating between the palace and rightist thugs in all the plots which had intimidated the nation early in the 1930's. The misplaced medical mercy shown to him confirmed the automatic presumption of the Japanese public that the war crimes trials would dispense more politics and propaganda than justice. To members of Japan's web society it was incredible that precisely twenty-eight of all the hundreds of retainers who had served the Throne in the previous two decades could be singled out as the master criminals most responsible for Japan's misfortunes. The International Military Tribunal was accepted, therefore, as just one of the many ceremonies of American democracy—of *demo-kurushi* or demo-suffering, as it was called—which would have to be lived through.

As the trials continued, however, many Japanese who had never traveled abroad were impressed by the evidence produced of Japanese savagery overseas. Bitterness at the superficiality of Allied fact finding, the inappropriate political biases of Allied historical interpretation, and the manifest self-righteousness of Allied law began to be tempered by sober horror at what Japan had done. The realization grew in Japan that the nation was convalescing from a sickness of evil and that both Japan and the world at large were better off because of her defeat.

Soldiers and diplomats who had traveled in previous years through the Co-Prosperity Sphere, and who had recoiled at what they saw, made sure that the public acknowledged the national guilt. Indeed Foreign Minister Shigemitsu, reporting to the palace after hearing MacArthur speak at the surrender-signing ceremony aboard the U.S.S. *Missouri* on September 2 1945, asked Hirohito to his face:

"Would it have been possible for us, if we had won, to embrace the vanquished with such magnanimity?"

Hirohito accepted the snide rebuke with a sigh and murmured, "Naturally would have been different."

Throughout the trials recognition of the fact that the kamikaze spirit was ιe of death and that the chewing-gum spirit of the G.I. was one of life ·adually seeped down into the Japanese mind. As the trials neared an end 1948, a Japanese newspaperman, reporting the consensus he found on ιe streets of Tokyo, observed: "If Japan had won we would be using slave bor to build bigger pyramids than the pharaohs. Instead we are erecting ·w factories with American bulldozers."

Having apologized many times individually and collectively for the wrongs ιey had done, most Japanese buttonholed by newspapermen in 1948 ex-:cted a reciprocal understanding and mercy from the International Mili-ry Tribunal in its verdict. Earlier, at the start of the trials, when U.S. οops had just created a favorable impression by their forbearance, goodwill ιd high spirits, MacArthur could have proclaimed almost any public figure Japan a war criminal and executed him out of hand, without being ques-οned. By 1948, however, the long historical exegesis of the trials had :monstrated beyond doubt what Japanese newspaper readers had always ιown: that Tojo and his colleagues in the dock were a sample of the war ιilty and could only be punished as a symbolic sacrifice to the angry ιirits of those whom Japan had wronged.

Accordingly, when the courtroom hearings ended and Doihara, Hirota, ιgaki, Kimura, Matsui, Muto, and Tojo were sentenced to hang, almost ι Japanese pronounced the judgment *hidoi,* harsh.

During their final months in Sugamo Prison, all seven of the condemned en, in obedience to samurai custom, gave clippings of their hair and nails · prison-visiting kin. These relics were already enshrined and revered on mily prayer shelves when—at a minute after midnight on the morning of ecember 23, 1948—the trap opened under Tojo and he fell to his death. is and the six other bodies were cremated and secretly disposed of by .S. prison wardens.

A Japanese lawyer who claimed to have had access to the funerary ovens ·ought scrapings of ash to General Matsui's family, saying that they were οrtions of the genuine remains of the hanged men. The lawyer's tiny boxes ' gray dust were buried on the Matsui estate behind the bronzed goddess of ercy, sculptured partly out of Yangtze River mud, at the shrine of morse, up on the hillside overlooking Atami and the sparkling waters of ιgami Bay where Hirohito pursued his marine biology. All the families of ιe deceased and thousands of other elder Japanese quickly accepted the lics as genuine and began to pay regular pilgrimages to the shrine with ·ayers that the mistakes of the war would never be repeated.

To most of the pilgrims the spirits on the hill were not martyrs but editors. Japan and the Emperor, it was felt, owed them an apology. They

had died to satisfy good American intentions. They should have b
avenged but it was impossible to take revenge on good intentions. Nea
of kin were forced to admit to the war criminal shades that the zeal
kamikaze spirit had been abandoned, that samurai ideals were dead,
that, for the time being, Japan must play the buffoon and lie low.

IMPERIAL CARETAKERS

Yoshida Shigeru, the former Peace Faction leader who had become
prime minister of occupied Japan, described his people's plight as "
comic helplessness of being Japanese." By this wry remark he meant c
that, during his term of office, all native Japanese political activity hac
be suspended and all talents devoted to circumventing or softening
reform directives, the "SCAPINS," which daily isued from MacArth
headquarters to be "Potsdammed" through the Diet onto the nation's
books. Except for a year-long interregnum in 1947–48 of well-contro
lower-class Socialist government, which embarrassed MacArthur but fa
to deter him from execution of his programs, Yoshida remained in cha
of the "comic helplessness" from May 1946 to December 1954.

In common kamikaze frustration and guilt at being alive, the Japan
were politically unified in defeat as they had not been in victory. No facti
of Army, Navy, and civilian bureaucrats were left to bicker with one
other. All were hungry together. And so, despite the best ideological fe
lizers which MacArthur could plow in, only one middle-of-the-furr
party would grow in Japan, and that was Yoshida's, the Liberal-Democr
Party. It made Japan a more perfect one-party state than Prince Konoye I
ever been able to achieve through his gang-sponsored, secret-police-s
ported Imperial Rule Assistance Association. The Liberal-Democratic lal
however, covered a multitude of sects and schisms. It included both the
Constitutionalist Party, the *Seiyukai,* and the *Seiyukai*'s loyal oppositi
the progressive, imperial anti-Constitutionalist *Minseito.*

Beneath its bland surface Yoshida's party was still fundamentally flav
by the same kind of disagreements which had divided the Strike-North a
Strike-South groups in prewar Japan. In the warrior caste of the samu
many were individualists and traditionalists who persisted in seeing mode
ization and collectivism as the main threats to Japan's heritage. They ma
tained the Strike-North position that the Russian ideology from across
western sea was the most subversive for Japan. The less specialized, I
military-minded nobles of Court rank, above the samurai, continued to
the main danger toward the east in the land of Commodore Perry. It v
there that people were controlled by financial rather than family status,
wages rather than religion, by the chance to earn ease rather than
opportunity to gain salvation through service to a lord. Individualism for
working classes was still anathema to Court nobles, and Russian comr

nism continued to seem far less destructive of the Japanese social fabric of family allegiances than did the anti-socialism of American Protestants.

In the postwar era, as before the war, the scions of samurai outnumbered those of Court nobles. In 1954, when the Occupation had come to an end and the Korean War had restored economic health to Japan, political strife awakened within the Liberal-Democratic Party. The majority unseated Yoshida and replaced him with Hatoyama Ichiro, the Strike-North partisan of General Araki and Prince Saionji, who as education minister from 1931 to 1934 had led the attack upon Prince Konoye's professorial imperial apologists, the organ theorists.

Between December 10, 1954, and December 23, 1956, under constant attack from the scholars and publicists whom he had once offended, Hatoyama formed and dissolved three Cabinets. He had the votes but not the influence to stay in office. As historians, since the Occupation, have not been able to draw upon subpoenaed diaries, the mechanics of Hatoyama's downfall remain hidden. Since his retirement, however, Japan has been ruled again by prime ministers possessing Hirohito's confidence: first by Kishi Nobusuke, the former minister of commerce in the wartime Tojo Cabinet, then by Ikeda Hayato, former finance minister in the Yoshida and Kishi Cabinets, then by Kishi's younger brother, Sato Eisaku.[11]

Sato and Kishi, who have dominated the ruling Liberal-Democratic Party since 1957, hail from the same south-Choshu area of fishing villages and belong to the same network of impecunious samurai families as did Emperor Meiji's great Constitutionalist prime minister, Ito Hirobumi. As Ito's heirs, they hark back to the Meiji era and command allegiances which antecede pro and anti Constitutionalist or Strike-North, Strike-South factionalism. Under their tutelage Japan has pursued the traditional foreign policy of Ito and the Constitutionalists: expansion abroad by peaceful means only—by economic opportunism, by cultural promotion, and by not so much as a ripple of military muscle.

FACTORY POWER

At the end of the war Japanese felt that American production of aircraft carriers and airplanes had overwhelmed the homeland despite the superior spiritual prowess of Japanese warriors. As a family they resolved that Japan would never go to war again without overwhelming material strength. The peaceful policies of Kishi and Sato have started Japan moving toward such strength—moving with a swiftness that is the wonder of the economists of other nations.

Japan has passed France, Great Britain, and West Germany to become, economically, the world's third most powerful state. In the lands and

---

[11] Kishi was born a Sato and adopted by the Kishi family. His father, conversely, had been born a Kishi and adopted by the Sato family.

islands which Hirohito once hoped to dominate by force, Japanese trade
reigns supreme. Filipinos, Indonesians, and even Australians depend on
Japanese salesmen for most of the manufactured goods they import and
on Japanese buyers for most of the raw materials they export.

Japan has become a great factory. Pylons strut across her green hills. The
concrete of superhighways lies heavy on her paddy lands. A belch of
smoke, which darkens the poetic heart of the samurai, threatens to blot
out the sacred sun. Opinions differ as to the outcome. Some Western economic analysts say that problems of pollution will ultimately halt Japan's
growth. Others say that Prime Minister Sato and the board of what is
anxiously called Japan Inc. have simply not yet dealt with pollution. Until
1965 the per-capita income of Japanese was held below $500 a year.
Then, in the next five years, when there began to be a little room in
Japan's factory building program to pay the builders, the per-capita income abruptly trebled to over $1,500 a year. If pollution has to be re-
duced, it may be that workers will temporarily go without raises again
while money is being invested in smoke and waste control.

Barring any sudden breakdown in Japan's well-collected mercantile
genius, Western economists agree that by 1980 the Japanese gross national
product will exceed that of the Soviet Union and before the year 2000 that
of the United States.

Neither the half-free American economy nor the rigidly planned Soviet
economy has been able to match the Japanese growth rate except fitfully.
Bureaucratic shortsightedness recurrently bogs down Soviet booms in bottlenecks and surpluses. U.S. spurts peak out in runaway opportunism, inflation, and technological unemployment. Japan, by comparison, has shown
an uncanny ability, through a spirit of internal co-operation and cohesion,
to damp out economic fluctuations. Japanese industrialists have regularly
worked together for the sake of the nation while still competing for the
sake of themselves. Japanese workers have regularly foregone spendthrift
consumption in favor of saving and have worked long hours for fringe
benefits rather than quick purchasing power.

Japan's astonishing economic growth in the 1950's and 1960's is no
new or passing phenomenon. It is simply a resumption of Japan's equally
astonishing development from 1867 to 1944. The American B-29's caused
a temporary setback, costing a decade of hard work, but from the grand
view of the economist, Japan, since she started from a state of medieval
technology and monetary bankruptcy in 1867, has continued to increase
her wealth more steadily and rapidly than any other power—and this
despite her cramped area, dense population, and acute lack of natural
resources.

The secret of Japan's achievement has been her stern, hierarchic family
system of government, combining as it does many of the most galvanizing
features of individualism as well as collectivism. Young Japanese have

regularly shown great initiative, secure in the belief that parents will excuse and a supreme parent, the Emperor, will sanction their acts. Old Japanese, even the most rich and greedy, have conferred, compromised, and worked together like brothers. Simple methods, realistic goals, and a sense of mission—of "God with us"—continue to inspire even the hypermodern Japan of the 1970's. As a result its bullet trains run on time and its videotape recorders work smoothly. Its public libraries and sewage systems are few, but its exchequers overflow with the hardest currencies of international exchange and its super-cities contain almost no slums.[12]

Prime Minister Sato personally presides over Japan's Supreme Trade Council on which the wizened, hard-eyed bankers and industrialists of Japan sit to agree upon annual national goals and division of world markets. The great cartels, which were officially broken up by MacArthur, continue to act as well-integrated units. The directors of the fragment companies of the Mitsui combine, for instance, all occupy the same building, consult with one another over private phone lines and across private corridors, and remain loyal to the dictates of the Mitsui family.

The Sato government holds all the big-business families together in a super-family. It grants them preferential credit, tax incentives, and insurance in all their overseas investments. Inter-cartel meetings of managers are held regularly, under government auspices, to agree upon price-fixing and sales propaganda in foreign lands. Japan's growing foreign-aid program is carefully discussed with export division managers so that it will dovetail with over-all economic planning, creating long-term credits and raw-material processing capacity in areas abroad where Japanese traders see market potential. The Japanese government owns a profit-making corporation called JETRO which supplies overseas advertising to Japanese firms and sells them information about favorable foreign investment opportunities. Sato's Supreme Trade Council not only helps to set the annual goals of Japanese economic expansion but also advises on the means by which the cartels will be most willing to achieve the goals.

Since the war the great Japanese merchant families, who a century ago were just above untouchables in caste, have all been privileged to form ties of marriage with the Court nobility or with the imperial family itself. Today the men who sit on Sato's council consider themselves aristocrats. They have been let into the "inner circle" as they never were before the war. They are now part of the elite in the most nearly tribal society which

---

[12] Broad areas of Tokyo, Osaka, and a few other large cities are covered with crowded shacks which appear to the casual tourist to be no better than slum dwellings. Nor are they except in one important psychological respect. Each shack has a tiny garden a yard or two square, and almost all the inmates of the shacks have bank or postal savings accounts. Almost none of the slum dwellers are on relief and few of them are even supported by relatives. Only in the 1960's did the municipal governments of Tokyo and Osaka begin to acknowledge that their shanty towns presented any social problem at all.

has adapted to the upheavals of the last two thousand years. As such they have adopted the imperial mission which is to defend Japan's ghostly heritage from molestation by the outside world.

MacArthur hoped to change the religious mission of the Japanese upper classes by his benign occupation of Japan. But he elevated Yoshida and other leading enemies of the United States to high office and he persecuted the less well-born enemies of Russia, even putting the political leader of the Strike-North movement, General Araki, in prison as a war criminal. As Prime Minister Yoshida observed: "The Occupation was hampered by its lack of knowledge, and even more so perhaps by its generally happy ignorance of the amount of requisite knowledge it lacked."

THE SILENT EMPEROR

In developing his blind spot toward the Emperor, MacArthur accepted views handed down to him by Ambassador Grew and other prewar diplomats. He then refused to consider and, by suppressing evidence, prevented others from considering, the truth about the Emperor as it might have been revealed in captured documents. That a mere mortal could fill the role of god, leaving unsatisfied the need for a larger, omnipotent, omnipresent Being, exceeded the imagination of MacArthur and many other Christian thinkers.

MacArthur was shrewd in seeing Hirohito as an indispensable helpmate in reforming Japan. MacArthur was shortsighted in believing that Hirohito could be emasculated by forgiveness and forgetfulness. It did not hurt Hirohito to have underlings take the blame for him, for that was customary in Japan at any time. It did hurt MacArthur, however, to make light of Western science and justice by strapping blinders on the International Military Tribunal for the Far East.

Had MacArthur been wiser and stronger he might have insisted that the trial of minor war criminals—of concentration camp commandants and secret-police torturers—was enough, and that the punitive sentiments of politicians in Washington and Canberra should not be extended to policy-shaping members of Hirohito's retinue. Indeed, if he had been supremely wise and strong, he might have insisted that the roughly $9 million spent on trying Tojo and his colleagues be used instead for a nonpunitive inquiry into the mechanics of leadership which had led Japan to offend the world. Truth, in short, could have been pursued, could have been put on record, and could have provided the Japanese people with more reliable clues to self-government than any of the fragile American relationships with Japanese aristocrats which MacArthur left behind him.

Now that MacArthur has passed into history, events have left Hirohito still warmly enshrined in the hearts of his tribe. A majority of Japanese still feel the imperial taboo and speak of their ruler only with great diffidence. Some politicians are willing to comment snidely upon Hirohito in private, but they do so more to suggest their noble birth and cosmopolitan independence than because they feel any irreverence. Some plebeian Marxists make theoretical statements against the institution of the Throne but seldom dare to attack Hirohito personally except through veiled, technically inoffensive hints. For instance, one of the most scurrilous booklets of anti-imperial propaganda, which may be bought at left-wing bars in Tokyo, is a handsomely boxed pamphlet containing ninety-nine identical pictures of Hirohito, looking his coldest, most sneering, and least lovable. Not a word illuminates this protest except a title and a designation of publisher: "Portrait of our Imperial Parent; Imperial Household Ministry." [13]

Since the end of the war, Hirohito has said little and allowed his public image to be rewrought by competent professional image-makers. In the early days of the Occupation, Prince Higashikuni, the prime minister for the surrender, apologized to the nation for unsuccessful imperial family leadership. Hirohito followed the apology with a tour of provincial areas. It was widely reported that when one of MacArthur's aides had tried to shake his hand he bowed graciously and said, "Let's do it this way, in the Japanese style, without touching." On his tour, however, he adopted the new American style and shook hands vigorously with his native Japanese constituents. Those who made contact with the divine hand were awed; a few of them were startled into attempts at conversation. Hirohito became famous for the unvarying words of his noncommittal response: *Ah so desuka?* "Oh, is that so?"

The Japanese masses supposed that in his bows and handshakes Hirohito was wearing a hair shirt before the world and drinking gall. The symbol of Hirohito's humiliation came to be the famous photograph showing MacArthur in casual khaki standing head and shoulders above the newly nondeified god-king in his seedy wartime morning clothes. Whether Hirohito felt his shame as keenly as others felt it for him may be doubted. In any case he endured it with good spirits and benefited by the fact that all Japanese felt sorry for him. Never before had he occupied such a warm place in the affection of his subjects.

Hirohito continued to do public penance throughout the seven years of the Occupation. In 1946 he was forced to dissolve the imperial family holding company and give most of his fortune back to the people. Throughout the war crimes trials, he read every word of testimony and legal

---

[13] Supporters of the Throne are sensitive about Hirohito's appearance. In 1968 a cosmopolitan young Japanese publisher, the son of one of the diplomats who represented Hirohito at the signing of surrender on the battleship *Missouri* in 1945, read a part of the work in hand with a view to having it translated for the home market. He reached the description of the Emperor at the August 9, 1945, conference (in Chapter 2) and slapped the manuscript down in anger. "This book," he said, "will never be published in Japan. You cannot describe the Emperor so."

wrangling and occasionally asked his courtiers to insert corrections in the record through Court-controlled witnesses. In 1947, after many unavailing evasions, he was compelled to let his uncles and cousins be demoted to the rank of commoners. In 1948, when sentence was about to be passed on Tojo and the other major war criminals, he threatened again, as he had at the start of the trials, to abdicate. MacArthur made concessions in other matters but refused to interfere with the judgment of the Allied jurists presiding on the tribunal. Having gained a little leverage, Hirohito, after all, sent MacArthur a pledge that he would not abdicate.

Having made his gestures of penitence and resistance, Hirohito took a new suit into his wardrobe for the first time since the war and settled down to live out the last three years of the American Occupation in apparent preoccupation with his hobby of marine biology. When the Occupation ended in 1952 he gradually and guardedly resumed a part in national affairs. How large a part will not be known for a generation or more until publication of some of the relevant documents. A little is known already, however.

Under the pretext of advising the Imperial Household Ministry, retired prime ministers and other public figures have reconstituted a near facsimile of the Privy Council which MacArthur abolished in 1945. As a "symbol of state" Hirohito retains the duty of putting his seal upon some 10,000 government documents annually. Since 1957 he has demanded, in exchange for discharge of this duty, that he receive regular briefings, at least once a week, from the prime minister. In the more than fourteen years of the Sato brothers' stewardship of the nation, his "imperial questions" have been seriously considered and respected.

PRIVY POCKETING

During his silence, Hirohito has been quietly gathering the major ingredient of private power: money. At the end of the war his family holdings stood at about three billion yen with an official value of less than a $100 million and a real value of $400 to $500 million. A small fraction of the fortune was in greatly depreciated bank deposits. About a tenth of it—a capital investment greater than that of any of the cartels except Mitsui [14]— was in damaged war factories. The bulk of it was in undepreciated land, gold, and jewels. SCAP succeeded in taking away about two thirds of this treasure and giving it to the Japanese government. Almost all the rest had been entrusted, during the closing months of the war, to loyal trustees. Acknowledging the impossibility of tracing all this buried wealth, SCAP

---

[14] The eleven branches of the Mitsui family held 390 million yens' worth of capital goods; the two branches of the Iwasaki's, who ran Mitsubishi, held 175 millions; the Sumitomo's held 315 millions; and the Imperial Household Ministry somewhat more than 330 millions.

made it illegal for the Emperor, in the years ahead, to accept gifts of any size.

Socialists in the Diet have periodically investigated the transactions of the Imperial Household Ministry in an effort to enforce the law, but adequate policing has not proved possible. It is estimated that the submerged imperial fortune, held in trust by loyal brokers, may now amount to considerably more than $1 billion.

In addition to his concealed assets, Hirohito has gradually amassed, by completely open means, a little gambling bankroll in the stock market, estimated to be from $40 to $50 million. Some of this money, which has grown quickly because of remarkable investment opportunities, represents repayment, through information, of some of the hidden imperial funds. The seed crystals from which it has grown, however, have been laid aside from the legal spending money alloted to Hirohito annually, by Diet vote, since 1947.

The Diet annually passes on three separate appropriations for the upkeep of the imperial family. The largest (some $12 million in 1970) goes to the upkeep of Hirohito's palaces and villas. A second (some $200,000 in 1970) goes to the support of the families of Hirohito's daughters and brothers, each of which receives a tax-free allowance of about $30,000 a year. The third appropriation goes into the privy purse of Hirohito and his son, Crown Prince Akihito, who reached the age of thirty-seven in December 1970. It, too, is tax free, but it represents almost pure profit because the imperial grounds and buildings, the imperial garages and marinas, the imperial tables and wardrobe, the imperial entertainments and protocols, and the imperial travel accounts are all covered by the separate, principal appropriation in support of the imperial household.

This mad money of Hirohito was set at a niggardly $22,000 a year in 1947.[15] By the end of the Occupation in 1952, it had been raised to $83,000, by 1965 to $189,000, by 1968 to $233,000, and by 1971 to over $300,000. Since the imperial allowance is all tax free, accessible and as good as the national exchequer, it enables Hirohito to stand pat with the largest of the cartels or to dive with the fastest plungers. Assisted by more than a score of investment counselors—a part of the permanent palace staff of about two thousand menials, chamberlains, guards, and experts— Hirohito has invested in the stock market wisely. (It is said that his portfolio is a bit heavy in electronics and hotels.)

In addition to giving Hirohito an annual raise in allowance, the Diet has also appropriated to Hirohito's use a number of special building funds

---

[15] Eight million yen with an official value of $160,000 and an actual value of about $22,000. It was one of the curiosities of the postwar Japanese economy that, as it recovered strength, MacArthur's experts gradually allowed the yen to seek its level on the market. As a result the yen was at first worth less and later more than its dollar quotation. I have used the factor of 360 to one for all post-1946 conversions.

which have been augmented by tax-deductible contributions from loyal subjects. In 1959 the villa of the Crown Prince was rebuilt. In 1962 Hirohito's wartime living quarters, the Imperial Library in the Fukiage Gardens, were expanded, modernized, and refurnished. In 1963 construction began on a new ceremonial palace to take the place of Emperor Meiji's magnificent edifice which had burned down on the night of May 25, 1945.

Completed in 1967, the new palace cost over $36 million. It is a handsome, modern concrete building with traditional roofs of green copper. Its seven wings, containing no less than 243,000 square feet of floor space, include a banqueting hall which can accommodate 3,000 guests. Its architect, Yoshimura Junzo, who also designed the Japanese house in New York's Museum of Modern Art, withdrew from the project in 1965, two years before its completion. It was claimed that he had aesthetic differences with Hirohito's chamberlains about some of the furnishings. In fact, after his departure, the underground areas of the palace, which include a 120-car garage, were redivided and greatly improved with vaults and stairways which do not appear in his original plans.

The new palace was considered such a success that Prime Minister Sato set aside another $2 million in 1968, to build Hirohito a new summer villa, with advanced marine research and communications facilities, on the least polluted, westernmost shores of Suruga Bay, near Shimoda, 110 miles from Tokyo.

DEMORALIZED PRINCELINGS

While Hirohito has silently prospered, his many kinsmen, who strutted about the Empire on inspections during the war years, have adjusted poorly to enforced retirement. Their undignified comments, carouses, cupidities, promiscuities, and other assorted incompetences as private citizens have repeatedly embarrassed the Throne and titillated a generation of Japanese tabloid readers.

Kanin Haruhito, the disentitled son of Prince Kanin Kotohito, former Army chief of staff, managed a "tourist agency," an "iron works," and two "trading companies" during the hectic giveaway years between 1945 and 1949. All four ventures operated at a loss, and Kanin's wife grew weary of her husband's role as a SCAP-palace pander. In her dissatisfaction she developed an intimacy with one of Kanin's former Army subordinates, a Mr. Takahashi. As she was, in her own right, a daughter of the noble Ichijo family and the headmistress of a fashionable girls' school, her dalliance excited gossip. After a showdown with the directors of the school, she abruptly walked out on all her former life and, in partnership with Mr. Takahashi, opened a successful coffeehouse on the Ginza in downtown Tokyo.

Another child of the late Prince Kanin, his fifth daughter Hanako, was married to the third son of the former Prince Fushimi, chief of the Navy General Staff. The two had been brought together for the first time on their wedding day after a courtship entirely by photograph. In 1951, after three children and twenty-four years of marriage, he was running a chicken farm on a vestige of his former properties and she, at home, was eking out the family budget by giving lessons in American dancing at their former princely villa. The menage fell in ruins on the night of July 18 when he returned from the chicken farm to stumble in upon her in the villa cloakroom making love to one of Hirohito's chamberlains, a Mr. Toda. After the divorce, she and Mr. Toda, at Hirohito's insistence, got married.

One of the family scandals touched Hirohito closely. On a bleak February morning in 1966 the grandson of Tokugawa Iesato, husband of Hirohito's third daughter, Kazuko, was discovered gassed and naked in a frowsy Tokyo walkup flat. Beside him lay the body of the proprietress of a bar called the Isaribi. A leaky gas fire had made sordid tragedy and public shame of an assignation which might have been held secretly, romantically, and safely in any proper princely villa of prewar days.

Through such revelations the Japanese middle classes—a rigidly proper group compared with either the Japanese upper or lower classes—have developed a jaundiced view of the lesser members of the imperial family. This view has helped to hold the many demoted princes in their new plebeian place. Former Prince Higashikuni, as the most forward and froward villain of the clan, has repeatedly tested the public to find out if it has yet relented at all.

After resigning as prime minister, Higashikuni pooled assets with March-Plot financier Tokugawa Yoshichika, the wartime director of Japan's Southeast Asian espionage headquarters at the Singapore museum and botanical gardens. Together they started an antique business. They made a successful failure out of their venture by putting nice Japanese pieces into the hands of influential Occupationaires. Then, in 1947, they declared themselves bankrupt and Higashikuni went on to new enterprises, chief of which was a religious sect which he named Ultra-Modern Cosmopolitan Buddhism.

To serve as high priest in his new religion Higashikuni took back into partnership the spiritual confidence man, Ohara Ryukai. Fifteen years earlier Ohara had supplied Higashikuni with the talking statue of the goddess of mercy which had figured in the Prayer Meeting Plot and others leading up to the February Mutiny of 1936. During the war Ohara had been imprisoned for five months for $400,000 worth of accumulated fraud. Notwithstanding his past record, Ohara still made an imposing chief priest. Ultra-Modern Cosmopolitan Buddhism spread rapidly and enjoyed a particular vogue in the spiritually starved ranks of retired servicemen.

In 1950 SCAP outlawed the "Higashikuni religion" as a subversive mili-

tary organization. Its Blue-Cloud-Mountain-Dragon-Sea Temple—a piece
of property which had formerly belonged to the Army's judge advocate—
was auctioned off to the highest bidder as seized contraband. In 1952, as
soon as the Occupation had ended, the new owner of the property brought
a complaint to court saying that minions of Prince Higashikuni were trying
to terrorize him and had just burned down his house. Higashikuni settled
out of court with a promise to cease and desist. A decade later, however,
in 1962, he had the aplomb to bring a countersuit of his own, claiming
that the land in question had been given to his family by Emperor Meiji
and remained his by divine disposition. The case dragged on through the
courts from June 1962 to February 1964. A Solomon of a judge finally
suggested that the only way to decide the divine rights of the matter
might be to call Hirohito into court for expert testimony. Higashikuni
promptly dropped his claim.

SHADOWS BEHIND CURTAINS

Half emancipated by the Occupation, half shackled by tradition, the
sensitive, literate, emotional Japanese public has been sorely tried and
torn by the demands made on its feelings since the war. It has repeatedly
demonstrated its affectionate loyalty to the Throne by oversubscribing
palace reconstruction schemes. At the same time it has repeatedly demonstrated its distrust of former imperial princes and of former Japanese Army
and Navy officers if they speak too resurgently or militantly. With fear of
the bad old days is coupled a genuine regard for the American G.I. and
for the democratic institutions he brought to Japan. On the other hand,
with traditional loyalty to Shinto and the Throne is coupled a doctrinaire
belief that Japan must someday, somehow avenge herself by besting the
United States. This conviction varies in emotional content from fierce
hatred to unhappy fatalism but it is widespread, and nothing that the most
good-natured G.I.'s might have done could ever have uprooted it.

Throughout the last twenty years most mass movements in Japan have
been mobilized as instruments of policy for dealing with the United States.
Demonstrations outside the U.S. Embassy in Tokyo have regularly featured
a platoon of vociferous leftists accompanied by regiments of common
folk who turn out because they enjoy demonstrating and because they
respond to the hints of policemen, ward heelers or student leaders. Rioters
may feel in need of expressing indignation, students may think they are
genuinely radical, but in politically sophisticated Japan they are mustered
by organizers who can usually be identified as the ambitious retainers of
staid public figures—men who express official horror at the disorders after
they have taken place.

In 1960 when the United States still needed bases in Japan for planes
and short-range missiles, Japanese mobs rioted obstreperously against re-

newal of the U.S.-Japanese Mutual Security Treaty, forcing cancellation of a visit to Japan by President Eisenhower. Nine years later in 1969, when the security treaty came up again for renegotiation, high-spirited students looked forward to staging the biggest and best riots in Japanese history. Their leaders had been planning novel escapades of protest for a full three years beforehand. When the time came, however, Liberal-Democratic bosses had the word spread that circumstances had changed since 1960; that ICBM's made bases in Japan a matter of convenience rather than necessity for the United States; and that the Mutual Security Treaty was now more to Japanese than American advantage. A single nationwide demonstration was staged in March 1969 in which 100,000 people participated. Thereafter the United States agreed to consider seriously the return to Japan of Okinawa and the Liberal-Democratic leadership discouraged further mob scenes.

After cancellation of the anti-American riots and extension of the security treaty, students in October 1969 expressed their disappointment by demonstrating violently against universities. Relative to the tens of thousands of students and policemen engaged, few heads were broken. For the first time since 1945, however, police boxes were smashed and tramcars turned over not for American benefit by a people united in defeat but for domestic benefit by genuine dissidents. The students had only vague ideas as to why they were protesting or by what chain of command they had been encouraged to protest. They felt a resentment, however, against the apparent fact that democracy was a sham and commoners were once more being manipulated as pawns in policy struggles taking place behind the scenes.

Since at least the early 1960's the fundamental question at issue within the inner sancta of Japan's closed society has been whether, and if so how, Japan should try to dominate her neighbors. Aged Strike-North partisans in the Self-Defense Forces and in the Liberal-Democratic Party have pleaded as ever for candor, for forthright rearmament, for open declaration of limited, practical, foreign-policy goals. In particular they have asked that Japan reach a negotiated understanding with the West, enabling her to take over most U.S. responsibilities in Asia and to compete on equal terms with Communist China for pan-Asian leadership.

Discredited remnants of the Emperor's Strike-South Faction, including all members of the imperial family, have carefully avoided offering any ultimate alternative to the program suggested by the Strike-North partisans. Rather they have piously supported Prime Minister Sato in his policy of all-out peaceful economic development. Some of them have admitted privately that they see no reason on the one hand for alarming the United States by an excess of candor and on the other for relieving the United States prematurely of its costly military burdens in the Orient. If Japan can continue to infiltrate foreign markets and outstrip the United States in rate of economic growth, there will eventually come a time, they say, when Japan can confront the land of Perry and MacArthur on equal terms. Then it will not be necessary to seek a negotiated understanding with the West; Japan's pre-eminence in Asia will be an accomplished fact.

During the last decade Japan's high-level secret introspections have found public expression in several incidents which no Western observer can know for sure how to interpret. In general, however, it is the heirs to the Strike-North heritage who encourage popular unrest for they are the partisans of international frankness and public discussion. Prime Minister Sato is on the side of silence. Hirohito's imperial kinsmen support Sato but do not object to an occasional incident as means of gauging popular sentiment.

One of the earliest outbreaks connected with the great debate was the "Three Nothings Incident" of 1961. Mikami Taku, the paroled Misty Lagoon flight lieutenant who in 1932 had shot Prime Minister Inukai through the head, resolved twenty-nine years later that "direct action" was once again needed to bring Japan to her senses. He approached members of the Self-Defense Forces for co-operation in a coup d'etat. They reported him to the police. When he was arrested he insisted that he had meant no harm and had only wanted to bring to nothing three great evils— bribery, taxes, and unemployment. For his "three nothings" he was appropriately sentenced to three years of imprisonment.

In 1932, when he assassinated Prime Minister Inukai, it had been hard to tell whether Mikami, in his headstrong idealism, was most under the influence of ex-Navy pilot Prince Yamashina, the Emperor's kinsman at the Misty Lagoon, or of War Minister Araki, the Strike-North leader. In June 1961, when he went to prison for the second time, it was still impossible to be sure for whom he acted, for he was still close both to retired General Araki and to former Prince Higashikuni.

On February 26, 1965, shortly after he emerged from prison, Mikami participated in a rightist rally which again raised many eyebrows. The occasion was the twenty-ninth anniversary of the February Mutiny of 1936. Mikami was guest of honor at the unveiling of a public monument in memory of the rebels. Beside him on the speakers' platform sat Sagoya Tomeo, who had shot Prime Minister Hamaguchi in 1930, and Blood Brother Konuma Tadashi, who had shot financier Inoue Junnosuke in 1932. Sagoya now read his given name as Yoshiaki and Konuma his as Hiromitsu but all present knew perfectly well who both men were.

The principal speaker that day was none other than the eighty-seven year-old former General Araki, still full of droll Shavian eloquence even after ten years in prison as a war criminal. Political connoisseurs took the strange get-together of aged assassins as a warning to Hirohito that Japanese idealism could no longer be used privily to intimidate but only publicly in frank and open discussion.

During the five years from 1965 to 1970 Prime Minister Sato's government undercut the outspoken Strike-North partisans by relaxing somewhat the stern thrift of Japan's economic revival and allowing some of the nation's earnings to be diverted from factory building to workers' wages. As a result taxable per-capita income and consumer spending both trebled. Almost every farmhouse gained its electric rice cooker and television antenna. Only idealistic students and samurai diehards could any longer complain of the direction in which the nation was heading.

In 1967, with little protest, an old national holiday was revived: February 11 or National Foundation Day. On this date, until disabused by MacArthur's men in 1948, Japanese had long celebrated Emperor Jimmu's mythical ascension to the Throne in 660 B.C. Now, on February 11, 1967, 100,000 pilgrims showed their approval of returning to old ways by journeying to the countryside outside Nara in the Kyoto area and paying homage at Emperor Jimmu's supposed tumulus.

LONE CRY OF ANGUISH

Nearly three more years of prosperity passed before the ill-conceived student riots of October 1969. These were directed very largely against the organ-theory academicians of the 1930's. When the public showed no sympathy for the rioters, it looked as if the old partisans of the Strike-North movement had fought and lost their last quixotic battle with the Japanese Establishment. One determined spirit, however, who had supported the students and shared their dissatisfactions, was not prepared to give up. Somehow nation and Emperor must be made to see the dangers of economic imperialism and to cherish the beauty of the old Japan. For months this solitary samurai considered the means of protest at his disposal and settled at last upon the traditional one, the ultimate gesture of sincerity, suicide. It was to be one of the most spectacular suicides in Japanese history.

The unlikely hero—or villain—in this act of self-destruction was none other than Japan's celebrated novelist Mishima Yukio. He was a man of good samurai family who had graduated during the war from Japan's most exclusive academy, the Peers' School. With sufferance, because of his manifest talent, he had gone on to become something of an eccentric. He furnished his house with the most ugly Western Victorian furniture. He was a homosexual. He kept a wife and two children. He had been repeatedly considered as a candidate by the Nobel Prize committee in Sweden. Since adolescence he had been haunted by memories of the kamikaze pilots of 1944–45 and by a sense of inadequacy in not having been one of them. According to his critics his writings apotheosized a life style of sex every night followed by suicide every morning.

A dramatist and actor as well as a novelist, Mishima was theatrical.

Words on the printed page were never enough for him; as proof of conviction, he demanded of himself deeds also. Having reached manhood at a time when all Japanese youths seemed hungry and small compared to U.S. Occupation troops, he made a fetish of body-building and succeeded in changing his appearance from that of a pale intellectual grub to that of a magnificently muscled Japanese adonis. With money from movies he outfitted a selection of his fans as an army—the *Tate-no-kai,* or Shield Society. Their gold braid and fancy dress struck some Japanese as a calculated mockery of militarism, but their sincerity seemed genuine. They decried the pall of smoke and self-deception settling on Japan; they lamented the loss of old Japanese cultural values; they criticized Hirohito for having never explained to the people frankly where he had been going in the war, why he had rejected a fight to the death at the end of the war, and what he looked for now after the war.

Novelist Mishima played with his following of toy soldiers by day and wrote furiously by night. Between 1948 and 1968 he published twenty novels, thirty-three plays, and over a hundred articles and short stories. In all his works he plowed one furrow deep: the theme of death and the need to sacrifice one's life for a cause, either through aggressive violence or introspective suicide.

Mishima idolized the young officers of the February 1936 Mutiny, the idealistic dupes of the Strike-North-Strike-South confrontation who had thrown away their lives in a vain appeal to the imperial conscience. In 1969 his sympathy for the 1936 rebels involved him in a controversy with a literary scion of the imperial family. This was the second-rate novelist Arima Yorichika, a son of Count Arima who had figured in imperial-family infiltration of left-wing groups during the 1930's. Arima maintained that the 1936 rebels "far from being misguided but pure revolutionaries were out-and-out murderers."

In late 1969, during his dispute with Arima, Mishima impressed his friends as being unusually despondent. He was weary of passive intellectual attainments. He was forty-four. He suffered from the crisis of middle age. He was working on the final volume of his most ambitious piece of fiction yet, a tetralogy called *The Sea of Fertility.* It was a bitter misanthropic title referring to one of the ill-named maria on the barren face of the moon.

As Mishima neared the end of his opus, draining himself of words, he sought to sweeten his imagination by involving himself in the student rallies and riots of October 1969. When they came to naught, his gloom deepened. One day in February 1970, a high-school student who was a complete stranger to him came to his house and waited at his gate for three hours to ask him a single question: "Sir, when are you going to kill yourself?"

Mishima reacted to the student as if he were an imperial messenger of the sort which had bidden men commit suicide in the days of the Tokugawa shoguns. Shortly after the visitation, he broached to his intimates in the

Shield Society his first tentative ideas for the melodramatic scheme which would answer the boy's question.

Under the extreme, lifelong pressure of Japan's feudalistic Mafia-style family society, many men have reached Mishima's state of spiritual exhaustion and have resolved on suicide as the only relief. Since Japanese are trained from childhood to be frugal and to be ambitious, every aspiring suicide always tries to gain a little immortality by making his death count for something. Mishima was no exception. He know from his American literary friends how little Japanese political indirection was appreciated in the West. He knew from a leading Strike-North partisan, his friend Nakasone Yasuhiro, the director of Japan's Self-Defense Forces, that the struggle for a frank foreign policy had been fought in the inner circles of government and had been lost. He also knew, from his study of the rebels of the February 1936 Mutiny, that the most telling way to embarrass the Throne was to die, calling for open international expression of Japanese feelings and for responsible direct rule by the traditional master of indirection, the Emperor.

And so Mishima, realizing that he was one of the best-known Japanese outside Japan—one known, moreover, for his cosmopolitanism and love of Western books and furniture—decided to make an unmistakable international sacrifice of himself. With a troupe of his theatrical soldiers of the Shield Society, he gained admittance on November 25, 1970, to the Ichigaya Headquarters of Japan's Self-Defense Forces. This was a place full of memories: the site of the prewar military academy, of the 1945 General Staff Offices, and of the postwar International Military Tribunal for the Far East. In 1970 its inner compound was surrounded by a sprawling complex of barracks and barriers. Any ordinary Japanese would have needed more than one officially stamped pass to enter the inner compound, but Mishima reached it without difficulty. So did half a dozen of his uniformed followers and also two Japanese news photographers.

Mishima and his men marched into the office of a friend, General Mashita Kanetoshi, tied him to a chair, threatened his aides with swords, and demanded that the officer corps of the Self-Defense Forces be assembled to hear a speech by Mishima. Helpless before the swords of Mishima's troupe, the armed M.P.'s guarding the headquarters went scurrying off to announce a muster over the public address system. In minutes 1,200 men, many of them officers, had gathered below the balcony from which Mishima was to hold forth. As cameras clicked Mishima strode forward. He delivered a ten-minute exhortation, begging Japan to return to the ways of her ancestors, to wipe the industrial smog from her green hills, to make the Emperor directly responsible for rule, to renounce the hypocrisy of pacifism written into the drably phrased Constitution which MacArthur had forced on Japan, to give up financially irresponsible dependence upon a U.S. "nuclear umbrella," and to admit forthrightly that the Self-Defense Forces were the best Army, Navy, and Air Force in Asia.

Despite the considerable co-operation which Self-Defense Force leaders had extended to Mishima, they had failed to give him a microphone with which to make his final words heard. Some of the 1,200 men gathered to hear him shouted *"Baka"* and *"Bakaro"* at him—"You idiot, you peasant" —and drowned out the logic of his eloquence. Mishima cut short his address, stalked back inside from the balcony, and turned to the difficult part of his gesture, for which he had done the most intensive psychological self-preparation. He knelt and ripped open his belly with a knife. One of his gold-braided retainers hacked and hacked again at his neck with a sword. When Mishima had finally been decapitated, his headsman knelt in turn, cut his own belly and was decapitated by a second retainer.

Many Japanese remarked upon the extreme sincerity and traditionalism of Mishima's suicide. The gory rite of decapitation by a second had been seldom practiced since the eighteenth century. Most of the important twentieth century suicides had made sure that they would be seconded by men who were good pistol shots or who knew how to cut into the carotid artery from the back of the neck.

Mishima's friends and admirers in the West could hardly believe the sacrifice he had made of his great talent. In the shocked obituaries which they wrote for New York, Paris, and London newspapers, they sought to explain his action in purely personal terms, acknowledging that they had never understood his political compulsions. None ventured to examine the merits of the cause for which he had killed himself.

In Japan an editorialist of the imperial faction, Yamamoto Kenkichi, was quick to point out that the act of violence made a Roman candle of Mishima's career, leaving "one flash in the darkness and nothing else." Novelist Arima of the imperial family contented himself with private observations to the effect that the futility of Mishima's death exposed the theatrical trumpery of the 1936 February Mutiny.

After the event the men of the Self-Defense Forces who were interviewed by newsmen all expressed regret that they had booed Mishima and showed admiration for his courage in acting upon his convictions. To a man, however, they continued to disagree with him. The Emperor, they insisted, should not and could not be held responsible for Japan—not in 1971 any more than in 1945. The MacArthur Constitution, they said, was right in defining him as a "symbol of state" rather than a living god.

"The Emperor should be a symbol," declared one sergeant, "a pillar the people of Japan can rely on in their hearts. He should not be in politics himself, nor should he be used by those who are in politics."

Despite the devout naïveté and historical ignorance manifested by such remarks, Japanese editorialists agreed in conclusion that the men of the Self-Defense Forces had proved themselves true individualists, true citizen soldiers, true products of postwar democracy.

At Mishima's funeral—a tolerant Buddhist affair attended by fashionable friends in maxis, minis, and bell-bottoms—one eulogist tried to break through the all-pervasive complacency by begging Hirohito "for even a single word [of comment on the suicide] from the imperial family."

On the balcony, and in his essays and articles for several years before mounting the balcony, Mishima had been asking Hirohito to break silence and say something meaningful and religious about the sacrifice of World War II. Hirohito had not responded then and he did not respond now. Instead, on January 5, 1971, forty days after Mishima's suicide, the Emperor appeared in public to officiate at the award-giving in the annual poetry-writing contest. The theme of the year was the word *ie,* meaning house or home or clan. Hirohito's own contribution to the contest was:

> Amid the cedars,
> I see a clump of houses,
> and then the cedars
> step out row after long row
> across the Tonami plain.[16]

Some Japanese opined that Hirohito, in this verse, had spoken out for pollution control on behalf of more trees and less houses; others insisted that he had spoken for continued breakneck economic development and for less trees and more houses. To all obvious intents and purposes Hirohito spoke not at all. The bright television lights seemed to bother him. He closed his eyes and seemed to be sleeping.

THE FUTURE

In 1931, when Japan invaded Manchuria and began her march toward Pearl Harbor, the United States did not have the military strength in the Orient to say her nay. As a result some five million human beings would die. This suffering, and all the present evils in Asia which stemmed from it, could probably have been averted if the United States had known how to contain Japan. The United States has since learned the lesson that deterrent military strength is a prerequisite to the containment of other nations. On a worldwide basis, however, no strength can ever suffice unless it is applied with mechanical advantage. To threaten an entire nation is to insult a people and gain more enemies than can ever be defeated. Far wiser is it to keep force as a basis for polite private conversations with the key leaders of a possible opponent.

If U.S. Intelligence agencies, backed by military force and speaking through the State Department, could have discreetly threatened to expose the machinations of the Throne at any time before September 1931, the

---

[16] A sacred wilderness area near the north coast in western Honshu.

Pacific half of World War II could most likely have been postponed indefinitely. Without bloodshed a situation could thereby have been achieved for U.S. interests in Asia which would certainly have been no worse than that which was achieved through much bloodshed.

Again in the 1970's U.S. leaders had to give grave thought to Japanese-American relations. The septuagenarian Hirohito was a spent samurai, who could not be a war leader again after the shame of 1945. He had carried himself well under the humiliation of defeat, but as long as he reigned, Japan would persevere in the ways of peace. In the fall of 1971 he planned to round out his *Showa* era by paying a flying visit to Bonn, Brussels, Paris, and London. He was scheduled to set out on September 27, the fiftieth anniversary of his report to the gods after his history-shaping 1921 European tour. Thereafter, it was rumored, he would turn over most state business to his son, Crown Prince Akihito, who would be thirty-eight in December 1971.

As tutor to the crown prince during the Occupation, Elizabeth Gray Vining gave Akihito a favorable report card as a bright, charming, and sensitive young man. According to courtiers, however, Mrs. Vining may have taken an indulgent view of her charge and may have closed her eyes to some of the tough, cynical ways of thought which had been trained into him during the first thirteen years of his life before her coming to Japan. Nonetheless it has been attributed to Mrs. Vining's tutelage that Akihito later broke precedent with tradition by marrying a commoner of no Court rank, the daughter of a wealthy cartel owner, whom he met on a tennis court. On trips abroad to Europe and the Philippines, Akihito has impressed foreign observers by his polish and understanding of local problems.

Like Hirohito before him, Akihito has inherited a religious duty in which vengeance has a part. Like Hirohito, too, he can be relied upon to do conscientiously whatever he believes he should do. Only the Japanese people, who are individually moral, courageous, and literate, can be expected to redirect national policy if it threatens to lead Japan again toward excesses. At the moment the people are busy enjoying the recent betterment in their lives. They are apathetic to calls upon both their conscience and their patriotism. Nevertheless, within the ceremonial formulas of the democracy which MacArthur left them, they will be asked soon to take sides in the debate about the goals or vengeance which Japan should ultimately pursue.

In the past men like Saionji, Araki, Matsuoka, and Mishima, who hoped to influence national policy making, have sacrificed themselves in the traditional Japanese manner—by passionately polite hints. They have failed to do more than embarrass their aristocratic patrons. If the Throne is to be made a true symbol of state and servant of majority interests in Japan criticism of it and of national policy may have to be expressed more explicitly in the future.

Many Japanese will try to dismiss from mind the ugly story told in this book, assuring themselves that it is a simplification. In a sense they will be right. Here the ideas of leaders have been put forward as the mainsprings of Japanese political action, whereas, in practice, Japanese tend to think of politics only in terms of personal ties between friends who have done favors for one another. If these pages have done scant justice to the complexities of allegiance and loyalty in Japan, perhaps they will stimulate Japanese historians to recount fully the personal relationships involved in the undoubted events of Hirohito's reign. Up to now Japanese explanations of the period have struck many Westerners as either allusively circumstantial or mystically broad.

To face reality, to earn the goodwill of neighboring peoples, and to make Asia a responsible fourth force which can stand apart from America, Russia, and Europe are hard tasks without glamor. They can be achieved only by exorcising the spell of the ancestors, by blowing away the heavy halo of taboo which encircles the Throne, and by shattering the devout silence which makes conspirators of all who enter service in the palace. Japanese know and dread the alternative, which is to dive back into the Pacific to grapple once again with Commodore Perry's leviathan.

GLOSSARY

Following is a descriptive list encapsulating or amplifying characters, events, groups, organizations, and geographical features mentioned in the text of *Japan's Imperial Conspiracy*. Offices and departments of the national government are described elsewhere, in the chart "Japan's Prewar Government" on pages 374–375. Relationships within the imperial family are delineated in the genealogical tables on pages 268–270. Names in capitals within the text are cross-references to other entries.

ANAMI KORECHIKA (1887–1945). Army officer, military academy classmate and protégé of Hirohito's uncles Prince HIGASHIKUNI and Prince ASAKA. From 1926 to 1933 he was Hirohito's favorite aide-de-camp. Thereafter, except for a brief term as vice war minister in 1939–40, he served mostly in the field, bringing morale to his men and firsthand knowledge back to Tokyo. In December 1944 he was recalled from his command in New Guinea and made war minister. He encouraged the attempted palace coup on the night of surrender, August 14, 1945, and then committed hara-kiri.

ANTI-COMINTERN PACT. Agreement between the Japanese and German governments, signed in Berlin on November 25, 1936, to act together against the spread of communism. Secret provisions of the pact bound each nation to assist the other economically and diplomatically if either waged war with Russia.

ANTI-CONSTITUTIONALIST PARTY (*Rikken Minseito*). Political party founded in 1927 by HAMAGUCHI OSACHI to offer organized, professionally managed opposition to the CONSTITUTIONALIST PARTY. Prince SAIONJI KINMOCHI recruited financial backing for it. After July 1940 the Anti-Constitutionalists, and the Constitutionalists as well, ceased to exist as parties and were replaced by the IMPERIAL RULE ASSISTANCE ASSOCIATION.

ARAKI SADAO (1877–1967). Army officer, protégé of Emperor Taisho, military academy classmate of HONJO SHIGERU and MAZAKI JINZABURO, and the most eloquent spokesman for the STRIKE-NORTH FACTION. An intelligence expert specializing in Russian affairs, he served in the St. Petersburg Embassy from 1909 to 1918, then with YONAI MITSUMASA in the Vladivostok Special Service

Organ during Japan's Siberian Intervention. In 1925–26 during the purge of the CHOSHU leadership from the Army, he commanded the secret police. Fallow years followed in which he ran the Army's staff college, gathered a group of supporters in the officer corps, and spoke out increasingly against the policies of the STRIKE-SOUTH FACTION. In December 1931, after the seizure of Mukden, he came into power as war minister with the Constitutionalists. For the next five years he fought a shifting battle with Hirohito on national policy and finally retired in defeat after the FEBRUARY MUTINY in 1936. Araki returned to prominence briefly as minister of education during the 1939 NOMONHAN INCIDENT. After World War II he submitted quietly to prosecution as a war criminal. Emerging from "life imprisonment" in 1955, he soon returned to his old ways and began to agitate for the strengthening of Japanese military power to deal with Russian threats. Until his death at ninety he kept various caches of secret state documents from the 1930's as guarantees for his continued health and freedom from persecution.

ARMY PURIFICATION MOVEMENT (*Seigun-ha*). An organization in the Army officer corps promoted in 1934–35 by Lieutenant General Count TERAUCHI HISAICHI. Its followers advocated strict obedience to orders and nonintervention in politics.

ASA-AKIRA, Prince Kuni III (1901–   ). Son of KUNIYOSHI, brother of Empress Nagako, childhood playmate of Hirohito. He graduated from the naval academy in 1921 and in 1925 married his second cousin Tomoko, daughter of Admiral Prince FUSHIMI HIROYASU. In 1942, as a rear admiral, he commanded the air squadron which supported the occupation of Timor. Later in the war he supported Prince TAKAMATSU in promotion of the kamikaze corps. In postwar Japan he ran the Kuni Perfume Company and a marriage brokerage. Later, as conditions eased, he became a gentleman farmer known for his sheep dogs and his orchids.

ASAHIKO, Prince Kuni (1824–1891). Son of KUNIYE, nineteenth Prince FUSHIMI. He became chief counselor to Emperor KOMEI and leading proponent of expelling Western barbarians from the Orient. Empress Nagako is his granddaughter.

ASAKA YASUHIKO, Prince (1887–   ). Eighth son of ASAHIKO and uncle of Hirohito. A professional Army officer, he was commander at Nanking in 1937 during the massive reprisal massacre which took about 140,000 Chinese lives. In the postwar era he was known as one of Tokyo's best golfers.

ASIA DEVELOPMENT BOARD (*Koa-in*). Established by Prince Konoye, then prime minister, in December 1938 to co-ordinate the economic exploitation of China. Major General SUZUKI TEI-ICHI was head of the Political Affairs Branch of the board.

BANZAI RIHACHIRO. Retired lieutenant general, veteran of Japanese intelligence in China, former advisor to Yuan Shih-kai in Peking. In the 1930's he became director of the "CIVILIAN SPY SERVICE."

BIG BROTHERS (*Ani-bun*). A descriptive term used by courtiers to designate a group of energetic aristocrats who were considered to be like elder brothers by Hirohito. All were nine to fifteen years older than he was. All had come often to his foster home to play with him as a child. All were PEERS' SCHOOL classmates either of his uncle Prince HIGASHIKUNI, born in 1887, or of his foster parent's son, KIDO KOICHI, born in 1889, or of Prince KONOYE FUMIMARO, the highest ranking noble of the Court clan of Fujiwara, born in 1891. At first, in addition to Higashikuni, Kido, and Konoye, the most influential of the Big Brothers were Fushimi family scions: Prince Asaka Yasuhiko, Prince Kitashirakawa Naruhisa, and Marquis Komatsu Teruhisa. Some other Big Brothers, who remained important in Hirohito's counsels until the close of World War II, were the Army officer Marquis Inoue Saburo; the courtiers Count Futara Yoshinori, Baron Harada Kumao, and Viscount Okabe Nagakage; also the diplomats Shigemitsu Mamoru and Tani Masayuki.

Black Dragon Society (*Kokuryu-kai*). A Japanese patriotic tong professing a credo of Asia for the Asiatics. The powerful underworld boss Toyama Mitsuru founded it in 1901 with the initial purpose of supporting Army Chief of Staff General Yamagata Aritomo's position that Japan should control all of Manchuria up to the Amur or Black Dragon River, the boundary between Manchuria and Siberia. Black Dragon lord Toyama was a patron of Sun Yat-sen, who met with Chinese exiles in Black Dragon headquarters in Tokyo to found a revolutionary party—the Kuomintang or KMT of Chiang Kai-shek. The Black Dragon Society later supported the Strike-North Faction in the Army, and its influence dwindled as that faction was gradually eliminated in the 1930's.

Blood Brotherhood (*Ketsumeidan*). Select group of apprentice spies trained for work in China as an adjunct of the Everyday Meiji Biographical Research Institute in Oarai. Agents belonging to the brotherhood acted as assassins in the killing of Inoue Junnosuke and Baron Dan in 1932.

Cabal. See Emperor's Cabal.

Cabinet Planning Board (*Kikaku-in*). The central organization controlling Japanese economic mobilization for World War II. For his part as chief of the board, retired Lieutenant General Suzuki Tei-ichi was found guilty of war crimes in 1948 and sentenced to life imprisonment.

Cherry Society (*Sakurakai*). An organization of Army junior officers, under the aegis of Army Intelligence chief General Tatekawa Yoshiji. It lobbied for conquest of Manchuria and larger military budgets in 1930. Some of its members were admitted to the Emperor's Cabal.

Chichibu, Prince (1902–1953). First brother of Hirohito. Often at odds with the Emperor, he sympathized with the Strike-North Faction in the February Mutiny of 1936.

Cho Isamu (1896–1945). Army fanatic, member of the Cherry Society and of the Emperor's Cabal. In 1931 he planned the October Plot. From August 1934 to July 1937 he was employed in drawing up plans for Japan's war with China. In December 1937 he was chief of staff for Prince Asaka outside Nanking and issued a notorious order for the prince: "Kill all prisoners." In the spring of 1938 he commanded the 74th Regiment in the border war with Russia known as the Lake Khasan Incident. During training of Strike-South forces in the summer of 1941, he served as vice chief of staff to General Yamashita Tomoyuki. On the eve of war he was assigned to the staff of General Count Terauchi Hisaichi in Saigon. Later in the war, July 1944, he became chief of staff of the 32d Army on Okinawa. There, in June 1945, having put up a good defense, he committed suicide rather than surrender.

Choshu. A large clan in the southwestern corner of the central island of Honshu, of which Mori was the leading family. When Emperor Komei enlisted Choshu support and advice in his struggle with the Tokugawa shogunate, clan leaders urged unification under the Emperor and a program of expansion on the Asiatic continent to create buffer zones between Japan and the West.

Choshu samurai led by General YAMAGATA ARITOMO dominated Emperor Meiji's new Imperial Army and monopolized key posts until its reorganization in 1924. Disgruntled Choshu officers and retired officers supplied much of the backing for the STRIKE-NORTH FACTION during the 1930's.

"CIVILIAN SPY SERVICE." A paramilitary espionage organization which coordinated and supplemented the work of the Army and Navy Intelligence departments of the Tokyo General Staffs. Its directorate, which worked out of the Imperial Palace through the fronts of charitable and cultural organizations, was mostly staffed by retired military intelligence officers. Its agents worked in the diplomatic corps of the Foreign Ministry and the marketing staffs of cartels engaged in foreign trade. Its network blanketed Asia and extended into all the major cities of the West. Founded by Emperor Meiji's Imperial Household Minister Count TANAKA MITSUAKI, the spy service was directed throughout most of Hirohito's reign by retired Lieutenant General BANZAI RIHACHIRO.

CONSTITUTIONALIST PARTY (*Rikken Seiyukai*). First important political party in Japan, founded in 1900 by Prime Minister ITO HIROBUMI, who hoped to create a counterbalance to the autocratic power of Emperor Meiji and a basis for constitutional party government. Constitutionalists in general favored economic rather than military expansion. In the Diet which had the power to veto increases in budgets, they sought to curtail military appropriations. Later leaders of the party were Prince SAIONJI KINMOCHI; Hara Takashi, prime minister in 1918–21 (when he was assassinated); and retired General Count Tanaka Gi-ichi, who attempted while prime minister in 1927–29 to moderate young Emperor Hirohito's aspirations for China.

CONTROL CLIQUE (*Tosei-hai*). The minority of the EMPEROR'S CABAL in the Army which remained loyal to him from 1930 to 1936 and supported him and the STRIKE-SOUTH FACTION in an anti-Western policy of expansion into Southeast Asia and Indonesia. The name Control Clique was meant to appeal to those who feared possible lack of self-control in Hirohito's policies for Japan. The dissident half of the Emperor's Cabal was the IMPERIAL WAY GROUP. Prominent members of the Control Clique were SUZUKI TEI-ICHI, DOIHARA KENJI, ITAGAKI SEISHIRO, TATEKAWA YOSHIJI, and KOISO KUNIAKI.

DOIHARA KENJI (1883–1948). Army officer, protégé of Prince KANIN, one of the ELEVEN RELIABLES, known as the "Lawrence of Manchuria." Throughout most of the 1920's he was attached to the General Staff, running espionage errands to eastern Siberia and North China. In March 1928 he was employed as a military advisor by Manchurian warlord Chang Tso-lin. In August 1931 he took charge of the Japanese Special Service Organ in Mukden, declaring himself mayor of the city on the morning of September 19 after the outbreak of the MANCHURIAN INCIDENT. He went on in November to become Special Service Organ chief in Harbin where he prepared for Japanese seizure of that city also. Doihara had a large part in the administration of the new puppet state of MANCHUKUO until 1937, when he abruptly began a second career as a respectable field officer, commanding the 14th Division and later the 5th Army in North China. In October 1940, assuming a professorial role, he was appointed principal of the military academy. In June 1941 he accepted the inspector generalship of military aviation. During the war he held successively three imposing commands of armies in rear areas. Doihara's earlier activities in Manchuria had not been forgotten, however. In 1948 he was convicted as a war criminal and hanged.

DOLLAR SWINDLE (*Doru-bai*). First element in the TRIPLE INTRIGUE of 1931–32. It was a financial maneuver advocated by the Emperor's close advisors among the BIG BROTHERS and the ELEVEN CLUB to win support from certain Japanese bankers and cartelists by inviting them to speculate in foreign currencies with advance knowledge of the government's intention to renounce the gold standard. The government fulfilled its pledge in late 1931, to the great financial disadvantage of the banking and industrial interests.

EAST ASIA ALL-ONE CULTURE SOCIETY (*Toa Dobun-kai*). Movement begun in Japan and extended to China by Fujiwara Prince Konoye Atsumaro, father of the future prime minister, Prince Konoye Fumimaro, to promote Japan's mission as the leader of Asian culture and politics.

ELEVEN CLUB (*Juichi-kai*). A group of about twenty PEERS' SCHOOL graduates of like mind and like age who met more or less regularly with Marquis KIDO KOICHI on the eleventh evening of each month. Most of them were courtiers or aristocratic bureaucrats; a few were military officers or diplomats. They discussed imperial policies, plans, and plots under consideration by Hirohito or by his official advisors. In either modifying or activating policy, they were extremely influential. Marquis Kido started the club in 1922, on November 11—the eleventh day of the eleventh month of the eleventh year in the reign of Emperor Taisho. The club held its last recorded session on January 11, 1945.

ELEVEN RELIABLES (*Jushu na jinsai no juichinin*). Junior Army officers thought trustworthy enough to approach as possible recruits for the EMPEROR'S CABAL by the THREE CROWS. Most prominent of the Eleven Reliables came to be TOJO HIDEKI, DOIHARA KENJI, KOMOTO DAISAKU, ISOGAI RENSUKE, ITAGAKI SEISHIRO, WATARI HISAO, and YAMAOKA SHIGEATSU.

EMPEROR'S CABAL (*Showa Rikukaigun no Chushin*). An elite cadre of intelligence officers recruited in the 1920's to work in secret for Hirohito's programs within the Army and Navy. The leaders of the cabal, brought together by Hirohito's uncle, Big Brother Prince HIGASHIKUNI in October 1921, were the THREE CROWS—Majors NAGATA TETSUZAN, Obata Toshiro, and Okamura Yasuji. They promptly enlisted a group of fellow junior officers known as the ELEVEN RELIABLES. The cabal's immediate goals were to modernize the Army and displace the old-line CHOSHU leadership. Further recruits came into the cabal through the UNIVERSITY LODGING HOUSE, the SUZUKI STUDY GROUP, and the CHERRY SOCIETY. Around 1930 the cabal split into the IMPERIAL WAY GROUP, which supported the STRIKE-NORTH FACTION, and the CONTROL CLIQUE, which supported the STRIKE-SOUTH FACTION.

EVERYDAY MEIJI BIOGRAPHICAL RESEARCH INSTITUTE (*Joyo Meiji Kinenkan*). Front organization in Oarai, 50 miles northeast of Tokyo, for co-ordinating intelligence supplied by the various branches of the "CIVILIAN SPY SERVICE." Nearby were two affiliated academies which trained agents for espionage work. The institute was organized by a longtime Court official, Count TANAKA MITSUAKI, who had been household minister to Emperor Meiji. Ostensibly it was a museum where scholars labored to prepare an official biography of Meiji. The institute was closed down and its staff moved elsewhere in 1932 when people began to point out that it had been deeply involved in the assassination of Prime Minister Inukai during the MAY FIFTEENTH INCIDENT.

FAKE WAR (*Shanhai ni kensei undo*). Second act in the TRIPLE INTRIGUE of 1931–32, a diversionary attack on the Chinese half of Shanghai in January 1932. In return for stopping it before it involved the Western segments of the city, the Japanese government expected that the League of Nations would abandon all thought of imposing economic sanctions against Japan for aggression in Manchuria. Expectations were fulfilled and the Fake War was brought to an end in March 1932.

FEBRUARY MUTINY (*Niniroku Jiken*). Armed uprising in Tokyo, organized by officers of the Army's crack 1st Division, who hoped to persuade Hirohito to change his national policy. They sought domestic reform and a return to the traditional values of the samurai ethic. They were set on by members of the STRIKE-NORTH and STRIKE-SOUTH factions, both of which hoped that the mutiny could be used to further their own political ends. In the early hours of February 26, 1936, soldiers of the 1st and 3d regiments led by two captains and nineteen lieutenants marched out of their barracks to kill "the evil men about the Throne." Assassination squads murdered Finance Minister Takahashi Korekiyko, Lord Privy Seal Admiral Viscount Saito, and General Watanabe Jotaro, inspector general of military education; they failed in attempts to kill Prime Minister Okada Keisuke and Hirohito's Grand Chamberlain Admiral SUZUKI KANTARO. Rural accomplices also failed in out-of-town attempts to murder former Lord Privy Seal Count MAKINO NOBUAKI and Prince SAIONJI KINMOCHI. The rebels occupied the center of Tokyo for three days before surrendering. Hirohito refused to bow to any of their demands, and after their suppression he demanded the resignation of most of the generals in the Army. He made a notable exception of General Count Terauchi of the ARMY PURIFICATION MOVEMENT, who became the next war minister. Two officer-leaders of the mutiny committed hara-kiri, thirteen others were executed by firing squad. In the months following, practically all officers of the Strike-North Faction were retired from the Army, and full-scale preparations were made to carry out Strike-South policies.

FUJIWARA. An imperial clan originating in the seventh century A.D. under the patronage of Emperor Tenji. Fujiwara princesses served as wives and concubines to emperors and Fujiwara princes acted as intimate advisors to the Throne for thirteen centuries. Two of the last of the Fujiwara princes were SAIONJI KINMOCHI (1849–1940) and KONOYE FUMIMARO (1891–1945).

FUSHIMI HIROYASU. Prince (1875–1947). Son of SADANARU, he was the twenty-second Prince Fushimi. He became an admiral and served Hirohito as chief of staff of the Navy from 1932 to 1941.

FUSHIMI, House of. A collateral branch of the imperial family, founded in the fourteenth century, which traditionally supplied husbands for the unwed daughters of emperors. Through the efforts of KUNIYE and ASAHIKO, its influence at Court increased greatly in the nineteenth century at a time when other imperial branch families were dying out for lack of male issue. Fushimi power reached its zenith in alliance with the SATSUMA clan and the Imperial Navy during the first half of the reign of Hirohito. A Fushimi princess, Nagako, daughter of Prince KUNIYOSHI, became Empress of Japan at her marriage to Hirohito in January 1924.

FUTARA YOSHINORI, Count (1886–   ). A member of Hirohito's boyhood BIG BROTHERS, later married to a cousin of the future Empress Nagako. He accompanied the Crown Prince on his European tour in 1921 and continued thereafter to serve as imperial public relations agent. He and SUZUKI KANTARO were largely responsible for creating the impression common in Western countries of Hirohito as a Westernized young liberal.

HAMAGUCHI OSACHI (1870–1931). Organized a new political party in 1927 to unite various factions opposed to the Constitutionalists. Shot by an assassin in November 1930, he was incapacitated and finally died in August 1931.

HARADA KUMAO, Baron (1888–1946). Prince SAIONJI KINMOCHI's political secretary, ELEVEN CLUB member, one of the BIG BROTHERS. His grandfather was Harada Kazumichi, an advisor of Emperor Meiji. He attended Kyoto University with other Big Brothers, graduating with KIDO KOICHI in 1915. Following Hirohito to Europe, he stayed on there to help Prince HIGASHIKUNI with intelligence work. Returning home, he became Prime Minister Kato Taka-aki's secretary in 1924. From 1926 to 1940, while acting as liaison between Hirohito and Prince Saionji, he wrote a nine-volume, 3,000-page record of his political transactions known as the "Saionji-Harada Memoirs."

HIGASHIKUNI NARUHIKO, Prince (1887–). Ninth son of Prince ASAHIKO, uncle of Hirohito, Army officer, BIG BROTHER. He managed the formation of the EMPEROR'S CABAL in 1921 and went on to play a personal part in almost every one of the plots, intrigues, and incidents of the next twenty-five years. At the end of the war, having achieved the rank of field marshal, he took responsibility for all he had wrought by becoming prime minister in the first two humiliating months after Japan's surrender.

HONJO SHIGERU (1876–1945). Army officer, protégé of Emperor Taisho, military academy classmate of General ARAKI SADAO. A China expert, he served as military advisor to North China warlord Chang Tso-lin from 1921 to 1924. In August 1931 he was made commander of the KWANTUNG ARMY to carry out the well-considered plans of the EMPEROR'S CABAL for the seizure of Manchuria. He fulfilled his assignment well and was rewarded with the post of chief aide-de-camp to Hirohito in April 1933. For the next three years he sought gently to persuade Hirohito to give up STRIKE-SOUTH aspirations. He failed. His nephew participated in the FEBRUARY MUTINY. And in March 1936, with many marks of imperial regard, he was forced to resign his position in the palace. Throughout the next nine years, however, he was summoned and consulted privately by the Emperor as a loyal dissident. On November 20, 1945, informed that he was about to be arrested as a major war criminal and tried for his part in the MANCHURIAN INCIDENT, he committed ritual suicide. Revealing extracts from diaries he kept during his service as chief aide-de-camp were published in Tokyo in 1967.

HONMA MASAHARU (1887–1946). Army officer, protégé of Prince CHICHIBU for whom he served repeatedly as aide-de-camp between 1927 and 1937. Though considered too pro-British by many of his fellow officers, he was valued for his fluent English. In 1932 he read and summarized for Emperor Hirohito the LYTTON COMMISSION Report, a 400-page document, in twenty-four hours. Put in charge of the invasion of the Philippines in 1941, he was reproved by the Emperor for failure to prevent MacArthur's forces from digging in on Bataan. His command authority was promptly pre-empted by Colonel TSUJI MASANOBU and a group of staff officers who came from Tokyo with imperial orders. The disgraced Honma sulked in his tent, virtually shorn of authority; it was he, however, who was executed for the Bataan death march by the Allies in 1946.

HO-UMEZU PACT. Agreement between China and Japan concluded by Chinese General Ho and the commander of the Japanese garrison at Tientsin, Strike-South General Umezu Yoshijiro, in June 1935. It provided that Chiang's troops in the North China province of Hopei be withdrawn—in the face of Japanese preparations to attack—leaving the North China area open to Japanese penetration and exploitation.

IMPERIAL RULE ASSISTANCE ASSOCIATION (*Taisei Yokusan-kai*). The m
party organized by Prime Minister Prince Konoye in 1940 to replace all ot
political parties in Japan.

IMPERIAL WAY GROUP (*Kodo-ha*). The antagonists of the CONTROL CLIQ
and the majority party in the EMPEROR'S CABAL. They became disaffected w
Hirohito's national strategy in the early 1930's and supported the STRI
NORTH FACTION in agitation for military preparations against Russia. Put do
by Hirohito in the FEBRUARY MUTINY, leaders of the Imperial Way Gro
were retired from the Army in 1936, but followers continued to resist impe
policies through the war and into the half century following the war. Princi
purged Imperial Way Group leaders were MAZAKI JINZABURO and one of
THREE CROWS, Obata Toshiro. Important unpurged sympathizers with
movement were ISHIWARA KANJI, YAMAMOTO ISOROKU, and YAMASH
TOMOYUKI.

ISHIWARA KANJI (1889–1949). Army officer admired for his intellectual b
liance but cordially detested by most of his peers for his religious preachi
uncompromising frankness, and self-righteous sense of mission. Ishiwara hea
his class at military academy and went on to staff college in 1915, only
years later. In the 1920's he served for four years as an instructor at the s
college and for three years as an attaché and intelligence agent in Berlin.
became a member of the SUZUKI STUDY GROUP and was accepted belate
into the EMPEROR'S CABAL. In October 1928 he was attached to the staff
the KWANTUNG ARMY to draw up plans for the seizure of Manchuria. Assis
by the salesmanship of ITAGAKI SEISHIRO, he saw his proposals accepted,
in 1931–32 he executed the military half of them with awesome efficien
From August 1935 to September 1937 he was employed, with many outspo
qualms, in supervising war planning for the conquest of central China. Dur
the FEBRUARY MUTINY of 1936 he insisted upon strict obedience to Hirohi
orders in dealing with the young mutineers. Having refused to side with eit
the STRIKE-NORTH or STRIKE-SOUTH factions, he survived the purges wh
followed the mutiny, but in the first year of the war with China he saw
worst fears confirmed and made himself increasingly unpopular by his crit
outbursts against imperial policy. After December 1938 he was relegated
garrison commands. Finally, in March 1941, he was retired to the rese
with the rank of lieutenant general. He returned briefly to prominence in 19
46 by making speeches for the government in exculpation of the Throne
accusation of General Tojo. The effort broke his health. During the war cri
trials the International Military Tribunal sent a deputation to take testim
from him on his sickbed. Assorted debilities, exacerbated by wartime ma
trition, ended his life in 1949.

ISOGAI RENSUKE (1886–1967). Army officer, one of the ELEVEN RELIABI
He conducted the preliminary negotiations for the HO-UMEZU PACT in 1
and acted as governor general of Hong Kong during World War II. After
war he was tried and judged guilty of war crimes by the Chinese, but
pardoned by Chiang Kai-shek through the intercession of TSUJI MASANOBU

ITAGAKI SEISHIRO (1885–1948). Army officer, one of the ELEVEN RELIAB
a tough, engaging, back-slapping specialist in China intelligence work. In N
1929 he was posted to the KWANTUNG ARMY to assist ISHIWARA KANJI p
ically in planning the seizure of Manchuria. In 1932 he ordered the incitem
for the FAKE WAR. From August 1932 to March 1937 he served on the Kw
TUNG ARMY staff as chief advisor on Manchukuoan affairs. In this capa

e shared with DOIHARA KENJI the responsibility for sore aggression and xploitation of the new colony. In the first year of the war with China he ommanded the 5th Division. As war minister from June 1938 to September 939 he presided over two disastrous border wars with Russia, the Lake .hasan affair and the NOMONHAN INCIDENT. Thereafter he served as a com- 1ander of rear-area armies in China, Korea, and Malaya. After the war he 'as tried for war crimes in Manchuria and hanged beside Doihara.

ro HIROBUMI (1841–1909). A Choshu samurai who became the leading ɔokesman of Japan during the reign of Emperor Meiji. He supervised the :rafting of the Constitution of 1889. As a gradual opponent of the war policies f General YAMAGATA ARITOMO he tried to avert the Russo-Japanese War. Vhile he was prime minister in 1900, he founded the CONSTITUTIONALIST ARTY. He was assassinated in Korea in 1909.

.MMU. The legendary first Emperor of Japan, or of YAMATO, who according ɔ tradition ascended the throne in 660 B.C. and according to archaeologists :igned in the first century A.D. All Japanese emperors are descended from im, though not all patrilineally or by primogeniture. Hirohito is accounted 1e one hundred and twenty-fourth of the line.

.ANIN KOTOHITO, Prince (1865–1945). Adopted son of Emperor KOMEI, :venth son of KUNIYE. Having outlived the last of his brothers, he ranked 'om 1923 to 1945 as the senior member of the imperial family. At the same me being a professional Army officer, a graduate of French military acad- mies, who had risen through the officer corps to the rank of field marshal, rince Kanin became the gray eminence of Japan's military establishment. .lways an activist, he presided over an attempt in 1916 to assassinate Chinese 'arlord Chang Tso-lin and occupy Manchuria. In 1921 he personally showed [irohito the World War battlefields of France. In the 1920's his protégés ATEKAWA YOSHIJI and KOISO KUNIAKE assisted their juniors, the THREE ROWS and the ELEVEN RELIABLES, in recruiting the EMPEROR'S CABAL. In ›ecember 1931, during the conquest of Manchuria, Prince Kanin accepted the .ghest post in the Army, that of chief of staff. He retained it throughout the 930's, while the war with China was undertaken, until October 1940. There- fter, in his late seventies, he remained at Hirohito's side, manipulating Army ders, until his death on May 21, 1945.

.AYA TSUNENORI, Prince (1900–   ). Grandson of ASAHIKO, first cousin of mpress Nagako, husband of a niece of Empress Dowager SADAKO, and child- ɔod playmate of Hirohito. In 1934 he and his wife paid a state visit to Hitler 1d returned admiring the Third Reich and supporting alliance with it. As a ɩajor general in 1943, he served on the faculty of the Army Staff College ɪpervising war strategy. After the war he occupied sinecures in the Taisho and 'isshin Life Insurance companies.

ɪDO KOICHI, Marquis (1888–   ). First of the BIG BROTHERS and founder : the ELEVEN CLUB. A diligent bureaucrat, he was responsible in the Ministry f Commerce and Industry for much of Japan's early industrial planning for ar. In 1930 he became secretary to the lord privy seal and in 1940 lord privy :al. He remained Hirohito's closest civilian advisor throughout the war. In)48 the International Military Tribunal sentenced him to life imprisonment; ɘ was paroled in 1956. His diaries were published in Japan in 1966.

.ITA IKKI (1882–1936). Political theorist whose major work, *The Fundamen- ·l Principles for the Reconstruction of the Nation,* provided many of the basic leas of Japanese fascism, particularly those of the STRIKE-NORTH FACTION.

After the FEBRUARY MUTINY he was executed for having written the manifes of the mutineers.

KMT. Abbreviation for the Kuomintang, political party in China ultimate headed by Chiang Kai-shek.

KOISO KUNIAKE (1880–1950). Army officer, intelligence specialist, protégé Prince KANIN, a senior member of the EMPEROR'S CABAL. As a General St. emissary to Inner Mongolia in 1915–17 he arranged for the Mongol invasi of Manchuria which was co-ordinated with the 1916 Japanese attempt on t life of Chinese warlord Chang Tso-lin. In the early 1920's he was responsit for seeing that aviation intelligence gathered by Japanese attachés in Euro was fully utilized in the development of a Japanese Army air force. In 19 he masterminded the MARCH PLOT. Vice war minister in 1932, command in chief of the Korean Army in 1935, minister of colonization in the Cabir in 1939 and 1940, governor general of Korea from 1942 to 1944, Koiso fina became prime minister in the desperate kamikaze months of July 1944 April 1945. After the war he died in prison while serving a life sentence as war criminal.

KOMEI, Emperor (1831–1867). The last Mikado of old Japan in whose rei, in 1853, U.S. Commodore Matthew Perry forced his way into Tokyo Bay cannon point. In the last fourteen years of his life, Komei cast about vair for vassals strong enough to expel the Western invaders, enforce Japan's tra tional policy of seclusion from the world, and preserve the sanctity of Japane shores—the religious trust handed down to him by his imperial ancestors. the course of his stubborn efforts Komei endorsed a long-range imperial poli for Japan: to cast out the barbarians and conquer a buffer zone in neighbori lands which would keep them from ever intruding again. By insisting on tl goal too early he demanded the impossible of his vassals. The martial samu clan of CHOSHU which had first suggested the goal to him was humiliated his insistence on immediate action. Leaders of the clan had him murder with the connivance of a sympathetic nobleman, Iwakura Tomomi. His fiftee year-old son MEIJI was accepted as his successor.

KOMOTO DAISAKU (1893–1954). One of the ELEVEN RELIABLES in the Arr officer corps. In 1928 he blew up a railroad car carrying Chang Tso-lin, t warlord of North China, and so launched Japanese aggression in the Mancl rian area, climaxed by the MANCHURIAN INCIDENT. Having taken responsibil for the assassination of Chang, he enjoyed a comfortable life as a member the board of directors of Japan's SOUTH MANCHURIAN RAILROAD. He died natural causes in his villa outside Kobe in 1954.

KONOYE FUMIMARO, Prince (1891–1945). Highest ranking FUJIWARA prin youngest of the BIG BROTHERS. As prime minister from 1937 to 1939, assumed responsibility for the war with China; as prime minister again in 194 41, he acquiesced in the Emperor's STRIKE-SOUTH plans, organized the IMI RIAL RULE ASSISTANCE ASSOCIATION, and prepared the way for totalitari government. Resigning in favor of TOJO HIDEKI in October 1941, Prin Konoye acted as titular leader of the PEACE FACTION during the war. On t eve of his arrest, after the war, as a major war criminal, he took poison. I Princeton-educated son Fumitaka, or "Butch," was sentenced to twenty-f years at hard labor by a Moscow court for war crimes against the Russia in Manchuria; he died in 1956 at Ivanova prison camp in Siberia. Prir Konoye's brother Konoye Hidemaro conducts the Tokyo Symphony Orchest

KUNIYE, Prince (1802–1875). Nineteenth Prince FUSHIMI, he was the adop son of Emperor Kokaku and the father of sixteen sons of his own. He w the progenitor of the entire modern imperial family except for the houses of Hirohito and his three brothers.

KUNIYOSHI, Prince Kuni II (1873–1929). Son of ASAHIKO, grandson of KUNIYE, father of Empress Nagako. He was an early advocate of air power and of germ warfare. One of his protégés was YAMAMOTO ISOROKU.

KURUSU SABURO (1888–1954). Career diplomat who negotiated the TRIPARTITE PACT and who was special envoy to Washington in November 1941 assigned to guide Ambassador NOMURA KICHISABURO in his negotiations with the U.S. State Department.

KWANTUNG ARMY (*Kanto-gun*). The portion of the Japanese Imperial Army stationed in Japan's KWANTUNG LEASEHOLD in Manchuria. Employed to protect Japanese interests on the Continent, it won a reputation as containing the toughest units in the Army. The success of Japan's invasion of Manchuria, begun with the MANCHURIAN INCIDENT, was largely the result of its effectiveness. At some points in their careers, most members of the EMPEROR'S CABAL served as staff officers with the Kwantung Army and came to be known, especially in the West, by the misleading euphemism of the "Kwantung Army gang."

KWANTUNG LEASEHOLD. Territory in southern part of Liaotung Peninsula, MANCHURIA, including ports of Dairen and Port Arthur. It was acquired by Japan after first Sino-Japanese War, 1895, and then relinquished under international pressure; China then leased the area to Russia. After the Russo-Japanese War it was occupied by Japan, and in 1915 Japan acquired a ninety-nine-year leasehold on it from China. It became the base for the KWANTUNG ARMY, the terminus for the SOUTH MANCHURIAN RAILROAD network, and the arsenal of Japanese strength on the Continent.

LYTTON COMMISSION. The League of Nations' Commission of Inquiry, headed by Lord Lytton of Great Britain, appointed to investigate the circumstances of Japan's invasion of MANCHURIA. The commission's conclusions, set forth in the Lytton Report, were that Japan's action was not in "self-defense" and that the subsequent state of MANCHUKUO did not result from any native independence movement. The report recommended that Manchuria be given an autonomous administration under Chinese sovereignty. The Lytton Report was adopted by the League over Japan's objection, in February 1933, and Japan's withdrawal from the League followed.

MACHIJIRI KAZUMOTO (1889–*c.* 1950). A well-connected Army officer, son of Count Mibu Motonaga who was a celebrated loyalist nobleman at the Court of Emperor Komei. He was the adopted son of Viscount Machijiri Kazuhiro, master of rituals at the Court of Hirohito, and brother of Count Mibu Motoyoshi who married the elder sister of Prince Higashikuni. Machijiri married Empress Nagako's first cousin Yukiko, the elder sister of Prince KAYA TSUNENORI. In 1919 Machijiri accompanied Prince HIGASHIKUNI to Europe where he helped to recruit the THREE CROWS and found the EMPEROR'S CABAL. Returning to Japan, he had command of artillery of the Imperial Guards in 1926 and became an aide-de-camp and liaison officer for Hirohito in 1930. He left the Emperor's side briefly after the FEBRUARY MUTINY in order to carry out a purge of dissident junior officers in the War Ministry. He left it again in October 1937 to take charge of the influential Military Affairs Bureau of the War Ministry during the personnel manipulations which preceded the Rape of Nanking. Other delicate assignments followed, some in the Army bureaucracy in Tokyo, others in command or staff posts with the armies in China. In the seven months before Pearl Harbor, Machijiri ran the Chemical

Weapons Branch of the Army which handled both gasses and gunpowders. During the war, from 1942 to 1944, he commanded Japan's garrison army in French Indochina. He retired from military life in May 1945 and died a few years later.

MAKINO NOBUAKI, Count (1862–1949). A member of the SATSUMA nobility, he was a principal companion of Crown Prince Hirohito on his European tour in 1921; as lord privy seal from 1925 until the end of 1935, he was the Emperor's principal advisor, closely involved in the intrigues to eliminate adherents of the STRIKE-NORTH FACTION from the Army and the government hierarchy.

MANCHUKUO. Japanese name for the pseudo-independent state set up in February 1932 and eventually comprising the three provinces of Manchuria and the province of Jehol.

MANCHURIA. Region in northeast China, including the Liaotung Peninsula or which Japan's KWANTUNG LEASEHOLD was situated. In the seventeenth century it had been the homeland of the Manchu conquerors of China. After the MANCHURIAN INCIDENT in September 1931 the Kwantung Army took it piece by piece and made it a slave state of Japan, renamed Manchukuo.

MANCHURIAN INCIDENT (*Manshu Jiken*). Japanese designation for the seizure of Mukden, capital of Manchuria, on the night of September 18, 1931, by th KWANTUNG ARMY; pretext for the attack was an explosion on the railway In reality the Japanese government, through assignments to various Arm officers, notably ISHIWARA KANJI, had been planning the conquest of Mar churia for more than two years.

MARCH PLOT (*Sangatsu Jiken*). Scheme devised in the early months of 193 by the Emperor's close supporters—principally Lord Privy Seal MAKIN NOBUAKI, his protégé Dr. OKAWA SHUMEI, and STRIKE-SOUTH FACTION office in the War Ministry and Army General Staff—to compromise the political moderate General Ugaki Kazushige, war minister and potential leader of th CONSTITUTIONALIST PARTY. The plotters involved Ugaki in a weird plan to sei the Diet and declare himself military dictator; the plan was never intend to be effected, but it was sufficient to incriminate Ugaki as disloyal to th Emperor. He was removed as war minister and appointed to the political harmless position of governor general of Korea. Intimidation of Army mo erates around Ugaki opened the way for militants to proceed with plans f the conquest of Manchuria.

MATSUOKA YOSUKE (1880–1946). American-educated diplomat, foreign mi ister who negotiated non-aggression pacts with both Germany and Russia a whose indecision concerning policies and intentions toward the United Sta led to his replacement in July 1941.

MAY FIFTEENTH INCIDENT (*Go-ichi-go Jiken*). Japanese designation for threatened coup d'etat which resulted in the assassination of Prime Minis Inukai on May 15, 1932. The assassination, promoted by the EMPEROR'S CAB and by the ELEVEN CLUB because of Inukai's opposition to substantial bud increases for the military, was the final act in the so-called TRIPLE INTRIGU in effect, it ended government by political party in Japan.

MAZAKI JINZABURO (1876–1956). Army officer, protégé of Emperor Tais military academy classmate of ARAKI SADAO and HONJO SHIGERU. Noted his loyalty and blunt honesty, he was put in charge of the 1st Regiment the Imperial Guards in July 1921 during the delicate months of Crown Pri

Hirohito's absence in Europe. He later became the leader of the IMPERIAL WAY GROUP in the EMPEROR'S CABAL. In 1931 he and his followers supported the war ministership of the urbane Strike-North leader Araki Sadao. Between 1932 and 1935, first as vice chief of staff, then as inspector general of military education, Mazaki feuded with Prince HIGASHIKUNI and repeatedly criticized palace policy making. In the summer of 1935 Chief of Staff Prince KANIN openly required him to resign as inspector general. As a consequence the schism deepened in the Emperor's Cabal and finally had to be dealt with in the bloody confrontation of the FEBRUARY MUTINY. After the mutiny Mazaki was interrogated for months by the secret police, refused to admit any guilt, went on a hunger strike, and was finally acquitted. He withdrew from public life and spent most of his last twenty years puttering about his ancestral estate on the island of Kyushu.

MEIJI, Emperor (1852–1912). Son of Emperor KOMEI, he completed the overthrow of the TOKUGAWA shogunate and effected the restoration of direct rule by the imperial house. During his reign Shinto was established as the state religion, industrialization and foreign trade were entrusted to the ZAIBATSU, and the buildup of the Imperial Army and Navy was climaxed by victory in the Russo-Japanese War of 1904–05. Meiji was succeeded by his son Yoshihito, Emperor TAISHO.

MIKASA, Prince (1915–   ). Third brother of Hirohito, Army officer, patron of TSUJI MASANOBU. After matriculating at the military academy in 1934, he specialized in tanks and graduated in 1936. He remained attached to the tactical communications headquarters of the cavalry throughout most of the war years. In 1944, as an associate member of the PEACE FACTION, he accepted a desk in the Office of Military Education to work with other junior officers who had been his classmates. In August 1945 a group of his charges staged the abortive palace coup on the night of surrender. During the Occupation he went back to school and became an "anthropologist" specializing in the ancient tombs of Babylon, Egypt, and Japan. He became known as the nonconformist of the imperial family, fond of wearing sports jackets and given to open-minded discussion of republican and proletarian views.

MILITARY ACADEMY PLOT (*Shikan-gakko Jiken*). Plan for an armed uprising in Tokyo, intended to arouse the Emperor to "renovate the nation," devised in November 1934 by a group of cadets at the military academy with the backing of Army staff officers who were partisans of former War Minister ARAKI SADAO and the STRIKE-NORTH FACTION. The plot was disclosed to the War Ministry by STRIKE-SOUTH FACTION spies in the academy—notably TSUJI MASANOBU—and its cadet leaders were put under arrest. However, the plans of the plotters were to become the basis for the FEBRUARY MUTINY in 1936.

MISTY LAGOON AIR DEVELOPMENT STATION. Naval air force training station, established under the command of YAMAMOTO ISOROKU, on Kasumi-ga-Ura, the Misty Lagoon, 30 miles northeast of Tokyo. Its function was to train Navy pilots in torpedo-bombing techniques in preparation for aircraft-carrier operations. A group of Misty Lagoon fliers assassinated Prime Minister Inukai during the MAY FIFTEENTH INCIDENT.

NAGATA TETSUZAN (1883–1935). Army officer who assumed leadership of the EMPEROR'S CABAL in the 1920's and came to be known as the first of the THREE CROWS. As a major general in 1932 he headed the Intelligence Department of the Army General Staff, then in 1934 became chief of the Military Affairs Bureau in the War Ministry. In 1935 he was assassinated because he

was opposed to plans for war with China and because his part in the MARC
PLOT, exposed by Strike-North generals, had grown embarrassing to th
Emperor.

NASHIMOTO MORIMASA, Prince (1874–1951). Fourth son of ASAHIKO and eld(
half-brother of Hirohito's two uncles Prince ASAKA and Prince HIGASHIKUN
He graduated from military academy in 1896; studied and traveled—incognit(
under the name of Nagai—in Europe 1903–04 and 1906–09; rose to the ran
of colonel in 1910, general in 1923, and field marshal in 1932. In 1936, du
ing the FEBRUARY MUTINY, he ingratiated himself with Hirohito by his u
questioning loyalty at a time when imperial family councils were divided. I
May 1937, on a visit to Tojo in Manchuria, he secured a pledge of co-oper
tion in the planned war with China from dissident Strike-North elemen
remaining in the KWANTUNG ARMY. He was rewarded in October 1937 b
appointment to the remunerative sinecure of lord custodian of national shrin
and chief priest of the sun goddess at Ise Shrine. Second to none in th
spiritual realm and second only to Prince KANIN in the Army, he continue
as one of Hirohito's closest family advisors until October 1945. Then he w
arrested and held for six months as MacArthur's hostage during negotiatio
of changes in Japan's fundamental laws and institutions.

NATIONAL FOUNDATION SOCIETY (*Kokuhonsha*). Right-wing nationalistic orga
ization of businessmen and labor leaders, which sometimes applied brakes
imperial policy making in the 1930's. Its director, Baron Hiranuma Kiichir
was prime minister during the NOMONHAN INCIDENT in 1939 and president
the Privy Council from March 1936 to January 1939 and again from April
August 1945.

NATIONAL PRINCIPLE GROUP (*Kokutai Genri-ha*). An organization of disside
Army junior officers concerned with the Army's role in politics and the co
flicts between the STRIKE-NORTH and STRIKE-SOUTH factions. The organize
were in sympathy with the officers involved in the MILITARY ACADEMY PLOT
November 1934 and were to be the leaders of the FEBRUARY MUTINY in 193

NATIVE-LAND-LOVING SOCIETY (*Aikyojuku*). Commune of philosophic farmer
followers of Tolstoyan doctrines, which maintained a co-operative located
the region between Oarai and Mito. Prince Konoye and Prince HIGASHIKU
arranged an endowment for the society in 1930.

NOMONHAN INCIDENT. A major border conflict fought in Manchuria with th
Soviet Union in 1939. Though hushed up at the time, it involved tens of tho
sands of troops and cost the Japanese Army thousands of lives. The Japane
troops who provoked it were soundly defeated. As a result the STRIKE-NORT
FACTION in Japan was discredited.

NOMURA KICHISABURO (1877–1964). Retired admiral, ambassador to th
United States in 1941 who conducted the final Japanese negotiations with th
State Department before the attack on Pearl Harbor.

OCTOBER PLOT (*Jugatsu Jiken*). Scheme promoted by the Emperor's B
BROTHERS and their supporters in the Army, in October 1931, to create
impression at the League of Nations that the Japanese government was
danger of a coup d'etat by militarists. Certain young Army officers were e
couraged to enlist in a synthetic plot, devised by Lieutenant Colonel Hashimo
Kingoro and Intelligence Major CHO ISAMU, to assassinate the prime minist
and members of his Cabinet. The plotters were duly exposed (but mere
placed under house arrest), and the government was able to announce
escape.

HTANI KOZUI (1876–1948). Maternal uncle of Emperor Hirohito by mar-
age, an early supporter of the STRIKE-SOUTH FACTION, and Buddhist mission-
y in the East Indies and Malaya. His friendship with the sultan of Johore
lped to make possible the swift capture of Singapore in February 1942.

KAWA SHUMEI (1886–1957). Propagandist and ideologist for the STRIKE-
)UTH FACTION and one of the top operatives in the "CIVILIAN SPY SERVICE."
e was a doctor of philosophy (Tokyo Imperial University) and a linguist
roficient in English, French, German, Sanskrit, Arabic, and several other
nguages. He worked as an intelligence agent in China for the Army General
aff from 1911 to 1918. In the 1920's he was director of the UNIVERSITY
ODGING HOUSE. A protégé of Count MAKINO NOBUAKI, he figured in the
[ARCH PLOT, the OCTOBER PLOT, the BLOOD BROTHERHOOD, and the MAY
IFTEENTH INCIDENT. As a defendant in the war crimes trials in Tokyo in 1946
e escaped sentence by feigning insanity.

SHIMA HIROSHI (1886–   ). Chief negotiator with Hitler from 1934 to
)45; officially ambassador to Germany from 1938 to 1939 and again from
)40 to 1945.

ALACE SHRINE (*Kashikodokoro*). The trio of Shinto shrines on the grounds
the Imperial Palace where Emperor Hirohito worshipped his ancestors and
d obeisance to replicas of the three sacred treasures of the imperial regalia:
e mirror of the sun, the necklace of agriculture, and the sword of war.
emnants of the originals of the three treasures are housed in shrines in the
ovinces. The sword, enshrined on a piece of sacred ground in the city of
agoya, was destroyed by a U.S. bomb in 1945.

ANAY INCIDENT. The sinking of the U.S. gunboat *Panay* in the Yangtze River,
ecember 12, 1937, by Japanese artillery commanded by Colonel Hashimoto
ingoro during the campaign to capture Nanking. President Franklin Roose-
elt and American Ambassador Joseph E. Grew protested vigorously, and the
suing international crisis probably deterred Japan from its planned attack
a Hong Kong. (Colonel Hashimoto of the OCTOBER PLOT, a protégé of the
en Prime Minister KONOYE FUMIMARO, later became executive director of the
IPERIAL RULE ASSISTANCE ASSOCIATION.)

EACE FACTION. A group of General Staff officers, diplomats, and politicians
ho in 1944 and 1945 drew up detailed plans for the contingency of defeat.
ounded in 1939 by Navy Captain Takagi Sokichi and Army Colonel Matsu-
ni Makoto in the General Staffs, the group was gradually expanded during
e war under the titular leadership of Prince KONOYE FUMIMARO, the active
adership of YOSHIDA SHIGERU, and over-all supervision of KIDO KOICHI.
rince MIKASA and Prince TAKAMATSU discussed its activities regularly with
irohito at a weekly gathering of the imperial family to watch newsreels in
e palace. By the end of the war the Peace Faction's organization included
aders from all spheres of Japanese life, and its planning covered everything
om demonstrations of protest at the surrender to planes held in readiness for
e transportation of peace negotiators.

EERS' SCHOOL (*Gakushuin*). Organized by Emperor Kokaku in 1821 (re-
rganized and named in 1877), to educate the sons of royalty and nobility for
les in government. The school provided Hirohito's formal education between
e ages of eight and fourteen; its headmaster was General Nogi Maresuke,
ommander of Japanese forces in the assault on Port Arthur in the Russo-
panese War. After World War II the school was opened to gifted common-

ers, and Crown Prince Akihito studied there under the tutelage of an Amer
can, Elizabeth Gray Vining.

PRAYER MEETING PLOT (*Shimpeitai Jiken*). Scheme to blackmail groups of tl
Emperor's political opponents devised by Lieutenant General Prince HIGASH
KUNI, prominent Big Brother and uncle of Hirohito, in the summer of 193
The absurd plot—to assemble several thousand rightists in the guise of pilgrin
at the Meiji Shrine in Tokyo for prayer and the Emperor's blessing, after whic
they would proceed to terrorize the capital with a series of political assassin
tions—was never intended to succeed; its purpose was to embarrass the spoi
sors enlisted for it by Prince HIGASHIKUNI, all of whom represented interes
allied with the STRIKE-NORTH FACTION.

SADAKO, Empress Dowager (1885–1951). Wife of Emperor Taisho and moth
of Emperor Hirohito. A strong and gracious woman, she disapproved of Hir
hito's warlike policies and made her palace a salon for aristocrats who soug
to keep him from going to war and later from continuing it.

SADANARU, Prince (1858–1923). Twenty-first Prince FUSHIMI, fourteenth si
of KUNIYE. He was a French-educated apostle of Westernized military orgar
zation for Japan and served as a field general in the 1894–95 war with Chir
and in the Russo-Japanese War of 1904–05. He was lord privy seal from 191
to 1915, an intimate advisor of Emperor Taisho and one of his group of S:
PRINCES.

SAIONJI KINMOCHI, Prince (1849–1940). One of the authors of the Constit
tion of 1889, a leader of the CONSTITUTIONALIST PARTY (later he helped finan
the ANTI-CONSTITUTIONALIST PARTY), twice prime minister—finally the la
Constitutional father (*genro*). In 1921 he accepted the role of prime-ministe
maker, official advisor to the Emperor on the appointment of Cabinets. Un
his retirement in 1937 he represented to many Japanese the last liberal Wes
ernizing influence in prewar Japan.

SATSUMA. A large clan in the island of Kyushu, of which Shimazu was tl
dominant family and Kagoshima the hereditary stronghold. A large proportic
of officers of the Imperial Japanese Navy in the decades leading up to Wor
War II were descendants of the old Satsuma clan, traditionally seamen-wa
riors.

SIX PRINCES. Intimates and advisors of Emperor Taisho, including SADANAR
twenty-first Prince FUSHIMI, and his brothers Prince ASAHIKO and Prin
KANIN. They plotted the unsuccessful attempt to assassinate Chang Tso-li
warlord of Manchuria, in 1916, favored the invasion of Siberia during Woi
War I, and opposed the Choshu policies of Army Chief of Staff Gener
YAMAGATA ARITOMO.

SORGE SPY RING. Masterminded by German intellectual Richard Sorge tl
ring provided liaison between the Russian and Japanese governments in tl
1936–41 period and in effect helped to maintain peace between the two cou
tries. One of Sorge's sources in Tokyo was Saionji Kinkazu, leftist grandsi
of Prince SAIONJI KINMOCHI; another was Ozaki Hotsumi, Marxist intellectu
and a protégé of Prince Konoye Atsumaro, father of Prince KONOYE FUN
MARO. Both men remained loyal to the Emperor while at the same time bei
in a position to assure the Kremlin that the STRIKE-NORTH FACTION would n
wage war against Russia. Foreigner Sorge and commoner Ozaki were execut
as spies in Tokyo in 1944 but aristocrat Saionji Kinkazu was spared; in tl
1960's he was Japan's representative in Communist Peking.

SOUTH MANCHURIAN RAILROAD (*Mantetsu*). A Japanese government corporation formed to build railroads on rights of way in Manchuria acquired in 1905 with the KWANTUNG LEASEHOLD. Railroad police garrisons along the rights of way kept the lines of track open for the KWANTUNG ARMY so that Japanese influence in Manchuria, from 1905 to 1931, could never be denied. At all important junctions on the railroad a Kwantung Army military mission or Special Service Organ operated through local hirelings to keep a finger on local political pulses. Engineers of the railroad later facilitated Japanese Army movements by repairing or laying track across the China and through the Burmese and Sumatran jungles.

SOUTHWARD MOVEMENT SOCIETY (*Nampo-kai*). A branch of the "CIVILIAN SPY SERVICE," utilizing Japanese commercial travelers and Japanese emigrants to Southeast Asia. It was set up in Taiwan in 1934, soon after Strike-South General Count Terauchi Hisaichi took command of Army forces there. Information about Malaya, the Dutch East Indies, and the Philippines supplied by the society's agents was used by Army staff officers in 1941 in planning the military campaigns which opened the war.

STRIKE-NORTH FACTION (*Hokushin-pa*). Proponents of the idea that Japan must devote all her military energies to preparing for an inevitable war with Communist Russia. A few of the Strike-North Faction, particularly the leaders of the IMPERIAL WAY GROUP in the Army, had a genuine ideological phobia against communism; many more, however, simply hoped that by turning Japanese belligerence against Russia, Japan could remain on friendly terms with the West. These pacifists in war paint included some of the noisiest CONSTITUTIONALIST PARTY politicians who spoke for a Strike North in the Diet.

STRIKE-SOUTH FACTION (*Nampo-ha*). The minority in the Japanese establishment which dared, under the leadership of Hirohito, to insist upon a national policy of expansion into the rich lands of Southeast Asia and Indonesia, thereby incurring the antagonism of the colonial Western powers, The Netherlands, France, Great Britain, and the United States. Historically the first advocates of a Strike South were the lords of the SATSUMA clan and their in-law allies at Court, the imperial branch family of FUSHIMI, with which Hirohito allied himself by his marriage to Empress Nagako in 1924. Satsuma-clan and Fushimi-family kinsmen dominated the Japanese Imperial Navy which carried out the Strike South in 1941 and 1942. In the Army the CONTROL CLIQUE in the EMPEROR'S CABAL fought for the Strike South against the IMPERIAL WAY GROUP. They were backed by industrialists who had foreign trade interests in Indonesia and the South Seas and by priests of the imperial family who believed that Emperor Jimmu, the progenitor of the imperial line, had come from the south. Most important, they were supported by Hirohito himself, who saw no profit for empire building except in the islands of the south where there were rubber, oil, and room for colonists.

SUGIYAMA HAJIME (1880–1945). Army officer, protégé of Prince KANIN, a senior member of the EMPEROR'S CABAL, nicknamed "Bathroom Door" for his noncommittal facial expression. In 1912 he drew up the first General Staff contingency plan for the capture of Singapore. In the 1920's he handled procurement for the fledgling Japanese Army air force. After assisting in the MARCH PLOT and MANCHURIAN INCIDENT, he rose to vice chief of staff in 1934 and war minister in 1937 during the first year of the war with China. In 1940 he followed Prince Kanin as Army chief of staff, a post which he would continue to fill until February 1944. From July 1944 to April 1945 he was again war minister. After the surrender in August 1945 both he and wife committed ritual suicide. A volume of his memoranda written during term as wartime chief of staff was published in Tokyo in 1967.

SUZUKI KANTARO (1867–1948). Admiral, chief of the Navy General St 1925–29, and grand chamberlain to the Emperor 1929–36. Severely wound in the FEBRUARY MUTINY, he remained an advisor to Hirohito but withdr from public office. In April 1945, at the age of seventy-seven, he was su moned by Hirohito to be prime minister, and he smoothly operated the mestic political machinery during Japan's surrender.

SUZUKI STUDY GROUP (*Kenkyu-kai*, later *Mumei-kai* and *Isseki-kai*). Ar officers under the direction of (then) Major SUZUKI TEI-ICHI who prepar position papers in 1927 urging that North China warlord Chang Tso-lin disposed of and his province of Manchuria acquired by Japan. The group cluded ISHIWARA KANJI, several graduates of the UNIVERSITY LODGING HOU and two of Hirohito's aides-de-camp, Viscount MACHIJIRI KAZUMOTO a ANAMI KORECHIKA.

SUZUKI TEI-ICHI (1888–   ). One of the most capable officers in the E PEROR'S CABAL, specialist in economics, and protégé of Marquis Inoue Sabu of the BIG BROTHERS. Having known Chiang Kai-shek at military acade in Tokyo in 1907–10, he was assigned from November 1920 to Decem 1926 to assist and observe Chiang during the latter's rise to power in the KM From 1927 to 1929 as a member of the operations section of the General St he successfully urged preparations for Japanese seizure of MANCHURIA. 1930 he was closely associated with Marquis KIDO KOICHI and the ELEV CLUB. From 1930 to 1933, first as an attaché in Peking, then as chief of China Squad, Military Affairs Bureau, War Ministry, he planned the mon oly-granting system which was used for the economic exploitation of M CHUKUO. After a brief stint as head of Army press relations, he was employ almost uninterruptedly from 1934 to 1941 in planning and executing the e nomic exploitation of China. From November 1937 to April 1938 he h charge of the organized sacking of Nanking. For the next three years he v the leading spirit in the ASIA DEVELOPMENT BOARD. In April 1941 he reti from the Army to become a minister of state in the second Konoye Cabi and head of the CABINET PLANNING BOARD. In this capacity he mobilized a administered Japan's war economy until the fall of Prime Minister Tojo July 1944. After the war the Allied Military Tribunal sentenced him to imprisonment, from which he was released in 1956.

TAISHO, Emperor (1879–1926). Son of Emperor MEIJI, father of Empe Hirohito. He was not a personal force during his reign; the policies of period, including Japan's participation in World War I, were largely det mined by his advisors, the SIX PRINCES. After 1921, when Taisho suffere stroke and consequent mental incompetence, Hirohito acted as Regent.

TAKAMATSU, Prince (1905–   ). Second brother of Hirohito, professio naval officer. From 1935 to 1945 he had a desk in the Navy General St offices. His intimacy with Admiral YAMAMOTO ISOROKU was largely resp sible for Japan's adoption of the Pearl Harbor attack plan. During the war was closely associated with the development of an Air Navy and the final sort to kamikaze tactics. After the war he was active in the affairs of Imperial Household Council and such cultural organizations as the Rebi Society, the Sericulture Association, the Red Cross, the Maison Fran Japonais, and the Japan Basketball Association.

TAKEDA TSUNEYOSHI, Prince (1909–   ). Grandson of Emperor Meiji and son of Meiji's sixth daughter, Masako, he was one of the ablest of Hirohito's generation in the imperial family. During World War II, as a major, later lieutenant colonel, he served as Hirohito's personal liaison officer to the Saigon-based staff of General Count TERAUCHI HISAICHI. After the war he escaped the financial pinch felt by some of his cousins and retired to his estate in Chiba, where he raised prize cattle and polo ponies.

TANAKA MEMORIAL. A report to the Throne by Prime Minister Tanaka Gi-ichi on the Far Eastern Conference of 1927, a meeting of Japanese Foreign Ministry officials and Army commanders from Korea and Manchuria to formulate policy for China and Manchuria. The actual text has been lost, but a Chinese version, widely circulated in translation in the West, presented the *Memorial* as Japan's blueprint for world conquest. Japanese sources, however, show that Tanaka's report was actually intended as a plea to the newly acceded Emperor Hirohito to pursue a policy of economic rather than military aggrandizement.

TANAKA MITSUAKI (1843–1939). As imperial household finance auditor, PEERS' SCHOOL director, assistant minister and then minister of the imperial household between 1891 and 1901, he became one of Emperor Meiji's closest confidants. During the last decade of Meiji's reign he established a single clearinghouse and co-ordinating directorship for Japan's proliferating autonomous espionage agencies. After Meiji's death, under guise of writing a definitive biography of Meiji, he moved most of the paper work of his "CIVILIAN SPY SERVICE" to a cover organization, the EVERYDAY MEIJI BIOGRAPHICAL RESEARCH INSTITUTE in Oarai, north of Tokyo. When the institute was closed following the MAY FIFTEENTH INCIDENT, he frequented the palace, took too proprietary an interest in Hirohito's sex life, and after his ninetieth birthday was eased out of Court circles with the excuse that he had become stone deaf.

TANGKU TRUCE. Agreement negotiated between Chiang Kai-shek's representatives and Major General Okamura Yasuji of the THREE CROWS in May 1933, following Japan's invasion of Jehol. The province was ceded to Japan and the area south of the Great Wall was declared a demilitarized zone.

TATEKAWA YOSHIJI (1880–1945). Army officer, master intriguer, protégé of Prince KANIN, and a senior member of the EMPEROR'S CABAL. He was commended by Emperor Meiji for conspicuous service as leader of a band of irregulars behind enemy lines during the 1904–05 war with Russia. After serving as an intelligence officer in Switzerland during World War I, he was appointed confidential secretary to War Minister Oshima Kenichi, the father of OSHIMA HIROSHI. During the purge of Choshu leadership from the Army in the mid-1920's, he handled the Europe-America desk in the General Staff. In 1928 he supervised the assassination of Chinese warlord Chang Tso-lin. In 1930 he sponsored the CHERRY SOCIETY. In September 1931, when he had become a lieutenant general, he carried secret imperial instructions to Mukden and closed his eyes approvingly when the MANCHURIAN INCIDENT broke out. In 1939, having retired from the Army, he was appointed ambassador to the Soviet Union and conducted the preliminary negotiations for the Soviet-Japanese Non-Aggression Pact. Returning to Japan in 1942, he assumed leadership of the youth corps of the IMPERIAL RULE ASSISTANCE ASSOCIATION. He died on the eve of his arrest as a war crimes suspect in September 1945.

TERAUCHI HISAICHI, Count (1879–1946). Son of Field Marshal Terauchi Masatake who was war minister throughout the last nine years of Emperor

Meiji's reign and prime minister for Emperor Taisho from 1916 to 1918
Hisaichi, the son, overcame an undistinguished early start in the Army b
coming out for an end to factionalism in the Army and an unquestioning obe
dience to imperial orders. He founded the ARMY PURIFICATION MOVEMEN
and after the FEBRUARY MUTINY in 1936 he was appointed war minister t
purge adherents of the IMPERIAL WAY GROUP and the STRIKE-NORTH FACTIO
from the Army officer corps. Still the martinet, he presided from Saigon a
commander in chief of all Japanese armies in the Southwest Pacific area fror
1941 to 1945. His uninspired leadership and harsh disciplinarian spirit wa
responsible in part for the failure of samurai chivalry during the war year
When the end of the war came he was too sick to attend surrender ceremonie
or be arrested as a war criminal.

THREAT OF COUP D'ETAT. Third element in the TRIPLE INTRIGUE of 1931–32
Political activists and espionage agents of the BLOOD BROTHERHOOD and th
NATIVE-LAND-LOVING SOCIETY along with a cadre of officer-pilots from th
Navy's MISTY LAGOON AIR DEVELOPMENT STATION were recruited by th
Emperor's inner circle of BIG BROTHERS and ELEVEN CLUB members to exe
cute a series of political assassinations which were climaxed by the murder c
Prime Minister Inukai in the MAY FIFTEENTH INCIDENT. The earlier OCTOBE
PLOT had also been intended to give the impression of dangerous instabilit
in Japan's internal affairs, but the Threat of Coup d'Etat was more convincin
It persuaded many foreign observers to be patient with Japan and many dc
mestic onlookers to fear for their lives.

THREE CROWS. The first and foremost officers of the EMPEROR'S CABAL, re
cruited in Europe by Prince HIGASHIKUNI in 1921: NAGATA TETSUZAN, Obat
Toshiro, and Okamura Yasuji, of whom Nagata was to be the most influer
tial. All three were trained in military intelligence and were serving in Europ
at Japanese embassies as attachés. Their immediate assignment was to formu
late plans to mechanize the Imperial Army and to purge it of CHOSHU leade
ship. During their first meeting in Baden-Baden, Germany, in October 1921
the three officers chose the ELEVEN RELIABLES. Nagata was eventually assa
sinated; Obata broke with the cabal in the 1930's in disagreement with i
objectives; Okamura went on to become an army commander in China, ac
visor later to Chiang Kai-shek, and after the war a leader in the organizatio
of Japan's Self-Defense Forces.

TOGO HEIHACHIRO (1847–1934). Admiral in command of the Japanese flee
during the Russo-Japanese War, popular hero of the decisive victory of Tsu
shima Strait in 1905, and later chief of Crown Prince Hirohito's board c
tutors. In the early 1930's he became estranged from Hirohito and a sympa
thizer with the STRIKE-NORTH FACTION. His son Togo Minoru rose to the ran
of rear admiral in the war and afterward served as a night watchman ;
Yokosuka Naval Base, standing guard over U.S. submarines and destroyer

TOGO SHIGENORI (1881–1950). Career diplomat, son of a SATSUMA cla
samurai. He was second secretary in the Japanese Embassy in Berlin in 1920
counselor there in 1929, and ambassador in 1937–38. He was appointed for
eign minister in the Cabinet of TOJO HIDEKI in October 1941 and was re
placed in September 1942; he was foreign minister again in 1945, in the sur
render Cabinet of SUZUKI KANTARO. He died in St. Luke's Hospital in Toky
in 1950 while serving a twenty-year sentence as a war criminal. He and h
German wife, whom he married in 1920, had one daughter; he adopted he
husband, Togo Fumihiko, who became consul general in New York in 196

Tojo HIDEKI (1884–1948). Army officer and World War II prime minister. He was a protégé of Prince KANIN, who had studied and toured in Europe with Tojo's father, later a lieutenant general. Through the prince Tojo became one of the original members of the EMPEROR'S CABAL and was chosen as one of the ELEVEN RELIABLES. He graduated from the military academy with highest honors and won a place in the 3d Regiment of the Imperial Guards in 1908; in 1916 he became adjutant to War Minister Oshima Kenichi, father of OSHIMA HIROSHI. During the 1920's and early 1930's he rose steadily but inconspicuously as the protégé and shadow of NAGATA TETSUZAN. After Nagata was assassinated in 1935, Tojo was taken under wing by Prince NASHIMOTO and immediately appointed commander in chief of the secret police in Manchukuo. In March 1937 he was made chief of staff of the KWANTUNG ARMY. He became vice war minister in May 1938 and war minister in July 1940. He succeeded Prince KONOYE FUMIMARO as prime minister in October 1941 and took responsibility for leading Japan into war with the United States. After resigning as prime minister, war minister, and Army chief of staff in July 1944, he remained an active advisor to the Throne until the end of the war. Under Allied arrest and prosecution for more than three years, October 1945 to December 1948, he defended himself ably and went to his hanging bravely.

TOKUGAWA. Clan that provided the shoguns between 1603 and 1868, beginning with Tokugawa Ioyasu (1542–1616). The Tokugawa shogunate ended when the fifteen-year-old Emperor MEIJI announced restoration of direct rule by the imperial family and enforced it with the aid of the CHOSHU and SATSUMA clans by defeating the last shogun, Tokugawa Yoshinobu, Lord of Mito, in a battle near Kyoto. Thereafter the Emperor moved the capital of Japan from Kyoto to the old Tokugawa stronghold of Tokyo (Edo). Tokugawas continued to take part in Court life and political intrigue; Baron Tokugawa Yoshichika financed the MARCH PLOT in 1931 and directed espionage activities in Southeast Asia during World War II from Singapore.

TOYAMA MITSURU (1855–1944). Patron-founder of the BLACK DRAGON SOCIETY and leader of the underworld in Japan from about 1890 to about 1936. Discredited finally because of his insistence upon fighting Russia and avoiding war with the Western powers, he yet remained a hero of the Japanese masses and was consulted by Prince HIGASHIKUNI for political advice as late as 1940.

TRIPARTITE PACT. Agreement made by Japan, Germany, and Italy (signed September 27, 1940) in which the three powers pledged, for ten years, "to assist one another with all political, economic, and military means."

TRIPLE INTRIGUE (*Sanbo no sanbo*). Designation for the crucial events in Japanese politics in 1931–32: the DOLLAR SWINDLE, the FAKE WAR, and the THREAT OF COUP D'ETAT.

TSINGTAO LEASEHOLD. Enclave including the port city of Tsingtao on the south coast of Shantung Peninsula in northeastern China, leased to Germany in 1898. Japan took it from Germany in 1914, returned it to China in 1922, and reoccupied it from 1937 to 1945.

TSUJI MASANOBU (1901–1961 or later). Army fanatic recruited by the EMPEROR'S CABAL through the CHERRY SOCIETY in 1930; later mentor and protégé of Prince MIKASA. In 1934, during Mikasa's term at military academy, Tsuji was an instructor there and exposed the MILITARY ACADEMY PLOT. He went on to prove himself a tough, zealous, brilliant staff officer in Manchuria and North China. In November 1940 he was attached to the command of the

Taiwan Army to draw up plans for the conquest of Malaya. In February 194 on the staff of General YAMASHITA TOMOYUKI, he saw his plans come t fruition in the Japanese capture of Singapore. A month later, reposted a chief of the Operations Squad, General Staff, he was in the Philippines whei he took part in the capture of Bataan and then supervised the Death Marcl Later the same year, in October, he was on Guadalcanal directing vain Japi nese efforts to dislodge the U.S. Marines. In August 1943 he was reposted t China in charge of secret but unsuccessful peace negotiations with Chiar Kai-shek. In July 1944, after the collapse of Japan's invasion of India, he wi sent south to shore up the morale of the Burma Area Army. At war's end I went underground in Bangkok and through contacts in the Chinese secr police was smuggled out to Chungking. There he assisted in staff planning fi Chiang's war with the Communists. As soon as danger had passed that I would be tried for war crimes in Japan, he returned home, wrote bestselle: entitled *Underground Escape, Singapore, Nomonhan,* and *Guadalcanal,* ar was elected to the Diet in 1952, 1954, and 1956. He mysteriously vanishe in 1961 while visiting Hanoi.

TWENTY-ONE DEMANDS. The substance of a bold diplomatic note presented t the new Republic of China by Japanese Foreign Minister Kato Taka-aki : January 1915. China had no recourse but to accede to most of the deman(until they could be renegotiated with arbitration by the Western powers at tl peace conferences following World War I. In consequence China conceded t Japan the right to occupy the TSINGTAO LEASEHOLD, to build a railroad inlai from Tsingtao to Tsinan, to occupy the KWANTUNG LEASEHOLD for an add tional ninety-nine years, and to exercise control of Chinese iron mines as cc lateral for Japanese loans to China. A final group of demands caused su(international stir that Japan withdrew them; they would have forced China accept Japanese advisors in political, military, and economic affairs and allow Japanese railroad building throughout central China. Twenty years lat Chiang Kai-shek's refusal to grant a similar set of demands brought on tl 1937–45 Sino-Japanese War.

UGAKI KAZUSHIGE (1869–1956). Army general who as war minister in 192(25 carried out the plans devised by staff officers of the EMPEROR'S CABAL fi reorganizing the Army. Later, taking a moderate position between the extrer ists of the STRIKE-NORTH and STRIKE-SOUTH factions, he acquired a larį following in the Army officer corps and was courted by both political parti as a potential prime minister who might keep the Army from executing i planned seizure of Manchuria. Before he could realize his political ambitior however, he was compromised by the MARCH PLOT in 1931. Consoled by tl post of governor general of Korea from 1931 to 1936, he was rebuffed in second attempt to become prime minister in 1937. In 1938 he served for foi months as foreign minister in the first Konoye Cabinet. After the war Ugai sat in the Upper House of the Diet from 1953 until his death.

UNIVERSITY LODGING HOUSE (*Daigaku-Ryo*). Cover name for the indoctrin tion center for junior Army officers established on the Imperial Palace groun soon after Hirohito became Regent. The purpose of the Lodging House w to educate carefully chosen officers in ideology, strategy, and tactics for tl expansion of the Japanese Empire into neighboring lands. Organization ai curriculum were entrusted to Dr. OKAWA SHUMEI.

WATARI HISAO (1885–1939). Army officer, one of the ELEVEN RELIABLES, specialist in Anglo-American intelligence. Assigned in 1932 as guide to tl

LYTTON COMMISSION, he made heroic but unavailing efforts to show the Commission only the bright side of Japanese rule in MANCHUKUO. He died, a major general, in China in 1939.

YAMAGATA ARITOMO, Count (1838–1922). Army general and leader of the CHOSHU clan. He was the principal architect of the Imperial Army as it was developed during Emperor Meiji's reign. His concepts of military strategy for Japan became the basis of policies pursued by the STRIKE-NORTH FACTION.

YAMAMOTO ISOROKU (1884–1943). Naval officer and protégé of Empress Nagako's father, Prince KUNIYOSHI. Trained in the Russo-Japanese War and later in the naval staff college, Harvard University, and the Japanese Embassy in Washington, he played a leading role in the development of the Japanese naval air force. In 1924 he took charge of the MISTY LAGOON AIR DEVELOPMENT STATION. In 1929–30 he attended the naval limitations negotiations in London. In late 1934 he led another delegation to London where he announced Japanese abrogation of the Naval Limitations Treaty. In 1936–39 he was Navy vice minister, and from 1939 on he was commander in chief of the Combined Fleet. In his last command he planned and executed the daring attack on Pearl Harbor. In April 1943 President Roosevelt had him ambushed and shot down by U.S. Army Air Force pilots while he was on an inspection flight in the Solomon Islands.

YAMAOKA SHIGEATSU (1884–   ). Army officer, one of the ELEVEN RELIABLES. A Shinto fanatic, with great faith in the spirits' inhabiting cold steel, he was responsible for the Japanese Army regulation that all officers must own swords. He was implicated in the murder of NAGATA TETSUZAN in 1935. He sympathized with the STRIKE-NORTH FACTION, became increasingly an embarrassment to his seniors, and was finally discharged from the Army in 1939.

YAMASHITA TOMOYUKI (1888–1946). Army general, the "Tiger of Malaya," who captured Singapore in February 1942. An intelligence specialist in German, he was brought into the EMPEROR'S CABAL through early acquaintance with TOJO HIDEKI and later membership in the SUZUKI STUDY GROUP. Before the FEBRUARY MUTINY he played a difficult part in leading on the rebels, for which Hirohito later sent him a secret commendation. Thereafter Yamashita became chief of staff in North China in 1938 and inspector general of Army aviation in 1940. In 1941 he led a delegation of officers to Germany to meet with Hitler and study *Wehrmacht* methods. Later that year he took charge of the training of the troops that were to be used in the invasions of Malaya, the Philippines, and Indonesia. After capturing Singapore he differed with Hirohito and was rusticated to command of the First Army Group in MANCHUKUO. In September 1944 he was posted to the Philippines, where he directed a brilliant defensive campaign against superior U.S. forces. In February 1946, after a trial much criticized by U.S. jurists, he was hanged as a war criminal.

YAMATO. The name for the early imperial realm in Japan which encompassed the fertile valleys from the harbor of modern Osaka inland to modern Kyoto.

YONAI MITSUMASA (1880–1948). Naval Intelligence officer specializing in Russian. He was chief of Special Service Organs in Vladivostok in 1918–19, the first year of Japan's Siberian intervention. Alternating between sea duty and intelligence posts, he rose to be Navy minister, 1937–39, and prime minister January–July 1940. Although opposed to the war with the United States, he returned to the Cabinet to serve as Navy minister and preside over the sinking of the Japanese fleet from July 1944 to December 1945. Thereafter he gave evidence at the war crimes trials in Tokyo. Because of his deceptively frank manner he was known to Japanese as "the goldfish minister" and "the lamp shining in daylight."

YOSHIDA SHIGERU (1878–1967). Diplomat and celebrated postwar prime minister of Japan. He was a member of the Takenouchi family, which was related by marriage to the imperial family through a daughter of Prince ASAHIKO, Yoshida grew up in Court circles and married a daughter of Count MAKINO NOBUAKI. He was first secretary in the Japanese Embassy in London in 1921 and was in Gibraltar to welcome Crown Prince Hirohito on his way to England. As consul general in Tientsin and later in Mukden in the 1920's, he played a leading part in formulating imperial policy regarding the Chinese revolution, Chiang Kai-shek, and Mao Tse-tung. In 1928 he tried to persuade the KWANTUNG ARMY to seize Manchuria. In 1933 he launched the first political agitation for a STRIKE-SOUTH policy. From 1936 to 1939 Yoshida was ambassador to Great Britain. Throughout the war he served in Japan as a member of the PEACE FACTION. Having been arrested by the secret police in 1945, he was deemed pure of war guilt by SCAP investigators. He then served as foreign minister from September 1945 until May 1947 and concurrently as prime minister from May 1946 to May 1947. He was appointed prime minister again in October 1948 and continued in office until December 1954. Historians generally credit him with Japan's successful accommodation to the Allied Occupation and the nation's subsequent resurgence as a first-class power.

ZAIBATSU. Any large Japanese family holding company, equivalent to a cartel in Western countries. The three great *zaibatsu* in twentieth century Japan have been Mitsui, belonging to the eleven branches of the Mitsui family; Mitsubishi, belonging to the Iwasakis; and Sumitomo, belonging to the Sumitomos. Together with the Imperial Household Ministry, which administers investments for the Throne, these three *zaibatsu* have controlled Japanese banking, heavy industry, and foreign trade both before and after World War II.

NOTES

In what follows I have not cited sources for personnel information or for conclusions drawn from knowing the employment and whereabouts of my characters at a given moment. I have collected this information little by little in my own card files. I have transcribed much of it from manuscript materials ("Notebooks" and "Personnel Records") lent to me by Hata Ikuhiko. Some I have filled in from casual references in the Japanese literature. The rest is available in the personnel records or lists of officeholders reproduced in the appendices of Harada's memoirs, of *Taiheiyo senso e no michi,* and of Hata's *Gun fuashizumu* and *Nichu senso.* A little personnel information may also be found in the annual *Daijin-mei jiten* [Dictionary of Illustrious Men] published by Heibon-sha; in *Who's Who in Japan,* published biennially from 1912 to 1944; and in IPS Document 1606.

The numbers at the beginning of Notes refer to page numbers in the text. Unnumbered notes following refer to material on the page as specified.

1. Rape of Nanking

There are no general accounts of this unchronicled but notorious episode in history. Except as specifically noted, my account follows Hata, *Nichu senso-shi,* 280–86, for military details; Timperley, *Japanese Terror in China,* and Hsu, *War Conduct of the Japanese,* for atrocity details; *Asahi* (both eds.) and the "Personnel Records" of Army, Navy, and Foreign Ministry officers compiled by Hata for comings and goings at the front. The Shimada and Usui volumes of *Gendai-shi shiryo* provide most of the extant Army documentation; Kido, *Nikki,* provides most of the insight into "the Center." I have chosen between minor textual differences in Timperley and Hsu by reference to papers at the National War Memorial in Canberra which appear to be mimeographed copies of original letters written by Western observers in Nanking during the rape. Many observers gave testimony and affidavits to the International Military Tribunal for the Far East (IMTFE).

I am indebted to Penelope Bergamini, Valle Fay, and Sharon Corsiglia for their assistance in the preparation of these citations.

From its "Proceedings" (microfilm, Yale Law School Library) I have consulted pp. 2624 ff., Minor S. Bates; pp. 4460 ff., George A. Fitch; pp. 3900 ff., John Magee; pp. 4470 ff., James McCallum; pp. 4450 ff., Lewis S. C. Smythe; and pp. 2527 ff., Robert O. Wilson. The notes of German observers John H. D. Rabe and General Alexander Ernst von Falkenhausen (Library of Congress microfilm WT5, pp. 4459-69) provided most useful and dispassionate corroboration of the Americans' accounts. In addition to specifically cited sources I have consulted: Ando, "Sense to kazoku"; Chamberlain; Hashimoto Kingoro, "Iwazumogana no shirushi" [A Record of Matters Better Left Unsaid], *Jinbutsu Orai*, March, 1966; Hata, "Higeki," in *Himerareta Showa-shi;* Imai Sei-ichi, "Misshitsu"; Ito Takeo; Nakano; *Taiheiyo senso e no michi,* 3; Harold S. Quigley, *Far Eastern War, 1937-1941* (Boston: World Peace Foundation, 1942); Yabe; and Yokoyama Taketsune, *Matsui Taisho den* [General Matsui's Story] (Tokyo: Kakko-sha, 1938).

5 A Japanese private . . . into the bushes to urinate: Morishima, 131.

6 Hirohito had directed his General Staff; see *Taiheiyo senso,* 8:214–16, also Chs. 17–19 of work in hand. All Japanese Army operation plans were drawn up in the offices of the General Staff and were personally approved by Hirohito. Then they were forwarded to commanders in the field with specific directions—also approved by Hirohito—defining the latitude for personal initiative which would be tolerated on the part of officers at the front; Gen. Seijima Ryuji, IMTFE "Proceedings," 8111 ff.

War with China part of the national program: see Chs. 5, 6.

By the 1920's, Hirohito had decided: my interpretation of the events recorded in Chs. 7–9.

Chiang ceased to co-operate before 1930; see Suzuki Tei-ichi in *Himerareta,* 20–25.

7 Matsui's visit to Emperor: *Asahi,* Aug. 16, 1937. Details of palace protocol from Honjo and Kido, *Nikki;* palace interior and grounds, Terry and Vining. I discussed Matsui's feelings and opinions with his relative, the priestess at Atami, and have drawn on accounts of his personality by Ito Kanejiro and Abend, *Life in China.*

8 A great honor for Matsui: Ito Kanejiro, 1:209, gives a circumspect but revealing discussion of Matsui's character.

Matsui's plots to prevent war: Harada, 6:62, and interview with former colonel in the secret police.

9 Matsui a devout Buddhist: Abend, *Life in China,* 268–85.

10 Matsui to Konoye: *Konoye Memoirs,* 320 (passage referred to here is in penciled notes or rough draft written by Konoye's secretary Ushiba Tomohiko, some years after 1937); see also Suda, 110 ff.

11 Chiang saved his best troops: he used over 400,000 men at Shanghai; Liu, 198.

Prince Higashikuni as head of Army Air Force: *Asahi,* Aug. 14, 1937; also June 9, 1937.

Five divisions: (the 9th, 13th, 101st, 3d, 11th); U.S. Army Forces Far East, *Japanese Monograph* No. 7, 12–14.

12 Grand Imperial Headquarters: Imai Sei-ichi, "Misshitsu," 78 ff.; Usui, *Gendai-shi,* 9:384; see also Crowley, 356–57.

Ishiwara and plans for Manchuria: see his entry in *Nihon jinbutsu-shi taikei* [Japan Biographical Outlines] (Tokyo: Asakura Shobo, 1960).
Toa Renmei: Fujimoto, 187.

13 *Koa Domei,* ibid.
Shimomura Sadamu and drive on Nanking: for his own version, see Usui, *Gendai-shi,* 9:379 ff.
Pledged themselves to Hirohito personally: see Ch. 7.
Two young officers: Col. Muto Akira and Lt. Col. Kimihira Masatake. They had been chiefs of Operations Section and Operations Squad in the Army General Staff; they now became vice chief of staff and assistant vice chief to Gen. Matsui. See Hata, *Nichu,* appendices.
Suzuki attached to 16th Div.: November 1, 1937, IMTFE "Proceedings," 2355; Hata, *Nichu,* 362, and *Gun juashizumu,* 351. This was an odd posting, for the orders reproduced in Shimada, *Gendai-shi,* 8, show that the 16th Div. already had a Col. Nakasawa as its chief of staff. He was a former Army medical school instructor, *Rikugun jitsueki teinen meibo* Sept. 1929, 255. Nakasawa was described simply by retired Lt. Gen. Fujisawa Shigezo as "a torturer" (interview).
Suzuki one of Army men whom Hirohito relied on most: Kido, *Nikki,* and Harada, *passim.*

14 Testimony on Suzuki's trips to war front: Lt. Gen. Fujisawa Shigezo (interview) remembers seeing him in Shanghai; Suzuki himself implied to IMTFE that he never left Kyoto, "Proceedings," 35172 ff. Repeated inquiries by me in Kyoto veterans' circles in 1965–66 failed to turn up anyone who remembered seeing Suzuki in Kyoto in 1937. For the staff of the Kyoto headquarters of the 16th Div. under Lt. Gen. Nakaoka Yataka, see Usui, *Gendai-shi,* 9:213.
Suzuki as intermediary: interview with retired major general, privileged source. See also Usui, *Gendai-shi,* 9:308.
Hirohito's rescript: IMTFE, "Judgment," ch. 5, part B, 700–701.
In late October a second flotilla: Hirohito's orders to Lt. Gen. Yanagawa dated Oct. 20, Usui, *Gendai-shi,* 9:213.

15 Half the men purged from the army: Matsui, interrogation March 8, 1946, IMTFE, "Proceedings," 3460.
Yanakawa quoted: letter dated Oct. 7, 1937. The Japanese text: *Kimi yasunze yo sudeni sugitari sanzu no kawa tenkoku no mon o hiraku mokusho no ma.*
Morning of November 5: this and two paragraphs following based on Hata, *Nichu,* pp. 282 ff., supplemented by Ito Kanejiro, 1:33, 38, 57–59; 2:110 ff.; and Moritaka, 5:41–43.
Yanagawa's *tanka*: Ito Kanejiro, 1:59: *Asagiri no/mada hareyaranu/sono naka ni/kyujippun no/machi-tosakana.//Okimi no/makase no manimani/ yukumichi ni/kyo no nagame wa/tada namida nari.*

16 Advertising balloons: *Taiheiyo senso* 4:32; Moritaka, 5:42.
Provincial Chinese levies: Liu, 199.
6th Div.: a tough unit traditionally recruited from the lowest class of peasants in the Kyoto area; Hata, interview.
Lt. Gen. Tani "galloping off": Ito Kanejiro, 1:333.
British correspondent quoted: Timperley, 72. He was correspondent in China for the *Manchester Guardian.*

17 Nakajima a "hard man": Hata, *Nichu,* 286.

"An expert marksman": quotation from Ito Kanejiro, 106–7.
"Nakajima drank": Tanaka, interview.
"After we broke out of Shanghai": retired Lt. Gen. Fujisawa, interview.
Claim of 390,000: Hata, *Nichu,* 285.
Lines drawn on map: Usui, *Gendai-shi,* 9:387; Hata, *Nichu,* 283–84.

19 Emperor's order: relayed through Prince Kanin, Usui, *Gendai-shi,* 9:390.
Tada's disapproval of attack: Tada was backed by Col. Kawabe Tora-shiro, chief of War Guidance Section of General Staff, who was on an inspection trip to the front, advising postponement of the attack in his telegraphic dispatches; Hata, *Nichu,* 284. Shimomura was backed by Muto Akira, Kimihira Masatake, and Matsui's chief of staff, Tsukada Osamu, later chief of staff for Gen. Terauchi in World War II; Hata, ibid., 283–84, 343; Horiba, 109 ff; Usui, *Gendai-shi,* 9:380.
Shimomura and Tada: for Shimomura's account of his coaxing, as told here and on next page, Usui, *Gendai-shi,* 9:387 ff.
First cable to Matsui: Hata, *Nichu,* 343; see also Usui, *Gendai-shi,* 9:392.
Second cable: ibid.

20 Thrust across the Tai-Hu: see Operations Log of 9th Div., repro-duced in Usui, *Gendai-shi,* 9: 230 ff.

22 Japanese terms summarized: Jones, 60, n.4.
Chiang ends negotiations: J. T. C. Liu, "German Mediation in the Sino-Japanese War, 1937–38," *Far Eastern Quarterly,* Feb. 1949, 16; also Dirk-sen to Neurath, Dec. 7, 1937, in *Documents on German Foreign Policy, 1937–45,* series D, Vol. 1, 799 (Washington, Gov't Printing Office, 1949).
Chiang leaves Nanking, Dec. 7: Hollington K. Tong, *Dateline: China* (New York: Rockport Press, 1950), 31–48.

23 Prince Asaka's attitude "not good": Kido, *Nikki,* 468.
"To sparkle before the eyes of the Chinese": Nakayama Yasuto, testi-mony to IMTFE, "Proceedings," 21893; see also 33081 ff., 37238 ff., 32686 (Canberra) ff.
Matsui's commandments: ibid., 47171–73.
Asaka's arrival at the front: IMTFE Exhibit #2577 (Canberra), 4.
Nakajima wounded: *Asahi,* Dec. 8, 1937.
Nakajima's report to Prince Asaka: Tanaka, interview.
Orders issued from Asaka's headquarters: Tanaka, *Sabakareru* 44–45; see also Harada, 7:152; Ando, "Senso to kazoku," part 2, 86.

24 Hirohito described: Harada, 6:87–88.
Prince Konoye protests: Kido, *Nikki,* 602–03.
Konoye quoted: ibid.

25 Konoye quoted: Kido, *Nikki,* 608; see also Harada, 6:171, 175, for insight into Hirohito's state of mind.
Hirohito's orders to attack Canton: Usui, *Gendai-shi,* 9:222.
Sinking of the *Panay*: this and next three paragraphs based on IMTFE "Proceedings," 3520–3552, also 21362–435, 3466 ff., 38181 ff.

27 That Roosevelt's message might presage a declaration of war: Butow, *Tojo,* 389, n.46.
Grew and *Panay* incident: Grew, *Ten Years,* 204–213.

Yamamoto accepts responsibility: Harada, 6:189; also 183 in which Yamamoto tells of meeting between Navy Minister Yonai and Prime Minister Konoye when Yonai went to dine with Hirohito on December 11, the day before the *Panay* was sunk.

28 30,000 troops embarked: retired Lt. Gen. Fujisawa, interview; Usui, *Gendai-shi*, 9:222.

Presumption that Konoye sent messenger to Hashimoto: see, e.g., Matsui's explanation of Hashimoto's motives in Abend, *Life in China*, 273.

Konoye's emissary mistakenly apprehended: retired Maj. Gen. Kajiura Ginjiro, interview; also Suda, 112.

Konoye quoted: Harada, 6:180.

Statement drafted by Hirohito's kinsman Machijiri: Horiba, 110; in observance of the imperial taboo, Horiba identifies Machijiri by office rather than by name. That Machijiri is meant, however, is clear from Hata, *Gun fuashizumu*, 357, and *Nichu*, 347. For Horiba's credentials, ibid., 365.

"Hate-China" Villa: a typical Japanese pun. The house was known as Tekigai-so or Outside Ogikubo Villa. *Tekigai* written with different characters, however, means "anger against enemies."

800,000 had fled upriver: Smythe et al, 4.

Rearguard of about 100,000: ibid., introduction, i.

Brick walls of Nanking: description of Nanking from J. Van Wie Bergamini, verbal.

29 Behavior of Chinese troops in Nanking: Rev. James McCallum's journal for Dec. 19, 1937, quoted in introduction to Smythe; IMTFE "Proceedings," 47174–175, 4470 ff.

Matsui's contribution of $3,000: equivalent to $10,000 Chinese. Hidaka Shunrokuro's testimony to IMTFE, "Proceedings," 21465; letter of Jan. 7, 1938, from Nanking Safety Zone Committee to Fukuda Tokuyasu of the Japanese Embassy in Nanking, Timperley, 193–94.

Twenty-two Westerners remaining in Nanking: count from Gen. Alexander von Falkenhausen memoranda, Jan. 15 and Feb. 10, 1938, to German Foreign Minister Baron von Neurath, via German Embassy in Hankow, found in German Foreign Office file of memoranda and telegrams, Nov. 1936–March 1938, IPS Document No. 4039, Library of Congress microfilm WT-5, 4462–69. Germans: John H. D. Rabe of the Siemans Co., Christian Kröger of Carlowitz & Co., Eduard Sperling of the Shanghai Insurance Co., Rupert Hatz, R. Hempel, Auguste Gounan. Americans: university professors Minor Searle Bates, Charles Riggs, and Lewis S. C. Smythe; J. V. Pickering of Standard Oil; physicians C. S. Trimmer and Robert O. Wilson; Y.M.C.A. secretary George A. Fitch; missionaries Rev. John Magee, Rev. Ernest H. Forster, Rev. James McCallum, Rev. W. P. Mills, Rev. Hubert L. Sone, Miss Minnie Vautrin, Mrs. Paul de Witt Twinem, Miss Grace Bauer. An Englishman: P. H. Munroe-Faure of British Asiatic Petroleum. Not included in Falkenhausen's count were two Russians and three other unidentified Europeans. See also Timperley, 25.

9th Div. on Dec. 9: Operations Log of 9th Div., Usui, *Gendai-shi*, 9:230 ff.

Leaflets dropped from planes: Nakayama Yasuto, testimony to IMTFE, "Proceedings," 21895 ff., 47173–175.

Prince Asaka described: *Asahi*, Feb. 24, 1938; date, ibid., Feb. 8, 1938.

31 Nanking noodles: *Asahi* (Tokyo ed.), Dec. 11, 1937.

Spotters in two blimps: Timperley, 24.
Y.M.C.A. secretary George Fitch quoted: ibid., 26.

32 Saké issued to sailors: Hashimoto Kingoro, testimony to IMTFE, "Proceedings," 3532 ff.
Chinese soldiers mingling with refugees: Timperley, 27, 171.
Report written by Gen. Alexander von Falkenhausen: cited in full in note on page 29.

33 Fitch quoted: Timperley, 26–27.
Matsui's parade route: Nakayama Yasuto, testimony to IMTFE, "Proceedings," 21899–907; Okada Takashi, testimony, ibid. (Canberra) 32738; Nakasawa Mitsuo testimony, ibid. (Canberra), 32623–627.
Buddhist chaplains' prayers: defense summation for Matsui, IMTFE, "Proceedings," 47177–183.
Japanese troops returned as ordered: Nakayama, testimony, ibid., 47174–175; Hidaka Shunrokuro, ibid., 21448–466.
A dozen Chinese women: extrapolation from Safety Zone Committee complaint no. 211, in Timperley, 162; complaint no. 178, ibid., 158; McCallum's testimony to IMTFE, "Proceedings," 4480 ff.; Bates's diary for Dec. 21, 1937, ibid., 2639 ff.; see also complaint no. 5, Hsu, 130, and Magee testimony, IMTFE "Proceedings," 3918 ff.
Drunk and disorderly on a bender: case no. 219, Timperley, 161, amplified by Magee testimony to IMTFE. "Proceedings," 3910 ff.
American missionary quoted: in a letter by Lewis S. C. Smythe, Dec. 15, 1937, Timperley, 19.
Three hundred civilians dead: Smythe et al, Table 4.
Western newsmen plan to leave: Hsu, 160, 162, 164–65.

34 Falkenhausen quoted: his report cited in full in note on page 29.
Nakajima's assignment from Prince Asaka: Hata, *Nichu*, 286.
Muto's "responsibility for billeting": Nakayama; testimony to IMTFE, "Proceedings," 21905–06, 21913–15.
Secret policemen supervising looting and standing guard while soldiers raped women: case nos. 81 and 94, Timperley, 147, 151; Smythe quoted, ibid., 19, 52, 56; also Fitch quoted, ibid., 37.

35 Muto's manpower: Usui, *Gendai-shi*, 9:214–15.
Water not turned on until Jan. 7: Falkenhausen, report cited in full in note on page 29; also Fitch quoted, Timperley, 24.
Magee's film circulated by America First organizations: Tong, 47.

36 Fitch quoted: Hsu, 163.
Men planted neck deep in earth: Tong, 48, confirmed and amplified at my request by Office of Information, Republic of China, Taiwan.
Smythe quoted: Timperley, 19.

37 Army storage shed containing two hundred pianos: Bates's testimony to IMTFE, "Proceedings," 2630 ff.
High officers, including Nakajima: Tanaka, interview.

38 Men "buried" in river clung to reeds for hours: see, e.g., affidavit of Chinese medical corpsman Captain Liang Ting-fang, IMTFE "Proceedings," 3370 ff.

39 Entombment of Sun Yat-sen: Jansen, 1–5.
Col. Hashimoto in Matsui's cavalcade: Abend, *Life in China*, 271.
Drunken laughter of soldiers at victory parade: *Showa no Kiroku* [The

Showa Record], Nihon Hoso Kaisha [Japan Broadcasting Corp.] (Tokyo: NHK Sabisu Senta, Oct. 1965).

40 Muto's promise to consider accommodations in countryside: IMTFE Exhibit No. 2577; Nakayama, testimony, IMTFE "Proceedings," 21899–907.
Matsui quoted (lines 11–16): Okada Takashi, testimony, IMTFE, ibid. (Canberra), 32738.
Matsui's press release quoted: ibid., 3510–11.
Memorial service at Nanking airport: ibid., 47183–87, 21901–07.
Matsui's poem: Ito Kanejiro, 1:212.

41 Matsui to his Buddhist confessor: Hanayama, 186.
Matsui quoted on China war: Okada Takashi, testimony, IMTFE "Proceedings" (Canberra), 32749 ff.
Prince Asaka's headquarters then 30 miles from Nanking: Iinuma Mamoru, testimony, ibid., 32655, 32673.
Matsui sent back to Shanghai: Nakayama Yasuto, testimony, ibid., 21907–916; Kazue Sakaibara, testimony, ibid., 32686; Okada Takashi, testimony, ibid., 32752.

42 One of Americans at Nanking quoted: Rev. John Magee, testimony, ibid., 3900 ff.
Thermit and strips of paper: John Rabe, Library of Congress microfilm WT 5, 4459–62.
Fitch cited: Timperley, 35.
Chinese soldiers in hiding, not 6,000 but 20,000: ibid., 27, 38; Hsu, 161, 171.

43 Muto quoted: testimony, IMTFE "Proceedings" (Canberra), 3552 ff.
114th, 6th, 9th divs. withdrawn: Nakasawa Mitsuo, testimony, ibid., 32623–627.
Prince Asaka in Nanking Dec. 25 to February 10: Iinuma Mamoru, testimony, ibid., 32673.
Matsui to Abend: Abend, *Life in China,* 270–73.
Matsui to Asaka's chief of staff: IMTFE Exhibit No. 2577; "Proceedings" (Canberra), 47187 ff.
Matsui to Japanese diplomat: Hidaka Shunrokuro; see his testimony, ibid., pp. 21448 ff.
"I considered that the discipline was excellent": Matsui, interrogation, March 8, 1946, ibid., 3459 ff.

44 Prince Kaya "talked earnestly to second lieutenants": *Asahi* (Osaka ed.), Jan. 20, 1938.
A third of the city destroyed by fire: Rabe, Library of Congress microfilm WT5, 4459–62.

45 Summary of economic distress: from findings reported in Smythe.
Nanking veterans' reports, War Ministry's suppression orders: IPS No. 625 Supplement, Library of Congress microfilm WT5, 641–43.
Nanking "the ten-year shame": Horiba, 109 ff.
Japanese spokesmen's claims at war crime trials re Nanking: defense summation for Matsui, IMTFE "Proceedings," 47187 ff.

46 Hirohito's "extreme satisfaction" expressed to Prince Kanin: *Asahi* (Tokyo ed.), Dec. 15, 1937.

Prince Kanin's telegram: ibid.

Hirohito presented silver vases to Matsui, Asaka, and Yanagawa: *Asahi* (Tokyo ed.), Feb. 27, 1938.

Three other members of imperial family: Prince Higashikuni, Prince Kaya, Prince Takeda II; see *Asahi,* March 8, 25, Apr. 4, May 31, June 20, Aug. 30, Oct. 28, Nov. 4, Dec. 22, 1938.

47 Matsui quoted: Hanayama, 186. On the night of his execution Matsui said: "I sincerely appreciate the infinite grace of the Throne. It happens that I have come to be sacrificed for the Nanking Incident" (ibid., 255).

48 Four million corpses: my own estimate including more than one million Japanese, two and a half million Chinese, and more than 100,000 Americans (in the Pacific theater).

2. A-Bomb

For this chapter, in addition to sources cited or listed in the bibliography, I have drawn for background on: Ronald William Clark, *The Birth of the Bomb* (New York: Horizon Press, 1961); *Hiroshima Plus 20,* by the editors of *The New York Times* (New York: Delacorte Press, 1965); and William Bradford Huie, *Hiroshima Pilot* (New York: G. P. Putnam's Sons, 1964).

49 HIROSHIMA: details of bombing mission, Amrine, 152–55, 176–79, 199–202; description of Hiroshima, John Hersey, *Hiroshima* (New York: Alfred A. Knopf, 1946); deaths, *Genshi bakudan saigai chosa hokoku-shi* [Collected A-Bomb Damage Investigation Reports] (Tokyo: Nihon Gakujutsu Shinkokai, 1953, 1961), 19 ff.

51 NAGASAKI: details of *Bock's Car* flight, Craig, 75–88, 90–97; description of Nagasaki and details of attack, Robert Trumbull, *Nine Who Survived Hiroshima and Nagasaki* (Rutland, Vt., and Tokyo: Charles E. Tuttle Co., 1957), Pt. 2, *passim.*

52 William L. Laurence quoted: Feis, *Japan Subdued,* 116, n.5.

53 N.1: crewmen of the bomb plane deny it: see Craig, 85–86, description of flight over Kokura, based on his interviews with crew members.

54 Clear blue sky: Trumbull, *Nine Who Survived,* 111: Nagai Takashi, *We of Nagasaki* (New York: Duell, Sloan & Pearce, 1951), 102, 146; among accounts in Japanese, Gembaku Kokunai, *Hiroku daitoa senshi* (Tokyo: Fuji Shoen, 1953), 330, 340.

55 N. 2: bombardier's two-mile miss: telephone interview, Kermit Beehan; *Bock's Car*'s radio message to Tinian, quoted, Craig, 97.

57 Stimson to Truman, Apr. 25, 1945: Stimson's memorandum in his article, "The Decision to Use the Atomic Bomb," *Harper's* magazine, February 1947.

Truman in his memoirs: *Year of Decisions* (1955), quoted, Amrine, 53.

May 1, Grew met with Stimson and Forrestal, Forrestal quoted: Feis, *Japan Subdued,* 15.

58 Truman's statement of May 8: ibid., 16.

Truman wrote to his family: *Year of Decisions,* quoted, Amrine, 79.

Stalin to Hopkins, "give them the works": Robert Sherwood, *Roosevelt and Hopkins,* 903–4, quoted in Feis, *Japan Subdued,* 18.

58–60 Interim Committee: ibid., 30–40.

60 Scientists' answer: Amrine, 108.
Franck Committee: Feis, *Japan Subdued*, 40–44.
Edward Teller quoted: by William L. Laurence in *N. Y. Times* News Service dispatch, Aug. 1965.

61 Navy peace mission: see note on page 72.
Okamoto's mission: for a full account see Tatamiya, 115–42.

62 Navy and Army reports: Butow, *Japan's Decision*, 22, 26.
Kido conceded war was lost: Kido, *Nikki*, 1078–79.

63 "Peace Faction": That the Peace Faction's assignment was contingency planning for defeat is my own interpretation of the evidence. I explained it in 1966 to Koizumi Shinzo, the courtier who had charge of the education of Crown Prince Akahito, and he did not demur. To my mind the salient considerations are as follows: Col. Matsutani Makoto and Rear Adm. Takagi Sokichi were assigned to work on contingency planning for defeat from 1940 onward (Hata, interview; also Butow, *Japan's Decision*, 20–22, 26–27, 38–40, 83 n.3). Takagi, in particular, maintained close liaison thereafter with civilian members of the Peace Faction (see, e.g., Harada, 8:316–18, 365–69, 379). The civilian Peace Faction leaders, Konoye and Yoshida, maintained close liaison with Hirohito's right hand, Lord Privy Seal Kido, and with Kido's secretary and successor, Matsudaira Yasumasa (Kido, *Nikki*, e.g., 945–47, 967–68, 1005, 1024–25, 1056–57, 1109–10). Princes Higashikuni, Kaya, Mikasa, and Takamatsu were all involved in Peace Faction schemes at one time or another during the war (see, e.g., Butow, *Japan's Decision*, 14 n.18; Coox, 8, 100, 126; Toland, *Rising Sun*, 824; Kido, *Nikki*, 1003–5, 1057–59). They met informally with Hirohito during the war years at weekly palace newsreel showings (Ando, "Senso to kazoku," Pt. 2, 89). Peace Faction members were responsible for creating the postwar illusions that Hirohito was a pawn of militarists and that the Peace Faction itself had to operate in a clandestine manner for fear of police persecution. The first illusion is belied by Chief Aide-de-Camp Honjo in his *Nikki* (see my notes to Chs. 17–21) and by Chief of Staff Sugiyama in his *Memo* (see my notes to Chs. 24–29). The second illusion is belied by such considerations as the following: As *naidaijin* and former *naimudaijin* (lord privy seal and former home minister), Kido Koichi had unsurpassed control of Japan's police apparatus. (In Japan proper, as the Sorge case demonstrated, the military secret police or *kempei* remained biddable colleagues of the metropolitan police and subordinates of the Thought Police or *tokko*.) The Peace Faction held receptions openly and on a lavish scale to recruit volunteers for special assignments (Kato Masuo, 15). By renting space in the Dai Ichi Building (testimony of Okada Keisuke, IMTFE "Proceedings," 29259–63), the Peace Faction shared quarters with local Army Area Headquarters which supervised discipline throughout the Tokyo area during the days before and after the surrender.
Former foreign minister to Kido: *Nikki*. 1206. The speaker was Togo Shigenori, who returned to the Cabinet as foreign minister in April 1945.

64 Mass arrest of Peace Faction members (the so-called Badoglio incident): my interpretation of the evidence. Yabe, 2:45 ff., demonstrates that only Kido could have supplied the information on which the police based their charges against Konoye and Yoshida. The terms of the wartime rela-

tionship between Kido and Konoye-Yoshida (Kido, *Nikki,* 933–1171 *passim*) make it inconceivable that Kido could have betrayed his friends out of animosity or indiscretion.

Konoye's "diary": published as *Konoye Nikki* (Tokyo: Kyodo Tsushinsha, 1968).

N. 3: Information from several interviews, but see Takeda, *Seiji-ka,* 99.

65 "Memorial to the Throne," read to Hirohito: Kido, *Kankei bunsho,* 495–98. Butow, *Japan's Decision,* 47–50, gives translation from which quotations here have been taken; see also his note (54, on p. 47) on the Konoye text.

Hirohito's underground retreat: Imai Sei-ichi, "Misshitsu no naka," 78 ff.

66 THE GREAT BLUFF: this section based on Kido, *Nikki,* as cited, and interviews with Koizumi Shinzo and another palace official.

Hirohito would abdicate: Vining, *Crown Prince,* 170. Mrs. Vining, as tutor to Crown Prince Akihito, was living in the palace in the war-crimes trial period and was acquainted with the Emperor's inner circle.

67 Details of palace grounds and interior: ibid., *passim.*

67–68 "The American fleet," Hirohito said: discussion between Emperor and Kido based on *Nikki,* 1134.

68 "The situation is extremely grave": for the basis of Emperor's statement, see a joint Army-Navy Report on War Prospects, Jan. 1945, reproduced in *Translations,* 1: No. 15.

He became a willing cog: see Kido, *Statements,* 2:175, "I perceived that an important resolution was being formed in his mind, and after that I exchanged opinions with the Emperor still more intimately."

69 Kido's poem: *Nikki,* 1167.

Hirohito gave private audiences: The best known of the Emperor's interviews is that with Prince Konoye, and the most revealing account of it may be found in Hayashi, *Nihon shusen-shi,* 19 ff. For Kido's memoranda on seven of the audiences see his *Kankei bunsho,* 492–510. I have assumed that in addition to those seven audiences of state Hirohito also gave unofficial audiences to some or all of the prominent Japanese who stopped by in Kido's office during February and March (see Kido, *Nikki,* 1169–84 *passim*).

69–70 Hirohito's audience with Koiso: Kido, *Nikki,* 1180.

70 Koiso's resignation: for additional resignation reasons see Hayashi Shigeru et al, 2:45.

Kido spent the next two weeks: *Nikki,* 1181–94.

Hirohito accepted Kido's recommendation: ibid.

71 Hirohito quoted re Suzuki: Matsudaira Yasumasa, *Statements,* 2: 418–24.

"A peace prime minister": In the officer corps, War Minister Anami was known to have been given the mission of ending the war; Maj. Gen. Nagai Yatsuji, *Statements,* 2:616.

Suzuki "given to understand": Butow, *Japan's Decision,* 67. See also Matsudaira, *Statements,* 2:418: "The Emperor told me after the war, 'I was aware of Suzuki's sentiments . . . and I was convinced that he understood my sentiments.'"

Grew asking for Japan to be reassured: Feis, *Japan Subdued,* 15–16.

71–72 Home minister, education minister consulted with Kido: *Nikki,* 1197.

On May 1, Hirohito warned Kido: ibid., 1198.

Kido went through family strong room: ibid., 1199.

Fujimura's dealings with O.S.S.: Fujimura, *Statements,* 1:135–58.

Pressure mounted on Navy General Staff: for one case of pressure see Hayashi Shigeru et al, 2:128-29.

72–73 Prince Takamatsu came to the palace: Kido, *Nikki,* 1201–2.

Prince Kanin's death: *Asahi,* May 22, 1945.

Fire raid destroyed ministries, ignited Outer Palace roof: Kido, *Nikki,* 1203.

N. 6: O.S.S. dropped Fujimura: Brooks, 133.

74 Cabinet resolved not to leave capital: Kido, *Nikki,* 1208–9.

Council in the Imperial Presence: Hasunuma Shigeru, *Statements,* 1:295–302; Matsudaira Yasumasa, ibid., 2:417–31.

75 Hirohito, "A concealed clause": Matsudaira Yasumasa, *Statements,* 2:425. In Matsudaira's further statement, note: "The Emperor consistently continued his efforts and scheming, but since most of this was behind the scenes and the matters handled were very minute, it would be difficult to explain them in detail here."

Kido drafted a written plan: *Nikki,* 1209; *Statements,* 2:171–84. Matsudaira Yasumasa, ibid., 2:418, says of Kido's plan: "Among my duties as secretary to the Lord Keeper of the Privy Seal, the task of submitting intelligence reports to him was particularly important. Both he and I were of the impression that, since the military had started the war, they no doubt had some definite plan for ending it. Since such a plan would be top secret I assumed that the military had kept it even from the Lord Keeper of the Privy Seal. Moreover, the Emperor never discussed matters pertaining to the High Command with Kido."

75–76 Kido arranged meeting of Big Six . . . confirmed at meeting in Imperial Presence: Kido, *Nikki,* 1211–13.

76 Through intermediary: Hayashi Shigeru et al, 2:133–34.

On Independence Day: Feis, *Japan Subdued,* 46.

Fresh intelligence from Switzerland: Tatamiya, 119–29.

77 Kido summoned Prime Minister Suzuki: Kido, *Nikki,* 1215.

Suzuki Tei-ichi came to palace: ibid., 1216.

Hirohito's private audience with Konoye: ibid., 1216–17.

77–78 Togo-Sato cables: texts given here are based on U.S. Intelligence intercepts which were seen by government officials at Potsdam (texts in Butow, *Japan's Decision,* 130, citing *The Forrestal Diaries,* ed. Walter Millis); I believe the originals (Togo to Sato, No. 891; Sato to Togo, No. 1382; Togo to Sato, No. 893) repose in the Japanese Diet Library among *Gaimusho* (Foreign Ministry) papers collectively entitled *Teikoku no taibei seisaku kankei no ken* (Imperial Policy Vis-à-vis the United States). A fuller translation of Nos. 1382 and 893, made from *Magic* intercepts, may be found on National Archives Microfilm No. 8-5.1 CA, "Translations of Japanese Documents" (vol. 2, no. 9, "Japanese Foreign Ministry Radios exchanged between Togo and Sato from 12 July to 7 August 1945," Document No. 57938). In Sato to Togo where the version quoted reads

"Japan is defeated . . . We must face that fact and act accordingly," the version supplied for Document No. 57938 by the Allied Translator and Interpreter Service has, "If it is correct to assume the war situation has taken an extremely unfavorable turn since [the Imperial Conference of June 8], the government must make a crucial decision."

Negotiations with Russia: see Togo Shigenori, *Statements,* 4:237–78; Togo, 294–308.

79 Efforts of Grew and others re a warning of atomic holocaust: Feis, *Japan Subdued,* 25–26.

"Baby born satisfactorily": reports and reactions to A-bomb detailed, ibid., 63 and note.

Churchill on July 22 to Stimson: Stimson diary for July 22, 1945, quoted, ibid., 75.

Churchill, "was never even an issue": *Second World War,* 6:553.

80 Eisenhower remembered later: quoted, Amrine, 169; see also Feis, *Japan Subdued,* 178, n. 1.

Stimson, "in the manner best calculated": quoted, ibid., 173. Operational order: quoted, ibid., 88.

Truman, "I casually mentioned to Stalin": *Year of Decisions,* 416; cited, ibid., 89–90.

Stalin four days later: ibid., 98.

Potsdam Declaration: text in U.S. Dept. of State, *Occupation of Japan: Policy and Progress,* 1946.

"to us . . . just something to be ignored": my translation from Obata, 7:327.

81 Broadcast on July 28: Zacharias, 421–22.

Togo cable, Aug. 2: *Translations,* 2: no. 9.

"The whole city . . .": Kawabe Torashiro, *Statements,* 2:98–100.

Hirohito and Kido met in Imperial Library: *Nikki,* 1222.

82 Japan's atomic research effort: Yanaga, *Since Perry,* 623.

Kido urged the Emperor: *Nikki,* 1222.

Hirohito to Togo, ". . . tell Prime Minister Suzuki . . .": ibid.

August 8 in Tokyo: for an account of events see "Fateful 8 August," *Translations,* 3: no. 1.

"blew Joey off the fence"; *N.Y. Times,* Aug. 9, 1945.

Sato's appointment with Molotov: Brooks, 172, based on Togo Shigenori, *Statements,* 4:285–89.

83 Lt. Marcus McDilda: his story told by Craig, 73–74.

83–89 Big Six meeting followed by council in the Imperial Presence (pages 85–89): Hasunuma Shigeru, *Statements,* 1:295–302; Hoshina Zenshiro, ibid., 1:480–86; Ikeda Sumihisa, ibid., 1:551–57; Kido, *Nikki,* 1223. See also Butow, *Japan's Decision,* 167–77.

84 "A cruel thing to say": Craig, 148.

85 Anami's career: Hata's "Personnel Records."

Expertise in *kendo,* personal habits: Brooks, 44–45.

86 Baron Hiranuma might be invited: see Miyazaki Shuichi, *Statements,* 2:543.

Kido assured Hirohito re Hiranuma: *Nikki,* 1222, 1223.

At 11:25 P.M.: ibid., 1223.

87 Hirohito unkempt and haggard-looking: my translation from Oya,

Ichiban nagai hi, 24.

Secretary Sakomizu Hisatsune's uncanny feeling: This somewhat fanciful reconstruction is based on the evidence of the painting itself (see paragraph below, in text) and on a remark by Sakomizu (*Statements,* No. 61476) to the effect that he felt himself already in the spirit world. He redescribed the scene in the bunker often after the war to friends in Tokyo, and two of them, Tony Kase and a privileged source, told me that my version sounded right.

88 Hiranuma, "In accordance with . . .": Miyazaki Shuichi, *Statements,* 2:550.

90 Japan's note: text in Butow, *Japan's Decision,* Appendix D.

Canberra cabled London: Australia, "Cablegrams, 1945–1946," No. 225 to London, Aug. 9, 1945.

Second cable: ibid., No. 1138 to Washington, Aug. 9, 1945.

91–92 Byrnes's Note: Butow, *Japan's Decision,* Appendix E.

92 At 5:30 that morning: account here follows that given in Brooks, 215–16, 218–19.

93–94 Foreign editor of Domei and Navy captain: Brooks, 216–17, also 228–29, based on interviews with editor Hasegawa Saiji.

"a menial belonging to . . .": Brooks, 216, has *reizoku* as the word used by the Domei editor to translate the crucial phrase in the Byrnes note ("the Emperor . . . shall be subject to"); he gives the English meaning as "subordinate to." The word *reizoku,* however, is a strong one, implying vassalage or even serfdom.

At 8:20 A.M. Army and Navy chiefs met: Hasunuma Shigeru, *Statements,* 1:295–302.

At 11:00 A.M. Togo at palace: Kido, *Nikki,* 1225; Togo, 324–25.

Anami, audience with Hirohito: Kido, *Nikki,* 1224.

Hiranuma received by Hirohito on Sunday: ibid., 1225.

95 Anami encouraged group to stage rebellion: Ida Masatake, *Statements,* 1:511.

Lt. col. of secret police, Tsukamoto Makoto: see his account in *Statements,* 4:413–17; see also Craig, 139–41.

96 Now did begin, in earnest, to plot coup d'etat: Tsukamoto Makoto, *Statements,* 4:413; Ida Masatake, *Statements,* 1:510–19.

97 Kido, "stricken with consternation": *Nikki,* 1225.

Council in the Imperial Presence, Aug. 14: ibid.

Hirohito's remarks as basis for imperial rescript: ibid.; also, Kido, IMTFE "Proceedings," 31191–94.

98 Anami told subordinates to abandon coup: Oya, *Longest Day,* 77; Takeshita Masahiko, *Statements,* 4:75.

Kido received visit from Prince Mikasa: Kido, *Nikki,* 1225.

Prince Konoye called on Kido: ibid.

Lt. Gen. Mori saw Emperor's chief aide-de-camp: The aide, Gen. Hasunuma Shigeru, gave account of events of Aug. 14 in *Statements,* 1:295–302; Oya, *Ichiban nagai hi,* 82, quotes Gen. Hasunuma, for which I have given my own translation.

98–99 Gen. Tojo's son-in-law, Tojo's visit to Anami: Oya, *Longest Day,* 156.

Difference of opinion between Anami and Yonai: ibid., 155–56.

99–100 Emperor's wishes communicated to Yonai: ibid., 165–66.

100 Emperor emended Anami's insertion: ibid., 166.

100–101 Arao remained to talk with Anami: Oya, *Ichiban nagai hi,* 102–3.

101–111 Reactivation of coup d'etat plans: narrative of officers' actions between 9:30 P.M. Aug. 14 and approx. 7:30 A.M. Aug. 15, including the suicide of War Minister Anami, based on: Ida Masataka, *Statements,* 1:510–19; Hayashi Saburo, ibid., 1:391–411; Takeshita Masahiko, ibid., 4:68–86; Oya, *Ichiban nagai hi,* 104–200 (and English version, *Japan's Longest Day,* 300-350); Brooks, 303–351; Craig, 181–201.

101 A fake coup: This interpretation—my own—of the evidence seems to me an inevitable consequence of the assumption that Japanese, and particularly Japanese in a position to know, behave logically in order to achieve practical ends. The opposite assumption, that Japanese leaders are irrational or that they put up with irrational behavior on the part of their subordinates, strikes me as difficult to reconcile with Japanese achievements. In this case, the behavior of all the participants in the coup achieved what most concerned them: the protection of the Emperor from American prosecution. No single piece of evidence in extenuation of the Emperor has been cited more frequently than his supposed helplessness in the face of the coup that night.

102 Togo reads lengthy postscript: text quoted, Togo, 336–37.
Anami to Togo: ibid., 335.

102–103 Anami to Suzuki: Sakonji Seizo, *Statements,* 3:191–98.

103 Recording session: Oya, *Ichiban nagai hi,* 120–21; *Longest Day,* 209–12.

106 A few minutes later Hatanaka shot Mori: Ida Masatake, *Statements,* 1:511, says shooting occurred at 2 A.M. I have followed Ida's chronology except in this particular; other sources indicate that the shot was fired earlier.

108 Chamberlain Tokugawa Yoshihiro: see his account in *Statements,* 4:295–300.

109 Anami's poem: *O-okimi no/fukaki megumi ni/abishi mi wa/i-i nokosubeki/kata koto mo nashi*; Oya, *Ichiban nagai hi,* 144.

111 Last days of Gen. Tanaka Shizichi: Tsukamoto Kiyoshi, *Statements,* 4:410–12.

112 Text of imperial rescript: U.S. Dept. of State, *Occupation of Japan: Policy and Progress,* 1946; also in USAFFE, "Japanese Monograph" No. 119, along with Hirohito's exhortations at the moment of defeat to the Army and Navy.

3. Defeat

116 Kido consulted only Hiranuma: Kido, *Nikki,* 1226–27.
Hiranuma's teeth: Oya, *Longest Day,* 320.

117 Higashikuni bargained with Hirohito: Ando, "Senso to kazoku," Pt. 1; Kido, *Nikki,* 1226–27.

119 "disposal of government goods": Army order no. 363, top secret, Aug. 17, 1945, IPS Document No. 539.

119–120 The $10-billion give-away and later Diet investigation: Gayn, 156, 496.

120 Ishiwara's anti-Tojo stumping: ibid., 67–68.
Tojo's consideration for menials: *Asahi,* Dec. 22, 1965.
Underground web of clubs and caches: Brines, 104; Gayn, 46, 88, 136, 154.
$2 billion sunk in Tokyo harbor: Singapore *Times,* Apr. 9, 10, 1946.

120–121 Time capsule on Kanawa: Alan S. Clifton, *Time of Fallen Blossoms* (London: Cassell & Co., 1950), 28–32.

121 Fears of U.S. vengeance: see, e.g., Hayashi Shigeru et al, 1:84; Imai Sei-ichi, "Kofuku to iu genjitsu," 74.

122 Secret police assigned to traffic beats: Kido, *Nikki,* 1228–29; Gayn, 51.
Sadist Brown and observer Tokugawa: Bush, *Circumstance,* 183, 256.
"flames of burning documents": Kodama, 173.
Destruction of destruction orders: IPS Document No. 539.

123 Empress Dowager's help enlisted: Koizumi, interview.
Refurbishing foreign embassies: see, e.g., Piggott, 367.
Perry's plaque restored: Imai Sei-ichi, "Kofuku," 75.
Konoye, Ban, and the R.A.A.: Sumimoto, 59; Gayn, 233–41.

123–124 Munitions factory turned into "Willow Run": Gayn, 212–16.

124 One-yen-a-year men: Sumimoto, 58; also Kido, *Nikki,* 1222, 1229–30.
Well-born lady translators: Sumimoto, 58; Gayn, 178–79; Wildes, 35.
Diehards quieted: Butow, *Japan's Decision,* 223, n. 28; Ando, "Senso to kazoku," Pt. 1, 87.

124–131 MISSION TO MANILA: except as cited, this section based on USAFFE "Japanese Monograph" No. 119, 15–17; Kawabe Torashiro, *Statements,* 2:91–97, 107–8; Matsumoto Shunichi, ibid., 2:444–50; Ohmae Toshikazu, ibid., 3:59; Okazaki Katsuo, ibid., 145–46; Craig, 237–49.

126 Kawabe reported to Hirohito: Kido, *Nikki,* 1228 (Aug. 21, 1945).

126–129 On differences in Allied thinking on postwar policy for Japan: Far Eastern Advisory Commission, A4–9, unlettered appendix; Australia, "Cablegrams 1945–1946"; Feis, *Japan Subdued,* 147–52 and *passim;* Wildes, 3, 71; Price, 2, 187 ff.

127 MacArthur, "something out of mythology": Lee, 178.

129 MacArthur disregarded suggestions: MacArthur, 283.
MacArthur's background: Gunther, 31–44.
MacArthur-Willoughby policy for Japan: Eichelberger, 260; MacArthur, 282; Wildes, 72.
MacArthur on the Japanese sickness: Frazier Hunt, *Untold Story of Douglas MacArthur* (New York: Devin-Adair, 1954), 338–39.

130 MacArthur's proposal to land at once in Tokyo: see Hunt, 395.
Sketch of Willoughby: Gunther, 72, 74, 75.
Willoughby's biases: Charles A. Willoughby, *Maneuver in War* (Harris-

burg, Pa.: Military Service Publishing Co., 1939), 235.
"shatteringly simple formula": Willoughby and Chamberlain, 310.

131 Sketch of Whitney: Gunther, 71, 73.
"We blackmailed Japan": Claude Monnier. "Working Paper on Constitutional Revision in Japan, 1945–46" (Ph.D. dissertation, University of Geneva, April 1964), 16–17.
"United States Initial Post-Surrender Policy for Japan": text in Maki, 124–32; also Martin, 123–150.

132 Kamikazes asked to kill selves before Americans: Arisue Seizo, *Statements,* 1:69.
Early landing at Atsugi by daredevil: Morison, 14:359.

132–133 Reception at Atsugi, Shinagawa hospital: Kato Masuo, 256 ff.; Craig, 285 ff.; *N.Y. Times,* Sept. 2, 1945.

133 P.O.W.'s evacuated: ibid., Sept. 1, 7, 1945.
Second day of occupation: Willoughby and Chamberlain, 294.
Admirals trying to beat MacArthur ashore: Eichelberger, 263.
Churchill on MacArthur's personal landing at Atsugi: quoted, Willoughby and Chamberlain, 295.
MacArthur landed and motored to Yokohama: Craig, 292 ff.; Whitney, 215 ff.

134 Yokohama's only egg: Sheldon, 29.
U.S. reporters to Tokyo: Brines, 23, 26; Kato Masuo, 259.
Police reports shown to Hirohito: Kido, *Nikki,* 1230–31.
G.I. crime rate revealed therein: *Asahi Journal,* Jan. 30, 1966, 74.

134–135 Considerations of Hirohito: Kido, *Nikki,* 1229–30, supplemented by interviews with Koizumi and the most aristocratic of my privileged sources.

135 Hirohito's threats to abdicate: MacArthur, 288.
Hirohito loath to hand over war crime suspects: Kido, *Nikki,* 1230–31.

136 Kido advised against abdication: ibid.
Higashikuni called on MacArthur: Ando, "Senso to kazoku," Pt. 1; also Whitney, 247.
MacArthur waited for Hirohito overture: MacArthur, 287.
Occupation proceeded apace: Eichelberger, 264 ff.
Wainwright and Percival: Whitney, 216 ff.

137 Difficulty in finding Japanese to sign surrender: Imai Sei-ichi, "Kofuku," 74–75.
On the *Missouri*: Whitney, 217 ff. (an account written by Kase for Whitney, later included in his own *Journey to the "Missouri"*) ; also Shigemitsu, 374.
Shigemitsu began negotiations with MacArthur: ibid., 375–76; Willoughby and Chamberlain, 302.
Hirohito's address to the Diet: *N.Y. Times,* Sept. 4, 1945; Willoughby and Chamberlain, 301; MacArthur, 280.

138 Konoye to Kyoto: Sumimoto, 131, 185.
Official U.S. occupation of Tokyo: *N.Y. Times,* Sept. 6, 8, 11, 1945; Craig, 312–13.

139 Japanese atrocities: see, e.g., Lord Russell, 66, 77, 180–86; John B. Powell testimony, IMTFE "Proceedings," 3268 ff., 3277 ff.

Konoye and Shigemitsu suggested as criminals: *N.Y. Times,* Sept. 9, 1945.

140–141 Tojo's arrest: Butow, *Tojo,* 446–67; Craig, 315–17; *N.Y. Times,* Sept. 12, 13, 1945.

141 A 32-caliber Colt: some writers say a Colt .38. Its serial number was 535330.

"All the so-called war criminals . . .": Kido, *Nikki,* 1234.

141–142 Shimada's arrest: *N.Y. Times,* Sept. 13, 1945.

"Government . . . of nonmilitary elements . . . trembling under threats from the Black Dragon": ibid., Sept. 12, 1945.

142–143 Black Dragon: for history of the society see Byas, *Govt. by Assassination,* 193–202; also Jansen, 33–102 and *passim;* for list of its actual members, see Storry, *Double Patriots,* 312–13.

143 Two of the men mentioned had never belonged to society: Kato Genchi, Hashimoto Kingoro. A third already dead: Uchida Ryohei, A fourth, Tojo's victim: Nakano Seigo. Three others no longer members: Hirota Koki, Kikuchi Toyosaburo, Ogata Taketora.

Konoye visit to MacArthur, Sept. 13: Yabe, 2:581; Shigemitsu, 379; Kido, *Nikki,* 1234. Eichelberger quoted: *N.Y. Times,* Sept. 14, 1945.

Kido saw most suspects before their arrest: Kido, *Nikki,* 1227–35.

Baldwin on Emperor as junior partner: *N.Y. Times,* Sept. 14, 1945; Higashikuni quoted on forgetting Pearl Harbor and Hiroshima: ibid.

144 Eichelberger and MacArthur criticized: *N.Y. Times,* Sept. 17, 1945.

Suzuki's outrageous lie: quoted, ibid., Sept. 16, 1945.

Willoughby accepted idealized account of Emperor: Willoughby and Chamberlain, 291.

Shigemitsu replaced by Yoshida: see Higashikuni, *Watashi,* 169.

145 MacArthur moved to Embassy and Dai Ichi Bldg. in Tokyo: Whitney, 227–32; Gunther, 52.

Higashikuni's first press conference: *N.Y. Times,* Sept. 19, 1945.

Sen. Russell's wish to try the Emperor: Singapore *Times,* Sept. 20, 1945; *N.Y. Times,* Sept. 19, 1945.

146 Higashikuni's Sept. 20 call on MacArthur: Ando, "Senso to kazoku," Pt. 1, 87–88.

Sept. 25, Japanese allowed to use short-wave bands: Singapore *Times,* Sept. 25, 1945.

Hirohito met the press: Kido, *Kankei bunsho,* 512–14; *N.Y. Times,* Sept. 25, 1945.

Headlined the next day: that is, on the morning of Sept. 25 New York time, the night of Sept. 25 Tokyo time.

Palace disavowal of Kluckhohn's report: *N.Y. Times,* Sept. 29, 1945; Singapore *Times,* Sept. 27, 1945.

Hirohito rehearsed for meeting: Kido, *Nikki,* 1237.

147 Hirohito's meeting with MacArthur, 287–88.

148 Hirohito's conversation with MacArthur: a composite drawn from several of MacArthur's own accounts to interviewers. The most complete version is given in Far Eastern Commission, Australian Delegation, Interim Report, Feb. 11, 1946. I have also made use of an account of the meeting

in the possession of Otis Cary and MacArthur's own *Reminiscences,* Mac-Arthur's final remarks, asking for Hirohito's advice, are from Hirohito's own report immediately afterward to Kido (*Nikki,* 1237). See also Willoughby and Chamberlain, 327.

149 Japanese attempts to suppress Hirohito-MacArthur photograph: Wildes, 77.
Hirohito's glee: Kido, *Nikki,* 1237–38; 1243.

149–152 FIRST QUARREL: this section a synthesis drawn from Yabe, 581 ff.; Sumimoto, 132–33; Hayashi Masayoshi, 266 ff.; Kido, *Nikki,* 1239–40; Yoshida, 64–68; *N.Y. Times,* Oct. 7, 10–14, 18, Dec. 2, 1945; MacArthur, 305; interviews with Koizumi and Tanaka.

152 Occupation now manned by fresh recruits: *N.Y. Times,* Oct. 16, 1945.
MacArthur's disenchantment with all occupation armies: MacArthur, 282.

153 "widespread promiscuous relationship": Sheldon, 120.
Yoshiwara ruins off limits: Craig, 296.

153–154 G.I. encounter like an opium dream: verbal, from a personal friend who was engaged at the time to his present wife. A very similar story is told by Sheldon, 42 ff.

155 Ando Akira and his Dai-an club: Wildes, 36; Sheldon, 145.

155–156 Entertainments and investment opportunities: Wildes, 35–36; Gayn, 178–79; Sumimoto, 304; Matsumoto, interview.

157 Burma-Thailand railway figures: Wakefield, 176.
Class A Criminals charged with "conspiracy," etc.: IMTFE "Indictment."
Matsudaira felt out supposed criminals: Koizumi and aristocrat (privileged source) have both confirmed this statement. Tanaka Takayoshi, in interviews and in "Kakute Tenno," "Oni kenji," and *Sabakareru rekishi,* has provided a wealth of circumstantial detail that supports the statement. See also Kido, *Nikki,* 1137, 1153 (Aug. 25, 1944, Nov. 16, 1944).

158 Nashimoto's menial chores: Sugamo, *Senpan,* see n. 2 on page 1048, Epilogue; Kurzman, 246.

158–161 Kido's last month of freedom: *Nikki,* 1238–57.

159 Trip to Ise: ibid.; also Kido, *Kankei bunsho,* 139–40. In the latter Kido thought it good that the elderly spectators sat instead of kneeling in the prewar fashion. "The ties of the imperial family are invisible," he wrote, "beyond all theories about the problem of war responsibility. People with oxcarts bowed. Just before the train entered the Tsu station in Mie-ken a widow held up a picture of her late Army officer husband. I watched her face and thought, 'She is a true Japanese.' "
"I heard the news with a calm heart": Kido, *Nikki,* 1255.

161 Konoye's suicide: Gayn, 30 ff.
Kido disinfected: Sugamo, *Senpan,* see n. 2 on page 1048. Epilogue.
"Now that the dead wood has been removed": courtier was Matsudaira Yasumasa, quoted by Cornelius Ryan in London *Daily Telegraph,* Dec. 20, 1945.

162 Vories mission: interviews with William P. Woodard, who had access to Vories's diary kept by his widow, Mrs. Hitotsuyanagi Meireiru;

also with Roy Smith, who came to Japan at the same time as Vories and has since taught in Kobe; also Sumimoto, 131, 185.

163 Drafts of non-divinity proclamation: Far Eastern Commission, Australian Delegation, "Interim Report," Annex VII.
Shidehara's final revision: Sumimoto, 135–36.

163–164 Non-divinity proclaimed: Wakefield, 145; Holtom, 219.

164 Hirohito's poem of 1946: I am indebted to Kitagawa Hiroshi for the Japanese text; the translation is mine. See also Wakefield, 144; Brines, 98.

164–169 DICTATING DEMOCRACY: except as cited, this section based on Kido, *Nikki,* 1240–42; Kido, *Kankei bunsho,* 514–26; MacArthur, 300–1; *N.Y. Times,* Oct. 22, Nov. 2, 22, 1945.
MacArthur's requirements of new Constitution: Far Eastern Commission, Pacific Affairs Division, "Memorandum."

165–166 U.S. draft of Constitution forced through: ibid.; Whitney, 248 ff.; Gayn, 126–29.

167 Resignation of fifteen princes: *Straits Times,* Apr. 8, 1946.
Wake in the palace: Fujishima, 61.
Imperial fortune liquidated: Wildes, 82; Gayn, 136.
Constitution promulgated: for a complete text and a comparison with the old Constitution, see Borton, Appendix IV.
Self-Defense Force: interviews with Tony Kase and Hata Ikuhiko. Officers in the Self-Defense Force in the 1960's include the sons of World War II Prime Minister Tojo; of conqueror and commander in Indonesia, Lt. Gen. Imamura Hitoshi; of Class A war crimes defendant and wartime Military Affairs Bureau chief, Sata Kenryo; of 1928 War Minister Shirakawa Yoshinori; and of wartime P.O.W. administrator, Hamada Hitoshi.

168 Hirohito at Hiroshima: Brines, 91.

168–169 Differing Allied views on choice and culpability of war crime defendants: Far Eastern Advisory Commission, WC 5–401; see also Australia, "Cablegrams, 1945–1946."

169 MacArthur quoted on distaste for trying vanquished: MacArthur, 318.
MacArthur's wish to limit indictment to Pearl Harbor: *N.Y. Times,* Nov. 25, 1945.
MacArthur asked to be relieved of responsibility for trials: MacArthur, 318.

170 Keenan's character: Butow, *Tojo,* 496: William J. Sebald with Russell Brines, *With MacArthur in Japan: A Personal History of the Occupation* (New York: W. W. Norton, 1965), 157.
Keenan's statements to press: *N.Y. Times,* Nov. 16, Dec. 1, 7, 8, 15, 1945; also Singapore *Times,* Dec. 14, 1945.

171 Keenan's staff: Far Eastern Commission, Australian Delegation, "Interim Report," Annex VII, Report on war crimes prosecution progress, Jan. 7, 1946.

172 MacArthur's defense of Emperor, visit of Far Eastern Commission, and Australian members' report: Far Eastern Commission, Australian

Delegation, "Interim Report," Annex I.

174 Agreement on use of evidence by Japanese defense lawyers: Sumimoto, 314.

175–176 Keenan's star witness and assistant: Tanaka Takayoshi, "Kakute Tenno," "Oni kenji," and interviews.

176 Description of courtroom: John Luter dispatch no. 291, May 11, 1946, to *Time* magazine.
Statistics of trial: Webb Collection, "IMTFE papers covering a series of applications . . . ," item (f).

177 Webb's work and character: see Webb Collection, "Inward and outward correspondence with SCAP, Feb. 1946 to Feb. 1948," *passim*.
Webb to Evatt: Webb Collection, "Miscellaneous Correspondence, 1946–1948," reproduced in memorandum of Sept. 15, 1948, to Maj. Gen. Myron C. Cramer.
Comyns Carr on possible suppression of minutes of Imperial Headquarters meetings: IMTFE "Proceedings," 21685; see also 21680–690 in Canberra copy.

178 Keenan's attempt, Sept. 25, 1946, to exonerate Hirohito: IMTFE "Proceedings," 29303 ff.
Kido's diary eight days before Pearl Harbor: *Nikki,* 927–31.

179 Keenan's press leak: *N.Y. Times,* Sept. 26, 1945.
Webb's press leak: *North China Daily News,* Sept. 27, 1945.
Tojo's brother arrested: *N.Y. Times,* Oct. 12, 1947.

180 Logan in direct examination of Tojo, Dec. 31, 1947: IMTFE "Proceedings," 36520.
Tanaka arbitrates: "Oni kenji"; interviews.
Kido promised the Tojo family betterment: my own conclusion, confirmed by a friend in Kyoto who made inquiries on my behalf of Mrs. Tojo whom he knew socially.
Keenan's entertainment in Atami: Tanaka, "Oni kenji"; "Kakute Tenno."

181 Webb to MacArthur on *Life* article: Webb Collection, "Inward and Outward Correspondence with SCAP."
Quote from Webb's second draft of judgment circulated Sept. 17, 1948: Webb Collection, "IMTFE papers," item (e), 271–74.

182 Justice Bernard quoted: IMTFE, "Separate and Dissenting Opinions," Dissenting Opinion of the Justice from France, 20–23.
Keenan, "the sentences are stupid": Tanaka, "Oni kenji," 278.

4. Imperial Heritage

In writing this chapter I have tried to provide a guide to the Japanese past and at the same time to fit my findings about 1920–1945 into the whole context of Japanese history. For this purpose I have used only materials already available in English, pointing up in them features which seem to me to have been neglected.

For the lives of the emperors I have relied upon Richard Ponsonby-Fane's *Imperial House of Japan,* 28–116, 229–91, 295–332, 369–405; on his *Sovereign and Subject,* 19–84, 93–248; on his *Studies in Shinto and Shrines,* 1–135; and on his *The Vicissitudes of Shinto,* 81–117.

For the wider history of shoguns and people I have depended mainly upon G. B. Sansom's authoritative three-volume *History of Japan.*

For the early prehistoric and semihistorical periods I have used Komatsu Isao's archeological summary, *The Japanese People,* and J. E. Kidder's *Japan Before Buddhism.*

I have found most useful the translated excerpts from early Japanese works included in *Sources of Japanese Tradition,* compiled by Tsunoda Ryusaku, Wm. Theodore de Bary, and Donald Keene.

Other general histories which I have consulted: Storry's *A History of Modern Japan,* Leonard's *Early Japan,* Natori's *Short History of Nippon,* and *A History of East Asian Civilization,* vol. 2, by Fairbank, Reischauer, and Craig.

On specific facets which interested or puzzled me, I found help in Ballou's *Shinto,* Bunce's *Religions in Japan,* Gouverneur Mosher's *Kyoto: A Contemporary Guide* (Rutland, Vt., and Tokyo: Charles E. Tuttle Co., 1964), and Takeyoshi Yosaburo, *The Story of the Wako: Japanese Pioneers in the Southern Regions.* A. L. Sadler's biography of Ieyasu was also useful, and so was Oliver Statler's *Japanese Inn.*

My account of the introduction of firearms into Japan, on pages 206 ff., is based almost entirely on Noel Perrin's "Giving Up the Gun" in the *New Yorker* magazine (November 20, 1965).

5. The Coming of Perry

For the most part this chapter is based on accessible English-language sources which I have not thought it necessary to cite in detail: principally, Sampson, vol. 3, Beasley, Barr, Reynolds, Perry, Heuskens, Preble, Yanaga's *Japan Since Perry,* and the books of Statler and Ponsonby-Fane. In Ponsonby-Fane I have drawn particularly on *The Imperial House of Japan,* 115–29, 281–91, 332–38, 405–17, dealing respectively with emperors, shoguns, imperial consorts, and imperial mausolea; on *Sovereign and Subject,* 248–52 (Tokugawa Mitsukuni), and 252–60 (Iwakura Tomomi); on *The Vicissitudes of Shinto,* 119–21 (the civil war), 248–50 (Shimazu Nariaki), 320–24 (Prince Kitashirakawa Yoshihisa); and on *Visiting Famous Shrines in Japan,* 380–90 (Shimazu Nariakira).

In addition I have absorbed points of view and atmosphere from George Akita, *Foundations of Constitutional Government in Modern Japan, 1868–1900* (Cambridge, Mass.: Harvard University Press, 1967); R. P. Dore, *Education in Tokugawa Japan* (Berkeley and Los Angeles: University of California Press, 1965); Richard Hildreth, *Japan As It Was and Is,* 2 vols. (Chicago: A. C. McClure & Co., 1906); Arthur May Knapp, *Feudal and Modern Japan* (Yokohama: Kelly & Walsh, Ltd., rev. ed., 1906); Joseph H. Longford, *The Evolution of New Japan* (Cambridge: Cambridge University Press, 1913); and Albert M. Craig, *Choshu in the Meiji Restoration,* Harvard Historical Monographs, XLVII (Cambridge, Mass.: Harvard University Press, 1967).

221–222 Discussion of the House of Fushimi: interviews with Koizumi Shinzo and a member of the Ohtani family, supplemented by reference to Japanese biographical dictionaries and the genealogical charts in the works of Ponsonby-Fane.

226 Prince Asahiko: here and in what follows my account of Asahiko's activities is taken from the brief biography of him written by his grand-

son, Empress Nagako's brother, Higashifushimi Kunihide.

238 Lord I-i's assassination: here I have supplemented the account in Barr with that in Okakura Kakuzo, *The Awakening of Japan* (1904. New York: Japan Society, Inc., reprint, 1921), 135–36.

248–249 The killing of Komei: Murofushi, 34 ff., supplemented by Koizumi interview and Ninagawa Arato, *Tenno* (Tokyo, 1952), 105.

252 Meiji's birthplace: I am indebted to Otis Cary for pointing out the cottage to me.

254 The crowds knelt in waves: On his own entry into Edo a decade earlier Heuskens, 141, wrote, "an officer shaking his paper fan sufficed to cause hundreds of persons to step back."

258 Meiji amassed fourth largest concentration of capital: Kuroda, 135. Young Saionji teasing Yamagata: Harada, 4:66–67.

261 Origins of the Diet: Fukuzawa Yukichi, "The History of the Japanese Parliament," *Transactions of the Asiatic Society of Japan,* Tokyo, 1914, 577 ff.

262–264 LORD HIGH ASSASSIN: Byas, *Govt. by Assassination*, 173–88.

265 Meiji's celibate headquarters in Hiroshima: Akimoto, 291–92.

6. Hirohito's Boyhood

273–274 EARLY BABY: These four opening paragraphs are based on an interview with a nobleman of one of the "five families." I repeated the story to Koizumi Shinzo, former chief tutor for Crown Prince Akihito, Hirohito's son. He sighed, acknowledged that he had heard the same gossip, and shrugged it off, saying, "In those days almost anything was possible." For documentary corroboration of the story, see n. 1, page 274 in text.

Since 1758 all emperors begot by mistresses: Ponsonby-Fane, *Imperial House,* 16, 21, 22.

Yoshito's wedding: Baroness d'Anetham, *Fourteen Years of Diplomatic Life in Japan* (London, 1912), entry of that date.

274 N.2: see Piggott, 125; *Enthronement of the Emperor,* Futara, "The Life of the Emperor," 47; Fleisher, 21. Also note statement of Ponsonby-Fane, *Imperial House,* 337.

275–277 Hirohito's foster home: Tanaka Sogoro, *Tenno no kenkyu* [The Emperor's Studies] (Tokyo: Kawabe Shobo, 1951), 232–37; Koizumi, interviews.

277 Hirohito's first and last drink: Honjo, 254.

Kido Koichi's lineage: The most aristocratic of my sources gave me this story about Kido's mother. Support is lent to it by *Kido Nikki* in which Kido refers to his mother with unusual respect and to an elder relative of his mother as Chutaro-sama, a familiar given name coupled with a respectful *sama* suffix which Kido accords to no one else in his entire diary.

278 "Konoye? He was a nice man. When I was at Peers' School, I used to make him cry by teasing him, but I thought he was a very nice man." Higashikuni in interview by Matsumoto Seicho, *Bungei Shunju,* January 1968, 160 ff.

Sun Yat-sen in Japan: Jansen, 105–30.

278–283 FELLING GOLIATH: this section on the Russo-Japanese War, except as cited, based on Yanaga, *Since Perry*, 294–300; Hargreaves; and Thomas Cowen, *The Russo-Japanese War* (London: Edward Arnold, 1904).

279 Toyama's visit to Ito: Kuzu Yoshihisa, *Toa senkaku shishi kiden* [Stories and Biographies of East Asian Adventurers] (Tokyo: 1933–1936), 1:705, cited by Jansen, 109.

281 $65 million bribe: Post Wheeler and Hallie Erminie Rides, *Dome of Many-Colored Glass* (Garden City, N.Y.: Doubleday & Co., 1965), 306 ff.

282 Baltic Fleet lost at Tsushima Strait: Scherer, *Meiji Leaders*, 103.

283 Terms of Portsmouth Treaty unpopular in Japan: Yanaga, *Since Perry*, 311–17.

On rioting which made Katsura Cabinet resign: see Harrison, 187–89.

Only Hirohito's Big Brothers exulted in victory: based on interviews with Arthur W. Hummel and Roy Smith who were teaching in Japan at the time.

Yamagata warned war too much of a gamble: Takahashi Yoshio, *Sanko iretsu* [Three Examples of Distinguished Service] (Tokyo: Keibundo-sha, 1925), 90–145.

Ito in Korea and later his assassination: Yanaga, *Since Perry*, 343–45.

284–286 Princely ABC's: Tanaka Sogoro, *Tenno no kenkyu* (Tokyo: Kawabe Shobo, 1951), 232–37; Mosley, ch. 1; Scherer, *Meiji Leaders*, 83, 71–73, 96; Koyama, 87; Koizumi, interviews.

287–288 Matsumoto Seicho, interview with Higashikuni, *Bungei Shunju*, January 1968, 160 ff.

288 1911 rebellion against Manchu emperors in China: Jansen, 105–30; Yanaga, 348.

7. Crown Prince Hirohito

290–292 DEATH OF MEIJI: Mosley, 19–20; Gibney, 92; A. M. Young, *Recent Times*, 18; my interpretation of Nogi's motives in committing suicide, Kido, *Nikki*, 527–30.

292–296 TAISHO'S COUP: my interpretation, with which the most aristocratic of my sources heartily agrees. It is usually assumed that Taisho was a pawn of Katsura, but this sorts ill with the wreck which the premature coup made of Katsura's career or with Katsura's social position relative to that of Sadanaru and other elder princes of the blood. In short, because of the imperial taboo I conclude that Japanese have blamed Katsura, when the plain fact of the event is that Taisho attempted a sudden increase in direct imperial power. See Bush, *Land of the Dragonfly*, 93; Beasley, 182; Borton, 251; A. M. Young, *Recent Times*, Ch. 2; Fairbank et al, 559–63; Mosley, 21–22.

295 Formation of Yamamoto Cabinet: Harada 4:334–35.

Taisho, Kato, Saionji smoke: ibid., 4:38.

296–298 FINISHING SCHOOL: Tanaka Sogoro, *Tenno no kenkyu* [The Emperor's Studies] (Tokyo: Kawabe Shobo, 1951), 232–37; Jidai Kenkyu-kai, *Rising Japan* (Tokyo 1918), section II.

296 Professors' lectures "bland as *jagaimo*": Koizumi Shinzo, interview,

relaying story told by Kanroji Osanaga.

297 Hirohito's fascination for tactics and logistics: this was not generally appreciated until the publication of the *Sugiyama Memo* and *Honjo Nikki.*

298 Sugiura's lecture notes: Tanaka Sogoro, *Tenno no kenkyu,* 232–37.

301–302 1916 bomb attempt on Chang Tso-lin: Harada, 1:11–13.

302 SIBERIA: I have drawn this section from James William Morley, *The Japanese Thrust into Siberia, 1918* (New York: Columbia University Press, 1957), and from A. M. Young, *Recent Times,* 128–42, 177–87.

306 No. 2: Wilson's present to Flower Child: Omura Bunji, 351.

307 Tojo's prior association with Prince Higashikuni: Matsumoto Seicho interview with Higashikuni, *Bungei Shunju,* January, 1968, 160 ff.

308–312 COLOR-BLIND BRIDE: this section based on Murofushi, 158–60, Koyama, 22–35; Mosley, 35–51; Tsurumi, 6:259–261.

309 Prince Kuni's enthusiasms: Jidai Kenkyu-kai, *Rising Japan,* section III.

313 Futara to Toyama: Yatsuji Kazuo, in *Bungei Shunju,* Special Edition, 1956, 149.
Saionji Hachiro's thrashing: Murofushi, 158–60.

314–317 SALT AIR: Futara, 13–36, supplemented by biographical information about members of the retinue.

317–322 WAR FRONT TOURISM: this section is based on Futara, 36–182.

318 Lord Riddell's observations on Hirohito: Lord Riddell, *Intimate Diary of the Peace Conference and After, 1918–1923* (London: Victor Gollancz), 298, quoted in Piggott, 129. It is Piggott, also, 126, who tells the story about Hirohito and the Prince of Wales.

320 Busts in Hirohito's study: Vining, *Crown Prince,* 114.

321 Battlefields an obsession: see *Mainichi,* July 9, 1921.
Officer broke his pelvis: Colonel Heusch, *Le Temps,* June 26, 1921.
Paris-Zurich-Frankfurt intelligence triangle: Col. Eugene Prince, U.S. Army Intelligence, retired, interview.

322 Hara assassinated: A. M. Young, *Recent Times,* 249–50.
Konoye given advance notice of assassination: Harada, 1:220–21.

323 Higashikuni organizing cabal: my own deduction, corroborated by the most aristocratic of my sources and not denied by either Tanaka or Koizumi when I asked them about it. For further corroboration consider Higashikuni, *Watashi,* 19.

323–326 Cabal's first meeting: Takahashi, 142 ff., citing Takamiya, *Gunkoku.* Although the meeting has not previously been mentioned in English, I met no official figure in Japan who did not already know of its occurrence when I mentioned it. The descriptive details supplied here are drawn from interviews and from knowledge of Baden-Baden.
That week Pétain in Baden-Baden area: *Le Temps,* Oct. 22, 1921.
Nagata's parentage: Ito Kanejiro, 1:136–38; description of his appearance and that of other plotters my own from photographs.
324 Obata's character and attainments: ibid., 1:356, supplemented by

Fujisawa interviews.

325 Okamura: ibid., 2:310.
Okamura to "historical" section: *Mainichi*, March 21, 1963.

326–328 A FUNNY HAPPENING: the main event of this section, the car crash, is based on *Asahi* (Osaka ed.), April 3, 4, and 7, 1923. For some details and minor discrepancies, see *Le Temps*, April 3, 4, 5, 7 and 8, 1923; also *Illustration*, April 7, May 5, 12, 1923.

328 Hirohito fell out of love with espionage: see, e.g., Harada, 7:234, which quotes Hirohito, in 1938, as saying: "Plots are very unreliable. The general rule is that they will all fail and that when one succeeds it must be regarded as a miracle."

8.   Hirohito as Regent

For this chapter, in addition to sources cited or listed in the bibliography, I have drawn for background on: J. Ingram Bryan, *Japan from Within: An Inquiry into the Political, Industrial, Commercial, Financial, Agricultural, Armamental and Educational Conditions of Modern Japan* (New York: Frederick A. Stokes, 1924); Fujiwara Akira, "Ugaki Kazushige to rikugun no kindaika" [Ugaki Kazushige and Modernization of the Army] (*Chuo Koron* 80, No. 8, 372 ff.); Kamada Taku-ichiro, *Ugaki Kazushige: A Biography* (Tokyo: Chuo Koron-sha, 1937); Nakayama Masaru, "Okawa Shumei to no Koto" [Okawa Shumei and His Affairs] (*Nagare*, February 1958); Kurihara Ken, *Tenno: Showa-shi oboegaki* [The Emperor: Notes on the Reign of Hirohito] (Tokyo: Yushin-do Bunka Shinsho, 1955); and Barclay Moon Newman, *Japan's Secret Weapon* (New York: Current Publishing Co., 1944).

329 Hirohito's party: Price, 22; Mosley, 70–71; interviews with the most aristocratic of my sources who was at the party.

330 Saionji's purpose on visit to Tokyo: Harada, 4:311.
Saionji not concerned about "looseness": Mosley, 29; also Honjo, 254.

331 Confirmed in office of *Genro*: Saionji had been appointed unofficially to the ranks of the *genro* by Emperor Taisho in 1913; Kido, *Nikki*, 207; Harada, 4:333–34.

331–334 PALACE PLOT SCHOOL: except as cited, this section based on "Brocade Banner," 14, 23; Ohtani, *Kempei-shi*, 71–72.

332 Social Problems Research Institute: *Shakai mondai kenkyu-sho;* Ohtani, *Kempei-shi*, 71.
Purpose of Lodging House: Tanaka MS, "Okawa Shumei hakushi."
Headmastership delegated to Dr. Okawa (assisted by Yasuoka Masaatsu): Ohtani, *Kempei-shi*, 71, and Tsurumi et al, 4:99.
On Makino-Okawa relationship: see Ohtani, *Kempei-shi*, 71; "Brocade Banner," 38; Tanaka MS, "Okawa Shumei hakushi."
Okawa's education: "Brocade Banner," 11–16; Hayashi Fusao, 123–24.

332–333 Credo published in *War Cry*: "Brocade Banner," 13.

333 Okawa discovered Kita in 1918: Hayashi Fusao, 148.
Kita's ideas summarized: "Brocade Banner," 12–13; Ohtani, *Kempei-shi*, 71, 89–91.
Chichibu's friend who made edition of Kita's work: Nishida Chikara.

Kita's sutra for Hirohito: Yatsuji Kazuo, "Showa o shinkan shita Kita Ikki" [Kita Ikki, the Man Who Shook the Reign of Hirohito], *Bungei Shunju* (Special Ed., Feb. 1956), 148.

Curriculum directed by Okawa: IPS Documents Nos. 687 and 689 give excerpts from Okawa's own writings during his term as headmaster. In one of them he refers to the Lodging House as the "Colonial University." In another, an appreciation of the 19th century agronomist-philosopher Sato Nobuhiro, dated Feb. 20, 1924, Okawa wrote: "According to Sato's belief, the first country to be created was Japan. Therefore Japan is the foundation of all other countries. From the beginning it has been the mission of him who rules our Empire to give peace and satisfaction to all peoples. Accordingly, he has established a most concrete geopolitical philosophy in which the means are expounded for fulfilling Japan's heavenly mission of reigning over the world." Okawa went on to specify the first steps as securement of control over eastern Siberia, the South Sea islands, and world trade.

334 Col. Sugiyama's comic dance recalled: letter of March 6, 1945, from Harada to Kido, in Kido, *Kankei bunsho*, 630–32.

335 Disaster of Yokohama earthquake: Bush, *Land of Dragonfly*, 140–43; A. M. Young, *Recent Times*, 295–306.

N. 2: *Scientific American*, Supplement No. 1293, May 26, 1900.

336 Yuasa and Osugi's death: Kido, *Nikki*, 507.

337 Assassination attempt: Ohtani, *Kempei-shi*, 60 ff.; Murofushi, 191–93.

337–338 Namba's father, and the gun used by Namba: Tsurumi et al, 5:119; also Murofushi, 191–93.

N. 3: On Higashikuni's equerry Yasuda, see Kido, "The Circumstances Before and After the Resignation of the Third Konoye Cabinet," IPS Document No. 2 (Library of Congress microfilm WT 6).

338 Ugaki Kazushige, a man of the people: for characterizations of Ugaki, see Bush, *Land of Dragonfly*, 144; A. M. Young, *Recent Times*, 307; Yanaga, *Since Perry*, 403 ff.

339 Ugaki as tutor to Hirohito: Tanaka Sogoro, *Tenno no kenkyu* [The Emperor's Studies] (Tokyo: Kawade Shobo, 1951), 232–37.

Ugaki in diary: quoted, Takeda, 1.

Princess Nagako studied under special tutors: Koyama, 10–34.

Nagako carried a fan: see Koyama, 42.

339–340 Wedding ceremonies: Mosley, 87–90; Koyama, 41–49; attended by Toyama Mitsuru: Bush, *Land of Dragonfly*, 133.

340 "We face a Satsuma clan conspiracy": Ohtani, *Rakujitsu*, 82–83.

Ugaki's shuffle of Choshu and Satsuma generals: My account of the Army purge is based on lists of generals who resigned, as given in *Mainichi* at the time, and Hata's "Personnel Records" concerning repostings. For similar conclusions based on independent approaches, see Ohtani, *Kempei-shi*, 15; Kennedy, *Japan and Her Defense Forces*, 104–25, 169–73; Crowley, 87–88; Takeda, 7.

341 33,894 men and 6,089 horses: Ohtani, *Kempei-shi*, 15.

342 NEW STAR IN CHINA: except as cited, this section based on Ekins and Wright, 16–23; Clubb, 144; Liu, 5–35.

Since 1920 Suzuki assigned to Chiang as advisor: For Suzuki Tei-ichi's experiences in China, see his testimony, IMTFE "Proceedings," 35172–185; also his "Hokubatsu," in *Himerareta, 23–24.*

N. 5: see Inoue's testimony, IMTFE "Proceedings," 35158 ff.

345–346 Anami's party for Lodging House graduates and their discussion: Tanaka MS, "Okawa Shumei hakushi."

9. Hirohito as Emperor

348–352 Hirohito's regimen: Suzuki Kantaro, *Gonichi no ittan,* 13 ff.; *Enthronement of the Emperor,* Futara Yoshinori, "The Life of the Emperor," 47–51; Byas, *Govt. by Assassination,* 300–301, 313–17; Fleisher, 17–20; Price, 17, 19–20.

350 Hirohito met with Privy Council every Wednesday: *Enthronement of the Emperor,* Futara's article, 50; *Japan Year Book, 1944–45,* 7, 118.

352 Emperor's function at religious rites, details of ceremonies: Ponsonby-Fane, *Studies in Shinto,* 1–136 *passim; Enthronement of the Emperor,* Hoshino Teruouki, "Ceremonies Throughout the Year," 66–70; *Japan Year Book, 1944–45,* 581–86; Byas, *Govt.,* 313–17.

352–353 Higashikuni returned "incognito" from Paris after word of Taisho's death: *N.Y. Times,* Jan. 12, 1927.
Went on to Asia for intelligence duties: interview, Koizumi; cp. Ohtani, *Kempei-shi,* 563.

354 Chiang blamed troops' excesses on Bolshevik agitators; troops burn consulates in Nanking; expeditionary force halted by Japan's refusal to join: Yanaga, *Since Perry,* 452–53; Abend, *Life in China,* 49–50; Shidehara Kijuro, testimony, IMTFE "Proceedings," 1349.
Foreign enclaves in largest Chinese cities: see esp. Murphey, 1–66, on Shanghai.
West had invested more than $2 billion: see, e.g., Boake Carter and Thomas Healy, *Why Meddle in the Orient?* (New York: Dodge Publishing Co., 1938), 173–75.

355 Chiang Kai-shek's struggle with Communists, climaxed by Black Tuesday and split in KMT: Ekins and Wright, 43–57; Liu, 36–52; Clubb, 135–37.
Chiang's government at Nanking: Liu, 48.

356 Sun Yat-sen's widow went into exile in Europe: Ekins and Wright, 54–55.
Tanaka Gi-ichi career and policies: A. M. Young, *Imperial Japan,* 46–47; Scalapino, 232, 235: Shimada, 53.

357 "I promise to co-operate with Chang Tso-lin": Tanaka quoted, Yoshihashi, 14.
Suzuki study group: Parent organization was the *Nagata kurabu* (Nagata club), Harada, 9:3. For the study group or *kenkyu-kai* phase of the association, see Tanaka Kiyoshi as quoted in "Brocade Banner," 22. Later names for the same group were *Mumei-kai* (Nameless Society) and *Isseki-kai* (One-Evening Society); Takahashi, 142–46. For other details see *Himerareta,* 180, and Ogata, 26.
Chang Tso-lin's reply to Tanaka: Shigemitsu, 47.

Chang's new policy; ibid., 47; Yoshihashi, 21; Clubb, 140.

358 FAR EASTERN CONFERENCE: except as cited, this section based on *Taiheiyo senso e no michi,* 1:289–90; Ogata, 15, 196–98; Yoshihashi, 21–26.

Suzuki's recollections of his address, quoted: Yamaura Kanichi, *Mori kaku* (Tokyo, 1941), 599–601.

Muto-Tanaka exchange: Yamaura, *Mori kaku,* 636–37, quoted, Yoshihashi, 26; Muto's reputation as "the Silent" (*mono iwanu shogun*), his obituary in *Mainichi,* Feb. 28, 1933.

359 *Tanaka Memorial*: text in Crow, 22–112; see also Shigemitsu, 45–46; K. K. Kawakami, *Japan Speaks on the Sino-Japanese Crisis* (New York: The Macmillan Co., 1932), 145–46, and introduction by Inukai Tsuyoshi, xi-xii.

CHIANG GOES A-WOOING: except as cited, this section based on Ekins and Wright, 58–66; Clubb, 141; Jansen, 199–201 and 254 n. 54; Yoshihashi, 34 and n.

N. 7: Crow, 36–38.

360 Tanaka, "Our government is taking the position . . .": Takakura Tetsuichi, ed., *Tanaka Gi-ichi denki* (Tokyo, 1960), 2:740.

Muto refused to accept Yoshida's proposal to cut Peking-Mukden railroad: Yoshihashi, 30–31.

Photograph of Chiang with Black Dragon leader Toyama: *Taiheiyo senso e no michi,* 2:207; see also Higashikuni, *Watashi,* 60. The photo is one of those reproduced in this volume.

361 Chiang's bargain: Naturally no official source states the basis for the Chiang-Japan understanding as explicitly as I have set it forth here. However, *Nihon gaiko nenpyo narabini shuyo monjo* [Chronology of Japan's Foreign Relations and Major Documents] (Tokyo: Diet Library, 1955), 2:105, does give the record of a conference between Prime Minister Tanaka and Chiang Kai-shek, Nov. 5, 1927. According to this record Chiang assured Tanaka that Japaneses interests would be duly respected should Japan assist in the achievement of the Kuomintang revolution; Ogata, 196.

Konoye resigned from Research Society (*Kenkyu-kai*), regarding it as dominated by reactionaries: Yabe, 1:118–20, 154, 168.

Col. Komoto Daisaku practiced dynamiting railroad bridges: Shimada, *Kanto gun,* 63.

361–362 March 1928 arrests of demonstrators, ultimate disposition of prisoners: Ohtani, *Kempei-shi,* 21–22.

Massacre of 7,000 Chinese at Tsinan: Yanaga, *Since Perry,* 455–56; A. M. Young, *Imperial Japan,* 39–40, 44; Abend, *Life in China,* 83. Special Service Organ agent was Nezu Masashi; *Dai Nihon teikoku no hokai* (Tokyo, 1961), 2:64. Hirohito sanctioned plan: Harada, 2:64, supplemented by interview with aristocratic source (privileged).

Prince Kanin's order to disarm Chang Tso-lin's troops: Usui Katsumi in *Himerareta showa-shi,* 29; see also Clubb, 143; Yoshihashi, 37–38.

Saionji's emissaries persuaded Tanaka to cancel scheduled disarming of Chang's troops: *Taiheiyo senso,* 1:306–8; Yoshihashi, 39–40, 42; "Brocade Banner," 19–20.

364 Komoto advised of plan to assassinate Chang Tso-lin, accepted

assignment to manage it himself: Hirano Reiji, *Manshu no inbosha* (Tokyo, 1959), 79–81, cited by Yoshihashi, 45; *Taiheiyo senso*, 1:308–9.

Chang telegraphed commanders his decision to withdraw to Manchuria: Watanabe, 89–93.

Preparations for bombing Chang's train: Murofushi, 209.

Chang sent "number-five wife" and others ahead: Shimada, *Kanto gun*, 64.

Maj. Giga remained on Chang's train: ibid., 65.

Train-watchers: *Taiheiyo senso*, 1:308–9; interview, Tanaka.

365 Details of bombing Chang's train: Murofushi, 210–13.

Manchurian guards killed, Russian-made bombs planted: Shimada, *Kanto gun*; 73ff.

Komoto's chief assistant: for Tomiya Tetsuo's career, see Tsurumi et al, 4:297–302.

Escaped Manchurian sentry told true story to Chang Hsueh-liang: Koyama, 98.

366 Banquet, June 13, and six notables at Hirohito's table: *Mainichi* (Osaka ed.), June 14, 1928.

366–367 Tanaka's visit to Saionji: Harada, 1:3–4, supplemented by interview with aristocrat (privileged source).

Mid-August, Gen. Mine's preliminary report: Ohtani, *Kempei-shi*, 563; Shimada, *Kanto gun*, 73 ff.; Tanaka Takayoshi, testimony, IMTFE "Proceedings," 1945–50.

Hirohito had telephone installed in study: *Mainichi* (Osaka ed.), Aug. 22, 1928.

Hirohito never identified himself on telephone: see, e.g., Harada, 1:94–95.

N. 9: Price, 16, and Fleisher, 20, were among journalists who initiated this misconception.

368 Kellogg-Briand Pact put Tanaka in disfavor with Emperor: Yanaga, *Since Perry*, 463–64; A. M. Young, *Imperial Japan*, 264.

Gen. Mine's second report on Chang Tso-lin killing: Harada, 1:5–11; *Taiheiyo senso*, 1:319–27; Shimada, *Kanto gun*, 73.

N. 10: Ishiwara had orders "to use force": IMTFE "Proceedings," 22170–180.

369 Enthronement: for ceremonies, traditions, etc., see *Enthronement of the Emperor, passim;* Ponsonby-Fane, *Imperial House*, 34–69: Mosley, 101–3; Vaughn, 181–90.

Chang Hsueh-liang's character: Kido eventually recognized his strengths; in Feb. 1932 he wrote in his diary, "Chang Hsueh-liang: complex personality, sensitive, cool, merciless, resolute" (*Nikki*, 136–37).

370 Anti-Chang handbill, excerpt: IMTFE "Proceedings," 19151.

Chang Hsueh-liang had Gen. Yang and railroad chief killed: Clubb, 152.

"believing that an opportunity will soon present itself": Vaughn, 118–19.

371 Komoto's memo ("Manmo taisaku no kicho") cited in Ogata, 198.

Hirohito's "august face would be muddy": Harada, 1:4.

Kido had worked on industrial mobilization plans: e.g., *Nikki*, 22, 26, 27, 68.

Motive for Kido's trip to America: interview, Koizumi.

371–372 Division chiefs' audiences with Hirohito: Harada, 1:8–9.

372 Tanaka's audience with Hirohito and his resignation: Harada, 1:9–11; *Taiheiyo senso,* 1:327; A. M. Young, *Imperial Japan,* 46–47. For insight into feelings about Tanaka's treatment, see Honjo, 160–61.
Col. Komoto posted to Kanazawa: "Brocade Banner," 19.

373 Maj. Giga: Several versions of the Giga story are extant. This one is confirmed by his son, Giga So-ichiro, a professor of economics at Osaka University, who is in possession of memoranda and notes left by his father. I am indebted to Maj. Giga's nephew Uemura Kazuhiko for having put me in touch with the son. See also Watanabe, *Bazoku,* 94–95.
Quote from Chinese Book of Rites: Shigemitsu, 49 and n.

10. Sea Power

380 Shidehara on assuming office: for full statement see *Asahi* (Tokyo ed.), July 10, 1929.
YOUNG ARMY GENIUS: This account, except as otherwise noted, follows Shimada, *Kanto gun,* 76, supplemented by Fujisawa Shigezo interviews.

381 Ishiwara: on his role and character see *Nihon jinbutsu-shi taikei* [Japan Biographical Outlines] (Tokyo: Asakura Shobo, 1960), 7; Shimada, *Kanto gun,* 79; Fujimoto, *Ningen,* 56–57, 67, 195, 203–4; Yoshihashi, 137; Ohtani, *Kempei-shi,* 430; Hata, *Gun,* 155; and Hata's "Personnel Records."

382 Ishiwara's book: it was entitled *The Ultimate World War*; Hayashi Fusao, 261.
Last week Kita Ikki had accused: "Brocade Banner," 15.

383–386 YOUNG NAVY GENIUS: Agawa, 3–18, 50–51; Potter, 3–22; Hata's "Personnel Records."

384 Secret naval development plan: Harada, 1:130.

387 Saionji's cautionary message: Harada, 1:18.

388 National defense question discussed in publication: "Brocade Banner," 26. See also Harada, 1:17 and 222.
Saionji opposed to official debate on national goals: ibid., 1:74–75.
N. 5: Phone interview with his son, Charles Allen Buchanan.

389 Japanese delegation dined with Hoover: *N.Y. Times,* Dec. 18, 19, 1929.
Yamamoto secretly met by Konoye: interviews with retired Navy commander, Tanaka, Matsumoto; see also Ohtani, *Kempei-shi,* 73–74.

391 Yamamoto and Takarabe acclaimed as conquerors: Harada, 1:54.
"Thank you for your pains": *Gokuro jyatta,* ibid., 1:70.
Crowds still cheered for Wakatsuki: ibid., 1:98.
Plan "agreed with actual development": Tanaka, interview.
Memorandum with plan: Harada, 1:130.

392 Ugaki's "sick-down strike": conversation with Tony Kase.
Saionji's tongue-in-cheek note to Ugaki: Ugaki diary quoted, Yoshihashi, 85. For another similar version see Harada, 1:82.

393 Eleven Club: Kido, *Kankei bunsho,* 97.
Kato accusing Count Makino: I have elided Kato's *cause célèbre,* but see Harada, 1:35, and Yoshihashi, 68–69.

N. 8: Kido, *Nikki,* 1165.

393–394 Kido-Konoye conversation at the golf club: as reconstructed by a fellow golfer over tea in locker room afterward and recorded and passed down to me through interview with banker's son. See also Kido, *Nikki,* 33.

394–395 Japan subject of intelligence annual report: "Brocade Banner," 22, and Yoshihashi, 101.

395 Three slogans of Nagata and the cabal: see Crowley, 88, 112.
"Scratching your toes": Harada, 1:148.
Treaty debate beginning to "vex" Hirohito: ibid., 1:176.

396 Detailed report on conquest of Manchuria: Shimada, *Kanto gun,* 81.
Too large a naval budget may "cause popular agitation": Harada, 1:210.

396–397 Killer Sagoya to Tokyo: Murofushi, 223–28.

397 Visit from Iogi Ryozo: "Brocade Banner," 9; Harada, 1:222 and note 9.
"Take good care of yourself": ibid., 1:219.

398 Hamaguchi shot: ibid., 1:219–20.
Assassin Sagoya: Kido, *Nikki,* 45–46, and Murofushi, 223–29.
Field headquarters (at Okayama): Kido, *Nikki,* 45–46.

11. March 1931

400 Saionji shocked and confused: Harada, 1:220.

401–402 According to a banker friend: Notes in possession of the banker's family; they were referred to by my informant in order to answer my questions. I have added some details, such as the Pall Mall cigarette, from Omura Bunji. Also, it may be that the attendant who followed him up the hill was his steward Kumagai Yasomi rather than his secretary Nakagawa Kojuro.

402 Saionji's comments regarding Ugaki: Harada, 1:226, 228.
Hirohito during return from maneuvers: Honjo, 257–58.

403 Harada's audience with Makino and his statement re Gen. Ugaki's value: Harada, 1:231–32.
To frame him for high treason: see for instance "Brocade Banner," 26.
N. 1: Honjo, 257–58, confirmed and explained by Koizumi Shinzo who heard the story from Suzuki Kantaro.

403–404 THE MARCH PLOT: The most important source of information about this dark affair appears to have been overlooked by Western historians: Okawa's *kempei* (secret police) interrogation paper reproduced in Harada, 9:344–53. Consequently an erroneous impression exists (see, for instance, Storry, *Double Patriots,* 63) that the bombs were returned to the military on March 8, 1931. In reality the bombs were kept by the civilian plotters and used to blackmail the Army until March 8, 1932. In this highly condensed account, I have also drawn on Nakano, 67–84; Murofushi, 229–32; Kido, *Nikki,* 147–48; Harada, 2:19, 22–30, 32, 37, 41–42, 44, 51, 55–56, 106, 111, 117–18, 121–24, 332–35; 4:299, 343, 348; 5:137; 6:14, 22, 78, 261; Ohtani, *Rakujitsu,* 34, 109–11; Hata, *Gun,* 27–31; "Brocade Banner," 28–32; Tokugawa Yoshichika's diaries as rendered in IPS Documents Nos. 2582, 2638, 2639, 2640; IMTFE "Proceedings," 1441–1605.

405 Ugaki accosted by Hashimoto: Cho Isamu, verbal, as reported by Tanaka, interview.
"Kemal Ataturk": ibid.
Tatekawa's advices to Ugaki: ibid.

405–406 Koiso, Nagata, and Nagata's "novel": Ohtani, *Rakujitsu*, 109–10; see also "Brocade Banner," 28.

406 The story of the bombs: Ohtani, *Rakujitsu*, 34; Murofushi, 231; Nakano, 74; Harada, 2:40, 55–56.

407 Ugaki's meeting with Col. Okamura: Nakano, 67 ff., reveals that Ugaki met him on January 13, 16, 21, and 24.
N. 6: IPS Document No. 517, citing an article by Iwabuchi Tatsuo in *Chuo Koron*, February 1946, says that Mazaki for this offense was rusticated to Taiwan.

408 $100,000: Harada, 9:344–45.
The night that compromised Ugaki: Harada, 4:348; Koiso's "memoirs" as cited in Hata, *Gun*, 29; Ugaki's diary as cited by Yoshihashi, 91 (a copy of the original is in the hands of Prof. James Morley of Columbia University); Harada, 2:44, 106, 111, 117–18; conversations with Hata Ikuhiko and Tanaka Takayoshi.
Plot had served its purpose: see, e.g., "Brocade Banner," 28–29.

409 March 2–6: Harada, 9:251; Hata, *Gun*, 27–31.
"This plot was not an ordinary one": IMTFE "Proceedings," 1627; also 1610–13, and Storry, *Double Patriots*, 62–63.
Ugaki at palace and Makino's promise of face-saving assignment: "Brocade Banner," 28–29; see also Makino's sly remark, Harada, 2:30.

409–410 Makino-Okawa blackmail of Army: "Brocade Banner," 38 and 28; Harada, 9:344–53; interview with Hata Ikuhiko. Details of Komoto's mediation and the financial settlement come from Harada, 9:346–49. See also "Brocade Banner," 31; IMTFE "Proceedings," 1402 ff., 1418 ff., 1441 ff.; Ohtani, *Rakujitsu*, 34, and Hata, *Gun*, 29, for some details.

410 Kido's visit to Saionji: based on verbal information from a source with access to the papers of Viscount Uramatsu Tomomitsu, a member of Kido's Eleven Club. Kido, *Nikki*, 65, states that the visit actually took place on March 10, after Ugaki had made his peace with Makino. That the two visits are one and the same is suggested by Kido's closing note: "Concerning Makino there was some very confidential talk until 11 p.m. Then I returned to Tokyo."
Makino "conducting . . . the March Plot . . . out of darkness into darkness": Kido, *Kankei bunsho*, 3.
Many important fish knew: see, for instance, Harada's raw, unprocessed notes on the March Plot, 9:112.

12. Seizure of Mukden

Two excellent studies have been written in English about the subject matter in this chapter, Ogata Sadako's *Defiance in Manchuria* and Yoshihashi Takehiko's *Conspiracy at Mukden*. In general, I have cited their summaries, which are liberally provided with source notes, rather than give my own citations.

411 A 10 per cent decrease: Kurzman, 110–13; Kido, *Nikki,* 78–80; see also Harada, 2:12, 82.

412 Hirohito had before him two plans: Crowley, 92, 107; *Taiheiyo senso,* 1:366–74; Yoshihashi, 137–43.

Began to find and make provocations: for details see Shimada, *Kanto gun,* 97; *Japan Chronicle,* July 22, Sept. 9, 16, 1931; IMTFE "Proceedings," 19195, 19210; Harada, 2:25-38, 41.

413 Regimental commanders at "map exercises": Honjo, 3–4.

Honjo's mustache: Fujisawa, interview.

Ugaki's conversation with Honjo: Honjo, 3, supplemented by interviews with Kajiura and Tanaka.

Ugaki's wire to Koiso: ibid.

Suzuki's arrival and conversation with Honjo: ibid.

415 Honjo's doubts and suspicions: my interpretation of entries in Honjo's diary, e.g., July 16, line 5; July 18, line 3; July 19, line 4; July 22, line 2; July 23, line 1.

Wakatsuki's special report: Harada, 2:9–12.

Chiang's speech and delegation from KMT: Vaughn, 261–62; *Japan Chronicle,* Sept. 16, 1931.

Saionji and the vice chamberlain: Harada, 2:12.

416 Chang Hsueh-liang hospitalized while field pieces set up: see Abend, *Life in China,* 150–51.

Pair of cannon in Mukden: Shimada, *Kanto gun,* 100–101; Yoshihashi, 133–34; Harada, 2:77; IMTFE "Proceedings," 1990.

417 Itagaki a consummate politician: description of Itagaki's role and character based on Morishima, *passim;* Ito Kanejiro, 1:234; 2:351; Shimada, *Kanto gun,* 75–84; Ogata, 42–50; Yoshihashi, 134–37.

418 Honjo at the Summer Palace: Honjo, 8. He had an audience afterward with Prince Kanin and a call late that night from Baden-Baden Reliable Isogai Rensuke of the 2d Dept. of the Office of the Inspector General of Military Education.

Commanders receive briefing: Honjo, 8–9.

Honjo closeted with Suzuki and Itagaki: this account, from interview with privileged source, differs slightly from Honjo's own, 9, in which he says he met Suzuki and Itagaki the next afternoon, Aug. 4, in his room at Tokyo's Station Hotel.

Secret meeting in offices of General Staff: Ogata, 56. Honjo, 9, reveals that, meanwhile, Minami was dining with him. Honjo met that day also with Okamura, Yasuji; and Mazaki Jinzaburo.

419 Minami quoted: Crowley, 109.

Asahi editorial: *Asahi* (Tokyo ed.), Aug. 8, 1931.

Spokesman asked Harada to warn Saionji: Harada, 2:40–41.

Visit of Wakatsuki to Saionji: Kido, *Nikki,* 96.

N. 1: ibid.

420 Tokyo papers received several thousand calls: Harada, 2:46.

Saionji's meeting with Minami: ibid., 52–53 and 9:123; Ogata, 58.

Emergency meeting: Yoshihashi, 115; Hanaya, 45–46.

Tatekawa's talk to his Intelligence officers: Yoshihashi, 115; further information from Tanaka, interview.

421 Tatekawa's telegram to Honjo: ibid.
Second telegram: Yamaguchi, 112.
Third telegram: *Taiheiyo senso,* 1:434.
Ishiwara's and Itagaki's doubts: Yoshihashi, 156–58; *Taiheiyo senso,* 1:436–37.

422 Honjo's movements: Honjo, p. 21; Tanaka, interview.
Tatekawa's train trip and reception in Mukden: *Taiheiyo senso,* 1:438; Yoshihashi, 158–59; IMTFE "Proceedings," 30261; Fujisawa and Tanaka, interviews.

423 At Special Service Organ office: Yoshihashi, 159–60; Fujisawa, interview; Morishima Morito's affidavit, IMTFE "Proceedings," 3004 ff.
Honjo at portrait painter's home: Honjo, 22; Giga Soichiro, interview.

424 Itagaki after phone call: ibid.
Railroad explosion: *Taiheiyo senso,* 1:438–39.
Army explanation of 10:40 express: Yoshihashi, 3, 165.
Skirmish at railroad track: ibid., 2–3.
Itagaki's orders: Fujisawa and Tanaka, interviews; Yoshihashi, 166–67

425 Tatekawa at the Literary Chrysanthemum: Kajiura, interview; Yoshihashi, 158–59.
Japanese soldiers occupied barracks: ibid., 3.
Honjo at Port Arthur: this and following three paragraphs a summary from Fujisawa, interview; IMTFE "Proceedings," 18890–92, 19111, 19326, 19518, 22119, 22237; Shimada, *Kanto gun,* 102–7; *Taiheiyo senso,* 1:436 ff.

426 Honjo transferred H.Q. to Mukden: Honjo, 22–23, 351–55; Yoshihashi, 167–68, 170.
Military success: Yoshihashi, 4–6; Honjo, 23, notes arrival of eight bombers and eight observation planes from Korea on afternoon of Sept. 20. Casualty figures, IMTFE "Proceedings," 19457.

427 Tatekawa in Mukden, Sept. 19: Fujisawa, interview.
Tatekawa delivers his message: IMTFE "Proceedings," 18901–5; Storry, *Double Patriots,* 81.
"altogether appropriate"; *shigoku dato,* Harada, 2:71.
"Restrict operations to south Manchuria": IMTFE "Proceedings," 18901–5, amplified by Tanaka, interviews.
Honjo's worrying: Kajiura, interview.

428 Meeting of principal advisors: Harada, 2:64–66; Kido, 100.

429 Minami, "non-aggravation does not necessarily mean non-enlargement": Harada, 2:64, 68; Takeuchi, 352.
Cable to commander in Korea: Tanaka, interview; Yoshihashi, 174; see also Mori, 56.
Honjo sent Tatekawa and Suzuki back to Tokyo: Honjo, 23.

430 Hirohito would personally take responsibility for ordering in Japan's Korean Army: My interpretation of events; see Privy Council meeting of Oct. 7, 1931, minutes in IPS Document No. 904. In my opinion, the strongest evidence for my interpretation is provided by the discussion in Harada 2:41 and 65. If in late July—almost two months before the event—the closest confidants of Hirohito were discussing the propriety

of moving troops without official imperial sanction, then it must be concluded that the officially unauthorized troop movements did have Hirohito's unofficial authorization. Otherwise Saionji and other liberals would have been able to persuade Hirohito to issue explicit orders to the Korean Army not to move. The events of the February Mutiny (see Chs. 20–21) demonstrate that Hirohito could have issued such an order and it would have been obeyed. Furthermore, Harada's observation that the Tsinan intervention had created a precedent for officially unauthorized troop movements indicates to me only that Hirohito had arranged for that troop movement also, knowing in advance that there would be a reprisal massacre for which the Throne must avoid official responsibility.

Johnson and memo: Rappaport, 25.

Forbes's return to U.S.: ibid., 26, and *N.Y. Times,* Feb. 27, 1932, ix, 2:7.

Stimson's cable: Rappaport, 26.

13. Dollar Swindle

433 Hirohito's post-mature birth: see note on page 273.

434–435 Excerpts from Vespa, 45–62.

435 Takeda Nukazo: data from Hata's "Personnel Records."

436 DINNER AT KIDO'S: this section based on the brief entry in Kido, *Nikki,* 101, supplemented by interviews with a privileged source who had access to the papers left by Big Brother Viscount Uramatsu. It seems to me to be corroborated by events, by Kido, 114–15, and by Harada, 2:72, 76, 84–86, 90, 93–94, 114, 126–28, 130–31, and esp. 156 and 164–67.

437 Hirohito on Hoover's moratorium: Kido, *Nikki,* 91.

"Save the League's face": Uchida Yasuya's phrase; see Harada, 2:93.

438 Okawa and Army bombs: see note on pages 403–4 and Harada, 2:55–56.

Konoye and Higashikuni endowment: Storry, *Double Patriots,* 96–101, and Byas, *Govt. by Assassination,* 39 ff.

439 Misty Lagoon unit an elite: see Sakai Saburo, 29–38.

Secret policeman Amakasu in Harbin: Ogata, 67–68; Pernikoff, *passim.*

439–441 Henry Pu-Yi taken to Manchuria: Pu-Yi, 219–21, supplemented by interviews with Tanaka.

440 Pu-Yi's "audience hall": a similar description is in Harry Carr, *Riding the Tiger: An American Newspaperman in the Orient* (Boston: Houghton Mifflin Co., 1934), 91.

A messenger: Kamizumi Toshi-ichi rather than Kaeisumi Toshi-ichi as Pu-Yi reports.

441 EASTERN JEWEL: this section based on Tanaka Takayoshi, "Shokai jihen," 82; his MS "Yoshiko"; and interviews with him. See also McAleavy, 160 ff. For details of Kawashima Naniwa's career, see Shimada, *Kanto gun,* 17–18, and Jansen, 137–40.

442–443 Itagaki quoted: Tanaka, "Shokai jihen," 182, and his "Yoshiko" give slightly different wordings.

443 Itagaki gave Tanaka $10,000: Watanabe, 118.

Saionji had gone to Kyoto: Harada, 2:52 ff.

443–444 Saionji's agent published letter accusing Makino of malfea-

sance: ibid., 90–91, 103.
Harada sent to Kyoto, Saionji's opinions recorded: ibid., 88.
Harada met with Kido, Makino, Suzuki: ibid. Note Saionji's refusal to
see Lt. Gen. Banzai Rihachiro of the Spy Service, Oct. 15; ibid., 93–94.

445 Harada in Kyoto with Saionji: ibid., 88–92; Koyama, 104.
"to refrain from action": Ogata, 69.
Ishiwara led air raid: Ishiwara entry in *Nihon Jinbutsu-shi Taikei*
[Japan Biographical Outline] (Tokyo: Asakuro Shobo, 1960); see Fujimoto, 67. He also spoke of severing relations between the Kwantung Army
and Japan and of abandoning Japanese citizenship; Ogata, 94.
October Plot: Harada, 2:91, 99–100.

446 Suzuki, Hashimoto, Cho involved in plot: Storry, *Double Patriots*,
89.
Cho's October plan and quote: Murofushi, 229–32.
[the commander of the Misty Lagoon Air Station]: "Brocade Banner,"
144.

447 To gain a blackmail hold on Araki: Kido, *Nikki*, 113, reveals that
the Eleven Club met on Oct. 13 to discuss the Army's growing espousal
"of a so-called Strike-North continental policy." Kido expressed disgust
with the Army's stupidity. According to IPS Document 517—an English-
language version of an Iwabuchi Tatsuo article in *Chuo Koron* of Feb.
1946—the Strike-North ideologist, Kita Ikki, offered to contribute in the
October Plot by organizing demonstrations in Hibiya Park. His help, however, was not accepted because he and Mori Kaku were believed "to have
a counterplot" for "avenging Tanaka Gi-ichi."
Araki quoted: Harada, 2:107.
Araki's talk with Hashimoto and Cho: Murofushi, 229–32.
Arrest of eleven officers in plot: ibid.; "Brocade Banner," 114.
Okawa quoted re October Plot: Murofushi, 232.
Saionji went to villa in Okitsu: Harada, 2:101, 103.
Koiso's talk with Saionji on train: ibid., 105, supplemented by interview
with privileged source, a banker.

448 Saionji's surrender was announced at dinner: Harada, 2:94. The
announcement was made by South Manchuria Railroad president Uchida
Yasuya; for his mission in Tokyo at that time, see Ogata, 83–85, also A.
M. Young, *Imperial Japan*, 99–100.
Saionji waited until Oct. 30: Harada, 2:108.
Saionji's health ignored: Inoki, interview.
Saionji met Makino Nov. 2, their exchange: ibid., 2:112, 114.

449 Saionji's visit with Emperor: ibid., 115–16.
Invasion ordered on Oct. 30: Honjo, 26.
Honjo dispatched engineers: ibid.
Kwantung Army's move on Tsitsihar: *Taiheiyo senso*, 2:49 ff.; A. M.
Young, *Imperial Japan*, 102–5, 145–46; Ito Kanejiro, 359; Harada, 2:134–
35; Rappaport, 82.

450 Doihara's visit to Pu-Yi villa: Pu-Yi, 1:225–28; Tanaka, interview.
See also IMTFE "Proceedings," 4373–374.
Eastern Jewel's visit to Doihara: Tanaka, "Yoshiko," and interview.
Doihara's account: corroborated by Fujisawa, interview.

451 Efforts to get Pu-Yi to Mukden: Pu-Yi, 1:228–29; see also

Tanaka, "Yoshiko."

Doihara engineered riots in Tientsin: IMTFE "Proceedings," 4394–97; Pu-Yi, 1:229–30; Harada, 2:126; Zumoto, 65–68.

Pu-Yi's flight: Pu-Yi, 1:231. An alternate version, circulated at the time by Doihara and often repeated (e.g., McAleavy, 202), had it that Pu-Yi was smuggled out of the "Quiet Garden" in a *nagabitsu,* a wooden tub for dirty laundry. For the occasion on which Doihara did resort to this strategem, see Ronald Seth, *Secret Servants: A History of Japanese Espionage* (New York: Farrar, Straus & Cudahy, 1957), 122–24.

452 Pu-Yi's escape: Pu-Yi, 1:232–40.

His wife joined him: Tanaka, interview; see also McAleavy, 203.

Arrangements handled by Prince Chichibu: Harada, 2:147.

453 Politics and financial maneuvers: based on Harada, 2:127–31, 135, 138–41, 144, 146, 149–56; O. D. Russell, 243 ff.

Saionji, "It is like a bank": Harada, 2:135–36.

League debated for a month: Rappaport, 68 ff.

Hirohito and fireflies: Kinoshita Michio, "Gunkan haruna kokanpan-jo ni haisu seinaru isshun no kokei" [One-Instant Scene of Reverence on the Quarterdeck of the Battleship *Haruna*]. *Fujin no Tomo,* June, 1939.

Toyama's opinion: Harada, 2:146.

454 League's decision: Rappaport, 76–77.

Herald Tribune's editorial: Dec. 10, 1931.

Black Dragon hireling: Adachi Kenzo; see Storry, *Double Patriots,* 313.

Saionji's opinion: Harada, 2:152–55.

Inukai's qualifications: Jansen, *passim;* A. M. Young, *Imperial Japan, passim.*

Harada's exchange with Kido: Harada, 2:156; Kido, *Nikki,* 120.

455 CASHING IN: this section based on Harada, 2:164–67; Kido, *Nikki,* 147; O. D. Russell, 247–51; Vaughn, 181–90.

14. Fake War

456 In China an envoy of Inukai: IMTFE "Proceedings," 1480. For details of the envoy, Kayano Chochi, see Jansen, 200 and *passim,* also "Proceedings," 1478–1522. For other peace efforts of Inukai, see Crowley, 158. Storry, *Double Patriots,* 109 ff., presents a factually accurate but strained interpretation of Kayano's mission.

Frigidly formal audience: Kido, *Nikki,* 120, makes a point of the fact that the audience lasted only thirteen minutes.

Cabinet met immediately: Araki's affidavit, IMTFE Exhibit 1880.

Gen. Kanaya Hanzo resigned: *Asahi* (Tokyo ed.), Dec. 16, 18, 1931.

Triumvirate agreed to nominate Minami: ibid., Dec. 23, 1931.

Process of Prince Kanin's appointment: my interpretation of Kido, *Nikki,* 121–23, and Harada, 2:197.

457 Kanin's appointment celebrated: *Asahi* (Tokyo ed.), Jan. 31, 1932; Harada, 2:175–77.

Sun Fo: he was then prime minister of China; Rappaport, 125. On his mission see Clubb, 194–95, and A. M. Young, *Imperial Japan,* 96.

457–458 Eastern Jewel in Shanghai: Tanaka, "Yoshiko," and interviews.

I Pong-chang's trip to Tokyo: Murofushi, 234; Ohtani, *Kempei-shi,* 63.

Itagaki flew to Tokyo: Honjo, 60; Tanaka, interview.

Western reaction to renewed aggression: Rappaport, 83–94; Westel W. Willoughby, *Japan's Case Examined* (Baltimore: Johns Hopkins Press, 1940), 12–13.

Stimson's note: *Foreign Relations, U.S.: Japan, 1931–1941,* 3:7–8. The note was sent to Ambassador Forbes at noon Jan. 7 Washington time, 2 A.M. Jan. 8, Tokyo time.

459 Assassination attempt: Murofushi, 233–35.

Assassin sentenced to death: according to "Brocade Banner," the sentence was not carried out; instead I Pong-chang supposedly recanted and became a loyal Japanese agent.

Kido on assassination: *Nikki,* 127–28.

Reactions of Ikki and Hirohito: Harada, 2:173, 184–88.

460 Saionji's comment: Harada, 2:189.

Japanese riot in Shanghai: A. M. Young, *Imperial Japan,* 133–34; Tanaka, interview.

GHOST HOUSE: this section based on "Brocade Banner," 40–44 and 16; Murofushi, 237–41; Harada, 2:304–5; Crowley, 174; and interviews with retired Navy commander.

461 Re Spider Tanaka: Hata, *Gun,* 49 says that priest Inoue Nisho was a direct protégé of old Tanaka. He adds that Inoue Nisho had had contact with the flight officers at the Misty Lagoon Air Station since Aug. or Sept. of 1930.

462 Inoue as intimate of Konoye and Higashikuni: see Inoue's entry in *Japan Biographical Encyclopedia and Who's Who* (Tokyo: Rengo Press, 1958), 384; see also Kido, *Nikki,* 844, 849, 861, 867, 869.

463 Itagaki's telegram to Tanaka: Tanaka, "Yoshiko."

Itagaki's report to Hirohito: Kido, *Nikki,* 128–29.

On receipt of Col. Itagaki's telegram . . .: this and following paragraph based on Tanaka, "Yoshiko" and "Shokai jihen," 181 ff.; Watanabe, 118 ff.

464 Tanaka and Shigeto and Mitsui representative: Ramifications of this incident finally led to murder of Mitsui industrialist Muto Sanji on March 9, 1934. I wish someone would unravel the complete story; some of the relevant references are Harada, 2:144, 153; O. D. Russell, 244; A. M. Young, *Imperial Japan,* 218–21.

Subsequent events in Shanghai: ibid., 136; Zumoto, 109–10.

22,000,000 yen: My source, a banker, states that the request was made on the day the Diet recessed, i.e., Jan. 21. Harada, 2:179, reports Inukai's conversation with Dan in his entry for Jan. 18; O. D. Russell, 255, seems to put the scene at a later date, Mar. 2. Kido, *Nikki,* 130–36, provides a context which strongly suggests that the conversation took place on or about the date stated (Jan. 21). Note that Harada's entries are curiously muddled in this month and that there are differences of more than translation between the published Japanese text and the English-language version prepared for the U.S. Army Far East Command in 1947.

464–465 Inukai hoped to establish Manchuria as a nation: Harada, 2:231, also 200–201, 211–14; Kido, *Nikki,* 134.

Hirohito's willingness to accept compromise: Inukai Ken's testimony, IMTFE "Proceedings," 1540–45, states that Inukai was ready to ask Hirohito to issue such an order.

Baron Dan promised to consider proposal: Harada, 2:178–79, 181.
Makino's warning to Saionji: Kido, *Nikki,* 131, 133.

465–469 COMMENCEMENT OF HOSTILITIES: this section based on Zumoto, 107–38; Abend, *Life in China,* 186–93; Vaughn, 313–15; A. M. Young, *Imperial Japan,* 135–38; IMTFE "Proceedings," 3245 ff.

466 Mayor Wu notified Adm. Shiozawa: IMTFE "Proceedings," 3286.
Abend's exchange with Adm. Shiozawa: *Life in China,* 187, also his *Can China Survive?,* 155–57.

467 By 7 A.M. planes were strafing and bombing Chapei: John B. Powell testimony, IMTFE "Proceedings," 3245–52.

468 Launching of Chiang's warship in Tokyo: Kennedy, *Problem of Japan,* 165–67.
"mufti army": *ben-i-tai,* Harada, 2:206.
In Tokyo Hirohito was gravely worried: this passage based on Kido, *Nikki,* 139; Harada, 2:201. See also Minami's report to the Throne, Jan. 28, 1932, Kido, *Nikki,* 132, and Hirohito's refusal to delegate any authority even in appointments of home guard commanders, ibid., 145, 149.

469 "sit big as a mountain": ibid., 129.
Household Ministry's announcement of Prince Fushimi's appointment: *Asahi* (Tokyo ed.), Feb. 3, 1932; see also Harada, 2:197–99.
N. 3: ibid., 197, 304; Murofushi, 275.

15. Government by Assassination

470 BLESSING THE KILLERS: this section based on "Brocade Banner," 40–44, and Murofushi, 237–41.

471 Foreign minister offered Western diplomats opportunity to mediate: Harada, 2:200; Rappaport, 127–29; Crowley, 162–64.
Makino told Inukai: Kido, *Nikki,* 134.
Stimson would not co-operate: Rappaport, 127–29.

471–472 War minister briefed by finance minister: Harada 2:201–6, 208; also Kido, *Nikki,* 136.

472 Hirohito directed Inukai to reject . . . green again: My summation based on what happened and on Hirohito's audiences that morning as reported, ibid., 135.
On Saturday morning, February 6: this paragraph based on "Brocade Banner," 42, and Harada, 2:204.
Commander Fujii: The departed ringleader, according to Mori, 1:40, was a graduate of the University Lodging House in the palace.

473 Army landed brigade of 10,000: Zumoto, 142.
Hirohito gave his personal instructions: Kido, *Nikki,* 136–37.
"lecture in the Imperial Study . . .": Harada, 2:208.
Matsuoka expressed the opinion: Kido, *Nikki,* 136–37; the younger-older brother illustration of "the Darwinian principle" is added from a later speech of Matsuoka reported in the newspapers.
Saionji's comment: Harada, 2:208.
Hirohito's audience with Lt. Gen. Banzai: Kido, *Nikki,* 137.
Banzai the immediate superior of Friar Inoue: Byas, *Govt. by Assassination,* 57; A. M. Young, *Imperial Japan,* 190.

Banzai left Hirohito at two o'clock: Kido, *Nikki,* 137.
Two hours later Konuma received a messenger: Murofushi, 237.
Konuma described: ibid., 240.

474 Details of Inoue Junnosuke's assassination: ibid., 237–38.
Friar Inoue moved his base to student hostel: "Brocade Banner," 42.
Honma had been Inoue's colleague, ran elementary school: ibid.
In his new headquarters . . .: this paragraph, ibid., 43.
Kido lunched with Arima and Harada: Kido, *Nikki,* 137. Kido's mention of Inoue Junnosuke's murder is brief; Harada's is briefer. Yet Fleisher, 66–69, tells of being present at a dinner party with Harada on the night Inoue was shot. The diplomatic elite of Tokyo were also present. The news of the assassination spread swiftly by whisper as embassy couriers arrived one after another at the door with urgent messages for their chiefs of mission. In the view of all present Harada walked across the room to relay the news to Imperial Household Minister Baron Ikki Kitokuro. Ikki reacted not at all except by rocking back and forth on his heels.

475 Board of Fleet Admirals and Field Marshals met: Harada, 2:209.
"burst of power": ibid., 213.
Election campaign issue and slogans: O. D. Russell, 251–52.
N. 3: Harada 9:351–52, supplemented with details about Tokugawa and Ohtani reported elsewhere in these pages.

476 "Constitutional Protection Movement": *Goken undo.* Kido, *Nikki,* 169, supplemented by interviews with privileged source (a banker).
Honjo refused bribe offer: Honjo, 75; interview with Kajiura.
Feb. 19 meeting of Eleven Club: Kido, *Nikki,* 140.

476–478 Dinner meeting of Kido and Konoye with Inoue Saburo: ibid., 140–41 (exegesis courtesy of source with access to Uramatsu papers).
N. 4: Harada, 2:219.

478 As anticipated, the people elected Constitutionalists: Scalapino, 242; Crowley, 169.
Harada told Saionji of purposes of planned coup d'etat, and Saionji's comment: Harada, 2:219–21.
Saionji knew there would be no coup d'etat, had reached own understanding with Araki: my interpretation of Harada, 2:221–36 *passim.*

479 Inukai exchanging cables with Chiang: e.g., Harada, 2:230–31.
Big Brothers spread excited gossip: e.g., ibid., 2:225.
Konoye's visit with Saionji: ibid., 2:226.
Harada at Okitsu with Saionji's comment: ibid., 2:227.

480 Stimson's letter to Sen. Borah: Rappaport, 141.
Inukai proposed Baron Dan as envoy, and Koiso's interview with Dan: Harada, 2:230, supplemented by interviews with Tanaka. For other attempts to intimidate Dan see A. M. Young, *Imperial Japan,* 719.
Friar Inoue selected Hisanuma to assassinate Dan: Murofushi, 243.

481 Saionji decided time had come to declare himself: Harada, 2:231–33, supplemented by reference, through an intermediary, to notes left by a banker close to Saionji.
Saionji quoted: Harada, 2:232–33.
VICTORY IN SHANGHAI: this section based on Zumoto, 163–66 and Chart 3; Yanaga, *Since Perry,* 557–59; IMTFE "Proceedings," 28135–138.

482 Three privates' suicide charge: The *nikudan* or "human bullets" became a legend: see, e.g., Vaughn, 325, and A. M. Young, *Imperial Japan,* 141–42.

Major who felt responsible: Maj. Soga; Vaughn, 326.

482–483 Eastern Jewel's role with 11th Div.: Tanaka, "Yoshiko," also *Taiheiyo senso,* 2:138.

482 N. 6: Zumoto, 163, 167, and interviews with Fujisawa.

483 LEAGUE'S WELCOME: this section based on IMTFE "Proceedings," 1713; Rappaport, 180; *N.Y. Times,* Feb. 29–Mar. 7, 1932.

484 N. 7: Lindbergh had annoyed Japanese authorities; had been entertained by Kido's brother: A. M. Young, *Imperial Japan,* 265.

485 Dan's connections with U.S.: Yanaga, *Since Perry,* 177; Fleisher, 68; Byas, *Govt. by Assassination,* 30.

Meeting of Mitsui directors, their dividend rate, Mitsui refusal to participate in government bond issue: O. D. Russell, 253–55.

A Browning delivered to Hisanuma: "Brocade Banner," 42.

486 Dan's dinner party: Fleisher, 66–69.

Assassin Hisanuma went to Funabashi Beach: "Brocade Banner," 42.

Harada, before entraining: Harada, 2:234.

Dan at banquet for League's commission: O. D. Russell, 256–57.

Details of assassination of Baron Dan: Murofushi, 242–44.

Saionji and Harada on train: Harada, 2:234–35.

N. 8: Harada, 1: Plate 3. This photo is one of those reproduced in this volume.

487 Saionji's visitors: Harada, 2:235–36.

As a son is expected . . .: this paragraph based on Harada, 2:236–39.

March 8, smoke bombs returned: Harada, 9:346–47. See also Hata, *Gun,* 29; Ohtani, *Rakujitsu,* 34; IMTFE "Proceedings," 1416.

Saionji met Araki for first time: Harada, 2:236.

Police chief began to make arrests: ibid., 2:237.

Friar Inoue taken to jail, Okawa left at liberty: "Brocade Banner," 43.

487–488 Saionji insisted only that the killing cease . . .: this and following five paragraphs based on Harada 2:238–48 and Kido, *Nikki,* 151–52.

488 $8-million bond issue and $7-million loan (22 million and 20 million yen): newspaper reports. For the negotiations concerning the Mitsui payoff, Harada, 2:256–57, 327–28, and 9:138.

Okawa gave flight lieutenant $500: Harada, 2:306.

488–489 April 4 meeting of Eleven Club: Kido, *Nikki,* 153–54; Harada, 2:252–53.

489 Lord Lytton described: Rappaport, 179.

Saionji and Lord Lytton: Harada, 2:312–13.

Lytton commissioners to be in Mukden April 21: Honjo, 98; IMTFE "Proceedings," 1713.

The former Japanese ambassador to the Soviet Union: Tanaka Tokichi. See Kido, *Nikki,* 161–64; Harada, 2:284; Honjo, 90, 92, 93, 98, 102.

Col. Watari Hisao detached to be advance man: Kajiura, interview, and Honjo, 47, 98. "Advance man" is perhaps the wrong term. On Nov. 24, 1931, Secretary of State Stimson wired Geneva his backing for the draft resolution proposing a commission of inquiry. Watari then visited Honjo in Manchuria on Nov. 28 to advise him on steps to be taken. Thereafter Watari dogged the heels of Lord Lytton himself and did not return to Manchuria until he came with the Commission of Inquiry in April 1932. In short, "tour director" might be a better description of Watari's position.

Piggott's appreciation of Watari quoted: Piggott, 266.

489–490 Japanese preparations in Manchuria: details from Pernikoff, 120–23, and Vespa, 147–64.

491 Activities of Watari and Obata: Honjo, 98 (entry for Apr. 20, 1932) and 96 (Apr. 15), supplemented by interviews.

492 Suzuki's position papers: Kido, *Nikki,* 157–58; interviews.

Matsuoka's audience with Hirohito: Kido, *Nikki,* 158–59; Harada, 2:270.

Saionji's comments: Harada, 2:273.

Suzuki's second position paper: ibid., 274.

493–494 Arrangements with Honjo: this section based on Honjo, 101–5, supplemented by Harada, 2:307 and various interviews.

495–496 AT A COUNTRY INN: this reconstruction is based on Byas, *Govt. by Assassination,* 22; Kido, *Nikki,* 279; Hato, *Gun,* 54; and on a field trip of my own to Tsuchiura in 1966. See also Harada, 2:234, 349, and Kido, *Nikki,* 187–90 (esp. last line on 189). This Kido passage raises the question whether Prince Higashikuni may not have come to the inn with Tachibana.

Okawa turned over 2,000 yen: Harada, 2:306.

496 Wanted to act on day Charlie Chaplin was arriving: see also Murofushi, 253–54.

496–497 Kido's information from Makino: Kido, *Nikki,* 161–62.

Harada took a train to Shizuoka . . .: Harada, 2:283–84.

Kido went to his golf club . . .: Kido, *Nikki,* 162.

Fliers, cadets, naval lt. went to Yasukuni Shrine: "Brocade Banner," 44.

497–498 At Yasukuni Shrine: this and following three paragraphs based on Byas, *Govt. by Assassination,* 22–24, and 28, supplemented by Ponsonby-Fane, *Vicissitudes of Shinto,* 130–32, and by *Terry's Guide* (1920 ed.), 155–57. The figure 126,363 heroes is from Ponsonby-Fane, *Vicissitudes,* 125, and *Studies in Shinto,* 526.

499 Second group of plotters: "Brocade Banner," 45.

First group of assassins in prime minister's residence: The narrative begun here and completed mid-page 501 based on Murofushi, 247–50; Byas, *Govt. by Assassination,* 24–26; Kido, *Nikki,* 162; Harada, 2:286–87. Note Harada's report that the assassins had a plan of the residence and that their entry may have been facilitated by secret policemen letting them in.

N. 14: Akimoto, *Japanese Ways,* 154–68; *Terry's Guide* (1920 ed.), 186–87.

501 "Call them back": Murofushi, 251.

Inukai's wounds and treatment: ibid., 251–52; also Kido, *Nikki,* 162, and Fleisher, 73.

At 7 P.M.: this and following three paragraphs based on "Brocade Banner," 44–46; Byas, *Govt. by Assassination,* 26, 30; also *N.Y. Times,*

May 16–18, 1932.

502 Inukai's shot of blood: Kido, *Nikki,* 162–63.
Kido's telephone calls: ibid.

502–503 Harada's conversation with Saionji: Harada, 2:283–8, interpreted in the light of Saionji's request for more information and of Harada's call to Kido the next morning (Kido, *Nikki,* 163) asking for help in making Saionji come up to Tokyo.

503 Kido reported to Makino: Kido, *Nikki,* 162–63.
Hirohito dispatched his personal physician: ibid.

503–504 THREAT OF MUTINY: this section based on Hata, *Gun,* 59 n. 8; Umashima, 19–20; Byas, *Govt. by Assassination,* 27.

504 Chief aide-de-camp informed Hirohito: interviews.
Kido drove to prime minister's residence: Kido, *Nikki,* 162.
"I feel a little better": Murofushi, 252.
Kido at his residence, then at palace: Kido, *Nikki,* 162–63.
Facts of Inukai's death: "Brocade Banner," 45–46.

505-507 STERN REPRESSION: this section based on Kido, *Nikki,* 163–65, also Harada, 2:284–85.

507–509 THE NEW REGIME: this section is taken from Harada, 2:285–97; from Kido, *Nikki,* 164–70; and from Harada, 9:138–39.
Appointments needed only to be confirmed: Harada, 9:138, last 2 lines—an interpretation of Harada's elliptic notes.

508 Hirohito to Suzuki for Saionji: quoted, Kido, *Nikki,* 169. Harada, 2:288, gives the "honeyed" version mentioned below.
"They cannot be arrested": quoted, Kido, *Nikki,* 168.

509 So ended Japan's experiment . . .: Ogata, 155, goes so far as to say that one of the chief motives for killing Inukai was a radio address he made on May 1 pledging to preserve political-party rule at all costs.

510 Hitler assassinated fifty-one opponents: William Shirer, *The Rise and Fall of the Third Reich* (New York: Simon & Schuster, 1960; Fawcett Crest Book, 1962), 266; 206.
Equivalent of a Japanese college education: A strong statement, perhaps, because some Westerners did take degrees at Japanese universities. The fluency and cultural appreciation of a native Japanese graduate, however, were not to be matched.
Osaka editor told American correspondent: Vaughn, 345.
Orchids and apathy at Inukai's funeral: *N.Y. Times,* May 19, 1932.
Honjo quoted: Honjo, 106.

511 Okawa with procurator and telephone calls: Harada, 2:305–6; "Brocade Banner," 38.

512 Okawa arrested in Tsuchiura: ibid.
His secretary arrested: Harada, 2:312–13.
Baron Tokugawa interrogated: ibid., 310, 332–33.
Tachibana, escape, book quoted: Byas, *Govt. by Assassination,* 69; "Brocade Banner," 46.
He turned himself over to Kwantung Army military police: Harada, 2:332.
Toyama's secretary negotiated his arrest: ibid., 369.
Hidezo placed himself in police custody Nov. 5: "Brocade Banner,"

47; Grew, *Ten Years,* 69.

Police attack on Socialist and Communist leaders' meeting: U.S. Army Far East, Intelligence Rept. "Left Wing, Right Wing," 27 ff.; Harada, 2:296.

Prince Konoye at Blood Brotherhood accessory's funeral: A. M. Young, *Imperial Japan,* 189.

All but six were free men by end of 1935: "Brocade Banner," 54–56.

513 Prince Yamashina's "nervous breakdown": Koizumi, interview; see also Kido, *Nikki,* 271.

Commander Inoue retired to the reserve: interview with retired Navy commander.

Meiji Institute turned into museum: Kido, *Nikki,* 188.

Higashikuni scandal: Harada, 2:344, 349.

Scandal hushed up with difficulty: ibid., 8:305.

Makino and writers of anonymous letters: Ohtani, *Kempei-shi,* 85; also Murofushi, 261–63.

Okawa carried letters signed by Makino: "Brocade Banner," 38.

Inukai's letter to Toyama: Vaughn, 341–42.

514 Friar Inoue's subsequent career: "Brocade Banner," 54; Kido, 844, 849, 861, 867, 869; *Japan Biog. Encl.* (1958), 384.

Flight Lt. Mikami: "Brocade Banner," 54; *Asahi,* June 5, 1961; and Feb. 26, 1965.

Eastern Jewel's later career: Tanaka, "Yoshiko"; McAleavy, 213–14; Tsuji, *Underground Escape,* 233–34. See also Kido, *Nikki,* 238–39 (May 23 and 30, 1933): is Kido really talking about lessons he is taking in the art of dramatic declamation, or about Eastern Jewel (Yuang Kuei-fei), General Kawashima Yoshiyuki, and a sumo wrestler named Takasago?

16. Outcast Nation

516 New American ambassador: Grew, *Ten Years,* 13–14.

517 Grew shooting a tiger, other details: *N.Y. Times,* Jan. 24, Feb. 10, 1932.

Grew's arrival: Grew, *Ten Years,* 17–21.

Impressed by courtiers, esp. Makino: ibid., 38–39.

518 Grew's diary quoted: ibid., 76.

OPERATION CONCUBINE: This section is based on interviews with the same nobleman who gave me the details of Early Birth on page 271. Again I checked the story with Koizumi Shinzo and he did not deny it. A partial version of the intrigue may be found in Koyama, 73–87, and in Mosley, 104–7 and 116–18. My account adds the artificial insemination episode and definite dating. I have based my chronology on a plenitude of relevant but obscure references in the diaries, including Kido, *Nikki,* 185–91 and 123, and Harada, 8:305 and 2:344–55. I have taken as corroboration of the artificial insemination episode all references in Kido to *Taichu Tenno* or Inside-the-Womb Emperor. He introduces this term in his entry for May 11, 1931 (Kido, 76) and last uses it on Nov. 27, 1937 (ibid., 605). *Taichu Tenno* is an ancient euphemism of Court diarists for any particularly private and personal affairs of an emperor. That Kido revived it as a specific code term for the test-tube prince seems to me clear for a number of reasons. First, Inside-the-Womb Emperor was extremely apposite. Second, neither Harada nor Honjo used it in their diaries. Third, Kido wrote straightforwardly of "the Emperor's personal problems" when that was what he meant. Fourth, Kido used the term last in 1937 when the test-tube prince should have reached adoption age. Fifth, Kido did not use the term again in the years 1938–45 when the Emperor continued to have many personal problems. And sixth, at his first use of the term in Nov. 1931, Kido wrote explicitly about "the problem of Inside-the-Womb Emperor's succession to the Throne." That this person was not some ancient pretender being considered for reinstatement in the imperial pantheon I am assured by absence of any reference to him in the authoritative works of Richard Ponsonby-Fane (see Bibliography).

520 Hirohito "too staid": Koyama, 76.

521 Tanaka's falling out with Higashikuni: Kido, *Nikki,* 190.
"I cannot believe you": Koyama, 82.

522 "I know everything": ibid., 85.
Empress and the illegitimate heir: ibid., 89–90.
N. 3: Harada, 9:139.

522–523 Gen. Ma's pretended sell-out: A. M. Young, *Imperial Japan,* 146–48.

523 Ma embarrassment to Japanese: summary of Honjo, 98–106.
Undercover messages to Lytton: Vespa, 161–63.
Russian student caught and killed: Pernikoff, 127.
Lytton retired to Peking: Rappaport, 180; *N.Y. Times,* June 5. 1932.
Report of Ma's death: A. M. Young, *Imperial Japan,* 148–50.

524 Honjo's ideas on development of Manchuria: interviews with Fujisawa and Kajiura.
Relocation of 25,000 Chinese families: Pernikoff, 102.

525 Farmers used for bayonet practice, described: ibid., 241.

525–526 Experiences of Oleg Volgins: ibid., 32, 47, 261–67.

526 166 technocrats dispatched, July 1932: testimony of Tanaka Shizuka, IMTFE "Proceedings," 20459 ff.
Aviation company an extension of Air Forces: ibid., 28312 and 2708.
Industrial development of Manchuria: this and following 2 paragraphs based on Chamberlain, 27 ff., and on Scherer, *Manchukuo,* 50–56.

527 Amleto Vespa quoted: Pernikoff, 74.
"Japan is poor": Vespa, 89.
Concessions sold to guilds of vice experts: details in Vespa, 231–65.
Japanese had healthy fear of dope addiction: this and following 4 paragraphs based on Frederick Merrill, 3–9, 72–110.

528 Reporter paid twenty coppers: Edgar Snow, in *Saturday Evening Post* article, Feb. 24, 1934.
Brothels, other rackets: Pernikoff, 98; Vespa, 102, 255–59, 272–75.

529 Manchukoans paid and paid again: Pernikoff, 143; Vespa, 25.
The friends of Hirohito . . . realized a substantial part of the profits and plowed it back: my own summary of evidence from many sources.
Chamberlain from Court in Manchukuo: from Aug. 1932 to Apr. 1934; see Kido, *Nikki,* 186, 321, and Iriye Kanichi in *Who's Who in Japan,* 1933–34 ed.
"like a miniature garden": Ogawa Masao, interview.

529–530 Plan of the puppet state: IMTFE "Proceedings," 2903–3001. For a succinct diagram of it, see Kido, *Kankei bunsho*, 163.

530 REPORT TO THE LEAGUE: most of this section is taken from dispatches of Hallett Abend and Hugh Byas in *N.Y. Times* during Aug. and Sept. 1932; Rappaport, Ch. 7; and memorandum from George H. Blakeslee to Stanley Hornbeck, U.S. State Dept., 14, 1932, reproduced in Rappaport, Appendix.
N. 5; *N.Y. Times*, Jan. 24, 1932.

532 Honma's translation: Hata Ikuhiko, interview; "Honma Trial Proceedings" in National War Memorial, Canberra.
Known as "linguist with the red nose": Ito Kanejiro, 1:203.

532 "The effect of . . .": *Appeal by the Chinese Government: Report of the Commission of Inquiry* (League of Nations Publication VII, Political, 1932. Series VII, No. 12), 107.
"without declaration of war": ibid., 127.

533 Foreign Office spokesman quoted: Byas, in *N.Y. Times*, Sept. 6, 1932; see also FO quotes from report in *Times*, Sept. 9, and Uchida's good summary of report as quoted in Sept. 10 issue.
"no secret clauses," terms "less onerous": Byas in *N.Y. Times*, Sept. 3, 1932.
Secret protocol re Manchukuo: IMTFE "Proceedings," 2982 ff. In three other secret protocols (ibid., 29789 ff.) Manchukuo agreed to bear the cost of building communication and other facilities; to grant its Japanese advisors full extraterritorial rights; and to adjudicate all differences with Japan on the basis of the Japanese rather than the Chinese text of relevant treaties, contracts, and understandings.

533–534 Plenary session of Privy Council: IMTFE "Proceedings," 2972 ff.

534 Rumor re conquest of Jehol: A. M. Young, *Imperial Japan*, 161–63.

535–536 Suzuki's embassy to Chiang Kai-shek: Suzuki-Huang conversations, Harada, 3:72–73, and interviews with Tanaka; see also Harada, 2:403, and A. M. Young, *Imperial Japan*, 202–3.

536 For final months of Japan's participation in League of Nations debate, see *N.Y. Times*, Nov. 1932-Jan. 1933.
Harada quoted: 2:421.
Details of Shanhaikwan Incident: *N.Y. Times*, Jan. 3, 1933; also Harry Carr, *Riding the Tiger: An American Newspaperman in the Orient* (Boston: Houghton Mifflin, 1934), 123–29.

537 General Staff would abide by Hirohito's pledge to Chiang: Honjo, 160, and Harada, 2:427-28. See also Harada, 2:419, 422–23, 426, 430 for the circumstances.
Mafia-style meeting: Harada, 3:4–5. The meeting took place in the evening at Hiranuma's home. The Black Dragon Society was represented by Nakano Seigo, the extreme rightist and apologist for Hitler who would be forced by Tojo to commit suicide during World War II. At the end of the meeting Hiranuma said to Konoye: "As for our China policy, I believe we must strike to the south. I have listened to Ambassador Yoshida's views and I am in complete accord." For students of Yoshida Shigeru it could

be pointed out that Harada's pages give considerable detail on the unity of Lord Privy Seal Makino and his son-in-law, Yoshida, with the Navy and the Satsuma clan. In this connection see also Yoshida's bellicose attitude toward Chang Tso-lin mentioned earlier herein, page 360; and Kido, *Nikki,* 215–16.

538 On Feb. 10, 1933: Kido, ibid., 216, gives a slightly different account. My source for this paragraph has been described earlier, on pages 271 and 518. At this juncture he withdrew from active participation in Hirohito's circle. His access to inside information, however, continued for several years thereafter and will be reflected occasionally in the notes that follow.

Cabinet meeting on League question: summary based on Harada 2:428–33 and 3:3–4, supplemented by interviews. It may be that the conference occupying Araki, mentioned by Harada, was a liaison conference rather than a Cabinet meeting. It may also be that the Cabinet meeting of February 13, which passed on the Jehol operation, had also approved withdrawal from the League and that Araki on Feb. 17 was simply informing the General Staff. In any case a day or two later, Harada could write about the League question with finality: "Our attitude has been decided upon."

539 League Assembly meeting: based on *N.Y. Times,* Feb. 25, 1933, dispatch by Clarence Streit.

17. North or South?

The interpretation implicit in this chapter title—one basic to this book —is confirmed by unusually explicit diary entries by Kido and by Harada in late 1932 and early 1933. Kido, *Nikki,* 215–16, stated plainly on January 25, 1933: "The Army expounds a policy of hostility toward Russia while the Navy calls for commencement of war between Japan and America." Harada echoed this realization and went on (Harada, 3:3–5) to explain how Lord Privy Seal Makino, in alliance with the Navy, the Satsuma clan, Hiranuma and the underworld, hoped to "control the Army" and persuade it that "we must strike south." Kido, too, noted the Makino-Navy alliance, and shortly therefater (*Nikki,* 226–27), he observed realistically that certain Strike-North leaders "are thinking of government directly by the Emperor. Makino says that on this point we must be extremely careful."

545 PSHAW: this section based on Takeda, 65–66, and *N.Y. Times* for Feb. 22, Mar. 1, 3, and 9, 1933; see also Hata, *Gun,* 73.

546 THE STRIKE-NORTH LEADER: this section is based upon Araki's own many speeches reported in both the Japanese and Western press. I have added little new except in my interpretation: this being that Araki was a sympathetic character and that his warlike bluster was a political stratagem by which he hoped to keep enough influence to prevent Japan from fighting America.

547 Araki's hostility to Russia: Takeda, 45–46.

Araki's file: interviews with Tanaka and with Araki's grandson. My explanation of its contents is deduced from Araki's previous career and relationships with the Throne.

Araki had first realized: my inference from remark of retired Lt. Gen. Fujisawa.

548 RED SMEAR: based on Kido, *Nikki,* 206, 238–42, 244, 246–48.

Mossbacked old baron: Kikuchi Takeo, a nephew-in-law of Education Minister Hatoyama. His charge was taken up in the Diet by Miyazawa Yutaka. Yanaga, *Since Perry,* 507.

549 To stop Araki's witch hunt: A. M. Young, *Imperial Japan,* 247. Keio Prof. Muneda Muneyoshi's attack on Kyoto Prof. Takikawa Yukitoki: Yanaga, *Since Perry,* 506; "Brocade Banner," 57.

Unorthodox view of adultery: Johnson, 88; see also Takikawa's *Chuo Koron* articles excerpted in IPS Document No. 3014.

Professor charged with heresy: "Brocade Banner," 59–60.

Emperor a part of or transcending?: see note on page 591.

550 Slurs against Okawa and Makino: "Brocade Banner," 57.

Kyoto University backs down: ibid., 59–60.

551 Hirohito on Napoleon: Honjo, 241.

Hirohito sent Mazaki to front: ibid., 159, 242.

Higashikuni accused Mazaki: Matsumoto Seicho's interview with Higashikuni, *Bungei Shunju,* Jan. 1968, 160 ff.; Harada, 3:63–64.

Mazaki trying to subvert Higashikuni's servants: Harada, 3:84, 72.

Hirohito-Chichibu argument: This episode is reported (Honjo, 163) without date; my most knowledgeable of aristocratic contacts said, "May, Showa eight." I have fixed the date at May 21 because of Kido's entry the next day (*Nikki,* 238). An earlier entry, March 8 (ibid., 224), would indicate that the scene might have occurred in Feb. 1933.

"I will reserve my absolute power . . .": Honjo, 163.

Kido and Konoye to see Chichibu: *Nikki,* 163.

552 Araki expanded Red smear: ibid., 238, 266.

Education Minister Hatoyama orders university: "Brocade Banner," 60.

Leading strategists met: Harada, 3:88.

ENEMY NUMBER ONE: this section based on Ohtani, *Rakujitsu,* 127–29, also his *Kempei-shi,* 226–28, supplemented by interviews with Fujisawa; Harada, 3:88.

553 This juncture reached June 2: Harada, 3:91.

554 Kido golfs with Saionji Kinkazu: *Nikki,* 239, 247, supplemented by interview with Matsumoto.

Kido and political left: ibid.; Johnson, 17 n.; *Nikki,* 249–50 (also 240–48).

555 Kido compiled roster of aristocrats: *Nikki,* 259–63, 287.

Kido versus Tokugawa Iesato: ibid., 270, 291, 300–301.

Higashi-Fushimi demoted: interview with member of Ohtani family; see also Kido, *Nikki,* 266.

Palace retainers pensioned: ibid., 249, 275.

GO-STOP INCIDENT: *Mainichi* (Osaka ed.), July 29, 1933; Yanaga, *Since Perry,* 509; Harada, 3:190.

556–560 PRAYER MEETING PLOT: this section based on Murofushi, 272–77; "Brocade Banner," 39–52; Byas, *Govt. by Assassination,* 213–25; Harada, 2:26 (n.), 3:100–102, 139–40, 148–50, 179, 4:155, 9:168; Kido, *Nikki,* 265–66, 269, 436, 470. See also 337 and Kido, *Kankei bunsho,* 404–5.

559 Fujita an undercover agent: Johnson, 109; Harada, 3:102, 149–59, 8:386. For Fujita's part in Sorge spy case later, see page 559.
Proroguing trial of Blood Brotherhood: A. M. Young, *Imperial Japan,* 191; Byas, *Govt.,* 50; *Asahi,* Mar. 28, 1934.

560 Hirohito thinking of abdication: Kido, *Nikki,* 246. That same day Kido, Harada, and two other young bureaucrats of the Eleven Club lunched with Prince Higashikuni at the Tokyo Club. They discussed with him a snide suggestion which had recently been made to reporters by Gen. Tanaka Kunishige, one of Gen. Araki's partisans. His Excellency Higashikuni, said Tanaka, should consider giving up his rank as a prince so that he would be eligible to run for prime minister. The prince told Kido: "I do not know Gen. Tanaka personally. However, I think no one would pay any attention to me if I descended to commoner status." Said Kido, "I am greatly relieved."
Settlement of Red smear: Kido, *Nikki,* 246–47; 249–54.

561 Reposting of Strike-North officers: my analysis of the shuffle based on Hata's personnel records and on replies to inquiries during interviews with Fujisawa and Kajiura.
Silent Muto asked for mercy toward Manchukuoans: Vespa, 109.
Muto's poem: *Mainichi* (Osaka ed.), July 27, 1933; my own translation.

561–562 Barony for Muto: Honjo, 244; also Harada, 3:108, and Kido, *Nikki,* 247, 255.

562 Hishikari and the press: *Mainichi* (Osaka ed.), July 28, 1933.

562–566 THE KASPÉ KIDNAPPING: this section based on Petya Balakchine, *Finale vi Kitaya: vosnik-novenive, razvitiye y ischez noveniye beloi emigrantzii na Dalnyem Vostokye* [Finale in China: formation, development, and disintegration of the White Russian immigration in the Far East] (Munich, Georg Butow, 1959): 110–122, 210 ff.; Pernikoff, 187–216; Vespa, 205–30. Balakchine is the most detailed; it is based on a manuscript by a certain Martinoff who is said by Vespa to have been one of the main organizers of the kidnapping.

566 Midwives and doctors agreed: Koyama, 90–91.
Hirohito and Nagako on beach: Honjo, 244–45.
Eleven Club party: Kido, *Nikki,* 249.
Prince Fushimi wanted change in regulations: ibid.; Honjo, 163–66; also Agawa, 119–20.

566–567 Army staged air raid drills: Kido, *Nikki,* 250; Honjo, 245–46; Koizumi, interview.

567 Hirohito on board the *Hiei:* Honjo, 246–47.
Croquet game: ibid.
Meeting with Cabinet ministers, Aug. 30: ibid., 247.
568 Princes unpopular at clubs: Kido, *Nikki,* 254.
Hirohito gives Honjo lesson on yacht: Harada, 3:132–33.
Change in naval regulations should be kept secret: Honjo, 163.
Hirohito on Dutch navy: ibid., 249.

569 "We will expand": Harada, 3:158.
"There is no middle way": ibid.
Big Brothers at Chinese feast: ibid., 3:164.

Oct. 20 Cabinet meeting: Harada, 3:158, 168–69.

570 Defendants coached by police minions: see, e.g., Harada, 3:113.
Army court-martial: A. M. Young, *Imperial Japan*, 191; Byas, *Govt. by Assassination*, 47.
Navy court-martial: ibid., 44–46; Young, 191; Harada, 3:180.
Civilian trial: Byas, *Govt. by Assassination*, 66, 70–71.
Blood Brotherhood trial: ibid., 60; A. M. Young, *Imperial Japan*, 198.

571 Support expressed for Native-Land-Lovers: "Brocade Banner," 47;
A. M. Young, *Imperial Japan*, 173.
Army cadets released: "Brocade Banner," 55; Harada, 3:147.
Sentences of others: A. M. Young, *Imperial Japan*, 195–97.
Araki hoped for outcry against Hirohito: see Harada, 3:188, 192, 201.
Hirohito after previous accouchement: Price, 27–28.

572 "It's a boy": Harada, 3:208.
"Problem has been solved": Kido, *Nikki*, 294.
Political parties' get-together: Harada, 3:206–7, supplemented by
Matsumoto, interview.
"it is time for Araki to quit": Harada, 3:210.
Saionji exhausted: ibid., 211.
Maj. Gen. Nagata renewed position-paper work: Tanaka, interview;
also Crowley, 207–8, 263.
On Jan. 7 Kido and others met at Konoye's villa: Harada, 3:211, sup-
plemented by source with access to Uramatsu papers. Kido, oddly, makes
no mention of this gathering in his diary.
Hirohito agreed to proclaim an amnesty: Harada, 3:211.

573 Saito-Hirohito exchange: ibid., 216–17.
Araki sequestered himself in the hospital: Ohtani, *Rakujitsu*, 89–93;
Harada, 3:217–19. Prime Minister Saito expressed a wish to visit Araki
and make him change his mind, but Kido warned him on the phone that
if he did that he might not be able to see the Emperor again for fear of
giving Hirohito Araki's pneumonia.
ZERO: basic references for this section, Kido, *Nikki*, 300, 308 and
Harada, 3:239, 241.

574 Herbert Smith's role: retired Navy commander, interview, also
Potter, *Yamamoto*, 23. I am indebted to John R. Cuneo for full identifica-
tion of Smith as the designer of the Sopwith Camel.
LET THEM EAT CAKE: basic source for this section is Honjo, 184–85.
Disastrous year agriculturally: Inoki Masamichi, interview, citing article
by Cho Yukio, *Asahi Journal*, Apr. 25, 1965.
Sent chamberlains to inspect: Honjo, 243.
Apply pressure to Mitsui cartel: O. D. Russell, 298, supplemented by
interviews with Koizumi, Inoki.

18. Organ or God?

576 Celebration in honor of Crown Prince Akihito: Grew, *Ten Years*,
113–14.

577 Japanese "astonishingly capable of fooling themselves": ibid., 81.
Grew's conclusion: ibid., 128.
Hayashi prohibited slogan "Crisis of 1936": Crowley, 207.

Imperial Way (*Koda-ha*) and Control (*Tosei-ha*): see Ohtani, *Raku-jitsu,* 71–76.

578 The Kayas' embassy: *Mainichi* (Osaka ed.), March 9, 1934; July 1, 1934; Sept. 18, 1934.

A NOT-SO-MEDIEVAL SCANDAL: except as cited, this section based on Harada, 3:224, 228, 232, 236–37, 241, 244, 255, 269, 271, 284, 286–87, 308, 314.

Northern and southern dynasties both of same blood: Honjo, 204.

579 Saionji's visit to the palace: Honjo, 234; see also Harada, 8:303–4.

Kido and Harada agreed on Okada as next prime minister: Kido, *Nikki,* 329–30.

Appointment of Okada Cabinet: ibid., 343–45. For the slow, cynical preparations, see Harada, 8:321–48.

580 Friend to Saionji, "You have covered a boil . . .": Omura Bunji, 408.

Hirohito required new prime minister to reratify decision to expand south: Harada, 4:16; see also ibid., 453.

580–581 Hirohito's difficulties with Navy: my summary interpretation drawn largely from Harada, 4:16–28 and Honjo, 190–95. Yamamoto's appointment in November 1933, from interview with retired Navy commander. The appointment was not made official until June 1934 but the earlier date fits well with the Honjo, Kido, and Harada diaries—see especially Honjo, 171, and Harada, 3:191. In the latter is also admitted the situation in regard to shipbuilding.

581 Hirohito, "If the treaty must be abrogated . . .": Harada, 4:22.

Hirohito personally dictated instructions for Yamamoto: Kido, *Nikki,* 354; Harada, 4:50–51.

Hirohito approved instructions as drafted: Harada, 4:67–69; Honjo, 194–95.

Yamamoto's American press conference and his later one in England: Agawa, 23–25; Potter, *Yamamoto,* 23–25.

582 Hirohito authorized abrogration of treaty "at earliest moment": Honjo, 197–98.

"I am smaller than you": Potter, *Yamamoto,* 25.

582–583 Last month of London conference: Harada, 4:144–51.

Army Purification Movement or *Seigun-ha*: Crowley, 254–55; Yanaga, *Since Perry,* 510. Although he stood behind the *Seigun-ha* Terauchi delegated leadership to Hashimoto Kingoro. Later (interview, Fujisawa) he was obliged to turn on his own creature and purge the Purification Movement along with other Army factions.

583–584 Terauchi's mission to Taiwan: interview, Tanaka. On review of my notes I find that my text is in error on last line of page 583 and first on 584. It should read: ". . . from October 1 to October 18, 1934, Imperial Army elder Field Marshal Prince Nashimoto visited Terauchi's command . . ." Nashimoto ranked second in seniority to Chief of Staff Prince Kanin in the Army and in the imperial family as well.

584 Manchukuo Structure Plan: Harada, 4:72–79; Nagata's position, ibid., 74–75. See also ibid., 97, 103, 145.

Booklet on war fathering creation: IPS Documents Nos. 717 and 3089,

Kokubo no hongi to sono kyoka no teisho; Crowley, 208; Harada, 4:91.

585 War Minister Hayashi assured businessmen: Harada, 4:119.
Hirohito bivouacked with Asaka: Honjo, 197.
Maneuvers: Ito Kanejiro, 1:182, 356–57, supplemented by Fujisawa, interview. Young officers at war minister's residence: Harada, 4:132.

585–586 Suicide at Middle School: Honjo, 258–59.

586–587 THE MILITARY ACADEMY PLOT (or "November Plot"): this section based on Ohtani, *Rakujitsu,* 114–17; IPS Document No. 1416; Harada, 4:141–42, 155; see also Yanaga, *Since Perry,* 512.

586 N. 1: Honjo, 259.

588 Resolution of Inner Cabinet, "For the time being . . .": Japanese Foreign Ministry Archives, *Teikoku no tai-shi seisaku kankei no ken* ("Matters Relating to Imperial Policy Against China"), v. 3 of 1933–1937 series, appendix; cited in Crowley, 201.
Power play could be expected: Harada, 4:153.
"names of the imperial family appear constantly": ibid., 155.
Budget battle: ibid., 107–95, *passim.*

588–589 National Principle Group (*Kokutai genri-ha*) and their catechism: Crowley, 263–65.
Kido's assessment of feelings and factions in Army: *Nikki,* 389–90.
Secret police briefs reported group "resolved to take political power": Harada, 201–2.
Attack on Ikki planned: Harada, 4:202–3.
Baron Kikuchi began defamation of Ikki: Yanaga, *Since Perry,* 507.
Minobe's two articles: Harada, 2:404, 3:218; Kido, *Nikki,* 202; Crowley, 209. The first was a five-part series in *Asahi,* Jan. 18–22, 1934, *Seito seiji no shorai* ("The Future of Political Parties"); the second, *Rikugun-sho hatten no kokubo-ron o yumu* (Perusing the Discussion of National Defense as Developed by the War Ministry), *Chuo Koron,* Nov. 1934.

590–591 Emperor did not transcend the state but was merely an organ of state: for a good summary of Japanese legal thoughts on the status of the Emperor, see Joseph Pittau, *The Meiji Political System* (Studies in Japanese Culture, Tokyo: Sophia University, 1963).

591 Prof. Minobe's speech: text in appendix, Harada, 4:455; translation of most of it is included in Tsunoda, 746–53.

591–592 Maj. Gen. Eto charged Minobe with lèse majesté: "Brocade Banner," 59–61.

592 On saluting Pu-Yi: Honjo, 201–2.

593 "Of course my ranking is different . . .": Honjo, 203.
Konoye decided to withdraw resolution: Harada, 4:213.
Omoto-kyo threat: Kido, *Nikki,* 385–87; 416–17; Harada, 4:160–62, 288.
"the Diet should be burned to the ground": Harada, 4:220.
Ikki beaten by thugs hired by relative of Kikuchi: Ohtani, *Kempei-shi,* 566; "Brocade Banner," 61.

593–594 Kido tried to persuade Minobe to resign: Harada, 4:216–17, 226, 228.
Commanders at palace for individual briefings from Hirohito: Honjo,

205–7; Harada, 4:227; Yanaga, *Since Perry*, 508.

Mazaki circulated memorandum, "The organ theory is incompatible . . .": ibid.

Hirohito, "Does the Army hope . . .": Honjo, 205–7.

594–595 "In his statement Mazaki calls me the *shutai* . . .": ibid. N. 3: Honjo, 261–62.

595 Hirohito asked Terauchi to help discipline the Army and end the organ-theory attack: Harada, 4:227–28, 231.

Apr. 18, Hirohito asked Fushimi for Navy policy: Honjo, 212–13.

Veterans' clubs petition explaining evils of organ theory: Harada, 4:241.

"Will it be all right . . .": Honjo, 207.

595–596 Hirohito had been called a liar, withdrew for six days; exchange with Honjo, "The Army is acting against my will . . .": Honjo, 207–8.

596–597 Hirohito itemized his objections to veterans' arguments: ibid.

597 Honjo maintained anti-organ agitation a philosophical debate, strengthening people's resistance to propaganda: ibid., 210–11.

Hirohito shocked by Navy Minister Osumi's show of disaffection: ibid.; Harada, 4:256–59, 268. (Harada, 4:246–47, already knew that "the Army and Navy have joined forces to start planning for operations in the South Seas, using Taiwan as their center." Note that his informants were Shigemitsu Mamoru, the later war's-end foreign minister, and Capt. Takagi Sokichi, the later ranking Navy member of the Peace Faction.)

597–598 Hirohito, "Men in the Navy . . . ," and Rear Adm. Idemitsu's reply: Honjo, 211–12, 262.

598–601 Through the Great Wall: except as cited, this section based on Crowley, 214–24; Honjo, 213–17; Harada, 4:256–66, *passim*; interview, Kajiura Ginjiro.

599 May 1, Prince Kaya off on tour of north China: *Mainichi* (Osaka ed.), June 28, 1935.

Staff officers at Tientsin accused Chinese magazine of lèse majesté: Harada, 4:286 n.

600 Terms of Ho-Umezu Pact: for effects of pact on Chinese see Chiang Mon-lin, *Tides from the West* (Taipei: China Publication Foundation, 1957), 204–5.

19. Purges of 1935

602 Ishiwara's hurried memo: see also Harada, 4:279–80.

603 "A Written Opinion on Purging the Army": *Shukugun ni kansuru ikensho*, by Capt. Muranaka Koji and Paymaster First Class Isobe Asakazu, IPS Document No. 3166 (National Archives Microfilm, WT79–WT80). For publication date see Harada, 4:302 (n.).

On the eve of the purge: Kajiura and Tanaka, interviews.

Hayashi and Prince Kanin visited Kwantung Army: Crowley, 260.

604–607 THE FIRING OF MAZAKI: entire section, including quotations, follows Ohtani, *Rakujitsu*, 73–102 (confirmed by Harada, 4:293–94, and Kido, *Nikki*, 418). Ohtani was in charge of the secret police squad detailed to monitor the affair, and he or one of his men hovered in earshot

of the conversations. The report he submitted afterward to his superior, the commandant of the secret police, was so detailed that it won him immediate promotion to the post of secret police chief for the Chiba area. Such reports were filed by the secret police commandant and made available to the palace on a need-to-know basis either through the civilian Office of the Lord Privy Seal or the military Office of Aides-de Camp, whichever was appropriate. Hirohito ordinarily appointed a new secret police commandant every eighteen months. The incumbent at this time was Lt. Gen. Tashiro Kanichiro.
N. 1: Kido, *Nikki,* 416–17.

607–609 RIPPLES AND THEIR CONTROL: this section, including quotations, based on Honjo, 220–222; also Harada, 4:295.

609 Nagata's position paper on using the Army for political purposes: a memorandum written in Aug. 1935 a few days before his death. In it Nagata wrote: "I believe it unjust to use the power of the Army for the purposes of the Restoration. . . . [It should be used] only at the direct order of the Emperor and only in its entirety." Shido Yasusuke, *Tetsuzan Nagata Chujo* [Lt. Gen. Nagata Tetsuzan] (Tokyo, 1938), 285–87, cited in Ogata, 200.

609–612 ARAKI'S REVELATIONS: except as cited, this section follows Ohtani, *Rakujitsu,* 102–13.
Yasuda and Aizawa old subordinates of Higashikuni: in 29th Regt., 2d Div., at Sendai; Matsumoto Seicho, interview with Higashikuni, *Bungei Shunju,* Jan. 1968, 161 ff.

612 On Matsui's resignation and missionary activities in China: see IMTFE "Proceedings," 2311 ff., and ibid., *passim,* Matsui's own testimony as indexed by Dull and Umemura.
Eleven Club meeting, July 26: Harada, 4:299; "Eleven Club" used loosely here; only the nucleus of Kido, Harada, and Konoye present.
Mazaki at Summer Palace: Honjo, 222–23.

613–616 NAGATA'S MURDER: except as cited, this section based on Murofushi, 280–86; Ohtani, *Rakujitsu,* 126–31; Harada, 6:291, 303, and 4:309; Byas, *Govt. by Assassination,* 95–118.

613 Aizawa went to see Prince Asaka: Harada, 4:355–56.

613–614 Prince Asaka arranged to see Hirohito: Kido, *Nikki,* 421.

614 Vice war minister begged Nagata to go abroad: Honjo, 226.

615 Kido expressed no regrets for Nagata's assassination: *Nikki,* 423–24.

615–616 Emperor's reaction to the murder: Honjo, 224.

616 Saionji's comment on Nagata's murder: Harada, 4:311.
Hayashi criticized: Ohtani, *Rakujitsu,* 129–30.
Nagata's funeral: Ito Kanejiro, 1:140–41.

617 Tojo given post of commandant of Kwantung Army's secret police: Higashikuni, interview with Matsumoto Seicho (*Bungei Shunju,* Jan. 1968, 160 ff.) took credit himself for Tojo's appointment. At the same time Higashikuni acknowledged that Tojo's patron was Gen. Abe Nobuyuki. Abe was a friend and protégé of Prince Nashimoto, his senior by one year at military academy. It would seem, therefore, that another source

(privileged) is correct in identifying Prince Nashimoto consistently as Tojo's main patron.

Hirohito took instant dislike to new war minister: see, e.g., Harada, 4:350.

Hirohito's instructions, "The Army must be the Emperor's Army . . .": ibid., 322–23.

Sept. 18, Minobe resigned from House of Peers: Yanaga, *Since Perry,* 507–8.

618 Kido recorded as fact that Higashikuni was paying Yasuda: Kido, *Nikki,* 266.

Okamura Yasuji's opinion re Chiang Kai-shek: Crowley, 231.

Finance Minister Takahashi's message to Saionji: Harada, 4:342–43.

618–619 Toyama's meeting an excuse for crackdown on Black Dragon Society: Byas, *Govt. by Assassination,* 198, 200.

619 Oct. 25, Lt. Gen. Nishio Toshizo's cable re propaganda for China war: IMTFE "Proceedings," 2277 ff.

Attempt to kill Minobe: Murofushi, 286–89; "Brocade Banner," 59–64.

619–620 Higashikuni told Harada of agitation for Prince Kanin's resignation: Harada, 4:352.

620 Saionji, "Ikki and Makino are still capable . . .": Kido, *Nikki,* 444–45.

20. February Mutiny

For this chapter, in addition to sources cited or listed in the bibliography, I have drawn for background on: Fukumoto Kameji, *Hiroku ni-ni-roku jiken shinso-shi* [True Story of the Secret Record of the February 26 Incident] (Tokyo: Ozei Shinbun-sha, 1958); Hashimoto Tetsuma, *Tenno to hanran shoko* [The Emperor and the Officers of the Rebellion] (Tokyo: Nihon Shuho-sha, 1954); Kono Tsukasa, ed., *Ni-ni-roku jiken* [The February 26 Incident] (Tokyo: Nihon Shuho-sha, 1957); Matsumura Hidetoshi, "Hochoku meirei to Ishiwara Kanji no yudan" [Obedience to Orders Decreed by the Emperor and the Brave Decision of Ishiwara Kanji] in *Tenno to hanran gun* (Tokyo: Nihon Shuho, March, 1957); Ohtani Keijiro, "Kempei no me de mita hanran shoko" [The Rebel Officers as Seen Through the Eyes of the Secret Police] in *Tenno to hanran gun*; Ohtani Keijiro, "Mazaki taisho muzai no giwaku" [Doubt as to the Innocence of General Mazaki] in *Tenno hanrun gun*; and *Ni-ni-roku jiken sanjunen kinengo* [February 26 Incident Thirtieth Anniversary Memorial Volume] (Tokyo: Shinseiryoku-sha, 1965).

In addition to the sources cited, I found Tateno's *Hanran* most useful for atmosphere. I am also indebted to his "Ni-ni-roku no nazo" and *Showa gunbatsu* for provocative ideas about the incitement and exploitation of the incident. Another background account I found helpful was Maeda Harumi, *Showa hanran-shi* [History of Rebellion in the Reign of Hirohito] (Tokyo: Nihon-sho Hosha, 1964). There is, of course, a voluminous Japanese literature on the rebellion, and it is impossible to do any research in Japan without being told many stories taken from this literature. The best guide that I know of to all *Ni-ni-roku* sources is Hata Ikuhiko, whose *Gun fuashizumu,* 131–202, includes a complete set of bibliographical notes.

622 Relations of rebel officers with Chichibu, Higashikuni, Asaka, Yamashita, and Okamura: Ohtani, *Kempei-shi,* 195–98, also his *Rakujitsu,* 174–76; "Brocade Banner," 78. For Chichibu's involvement, see especially Kono Tsukasa, "Ni-ni-roku jiken no nazo" and also his *Ni-ni-roku jiken, passim.* As a close kinsman of Kono Hisashi, one of the rebels, Kono Tsukasa was long the head of the *Ni-ni-roku izoku-kai* or February Mutiny Bereaved Families Association.

623 "The gods, the Emperor, and the good earth . . .": Hata, *Gun,* 154. Yamashita failed to keep appointment: Ohtani, *Rakujitsu,* 174–76.
Dec. 20 protest meeting: Harada, 4:403; Storry, *Double Patriots,* 180–81. Mutiny plan in Kido's diary: *Nikki,* 452–53.
Defection of soldiers in Manchuria: Harada, 4:413; Kido, *Nikki,* 459–60; Tanaka, interview.

624 THE TALKING GODDESS: This section, not previously reported either in Western or Japanese secondary sources, is taken from Kido's memo on the police findings, Ohara-Shimazu case (Kido, *Nikki,* 527–29), and on Kido's diary entries (ibid., 456, 493–97, 500–501, 504–14, 516, 518, 526, 591). See also Harada, 5:154–55, 167.

625 N. 2: Koyama, 51–52; see also Murofushi, 195.

626 Higashikuni's stand-by sword arms: Kido, *Nikki,* 470–71; Harada, 4:413, 420; also "Brocade Banner," 71–72.

626–627 Aizawa trial: Yanaga. *Since Perry,* 513: Byas, *Govt. by Assassination,* 99–118; Kido, *Nikki,* 452–53; Takahashi, 32; "Brocade Banner," 71–73; Harada, 4:411.
N. 4: Kido, *Nikki,* 470–71.

627 Kido's research into Army feeling: *Nikki,* 459–60.

628 1936 elections: Scalapino, 381–82.

628–629 Preliminaries of mutiny up to Feb. 22: Takahashi, 32–37; Ohtani, *Kempei-shi,* 89–91.

629 P-day minus four: Takahashi, 37.
P-day minus three: ibid., 34, 40; "Brocade Banner," 74.
Feb. 24, P-day minus two: ibid., 73–74, 134; Takahashi, 35–36; Harada, 5:300. After the war Usawa became the defense lawyer for Matsui Iwane and Shiratori Toshio at the International Military Tribunal; "Brocade Banner," 146.
Saionji warned he was to be assassinated: The various accounts conflict as to when Saionji received this warning. The best and most aristocratic of my verbal sources states positively that Saionji removed himself from harm's way on the day before the rising. Kodama Yoshio, a rightwing jailbird with excellent underworld sources of information, also felt that Saionji had received adequate prior notice of the rising (Kodama, 54). A. M. Young, *Imperial Japan,* 277, understood that Saionji "warned by a telephone call . . . claimed the hospitality of the Chief of Police for the night." Byas, another Western newsman with usually reliable information, states only that Saionji "was hastily taken to a place of safety by the Governor of the prefecture where he lived, and if the rebels intended to kill him, they were baffled"; *Govt.,* 121. "Brocade Banner," compiled by U.S. Intelligence agents after the war from Japanese secret police files, implies that Saionji was not warned until some time between 6 and 7 A.M. on the morning of the killings (143). Latter-day Japanese investigators,

including Murofushi and Takahashi, also indicate that Saionji had only just enough time to escape. Harada, 5:36, 300, however, reveals that Saionji was warned by telegram on Feb. 25. His informant, Usawa Fusa-aki, had learned of the conspiracy the day before, Feb. 24 ("Brocade Banner," 143). "Brocade Banner" further states that Gen. Mazaki awakened Usawa shortly after 4 A.M. on Feb. 26 and put him on the 5:30 train to Okitsu. I interpret this to mean that Usawa arrived in Okitsu before 7 A.M. and that he came to make sure that Saionji had heeded the warnings sent a day earlier. Then, apparently, he found no one at Saionji's "Sit-and-Fish" Villa except a few servants such as the maid who answered the phone when Kido called at 6:40. Kido's behavior seems to support this conclusion. In *Kankei bunsho*, 4–5, he reveals that he knew on Feb. 2, 1936, that the 1st Div. intended to rise and kill the elder statesmen. He apparently waited until 6:40 A.M. on Feb. 26 to phone a warning to Saionji. He was then told that Saionji was peacefully sleeping and need not be disturbed. A year later (*Nikki*, 535) Kido learned by phone from Makino that news of the mutiny's definite commencement had reached Gen. Mazaki "not at 8 A.M. as previously stated but at about 3 A.M.—and this is corroborated by the chauffeur." In short, it would seem that by the date of this entry, Jan. 12, 1937, Kido and Makino were still trying to find out whom to blame for Saionji's escape.

N. 7: Harada, 5:300.

630 Saionji's escape: A. M. Young, *Imperial Japan*, 277–78, corroborated by interview with the son of a banker who was a close friend of Saionji.

Polishing the manifesto: "Brocade Banner," 74; Takahashi, 27–28.

Evening, Feb. 24–morning, Feb. 25: ibid., 34–35; Murofushi, 310–11.

Mazaki at Aizawa trial: *Asahi*, Feb. 26, 1936; A. M. Young, *Imperial Japan*, 276.

Resentment in 1st Div. barracks: Takahashi, 37–38.

BLOODSHED AT LAST: this section, except as cited, based on "Brocade Banner," 73–94; Takahashi, 46–60; Murofushi, 290–313; Byas, *Govt. by Assassination*, 119–22; Fleisher, 69–88; A. M. Young, *Imperial Japan*, 276–80.

633 Ishiwara's sortie from General Staff offices: Hata, *Gun*, 154–55. Saito's night before at the Grews: Grew, *Ten Years*, 157.

634 Suzuki's delicate wound: Agawa, 88.

636 Makino's rescue by his granddaughter: Grew, *Ten Years*, 157–58. N. 8: by count from Takahashi, 46–49.

637 Story which diaries expose as false: compare Kido, *Nikki*, 464–79; Harada, 5:3–22; and Honjo, 235–38, 266–67, 271–99, with the accounts of the February Mutiny preserved in Grew, *Ten Years*; Craigie; Byas, *Govt. by Assassination*; Fleisher; and A. M. Young, *Imperial Japan* (as cited). Honjo-Hirohito exchange, Feb. 25: Honjo, 234–35.

21. Suppression

638–639 Honjo, 5 to 8 A.M., Feb. 26: Honjo, 271–72. In Honjo's reply, on page 639, I have compressed thoughts which Honjo in his own version wrote down as if he wished he had voiced them.

639 Kido and Harada to 8 A.M.: Kido, *Nikki*, 464–66; Harada, 5:3–4.

Kido's phone call to Saionji: Kido's three-line description of this call was unaccountably left out of the translation—marked "in full"—of this entry which was prepared for presentation at the IMTFE.

Harada's two days in rebel territory (i.e., Feb. 26 and part of Feb. 27): Harada, 5:4.

"Shoot-at-sight" list: Ohtani, *Kempei-shi*, 191.

639–640 Kido at Inner Palace: *Nikki*, 464; description of accommodations there: Koizumi, interview.

640 Terms given Kawashima: "Brocade Banner," 75 ff.; Takahashi, 58–60.

Prince Fushimi's audience with Emperor: Kido, *Nikki*, 464. At 8 A.M.: Honjo, 272; see also Agawa, 94; Honjo, 273.

641 Kawashima at palace: ibid., 272; also Byas, *Govt. by Assassination*, 123.

Manifesto: Takahashi, 25–26. In this translation·I have tried to reproduce the flavor as well as the sense.

642 Hirohito's reply to Kawashima: Kido, *Nikki*, 464, gives the first two sentences of this reply and Honjo, 272, the last sentence.

642–646 FIRST DAY OF SIEGE: this section based on Honjo, 272–74; Kido, *Nikki*, 464–66; "Brocade Banner," 81–82, 86–88; Takahashi, 58–64, 69–72, 78–90; Hata, *Gun*, 152–55; interviews with Koizumi.

646–649 THE SECOND DAY: except as cited, this section based on Honjo, 274–76; Kido, *Nikki*, 466–67; Takahashi, 78–90 *passim*, also 93–99; "Brocade Banner," 87–88.

646 "to strangle me with a silken cord and . . .": for clarity I have doubled the Emperor's image, which was literally "to strangle my head with soft cotton"—*mawata ni te Chin ga kobe o shimuru ni hitoshiki yukinari*; Honjo, 276.

647 Hirohito willing to go down to barricades himself: Honjo, 235 and 276, gives two slightly different versions of this scene.

Peers' Club and stopping of Harada: Ohtani, *Kempei-shi*, 191–92.

Chichibu and Imperial Family Council: ibid., 195–98, supplemented by interviews with Koizumi Shinzo; Kido, *Nikki*, 466; and Higashikuni in Matsumoto interview, *Bungei Shunju*, January 1968, 160 ff.

N. 3: Ideograph for *Chin*: I am indebted for this charming etymology to Kitagawa Hiroshi.

648 Chichibu and Nonaka suicide: "Brocade Banner," 146.

Hirohito's evaluation of his kinsmen: Kido, *Nikki*, 468.

N. 4: Imperial House Law: *The Japan Year Book*, 1944–45, 809 ff.

649 THE THIRD DAY: except as cited, this section based on Honjo, 276–79; Kido, *Nikki*, 466–67; Takahashi, 99–104.

650 Honjo aged years that day: Ito Kanejiro, 2:68.

Ishiwara, "We shall attack": see his entry in *Nihon Jinbutsu-shi Taikei* [Japan Biographical Outline] (Tokyo: Asakura Shobo, 1960), vol. 7.

Rebel response to pleas: see *Bungei Shunju*, January 1966, 263.

651 Hirohito accused the Army of insubordination: In *Honjo Nikki* as published this scene is reported as of this hour and date (4:30 P.M., Feb. 28) in two different places (236, 278); in relating the conversation here,

I have put the two accounts together.

653 Ishiwara confronted Araki: Agawa, 6.
HIROHITO'S SETTLEMENT: except as cited, this section based on Honjo,
279–300; Kido, *Nikki,* 468–78; Harada, 5:6–22; Takahashi, 104–118.
Nonaka's suicide: "Brocade Banner," 146.

654 Hirohito in uniform: Honjo, 266–67, 283.

656 Addition of seven divisions: Hata, "Notebooks"; Tanaka, interview.

657 Kanin's explanation of purges: my own translation of Harada,
5:10.
2,000 noncommissioned officers to Army reserve: Ohtani, *Kempei-shi,*
212; also Crowley, 274.

658 Mazaki's hunger strike: Kido, *Nikki,* 535.
Araki's assessment of Mazaki's pardon: Takahashi, 203.

659 Yamashita's reassuring note from Hirohito: Potter, *Soldier Must
Hang,* 22; supplemented by Hata's "Notebooks," corroborated by interview
with Fujisawa, who served under Yamashita in the Philippines.
Rebels' one-hour trials: Ohtani, *Kempei-shi,* 214–17.
Last words of executed rebels: Takahashi, 192–200; also "Brocade
Banner," 90.

22. Neutralizing Russia

663–664 DROWNING A RADIO: this section based on Klausen's own
account in interrogations, as cited in Deakin and Storry, 207.

664 Significance of Sorge ring: see Johnson, ch. 7, esp. 153–55.
Sorge a middle-class intellectual, Russian mother, served in World War
I: Johnson, 69.
Acknowledged Hero of Soviet Union in 1964: Deakin and Storry, 350.

665 Sorge joined party in 1920, became agent for Comintern: Johnson,
71–72.
Reassigned to Red Army Intelligence, sent to Shanghai: ibid., 73–74.
Sorge met future Japanese agents in Shanghai: Deakin and Storry, 75.
Communist paymaster in Shanghai arrested, Sorge closely watched:
ibid, 91–92.
Sorge's mission in Japan, his preparations in Germany: ibid., 95–103.
Established close relations with German Embassy in Tokyo: Johnson,
140–42.
American Japanese joined Sorge, arranged meetings with Japanese lib-
erals and leftists: Johnson, 94–95, 105.

666 Sorge obtained Klausen for radio work; he built equipment, estab-
lished contact with Russian station in Siberia in Apr. 1936: Deakin and
Storry, 156 ff.; Johnson, 101–2.
Delegation to Yosemite: Johnson, 111–13.

667 Saionji Kinkazu consulted on Communist problems: My interpretation of young Saionji's role here and later was first suggested to me by
Matsumoto Shigeharu. I asked him how it was that Saionji had escaped
severe punishment for his involvement with Sorge's Soviet spy ring and he
replied that since Konoye always encouraged his advisors to keep in touch
with all shades of political opinion, it would have been unfair to punish
Saionji for doing what was expected of him. Later I asked Koizumi Shinzo

about young Saionji's pardon and he observed that upper-class Japanese looked upon spying somewhat differently from Westerners; that they could not imagine one of their number being a traitor; that the relationship of Saionji and even of Ozaki to the Sorge ring could be considered a form of international mediation or public relations rather than of spying or treason.

Still later I asked the most aristocratic of my sources about Saionji, and he replied in his outspoken fashion that in the inner circle Saionji was considered a valuable pipeline to Stalin.

Analysis of Kido's diary supports these statements. In the entire period between 1930 and 1945 Kido reported meeting with young Saionji exactly twenty-two times on July 10 and Aug. 1, 1932; on March 25, June 3, June 10, July 22 and Sept. 16, 1933; on March 16 and Nov. 1, 1934; on March 10, 1936; on July 13, Aug. 31, Sept. 2, Sept. 16 and Oct. 25, 1937; on Apr. 25 and July 23, 1938; on June 9, 1939; on Nov. 24 and Dec. 2, 1940; and on March 3 and Nov. 24, 1941. From Kido's brief entries on these meetings, supplemented by interviews, I have pieced together a tentative history of the Kido-Saionji relationship. At the first two meetings Kido made use of Saionji's knowledge of English and his Oxford connections to get information on the attitudes of the Lytton commissioners who were then drafting their famous report. At the third meeting, Kido and Saionji discussed British attitudes to Japan's withdrawal from the League of Nations. The next four meetings were all concerned with Araki's Red smear and Kido's attempts to dig up material for counter-blackmail. By this juncture Saionji had proved his skill and loyalty as an agent of the Throne and on Dec. 26, 1933, and Jan. 10, 1934, Kido discussed with Harada a long-term assignment for young Saionji as an advisor on left-wing matters to Prince Konoye. At the eighth meeting, in March 1934 Kido discussed the assignment with Saionji. At the ninth, the following November, Saionji met with several members of the Eleven Club to celebrate the successful defamation and overthrow of Konoye's rival in the House of Peers, Tokugawa Iesato. By the next, the tenth meeting, in March 1936, Saionji had already infiltrated leftist circles and was instructed on the line he should take at Yosemite. The next five meetings took place in 1937 when war had broken out with China and when Saionji was a member of Prime Minister Konoye's kitchen cabinet. Out of them came Ozaki's reports to Sorge and Sorge's reports to Stalin on Japanese intentions in China. The sixteenth meeting, in April 1938, had the effect of explaining Japan's mobilization to Stalin. The seventeenth, in July 1938, in effect assured Stalin that the Lake Khasan incident would not be allowed to escalate into war; the eighteenth, in June 1939, did the same for the Nomonhan incident. Then in November-December 1940 followed the only two social meetings of the entire Kido-Saionji relationship and both were purely formal, having to do with the death and funeral of old Prince Saionji. Finally, on March 3, 1941, Kido met young Saionji to instruct him on his duties as a companion to Matsuoka on his European trip. The last meeting was held at old Saionji's tomb on the anniversary of his death. Since the rest of the Sorge ring had been arrested, it marked the funeral of the Saionji-Kido association. Thereafter Kido discussed Saionji with others and exerted influence on Saionji's behalf but held no more recorded meetings with him.

Ozaki's youth: Johnson, 22–23; Koizumi, interview; for background on Japanese in Taiwan, see Jansen, 83.

Ozaki at university: Johnson, 26.

His postgraduate work: ibid., 32.
Trained as journalist, sent to Shanghai: Johnson, 34, 40.
Ozaki and Agnes Smedley: Deakin and Storry, 70–71.

668 Sorge and Ozaki: Johnson, 67; their beliefs, ibid., 1–4.
For six years Ozaki knew Sorge as "Johnson": ibid., 67, 87.
Sorge's intermediary met Ozaki in deer park, Nara: ibid., 11.
Report of 1936 Army Mutiny: in obi, *Gendai-shi*, 2: 137.

669 Kawai Teikichi's spy career: Johnson, 79–80, 90, 109.
Ozaki joined group around Prince Konoye: ibid., 115–20.
Ozaki learned "Johnson" was Sorge, Sept. 1936: Deakin and Storry, 187.
Ozaki became member of Konoye's Showa Research Society: Johnson, 120.
Kido and Saionji Kinkazu: see note on page 667.

670–671 INNER MONGOLIA: this section based on Tanaka MS, "Yoshiko," IPS Documents 724, 1634.
Mongol horsemen massacred Japanese officers: *N.Y. Times,* Dec. 10, 1936.
Prince Teh proclaimed loyalty to Chiang Kai-shek: ibid., Dec. 12, 1936.

671–674 THE GENERALISSIMO KIDNAPPED: except as cited, this section based on Ekins and Wright, 155–76; Snow, 397–431; Chiang Kai-shek, *A Summing Up at Seventy: Soviet Russia in China* (London: George C. Harrap, 1957), 72–79.

672 Details of kidnapping: Chiang's own account as related to Abend; *Life in China,* 233–35.
Chiang family gave news to Abend of *N.Y. Times:* ibid., 226–31.
Donald arrived in Sian on Dec. 14: for dating of his and others' arrivals, I have followed *N.Y. Times,* Dec. 14, Dec. 21, 1936.

674 Chang Hsueh-liang in Taiwan: my personal correspondence with James Chen, an aide to Chiang Kai-shek.
ALLIANCE WITH HITLER: except as cited, this section based on Presseisen, 87–119, and Iklé, 21–50.
Goebbels' Bureau of Race Investigation quoted: Iklé, 28.

675 Ott on Schleicher's staff: Presseisen, 68.
Ott liaison officer in Nagoya: Deakin and Storry, 101, 138; Hata, "Notebooks" and interview.
Oshima's career: summarized in Presseisen, 69.

676 Secret protocols in Anti-Comintern Pact and Stalin's knowledge of them: Iklé, 38–39.
Sorge had reported on pact: Deakin and Storry, 185 ff.
Sorge met Ott in Nagoya, had served in same German division: ibid., 138.
Sorge reported on Kwantung Army strength and opinion that no Strike North was pending: ibid., 185.
Soviet government delivered calculated slap to Japan: Iklé, 40.

676–680 BLOCKING UGAKI: except as cited, this section based on Kido, *Nikki,* 537–40; Harada, 5:235–47, 248–59 *passim*; Hata, *Gun,* 184–91.

679 Ugaki's search for war minister and Terauchi's counter-moves, Monday and Tuesday: Umezu papers and interrogations cited in IMTFE "Proceedings," 15797 ff.

680 Journalist who advised assassination of Prince 'Kanin: Ohtani, *Kempei-shi*, 250–51.

680–682 SAIONJI DROPS OUT: except as cited, this section based on Kido, *Nikki*, 540–44, 559, supplemented by interviews with banker's son.

681 Saionji on Higashikuni's air force command: Harada, 5:279.

682 Chichubu's departure for England: *Asahi* (Osaka ed.), March 19, 1937; the words of his equerry beforehand: Ito Kanejiro, 1:204.

683–684 KONOYE: this sketch based on Yabe Teiji's authoritative biography of Konoye.

684–686 MARCO POLO'S BRIDGE: to this famous chapter in history, most of which is a matter of record, I have added the Nashimoto-Tojo episode. I noticed the coincidence of Nashimoto's trip as later reported in Japanese newspapers, with the sending of Tojo's telegram. Then I asked retired Maj. Gen. Kajiura Ginjiro about Nashimoto's entertainment at Hsinking (Long Spring Thaw). He assumed that I knew of the episode through prior official statements at the IMTFE, and having been present at the banquet, he gladly gave me the details I have used here. The Japanese text of the Tojo telegram is in IMTFE Exhibit 672.

685 Tojo accompanied Nashimoto as far as Kyushu: *Asahi* (Osaka ed.), June 10, 1937.
Higashikuni's inspection trip to Taiwan: ibid., June 9, 18, 19, 1937.
Army bargain, Saionji Kinkazu informed, Chichibu's message from London: my interpretation of Kido, *Nikki*, 575–78, and Harada, 6:25–28, corroborated by Tanaka interviews.

686 In Chapter 1: see note on page 5.
Konoye's protestations of peaceful intent: see also Ohtani, *Kempei-shi*, 274–75.

686–687 Kido into Cabinet: *Nikki*, 595–91.

687 German desire to mediate Sino-Japanese dispute: Presseisen, 129.
Hirohito refused to offer realistic peace terms: he was encouraged by Kido, who led the fight to "keep the terms abstract"; IMTFE "Proceedings," 30836–837.
No settlement but complete mastery: see Sugiyama, 2:327 for "Basic Policy in re China Incident," adopted Jan. 11, 1938.
Konoye's suggestion to threaten China politically: see also Horiba, 109–11, on role of Military Affairs Bureau Chief Machijiri.
General Staff opposed ultimatum: Usui, *Gendai-shi*, 9:841; Harada, 6:203–8.
Kanin suppressed opposition: Ohtani, *Kempei-shi*, 278; for other instances of old Kanin's continuing activity and influence, see ibid., 282–84.

688 Hirohito did not want to end war: "Why is the General Staff so eager to stop the war?" he asked, Harada, 6:207–8. He was much influenced by Kido, for whose position see ibid., 193 and 209–10. See also ibid., 7:97–100, for handling of Chichibu and Ishiwara, who agreed with General Staff.
Navy position on China war: Usui, *Gendai-shi*, 9:842.

689 Higashikuni and Machijiri in their new commands: Hata, *Nichu,* 291.

For a flattering account of Higashikuni's campaigning, see Ikeda Genji, *Higashikuni Shireikan-miya* [Higashikuni, the Commander-Prince] (Tokyo: Masu Shobo, 1943).

690 BREACHING THE MATANG BOOM: interviews with J. Van Wie Bergamini, Hata, Tanaka.

691 A SOVIET DEFECTOR: this section based on Johnson, 148–49; Deakin and Storry, 199–203; interviews with Tanaka.

N. 9: Itagaki recalled to become war minister, see *Taiheiyo senso,* 4:47.

692 AN UNAUTHORIZED INCIDENT: military details in this section drawn from IMTFE "Proceedings," 38290 ff.; 22575–638; 7773 ff.

Lake Khasan incident plotted by Tada: Harada, 6:300–35, and 7:1–47, coupled with Prince Chichibu's trip to China May 2–18 (*Asahi,* June 20, 1938), suggests to me that Hirohito may have enabled the Lake Khasan incident to take place as a device for discrediting the Strike-North Faction.

Tojo's cable to 19th Div. commander: Tsunoda, *Gendai-shi,* 10:4.

693 Kanin and Itagaki, Itagaki and Hirohito: these three paragraphs based on Tsunoda, *Gendai-shi,* 10:xxxiv–vi, and Harada, 7:50–54, 61. I have followed an interview source in inserting the Emperor's remark about Itagaki's stupidity (*Omae gurai atama no warui mono wa nai*); according to Harada, 8:13, it was actually made on a similar occasion a year later.

694 Ozaki's report to Sorge that the Lake Khasan incident would stop short of war: Obi, *Gendai-shi,* 2:165, also 85.

Significance of Ott's appointment as ambassador: Deakin and Storry, 101, 138; Hata, "Notebooks"; Kido, *Nikki,* 638. Sorge's own appointment, Johnson, 140, 143.

694–95 Sorge's mission to Hong Kong and Manila, his motorcycle accident and its sequel: Deakin and Storry, 197–99.

696 THE LAKE KHASAN MUTINY: military details in this section from IMTFE "Proceedings," 38290 ff.; 22575–638; 7773 ff.

Mission of Tanaka and Cho at Lake Khasan: my synthesis from Tanaka, interviews; his *Sabakareru,* 44; Hata's "Notebooks"; Harada, 7:61.

Bare display of courage by Tanaka and Cho: Ito Kanejiro, 2:274, also 1:43.

Stalin reassured, Blücher imprisoned, report to Berlin photographed: Johnson, 146–49; Deakin and Storry, 200.

697–698 Wang Ching-wei left Chunking, was later abducted: Usui, *Gendai-shi,* 9:624–25; IPS Document No. 1005. See Miwa Kimitada, "The Wang Ching-wei Regime and Japanese Efforts to Terminate the China Conflict." In *Studies in Japanese Culture,* edited by Joseph Roggendorf (Tokyo: Sophia University Press, 1963).

698 Ozaki Hotsumi, "The New National Structure," *Contemporary Japan,* Oct. 1940, cited in USAFFE, "Left Wing, Right Wing: Japanese Proletarian Politics"; Sorge-Ozaki conversation about it: Johnson, 120.

699 Konoye's resignation and its purpose: see Harada, 7:250–59.

Takamatsu at Hainan: *Asahi* (Osaka ed.), March 1, 1939.

700 Hitler pressed for alliance: Iklé, 78–88.

701–702 Hirohito's provisional acceptance of alliance and Hitler's rejection: ibid., 711–15; Tanaka and Koizumi, interviews; Iklé, 87–102.
Hirohito's turmoil over alliance with Hitler, Kido, *Nikki,* 710–11.

702 NOMONHAN (1): this section based on IMTFE "Proceedings," 7854, and testimony of Maj. Afimogen Erastovich Bykov, ibid., 38359 ff.; see also ibid., 22594–718; 23011 ff.; 23025 ff.

703 Hitler signed with Mussolini, Japan excluded: Iklé, 113–14.
NOMONHAN (2): Bykov testimony, IMTFE "Proceedings," 38359–385.

704 Significance of Azuma, Yamagata, and young Higashikuni: Hata, "Notebooks"; Tsunoda, *Gendai-shi,* 10:81; *Asahi,* March 20, 1942.

705 Ozaki took job under Okawa: Deakin and Storry, 249.
Kido to Saionji, Saionji to Sorge, Sorge to Moscow: Obi, *Gendai-shi,* 1:50, 2:86, 169–70; also Deakin and Storry, 202–3; Johnson, 150–52.

705–706 Zhukov in Mongolia: Georgy K. Zhukov, *Marshal Zhukov's Greatest Battles,* intro. by Harrison E. Salisbury (New York: Harper & Row, 1969), 7–8.

706 Young Higashikuni's desertion: Tsunoda, *Gendai-shi,* 10:81; also Kido, *Nikki,* 1105 (entry for May 9, 1944).
Zhukov's offensive: see Zhukov, *Greatest Battles,* Intro., 7–8; IMTFE "Proceedings," 7854; Johnson, 150.

707 "Japanese not good at armor": Zhukov to Gen. Bedell Smith at end of war, quoted, Zhukov, *Greatest Battles,* Intro., 8.
Kido's and Hiranuma's reactions to pact: Kido, *Nikki,* 741–42.
Hitler's tirade against Hirohito: Iklé, 133.

708 Nakajima embassy to Nomonhan: Ishiwara Kanji, testimony, IMTFE "Proceedings," 22594 ff.
Suicide of some Japanese commanders: Imai Sei-ichi, "Nomonhan jiken," 76 ff.

23. Joining the Axis

709 Twelve new divisions added: Hata, "Notebooks."
Grew's speech, Oct. 19, 1939: Grew, *Ten Years,* 251–56.
Speech discussed by Emperor's circle: ibid., 258–59.

710 Diet members formed League for Waging Holy War: Yanaga, *Since Perry,* 543–44.
Hirohito sent emissary to Marquis Kido: Kido, *Nikki,* 783.
Kido had advised Konoye re I.R.A.A.: ibid., 744–83.
He acknowledged to his diary: ibid., 784.
Kido put pressure on politicians: ibid., 784–86.

710–711 Kido, Konoye, Arima agreed on postponement of announcement of New Structure: ibid., 787–88.

711 Finished plans for New Structure, invested as lord privy seal: ibid., 788. See also Harada, 8.250–51, wherein Saionji refused to give ceremonial endorsement to Kido's appointment.

711–712 Hirohito read position papers describing Japan's "fateful juncture," "golden opportunity": see, e.g., IMTFE "Proceedings," 6975–7001, and IPS Document No. 1987.

712 Emperor's visit to tombs of his ancestors: Kido, *Nikki,* 791–92.
Emperor asked questions about Italy's entry into war: ibid., 792.
Kido and Hirohito discussed French and Dutch colonies during dinner at Kyoto Palace: ibid.
Pact with Thailand a means to infiltrate French Indochina: IMTFE "Proceedings," 6869–75; Frederick Whyte, *Japan's Purpose in Asia and the Pacific* (Melbourne: Oxford University Press, 1942).

713 Kido advised Yonai's Cabinet members to resign, urged vice foreign minister to speed negotiations: Kido, *Nikki,* 792.
Tani's conversations with French ambassador: Negotiations between Tani and Arsène-Henry for further concessions in French Indochina continued through Sept.: IMTFE "Proceedings," 6875–6924; Harada, 8: 266–67.
Meeting at Changsha of Chiang's deputy and Japanese vice chief of staff: Kido, *Nikki,* 802–3, 808, 810–11, 816–17, and thereafter *passim.*

714 Japanese encounters with Chiang's forces arranged in advance: interviews with Kajiura Ginjiro (he had command of Japanese salient farthest up Yangtze River during most of the war).

714–715 Prince Asaka assured Hirohito that British were losing, recommended combined air force: Kido, *Nikki,* 795.

715 Hirohito approved Konoye's Cabinet choices: ibid., 797–98.
Kido suggested Anami stay on as vice war minister: ibid., 799.
Kido recommended Konoye as prime minister: ibid. 805–7.
Tojo learned of his selection on return to Tokyo: Butow, *Tojo,* 142.
"a high-degree defense state": propaganda slogan of editorialists at the time.

715–716 Saionji comment, "like inviting a robber": Harada, 7: 366.
THE NEW ORDER: Konoye's program is set forth in detail in Harada, 8: 338–45.
Matsuoka's American experiences: Fleisher, 46–47.
Grew's conversation with Matsuoka: Grew, *Ten Years,* 279–80.
July 26, 1940, new Cabinet adopted program: Sugiyama, 1: 7–10.

717 Hirohito planned to remove members of imperial family from positions of responsibility: Kido, *Nikki,* 811.
Important ministers of Cabinet met with chiefs of staff to ratify program: Harada, 8: 299–302.
This "liaison conference" first in two years: Sugiyama, 1: 6.
Staff officers' plan, "Main Japanese Policy Principles": *Taiheiyo senso,* 8: 322–24.

718 Tojo protested to Kido: Kido, *Nikki,* 812.
Hirohito's analysis of Cabinet's difficulties: ibid., 812–13.

719 Concubines would no longer have telephones: Grew, *Ten Years,* 284.
Saionji re Japanese press writing "like drunkards": Harada, 7: 282.
THE COX CASE: sources for this incident are Fleisher, 123: 308–9; Morin, 60; Craigie, 111–12; IPS Document No. 1533; obi, *Gendai-shi,* 1: 192.
Hirohito ready to reconsider tripartite military alliance: Iklé, 154.
N. 6: see, e.g., Higashikuni, *Watashi,* 59, and Matsumoto Seicho's article

in *Bungei Shunju*, January 1938, 160 ff. Re Kido's continued communication with Toyama: *Nikki*, e.g., 844, 849, 861, 867, 869.

720 Japanese must suppress pro-British sentiments: Iklé, 167.

721 Konoye government "marking time": Grew, *Ten Years*, 283.
Stahmer at Japanese Embassy: Iklé, 168.
Matsuoka consulted Emperor on replacement of diplomats abroad: Kido, *Nikki*, 816; see also IMTFE Exhibit 548.

721–722 Agreement between Matsuoka and Vichy French ambassador Arsène-Henry: This may have been reached on Aug. 20 but I err in saying that it was signed then; the signing took place on Aug. 30 (Kido, *Nikki*, 818; Grew, *Ten Years*, 286–87). Col. Cho Isamu was dispatched to Indochina in late August and Gen. Tominaga Kyoji in early September (Tanaka, interview; Hata, "Notebooks"). My interpretation of the gallant Japanese effort to save French honor is based on interviews with Tanaka and Koizumi. A German transcript of a September 20 telephone call from Gen. Boyen of the French Armistice Commission to his German opposite number, Gen. Stülpnagel, reveals that the French gesture of resistance was reported in advance to the Reich (IMTFE "Proceedings," 6968–75). For other details of the Franco-Japanese negotiations see IPS Document No. 985 on Library of Congress Microfilm WT-26 and "Proceedings," 6801–6975. The latter, 6875 ff., contains an exchange that expresses perfectly the spirit of the talks. Ambassador Arsène-Henry said, "The Japanese request is one-sided." The chief Japanese negotiator, Vice Foreign Minister Tani Masayuki of the Eleven Club, replied, "That is natural. That is why we are able to negotiate."

722 Saionji on the Emperor's fading aura in approving the Tripartite Pact: Harada, 8:330. Of Matsuoka, who had negotiated the pact. Saionji spoke more gently: "It would do Matsuoka good to go crazy, but unfortunately for him he is more likely to regain his sanity."
New Navy minister "easy to talk to": Harada, 8:331.

723 Hirohito's private acceptance of pact on Sept. 4: Harada, 8:368 (also 335) and Kido, *Nikki*, 819, supplemented by interview with Koizumi. Also that day Hirohito attended graduation ceremonies at the military academy and received news of young Prince Kitashirakawa Nagahisa's death in a plane crash.
Hirohito's talk with Kido about German bombing: Kido, *Nikki*, 820.
Sept. 9, Hirohito unexpectedly at liaison conference: Harada, 8:348–49.

724 Matsuoka and Stahmer conversed in English: Iklé, 171.
Sept. 13, Hirohito studied text of pact four and a half hours: interview, Koizumi; see also Kido, *Nikki*, 821.
Hirohito's editing of text: ibid., 823–24.
Unofficial liaison conference of Sept. 14: Harada, 8:369.

725 Hirohito asked Kido to call conference in Imperial Presence: Kido, *Nikki*, 822.

725–727 Conference of Sept. 19: Sugiyama, 1:41–55: Ike, 4–13.

727 Matsuoka's ultimatum of Sept. 19: IPS Document No. 985.
Tominaga Kyoji arranged invasion: Imai Sei-ichi, "Misshitsu no naka no konran," 78 ff.

728 Tripartite Pact signed in Berlin: The procedure and date, as well

as the text of the pact, had been passed upon by Hirohito at the conference in the Imperial Presence of Sept. 19. Sugiyama, 1:42–43, gives the Japanese text of the pact; for an English text see F. C. Jones, 469–70.

729 Hirohito felt as if he were looting a store during a fire: Kido, *Nikki,* 854. "Really," he said, "we should not exploit this time when others are weak as if we were robbers at a fire. Personally I don't like it. It doesn't fit my principles. Now, however, when we face crisis, I have no choice."

Hirohito approved pact out of fear of assassination: Grew, *Ten Years,* 300.

730 Harada made contribution to imperial cover story by producing so-called Saionji-Harada Memoirs: my interpretation of Harada, 1:3–9 (Introduction) and 297–303, which includes account of removal of manuscript to Prince Takamatsu's villa.

Saionji understood journal was kept to show Emperor complexities of politics: So Hirohito told the professional writer Satomi Ton who had helped with matters of style in writing the diary. The occasion was a dinner for the Belles Lettres Society in Sept. 1948; see Abe Nose, ed., *Tenno no insho* (Tokyo: Sogen-sha, 1949), 24–25.

Special ceremony at Palace Shrine, Oct. 17: Kido, *Nikki,* 830.

731 Yamamoto raising funds in Osaka: Harada, 8:380.
Hirohito 2600th birthday speech: Byas, *Govt. by Assassination,* 296.
Takamatsu broadcast: Harada, 8:393–94.
DEATH OF SAIONJI: this section based on Harada, 8:394–99.
Kido went to Okitsu to express Emperor's regrets: Kido, *Nikki,* 838.

732 Kido met Saionji Kinkazu at funeral: ibid.
Sorge had had to rely on German Embassy sources entirely: Deakin and Storry, 223.
Sorge's Communist ties discovered, but Nazi Press Dept. head decided to keep contact with him: Johnson, 12, 171.
Schellenberg sent Gestapo Colonel Josef Meisinger to watch Sorge: ibid., 172.
Meisinger had part in rape of Warsaw: Deakin and Storry, 314.
Meisinger revealed suspicions about Sorge to secret police; aristocrats around Court cut connections with him: Johnson, 172.

732–733 Young Saionji spurned Australia for rightest cell: Harada, 8:325.

733 Kido's long view, Dec. 3: Kido, *Nikki,* 840.

733–734 Yamamoto's forebodings: Harada, 8:365–66.

24. Passive Resistance

736 Yamamoto taunted code experts for new Admirals' Code: interview, Okumiya; Farago, 106–7.

Yamamoto communicated with Hirohito through Prince Takamatsu re Pearl Harbor plan: Kido, *Nikki,* 836, as explained by former Navy commander (privileged source). The explanation is corroborated by the delicate handling of the story in Agawa, 206–8. Agawa states that the *naimei* or "inside orders" for Genda to make his study were not passed on to Yamamoto "formally" until Jan. 7, 1941. Agawa suggests that the cause for the delay may have been related to the indiscretion of a junior officer who told a Peruvian Embassy official about rumors that Japan meant to attack Pearl Harbor. Ambassador Grew heard the warning in late Jan. and relayed it to Washington, where it was discussed (Grew, *Ten Years*, 318; Farago, 135–37). In the meantime, however, Genda had received his assignment. Evidently the officers around Prince Takamatsu had already decided that the security breach would have no repercussions. The fate of the indiscreet junior officer is unknown. For further details on the close relationship between Yamamoto and Prince Takamatsu, see Agawa, 108–9; see also Potter, *Yamamoto*, 53–57, and Farago, 136, for other English-language accounts of the Pearl Harbor plan.

737–739 UNIT 82: this section based on ATIS Rept. No. 131 ("Japan's Decision to Fight") ; Tsuji, *Singapore*, 3–71; Farago, 119–123.

N. 1. "In January 1941 . . . Emperor ordered Onishi to research Hawaii attack": Sugiyama, 1:370: *Ichigatsu Yamamoto GF chokan ni tai su Hawai kogeki no kenkyu o Onishi shosho ni kamei su.* Takao Akiyama, who translated *The Tale of Genji* for U.S. television, gave me this translation. As a student of Court Japanese, and one old enough to remember the idiom of 1941, he states flatly that the expression *kamei su* is absolutely unambiguous in this context and means "the Emperor ordered."

738 Count Ohtani's career: interview with member of Ohtani family. Ohtani had been expelled from Java: Harada, 5:127–28.
For Ohtani's Strike-South credentials, see his 1936 entry in *Who's Who in Japan.*
Tsuji and colleagues made flights over Southeast Asia: ATIS Rept. No. 131.

739 "In the first six to twelve months of a war . . .": interview with Matsumoto Shigeharu; Potter, *Yamamoto*, 41, 43. There are several prime sources for Yamamoto's sentiments which indicate that he voiced them on several occasions in roughly the same words from the summer of 1940 to the fall of 1941.
Worthless paper money "made ideal spills": Koizumi Shinzo, interview.
Army not budgeted in 1941 for new divisions: Kido, *Nikki*, 850.

739–740 Numbers of divisions: Hata, "Notebooks." These notes give the dates on which divisional commanders and chiefs of staff were first posted to the command structures of divisions. Although some divisions may have remained skeletal for months after they had headquarters, the Japanese reservist system was such that any one of the divisions could be activated and put in the field within six weeks of the receipt of battle orders. Here and elsewhere, therefore, I have followed Hata's notes and counted divisions by the dates of the establishment of their command structures. Historians familiar with "Report Concerning the Expansion of the Japanese Ground Forces from 1921 to 1941" (*Translations*, 2, No. 29, National Archives Microfilm 8-5.1 CA) may find that I count some divisions as forces to be reckoned with before their official mobilization as acknowledged by Japanese officers in postwar interrogations. Counts based on Hata's notes, however, seem to me to be more realistic.

740 Diet cut appropriations for I.R.A.A.: Tolischus, *Tokyo Record*, 83–86.
Count Arima resigned, replaced by Gen. Yanagawa Heisuke: ibid.

741 Nomura wanted no part of "act which might disgrace nation":

Harada, 8:377–78; see also ibid., 361–63.

Hirohito assured Nomura: Kido, *Nikki,* 835, but see also Harada, 8:387–88.

743 Feb. 3 liaison conference: Sugiyama, 1:173–77.

German military attachés showed Japanese visitors how to take Singapore: Deakin and Storry, 223.

744 Feb. 7, Hirohito's discussion with Kido re German-Russian war: Kido, *Nikki,* 855.

March 3 meeting between Kido and Saionji Kinkazu: ibid., 859, supplemented by interview with Matsumoto Shigeharu.

Saionji reported back to Ozaki: Deakin and Storry, 224; Johnson, 152; Obata, *Kindai,* 57–59. Obi, *Gendai-shi,* vols. 1–3, contains a good deal of information on Sorge's reports regarding the Matsuoka trip. See especially the thirtieth and fortieth interrogations of Sorge by the procurator.

745 Hirohito gave audience to Matsuoka, March 11: Kido, *Nikki,* 861.

Matsuoka in Berlin: Feis, *Pearl Harbor,* 180–84; Tolischus, *Record,* 106–7; Presseisen, 289–93; Deakin and Storry, 224.

Hitler quoted re German objectives: Basic Army Order No. 24, March 5, 1941, cited in Feis, *Pearl Harbor,* 183.

Matsuoka four days with Ribbentrop, two interviews with Hitler: Presseisen, 289.

Matsuoka reported Hitler's comments: Kido, *Nikki,* 861.

746 Dr. Paul Schmidt quoted re Matsuoka: William Shirer, *The Rise and Fall of the Third Reich* (New York: Simon & Schuster, 1960; Fawcett Crest Book, 1962), 1144.

Matsuoka's exchanges with Ribbentrop: Presseisen, 289–91.

"If Japan gets into a conflict with the United States": Shirer, 1146.

746–750 HUGGING THE BEAR: except as cited this section based on Feis, *Pearl Harbor,* 186–87, and Presseisen, 293–95.

748 Steinhardt's report: telegram from Steinhardt to Secretary of State, March 24, 1941, *Foreign Relations, U.S.: Japan, 1931–1941,* 2:143–45.

Sorge explained neutrality pact to Red Army Intelligence: Johnson, 152; Deakin and Storry, 224.

Matsuoka lectured Stalin on *Hakko Ichiu:* Sugiyama, 1:201: Ike, 20–23; report of liaison conference, Apr. 22, 1941, during which Matsuoka gave account of his visits in Moscow.

Trans-Siberian express held for Matsuoka: Kase, 159.

749–750 "Banzai for the Emperor!": details of Stalin-Matsuoka exchange at celebration of pact from Tolischus. *Record,* 106–7, as reported by members of Matsuoka's party on return from Moscow.

750–753 KONOYE'S PEACE PLOT: account of the efforts of the Maryknoll Fathers, see *Taiheiyo,* 8, final document, for memo drawn up by Ikawa Tadao and Father Drought which began negotiations. The rest of my account is taken from Farago, 172–88; Robert J. C. Butow, "The Hull-Nomura Conversations: A Fundamental Misconception," *American Historical Review,* 65:4 (July 1960), 822–36; Konoye Memoirs, IPS Document No. 3 (Library of Congress Microfilm WT6, 329 ff.); Bishop Walsh to IMTFE, Exhibit 3441; see also Ike, xx-xxiii.

754 Matsuoka received immediately by Hirohito: Kido, *Nikki*, 870. Cf. Konoye, "Memoirs," which suggests that Matsuoka merely stopped at *Nijubashi* to do obeisance.

Matsuoka "recovered from fatigue": Kido, *Nikki*, 871. Kido and Konoye were also indisposed at the same time, and Hirohito sent a courtier to Kido asking whom he was expected to turn to for advice.

Procrastination would make U.S. distrustful: Sugiyama, 203–5.

May 8 liaison conference: ibid., 205–7; Ike, 27–31. Prof. Ike's book, *Japan's Decision for War*, contains translations of liaison conferences and conferences in the Imperial Presence from April to December 1941. They are based on the Japanese text reproduced in *Taiheiyo*, 8. *Sugiyama Memo* from which the materials in *Taiheiyo* were drawn was not available to Prof. Ike when he began his work. Conversely I read *Sugiyama Memo* and drafted this and following chapters before Prof. Ike's book came to my attention. In my final text I have followed, for the most part, Prof. Ike's wording and am greatly indebted to him for the precision and polish of his translations. In one or two passages I have kept my own rough translation because I felt it better mirrored the roughness of the original.

755 Hirohito questioned Kido on "how to fathom Matsuoka": *Nikki*, 873.

Konoye and military chiefs discussed Matsuoka: Sugiyama, 213.

Hirohito to Konoye re considering replacement for Matsuoka: Konoye, "Memoirs."

755–759 MATSUOKA'S TREASON: this section based on Farago, 191–201.

758 Matsuoka's report persuading Hirohito and Navy Staff that Code Purple remained secure: interview, Matsumoto Shigeharu; see also Kido, *Nikki*, 873.

759 Matsuoka's campaign of double talk: see, e.g., his personal message to Molotov reported in Sugiyama, 1:295.

Matsuoka cabled Nomura revised version of "draft proposal": Ike, 31.

Grew considered Matsuoka's harangue "bellicose": *Foreign Relations, U.S.: Japan, 1931–1941*, 2: 146–48; see also *Ten Years*, 337.

Liaison conferences, May 12 and 15: Sugiyama, 1:207–11; Ike, 31–36. Ike dates the 23d liaison conference May 13, but Sugiyama, 207 and *Taiheiyo*, 8:416, agree that it was held on May 12.

760–761 Liaison conference of May 22: Sugiyama, 1:211–15; Ike, 36–43.

760 N. 10: Prince Takamatsu as *Bo*: I discussed this identification with Koizumi and Tanaka; Koizumi's only response was that he had heard the same account, but Tanaka declined to comment on the grounds that Takamatsu was a Navy man and therefore outside his field of expertise.

761–762 Liaison conference of May 29: Sugiyama, 1:215–17; Ike, 43–46.

Matsuoka's anti-British feelings: see, e.g., Kido, *Nikki*, 877–78.

762 Oshima's cable: ibid., 879.

June 6 liaison conference: ibid.; see Sugiyama, 1:218.

Conference on June 7: Sugiyama, 1:218–20; Ike, 46–47.

Matsuoka-Takamatsu exchange, June 12: Sugiyama, 1:220–22; Ike, 52–53.

Substance of General Staff document "Concerning the South": Ike, 51. Matsuoka on Indochina policy, conference of June 16: Sugiyama, 1:222–25; Ike, 53–56.

765 Matsuoka asked for invasion of Siberia, Hirohito ordered Kido to investigate his "true intentions": Kido, *Nikki,* 884–85.
Hirohito's discussion with Sugiyama, June 25: Sugiyama, 1:228–31.

765–766 Substance of position papers: ibid., 231–40.

766 Matsuoka discussed Russo-German war at conference of June 25: ibid., 225–28; Ike, 56–60.

766–768 Conferences of June 26, 27, 28, 30, July 1: Sugiyama, 1:240–50; 251–52; Ike, 60–77.

767 Supreme War Council meeting, night of June 30: Sugiyama, 1:250–51.

768 Roosevelt's letter to Ickes: quoted, Feis, *Pearl Harbor,* 206.

769–770 July 2, conference in the Imperial Presence: Sugiyama, 1:254–64; Ike, 77–90.

771 Japanese domestic atmosphere tense, high schools and universities closed: Kido, *Nikki,* 890.
Matsuoka considered Hull had personally attacked him: Ike, 93.
Liaison conference of July 12: Sugiyama, 1:269–73; Ike, 98–103.

772 Matsuoka withheld Japanese draft: Ike, 103–4.
Konoye's discussion with Hirohito and agreement that Cabinet should resign: Kido, *Nikki,* 890.
Hirohito's audience with Lt. Gen. Yamashita: ibid., 891.

773 Hirohito directed Konoye to form new Cabinet, presided at investiture, July 18: ibid., 891–92.

774 Matsuoka after the war: In Sept. 1945 he composed a half-coherent statement in English (handwritten, IPS Document No. 491, Library of Congress Microfilm WT4) which lays bare his heartbreak. In it he bows to the will of the Emperor and calls the war with the U.S. "inevitable under the circumstances."

25. Konoye's Last Chance

774–775 Liaison conference of July 21: Sugiyama, 1:273–74; Ike, 103–7.

775 "Subjugated the city peacefully": Kido, *Nikki,* 894.
Drawing of battle lines: reactions in Tokyo, Tolischus, *Record,* 173.
Hirohito sensed danger of fatalism, his warning to Sugiyama, and the latter's daybook quoted: Sugiyama, 1:276–84.

775–776 July 29 meeting of Nagano with Hirohito: ibid.

776 July 30 exchange between Hirohito and Nagano: Kido, *Nikki,* 895–96.
Kido's discussion with Hirohito of alternatives: ibid., 899–900.
Quotes, July 22–29: Sugiyama, 1:276–84.

777 Matsuoka quoted: Tolischus, *Record,* 172.
Konoye to Kido, Aug. 25: *Nikki,* 897–98.

Memorandum of Aug. 22 noted by Sugiyama on Oct. 30: Sugiyama, 1:370.

778 Army plans: Tsuji, *Singapore,* 21–22.
Massive troop movements to Manchuria: see Sugiyama, 1:291.
Yamashita began two months of intensive exercises: ATIS Rept. No. 131.
Sorge re build-up in Manchuria: Johnson, 139.
Sorge reported on Aug. 15: ibid., 157.

779 Early Oct. report to Moscow from Sorge: ibid., 158.
Memos GZ–1 and GZ–4: Farago, 211–12.
Hirohito commenced his review: interview with retired Navy commander.
Navy's war planning: testimony of Adm. Nagano, IMTFE "Proceedings," 10189; ATIS Rept. No. 131.

779–780 Yamamoto's presentation at Naval Staff College: ibid.
Liaison conference of Aug. 16: Sugiyama, 1:297; Ike, 121–24.

780–781 Sept. meeting at Naval Staff College: ATIS Rept. No. 131; interview with retired Navy commander; some details from *Translations,* 1: No. 11 and No. 21, "Naval War Games of Sept. 1941 at Naval War College," (National Archives Microfilm 8–5.1 CA).

781 Liaison conference of Sept. 3: Sugiyama, 303–5; Ike, 129–33.

781–783 From 6 P.M. (Sept. 3) to 10 A.M. Sept. 6: my account weaves together Sugiyama, 1:309–11, and Konoye's "Memoirs"; see also Tiedemann, 142–44.

783–786 Conference in the Imperial Presence, Sept. 6: Sugiyama, 1:306–9, 311–30; Ike, 133–63.

786 Meeting of Konoye with Grew: Feis, *Pearl Harbor,* 271; Grew, *Ten Years,* 367.

787 Excerpt from Grew's diary: ibid., 368–69.

788 Decision by staff admirals in favor of Yamamoto's map exercise, Sept. 10–12: ATIS Rept. No. 131.
Marquis Komatsu's banquet: Kido, *Nikki,* 906.
Sept. 9, Yamamoto gave presentation to umpires: ATIS Rept. No. 131 indicates that Yamamoto spent Sept. 6 and 7 convincing fellow officers that his plan was the best of several possible Pearl Harbor attack plans, then that from Sept. 9 to Sept. 12 he demonstrated his plan in detail. The last three days of the demonstration are described in detail by Tomioka Sadatoshi, *Statements,* 4:300–307.
Hirohito's exchange with Sugiyama that afternoon (of Sept. 9): Sugiyama, 1:331.
Call-up of the reserve, Hirohito quoted: ibid.

788–789 Yamamoto's map exercise: ATIS Rept. No. 131.

789 Yamamoto's activities, Sept. 13–21, and preparation of Order No. 1: ibid.
N. 4: The yeoman, from whose recollections most of ATIS Rept. No. 131 was constructed, had one of those prodigious memories that are so frequently encountered in brains formed by training in the Sino-Japanese writing system. After the war, when charred fragments of Yamamoto's

Order No. 1 were resurrected from the Tokyo city dump, the yeoman's recollection of it was found to be letter perfect except for a few stray prepositions and relative pronouns. (This note courtesy of Otis Cary.)

790 Konoye began to think of resigning: Kido, *Nikki,* 906–7.
On Sept. 18 four toughs attacked Konoye's car: "Brocade Banner," 102.
Konoye at liaison conference of Sept. 20: Sugiyama, 1:334–41; Ike, 173–76.
Sept. 26 exchange between Konoye and Kido: Kido, *Nikki* 909.
Hirohito asked Kido to investigate U.S. rubber supplies: ibid., 910.

791 Hirohito taken up with maneuvers at Army War College: Hattori Takushiro, *Statements,* 1:341; Kido, *Nikki* 911; interview with retired Navy commander.
Konoye begged Grew and the Emperor for help: Grew, *Ten Years,* 387–89; Kido, *Nikki,* 911.
Oct. 9 statements of Kido to Konoye: ibid., 912.
Hirohito consults Prince Fushimi: ibid., 913.

792 Hirohito approved combined Army-Navy command for Southern Regions: ATIS Rept. No. 131.
Hirohito admitted no hope in diplomacy: Kido, *Nikki,* 914.
Konoye's message to Roosevelt via Bishop Walsh: Farago, 222.
Kido and Tojo reached an agreement: *Nikki,* 914–15; Konoye, "Memoirs".
Tojo and Oikawa at meeting Oct. 12: Kido, *Nikki,* 913–14. This was apparently not a formal Cabinet meeting, but among those present were the prime, foreign, war, and Navy ministers, Suzuki Tei-ichi of the Cabinet Planning Board, and Cabinet Secretary Tomita Kenji. The meeting was held at Konoye's Ogikubo villa.

792–793 Tojo's report of his conversation with Kido: Sugiyama, 350–51.

793 Cabinet change seemed inevitable: Kido, *Nikki,* 915; Konoye, "Memoirs" (section entitled "On the Resignation of the Third Konoye Cabinet," Library of Congress Microfilm WT6) ; Kido, 3 (*Kankei bunsho*) : 488–92.
Prince Higashikuni receives Konoye: Ando, "Senso," Pt. 1; Matsumoto Seicho, *Bungei Shunju,* January 1968, 161 ff.
Tojo's private audience with Hirohito: Kido, *Nikki,* 916. I have assumed that the conversation Tojo had with Kido at 3 P.M. was substantially the same as one that he had just had with Hirohito; see also Kido, *Kankei bunsho,* 488–92.

794 Kido's consultation with the *Jushin:* Kido, *Nikki,* 917–18, and *Kankei bunsho:* 481–88; Kase, 53–56.
Hirohito dismisses Oikawa: ibid.
N. 6: "Brocade Banner," 109; Tolischus, *Record,* 227–28.

795 Hirohito promoted Tojo to full general: Sugiyama, 1:352.
Hirohito to Kido, "You cannot catch a tiger": *Nikki,* 918; see also Sugiyama, 1:353.

26. Pearl Harbor

For this chapter, in addition to sources cited or listed in the bibliography,

I have drawn for background on: A. J. Barker, *Pearl Harbor* (New York: Ballantine Books, 1969); Fujisawa Chikao, *Kotonarism: An Introduction to the Study of Japanese Global Philosophy or Kotonarism* (Tokyo: The Society for the Advancement of Global Democracy, 1954), an extraordinary postwar exposition of Japanese ideology by a prewar propagandist; Ohashi Hideo, "Watashi wa Zoruge o toraeta" [I Arrested Sorge] (*Sunday Mainichi,* July 2, 1961); Maeda Minoru, ed., *Nanpo to kokumin no kakugo* [The Strike South and the Resolution of the People] (Tokyo: Nanpo Mondai Kenkyu-sho, 1941) [Strike South Problems Research Institute]; Sakamaki Kazuo, *I Attacked Pearl Harbor* (New York: Associated Press, 1949); and Sugimori Hisahide, "Tojo Hideki: Hitoware o jotohei to yobu" [Tojo Hideki: They make fun of him by calling him a first-class private], in *Bungei Shunju,* Special Edition No. 95, April 1966, 116 ff.

798 Sorge's Arrest: This section is based on Johnson, 168–99, and Deakin and Storry, 248–80.
Ito an informer: Johnson, 175–77.

799 Ozaki waited stoically: he described his "premonition" and preparations for arrest in a statement written in prison, quoted, Deakin and Storry, 252.
Sorge on evening of Oct. 17: Klausen quoted, ibid., 253.
Arrest of Sorge: ibid., 254.

801 Liaison conference of Oct. 23: Sugiyama, 1:353–54; Ike, 184–87.

801–802 Daily liaison conferences: Sugiyama, 1:354–62; Ike, 187–99.

803 Formation of the Peace Faction: Kido, *Nikki,* 920–21, supplemented by interview with Matsumoto Shigeharu.
Liaison conference of Oct. 30: Sugiyama, 1:336–62; Ike, 196–99.
Tojo breakfasted with Sugiyama: Sugiyama, 1:370–72.

803–804 Liaison conference of Nov. 1: ibid., 1:372–86; Ike, 199–207.

805 Kaya phoned: Sugiyama, 1:386.
Togo held out: ibid.
Tojo's audience with Hirohito: ibid., 386–87.
At 5 P.M.: Kido, *Nikki,* 921.
Nagano received his copy of Order Number One: ATIS Research Rept. No. 131.
Preamble quoted: ibid.

806 Quotations from order: ibid.
By the evidence of his own memoranda: Sugiyama interleafed his memorandum on the subject from the Navy at the beginning of his entry for Nov. 1: see Sugiyama, 1:370.

806–808 Meeting of Nagano and Sugiyama with Hirohito: Sugiyama, 387–88.

806 N. 3: Butow, *Tojo,* 375 n. 24. Prof. Butow's conclusion is consistent with the fact that, according to ATIS No. 131, only two of the 300 copies of Order No. 1 were distributed to the Army. These presumably went to Terauchi and Sugiyama, the two officers with the most need to know.

807 The Emperor's copy of any major military order was regularly

submitted to him by the appropriate aide-de-camp before he was called upon to discuss it with either of his chiefs of staff. In this instance Hirohito had apparently received his copy of Order No. 1 late on Nov. 1, for early the next morning he phoned his Navy brother, Takamatsu, with a question regarding plans vis-à-vis the United States: Kido, *Nikki,* 921.

808 Nagano's meeting with Kuroshima: Potter, *Yamamoto,* 68–69.

808–812 THE WAR COUNCIL ASSENTS: This section, including all quotations, is taken from Sugiyama, 1:388–406.

812–816 THE FORMAL WAR DECISION: This section is based on Sugiyama, 1:406–30, supplemented by Ike, 208–39.

816 Hirohito approved dispatch of Kurusu: Kido, *Nikki,* 921.

817 Clipper was kept waiting: Moore, 258.

Hirohito assumed incognito to attend *gozen heigo*: Tanaka, in interview, first mentioned that the Emperor was said to have reviewed the fleet secretly before Pearl Harbor; Koizumi, in interviews, did not deny the rumor. I deduced the dates from Kido's diaries and mentioned the episode as if it were well known and proven in an interview with the retired Navy commander; he said he was unsure of the details but suggested those used in the account here. Later the publication of *Sugiyama Memo* convinced me that the Emperor's review had indeed taken place in the period described.

Chiefs of staff met with Hirohito immediately after Nov. 5 conference: Sugiyama, 1:431.

818 Hirohito to Hayama at 10 A.M. Nov. 7: Kido, *Nikki,* 922–23, and preceding note on *gozen heigo.*

Eighty-three pages of tables: Sugiyama, 1:433–516.

819 December 8 the day of attack: ATIS Research Rept. No. 131; Hashimoto, 1–5.

Nagumo orders captains to "complete battle preparations"; ibid.

First of twenty-seven: ibid.

Most of Pearl Harbor task force had gathered, by Nov. 14: Farago, 267; and interview, retired Navy commander; ATIS Research Rept. No. 131; Hashimoto, 4–5; Potter, 78.

FLEET DISPATCH: Material in this section is drawn from ATIS Research Rept. No. 131; Farago, 267–68; Hashimoto, 1–5; Potter, 78; interview with retired Navy commander.

820 Joseph W. Ballantine quoted: text of memo in Trefousse, 304–6.

821 In World War II, it was planned: quotations from "Land Disposal Plan in the Greater Asia Co-Prosperity Sphere," IMTFE Exh. 1334; text in Storry, *Double Patriots,* 317–19.

821–822 Liaison conference of Nov. 20: Sugiyama, 1:525–28; Ike, 249–53.

822 Togo cable: IMTFE "Proceedings," 10399.

823 Stimson's diary: entry for Nov. 25, 1941, quoted in Feis, *Pearl Harbor,* 314.

25,000 Japanese troops: ibid., 315.

The President "fairly blew up—": Stimson's diary for Nov. 26, 1941, reproduced in Trefousse, 141.

Hirohito to Kido: Kido, *Nikki,* 925, and Sugiyama, 1:532.

824 Received radio message: Hashimoto Mochitsuru, 5.
Nomura and Kurusu, cable to Tokyo: quoted, Millis, 244.
"I have washed my hands of it": Hull as recorded in Stimson's diary for Nov. 27, 1941, entry reproduced in Trefousse, 141.
Fleet began to sail from Hitokappu Bay: IMTFE "Proceedings," 10425.
"the final alert": Stimson's diary for Nov. 27, Trefousse, 142.

825 Stark's message: quoted, Millis, 250.
Kimmel and Short agreed to plan: Kimmel's testimony to Joint Committee, Trefousse, 35.
Halsey was ordered to depart for Wake: Kimmel's testimony, quoted, Millis, 268.
Kimmel later testified: testimony reproduced in Trefousse, 36.
Gen. Short's cable: ibid., 65.

826 June 1940 order: ibid., 62.
Maj. Gen. Martin supervised study: Millis, 63.

827 Grew's warning, Jan. 27, 1941: *Ten Years,* 318; quoted, Millis, 33–34.
Forwarded to Kimmel: ibid., 34.

827–828 Kurusu's trans-Pacific telephone conversation: IMTFE "Proceedings," 10430 ff.

829 War Cabinet meeting, Nov. 28: Stimson's testimony to Joint Committee, reproduced in Trefousse, 133.
Tojo's objections: Butow, *Tojo,* 344, n. 58.

829–830 Elder Statesmen's Conference: Kido to IMTFE, Exhibit 1966, Trefousse, 250–51.

830 Liaison conference of Nov. 29: Sugiyama, 1:535–38; Ike, 260–62.
Kido at residence of Prince Takamatsu: Kido, *Nikki,* 927–28.
Hirohito, after hearing message from Takamatsu: ibid.
Kido's reply: ibid.
Hirohito sees Tojo, Shimada, Nagano: ibid.
Hirohito, "Instruct Prime Minister Tojo": ibid.
Kido wrote in his diary: ibid.

831–832 Conference in the Imperial Presence, Dec. 1, 1941: Sugiyama, 1:539–44; Ike, 262–83.
Hirohito to Sugiyama: Sugiyama, 1:544.

833 "Climb Mount Niitaka": ATIS Rept. 131.
Kimmel-Layton exchange: Layton's testimony to Joint Committee, quoted, Millis, 297.
Ciano's diary entry: extract in Trefousse, 271.

834 Foote burning code books: his testimony to Joint Committee, Farago, 303.
Japanese task force left Samah harbor: Tsuji, *Singapore,* 72–78; Tsuji had made a flying trip to Tokyo the week before to defend his plans against last-minute alterations, Sugiyama, 1:5–6.
N. 6: Ciano diary, Trefousse, 272.

835 Liaison conference, Dec. 6: Sugiyama, 1:565, identifies the meeting of Dec. 6 as the 75th liaison conference. On pages 563–65 he has

identified another meeting, Dec. 4, as the 75th liaison conference. *Taiheiyo senso,* 8:611–13, agrees that both meetings should be called the 75th liaison conference. *Taiheiyo*'s text, however, omits a mysterious typographic symbol (two concentric circles) which appears in the original Sugiyama version, identifying the speaker of a deadlock-breaking statement near the end of the second half of the conference on Dec. 6. To judge by internal evidence, the 75th liaison conference met for two hours on Dec. 4 and broke up after failing to agree on anything of substance except the proper protocol to use in announcing the war to Pu-Yi, the Manchukoan puppet emperor. On Dec. 6, after two days of back-room consultation, the conference reconvened at 10 A.M. to consider the rest of its agenda. The timing of the note to Hull was conceded without much debate, but then both Army and Navy officials expressed their lingering doubts about the war in an argument as to what to tell Hitler. The Army, Russophobic as always, wanted to promise Hitler that Japan, by making war on the United States, would cut off American aid to Russia through Vladivostok; the Navy insisted that it would do nothing to interdict U.S. aid to Russia because the possibility of antagonizing Russia was more than Japan could risk during her Strike South. At 3 P.M. the bickering was recessed briefly, then resumed in a session that lasted until 6:30. Late in the afternoon the person identified by the two concentric circles made a "decision" to adopt a suggestion of Finance Minister Kaya and to tell Hitler simply, "We hope you will understand, but, as long as we must avoid a confrontation with Russia, we cannot co-operate fully with you while still carrying out our military operation in the South." Having made this single utterance, the speaker was rewarded by seeing the proceedings brought to a speedy conclusion.

Japanese reply to Hull's Nov. 26 statement: Millis, 322.
Consulted privately: Millis, 219–20.

836 Roosevelt's message: text reproduced in Grew, *Ten Years,* 421–23.
Roosevelt's memo to Hull: Millis, 319.

837 Decipherment of fourteen-part note: Kramer's testimony to Joint Committee, Trefousse, 196–200.
Roosevelt and Hopkins: Schulz's testimony to Joint Committee, ibid., 220–25.
Nagumo listening to local Hawaiian stations: Millis, 331.
Flag of Admiral Togo: Zacharias, 250.

838 Grew received cable late in evening: *Ten Years,* 420.
At 6:15 P.M.: Kido, *Nikki,* 932.

839 Typing the note: Feis, *Pearl Harbor,* 341.

840 Marshall's cable to Short: Marshall's testimony to Joint Committee, Trefousse, 178–79.
Grew's efforts to deliver Roosevelt's message: *Ten Years,* 420–21.
Togo's reply: Togo, 219.
Togo's telephone call to Kido: ibid., 220; Kido, *Nikki,* 932.
Japanese bluejackets in Shanghai: testimony of Frederick Charles Parr, IMTFE "Proceedings," 10608–38.

841 Kido drives to Imperial Library: Kido, *Nikki,* 932.
Hirohito listening to radio: ibid., amplified by interview with a retired lieutenant general who in 1941 was attached to Imperial Headquarters. Another informant, Koizumi Shinzo, said: "I believe that, like most people

in the palace, the Emperor was listening to the radio. He had a short-wave set in his study, and I have heard that he listened to the actual transmissions from Malaya."
Roosevelt in Oval Study with Hopkins: Davis and Lindley, 4.

842 Hirohito and Togo discuss Roosevelt's message: Togo, 221.
At 3:15 P.M. Togo left: ibid.
Kido lingered for fifteen minutes: Kido, *Nikki*, 932.
TIGER, TIGER: This section is based on Lord, *Day of Infamy*; Karig and Kelley, 22–96; Millis; Morison, 3:80–146.

843 Fuchida quoted: Potter, *Yamamoto*, 98.

844 Hirohito dismissed Kido: Kido, *Nikki*, 932.

847 Casualties at Pearl Harbor: Morison, 3:126. Another count was given by Adm. James O. Richardson to IMTFE: 1,999 sailors, 109 Marines, 234 soldiers, and 188 U.S. planes.
Bellinger's signal: Morison, 3:101.

848 Roosevelt receiving news of Pearl Harbor: Davis and Lindley, 5.
Hull's last meeting with Nomura and Kurusu: ibid., 15–18.
N. 10: IMTFE "Proceedings," 11311 ff.

849 Halsey quoted: Morison, 3:212.

27. The Strike South

For this chapter, in addition to sources cited or listed in the bibliography, I have drawn for background on: David Bernstein, *The Philippine Story* (New York: Farrar, Straus & Co., 1947), circumspect but interesting account of President Manuel Quezon during the fall of the Philippines and the years of government in exile; Russell Braddon, *The Naked Island* (London: Werner Laurie, 1952), Singapore and the Burma-Thai railroad illustrated by Braddon's famous fellow prisoner, Ronald Searle; Eugene Burns, *Then There Was One: The U.S.S. Enterprise and the First Year of the War* (New York: Harcourt, Brace & Co., 1944); Paul Carano and Pedro C. Sanchez, *A Complete History of Guam* (Rutland, Vermont, and Tokyo: Chas. E. Tuttle Co., 1964); Don Congdon, ed., *Combat: Pacific Theater, World War II* (New York: Dell Publishing Co., 1958), an anthology of firsthand war experiences. Frank Wesley Craven and James Lea Cate, eds., *Plans and Early Operations: January 1939 to August 1942*, The Army Air Force in World War II, Vol. 1 (Chicago: University of Chicago Press, 1948); Ralph Goodwin, *Passport to Eternity* (London: Arthur Barker, Ltd., 1956), the fall of Hong Kong; John Hersey, *Men on Bataan* (New York: Knopf, 1942); Stanley Johnston, *Queen of the Flat-tops: The U.S.S. Lexington and the Coral Sea Battles* (New York: E. P. Dutton & Co., 1942); Edgar McInnis, *The War, Third Year* (London, Toronto, New York: Oxford University Press, 1942); Ronald McKie, *Proud Echo* (Sydney: Angus and Robertson Ltd., 1953), firsthand account of the Battle of Sunda Strait and the sinking of the *Perth*; John F. Moyes, *Mighty Midgets* (Sydney: N.S.W. Bookstall Co., 1946), small craft naval actions in the seas north of Australia; Munebi Matsuharu, Hankushi Takashi, and Tominaga Kengo, *Daitoa-sen ni-shi* [Japanese Bulletins from the Greater East Asia War] 1, December 8, 1941-April 7, 1942; II, April 8,

1942-August 7, 1942 (Tokyo: Asahi Shinbun-sha, 1942); Rohan D. Rivett, *Behind Bamboo: An Inside Story of the Japanese Prison Camps* (Sydney: Angus & Robertson Ltd., 1946), containing an account of the Sunda Straits battle; R. W. Volckmann, *We Remained* (New York: W. W. Norton & Co., 1954); Robert Ward, *Asia for the Asiatics? The Techniques of Japanese Occupation* (Chicago: University of Chicago Press, 1945), by the U.S. consul in Hong Kong in 1941; Osmar White, *Green Armour* (Sydney: Angus and Robertson Ltd., 1942), firsthand account of Australian defense of New Guinea; W. L. White, *They Were Expendable* (New York: Harcourt, Brace & Co., 1942); and Malcolm Wright, *If I Die: Coastwatching and Guerrilla Warfare Behind Japanese Lines* (Melbourne: Landsdown Press, 1965), adventure on the island of New Britain.

853 Excerpt from Kido's diary: Kido, *Nikki*, 932–33.

854 Invasion at Singora: Tsuji, *Singapore*, 82–88.
Landing at Kota Bharu and Japanese sapper's action: ibid., 95.
Fog over air bases in Taiwan: Sakai Saburo, 71.
Japanese Army pilots damaged Baguio: Ind, 91–105.

855 Brereton urged take-off of B-17's and MacArthur's refusal: Brereton, 38–39.
At 10 A.M. in Taiwan, fog lifted: Sakai Saburo, 71.

855–856 Account of air attacks on Clark Field based on Brereton, 39–43; Morison, 3:170–71; Allison Ind, Bataan: *The Judgment Seat* (New York: The Macmillan Co., 1944), 91–105.

856 Account of one Japanese air ace and quotation: Sakai Saburo, 72–73.
Sakai's tribute to the B-17: ibid., 85.

857 Only a cloud marred the day: see Emperor's remarks to Sugiyama on Feb. 13, 1942; Sugiyama, 2:26.
British destruction in Borneo oil fields: Wigmore, 180.

858 Attack on Guam: Morison, 3:185–86.
Japanese landings at Aparri and Vigan: Kawagoe Moriji, *Statements*, 2:155 ff.; Nakajima Toshio, ibid., 638–41.
CONTROL OF THE OCEAN: this section based on Gill, 476–83; Grenfell, 109–36; Wigmore, 141–45, with some details from O. D. Gallagher, *Retreat in the East* (London: George C. Harrap & Co., 1942).

859 "Churchill's yacht": Gallagher, 45.

861 "We are off to look for trouble": message posted in *Repulse*, quoted, Gallagher, 45.
"At dawn": ibid., 49.

864 "Bloody good shooting": CBS correspondent Cecil Brown, in Don Congden, ed., *Combat: The War with Japan* (New York: Dell Publishing Co., 1962), 23.
Officers had never seen such bombing: Gallagher, 60.
"We have completed our task": ibid., 70.
News of victory reached Hirohito at 3 P.M.: Kido, *Nikki*, 933.

867 "Hup, hup, hooray!": ibid.

868 114th Regt. required 550 trucks: Tsuji, *Singapore*, 207–9.

869 Cuff links from Prince Mikasa: Tsuji, *Underground Escape,* 77.
Prince Takeda sent to Saigon: *Asahi,* Nov. 20, 1942.
N. 2, death of Prince Nagahisa: *Asahi,* Sept. 6, 1940.

870 Excerpt from *Just Read This*: ATIS Document No. 7396.

871 MALAYA'S JITRA LINE: this section based on Wigmore, 137–52,
and Tsuji, *Singapore,* 107–25.

872 Bicycle troops: operations described in Tsuji, *Singapore,* 183–85.

873 WAKE: this section based on Morison, 3:223–54.

874 HONG KONG: this section based on Wigmore, 170–76; Strategicus,
The War Moves East (London: Faber & Faber, 1942); James Bertram,
Beneath the Shadow (New York: John Day Co., 1947), 78–96.
Japanese terror at field hospital in St. Stephen's College: testimony of
James Barnett, IMTFE "Proceedings," 13112 ff.

877–887 LUZON: this section and the following MANILA and THE
DEFENSE OF BATAAN are based, except as specifically cited, on Hattori,
278–83 (plus separate folio of annotated maps); on Hattori (he was chief
of operations in the Army General Staff) in *Statements,* 1:315–90; on
other officers' statements, ibid., 2:115–36, 393–96, 576–77, 627–30,
638–44, 657–60, 661–68; ibid., 3:80–97, 110–17, 152–59; ibid; 4:369–
82, 544–51; 552–57; and on Agoncillo, 1:124–62, and Toland, *But Not
in Shame,* 124–93.

877–878 Seventy-three convoys: Kawagoe Moriji, *Statements,* 2:122–35;
Ohmae Toshikazu, ibid., 3:60–63.
N. 4; Japanese commanders claimed only 15,000 troops landed: for
data and reasons see, e.g., Kawagoe, Morioka, Ohyabe, Onumu, Towatari,
Statements, 2:117, 578; 3:81, 153; 4:375.

878–879 Fall-back of Gen. Wainwright's forces: this and following two
paragraphs, personal knowledge refreshed by conversations with my father,
J. Van Wie Bergamini, and reference to the diaries of my mother, Clara
D. Bergamini.

879 Honma on ramp of barge: Agoncillo, 1, plate opp. p. 87.
Landings at Lamon Bay and Legaspi: Morioka Susumu, *Statements,*
2:576–77.
N. 6, 7: Ohyabe Shozo, *Statements,* 3:81.
N. 8: Kawagoe Moriji, *Statements,* 2:117; interview with Fujisawa.
N. 9: Nara Akira, *Statements,* 2:662.

880 MacArthur announced decision to Quezon Dec. 23: see Agoncillo,
1:79. Maeda Masami, *Statements,* 2:393, says Gen. Honma knew of decision through spies by Dec. 25.
Message from Quezon to Japanese colonel: see note on pages 878–79.

881 Sugiyama to Honma re Philippines command: Kojima, 1:182–85.

882 On withdrawal to Bataan: Haba Hikaru, *Statements,* 1:195; Nakayama Makoto, ibid., 2:657–60.
Kido interviewed Lt. Gen. Tanaka: Kido, *Nikki,* 936; Agoncillo, 1:358.

882–883 Hirohito urged Sugiyama to abbreviate timetable: Hattori,
Statements, 1:315–16.

883 Honma's staff officers had protested: Maeda Masami, *Statements,*
2:393; Nakajima Yoshio, ibid., 2:638–44.

Terauchi's message to Honma, transmitted verbally: Arao Okikatsu, *Statements*, 1:44–46; Ishii Masami, ibid., 587; Maeda Masami, ibid., 2:393–96.

Prince Takeda sent to Manila: *Asahi*, Jan. 20, 1942; Ishii Masami, *Statements*, 2:588.

Takeda communicated "real situation in the Philippines" to Hirohito: ibid., supplemented by interview with retired lieutenant general.

884 Cable to Honma, his discussion with Takeda: "Honma Trial Transcript" (National War Memorial, Canberra) 3:225–27; Maeda Masami, *Statements*, 2:393–96.

Lt. Gen. Nara Akira a kinsman of Nara Takeji: Koizumi, interview.

Nara's attack on Abucay line: According to Hattori, *Statements*, 1:383, the official order for the attack was Imperial General H.Q. Army Directive No. 1076. According to retired Lt. Gen. Fujisawa Shigezo, directives with this designation were *taimei* or Great Orders, which had to be not only reported to Hirohito by his aides-de-camp but actually stamped with Hirohito's personal seal of state. The series of which this was No. 1076 had started with the various orders for Dec. 8, 1941; in other words, in a little over a month, Hirohito had personally issued over a thousand orders to the Army alone.

885 Honma's meeting with Gen. Staff officers from Tokyo: Kojima, 1:182–85.

886 "an old carp . . . must be fished patiently": Fujisawa, interview. Eisenhower had "studied dramatics under MacArthur": quoted, Lee, 99. Eisenhower's staff study: Long, *MacArthur*, 74–75.

887–890 RETREAT FROM MALAYA: this section based on Percival; Tsuji, *Singapore;* Wigmore, 337–81; Attiwill, *passim.*

On Japanese planning for advance on New Zealand and Samoa, see Takahashi Chikaya, *Statements*, 4:34–37.

888 Churchill's complaint re Singapore's guns: 4:50–51.

890–896 SINGAPORE'S AGONY: this section based on Percival, 272–301; Tsuji, *Singapore;* Wigmore, 337–81; Attiwill, *passim.*

Situation at Imperial Headquarters, Tokyo: interview with retired Navy commander.

Liaison conference of Feb. 4: Sugiyama, 2: Intro. 11–13.

891 Hirohito's briefing protracted many hours: interview with retired Navy commander.

Hirohito's conference with Sugiyama, Feb. 9: Sugiyama, 2:22.

For a more detailed account of Yen's position, see George E. Taylor, *The Struggle for North China* (New York: Institute of Pacific Relations, 1940).

General Staff kept a Yen file: interview with Tanaka Takayoshi.

892 Yen's name a code word: interview with Tanaka Takayoshi. The first Yen Hsi-shan operation—a hunt of Yen's men from airplanes—is described in Harada, 2:36.

"The Yen Hsi-shan treatment": interviews with Tanaka and Fujisawa; also see Kido's references to Yen Hsi-shan operations in 1940–41, *Nikki*, 843, 847, 886, 901, 902, 907, 920.

892–893 Hirohito's conference with Sugiyama, Feb. 9 (continued):

Sugiyama, 2:22–23.
Sugiyama discussed situation with aides: interview with retired officer.
Excerpt from Tsuji: *Singapore,* 258, supplemented by interview with Fujisawa.
Tsuji's reference to reduction of Taiyuan Sheng: for Prince Kanin Haruhito's and Prince Takeda's parts in this earlier atrocity, see *Asahi,* Mar. 20, 1942.
Japanese action at Alexandra Barracks Hospital: Tsuji, *Singapore,* 259–65.

896–897 Kido had warned Hirohito: *Nikki,* 943–44; see also Kido Koichi, *Statements,* 2:195, "The Emperor wore an expression as if to say, 'I wonder if Kido knows what he is saying.' "

897 Hirohito's statement to Tojo: Kido, *Nikki,* 945.
The next morning Hirohito informed Kido: ibid., 946.
Hirohito had watched newsreels: ibid., 944.

898–899 Plans to invade Australia: Hattori, *Daitoa,* and *Statements,* 1:357–58; interview with retired Navy commander.

899–900 Liaison conference of Feb. 23: Sugiyama, 2:30–33.

900 N. 14: Sugiyama, 2:32.

901 Liaison conference of March 7: Sugiyama, 2:12.
Excerpt from Kido's diary: *Nikki,* 949–50.

902 N. 15: Sugiyama, 2:60.

904 Hirohito's attitude to Hong Kong disclosures: Kido, *Nikki,* 950.

904–906 On the capture of Bataan: Akiyama Monjiro, *Statements,* 1:18–20; Nara Akira, ibid., 2:661–68; Onuma Kiyoshi, ibid., 3:152–59; Ohyaba Shozo, ibid., 3:80–97; Oishi Hiromi, ibid., 3:110–117; Yoshida Motohiko, ibid., 4:544–51.

906–909 THE DEATH MARCH: this section based on Agoncillo, 1:198–231; Dyess, 61–132 *passim;* IMTFE "Proceedings," 12578–738; Toland, *Not in Shame,* 70–104; Tsuji, *Guadarukanaru.*
Brig. Gen. Steve Mellnik, U.S.A. Ret., in his *Philippine Diary, 1939–1945* (New York: Van Nostrand Reinhold Co., 1969), tells of acting as guide after the fall of Corregidor to a Japanese colonel who would appear almost certainly to have been the redoubtable Tsuji himself.
A few commanders refused to be bullied: Imai Takeo, 184 ff.

909 Kido knew Korematsu well: Kido records in *Nikki* over 100 meetings with him.

910 Kido's talk with the Empress Dowager and the botanical ramble: Kido, *Nikki,* 956, supplemented by interview, Koizumi Shinzo.

910–912 Doolittle raid: see James Merrill, *passim.*

912 Tojo defended captured U.S. airmen: see esp. testimony even of Tojo's arch rival, Tanaka Takayoshi, IMTFE "Proceedings," 14387–402.

913 Orders: USAFFE, "Japanese Monograph" No. 71, 86–87; see also 87–118.
Destruction in Chekiang and Kiangsi: James Merrill, 160.

914 Armada dispatched to Midway: on interrelationship of Doolittle raid and Midway attack, see Agawa, 271–72.

THE DEATH OF CORREGIDOR: this section based on Yoshida Motohiko, *Statements*, 4:552–57, and Mellnik, *Philippine Diary*, 135–55.

915–916 Prince Higashikuni's son on tour of southern areas: *Asahi*, May 17, 27, 1942.

916–920 THE CORAL SEA: this section based mainly on Morison, 4:21–64; Ito Masanori, 52–53; Toland, *But Not in Shame*, 369–73.

920–933 MIDWAY: this section based on Morison, 4:69–159; Lord, *Incredible Victory*; Fuchida et al; Tuleja; and Toland, *But Not in Shame*, 373–98.

931–932 Attack of *Yorktown* and *Enterprise* dive bombers: Who bombed what has been the source of controversy. On review I have accepted the reconstruction by Walter Lord in *Incredible Victory*, 289–95, which seems to me best to accommodate the largest number of details in the accounts of Japanese as well as American eyewitnesses.

28. Crumbling Empire

For this chapter, in addition to sources cited or listed in the bibliography, I have drawn for background on: A. G. Allbury, *Bamboo and Bushido* (London: Robert Hale, 1955), firsthand account of work on the Burma-Thai railroad; Benedict R. O'G. Anderson, "Japan the Light of Asia" (Ph.D. dissertation, Yale University, 1964), Japanese policies in Indonesia; Corey Ford, *Short Cut to Tokyo: The Battle for the Aleutians* (New York: Charles Scribner's Sons, 1943); Frank Foster, *Comrades in Bondage* (London: Skeffington and Son, Ltd., n.d. [1946], fall of Java and Burma-Thai railroad; Ernest Gordon, *Through the Valley of the Kwai* (New York: Harper and Brothers, 1962); Agnes Newton Keith, *Three Came Home* (Boston: Little, Brown & Co., 1947); K. P. MacKenzie, *Operation Rangoon Jail* (London: Christopher Johnson Ltd., 1954), Japanese prisoners in Burma; William H. McDougall, Jr., *By Eastern Windows: The Story of a Battle of Souls and Minds in the Prison Camps of Sumatra* (London: Arthur Barker Ltd., 1951); Nakamura Aketo, *Hotoke no shireikan: Chu-tai kaiso-roku* [Buddha's Commander: Reminiscences of Garrison Duty in Thailand] (Tokyo: Nihon Shuho-sha, 1958); *Reconquest: An Official Record of the Australian Army's Successes in the Offensives against [New Guinea] September 1943–June 1944* (Director General of Public Relations, Under Authority of Sir Thomas Blamey, C-in-C, Australian Military Forces); Alfred A. Weinstein, *Barbed-Wire Surgeon* (New York: The Macmillan Co., 1948), efforts of a doctor in Camp O'Donnell and Cabanatuan; and Desmond Wettem, *The Lonely Battle* (London: W. H. Allen & Co., 1960), adventure of HMS *Petrel* crewman who hid out in Shanghai and evaded capture for four years.

934 Sumo-wrestling image: letter from Yamamoto Eisuke to Kido, June 5, 1943 (the day of Adm. Yamamoto Isoroku's funeral—no relation), Kankei bunsho, 596–97: "Japan was a small sumo-wrestler of good technique fighting a grand champion of great weight. Instead of waiting for the usual limbering-up ceremonies, the little wrestler attacked and almost pushed the champion out of the ring . . . but the grand champion staggered back at the edge of the ring, planted his feet firmly, and slowly began to come forward."

935 Kido persuaded him Throne not yet so desperate: *Nikki,* 967–68.
Kido received visit from Yoshida: ibid.
Peace Faction: see note on page 64 (in Ch. 2 of Notes).
Dec. 16, 1941, Kido talked with Konoye: Kido, *Nikki,* 934.
Konoye met again, Jan. 20, with Kido: ibid., 941.
Harada reported to Kido on police opinion of Saionji Kinkazu: ibid., 942–43.
Hirohito discussed Sorge case with Home Minister Yuzawa: ibid., 951.
Saionji Kinkazu interrogated: Johnson, 199; Deakin and Storry, 292. After the war Saionji became Japan's unofficial ambassador to Communist China. When he returned to Japan in 1969 he set out to act as a bridge between Peking and the West. He appeared conspicuously in photographs of the Chinese Ping-Pong team which accompanied a U.S. team on a widely publicized good will tour of China in 1971. Moreover, a Japanese diplomat has told me that he played a leading role as intermediary in the Washington-Peking negotiations that preceded the Ping-Pong rapprochement. Once branded a spy, Saionji Kinkazu was at last being appreciated for his true forte as an international go-between.

937 Kido's frank conversation with Konoye: *Nikki,* 951.

937–938 Konoye's proposed peace trip to Europe, Yoshida's letter: ibid., 967–68.

939 Landings on Guadalcanal: Morison, 4:283–91.
On surprise caused by Guadalcanal landings in ranks of palace staff officers: Takahashi Chikaya, *Statements,* 4:34–37. In Sugiyama, 2: Intro., 15, the news is described as coming like "cold water in a sleeper's ear."

940 Australian coast-watcher saw Japanese planes approaching: Morison, 4:292.

940–941 Sakai's adventure: Sakai Saburo, 218–34.

941 N.1: Raymond F. Toliver and Trevor J. Constable, *Fighter Aces* (New York: The Macmillan Co., 1965), 338, 343, 345.

943 Battle of Savo Island: Morison, 5:17–64; Collier, 278–86.

943–944 Guadacanal routine: Morison, 5, is basic source; many details from Griffith.

945 Hirohito gave lunch to Nomura and Kurusu: Kido, *Nikki,* 979.
Hirohito proposed Tojo as foreign minister: ibid., 980–81.
Hiranuma's audience with the Emperor: ibid., 982.

947 Battle of the Eastern Solomons: Morison, 5:79–107.

948 New troops commanded by Maj. Gen. Hyakutake Seikichi: on this and following imperial interventions in the Guadalcanal battle, see *Translations,* 3, No. 3, "Truth of the Guadalcanal Battle."
Hirohito informed Kido that counterattack had failed: Kido, *Nikki,* 983–84.
Saratoga torpedoed: Morison, 5:111–13.
Casualties in Hyakutake's bayonet charges: Griffith, 121.
Japanese submarine damage: Morison, 5:130–38.
U.S. troops got adequate supplies: Griffith, 130.

949 Maruyama's attack: Griffith, 168–73.

950 "second attack has failed"; Kido met Konoye at hospital; new

ambassador to Rome: Kido, *Nikki,* 989–91.

951 Halsey on Guadalcanal; "Kill Japs": Griffith, 188.
Naval Battle of Guadalcanal: Morison, 5:225–82.
Hirohito ordered Adm. Komatsu to use submarines for supply: Hashimoto, 61; Kido, *Nikki,* 994–95.

952 Kido heard news of naval battle at concert: ibid., 995; *Asahi* (Tokyo ed.), Nov. 18, 1942.
Battle of Tassafaronga: Morison, 5:296–315; Griffith, 217–21.

953 I-boats modified for freight duty: Hashimoto, 62–63.

954 Empress Dowager's return: Kido, *Nikki,* 998 (Dec. 6, 1942). For negotiations with Sadako see Kido's entries of Apr. 17, July 11, Aug. 29, Sept. 18–21, 23, Nov. 10, 13, 16, 17, 19, 1942.
Hirohito's celebration of start of second war year: ibid., 999.
Dec. 9 liaison conference: Sugiyama, 2:191.

955–956 Kido and Hirohito to Ise Shrine: Kido, *Nikki,* 999–1000; details of shrine and ceremony, *Enthronement,* 71–74.

956 Decision on Guadalcanal at meeting Dec. 31, Hirohito's statement: Sugiyama, 2, Intro., 18.

957 Japanese evacuation of Guadalcanal, Feb. 1–7, 1943: Griffith, citing Japanese Gen. Miyazaki.

959 Kido's reasons for continuing war: my analysis based on reading of Kido, *Nikki,* for years 1943 and 1944; in early 1943, e.g., see entries for Feb. 4 and 23.; also interviews with Koizumi and most aristocratic of privileged sources.

960 To eat the flesh of Americans: there were several cases in the Marianas, IMTFE "Proceedings," 15033 ff.
Prisoner of war statistics: ibid., 14901.

961 Japan's policy on prisoners, Prisoner of War Information Bureau: IPS Document No. 814 contains extracts from Imperial Ordinance No. 1182 establishing P.O.W. camps and from Imperial Ordinance N. 1246 on the P.O.W. Information Bureau. Unfortunately IPS Document No. 1303 containing all imperial ordinances regarding prisoners of war remains classified; it is described in Library of Congress microfilm reels WT1-WT5 (Analyses of IPS Document Nos. 1–4097) but the text is not available. IPS Document No. 857 containing the incidental notebooks of Gen. Tamura Hiroshi when he was head of the P.O.W. Information Bureau is also classified. In general U.S. files on P.O.W.'s were classified in 1945. They must be voluminous because a sympathetic librarian at the War Documents Center in Alexandria, Va., once read me the U.S. government dossier kept on my family during the years when we were prisoners of the Japanese.

962 Tojo's P.O.W. proposal on behalf of Doolittle captives: Tanaka Takayoshi, testimony, IMTFE "Proceedings," 14285 ff.; for date of War Ministry meeting see ibid., 14379; for slogan "no work, no food" see telegram of June 5, 1942, from chief of P.O.W. Control Bureau to chief of staff, Taiwan Army, ibid., 14361. Uemura's objections are stressed by Tanaka, ibid., 14374.

963 Treatment of Wake prisoners: ibid., 14970 ff.

Prisoners as writers and announcers for Tokyo radio: IPS Document No. 975; James Bertram, in *Beneath the Shadow* (New York: John Day Co., 1947), 138–44, describes attempts to persuade him to join the staff of Tokyo Rose when he was a prisoner in the notorious Omori concentration camp. He was interrogated in the guardhouse there by the head of the Army Press Section's Cultural Program. This was a former Oxford acquaintance, the son of Marquis Ikeda, Empress Nagako's first cousin.

964 Tojo's statement to Zentsuji commandant: document introduced in evidence, IMTFE "Proceedings," 14424.

Tojo's address to P.O.W. camp commandants, June 25, 1942: ibid., 14427.

Police report on parade of P.O.W.'s in Pusan: ibid., 14518 ff.

966 Incident at Changi: Wigmore, 522–23.

Hirohito approved in principle of Burma-Thailand rail link: affidavit of Wakamatsu Tadakazu, IMTFE "Proceedings," 14633, stated that "Southern Army requested and Imperial General Headquarters decided" to build railroad in first half of 1943.

967–971 Prisoners from Singapore began work on railroad in Oct. 1942: many details of prisoners' treatment and conditions from Wigmore, 541–92.

971 Casualties of Burma-Thailand railroad: ibid., 588.

Roosevelt sanctioned assassination of Yamamoto: Davis, 16–17.

972 Lockheed Lightnings as match for Zeroes: Caidin, *Zero Fighter*, 140.

973 Action at Japanese beachheads on Guadalcanal: Morison, 5: 41–50.

Hirohito's audience with Gen. Sugiyama Jan 9: Sugiyama, 2: Intro., 19.

Battle of the Bismarck Sea: Morison, 5: 54–65.

974 Hirohito to Sugiyama March 3: Sugiyama, 2: Intro., 19–20.

975 Air strikes on Guadalcanal directed by Adm. Yamamoto from Rabaul: Morison, 5: 118–25.

Message announcing Yamamoto's itinerary: text of intercepted message in Davis, 6–7; Agawa, 309.

Yamamoto at flight officers' party, evening of Apr. 13: Davis, 103.

976 Yamamoto's exchange with Lt. Gen. Imamura: ibid., 105–6.

977 Adm. Nimitz and Comdr. Layton: ibid., 5–8; Morison, 6: 128–29, has concise account of the role of Nimitz.

Nimitz's message to Halsey and reply: Davis, 9–11.

Capt. Zacharias and Secretary Knox: ibid., 15, 19–20.

Operation Vengeance: order quoted, Potter, *Yamamoto*, 303–4; preparations, Davis, 116–142.

978 Details of flight and death of Yamamoto: ibid., 142–53; 160–70; 175–76.

979 Kido, "I felt shock and bitter grief": *Nikki*, 1029.

979–980 Yamamoto's funeral ceremonies: Agawa, 325–27.

980 Yamamoto's poems: adapted from Davis, 147, 199. I have retranslated the first to agree with the meter of the original and have somewhat condensed the second.

Kido attended funeral: *Nikki*, 1030.

N. 9: ibid., 1047.

981 Col. Tsuji Masanobu's career: see his book *Guadarukanaru, passim.*

982 Kido's report of Emperor's session with Tojo, subsequent changes in government: Kido, *Nikki,* 1005-9.

Kido continued contingency preparations for defeat: ibid., 1010, 1018.

983 Pipeline from Hirohito to Chiang Kai-shek: ibid., 1056 (entries for Sept. 22–23, 1943); also Shigemitsu, 287–90.

Konoye reported Mme. Chiang's information from Washington: Kido, *Nikki,* 1025.

983–984 Japan would honor diplomatic commitments, if necessary Hirohito would appoint imperial prince as prime minister: ibid., 1028.

Communism as threat, Japanese anti-Communists and Strike-North partisans brought back into government: Kido, *Nikki,* 1024.

N. 12: Tanaka MS, "Yoshiko": McAleavy, 243–46.

984 Kido discussed situation with Prince Takamatsu: Kido, *Nikki,* 1029.

Conference of puppet leaders discussed by Hirohito with Kido: ibid., 1030.

What to do with Hong Kong: The decision was finally to use Hong Kong as a counter in bargaining with Chiang; conference in the Imperial Presence, Sugiyama, 2:409.

ATTU: except as cited this section based on Morison, 7:41–50, and Howard Handleman, *Bridge to Victory: Story of the Reconquest of the Aleutians* (New York: Random House, 1954).

986 "I sincerely bowed . . .": Kido, *Nikki,* 1032.

Hirohito complained to Sugiyama: Sugiyama, 2: Intro., 20.

Tojo's audience with Hirohito and his warning that now Japan fought alone: Kido, *Nikki,* 1033–34; see also 1043.

Hirohito to Sugiyama on Attu tragedy: Sugiyama, 2: Intro., 20–21.

987 Emperor commended Sugiyama for success of raid in China: ibid., 21–22.

Kido found "ideas of great interest" in *War and Peace*: Kido, *Nikki,* 1041–42.

988 Hirohito summoned Adm. Komatsu, who reported Solomons could not be held: ibid., 1037–38; interview with retired Navy commander.

Hirohito at Imperial Headquarters, gave Tojo message for commanders in Solomons: Sato, "Tojo Hideki to daitoa senso," 390 ff. Hirohito's angry speech to Tojo: Sugiyama, 2: Intro., 23–24.

Tojo in Rabaul: Sato, "Tojo Hideki to daitoa senso," 390 ff.

989 Kido's efforts on behalf of air power: see, e.g., *Nikki* entries for July 6, 13, and Aug. 8, 11, 18, 20, 1943.

Chichibu's aide to co-ordinate peace dealings with Chiang: ibid., 1038. A participant in the venture was Col. Matsutani Makoto, the Army's contingency peace planner: Kase, 75–76; Butow, 26 n. 52.

Kido warned Hirohito, July 25, on Axis partners: Kido, *Nikki,* 1043.

Maj. Gen. Matsumoto advised Kido of police interest in peace plots: ibid., 1044.

990 Hirohito's exchange with Sugiyama, Aug. 5: Sugiyama, 2: Intro., 24–26.

Hirohito, "Can't we take offensive?" and substance of General Staff report on dubious possibilities for counteroffensive: ibid.

Intelligence studies prescribed events that took place: one of the outspoken statements of the most aristocratic of my sources; see also note on page 63.

Adm. Nomura Naokumi reported to Hirohito on serious situation in Germany: Kido, *Nikki,* 1046.

Hirohito at liaison conference Sept. 9: ibid., 1051.

992 Hirohito on transfer of divisions to Taiwan and Philippines and his arguments to Army chiefs on U.S. submarine operations: ibid., 1051–52; interview with retired Lt. Gen. Fujisawa.

Emperor quoted proverb to justify refusal to reinforce Marshalls: Kido, *Nikki,* 1052 (entry of Sept. 10, 1943).

Hirohito's private audience with Wang Ching-wei: ibid., 1055–56; see also 1053 (entry of Sept. 17, 1943). His comment afterward to Kido: ibid. 1056.

993 Dr. Okawa Shumei suggested to Kido that projected Higashikuni Cabinet have Lt. Gen. Ishiwara Kanji as advisor: ibid., 1057.

Okawa wanted matter discussed with Count Makino: ibid.

Makino finally came to Kido: ibid., 1075.

Suzuki Tei-ichi allowed to retire: ibid., 1060.

994 Prince Mikasa on China situation and leaders: ibid., 1061–62.

Nakano's assassination plot, details of Terai's spree and arrest: ibid., 1064 (entry of Oct. 21, 1943).

Nakano's suicide and rumors about it: ibid., 1065; Yanaga, *Since Perry,* 613.

995 Prince Mikasa and Lt. Gen. Anami went south Nov. 4: Kido, *Nikki,* 1067.

995–996 Meeting of Greater East Asia Conference, Tojo's views and comments: Kido, *Nikki,* 1064, 1066–67; Shigemitsu, 293–94; news reports in *Mainichi, Asahi, Syonan Times;* observation about the lack of braziers for representatives of conquered countries from interview with Tanaka.

996 Hirohito gave lunch in palace to delegates: Kido, *Nikki,* 1067.

Nov. 19, Kido received Takagi's pessimistic report and heard of Matsutani's view that Japan might be decimated: ibid., 1070; interview with retired Navy commander; Butow, *Japan's Decision,* 20–21, 26–27.

Higashikuni's recruiting lunch, Kido's conference with Hirohito on Takagi's report, negotiations between Wang and Chiang broken off: Kido, *Nikki,* 1070–72.

996–997 Hirohito visited Yamamoto's tomb, Kido at Prince Saionji's: ibid., 1073.

997 Count Kabayama reported on U.S. feelings about Pacific war: ibid., 1075. Hirohito's own appraisal of war prospects, his conclusions conveyed to Kido Jan. 4, and Kido's memorandum of Jan. 6: ibid., 1075–78.

997–998 Substance of Kido's "blueprint for postwar Japan": ibid., 1078–79.

29.   The Fall of the Homeland

For this chapter, in addition to sources cited or listed in the bibliography, I have drawn for background on: W. G. Burchett, *Wingate Adventure* (Melbourne: F. W. Cheshire, 1944); Claude A. Buss, "Inside Wartime Japan" (*Life*, January 24, 1944); Dorothy Guyot, "The Burma Independence Army: A Political Movement in Military Garb" (Paper read at Association for Asian Studies meeting, San Francisco, April 2, 1965); Tom Harrison, *World Within: A Borneo Story* (London: The Cresset Press, 1959); A. V. H. Hartendorp, *The Santo Tomas Story* (New York: McGraw Hill, 1964); Vern Haughland, *The AAF Against Japan* (New York: Harper and Brothers, 1948); Hayashi Saburo, *Taiheiyo Senso Rikusen Gaishi* [A History of Land Warfare Conditions in the Pacific War] (Tokyo: Iwanami Shinsho, 1951); Harold Riegelman, *Caves of Biak: An American Officer's Experiences in the Southwest Pacific*, with prefaces by Robert Eichelberger and Hu Shih (New York: Dial Press, 1955); Frederic Stevens, *Santo Tomas Internment Camp*, foreword by Douglas MacArthur (Limited private edition printed at Stratford House, 1946); Usui Katsumi, "Kuten suru senryo seisaku: Daitoa kaigi" [Vain Occupation Policy: The Greater East Asia Conference] *Asahi Jyanaru* (Asaki Journal), 7, No. 45 (30 October 1965), 74 ff.

1001 U.S. Fleet for Gilberts invasion: Morison, 7, Appendix II.
Makin and Tarawa: ibid., 7:121–74.
Marshalls: ibid., 7:230–304.

1001–1004 AIR NAVY: this section based on Kido, *Nikki*, 1082–87, supplemented by interviews with retired Navy commander; also Kido, *Nikki*, 104 (May 1, 1944).

1004 THE "CHUNGKING MANEUVER": Kido, *Nikki*, 1088; Hayashi Shigeru et al, 2:39–46; Matsumoto interviews; also Butow, *Japan's Decision*, 51–54.

1004–1006 SACKING THE STAFF: Kido, *Nikki*, 1089–90; Sugiyama, 2: Intro., 27–28, 32–33.

1006 Press acknowledged direct imperial guidance: *Asahi*, Feb. 27, 1944.
Aircraft production: U.S. Strategic Bombing Survey, *Summary Report*, 9; goals: Kido, *Nikki*, 1087.

1007 Attack on Kohima: Slim, 254–95; Collier, 413–17.
Casualty reports from Japanese sources: Kojima, 2:143–59; Hattori, 989–93.

1008 MacArthur cuts off Rabaul: Bougainville casualties, Morison, 7:430.
Biak and Noemfoor casualties; Morison, 133–40.
Hirohito quick to realize: my interpretation of his immediate consideration of a more popular and pro-American cabinet; see memorandum of June 15, 1944, Kido, *Nikki*, 1110–111.
Battle of the Philippine Sea: ships engaged, Morison, 8, Appendices II and III; ships lost: ibid., 8:233, and Inoguchi et al., 25.

1009 Jo's radiogram, including its text: Inoguchi et al., 27–29; his career, Zacharias, 182.

1009–1011 Hirohito considers Jo's idea; blames Shimada for Philippine Sea disaster; gives tentative authorization for kamikaze program: Kido, *Nikki*, 1112–113, supplemented by interviews with retired Navy commander.

1010 Planes lost in operational use: U.S. Strategic Bombing Survey, *Summary Report,* 9.

1011 Political objections to kamikaze idea: "Handling of Special Air Attacks by the High Command," Kawabe Torashiro, *Statements,* 2:67–68. Okamura also pleads for kamikaze: Inoguchi et al, 139–40.

1012 Saipan population: Morison 8:152.
Camp for surrendering Japanese: Morison, 8:339; Otis Cary, interview.
Despite Tojo, Saipan suicides encouraged: Kido, *Nikki,* 1114 (July 1); also 1112–113.

1013 Nagumo suicide: Toland, *Rising Sun,* 511–12.
Main garrison dead: Morison, 8:336.
Civilian suicides: ibid., 338.
Total casualties: ibid., 339.
Guan casualties: ibid., 401.
Tinian: ibid., 364.
Tinian casualties: ibid., 369.

1013–1015 Tojo ousted, Hirohito withdraws from limelight: this summary is drawn from Kido, *Nikki,* 1115–129.
Ohka program: Nakajima et al, 140–41.
Peace Faction opposition: Kido, *Nikki,* 1137.

1016 Final Strategy Japan: Morison, 12:9–11.
Morotai: ibid., 24.
Peleliu: ibid., 35–36; 41–43.
Murai identified: Hata's "Personnel Records"; see also Maj. Frank O. Hough, *The Assault on Peleliu,* (U.S. Marine Corps, Historical Division H.Q., 1950), Appendix F, "Mission of Murai."

1017 SHO: Hattori, 673–89.
Yamashita Cabinet avoided, Yamashita reposted: Kido, *Nikki,* 1143–144.
Yamashita at Fort McKinley: Potter, *Soldier Must Hang,* 110.

1018 Halsey's fast carrier task force: Morison, 12:50.
Taiwan air strike: ibid., 104, 106.
U.S. armada: ibid., Appendix I, 113.
Morishima to Moscow: Kido, *Nikki,* 1146.

1019 Rescript on Taiwan air disaster: Kido, *Nikki,* 1148 (entries for Oct. 16, 18, and 19, 1944).
Hirohito and Onishi: retired Navy commander explained that the imperial messenger *(gosai)* mentioned by Kido in his entry for October 19, *Nikki,* 1148, is Onishi.
Onishi's words at Mabalacat: Inoguchi et al, 7.
Admiral Arima's example: ibid., 37 and n.
"Chances of scoring a hit": ibid., 8.

1019–1029 Battle of Leyte Gulf: Ito, 120–79; Morison, 12:159–338; d'Albas, 301–35; Inoguchi et al, 47–78, on kamikaze operations.

1020 Landings at Leyte: Morison, 12:130–38.
"Southward Movement of Ozawa Decoy Force," *Translations,* 3; No. 5.
Onishi at Mabalacat: Inoguchi et al, 19.

1025 Battle of the escort carriers: Morison, 12:242–88.

1029 Fate of derelicts: *Nachi*, ibid., 239; *Kiso*, ibid., 356; *Kongo*, ibid., 410; *Kumano*, ibid., 357.

Total losses, Japanese and American: ibid., Appendix II (Japanese) and Appendix I (U.S.).

1029–1030 Emperor's message to kamikaze: Kido, *Nikki*, 1148; interview with retired Navy commander; Inoguchi et al, 64.

1030 Leyte casualties: Morison, 12:397; Toland, *Rising Sun*, 607.
Luzon casualties: Smith, Appendix H, 692, 694.
Iwo casualties: Morison, 14:68–69.
Incendiary raids: Berger, 145.
Okinawa casualties: U.S. Strategic Bombing Survey, *Campaigns of Pacific War*, 331; Appleman et al, 473.

1031 N. 7: Survey on Japan's will to fight: U.S. Strategic Bombing Survey, *Effects of Strategic Bombing on Japanese Morale*, also *Summary Report*, 21.

1032 Warning leaflets: Berger, 146, 149.
Hirohito's bleak personal prospects: Coox, 100; Koizumi interview. It may be that Hirohito did not seriously entertain any thoughts of suicide or abdication. He knew, however, that some of his samurai retainers would expect one or the other of him as a matter of honor.
Lingayen Gulf landing: Morison, 13:123–30, 193–96.

1033 15,000 Japanese sailors and Marines to Manila: ibid., 196–97.
Intramuros casualties: Smith, 306–7.
Japanese intentions for war prisoners: see, e.g., telegram entitled Army Asia (Secret) No. 2257 introduced in evidence, "Proceedings," 14533; or Taikoku Camp document on "final disposition" introduced ibid., 14725, or file of radio messages concerning "release without record" from chief P.O.W. administrator, Tokyo, to chief of staff, Taiwan Army, IPS Document No. 2697.
Palawan massacre: Lord Russell, 88–91.

1034 The prison hulks: ibid., 93–107.

1035 Vice war minister telegram on war prisoners: IPS Document No. 2697.

1036 Kamikaze spirit and effectiveness: e.g., Suzuki Kantaro quoted in Inoguchi et al, 189–90.
"Death without meaning": Sakai Saburo, 319; also 306, 309.
Flight described in detail: ibid., 302–25.

1037 Details of March 9 raid: Berger, 127–31.

1038 Fire raid casualties: Kato, 215, 224.
Hirohito moved underground: Coox, 24.

1038–1039 Hirohito on March 9: ibid., 28.
N. 10: Poison gas proposal: Newcomb, 240.

1039 Spare Imperial Palace: Toland, *Rising Sun*, 744.
Kido advised informal visit to ruins: Kido, *Nikki*, 1176–177.
N. 11: U.S. Strategic Bombing Survey, *Japanese Morale*; also *Summary Report*, 21.

1040 *Yamato* lost: Ito Masanori, 184–90.
Details of Cho's death: Tanaka interview; see also Appleman, et al,

Okinawa, the Last Battle, United States Army in World War II: The War in the Pacific, vol. 1 (Washington, D.C.: Department of the Army, Office of the Chief of Military History, 1948).

1041 In Japanese the equivalent of "it never rains but it pours" is "while crying stung by a bee on the face." On top of the fire bombing the atomic bomb stung cruelly. Kato, *Lost War,* 217.

1042 "Emperor . . . retained the people's faith": *Summary Report,* 21. Imperial Family Council: Kido, *Nikki,* 1225; see also Coox, 126.

1042–1043 Anami's visit to Prince Mikasa: Craig, 148; Toland, *Rising Sun,* 824.

1043–1044 Installation of Lincoln's bust: Oya, *Ichiban nagai hi,* 202; Oya, *Longest Day,* 312. (The choice of words in the Japanese text seems to me to convey a richer feeling of belly talk and belly laughter than that of the English text.)

Epilogue: New Clothes

This brief review of Japanese events since 1945 is based on the common record of news reports and on conversations with Japanese. I have cited below a few specific sources for details which seem to me to have gone unappreciated. Essentially my account is an interpretation of events —an opinion, if you will—suggesting the relevance of what has gone before in these pages to what may come after. I have drawn on no state papers and no diaries of statesmen because none are available. I look forward, however, to the gradual opening of such records in the years and decades ahead.

1045 Japanese arsenals turned over to native patriots: e.g., see *N.Y. Times,* Sept. 9, 1945, and Singapore *Times,* Nov. 20, Dec. 12, 1945.

1046 Cheat-the-enemy tactics: see Tsuji, *Underground Escape,* 1–90. N. 1. from interviews with retired Maj. Gen. Kajiura Ginjiro.

1047 6,000 Japanese prisoners attacked by tribesmen on Borneo: K. G. Tregonning, *A History of Modern Sabah (North Borneo, 1881–1963),* 2d ed. (Singapore: University of Malaya Press, 1965), 217–221.

1049 HANGING THE TIGER: this section based on "Yamashita Trial Proceedings" (unpublished papers, National War Memorial, Canberra), *passim.* See also Potter, *Soldier Must Hang,* 170–97, and Reel, *passim.*

1050 News reports quoted: Potter, 180.
Yamashita took pains to remove U.S. prisoners from Baguio: author's experience; Watanabe Hiroshi, *Statements,* 4:448–53; see also Todani Naotoshi, *Yama Yukaba Kusamusu Shikabane* [Walk in the Mountains, Rot as a Corpse in the Grass] (Osaka: Bunsho-in, 1965), *passim.*

1051–52 Yamashita in his own defense: excerpted from Yamashita's final statements to the court, *N.Y. Times,* Dec. 1, 1945.
N. 5: Taylor quoted: Neil Sheehan article, *N.Y. Times,* Jan. 9, 1946; Reel protested: letter to *N.Y. Times,* Jan. 19, 1946. See also *Newsweek,* Feb. 22, March 22, 1946.

1052–1053 Justice Frank Murphy quoted: *N.Y. Times,* Feb. 5, 1946.

1053–1054 Gen. MacArthur's statement on the Yamashita case:

Reminiscences, 295–96.

1054 Gen. Yamashita's last hours: Potter, *Soldier Must Hang,* 194.
CUTTING OFF THE NOSE: this section based on "Honma Trial Proceedings" (unpublished papers, National War Memorial, Canberra).

1055 Honma's American lawyers active in his defense: Toland, *Rising Sun,* 320 n.
Justice Murphy quoted: ibid.
MacArthur defended verdict: *Reminiscences,* 296–98.

1056 Honma's last letter to his children: Toland, *Rising Sun,* MacArthur quoted: 298.

1059 Okawa's behavior at trial opening: John Luter, Dispatch No. 284 to *Time* magazine; in Okawa's ravings Luter included: "Do you know Happy Chandler? I'm going into business with him."
Okawa raved to reporters: Gayn, *Japan Diary,* 209; *Newsweek,* May 13, 1946, cited in Butow, *Tojo,* 485.

1060 Official diagnosis of Okawa: ibid., 486.
Many Japanese impressed by evidence of savagery: Takeda, 120–23.
Shigemitsu asked Hirohito to his face: Kase Toshikazu, in *N.Y. Times,* Sept. 2, 1970; see also his *Journey to the "Missouri,"* 220 ff.

1061 A Japanese newspaperman observed: Tony Kase, interview.
Japanese attitudes at beginning of trial, and judgment declared *hidoi*: Carl Mydans, Dispatch No. 770 to *Life* International, Nov. 13, 1948.

1062 "the comic helplessness of being Japanese": Faubion Bowers (a personal aide-de-camp to MacArthur, 1945–46), "How Japan Won the War," *N.Y. Times Magazine,* Apr. 30, 1970, 39. See also Yoshida, 59.

1063 FACTORY POWER: In this brief recital of Japan's economic resurgence I have consulted Louis Kraar, *Fortune,* Sept. 1970, 126; Takashi Oka, *N.Y. Times,* Jan. 5, 1970; "What Makes Japanese Business Grow," Boston Consulting Group (unpublished printed material); "The Japanese Economy: A Continuing Miracle?" *Interplay,* Dec. 1969/Jan. 1970; James C. Abegglen, "The Economic Growth of Japan," *Scientific American,* March 1970, 31.

1065 Merchant families have ties of marriage to nobility: for a full account of merchant-noble intermarriage see Suzuki Yukio, esp. the genealogies.

1066 "Occupation was hampered by its lack of knowledge . . .": quoted, in Bowers, "How Japan Won the War," 37. The extent of U.S. ignorance remains a moot point. Gen. MacArthur's Staff, *Historical Report of Operations in the Southwest Pacific Area,* completed in 1951, told the story from the general's point of view (vol. 1) and from captured documents by the Japanese commanders (vol. 2); it has remained classified. Morison, 12:ix, says of it: "Only three copies were printed (and don't ask me where I saw one, I can't tell!)."
Roughly $9 million spent on war crime trials: Carl Mydans, Dispatch No. 770 to *Life* International, Nov. 13, 1948.

1068 PRIVY POCKETING: this section based on Kuroda, 185 ff., supplemented by *N.Y. Times,* Dec. 27, 1967, Dec. 27, 1968, Jan. 25, 1970.

1070 Another $2 million to build new summer villa for the Emperor:

N.Y. Times, Jan. 13, 1968.

Kanin and Fushimi scandals: Fujishima, 62 ff.

1071 Proprietress of the Isaribi: *Shukan Asahi,* Feb. 11, 1966, 15.

1071–1072 Ohara and Higashikuni religion: Fujishima, 68; Matsumoto Seicho, interview with Higashikuni, *Bungei Shunjo,* Jan. 1968, 170 ff.

1074 "Three Nothings Incident," Mikami Taku, and rightist rally of Feb. 26, 1965: Murofushi, 247–49.

Get-together of assassins a warning: interview with retired lieutenant general.

1075 National Foundation Day revived: *N.Y. Times,* Feb. 11, 1967.

LONE CRY OF ANGUISH: this section based on Donald Keene, "Mishima," *N.Y. Times Book Review,* Jan. 3, 1971, 5; *Time* magazine, Dec. 7, 1970, 32–37; Takashi Oka, "Japan's Self-Defense Force Wins a Skirmish with the Past," *N.Y. Times Magazine,* Feb. 28, 1971.

1076 Mishima involved in controversy with son of Count Arima: conversation with Tony Kase; also Oka, in *N.Y. Times,* June 1, 1970.

1078 Novelist Arima's opinion of Mishima's death: private correspondence.

"The Emperor should be a symbol": Staff Sergeant Amma Takaji quoted by Oka, *N.Y. Times Magazine,* Feb. 28, 1971.

1079 Hirohito's poem: *Asahi,* Jan. 6, 1971.

BIBLIOGRAPHY

Abend, Hallett. *Chaos in Asia.* New York: Ives Washburn, 1939.

————. *My Life in China, 1926–41.* New York: Harcourt, Brace, 1943. Abend was correspondent for *The New York Times* in China.

———— and Billingham, Anthony J. *Can China Survive?* New York: Ives Washburn, 1936.

Agawa Hiroshi, *Yamamoto Isoroku.* Tokyo: Shincho Shahan, 1965. Anecdotal and disorganized, but the most authoritative Japanese biography.

Agoncillo, Teodoro A. *The Fateful Years: Japan's Adventure in the Philippines, 1941–45.* 2 vols. Quezon City, Philippines: R. P. Garcia Publishing Co., 1965.

Aikawa Gisuke. "Manshu keizai shikai no ki-pointo" [Key Points of Manchurian Financial Management]. In *Himerareta Showa-shi.*

Akimoto Shunkichi. *Exploring the Japanese Ways of Life.* Tokyo: Tokyo News Service, 1961. A compendium of cultural and historical lore by a Japanese connoisseur.

Allen, G. C. *A Short Economic History of Modern Japan.* London: George Allen and Unwin, 1962.

Amrine, Michael. *The Great Decision: The Secret History of the Atomic Bomb.* New York: G. P. Putnam's Sons, 1959. Well-researched, well-written reconstruction.

Ando Yoshio. "Senso to kazoku" [*The War and the Imperial Family*]. Part 1, *Ekonomisuto,* August 31, 1965, pp. 85 ff. (interview with Prince Higashikuni); Part 2, ibid., February 22, 1966, pp. 84 ff. (interview with Prince Mikasa); Part 3, ibid., March 1, 1966, pp. 84 ff. (interview with Prince Mikasa).

————, ed. *Showa keizai-shi e no shogen* [Evidence Pertaining to Economic History in the Reign of Hirohito]. Tokyo: Mainichi Shinbun-sha, 1966.

Araki Sadao. "Doran Showa ni tatsu tenno" [The Emperor Stood Forth

During a Disturbance of His Reign]. In *Tenno hakusho* [White Paper on the Emperor], *Bungei Shunju,* October, 1956.

————. "Nikka jihen totsunyu made" [Up Until Japan Rushed into the China Incident]. In *Himerareta Showa-shi.*

Asahi, Tokyo and Osaka editions. One of Japan's two leading daily newspapers.

Asahi. *Juyo shimen no shichijugo-nen: Meiji juni-nen—Showa nyukyu-nen* [Momentous News Columns of Seventy-five Years: 1879–1954]. Tokyo: Asahi Shinbun-sha, 1954.

ATIS. See United States of America, Supreme Command for Allied Powers, Far East: Allied Translator and Interpreter Section.

Attiwill, Kenneth. *The Singapore Story.* London: Frederich Muller, 1959. Scathing comment by a participant.

Australia, Commonwealth of, Department of External Affairs. "Cablegrams, 1945–1946." Unpublished material on file at Commonwealth Archives, Canberra.

Ballou, Robert O. *Shinto: The Unconquered Enemy.* New York: Viking Press, 1945.

Barr, Pat. *The Coming of the Barbarians: The Opening of Japan to the West, 1853–1870.* New York: E. P. Dutton & Co., 1967.

Beasley, W. G. *The Modern History of Japan.* New York: Frederick A. Praeger, 1963. Outstanding on the period 1853–1868.

Benda, Harry J. *The Crescent and the Rising Sun: Indonesian Islam under the Japanese Occupation, 1942–1945.* The Hague: W. van Hoeve Ltd., 1958.

Benedict, Ruth. *The Chrysanthemum and the Sword.* Boston: Houghton Mifflin, 1946. An anthropological classic.

Bennett, H. Gordon. *Why Singapore Fell.* Sydney: Angus and Robertson, 1944. By the commander of Australian forces in Malaya.

Berger, Carl. *B-29: The Superfortress.* New York: Ballantine Books, 1970.

Borg, Dorothy: *The United States and the Far Eastern Crisis of 1933–1938.* Cambridge, Mass.: Harvard University Press, 1964.

Borton, Hugh. *Japan's Modern Century.* New York: The Ronald Press, 1955. An over-all social and economic history since 1850.

Brereton, Lewis H. *The Brereton Diaries: 3 October 1941–8 May 1945.* New York: William Morrow & Co., 1946. Brereton was U.S. Army Air Corps commander in the Philippines, 1941.

Brines, Russell. *MacArthur's Japan.* Philadelphia: J. B. Lippincott Co., 1948. An able journalist's return to Japan in 1945–46.

"Brocade Banner". See United States Army, Far East Command, Intelligence, Civil Intelligence Section.

Brooks, Lester. *Behind Japan's Surrender: The Secret Struggle That Ended an Empire.* New York: McGraw-Hill Book Co., 1968. Reflects valuable interviewing of living protagonists.

Bullock, Cecil. *Etajima: The Dartmouth of Japan.* London: Sampson Low, Marston & Co., 1942. The Japanese Naval Academy.

Bunce, William K., ed. *Religions in Japan: Buddhism, Shinto, Christianity.* Rutland, Vt., and Tokyo: Charles E. Tuttle Co., 1955.

Bush, Lewis. *Clutch of Circumstance.* Tokyo: Bungei Shunju, 1956. Japanese concentration camps through the eyes of a Japanophile.

————. *Japanalia.* 4th ed., rev. and enl. New York: David MacKay Co., 1959. A useful glossary to things Japanese.

————. *Land of the Dragonfly.* London: Robert Hale, 1959. A short history of Japan.

Butow, Robert J. C. *Japan's Decision to Surrender.* Hoover Library on War, Revolution and Peace, Publication No. 24. Stanford, California: Stanford University Press, 1954. Readable, a model of documentation, based largely on IMTFE materials.

————. *Tojo and the Coming of the War.* Princeton, N.J.: Princeton University Press, 1961. The most detailed account available in English of the years 1936–45 from the Japanese point of view.

Byas, Hugh. *Government By Assassination.* New York: Alfred A. Knopf, 1942. A classic by the prewar *New York Times* correspondent in Tokyo.

————. *The Japanese Enemy: His Power and His Vulnerability.* New York: Alfred A. Knopf, 1942.

Caidin, Martin. *The Ragged, Rugged Warriors.* New York: E. P. Dutton & Co., 1966. Bataan.

————. *Zero Fighter.* With introduction by Sakai Saburo. New York: Ballantine Books, 1969.

Chamberlain, William Henry. *Japan Over Asia.* Boston: Little, Brown & Co., 1938. Temperate account of Japanese aggression in China, 1928–37.

Churchill, Winston S. *The Second World War.* 4, The Hinge of Fate; 5, Closing the Ring; 6, Triumph and Tragedy. Boston: Houghton Mifflin Co., 1950, 1951, 1953.

Ciano, Galeazzo. *Ciano Diaries, 1939–1945.* Edited by Hugh Gibson. Garden City, N.Y.: Doubleday & Co., 1946.

Clubb, O. Edmund. *20th Century China.* New York: Columbia University Press, 1946. A history by a U.S. Foreign Service officer with twenty years' experience in China.

Cohen, Jerome B. *Japan's Economy in War and Reconstruction.* Minneapolis: University of Minnesota Press, 1949.

Collier, Basil. *The War in the Far East, 1941–1945: A Military History.* New York: William Morrow and Co., 1969.

Coox, Alvin. *Japan: The Final Agony.* New York: Ballantine Books, 1970. Last year of the war by a Japan expert who has interviewed many of the participants.

Craig, William. *The Fall of Japan.* New York: Dial Press, 1967. A journalistic reconstruction that benefits from astute interviewing of surviving participants.

Craigie, Sir Robert. *Behind the Japanese Mask.* London: Hutchinson & Co., 1945. Craigie was British ambassador in Tokyo before the war.

Cresswell, H. T., Hiroka, J., and Namba, R. *A Dictionary of Military Terms (English-Japanese and Japanese-English).* American ed. Chicago: University of Chicago Press, 1942.

Crow, Carl, ed. *Japan's Dream of World Empire: The Tanaka Memorial.* 3rd ed. New York: Harper & Brothers, 1942.

Crowley, James B. *Japan's Quest for Autonomy: National Security and Foreign Policy 1930–1938.* Princeton, N.J.: Princeton University Press, 1966. A scholarly study which contains new material drawn from Japanese military position papers written in the early 1930's.

D'Albas, Andrieu. *Death of a Navy: Japanese Naval Action in World*

War II. New York: The Devin-Adair Co., 1957.

Davis, Burke. *Get Yamamoto.* New York: Random House, 1969.

Davis, Forrest, and Lindley, Ernest K. *How War Came: An American White Paper from the Fall of France to Pearl Harbor.* New York: Simon and Schuster, 1942. A lively, well-researched account of doings in the White House just before the war.

Deakin, F. W., and Storry, G. R. *The Case of Richard Sorge.* New York: Harper & Row, 1966. A semipopular account of the Sorge case by two British scholars, good in its review of the German documentation.

Dexter, David. *The New Guinea Offensives.* Vol. VI, Series 1 (Army), Australia in the War of 1939–1945. Canberra: Australian War Memorial, 1961.

Dull, Paul S., and Umemura, Michael Takaaki. *The Tokyo Trials: A Functional Index to the Proceedings of the International Military Tribunal for the Far East.* Ann Arbor, Mich.: University of Michigan Press, 1957.

Dyess, Wm. E. *Death March from Bataan.* Sydney: Angus and Robertson Ltd., 1945. One of the best of many firsthand accounts.

Eichelberger, Robert L. *Our Jungle Road to Tokyo.* New York: Viking Press, 1950.

Ekins, H. R., and Wright, Theon. *China Fights for Her Life.* New York: McGraw-Hill, Whittlesey House, 1938. Hard-boiled, journalistic, full of information.

Elsbree, Willard H. *Japan's Role in Southeast Asian Nationalist Movements, 1940–45.* Cambridge, Mass.: Harvard University Press, 1953.

Enthronement of the One Hundred Twenty-fourth Emperor of Japan. Edited by Benjamin W. Fleisher. Tokyo: Japan Advertiser, 1928.

Fairbank, John K., Reischauer, Edwin O., and Craig, Albert M. *East Asia: The Modern Transformation.* Vol. II, *A History of East Asian Civilization.* Boston: Houghton Mifflin Co., 1964. A useful over-all textbook.

Far Eastern Advisory Commission, Australian Delegation. Unpublished papers, Commonwealth Archives, Canberra. I-3: "Events Concerning Japan, August 20–December 30, 1945."

————. A4-9, Appendix A: Memoranda from Truman to MacArthur.

————. A4-9, unlettered appendix: Intelligence summary of American leaders' views regarding Emperor.

————. A7: New Zealand General Policy with Regard to Japan.

————. WC 1-1/5: Deliberations on directives of U.S. Joint Chiefs of Staff.

————. WC 5-401: On Japanese War Criminals.

Far Eastern Commission, Australian Delegation. Unpublished papers, Commonwealth Archives, Canberra. "Interim Report, 11 February 1946." Annex I: Notes by W. D. Forsyth on talk with MacArthur, Tuesday, January 29, 1946, 11.40 AM–1.40 PM, Dai Ichi Building.

————. Ibid., Annex II: Summary of Principal Orders by S.C.A.P. to Japanese Government.

————. Ibid., Annex VII: Miscellaneous Notes by Members of the Australian Delegation.

Far Eastern Commission, Pacific Affairs Division. "Memorandum to Acting Secretary on Reform of the Japanese Constitution, 18 March 1946."

Farago, Ladislas. *The Broken Seal: The Story of "Operation Magic" and the Pearl Harbor Disaster*. New York: Random House, 1967. A readable account that reflects acquaintance with intelligence information that is not found elsewhere. Farago was in charge of research and planning in the psychological warfare branch of the Office of Naval Intelligence during the last two years of the war.

Feis, Herbert. *The China Tangle: The American Effort in China from Pearl Harbor to the China Mission*. Princeton, N.J.: Princeton University Press, 1953.

————. *Japan Subdued: The Atomic Bomb and the End of the War in the Pacific*. Princeton, N.J.: Princeton University Press, 1961. Like Morison, Feis combines diplomacy and discretion with good writing and the highest order of scholarship.

————. *The Road to Pearl Harbor: The Coming of the War Between the United States and Japan*. Princeton, N.J.: Princeton University Press, 1950.

Fleisher, Wilfrid. *Volcanic Isle*. Garden City, N.Y.: Doubleday, Doran & Co., 1941. A firsthand account of Tokyo before the war by one of the few Western editors who continued to publish there until 1940.

Fuchida, Mutsuo and Okumiya Masatake. *Midway: The Japanese Navy's Story*. Annapolis, Md.: United States Naval Institute, 1955. By members of the Japanese Navy General Staff who participated in Midway.

Fujimoto Harutake. *Ningen Ishiwara Kanji* [Ishiwara Kanji as a Human Being]. Tokyo: Taisen Sangyo-sha, 1959.

Fujishima Taisuke. *Nihon no joryu shakai* [Japan's High Society]. Tokyo: Kobun-sha, 1965. An exposé by an insider.

Futara Yoshinori, Count, and Sawada Setsuzo. *The Crown Prince's European Tour*. English ed. Osaka: Osaka Mainichi Publishing Co., 1926.

Gayn, Mark J. *Japan Diary*. New York: William Sloane Associates, 1948. A firsthand account of the early days of the Occupation by a journalist who had worked in Japan before the war.

Gendai-shi shiryo: see Shimada Toshihiko; Obi Toshihito; Usui Katsumi; Tsunoda Jun.

Gibbs, John M. "On Prisoner of War Camps in Japan and Japanese Controlled Areas as Taken from Reports of Interned American Prisoners." Mimeographed report, dated 31 July 1946, prepared for the American Prisoner of War Information Bureau, Liaison and Research Branch.

Gibney, Frank. *Five Gentlemen of Japan: The Portrait of a Nation's Character*. New York: Farrar, Straus and Young, 1953.

Gill, G. Hermon. *Royal Australian Navy, 1939–42*. Vol. I, Series 2 (Navy), Australia in the War of 1939–1945. Canberra: Australian War Memorial, 1957.

Grenfell, Russell. *Main Fleet to Singapore*. London: Faber and Faber, Ltd., 1951.

Grew, Joseph C. *Ten Years in Japan*. New York: Simon & Schuster, 1944. Grew was U.S. ambassador in Tokyo from 1932 to Pearl Harbor.

————. *Turbulent Era: A Diplomatic Record of Forty Years, 1904–1945*. 2 vols. Boston: Houghton Mifflin, 1952.

Griffith, Samuel B., II. *The Battle for Guadalcanal*. Philadelphia: J. B. Lippincott Co., 1963. A Marine officer's research into the campaign in which he took part.

Guillain, Robert. *Le peuple japonais et la guerre: Choses vues 1939–*

1946. Paris: Juilliard, 1947. A perceptive journalistic view from the Left Bank.

Gunther, John. *Riddle of MacArthur: Japan, Korea and the Far East.* New York: Harper & Brothers, 1951.

Hanaya Tadashi. "Manshu jihen wa koshite keikaku sareta" [A Plan Was Made for Bringing About the Manchurian Incident]. In *Himerareta Showa-shi.*

Hanayama Shinsho. *The Way of Deliverance: Three Years With the Condemned Japanese War Criminals.* New York: Charles Scribner's Sons, 1950. By the Buddhist priest who shrove them.

Harada Kumao. *Saionji-ko to seikyoku* [Prince Saionji and the Political Situation]. 8 vols. Tokyo: Iwanami Shoten, 1950–1956. These are the original for United States Army, Far East Command, Civil Intelligence Section, Special Report "Saionji-Harada Memoirs." Also, *Saionji-ko to Seikyoku Bekkan,* a supplementary volume to the above, containing index, Harada's original notes, appendices on the period 1927–1929 and 16 valuable source telegrams, position papers etc.

Hargreaves, Reginald. *Red Sun Rising: The Siege of Port Arthur.* Philadelphia and New York: J. B. Lippincott Co., 1962.

Harrison, E. J. *Fighting Spirit of Japan.* London: W. Foulsham & Co., Ltd., n.d. An early account of judo, kendo, and other Japanese warrior exercises by an enthusiast.

Hashimoto Mochitsura. *Sunk: The Story of the Japanese Submarine Fleet 1942–1945* (tr. by E. H. M. Colegrave). London: Cassell and Company Ltd., 1954.

Hata Ikuhiko. *Gun fuashizuma* [Army Fascism]. Tokyo: Kawade Shobo, 1962. A historian trained in Western methods of documentation, who is employed by the Japanese Self-Defense Forces.

————. *Nichu senso-shi* [History of the Sino-Japanese War]. Tokyo: Kawade Shobo, 1961. Concise and well documented.

————. "Higeki no Showa-shi" [The Tragedy of Hirohito's Reign]. In *Himerareta Showa-shi.*

————. "Notebooks." Manuscript materials containing names of Japanese military attachés by city and the commanders and chiefs of staff of Imperial Guards Divisions and Divisions 1 through 43, Japanese Imperial Army, 1900–1945; also names of commanders and chiefs of staff of Divisions 44 through 116, Area Army commanders and chiefs of staff, and the Army officer corps seniority list for Sept. 1944.

————. "Personnel Records." Postings by date of leading Japanese Army and Navy officers. Many of these career summaries are reproduced in appendices to his *Gun fuashizuma* and *Nichu senso-shi;* many others, mostly incomplete, are in manuscript.

Hattori Takushiro. *Daitoa senso zen-shi* [Complete History of the Greater East Asia War], revised by Naruse Yasushi. One volume, divided into 11 books and appendix, plus separate folder of maps and charts. Tokyo: Hara Shobo, 1965. Hattori was confidential secretary to Gen. Tojo Hideki, 1941–43, then chief of the Operations Section of the Army General Staff.

Hayashi Fusao. *Daitoa senso koteiron* [Affirmative Discussion of the Greater East Asia War]. Tokyo: Bancho Shobo, 1965.

Hayashi Masayoshi, ed. *Himerareta Showa-shi* [Hidden History of

Hirohito's Reign]. Tokyo: Mainichi Shimbun-ki, 1965.

Hayashi Shigeru, Ando Yoshio, Imai Sei-ichi, and Oshima Taro. *Nihon Shusen-shi.* 3 vols. [The History of the End of Japan's War]. Tokyo: Yomiuri Shimbun-sha, 1965.

Heusken, Henry. *Japan Journal, 1855–1861.* Trans. and ed. by Jeannette C. Van der Corput and Robert A. Wilson. New Brunswick, N.J.: Rutgers University Press, 1964.

Higashifushimi Kunihide. *Asahiko shinno ryakureki* [A Brief Biography of Prince Asahiko]. Kyoto: Privately printed, 1965. A scholarly monograph based on family recollections, written by Empress Nagako's brother about the activities of his grandfather, Prince Asahiko, who was chief advisor to Emperor Komei at the time of the coming of Perry.

Higashikuni Naruhiko. *Higashikuni nikki* [Higashikuni Diary]. Tokyo: Tokuma Shoten, 1968.

————. *Watashi no kiroku* [My Personal Diary]. Tokyo: Toho Shobo, 1947.

Himerareta Showa-shi [Hidden History of the Reign of Hirohito], *Bessatsu Chisei No. 5.* Tokyo: Kawade Shobo, 1956. A collection of articles by leading participants in the events of 1928–1945, cited by author: Aikawa Gisuke; Araki Sadao; Hanaya Tadashi; Imamura Hitoshi; Ito Nobufumi; Katakura Tadashi; Okawa Kanji; Suzuki Tei-ichi; Takamiya Taihei; Tanaka Takayoshi; Toyoshima Fusataro; Tsuji Masanobu; Usui Katsumi.

Holtom, D. C. *Modern Japan and Shinto Nationalism: A Study of Present Day Trends in Japanese Religions.* Rev. Ed. Chicago: University of Chicago Press, 1947.

Honjo Shigeru. *Honjo nikki* [Honjo Diaries]. Tokyo: Hara Shobo, 1967.

Horiba Kazuo. *Shina jihen senso shido-shi* [History of the Conduct of the War in the China Incident]. 2 volumes plus separate folder of maps. Tokyo: Jiji Press, 1962.

Hozumi Nobushige, Baron. *Ancestor-Worship and Japanese Law.* 5th ed. rev. Tokyo: The Hokuseido Press, 1940.

Hsu Shu-hsi. *The War Conduct of the Japanese.* Political and Economic Studies No. 3, Council of International Affairs. Hangkow and Shanghai: Kelley & Walsh Ltd., 1938. Eyewitness accounts of Japanese atrocities in China.

Ike Nobutaka, ed. and transl. *Japan's Decision for War: Records of the 1941 Policy Conferences.* Stanford, Calif.: Stanford University Press, 1967. Translated from portions of *Sugiyama Memo,* q.v. as reproduced in *Taiheiyo senso,* 8 q.v.

Iklé, Frank William. *German-Japanese Relations 1936–1940.* New York: Bookman Associates, 1956.

Imai Sei-ichi. "Kampaku seiji no gosan: Konoye naikaku" [Miscalculations of the Emperor's Political Advisors: Konoye Cabinet]. *Asahi Jyanaru* [Asahi Journal] 7 No. 32 (1 Aug. 1965), pp. 74 ff.

————. "Kofuku to iu genjitsu—senryo kenryoku to no shukkai" [Realities of What Was Called Surrender—The Occupation Authorities and Their Encounters]. *Asahi Jyanaru* [Asahi Journal] 8 No. 5 (30 Jan. 1966), pp. 74 ff.

————. "Nomonhan jiken" [The Nomonhan Incident]. *Asahi Jyanaru* [Asahi Journal] 7 No. 36, (29 August 1965), pp. 76 ff.

————. "Misshitsu no naka no konran—daihonei" [Confusion in the

Secret Chamber—Imperial Headquarters]. *Asahi Jyanaru* [Asahi Journal] 7 No. 49 (28 Nov. 1965), pp. 78 ff.

Imai Takeo. *Shina jihen no kaiso* [Reminiscences of the China Affair]. Tokyo: Misuzu Shobo, 1964.

Imamura Hitoshi. "Manshu hi o fuku goro" [When the Manchurian Fire Broke Out]. In *Himerareta Showa-shi*.

IMTFE "Proceedings." See International Military Tribunal for the Far East.

Inoguchi Rikihei and Tadashi Nakajima, with Roger Pineau. *The Divine Wind: Japan's Kamikaze Force in World War II*. Annapolis, Md.: United States Naval Institute, 1958.

Inoki Masamichi. "The Civil Bureaucracy in Japan." In *Political Modernization in Japan and Turkey,* edited by Robert E. Ward and Dankwart A. Rustow. Princeton, N.J.: Princeton University Press, 1964.

International Military Tribunal for the Far East (IMTFE). "Exhibits," (also called "Documents Presented in Evidence"); Prosecution Exhibits Nos. 1–2282, Defense Exhibits Nos. 2283–3915. Mimeographed. Author used complete, bound, indexed set in the National War Memorial, Canberra, and incomplete set in the Yale Law School Library.

————. "Hearings in Chambers." In the National War Memorial, Canberra.

————. "Judgment." In the National War Memorial, Canberra.

————. "Proceedings" (before matters to be stricken from record were struck). Bound, indexed copies of mimeographed transcript. In the National War Memorial, Canberra.

————. "Proceedings" (after matters to be stricken from record were struck). 48,412 pp. on microfilm. In the Yale Law School Library, New Haven, Conn.

————. "Separate and Dissenting Opinions." In the National War Memorial, Canberra.

————. International Prosecution Section. Summaries and extracts of 4,096 documents collected by the International Prosecution Section, cited as IPS No. 1 . . . IPS No. 4,096. Of these, 2,282 were presented in evidence as "Exhibits." Microfilms WT1–WT94, Library of Congress.

Interviews. Koizumi Shinzo, former chief tutor to Crown Prince Akahito. Major General Tanaka Takayoshi, retired, star witness for the International Military Tribunal for the Far East. Lieutenant General Fujisawa, retired, staff officer and air-to-ground communications specialist; served in Manchuria, China, Tokyo General Staff, and finally as a divisional commander under Yamashita in the Philippines. Major General Kajiura Ginjiro, retired, staff officer and field commander in Manchuria in the early 1930's, after 1937 a field commander in China. Matsumoto Shigeharu, former member of Prince Konoye's brain trust. Tony Kase, the son of Kase Toshikazu who as secretary to Foreign Minister Shigemitsu attended the signing of surrender in 1945. Privileged sources: banker's son, who had access to the papers of one of Prince Saionji's closest friends; retired Navy commander, a wartime member of the Japanese Navy General Staff and friend of Prince Takamatsu; Uramatsu contact, who had access to the papers of a member of Kido's Eleven Club; most aristocratic source, a Fujiwara scion who knew Hirohito as a boy and young man.

IPS Documents. See International Military Tribunal for the Far East,

International Prosecution Section.

Ito Kanejiro. *Gunjin Washi ga kuni sa* [Military Men of My Native Land]. 2 vols. Tokyo: Kyo no Mondai-sha, 1939.

Ito Masanori. *The End of the Imperial Japanese Navy.* Translated by Andrew Y. Kuroda and Roger Pineau. New York: Norton, 1962.

Ito Nobufumi. "Manshu jihen boppatsu to kokusai renmei" [The Manchurian Incident and the League of Nations]. In *Himerareta Showa-shi.*

Ito Takeo. *Problems in the Japanese Occupied Areas in China.* Japanese Council, Institute of Pacific Relations, Tokyo, 1941.

Iwabuchi Tatsuo. *Gunbatsu no keifu* [A Genealogy of Army Factions]. Chuokoron-sha, 1948.

Jansen, Marius B. *The Japanese and Sun Yat-sen.* Cambridge, Mass.: Harvard University Press, 1954. An admirable study, taken from Japanese sources, of Japan's Pan-Asian aspirations in the 1880–1930 period.

Japan Year Book, 1944–45. Published by The Foreign Affairs Association of Japan.

Johnson, Chalmers. *An Instance of Treason: Ozaki Hotsumi and the Sorge Spy Ring.* Stanford, Calif.: Stanford University Press, 1964. Exciting scholarly account of the Sorge spy ring based on Japanese police files.

Johnston, B. F. *Japanese Food Management in World War II.* Stanford, Calif.: Stanford University Press, 1953.

Johnston, Reginald F. *Twilight in the Forbidden City.* London: Victor Gollancz, 1934. Johnston was the tutor of Pu Yi, last emperor of China and puppet emperor of Manchuria.

Jones, F. C. *Japan's New Order in East Asia: Its Rise and Fall, 1937–45.* London: Oxford University Press, 1954.

Kajima Morinosuke. *Emergence of Japan as a World Power, 1895–1925.* Rutland, Vt., and Tokyo: Charles E. Tuttle Co., 1968.

Kamiyama Shigeo. *Tenno-sei ni kansuru riron-teki mondai* [Theoretical Problems Concerning the Emperor System]. Tokyo: Ashi-kai, 1947.

Kaneko Harushi. *Tenno-ke no sugao* [The Face of the Imperal Family]. Tokyo: Imperial Household Ministry, 1962.

Kanichi dai jiten [Sino-Japanese Dictionary]. Newly revised by Miyanokochi Kentaro. Tokyo: Obun-sha, 1957.

Kanroji Osanaga. "Tenno to uta to uma to" [The Emperor and Poems and Horses]. *Shuken Asahi,* 6 January 1967, pp. 52 ff.; 13 January 1967, pp. 40 ff.; 26 January 1967, pp. 31 ff.; 27 January 1967, pp. 32 ff. Jottings by one of Hirohito's favorite chamberlains.

Karig, Walter, and Kelley, Welbourn, eds. *Battle Report: Pearl Harbor to Coral Sea.* Vol. 1, Battle Report Series. New York: Rinehart & Co., 1944.

————; Harris, Russel L.; and Manson, Frank A., eds. *Battle Report: The End of an Empire.* Vol. IV, Battle Report Series. New York: Rinehart & Co., 1948.

Kase Toshikazu. *Journey to the "Missouri."* Edited by Davis Nelson Rowe. New Haven, Conn.: Yale University Press, 1952. Readable explanation of the war by a diplomat of the Peace Faction who attended the surrender aboard the *Missouri.*

Katakura Tadashi. "Ugaki naikaku ryuzan-su" [Aborting the Ugaki Cabinet]. In *Himerareta Showa-shi.*

Kato Hidetoshi. "Jisatsu seishin ni kaketa koku un—tokko-tai" [When the Nation's Destiny Was Staked on the Spirit of Suicide: The Special

Attack Forces]. *Asahi Jyanaru* [Asahi Journal] 7 No. 53 (26 December 1965), pp. 74 ff.

————. "Nihonteki na, amari ni nihonteki na—zero sen" [Japanese, too Japanese—the Zero Fighter] *Asahi Jyanaru* [Asahi Journal] 7 No. 47 (17 November 1965), pp. 46 ff.

Kato Masuo. *The Lost War: A Japanese Reporter's Inside Story.* New York: Alfred A. Knopf, 1946. Recollections of Washington in 1941 and Tokyo in 1945.

Kawai Kazuo. *Japan's American Interlude.* Chicago: University of Chicago Press, 1960.

Kennedy, Malcolm. *A History of Japan.* London: Weidenfeld & Nicolson, 1963. Kennedy was long an attaché at the British Embassy in Tokyo as a specialist in military intelligence.

————. *The Problem of Japan.* London: Nisbet & Co., 1935.

————. *Some Aspects of Japan and Her Defense Forces.* Kobe: J. L. Thompson & Co., 1928.

Kidder, Jonathan Edward. *Japan Before Buddhism.* New York: Frederick A. Praeger, 1959.

Kido Koichi. *Kido Koichi nikki* [Kido Koichi's Diaries]. 2 vols. (paged consecutively). Tokyo: Tokyo University Press, 1966.

————. *Kankei bunsho* [Additional Writings]. Tokyo: Tokyo University Press, 1966.

Kirby, S. Woodburn, et al. *The War Aganst Japan.* Vol. II, India's Most Dangerous Hour; Vol. IV, The Reconquest of Burma. History of the Second World War, United Kingdom Military Series, edited by Sir James Butler. London: Her Majesty's Stationery Office, 1958, 1965.

Knollwood, James L., and Shek, Emily L. "On Prisoner of War Camps in Areas other than the Four Principal Islands of Japan." Mimeographed report, dated 31 July 1946, prepared for American Prisoner of War Information Bureau, Liaison and Research Branch.

Kodama Yoshio. *I Was Defeated.* Tokyo: Robert Booth and Taro Fukuda, 1951. Memoir by a right-wing activist.

Kojima Noboru. *Taiheiyo Senso* [The Pacific War]. 2 vols. Tokyo: Chuo Koron-sha, 1966.

Komatsu Isao. *The Japanese People: Origins of the People and the Language.* Tokyo: Kokusai Bunka Shinkokai [The Society for International Cultural Relations], 1962.

Kono Tsukasa. "Ni-ni-roku jiken no nazo" [The Riddle of the February 26 Incident]. In *Himerareta Showa-shi.*

Konoye Fumimaro. *Nikki* [Diary]. Tokyo: Kyodo Tsushin-sha, 1968. A fragment, written during the summer of 1944.

————, with Uchiba Tomohiko. "Memoirs." English and Japanese texts, including repetitions, rough drafts, and handwritten corrections in margins in English by the author (IPS Documents Nos. 3, 570, 849, 850, 1467). Library of Congress microfilm WT6. Konoye's final text, in English, is reprinted in U.S. Congress, Joint Committee on the Investigation of the Pearl Harbor Attack, Hearings, Part 20, 3985 ff. It is also found in IMTFE Exhibit 173. The original was written, probably in English, in the spring of 1942; a Japanese version was produced the following year. An afterthought entitled "Concerning the Triple Alliance" was penned in May 1945.

Koop, Albert J., and Inada Hogitaro. *Japanese Names and How to Read Them*. London: Routledge & Kegan Paul, Ltd., 1923 (reissued 1960).

Koyama Itoko. *Nagako, Empress of Japan*. New York: John Day Co., 1958. A revealing public relations effort by the daughter of a courtier.

Kuroda Hisata. *Tenno-ke no zaisan* [Imperial Family Finances]. Tokyo: San-ichi Shobo, 1966. A quiet, factual exposé by an economist.

Kurzman, Dan. *Kishi and Japan: The Search for the Sun*. New York: Ivan Obolensky, 1960.

Lee, Clark. *Douglas MacArthur: An Informal Biography*. New York: Henry Holt & Co., 1952.

Leonard, Jonathan Norton. *Early Japan*. New York: Time-Life Books, 1968.

Liu, F. F. *A Military History of Modern China, 1924–1949*. Princeton, N.J.: Princeton University Press, 1956.

Long, Gavin. *The Final Campaigns*. Vol. VII, Series 1 (Army), Australia in the War of 1939–1945. Canberra: Australian War Memorial, 1963.

————. *MacArthur as Military Commander*. New York: Van Nostrand Reinhold Co., 1969.

Lord, Walter. *Day of Infamy*. New York: Holt, Rinehart & Winston, 1961.

————. *Incredible Victory*. New York: Harper & Row, 1967. An admirable reconstruction of a moment in history based on exhaustive interviewing.

MacArthur, Douglas. *Reminiscences*. New York: McGraw-Hill Book Co., 1964.

McAleavy, Henry. *A Dream of Tartary: The Origins and Misfortunes of Henry Pu Yi*. London: George Allen and Unwin, Ltd., 1963.

McCarthy, Dudley. *South-West Pacific Area—First Year: Kokoda to Wau*. Vol. V, Series 1 (Army), Australia in the War of 1939–1945. Canberra: Australian War Memorial, 1959.

Mainichi, Tokyo and Osaka editions. One of Japan's two leading daily newspapers.

Mainichi, "Nihon no senreki" [Japan's War Calendar]. *Mainichi Gurafu* [Mainichi Graphic] 1 August, 1965. A special issue of Japanese war photographs previously suppressed by censorship.

Maki, John M. *Conflict and Tension in the Far East: Key Documents, 1894–1960*. Seattle: University of Washington Press, 1961.

Martin, Edwin M. *The Allied Occupation of Japan*. New York: American Institute of Pacific Relations, 1948.

Maruyama Masao. *Thought and Behavior in Modern Japanese Politics*. Edited by Ivan Morris. London: Oxford University Press, 1963.

Mendelssohn, Peter de. *Japan's Political Warfare*. London: George Allen & Unwin Ltd., 1944.

Merrill, Frederick T., *Japan and the Opium Menace*. New York: Institute of Pacific Relations and the Foreign Policy Association, 1942.

Merrill, James M. *Target Tokyo: The Halsey-Doolittle Raid*. Chicago: Rand McNally & Co., 1964.

Millis, Walter. *This is Pearl! The United States and Japan—1941*. New York: William Morrow & Co., 1947.

Mook, Hubertus J. van. *The Netherlands Indies and Japan: Battle on*

Paper, 1940–1941. New York: W. W. Norton & Co., 1944.

Moore, Frederick. *With Japan's Leaders: An Intimate Record of Fourteen Years as Counsellor to the Japanese Government, Ending Dec. 7, 1941.* New York: Charles Scribner's Sons, 1942.

Mori Shozo. *Tsumuji kaze niju-nen* [Twenty-Year Whirlwind]. 2 vols. Tokyo: Masu Shobo, 1947.

Morin, Relman, *Circuit of Conquest.* New York: Alfred A. Knopf, 1943.

Morishima Morito. *Inbo ansatsu gunto* [Plots, Assassinations, and Long Swords]. Tokyo: Iwanami Shoten, 1950. A lively history of assassination and intimidation in Japan by a painstaking journalist who has interviewed more surviving witnesses than any Westerner could.

Morison, Samuel Eliot. *History of United States Naval Operations in World War II.* 3, The Rising Sun in the Pacific, 1931–April 1942; 4, Coral Sea, Midway and Submarine Actions, May 1942–August 1942; 5, The Struggle for Guadalcanal, August 1942–February 1943; 6, Breaking the Bismarcks Barrier, 22 July 1942–1 May 1944; 7, Aleutians, Gilberts and Marshalls, June 1942–April 1944; 8, New Guinea and the Marianas, March 1944–August 1944; 12, Leyte, June 1944–January 1945; 13, The Liberation of the Philippines: Luzon, Mindanao, the Visayas, 1944–1945; 14, Victory in the Pacific, 1945; 15, Supplement and General Index. Boston: Little, Brown & Co., 1948–1962.

Moritaka Shigeo, ed. *Daitoa senso shashin-shi* [Photographic History of the Greater East Asia War]. 8 vols. Tokyo: Fuji Shoen, 1954.

Morrison, Ian. *Malaya Postscript.* Sydney: Angus and Robertson Ltd., 1943. Fall of Singapore, by a correspondent for *The Times* of London.

Morton, Louis. *Strategy and Command: The First Two Years.* United States Army in World War II: The War in the Pacific, vol. 10. Washington, D.C.: Department of the Army, Office of the Chief of Military History, 1962.

Mosley, Leonard. *Hirohito, Emperor of Japan.* New York: McGraw-Hill Book Co., 1966. A hasty journalistic account, with numerous inaccuracies, but valuable for the information it contains stemming from Kanroji Osanaga, long Hirohito's assistant grand chamberlain.

Murofushi Tetsuro. *Nihon no terorisuto* [Japan's Terrorists]. Tokyo: Kobunsho, 1963.

Murphey, Rhoads. *Shanghai: Key to Modern China.* Cambridge, Mass.: Harvard University Press, 1953.

Mydans, Carl. *More Than Meets the Eye.* New York: Harper & Brothers, 1959.

Nakano Masao. *Hashimoto taisa no shuki* [Colonel Hashimoto (Kingoro)'s Notes]. Tokyo: Misuzu Shobo, 1963.

Natori Junichi. *A Short History of Nippon.* Tokyo: Hokuseido Press, 1943.

Newcomb, Richard F. *Iwo Jima.* New York: Holt, Rinehart & Winston, 1965.

Nihon Kokusai Seiji Gakkai [Japan Association of International Relations]. *Taiheiyo senso e no michi* [Road to the Pacific War]. 8 vols. 1, *Manshu jihen zen'ya* [Eve of the Manchurian Incident]. 2, *Manshu jihen* [Manchurian Incident]. 3, *Ni-chu senso* (jo) [Sino-Japanese War, Part I]. 4, *Ni-chu senso* (ge) [Sino-Japanese War, Part II]. 5, *Sankoku domei: Nichi-so churitsu joyaku* [Tripartite Alliance: Soviet-Japanese Neutrality

Pact]. 6, *Nanpo shinshutsu* [Southward Advance]. 7, *Nichi-bei kaisen* [Opening of War with America]. 8, *Bekkan shiryohen* [Supplement of Source Materials]. Tokyo: Asahi Shinbun-sha, 1963.

Nu Thakin (U Nu), *Burma Under the Japanese: Pictures and Portraits.* London: Macmillan & Co., 1954.

Obata Tokushiro. *Kendai no senso* [Wars of Modern Times], vols. 6 and 7, *Taiheiyo senso* [The Pacific War]. Tokyo: Jimbutsu Orai-sha, 1966.

Obi Toshihito, ed. *Gendai-shi shiryo* [Source Materials on Modern History], vols. 1–3, *Zoruge jiken* [The Sorge Incident]. Tokyo: Misuzu Shobo, 1963.

Ogata, Sadako N. *Defiance in Manchuria: The Making of Japanese Foreign Policy, 1931–1932.* Berkeley and Los Angeles: University of California Press, 1964.

Ohtani Keijiro. *Rakujitsu no josho: Showa rikugun-shi* [The Beginning of Sunset: History of the Japanese Army in the Reign of Hirohito]. Tokyo: Yakumo Shoten, 1959.

————. *Showa kempei-shi* [History of the Secret Police During the Reign of Hirohito]. Tokyo: Misuzu Shobo, 1966.

Okamoto Aisuke. "Jusan-nin no gozen bansan" [Thirteen Men Who Dined with the Emperor]. In *Tenno hakusho* [White Paper on the Emperor]. Tokyo: Bungei Shunju, 1956.

Okawa Kanji. "Himerareta tai-bei choho katsudo" [Hidden Activity in Circulating Anti-American News]. In *Himerareta Showa-shi.*

Omura Bunji. *The Last Genro: Prince Saionji, The Man Who Westernized Japan.* Philadelphia: J. B. Lippincott Co., 1938.

Omura Takeshi. *Saionji-ko nozo-tsutae* [Prince Saionji in the Full Moon of Life]. Tokyo: Denki Kanko-kai, 1937.

Oya Soichi. "Ishiwara Kanji to manshu kenkoku" [Ishiwara Kanji and the Founding of Manchukuo]. *Chuo Koron* 80, No. 8 (August 1965), pp. 378 ff.

————. *Nihon no ichiban nagai hi* [Japan's Longest Day]. Tokyo: Bungei Shunju, 1965.

————. *Japan's Longest Day.* English-language edition of the above; see Pacific War Research Society.

Ozaki Yoshiharu. *Rikugun o ugokashita hito* [The Men Who Moved the Army]. Odawara: Hachi-ko-do Shoten, 1960.

Pacific War Research Society, comp. *Japan's Longest Day.* Tokyo and Palo Alto, Calif.: Kodansha International Ltd., 1968.

Patrick, W. D. "Planning Conspiracy. In Relation to Criminal Trials and Specially in Relation to This Trial. 17 February, 1947." Sir William Webb Collection. National War Memorial, Canberra.

Percival, A. E. *The War in Malaya.* London: Eyre and Spottiswoode, Ltd., 1949.

Pernikoff, Alexandre. *Bushido: The Anatomy of Terror.* New York: Liveright, 1943.

Perry, Matthew Calbraith. *The Japan Expedition, 1852–1854; The Personal Journal of Commodore Matthew C. Perry.* Edited by Roger Pineau. Washington, D.C.: Smithsonian Institution Press, 1968.

Piggott, F. S. G. *Broken Thread: An Autobiography.* Aldershot (England): Gale & Polden Ltd., 1950.

Ponsonby-Fane, Richard A. B. *Imperial House of Japan.* Kyoto:

Ponsonby Memorial Society, 1959.

————. *Sovereign and Subject*. Kyoto: Ponsonby Memorial Society, 1962.

————. *Studies in Shinto and Shrines*. Kyoto: Ponsonby Memorial Society, 1962.

————. *The Vicissitudes of Shinto*. Kyoto: Ponsonby Memorial Society, 1963.

————. *Visiting Famous Shrines in Japan*. Kyoto: Ponsonby Memorial Society, 1964.

Potter, John Deane. *A Soldier Must Hang: The Biography of an Oriental General*. London: Frederick Miller Ltd., 1963.

————. *Yamamoto: The Man Who Menaced America*. New York: The Viking Press, 1965.

Prasad, S. N.; Bhargava, K. D.; and Khera, P. H. *The Reconquest of Burma*. 2 vols. Official History of the Indian Armed Forces in the Second World War (1939–1945), Bisheshwar Prasad, general editor. India and Pakistan: Combined Inter-Service Historical Section, 1958.

Preble, George Henry. *The Opening of Japan: A Diary of Discovery in the Far East, 1853–1856*. Norman, Okla.: University of Oklahoma Press, 1962.

Presseisen, Ernst L. *Germany and Japan: A Study in Totalitarian Diplomacy, 1933–1941*. The Hague: Martinus Nijhoff, 1958.

Price, Willard. *Japan and the Son of Heaven*. New York: Duell, Sloan & Pearce, 1945.

Pu Yi, Aisin Gioro. *From Emperor to Citizen*. 2 vols. Peking: Foreign Language Press, 1964, 1965.

Rappaport, Armin. *Henry Stimson and Japan, 1931–1933*. Chicago: University of Chicago Press, 1963.

Reel, A. Frank. *The Case of General Yamashita*. Chicago: University of Chicago Press, 1949.

Reynolds, Robert L., and the Editors of American Heritage. *Commodore Perry in Japan*. New York: American Heritage Publishing Co., 1963.

Romulo, Carlos P. *I Saw the Fall of the Philippines*. London: George C. Harrap & Co., 1943.

Roth, Andrew. *Japan Strikes South*. New York: American Council, Institute of Pacific Relations, 1941.

Russell, Lord, of Liverpool. *The Knights of Bushido: The Shocking History of Japanese War Atrocities*. New York: E. P. Dutton & Co., 1958. One-dimensional shocker but solidly based on IMTFE evidence.

Russell, Oland D. *The House of Mitsui*. Boston: Little, Brown & Co., 1939.

Sakai Tsune. "Heika no go-kenkyu no" [Concerning the Researches of His Majesty]. *Shukan Asahi*. January 27, 1967, pp. 53 ff.

Sakai Saburo with Martin Caidin and Fred Saito. *Samurai!* New York: E. P. Dutton & Co., 1957.

Sansom, Sir George Bailey. *A History of Japan*. 3 vols. Stanford, Calif.: Stanford University Press, 1958.

Sadler, A. L. *The Maker of Modern Japan: The Life of Tokugawa Ieyasu*. New York: W. W. Norton, 1937.

Sato Kenryo. "Tojo Hideki to daitoa senso no sekinin" [Tojo Hideki and the Responsibility for the Greater East Asia War]. *Chuo Koron*, 80

No. 8 (August 1965) pp. 390 ff.

————. *Tojo Hideki to taiheiyo senso* [Tojo Hideki and the Pacific War]. Tokyo: Bungei Shunju, 1960.

Scalapino, Robert A. *Democracy and the Party Movement in Prewar Japan*. Berkeley: University of California Press, 1952.

Scherer, James A. B. *Manchukuo: A Bird's Eye View*. Tokyo: The Hokuseido Press, 1933.

————. *Three Meiji Leaders*. Tokyo: Hokuseido Press, 1936.

Sheldon, Walter J. *The Honorable Conquerors: The Occupation of Japan 1945–1952*. New York: Macmillan, 1965.

Sherrod, Robert Lee. *Tarawa: The Story of a Battle*. New York: Duell, Sloan and Pearce, 1945.

Shigemitsu Mamoru. *Japan and Her Destiny: My Struggle for Peace*. New York: E. P. Dutton & Co., Inc., 1958.

Shimada Toshihiko. *Kanto gun*. [The Kwantung Army]. Tokyo: Chuo Koron-sha, 1965.

————, ed., with Inaba Masao. *Gendai-shi shiryo* [Source Materials on Modern History], vol. 8, *Nichu senso I* [Sino-Japanese War I]. Tokyo: Misuzu Shobo, 1964.

Shin sekai chizu [New World Atlas]. Tokyo: Zenkoku Kyoiku Tosho, 1965.

Slim, Viscount Sir William. *Defeat into Victory*. New York: David MacKay Co., 1961.

Smith, Robert Ross. *Triumph in the Philippines*. United States in World War II: The War in the Pacific, vol. 10. Washington, D.C.: Department of the Army, Office of the Chief of Military History, 1963.

Smythe, Dr. Lewis S. C., and others. *War Damage in Nanking Area, December 1937 to March 1938*. Nanking: Nanking International Relief Committee, 1938.

Snow, Edgar. *Red Star Over China*. London: Victor Gollancz, Ltd., 1937, reissued 1963.

Statements: See United States Army, Far East Command, Historical Section.

Statler, Oliver. *The Black Ship Scroll. An Account of the Perry Expedition at Shimoda in 1854 and the Lively Beginnings of People-to-People Relations Between Japan and America*. Rutland, Vt., and Tokyo: Charles E. Tuttle Co., 1963.

————. *Japanese Inn*. New York: Random House, 1961.

————. *Shimoda Story*. New York: Random House, 1969.

Stimson, H. L. *The Far Eastern Crisis: Recollections and Observations*. New York: Harper & Brothers, 1936.

Stimson, Henry L., and McGeorge Bundy. *On Active Service in Peace and War*. New York: Harper & Brothers, 1948.

Storry, Richard. *Double Patriots: A Study of Japanese Nationalism*. London: Chatto and Windus, 1957.

————. *A History of Modern Japan*. Harmondsworth, England: Penguin Books, Ltd., 1960.

Stuart, John Leighton. *Fifty Years in China*. New York: Random House, 1954. Memoirs of a missionary-educator who served as U.S. ambassador to China, 1946–52.

Suda Teichi. *Kazami Akira to sono jidai* [Kazami Akira and Those

Times]. Tokyo: Misuzu Shobo, 1965.

Sugamo no homu-in kai [Legal Affairs Commission of Sugamo War Criminals]. *Senpan saiban no jisso* [The Real Facts of the War Crime Trials]. Privately printed, n.d. but *c.* 1960.

Sugiyama Hajime (Gen). *Sugiyama Memo* [Sugiyama's Memoranda]. 2 vols. Tokyo: Hara Shobo, 1967. Papers of Japan's wartime Army Chief of Staff.

Sumimoto Toshio. *Senryo hiroku* [Secret Report of the Occupation]. Tokyo: Mainichi Shinbun-sha, 1965. Libelous but based on conscientious interviewing.

Suzuki Kantaro. "Arashi ni jijucho hachinen" [Eight Years as Grand Chamberlain in the Storm]. In *Tenno hakusho* [White Paper on The Emperor]. Tokyo: Bungei Shunju, 1956.

————. *Konjo tenno gonichijo no ittan* [One Aspect of the Present Emperor's Everyday Life]. Tokyo: Imperial Household Ministry, October 30, 1940.

Suzuki Tei-ichi. "Hokubatsu to Chiang-Tanaka mitsuyaku" [The Strike North and the Chiang-Tanaka Agreement]. In *Himerareta Showa-shi*.

Suzuki Yasuzo. *Hikaku kenno-shi* [Comparative Constitutional History]. Tokyo: Keiso Shobo, 1931.

Suzuki Yukio. *Keibatsu* [Financial Cliques]. Tokyo: Kobun-sha, 1965.

Taiheiyo senso e no michi. See Nihon Kokusai Seiji Gakkai.

Takagi Sokichi. "Chishikijin to kaigun to senso" [The Intellectuals and the Navy and the War]. *Bungei Shunju* 40 No. 1 (January 1966), pp. 262 ff. An assessment of Japanese naval intelligence in World War II.

————. *Taiheiyo Kaisen-shi* [Naval History of the Pacific War]. Tokyo: Iwanami Shinsho, 1949.

Takahashi Masae. *Ni-ni-roku jiken.* [The February Twenty-sixth Incident]. Tokyo: Chuo Koron-sha, 1965.

Takamiya Taihei. *Gunkoku taiheiki* [Pacific Record of a Nation]. Tokyo: Takenawa-to-sha, 1951. Revelations about the Japanese Army by one of its veteran military correspondents.

————. "Rikugun o nibun shita kodoha-toseiha" [The Imperial Way and Control Faction Army Split]. In *Himerareta Showa-shi*.

Takeda Taijun. *Seiji-ka no bunsho* [Notes on Politicians]. Tokyo: Iwanami Shinsho, 1960. Recollections of a Japanese publicist who served in Shanghai during the 1930's.

Takeyoshi Yosaburo. *The Story of the Wako: Japanese Pioneers in the Southern Regions*. Translated by Watanabe Hideo. Tokyo: Kenkyusha Ltd., 1940.

Takeuchi, Tatsuji. *War and Diplomacy in the Japanese Empire*. Garden City, N.Y.: Doubleday, Doran & Co., 1935.

Tamura Yoshio, ed. *Hiroku daitoa sen-shi* [Secret History of the Greater East Asia War]. 12 vols. Tokyo: Fuji Shoen, 1953.

Tanaka Memorial. See Crow, Carl.

Tanaka Shinichi. "Ishiwara Kanji to Tojo Hideki" [Ishiwara Kanji and Tojo Hideki]. *Bungei Shunju* 44 No. 1 (January 1966) pp. 262 ff.

Tanaka Takayoshi (Ryukichi). "Kakute tenno wa muzai to natta" [Thus It Turned Out That the Emperor Was Innocent]. *Bungei Shunju* 43 No. 8 (August 1965) pp. 198 ff.

————. *Nihon gunbatsu anto-shi* [History of Secret Strife Among

Japanese Army Factions]. Tokyo: Seiwa-do, 1947.

―――――. "Oni kenji, Keenan" [Devil's Lawyer, Keenan]. *Bungei Shunju* 43 No. 10 (October 1965) pp. 274 ff.

―――――. *Sabakareru rekishi: Haisen hiwa* [History of Being Judged: The Secret Story of Defeat]. Tokyo: Shimpu-sha, 1948.

―――――. "Shokai jihen wa koshite okosareta" [The Outbreak of the Shanghai Incident was Promoted]. In *Himerareta Showa-shi.*

―――――. "Okawa Shumei hakushi to rikugun." Dr. Okawa Shumei and the Army. Manuscript chapter of a book, which Tanaka was kind enough to let me photostat.

―――――. "Yoshiko." Unpublished manuscript on Tanaka's relationship with Kawashima Yoshiko or Eastern Jewel. Lent to author.

Tanin, O., and Yohan, E. *When Japan Goes to War.* New York: International Publishers, 1936.

Tatamiya Eitaro. *Daitoa senso shimatsu-ki jiketsu hen* [A Collection of Circumstantial Accounts of Greater East Asia War Suicides]. Tokyo: Keizai Orai-sha, 1966.

Tateno Nobuyuki. *Hanran* [Rebellion]. Tokyo: Rokukyo, 1952. Evocative historical novel about the February Mutiny; the author was a member of Konoye's circle.

―――――. "Ni-ni-roku jiken no nazo" [Riddle of the February 26 Incident]. In *Tenno to hanran gun* [The Emperor and the Rebel Troops]. Nihon Shuho, March 1957.

―――――. *Showa gunbatsu: Gekido-hen* [Army Factions in the Reign of Hirohito: An Anthology of Upheaval]. Tokyo: Kodan-sha, 1963.

Terasaki, Gwen. *Bridge to the Sun.* London: Michael Joseph, Ltd., 1958.

Terry, T. Philip. *Terry's Guide to the Japanese Empire.* Boston: Houghton-Mifflin Co., 1920.

Tiedemann, Arthur. *Modern Japan.* Rev. ed. Princeton, N.J.: D. Van Nostrand Co., Inc., 1962.

Timperley, H. J. *Japanese Terror in China.* New York: Modern Age Books, 1958. (A collection of eyewitness accounts.)

Togo Shigenori. *The Cause of Japan.* Translated and edited by Togo Fumihiko and Ben Bruce Blakeney. New York: Simon & Schuster, 1956. By the man who was former minister in December 1941 and again in August 1945.

Toland, John. *But Not in Shame: The Six Months After Pearl Harbor.* New York: Random House, 1961.

―――――. *The Rising Sun.* New York: Random House, 1970.

Tolischus, Otto D. *Through Japanese Eyes.* New York: Reynal & Hitchcock, 1945.

―――――. *Tokyo Record.* New York: Reynal and Hitchcock, 1943. A day-by-day account of 1941 by a correspondent for *The New York Times.*

Toyama Shigeki, Imai Sei-ichi, and Fujiwara Akira. *Showa-shi* [History of the Reign of Hirohito]. Tokyo: Iwanami Shoten, 1962.

Toyoshima Fusataro. "Chosen gun ekkyo shingekisu!" [In Crossing the Border the Korean Army Charged!]. In *Himerareta Showa-shi.*

Translations. See United States Army, Far East Command, Historical Section.

Trefousse, Hans Louis, ed. *What Happened at Pearl Harbor: Documents Pertaining to the Japanese Attack of December 7, 1941, and Its Back-*

ground. New York: Twayne Publishers, 1958.

Tsuji Masanobu. "Futari do daitoa shidosha—Ishiwara Kanji to O Chomei" [The Two Leaders of Greater East Asia—Ishiwara Kanji and Wang Ching-wei]. In *Himerareta Showa-shi.*

————. *Guadarukanaru.* Nara: Tamba-shi, 1950.

————. *Jugo tai ichi: Biruma no shito* [Fifteen Against One: Life-and-Death Struggle in Burma]. Tokyo: Kanto-sha, 1950.

————. *Nomonhan.* Tokyo: A-To Shobo, 1950.

————. "Senkakusha Ishiwara Kanji" [Ishiwara Kanji, Pioneer]. In *Fusetsu jinbutsu tokuhon* [Primer on Personalities in a Blizzard]. Tokyo: Bungei Shunju-sha, 1955.

————. *Singapore: The Japanese Version.* Translated by Margaret E. Lake. Edited by H. V. Howe. New York: St. Martin's Press, 1960.

————. *Underground Escape.* Translated from the Japanese. Tokyo: Robert Booth and Taro Fukada, 1952.

Tsunoda Jun, ed. *Gendai-shi shiryo* [Source Materials of Modern History], vol. 10, *Nichu senso III* [Sino-Japanese War III]. Tokyo: Misuzu Shobo, 1964.

Tsunoda, Ryusaku; de Bary, Wm. Theodore; and Keene, Donald, compilers. *Sources of Japanese Tradition.* Introduction to Oriental Civilizations, edited by Wm. Theodore de Bary. New York: Columbia University Press, 1958.

Tsurumi Shunsuke, Hashikawa Bunzo, Imai Sei-ichi, Matsumoto Sannosuke, Kamishima Jiro, Abe Osamu. *Nihon no hyakunen* [Japan's Century]. 10 vols. Tokyo: Chikuma Shobo, 1964. Most authoritative history of modern Japan.

Tuleja, Thaddeus V. *Climax at Midway.* New York: W. W. Norton & Co., 1960.

Ugaki Kazushige. *Ugaki nikki* [Ugaki Diary]. Tokyo: Asahi Shinbun-sha, 1954.

Ugaki Matome. *Senso roku: Ugaki Matome nikki* [Seaweed War: Ugaki Matome's Diary]. 2 vols. Tokyo: Kyodo, 1953.

Umashima Takeshi. *Gunbatsu anto hishi* [Secret History of Hidden Factional Feuds in the Army]. Tokyo: Kyodo, 1946.

United States Army Air Forces. *Mission Accomplished:* Interrogations of Japanese Industrial, Military and Civil Leaders of World War II. Washington, D.C.; Government Printing Office, 1946.

————. "Third Report of the Commanding General of the Army Air Forces to the Secretary of War, 12 November 1945." Mimeographed.

United States Army, Army Forces Pacific, Psychological Warfare Branch. Special Report No. 4, 22 July 1945: "The Emperor of Japan." Mimeographed.

————. Special Report No. 5, 23 July 1945: "Inside Japan—Youth Pawn of Militarists." Mimeographed.

United States Army, Far East Command, Historical Section. "Interrogations of Japanese Officials on World War II." 2 vols. Mimeographed.

————. "Statements of Japanese Officials on World War II." 4 vols. Mimeographed. National Archives microfilm no. 8–5.1 AD 4; page references in Notes are to this microfilm.

————. "Translations of Japanese Documents." 3 vols. Mimeographed. National Archives microfilm 8–5.1 CA; page references in Notes are to the pagination in this microfilm.

United States Army, Far East Command, Intelligence, Civil Intelligence Section. "The Brocade Banner: The Story of Japanese Nationalism." Special Report. Mimeographed. 1946.

————. "Left Wing, Right Wing: Japanese Proletarian Politics." Special Report. Mimeographed. 1946.

————. "Saionji-Harada Memoirs." [Rough English translation of Harada Kumao's *Saionji-ko to Seikyoku,* q.v.] 25 vols. Mimeographed. 1947.

————. "War Politics in Japan." Special Report. Mimeographed. 1946.

United States Army Forces Far East. Numbered, mimeographed "Japanese Monographs" distributed by Department of the Army, Office of Military History, 1952–1956. a) No. 24: "History of the Southern Army." b) No. 70: "China Area Operations Record, July 1937–November 1941." c) No. 71: "Army Operations in China, December 1941–December 1943." d) No. 72: "Army Operations in China, January 1944–August 1945." e) No. 119: "Outline of Operations Prior to Termination of War and Activities Connected with the Cessation of Hostilities." f) Nos. 144, 145, 147, 150 & 152: "Political Strategy Prior to Outbreak of War."

United States Army, Supreme Command for the Allied Powers, Far East: Allied Translator and Interpreter Section. (Mimeographed translations of documents captured from the Japanese.) Bulletin No. 234: "British Malaya, Military Geography and Supplement, 30 April 1940"; "Dutch East Indies, Military Geography and Supplement, 1 November 1940"; "British Borneo, Military Geography and General Description, 30 August 1941"; "Aeronautical Map of Borneo and Java, February 1941."

————. Bulletin No. 567: containing inter alia "Diary of a Japanese Soldier on Wewak, 30 August 1943."

————. Document No. 7396: "Just Read This and the War is Won."

————. Documents Captured in Hollandia: containing inter alia "Intelligence Reports of the Kami Organization, Special Service Organ, New Guinea, 20 December 1943–14 March 1944."

————. Enemy Publications No. 6, 27 March 1943: containing inter alia, a) "Naval Operations in Hawaii and Malaya (from *Bungei Shunju*)"; b) "Sinking the Prince of Wales, by Hayashi Noboru;" c) "Sinking the Prince of Wales, by Murakami Tsutae."

————. Enemy Publications No. 32, 11 August 1943: "The Taking of Java, February–March, 1942, by an unidentified lieutenant colonel."

————. Enemy Publications No. 56, 21 November 1943: "Characteristics of American Combat Methods on Guadalcanal, 4 March 1943."

————. Enemy Publications No. 64, 1 December 1943: "Summary of American Combat Methods as Observed by Staff Officer Sugita While Attached Temporarily to U.S. Army: Pamphlet Issued 25 September 1942 by Oki Group Headquarters."

————. Enemy Publications No. 111, 30 March 1944: "Japanese Study of Jungle Combat, Captured in New Guinea."

————. Enemy Publications No. 278, 11 January, 1945: "Malaya Campaign by Yokoyama Ryu-ichi, 8 October 1942, Captured in Lae Area on 19–20 December 1943."

————. Enemy Publications No. 359, 28 April 1945: "Guerrilla Warfare in the Philippines (Intelligence Reports of the Watari Army Group)."

————. Enemy Publications No. 371, 13 May 1945: "Morale and Economy in Japan from Letters to a Soldier (Correspondence of Nagamitsu Isami of Oka 10413 Force, 21 April 1943–6 June 1944, Captured 23 January 1945 in Pozzarubio, Luzon)."

————. "Horii Tomitaro's Message to His Troops, 4 December 1941."

————. "Kawakita Katsumi's Account of Pearl Harbor Attack."

————. "Matsuura Saga-ei's Diary of Attack on Guam."

————. Research Report No. 65, Supplement No. 1, 29 March 1945: "Japanese Knowledge of Allied Activities."

————. Research Report No. 69, 6 February 1944: "Ration Supply System and Ration Scale of Japanese Land Forces in Southwest Pacific Area."

————. Research Report No. 72, Supplement No. 2, 23 June 1945: "Japanese Violations of the Laws of War."

————. Research Report No. 76. Part I, 4 April 1944: "Self-Immolation as a Factor in Japanese Military Psychology."

————. Ibid., Part II, 21 June 1944: "The Emperor Cult as a Present Factor in Japanese Military Psychology."

————. Ibid., Part III, 30 October 1944: "The Warrior Tradition as a Present Factor in Japanese Military Psychology."

————. Ibid., Part IV, 7 February 1945: "Prominent Factors in Japanese Military Psychology."

————. Ibid., Part V, 24 February 1945: Superstitions as a Present Factor in Japanese Military Psychology."

————. Ibid., Part VI, 10 October 1945: "Defects Arising from the Doctrine of 'Spiritual Superiority' as Factors in Japanese Military Psychology."

————. Research Report No. 119, 28 February 1945: "The Japanese Military Police Service."

————. Research Report No. 122, 19 April 1945: "Antagonism Between Officers and Men in the Japanese Armed Forces."

————. Research Report No. 123, 20 April 1945: "Control by Rumor in the Japanese Armed Forces."

————. Research Report No. 126, Part I, 26 April 1945 & Part II, 11 May 1945: "Hoko—the Spy-Hostage System of Group Control—the Clue to Japanese Psychology."

————. Research Report No. 131, 1 December 1945: "Japan's Decision to Fight."

————. Research Report No. 132, 1 December 1945: "The Pearl Harbor Operation."

————. Special Report No. 72, Supplement No. 1, 19 March 1945: "Diary of [Japanese Army Interpreter] Horikoshi Hiroshi of 65th Brigade Headquarters, Baguio, on Capture of Bataan."

United States Congress, Joint Committee on the Investigation of the Pearl Harbor Attack. *Hearings.* 79th Cong. 2d Sess., Public Document No. 79716. 39 vols. Washington, D.C.: Government Printing Office. 1946.

United States Department of the Navy. *Heigo* [Japanese Military Terminology]. Mimeographed.

————. *Narrative of the Expedition of an American Squadron to the China Seas and Japan, performed in the years 1852, 1853, 1854, under the command of Commodore M. C. Perry.* 2 vols. Washington, D.C.: 1856.

United States Department of State. *Papers Relating to the Foreign Relations of the United States and Japan, 1931–1941.* 2 vols. Washington, D.C.: Government Printing Office, 1943.

————. *Occupation of Japan: Policy and Progress.* Washington: Government Printing Office, 1946.

————. *Trial of Japanese War Criminals.* Publication 2613, Far Eastern Series 12. Washington, D.C.: Government Printing Office, 1946.

United States Department of War, Military Intelligence Service. "Campaign Study No. 3: Japanese Land Operations." Mimeographed.

United States Navy, Office of Naval Operations. *Japanese Military Administration in Taiwan* (Civil Affairs Handbook Op. Nav. 50–E–14. Washington, D.C.: 10 August 1944.

————. *U.S. Navy at War, 1941–1945: Official Reports to the Secretary of the Navy* by Ernest J. King. Department of the Navy, 1946.

United States Navy, Office of Public Relations. "Communiques 1–300 and Pertinent Press Releases December 10, 1941 to March 5, 1943." Mimeographed.

United States Office of Strategic Services (O.S.S.). Research and Analysis Branch. *Japanese Administration of Occupied Areas—Burma* (Army Service Forces Manual M354–18A). Washington, D.C.: Government Printing Office, 1944.

————. *Japanese Administration of Occupied Areas—Malaya* (Army Service Forces Manual M354–18B). 1944.

————. *Japanese Administration of Occupied Areas—Philippine Islands* (Army Service Forces Manual M354–18C). 1944.

————. *Japanese Administration of Occupied Areas—Thailand* (Army Service Forces Manual M354–18E). 1944.

United States Strategic Bombing Survey. *Campaigns of the Pacific War.* Washington, D.C.: Government Printing Office, 1946.

————. *The Effects of the Atomic Bombs on Hiroshima and Nagasaki.* 1946.

————. *Japan's Struggle to End the War.* 1946.

————. *Summary Report (Pacific War).* 1946.

United States Strategic Bombing Survey, Civil Analysis Division. *Study No. 10: Summary Report Covering Air Raid Protection Allied Subjects Japan.* 1946.

————. *Study No. 11: Final Report Covering Air Raid Protection Allied Subjects Japan.* 1946.

United States Strategic Bombing Survey, Military Analysis Division. *Study No. 62: Japanese Air Power.* 1946.

————. *Air Campaigns of the Pacific War.* 1947.

United States Strategic Bombing Survey, Military Defense Division. *Field Report Covering Air Raid Protection and Allied Subjects in Kyoto, Japan.* 1947.

United States Strategic Bombing Survey, Morale Division. *The Effects of Strategic Bombing on Japanese Morale.* 1947.

United States Strategic Bombing Survey, Naval Analysis Division. *Interrogations of Japanese Officials.* 2 vols. 1946.

————. *The Reduction of Truk.* 1947.

————. *The Allied Campaign Against Rabaul.* 1946.

_____. *The Effect of the Incendiary Bomb Attacks on Japan: A Report on Eight Cities* (Study No. 90). 1946.

United States Strategic Bombing Survey, Urban Areas Division. *The Effects of Air Attack on the Japanese Urban Economy*. 1947.

_____. *The Effects of Air Attack on Osaka, Kobe and Kyoto*. 1947.

Usami Seijiro, ed., and Rekishigaku kenkyukai [Historical Research Society]. *Taiheiyo senso-shi* [Pacific War History]. 5 vols.: Manchuria, China, Pacific I, Pacific II, Peace Making. Tokyo: Toyo Keizai Shimposha, 1953.

Usui Katsumi. "Cho Saku-rin bakushi no shinso" [The Truth About Chang Tso-lin's Death by Bombing]. In *Himerareta Showa-shi*.

_____. "Dai Nihon teikoku no shushifu: Potsudamu sengen judaku" [A Period to the Japanese Empire: Acceptance of the Potsdam Declaration]. *Asahi Jyanaru* (Asahi Journal) 8, No. 3 (16 January 1966), pp. 74 ff.

_____, ed., with Inaba Masao. *Nichu senso II* [Sino-Japanese War II], vol. 9, *Gendai-shi shiryo* [Sources of Modern History]. Tokyo: Misuzu Shobo, 1964.

Uyehara, Cecil H., comp. *Checklist of Archives in the Japanese Ministry of Foreign Affairs, Tokyo, Japan, 1868–1945*. Washington, D.C.: Library of Congress, 1954.

Vaughn, Miles W. *Under the Japanese Mask*. London: Lovat Dickson Ltd., 1937.

Vespa, Amleto. *Secret Agent of Japan*. Boston: Little, Brown & Co., 1938.

Vinacke, Harold M. *A History of the Far East in Modern Times*. 6th ed. New York: Appleton-Century-Crofts, 1959.

Vining, Elizabeth Gray. *Return to Japan*. Philadelphia: J. B. Lippincott Co., 1960.

_____. *Windows for the Crown Prince*. Philadelphia: J. B. Lippincott Co., 1952.

Wakefield, Harold. *New Paths for Japan*. New York: Oxford University Press, 1948. A scholarly account of the early days of the Occupation.

Wartime Legislation in Japan: A Selection of Important Laws Enacted or Revised in 1941. Translated and compiled by the Overseas Department, *Domei Tsushin-sha*. Tokyo: Nippon Shogyo Tsushin-sha, n.d.

Watanabe Ryusaku. *Bazoku* [Bandits on Horseback]. Tokyo: Chuo Koron-sha, 1964. An excellent journalistic reconstruction of Japanese fifth-column work in North China, Manchuria, and Mongolia.

Webb, Sir William. Collection of mimeographed and handwritten papers at the National War Memorial, Canberra. File entitled: "I.M.T.F.E. papers covering a series of applications made to the Tribunal on matters of evidence by the Defense and Prosecution and on general matters arising out of the conduct and administration of the Tribunal." Inter alia: a) Medical report on Matsuoka, May 14, 1946; b) Plea to introduce extracts from the diary of Marquis Kido Koichi (I.P.S. Document No. 1632); c) Tokyo Charter; d) MacArthur's charge to the Tribunal, January 19, 1946; e) "Conclusions," a folder containing various drafts of the dissenting paragraphs which Chief Justice Webb appended to the I.M.T.F.E.'s *Judgment;* f) "The surrender of Japan," Chief Justice Webb's chronology of the trial, including notes on Okawa's dismissal; Matsuoka's death, June 27, 1946; Nagano's death, January 5, 1947; and statistics of trial.

————. File entitled "Inward and outward correspondence with S.C.A.P., February 1946 to February 1948." Inter alia: a) To MacArthur, February 27, 1946, on lodgings; b) To MacArthur, February 11, 1948, on article in *Life* Magazine.

————. File entitled "Miscellaneous correspondence 1946–1948. Inter alia: a) Major General Myron C. Cramer to Webb, June 15, 1948; b) Webb to Cramer, July 8, 1948; c) Webb to Cramer, September 15, 1948; d) Webb to Cramer, October 4, 1948, morning; e) Webb to Cramer, October 4, 1948, afternoon.

————. File entitled "President Webb to all judges—miscellaneous, May 1946 to December 1947, and January 1948 to November 1948." Inter alia: "Revised *Judgment*, September 17, 1948.

————. File entitled "Private letters to Sir William Webb concerning trial and fate of war criminals, January 1946 to May 1948." Inter alia: a) Unsigned letter of June 17, 1946 from Christian in Fukuoka on character of Tojo and of Tojo's brother, Ito Hishi; b) Letter from W. A. Wootton, Australian Legation, Shanghai, containing clipping from North China Daily News of September 27, 1947.

Whitney, Courtney. *MacArthur: His Rendezvous with History.* New York: Alfred A. Knopf, 1956.

Wigmore, Lionel. *The Japanese Thrust.* Vol. IV, Series 1 (Army), Australia in the War of 1939–1945. Canberra: Australian War Memorial, 1959.

Wildes, Harry Emerson. *Typhoon in Tokyo: The Occupation and its Aftermath.* New York: The Macmillan Co., 1954.

Willoughby, Charles A., and Chamberlain, John. *MacArthur, 1941–1951.* New York: McGraw-Hill Book Co., 1954.

Wu, Felix L., ed. *The Asia Who's Who, 1958.* Hong Kong: Pan-Asia Newspaper Alliance, 1958.

Yabe Teiji. *Konoye Fumimaro.* A biography, 2 vols. Tokyo: Kobundo, 1952.

Yamaguchi Shigeji. *Higeki no shogun: Ishiwara Kanji* [Tragedy's General: Ishiwara Kanji]. Tokyo: Sekai-sha, 1952.

Yanaga Chitoshi. *Japan Since Perry.* New York: McGraw-Hill Book Co., 1949.

————. *Japanese People and Politics.* New York: John Wiley & Sons, 1956.

Yatsuji Kazuo. *Showa jinbutsu hiroku* [A Memoir on Leading Figures of Hirohito's Reign]. Tokyo: Shinkigen-sha, 1954.

Yoshida Shigeru. *The Yoshida Memoirs: The Story of Japan in Crisis.* Translated by Yoshida Kenichi. Boston: Houghton Mifflin Co., 1962.

Yoshihashi Takehiko. *Conspiracy at Mukden: The Rise of the Japanese Military.* New Haven, Conn.: Yale University Press, 1963.

Young, A. Morgan. *Imperial Japan: 1926–1938.* New York: William Morrow & Co., 1938.

————. *Japan in Recent Times, 1912–1926.* New York: William Morrow & Co., 1929.

Young, John, comp. "Checklist of Microfilm Reproduction of Selected Archives of the Japanese Army, Navy and Other Government Agencies, 1868–1945." Mimeographed. Washington, D.C.: Georgetown University Press, 1959.

Zacharias, Ellis M. *Secret Missions: The Story of an Intelligence Officer.* New York: G. P. Putnam's Sons, 1946.

Zumoto Motosada, *Sino-Japanese Entanglements, 1931–1932: A Military Record.* Tokyo: Herald Press, n.d. [1932]. Slanted for propaganda purposes but valuable for military details.

INDEX

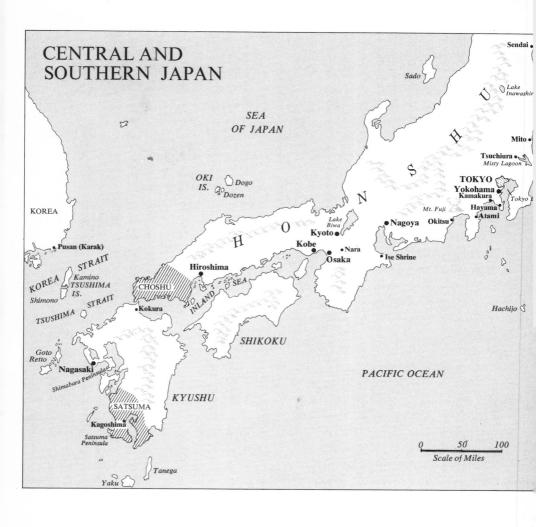